Lecture Notes in Computer Science   13161

More information about this subseries at https://link.springer.com/bookseries/7410

Steven D. Galbraith (Ed.)

Topics in Cryptology – CT-RSA 2022

Cryptographers' Track at the RSA Conference 2022
Virtual Event, March 1–2, 2022
Proceedings

 Springer

Editor
Steven D. Galbraith 🆔
University of Auckland
Auckland, New Zealand

ISSN 0302-9743   ISSN 1611-3349 (electronic)
Lecture Notes in Computer Science
ISBN 978-3-030-95311-9   ISBN 978-3-030-95312-6 (eBook)
https://doi.org/10.1007/978-3-030-95312-6

LNCS Sublibrary: SL4 – Security and Cryptology

This Springer imprint is published by the registered company Springer Nature Switzerland AG
The registered company address is: Gewerbestrasse 11, 6330 Cham, Switzerland

Preface

The RSA conference has been a major international event for information security experts since its inception in 1991. It is an annual event that attracts several hundred vendors and over 40,000 participants from industry, government, and academia. Since 2001, the RSA conference has included the Cryptographers' Track (CT-RSA). This track, essentially a sub-conference of the main event, provides a forum for the dissemination of current research in cryptography. This volume represents the proceedings of the 2022 edition of the Cryptographers' Track at the RSA Conference.

On the original submission deadline there were 56 submissions. The deadline was extended by about 10 days and the final number of submissions was 87. As always, the selection process was challenging. The submissions were anonymous (double-blind review), and each submission was assigned to at least three reviewers. We followed the IACR policy on conflicts of interest. We used EasyChair for the submission and review process. At the conclusion of the review and discussion phase there were 20 accepted papers and five conditionally accepted papers. This is an acceptance rate of 28.7%. Subsequently one of the conditionally accepted papers was withdrawn by the authors, so the final conference program comprised 24 papers.

I am thankful to all Program Committee members for producing high-quality reviews and for actively participating in discussions. My appreciation also goes to all external reviewers. I am also grateful to those Program Committee members who checked the conditionally accepted submissions.

I am grateful to Kenny Paterson (the CT-RSA 2021 Program Chair) and Moti Yung (Chair of the CT-RSA Steering Committee) for their wisdom. I also thank Lukas Zobernig for setting up the conference webpage and for help with processing the final versions of the papers for publication.

This year the conference took place online as a virtual conference on March 1–2, 2022.

My sincere thanks go to the Springer team for their assistance in preparing and producing these proceedings. Last but not least, on behalf of all CT-RSA participants, I would like to thank Tara Jung and Britta Glade who acted as RSA Conference liaison to the Cryptographer's Track. I am very grateful to them for all the work they did in helping to organize both the in-person conference and also the online conference.

December 2021   Steven D. Galbraith

Organization

Program Chair

Steven D. Galbraith   University of Auckland, New Zealand

Program Committee

Masayuki Abe	NTT Laboratories, Japan
Gorjan Alagic	University of Maryland, USA
Man Ho Au	University of Hong Kong, Hong Kong
Shi Bai	Florida Atlantic University, USA
Paulo Barreto	University of Washington, USA
Lejla Batina	Radboud University, The Netherlands
Josh Benaloh	Microsoft Research, USA
Nina Bindel	University of Waterloo and Institute for Quantum Computing, Canada
Olivier Blazy	Ecole Polytechnique, France
Ran Cohen	Northeastern University, USA, and IDC Herzliya, Israel
Gareth T. Davies	Bergische Universität Wuppertal, Germany
Jean Paul Degabriele	TU Darmstadt, Germany
Prastudy Fauzi	Simula UiB, Bergen, Norway
Luca De Feo	IBM Research Europe – Zürich, Switzerland
Pierrick Gaudry	CNRS, Nancy, France
Qian Guo	Lund University, Sweden
Helena Handschuh	Rambus Cryptography Research, USA
Stanislaw Jarecki	University of California, Irvine, USA
Shuichi Katsumata	AIST, Japan
Marcel Keller	CSIRO Data61, Australia
Veronika Kuchta	University of Queensland, Australia
Joseph Liu	Monash University, Australia
Anna Lysyanskaya	Brown, USA
Giorgia Azzurra Marson	NEC Labs Europe, Germany
Willi Meier	University of Applied Sciences and Arts Northwestern Switzerland (FHNW) Windisch, Switzerland
Brice Minaud	Inria and ENS, France
Tarik Moataz	MongoDB, USA

Khoa Nguyen	Nanyang Technological University, Singapore, and University of Wollongong, Australia
Bertram Poettering	IBM Research Europe – Zürich, Switzerland
David Pointcheval	ENS, France
Bart Preneel	KU Leuven, Belgium
Mike Rosulek	Oregon State University, USA
Adeline Roux-Langlois	University of Rennes, CNRS, IRISA, France
Arnab Roy	University of Klagenfurt, Austria
Reihaneh Safavi-Naini	University of Calgary, Canada
Yu Sasaki	NTT Laboratories, Japan
Abhi Shelat	Northeastern University, USA
Luisa Siniscalchi	Aarhus University, Denmark
Nigel Smart	KU Leuven, Belgium
Willy Susilo	University of Wollongong, Australia
Qiang Tang	University of Sydney, Australia
Jacques Traoré	Orange Labs, France
Fernando Virdia	ETH Zürich, Switzerland

External Reviewers

Sepideh Avizheh	Vukašin Karadžić	Willy Quach
Ward Beullens	Yashvanth Kondi	Yuan Quan
Vincenzo Botta	Xinyu Li	Paul Rösler
Katharina Boudgoust	Fukang Liu	Partha Sarathi Roy
Maxime Buser	Xingye Lu	Rajeev Anand Sahu
Wouter Castryck	Lin Lyu	Olivier Sanders
Long Chen	Mark Marson	Peter Scholl
Liron David	Sarah McCarthy	Jan Schoone
Denis Diemert	Ian McQuoid	Gaurav Sharma
Jan Peter Drees	Marine Minier	Manasi Shingane
Abhraneel Dutta	Dustin Moody	Benjamin Smith
Thomas Espitau	Tran Ngo	Hadi Soleimany
Mojtaba Fadavi	Luca Notarnicola	Patrick Struck
Hanwen Feng	Arne Tobias Ødegaard	Zhimei Sui
Danilo Francati	Bo Pang	Anupama Unnikrishnan
Benedikt Gierlichs	Kenny Paterson	Michiel Van Beirendonck
Jérôme Govinden	Hilder V. L. Pereira	Haiyang Xue
Vincent Grosso	Jeroen Pijnenburg	Rupeng Yang
Martha Norberg Hovd	Lucas Prabel	Zuoxia Yu
Senyang Huang	Nitin Pundir	Shang Zehua
Floyd Johnson	Chen Qian	Yongjun Zhao

Contents

Multicast Key Agreement, Revisited

Alexander Bienstock[1]($\boxtimes$), Yevgeniy Dodis[1], and Yi Tang[2]

[1] New York University, New York, USA
{abienstock,dodis}@cs.nyu.edu
[2] University of Michigan, Ann Arbor, USA
yit@umich.edu

Abstract. Multicast Key Agreement (MKA) is a long-overlooked natural primitive of large practical interest. In traditional MKA, an omniscient *group manager* privately distributes secrets over an untrusted network to a dynamically-changing set of group members. The group members are thus able to derive shared group secrets across time, with the main security requirement being that only current group members can derive the current group secret. There indeed exist very efficient MKA schemes in the literature that utilize symmetric-key cryptography. However, they lack formal security analyses, efficiency analyses regarding dynamically changing groups, and more modern, robust security guarantees regarding user state leakages: *forward secrecy* (FS) and *post-compromise security* (PCS). The former ensures that group secrets prior to state leakage remain secure, while the latter ensures that after such leakages, users can quickly recover security of group secrets via normal protocol operations.

More modern Secure Group Messaging (SGM) protocols allow a group of users to asynchronously and securely communicate with each other, as well as add and remove each other from the group. SGM has received significant attention recently, including in an effort by the IETF Messaging Layer Security (MLS) working group to standardize an eponymous protocol. However, the group key agreement primitive at the core of SGM protocols, Continuous Group Key Agreement (CGKA), achieved by the TreeKEM protocol in MLS, suffers from bad worst-case efficiency and heavily relies on less efficient (than symmetric-key cryptography) public-key cryptography. We thus propose that in the special case of a group membership change policy which allows a *single* member to perform all group additions and removals, an upgraded version of classical Multicast Key Agreement (MKA) may serve as a more efficient substitute for CGKA in SGM.

We therefore present rigorous, stronger MKA security definitions that provide increasing levels of security in the case of both user and group manager state leakage, and that are suitable for modern applications, such as SGM. We then construct a formally secure MKA protocol with strong efficiency guarantees for dynamic groups. Finally, we run experiments

The full version [9] is available as entry 2021/1570 in the IACR eprint archive.

A. Bienstock—Partially supported by a National Science Foundation Graduate Research Fellowship.

Y. Dodis—Partially supported by gifts from VMware Labs and Google, and NSF grants 1619158, 1319051, 1314568.

S. D. Galbraith (Ed.): CT-RSA 2022, LNCS 13161, pp. 1–25, 2022.
https://doi.org/10.1007/978-3-030-95312-6_1

which show that the left-balanced binary tree structure used in TreeKEM
can be replaced with red-black trees in MKA for better efficiency.

1   Introduction

Multicast Key Agreement. Multicast Key Agreement (MKA) is a natural primitive of large practical interest that has not received much attention recently. In
MKA, there is an omniscient *group manager* that privately distributes secrets
through *control messages* over an untrusted network to a dynamically-changing
set of group members. The secrets delivered via these control messages allow
group members to derive shared group secrets across time. The main security
requirement is that users added to the group are not able to derive old group
secrets while users removed from the group are not able to derive new group
secrets. Traditionally, these derived group secrets could then be used in some
higher-level application, such as digital rights management (DRM) for PayTV,
in which the group manager could broadcast content privately to users in a
unidirectional manner.

There are several works in the literature that propose and study practical
MKA protocols [15,19,23,31,33,35], the best of which achieve $O(\log n_{\max})$ worst-
case communication complexity, where $n_{\max}$ is the maximum number of users
ever in the group. Moreover, all of these protocols utilize efficient *symmetric-key*
cryptography for the control messages of each operation.

However, prior practical multicast works did *not* (i) provide formal security
models or proofs, (ii) resolve efficiency issues regarding dynamically changing
groups, nor, importantly, (iii) achieve more modern, robust security notions,
such as privacy surrounding leakages of user secret states. With respect to a
user secret state leakage, optimal security requires:

- *Forward Secrecy* (FS): All group secrets that were generated before the leakage should remain secure.
- *Post-Compromise Security* (PCS): Privacy of group secrets should be quickly
  recovered as a result of normal protocol operations.

Most of these prior schemes base off of the Logical Key Hierarchy (LKH)
from [33,35]. In these schemes, symmetric keys are stored at the nodes of a tree
in which users are assigned to leaf keys and the group secret is the key at the
root. The tree invariant is that users only know the keys at the nodes along the
path from their leaf to the root. Thus in its simplest form, if, for example, a user
is removed, the group manager simply removes their leaf, refreshes the other
keys at the nodes along the path from their leaf to the root, and encrypts these
keys to the children of the corresponding nodes on the path. This strategy thus
achieves $O(\log n_{\max})$ communication and computational complexity.

We state the efficiency in terms of $n_{\max}$, since these schemes never address
exactly how the tree should be balanced if many users are added or removed
from the group. In order to achieve optimal efficiency of the scheme according to
the lower bound of Micciancio and Panjwani [22], i.e., have communication and

computational complexity of $O(\log n_{\text{curr}})$, where n_{curr} is the current number of users in the group, the tree must remain balanced after such operations. However, this complicates the tree invariant: how should it be maintained so that security is achieved? Users should never occupy interior nodes nor retain information for old leaf-to-root paths. The first column of Table 1 summarizes the properties of traditional practical MKA constructions.

New Applications: Single Administrator Secure Group Messaging. We observe that today, MKA has several more modern applications, including:

1. Adapting the classical use case of DRM to more modern purposes, such as live streaming on the internet (e.g., twitch), or
2. Communicating with resource-constrained IoT devices [26], or
3. Enabling *Secure Group Messaging* (SGM) among the group members.

Here, we focus on SGM and first provide some background: End-to-end Secure Messaging protocols allow two parties to exchange messages over untrusted networks in a secure and asynchronous manner. The famous double ratchet algorithm of the Signal protocol [24] achieves great security and efficiency in this setting, and is now the backbone of several popular messaging applications (e.g., Signal, WhatsApp, Facebook Messenger Secret Conversations, etc.) which are used by billions of people worldwide.

However, allowing *groups* of users to efficiently exchange messages over untrusted networks in a secure manner introduces a number of nontrivial challenges. Such SGM protocols have begun to receive more attention recently: e.g., the IETF has launched the message-layer security (MLS) working group, which aims to standardize an eponymous SGM protocol [5]. In the SGM setting, users share evolving group secrets across time which enable them to asynchronously and securely communicate with each other. Furthermore, they are allowed to asynchronously add and remove other users from the group. However, in practice, groups typically utilize some stable policy to determine membership change permissions.

The key agreement primitive at the center of SGM is called Continuous Group Key Agreement (CGKA) [1,3,32] and is achieved by the TreeKEM protocol in MLS [8], among others (e.g., [3,34]). Much like MKA, CGKA requires end-to-end security of the evolving group secrets which can only be known by current group members, but also FS and PCS with respect to user state leakages. Furthermore, asynchronous dynamic operations can be performed by any user. It is a hard problem to design CGKA protocols from minimal security assumptions that are efficient. All current practical CGKA constructions require $\Omega(n_{\text{curr}})$ communication in the worst-case, due to complications regarding user-performed dynamic operations.[1] A definitively bad situation is immediately following the creation of a CGKA group: if many users remain offline for a long time after creation,

---

[1] Most constructions informally claim to have "fair-weather" $O(\log n_{\text{max}})$ communication complexity [2], i.e., in some (undefined) *good* conditions, they have $O(\log n_{\text{max}})$ communication.

communication complexity may remain $\Omega(n_{\text{curr}})$ during this time (for example, if the creator performs updates), since only a few users will have contributed secrets to the group. Additionally, all current CGKA protocols heavily rely on public-key cryptography (which is of course less efficient than symmetric-key cryptography).

Although CGKA is usually the best way to distribute keys amongst group members in the SGM setting, due to its strong functionality guarantees, it clearly suffers from the above deficiencies. Therefore, more efficient alternatives should be provided for special cases. One such realistic setting is when the policy for group membership changes only permits a single group member (administrator) to add and remove users. In this case, we posit that a great substitute for CGKA is (a stronger version of) MKA. Therefore, a main contribution of this paper, upon which we elaborate in the next subsection of the introduction, is providing a strong formal model of MKA that is suitable for modern uses such as SGM, and then constructing a protocol which efficiently achieves the security of this model. This protocol does not heavily rely on public-key cryptography as in CGKA, and has much more efficient $O(\log n_{\text{curr}})$ communication for operations as opposed to $\Omega(n_{\text{curr}})$ communication in the worst-case for CGKA. Table 1 compares the properties of traditional MKA in the literature with CGKA and our more secure, and efficient, MKA protocol.

We emphasize that the group manager in MKA (who is the single member of the SGM group with membership change privileges) only generates the secrets of the group and the control messages by which they are distributed, and can (should) be viewed as completely divorced from the central delivery server that is usually a part of SGM protocols such as MLS. Therefore, for example, the group manager does not need to be always online and the group secrets remain private from the delivery server, thus providing proper end-to-end security for SGM. Furthermore, despite the fact that the group manager performs all membership change operations, actual SGM communications remain asynchronous by using the group secret from MKA for the Application Key Schedule, as is usually done with CGKA in MLS [5].

Group Authenticated Key Exchange. MKA and CGKA are closely related to the setting of Group Authenticated Key Exchange (GAKE) (e.g., [12–14,21]). In GAKE, several (possibly overlapping) groups of users work together to establish independent group keys across time. Formal models, constructions, and proofs for GAKE indeed exist that consider FS and PCS. However, all such constructions involve a large amount of interaction, requiring many parties to be online, which is undesirable for the MKA and SGM settings.

1.1 Contributions

Multicast Key Agreement with Optimal User Security. This paper provides a more rigorous study of practical MKA constructions by first providing a formal security definition (based on that of [1] for CGKA) which guarantees correctness and privacy of the protocol, as well as PCS and FS for users. Moreover, our

Table 1. A comparison of some properties of the traditional MKA construction in the literature, CGKA constructions, and our optimal MKA construction. The top half showcases the efficiency advantages of both traditional and our MKA, while the bottom showcases the functionality advantages of CGKA, and the added security and efficiency of our MKA with respect to traditional MKA.

	Traditional MKA	CGKA	Our MKA
Efficiency	$O(\log n_{\max})$	$\Omega(n_{\mathrm{curr}})$ ("fair-weather" $O(\log n_{\max})$)	$O(\log n_{\mathrm{curr}})$
Heavy Use of Public-Key Cryptography	no	yes	no
Add/Remove	group mgr	anybody[a]	group mgr
Members PCS/FS	no/no	yes/yes	yes/yes
Group Mgr PCS/FS	no/no	N/A	weak[b]/yes
Group Mgr Local Storage	$\Omega(n_{\mathrm{curr}})$	N/A	$O(1)$

[a] Although in formal definitions of CGKA constructions, any group member can perform add and remove operations, in practice, a stable policy is needed.
[b] PCS against group manager corruptions in our construction requires every group member at the time of corruption to be either removed or updated.

definition allows for partially active security, meaning the delivery service can send control messages to users in arbitrarily different orders (with arbitrary delays), but cannot inject or modify control messages. We additionally allow for *adaptive* adversaries, achieving security proofs with quasipolynomial loss in the standard model, and polynomial loss in the random oracle model, using the proofs of Tainted TreeKEM (a CGKA protocol) in [3] as a template.

We then provide a secure and efficient construction of the primitive based on LKH that instead utilizes *generic* tree structures. This protocol moreover utilizes (dual) pseudorandom functions (dPRFs) [6] and an *Updatable Symmetric Key Encryption* (USKE) primitive [7] (which is the symmetric analog to Updatable Public Key Encryption (UPKE) [1,17,20]) to allow for optimal FS by refreshing keys in the tree as soon as they are used as an encryption secret key.

Furthermore, we show that if the tree structure used is a left-balanced binary tree (LBBT), as in most CGKA constructions, then the computational and communication complexity of operations besides creation are $O(\log n_{\max})$. However, we show that if the protocol uses 2–3 trees or red-black trees (RBTs), this complexity improves to $O(\log n_{\mathrm{curr}})$, thus achieving optimal communication complexity according to the lower bound of [22]. Indeed, we implement our construction which shows empirically that this theoretical difference between $n_{\max}$ and n_{curr} makes RBTs more efficient than LBBTs in practice.[2] In Sect. 4.4, we illustrate

---

[2] See https://github.com/abienstock/Multicast-Key-Agreement for the code.

that in the average case, where updates are performed more often than additions and removals (which occur at the same rate), RBTs are the most efficient out of the three trees. Furthermore, in an event in which group membership drastically decreases, LBBTs are much less efficient than both RBTs and 2–3 trees after this decrease. Even if group membership gradually decreases over time, RBTs are still the most efficient of the three.

Adding Security for Group Manager Corruptions. We then add to the security definition of MKA to allow for corruptions of the group manager state. Despite these corruptions, our definition still demands immediate FS, i.e. all group secrets before the corruption should remain secure, and eventual PCS, i.e. after the group manager has updated or removed all of the members of the group at the time of the corruption, future group secrets should be secure. While our above construction already achieves this stronger definition, it relies on the group manager to store the keys at each node of the tree. Such a requirement assumes that the group manager has the capability to locally store such large ($\Omega(n_{curr})$) amounts of data, as well as handle availability, replication, etc. In an effort to reduce the local storage of the group manager and securely outsource storage of the tree to an untrusted remote server, we use the recent work of [10], who formalize the notion of *Forward Secret encrypted RAM* (FS eRAM) and apply it to MKA.[3] Intuitively, the security of FS eRAM only allows the adversary to obtain secrets currently at the nodes of the MKA tree upon corruption of the group manager, while past secrets at the nodes remain secure.

The work of [10] focuses on a lower bound for FS eRAM and only sketches its application to MKA, with similar limitations as the prior works on MKA (no formal analysis of security or dynamism). We therefore provide a similar result with a fully formal argument that achieves the security of the modified MKA definition, while retaining asymptotic communication and computational complexity of our original MKA scheme. Moreover, it enables the group manager to separate her state into $O(1)$ local storage and $O(n_{curr})$ remote storage. The third column of Table 1 shows the properties of our second construction.

Optimal PCS for Group Manager Corruptions. The security notion described above allows us to retain the use of efficient symmetric-key encryption for control messages, while achieving good, but not optimal, eventual PCS for group manager corruptions. Indeed, we show in the full version [9] that to obtain optimal PCS, i.e., security after one operation following a group manager corruption, public-key encryption is necessary. Then we show that achieving optimal PCS (and all the other properties described above) with public-key encryption is easy: In our construction, we simply replace USKE with UPKE (and the group manager only remotely, not locally, stores the public keys at the tree nodes).

---

[3] FS eRAM is also known in the literature as, e.g., "secure deletion" [4,25,27–29], "how to forget a secret" [16], "self-destruction" [18], and "revocability" [11].

2   Preliminaries

In this section we introduce some basic concepts on top of the standard notions of graph-theoretic trees. For the standard definitions of PRGs, dual PRFs and CPA-secure symmetric-key encryption, see the full version [9].

For our purposes, every node in a tree has a unique identifier ℓ. For every node in a tree, there is a unique path from (and including) the node to the root of the tree, referred to as its *direct path*. The set of siblings of all nodes along the direct path of node v is the *copath* of v. We refer to a connected subgraph of the tree that includes the root as a *skeleton* of the tree. For any skeleton, its *frontier* consists of those nodes in the tree that are not in the skeleton but have edges from nodes in the skeleton.

3   Multicast Key Agreement

A Multicast Key Agreement (MKA) scheme allows for a group manager to distribute secret random values to group members which they can use to obtain shared key material for some higher-level protocol. The manager (and only the manager) can make changes to the group, i.e. add and remove members, as well as help *individual* parties in the group update their secrets, if needed. There are many options for what a higher-level protocol can do with the shared group key material from the MKA scheme, as stated in the introduction.

In this section, we formally define the syntax of MKA schemes and introduce a security notion that captures correctness, key indistinguishability, as well as forward secrecy and post-compromise security for group members, even with a partially active and adaptive adversary that can deliver control messages in an arbitrary order for each user.

3.1   MKA Syntax

Before we formally define the syntax of MKA, observe that the group manager will often need to communicate secrets to users with whom she does not share any prior secrets (e.g., when adding them). Indeed, there are many primitives that require such delivery of secrets with no prior shared secrets – e.g., CGKA, Identity-Based Encryption (IBE), Broadcast Encryption (BE), etc. – and all do so using a secure channel (which may be compromised by an adversary on-demand). In modern SGM literature, this channel is usually implemented by a Public Key Infrastructure (PKI), since the parties anyway need a PKI to authenticate each other. For our setting, where all control messages are sent by a single party (much like IBE and BE), we take a more traditional route by not explicitly including a PKI for the secure channel used to deliver secret keys. Instead, we simply model separate *out-of-band* channels from the group manager to each user for such messages (which will indeed often be implemented via a PKI). In the definition, all *out-of-band values* k_{ID} output by group manager algorithms are *small* (security parameter size), and will be sent over the corresponding individual out-of-band channel from the group manager to user ID. Moreover, any out-of-band values input by the user process algorithm will have been retrieved from their corresponding out-of-band channel from the group manager.

Definition 1 (Multicast Key Agreement (MKA)). *An* MKA *scheme* M = (Minit, Uinit, create, add, rem, upd, proc) *consists of the following algorithms:*[4]

- Group Manager Initialization: Minit *outputs initial state* Γ.
- User Initialization: Uinit *takes an ID* ID *and outputs an initial state* γ.
- Group Creation: create *takes a state* Γ *and a set of IDs* G = {$ID_1, \ldots, ID_n$}, *and outputs a new state* Γ', *group secret* I, *control message* T, *and dictionary* K[·], *which stores a small user out-of-band value for every* ID $\in$ G.
- Add: add *takes a state* Γ *and an ID* ID *and outputs a new state* Γ', *group secret* I, *control message* T, *and a small out-of-band value for* ID, k_{ID}.
- Remove: rem *takes a state* Γ *and an ID* ID *and outputs a new state* Γ', *group secret* I, *and a control message* T.
- Update: upd *takes a state* Γ *and an ID* ID *and outputs a new state* Γ', *group secret* I, *control message* T, *and a small out-of-band value for* ID, k_{ID}.
- Process: proc *takes a state* γ, *a control message* T *sent over the broadcast channel, and an (optional) out-of-band value* k, *and outputs a new state* γ' *and a group secret* I.

One uses a MKA scheme as follows: Once a group is established by the group manager using create, the manager may call the add, rem, or upd algorithms. We note that including an explicit upd algorithm for users enables better efficiency than the alternative – removing a user and immediately adding her back. After each operation performed by the group manager, a new *epoch* is instantiated with the corresponding group secret computed by the operation. It is the implicit task of a delivery server connecting the group manager with the members to relay the *control messages* to all current group members. The delivery server can deliver any control message output by the group manager to any user, at any time. Additionally, the group manager may (directly) send certain members secret values over the out-of-band channel. Whenever a group member receives a control message and the corresponding out-of-band secret from the group manager (if there is one), they use the proc algorithm to process them and obtain the group secret I for that epoch.

3.2 MKA Efficiency Measures

We introduce four measures of efficiency for MKA schemes. These efficiency measures are in terms of the number of group members at a certain epoch,

---

[4] We could easily allow for batch operations – as the latest MLSv11 draft does through the "propose-then-commit" framework [5] – which would be more efficient than the corresponding sequential execution of those operations, but we choose not to for simplicity. We also note that updating one user at a time in case of their corruption is of course much more efficient (and just as secure) than updating the whole group in case just that user was corrupted.

n_{curr}, and the maximum number of group members throughout the execution of the protocol, n_{max}. The first is that of worst-case space complexity of the group manager state, i.e. the size of Γ, which we refer to as $s(n_{curr}, n_{max})$. The second is that of worst-case communication complexity of control messages output by the group manager for add, rem, and upd operations, which we refer to as $c(n_{curr}, n_{max})$. The third is that of worst-case time complexity of group manager add, rem, and upd operations, which we refer to as $t_1(n_{curr}, n_{max})$. The fourth is that of worst-case time complexity of user proc process algorithms for control messages output by group manager, which we refer to as $t_2(n_{curr}, n_{max})$. In our construction, using specific tree structures in Sect. 4, the worst-case space complexity of a user, i.e. the size of γ, is proportional to $t_2(n_{curr}, n_{max})$. We will often refer to these measures without writing them explicitly as functions of n_{curr} and n_{max} (and will sometimes informally conflate n_{curr} and n_{max} into a single value, n, for simplicity).

3.3 MKA Security

We now introduce the formal security definition for MKA schemes that ensures optimal security for group members against adaptive and partially active adversaries. The basic properties any MKA scheme must satisfy for this definition are the following:

- *Correctness even with partially active adversaries*: The group manager and all group members output the same group secret in all epochs, once the group members have eventually received all control messages in order (with different messages possibly arbitrarily ordered in between).
- *Privacy*: The group secrets look random given the message transcript.
- *User Forward Secrecy (FS)*: If the state of any user is leaked at some point, all previous group secrets remain hidden from the attacker.
- *User Post-compromise Security (PCS)*: Once the group manager performs updates for every group member whose state was leaked, group secrets become private again.

All of these properties are captured by the single security game presented in Fig. 1, denoted by user-mult. In the game the attacker is given access to oracles to drive the execution of the MKA protocol. We note that the attacker is not allowed to modify or inject any control messages, but again, they can deliver them in any arbitrary order. This is because we assume MKA will be used in a modular fashion, and thus, whichever higher-level application it is used within will provide authentication (as is also assumed for CGKA). However, we do assume that the attacker sees all broadcast control messages and can corrupt out-of-band messages.

Epochs. The main oracles to drive the execution of the game are the oracles for the group manager to create a group, add users, remove users, and update individual users' secrets, as well as the oracle to deliver control messages to users,

```
init():                          create-group(G):                deliver(t_d, ID):
  b ←_$ {0,1}                      req t = 0                        req t ≥ t_d
  Γ ← Minit()                      t++                              (γ[ID], I) ← proc(γ[ID],
  ∀ID : γ[ID] ← Uinit(ID)          (Γ', I, T, K) ←                     M[t_d, ID], (K[t_d, ID]))
  t ← 0, ep[·] ← −1                   create(Γ, G)                  if (t_d = ep[ID] + 1 ∨
  chall[·] ← false                 I[t] ← I                          (ep[ID] = −1 ∧
  G[·], I[·], K[·] ← ε             G[t] ← G                           added(t_d, ID))):
  pub M[·] ← ε                     for every ID ∈ G[t]:               if removed(t_d, ID):
                                     M[t, ID] ← T                       ep[ID] ← −1
add-user(ID):                        K[t, ID] ← K[ID]                   return
  req t > 0 ∧ ID ∉ G[t]                                             else if I ≠ I[t_d]:
  t++                           remove-user(ID):                       win
  (Γ', I, T, k) ←                  req t > 0 ∧ ID ∈ G[t]            if added(t_d, ID):
     add(Γ, ID)                    t++                                ep[ID] ← t_d
  I[t] ← I                         (Γ', I, T) ← rem(Γ, ID)          else:
  G[t] ← G[t − 1] ∪ {ID}           I[t] ← I                           ep[ID] ++
  for every ID' ∈ G[t]:            G[t] ← G[t − 1] \ {ID}
    M[t, ID'] ← T                  for every ID' ∈ G[t − 1]:      reveal(t_r):
  K[t, ID] ← k                       M[t, ID'] ← T                  req I[t_r] ≠ ε ∧ ¬chall[t_r]
                                                                    chall[t_r] ← true
update-user(ID):                 chall(t*):                         return I[t_r]
  req t > 0 ∧ ID ∈ G[t]            req I[t*] ≠ ε ∧ ¬chall[t*]
  t++                              I_0 ← I[t*]                     corrupt(ID):
  (Γ', I, T, k) ←                  I_1 ←_$ I                        return γ[ID]
     upd(Γ, ID)                    chall[t*] ← true
  I[t] ← I                         return I_b                     corrupt-oob(t_o, ID):
  G[t] ← G[t − 1]                                                   return K[t_o, ID]
  for every ID' ∈ G[t]:
    M[t, ID'] ← T
  K[t, ID] ← k
```

Fig. 1. Oracles for the MKA security game user-mult for a scheme M = (Minit, Uinit, create, add, rem, upd, proc). Functions added and removed are explained in the text.

i.e. **create-group, add-user, remove-user, update-user, deliver.** The first four oracles allow the adversary to instruct the group manager to initiate a new epoch, while the deliver oracle advances group members to the next epoch in which they are a group member, if in fact the message for that epoch is the one being delivered. The game forces the adversary to initially create a group, and also enables users to be in epochs which are arbitrarily far apart.

Initialization. The **init** oracle sets up the game and all variables needed to keep track of its execution. The game initially starts in epoch $t = 0$. Random bit b is used for real-or-random challenges, Γ stores the group manager's current state, and γ is a dictionary which keeps track of all of the users' states. The dictionary ep keeps track of which epoch each user is in currently (-1 if they are not in the group). Dictionaries **G** and **I** record the group members in each epoch, and the group secret of each epoch, respectively. Dictionary chall is used to ensure that the adversary cannot issue multiple challenges or reveals per epoch. Additionally, K records any out-of-band random values that the group manager needs to send to any of the group members for each epoch. Finally, M records all control messages that the group manager associates with group members for each epoch; the adversary has read access to M, as indicated by **pub**.

Operations. When the adversary calls any of the oracles to perform operations to define a new epoch t, the resulting control messages for group members ID are stored in M with the key (t, ID). Additionally, any associated out-of-band values for ID are stored in K with the key (t, ID). The oracle **create-group** causes the group manager to create a group with members $\mathsf{G} = \{\mathsf{ID}_1, \ldots, \mathsf{ID}_n\}$, only if $t = 0$. Thereafter, the group manager calls the group creation algorithm and produces the resulting control message and out-of-band values for their respective users. In each of the oracles **add-user**, **remove-user**, and **update-user**, the **req** statements checks that the call is proper (e.g., that an added ID was not already in the group); exiting the call if not. Subsequently, the oracles call the corresponding MKA algorithms, and store the resulting control messages (and possibly out-of-band values) in M (and K).

Delivering Control Messages and Out-of-Band Values. The oracle **deliver** is called with the same arguments (t_d, ID) that are used as keys for M and K. The associated control message (and possibly out-of-band value) is retrieved from M (and K) and run through proc on the current state of ID. The security game then checks that this is the next message for ID to process, i.e., either ID is in epoch $t_d - 1$, or was added to the group in epoch t_d, as checked by the function: $\mathsf{added}(t_d, \mathsf{ID}) := \mathsf{ID} \notin \mathbf{G}[t_d - 1] \wedge \mathsf{ID} \in \mathbf{G}[t_d]$. If so, the game first checks if ID is removed from the group in epoch t_d, as checked by the function: $\mathsf{removed}(t_d, \mathsf{ID}) := \mathsf{ID} \in \mathbf{G}[t_d - 1] \wedge \mathsf{ID} \notin \mathbf{G}[t_D]$. In this case, the game sets the epoch counter for ID to -1. Otherwise, the game requires that the group secret I which is output by $\mathsf{proc}(\gamma[\mathsf{ID}], M[t_d, \mathsf{ID}], (K[t_d, \mathsf{ID}]))$ is the same as the secret output by the group manager for that epoch. If it is not, the instruction **win** reveals the secret bit b to the attacker (this ensures correctness). Finally, the epoch counter for ID is set to t_d. Note: although the security game only requires correctness for control messages that are eventually delivered in order, the adversary can choose to deliver them in arbitrary order, and users must immediately handle them.

Challenges, Corruptions, and Deletions. In order to capture that group secrets must look random and independent of those for other rounds, the attacker is allowed to issue a challenge $\mathbf{chall}(t^*)$ for any epoch *or* use $\mathbf{reveal}(t_r)$ to simply learn the group secret of an epoch.

We model forward secrecy and PCS by allowing the adversary to learn the current state of any party by calling the **corrupt** oracle. Through such corruptions, the security game also prohibits the phenomenon called *double joining*: In the specification of a protocol, users may delete certain secrets from their state, when they are deemed to be useless. However, a user could decide to act maliciously by saving all of these old secrets. Double joining is the phenomenon in which a user has been removed from the group in some epoch, but perhaps they have saved some secrets that allow them to still derive the group secret for future epochs. In fact, since the group manager handles all operations, this is the *only* way that users can act maliciously. The **corrupt** oracle on its own prohibits double joining because if the adversary corrupts some user ID in epoch t and removes them in some later epoch $t' > t$ without calling the update oracle before t', the group secret for epoch t' (and all later epochs for which ID is still not a group member) should be indistinguishable from random. This should hold even though the adversary can save all information ID can derive from their state at epoch t and control messages through time t'.

We also allow the adversary to corrupt out-of-band messages sent to a user in a given epoch by querying the **corrupt-oob** oracle. Note that since we do not explicitly require the out-of-band channel to be implemented in a particular way, the adversary can only corrupt individual messages. However, if for example a PKI is used without PCS after corruptions to implement the out-of-band channel, then the adversary in user-mult can simply repeatedly query the **corrupt-oob** oracle. Our modeling choice abstracts out the corruption model of the out-of-band channel, allowing the adversary to decide the consequences of corruption at a given time.

Avoiding Trivial Attacks. We prevent against trivial attacks by running the **user-safe** predicate at the end of the game on the queries $q_1, \ldots, q_q$ in order to determine if the execution had any such attacks. The predicate checks for every challenge epoch t^* if there is any ID $\in \mathbf{G}[t^*]$ that was corrupted in epoch $t < t^*$; or who was added in epoch $t < t^*$ and whose corresponding out-of-band message for that add was corrupted. If so, the predicate checks if the user was not removed by the group manager or did not have her secrets updated by the group manager for an operation whose corresponding out-of-band message is not later corrupted, after t and before or during t^*.

If this were true, then the attacker could trivially compute the group secret in the challenge epoch t^* by using the state of corrupted user ID, or her corrupted out-of-band message, in epoch t and the broadcast control messages and/or future corrupted out-of-band messages. The predicate is depicted in Fig. 2, which uses the function q2e(q), that returns the epoch corresponding to query q. Specifically if $q = \textbf{corrupt}(ID)$, if ID is a member of the group when q is made, q2e(q) corresponds to ep[ID], otherwise, q2e(q) returns $\perp$.[5] If $q = \textbf{corrupt-oob}(t, ID)$, then q2e($q$) = t. For $q \in \{\textbf{update-user}(ID), \textbf{remove-user}(ID)\}$, q2e($q$) is the epoch defined by the operation.

Observe that this predicate achieves optimal security for users. For forward secrecy, if an adversary corrupts a user that is currently at epoch t, for every epoch $0 < t' \leq t$, the group secret is indistinguishable from random. For PCS, if the adversary corrupts a user that is currently at epoch t, or their out-of-band channel at epoch t if they are added in epoch t, once the group manager

---

[5] Any expression containing $\perp$ evaluates to false.

---

user-safe($q_1, \ldots, q_q$):
    for (i, j) s.t. $q_i = \textbf{corrupt}(\textsf{ID}) \vee (q_i = \textbf{corrupt-oob}(t, \textsf{ID}) \wedge$
    $\textbf{added}(t, \textsf{ID}))$ for some $t, \textsf{ID}$ and $q_j = \textbf{chall}(t^*)$ for some t^*:
        if $\textsf{q2e}(q_i) < t^* \wedge \nexists l$ s.t. $0 < \textsf{q2e}(q_i) < \textsf{q2e}(q_l) \leq t^* \wedge$
        $((q_l = \textbf{update-user}(\textsf{ID}) \wedge \nexists m > l$ s.t.
          $q_m = \textbf{corrupt-oob}(\textsf{q2e}(q_l), \textsf{ID})) \vee q_l = \textbf{remove-user}(\textsf{ID}))$:
          return 0
    return 1

Fig. 2. The **user-safe** safety predicate determines if a sequence of calls $(q_1, \ldots, q_q)$ allows the attacker to trivially win the MKA game.

updates their secrets in some epoch $t' > t$ for which the corresponding out-of-band message is not corrupted (and does the same for every other corrupted user), the group secret is indistinguishable from random. Additionally, double-joins are prohibited, since once a user is removed from the group, even if their state is corrupted before the removal, the group secret of all future epochs in which the user is not a group member are indistinguishable from random.

Advantage. In the following, a $(t, q_c, n_{\max})$-*attacker* is an attacker $\mathcal{A}$ that runs in time at most t, makes at most q_c challenge queries, and never produces a group with more than $n_{\max}$ members. The attacker wins the MKA security game user-mult if he correctly guesses the random bit b in the end *and* the safety predicate **user-safe** evaluates to true on the queries made by the attacker. The advantage of $\mathcal{A}$ against MKA scheme M is: $\textsf{Adv}^{\textsf{M}}_{\textsf{user-mult}}(\mathcal{A}) := \left| \Pr[\mathcal{A} \text{ wins}] - \frac{1}{2} \right|$.

Definition 2 (MKA User Security). *A MKA scheme* M *is* $(s, c, t_1, t_2, t', q_c, n_{max}, \varepsilon)$-*secure in* user-mult *against adaptive and partially active attackers, if for all* (t', q_c, n_{max})-*attackers,* $\textsf{Adv}^{\textsf{M}}_{\textsf{user-mult}}(\mathcal{A}) \leq \varepsilon$, *and the complexity measures of the group managers and users are* s, c, t_1, t_2.

4 MKA Construction

Our MKA construction is similar to LKH [33,35] described in the introduction, in which the group manager stores for each epoch, the whole tree with the group secret at at the root, keys at all other nodes, and n users at the leaves (with no extra leaves). We call this tree the *MKA tree* and it has $O(n)$ values in total for most commonly used trees. Observe that the group manager should be expected to store $\Omega(n)$ amount of information, since she must minimally be aware of the group members. Users only need to store in their state the secrets along their direct path, which we will show is size $O(\log(n))$ for most *balanced* trees.

4.1 MKA Trees

Below, we describe operations on MKA trees needed for our construction. In addition to modifying the tree, for the purposes of our MKA construction, each operation also returns a skeleton (refer back to Sect. 2 for a definition of skeleton and frontier). This skeleton consists of any new nodes added to the tree, as well as any nodes in the original tree whose subtree (rooted at that node) has been modified (i.e., a node has been removed from or added to it by the operation), and their edges to each other. Every edge in the skeleton is labeled with a color *green* or *blue* with the requirement that for each node v in the skeleton, at most one of its edges to its children can be colored green. When we specify the cryptographic details of our MKA scheme, if an edge is blue, it means that the secret at the parent will be encrypted under a key at the child, whereas if an edge is green, it means that the secret at the parent will be generated using a dPRF computation on a key at the child.[6] A tree has the following operations:

- *Initialize.* The $\tau_{\mathsf{mka}} \leftarrow \text{INIT}(\ell_1, \ldots, \ell_n)$ operation initializes τ_{mka} with n leaves labeled by $(\ell_1, \ldots, \ell_n)$ (which will be user IDs).
- *Add.* The $\text{ADD}(\tau_{\mathsf{mka}}, \ell)$ operation adds a leaf to the tree τ_{mka} labeled by ℓ (ID of added user).
- *Remove.* The $\text{REMOVE}(\tau_{\mathsf{mka}}, \ell)$ operation removes the leaf from the tree τ_{mka} with label ℓ (ID of user to be removed).

MKA Tree Efficiency Measures. We say a node in a MKA tree is *utilized* in a given epoch if it contains a secret. We assume w.l.o.g., that every interior node of a MKA tree is utilized, since otherwise, a needless efficiency decrease would result. We refer to a MKA tree τ_{mka} as a $(s_{\text{tree}}(n, m), s_{\text{skel}}(n, m), d(n, m), \deg(\tau_{\mathsf{mka}}))$-*tree* if it has degree of nodes bounded by $\deg(\tau_{\mathsf{mka}})$ and given that it contains at *maximum* m leaves throughout its existence: with n utilized leaves in any configuration it has depth $d(n, m)$, $s_{\text{tree}}(n, m)$ total nodes in the worst case and skeletons formed by ADD or REMOVE operations with total number of nodes $s_{\text{skel}}(n, m)$ in the worst case. In terms of our MKA scheme, $m = n_{\max}$ is the maximum number of users in the group throughout the execution of the protocol and $n = n_{\text{curr}}$ is the number of users in the group at a given epoch. We will often refer to these measures without writing them explicitly as functions of m and n. It will become clear in our construction below that measure s_{tree} upper bounds MKA efficiency measure s and measure s_{skel} upper bounds MKA efficiency measures c, t_1, t_2 as described in Sect. 3.2 for constant-degree trees.

See the full version [9] for the implementation details and efficiency of three types of trees that can be used in our MKA construction: LBBTs, 2–3 trees, and left-leaning red-black trees (LLRBTs) [30]. There we show that LBBTs are $(O(m), O(\log m), O(\log m), 2)$-trees, 2–3 trees are $(O(n), O(\log n), O(\log n), 3)$-trees, and LLRBTs are $(O(n), O(\log n), O(\log n), 2)$-trees.

4.2 GUS MKA Protocol

We now describe the cryptographic details of an MKA scheme utilizing a generic tree structure that achieves security with respect to the user-mult game. We

---

[6] Where we use the standard PRF security of a dPRF dprf on the child's key (see the full version [9]).

denote the scheme GUS (for Generic User Security). GUS makes (black-box) use of a dPRF dprf and an Updatable Symmetric Key Encryption (USKE) scheme uske = (UEnc, UDec). USKE is the symmetric analog to the well-known Updatable Public Key Encryption primitive used in the Secure Messaging Literature [1,17,20]. USKE schemes compute a new key after each encryption (resp. decryption) such that if the newest key is exposed, then all plaintexts encrypted under previous versions of the key remain secure. In the full version [9], we formally define IND-CPA* security for USKE and show a simple construction which achieves it, using a PRG and one-time pad encryption (our security notion and construction are quite similar to that of [7]).We use USKE in GUS to obtain forward secrecy: Essentially, each node v in the MKA tree τ_{mka} for a given epoch t will store a key k which the manager can use to communicate to the users at the leaves of the subtree rooted at v information needed to derive the group secret. If the operation for t causes some information to be encrypted to some node key k, k must be refreshed (as in USKE): if k is not refreshed, in epoch $t + 1$, an adversary can corrupt any user storing k and break FS by regenerating the group secret for epoch t.

GUS is depicted in Fig. 3. Note that the group manager's state only consists of the current epoch t and the MKA tree for the current epoch t, which we denote as τ_{mka}. Each user ID stores the current epoch which they are in, t_{ME}, as well as the secrets of their direct path in τ_{mka} at t_{ME}, which we denote as P_{ID}, and refer to as their *secret path*.

GUS MKA Group Manager Operations. Here we define operations with generic trees for how the group manager creates the group, adds and removes members, and updates key material for members. In initialization, the group manager simply initializes her MKA tree to be empty, and her epoch $t \leftarrow 0$.

Skeleton Secret Generation. We first describe a procedure to generate the secrets and any corresponding ciphertexts for a skeleton. The procedure $(I, \mathsf{K}, \mathsf{CT}, \tau'_{mka}) \leftarrow \texttt{SecretGen}(\mathsf{skeleton}, \tau_{mka})$ first initializes sets $\mathsf{CT}[\cdot] \leftarrow \bot, \mathsf{K}[\cdot] \leftarrow \bot$ then recursively for each node v in skeleton starting with its leaves:

1. If v is a leaf of skeleton or a node for whom all edges to its children are labeled *blue* in skeleton, the procedure samples a random value k_s and computes $(k_p \| k'_{d,v} \| k_{e,v}) \leftarrow \mathsf{dprf}(k_s, k_{d,v}),$[7] where $k_{d,v}$ is the current dPRF key at v (if it exists, $\bot$ otherwise), $k_{e,v}$ will be the new encryption key at v, $k'_{d,v}$ will be the new dPRF key at v, and k_p may be used for the parent of v. Then:
   (a) The group manager writes $(k'_{d,v}, k_{e,v}, \ell_v)$ to node v of τ_{mka}, where ℓ_v is either a new value if v is new, or its old value otherwise.
   (b) Additionally, if v was a leaf node of τ_{mka}, the manager sets $\mathsf{K}[\mathsf{ID}] \leftarrow k_s$, for the label ID of v.
2. Otherwise, it uses the key k_s (labeled as k_p above) obtained from the child whose edge from v is *green* and does the same.

---

[7] We only need to use a dPRF at leaves of the MKA tree for updates in which the corresponding oob message is corrupted (we could use a PRG elsewhere), but we use one at all nodes, for all operations, for simplicity.

GUS-Minit):
  $\tau_{\text{mka}} \leftarrow \perp, t \leftarrow 0$

GUS-Uinit(ID):
  $\text{ME} \leftarrow \text{ID}, P_{\text{ME}} \leftarrow \perp, t_{\text{ME}} \leftarrow -1$

GUS-create($G = (\text{ID}_1, \ldots, \text{ID}_n)$):
  $t + +$
  $(\tau_{\text{mka}}, \text{skeleton}) \leftarrow \text{INIT}(\tau_{\text{mka}}, G)$
  $(I, \text{K}, \text{CT}, \tau_{\text{mka}}) \leftarrow$
    $\text{SecretGen}(\text{skeleton}, \tau_{\text{mka}})$
  $T \leftarrow (t, \text{create}, -1, \text{skeleton}, \text{CT})$
  return (I, T, K)

GUS-add(ID):
  $t + +$
  $(\tau_{\text{mka}}, \text{skeleton}) \leftarrow \text{ADD}(\tau_{\text{mka}}, \text{ID})$
  $(I, \text{K}, \text{CT}, \tau_{\text{mka}}) \leftarrow$
    $\text{SecretGen}(\text{skeleton}, \tau_{\text{mka}})$
  $T \leftarrow (t, \text{add}, \text{ID}, \text{skeleton}, \text{CT})$
  $k_{\text{ID}} \leftarrow \text{K}[\text{ID}]$
  return (I, T, k_{ID})

GUS-rem(ID):
  $t + +$
  $(\tau_{\text{mka}}, \text{skeleton}) \leftarrow$
    $\text{REMOVE}(\tau_{\text{mka}}, \text{ID})$
  $(I, \text{K}, \text{CT}, \tau_{\text{mka}}) \leftarrow$
    $\text{SecretGen}(\text{skeleton}, \tau_{\text{mka}})$
  $T \leftarrow (t, \text{rem}, \text{ID}, \text{skeleton}, \text{CT})$
  return (I, T)

GUS-upd(ID):
  $t + +$
  $\text{skeleton} \leftarrow \text{SkelGen}(\tau_{\text{mka}}, \text{ID})$
  $(I, \text{K}, \text{CT}, \tau_{\text{mka}}) \leftarrow \text{SecretGen}(\text{skeleton}, \tau_{\text{mka}})$
  $T \leftarrow (\text{ID}, \text{skeleton}, \text{CT})$
  $k_{\text{ID}} \leftarrow \text{K}[\text{ID}]$
  return (I, T, k_{ID})

GUS-proc($T = (t, \text{op}, \text{ID}, \text{skeleton}, \text{CT}), (k_{\text{ID}})$):
  if $t_{\text{ME}} = t - 1 \vee (t_{\text{ME}} = -1 \wedge$
    $\text{op} \in \{\text{create}, \text{add}\} \wedge \text{ID} \in \{-1, \text{ME}\})$:
    if $\text{op} = \text{rem} \wedge \text{ID} = \text{ME}$:
      $t_{\text{ME}} \leftarrow -1$
    else:
      $t_{\text{ME}} + +$
      $(P_{\text{ME}}, I) \leftarrow \textbf{proc}(T, (k_{\text{ID}}))$
    return I

$\textbf{proc}(T = (t, \text{op}, \text{ID}, \text{skeleton}, \text{CT}))$:
  $(k_p, \ell_v) \leftarrow \text{GetEntrySecret}(P_{\text{ME}}, v_{\text{ME}}, \text{CT},$
    $\text{skeleton})$
  $(P_{\text{ME}}, I) \leftarrow \text{PathRegen}(P_{\text{ME}}, \ell_v, \text{skeleton}, k_p,$
    $\text{CT})$
  return (P_{ME}, I)

$\textbf{proc}(T = (t, \text{op}, \text{ME}, \text{skeleton}, \text{CT}), k_{\text{ME}})$:
  $(P_{\text{ME}}, I) \leftarrow \text{PathRegen}(P_{\text{ME}}, \text{ME},$
    $\text{skeleton}, k_{\text{ME}}, \text{CT})$
  return (P_{ME}, I)

Fig. 3. Generic construction of multicast scheme GUS that achieves security in the user-mult security game.

3. For every child u of v that has a *blue* edge from v or is a *utilized* node in the frontier of skeleton, it retrieves $(k_{d,u}, k_{e,u}, \ell_u)$ from node u, computes $(k'_{e,u}, c) \leftarrow \text{UEnc}(k_{e,u}, k_s)$, $\text{ct} \leftarrow (c, \ell_v, \ell_u)$, sets $\text{CT}[u] \leftarrow \text{ct}$, and lastly writes $(k_{d,u}, k'_{e,u}, \ell_u)$ to node u.
4. If v is the root, it sets $I \leftarrow \text{dprf}(k_p, \perp)$.

Group Operations. To create a group $G = (\text{ID}_1, \ldots, \text{ID}_n)$, the manager first increments t then calls $(\tau'_{\text{mka}}, \text{skeleton}) \leftarrow \text{INIT}(\tau_{\text{mka}}, G)$, which initializes the tree with the IDs in G at its leaves in τ_{mka} and returns the skeleton (which will be the whole tree). Then they call $(I, \text{K}, \text{CT}, \tau''_{\text{mka}}) \leftarrow \text{SecretGen}(\text{skeleton}, \tau'_{\text{mka}})$ to generate secrets and ciphertexts for skeleton, set $T \leftarrow (t, \text{create}, -1, \text{skeleton}, \text{CT})$ and return (I, T, K).

To add a user ID to the group, the manager first increments t then calls $(\tau'_{\text{mka}}, \text{skeleton}) \leftarrow \text{ADD}(\tau_{\text{mka}}, \text{ID})$, which adds a leaf for ID to τ_{mka}. Then they call $(I, \mathsf{K}, \mathsf{CT}, \tau''_{\mathsf{mka}}) \leftarrow$ SecretGen(skeleton, τ'_{mka}) to generate new secrets and ciphertexts for skeleton, set $T \leftarrow (t, \mathsf{add}, \mathsf{ID}, \mathsf{skeleton}, \mathsf{CT})$ and oob value $k_{\mathsf{ID}} \leftarrow$ $\mathsf{K}[\mathsf{ID}]$, and return (I, T, k_{ID}).

To remove a group member ID from the group, the group manager increments t then calls $(\tau'_{\mathsf{mka}}, \mathsf{skeleton}) \leftarrow \text{REMOVE}(\tau_{\mathsf{mka}}, \mathsf{ID})$, which removes the leaf for ID from τ_{mka}. Then they call $(I, \mathsf{K}, \mathsf{CT}, \tau''_{\mathsf{mka}}) \leftarrow$ SecretGen(skeleton, τ'_{mka}) to generate new secrets and ciphertexts for skeleton, set $T \leftarrow (t, \mathsf{rem}, \mathsf{ID}, \mathsf{skeleton}, \mathsf{CT})$, and return (I, T).

To update the secrets of a group member ID, the group manager first increments t, then, in the procedure skeleton $\leftarrow$ SkelGen($\tau_{\mathsf{mka}}, \mathsf{ID}$), forms the skeleton skeleton, consisting of the nodes on the direct path of v_{ID} (the leaf occupied by ID) and its frontier being the copath of v_{ID}. They do so by traversing the direct path of v_{ID}, and for each node v besides v_{ID}, they color the edge to the child of v on the direct path as green. Then they call $(I, \mathsf{K}, \mathsf{CT}, \tau'_{\mathsf{mka}}) \leftarrow$ SecretGen(skeleton, τ_{mka}) to generate new secrets and ciphertexts for skeleton, set control message $T \leftarrow (t, \mathsf{up}, \mathsf{ID}, \mathsf{skeleton}, \mathsf{CT})$ and out-of-band value $k_{\mathsf{ID}} \leftarrow \mathsf{K}[\mathsf{ID}]$, and return (I, T, k_{ID}).[8]

GUS MKA User Operations. Here we define operations for how group members process changes that the group manager makes to the group, in an effort to recover the group secret. In initialization, users simply set $\mathsf{ME} \leftarrow \mathsf{ID}$ for input ID ID, $P_{\mathsf{ME}} \leftarrow \perp$, and $t_{\mathsf{ME}} \leftarrow -1$.

Path regeneration. When processing operations, users will have to regenerate secret pairs in P_{ID}. The procedure $(P_{\mathsf{ID}}, I) \leftarrow$ PathRegen($P_{\mathsf{ID}}, \ell_w, \mathsf{skeleton}, k_s, \mathsf{CT}$):

1. First finds w corresponding to the label ℓ_w in skeleton and then traverses the direct path of w in skeleton to the root v_r, while at each node u:
   (a) Computes $(k_p \| k'_{d,u} \| k_{e,u}) \leftarrow \mathsf{dprf}(k_s, k_{d,u})$, where $k_{d,u}$ is the current encryption key at u (if it exists, $\perp$ otherwise) and writes $(k'_{d,u}, k_{e,u}, \ell_u)$ to u in P_{ID}.
   (b) Then, if the edge in skeleton from u to its parent v is blue, the procedure:
       i. Retrieves $\mathsf{CT}[u] = (c, \ell_v, \ell_u)$ then computes $(k'_p, k'_{e,u}) \leftarrow \mathsf{UDec}(k_{e,u}, c)$, and writes $(k'_{d,u}, k'_{e,u}, \ell_u)$ to u.
       ii. In this case, k'_p is used at v, i.e. $k_s \leftarrow k'_p$.
   (c) Otherwise, k_p is used at v, i.e. $k_s \leftarrow k_p$.
2. Lastly, it returns $I \leftarrow \mathsf{dprf}(k_p, \perp)$, where k_p was generated at the root v_r.

Processing Control Messages. A user processing a control message $T = (t, \mathsf{op}, \mathsf{ID}, \mathsf{skeleton}, \mathsf{CT})$ first checks that either 1. $t_{\mathsf{ME}} = t-1$; or 2. $t_{\mathsf{ME}} = -1 \wedge \mathsf{op} \in \{\mathsf{create}, \mathsf{add}\} \wedge \mathsf{ID} \in \{-1, \mathsf{ME}\}$. If not, they stop processing. Otherwise, they first check if $\mathsf{op} = \mathsf{rem} \wedge \mathsf{ID} = \mathsf{ME}$; if so, they set $t_{\mathsf{ME}} \leftarrow -1$ and stop processing.

Otherwise, they increment t_{ME}. Then if $\mathsf{ID} \in \{-1, \mathsf{ME}\}$, that user needs to completely refresh their secret path P_{ME} as a result of processing the

---

[8] Note: we do not actually have to include the skeleton, since the tree does not actually change after updates, but we do for ease of exposition. It should not affect the complexity of the scheme since its size should be proportional to that of CT.

operation from which T was generated. Using the dPRF key k_{ME} (sent via an out-of-band channel) for the leaf v_{ME}, the user computes $(P_{ME}, I) \leftarrow$ PathRegen$(P_{ME}, ME, \text{skeleton}, k_{ME}, CT)$ and returns I.

Otherwise, if ID $\notin \{ME, -1\}$, she needs only change part of her secret path P_{ME} as a result of processing the operation on ID from which T was generated. She:

1. First finds the node u that is on the direct path of her corresponding leaf v_{ME} and is in the frontier of skeleton.
2. Then retrieves the ciphertext $(c, \ell_v, \ell_u) \leftarrow CT[u]$.
3. Next, retrieves $(k_{d,u}, k_{e,u}, \ell_u)$ from u and computes $(k_p, k'_{e,u}) \leftarrow$ UDec$(k_{e,u}, c)$ to obtain the dPRF key k_p used at the parent v of u, then writes $(k_{d,u}, k'_{e,u}, \ell_u)$ to u.

We call this operation $(k_p, \ell_v) \leftarrow$ GetEntrySecret$(P_{ME}, v_{ME}, CT, \text{skeleton})$. They then compute $(P_{ME}, I) \leftarrow$ PathRegen$(P_{ME}, \ell_v, \text{skeleton}, k_p, CT)$ and return I.

4.3 Security of GUS MKA Protocol

Theorem 1 (security of GUS). *Let Q be the number of queries an adversary makes to the oracles of the user-mult game. Assume* dprf *is a $(t_{dprf}, \varepsilon_{dprf})$-secure pseudorandom generator,* uske *is a $(t_{cpa*}, \varepsilon_{cpa*})$-CPA*-secure USKE scheme, and τ_{mka} is a $(s_{tree}, s_{skel}, d, \deg(\tau_{mka}))$-tree. Then,* GUS *is a $(s_{tree}, \deg(\tau_{mka}) \cdot s_{skel}, \deg(\tau_{mka}) \cdot s_{skel}, s_{skel}, t, q_c, n_{max}, \varepsilon)$-secure MKA protocol with respect to the* user-mult *security game for $\varepsilon \in \{\varepsilon_S, \varepsilon_{RO}\}$, where $t \approx t_{dprf} \approx t_{cpa*}$. In the standard model, $\varepsilon_S = q_c(Q \cdot \varepsilon_{dprf} + 2\varepsilon_{cpa*} \cdot \deg(\tau_{mka})) \cdot (2 \deg(\tau_{mka}))^d \cdot Q^{(\deg(\tau_{mka}) \cdot d + 1)}$. In the random oracle model, $\varepsilon_{RO} = q_c(\varepsilon_{cpa*} \cdot 2(s_{tree} \cdot Q)^2 + \text{negl})$.*

The proof of Theorem 1 is provided in the full version [9].

Corollary 1.

1. *If the tree used in the* GUS *protocol is a LBBT, then* GUS *is a $(O(n_{max}), O(\log n_{max}), O(\log n_{max}), O(\log n_{max}), t, q_c, n_{max}, \varepsilon)$-secure MKA protocol, where $\varepsilon_S = O(q_c n_{max}^2 \cdot Q^{2\log(n_{max})+1} \cdot (Q\varepsilon_{dprf} + \varepsilon_{cpa*}))$ and $\varepsilon_{RO} = O(q_c \varepsilon_{cpa*} \cdot (n_{max}Q)^2)$.*
2. *If the tree used in the* GUS *protocol is a 2–3 tree or LLRBT, then* GUS *is a $(O(n_{curr}), O(\log n_{curr}), O(\log n_{curr}), O(\log n_{curr}), t, q_c, n_{max}, \varepsilon)$-secure MKA protocol, where $\varepsilon_S = O(q_c n_{curr}^3 \cdot Q^{2\log(n_{curr})+1} \cdot (Q\varepsilon_{dprf} + \varepsilon_{cpa*}))$ and $\varepsilon_{RO} = O(q_c \varepsilon_{cpa*} \cdot (n_{max}Q)^2)$.*

Proof. In the full version [9], we show that LBBTs are $(n_{max}, \log n_{max}, \log n_{max}, 2)$-trees, 2–3 trees are $(n_{curr}, \log n_{curr}, \log n_{curr}, 3)$-trees and LLRBTs are $(n_{curr}, \log n_{curr}, \log n_{curr}, 2)$-trees. The results follow easily from this. $\square$

4.4   Comparison of Trees in GUS

Here we compare the performance of GUS using LBBTs, 2–3 trees, and *restricted* LLRBTs empirically (see the full version [9] for the details of these trees; we use restricted instead of normal LLRBTs simply because they give empirically slightly better performance).[9] We simulate GUS with the different trees on a randomized sequence of Add/Remove/Update operations, starting from a certain initial group size. The measure we adopt is the number of encryptions per operation, which encapsulates the goal of reducing communication for bandwidth-constrained devices.

Following [3] in the TreeKEM context, the scales of the simulations we conduct are represented by tree sizes $2^3, 2^4, \ldots, 2^{14}$; for simulation with tree size 2^i, the initial group size is 2^{i-1}, and the number of operations is $10 \cdot 2^i$, where each operation is sampled to be an Add/Remove/Update operation with ratio 1:1:8 (and the user to be removed/updated is chosen uniformly at random from current group members), as one expects updates to be more frequent.

As shown in the graph at the top left of Fig. 4, although 2–3 trees have better worst-case complexity $O(\log n_{\mathrm{curr}})$ than the complexity $O(\log n_{\mathrm{max}})$ of LBBTs, they empirically suffer, likely from the large overhead introduced by degree-3 nodes. Moreover, although restricted LLRBTs are isomorphic to 2–3 trees, they lead to dramatically improved efficiency in terms of number of encryptions, outperforming both 2–3 trees and LBBTs in a stable manner, likely due to improved asymptotic complexity and also retention of degree-2 nodes.

To see the difference between worst-case $O(\log n_{\mathrm{curr}})$ and $(\log n_{\mathrm{max}})$ complexity, we repeated the simulations, but this time before performing the operations with 1:1:8 ratio, we first remove a random choice of 99% of the users from the group (and consequently the number of operations becomes $0.1 \cdot 2^i$). Removing a large number of users can happen in practice, e.g., after a popular event or livestream has concluded. As shown in the graph at the top right of Fig. 4, this time both 2–3 trees and LLRBTs, which have worst-case complexity $O(\log n_{\mathrm{curr}})$, have better performance in accordance with the decrease of the group size, while the performance of LBBTs, which have worst-case complexity $O(\log n_{\mathrm{max}})$, does not improve even once the group becomes 99% smaller.

To provide more evidence that $O(\log n_{\mathrm{curr}})$ instead of $O(\log n_{\mathrm{max}})$ complexity makes a difference, we conduct additional simulations with initial tree size 2^{14} while increasing the probability of Remove operations from the previous 10% to as large as 12.5% (and decreasing the probability of Add operations so that the 80% probability of Update operations remains). Thus, in these experiments the group size has a decreasing trend during the execution of the operations.[10] As can be observed in the graph at the bottom of Fig. 4, both 2–3 trees and LLRBTs (complexity $O(\log n_{\mathrm{curr}})$) benefit from the decreasing trend of group

---

[9] See https://github.com/abienstock/Multicast-Key-Agreement for the code.

[10] Note that 12.5% is the threshold such that the group size does not approach zero in expectation, as the number of operations $10 \cdot 2^i$ is 20 times more than the initial group size 2^{i-1} and thus the difference between the probabilities of Remove and Add operations needs to be less than $1/20 = 5\%$.

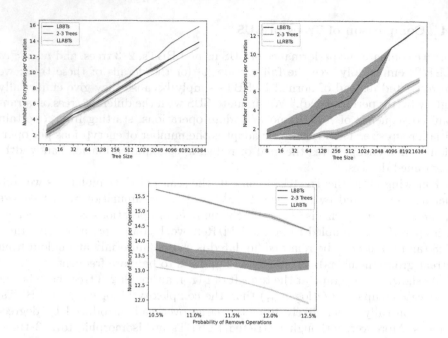

Fig. 4. Top Left: number of encryptions per operation of GUS using different trees in simulations with different initial tree sizes. Top Right: same as top left, except that at the beginning of simulations a random choice of 99% of the users are removed. Bottom: number of encryptions per operation of GUS using different trees in simulations with initial tree size 2^{14} and different probabilities of Remove operations. The bands illustrate one standard deviation under 8 independently repeated experiments.

size, while LBBTs (complexity $O(\log n_{\max})$) hardly benefit. Besides, the variance when using LBBTs is dramatically larger than 2–3 trees and LLRBTs, which verifies that the performance of LBBTs is highly sensitive to the actual choices of removed users and cannot directly benefit from the decreasing trend of group size. Moreover, the performance of LLRBTs is stable and is better than that of LBBTs by roughly at least twice the huge standard deviation, which further verifies that LLRBTs outperform LBBTs in a stable manner.

5   Adding Security for Group Manager Corruptions

In this section, we introduce a security definition that requires both security with respect to user corruptions, and FS and eventual PCS for group manager corruptions: If the secret state of the group manager is leaked at some point, all previous group secrets remain hidden from the attacker. Furthermore, once every user has their secrets updated by the group manager or is removed from the group after her corruption, all future group secrets remain hidden.

Before we formally define this security, we observe that our GUS construction indeed already achieves it – the MKA tree only stores unused USKE keys and thus the adversary learns nothing about old group secrets from corrupting the group manager (eventual PCS also trivially follows). However, the group manager has large *local* storage in GUS (the whole MKA tree), which is undesirable. Therefore, in the full version [9] (due to space limitations) we slightly modify our GUS construction to create our GMS (Generic Manager Security) construction, which has the above security, but $O(1)$ *local* storage and $O(n)$ *remote* storage for the group manager. We show how the group manager can use Forward Secret Encrypted RAM [10] (FS eRAM) in the GUS MKA scheme to achieve this. Intuitively, FS eRAM allows a client to securely outsource data storage to some remote server such that if the client's secret storage is leaked, in addition to the outsourced (encrypted) data, then all previously overwritten data remains secure. Canonical FS eRAM schemes allow for $O(1)$ local storage, $O(n)$ remote storage, and only introduce $O(\log n)$ overhead for Read() and Write() operations. Thus, GMS simply uses FS eRAM to outsource storage of the MKA tree, and does everything else as in GUS, so that corruptions of the group manager are forward secret (and eventual PCS trivially follows). Therefore, group manager local storage is $O(1)$, group manager remote storage is $O(n)$, computational complexity of the group manager becomes $O(\log^2 n)$,[11] and all other efficiency measures from GUS stay the same (namely $O(\log n)$ communication).

Although eventual PCS as defined in the security definition may be less than ideal, it allows us to use only symmetric-key encryption for control messages. We in fact show in the full version [9] that public-key encryption is necessary for optimal PCS, i.e., security after one operation following a group manager corruption. Then, we show that achieving optimal PCS (and all the other properties described above) with public-key encryption is easy: In our construction, we simply replace USKE with UPKE (and the group manager only remotely stores the public keys at the tree nodes; with no local storage).

5.1   Group Manager State Separation and Efficiency Measures

For such added properties, we separate the state MKA group manager state Γ into two components: the secret (local) state, Γ_{sec}, which the attacker can only read upon state corruption of the group manager, and public (remote) state Γ_{pub}, for which the attacker *always* has read access. We will use $s_1(n_{\mathrm{curr}}, n_{\mathrm{max}})$ to refer to the worst-case Γ_{sec} space complexity in a group with n_{curr} users currently and n_{max} maximum users across all epochs of the protocol execution. We will also use $s_2(n_{\mathrm{curr}}, n_{\mathrm{max}})$ to refer to the corresponding worst-case Γ_{pub} space complexity.

5.2   MKA Security with Group Manager FS and Eventual PCS

To obtain security with respect to group manager corruptions, in addition to the security captured by user-mult, we create a new security game mgr-mult, in which we add to the user-mult game an additional oracle **mgr-corrupt**, which

---

[11] In the full version [9], we also show how to retain GUS's $O(\log n)$ computational complexity.

simply returns the secret state of the group manager to the adversary. Observe that there are now more trivial attacks which the adversary can use to win mgr-mult (e.g., corrupting the group manager and then challenging before every user has been updated or removed from the group). We therefore check a new **mgr-safe** predicate at the end of the game on the queries $q_1, \ldots, q_q$ in order to determine if the execution had any trivial attacks. In addition to that which **user-safe** checks for, **mgr-safe** also checks for every challenge epoch t^* if the group manager was corrupted in some epoch $t < t^*$, and there was any $ID \in G[t]$ that did not have its secrets updated by the group manager (in an operation for which the oob to ID is not corrupted), and was not removed by the group manager, after the corruption, but before t^*.

mgr-corrupt():	**mgr-safe($q_1, \ldots, q_q$):**
return Γ_{sec}	for (i, j) s.t. $q_i = $ **mgr-corrupt**(), $q_j = $ **chall**(t^*) for some t^*:
	if q2e(q_i) $< t^*$ and $\exists ID \in G[$q2e$(q_i)]$ s.t. $\nexists l$ s.t.
	$0 < $ q2e$(q_i) < $ q2e$(q_l) \leq t^* \wedge ((q_l = $ **update-user**(ID) $\wedge$
	$\nexists m$ s.t. $q_m = $ **corrupt-oob**(q2e(q_l), ID)) $\vee$
	$q_l = $ **remove-user**(ID)):
	return 0
	return **user-safe**($q_1, \ldots, q_q$)

Fig. 5. Oracle and **mgr-safe** safety predicate introduced in the MKA security game mgr-mult for a scheme M = (Minit, Uinit, create, add, upd, proc) to capture forward secrecy and eventual PCS for the group manager, as well as prevent trivial attacks.

Figure 5 denotes both of these changes. The predicate **mgr-safe** uses q2e() to additionally return the epoch corresponding to a query to $q = $ **mgr-corrupt**(). In this case, q2e(q) corresponds to the epoch t that the group manager is in when the query is made (i.e., the epoch defined by the most recent group manager operation **create-group**, **add-user**, **remove-user**, **update-user**).

Advantage. A (t, q_c, n_{max})-*attacker* $\mathcal{A}$ and $\mathsf{Adv}^{M}_{mgr-mult}(\mathcal{A})$ are defined in the same manner as in Sect. 3.3.

Definition 3 (MKA Security with Group Manager FS and Eventual PCS). *A MKA scheme* M *is* $(s_1, s_2, c, t_1, t_2, t', q_c, n_{max}, \varepsilon)$-*secure in* mgr-mult *against adaptive, partially active attackers, if for all* (t', q_c, n_{max})-*attackers,* $\mathsf{Adv}^{M}_{mgr-mult-na}(\mathcal{A}) \leq \varepsilon$, *and the efficiency measures of the group manager and users are* s_1, s_2, c, t_1, t_2 *as defined in Sects. 3.2 and 5.1.*

References

1. Alwen, J., Coretti, S., Dodis, Y., Tselekounis, Y.: Security analysis and improvements for the IETF MLS standard for group messaging. In: Micciancio, D., Ristenpart, T. (eds.) CRYPTO 2020, Part I. LNCS, vol. 12170, pp. 248–277. Springer, Cham (2020). https://doi.org/10.1007/978-3-030-56784-2_9

2. Alwen, J., Coretti, S., Jost, D., Mularczyk, M.: Continuous group key agreement with active security. In: Pass, R., Pietrzak, K. (eds.) TCC 2020, Part II. LNCS, vol. 12551, pp. 261–290. Springer, Cham (2020). https://doi.org/10.1007/978-3-030-64378-2_10

3. Alwen, J., et al.: Keep the dirt: tainted treekem, adaptively and actively secure continuous group key agreement. In: 2021 IEEE Symposium on Security and Privacy (SP). IEEE (2021)

4. Bajaj, S., Sion, R.: Ficklebase: looking into the future to erase the past. In: 2013 IEEE 29th International Conference on Data Engineering (ICDE), pp. 86–97. IEEE

5. Barnes, R., Beurdouche, B., Millican, J., Omara, E., Cohn-Gordon, K., Robert, R.: The Messaging Layer Security (MLS) Protocol. Internet-Draft draft-ietf-mls-protocol-11, Internet Engineering Task Force, December 2020, work in Progress

6. Bellare, M., Lysyanskaya, A.: Symmetric and dual PRFs from standard assumptions: A generic validation of an HMAC assumption. Cryptology ePrint Archive, Report 2015/1198 (2015). https://eprint.iacr.org/2015/1198

7. Bellare, M., Yee, B.: Forward-security in private-key cryptography. In: Joye, M. (ed.) CT-RSA 2003. LNCS, vol. 2612, pp. 1–18. Springer, Heidelberg (2003). https://doi.org/10.1007/3-540-36563-X_1

8. Bhargavan, K., Barnes, R., Rescorla, E.: TreeKEM: Asynchronous decentralized key management for large dynamic groups (2018). https://mailarchive.ietf.org/arch/msg/mls/e3ZKNzPC7Gxrm3Wf0q96dsLZoD8

9. Bienstock, A., Dodis, Y., Tang, Y.: Multicast key agreement, revisited. Cryptology ePrint Archive, Report 2021/1570 (2021). https://eprint.iacr.org/2021/1570

10. Bienstock, A., Dodis, Y., Yeo, K.: Forward secret encrypted RAM: lower bounds and applications. In: Nissim, K., Waters, B. (eds.) TCC 2021, Part III. LNCS, vol. 13044, pp. 62–93. Springer, Cham (2021). https://doi.org/10.1007/978-3-030-90456-2_3

11. Boneh, D., Lipton, R.J.: A revocable backup system. In: USENIX Security Symposium, pp. 91–96 (1996)

12. Bresson, E., Chevassut, O., Pointcheval, D.: Provably authenticated group Diffie-Hellman key exchange—the dynamic case. In: Boyd, C. (ed.) ASIACRYPT 2001. LNCS, vol. 2248, pp. 290–309. Springer, Heidelberg (2001). https://doi.org/10.1007/3-540-45682-1_18

13. Bresson, E., Chevassut, O., Pointcheval, D.: Dynamic group Diffie-Hellman key exchange under standard assumptions. In: Knudsen, L.R. (ed.) EUROCRYPT 2002. LNCS, vol. 2332, pp. 321–336. Springer, Heidelberg (2002). https://doi.org/10.1007/3-540-46035-7_21

14. Bresson, E., Chevassut, O., Pointcheval, D.: Security proofs for an efficient password-based key exchange. In: Jajodia, S., Atluri, V., Jaeger, T. (eds.) ACM CCS 2003, pp. 241–250. ACM Press, Washington, DC, 27–30 October 2003

15. Canetti, R., Garay, J., Itkis, G., Micciancio, D., Naor, M., Pinkas, B.: Multicast security: a taxonomy and some efficient constructions. In: IEEE INFOCOM 1999. Conference on Computer Communications. Proceedings. Eighteenth Annual Joint Conference of the IEEE Computer and Communications Societies. The Future is Now (Cat. No.99CH36320), vol. 2, pp. 708–716 (1999)

16. Di Crescenzo, G., Ferguson, N., Impagliazzo, R., Jakobsson, M.: How to forget a secret. In: Meinel, C., Tison, S. (eds.) STACS 1999. LNCS, vol. 1563, pp. 500–509. Springer, Heidelberg (1999). https://doi.org/10.1007/3-540-49116-3_47

17. Dodis, Y., Karthikeyan, H., Wichs, D.: Updatable public key encryption in the standard model. In: Nissim, K., Waters, B. (eds.) TCC 2021, Part III. LNCS, vol. 13044, pp. 254–285. Springer, Cham (2021). https://doi.org/10.1007/978-3-030-90456-2_9

18. Geambasu, R., Kohno, T., Levy, A.A., Levy, H.M.: Vanish: increasing data privacy with self-destructing data. In: USENIX Security Symposium, vol. 316 (2009)

19. Harney, H., Muckenhirn, C.: RFC2093: Group Key Management Protocol (GKMP) Specification (1997)

20. Jost, D., Maurer, U., Mularczyk, M.: Efficient ratcheting: almost-optimal guarantees for secure messaging. In: Ishai, Y., Rijmen, V. (eds.) EUROCRYPT 2019, Part I. LNCS, vol. 11476, pp. 159–188. Springer, Cham (2019). https://doi.org/10.1007/978-3-030-17653-2_6

21. Katz, J., Yung, M.: Scalable protocols for authenticated group key exchange. In: Boneh, D. (ed.) CRYPTO 2003. LNCS, vol. 2729, pp. 110–125. Springer, Heidelberg (2003). https://doi.org/10.1007/978-3-540-45146-4_7

22. Micciancio, D., Panjwani, S.: Optimal communication complexity of generic multicast key distribution. In: Cachin, C., Camenisch, J.L. (eds.) EUROCRYPT 2004. LNCS, vol. 3027, pp. 153–170. Springer, Heidelberg (2004). https://doi.org/10.1007/978-3-540-24676-3_10

23. Mittra, S.: Iolus: A framework for scalable secure multicasting. In: Proceedings of the ACM SIGCOMM 1997 Conference on Applications, Technologies, Architectures, and Protocols for Computer Communication, SIGCOMM 1997, pp. 277–288. Association for Computing Machinery, New York (1997)

24. Perrin, T., Marlinspike, M.: The double ratchet algorithm (2016). https://signal.org/docs/specifications/doubleratchet/

25. Peterson, Z.N., Burns, R.C., Herring, J., Stubblefield, A., Rubin, A.D.: Secure deletion for a versioning file system. In: FAST, vol. 5 (2005)

26. Porambage, P., Braeken, A., Schmitt, C., Gurtov, A., Ylianttila, M., Stiller, B.: Group key establishment for enabling secure multicast communication in wireless sensor networks deployed for IoT applications. IEEE Access 3, 1503–1511 (2015)

27. Reardon, J., Basin, D., Capkun, S.: Sok: secure data deletion. In: 2013 IEEE Symposium on Security and Privacy, pp. 301–315. IEEE (2013)

28. Reardon, J., Ritzdorf, H., Basin, D., Capkun, S.: Secure data deletion from persistent media. In: Proceedings of the 2013 ACM SIGSAC Conference on Computer and Communications Security, pp. 271–284 (2013)

29. Roche, D.S., Aviv, A., Choi, S.G.: A practical oblivious map data structure with secure deletion and history independence. In: 2016 IEEE Symposium on Security and Privacy (SP), pp. 178–197. IEEE (2016)

30. Sedgewick, R.: Left-leaning red-black trees (2008)

31. Sherman, A.T., McGrew, D.A.: Key establishment in large dynamic groups using one-way function trees. IEEE Trans. Softw. Eng. 29(5), 444–458 (2003)

32. Tselekounis, Y., Coretti, S., Alwen, J., Dodis, Y.: Modular design of secure group messaging protocols and the security of MLS. In: ACM CCS 2021 (2021)

33. Wallner, D., Harder, E., Agee, R.: RFC2627: Key management for multicast: Issues and architectures (1999)

34. Weidner, M., Kleppmann, M., Hugenroth, D., Beresford, A.R.: Key agreement for decentralized secure group messaging with strong security guarantees. Cryptology ePrint Archive, Report 2020/1281 (2020). https://eprint.iacr.org/2020/1281

35. Wong, C.K., Gouda, M., Lam, S.S.: Secure group communications using key graphs. In: Proceedings of the ACM SIGCOMM 1998 Conference on Applications, Technologies, Architectures, and Protocols for Computer Communication, SIGCOMM 1998, pp. 68–79. Association for Computing Machinery, New York (1998)

A Pairing-Free Signature Scheme from Correlation Intractable Hash Function and Strong Diffie-Hellman Assumption

Benoît Chevallier-Mames[✉]

Zama, 41 Boulevard Malherbes, 75008 Paris, France
benoit.chevalliermames@zama.ai
https://zama.ai

Abstract. Goh and Jarecki (Eurocrypt 2003) showed how to get a signature scheme from the computational Diffie-Hellman assumption, and they introduced the name EDL for signatures of this type. The corresponding EDL family of signature schemes is remarkable for several reasons: elegance, simplicity and tight security. However, EDL security proofs stand in the random oracle model, and, to the best of our knowledge, extending this family without using an idealization of hash functions has never been successful.

In this paper, we propose a new signature scheme belonging to the EDL family, which is simple, natural and efficient, without using the random oracle model. Our scheme is based on the very same assumption than the Boneh-Boyen scheme, namely the strong Diffie-Hellman assumption, with the precision that our groups are not bound to being bilinear. We also make use of a correlation-intractable hash function, for a particular relation related to discrete-logarithm.

In addition to the theoretical interest of extending the EDL family without the random oracle model, our scheme is also one of the very few schemes which achieve discrete-log security properties without relying on pairings.

Keywords: Public-key cryptography · Signature schemes · Standard model · Random oracle model · Correlation intractability · Discrete logarithm problem · Diffie-Hellman problem · EDL signature scheme · Boneh-Boyen signature scheme

1 Introduction

Signature schemes have existed since the introduction of public key cryptography [26] and constitute one of the most essential tools in the cryptographic toolbox. Among the various families of schemes that prevail, the so-called online/off-line signatures have the nice property that one can precompute a part

© The Author(s), under exclusive license to Springer Nature Switzerland AG 2022
S. D. Galbraith (Ed.): CT-RSA 2022, LNCS 13161, pp. 26–48, 2022.
https://doi.org/10.1007/978-3-030-95312-6_2

of the signature beforehand, independently from the signed message, and complete the signature generation very quickly once the message is known. Most signature schemes derived from the Fiat-Shamir heuristic [31] are inherently on-line/off-line signature schemes. These schemes are of particular interest in implementations, especially in constrained environments, and have numerous applications. Fortunately, there exist generic constructions that one can use to transform any signature scheme into an on-line/off-line scheme [66] based on chameleon hashing [52].

Before the advancement of (reductionist) provable security, designing a seemingly secure signature scheme was mainly an art, but with the steady accumulation of knowledge, security definitions and constructions [41,42] have been more and more precise, up to the point where the security of a signature scheme can be formally proven under the assumption that some algorithmic problem is hard to solve [67]. Classically, provably secure signatures divide into two categories: the ones based on integer factoring such as RSA [61,62], and the ones based on the discrete log and Diffie-Hellman problems [30,64]. A fundamental breakthrough in security proving has been the now widely adopted Random Oracle (RO) model [4,5], a paradigm that models hash functions used in schemes as randomly chosen functions. The RO model made it possible to prove the security of discrete-log based signature schemes such as Schnorr under the discrete-log assumption thanks to the so-called forking lemma technique [59]. A critical feature of security proofs, however, resides in the "quality" of the reduction that goes along with the proof. A security reduction is said to be tight when its success probability is close to the adversary's success probability, otherwise it is said to be loose [54]. Carefully assessing the tightness of a reduction allows to give concrete security parameters for which the proof results in a meaningful security assurance [5,20,65].

The fact that RO-based security proofs do not imply that a scheme is secure in the real world is known for a long time [14,15,40]. Other works have shown that separations between the RO and the standard models also apply on non-pathological signature schemes such as Schnorr [58] and RSA [27,57]. These limitations as well as the wide adoption of pairings [2,9,10,49] in cryptographic design have empowered the search for new schemes that achieve provable security in the standard model. This has resulted in the appearing of new intractability assumptions such as the strong RSA assumption [25,36] or the strong Diffie-Hellman assumption on bilinear groups [6].

Even though numerous signature schemes are known today which security is proven either in the RO model [10,37,43,60,70] or[1] in the standard model [11,12,23,29] (see also [19,32,45–47,53]), it is striking to observe that, excluding the use of pairings, very few discrete-log-based signature schemes were proven secure in the standard model. This includes notably the generic construction of signature schemes from one-way functions [56,63], [22] (whose signature size grows logarithmically with the number of signatures) and the generic trans-

---

[1] We remark that other hash function idealizations or instantiations have also been investigated, *e.g.,* in [34,45].

formation to turn an identity-based encryption (IBE) scheme into a signature scheme [8,69] with pairing-free but inefficient IBE proposed in [28]. We can also list more recent schemes as [1,33] with their proofs based on the DDH assumption in the *non-programmable* random oracle model.

Contribution. This paper introduces a new, pairing-free signature scheme, which extends the EDL scheme and its variants [16,18,38,39,48,51] which are proven under the computational Diffie-Hellman assumption in the random oracle model. For our construction, we notably borrow ideas to Boneh-Boyen signature scheme [6,7], whose security proof is based on the strong Diffie-Hellman (SDH) assumption in the standard model.

At a high-level view, the basic idea behind our construction is to prove that some group element h is a solution of the SDH problem, *i.e.*, that

$$h = g^{\frac{1}{x+\alpha}}$$

for known g, α and secret (but committed) x. On its own, this part is similar to the Boneh-Boyen scheme. However, while Boneh-Boyen signatures use a bilinear map to prove that h is well-formed, we rather use proofs of equality of discrete logs for the same purpose, as other schemes in the EDL family. As explained further in our security proof, we ensure equality of discrete logs, unless a very unlikely type of collision (that we link to the notion of *correlation-intractability* [14]) is found within one of the hash functions, which is typical to EDL proofs.

We mention that our scheme runs two independent instances of a simpler scheme and is therefore reminiscent to twin signatures [55] even though the final signature is obtained in a specific way. Previous schemes like [25] have also used the principle of a double key and (somehow) a signature which is like the concatenation of two independent-key related underlying signatures. Finally, our scheme has strong connections with OR-proofs [1,24,33], since our security proof is essentially a proof of discrete-log equality in at least one of the two independent instances.

Road-map. The rest of this paper is organized as follows: the next section provides some background on signatures and intractability assumptions. Section 3 describes the EDL and Boneh-Boyen signature schemes, as well as other relevant state of the art regarding pairing-free discrete-log signature schemes. Section 4 is the core of our paper: we describe our new signature scheme and provide a tight security proof based on the strong Diffie-Hellman assumption and the hash function intractability. We finally conclude in Sect. 5.

2   Definitions

This section provides some rather informal background on signature schemes and security notions attached to these. Most of these definitions are classical.

We also define the intractability assumptions on which are based the security proofs of the EDL and Boneh-Boyen signature schemes.

2.1 Signature Schemes

A signature scheme $\mathsf{Sig} = (\mathsf{SetUp}, \mathsf{GenKey}, \mathsf{Sign}, \mathsf{Verify})$ is defined by the four following algorithms:

- The *set-up algorithm* SetUp. On input 1^k, algorithm SetUp produces some common parameters.
- The *key generation algorithm* GenKey. On input 1^k, algorithm GenKey produces a pair $(\mathsf{pk}, \mathsf{sk})$ of matching public (verification) and private (signing) keys.
- The *signing algorithm* Sign. Given a message m in a set of messages $\mathcal{M}$ and a pair of matching public and private keys $(\mathsf{pk}, \mathsf{sk})$, Sign produces a signature σ. Often, the signing algorithm is probabilistic.
- The *verification algorithm* Verify. Given a signature σ, a message $m \in \mathcal{M}$ and a public key pk, Verify tests whether σ is a valid signature of m with respect to pk.

Several security notions have been defined about signature schemes, mainly based on the seminal work of Goldwasser, Micali and Rivest [41,42]. It is now customary to ask for the impossibility of existential forgeries, even against adaptive chosen-message adversaries:

- An *existential forgery* is a signature, valid and generated by the adversary, corresponding to a message which was never submitted to the signature oracle. The corresponding security notion is called *existential unforgeability* (EUF).
- The verification key is public, including to the adversary. But more information may also be available. The strongest kind of information is definitely formalized by the *adaptive chosen-message attacks* (CMA), where the attacker can ask the signer to sign any message of its choice, in an adaptive way.

As a consequence, we say that a signature scheme is *secure* if it prevents existential forgeries, even under adaptive chosen-message attacks (EUF-CMA). This is measured by the following success probability, which should be negligibly small, for any adversary $\mathcal{A}$ which outputs a valid signature σ on a message m that was never submitted to the signature oracle, within a "reasonable" bounded running-time and with at most q_s signature queries to the signature oracle:

$$\mathsf{Succ}_{\mathsf{Sig}}^{\mathsf{EUF-CMA}}(\mathcal{A}, q_s) = \Pr \left[\begin{array}{c} (\mathsf{pk}, \mathsf{sk}) \leftarrow \mathsf{GenKey}(1^k), (m, \sigma) \leftarrow \mathcal{A}^{\mathsf{Sign}(\mathsf{sk}; \cdot)}(\mathsf{pk}) : \\ \mathsf{Verify}(\mathsf{pk}; m, \sigma) = \mathrm{TRUE} \end{array} \right].$$

When the signature generation is not deterministic, several signatures may correspond to the same message. In this case, we do not consider the attacker successful when it outputs a second signature on a message already submitted to the signature oracle. Being given a message-signature pair (m, σ), providing a second signature σ' on the same message m is captured by the adversarial goal of *malleability* [68].

2.2   Intractability Assumptions

Let us consider a cyclic (multiplicatively written) group $\mathbb{G}$ of prime order q generated by g, i.e., $\mathbb{G} = \{g^i, i \in \mathbb{Z}_q\}$.

DL. Solving the discrete log problem in $\mathbb{G}$ consists, given g and $y = g^x$ for some unknown random integer $x \in \mathbb{Z}_q$, in finding the value of $\mathsf{DL}_g(y) = x$.

CDH. Solving the (computational) Diffie-Hellman (CDH) problem is as follows:[2] given (g, g^a, g^x) for unknown random integers $a, x \in \mathbb{Z}_q$, one must compute the group element g^{ax}.

q-SDH (bilinear setting) [6,7]. Let $\mathbb{G}_1$, $\mathbb{G}_2$ and $\mathbb{G}_T$ be three multiplicative groups of prime order q and $e : \mathbb{G}_1 \times \mathbb{G}_2 \to \mathbb{G}_T$ an admissible bilinear map [3, 10,35,44]. The q-strong Diffie-Hellman problem (q-SDH) consists in computing a pair

$$(\alpha, g_2^{\frac{1}{x+\alpha}})$$

given a $(q+2)$-tuple $(g_1, g_1^x, ..., g_1^{x^i}, ..., g_1^{x^q}, g_2, g_2^x)$, for a random integer $x \in \mathbb{Z}_q$, generators g_1 and g_2 of $\mathbb{G}_1$ and $\mathbb{G}_2$ respectively, and a security parameter q. The q-SDH problem on bilinear groups was further studied in [7,17]. Note that g_2, g_2^x may be omitted in the input tuple when $\mathbb{G}_1 = \mathbb{G}_2$.

In this work, we make use of the q-SDH in a general, non-bilinear context.

q-SDH (general setting) [6,7]. Solving q-SDH in the general setting consists in computing a pair

$$(\alpha, g^{\frac{1}{x+\alpha}})$$

given a q-tuple $(g, g^x, ..., g^{x^i}, ..., g^{x^q})$, for a random integer $x \in \mathbb{Z}_q$ and a security parameter q. Note that deciding whether a solution for the bilinear q-SDH problem is valid is easy since the pairing provides a straightforward way to verify it. This is however not the case in the general setting, meaning that q-SDH admits a non-trivial decisional variant.

In particular, q-SDH in the general setting is *non-falsifiable*. However, as shown in Sect. 4.4, with auxiliary information (the (s_i, c_i)'s of the scheme described in Sect. 4.2), one can efficiently decide if a pair is a valid q-SDH pair.

3   Prior Art

We now review signatures schemes that enjoy a tight EUF-CMA security under the discrete-log-related complexity assumptions discussed above. In this section, ℓ_p, ℓ_q, and ℓ_r denote security parameters. The schemes make use of cyclic groups $\mathbb{G}$ (resp. $\mathbb{G}_1$ and $\mathbb{G}_2$) of prime order q generated by g (resp. g_1 and g_2) where q is a ℓ_q-bit prime. We assume that elements of $\mathbb{G}$ (resp. $\mathbb{G}_1$ and $\mathbb{G}_2$) can be represented as binary strings in $\{0,1\}^{\ell_p}$. The set of messages to be signed is denoted $\mathcal{M}$.

---

[2] Whether DL and CDH are equivalent is actually an open question.

3.1   The EDL Family of Signatures

The EDL[3] signature scheme, independently proposed in [16,48], is defined as follows.

Set-up: Let two hash functions, $\mathcal{H} : \mathcal{M} \times \{0,1\}^{\ell_r} \to \mathbb{G}$ and $\mathcal{G} : \mathbb{G}^6 \to \mathbb{Z}_q$.

Key generation: The private key is a random number $x \in \mathbb{Z}_q$. The corresponding public key is $y = g^x$.

Signature: To sign a message $m \in \mathcal{M}$, one first randomly chooses $r \in \{0,1\}^{\ell_r}$, and computes $h = \mathcal{H}(m,r)$ and $z = h^x$. Follows a proof of logarithm equality that $\mathsf{DL}_h(z) = \mathsf{DL}_g(y)$: for a random number $k \in \mathbb{Z}_q$, one computes $u = g^k$, $v = h^k$, $c = \mathcal{G}(g,h,y,z,u,v)$ and $s = k + cx \bmod q$. The signature on m is $\sigma = (z,r,s,c)$.

Verification: To verify a signature $\sigma = (z,r,s,c) \in \mathbb{G} \times \{0,1\}^{\ell_r} \times \mathbb{Z}_q^2$ on a message $m \in \mathcal{M}$, one computes $h = \mathcal{H}(m,r)$, $u = g^s y^{-c}$ and $v = h^s z^{-c}$. The signature σ is accepted iff $c = \mathcal{G}(g,h,y,z,u,v)$.

In the random oracle model, the chosen-message security of EDL reduces to the security of the computational Diffie-Hellman problem [38], by showing that the EDL scheme is a proof that $\mathsf{DL}_h(z) = \mathsf{DL}_g(y) = x$. The scheme yields signatures of $(\ell_p + 2\ell_q + \ell_r)$ bits (for typical setting, $\ell_r = 111$). In its classical use, the scheme cannot be used with precomputations (*a.k.a.* coupons) before knowing the message, but, as noted by Goh and Jarecki, one can use the technique of [66] based on chameleon hash functions [52] to transform this signature into a signature with coupons, at the price of larger signatures.

The Katz-Wang Variants. In [51][4], Katz and Wang proposed two variants of EDL, one based on DDH assumption, and the other which yields shorter signatures still with tight relation to the CDH problem.

Being relatively generic to signature schemes with randomness,[5] the idea of Katz and Wang is to remove the *randomness* of r, and to replace it by *unpredictability*. Namely, r is replaced by a bit b that can only be computed by the signer (*e.g.*, b is the result of a pseudo-random function, under a secret key included in the signing key):[6] the signatures are then (z,b,s,c), and so are shorter than EDL signatures by 110 bits. This modification gives a signature scheme with a signature length of $(\ell_p + 2\ell_q + 1)$ bits. In this scheme, as in EDL, only u can be computed off-line, and so the on-line part of the signature is two modular exponentiations in $\mathbb{G}$.

---

[3] The name EDL was proposed in [38], based upon the fact that the scheme is a proof of equality of discrete-logarithms.

[4] A remarkable unification of [38,51] papers appeared in [39].

[5] Notably, the very same idea can be applied on Probabilistic RSA-FDH to get a tight signature scheme with a single extra bit.

[6] In other words, in EDL, signing few times the same message would result in different random numbers r, while doing the same with Katz-Wang scheme would give always the same bit b.

The Chevallier-Mames Variant. In [18], another EDL variant was proposed. The main modification is how the value h is computed. Instead of being $h = \mathcal{H}(m, r)$ as in EDL or $h = \mathcal{H}(m, b)$ as in Katz-Wang scheme, one sets $h = \mathcal{H}(u)$.

Set-up: Let two hash functions, $\mathcal{H} : \mathbb{G} \to \mathbb{G}$ and $\mathcal{G} : \mathcal{M} \times \mathbb{G}^6 \to \mathbb{Z}_q$.

Key generation: The private key is a random number $x \in \mathbb{Z}_q$, while the corresponding public key is $y = g^x$.

Signature: To sign a message $m \in \mathcal{M}$, one first randomly chooses $k \in \mathbb{Z}_q$, and computes $u = g^k$, $h = \mathcal{H}(u)$, $z = h^x$ and $v = h^k$. Next, one computes $c = \mathcal{G}(m, g, h, y, z, u, v)$ and $s = k + cx \bmod q$. The signature on m is $\sigma = (z, s, c)$.

Verification: To verify a signature $\sigma = (z, s, c) \in \mathbb{G} \times \mathbb{Z}_q^2$ on a message $m \in \mathcal{M}$, one computes $u = g^s y^{-c}$, $h = \mathcal{H}(u)$, and $v = h^s z^{-c}$. The signature σ is accepted iff $c = \mathcal{G}(m, g, h, y, z, u, v)$.

The signatures are a little bit smaller than the EDL's ones: they are only $(\ell_p + 2\ell_q)$-bit long. Interestingly, this scheme natively allows on-line/off-line signature scheme, i.e., without affecting the efficiency of the signature or of the verification nor the signature size. The scheme remains tightly related to the computational Diffie-Hellman problem, still in the random oracle model.

Proving Equality of Discrete Logs. A common part of the respective proofs of the previous schemes (see [18,39] for more details) consists in showing that it is very unlikely that the forger can provide a valid signature with $u = g^k$, $v = h^{k'}$ and $z = h^{x'}$ with $k \neq k'$ or $x \neq x'$. More precisely, the forger would need to find (m, k, k', x') such that[7]

$$c = \mathcal{G}(m, g, h, y, z, u, v) = \mathcal{G}(m, g, h, y, h^{x'}, g^k, h^{k'}) = \frac{k - k'}{x' - x} \bmod q$$

which is doable only with a probability $\frac{q_{\mathcal{G}}}{q}$ if $\mathcal{G}$ is assumed to be a random oracle and $q_{\mathcal{G}}$ is the number of requests to $\mathcal{G}$ oracle.

Remark that previous equation can be rewritten as follows, if one defines $\beta = \mathsf{DL}_g(h)$:

$$c = \mathcal{G}(m, g, g^\beta, g^x, g^{\beta x'}, g^k, g^{\beta k'}) = \frac{k - k'}{x' - x} \bmod q$$

which can also be seen as

$$\mathcal{G}(m, g, g^{a_1}, g^{a_2}, g^{a_3}, g^{a_4}, g^{a_5}) = \frac{a_4 - a_5/a_1}{a_3/a_1 - a_2} = \frac{a_1 a_4 - a_5}{a_3 - a_1 a_2} \bmod q$$

In our scheme, we formalize the notion of *discrete-log collision resistant* hash function (in Sect. 4.3) and use it to prove the security of our scheme (in Sect. 4.4).

---

[7] Strictly, the equality is for Chevallier-Mames variant; for EDL or Katz-Wang, m is not an input of $\mathcal{G}$, without changing anything to the analysis.

3.2   Boneh-Boyen Signatures

In [6,7], a completely different way to prove that a tuple is a Diffie-Hellman tuple was used: the pairing.

Set-up: Let $\mathbb{G}_1$, $\mathbb{G}_2$ and $\mathbb{G}_T$ be three groups whose prime order is q, for which it exists an efficient pairing $e : \mathbb{G}_1 \times \mathbb{G}_2 \to \mathbb{G}_T$.

Key generation: Let g_1 and g_2 be two random generators of $\mathbb{G}_1$ and $\mathbb{G}_2$. Let x, y be two random integers of $\mathbb{Z}_q$. Let $u = g_2{}^x$, $v = g_2{}^y$, $z = e(g_1, g_2)$. The private key is (x, y, g_1) and the corresponding public key is (g_2, u, v, z).

Signature: To sign a message $m \in \mathbb{Z}_q$, one first randomly chooses $r \in \mathbb{Z}_q$ $(r \neq -\frac{x+m}{y})$, and computes $s = g_1^{\frac{1}{x+m+y \cdot r}}$. The signature on m is $\sigma = (s, r)$.

Verification: To verify a signature $\sigma = (s, r) \in \mathbb{G}_1 \times \mathbb{Z}_q$ on a message $m \in \mathcal{M}$, one checks that $e(s, u \cdot g_2{}^m \cdot v^r) = z$. If true, the signature σ is accepted.

Boneh-Boyen signature scheme has the following notable differences with EDL variants: its security is based on q_s-SDH problem (where q_s is the number of signature queries), and does not require the random oracle model. A security proof in the standard model rather than the RO model is arguably an important improvement over pre-existing schemes. However, we stress that the result was mainly achieved thanks to the use of pairings. Evaluating a pairing at verification time may result in a slower and more complicated implementation as opposed to when only common group operations are performed.

3.3   Existing Pairing-Free Discrete-Log Signature Schemes in the Standard Model

In the set of signature schemes provably secure under a discrete-log-kind assumption, it is remarkable that most schemes rely on pairing. We succinctly describe here two schemes which are pairing-free but significantly less efficient than the scheme we propose in Sect. 4.2.

First, it is a classical result that signature schemes can be generically built from one-way functions [56,63]. This type of construction is however particularly inefficient in term of signature size.

Cramer-Damgård Scheme. In [22], Cramer and Damgård have shown a generic construction, which can be instantiated for the discrete-log case as described in their Sect. 6. The principle relies on the following zero-knowledge protocol.

Key generation: Let d be a security parameter. Let x_i be random elements of $\mathbb{Z}_q$, and $y_i = g^{x_i}$, for $i \in \{0, ..., d-1\}$. The private key is $\{x_i\}$ and the corresponding public key is $\{y_i\}$.

Commit: The prover generates a random $k \in \mathbb{Z}_q$ and sends $u = g^k$ to the verifier.

Challenge: The verifier generates random $c_i \in \mathbb{Z}_q$ for $i \in \{0, ..., d-1\}$, and sends them to the prover.

Answer: The prover computes $s = k + \sum_{i=0}^{d-1} c_i \cdot x_i \bmod q$ and sends s to the verifier.

Verification: Finally, the verifier checks whether $g^s = u \cdot \prod_{i=0}^{d-1} y_i^{c_i}$.

With the use of an authentication tree, Cramer and Damgård get a signature scheme whose signature size is $\mathcal{O}(\ell_p \cdot \log(q_s))$. The number of exponentiations to compute or verify the signature also depends on the depth of the tree.

Generic transformation from an identity-based encryption scheme into a signature scheme. Another possibility to have a scheme based on a discrete-log assumption without relying on pairings is to use the generic transformation from an identity-based encryption scheme into a signature scheme, that was proposed by Boneh and Franklin in seminal [8] (see [69] as well). Regarding the purpose of this paper, this generic transformation can be combined with pairing-free scheme proposed in [28] to get a signature scheme. However, as remarked by Döttling and Garg, the scheme is particularly inefficient.

3.4 OR-Based Signature Schemes

OR-proofs [24] are one of the fascinating techniques used to achieve security proofs, which was notably recently used to achieve signatures schemes as in [1, 33]. In this section, we remind the reader of the first construction, which can notably be instantiated to get a scheme based on the DDH assumption in the non-programmable random oracle, in a scheme comparable to ours.

Fischlin, Harasser and Janson scheme. The principle is to have two Sides 0 and 1, with their respective DDH tuple $(y_i, h_i, z_i) = (g^{x_i}, g^{a_i}, g^{a_i \, x_i})$. One Side $b \in \{0, 1\}$ is the preferred side. Roughly, the non-preferred side will be completely simulated (and so x_{1-b} is not needed in the signature processing), while the Side b will go in a process very close to Katz-Wang DDH scheme [51]. However, for the security of the construction, the role of the two sides remains completely symmetric, such that they are non distinguishable.

Set-up: Let a hash function $\mathcal{H} : \{0,1\} \times \mathbb{G}^7 \times \mathbb{G}^2 \times \mathcal{M} \to \mathbb{Z}_q$.

Key generation: Let b be a random bit and $\tilde{b} = 1 - b$. Let g and h_b be two generators of $\mathbb{G}$ and x_b be a scalar of $\mathbb{Z}_q$. Let $(y_b, z_b) = (g^{x_b}, h_b^{x_b})$. Finally, let $(g, y_{\tilde{b}}, h_{\tilde{b}}, z_{\tilde{b}})$ be another random DDH tuple. The private key is (b, x_b) while the public key is $\mathrm{pk} = (g, y_0, y_1, h_0, h_1, z_0, z_1)$.

Signature: To sign a message $m \in \mathcal{M}$, one first pick a random $k_b \in \mathbb{Z}_q$, then compute $u_b = g_b^{k_b}$ and $v_b = h_b^{k_b}$, which is the commitment of the Side b. Then, the Side $\tilde{b}$ is completely simulated by picking a random $s_{\tilde{b}} \in \mathbb{Z}_q$, and computing $c_{\tilde{b}} = \mathcal{H}(b, \mathrm{pk}, u_b, v_b, m)$, $u_{\tilde{b}} = g_{\tilde{b}}^{s_{\tilde{b}}} y_{\tilde{b}}^{-c_{\tilde{b}}}$ and $v_{\tilde{b}} = h_{\tilde{b}}^{s_{\tilde{b}}} z_{\tilde{b}}^{-c_{\tilde{b}}}$. Finally, the Side b is completed, by computing $c_b = \mathcal{H}(\tilde{b}, \mathrm{pk}, u_{\tilde{b}}, v_{\tilde{b}}, m)$ and $s_b = k_b + c_b x_b \bmod q$. The signature is $\sigma = (s_0, s_1, c_0, c_1)$.

Verification: To verify a signature $\sigma = (s_0, s_1, c_0, c_1) \in \mathbb{Z}_q^4$ on a message $m \in \mathcal{M}$, one computes $u_0 = g_0{}^{s_0} y_0{}^{-c_0}$, $u_1 = g_1{}^{s_1} y_1{}^{-c_1}$, $v_0 = h_0{}^{s_0} z_0{}^{-c_0}$ and $v_1 = h_1{}^{s_1} z_1{}^{-c_1}$. The signature is accepted iff $c_0 = \mathcal{H}(1, \mathrm{pk}, u_1, v_1, m)$ and $c_1 = \mathcal{H}(0, \mathrm{pk}, u_0, v_0, m)$.

The fundamental principle in this construction is that the commitment (u, v) used in the computation of c is the commitment from the other side, which allows the author of [33] to prove that their scheme has a tight security on the DDH in the non-programmable random oracle model.

Regarding efficiency, we can note that the signature size is $4\ell_q$ and that some parts of the computations (more precisely u_b and v_b) can be done before the message is known. Let us remark however that it is also possible for the signer to know the discrete logarithm $x_{\bar{b}}$ as well, not to have to simulate the Side b, in order to be able to precompute $u_{\bar{b}}$ and $v_{\bar{b}}$ as well.

4   Our Signature Scheme

4.1   Intuition of the Design

In this section, we explain how we finally came to our design, to explain its difference with previous state of the art, and why we had to do these changes.

From the beginning, we wanted to extend the EDL family described in Sect. 3.1 to the standard model. However, this will is blocked in its early steps by the fact that, in these schemes, h is the output of the hash function $\mathcal{H}$—although the exact form of h is different from one scheme to the other—and that there is some h^x to compute: without the random oracle model, it seems impossible to compute such quantities during the signature queries, unless by having the secret key x. In other words, it seems at first glance that $\mathcal{H}$ *has* to be a random oracle to allow the security reduction to compute pairs of the form (h, h^x) without key x.

Inversing the problem. To be able to achieve security without the random oracle model (and notably, the programmability property), we had to fundamentally change the design, and notably, we somehow *inversed the problem*, by—let's say—"making h hard to compute" and "z simple to deduce". For this, we borrow ideas from [6] and notably make use of a q_s-SDH instance to essentially replace the random oracle.

To this end, we now pose $h = g^{\frac{1}{x+\alpha}}$ for some α (which requires the secret key x to be computed) and see that $z = h^x$ is easy to compute since

$$z = g^{\frac{x}{x+\alpha}} = g \cdot h^{-\alpha}.$$

Therefore, being given h, if one can prove that z defined by $z = g \cdot h^{-\alpha}$ is such that $z = h^x$ then the well-formedness of h—i.e., , the fact that $h = g^{\frac{1}{x+\alpha}}$—is automatically proven. As should be already clear to the reader, we are using technique a-la EDL to prove that $z = h^x$.

Checking equality of logarithms. However, our goal is still not achieved: the second complicated part is to be able to prove that the two logarithms $\mathsf{DL}_g(y)$ and $\mathsf{DL}_h(z)$ are equal (to answer signature queries), but at the same time, from the signature forge, to learn something (to answer the q_s-SDH challenge).

In the random-oracle proofs, achieving these two things at the same time is easy, since one can simulate thanks to the random oracle model, and simultaneously, know a new $z = h^x$ from the forge, to solve the CDH problem. Very informally,[8] during signature queries, the random oracle allows to take random s, c and deduce u, v, h, z from these quantities, and still "close the loop", *i.e.*, make that $c = \mathcal{G}(m, g, h, u, v, y, z)$. In the standard model, on the contrary, $\mathcal{G}$ function cannot be bent to our will.

Consequently, a second major change of design in our scheme as compared to the rest of the EDL family is to have a double-key mechanism. We have two sides (see the full description in our next section), which are linked together by a new degree of liberty e. In the security proof, the reduction knows one (and only one) of the two keys, and can simulate the unknown side a bit like in the random oracle model, and complete the signature with the known key. For this aspect of the design and of the proof, we are very close to the OR-based schemes described in Sect. 3.4. As we will show in the security proof, the known side is indistinguishable for the adversary, and even with this new degree of liberty, the security reduction can turn the forge into an answer to the q_s-SDH challenge.

4.2   Description

Our scheme is made of two instances of the same flow, which we will call Side 0 and Side 1. Note that this almost entirely symmetric design presents some similarities with the approach undertaken with twin signatures [55] or other schemes as [1, 25, 33].

The signature scheme is depicted as follows.

Set-up: Let ℓ_p and ℓ_q denote security parameters. Select a cyclic group $\mathbb{G}$ of prime order q. Let $\mathbb{G}^\diamond$ be equal to $\mathbb{G}\backslash\{1\}$. Finally, select two hash functions, $\mathcal{H}: \mathbb{G}^2 \to \mathbb{Z}_q$ and $\mathcal{G}: \mathcal{M} \times \mathbb{G}^{11} \to \mathbb{Z}_q$.

Key generation: Let g, g_0 and g_1 be three random generators of $\mathbb{G}$. The private key is made of two random numbers $(x_0, x_1) \in \mathbb{Z}_q^2$. The corresponding public key is (g, g_0, g_1, y_0, y_1) with $y_0 = g^{x_0}$ and $y_1 = g^{x_1}$.

Signature: To sign a message $m \in \mathcal{M}$, randomly select $(k_0, k_1, e) \in \mathbb{Z}_q^3$, and then proceed as follows

---

[8] The reader is referred to original papers [18, 38, 39, 51] for more formal proofs.

Side 0

$u_0 = g^{k_0}$

$$\alpha = \mathcal{H}(u_0, u_1)$$

$h_0 = g_0^{\frac{1}{x_0 + \alpha}}$

$v_0 = h_0^{k_0}$

$z_0 = h_0^{x_0}$

$$d = \mathcal{G}(m, g, h_0, y_0, z_0, u_0, v_0$$
$$h_1, y_1, z_1, u_1, v_1)$$

$c_0 = d + e \bmod q$

$s_0 = k_0 + c_0 \cdot x_0 \bmod q$

Side 1

$u_1 = g^{k_1}$

$h_1 = g_1^{\frac{1}{x_1 + \alpha}}$

$v_1 = h_1^{k_1}$

$z_1 = h_1^{x_1}$

$c_1 = -e \bmod q$

$s_1 = k_1 + c_1 \cdot x_1 \bmod q$

If $\alpha + x_0 = 0 \bmod q$ or $\alpha + x_1 = 0 \bmod q$, other randoms are picked. The signature on m is $\sigma = (h_0, s_0, c_0, h_1, s_1, c_1)$.

Verification: To verify a signature $\sigma = (h_0, s_0, c_0, h_1, s_1, c_1) \in \mathbb{G}^\diamond \times \mathbb{Z}_q^2 \times \mathbb{G}^\diamond \times \mathbb{Z}_q^2$ on a message $m \in \mathcal{M}$, one computes

$u_0 = g^{s_0} y_0^{-c_0}$

$$\alpha = \mathcal{H}(u_0, u_1)$$

$z_0 = g_0 \cdot h_0^{-\alpha}$

$v_0 = h_0^{s_0} z_0^{-c_0}$

$u_1 = g^{s_1} y_1^{-c_1}$

$z_1 = g_1 \cdot h_1^{-\alpha}$

$v_1 = h_1^{s_1} z_1^{-c_1}$

$$d = \mathcal{G}(m, g, h_0, y_0, z_0, u_0, v_0,$$
$$h_1, y_1, z_1, u_1, v_1)$$

The signature is accepted iff $c_0 + c_1 = d \pmod q$.

As shown later, signatures as per our scheme provide a proof that either $\mathrm{DL}_{h_0}(z_0) = \mathrm{DL}_g(y_0)$ or $\mathrm{DL}_{h_1}(z_1) = \mathrm{DL}_g(y_1)$ or both. One can note that this "one of the DL-equalities holds" is exactly what one needs to create a ring signature, and notably, we can see our construction as a kind of ring signature with only two virtual signers, one per side.

As explained later, we base our security proof on the property that one of the two sides can be perfectly simulated but not both at the same time.

Correctness. The scheme is consistent since, if the signature is well formed, for $\delta \in \{0, 1\}$,

$$h_\delta = g_\delta^{\frac{1}{x_\delta + \alpha}}, \text{ for } \alpha = \mathcal{H}(u_0, u_1).$$

It follows that $z_\delta = h_\delta^{x_\delta} = g_\delta^{\frac{x_\delta}{x_\delta + \alpha}} = g_\delta^{\frac{x_\delta + \alpha - \alpha}{x_\delta + \alpha}}$, and consequently $z_\delta = g_\delta \cdot h_\delta^{-\alpha}$.

Discussion. The main features of our scheme is that it does not rely on pairings and, at the same time, achieves chosen-message security (without the random-oracle model) with a tight reduction. Our signatures are $2\ell_p + 4\ell_q$ bits. Our construction also inherently supports on-line/off-line precomputations, *i.e.*, one can perform most of the computations *before* knowing the message m: only remains the computation of (c_0, c_1, s_0, s_1) once the message is finally known.

A comparison with schemes of Sect. 3 could be the following:

– as opposed to the EDL family of schemes of Sect. 3.1, our scheme does not need the random oracle model
– as opposed to Boneh-Boyen scheme of Sect. 3.2, our scheme does not use pairings
– our scheme is more efficient than generic constructions of Sect. 3.3.

A comparison with OR-based schemes of Sect. 3.4 shows that results are pretty close. [33] scheme is based on the DDH assumption, which is more classical than the SDH assumption we use in our scheme (which, in a pairing-free group, is non-falsifiable). However, SDH is a computational problem while DDH is a decisional problem. Also, even if SDH is non-falsifiable, we argue in Sect. 4.4 that, with the auxiliary (s_i, c_i)'s information of our scheme, one can check that whether a pair is a valid SDH pair or not. Regarding the security model, the non-programmable random-oracle model used in [33] is slightly stronger than simply assuming correlation intractability of the hash function as we do. Finally, [33] signature size is smaller than our signature size.

4.3   Introducing Discrete-Log Collisions

Let us start with a definition.

Definition 1 (Discrete-log collisions). *Let $\mathcal{G}$ be a hash function mapping tuples of $\mathcal{M} \times \mathbb{G}^{n+1}$ to $\mathbb{Z}_q$. Let $\mathcal{F}$ be a function mapping vectors of $\mathbb{Z}_q^n$ to $\mathbb{Z}_q$. An algorithm is said to $(\varepsilon_{\mathsf{dlg},\mathcal{F}}, \tau)$-break the intractability of finding discrete-log collisions of $\mathcal{G}$ with respect to $\mathcal{F}$ if, being given a fresh random generator $g \in \mathbb{G}$,[9] it can find, with a probability $\varepsilon_{\mathsf{dlg},\mathcal{F}}$ and within a time τ, a tuple $(m, g, g^{a_1}, g^{a_2}, ..., g^{a_n})$ such that*

$$\mathcal{G}(m, g, g^{a_1}, g^{a_2}, ..., g^{a_n}) = \mathcal{F}(a_1, a_2, ..., a_n)$$

Such a tuple is called a discrete-log collision of $\mathcal{G}$ with respect to $\mathcal{F}$ and g.

Correlation-intractability. This security notion for hash function is actually an instantiation of so-called *correlation-intractability*. As introduced in [14], a hash function $\mathcal{G}$ is said correlation-intractable with respect to a relation $\mathcal{R}$ if it is computationally infeasible to exhibit u such that $(u, \mathcal{G}(u)) \in \mathcal{R}$.

In the case of Definition 1, the relation $\mathcal{R}_{\mathcal{F}}$ can be defined as follows. Since g is a generator, the function

$$\Lambda: \mathcal{M} \times \mathbb{G}^{n+1} \qquad\qquad \rightarrow \mathcal{M} \times \mathbb{G} \times \mathbb{Z}_q^n$$
$$(m, g, g^{a_1}, g^{a_2}, ..., g^{a_n}) \qquad\qquad \mapsto (m, g, a_1, a_2, ..., a_n)$$

is bijective. So, to any $u = (m, g, g^{a_1}, g^{a_2}, ..., g^{a_n})$ corresponds a unique $v = \Lambda(u) = (m, g, a_1, a_2, ..., a_n)$, and so a unique $w = (a_1, a_2, ..., a_n)$ which we note

---

[9] Notably, $\mathcal{F}$ and $\mathcal{G}$ definitions cannot suppose the generator g to be already defined.

as $w = \Lambda_a(u)$. We then say that $(u, v) \in \mathcal{R}_{\mathcal{F}}$ iff $v = \mathcal{F}(\Lambda_a(u))$. Remark that saying that $(u, \mathcal{G}(u)) \in \mathcal{R}_{\mathcal{F}}$ is the same as saying that u is a discrete-log collision of $\mathcal{G}$ with respect to $\mathcal{F}$.

Building a hash function whose correlation-intractability is formally proved is out of scope of this paper.[10] Instead, in our scheme, we use a hash function $\mathcal{G}$, and show that a potential forge can be turned into showing that $\mathcal{G}$ is *not* correlation-intractable (or some other hard problem is solved, see Sect. 4.4).

Checking discrete-log collisions. One could note that verifying that a given tuple is a valid discrete-log collision may be achieved in two ways: one way is to provide the tuple $(m, a_1, a_2, ..., a_n)$, *i.e.,* to disclose all the discrete logarithms $a_1, a_2, ..., a_n$. However, if the analytic form of $\mathcal{F}$ is simple enough (*e.g.,* our function $\mathcal{F}_0$ below), a verification that the collision is valid can be performed "in the exponents", *i.e.,* by providing proofs of equations followed by the inputs (see Sect. 4.4, Case 2.1).

For any hash function, having resistance against discrete-logarithm collisions is actually a desirable property, even if not a classical one. As Λ is bijective, when computing $\mathcal{G}(m, g, i_1, i_2, ..., i_n)$ for any $(m, g, i_1, i_2, ..., i_n) \in \mathcal{M} \times \mathbb{G}^{n+1}$, there is only one target value $v = \mathcal{F}(\Lambda_a(m, g, i_1, i_2, ..., i_n))$ which can lead to a discrete-log collision. Furthermore, g is picked randomly after $\mathcal{F}$ and $\mathcal{G}$ are defined.[11] Thus, for cryptographic hash functions $\mathcal{G}$—notably but not only *non-programmable* random oracle hash functions [34]—, finding discrete-log collision should be hard.

Setting a particular $\mathcal{F}$ for our scheme. In this paper, we are only interested in $n = 10$ and function $\mathcal{F} = \mathcal{F}_0$ defined as follows, which is a purely modular rational function

$$\mathcal{F}_0(a_1, a_2, ..., a_{10}) = \frac{a_1 a_4 - a_5}{a_3 - a_1 a_2} + \frac{a_6 a_9 - a_{10}}{a_8 - a_6 a_7} \bmod q,$$

resulting in that a discrete-log collision can be verified by providing equations satisfied by $g^{a_1}, g^{a_2}, ..., g^{a_{10}}$ as shown in Case 2.1 of Sect. 4.4.

Relation to security proofs of EDL variants. Remarkably, the discrete-logarithm collision notion was already present in EDL security proofs [18, 38, 51], even if not explicitly defined (see as well the end of our Sect. 3.1). Notably, the authors of these papers were using $n = 5$ and

$$\mathcal{F}_1(a_1, a_2, ..., a_5) = \frac{a_1 a_4 - a_5}{a_3 - a_1 a_2} \bmod q.$$

---

[10] One may read [13, 21, 50] for state of the art on this area of research.

[11] If $\mathcal{F}$ and g were chosen by the solver, this latter could trivially pick any $(m, g, g^{a_1}, g^{a_2}, ..., g^{a_n})$, precompute $f = \mathcal{G}(m, g, g^{a_1}, g^{a_2}, ..., g^{a_n})$, and choose $\mathcal{F}(a_1, a_2, ..., a_n)$ as the constant function f.

4.4   Security Proof

In this section, we prove the security of our scheme under the q-SDH assumption over the group $\mathbb{G}$. Recall that $\mathbb{G}$ is an arbitrary prime-order group here, and is not required to admit a bilinear map.

Before proving the security theorem, we refer to a useful lemma whose proof can be found in [6,7].

Lemma 1 (Proof of Lemma 9, [7]). *Let f be the polynomial*

$$f(X) = \prod_{j=1}^{j=q_s} (X + \kappa_j)$$

for some κ_j in $\mathbb{Z}_q$, and let θ be a random integer in $\mathbb{Z}_q$. Given $\{g^{x^i}\}_{i=0,\dots,q_s}$, let us define g_0 as $g_0 = g^{\theta f(x)}$. It is easy to compute g_0 and $g_0^{\frac{1}{x+\kappa_i}}$ for any $i \in [1, q_s]$. Furthermore, if one is given $h = g_0^{\frac{1}{x+\alpha}}$ with $\alpha \neq \kappa_j$, then one can easily compute $g^{\frac{1}{x+\alpha}}$.

We now state:

Theorem 1. *Let $\mathcal{A}$ be an adversary against our scheme that returns an existential forgery under a chosen-message attack with success probability ε within time τ, after q_s queries to the signing oracle. Further assume that $\mathcal{H}$ and $\mathcal{G}$ are respectively $(\varepsilon_{\mathcal{H}}, \tau)$ and $(\varepsilon_{\mathcal{G}}, \tau)$-collision secure and that finding discrete-log collisions of $\mathcal{G}$ with respect to $\mathcal{F}_0$ is $(\varepsilon_{\mathsf{dl}_{\mathcal{G},\mathcal{F}_0}}, \tau)$-intractable, then the q_s-SDH problem over $\mathbb{G}$ can be solved with success probability ε' such that*

$$3\varepsilon' + 3\varepsilon_{\mathsf{dl}_{\mathcal{G},\mathcal{F}_0}} + \varepsilon_{\mathcal{G}} + \varepsilon_{\mathcal{H}} \geq \varepsilon$$

in time τ' with

$$\tau' \lesssim \tau + \mathcal{O}(q_s) \cdot \tau_0$$

where τ_0 is the time required to perform a group exponentiation in $\mathbb{G}$.

Our proof combines techniques from [6,38,39] with new ideas. Intuitively a signature in our scheme is a proof that either $\mathsf{DL}_{h_0}(z_0) = \mathsf{DL}_g(y_0)\ (= x_0)$ or $\mathsf{DL}_{h_1}(z_1) = \mathsf{DL}_g(y_1)\ (= x_1)$ (or both), or that a collision (including the discrete-log collision case) is found on one of the hash functions.

Proof (of Theorem 1). Our reduction is given a group $\mathbb{G}$ and a q_s-SDH challenge $\{g^{x^i}\}_{i=1,\dots,q_s}$. Let us call $\mu_i = g^{x^i}$, for $i \in [1, q_s]$.

The reduction algorithm uses an existential forger $\mathcal{A}$ against our signature scheme to solve this challenge, *i.e.*, to find $g^{\frac{1}{x+\alpha}}$ for some α or to find collisions of one of the three above types. The reduction picks a random integer $\delta \in \{0, 1, 2\}$ and runs the subroutine Simulation δ described below.

Simulation 0

In this simulation, we simulate the Side 0 of the signature scheme while knowing the private key associated with Side 1, *i.e.*, the simulator knows x_1 but not x_0. The subroutine poses $y_0 = \mu_1$, randomly picks $x_1 \in \mathbb{Z}_q$ and sets $y_1 = g^{x_1}$. If $y_1 = y_0$, we know that $x_0 = x_1$ and so the q_s-SDH challenge can be solved easily. Therefore we assume that $x_0 \neq x_1$. A random generator $g_1 \in \mathbb{G}$ is generated as well.

Initialization: The simulator prepares q_s random tuples $(s_{0,i}, c_{0,i}, k_{1,i}) \in \mathbb{Z}_q^3$ and computes

$$u_{0,i} = g^{s_{0,i}} y_0^{-c_{0,i}}$$
$$u_{1,i} = g^{k_{1,i}}$$
$$\alpha_i = \mathcal{H}(u_{0,i}, u_{1,i}).$$

The simulator checks whether one of the α_i's is actually equal to $q - x_0$, in which (unlikely) case, the simulator sets $x = q - \alpha_i$ and directly solves the q_s-SDH problem. Similarly, it checks that $\alpha_i \neq q - x_1$, in which case initialization is restarted. Thus we now assume that $\alpha_i + x_0 \neq 0 \bmod q$ and $\alpha_i + x_1 \neq 0 \bmod q$, and so are invertible modulo q.

Let f be the polynomial $f(X) = \prod_{j=1}^{j=q_s} (X + \alpha_j)$. Let $g_0 = g^{\theta f(x)}$, for a random $\theta \in \mathbb{Z}_q$. By Lemma 1, g_0 can be simply computed thanks to μ_i's.

Now the simulator runs $\mathcal{A}$ on the public key (g, g_0, g_1, y_0, y_1) and the public parameters $(q, \mathcal{G}, \mathcal{H}, \mathbb{G})$.

Simulating signature queries: Let $m_i \in \mathcal{M}$ be the i-th signature query. Simulator 0 behaves as follows. Using Lemma 1, $h_{0,i} = g_0^{\frac{1}{x_0 + \alpha_i}}$ is easily computed, without unknown secret x_0. The simulator then computes $z_{0,i} = g_0 h_{0,i}^{-\alpha_i}$ and $v_{0,i} = h_{0,i}^{s_{0,i}} z_{0,i}^{-c_{0,i}}$.

Now that all variables from Side 0 are simulated, the simulator uses x_1 to generate the variables from Side 1 as

$$h_{1,i} = g_1^{\frac{1}{x_1 + \alpha_i}}$$
$$v_{1,i} = h_1^{k_{1,i}}$$
$$z_{1,i} = h_1^{x_1}$$

Finally, the simulator computes $d_i = \mathcal{G}(m_i, g, h_{0,i}, y_0, z_{0,i}, u_{0,i}, v_{0,i}, h_{1,i}, y_1, z_{1,i}, u_{1,i}, v_{1,i})$ and set $c_{1,i} = d_i - c_{0,i} \bmod q$. Finally, $s_{1,i} = k_{1,i} + c_{1,i} \cdot x_1 \bmod q$ is derived.

As one can see, signature $(h_{0,i}, s_{0,i}, c_{0,i}, h_{1,i}, s_{1,i}, c_{1,i})$ is valid and distributed as a regular signature (notably, $\mathsf{DL}_{h_0}(z_0) = \mathsf{DL}_g(y_0)$ and $\mathsf{DL}_{h_1}(z_1) = \mathsf{DL}_g(y_1)$).

Simulation 1

In this simulation, we proceed exactly as in Simulation 0, except that variables from the two sides are swapped: Side 1 is simulated using the μ_i's and Side 0 is trivial since the key x_0 is known by the simulation.

Simulation 2

The purpose of this simulation is not to solve the SDH instance, but to find a discrete-log collision on $\mathcal{G}$. Thus, in this simulation, the simulator knows the two keys x_0 and x_1, and responds to the adversary's signature queries as per the definition of the signing procedure.

Solving the q_s-SDH problem or finding collisions

This completes the description of our three simulation subroutines. Note that the three routines yield perfectly simulated distributions and are indistinguishable from one another from the adversary's perspective. We now focus on what our reduction does assuming that a forgery is returned by the forger at the end of the game.

Let $\sigma = (h_0, s_0, c_0, h_1, s_1, c_1) \in \mathbb{G}^\circ \times \mathbb{Z}_q^2 \times \mathbb{G}^\circ \times \mathbb{Z}_q^2$ be the valid forgery on a new message[12] $m \in \mathcal{M}$. Our reduction algorithm easily computes the other variables $u_0, v_0, z_0, u_1, v_1, z_1, \alpha, d$ by following the verification procedure. The reduction then checks whether $\alpha = \alpha_i$ for some $i = 1, ..., q_s$. Several cases and sub-cases appear.

■ **Case 1: $\alpha = \alpha_i$.** This case can be subdivided into three sub-cases.

Case 1.1: $(u_0, u_1) \neq (u_{0,i}, u_{1,i})$. Then, (u_0, u_1) and $(u_{0,i}, u_{1,i})$ is a pair which forms a collision on $\mathcal{H}$ function. This probability is captured by $\varepsilon_{\mathcal{H}}$.

Case 1.2: $(u_0, u_1) = (u_{0,i}, u_{1,i})$ and $(c_0, c_1) \neq (c_{0,i}, c_{1,i})$. If $\delta \in \{0, 1\}$ and $c_\delta \neq c_{\delta,i}$, the reduction directly finds x and subsequently solves the q_s-SDH challenge: indeed, we have equations $u_\delta = u_{\delta,i}$, $u_{\delta,i} = g^{s_{\delta,i}} y_\delta^{-c_{\delta,i}}$ (from the signature queries) and $u_\delta = g^{s_\delta} y_\delta^{-c_\delta}$ (from the forge). Since δ is independent from the adversary, $\delta \in \{0, 1\}$ happens with a probability $\frac{2}{3}$ and $c_\delta \neq c_{\delta,i}$ knowing that $(c_0, c_1) \neq (c_{0,i}, c_{1,i})$ happens with a probability of $\frac{1}{2}$. This case probability is thus upper-bounded by the $3\,\varepsilon_{\text{SDH},1}$ term.

Case 1.3: $(u_0, u_1) = (u_{0,i}, u_{1,i})$ and $(c_0, c_1) = (c_{0,i}, c_{1,i})$. We know by the verification step that $d_i = c_{0,i} + c_{1,i} \bmod q$, and thus $d_i = d$. In other words,

$$(m, g, h_0, y_0, z_0, u_0, v_0, h_1, y_1, z_1, u_1, v_1)$$

and

$$(m_i, g, h_{0,i}, y_0, z_{0,i}, u_{0,i}, v_{0,i}, h_{1,i}, y_1, z_{1,i}, u_{1,i}, v_{1,i})$$

constitute a (classical) $\mathcal{G}$ collision.[13] This probability is captured by $\varepsilon_{\mathcal{G}}$. Summing up, we get

$$\varepsilon_{\mathcal{H}} + 3\,\varepsilon_{\text{SDH},1} + \varepsilon_{\mathcal{G}} \geq \varepsilon \cdot \Pr[\text{Case 1}]$$

■ **Case 2: $\alpha \neq \alpha_i$.** Since h_0 and h_1 are generators of $\mathbb{G}$ (this is notably the reason why we must check that they are not equal to 1 in the verification step), there exists a unique tuple $(k_0, k_0', k_0'', k_1, k_1', k_1'', x_0', x_1') \in \mathbb{Z}_q^2 \times \mathbb{Z}_q^\circ \times \mathbb{Z}_q^2 \times \mathbb{Z}_q^\circ \times \mathbb{Z}_q^2$ such that

---

[12] Hence, our scheme does not ensure strong existential unforgeability, but only existential unforgeability, which is sufficient in most usages.

[13] Remind that $m \neq m_i$, since the forgery is assumed to be valid.

$$u_0 = g^{k_0}, \qquad\qquad u_1 = g^{k_1}$$
$$v_0 = h_0^{k_0'}, \qquad\qquad v_1 = h_1^{k_1'}$$
$$z_0 = h_0^{x_0'}, \qquad\qquad z_1 = h_1^{x_1'}$$
$$h_0 = g^{k_0''}, \qquad\qquad h_1 = g^{k_1''}.$$

Our goal is to prove that, with overwhelming probability, either ($k_0 = k_0'$ and $x_0 = x_0'$) or ($k_1 = k_1'$ and $x_1 = x_1'$), or both. This is somehow similar to EDL's proofs. By the verification step, we know that (all computations being modulo q)

$$k_0 = s_0 - x_0 \cdot c_0, \qquad k_1 = s_1 - x_1 \cdot c_1$$
$$k_0' = s_0 - x_0' \cdot c_0, \qquad k_1' = s_1 - x_1' \cdot c_1$$

and that $c_0 + c_1 = \mathcal{G}(m, g, h_0, y_0, z_0, u_0, v_0, h_1, y_1, z_1, u_1, v_1)$.

Case 2.1: $x_0 \neq x_0'$ and $x_1 \neq x_1'$: if the Simulation 2 was not executed, the reduction aborts. Else, the reduction knows the two parts of the signing key x_0 and x_1, and can actually check that $z_0 \neq h_0^{x_0}$ and $z_1 \neq h_1^{x_1}$, i.e., that $x_0 \neq x_0'$ and $x_1 \neq x_1'$. Then, $c_0 = \frac{k_0 - k_0'}{x_0' - x_0} \bmod q$ and $c_1 = \frac{k_1 - k_1'}{x_1' - x_1} \bmod q$. This implies (modulo q)

$$\frac{k_0 - k_0'}{x_0' - x_0} + \frac{k_1 - k_1'}{x_1' - x_1} = \mathcal{G}(m, g, h_0, g^{x_0}, h_0^{x_0'}, g^{k_0}, h_0^{k_0'}, h_1,$$
$$g^{x_1}, h_1^{x_1'}, g^{k_1}, h_1^{k_1'})$$

or written differently

$$\frac{k_0 - k_0'}{x_0' - x_0} + \frac{k_1 - k_1'}{x_1' - x_1} = \mathcal{G}(m, g, g^{k_0''}, g^{x_0}, g^{x_0' k_0''}, g^{k_0}, g^{k_0' k_0''}, g^{k_1''},$$
$$g^{x_1}, g^{x_1' k_1''}, g^{k_1}, g^{k_1' k_1''})$$

or, in a more evocative form, with $k_0'' = a_1$ and $k_1'' = a_6$ not zero

$$k_0'' = a_1 \qquad\qquad k_1'' = a_6$$
$$x_0 = a_2 \qquad\qquad x_1 = a_7$$
$$x_0' = a_3/a_1 \qquad\qquad x_1' = a_8/a_6$$
$$k_0 = a_4 \qquad\qquad k_1 = a_9$$
$$k_0' = a_5/a_1 \qquad\qquad k_1' = a_{10}/a_6$$

and finally

$$\frac{a_1 a_4 - a_5}{a_3 - a_1 a_2} + \frac{a_6 a_9 - a_{10}}{a_8 - a_6 a_7} = \mathcal{G}(m, g, g^{a_1}, g^{a_2}, g^{a_3}, g^{a_4}, g^{a_5}, g^{a_6}, g^{a_7}, g^{a_8}, g^{a_9}, g^{a_{10}})$$

This provides a discrete-log collision on $\mathcal{G}$ function, for the function $\mathcal{F}_0$ defined in Sect. 4.3, or, in other words, proves that $\mathcal{G}$ is not correlation-intractable. The reduction cannot provide the a_i discrete logarithms, but this is not a problem, since the discrete-log collision can be checked without them, by giving away (x_0, x_1) and the equations followed by $(m, g, h_0, y_0, z_0, u_0, v_0, h_1, y_1, z_1, u_1, v_1)$. The probability of this event is counted by $3\,\varepsilon_{\mathsf{dl}_{\mathcal{G}}, \mathcal{F}_0}$.

<u>Case 2.2:</u> $x_\delta = x'_\delta$. Then, $z_\delta = h_\delta{}^{x_\delta}$ and $h_\delta = g_\delta{}^{\frac{1}{x+\alpha}}$. As the simulation actually executed is unknown to the adversary, this happens with probability $\frac{1}{3}$. Thanks to Lemma 1, the reduction can return $(\alpha, g^{\frac{1}{x+\alpha}})$ as our answer to the q_s-SDH problem.

Summarizing, we have

$$3\,\varepsilon_{\mathsf{dl}_{\mathcal{G}}, \mathcal{F}_0} + 3\,\varepsilon_{\mathsf{q-SDH},2} \geq \varepsilon \cdot \Pr[\mathsf{new}]$$

which proves the theorem.

5　Conclusion

In this paper, we have introduced a new signature scheme which is efficient and does not rely on pairings. Our scheme is provably secure under the strong Diffie-Hellman assumption and the correlation-intractability of the hash function. This scheme is our best attempt to extend the EDL family without the random oracle model.

An open question remains in how to reduce the size of our signatures and how to completely get rid of the assumption that finding discrete-log collisions for $\mathcal{G}$ function is intractable. More generally, one may try to extend EDL family in the standard model with other techniques, or to rely on weaker assumptions.

Acknowledgements. The author would like to thank the anonymous referees and Marc Fischlin for their useful remarks, Pascal Paillier and Marc Joye for their careful reading of this paper and finally Jeremy Bradley-Silverio Donato for his edits. More personal thanks go to Amal and Mathieu for their continuous support.

References

1. Abe, M., Ambrona, M., Bogdanov, A., Ohkubo, M., Rosen, A.: Non-interactive composition of sigma-protocols via share-then-hash. In: Moriai, S., Wang, H. (eds.) ASIACRYPT 2020, Part III. LNCS, vol. 12493, pp. 749–773. Springer, Cham (2020). https://doi.org/10.1007/978-3-030-64840-4_25
2. Barreto, P.S.L.M., Kim, H.Y., Lynn, B., Scott, M.: Efficient algorithms for pairing-based cryptosystems. In: Yung, M. (ed.) CRYPTO 2002. LNCS, vol. 2442, pp. 354–369. Springer, Heidelberg (2002). https://doi.org/10.1007/3-540-45708-9_23
3. Barreto, P.S.L.M., Naehrig, M.: Pairing-friendly elliptic curves of prime order. In: Preneel, B., Tavares, S. (eds.) SAC 2005. LNCS, vol. 3897, pp. 319–331. Springer, Heidelberg (2006). https://doi.org/10.1007/11693383_22

4. Bellare, M., Rogaway, P.: Random oracles are practical: a paradigm for designing efficient protocols. In: ACM Conference on Computer and Communications Security - ACM CCS 1993, pp. 62–73. ACM Press (1993)
5. Bellare, M., Rogaway, P.: The exact security of digital signatures-how to sign with RSA and Rabin. In: Maurer, U. (ed.) EUROCRYPT 1996. LNCS, vol. 1070, pp. 399–416. Springer, Heidelberg (1996). https://doi.org/10.1007/3-540-68339-9_34
6. Boneh, D., Boyen, X.: Short signatures without random oracles. In: Cachin, C., Camenisch, J.L. (eds.) EUROCRYPT 2004. LNCS, vol. 3027, pp. 56–73. Springer, Heidelberg (2004). https://doi.org/10.1007/978-3-540-24676-3_4
7. Boneh, D., Boyen, X.: Short signatures without random oracles and the SDH assumption in bilinear groups. J. Cryptol. **21**(2), 149–177 (2008). https://doi.org/10.1007/s00145-007-9005-7
8. Boneh, D., Franklin, M.: Identity-based encryption from the Weil pairing. In: Kilian, J. (ed.) CRYPTO 2001. LNCS, vol. 2139, pp. 213–229. Springer, Heidelberg (2001). https://doi.org/10.1007/3-540-44647-8_13
9. Boneh, D., Franklin, M.K.: Identity-based encryption from the Weil pairing. SIAM J. Comput. **32**(3), 586–615 (2003)
10. Boneh, D., Lynn, B., Shacham, H.: Short signatures from the Weil pairing. J. Cryptol. **17**(4), 297–319 (2004). https://doi.org/10.1007/s00145-004-0314-9
11. Camenisch, J., Lysyanskaya, A.: A Signature Scheme with Efficient Protocols. In: Cimato, S., Persiano, G., Galdi, C. (eds.) SCN 2002. LNCS, vol. 2576, pp. 268–289. Springer, Heidelberg (2003). https://doi.org/10.1007/3-540-36413-7_20
12. Camenisch, J., Lysyanskaya, A.: Signature schemes and anonymous credentials from bilinear maps. In: Franklin, M. (ed.) CRYPTO 2004. LNCS, vol. 3152, pp. 56–72. Springer, Heidelberg (2004). https://doi.org/10.1007/978-3-540-28628-8_4
13. Canetti, R., Chen, Y., Reyzin, L., Rothblum, R.D.: Fiat-Shamir and correlation intractability from strong KDM-secure encryption. In: Nielsen, J.B., Rijmen, V. (eds.) EUROCRYPT 2018, Part I. LNCS, vol. 10820, pp. 91–122. Springer, Cham (2018). https://doi.org/10.1007/978-3-319-78381-9_4
14. Canetti, R., Goldreich, O., Halevi, S.: The random oracle methodology, revisited (preliminary version). In: ACM Symposium on the Theory of Computing - STOC 1998, pp. 209–218. ACM Press (1998)
15. Canetti, R., Goldreich, O., Halevi, S.: The random oracle methodology, revisited. J. ACM **51**(4), 557–594 (2004)
16. Chaum, D., Pedersen, T.P.: Wallet databases with observers. In: Brickell, E.F. (ed.) CRYPTO 1992. LNCS, vol. 740, pp. 89–105. Springer, Heidelberg (1993). https://doi.org/10.1007/3-540-48071-4_7
17. Cheon, J.H.: Security analysis of the strong Diffie-Hellman problem. In: Vaudenay, S. (ed.) EUROCRYPT 2006. LNCS, vol. 4004, pp. 1–11. Springer, Heidelberg (2006). https://doi.org/10.1007/11761679_1
18. Chevallier-Mames, B.: An efficient CDH-based signature scheme with a tight security reduction. In: Shoup, V. (ed.) CRYPTO 2005. LNCS, vol. 3621, pp. 511–526. Springer, Heidelberg (2005). https://doi.org/10.1007/11535218_31
19. Chevallier-Mames, B., Joye, M.: A practical and tightly secure signature scheme without hash function. In: Abe, M. (ed.) CT-RSA 2007. LNCS, vol. 4377, pp. 339–356. Springer, Heidelberg (2006). https://doi.org/10.1007/11967668_22
20. Coron, J.-S.: On the exact security of full domain hash. In: Bellare, M. (ed.) CRYPTO 2000. LNCS, vol. 1880, pp. 229–235. Springer, Heidelberg (2000). https://doi.org/10.1007/3-540-44598-6_14

21. Couteau, G., Katsumata, S., Ursu, B.: Non-interactive zero-knowledge in pairing-free groups from weaker assumptions. In: Canteaut, A., Ishai, Y. (eds.) EURO-CRYPT 2020, Part III. LNCS, vol. 12107, pp. 442–471. Springer, Cham (2020). https://doi.org/10.1007/978-3-030-45727-3_15

22. Cramer, R., Damgård, I.: Secure signature schemes based on interactive protocols. In: Coppersmith, D. (ed.) CRYPTO 1995. LNCS, vol. 963, pp. 297–310. Springer, Heidelberg (1995). https://doi.org/10.1007/3-540-44750-4_24

23. Cramer, R., Damgård, I.: New generation of secure and practical RSA-based signatures. In: Koblitz, N. (ed.) CRYPTO 1996. LNCS, vol. 1109, pp. 173–185. Springer, Heidelberg (1996). https://doi.org/10.1007/3-540-68697-5_14

24. Cramer, R., Damgård, I., Schoenmakers, B.: Proofs of partial knowledge and simplified design of witness hiding protocols. In: Desmedt, Y.G. (ed.) CRYPTO 1994. LNCS, vol. 839, pp. 174–187. Springer, Heidelberg (1994). https://doi.org/10.1007/3-540-48658-5_19

25. Cramer, R., Shoup, V.: Signature schemes based on the strong RSA assumption. ACM Trans. Inf. Syst. Secur. (TISSEC) 3(3), 161–185 (2000)

26. Diffie, W., Hellman, M.E.: New directions in cryptography. IEEE Trans. Inf. Theory 22(6), 644–654 (1976)

27. Dodis, Y., Oliveira, R., Pietrzak, K.: On the generic insecurity of the full domain hash. In: Shoup, V. (ed.) CRYPTO 2005. LNCS, vol. 3621, pp. 449–466. Springer, Heidelberg (2005). https://doi.org/10.1007/11535218_27

28. Döttling, N., Garg, S.: Identity-based encryption from the Diffie-Hellman assumption. In: Katz, J., Shacham, H. (eds.) CRYPTO 2017, Part I. LNCS, vol. 10401, pp. 537–569. Springer, Cham (2017). https://doi.org/10.1007/978-3-319-63688-7_18

29. Dwork, C., Naor, M.: An efficient existentially unforgeable signature scheme and its applications. In: Desmedt, Y.G. (ed.) CRYPTO 1994. LNCS, vol. 839, pp. 234–246. Springer, Heidelberg (1994). https://doi.org/10.1007/3-540-48658-5_23

30. ElGamal, T.: A public key cryptosystem and a signature scheme based on discrete logarithms. IEEE Trans. Inf. Theory 31(4), 469–472 (1985)

31. Fiat, A., Shamir, A.: How to prove yourself: practical solutions to identification and signature problems. In: Odlyzko, A.M. (ed.) CRYPTO 1986. LNCS, vol. 263, pp. 186–194. Springer, Heidelberg (1987). https://doi.org/10.1007/3-540-47721-7_12

32. Fischlin, M.: The Cramer-Shoup strong-RSA signature scheme revisited. In: Desmedt, Y.G. (ed.) PKC 2003. LNCS, vol. 2567, pp. 116–129. Springer, Heidelberg (2003). https://doi.org/10.1007/3-540-36288-6_9

33. Fischlin, M., Harasser, P., Janson, C.: Signatures from Sequential-OR Proofs. In: Canteaut, A., Ishai, Y. (eds.) EUROCRYPT 2020. LNCS, vol. 12107, pp. 212–244. Springer, Cham (2020). https://doi.org/10.1007/978-3-030-45727-3_8

34. Fischlin, M., Lehmann, A., Ristenpart, T., Shrimpton, T., Stam, M., Tessaro, S.: Random oracles with(out) programmability. In: Abe, M. (ed.) ASIACRYPT 2010. LNCS, vol. 6477, pp. 303–320. Springer, Heidelberg (2010). https://doi.org/10.1007/978-3-642-17373-8_18

35. Freeman, D., Scott, M., Teske, E.: A taxonomy of pairing-friendly elliptic curves. J. Cryptol. 23(2), 224–280 (2010). https://doi.org/10.1007/s00145-009-9048-z

36. Gennaro, R., Halevi, S., Rabin, T.: Secure Hash-and-sign signatures without the random oracle. In: Stern, J. (ed.) EUROCRYPT 1999. LNCS, vol. 1592, pp. 123–139. Springer, Heidelberg (1999). https://doi.org/10.1007/3-540-48910-X_9

37. Girault, M.: Self-certified public keys. In: Davies, D.W. (ed.) EUROCRYPT 1991. LNCS, vol. 547, pp. 490–497. Springer, Heidelberg (1991). https://doi.org/10.1007/3-540-46416-6_42

38. Goh, E.-J., Jarecki, S.: A signature scheme as secure as the Diffie-Hellman problem. In: Biham, E. (ed.) EUROCRYPT 2003. LNCS, vol. 2656, pp. 401–415. Springer, Heidelberg (2003). https://doi.org/10.1007/3-540-39200-9_25

39. Goh, E.-J., Jarecki, S., Katz, J., Wang, N.: Efficient signature schemes with tight reductions to the Diffie-Hellman problems. J. Cryptol. **20**(4), 493–514 (2007). https://doi.org/10.1007/s00145-007-0549-3

40. Goldwasser, S., Kalai, Y.T.: On the (in)security of the Fiat-Shamir paradigm. In: FOCS, pp. 102–113. IEEE Computer Society (2003)

41. Goldwasser, S., Micali, S., Rivest, R.L.: A "paradoxical" solution to the signature problem (extended abstract). In: Symposium on Foundations of Computer Science - FOCS 1984, pp. 441–448. IEEE Press (1984)

42. Goldwasser, S., Micali, S., Rivest, R.L.: A digital signature scheme secure against adaptive chosen-message attacks. SIAM J. Comput. **17**(2), 281–308 (1988)

43. Guillou, L.C., Quisquater, J.-J.: A practical zero-knowledge protocol fitted to security microprocessor minimizing both transmission and memory. In: Barstow, D., et al. (eds.) EUROCRYPT 1988. LNCS, vol. 330, pp. 123–128. Springer, Heidelberg (1988). https://doi.org/10.1007/3-540-45961-8_11

44. Hess, F., Smart, N.P., Vercauteren, F.: The eta pairing revisited. IEEE Trans. Inf. Theory **52**(10), 4595–4602 (2006)

45. Hofheinz, D., Kiltz, E.: Programmable hash functions and their applications. J. Cryptol. **25**(3), 484–527 (2012)

46. Hohenberger, S., Waters, B.: Realizing Hash-and-sign signatures under standard assumptions. In: Joux, A. (ed.) EUROCRYPT 2009. LNCS, vol. 5479, pp. 333–350. Springer, Heidelberg (2009). https://doi.org/10.1007/978-3-642-01001-9_19

47. Hohenberger, S., Waters, B.: Short and stateless signatures from the RSA assumption. In: Halevi, S. (ed.) CRYPTO 2009. LNCS, vol. 5677, pp. 654–670. Springer, Heidelberg (2009). https://doi.org/10.1007/978-3-642-03356-8_38

48. Jakobsson, M., Schnorr, C.P.: Efficient oblivious proofs of correct exponentiation. In: Communications and Multimedia Security - CMS 1999. IFIP Conference Proceedings, vol. 152, pp. 71–86. IFIP (1999)

49. Joux, A.: A one round protocol for tripartite Diffie–Hellman. In: Bosma, W. (ed.) ANTS 2000. LNCS, vol. 1838, pp. 385–393. Springer, Heidelberg (2000). https://doi.org/10.1007/10722028_23

50. Kalai, Y.T., Rothblum, G.N., Rothblum, R.D.: From Obfuscation to the Security of Fiat-Shamir for Proofs. In: Katz, J., Shacham, H. (eds.) CRYPTO 2017. LNCS, vol. 10402, pp. 224–251. Springer, Cham (2017). https://doi.org/10.1007/978-3-319-63715-0_8

51. Katz, J., Wang, N.: Efficiency improvements for signature schemes with tight security reductions. In: ACM Conference on Computer and Communications Security - ACM CCS 2003, pp. 155–164. ACM Press (2003)

52. Krawczyk, H., Rabin, T.: Chameleon signatures. In: Network and Distributed System Security Symposium - NDSS 2000, pp. 143–154 (2000)

53. Kurosawa, K., Schmidt-Samoa, K.: New online/offline signature schemes without random oracles. In: Yung, M., Dodis, Y., Kiayias, A., Malkin, T. (eds.) PKC 2006. LNCS, vol. 3958, pp. 330–346. Springer, Heidelberg (2006). https://doi.org/10.1007/11745853_22

54. Micali, S., Reyzin, L.: Improving the exact security of digital signature schemes. J. Cryptol. **15**(1), 1–18 (2002). https://doi.org/10.1007/s00145-001-0005-8

55. Naccache, D., Pointcheval, D., Stern, J.: Twin signatures: an alternative to the hash-and-sign paradigm. In: ACM Conference on Computer and Communications Security - ACM CCS 2001, pp. 20–27. ACM Press (2001)

56. Naor, M., Yung, M.: Universal one-way hash functions and their cryptographic applications. In: 1989 Proceedings of the 21st Annual ACM Symposium on Theory of Computing, pp. 33–43. ACM (1989)
57. Paillier, P.: Impossibility proofs for RSA signatures in the standard model. In: Abe, M. (ed.) CT-RSA 2007. LNCS, vol. 4377, pp. 31–48. Springer, Heidelberg (2006). https://doi.org/10.1007/11967668_3
58. Paillier, P., Vergnaud, D.: Discrete-log-based signatures may not be equivalent to discrete log. In: Roy, B. (ed.) ASIACRYPT 2005. LNCS, vol. 3788, pp. 1–20. Springer, Heidelberg (2005). https://doi.org/10.1007/11593447_1
59. Pointcheval, D., Stern, J.: Security proofs for signature schemes. In: Maurer, U. (ed.) EUROCRYPT 1996. LNCS, vol. 1070, pp. 387–398. Springer, Heidelberg (1996). https://doi.org/10.1007/3-540-68339-9_33
60. Poupard, G., Stern, J.: Security analysis of a practical "on the fly" authentication and signature generation. In: Nyberg, K. (ed.) EUROCRYPT 1998. LNCS, vol. 1403, pp. 422–436. Springer, Heidelberg (1998). https://doi.org/10.1007/BFb0054143
61. Rabin, M.O.: Digital signatures and public-key functions as intractable as factorization. Technical Report MIT/LCS/TR-212, MIT Laboratory for Computer Science, January 1979
62. Rivest, R.L., Shamir, A., Adleman, L.M.: A method for obtaining digital signatures and public-key cryptosystems. Commun. ACM **21**(2), 120–126 (1978)
63. Rompel, J.: One-way functions are necessary and sufficient for secure signatures. In: 1990 Proceedings of the 22nd Annual ACM Symposium on Theory of Computing, pp. 387–394. ACM (1990)
64. Schnorr, C.P.: Efficient signature generation by smart cards. J. Cryptol. **4**(3), 161–174 (1991). https://doi.org/10.1007/BF00196725
65. Seurin, Y.: On the exact security of Schnorr-type signatures in the random oracle model. In: Pointcheval, D., Johansson, T. (eds.) EUROCRYPT 2012. LNCS, vol. 7237, pp. 554–571. Springer, Heidelberg (2012). https://doi.org/10.1007/978-3-642-29011-4_33
66. Shamir, A., Tauman, Y.: Improved online/offline signature schemes. In: Kilian, J. (ed.) CRYPTO 2001. LNCS, vol. 2139, pp. 355–367. Springer, Heidelberg (2001). https://doi.org/10.1007/3-540-44647-8_21
67. Stern, J.: Why provable security matters? In: Biham, E. (ed.) EUROCRYPT 2003. LNCS, vol. 2656, pp. 449–461. Springer, Heidelberg (2003). https://doi.org/10.1007/3-540-39200-9_28
68. Stern, J., Pointcheval, D., Malone-Lee, J., Smart, N.P.: Flaws in applying proof methodologies to signature schemes. In: Yung, M. (ed.) CRYPTO 2002. LNCS, vol. 2442, pp. 93–110. Springer, Heidelberg (2002). https://doi.org/10.1007/3-540-45708-9_7
69. Waters, B.: Efficient identity-based encryption without random oracles. In: Cramer, R. (ed.) EUROCRYPT 2005. LNCS, vol. 3494, pp. 114–127. Springer, Heidelberg (2005). https://doi.org/10.1007/11426639_7
70. Zhang, F., Safavi-Naini, R., Susilo, W.: An efficient signature scheme from bilinear pairings and its applications. In: Bao, F., Deng, R., Zhou, J. (eds.) PKC 2004. LNCS, vol. 2947, pp. 277–290. Springer, Heidelberg (2004). https://doi.org/10.1007/978-3-540-24632-9_20

Faster Isogenies for Post-quantum Cryptography: SIKE

Rami Elkhatib, Brian Koziel$^{(\boxtimes)}$, and Reza Azarderakhsh

PQSecure Technologies, LLC, Boca Raton, FL, USA
{rami.elkhatib,brian.koziel,razarder}@pqsecurity.com

Abstract. In the third round of the NIST PQC standardization process, the only isogeny-based candidate, SIKE, suffers from slow performance when compared to other contenders. The large-degree isogeny computation performs a series of isogenous mappings between curves, to account for about 80% of SIKE's latency. Here, we propose, implement, and evaluate a new method for computing large-degree isogenies of an odd power. Our new strategy for this computation avoids expensive recomputation of temporary isogeny results. We modified open-source libraries targeting x86, ARM64, and ARM32 platforms. Across each of these implementations, our new method achieves 10% and 5% speedups in SIKE's key encapsulation and decapsulation operations, respectively. Additionally, these implementations use 3% less stack space at only a 48 byte increase in code size. Given the benefit and simplicity of our approach, we recommend this method for current and emerging SIKE implementations.

Keywords: Isogeny-based cryptography · Post-quantum cryptography · SIKE · Isogeny computations

1 Introduction

Quantum computing technology is heralded as the next big leap in processing powers. This new type of computer will allow humanity to solve a wealth of difficult problems in applications such as medicine, finance, and data analytics. However, the dark side of these new quantum computers is that they are capable of breaking the foundational cryptography that secures the internet and our digital infrastructure. Namely, today's deployed public-key cryptosystems are protected by the difficulty to compute discrete logarithms and factorization, both of which are infeasible for classical computers once the numbers become large. However, in 1994, Peter Shor proposed a polynomial-time algorithm that can break these hard problems in conjunction with a large-scale quantum computer [44]. It is unclear when a large enough quantum computer will emerge, so there exist many estimates ranging from a few years to several decades.

With quantum computer fears in mind, the US National Institute for Standards and Technology (NIST) has initiated a post-quantum cryptography (PQC) standardization process for public-key cryptosystems [46]. Started in 2017, the

S. D. Galbraith (Ed.): CT-RSA 2022, LNCS 13161, pp. 49–72, 2022.
https://doi.org/10.1007/978-3-030-95312-6_3

standardization effort is currently in its third round, cutting the original 69 submissions to just 15. Quantum-safe schemes fall into a number of categories ranging from lattices, codes, hashes, multi-variate equations, and isogenies. Unfortunately, there are no clear "drop-in replacements" for today's currently deployed technology. Each of the proposed quantum-resilient schemes feature performance, size, communication, and security tradeoffs.

This work focuses on optimizations to the NIST PQC candidate SIKE, which is based on the hardness of finding isogenies between supersingular elliptic curves. SIKE is currently a third round alternative scheme for key encapsulation mechanisms. SIKE is lauded for its small public keys, straightforward parameter selection, immunity to decryption errors, and understanding of its generic attacks. However, SIKE is an order of magnitude slower than lattices and other schemes and many are requiring further examination of its foundational security. Nevertheless, SIKE's small key and ciphertext sizes enable some applications that can take the hit to performance. NIST sees SIKE "as a strong candidate for future standardization with continued improvements." [2]

In this work, we present a faster method for computing the large-degree isogeny in SIKE for isogenies of an odd power. As we have observed, current open source implementations of SIKE such as that in the SIKE submission [5] or Microsoft's SIDH Library [15] utilize a slow strategy for computing large-degree isogenies that require a mix of 2 and 4-isogenies. Our new strategy modifies this strategy, achieving a nice speedup in SIKE's key generation and decapsulation operations. Currently, this applies to only the NIST Level 3 SIKE parameter set. However, new security analyses have proposed additional SIKE parameter sets for which we can and do apply this large-degree isogeny method.

Our contributions:

- We propose a new method for computing large-degree isogenies of an odd power.
- We provide explicit algorithms and formulas to speed up these large-degree isogenies.
- We implement, deploy, and evaluate our methodology on x86, ARM64, and ARM32 platforms.
- We achieve 10% and 5% speedups in SIKEp610's key encapsulation and decapsulation, respectively, with approximately a 3% improvement in stack usage in our experimental results.

2   Preliminaries: Isogenies on Elliptic Curves

In this section, we provide a brief overview of the large-degree isogeny and its use in SIKE.

2.1   Isogeny-Based Cryptography

History. Primarily, isogeny-based cryptography has focused on the use of isogenies on elliptic curves in cryptosystems. An isogeny is a non-constant rational map between elliptic curves that is also a group homomorphism. The use of isogenies for a cryptosystem was first proposed in independent works by Couveignes [17] and Rostovtsev and Stolbunov [41] that were first published in 2006. These works proposed an isogeny-based key-exchange based on the hardness to compute isogenies between ordinary elliptic curves. Initially, these were believed to be resistant to quantum attacks. However, in 2010, Childs, Jao, and Soukharev [13] proposed a new quantum subexponential algorithm that computes isogenies between ordinary curves, thus breaking these schemes. In 2009, Charles, Lauter, and Goren [12] proposed an isogeny-based hash function that was based on the hardness to compute isogenies between supersingular elliptic curves which creates an expander graph. Then, in 2011, Jao and De Feo [27] modified the original isogeny-based key-exchange to now also utilize supersingular elliptic curves, creating the Supersingular Isogeny Diffie-Hellman (SIDH) key-exchange. Interestingly, the quantum algorithm from Childs, Jao, and Soukharev [13] relies on a commutative endomorphism ring. Ordinary elliptic curves have a commutative endomorphism ring, making them vulnerable, while supersingular elliptic curves have a non-commutative endomorphism ring. SIKE is an IND-CCA2 upgrade of SIDH that was submitted to the NIST PQC standardization process in 2017 [6]. Since the inception of SIDH in 2011 to the 4 years of SIKE in the NIST PQC process, these supersingular isogeny-based schemes remain unbroken.

Since the emergence of SIDH, many facets have isogeny-based cryptography have been explored through research. Many researchers have investigated security foundations from the isogeny hard problems [1,16,24,28] to side-channel attacks [26,31,32,47]. On the application side, we have seen the use of SIDH/SIKE public key compression [7,14,39,40], new isogeny-based digital signatures schemes [25,49], isogeny-based hybrid key exchange [9,15], isogeny-based password authenticated key exchange [8,45], and new isogeny-based key agreement with CSIDH [11]. Among isogeny-based cryptosystem implementations, we have seen a wealth of implementations including software [3,15,18,23,36,42,43], hardware [19,20,22,30,33–35], and even software-hardware co-design [21,38].

Elliptic Curves. Isogeny-based cryptography can be thought of as an extension of elliptic curve cryptography. Both operate on elliptic curves defined over finite fields. However, rather than stick to a single elliptic curve, isogenies on elliptic curves focus on the relationship between elliptic curves.

We define an elliptic curve E over a finite field $\mathbb{F}_q$ as the collection of all points (x, y) as well as the point at infinity that satisfy the short Weierstrass curve equation:

$$E/\mathbb{F}_q \ : \ y^2 = x^3 + ax + b$$

where $a, b, x, y \in \mathbb{F}_q$. By defining a method for adding points using geometry, this collection forms an abelian group over addition. The scalar point multiplication is a repeated use of point addition such that $Q = kP$, where $k \in \mathbb{Z}$ and

$P, Q \in E$. Given P and k, it is simple to compute $Q = kP$ via a sequence of point additions and point doublings. However, as the order of the elliptic curve E becomes very large (such as 2^{256}), finding k when given Q and P becomes infeasible for classical computers. Unfortunately, a large-scale quantum computer can efficiently solve this problem by using Shor's algorithm [44].

Isogenies. An elliptic curve isogeny over $\mathbb{F}_q$, $\phi : E \to E'$ is defined as a nonconstant rational map from $E(\mathbb{F}_q)$ to $E'(\mathbb{F}_q)$ that preserves the point at infinity. Isogenies between elliptic curves can be computed over a kernel, $\phi : E \to E/\langle ker \rangle$, by using Vélu's formulas [48]. The degree of an isogeny is its degree as a rational map. Large-degree isogenies of the form ℓ^e can be computed by chaining e isogenies of degree ℓ. Lastly, an elliptic curve's j-invariant acts as an identifier of its isomorphism class. An isogeny moves from one elliptic curve isomorphism class to another isomorphism class.

Isogeny-based cryptography relies on the difficulty to compute isogenies between elliptic curves. For $\phi : E \to E'$, it is simple to compute an isogeny from E to E' given a finite kernel. However, when only given E and E', it is difficult to find the isogenous mapping between elliptic curves. SIDH and SIKE compute ϕ as a sequence of small-degree isogenies. This problem can be visualized as a walk on an isogeny graph of degree ℓ where each node represents an isomorphism class and the edges are isogenies of degree ℓ. For supersingular elliptic curves $E(\mathbb{F}_q)$, $q = p^2$, there are approximately $p/12$ isomorphism classes. For an isogeny graph over base degree ℓ, this is a complete graph where each node has $\ell + 1$ unique isogenies up to isomorphism of degree ℓ. SIDH and SIKE perform an isogeny walk by computing a large-degree isogeny of the form ℓ^e. In this walk, there are e steps of ℓ-degree isogenies.

Isogeny-Friendly Primes. SIDH and SIKE utilize a prime of the form $p = \ell_A^{e_A} \ell_B^{e_B} f \pm 1$, where ℓ_A and ℓ_B are small primes, e_A and e_B are positive integers, and f is a small cofactor to make the number prime. This prime is used to find a supersingular elliptic curve $E_0(\mathbb{F}_{p^2})$ and find torsion bases $\{P_A, Q_A\}$ and $\{P_B, Q_B\}$ that generate $E_0[\ell_A^{e_A}]$ and $E_0[\ell_B^{e_B}]$, respectively. Curve E_0 has order $\#E_0 = (p \mp 1)^2$ which has a smooth order so that rational isogenies of exponentially large degree can be computed efficiently as a chain of low-degree isogenies. Alice performs her large-degree isogeny ϕ_A over the ℓ_A isogeny graph and Bob performs his large-degree isogeny ϕ_B over the ℓ_B isogeny graph.

The core Diffie-Hellman principle of SIDH and SIKE is that Alice and Bob each separately perform their large-degree isogenies over ℓ_A and ℓ_B graphs, respectively, exchange the resulting curve and a few extra points, and then perform their large-degree isogeny over the other party's public key. Both parties will have new elliptic curves for which ℓ_A and ℓ_B isogeny walks were performed, so Alice and Bob can use the elliptic curve's j-invariant as a shared secret. Since Alice and Bob perform separate walks, the SIDH and SIKE schemes are as strong as the weaker isogeny graph to attack. For security, it is desirable that $\ell_A^{e_A} \approx \ell_B^{e_B}$.

Table 1. SIKE parameter sets for each NIST security level [5]. All sizes are in bytes.

SIKE Scheme	Security Level	As Strong as	Prime Form	Secret Key	Public Key	Cipher Text	Shared Secret
SIKEp434	NIST level 1	AES128	$p_{434} = 2^{216}3^{137} - 1$	374	330	346	16
SIKEp503	NIST level 2	SHA256	$p_{503} = 2^{250}3^{159} - 1$	434	378	402	24
SIKEp610	NIST level 3	AES192	$p_{610} = 2^{305}3^{192} - 1$	524	462	486	24
SIKEp751	NIST level 5	AES256	$p_{751} = 2^{372}3^{239} - 1$	644	564	596	32

Table 2. SIKE parameter sets for each round. "Level" indicates the NIST security level of the prime for the NIST round. [5]

Parameter Set	Prime Form	NIST Standardization Round			
		Round 1	Round 2	Round 3	Proposed in [37]
SIKEp434	$2^{216}3^{137} - 1$		Level 1	Level 1	
SIKEp503	$2^{250}3^{159} - 1$	Level 1	Level 2	Level 2	
SIKEp610	$2^{305}3^{192} - 1$		Level 3	Level 3	
SIKEp751	$2^{372}3^{239} - 1$	Level 3	Level 5	Level 5	
SIKEp964	$2^{486}3^{301} - 1$	Level 5			
SIKEp377 [37]	$2^{191}3^{117} - 1$				Level 1
SIKEp546 [37]	$2^{273}3^{172} - 1$				Level 3
SIKEp697 [37]	$2^{356}3^{215} - 1$				Level 5

2.2 Supersingular Isogeny Key Encapsulation

The Supersingular Isogeny Key Encapsulation (SIKE) mechanism [5] allows for an IND-CCA2 key establishment between two parties. In this scheme, Alice and Bob want to agree on a shared secret. To accomplish this, Alice and Bob perform their own isogeny walks over separate isogeny graphs. SIKE is protected by the computational supersingular isogeny (CSSI) problem [1].

SIKE API. SIKE is a key encapsulation mechanism split into three operations: key generation, key encapsulation, and key decapsulation. In the SIKE protocol, Bob wants to agree on a shared secret with Alice. He begins the protocol by performing key generation, where a secret key and public key are generated. He sends this public key to Alice over a public channel. Alice, upon receiving Bob's public key, performs key encapsulation to generate a ciphertext and shared secret. Alice then sends her ciphertext to Bob, again over a public channel. Bob then finalizes this protocol by performing key decapsulation over his secret key and Alice's ciphertext, generating a shared secret. From there, Alice and Bob can utilize this shared secret to exchange encrypted communications.

SIKE Parameters. The primary computations in SIKE include a double-point multiplication, large-degree isogeny, and SHAKE256 hashing. For efficiency and simplicity, SIKE fixes a prime of the form $p = 2^{e_A}3^{e_B} - 1$ where $2^{e_B} \approx 3^{e_B}$. The sizes of these isogeny graphs are the primary metric for SIKE's security strength.

Based on known cryptanalysis and known attacks, the SIKE team has proposed SIKE parameter sets of the form SIKEpXXX, where "XXX" is the size of the prime in bits. Each SIKE parameter set targets a NIST Security Level from 1 to 5. NIST Security Level 1 is considered as hard to break as a brute-force attack on AES128, Level 2 is as hard as finding a hash collision of SHA256, Level 3 is as hard as a brute-force attack on AES192, and Level 5 is as hard as a brute-force attack on AES256. Interestingly, SIKE's prime sizes have decreased in size over the course of the NIST PQC standardization process, showing that the CSSI problem was harder than originally thought.

SIKE's strongest advantage is its small public keys and ciphertexts. We summarize SIKE's round 3 parameter sets in Table 1. The communication overhead is for the uncompressed SIKE scheme. The compressed SIKE scheme further reduces the public key and ciphertext by almost half. Compared to other schemes, SIKE has the smallest public keys and almost the smallest ciphertext. Only Classic McEliece [10] has a smaller ciphertext. Kyber [4] is a lattice-based scheme with fairly small public keys, but SIKE's public keys and ciphertexts are more than half of Kyber's size for an equivalent security level. For instance, Kyber Security Level 1 has an 800 byte public key and 768 byte ciphertext.

SIKE Primes. In Table 2, we summarize the SIKE parameter sets for the NIST PQC standardization process. Based on cryptanalysis of [1,16] and the like, it was deemed that SIKE's Round 1 parameters were too conservative, so they were reduced for Round 2 and beyond. We also added the proposed primes from [37] as it is another work that considers the CSSI problem harder than expected, resulting in even smaller primes.

For these results, we note that SIKE parameters are not permanent and could continue to change based on security analysis. When searching for SIKE primes, there are also limited options. When choosing a random form for p, it is desirable that $2^{e_A} \approx 3^{e_B}$ so that low-level modular arithmetic is more efficient and there are fewer isogenies to perform. Based on the prime number theorem, there is approximately a $\frac{1}{\ln x}$ chance that a random integer x is prime. If we only choose odd numbers by using the form $2^{e_A} 3^{e_B} - 1$, then there is a $\frac{2}{\ln x}$ chance that the number is prime. In practice, this means that a 400-bit candidate has a 1 in 139 chance of being prime and a 700-bit candidate has a 1 in 243 chance of being prime.

3 Proposed Method for Large-Degree Isogenies of Odd Power Degree

In this section, we propose a new method to compute the large-degree isogeny operation in SIKE. This method can be applied to any scheme that computes a large-degree isogeny of an odd power of the form ℓ^{2k+1}, where k is an integer. In terms of the parameter schemes presented in Table 2, this applies to each prime, as every prime has at least one of the 2-isogeny or 3-isogeny graph sizes of an odd power. However, this is only if it is more efficient to perform the large-degree isogenies as a chain of ℓ^2 isogenies rather than ℓ isogenies, which is the

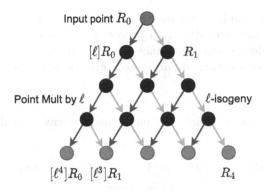

Fig. 1. Visualization of the large-degree isogeny computation.

case for the 2-isogeny graphs, where practitioners compute it as a sequence of 4-isogenies. Thus, this method specifically applies to the SIKE schemes SIKEp610, SIKEp377, and SIKEp546 where the 2-isogeny graph has an odd power.

3.1 Large-Degree Isogenies

First, we review how the large-degree isogeny is traditionally performed. This computation accounts for 80% of the latency in SIDH and SIKE operations. Given a large-degree isogeny of the form ℓ^e, we compute this by chaining together e isogenies of degree ℓ. For a base curve E_0 and kernel point $R_0 = R$ of order ℓ^e we compute e isogenies of degree ℓ as follows:

$$E_{i+1} = E_i/\langle \ell^{e-i-1}R_i \rangle, \quad \phi_i : E_i \to E_{i+1}, \quad R_{i+1} = \phi_i(R_i) \tag{1}$$

This computation can be visualized as traversing an acyclic graph in the shape of a triangle starting from the kernel point (R_0) to each of the leaves $(\ell^{e-i-1}R_i)$ as is shown in Fig. 1. Here, we are computing an isogeny of degree ℓ^5 by starting at the purple kernel node of order ℓ^5 and traversing to each of the green leaf nodes that has order ℓ with which we can compute an ℓ isogeny. When traversing this graph, there is an uneven cost to move left by computing a point multiplication by ℓ and to move right by evaluating an ℓ-degree isogeny over a point.

The simplest method to traverse this graph is the multiplication-based strategy with complexity $O(e^2)$ [27], which is the same as Eq. 1. However, the only requirement for the large-degree isogeny is that an isogeny is computed at each of the leaf nodes. Thus, one can save specific points that act as a pivot to dramatically reduce the number of point multiplication and isogeny evaluations. As was first proposed in [18], optimal strategies can be devised as one of the least cost, with complexity $O(e \log e)$. The key insight when finding an optimal strategy is that an optimal strategy is composed of two optimal sub-strategies. The standard method to perform the large-degree isogeny is to utilize a precomputed strategy, whereby we cycle through the following steps until all ℓ-isogenies are computed.

1. Perform point multiplications by ℓ to traverse left to reach a leaf node, while storing pivot points according to a precomputed strategy
2. Compute an ℓ-degree isogeny to move from E_i to E_{i+1}
3. Evaluate ℓ-degree isogenies on all stored pivot points, translating them from E_i to E_{i+1}

Table 3. Fastest known point arithmetic and isogeny formulas for 2 and 4 isogenies [5].

Operation	$\#\mathbb{F}_{p^2}$ Add	$\#\mathbb{F}_{p^2}$ Sub	$\#\mathbb{F}_{p^2}$ Mult	$\#\mathbb{F}_{p^2}$ Sqr
2-Isogenies				
Point Doubling	2	2	4	2
Compute 2 Isogeny	0	1	0	2
Evaluate 2 Isogeny	3	3	4	0
4-Isogenies				
Point Quadrupling	4	4	8	4
Compute 4 Isogeny	4	1	0	4
Evaluate 4 Isogeny	3	3	6	2

Why 4 Isogenies? The simple reason that 4 isogenies are used instead of 2 isogenies is that 4 isogenies are more efficient. The cost of the fastest known isogeny formulas are shown in Table 3. In this table, each isogeny operation is made up of point multiplication by ℓ, computing an ℓ isogeny that performs a mapping between curves, and evaluating an ℓ isogeny that maps a point to a new isogenous curve. Also in this table, the most important computations are $\mathbb{F}_{p^2}$ multiplications and $\mathbb{F}_{p^2}$ squarings that require expensive field multiplications. In the SIKE landscape, $\mathbb{F}_{p^2}$ multiplications require 3 modular multiplications and $\mathbb{F}_{p^2}$ squarings require 2 modular multiplications. When comparing the cost of formulas, evaluating two 2-isogenies requires 8 $\mathbb{F}_{p^2}$ multiplications while evaluating a single 4-isogeny requires 6 $\mathbb{F}_{p^2}$ multiplications and 2 $\mathbb{F}_{p^2}$ squarings. Thus, 4-isogenies require 2 fewer field multiplications here. In the case of large-degree isogenies, hundreds of isogeny evaluations are performed, meaning that saving a few modular multiplications each step is valuable. Otherwise, 3 isogenies are known to be faster than 9 isogenies and larger isogeny algorithms are less explored as the costs of larger base degree isogenies do not scale well. The results of this paper are specifically applied to 2 and 4 isogenies, but given advances in isogeny formulas, could apply to other base degrees.

3.2   Large-Degree Isogenies of an Odd Power

Since large-degree isogenies of base degree 4 are faster than that of base degree 2, computing large-degree isogenies of the form 2^{2k} is preferred. However, given the limited availability of SIKE primes, such SIKE-friendly primes may not exist.

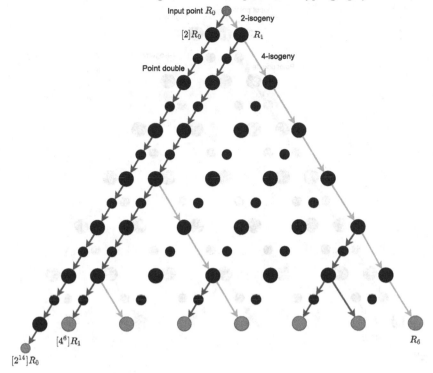

Fig. 2. Visualization of the state-of-the-art [5] methodology to compute large-degree isogenies of an odd power.

When computing large-degree isogenies of the form 2^{2k+1}, at least one 2-isogeny must be computed.

There are a few options for performing large-degree isogenies of an odd power. The simplest option may be to just skip the 2-isogeny. However, this weakens the security of the 2-isogeny graph and should only be done if the 2-isogeny graph is larger than the 3-isogeny graph, i.e. $2^{e_A} \gg 3^{e_B}$.

Current Methodology. Currently, the SIKE submission [5] and other libraries perform the 2^{2k+1} isogeny by performing an initial 2-isogeny, and then proceeding with an optimized large-degree isogeny of base degree $2^{2k} = 4^k$. Thus, this approach starts with the point multiplication-based strategy and then proceeds with the optimized strategy.

A visualization of this approach is shown in Fig. 2 with a toy example. Although the Figure shows the computation of a 2^{15} large-degree isogeny, it is simple to adapt this figure for ℓ and ℓ^2 isogenies for a different base degree. We use similar colors and representation as Fig. 1. Here, a small-sized node represents a point of an odd power 2^{2k+1} and a medium-sized node represents a point of an even power $2^{2k} = 4^k$. Thus, we still traverse to the green leaf nodes, but we have the option to compute 2 or 4 isogenies at the leaves. Since 4-isogenies

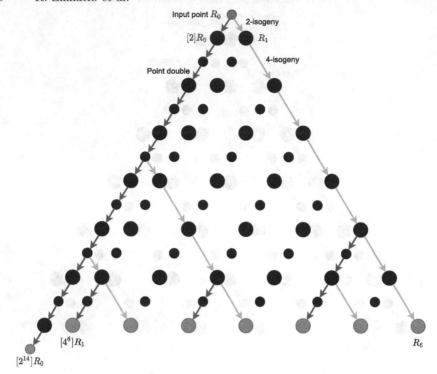

Fig. 3. Visualization of the proposed methodology to compute large-degree isogenies of an odd power.

are preferred, the example strategy utilizes seven 4-isogenies and one 2-isogeny to compute the 2^{15} large-degree isogeny.

As Fig. 2 shows, there is a large amount of recomputation needed to compute the large-degree isogeny. Namely, this strategy performs two traversals from the top node to the left-most node. Of the 33 point doublings in this Figure, 27 point doublings are computed for the first 2-isogeny and subsequent 4-isogeny.

Proposed Methodology. To dramatically reduce this wasted traversal, our proposed fix is to store pivot points on the first traversal to the left, as is shown in Fig. 3. In order to make this work, we need to store pivot points of an odd power order 2^{2k+1} that correspond to the point multiples used in the optimized 4-isogeny strategy. After performing the first 2-isogeny, we push each of these pivot points through the 2-isogeny, incrementing their order to $2^{2k} = 4^k$. Thus, we can then continue with an optimized 4-isogeny as normal.

Improvement. Between Figs. 2 and 3, we showed two different methods for computing the large-degree isogeny 2^{15}. The state-of-the-art method requires 33 point doublings, 1 2-isogeny, and 11 4-isogenies, whereas the new method requires

22 point doublings, 3 2-isogenies, and 11 4-isogenies. Thus, for this toy example, our proposed method exchanges 10 point doublings for 2 additional 2-isogeny evaluations. Based on the cost of current isogeny formulas shown in Table 3, this saves 16 $\mathbb{F}_{p^2}$ multiplication operations and 20 $\mathbb{F}_{p^2}$ squaring operations. When applied to something like SIKEp610, one sample strategy comparison showed that our new method exchanges 303 point doubling operations for 5 additional 2-isogeny point evaluations.

Discussion. With this proposed methodology, we chose the same policy of performing the 2-isogeny first. This is primarily because once done, no more of the (slower) 2-isogeny operations need to be performed in the middle of the large-degree isogeny. One interesting consideration was the use of mixing 2 and 4-isogeny operations. For example, one could perform about half of the isogeny computations and then the 2-isogeny. This makes the algorithm more complex and did not provide any real benefit from our analysis as the more 2-isogeny arithmetic you use, the more the large-degree isogeny slows down. Lastly, one could use a mix of 2 and 4-isogenies to compute new representations of pivot points. We did not find any benefit, but leave this open for further investigation.

4 Proposed Explicit Formulas for Large-Degree Isogenies

In this section, we propose a new algorithm and method to perform the large-degree isogeny within SIKE or SIDH. Although we directly apply this algorithm to the large-degree isogeny of odd power over base degree 2 for SIKE, we generalize this algorithm for any large-degree isogeny of a single base degree.

4.1 Proposed Efficient Algorithm for Large-Degree Isogenies with a Remainder

The large-degree isogeny computes an isogeny of degree ℓ^e by chaining together e isogenies of degree ℓ. Typically, ℓ is a small prime such as 2 or 3. When isogeny operations over degree ℓ^x, where x is a positive integer, are more efficient than performing x ℓ-isogenies, then ℓ^x isogenies should be used. However, when e is not divisible by x, there will be a remainder r. Thus, we represent $\ell^e = \ell^{x \cdot \lfloor e/x \rfloor + r}$, where $r = e \bmod x$.

For this algorithm we assume that the computations for ℓ^x isogeny computations, ℓ^x isogeny evaluations, and scalar point multiplications by ℓ^x will speed up the large-degree isogeny operation over other powers of ℓ. An isogeny computation computes an isogenous mapping between two elliptic curves given a kernel and an isogeny evaluation uses an isogenous mapping to map a point on one elliptic curve to its new representation on the isogenous curve. As is used by efficient SIDH and SIKE implementations, we can precompute an optimized strategy to traverse the large-degree isogeny computation as is shown in Figs. 2 and 3. This significantly improves the complexity of the large-degree isogeny. For our large-degree isogeny with a remainder algorithm, we only need to precompute the optimized strategy for a large-degree isogeny of the form $\ell^{x \cdot \lfloor e/x \rfloor}$. Although there are several methods to store a strategy, the strategy simply represents the number of point multiplications to traverse left. In most implementations, this is stored as a series of e positive integers. When using isogenies of base degree ℓ^x, we only need to store e/x positive integers.

New Large-Degree Isogeny Algorithm. Our proposed algorithm for large-degree isogenies with a remainder is shown in Algorithm 1. In general, the method boils down to computing the remainder isogeny ℓ^r first by computing a series of point multiplications by ℓ^x up to $\ell^{x \cdot \lfloor e/x \rfloor}$ where we store the pivot points along the way. These point multiplications produce a point of order ℓ^r for which an ℓ^r isogeny can be computed. After the ℓ^r isogeny, the remaining $\ell^{x \cdot \lfloor e/x \rfloor}$ isogenies can then be computed using an optimal strategy based on the latency of ℓ^x isogeny evaluations and point multiplications by ℓ^x.

Algorithm 1 uses a very similar format as the large-degree isogeny formulas found in the SIKE submission. [5]. We note that we use D to represent a deque, or double-ended queue, where each data element contains an index representing a point and the order of the point. h represents the remaining number of ℓ^x scalar point multiplications that could be applied, so $h = 1$ indicates the point is of order ℓ^x. Indeed, Lines 1 to 3 and Lines 18 to 35 are roughly equivalent to the state-of-the-art [5]. Lines 4 to 17 compute the remainder isogeny ℓ^r in a similar fashion as Lines 18 to 35, however only one isogeny needs to be computed. Specifically, Lines 4 through 9 perform the point multiplications by ℓ^x according to the large-degree isogeny strategy, Lines 10 to 11 compute the ℓ^r isogeny, and Lines 13 to 17 apply the ℓ^r isogeny to all stored pivot points.

Although we do not describe how to compute the ℓ^r isogeny, it can be computed in whatever the most efficient method is, whether that is a combination of smaller isogenies or a single ℓ^r isogeny. For simplicity, Algorithm 1 assumes that the ℓ^r isogeny is computed in one go. If multiple smaller isogenies are computed, then the Lines 11 through 17 of the algorithm simply need to be revised such that smaller point multiplications are performed to get a kernel point, whereby each smaller isogeny computation over the kernel is followed by a smaller isogeny evaluation over each stored pivot point.

Strategy Considerations. Interestingly, we found that only an optimal strategy needs to be made for the $\ell^{x \cdot \lfloor e/x \rfloor}$ large-degree isogeny. When applying the $\ell^{x \cdot \lfloor e/x \rfloor}$ strategy to a kernel point of order $\ell^{x \cdot \lfloor e/x \rfloor + r}$, the first series of scalar point multiplications will find pivot points of the order ℓ^{kx+r} where k is some positive integer whereas applying the strategy to a kernel point of order $\ell^{x \cdot \lfloor e/x \rfloor}$ will produce points of the order ℓ^{kx}. Thus, after applying the ℓ^r isogeny to the pivot points generated with the kernel point of order $\ell^{x \cdot \lfloor e/x \rfloor + r}$, we will naturally have pivot points of the order ℓ^{kx} as we need. The only caveat is that we need to perform one additional ℓ^x scalar point multiplication before the ℓ^r isogeny so that the point actually has order ℓ^r. Our Algorithm accounts for this by performing point multiplications until $h = 0$ rather than $h = 1$, as is done in Line 4. Furthermore, after the ℓ^r isogeny evaluations, we do not update the h indices in the deque as an ℓ^x isogeny has not been performed.

Algorithm 1: Computing and evaluating an ℓ^e-isogeny with remainder

---

function ℓ_e_iso

    Static Parameters: Integer e from public parameters, Integer x for fastest ℓ^x isogenies, Integer $r = e \bmod x$, a *strategy* $(s_1, \ldots, s_{\lfloor e/x \rfloor - 1}) \in (\mathbb{N}^+)^{\lfloor e/x \rfloor - 1}$

    Input: Curve E_0 and point S on E_0 with exact order $\ell^e = \ell^{x \cdot \lfloor e/x \rfloor + r}$

    Output: Curve $E = E_0/\langle S \rangle$ by computing e isogenies of degree ℓ

1 Initialize empty deque D
2 push$(D, (\lfloor e/x \rfloor, S))$
3 $E \leftarrow E_0, i \leftarrow 1, h \leftarrow \lfloor e/x \rfloor$
4 **while** $h \neq 0$ **do**
5     $(h, R) \leftarrow$ pop(D)
6   push$(D, (h, R))$
7   **for** $j \leftarrow 0$ **to** s_i **do**
8         $R \leftarrow$ mult_by_$\ell^x(R, E)$
9   push$(D, (h - s_i, R)), i \leftarrow i + 1$
10 $(h, R) \leftarrow$ pull(D)
11 $(E', \phi) \leftarrow$ compute_ℓ^r_iso(E, R)
12 Initialize empty deque D'
13 **while** D *not empty* **do**
14     $(h, R) \leftarrow$ pull(D)
15     $R \leftarrow$ evaluate_ℓ^r_iso(E', ϕ, R)
16   push$(D', (h, R))$
17 $D \leftarrow D', E \leftarrow E'$
18 **while** D *not empty* **do**
19     $(h, R) \leftarrow$ pop(D)
20   **if** $h = 1$
21         $(E', \phi) \leftarrow$ compute_ℓ^x_iso(E, R)
22   Initialize empty deque D'
23   **while** D *not empty* **do**
24             $(h, R) \leftarrow$ pull(D)
25             $R \leftarrow$ evaluate_ℓ^x_iso(E', ϕ, R)
26   push$(D', (h - 1, R))$
27         $D \leftarrow D', E \leftarrow E'$
28   **elif** $0 < s_i < h$
29   push$(D, (h, R))$
30   **for** $j \leftarrow 0$ **to** s_i **do**
31             $R \leftarrow$ mult_by_$\ell^x(R, E)$
32   push$(D, (h - s_i, R)), i \leftarrow i + 1$
33   **else**
34   **Error:** Invalid strategy
35 **return** $E = E_0/\langle S \rangle$

Complexity. For a large-degree isogeny of degree ℓ^e, this proposed Algorithm features the same $O(e \log e)$ complexity as the original use of optimized strategies proposed in [18]. However, when the fastest base degree isogeny ℓ^x has an x which is not a divisor of e, this method efficiently performs the ℓ^r isogeny in complexity $O(e)$ and has already stored pivot points for the following $\ell^{x \cdot \lfloor e/x \rfloor}$ large-degree isogeny in complexity $O(e \log e)$. This Algorithm also does not change the size of the precomputed strategy.

4.2 Proposed Faster 2-Isogeny Formulas for Large-Degree Isogenies

In the SIKE submission [5] and similar SIKE libraries, we noted that the 2-isogeny formulas are not optimized for the scenario when multiple 2-isogeny evaluations are performed. Thus, we propose new and faster 2-isogeny formulas for this case that can be used in conjunction with our large-degree isogeny algorithm to accelerate the large-degree isogeny in SIKE parameters such as SIKEp610. Specifically, SIKEp610 performs a large-degree isogeny of degree 2^{305} which can be rewritten as $2^{2 \cdot 152 + 1} = 4^{152} 2$. Our optimized formulas slightly alter the 2-isogeny APIs, moving computations over a point of order 2 from the 2-isogeny evaluation function to the 2-isogeny computation function, resulting in fewer field addition and subtractions when multiple 2-isogeny evaluations are performed.

For the following optimized formulas, we operate on Montgomery curves of the form $E/\mathbb{F}_q \; : \; by^2 = x^3 + ax^2 + x$. Similar to short Weierstrass curves, Montgomery curves are the set of all points (x, y) as well as the point at infinity that satisfy this equation. This curve is defined over the finite field $\mathbb{F}_q$, so, $b, y, x, a \in \mathbb{F}_q$.

There are additional representations of this curve for SIDH and SIKE to reduce the complexity of isogeny and point arithmetic. Notably, the introduction of a projective "C" term is used so that isogenies can be performed without inversions until the very end of a large-degree isogeny. The following formulas fix the b coefficient to 1 and simplify the Montgomery form to $E/\mathbb{F}_q \; : \; y^2 = x^3 + ax^2 + x$. Next, we denote the projective representation $(A \; : \; C)$ to denote the equivalence $(A \; : \; C) \sim (a \; : \; 1)$. Rather than keep track of A and C, the following equations represent the Montgomery curve with the values $(A_{24}^+ \; : \; C_{24})$ $\sim (A + 2C \; : \; 4C)$. Lastly, elliptic curve points are represented in the Kummer projective representation $(X \; : \; Z)$ where $x = X/Z$ and the y-coordinates are dropped.

2-Isogeny Computation. Our new 2-isogeny computation formula is shown in Algorithm 2. The 2-isogeny computation uses an input curve E and point of order 2 on the input curve $P_2 = (X_2 \; : \; Z_2)$ to compute a 2-isogenous elliptic curve E' such that $\phi \; : \; E \rightarrow E/\langle P_2 \rangle = E'$. Similar to the SIKE submission's formulas [5], the output curve is represented with coefficients $(A_{24}^+ \; : \; C_{24}) \sim (A' + 2C' \; : \; 4C')$, where A' and C' are the projective coefficients on curve E'. Our new formula adds new computations for constants K_1 and K_2 which are used in the 2-isogeny evaluation formula. The total cost of this computation is $2S + 3A$, where S is the cost of $\mathbb{F}_{p^2}$ squaring and A is the cost of $\mathbb{F}_{p^2}$ addition/subtraction.

Algorithm 2: Computing the 2-isogenous curve

function 2_iso_curve

    Input: $P_2 = (X_{P_2} \ Z_{P_2})$, where P_2 has exact order 2 on Montgomery curve $E_{A,C}$

    Output: $(A_{24}^+ : C_{24}) \sim (A' + 2C' \ 4C')$ corresponding to $E_{A',C'} = E_{A,C}/\langle P_2 \rangle$, and

        constants $(K_1, K_2) \in (\mathbb{F}_p^2)^2$

1 $A_{24}^+ \leftarrow X_{P_2}^2$,   3 $A_{24}^+ \leftarrow C_{24} - A_{24}^+$,   5 $K_2 \leftarrow X_{P_2} + Z_{P_2}$,

2 $C_{24} \leftarrow Z_{P_2}^2$,   4 $K_1 \leftarrow X_{P_2} - Z_{P_2}$,   6 **return** $A_{24}^+, C_{24}, (K_1, K_2)$

Algorithm 3: Evaluating a 2-isogeny at a point

function 2_iso_eval

    Input: Constants $(K_1, K_2) \in (\mathbb{F}_p^2)^2$ from 2_iso_curve, and $Q = (X_Q : Z_Q)$ on

        Montgomery curve $E_{A,C}$

    Output: $(X_Q' : Z_Q')$ corresponding to $Q' \in E_{A'/C'}$, where $E_{A'/C'}$ is the curve

        2-isogenous to $E_{A/C}$ output from 2_iso_eval

1 $t_0 \leftarrow X_Q + Z_Q$,   4 $t_1 \leftarrow t_1 \cdot K_2$,   7 $X_Q' \leftarrow t_2 \cdot X_Q$,

2 $t_1 \leftarrow X_Q - Z_Q$,   5 $t_2 \leftarrow t_1 + t_0$,   8 $Z_Q' \leftarrow t_0 \cdot Z_Q$,

3 $t_0 \leftarrow t_0 \cdot K_1$,   6 $t_0 \leftarrow t_1 - t_0$,   9 **return** $Q' = (X_Q' : Z_Q')$

2-Isogeny Evaluation. Our new 2-isogeny evaluation formula is shown in Algorithm 3. The 2-isogeny evaluation pushes a point $Q = (X_Q : Z_Q)$ on elliptic curve E to its 2-isogenous representation $Q' = (X_{Q'} : Z_{Q'})$ on elliptic curve E' by using 2-isogeny constants outputted in the 2-isogeny computation. Our new formula no longer needs the point of order 2 to evaluate the 2-isogeny. We remark that this formula requires three temporary registers whereas the previous formula required four. The total cost of this computation is $4M + 4A$, where M is the cost of $\mathbb{F}_{p^2}$ multiplication and A is the cost of $\mathbb{F}_{p^2}$ addition/subtraction.

Table 4. Complexity of newly proposed 2-isogeny formulas versus the state-of-the-art.

Operation	#$\mathbb{F}_{p^2}$ Add	#$\mathbb{F}_{p^2}$ Sub	#$\mathbb{F}_{p^2}$ Mult	#$\mathbb{F}_{p^2}$ Sqr	#Temporary Values
SIKE Submission [5]					
Compute 2 Isogeny	0	1	0	2	0
Evaluate 2 Isogeny	3	3	4	0	4
This Work					
Compute 2 Isogeny	1	2	0	2	0
Evaluate 2 Isogeny	2	2	4	0	3

Efficiency of New Formulas. We summarize the cost of our 2-isogeny formulas versus the SIKE submission's [5] in Table 4. Our new formulas swap out an $\mathbb{F}_{p^2}$ addition and $\mathbb{F}_{p^2}$ subtraction from the evaluate 2 isogeny formula to the compute 2 isogeny formula. Since 4 isogenies are more efficient than 2-isogenies, it is expected that we will only ever compute a single 2-isogeny. However, with our new method we will evaluate multiple 2-isogenies, resulting in saving several $\mathbb{F}_{p^2}$ additions and subtractions. Interestingly, our proposed method uses fewer temporary registers in the 2-isogeny evaluation formula. As we see in our stack usage, this actually reduces the total stack usage of the SIKE operations that perform a large-degree isogeny of base degree 2. Given that this revision of formulas reduces stack size, we recommend its use even if our large-degree isogeny algorithm is not employed.

5 Benchmarking and Evaluation

Benchmarking Platforms. With this new method for large-degree isogenies of an odd power, we set out to benchmark it on various platforms. To target different computing capabilities, we chose SIKE implementations based on x86-64, ARM64, and ARM32. Our x86-64 platform was on an X1 Carbon 7th Generation laptop running an Intel Core i7-8565U processor at 1.8 GHz. Our ARM64 platform was a Raspberry Pi 4B device with 8 GB of RAM running an ARM Cortex-A72 processor at 1.5 GHz. Lastly, our ARM32 platform is the STM32F407 Discovery Kit which runs an ARM Cortex-M4 processor at up to 168 MHz. Although we only benchmark on software platforms, our improvements to the large-degree isogenies will most likely provide similar speedups to hardware and software-hardware designs.

x86/ARM64 Benchmarking. For the x86 and ARM64 devices, we used Microsoft's SIDH library [15] v3.4[1] as a base. This provides both SIDH and SIKE implementations for each of the SIKE parameter sets. Importantly, this provides optimized low-level arithmetic for both x86 and ARM64 devices. For the x86 implementation, we disabled TurboBoost. The X1 Carbon 7th Generation device was running Ubuntu 20.04 and the Raspberry Pi 4 is running Raspberry Pi OS (64 bit) release built on May 28, 2021. Although the 64-bit Raspberry Pi OS is still in beta, the ability to employ optimized ARM64 assembly improves performance. Both platforms utilized GNU GCC version 9.3.0 and were compiled with -O3.

ARM32 Benchmarking. On the ARM32 side, we used PQCRYPTO's open-source pqm4 [29] library[2]. The pqm4 library provides a benchmarking and testing framework for evaluating post-quantum schemes. It includes ARM Cortex-M4 implementations of schemes such as SIKE with hand-optimized assembly. In addition, there are simple benchmarking capabilities to analyze performance, stack usage, and code-size. Our numbers are obtained with the toolchain `arm-none-eabi-gcc` `9.2.1`. We note that for speed benchmarking, the Cortex-M4 is locked to 24 MHz to avoid wait cycles caused by the memory controller.

---

[1] Commit @effa607 of https://github.com/microsoft/PQCrypto-SIDH.
[2] Commit @844e7ca of https://github.com/mupq/pqm4.

Library Modifications. Both of these above libraries utilize code that originated in Microsoft's SIDH library and was extended for the SIKE submission [5]. The basic framework of the libraries, such as the directory structure or function names are generally consistent. Of the four NIST implementations in SIKE's round 3 package, this new method applies only to SIKEp610, which is at NIST Level 3. When upgrading these implementations for our new method of computing a large-degree isogeny, we only edited the ec_isogeny.c for new 2-isogeny formulas, P610.c for a new large-degree strategy, and sidh.c for Alice's large-degree isogeny algorithm. All other files were left untouched.

Table 5. Speedups achieved for SIKEp610 using newly proposed large-degree isogeny method.

Work	Timings [ms]				Timings [$cc \cdot 10^6$]			
	KeyGen	Encap	Decap	E + D	KeyGen	Encap	Decap	E + D
x86-64 i7-8565U @ 1.8 GHz								
Prior	9.5	17.1	17.3	34.5	17.0	30.9	31.2	62.0
This Work	9.5	15.6	16.5	32.0	17.0	28.0	29.7	57.7
Improvement	–	10.5%	4.8%	7.5%	–	10.5%	4.8%	7.5%
ARM64 ARM Cortex-A72 @ 1.5 GHz								
Prior	32.8	60.3	60.6	120.9	49.2	90.4	90.9	181.4
This Work	32.8	54.7	57.9	112.6	49.2	82.1	86.8	168.9
Improvement	–	10.2%	4.8%	7.4%	–	10.2%	4.8%	7.4%
ARM32 ARM Cortex-M4 @ 24 MHz								
Prior	4,972	9,139	9,196	18,335	119.3	219.3	220.7	440.0
This Work	4,972	8,295	8,774	17,069	119.3	199.1	210.6	409.9
Improvement	–	10.2%	4.8%	7.4%	–	10.2%	4.8%	7.4%

Table 6. Stack and code size improvements on ARM Cortex-M4 for SIKEp610 using newly proposed large-degree isogeny method.

Work	Stack [Bytes]			Code size [Bytes]		
	KeyGen	Encap	Decap	.text	.data	.bss
ARM32 ARM Cortex-M4 @ 24 MHz						
Prior	10,528	10,952	11,416	29,936	0	0
This Work	10,528	10,624	11,088	29,984	0	0
Improvement [value]	–	328	328	−48	–	–
Improvement [%]	–	3.1%	3.0%	−0.16%	–	–

P610 Speedups. First, we summarize our performance improvements for SIKEp610 in Table 5. These results target the three major SIKE operations, including key generation, key encapsulation, and key decapsulation. The "E +

D" column is the sum of the key encapsulation and key decapsulation timings. Since key generation generally only needs to be performed once, the "E + D" time has been used as an effective measure of SIKE's performance when deployed. Across the board, key encapsulation is improved by just over 10% and key decapsulation is improved by just less than 5%, resulting in "E + D" improvement of about 7.5%.

P610 Stack and Code Size. In Table 6, we utilize pqm4 to analyze the stack usage and code size of our implementation. Interestingly, our approach reduces the stack usage by 3% for both key encapsulation and decapsulation. Our modifications do include 48 additional bytes for code size, but this is a neglible amount. Based on the analysis of our new 2-isogeny formulas, we believe our revised 2-isogeny computation and evaluation formulas are the primary reason for stack usage improvement. Furthermore, our changes actually impacted the max stack usage, which means that the large-degree isogeny over base degree 2 consumes the most stack within both key encapsulation and decapsulation.

Table 7. Speedups achieved for SIKEp610_compressed using newly proposed large-degree isogeny method.

Work	Timings [ms]				Timings [$cc \cdot 10^6$]			
	KeyGen	Encap	Decap	E + D	KeyGen	Encap	Decap	E + D
x86-64 i7-8565U @ 1.8 GHz								
Prior	17.2	24.1	18.5	42.6	30.9	43.4	33.3	76.7
This Work	16.3	24.1	17.6	41.7	29.3	43.4	31.7	75.1
Improvement	5.4%	–	5.0%	2.1%	5.4%	–	5.0%	2.1%

Table 8. Speedups achieved for SIKEp377 and SIKEp546 on x86-64 i7-8565U platform @ 1.8 GHz using newly proposed large-degree isogeny method.

Work	Timings [ms]				Timings [$cc \cdot 10^6$]			
	KeyGen	Encap	Decap	E + D	KeyGen	Encap	Decap	E + D
SIKEp377								
Prior	2.7	5.0	5.0	9.9	4.81	8.92	8.93	17.8
This Work	2.7	4.5	4.7	9.2	4.81	8.07	8.52	16.6
Improvement	–	10.5%	4.8%	7.5%	–	10.5%	4.8%	7.5%
SIKEp546								
Prior	7.2	13.1	13.2	26.3	12.9	23.6	23.7	47.3
This Work	7.2	11.8	12.5	24.3	12.9	21.3	22.5	43.8
Improvement	–	10.9%	5.5%	8.1%	–	10.9%	5.5%	8.1%

P610 Compressed Speedups. As a further testament to the robustness of our method, we apply it to the SIKEp610_compressed scheme with results shown in

Table 7. SIKE with key compression actually swaps the order of 2 and 3 isogenies. Now, key generation and key decapsulation perform the isogeny of base degree 2. Compared to the uncompressed scheme, SIKEp610_compressed only computes two large-degree isogenies of base degree 2, one in key generation and one in key decapsulation, whereas SIKEp610(_uncompressed) computes three large-degree isogenies of base degree 2, two in key encapsulation and one in key decapsulation. Our results agree with this fact and show a 5.4% improvement in key generation and a 5.0% improvement in key decapsulation, leading to an "E + D" speedup of about 2.1%.

New P377 and P546 Speedups. Next, we apply our work to the newly proposed SIKE parameters featured in [37]. SIKEp377 and SIKEp546 are new parameter sets targeted at NIST Security Level 1 and 3, respectively. Since this work only provided implementations targeting x86 implementations, we only benchmarked it for our x86 platform. SIKEp377 and SIKEp546 timing results are summarized in Table 8. When comparing these results to the SIKEp610 results, the same 10% improvement for key encapsulation and 5% improvement for key decapsulation are achieved. These numbers are so close most likely because all three implementations feature a similar point multiplication to point evaluation ratio which is used for finding a large-degree isogeny strategy.

Table 9. Evaluation of SIKE performance scaling as prime size increases on x86-64 i7-8565U platform @ 1.8 GHz. Note that SIKEp377, SIKEp546, and SIKEp610 employ our revised large-degree isogeny method.

SIKE Parameter Set	Timings [ms]				Timings [$cc \cdot 10^6$]			
	KeyGen	Encap	Decap	E + D	KeyGen	Encap	Decap	E + D
SIKEp377	2.7	4.5	4.7	9.2	4.81	8.07	8.52	16.6
SIKEp434	3.8	6.2	6.7	12.9	6.90	11.2	12.1	23.2
SIKEp503	5.2	8.5	9.2	17.7	9.37	15.4	16.5	31.9
SIKEp546	7.2	11.8	12.5	24.3	12.9	21.3	22.5	43.8
SIKEp610	12.7	21.4	22.7	44.1	22.9	38.6	40.8	79.4
SIKEp751	15.8	25.4	27.3	52.8	28.4	45.8	49.2	95.0

SIKE Performance Scaling. As a final evaluation of our method, we examine the scaling of SIKE performance as the prime size increases. We summarize the results of all SIKE implementations on our x86 platform in Table 9. Our new large-degree isogeny method applies to SIKEp377, SIKEp546, and SIKEp610. All other schemes have been left unchanged and their performance is only to analyze scaling. For instance, prior SIKE results in the SIKE submission [5] show that key encapsulation is several percent faster than key decapsulation. This trend did not fit for SIKEp610, where key encapsulation and decapsulation results were almost the same. Since our new method accelerates SIKEp610 encapsulation by 10% and decapsulation by 5%, our results now show a several percent gap between encapsulation and decapsulation.

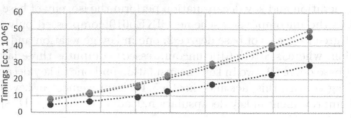

Fig. 4. Performance of SIKE versus the size of its prime on x86 platforms.

We visualize the SIKE performance scaling results as a graph in Fig. 4. As a trendline, we added a polynomial of order 2, which generally fits well. This is to be expected as the size of the prime dictates the low-level modular arithmetic as well as the size of the large-degree isogeny. Low-level modular arithmetic is $O(p^2)$ for a prime p and the large-degree isogeny is $O(e \log e)$, where $e = p/2$. Thus, a combined complexity of about $O(p^3 \log p)$ is achieved. The only blip in the performance graph is for SIKEp503, which may be because 512 bits fits very well in modern processors when computing modular multiplication.

6   Conclusion

In this paper, we proposed, implemented, and evaluated a new method for computing large-degree isogenies of an odd power. Our results accelerated uncompressed SIKEp610 key encapsulation and decapsulation operations by about 10% and 5%, respectively, also with a 3% improvement in stack usage. This proposed method is both simple to implement and applicable to a variety of SIKE applications. Besides SIKE parameter sets, we applied this method to newly proposed SIKE parameter sets and SIKE key compression. Given the benefit and simplicity of our approach with very few drawbacks, we recommend this method for current and emerging SIKE implementations.

Acknowledgment. The authors would like to thank the reviewers for their comments.

Intellectual Property Disclosure

Some of these techniques may be covered by US and/or international patents.

References

1. Adj, G., Cervantes-Vázquez, D., Chi-Domínguez, J.J., Menezes, A., Rodríguez-Henríquez, F.: On the cost of computing isogenies between supersingular elliptic curves. In: Cid, C., Jacobson, M., Jr. (eds.) SAC 2018. LNCS, vol. 11349, pp. 322–343. Springer, Cham (2019). https://doi.org/10.1007/978-3-030-10970-7_15
2. Alagic, G., et al.: Status Report on the Second Round of the NIST Post-Quantum Cryptography Standardization Process. NIST IR 8309 (2020)
3. Anastasova, M., Azarderakhsh, R., Kermani, M.M.: Fast strategies for the implementation of SIKE round 3 on ARM Cortex-M4. IEEE Trans. Circuits Syst I Regular Papers **68**, 1–13 (2021)
4. Roberto Avanzi, et al.: Crystals-kyber: Algorithm specifications and supporting documentation (version 2.0). Submission to the NIST Post-Quantum Standardization project (2019)
5. Azarderakhsh, R., et al.: Supersingular Isogeny Key Encapsulation. Submission to the NIST Post-Quantum Standardization project (2020)
6. Azarderakhsh ,R., et al.: Supersingular Isogeny Key Encapsulation. Submission to the NIST Post-Quantum Standardization Project (2017)
7. Azarderakhsh, R., Jao, D., Kalach, K., Koziel, B., Leonardi, C.: Key compression for isogeny-based cryptosystems. In: Proceedings of the 3rd ACM International Workshop on ASIA Public-Key Cryptography, pp. 1–10 (2016)
8. Azarderakhsh, R., Jao, D., Koziel, B., LeGrow, J.T., Soukharev, V., Taraskin, O.: How not to create an isogeny-based PAKE. In: Conti, M., Zhou, J., Casalicchio, E., Spognardi, A. (eds.) ACNS 2020, Part I. LNCS, vol. 12146, pp. 169–186. Springer, Cham (2020). https://doi.org/10.1007/978-3-030-57808-4_9
9. Azarderakhsh, R., El Khatib, R., Koziel, B., Langenberg, B.: Hardware deployment of hybrid PQC. Cryptology ePrint Archive, Report 2021/541 (2021). https://ia.cr/2021/541
10. Bernstein, D.J., et al.: Classic McEliece: conservative code-based cryptography. Submission to the NIST Post-Quantum Standardization project (2019)
11. Castryck, W., Lange, T., Martindale, C., Panny, L., Renes, J.: CSIDH: an efficient post-quantum commutative group action. In: Peyrin, T., Galbraith, S. (eds.) ASIACRYPT 2018, Part III. LNCS, vol. 11274, pp. 395–427. Springer, Cham (2018). https://doi.org/10.1007/978-3-030-03332-3_15
12. Charles, D.X., Lauter, K.E., Goren, E.Z.: Cryptographic hash functions from expander graphs. J. Cryptol. **22**(1), 93–113 (2009). https://doi.org/10.1007/s00145-007-9002-x
13. Childs, A.M., Jao, D., Soukharev, V.: Constructing elliptic curve isogenies in quantum subexponential time. J. Math. Cryptol. **8**(1), 1–29 (2014)
14. Costello, C., Jao, D., Longa, P., Naehrig, M., Renes, J., Urbanik, D.: Efficient compression of SIDH public keys. In: Coron, J.-S., Nielsen, J.B. (eds.) EUROCRYPT 2017, Part I. LNCS, vol. 10210, pp. 679–706. Springer, Cham (2017). https://doi.org/10.1007/978-3-319-56620-7_24
15. Costello, C., Longa, P., Naehrig, M.: Efficient algorithms for supersingular isogeny Diffie-Hellman. In: Robshaw, M., Katz, J. (eds.) CRYPTO 2016, Part I. LNCS, vol. 9814, pp. 572–601. Springer, Heidelberg (2016). https://doi.org/10.1007/978-3-662-53018-4_21
16. Costello, C., Longa, P., Naehrig, M., Renes, J., Virdia, F.: Improved classical cryptanalysis of SIKE in practice. In: Kiayias, A., Kohlweiss, M., Wallden, P., Zikas, V. (eds.) PKC 2020, Part II. LNCS, vol. 12111, pp. 505–534. Springer, Cham (2020). https://doi.org/10.1007/978-3-030-45388-6_18

17. Couveignes, J.-M.: Hard homogeneous spaces. Cryptology ePrint Archive, Report 2006/291 (2006)
18. De Feo, L., Jao, D., Plût, J.: Towards quantum-resistant cryptosystems from supersingular elliptic curve isogenies. J. Math. Cryptol. **8**(3), 209–247 (2014)
19. El Khatib, R., Azarderakhsh, R., Mozaffari-Kermani, M.: Optimized algorithms and architectures for montgomery multiplication for post-quantum cryptography. In: Mu, Y., Deng, R.H., Huang, X. (eds.) CANS 2019. LNCS, vol. 11829, pp. 83–98. Springer, Cham (2019). https://doi.org/10.1007/978-3-030-31578-8_5
20. Elkhatib, R., Azarderakhsh, R., Mozaffari-Kermani, M.: Highly optimized montgomery multiplier for SIKE primes on FPGA. In: 2020 IEEE 27th Symposium on Computer Arithmetic (ARITH), pp. 64–71, (2020)
21. Elkhatib, R., Azarderakhsh, R., Mozaffari-Kermani, M.: Accelerated RISC-V for post-quantum SIKE. Cryptology ePrint Archive, Report 2021/597 (2021). https://ia.cr/2021/597
22. Farzam, M.-H., Bayat-Sarmadi, S., Mosanaei-Boorani, H.: Implementation of supersingular isogeny-based Diffie-Hellman and key encapsulation using an efficient scheduling. IEEE Trans. Circuits Syst. **67**(12), 4895–4903 (2020)
23. Faz-Hernández, A., López, J., Ochoa-Jiménez, E., Rodríguez-Henríquez, F.: A faster software implementation of the supersingular isogeny Diffie-Hellman key exchange protocol. IEEE Trans. Comput. **67**(11), 1622–1636 (2017)
24. Galbraith, S.D., Petit, C., Shani, B., Ti, Y.B.: On the security of supersingular isogeny cryptosystems. In: Cheon, J.H., Takagi, T. (eds.) ASIACRYPT 2016, Part I. LNCS, vol. 10031, pp. 63–91. Springer, Heidelberg (2016). https://doi.org/10.1007/978-3-662-53887-6_3
25. Galbraith, S.D., Petit, C., Silva, J.: Identification protocols and signature schemes based on supersingular isogeny problems. In: Takagi, T., Peyrin, T. (eds.) ASIACRYPT 2017, Part I. LNCS, vol. 10624, pp. 3–33. Springer, Cham (2017). https://doi.org/10.1007/978-3-319-70694-8_1
26. Gélin, A., Wesolowski, B.: Loop-abort faults on supersingular isogeny cryptosystems. In: Lange, T., Takagi, T. (eds.) PQCrypto 2017. LNCS, vol. 10346, pp. 93–106. Springer, Cham (2017). https://doi.org/10.1007/978-3-319-59879-6_6
27. Jao, D., De Feo, L.: Towards quantum-resistant cryptosystems from supersingular elliptic curve isogenies. In: Yang, B.-Y. (ed.) PQCrypto 2011. LNCS, vol. 7071, pp. 19–34. Springer, Heidelberg (2011). https://doi.org/10.1007/978-3-642-25405-5_2
28. Jaques, S., Schanck, J.M.: Quantum cryptanalysis in the RAM model: claw-finding attacks on SIKE. In: Boldyreva, A., Micciancio, D. (eds.) CRYPTO 2019, Part I. LNCS, vol. 11692, pp. 32–61. Springer, Cham (2019). https://doi.org/10.1007/978-3-030-26948-7_2
29. Kannwischer, M.J., Rijneveld, J., Schwabe, P., Stoffelen, K.: PQM4: Post-quantum crypto library for the ARM Cortex-M4. https://github.com/mupq/pqm4
30. Koziel, B., Ackie, A., El Khatib, R., Azarderakhsh, R., Kermani, M.M.: SIKE'd up: fast hardware architectures for supersingular isogeny key encapsulation. IEEE Trans. Circuits Syst. I Regul. Pap. **61**, 1–13 (2020)
31. Koziel, B., Azarderakhsh, R., Jao, D.: An exposure model for supersingular isogeny Diffie-Hellman key exchange. In: Smart, N.P. (ed.) CT-RSA 2018. LNCS, vol. 10808, pp. 452–469. Springer, Cham (2018). https://doi.org/10.1007/978-3-319-76953-0_24
32. Koziel, B., Azarderakhsh, R., Jao, D.: Side-channel attacks on quantum-resistant supersingular isogeny Diffie-Hellman. In: Adams, C., Camenisch, J. (eds.) SAC 2017. LNCS, vol. 10719, pp. 64–81. Springer, Cham (2018). https://doi.org/10.1007/978-3-319-72565-9_4

33. Koziel, B., Azarderakhsh, R., Mozaffari-Kermani, M.: Fast hardware architectures for supersingular isogeny Diffie-Hellman key exchange on FPGA. In: Dunkelman, O., Sanadhya, S.K. (eds.) INDOCRYPT 2016. LNCS, vol. 10095, pp. 191–206. Springer, Cham (2016). https://doi.org/10.1007/978-3-319-49890-4_11

34. Koziel, B., Azarderakhsh, R., Mozaffari-Kermani, M.: A high-performance and scalable hardware architecture for isogeny-based cryptography. IEEE Trans. Comput. **67**(11), 1594–1609 (2018)

35. Koziel, B., Azarderakhsh, R., Mozaffari-Kermani, M., Jao, D.: Post-quantum cryptography on FPGA based on isogenies on elliptic curves. IEEE Trans. Circuits Syst. I Regul. Pap. **64**(1), 86–99 (2017)

36. Koziel, B., Jalali, A., Azarderakhsh, R., Jao, D., Mozaffari-Kermani, M.: NEON-SIDH: efficient implementation of supersingular isogeny Diffie-Hellman key exchange protocol on ARM. In: Foresti, S., Persiano, G. (eds.) CANS 2016. LNCS, vol. 10052, pp. 88–103. Springer, Cham (2016). https://doi.org/10.1007/978-3-319-48965-0_6

37. Longa, P., Wang, W., Szefer, J.: The cost to break SIKE: a comparative hardware-based analysis with AES and SHA-3. In: Malkin, T., Peikert, C. (eds.) CRYPTO 2021, Part III. LNCS, vol. 12827, pp. 402–431. Springer, Cham (2021). https://doi.org/10.1007/978-3-030-84252-9_14

38. Massolino, P.M., Longa, P., Renes, J., Batina, L.: A compact and scalable hardware/software co-design of SIKE. IACR Trans. Crypt. Hardw. Embed. Syst. **2020**, 245–271 (2020)

39. Naehrig, M., Renes, J.: Dual isogenies and their application to public-key compression for isogeny-based cryptography. In: Galbraith, S.D., Moriai, S. (eds.) ASIACRYPT 2019, Part II. LNCS, vol. 11922, pp. 243–272. Springer, Cham (2019). https://doi.org/10.1007/978-3-030-34621-8_9

40. Pereira, G.C.C.F., Barreto, P.S.L.M.: Isogeny-based key compression without pairings. In: Garay, J.A. (ed.) PKC 2021, Part I. LNCS, vol. 12710, pp. 131–154. Springer, Cham (2021). https://doi.org/10.1007/978-3-030-75245-3_6

41. Rostovtsev, A., Stolbunov, A.: Public-key cryptosystem based on isogenies. Cryptology ePrint Archive, Report 2006/145 (2006)

42. Seo, H., Anastasova, M., Jalali, A., Azarderakhsh, R.: Supersingular isogeny key encapsulation (SIKE) round 2 on ARM Cortex-M4. IEEE Trans. Comput. **70**, 1705–1718 (2020). https://www.computer.org/csdl/journal/tc/2021/10/09190059/1mYZi2oUoWk

43. Seo, H., Sana, P., Jalal, A., Azarderakhsh, R.: Optimized implementation of SIKE round 2 on 64-bit ARM Cortex-A processors. IEEE Trans. Circuits Syst. I Regul. Pap. **67-I**(8), 2659–2671 (2020)

44. Shor, P.W.: Algorithms for quantum computation: discrete logarithms and factoring. In: 35th Annual Symposium on Foundations of Computer Science (FOCS 1994), pp. 124–134 (1994)

45. Taraskin, O., Soukharev, V., Jao, D., LeGrow, J.T.: Towards isogeny-based password-authenticated key establishment. J. Math. Cryptol. **15**(1), 18–30 (2021)

46. The National Institute of Standards and Technology (NIST). Post-quantum cryptography standardization, 2017–2018. https://csrc.nist.gov/projects/post-quantum-cryptography/post-quantum-cryptography-standardization

47. Ti, Y.B.: Fault attack on supersingular isogeny cryptosystems. In: Lange, T., Takagi, T. (eds.) PQCrypto 2017. LNCS, vol. 10346, pp. 107–122. Springer, Cham (2017). https://doi.org/10.1007/978-3-319-59879-6_7

48. Vélu, J.: Isogénies entre courbes elliptiques. Comptes Rendus de l'Académie des Sciences Paris Séries A-B **273**, A238–A241 (1971)
49. Yoo, Y., Azarderakhsh, R., Jalali, A., Jao, D., Soukharev, V.: A post-quantum digital signature scheme based on supersingular isogenies. In: Kiayias, A. (ed.) FC 2017. LNCS, vol. 10322, pp. 163–181. Springer, Cham (2017). https://doi.org/10.1007/978-3-319-70972-7_9

Fully Projective Radical Isogenies in Constant-Time

Jesús-Javier Chi-Domínguez[1] and Krijn Reijnders[2(✉)]

[1] Cryptography Research Centre, Technology Innovation Institute, Abu Dhabi,
United Arab Emirates
`jesus.dominguez@tii.ae`
[2] Radboud University, Nijmegen, The Netherlands
`krijn@cs.ru.nl`

Abstract. At PQCrypto-2020, Castryck and Decru proposed CSURF (CSIDH on the surface) as an improvement to the CSIDH protocol. Soon after that, at Asiacrypt-2020, together with Vercauteren they introduced radical isogenies as a further improvement. The main improvement in these works is that both CSURF and radical isogenies require only one torsion point to initiate a chain of isogenies, in comparison to Vélu isogenies which require a torsion point per isogeny. Both works were implemented using non-constant-time techniques, however, in a realistic scenario, a constant-time implementation is necessary to mitigate risks of timing attacks. The analysis of constant-time CSURF and radical isogenies was left as an open problem by Castryck, Decru, and Vercauteren. In this work we analyze this problem. A straightforward constant-time implementation of CSURF and radical isogenies encounters too many issues to be cost effective, but we resolve some of these issues with new optimization techniques. We introduce projective radical isogenies to save costly inversions and present a hybrid strategy for integration of radical isogenies in CSIDH implementations. These improvements make radical isogenies almost twice as efficient in constant-time, in terms of finite field multiplications. Using these improvements, we then measure the algorithmic performance in a benchmark of CSIDH, CSURF and CRADS (an implementation using radical isogenies) for different prime sizes. Our implementation provides a more accurate comparison between CSIDH, CSURF and CRADS than the original benchmarks, by using state-of-the-art techniques for all three implementations. Our experiments illustrate that the speed-up of constant-time CSURF-512 with radical isogenies is reduced to about 3% in comparison to the fastest state-of-the-art constant-time CSIDH-512 implementation. The performance is worse for larger primes, as radical isogenies scale worse than Vélu isogenies.

Keywords: Isogeny-based cryptography · CSIDH · Constant-time implementation · CSURF · Radical isogenies

The European Commission initially supported this work through the ERC Starting Grant 804476 (SCARE), while J. J. Chi-Domínguez was a postdoctoral researcher at Tampere University.

S. D. Galbraith (Ed.): CT-RSA 2022, LNCS 13161, pp. 73–95, 2022.
https://doi.org/10.1007/978-3-030-95312-6_4

1   Introduction

The first proposal of an isogeny-based Diffie-Hellman key exchange was done by Couveignes [13] and centered on the action of an ideal class group on a set of ordinary elliptic curves. Later Rostovtsev and Stolbunov [23,24] independently rediscovered it and recognized its potential as a possible post-quantum candidate. In the last decade, isogeny-based key exchange developed further, notably with SIDH in [2,14,16]. In Asiacrypt 2018, Castryck, Lange, Martindale, Panny, and Renes introduced CSIDH (a *non-interactive* key exchange) as a reformulation of the Couveignes-Rostovtsev-Stolbunov system using supersingular curves defined over a prime field [9]. With the hope to improve the performance of CSIDH, Castryck and Decru proposed CSURF, which exploits 2-isogenies [7] on the surface of the isogeny graph. Later on, Castryck, Decru, and Vercauteren in Asiacrypt 2020 expanded on the ideas in CSURF to construct isogenies with small odd degree based on radical computations (N-th roots) [8]. Using radical isogenies, they claimed a speed-up of about 19% over CSIDH-512, however both of the implementations in [7,8] focus on non-constant-time instantiations. In particular, Castryck, Decru, and Vercauteren left the analysis of a constant-time implementation of CSURF and radical isogenies as an open problem. A constant-time algorithm refers to an algorithm whose running time is independent of (or uncorrelated with) the secret input. This implies the variability in the running time depends on randomness and not on the leakage of information on secret values.

Dealing with constant-time implementations of CSIDH (and CSURF) can be tricky as there are multiple approaches, such as using dummy isogenies or a dummy-free approach. The first constant-time CSIDH instantiation is the procedure using dummy isogenies proposed by Meyer, Campos, and Reith in [18], later improved by Onuki *et al.* in [20]. Subsequently, Cervantes-Vázquez *et al.* proposed a dummy-free variant of CSIDH [10], and more recently, Banegas *et al.* presented CTIDH [3]. This covers the literature that we are aware of.

The general idea to make CSIDH implementations run in constant-time is to perform a fixed number m of isogenies of a certain degree ℓ_i, independent of the secret key e_i. For example, take the CSIDH-512 prime $p = 4 \cdot \prod_{i=1}^{74} \ell_i - 1$, where ℓ_1 up to ℓ_{73} are the smallest 73 odd prime numbers and $\ell_{74} = 587$. Let $E/\mathbb{F}_p: y^2 = x^3 + Ax^2 + x$ be a supersingular Montgomery curve with $(p+1)$ rational points. Assuming we require exactly $m = 5$ isogenies per ℓ_i, then our key space corresponds with the integer exponent[1] vectors $(e_1, \ldots, e_{74}) \in [\![-m \mathbin{..} m]\!]^{74}$. A dummy-based variant of constant-time CSIDH performs $|e_i|$ secret ℓ_i-isogenies and then proceeds by performing $(m - |e_i|)$ dummy-isogenies. The ℓ_i-isogeny kernel belongs to either $E[\pi - 1]$ or $E[\pi + 1]$, which is determined by the sign of e_i. A dummy-free variant (which prevents e.g. fault injection attacks) does not perform the $(m - |e_i|)$ dummy-isogeny constructions, but instead requires e_i to have the same parity as m. It then alternates between using kernels in

---

[1] The word *exponent* comes from the associated group action, see Sect. 2.2.

$E[\pi - 1]$ and $E[\pi + 1]$ in such a way that one effectively *applies* e_i isogenies while *performing* m isogenies.

The experiments presented in [8] suggest a speed-up of about 19% when using radical isogenies instead of Vélu's formulas (for a prime of 512 bits). As mentioned above, these experiments focused on a non-constant-time Magma implementation for both the group-action evaluation and the chain of radical isogenies. More specifically, the Magma-code implementation of [8] performs field inversions in variable time depending on the input. Furthermore, the implementation computes exactly $|e_i|$ ℓ_i-radical isogenies, where $e_i \in [\![-m_i \,..\, m_i]\!]$ is a secret exponent of the private key (for instance when $e_i = 0$ the group action is trivial). Clearly, when measuring random non-constant time instances of CSURF or radical isogenies the average number of ℓ_i-radical isogenies to be performed is $\frac{m_i}{2}$, whereas in constant-time implementations the number of isogenies of degree ℓ_i is the fixed bound m_i.

A straightforward constant-time implementation of CSURF and radical isogenies would replace all non-constant-time techniques with constant-time techniques. This would, however, drastically reduce the performance of CSURF and radical isogenies, as inversions become costly and we need to perform more (dummy) isogenies per degree. Furthermore, radical isogenies currently do not use relatively 'cheap' Vélu isogenies of low degree because they are replaced by relatively expensive radical isogenies. Such an implementation would be outperformed by any state-of-the-art CSIDH implementation in constant-time.

Contributions. In this paper, we are interested in constant-time implementations of CSURF and radical isogenies. We present two improvements to radical isogenies which reduce their algorithmic cost. Then, we analyze the cost and efficiency of constant-time CSURF and radical isogenies, and benchmark their performance when implemented in CSIDH in number of finite field multiplications. More concretely, our contributions are

1. *fully projective radical isogenies*, a non-trivial reformulation of radical isogenies in projective coordinates, and of the required isomorphisms between curve models. This allows us to perform radical isogenies without leaving the projective coordinates used in CSIDH. This saves an inversion per isogeny and additional inversions in the isomorphisms between curve models, which in total reduces the cost of radical isogenies in constant-time by almost 50%.
2. a *hybrid strategy* to integrate radical isogenies in CSIDH, which allows us to 're-use' torsion points that are used in the CSIDH group action evaluation to initiate a 'chain' of radical isogenies, and to keep cheap low degree Vélu isogenies. This generalizes the 'traditional' CSIDH evaluation, optimizes the evaluation of radical isogenies, and does not require sampling an extra torsion point to initiate a 'chain' of radical isogenies.
3. a *cost analysis* of the efficiency of radical isogenies in constant-time, which describes the overall algorithmic cost to perform radical isogenies, assuming the aforementioned improvements. We show that, although these improvements greatly reduce the total cost in terms of finite field operations, radical

isogenies of degree 5, 7, 11 and 13 are too costly in comparison to Vélu and $\sqrt{}$élu isogenies. We conclude that only radical isogenies of degree 4 and 9 are an improvement to 'traditional' CSIDH. Furthermore, we show that radical isogenies scale worse than Vélu isogenies with regards to the size of the base field, which reduces the effectiveness of CSURF and radical isogenies in comparison to CSIDH for large primes.

4. the *first constant-time implementation* of CSURF and radical isogenies, optimized with concern to the exponentiations used in radical isogenies, and optimal bounds and approximately optimal strategies as in [12,14,15], which allow for a more precise comparison in performance between CSIDH, CSURF and implementations using radical isogenies (CRADS) than [7,8]. Our Python-code implementation allows isogeny evaluation strategies using both traditional Vélu and $\sqrt{}$élu formulas, as well as radical isogenies and 2-isogenies (on the surface), and can thus be used to compare CSURF and CRADS against a state-of-the-art constant-time implementation of CSIDH.

5. a *performance benchmark* of CSURF and CRADS in comparison to 'traditional' CSIDH, in total finite field operations. Our benchmark is more accurate than the original benchmarks from [7,8] and shows that the 5% and 19% speed-up (respectively) diminishes to roughly 3% in a precise constant-time comparison. These results gives a detailed view of the performance of radical isogenies in terms of finite field operations, and their performance when increasing the size of the base field. We show that in low parameter sets, with the additional cost of moving to constant-time, CSURF-512 and CRADS-512 perform a bit better than CSIDH-512 implementations, with a 2.53% and 2.15% speed-up respectively. Additionally, with the hybrid strategy this speed-up is slightly larger for small primes. However, we get no speed-up for larger base fields: For primes of 1792 bits and larger, CSIDH outperforms both CSURF and CRADS due to the better scaling of Vélu isogenies in comparison to radical isogenies.

The (Python) implementation used in this paper is freely available at

https://github.com/Krijn-math/Constant-time-CSURF-CRADS.

The results from the benchmark answer the open question from Castryck, Decru, and Vercauteren in [8]: in constant-time, the CSIDH protocol gains only a small speed-up by using CSURF or radical isogenies, and only for small primes. Even stronger, our hybrid strategy shows that radical isogenies require significant improvements to make them cost effective, as computing a radical per isogeny is in most cases too expensive. Our results illustrate that constant-time CSURF and radical isogenies perform worse than large CSIDH instantiations (i.e. $\log(p) \geq 1792$), at least at the level of finite field operations.[2]

---

[2] We explicitly do not focus on performance in clock cycles; a measurement in clock cycles (on our python-code implementation) could give the impression that the underlying field arithmetic is optimized, instead of the algorithmic performance.

Outline. In Sect. 2, we recap the theoretical preliminaries on isogenies, CSIDH, CSURF, and radical isogenies. In Sect. 3, we introduce our first improvement: fully projective radical isogenies. This allows us to analyse the effectiveness and cost of constant-time radical isogenies in Sect. 4. Then we improve the integration of radical isogenies in CSIDH in Sect. 5, using a hybrid strategy. In Sect. 6, we benchmark constant-time CSIDH, CSURF and CRADS in terms of finite field operations, using state-of-the-art techniques for all three. Finally, in Sect. 7 we present our conclusions concerning the efficiency of radical isogenies in comparison to CSIDH in constant-time.

2 Preliminaries

In this section we describe the basics of isogenies, CSIDH, CSURF and radical isogenies.

Given two elliptic curves E and E' over a prime field $\mathbb{F}_p$, an isogeny is a morphism $\varphi : E \to E'$ such that $\mathcal{O}_E \mapsto \mathcal{O}_{E'}$. A separable isogeny φ has a degree $\deg(\varphi)$ equal to the size of its kernel, and for any isogeny $\varphi : E \to E'$ there is a unique isogeny $\hat{\varphi} : E' \to E$ called the *dual isogeny*, with the property that $\hat{\varphi} \circ \varphi = [\deg(\varphi)]$ is the scalar point multiplication on E. A separable isogeny is uniquely defined by its kernel and *vice versa*; a finite subgroup $G \subset E(\overline{\mathbb{F}_p})$ defines a unique separable isogeny $\varphi_G : E \to E/G$ (up to isomorphism).

Vélu's formulas [25] provide the construction and evaluation of separable isogenies with cyclic kernel $G = \langle P \rangle$ for some $P \in E(\overline{\mathbb{F}_p})$. Both the isogeny construction of φ_G and the evaluation of $\varphi_G(R)$ for a point $R \in E(\overline{\mathbb{F}_p})$ have a running time of $O(\#G)$, which becomes infeasible for large subgroups G. A new procedure presented by Bernstein, De Feo, Leroux, and Smith in ANTS-2020 based on the baby-step giant-step algorithm decreases this cost to $\tilde{O}(\sqrt{\#G})$ finite field operations [4]. We write this procedure as $\sqrt{\text{élu}}$. This new approach is based on multi-evaluations of a given polynomial, although at its core it is based on traditional Vélu's formulas.

Isogenies from E to itself are *endomorphisms*, and the set of all endomorphisms of E forms a ring, which is usually denoted as $\text{End}(E)$. The scalar point multiplication map $(x, y) \mapsto [N](x, y)$ and the Frobenius map $\pi : (x, y) \mapsto (x^p, x^p)$ are examples of such endomorphisms over the finite field of characteristic p. In particular, the order $\mathcal{O} \cong \mathbb{Z}[\pi]$ is a subring of $\text{End}(E)$. An elliptic curve E is *ordinary* if it has a (commutative) endomorphism ring isomorphic to a suborder $\mathcal{O}$ of the ring of integers $\mathcal{O}_K$ for some quadratic number field K. A *supersingular* elliptic curve has a larger endomorphism ring: $\text{End}(E)$ is isomorphic to an order $\mathcal{O}$ in a quaternion algebra, and thus non-commutative.

2.1 CSIDH and Its Surface

CSIDH works with the smaller (commutative) subring $\text{End}_p(E)$ of $\text{End}(E)$, which are rational endomorphisms of a supersingular elliptic curve E. This subring $\text{End}_p(E)$ is isomorphic to an order $\mathcal{O} \subset \mathcal{O}_K$. As both $[N]$ and π are defined over $\mathbb{F}_p$, we get $\mathbb{Z}[\pi] \subset \mathrm{End}_p(E)$. To be more precise, the CSIDH protocol is based on the commutative action of the class group $\mathcal{C}\ell(\mathcal{O})$ on the set $\mathcal{E}\ell\ell_p(\mathcal{O})$ of supersingular elliptic curves E such that $\mathrm{End}_p(E)$ is isomorphic to the specific order $\mathcal{O} \subset \mathcal{O}_K$. The group action for an ideal class $[\mathfrak{a}] \in \mathcal{C}\ell(\mathcal{O})$ maps a curve $E \in \mathcal{E}\ell\ell_p(\mathcal{O})$ to another curve $[\mathfrak{a}] \star E \in \mathcal{E}\ell\ell_p(\mathcal{O})$ (see Sect. 2.2). Furthermore, the CSIDH group action is believed to be a *hard homogeneous space* [13] that allows a Merkle-Diffie-Hellman-like key agreement protocol with commutative diagram.

$$
\begin{array}{ccc}
E & \xrightarrow{\quad \mathfrak{a} \quad} & [\mathfrak{a}] \star E \\
\Big\downarrow{\scriptstyle \mathfrak{b}} & & \Big\downarrow{\scriptstyle \mathfrak{b}} \\
[\mathfrak{b}] \star E & \xrightarrow{\quad \mathfrak{a} \quad} & [\mathfrak{ab}] \star E
\end{array}
$$

The original CSIDH protocol uses the set $\mathcal{E}\ell\ell_p(\mathcal{O})$ with $\mathcal{O} \cong \mathbb{Z}[\pi]$ and $p = 3$ mod 4 (named the *floor*). To also benefit from 2-isogenies, the CSURF protocol switches to elliptic curves on the *surface* of the isogeny graph, that is, $\mathcal{E}\ell\ell_p(\mathcal{O})$ with $\mathcal{O} \cong \mathbb{Z}[\frac{1+\pi}{2}]$. Making 2-isogenies useful requires $p = 7 \mod 8$.

2.2　The Group Action of CSIDH and CSURF

The traditional way of evaluating the group action of an element $[\mathfrak{a}] \in \mathcal{C}\ell(\mathcal{O})$ is by using 'traditional' Vélu's [25] or $\sqrt{}$élu [4] formulas. The group action maps $E \to [\mathfrak{a}] \star E$ and can be described by the kernel $E[\mathfrak{a}]$ of an isogeny $\varphi_{\mathfrak{a}}$ of finite degree. Specifically, $[\mathfrak{a}] \star E = E/E[\mathfrak{a}]$ where

$$
E[\mathfrak{a}] = \bigcap_{\varphi \in \mathfrak{a}} \mathrm{Ker}(\varphi).
$$

In both CSIDH and CSURF, we apply specific elements $[\mathfrak{l}_i] \in \mathcal{C}\ell(\mathcal{O})$ such that $\mathfrak{l}_i^{\pm 1} = (\ell_i, \pi \mp 1)$ and ℓ_i is the i-th odd prime dividing $(p+1)$. For $\mathfrak{l}_i$, we have

$$
E[\mathfrak{l}_i^{\pm 1}] = E[\ell_i] \cap E[\pi \mp 1],
$$

where $P \in E[\ell_i]$ means P is a point of order ℓ_i and $P \in E[\pi \mp 1]$ implies $\pi(P) = \pm P$, so P is either an $\mathbb{F}_p$-rational point or a zero-trace point over $\mathbb{F}_{p^2}$. Thus, the group action $E \to [\mathfrak{l}_i^{\pm 1}] \star E$ is usually calculated by sampling a point $P \in E[\mathfrak{l}_i^{\pm 1}]$ and applying Vélu's formulas with input point P. A secret key for CSIDH is then a vector (e_i), which is evaluated as $E \to \prod_i [\mathfrak{l}_i]^{e_i} \star E$. CSURF changes the order $\mathcal{O}$ used to $\mathbb{Z}[\frac{1+\pi}{2}]$ to also perform 2-isogenies on the surface of the isogeny graph; these 2-isogenies do not require the sampling of a 2-order point but can instead be calculated by a specific formula based on radical computations.

Key space. Originally, the secret key $e = (e_i)$ was sampled from $[\![-m \mathrel{{.}{.}} m]\!]^n$ for some bound $m \in \mathbb{N}$. This was improved in [12,15,18] by varying the bound m per degree ℓ_i (a weighted L_∞-norm ball). Further developments with regards to improving the key space are presented in [19], using an $(L_1 + L_\infty)$-norm ball, and in CTIDH ([3]). These methods can give significant speed-ups. In their cores, they rely on (variations of) Vélu isogenies to evaluate the group action. In [7,8], the authors compare the performance of radical isogenies to CSIDH by using an unweighted L_∞-norm ball for CSIDH-512 versus a weighted L_∞-norm ball for the implementation using radical isogenies. This gives a skewed benchmark, which favors the performance of CSURF and CRADS. In this paper, to make a fair comparison to the previous work, we continue in the line of [12,15,18] by using *weighted* L_∞-norm balls for the implementations of CSIDH, CSURF and CRADS. It remains interesting to analyse the impact of radical isogenies in key spaces that are not based on weighted L_∞-norm balls. As radical isogenies can easily be made to have exactly the same cost per degree (with only slightly extra cost), they are interesting to analyse with respect to CTIDH.

2.3 The Tate Normal Form

CSURF introduced the idea to evaluate a 2-isogeny by radical computations. [8] extends this idea to higher degree isogenies, using a different curve model than the Montgomery curve. To get to that curve model, fix an N-order point P on E with $N \geq 4$. Then, there is a unique isomorphic curve $E(b,c)$ over $\mathbb{F}_p$ such that P is mapped to $(0,0)$ on $E(b,c)$. The curve $E(b,c)$ is given by Eq. (1), and is called the Tate normal form of (E, P):

$$E(b,c)/\mathbb{F}_p: y^2 + (1 - c)x - by = x^3 - bx^2, \quad b,c \in \mathbb{F}_p. \tag{1}$$

The curve $E(b,c)$ has a non-zero discriminant $\Delta(b,c)$ and in fact, it can be shown that the reverse is also true: for $b,c \in \mathbb{F}_p$ such that $\Delta(b,c) \neq 0$, the curve $E(b,c)$ is an elliptic curve over $\mathbb{F}_p$ with $(0,0)$ of order $N \geq 4$. Thus the pair (b,c) uniquely determines a pair (E,P) with P having order $N \geq 4$ on some isomorphic curve E over $\mathbb{F}_p$. In short, there is a bijection between the set of isomorphism classes of pairs (E,P) and the set of $\mathbb{F}_p$-points of $\mathbb{A}^2 - \{\Delta = 0\}$. The connection with *modular curves* is explored in more detail in [21].

2.4 Radical Isogenies

Let E_0 be a supersingular Montgomery curve over $\mathbb{F}_p$ and P_0 a point of order N with $N \geq 4$. Additionally, let $E_1 = E_0/\langle P_0 \rangle$, and P_1 a point of order N on E_1 such that $\hat{\varphi}(P_1) = P_0$ where $\hat{\varphi}$ is the dual of the N-isogeny $\varphi \colon E_0 \to E_1$. The pairs (E_0, P_0) and (E_1, P_1) uniquely determine Tate normal parameters (b_0, c_0) and (b_1, c_1) with $b_i, c_i \in \mathbb{F}_p$.

Castryck, Decru, and Vercauteren proved the existence of a function φ_N that maps (b_0, c_0) to (b_1, c_1) in such a way that it can be applied iteratively. This computes a chain of N-isogenies without the need to sample points of order N

per iteration. As a consequence, by mapping a given supersingular Montgomery curve $E/\mathbb{F}_p$ and some point P of order N to its Tate normal form, we can evaluate $E \rightarrow [\mathfrak{l}_i] \star E$ without any points (except for sampling P). Thus, it allows us to compute $E \rightarrow [\mathfrak{l}_i]^k \star E$ without having to sample k points of order N.

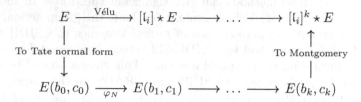

Notice that the top row and the bottom row of the diagram are isomorphic. The map φ_N is an elementary function in terms of b, c and $\alpha = \sqrt[N]{\rho}$ for a specific element $\rho \in \mathbb{F}_p(b, c)$: hence the name 'radical' isogeny. Over $\mathbb{F}_p$, an N-th root is unique whenever N and $p - 1$ are co-prime (as the map $x \mapsto x^N$ is then a bijection). Notice that this in particular holds for all odd primes ℓ_i of a CSIDH prime $p = h \cdot \prod \ell_i - 1$ for a suitable cofactor h. Castryck, Decru, and Vercauteren provided the explicit formulas of φ_N for $N \in \{2, 3, 4, 5, 7, 9, 11, 13\}$. For larger degrees the formulas could not be derived yet. They also suggest the use of radical isogenies of degree 4 and 9 instead of 2 and 3, respectively.

Later work by Onuki and Moriya [21] provides similar radical isogenies on Montgomery curves instead of Tate normal curves. Although their results are of theoretical interest, they only provide such radical isogenies for degree 3 and 4. For degree 3, the use of degree 9 radical isogenies on Tate normal curves is more efficient, while for degree 4 the difference between their formulas and those presented in [8] are negligible. We, therefore, focus only on radical isogenies on Tate normal curves for this work.

3 Fully Projective Radical Isogenies

In this section we introduce our first improvement to radical isogenies: *fully projective* radical isogenies. These allow to us bypass all inversions required for radical isogenies. We perform (a) the radical isogenies on Tate normal curves in projective coordinates, and (b) the switch between the Montgomery curve and the Tate normal curve, and back, in projective coordinates. (a) requires non-trivial work which we explain in Sect. 3.1, whereas (b) is only tediously working out the correct formulas. The savings are worth it: (a) saves an inversion per radical isogeny and (b) saves numerous inversions in overhead costs. All in all, it is possible to remain in projective coordinates throughout the whole implementation, which saves about 50% in terms of finite field operations in comparison to affine radical isogenies in constant time.

3.1 Efficient Radicals for Projective Coordinates

The cost of an original (affine) radical isogenies of degree N in constant-time is dominated by the cost of the N-th root and one inversion per iteration. We introduce projective radical isogenies so that we do not require this inversion. In a constant-time implementation, projective radical isogenies save approximately 50% of finite field operations in comparison to affine radical isogenies. A straightforward translation to projective coordinates for radical isogenies would save an inversion by writing the Tate normal parameter b (when necessary c) as $(X : Z)$. However, this comes at the cost of having to calculate both $\sqrt[N]{X}$ and $\sqrt[N]{Z}$ in the next iteration. Using the following lemma, we save one of these exponentiations.

Lemma 1. *Let $N \in \mathbb{N}$ such that $\gcd(N, p - 1) = 1$. Write $\alpha \in \mathbb{F}_p$ as $(X : Z)$ in projective coordinates with $X, Z \in \mathbb{F}_p$. Then $\sqrt[N]{\alpha} = (\sqrt[N]{XZ^{N-1}} : Z)$.*

Proof. As $\alpha = (X : Z) = (XZ^{N-1} : Z^N)$, we only have to show that the N-th root is unique. But N is co-prime with $p - 1$, so the map $x \mapsto x^N$ is a bijection. Therefore, the N-th root $\sqrt[N]{\rho}$ is unique for $\rho \in \mathbb{F}_p$, so $\sqrt[N]{Z^N} = Z$. $\qquad \square$

Crucially for radical isogenies, we want to compute N-th roots where $N = \ell_i$ for some i, working over the base field $\mathbb{F}_p$ with $p = h \cdot \prod_i \ell_i - 1$, and so for such an N we get $\gcd(N, p - 1) = 1$. This leads to the following corollary.

Corollary 1. *The representation $(XZ^{N-1} : Z^N)$ saves an exponentiation in the calculation of a radical isogeny of degree $N = \ell_i$ in projective coordinates.*

This brings the cost of a projective radical isogeny of small degree ℓ_i down to below $1.25 \log(p)$. Compared with affine radical isogeny formulas in constant-time, which cost roughly two exponentiations, such projective formulas cost approximately half of the affine ones in terms of finite field operations. The effect this has for degrees 2, 3, 4, 5, 7 and 9 can be seen in Table 1. A similar approach as Lemma 1 works for radical isogenies of degree $N = 4$.

3.2 Explicit Projective Formulas for Low Degrees

We give the projective radical isogeny formulas for three cases: degree 4, 5 and 7. For larger degrees, it becomes increasingly more tedious to work out the projective isogeny maps. In the repository, we provide formulas for $N \in \{2, 3, 4, 5, 7, 9\}$.

Projective isogeny of degree 4. The Tate normal form for degree 4 is $E : y^2 + xy - by = x^3 - bx^2$ for some $b \in \mathbb{F}_p$. From [8], we get $\rho = -b$ and $\alpha = \sqrt[4]{\rho}$, and the affine radical isogeny formula is

$$\alpha \mapsto b' = -\frac{\alpha(4\alpha^2 + 1)}{(2\alpha + 1)^4}.$$

Projectively, write α as $(X : Z)$ with $X, Z \in \mathbb{F}_p$. Then the projective formula is

$$(X : Z) \mapsto (X'Z'^4 : Z') \quad \text{with} \tag{2}$$
$$X' = (4X^2 + Z^2)XZ, \quad \text{and} \quad Z' = 2X + Z.$$

This isogeny is a bit more complex than it seems. First, notice that the denominator of the affine map is a fourth power. One would assume that it is therefore enough to map to $(X' : Z')$ and continue by taking only the fourth root of X' and re-use $Z' = \sqrt[4]{Z'^4}$. However, as $\gcd(4, p - 1) = 2$, the root $\delta = \sqrt[4]{Z'}$ is not unique. Following [8] we need to find the root δ that is a quadratic residue in $\mathbb{F}_p$. We can force δ to be a quadratic residue: notice that $(X' : Z'^4)$ is equivalent to $(X'Z'^4 : Z'^8)$, so that taking fourth roots gives $(\sqrt[4]{X'Z'^4} : \sqrt[4]{Z'^8}) = (\sqrt[4]{X'Z'^4} : Z'^2)$, where we have forced the second argument to be a square, and so we get the correct fourth root.

Therefore, by mapping to $(X'Z'^4 : Z')$ we compute $\sqrt[4]{-b'}$ as $(\sqrt[4]{X'Z'^4} : Z'^2)$ using only one 4-th root. This allows us to repeat Eq. (2) using only one exponentiation, without the cost of the inversion required in the affine version.

Projective isogeny of degree 5. The Tate normal form for degree 5 is $E : y^2 + (1 - b)xy - by = x^3 - bx^2$ for some $b \in \mathbb{F}_p$. From [8] we get $\rho = b$ and $\alpha = \sqrt[5]{\rho}$, and the affine radical isogeny formula is

$$\alpha \mapsto b' = \alpha \cdot \frac{\alpha^4 + 3\alpha^3 + 4\alpha^2 + 2\alpha + 1}{\alpha^4 - 2\alpha^3 + 4\alpha^2 - 3\alpha + 1}.$$

Projectively, write α as $(X : Z)$ with $X, Z \in \mathbb{F}_p$. Then the projective formula is

$$(X : Z) \mapsto (X'Z'^4 : Z') \quad \text{with} \tag{3}$$
$$X' = X(X^4 + 3X^3Z + 4X^2Z^2 + 2XZ^3 + Z^4), \quad \text{and}$$
$$Z' = Z(X^4 - 2X^3Z + 4X^2Z^2 - 3XZ^3 + Z^4).$$

Notice that the image is $(X'Z'^4 : Z')$ instead of $(X' : Z') = (X'Z'^4 : Z'^5)$, following Lemma 1. This allows us in the next iteration to compute $\sqrt[5]{b} = (\sqrt[5]{X} : \sqrt[5]{Z}) = (\sqrt[5]{X'Z'^4} : Z')$ using only one 5-th root. This allows us to repeat Eq. (3) using only one exponentiation, without the cost of the inversion required in the affine version.

Projective isogeny of degree 7. The Tate normal form for degree 7 is $E : y^2 + (-b^2 + b + 1)xy + (-b^3 + b^2)y = x^3 + (-b^3 + b^2)x^2$ for some $b \in \mathbb{F}_p$, with $\rho = b^5 - b^4$ and $\alpha = \sqrt[7]{\rho}$. However, the affine radical isogeny is already too large to display here, and the projective isogeny is even worse. However, we can still apply Lemma 1. The projective isogeny maps to $(X'Z'^6 : Z')$ and in a next iteration we can compute $\alpha = \sqrt[7]{\rho} = \sqrt[7]{b^5 - b^4}$ as $(\sqrt[7]{X^4Z^2(X - Z)} : Z)$.

3.3   Cost of Projective Radical Isogenies per Degree

In Table 1, we compare the cost of affine radical isogenies to projective radical isogenies. In Table 2, we compare the cost in switching between the different curve models for affine and projective coordinates.

In summary, fully projective radical isogenies are almost twice as fast as the original affine radical isogenies for constant-time implementations. Nevertheless, as we will see in the analysis of Sect. 4.1, the radical isogenies of degree 5, 7, 11 and 13 still perform worse than 'traditional' Vélu isogenies in realistic scenarios.

Table 1. Comparison between affine radical isogenies from [8] and the projective radical isogenies in this work. The letters $\mathbf{E}$, $\mathbf{M}$, $\mathbf{S}$, $\mathbf{A}$ and $\mathbf{I}$ denote exponentiation, multiplication, squaring, addition and inversion respectively. The last column expresses the ratio projective/affine in terms of finite field multiplications over $\mathbb{F}_p$ for a prime of 512 bits, using close-to-optimal addition chains for exponentiation and inversion, assuming $\mathbf{S} = \mathbf{M}$ and ignoring $\mathbf{A}$.

Degree	Affine ([8])	Projective (This work.)	Ratio projective/affine
2-isogeny	$\mathbf{E} + 4\mathbf{M} + 6\mathbf{A} + \mathbf{I}$	$\mathbf{E} + 3\mathbf{M} + 5\mathbf{S} + 10\mathbf{A}$	50.4%
3-isogeny	$\mathbf{E} + 6\mathbf{M} + 3\mathbf{A}$	$\mathbf{E} + 2\mathbf{M} + 10\mathbf{A}$	99.3%
4-isogeny	$\mathbf{E} + 4\mathbf{M} + 3\mathbf{A} + \mathbf{I}$	$\mathbf{E} + 6\mathbf{M} + 4\mathbf{S} + 3\mathbf{A}$	50.5%
5-isogeny	$\mathbf{E} + 7\mathbf{M} + 6\mathbf{A} + \mathbf{I}$	$\mathbf{E} + 8\mathbf{M} + 6\mathbf{S} + 18\mathbf{A}$	50.7%
7-isogeny	$\mathbf{E} + 24\mathbf{M} + 20\mathbf{A} + \mathbf{I}$	$\mathbf{E} + 14\mathbf{M} + 4\mathbf{S} + 64\mathbf{A}$	50.5%
9-isogeny	$\mathbf{E} + 69\mathbf{M} + 58\mathbf{A} + \mathbf{I}$	$\mathbf{E} + 61\mathbf{M} + 10\mathbf{S} + 202\mathbf{A}$	52.1%

Table 2. Comparison between the cost of different functions to switch curve models, necessary to perform radical isogenies. Affine results from [8] and projective results from this work.

Function	Affine ([8])	Projective (This work.)	Ratio projective/affine
Mont+ to Mont-	$\mathbf{E} + \mathbf{M} + \mathbf{S} + 2\mathbf{A} + \mathbf{I}$	$\mathbf{E} + 2\mathbf{M} + 2\mathbf{S} + 4\mathbf{A}$	50.1%
Mont- to Mont+	$\mathbf{E} + \mathbf{M} + \mathbf{S} + 2\mathbf{A} + \mathbf{I}$	$\mathbf{E} + 2\mathbf{S} + 4\mathbf{A}$	50.0%
Mont- to Tate4	$7\mathbf{M} + \mathbf{S} + \mathbf{A} + \mathbf{I}$	$5\mathbf{M} + 8\mathbf{S} + 7\mathbf{A}$	2.1%
Tate4 to Mont-	$2\mathbf{E} + 3\mathbf{M} + \mathbf{S} + 7\mathbf{A} + 2\mathbf{I}$	$2\mathbf{E} + 6\mathbf{M} + \mathbf{S} + 11\mathbf{A}$	50.1%
Full overhead CSURF	$7\mathbf{E} + 17\mathbf{M} + 6\mathbf{S} + 19\mathbf{A} + 5\mathbf{I}$	$7\mathbf{E} + 18\mathbf{M} + 16\mathbf{S} + 35\mathbf{A}$	58.5%
Mont+ to TateN	$\mathbf{E} + 9\mathbf{M} + \mathbf{S} + 11\mathbf{A} + \mathbf{I}$	$\mathbf{E} + 13\mathbf{M} + 7\mathbf{S} + 13\mathbf{A}$	51.1%
TateN to Mont+	$3\mathbf{E} + 20\mathbf{M} + 7\mathbf{S} + 34\mathbf{A} + \mathbf{I}$	$3\mathbf{E} + 33\mathbf{M} + 11\mathbf{S} + 65\mathbf{A}$	75.9%
Full overhead CRADS	$4\mathbf{E} + 34\mathbf{M} + 14\mathbf{S} + 54\mathbf{A} + 4\mathbf{I}$	$4\mathbf{E} + 54\mathbf{M} + 22\mathbf{S} + 83\mathbf{A}$	50.9%

4   Cost Analysis of Constant-Time Radical Isogenies

In this section, we analyze the cost and effectiveness of radical isogenies on Tate normal curves in constant-time. In a simplified model, the cost of performing n radical ℓ-isogenies can be divided into 4 steps.

1. Sample a point P on E_A of order ℓ;
2. Map (E_A, P) to the (isomorphic) Tate normal curve E_0 with $P \mapsto (0,0)$;
3. Perform the radical isogeny formula n times: $E_0 \to E_1 \to \ldots \to E_n$;
4. Map E_n back to the correct Montgomery curve $E_{A'} = [\mathfrak{l}]^n \star E_A$.

In each of these steps, the cost is dominated by the number of exponentiations ($\mathbf{E}$) and inversions ($\mathbf{I}$). Using Tables 1 and 2, in an affine constant-time implementation, moving to the Tate normal curve (step 2) will cost close to $1\,\mathbf{E} + 1\,\mathbf{I}$, an affine radical isogeny (step 3) costs approximately $1\,\mathbf{E} + 1\,\mathbf{I}$ per isogeny, and moving back to the Montgomery curve (step 4) will cost about $3\,\mathbf{E} + 1\,\mathbf{I}$.

Inversions. In contrast to ordinary CSIDH, radical isogenies would require these inversions to be constant-time, as the value that is inverted can reveal valuable information about the isogeny walk related to the secret key. Two methods to compute the inverse of an element $\alpha \in \mathbb{F}_p$ in constant-time are 1) by Fermat's little theorem[3]: $\alpha^{-1} = \alpha^{p-2}$, or 2) by masking the value that we want to invert with a random value $r \in \mathbb{F}_p$, computing $(r\alpha)^{-1}$ and multiplying by r again. Method 1 makes inversion as costly as exponentiation, while method 2 requires a source of randomness, which is an impediment from a crypto-engineering point of view. Using Fermat's little theorem almost doubles the cost of CSURF and of a radical isogeny in low degrees (2, 3, 4, 5, 7) and significantly increases the cost of a radical isogeny of degree 9, 11 or 13. Furthermore, such constant-time inversions increase the overhead of switching to Tate normal form and back to Montgomery form, which in total makes performing n radical isogenies less effective. Both methods of inversion are unfavorable from a crypto-engineering view, and thus we implement the fully projective radical isogenies from Sect. 3 to by-pass all inversions completely for radical isogenies.

Approximate cost of radical isogenies. We can now approximate the cost of evaluating fully projective radical isogenies in constant-time. We can avoid (most of) the cost of step 1 with a hybrid strategy (see Sect. 5). Projective coordinates avoid the inversion required in step 2 to move from the Montgomery curve to the correct Tate normal curve, and the inversion required in step 4 to move from the Tate normal curve back to the Montgomery curve. In step 3, projective radical isogenies save an inversion per isogeny, and so step 3 costs approximately n **E**. In total, performing n radical ℓ-isogenies therefore costs approximately $(n+4)\mathbf{E}$.

At first sight, this approximated cost does not seem to depend on ℓ. However, there is some additional cost besides the exponentiation per isogeny in step 3, and this additional cost grows with ℓ. But, the cost of an exponentiation is larger than $\log_2(p)$ **M** and so overshadows the additional cost. For more details, see Table 1. For this analysis, the approximated cost fits for small degrees.

The cost of exponentiation is upperbounded by $1.5 \log(p)$ by the (suboptimal) square-and-multiply method, assuming squaring (**S**) costs as much as multiplication (**M**). In total, we get the following approximate cost:

Lemma 2. *The cost to perform n radical isogenies (using Tate normal curves) of degree $\ell \in \{5, 7, 9, 11, 13\}$ is at least*

$$(n+4) \cdot \alpha \cdot \log_2(p),$$

*finite field multiplications (**M**) where $\alpha \in [1, 1.5]$ depends on the method to perform exponentiation (assuming $\mathbf{S} = \mathbf{M}$).*

4.1   Analysis of Effectiveness of Radical Isogenies

In this subsection, we analyze the efficiency of radical isogenies in comparison to Vélu isogenies, assuming the results from the previous sections. We argue that

---

[3] Bernstein and Yang [5] give a constant-time inversion based on gcd-computations. We have not implemented this, as avoiding inversions completely is cheaper.

the cost of $(n + 4) \cdot \alpha \cdot \log_2(p)$ from Lemma 2 for radical isogenies is too high and it is therefore not worthwhile to perform radical isogenies for degrees $5, 7, 11$ and 13. Degrees 2 and 3, however, benefit from the existence of radical isogenies of degree 4 and 9. Degree 4 and 9 isogenies cost only one exponentiation, but evaluate as two. This implies that performing radical isogenies is most worthwhile in degrees 2 and 3. We write $2/4$ and $3/9$ as shorthand for the combinations of degree 2 and 4, resp. degree 3 and 9 isogenies.

The three crucial observations in our analysis are

1. Current faster $\sqrt{\text{é}}$lu isogeny formulas require $\mathcal{O}(\sqrt{\ell^{\log_2 3}})$ field multiplications, whereas the cost of a radical isogeny scales as a factor of $\log_2(p)$ (for more details, see [1, 4]);
2. The group action evaluation first performs one block using $\sqrt{\text{é}}$lu isogeny formulas, and then isolates the radical isogeny computations. What is particularly important among these $\sqrt{\text{é}}$lu isogeny computations, is that removing one specific ℓ'-isogeny does not directly decrease the number of points that need to be sampled. Internally, the group action looks for a random point R and performs all the possible ℓ_i-isogenies such that $\left[\frac{p+1}{\ell_i}\right] R \neq \mathcal{O}$.
3. Replacing the smallest Vélu ℓ-isogeny with a radical isogeny could reduce the sampling of points in that specific Vélu isogeny block. This is because the probability of reaching a random point R of order ℓ is $\frac{\ell-1}{\ell}$, which is small for small ℓ. Additionally, the cost of verifying $\left[\frac{p+1}{\ell}\right] R \neq \mathcal{O}$ is about $1.5 \log_2\left(\frac{p+1}{\ell}\right)$ point additions $\approx 9 \log_2\left(\frac{p+1}{\ell}\right)$ field multiplications (for more details see [10]). In total, sampling n points of order ℓ costs

$$\texttt{sampling}(n, p, \ell) = 9 \left\lfloor \frac{n\ell}{\ell - 1} \right\rfloor \log_2\left(\frac{p+1}{\ell}\right) \mathbf{M}$$

$$\approx 9 \left\lfloor \frac{n\ell}{\ell - 1} \right\rfloor (\log_2(p) - \log_2(\ell))\mathbf{M}.$$

Nevertheless, using radical isogenies for these degrees does not save the sampling of n points, just a fraction of them. To be more precise, let $\ell' > \ell$ be the next smallest prime such that the group action requires n' ℓ'-isogenies and $\left\lfloor \frac{n\ell}{\ell-1} \right\rfloor \geq \left\lfloor \frac{n'\ell'}{\ell'-1} \right\rfloor$. Then the savings are given by their difference with respect to the cost sampling such torsion-points (see Eq. (4)).

$$9 \left(\left\lfloor \frac{n\ell}{\ell - 1} \right\rfloor - \left\lfloor \frac{n'\ell'}{\ell' - 1} \right\rfloor \right) (\log_2(p) - \log_2(\ell))\mathbf{M}. \tag{4}$$

Whenever $\left\lfloor \frac{n\ell}{\ell-1} \right\rfloor < \left\lfloor \frac{n'\ell'}{\ell'-1} \right\rfloor$, using radical isogenies does not reduce the number of points that need to be sampled.

As an example for the cost in a realistic situation, we take the approximately optimal bounds analyzed in [12, 20]. In both works, $\log_2(p) \approx 512$ and the first five smallest primes ℓ_i's in $\{3, 5, 7, 11, 13\}$ have bounds m_i that satisfy

$$\left\lfloor \frac{m_0 \ell_0}{\ell_0 - 1} \right\rceil = \left\lfloor \frac{m_1 \ell_1}{\ell_1 - 1} \right\rceil = \left\lfloor \frac{m_2 \ell_2}{\ell_2 - 1} \right\rceil = \left\lfloor \frac{m_3 \ell_3}{\ell_3 - 1} \right\rceil = \left\lfloor \frac{m_4 \ell_4}{\ell_4 - 1} \right\rceil.$$

Thus, there are no savings concerning sampling of points when including small degree radical isogenies. Clearly, performing n radical ℓ-isogenies becomes costlier than using $\sqrt{\text{élu}}$ isogenies, and thus the above analysis suggests radical isogenies need their own optimal bounds to be competitive. The analysis is different for degree 2 and 3, where we can perform 4-and 9-isogenies in $\lceil \frac{n}{2} \rceil$ radical computations instead of n computations. In fact, 4-isogenies directly reduces the sampling of points by decreasing the bounds of the other primes ℓ_i's. Nevertheless, performing n radical isogenies takes at least $(n+4)\log_2(p)$ field multiplications (Lemma 2), which implies higher costs (and then lower savings) for large prime instantiations. For example, a single radical isogeny in a 1024-bit field costs twice as much as a single radical isogeny in a 512-bit field, and in a 2048-bit field this becomes four times as much. These expected savings omit the cost of sampling an initial point of order ℓ_i, as we show in Sect. 5 how we can find such points with little extra cost with high probability.

4.2   Further Discussion

In this subsection, we describe the two further impacts on performance in constant-time and higher parameter sets in more detail: Radical isogenies scale badly to larger primes, as their cost scales with $\log(p)$, and dummy-free isogenies are more expensive, as we need to switch direction often for a dummy-free evaluation.

Radical isogenies do not scale well. Using the results in Tables 1 and 2, the cost of a single radical isogeny is approximately 600 finite field operations, with an overhead of about 2500 finite field operations for a prime of 512 bits. Thus, a CSURF-512 implementation (which uses 2/4- radical isogenies) or a CRADS-512 implementation (which uses 2/4- and 3/9- radical isogenies) could be competitive with a state-of-the-art CSIDH-512 implementation. However, implementations using radical isogenies scale worse than CSIDH implementations, due to the high cost of exponentiation in larger prime fields. For example, for a prime of 2048 bits, just the overhead of switching curve models is already over 8500 finite field operations, which is close to 1% of total cost for a 'traditional' CSIDH implementation. Therefore, CSIDH is expected to outperform radical isogenies for larger primes. In Sect. 6, we demonstrate this using a benchmark we have performed on CSIDH, CSURF, CRADS, and an implementation using the hybrid strategy we introduce in Sect. 5, for six different prime sizes, from 512 bits up to 4096 bits. These prime sizes are realistic: several analyses, such as [6,11,22], call the claimed quantum security of the originally suggested prime sizes for CSIDH (512, 1024 and 1792 bits) into question. We do not take a stance on this discussion, and therefore provide an analysis that fits both sides of the discussion.

Dummy-free radical isogenies are costly. Recall that radical isogenies require an initial point P of order N to switch to the right Tate normal form, depending on the direction of the isogeny. So, two kinds of curves in Tate normal form arise: P belongs either to $E[\pi - 1]$ or to $E[\pi + 1]$. Now, a dummy-free chain of radical isogenies requires (at some steps of the group action) to switch the direction of the isogenies, and therefore to switch to a Tate normal form where P belongs to either $E[\pi - 1]$ or $E[\pi + 1]$. As we switch direction $m_i - |e_i|$ times, this requires $m_i - |e_i|$ torsion points. That is, a dummy-free implementation of a chain of radical isogenies will require at least $(m_i - |e_i|)$ torsion points, which leaks information on e_i. We can make this procedure secure by sampling m_i points every time, but this costs too much. These costs could be decreased by pushing points through radical isogenies, however, this is still not cost-effective. In any case, we will only focus on dummy-based implementations of radical isogenies.

5   A Hybrid Strategy for Radical Isogenies

In this section we introduce our second improvement to radical isogenies: a *hybrid strategy* for integrating radical isogenies into CSIDH. In [8], radical ℓ-isogenies replace Vélu ℓ-isogenies, and they are performed before the CSIDH group action, by sampling a point of order ℓ to initiate a 'chain' of radical ℓ-isogenies. Such an approach replaces cheap Vélu ℓ-isogenies with relatively expensive radical ℓ-isogenies and requires finding a point of order ℓ to initiate this 'chain'. The hybrid strategy combines the 'traditional' CSIDH group action evaluation with radical isogenies in an optimal way, so that we do not sacrifice cheap Vélu isogenies of low degree and do not require another point of order ℓ to initiate the 'chain'. This substantially improves the efficiency of radical isogenies.

Concretely, in 'traditional' CSIDH isogeny evaluation, one pushes a torsion point T through a series of ℓ-isogenies with Vélu's formulas. This implies that at the end of the series of Vélu isogenies, such a point T might still have suitable torsion to initiate a chain of radical isogenies. Re-using this point saves us having to specifically sample a torsion point to initiate radical isogenies. Furthermore, with this approach we can do *both* radical and Vélu isogenies for such ℓ where we have radical isogenies. We show this hybrid strategy generalizes CSIDH, CSURF and CRADS (an implementation with radical isogenies) and gives an improved approach to integrate radical isogenies on Tate normal curves in CSIDH.

In this section, V refers to the set of primes for which we have Vélu isogenies (i.e. all ℓ_i), and $R \subset V$ refers to the set of degrees for which we have radical isogenies. Currently, $R = \{3, 4, 5, 7, 9, 11, 13\}$.

5.1   A Hybrid Strategy for Integration of Radical Isogenies

Vélu isogenies for degree ℓ_i with $i \in R$ are much cheaper than the radical isogenies for those degrees, as a single radical isogeny always requires at least one exponentiation which costs $O(\log(p))$. The downside to Vélu isogenies is that they require a torsion point per isogeny. However, torsion points can be re-used for Vélu isogenies of many degrees by pushing them through the isogeny, and so the cost of point sampling is amortized over all the degrees where Vélu isogenies are used. Thus, although for a single degree n radical isogenies are much cheaper than n Vélu isogenies, this does not hold when the cost of point sampling is distributed over many other degrees. The idea of our hybrid strategy is to do both types of isogeny per degree: we need to perform a certain amount of Vélu blocks in any CSIDH evaluation, so we expect a certain amount T_i of points of order ℓ_i. So, for $i \in R$, we can use $T_i - 1$ of these points to perform Vélu ℓ_i-isogenies, and use the last one to initiate the chain of radical ℓ_i-isogenies. Concretely, we split up the bound m_i for $i \in R$ into m_i^v and m_i^r. Here, m_i^v is the number of Vélu isogenies, which require m_i^v points of order ℓ_i, and m_i^r is the number of radical isogenies, which require just 1 point of order ℓ_i.

Thus, our *hybrid strategy* allows for evaluation of CSIDH with radical isogenies, in such a way that we can the following parameters

- for $i \in R$, m_i^r is the number of radical isogenies of degree ℓ_i,
- for $i \in V$, m_i^v is the number of Vélu/$\sqrt{}$élu isogenies of degree ℓ_i.

For $i \in R$, we write $m_i = m_i^v + m_i^r$ for simplicity. What makes the difference with the previous integration of radical isogenies, is that this hybrid strategy allows R and V to overlap! That is, the hybrid strategy does not require you to pick between Vélu *or* radical isogenies for $\{3, 5, 7, 9, 11, 13\}$. In this way, hybrid strategies generalize both CSIDH/CSURF and CRADS:

Lemma 3. *The CSIDH/CSURF group action evaluation as in [7,9], and the radical isogenies evaluation from [8] are both possible in this hybrid strategy.*

Proof. Take $m_i^r = 0$ for all $i \in R$ to get the CSIDH/CSURF group action evaluation, and take $m_i^v = 0$ for all $i \in R$ to get the radical isogenies evaluation.

In the rest of this section, we look at non-trivial hybrid parameters (i.e. there is some i such that both m_i^v and m_i^r are non-zero) to improve the performance of CSIDH and CRADS. As we can predict T_i (the number of points of order ℓ_i) in a full CSIDH group action evaluation, we can choose our parameter m_i^v optimally with respect to T_i: for $i \in R$, we take $m_i^v = T_i - 1$ and use the remaining point of order ℓ_i to initiate the 'chain' of radical ℓ_i isogenies of length m_i^r.

5.2   Choosing Parameters for Hybrid Strategy

As we explained above, the parameter m_i^v is clear given T_i, and we are left with optimizing the value m_i^r. Denote the cost of the overhead to switch curve models by c_{overhead} and the cost of a single isogeny by $c_{\text{single}}(\ell)$, then the cost of performing the m_i^r radical isogenies is clearly $c = c_{\text{overhead}} + m_i^r \cdot c_{\text{single}}(\ell_i)$ (see also Lemma 2). Furthermore, given m_i^v, the increase in key space is

$$b = \log_2 \left(\frac{2 \cdot (m_i^r + m_i^v) + 1}{2 \cdot m_i^v + 1} \right).$$

So, we can minimize c/b for a given m_i^v (independent of p). This minimizes the number of field operations per bits of security. Notice that for degree 3, the use of 9-isogenies means we get a factor $\frac{1}{2}$ for the cost of single isogenies, as we only need to perform half as many.

It is possible that the 'optimal' number m_i^r is higher, when c/b is still lower than in CSIDH. However, we heuristically argue that such an optimum can only be slightly higher, as the increase in bits of security decreases quite rapidly.

5.3   Algorithm for Evaluation of Hybrid Strategy

Evaluating the hybrid strategy requires an improved evaluation algorithm, as we need to re-use the 'left-over' torsion point at the right moment of a 'traditional' CSIDH evaluation. We achieve this by first performing the CSIDH evaluation for all $i \in V$ and decreasing m_i^v by 1 if a Vélu ℓ_i-isogeny is performed. If m_i^v becomes zero, we remove i from V, so that the next point of order ℓ_i initiates the 'chain' of radical isogenies of length m_i^r. After this, we remove i from R too.

Algorithm 1. High-level evaluation of hybrid strategy for radical isogenies

---

Input: $A \in \mathbb{F}_p$, a key $(e_1, \ldots, e_n)$, a set V (Vélu isog.) and a set R (radical isog.).
Output: $B \in \mathbb{F}_p$ such that $\prod [\mathfrak{l}_i]^{e_i} \star E_A = E_B$
1: **while** $m_i \neq 0$ for $i \in V \cup R$ **do**
2:     Sample $x \in \mathbb{F}_p$, set $s \leftarrow 1$ if $x^3 + Ax^2 + x$ is a square in $\mathbb{F}_p$, else $s \leftarrow -1$.
3:     Let $S = \{i \in V \cup R \mid m_i^v \neq 0, \text{sign}(e_i) = s\}$. **Restart** if S is empty.
4:     Let $k \leftarrow \prod_{i \in S} \ell_i$ and compute $T \leftarrow [(p+1)/k]P$.
5:     **for** $i \in S \cap V$ **do**
6:         Compute $Q \leftarrow [k/\ell_i]T$. If $Q = \infty$, **skip** this i and set $S \leftarrow S - \{i\}$.
7:         Compute $\phi : E_A \to E_B$ with kernel $\langle Q \rangle$ using Vélu.
8:         When $e_i \neq 0$, set $A \leftarrow B$, $T \leftarrow \phi(T)$, $e_i \leftarrow e_i - s$
9:         Set $m_i^v \leftarrow m_i^v - 1$ and set $S \leftarrow S - \{i\}$
10:        If $m_i^v = 0$, set $V \leftarrow V - \{i\}$
11:    **for** $i \in S \cap R$ **do**
12:        Compute $Q \leftarrow [k/\ell_i]T$. If $Q = \infty$, **skip** this i.
13:        Compute $E_B = [\mathfrak{l}_i]^{e_i} \star E_A$ using m_i^r radical ℓ_i-isogenies
14:        Set $A \leftarrow B$, $R \leftarrow R - \{i\}$, and **start over** at line 1
15: **return** A.

Effectively, for $i \in V \cap R$, we first check if we can perform a Vélu ℓ_i-isogeny in the loop in lines 5–9 (a Vélu block). If m_i^v of these have been performed, we check in lines 11–14 if the 'left-over' point Q has order ℓ_i for some $i \in S \cap R$, so that it can initiate the 'chain' of radical ℓ_i-isogenies in line 13. Algorithm 1 does not go into the details of CSURF (i.e. using degree 2/4 isogenies), which can easily be added and does not interfere with the hybrid strategy. Furthermore, Algorithm 1 does not leak any timing information about the secret values e_i, only on m_i, which is public information. For simplicity's sake, we do not detail many lower-level improvements.

6   Implementation and Performance Benchmark

All the experiments presented in this section are centred on constant-time CSIDH, CSURF and CRADS implementations, for a base field of 512-, 1024-, 1792-, 2048-, 3072-, and 4096-bits. To be more precise, in the first subsection we restrict our experiments to i) the most competitive CSIDH-configurations according to [12,15], ii) the CSURF-configuration presented in [7,8] and iii) the radical isogenies-configuration presented in [8] (i.e. without the hybrid strategy). As mentioned in Sect. 4, we only focus on dummy-based variants such as MCR-style [18] and OAYT-style [20]. The experiments using only radical isogenies of degree 2/4 are labelled CSURF, whereas the experiments using both radical isogenies of degree 2/4 and 3/9 are labelled CRADS. In the second subsection, we integrate the hybrid strategy to our experiments, and focus on dummy-based OAYT-style implementations. This allows us to compare the improvement of the hybrid strategy against the previous section. When comparing totals, we assume one field squaring costs what a field multiplication costs ($\mathbf{S} = \mathbf{M}$). Primes used are of the form $p = h \cdot \prod_{i=1}^{74} \ell_i - 1$, with $h = 2^k \cdot 3$. The key space is about 2^{256}.

On the optimal exponent bounds (fixed number of ℓ_i-isogenies required), the results from [15] give $\approx 0.4\%$ of saving in comparison to [12] (see Table 5 from [12]). The results from [15] are mathematically rich: analysis on the permutations of the primes and the (integer) convex programming technique for determining an approximately optimal exponent bound. However, their current Matlab-based code implementation from [15] only handles CSIDH-512 using OAYT-style prioritizing multiplicative-based strategies. Both works essentially give the approximate same expected running time, and by simplicity, we choose to follow [12], which more easily extends to any prime size (for both OAYT and MCR styles). Furthermore, all CSIDH-prime instantiations use the approximately optimal exponent bounds presented in [12].

To reduce the cost of exponentiations in radical isogenies, we used short addition chains (found with [17]), which reduces the cost from $1.5 \log(p)$ (from square-and-multiply) to something in the range $[1.05 \log(p), 1.18 \log(p)]$. These close-to-optimal addition chains save at least 20% of the cost of an exponentiation used per (affine or projective) radical isogeny in constant-time.

Our CSURF and CRADS constant-time implementations evaluate the group action by first performing the evaluation as CSIDH does on the floor of the isogeny graph, with the inclusion of radical isogenies as in Algorithm 1. Afterwards we move to the surface to perform the remaining 4-isogenies. So, the only curve arithmetic required is on Montgomery curves of the form $E/\mathbb{F}_p : By^2 = x^3 + Ax^2 + x$. Concluding, we compare three different implementations which we name CSIDH, CSURF and CRADS. The CSIDH implementation uses traditional Vélu's formulas to perform an ℓ_i-isogeny for $\ell_i \leq 101$ and switches to √élu for $\ell_i > 101$. The CSURF implementation adds the functionality of degree 2/4 radical isogenies, while the CRADS implementation uses radical isogenies of degree 2/4 and 3/9.

6.1   Performance Benchmark of Radical Isogenies

We compare the performance using a different keyspace (i.e., different bounds (e_i)) for CSIDH, CSURF, and CRADS than in [7,8], where they have used weighted L_∞-norm balls for CSURF and CRADS to compare against an unweighted L_∞-norm ball for CSIDH. Analysis from [12,15,18] shows that such a comparison is unfair against CSIDH. We therefore use approximately optimal keyspaces (using weighted L_∞-norm) for CSIDH, CSURF and CRADS.

Suitable bounds. We use suitable exponent bounds for approximately optimal keyspaces that minimize the cost of CSIDH, CSURF, and CRADS by using a slight modification of the greedy algorithm presented in [12], which is included in the provided repository. In short, the algorithm starts by increasing the exponent bound $m_2 \le 256$ of two used in CSURF, and then applies the exponent bounds search procedure for minimizing the group action cost on the floor (the CSIDH computation part). Once having the approximately optimal bounds for CSURF, we proceed in a similar way for CRADS: this time m_2 is fixed and the algorithm increases the bound $m_3 \in [\![1 .. m_2]\!]$ until it is approximately optimal.

Comparisons. The full results are given in Table 3. From Fig. 1a we see that CSURF and CRADS outperform CSIDH for primes of sizes 512 and 1024 bits, and is competitive for primes of sizes 1792 and 2048 bits. For larger primes, CSIDH outperforms both CSURF and CRADS. Using OAYT-style, CSURF-512 provides a speed-up over CSIDH-512 of 2.53% and CRADS-512 provides a speed-up over CSIDH-512 of 2.15%. The speed-up is reduced to 1.26% and 0.68% respectively for 1024 bits. For larger primes both CSURF and CRADS do not provide speed-ups, because radical isogenies scale worse than Vélu's (or $\sqrt{\text{élu}}$'s) formulas (see Sect. 4.2). This is visible in Fig. 1a and Fig. 1b.

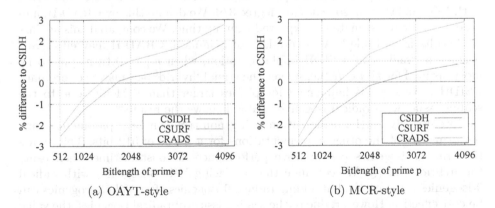

(a) OAYT-style   (b) MCR-style

Fig. 1. Relative difference between the number of finite field multiplications required for CSURF and CRADS in comparison to CSIDH. The percentage is based on the numbers in Table 3.

Table 3. Results for different prime sizes. The numbers are given in millions of finite field multiplications, and the results are the average over 1024 runs. The results count multiplication (**M**) and squaring (**S**) operations, assuming **S** = **M**. Numbers in bold are optimal results for that prime size.

Dummy-style	512-bits	1024-bits	1792-bits	2048-bits	3072-bits	4096-bits
CSIDH-OAYT	0.791	0.873	**0.999**	**1.039**	**1.217**	**1.361**
CSURF-OAYT	**0.771**	**0.862**	1.000	1.042	1.225	1.387
CRADS-OAYT	0.774	0.867	1.007	1.050	1.237	1.399
CSIDH-MCR	1.011	1.093	1.218	1.255	1.436	1.580
CSURF-MCR	0.980	1.074	1.211	1.253	1.443	1.594
CRADS-MCR	0.985	1.086	1.228	1.272	1.469	1.625

Furthermore, the approximately optimal bounds we computed show that the exponents m_2 and m_3 decrease quickly: from $m_2 = 32$ and $m_3 = 12$ for 512-bits, to $e_0 = e_1 = 4$ for 1792-bits, to $e_0 = e_1 = 2$ for 4096-bits. When using MCR-style CSURF and CRADS are slightly more competitive, although the overall cost is significantly higher than OAYT-style. Table 3 presents the results obtained in this benchmark and highlights the best result per parameter set. Notice that CSURF outperforms CRADS in every parameter set, which implies that replacing Vélu 3-isogenies with radical 9-isogenies is not cost effective.

6.2 Performance of Radical Isogenies Using the Hybrid Strategy

In this subsection, we benchmark the performance of radical isogenies when the hybrid strategy of Sect. 5 is used to integrate radical isogenies into CSIDH. Concretely, in comparison to the previous benchmark, we allow a strategy using both Vélu and radical isogenies for degree 3/9. We denote this by CRAD-H, and used our code to estimate the expected running time. We compared this against the results from Table 3. As a corollary of Lemma 3, CRAD-H may effectively become a 'traditional' CSIDH implementation, when $m_i^r = 0$ turns out to be most optimal for all $i \in R$ (i.e. we get the trivial 'hybrid' paramaters of ordinary CSIDH). We see this happening for primes larger than 1024 bits due to the scaling issues with radical isogenies. Table 4 shows the results[4].

Interestingly, an implementation using non-trivial hybrid parameters outperforms any of the other implementations for a prime of 512 bits. This shows that radical isogenies *can* improve performance in constant-time when using the hybrid strategy. We conclude that replacing Vélu 3-isogenies with radical 9-isogenies is too costly, but adding radical 9-isogenies after Vélu 3-isogenies can be cost effective. However, due to the scaling issues of radical isogenies, the value m_i^r quickly drops to 0 and we get trivial parameters for primes larger than 1024 bits, implying that traditional CSIDH performs better for large primes than any

---

[4] Only for OAYT-style. Using the code, we analysed the cost of m_i^r projective radical isogenies and m_i^v Vélu isogenies. The results are realistic; there are no extra costs.

Table 4. Results for different prime sizes. The first row is given in millions of finite field multiplications, counting multiplication (M) and squaring (S) operations, assuming $S = M$. The second row gives the speed-up in comparison to CSIDH. Trivial parameters are denoted by a superscript t.

CRAD-H	512-bits	1024-bits	1792-bits	2048-bits	3072-bits	4096-bits
Performance	0.765	0.861	0.999^t	1.039^t	1.217^t	1.361^t
Speed-up	3.3%	2.2%	-	-	-	-

implementation using radical isogenies, even when such an implementation does not have to sacrifice the cheap Vélu isogenies of small degree. We conclude that 'horizontally' expanding the degrees ℓ_i for large primes p is more efficient than 'vertically' increasing the bounds m_i using radical isogenies. Nevertheless, for small primes, our hybrid strategy for radical isogenies can speed-up CSIDH and requires only slight changes to a 'traditional' CSIDH implementation.

Remark. The CTIDH proposal from [3] is about twice as fast as CSIDH by changing the key space in a clever way: CTIDH reduces the number of isogenies by half compared to CSIDH, using this new key space, which requires the *Matryoshka structure* for Vélu isogenies. The radical part of CSIDH is isolated from the Vélu part, and this will be the same case for CTIDH, when using radical isogenies. The CTIDH construction decreases the cost of this Vélu part by approximately a factor half, but the radical part remains at the same cost. Hence, we heuristically expect that the speed-up of radical isogenies in CTIDH decreases from 3.3%, and may even become a slow-down.

7   Concluding Remarks and Future Research

We have implemented, improved and analyzed radical isogeny formulas in constant-time and have optimized their integration into CSIDH with our hybrid strategy. We have evaluated their performance against state-of-the-art CSIDH implementations in constant-time. We show that fully projective radical isogenies are almost twice as fast as affine radical isogenies in constant-time. But, when integrated into CSIDH, both CSURF and radical isogenies provide only a minimal speed-up: about 2.53% and 2.15% respectively, compared to state-of-the-art CSIDH-512. Furthermore, larger (dummy-based) implementations of CSURF and CRADS become less competitive to CSIDH as radical isogenies scale worse than Vélu or $\sqrt{}$élu isogenies. In such instances ($\log(p) \geq 1792$ bits) the use of constant-time radical isogenies even has a negative impact on performance.

Our hybrid strategy improves this performance somewhat, giving better results for primes of size 512 and 1024, increasing the speed-up to 3.3%, and making radical 9-isogenies cost effective. For larger primes however, our hybrid approach shows that $\sqrt{}$élu-isogenies quickly outperformed radical isogenies, as we get 'trivial' parameters for our hybrid strategy. We therefore conclude that, for larger primes, expanding 'horizontally' (in the degrees ℓ_i) is more efficient than expanding 'vertically' (in the bounds m_i).

Due to the large cost of a single exponentiation in large prime fields, which is required to compute radicals, it is unlikely that (affine or projective) radical isogenies can bring any (significant) speed-up. However, similar applications of modular curves in isogeny-based cryptography could bring improvements to current methods. Radical isogenies show that such applications do exist and are interesting; they might be more effective in isogeny-based cryptography in other situations than CSIDH. For example with differently shaped prime number p or perhaps when used in Verifiable Delay Functions (VDFs).

Acknowledgements. The authors would like to thank Simona Samardjiska, Peter Schwabe, Francisco Rodríguez-Henríquez, and anonymous reviewers for their valuable comments that helped to improve the technical material of this paper.

References

1. Adj, G., Chi-Domínguez, J., Rodríguez-Henríquez, F.: Karatsuba-based square-root Vélu's formulas applied to two isogeny-based protocols. IACR Cryptology ePrint Archive, p. 1109 (2020). https://eprint.iacr.org/2020/1109

2. Azarderakhsh, R., et al.: Supersingular isogeny key encapsulation. In: Third Round Candidate of the NIST's Post-Quantum Cryptography Standardization Process (2020). https://sike.org/

3. Banegas, G., et al.: CTIDH: faster constant-time CSIDH. Cryptology ePrint Archive, Report 2021/633 (2021). https://ia.cr/2021/633

4. Bernstein, D.J., De Feo, L., Leroux, A., Smith, B.: Faster computation of isogenies of large prime degree. IACR Cryptology ePrint Archive **2020**, 341 (2020)

5. Bernstein, D.J., Yang, B.: Fast constant-time GCD computation and modular inversion. IACR Trans. Cryptogr. Hardw. Embed. Syst. **2019**(3), 340–398 (2019). https://doi.org/10.13154/tches.v2019.i3.340-398

6. Bonnetain, X., Schrottenloher, A.: Quantum security analysis of CSIDH. In: Canteaut, A., Ishai, Y. (eds.) EUROCRYPT 2020. LNCS, vol. 12106, pp. 493–522. Springer, Cham (2020). https://doi.org/10.1007/978-3-030-45724-2_17

7. Castryck, W., Decru, T.: CSIDH on the surface. In: Ding, J., Tillich, J.P. (eds.) PQCrypto 2020. LNCS, vol. 12100, pp. 111–129. Springer, Cham (2020). https://doi.org/10.1007/978-3-030-44223-1_7

8. Castryck, W., Decru, T., Vercauteren, F.: Radical isogenies. In: Moriai, S., Wang, H. (eds.) ASIACRYPT 2020. LNCS, vol. 12492, pp. 493–519. Springer, Cham (2020). https://doi.org/10.1007/978-3-030-64834-3_17

9. Castryck, W., Lange, T., Martindale, C., Panny, L., Renes, J.: CSIDH: an efficient post-quantum commutative group action. In: Peyrin, T., Galbraith, S. (eds.) ASIACRYPT 2018. LNCS, vol. 11274, pp. 395–427. Springer, Cham (2018). https://doi.org/10.1007/978-3-030-03332-3_15

10. Cervantes-Vázquez, D., Chenu, M., Chi-Domínguez, J.J., De Feo, L., Rodríguez-Henríquez, F., Smith, B.: Stronger and faster side-channel protections for CSIDH. In: Schwabe, P., Thériault, N. (eds.) LATINCRYPT 2019. LNCS, vol. 11774, pp. 173–193. Springer, Cham (2019). https://doi.org/10.1007/978-3-030-30530-7_9

11. Chávez-Saab, J., Chi-Domínguez, J., Jaques, S., Rodríguez-Henríquez, F.: The SQALE of CSIDH: square-root vélu quantum-resistant isogeny action with low exponents. IACR Cryptology ePrint Archive 2020, 1520 (2020). https://eprint.iacr.org/2020/1520
12. Chi-Domínguez, J., Rodríguez-Henríquez, F.: Optimal strategies for CSIDH. IACR Cryptology ePrint Archive **2020**, 417 (2020)
13. Couveignes, J.M.: Hard homogeneous spaces. Cryptology ePrint Archive, Report 2006/291 (2006). http://eprint.iacr.org/2006/291
14. De Feo, L., Jao, D., Plût, J.: Towards quantum-resistant cryptosystems from supersingular elliptic curve isogenies. J. Math. Cryptol. **8**(3), 209–247 (2014)
15. Hutchinson, A., LeGrow, J., Koziel, B., Azarderakhsh, R.: Further optimizations of CSIDH: a systematic approach to efficient strategies, permutations, and bound vectors. Cryptology ePrint Archive, Report 2019/1121 (2019). https://ia.cr/2019/1121
16. Jao, D., De Feo, L.: Towards quantum-resistant cryptosystems from supersingular elliptic curve isogenies. In: Yang, B.-Y. (ed.) PQCrypto 2011. LNCS, vol. 7071, pp. 19–34. Springer, Heidelberg (2011). https://doi.org/10.1007/978-3-642-25405-5_2
17. McLoughlinn, M.B.: Addchain: cryptographic addition chain generation in go. Github Repository (2020). https://github.com/mmcloughlin/addchain
18. Meyer, M., Campos, F., Reith, S.: On Lions and Elligators: an efficient constant-time implementation of CSIDH. In: Ding, J., Steinwandt, R. (eds.) PQCrypto 2019. LNCS, vol. 11505, pp. 307–325. Springer, Cham (2019). https://doi.org/10.1007/978-3-030-25510-7_17
19. Nakagawa, K., Onuki, H., Takayasu, A., Takagi, T.: l_1-norm ball for CSIDH: optimal strategy for choosing the secret key space. Cryptology ePrint Archive, Report 2020/181 (2020). https://ia.cr/2020/181
20. Onuki, H., Aikawa, Y., Yamazaki, T., Takagi, T.: (Short Paper) a faster constant-time algorithm of CSIDH keeping two points. In: Attrapadung, N., Yagi, T. (eds.) IWSEC 2019. LNCS, vol. 11689, pp. 23–33. Springer, Cham (2019). https://doi.org/10.1007/978-3-030-26834-3_2
21. Onuki, H., Moriya, T.: Radical isogenies on montgomery curves. IACR Cryptology ePrint Archive 2021, 699 (2021). https://eprint.iacr.org/2021/699
22. Peikert, C.: He gives C-sieves on the CSIDH. In: Canteaut, A., Ishai, Y. (eds.) EUROCRYPT 2020. LNCS, vol. 12106, pp. 463–492. Springer, Cham (2020). https://doi.org/10.1007/978-3-030-45724-2_16
23. Rostovtsev, A., Stolbunov, A.: Public-key cryptosystem based on isogenies. IACR Cryptology ePrint Archive 2006, 145 (2006). http://eprint.iacr.org/2006/145
24. Stolbunov, A.: Constructing public-key cryptographic schemes based on class group action on a set of isogenous elliptic curves. Adv. Math. Comm. **4**(2), 215–235 (2010)
25. Vélu, J.: Isogénies entre courbes elliptiques. C. R. Acad. Sci. Paris Sér. A-B **273**, A238–A241 (1971)

Private Liquidity Matching Using MPC

Shahla Atapoor⬤, Nigel P. Smart(✉)⬤, and Younes Talibi Alaoui⬤

imec-COSIC, KU Leuven, Leuven, Belgium
{Shahla.Atapoor,nigel.smart,younes.talibialaoui}@kuleuven.be

Abstract. Many central banks, as well as blockchain systems, are looking into distributed versions of interbank payment systems, in particular the netting procedure. When executed in a distributed manner this presents a number of privacy problems. This paper studies a privacy-preserving netting protocol to solve the gridlock resolution problem in such Real Time Gross Settlement systems. Our solution utilizes Multi-party Computation and is implemented in the SCALE MAMBA system, using Shamir secret sharing scheme over three parties in an actively secure manner. Our experiments show that, even for large throughput systems, such a privacy-preserving operation is often feasible.

1 Introduction

Real Time Gross Settlement systems (RTGS systems for short) consist of fund transfer systems that permit banks to exchange transactions, where debiting the funds from the account of the source to credit them to the account of the destination (Settlement) is performed immediately (Real Time) if enough funds are available from the account of the source. The settlement of transactions happens individually (Gross), that is, the funds move (in electronical form as opposed to physical form) every time a transaction is performed.

RTGS systems are nowadays widely adopted as they reduce the risks associated with high-value payment settlements between participants. However, the immediate settlement of transactions increases the liquidity requirements for the participants, and as a consequence, banks will be exposed to the risk of not being able to settle transactions due to the lack of liquidity, and therefore settling their transactions will be postponed. This delay comes with a cost for both sources and destinations, especially for time-critical payments if they are not settled in due time. Moreover, such disturbances in the system may lead to *gridlock* situations, where a set of transactions cannot be settled as each transaction is waiting for another one to be settled (see Sect. 2).

To address such a situation, the parties involved could inject more liquidity into the system, but this comes with a cost if the additional liquidity was borrowed. Alternatively, *Liquidity Saving Mechanisms* (LSM for short) [23] can be

S. D. Galbraith (Ed.): CT-RSA 2022, LNCS 13161, pp. 96–119, 2022.
https://doi.org/10.1007/978-3-030-95312-6_5

employed, such as *multilateral netting*, which consists of simultaneously offsetting multiple transactions, to result in a single net position for the participants involved. This will eventually permit the unblocking some of the pending transactions if the net positions of the respective sources are positive. This process is generally carried out by a central entity, as RTGS systems are traditionally managed by the central banks of countries. That is, each country has its own RTGS system, but we may also have a shared RTGS system between more than one country, as the Target 2 system [21] operated by the Eurosystem.

Running the RTGS requires the central entity in charge to have sight over the balances of the participants as well as all payment instructions, which includes the source, destination, and the amount being transferred. Thus, this entity is trusted to preserve the confidentiality of this information. As a result, participants might be skeptical about submitting all their transactions to the RTGS. In order to eliminate this need for having a trusted entity, one could *decentralize* the RTGS system, by permitting the participants to exchange transactions, without having to disclose them to a central entity.

However, designing such an RTGS gives rise to three main challenges, namely how to guarantee (i) Correctness: while settling a transaction, the amount debited from the source is the same as the amount transferred to the destination; (ii) Fairness: The LSM process implemented should not favor a participant over the others. (iii) Privacy: Account balances and payment amounts, and possible source and destination identities should be kept private to the respective banks. These requirements are easy to achieve in a centralized system, as all the transactions are visible to the trusted central entity in charge of the RTGS, but in a decentralized payment system, one would expect that these tasks become a burden. In fact, one could imagine a fully decentralized solution where in the case of a gridlock, each participant notifies the banks it is planning to send transactions to (with the respective amounts), and based on this, each participant would determine the expected balance it would hold. Then each participant removes transactions from its queue till the expected balance becomes positive, and notifies the corresponding receivers about the deleted transactions. This will allow the participants to resolve the gridlock situation without the interference of a third party, but does not necessarily address the aforementioned challenges, particularly the privacy guarantee, as the participants cannot move forward from the gridlock situation, until all participants confirm that they have a positive balance, and this obviously depends on the transactions they are exchanging. Thus, it may occur that correlations can be drawn over the sender and receiver of a transaction, from the sequence of the parties that signal having a negative balance. It is thus not trivial how to construct a protocol that avoids such leakages, without introducing heavy computation that would make the RTGS impractical.

In this paper, we propose a *Multi-Party Computation* (MPC for short) based solution to perform the liquidity optimization for decentralized RTGS systems. In particular, we show that the task of managing the RTGS system can be assigned to a set of p entities, that will obliviously settle the incoming transactions, and update the (private) balances of the parties involved. The payments instructions and balances will remain hidden as long as less than $t + 1$ of these entities collude.

We show that these p entities will be capable of obliviously running the multilateral netting process. For this purpose, we distribute the gridlock resolution algorithm of [6] (See Sect. 2), providing three main versions: (i) sodoGR where the amount being transferred in transactions is held secret, while the source and the destination are revealed to the p entities; (ii) sodsGR where the amount and the source are secret whereas the destination is revealed to the p entities; (iii) ssdsGR where the source, destination, and the amount are all held secret;

We implemented our algorithms using the SCALE MAMBA framework [3], with $p = 3$ and $t = 1$, and we simulated an RTGS system running over time using the three aforementioned versions of gridlock resolution. For our simulation, we generated transactions drawn from a distribution similar to what is seen in real life. For one variant of our clearing methodology we found that, in the sodoGR and sodsGR cases, that transactions could be cleared in effectively real time, with no delay due to the secure nature of the processing. Only in the case of ssdsGR that we find a significant delay being introduced, which depends on the number of banks, the number of transactions per hour, and the overall liquidity within the system. In this case, we also allow a small amount of information leakage, since removing this leakage would cause an even greater delay being introduced.

Prior usage of MPC in financial applications has mainly focused on auctions, such as [5,8,9,29], for one shot auctions, and [4,13,14] for auctions running in Dark Markets. MPC was also used for privacy-preserving financial data analysis, such as [7] to conduct statistics over the performance of companies throughout the year or to compute the systemic risk between financial institutions such as in [2] and [25]. Also, [30] and [19] used MPC for detecting fraud between financial institutions, and [11] used MPC for privacy- preserving federated learning for financial applications.

Driven by the motivation of removing the central entity, various blockchain projects have also investigated the feasibility of a decentralized RTGS using blockchain combined with smart contracts, for example, the Jasper [17], Ubin [28] and Stella [22] projects, In [35] the authors provide a blockchain based solution, however it still relied on a central entity that checks the correctness of the multilateral netting process. In addition, while the source, destination, and amount of every transaction are hidden, the net positions during the multilateral netting process are revealed. Moreover, the multilateral process being an expensive operation is only executed whenever a pending transaction approaches its due time (if any).

More recently, another blockchain-based work was proposed in [12], which is the work most closely related to ours. In [12] homomorphic Pedersen commitments and Zero-knowledge proofs are used to remove the need of a central entity, as well as the need to reveal the net positions during the multilateral netting process. However, the basic protocol reveals the source and destination of every transaction. Hiding them is possible, but it would induce a factor of n to the cost

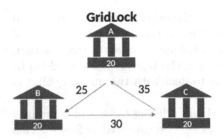

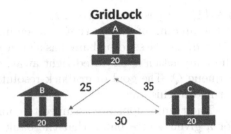

Fig. 1. The banks do not have enough liquidity to settle their transactions, as each bank is planning to send more than what it currently holds. However, a multilateral netting will result in positive net positions for all banks.

Fig. 2. The banks do not have enough liquidity to settle their transactions, as each bank is planning to send more than what it currently holds, and even multilateral netting will not result in positive net positions for all banks

of the protocol, where n is the number of participants in the RTGS. In addition, the protocol would still suffer from the issue described earlier about participants inferring correlations between senders and receivers, from the expected balances of the participants during the multilateral netting process.

The paper [12] does not provide any concrete runtimes, but simply gives execution times of the underlying cryptographic primitives. In comparison to our algorithm, with 100 banks and 9000 transactions, and a liquidity measure of $\beta = 0.1$ (see Sect. 4) one would need to execute approximately 1697 gridlock computations per hour. Our solution could achieve this with a delay of zero seconds, assuming we only secure the values and not the source and destination addresses. The algorithm in [12] would require around 63 minutes to process the transactions, and thus is not real time even with these relatively modest transaction levels.

2 Preliminaries

2.1 The Gridlock Resolution Problem

For a pictorial description of the problem see Figs. 1 and 2. The problem is to decide on a multilateral netting which will result in transactions being settled when this is possible. Such a multilateral netting may not be locally determinable by an individual entity, as it requires knowledge of the position of other entities and the transactions being processed. This problem can be modeled as a discrete optimization problem. In order to introduce it, we will base our definitions on [6] with some simplifications for ease of exposition.

Let n denote the number of banks using the RTGS system, with each bank i having an initial balance $B^i \geq 0$. A transaction is of the form $t = [s, a, r]$, where

$s \in \{1, \ldots n\}$ is the source of t, $r \in \{1, \ldots n\}$ is the destination of t, and $a > 0$ is the amount of money that s is sending to r. For a transaction $t = [s, a, r]$, if $B^s \geq a$, i.e. the sending bank has a large enough balance to cover the transaction, the transaction is executed right away, otherwise, the transaction t is added to a queue Q. The goal of gridlock resolution is to deal with the queue Q that is formed in this way.

The transactions are assumed to come with an ordering $t < t'$ which implies, for a given source bank, that the bank prefers t to be executed before t'. This ordering can be First-In-First-Out, that is, among the transactions hanging issued by bank i, no transaction can be addressed prior to the execution of all transactions that arrived before it.

We define $\mathsf{Sen}_U \subseteq \{1, \ldots, n\}$ to be the set of sources of transactions in a set $U \subseteq Q$. We also denote by U^i the set of the transactions in U coming from bank i, i.e. $U^i = \{t = (s, a, r) \in U \text{ s.t. } s = i\}$, and let us denote by m the size of Q. Let S_U^i and R_U^i denote respectively the amounts sent and received by bank i after running simultaneously a set of U transactions. Let B_U^i denote the balance of this bank after running these transactions. i.e., $B_U^i = B^i - S_U^i + R_U^i$.

The key two states for the queue are those of gridlock and deadlock. A gridlock is where there is a subset of transactions which can be executed, the term 'gridlock' is used here to distinguish it from the situation where the transactions clear without resorting to a queue.

Definition 2.1 (Gridlock). *A gridlock is a situation where among the transactions hanging in Q, there exists $U \subseteq Q$ and $U \neq \emptyset$, such that:*

$$\forall i \in \mathsf{Sen}_U, \ B_U^i \geq 0 \tag{1}$$

$$\forall i \in \mathsf{Sen}_U, \ \forall t \in U^i, \ \nexists t' \in Q^i \setminus U^i \quad \text{such that} \quad t < t' \tag{2}$$

A deadlock is where no transactions can be executed, with the current queue state.

Definition 2.2 (Deadlock). *A deadlock is a situation where $\nexists U \subseteq Q$ that satisfies the conditions of Definition 2.1*

The gridlock resolution problem is to find a subset of transactions in the queue which can be executed.

Definition 2.3 (The gridlock resolution problem). *The gridlock resolution problem consists of finding $\max_{U \subseteq Q} |U|$, such that (1) and (2) from Definition 2.1 hold*

This problem is NP-complete if no strict global ordering is given, and thus one needs to use approximate algorithms in order to solve it, such as the ones introduced in [31] and [24]. However, the problem is not NP-complete if the transactions are augmented with a strict ordering $<$ of execution, and in such a situation one can find an optimal solution in polynomial time.

The Gridlock Resolution Algorithm. The algorithm for gridlock resolution GR [6] proceeds in the following steps, with the formal definition of the algorithm being given in Fig. 3. We first empty the queue Q by moving all the transactions from Q to U. We then call a subroutine which computes the balances resulting from the set U. Thus we compute the amounts sent by the banks, i.e. $[S_U^1, \ldots, S_U^n]$, as well as the amounts received by the banks, i.e. $[R_U^1, \ldots, R_U^n]$. From this we can compute the balances as $[B_U^1, \ldots, B_U^n]$, from $B_U^i \leftarrow B^i + S_U^i - R_U^i$.

At this point, if all the balances of Sen_U are positive, the GR algorithm terminates with the set U. Otherwise, the last transaction for all sources i such that the balance B_U^i is negative is moved from U to the queue Q^1. The balances are recomputed for this new set U, and this process is repeated. If at some point the algorithm terminates with a set $U \neq \emptyset$, the transactions in U are executed, and the actual balances B^i are updated. If however $U = \emptyset$ then we have reached a deadlock and we need to wait for more transactions to come in before running the GR algorithm again.

The GR algorithm

Algorithm: Balance(U, B):
   On input of a list of transactions U and the current set of balances B this computes the new balances B_U^i for all $i \in [1, \ldots, n]$.
   (1) For $i \in [1, \ldots, n]$
       (I) $S^i \leftarrow \sum_{t=[s,a,r] \in U^i} a$
       (II) $R^i \leftarrow \sum_{t=[s,a,r] \in U \; s.t. \; r=i} a$
       (III) $B_U^i \leftarrow B^i - S^i + R^i$
   (2) Output $[B_U^1, \ldots, B_U^n]$

Algorithm : GR(Q):
   On input Q this algorithm finds is a solution $U \subset Q$ to the gridlock resolution problem, or it returns Deadlock.
   (1) $U \leftarrow Q$ and $Q \leftarrow \emptyset$
   (2) While $U \neq \emptyset$ do
       (I) $B_U \leftarrow$ Balance(U, B)
       (II) If all the balances in B_U are positive returns U.
       (III) Remove from U the last transaction sent by all of the banks for which $B_U^i < 0$, and place these transactions in Q
   (3) Return Deadlock

Fig. 3. The GR algorithm

2.2 Multiparty Computation (MPC)

MPC is a family of cryptographic techniques that allow a set of parties, to perform computation on their inputs, without having to reveal them. MPC was

---

[1] The algorithm from [6] removes just one transaction of a source with a negative balance at this point, but it is equivalent to removing one transaction from each source which has a negative balance.

introduced by Yao in [36], and was developed throughout the years. One family of MPC protocols, and the ones we will consider in this paper, are those based on secret sharing schemes. In these protocols, secrets are split among the p parties participating in the protocol using a secret sharing scheme. The computation on the shared secret is performed through communication between the parties. The function to be evaluated is expressed (to a first-order approximation) through a circuit consisting of addition and multiplication gates over a field $\mathbb{F}_q$, for a large prime q.

The specific underlying MPC protocol we will use is that of [32], this is a protocol which provides active security with abort. This means that an adversary may arbitrarily deviate from the protocol, but if he does so then with overwhelming probability the honest parties should abort the protocol. Whilst based on information-theoretic primitives, the protocol of [32] is computationally secure since it relies on hash functions and PRFs, etc. for efficiency (as well as TLS in the implementation we use in order to obtain secure channels).

MPC functionality $\mathcal{F}^P[\text{MPC}]$

The functionality runs with $\mathcal{P} = \{P^1, \ldots, P^p\}$ and an ideal adversary $\mathcal{A}$, that statically corrupts a set A of parties. Given a set I of valid identifiers, all values are stored in the form $(varid, x)$, where $varid \in I$.

Initialize: On input $(init, q)$ from all parties, the functionality stores $(domain, q)$,

Input: On input $(input, P^i, varid, x)$ from party P^i and $(input, P^i, varid, ?)$ from all other parties, with $varid$ a fresh identifier, the functionality stores $(varid, x)$ in memory.

Add: On command $(add, varid_1, varid_2, varid_3)$ from all parties, where $varid_1, varid_2$ are present in memory and $varid_3$ is not, the functionality retrieves $(varid_1, x)$, $(varid_2, y)$ and stores $(varid_3, x + y)$ in memory.

Multiply: On input $(multiply, varid_1, varid_2, varid_3)$ from all parties, where $varid_1, varid_2$ are present in memory and $varid_3$ is not), the functionality retrieves $(varid_1, x)$, $(varid_2, y)$ and stores $(varid_3, x \cdot y)$ in memory.

Output: On input $(output, varid, i)$ from all honest parties, where $varid$ is present in memory, the functionality retrieves $(varid, y)$ and outputs it to the environment. The functionality waits for input from the environment. If this input is Deliver then y is output to all parties if $i = 0$, or y is output to party i if $i \neq 0$. If the adversarial input is not equal to Deliver then $\varnothing$ is output to all parties.

Fig. 4. MPC functionality $\mathcal{F}^P[\text{MPC}]$

The protocol of [32] essentially allows the implementation of the arithmetic black box defined in Fig. 4. Note, as a shorthand in our protocols we will refer to the addition and multiplication operations as $\langle z \rangle \leftarrow \langle x \rangle + \langle y \rangle$ and $\langle z \rangle \leftarrow \langle x \rangle \cdot \langle y \rangle$, and the output operations as $z \leftarrow \text{Open}(\langle z \rangle)$ for open-to-all. We also define an operation $\text{Open}_E(\langle z \rangle, i)$ which opens the shared value $\langle z \rangle$ to the external bank i (by sending the players' shares of $\langle z \rangle$ to the external bank i.) This last operation is used to send data to external parties which is the output of the computation; this is identical as an opening to an internal player in terms of the ability for the environment to decide if the correct value is actually delivered.

The protocol of [32] is defined for arbitrary $\mathcal{Q}_2$ access structures, but in this paper, we will concentrate on the simpler subset of threshold access structures.

In a threshold access structure on p players, with threshold t, up to t players can collude. A Q_2 access structure in this threshold context is one for which $t < p/2$. Such honest majority protocols allow efficient multiplication of secret shared data.

In such a situation (threshold access structures with $t < p/2$) we can (and do in this paper) define the underlying secret sharing scheme via Shamir Secret Sharing. In Shamir Secret Sharing, the secret $x \in \mathbb{F}_q$ is encoded in the constant term of a polynomial $f_x(X)$ of degree t, i.e. $x = f_x(0)$, where t is the threshold considered. The share of each party i of the secret x is $x_i \in \mathbb{F}_q$, such that $f_x(i) = x_i$. From now on we will denote such a secret shared value x by $\langle x \rangle$. If $t + 1$ parties combine their shares by interpolation of the polynomial, they can recover the polynomial f_x and thus the secret x. We will write $\langle x \rangle$ for the sharing of x with this sharing.

Linear operations on the secret shared values can be performed via local operations, whilst the multiplication operations in our arithmetic black box are performed in an offline-online manner (since our protocol is based upon [32]). In an "offline" phase is where data that does not depend on player inputs or the function is pre-computed, and then in the "online" phase, the actual computation takes place. The protocol of [32] provides an efficient online phase, although the combined cost of the offline plus online phases can be less efficient than other protocol choices.

Up until now, we have considered the arithmetic black box of Fig. 4. This can be extended to cope with non-arithmetic operations in a standard manner. For example, in this work, we will represent integer values $x \in [-2^{K-1}-1, \ldots, 2^K-1]$ as elements of F_q, where $k \ll \log_2 q$. Comparison, and non-arithmetic operations, on such encoded integers, can then be performed using special purpose statistically secure sub-protocols such as those in [15,16,20]. The reader should note that comparison is more expensive to execute than multiplication; which is the opposite of what happens when computing in the clear.

At many points, we will need to read and write to an array of secret values, with an index which is also secret. To do this we make use of the naive Oblivious RAM (ORAM) implementation from [27]. We only require the naive methodology as our arrays will be relatively small, meaning the naive methodology will be faster for our example than the more elaborate variants given in [27]. The naive ORAM has at its heart a Demux function, which takes as input a secret x and a bound L, and outputs a list of bits $b_1, \ldots b_L$, such that $b_i = 1$ if $i = x$, and $b_i = 0$ otherwise.

Given this arithmetic black-box extended with the protocols for comparison and ORAM-style array lookup, we can implement algorithms securely. If the algorithm is correct and utilizes only the operations described above, then the secure implementation will inherit the security properties of the underlying MPC protocol. Particularly, if a server running the computation does not perform the required computation, this will be detected by the honest servers. The only issue which needs to be verified would be if the secure implementation opens any intermediate result, at this point one simply needs to verify that the opened value is something which is inherent in the application; i.e. it is a public value which we expect the algorithm to output to the parties. This is a topic which we will return to in the next section.

3   The Gridlock Resolution Algorithm with MPC

Executing the GRP algorithm totally obliviously, i.e. where the MPC engines know neither the amounts, the source addresses of each transaction, or the destinations, turns out to be very expensive. Thus as well as examining this situation we also examine two relaxed situations in which both the source and destination addresses are in the clear (i.e. open) (which we call sodoGR), and one in which the source addresses are in the clear, but the destination addresses are not (which we call sodsGR). We denote the fully oblivious version ssdsGR. In all situations, we ensure the privacy of the amount in the transactions and privacy of the banks' balances. The basic ideal functionality we aim to emulate is given in Fig. 5.

Gridlock Resolution Algorithm Functionality $\mathcal{F}^{type}[GRP]$

The functionality operates between n banks, p servers and an ideal adversary $\mathcal{A}$ that statically corrupts a set A of parties among the servers. We assume that the banks are acting honestly throughout the protocol.

The functionality is reactive in that it maintains a list of the unexecuted queue of transactions Q, and then updates this with the new incoming transaction I. The internal queue is updated with I and then the GRP algorithm described in figure Fig. 3 is executed. The set of executed transactions U is returned (or Deadlock), and these executed transactions are deleted from the internal queue Q for usage in the next call to $\mathcal{F}^{type}[GRP]$. We distinguish three versions of the functionality: where type is in $\{$sodoGR, sodsGR, ssdsGR$\}$

Initialize: The system is initialized with
- An empty queue of transactions Q.
- The current balances b_i for the banks.

InputTrans: On input $t = (s, a, r)$ from bank s, the functionality takes a fresh identifier id_t and associates it to the transaction t. If type $\neq$ ssdsGR and this transaction can be instantly executed, i.e. the balance of bank s is larger than a, then this transaction is executed (i.e. the functionality informs banks s and r of the amount a), otherwise the functionality also adds t to Q.
  In addition to this, the functionality may reveal to the servers some of the components of the transaction t depending on the type.
- If type = sodoGR, s and r are revealed to the servers.
- If type = sodsGR, s is revealed to the servers.
- Otherwise, i.e. type = ssdsGR, nothing is revealed to the servers.

Run: On input Run from the servers, the functionality processes Q, by executing the algorithm of Fig. 3. If the algorithm returns Deadlock then this is returned to the servers and the banks. If the algorithm returns a set of transactions U then the functionality informs the servers as to which transactions these values in U correspond to; and they are deleted from the current queue Q. For every transaction $t = (s, a, r)$ in U the functionality informs s and r about this transaction and the amount.

Fig. 5. Gridlock resolution algorithm functionality $\mathcal{F}^{type}[GRP]$

In Fig. 6 we present the algorithm to compute the balances, upon processing a list of payments Q, in our three different scenarios. The algorithms, make use

---

Algorithms for Balances

$\mathsf{Demux}_{\mathsf{sodsGR}}(Q)$
  On input of a list of transactions Q this produces the demux flags C for the destination
  addresses when the source addresses are in the clear
  (1) $C \leftarrow [\,]$.
  (2) For $t = [s, \langle a \rangle, \langle r \rangle]$ in Q :
      (I) $\langle \mathbf{c}^t \rangle \leftarrow \mathsf{Demux}(\langle r \rangle, n)$.
      (II) Append C by $\langle \mathbf{c}^t \rangle$.
  (3) Output C.

$\mathsf{Demux}_{\mathsf{ssdsGR}}(Q)$
  On input of a list of transactions Q this produces the demux flags for the recipient addresses
  C and the source addresses W
  (1) $C \leftarrow [\,]$, $W \leftarrow [\,]$.
  (2) For $t = [\langle s \rangle, \langle a \rangle, \langle r \rangle]$ in Q:
      (I) $\langle \mathbf{c}^t \rangle \leftarrow \mathsf{Demux}(\langle r \rangle, n)$.
      (II) $\langle \mathbf{w}^t \rangle \leftarrow \mathsf{Demux}(\langle s \rangle, n)$.
      (III) Append C by $\langle \mathbf{c}^t \rangle$ and C by $\langle \mathbf{w}^t \rangle$.
  (3) Output (C, W).

$\mathsf{Balance}([\langle B^i \rangle]_{i=1}^n, Q, X, C, W, \mathsf{type})$
This algorithm updates the balances $\langle B^i \rangle$ for every bank i, given a set of transactions $U \subset Q$ and
the operation type, $\mathsf{type} = \mathsf{sodoGR}, \mathsf{sodsGR}, \mathsf{ssdsGR}$. The set U is oblivious to the algorithm and
determined by an indicator set $X = [\langle x_t \rangle]_{t \in Q}$, such that $x_t = 1$ if and only if $t \in U$, otherwise
$x_t = 0$. The sets $C = [\mathbf{c}^t]_{t \in Q}$ and $W = [\langle \mathbf{w}^t \rangle]_{t \in Q}$ are derived from the Demux operations above,
when needed.

  (1) $\langle B_U^i \rangle \leftarrow \langle B^i \rangle$ for all $i \in [1, \ldots, n]$.
  (2) For $i \in [1, \ldots, n]$:
      (I) If $\mathsf{type} \neq \mathsf{ssdsGR}$ then $\langle S^i \rangle \leftarrow \sum_{t=(i, \langle a \rangle, *) \in Q^i} \langle a \rangle \cdot \langle x_t \rangle$.
      (II) else $\langle S^i \rangle \leftarrow \sum_{t=(\langle s \rangle, \langle a \rangle, \langle r \rangle) \in Q} \langle a \rangle \cdot \langle x_t \rangle \cdot \langle \mathbf{w}_i^t \rangle$.
      (III) If $\mathsf{type} = \mathsf{sodoGR}$ then $\langle R^i \rangle \leftarrow \sum_{t=(s, \langle a \rangle, r) \in Q, r=i} \langle a \rangle \cdot \langle x_t \rangle$.
      (IV) else $\langle R^i \rangle \leftarrow \sum_{t=(*, \langle a \rangle, \langle r \rangle) \in Q} \langle a \rangle \cdot \langle x_t \rangle \cdot \langle \mathbf{c}_i^t \rangle$.
      (V) $\langle B_U^i \rangle \leftarrow \langle B^i \rangle - \langle S^i \rangle + \langle R^i \rangle$.
  (3) Return $[\langle B_U^i \rangle]_{i=1}^n$.

Fig. 6. Algorithms for balances

of the Demux operation. Recall $\langle \mathbf{v} \rangle \leftarrow \mathsf{Demux}(\langle r \rangle, n)$, where we are guaranteed
that $1 \leq r \leq n$, produces a vector $\langle \mathbf{v} \rangle$ of size n such that each entry is a sharing
of zero, apart from entry r where we have a sharing of one. The i-th element of
$\langle \mathbf{v} \rangle$ will be denoted by $\langle \mathbf{v}_i \rangle$.

In Fig. 8 we present the algorithm for executing the Gridlock Resolution algorithm in our three cases. This utilizes the algorithm for computing balances from
Fig. 6, as well as the algorithm, in Fig. 7, which notifies the banks of their completed transactions. In the following paragraphs, we highlight aspects of these
algorithms in the three different situations.

Sources and Destinations are Open (sodoGR). For this version, computing
the receipts and payments is straightforward. That is, we know the source and
destination of every transaction, thus for every bank of Sen_Q, we know the

---

Method to Notify Participants of Executed Transactions

Notify($X, Q, C, W,$ type)

This algorithm notifies the participants about the executed transactions they sent/received. On input Q contains a set of transactions, X specifies (in the clear) the transactions in Q that were executed (signaled by a one bit), the sets C and W are derived from the Demux operation in Fig. 6.

(1) If type = sodoGR
  (I) For $t = [s, \langle a \rangle, r] \in Q$ such that $x_t = 1$.
    (A) Notify s and r about t and execute $\mathsf{Open}_E(\langle a \rangle, r)$.
(2) If type = sodsGR
  (I) For $t = [s, \langle a \rangle, \langle r \rangle] \in Q$ such that $x_t = 1$
    (A) Notify s about t, who can then update bank r about (s, a, r).
(3) If type = ssdsGR
  (I) For $i \in [1, \ldots, n]$ and $t = [\langle s \rangle, \langle a \rangle, \langle r \rangle] \in Q$ such that $x_t = 1$
    (A) Execute $\mathsf{Open}_E(\langle \mathbf{w}_i^t \rangle \cdot \langle s \rangle, i)$, $\mathsf{Open}_E(\langle \mathbf{w}_i^t \rangle \cdot \langle a \rangle, i)$, $\mathsf{Open}_E(\langle \mathbf{w}_i^t \rangle \cdot \langle r \rangle, i)$, $\mathsf{Open}_E(\langle \mathbf{c}_i^t \rangle \cdot \langle s \rangle, i)$, $\mathsf{Open}_E(\langle \mathbf{c}_i^t \rangle \cdot \langle a \rangle, i)$, and $\mathsf{Open}_E(\langle \mathbf{c}_i^t \rangle \cdot \langle r \rangle, i)$.

Fig. 7. Method to notify participants of executed transactions

amount of each transaction we need to add or subtract to its balance. Therefore, the algorithm for updating the balances (Fig. 6) is relatively cheap. However, we face two main obstacles for this version: (1) How to determine whether we have a solution for the problem without leaking which banks have negative balances? (2) In the case where we still do not have a solution, how can we remove transactions without leaking which ones, and without leaking their corresponding banks?

To address the first obstacle, in Fig. 8 we first compare the balances of the banks in an oblivious manner, by performing in step 5.II.A a secure comparison of all balances of Sen_Q, which will result in secret values $\langle h^i \rangle$. Each of these values is equal to one if the corresponding balance is negative, or equal to zero otherwise. Then in step 5.IV, we open $\langle z \rangle$ which is the product of $(1 - \langle h^i \rangle)$. Thus z will be one if all the balances are positive and therefore we found a solution or z will be zero in which case we need to continue removing transactions.

For the second obstacle, basically we need to touch every transaction so as to not leak which ones are being removed. We ensure this using the flags $\langle h^i \rangle$, which guarantee that we will be modifying the indicators of only the banks with negative balances,

Then in order to not reveal which transaction was removed for these banks, we use the indicators x_{t_j} to act as flags. Namely, step 5.VI.A.ii guarantees that we are setting to zero only the last indicator in the queue that has the value one, for the banks in question, i.e., the last transaction submitted to the RTGS among the ones that are still considered for the gridlock resolution. Note that within this step, we could have simply conducted secure comparisons in order to determine which indicator to modify. However, we implemented it as such purely for performance purposes, as multiplications are cheaper than comparisons. In order to detect a deadlock, we compute the product of $(1 - \langle x_t \rangle)$ in 5.VI.B and we open it, which will be equal to one if a deadlock occurs.

Finally, once a set of transactions are executed, we notify the corresponding sources and destinations using the algorithm Notify. For every transaction exe-

MPC variant of the Gridlock Resolution Algorithm

$GR(\langle B^i \rangle_{i=1}^n, Q, \text{type})$

Given a set of balances B_i and a queue of transactions this determines a subset of the transactions $U \subset Q$ which can be executed; where the set U is given by an indicator set X. If no such U exists it returns Deadlock, otherwise it returns the set of remaining transactions which have not been executed.

(1) $X \leftarrow [\langle x_t \rangle]_{t \in Q}$ with $\langle x_t \rangle \leftarrow 1$.
(2) $C, W \leftarrow \emptyset$.
(3) If type = sodsGR then $C \leftarrow \text{Demux}_{\text{sodsGR}}(Q)$.
(4) If type = ssdsGR then $(C, W) \leftarrow \text{Demux}_{\text{ssdsGR}}(Q)$ and $\text{CNT}_{\text{Deadlock}} \leftarrow 0$.
(5) Repeat
    (I) $[\langle B_U^i \rangle]_{i=1}^n \leftarrow \text{Balance}([\langle B^i \rangle]_{i=1}^n, Q, X, C, W, \text{type})$.
    (II) If type $\neq$ ssdsGR
        (A) For $i \in \text{Sen}_Q$ do $\langle h^i \rangle \leftarrow (\langle B_U^i \rangle < 0)$.
        (B) $\langle z \rangle \leftarrow \prod_{\{i \in \text{Sen}_Q\}} (1 - \langle h^i \rangle)$.
    (III) else
        (A) $\langle \text{Sender} \rangle \leftarrow 0$.
        (B) For $i \in \{1, \ldots, n\}$:
            (i) $\langle h^i \rangle \leftarrow (\langle B^i \rangle < 0)$
            (ii) $\langle f^i \rangle \leftarrow \langle h^i \rangle - \langle h^i \rangle \sum_{k=1}^{k=i-1} \langle f^k \rangle$
            (iii) $\langle \text{Sender} \rangle \leftarrow \langle \text{Sender} \rangle + i \cdot \langle f^i \rangle$
        (C) $\langle z \rangle \leftarrow \sum_{i=1}^n \langle f^i \rangle$
    (IV) $z \leftarrow \text{Open}(\langle z \rangle)$.
    (V) If $z = 1$ then
        (A) $x_t \leftarrow \text{Open}(\langle x_t \rangle)$ for $t \in Q$, and let $X' = [x_t]_{t \in Q}$.
        (B) Execute $\text{Notify}(X', Q, C, W, \text{type})$.
        (C) For $i \in [1, \ldots, n]$ execute $\langle B^i \rangle \leftarrow \langle B_U^i \rangle$.
        (D) $Q \leftarrow Q \setminus \{t\}_{t \in Q, x_t = 1}$.
        (E) Return Q.
    (VI) If type $\neq$ ssdsGR
        (A) For $i \in \text{Sen}_Q$
            (i) Let $t_1, \ldots, t_v$ denote the transactions in Q with source i ordered in time of receipt order.
            (ii) For $j = 1, \ldots, v - 1$ do
                (a) $\langle x_{t_j} \rangle \leftarrow (\langle x_{t_j} \rangle \cdot \langle x_{t_{j+1}} \rangle) \cdot \langle h^i \rangle + \langle x_{t_j} \rangle \cdot (1 - \langle h^i \rangle)$.
            (iii) $\langle x_{t_v} \rangle \leftarrow \langle x_{t_v} \rangle \cdot (1 - \langle h^i \rangle)$.
        (B) $\langle \text{Deadlock} \rangle \leftarrow \prod_{i \in \text{Sen}_Q, t \in Q^i} (1 - \langle x_t \rangle)$.
        (C) Deadlock $\leftarrow \text{Open}(\langle \text{Deadlock} \rangle)$.
    (VII) else
        (A) $\text{CNT}_{\text{Deadlock}} \leftarrow \text{CNT}_{\text{Deadlock}} + 1$
        (B) If $(\text{CNT}_{\text{Deadlock}} = m - 1)$:
            (i) Deadlock $\leftarrow 1$.
        (C) else
            (i) $\langle d \rangle \leftarrow 1$
            (ii) For j in $\{m, \ldots, 1\}$
                (a) $\langle y \rangle \leftarrow (\langle s_j \rangle = \langle \text{Sender} \rangle) \cdot \langle x_j \rangle \cdot \langle d \rangle$.
                (b) $\langle x_j \rangle \leftarrow \langle x_j \rangle - \langle y \rangle$.
                (c) $\langle d \rangle \leftarrow \langle d \rangle - \langle y \rangle$.
(6) Until Deadlock = 1.
(7) Return Deadlock.

Fig. 8. MPC variant of the gridlock resolution algorithm

cuted $t = [s, \langle a \rangle, r]$, this algorithm notifies s about the execution of transaction t, and notifies r of receiving a transaction by sending him the tuple (s, a). The amount a here was opened to r by having the p entities send their respective shares of $\langle a \rangle$ to him, who will reconstruct a from these shares. This way only r will learn a while the entities will not.

Sources are Open and Destinations are Secret (sodsGR). For this version, computing the payments needed by a party is straightforward as the sources of transactions are open, but computing the corresponding receipts we need to apply a Demux operation to compute the balances in Fig. 6. This is done only once at the beginning of the algorithm, at the expense of having to store the vectors C in memory all along with the computation. The rest of the computation proceeds as in the case sodoGR described above.

To notify participants about the execution of their transactions, we again use Notify. For every transaction executed $t = [s, \langle a \rangle, \langle r \rangle]$, this algorithm, in this case, notifies s of the execution of t, who can update r about the amount sent a.

Sources and Destinations are Secret (ssdsGR). This version is more challenging to address compared to the previous versions as we keep all the sources and destinations secret, thus we have to deal with some challenges. The alteration to compute the balances is similar to the case sodsGR. However, given that the sources are hidden from the system, the Gridlock Resolution algorithm needs to update all the n balances when looking for a solution, as opposed to only the balances of the sources in sodoGR and sodsGR, which is quite expansive.

The fact that the sources and destinations are hidden obliged us to radically change our strategy to remove transactions with negative balances. In fact, obliviously removing the last transaction of *all* sources which have a negative balance is expensive, as it would require $n \cdot m$ equality checks; where n is the number of banks and m is the number of transactions in Q. Therefore, for this version we remove only one transaction at each iteration, as this requires only m equality checks. To determine which transaction to remove, we compute the flags $\langle h_i \rangle$ in a similar way to sodoGR and sodsGR, then we compute the flags $\langle f_i \rangle$ in step 5.III.B.ii, which are all equal to zero, except for the first source who has a negative balance, in which case it is equal to one. These flags will be used to determine the sender $\langle \mathsf{Sender} \rangle$ for which we remove the last transaction. Removing this last transaction is done in step 5.VII where we iterate over all the transactions starting from the end and going backward, so as to switch the first encountered indicator x_j equal to one corresponding to a transaction issued by source $s_j = \mathsf{Sender}$. Ensuring that the indicators of other sources will not be modified while doing this operation is guaranteed by the term $\langle s_j \rangle = \langle \mathsf{Sender} \rangle$ in $\langle y \rangle$, thus when this equality test is equal to zero, y will be zero, and thus x_j will not be modified in step 5.VII.C.ii.a, and ensuring that only one indicator for Sender is switched from one to zero is guaranteed using the variable d, that is, once we reach the first indicator x_j for Sender that is equal to one, y will be equal to one in step 5.VII.C.ii.b, and d will be equal to zero. Once d becomes zero, y will always have the value zero, and thus no other indicator will change in step 5.VII.C.ii.b.

In addition, we introduce a counter $\mathsf{CNT}_{\mathsf{Deadlock}}$ into the algorithm in order to identify a deadlock. This counter is augmented by one each time we perform an iteration, and therefore we will have a deadlock when this counter reaches m.

Finally, we need to notify participants of the execution of their transactions. For every transaction executed $t = [\langle s \rangle, \langle a \rangle, \langle r \rangle]$, this algorithm sends to every bank i the opening of the values, $\{(\langle \mathbf{w}_i^t \rangle \cdot \langle s \rangle, \langle \mathbf{w}_i^t \rangle \cdot \langle a \rangle, \langle \mathbf{w}_i^t \rangle \cdot \langle r \rangle), (\langle \mathbf{c}_i^t \rangle \cdot \langle s \rangle, \langle \mathbf{c}_i^t \rangle \cdot \langle a \rangle, \langle \mathbf{c}_i^t \rangle \cdot \langle r \rangle)\}$ which are equal to $\{(0, 0, 0), (0, 0, 0)\}$ if t was not sent to i or received by i; equal to $\{(s, a, r), (0, 0, 0)\}$ if $i = s$; and equal to $\{(0, 0, 0), (s, a, r)\}$ if $i = r$.

3.1   Leakage

We now discuss the leakage our algorithms have in comparison to the ideal functionality given in Fig. 5. Given the underlying MPC system implements securely any algorithm, the only leakage which can arise is when our algorithms reveal information via an Open command. We assume that the ordering between transactions is public knowledge, which will be the case if the ordering is done purely in a first-in/first-out manner.

We first discuss each such operation in Fig. 8. The openings in the notify algorithm in Fig. 7 are all identical to values revealed by the ideal functionality.

In step 5.V.A the identifiers of which transactions, which are executed, are opened but this is also something which is leaked in our ideal functionality; thus this line provides no additional leakage over what the ideal functionality will leak.

In step 5.VI.C the algorithm reveals to all servers whether Deadlock has been reached. Again this is something which happens in our ideal functionality.

This leaves us with the opening in step 5.IV, which reveals the value of $\langle z \rangle$. This reveals whether on this iteration we should terminate with a solution or not, thus revealing this value reveals *the number of iterations* needed to solve the GRP problem or the number of iterations needed to reach Deadlock. In the first situation, this value is equal to the maximum number of transactions not executed by one of the banks when it is the source. Thus this information is always revealed by the functionality in the case where we have type = sodoGR or type = sodsGR. In the case of type = ssdsGR this value leaks to the p servers, but not to the n banks. In the case where Deadlock is output then the number of iterations reveals the maximum number of transactions with a given source. Thus this value does reveal some information about the distribution of transactions between banks at any given point in time, but we feel it is an acceptable leakage. Removing this leakage is possible, by essentially looping obliviously, in the case where we have type = ssdsGR, for a maximum number of iterations. This would make our implementation match the specifications of Fig. 5 for ssdsGR without inducing the aforementioned leakage, however, this would cause a huge performance penalty.

3.2   Experiments

We implemented the above three variants using the SCALE MPC system [3], which provides a convenient interface to access different secret sharing-based access structures, as well as the comparison and Demux operations discussed above. The experiments were performed using a setup using Shamir Secret Sharing between three parties, over a finite field of size 128 bits. This models the situation where the n banks outsource the computation to $p = 3$ entities, such that each bank trusts that only one of the three entities will act in a malicious manner. The reason for doing this is to avoid having to perform a secure computation with n servers, which will be prohibitively expensive for practical values of n. Of course we can outsource the computation to more than $p = 3$ entities, which will allow the n servers to tolerate more malicious entities, but this will increase the cost of the computation. We used three machines to perform the experiments, that is one machine for each entity. The machines used are 128GB of RAM, with an Intel i-9900 CPU, with a ping time of 0.098 ms between them.

We begin by examining the online phase runtimes of single runs of the algorithms of this section (without including the notification part of the participants about the execution of their transactions). In all experiments, we varied the number of banks n to have the values $\{8, 64, 128, 256, 512, 1024\}$, and the number of transactions m to have the values $\{10, 50, 100\}$. The m transactions were chosen in such a way that a solution will be found after $m/4$ iterations.

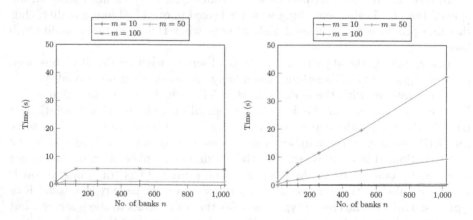

Fig. 9. Run times for sodoGR (left) and sodsGR (right).

sodoGR. The runtimes for this variant are shown in Fig. 9. As one can notice, the runtimes keep increasing when n increases, and stabilize when n becomes bigger than m; reaching a maximum of 5.7 s when considering $m = 100$ and $n \geq m$. This is because when $m \leq n$ we set the transactions in such a way that we only process the m banks that will be sources of the transactions. Therefore, when $m \leq n$ the algorithm will perform exactly the same amount of work as when $n = m$.

sodsGR. The runtimes for this experiment are also presented in Fig. 9. One sees that they grow as n increases, irrespective of m, when $m = 100$ growing to around 39 s for $n = 1024$. When $n \geq m$ the runtime increases, but at a slower pace than for $n < m$. This is due to the fact that once n reaches m, the only extra computation is the calculation of the Demux flags C over a bigger set for n, as we can set in this case m banks to be the sources of the transactions when $m \leq n$.

Since this variant needs to calculate the Demux flags, as well as performing more multiplications to compute the received values, for all values of n and m it is slower than sodoGR. For example in step 2.IV of the Balance algorithm in Fig. 6 we need to compute a multiplication by the Demux flag $\langle \mathbf{c}_t^i \rangle$, as opposed to performing a conditional multiplication (conditioned on where $r = i$) in step 2.III of the same algorithm.

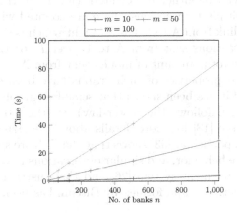

Fig. 10. Run times for ssdsGR.

ssdsGR. The runtimes for this variant are shown in Fig. 10. As one can see the runtimes keep increasing at the same rate even when $m \leq n$. This is related to the fact that sources are hidden from the algorithms. The runtimes are larger for this variant due to the fact that as explained in Sect. 3, the algorithm cannot exclude the banks that are not sources of the transactions hanging, therefore whenever a transaction is removed, the balances of all banks are calculated. Another thing that one can notice is that, the runtimes of ssdsGR are only twice the ones of sodsGR. This is actually related to how we chose transactions as explained earlier. That is, we chose transactions in such a way that we run $m/4$ iterations in step 5.VI/5.VII. We refer the reader to the next section for a more accurate comparison between the two algorithms.

4   Simulating an RTGS

Having so far provided latency values for single executions of our algorithms, we now turn to discussing are these latencies 'fast enough' in a real application. The latency depends not only on the number of banks n, but also on the number of unmet transfers in the queue Q, i.e. m. In a real system, the value of m can both increase and decrease over time, depending on the frequency of incoming transactions and the amount of liquidity in the system. In this section, we aim to simulate a realistic system and determine the cost of performing the liquidity matching in a privacy-preserving manner.

Simulating Transactions. Our first task is to simulate the banks and the transactions between them. The transactions exchanged between banks over a period of time L can be modeled as a directed graph, where nodes represent banks and edges among them represent the flow of the transactions, i.e. a link from bank A to bank B is formed if bank A sent a transaction to bank B over L. This graph can be either unweighted, that is, in the case that bank A sends to bank B multiple transactions, these are counted with only one link or weight. That is, the link from A to B has a weight which is determined by either the number of transactions sent from A to B over L, or the volume of these transactions, i.e., the total amount of money sent from A to B.

The structure and properties of such graphs have been extensively studied in the literature, and it has been shown that scale-free graphs (graphs for which the degree distribution follows the power-law) are the closest ones to model transaction graphs (see [18] for more details about the structural properties of scale-free graphs). In particular [33] shows that the Fedwire system in the United States has a scale-free behavior, and similar observations have been made for the Japanese inter-bank payment system [26] and the Austrian inter-bank market [10]. Even the transaction graph formed by Bitcoin has been shown to be scale-free [1].

Our simulation is controlled by a number of parameters: n the number of banks in the network, n_0 the number of 'central nodes' (see below), the total number of transactions M to be simulated, the time interval L over which we simulate the transactions, a parameter o giving the average number of transactions for each of the $n - n_0$ non-central nodes, a value for modifying the preferential attachment α (which we take to be 0.1), and a value β controlling the amount of liquidity in the system.

For our work, we utilized the simulator of [34] to generate the transaction graph. This simulator uses a tweaked version of the Barabasi-Albert model to generate scale-free graphs. In this simulation the graph is built by setting first n_0 central nodes among the n nodes, these central nodes are intended to send and receive transactions more than the remaining nodes; they correspond in the real world to the important banks in a network. This preference is guaranteed by at the beginning setting the preferential attachment v_i for these banks to be one, and for the remaining banks to be zero. The algorithm then proceeds to find a total number of $M = o \cdot (n - n_0)$ transactions $t_1, \ldots, t_M$.

These transactions $t_i = (s, a, r)$ are generated as follows: The source bank $s \in \{1, \ldots, n\}$ is selected with probability $v_s / \sum_{j=1}^{j=n} v_j$, the destination bank $r \in \{1, \ldots, n\}$ is selected with probability $v_r / \sum_{j=1}^{j=n} v_j$. If we obtain $s = r$ then a new value of r is sampled in the same way, until $s \neq r$. Whenever a transaction is generated, we update the preferential attachment for both the source and destination, by adding $\alpha = 0.1$ to v_s and v_r, and whenever o transactions are generated, we set the preferential attachment to be 1 for one of the banks that were not yet considered for sending or receiving transactions, i.e., a bank i that still has $v_i = 0$. The amount a is sampled by taking a value v from the normal distribution with mean 1 and standard deviation 0.2, and then setting $a = d \cdot \exp(v)$, where d is the minimum of the in-out degrees of the source and destination nodes s and r; this follows the methodology in [34]. It also means that transactions are likely to be larger from banks which are more central to the graph, a fact which is born out in practice.

To each transaction we assign a time of occurrence; for this, we assume that the M transactions are uniformly distributed over the time interval L. The order of the transactions is as in the simulation above, with transaction t_i entering the system at time τ_i, where we have $\tau_{i+1} - \tau_i \approx L/M$ for all i.

For the initial balances of the banks, these are set according to a parameter $\beta \in [0,1]$ that determines the amount of liquidity available in the system. That is, we calculate the lower and upper bounds of liquidity for each bank, where the lower bound L_i for bank i refers to the minimal initial balance that will allow the bank to settle all its transactions at the end of the time window, and the upper bound U_i refers to an initial balance that will allow the bank to settle immediately all its transactions without having to be placed in the queue U for the gridlock execution. Then the initial balance of bank i we set equal to $B^i = \beta \cdot (U_i - L_i) + L_i$.

In [34] it is claimed that the above algorithm is a good model for transaction graphs between banks. In particular, they discuss the Fedwire transaction graph. To get some idea of the sizes of the graph we note that Fedwire in 2008 had approximately $n = 7300$ participants[2] and the average daily volume of transfers in January 2021[3] was $803,413$ transactions. A smaller system is the Target2 system run by the European Central Bank, according to the annual report of 2019[4], the number of direct participant is $n = 1050$, with each participant originating on average $344,120$ transactions per day.

The Simulation. In our simulation, we assume that for sodoGR and sodsGR, two banks will settle an incoming transaction if it can be settled immediately, with unsettled transactions being passed to the queue Q for application of the Gridlock Resolution algorithm. For the case of ssdsGR, the only way a transaction can be settled is through the Gridlock Resolution algorithm. For the remaining transactions, we process them in one of two manners: In Version 1 each transaction is processed one at a time, it is cleared immediately if it can be, otherwise, it is added to the current queue Q. For the cases of sodsGR and ssdsGR, we run the GR algorithm if Q has more than one entry. For the case of sodoGR, we run the GR algorithm if the last incoming transaction (either settled or not) has as the destination one of the sources of the transactions in Q. In Version 2 we

---

[2] https://www.federalreserve.gov/paymentsystems/fedfunds_about.htm.

[3] https://www.frbservices.org/resources/financial-services/wires/volume-value-stats/monthly-stats.html.

[4] https://www.ecb.europa.eu/pub/targetar/html/ecb.targetar2019.en.html.

simulate the current time (according to how long previous executions of the GR algorithm take), we then add all transactions, which have arrived between the start of the previous execution of the GR algorithm and the end of the previous execution, to the queue Q, after clearing all which can be executed immediately. For the cases of sodsGR and ssdsGR, we then execute the GR algorithm if Q has more than one entry. For the case of sodoGR, we run the GR algorithm if at least one of the last incoming transactions (either settled or not) has as the destination one of the sources of the transactions in Q. These two variants are described in Fig. 11.

Simulation of RTGS

RTGSSimulation: Given a set of transaction $\mathsf{T} = \{(t_i, \tau_i)\}$ where t_i is the transaction and τ_i is the time stamp of this transaction execute:

(1) $Q \leftarrow \emptyset$, $\mathsf{T} \leftarrow \emptyset$, $\tau = 0$. The variable τ will define the current time in the simulation.

(2) While $\mathsf{T} \neq \emptyset$ do

   (I) If Version 1
     (A) Let (t_i, τ_i) denote element in T with the minimal value of τ_i.
     (B) $\tau \leftarrow \tau_i$ if $\tau < \tau_i$.
     (C) $\mathsf{T} \leftarrow \mathsf{T} \setminus \{(t_i, \tau_i)\}$.
     (D) $\mathcal{U} \leftarrow \{(t_i, \tau_i)\}$.

   (II) Else if Version 2
     (A) Let $\mathcal{U}$ denote all transactions in T with time $\tau_i < \tau$.
     (B) If $\mathcal{U} = \emptyset$ execute the above four steps for Version 1.
     (C) Else $\mathsf{T} \leftarrow \mathsf{T} \setminus \mathcal{U}$.

   (III) Start-timer; this is used to ensure we simulate time correctly.

   (IV) For all $(t, \tau_i) \in \mathcal{U}$
     (A) If type = sodoGR:
       (i) Write $t = [s, \langle a \rangle, r]$.
       (ii) $\langle z \rangle \leftarrow \langle B^s \rangle \geq \langle a \rangle$
       (iii) $z \leftarrow \mathsf{Open}(\langle z \rangle)$
       (iv) If $z = 1$ then
         1. $\langle B^s \rangle \leftarrow \langle B^s \rangle - \langle a \rangle$.
         2. $\langle B^r \rangle \leftarrow \langle B^r \rangle + \langle a \rangle$.
         3. Execute $\mathsf{Notify}(\{1\}, \{t\}, \emptyset, \emptyset, \mathsf{sodoGR})$.
       (v) Else $Q \leftarrow Q \cup \{t\}$.
     (B) Else if type = sodsGR:
       (i) Write $t = [s, \langle a \rangle, \langle r \rangle]$.
       (ii) $\langle z \rangle \leftarrow \langle B^s \rangle \geq \langle a \rangle$
       (iii) $z \leftarrow \mathsf{Open}(\langle z \rangle)$
       (iv) If $z = 1$ then
         (a) $\mathbf{v} \leftarrow \mathsf{Demux}(\langle r \rangle, n)$.
         (b) $\langle B^s \rangle \leftarrow \langle B^s \rangle - \langle a \rangle$
         (c) $\langle B^i \rangle \leftarrow \langle B^i \rangle + \langle a \rangle \cdot \mathbf{v}_i$ for $i \in [1, \ldots, n]$
         (d) Execute $\mathsf{Notify}(\{1\}, \{t\}, \mathbf{v}, \emptyset, \mathsf{sodsGR})$.
       (v) $Q \leftarrow Q \cup \{t\}$.
     (C) Else if type = ssdsGR:
       (i) $Q \leftarrow Q \cup \{t\}$.

   (V) If type = sodoGR and $\exists t_j = [s_j, \langle a_j \rangle, r_j] \in \mathcal{U}$ and $\exists t_k = [s_k, \langle a_k \rangle, r_k] \in Q \setminus \mathcal{U}$ such that $r_j = s_k$ then execute sodoGR(Q).

   (VI) Else if type = sodsGR then execute sodsGR(Q), running $\mathsf{Demux}_{\mathsf{sodsGR}}$ only on the new transactions in $\mathcal{U} \subset Q$, by keeping track of the prior executions.

   (VII) Else if type = ssdsGR then execute ssdsGR(Q), running $\mathsf{Demux}_{\mathsf{sodsGR}}$ and $\mathsf{Demux}_{\mathsf{ssdsGR}}$ only on the new transactions in $\mathcal{U} \subset Q$, by keeping track of the prior executions.

   (VIII) Stop-timer; let the elapsed time be denoted by τ_0.

   (IX) $\tau \leftarrow \tau + \tau_0$.

(3) Output the elapsed time τ needed to execute all the transactions.

Fig. 11. Simulation of RTGS

Leakage. Again we need to consider if there is any leakage of information from the Open operations in Fig. 11. The two lines, in steps 2.IV.A.iii and 2.IV.B.iii, open a value which indicates whether (in the cases of type = sodoGR and type = sodsGR respectively) a transaction can be executed immediately, without needing to be passed into a gridlock resolution process. This is something which our ideal functionality also leaks.

Experimental Results. We executed the above simulation, again with an MPC system of three players, over a simulation time window L of one hour, considering only the online phase, with three different levels of liquidity $\beta \in \{0.1, 0.5, 0.9\}$, and with $n_0 = 10$. We tested on different values of n and o, with n either 100 or 1000; a value of 1000 is approximately the number of direct participants in Target 2. Our values of o (which controls the number of transactions $M = o \cdot (n - n_0)$) where also chosen to approximate the number of transactions Target 2 deals with in an hour assuming transactions are uniformly distributed through the day (in this case only with $n = 100$).

We considered two main metrics to evaluate the performance: (i) How much time we exceed the time window L, i.e. was the value τ output by the simulation larger than the time window L, i.e. $E = \tau - L$. (ii) The average delay time for transactions. Each transaction (t, τ_i) is supposed to enter to the system in time τ_i, however, the system may not be able to address this transaction at time τ_i, but only at a later time τ_i', after finishing an ongoing gridlock computation. Thus the average delay time, in seconds, will be $D = \sum_{i=1}^{i=M} (\tau_i' - \tau_i)/M$. In a real system, one would desire that E is zero, or as close as possible (to ensure real time settlement of all transactions in a day) and that D is also as small as possible (to ensure individual transactions are not delayed too much). The results of our simulation are given in Table 1.

We can notice from the runtimes that the more liquidity we have, the faster the runtimes are. This is because liquidity affects how many times the gridlock computation takes place, as well as the size of the queues on which this computation happens. We can also notice that the slowest runtimes correspond (unsurprisingly) to the case where sources and destinations are hidden. Version 2 of the algorithm for clearing is much better and indeed seems to meet the operational requirements of E and D being close to zero, for all cases bar that of both sources and destinations being secret.

Table 1. Experimental results

			Version 1		Version 2	
			E	D	E	D
sodoGR	$\beta = 0.1$	$n = 100$, $M = 900$, $o = 10$	0	0	0	0
		$n = 100$, $M = 9000$, $o = 100$	0	307	0	0
		$n = 100$, $M = 45000$, $o = 500$	–	–	0	0
		$n = 1000$, $M = 9900$, $o = 10$	–	–	0	1
	$\beta = 0.5$	$n = 100$, $M = 900$, $o = 10$	0	0	0	0
		$n = 100$, $M = 9000$, $o = 100$	0	0	0	0
		$n = 100$, $M = 45000$, $o = 500$	–	–	0	0
		$n = 1000$, $M = 9900$, $o = 10$	–	–	0	0
	$\beta = 0.9$	$n = 100$, $M = 900$, $o = 10$	0	0	0	0
		$n = 100$, $M = 9000$, $o = 100$	0	0	0	0
		$n = 100$, $M = 45000$, $o = 500$	–	–	0	0
		$n = 1000$, $M = 9900$, $o = 10$	–	–	0	0
sodsGR	$\beta = 0.1$	$n = 100$, $M = 900$, $o = 10$	0	0	0	0
		$n = 100$, $M = 9000$, $o = 100$	18707	12030	0	0
		$n = 100$, $M = 45000$, $o = 500$	–	–	0	2
		$n = 1000$, $M = 9900$, $o = 10$	–	–	0	7
	$\beta = 0.5$	$n = 100$, $M = 900$, $o = 10$	0	0	0	0
		$n = 100$, $M = 9000$, $o = 100$	0	163	0	0
		$n = 100$, $M = 45000$, $o = 500$	–	–	0	0
		$n = 1000$, $M = 9900$, $o = 10$	–	–	0	5
	$\beta = 0.9$	$n = 100$, $M = 900$, $o = 10$	0	0	0	0
		$n = 100$, $M = 9000$, $o = 100$	0	0	0	0
		$n = 100$, $M = 45000$, $o = 500$	–	–	0	0
		$n = 1000$, $M = 9900$, $o = 10$	–	–	0	0
ssdsGR	$\beta = 0.1$	$n = 100$, $M = 900$, $o = 10$	0	63	0	0
		$n = 100$, $M = 9000$, $o = 100$	164556	102046	0	13
		$n = 100$, $M = 45000$, $o = 500$	–	–	1175	835
		$n = 1000$, $M = 9900$, $o = 10$	–	–	7426	5427
	$\beta = 0.5$	$n = 100$, $M = 900$, $o = 10$	0	0	0	0
		$n = 100$, $M = 9000$, $o = 100$	28646	14442	0	2
		$n = 100$, $M = 45000$, $o = 500$	–	–	0	8
		$n = 1000$, $M = 9900$, $o = 10$	–	–	4482	1784
	$\beta = 0.9$	$n = 100$, $M = 900$, $o = 10$	0	0	0	0
		$n = 100$, $M = 9000$, $o = 100$	0	0	0	0
		$n = 100$, $M = 45000$, $o = 500$	–	–	0	0
		$n = 1000$, $M = 9900$, $o = 10$	–	–	0	105

Acknowledgments. We would like to thank Cedric Humbert of the European Central Bank for suggesting we look into this problem, and answering various questions we had along the way. This work has been supported in part by ERC Advanced Grant ERC-2015-AdG-IMPaCT, by the FWO under an Odysseus project GOH9718N, and by CyberSecurity Research Flanders with reference number VR20192203.

References

1. Aspembitova, A., Feng, L., Melnikov, V., Chew, L.Y.: Fitness preferential attachment as a driving mechanism in bitcoin transaction network. PLoS One **14**, e0219346 (2019)
2. Abbe, E., Khandani, A.E., Lo, A.W.: Privacy-preserving methods for sharing financial risk exposures. CoRR abs/1111.5228 (2011)
3. Aly, A., et al.: SCALE and MAMBA v1.14: documentation (2021). https://homes.esat.kuleuven.be/~nsmart/SCALE/Documentation.pdf
4. Asharov, G., Balch, T.H., Polychroniadou, A., Veloso, M.: Privacy-preserving dark pools. In: Seghrouchni, A.E.F., Sukthankar, G., An, B., Yorke-Smith, N. (eds.) Proceedings of the 19th International Conference on Autonomous Agents and Multiagent Systems, AAMAS 2020, Auckland, New Zealand, 9–13, May 2020, pp. 1747–1749. International Foundation for Autonomous Agents and Multiagent Systems (2020)
5. Bag, S., Hao, F., Shahandashti, S.F., Ray, I.G.: SEAL: sealed-bid auction without auctioneers. IEEE Trans. Inf. Forensics Secur. **15**, 2042–2052 (2020)
6. Bech, M., Soramaki, K.: Gridlock resolution in payment systems. Danmarks Nationalbank Monetary Review, July (2001)
7. Bogdanov, D., Talviste, R., Willemson, J.: Deploying secure multi-party computation for financial data analysis. In: Keromytis, A.D. (ed.) FC 2012. LNCS, vol. 7397, pp. 57–64. Springer, Heidelberg (2012). https://doi.org/10.1007/978-3-642-32946-3_5
8. Bogetoft, P., et al.: Secure multiparty computation goes live. In: Dingledine, R., Golle, P. (eds.) FC 2009. LNCS, vol. 5628, pp. 325–343. Springer, Heidelberg (2009). https://doi.org/10.1007/978-3-642-03549-4_20
9. Bogetoft, P., Damgård, I., Jakobsen, T., Nielsen, K., Pagter, J., Toft, T.: A practical implementation of secure auctions based on multiparty integer computation. In: Di Crescenzo, G., Rubin, A. (eds.) FC 2006. LNCS, vol. 4107, pp. 142–147. Springer, Heidelberg (2006). https://doi.org/10.1007/11889663_10
10. Boss, M., Elsinger, H., Summer, M., Thurner, S.: Network topology of the interbank market. Quant. Financ. **4**(6), 677–684 (2004)
11. Byrd, D., Polychroniadou, A.: Differentially private secure multi-party computation for federated learning in financial applications. In: ICAIF 2020: The First ACM International Conference on AI in Finance, New York, NY, USA, 15–16, October 2020, pp. 16:1–16:9 (2020)
12. Cao, S., Yuan, Y., De Caro, A., Nandakumar, K., Elkhiyaoui, K., Hu, Y.: Decentralized privacy-preserving netting protocol on blockchain for payment systems. In: Bonneau, J., Heninger, N. (eds.) FC 2020. LNCS, vol. 12059, pp. 137–155. Springer, Cham (2020). https://doi.org/10.1007/978-3-030-51280-4_9
13. Cartlidge, J., Smart, N.P., Alaoui, Y.T.: Multi-party computation mechanism for anonymous equity block trading: a secure implementation of turquoise plato uncross. Cryptology ePrint Archive, Report 2020/662 (2020). https://eprint.iacr.org/2020/662

14. Cartlidge, J., Smart, N.P., Talibi Alaoui, Y.: MPC joins the dark side. In: Galbraith, S.D., Russello, G., Susilo, W., Gollmann, D., Kirda, E., Liang, Z. (eds.) ASIACCS 2019: 14th ACM Symposium on Information, Computer and Communications Security, pp. 148–159. ACM Press, Auckland, New Zealand 9–12, July 2019

15. Catrina, O., de Hoogh, S.: Improved primitives for secure multiparty integer computation. In: Garay, J.A., De Prisco, R. (eds.) SCN 2010. LNCS, vol. 6280, pp. 182–199. Springer, Heidelberg (2010). https://doi.org/10.1007/978-3-642-15317-4_13

16. Catrina, O., Saxena, A.: Secure computation with fixed-point numbers. In: Sion, R. (ed.) FC 2010. LNCS, vol. 6052, pp. 35–50. Springer, Heidelberg (2010). https://doi.org/10.1007/978-3-642-14577-3_6

17. Chapman, J., ans Scott Hendry, R.G., McCormack, A., McMahon, W.: Project jasper: are distributed wholesale payment systems feasible yet? https://www.finextra.com/finextra-downloads/newsdocs/fsr-june-2017-chapman.pdf

18. Cohen, R., Havlin, S., Ben-Avraham, D.: Structural Properties of Scale-free Networks, pp. 85–110. Wiley, Hoboken (2003)

19. Cozzo, D., Smart, N.P., Alaoui, Y.T.: Secure fast evaluation of iterative methods: with an application to secure pagerank. In: Paterson, K.G. (ed.) CT-RSA 2021. LNCS, vol. 12704, pp. 1–25. Springer, Cham (2021). https://doi.org/10.1007/978-3-030-75539-3_1

20. Damgård, I., Fitzi, M., Kiltz, E., Nielsen, J.B., Toft, T.: Unconditionally secure constant-rounds multi-party computation for equality, comparison, bits and exponentiation. In: Halevi, S., Rabin, T. (eds.) TCC 2006. LNCS, vol. 3876, pp. 285–304. Springer, Heidelberg (2006). https://doi.org/10.1007/11681878_15

21. ECB: Target 2. https://www.ecb.europa.eu/paym/target/target2/html/index.en.html

22. European Central Bank and Bank of Japan: Payment systems: liquidity saving mechanisms in a distributed ledger environment. https://www.ecb.europa.eu/pub/pdf/other/ecb.stella_project_report_september_2017.pdf

23. Galbiati, M., Soramaki, K.: Liquidity-saving mechanisms and bank behaviour. Bank of England, Bank of England working papers, July 2010

24. Guntzer, M.M., Jungnickel, D., Leclerc, M.: Efficient algorithms for the clearing of interbank payments. Eur. J. Oper. Res. **106**(1), 212–219 (1998)

25. Hastings, M., Falk, B., Tsoukalas, G.: Privacy-preserving network analytics, August 2020

26. Inaoka, H., Ninomiya, T., Taniguchi, K., Shimizu, T., Takayasu, H.: Fractal Network derived from banking transaction - an analysis of network structures formed by financial institutions. Bank of Japan Working Paper Series 04-E-4, Bank of Japan, April 2004

27. Keller, M., Scholl, P.: Efficient, oblivious data structures for MPC. In: Sarkar, P., Iwata, T. (eds.) ASIACRYPT 2014. LNCS, vol. 8874, pp. 506–525. Springer, Heidelberg (2014). https://doi.org/10.1007/978-3-662-45608-8_27

28. Monetary Authority of Singapore: Project Ubin: Cntral bank digital money using distributed ledger technology. https://www.mas.gov.sg/schemes-and-initiatives/Project-Ubin

29. Parkes, D.C., Rabin, M.O., Shieber, S.M., Thorpe, C.: Practical secrecy-preserving, verifiably correct and trustworthy auctions. Electron. Commer. Res. Appl. **7**(3), 294–312 (2008)

30. Sangers, A., et al.: Secure multiparty pagerank algorithm for collaborative fraud detection. In: Goldberg, I., Moore, T. (eds.) FC 2019. LNCS, vol. 11598, pp. 605–623. Springer, Cham (2019). https://doi.org/10.1007/978-3-030-32101-7_35
31. Shafransky, Y.M., Doudkin, A.A.: An optimization algorithm for the clearing of interbank payments. Eur. J. Oper. Res. **171**(3), 743–749 (2006)
32. Smart, N.P., Wood, T.: Error detection in monotone span programs with application to communication-efficient multi-party computation. In: Matsui, M. (ed.) CT-RSA 2019. LNCS, vol. 11405, pp. 210–229. Springer, Cham (2019). https://doi.org/10.1007/978-3-030-12612-4_11
33. Soramaki, K., Bech, M.L., Arnold, J., Glass, R.J., Beyeler, W.E.: The topology of interbank payment flows. Phys. A Stat. Mech. Appl. **379**(1), 317–333 (2007)
34. Soramaki, K., Cook, S.: Sinkrank: an algorithm for identifying systemically important banks in payment systems. Econ. Open-Access, Open-Assess. E-J. **7**, 2013–2028 (2013)
35. Wang, X., Xu, X., Feagan, L., Huang, S., Jiao, L., Zhao, W.: Inter-bank payment system on enterprise blockchain platform. In: 11th IEEE International Conference on Cloud Computing, CLOUD 2018, San Francisco, CA, USA, 2–7, July 2018, pp. 614–621. IEEE Computer Society (2018)
36. Yao, A.C.C.: How to generate and exchange secrets (extended abstract). In: 27th Annual Symposium on Foundations of Computer Science, pp. 162–167. IEEE Computer Society Press, Toronto, Ontario, Canada 27–29, October 1986

Approximate Homomorphic Encryption with Reduced Approximation Error

Andrey Kim[1,2], Antonis Papadimitriou[3], and Yuriy Polyakov[3](✉) ⓘD

[1] New Jersey Institute of Technology, Newark, USA
[2] Samsung Advanced Institute of Technology, Suwon, Republic of Korea
[3] Duality Technologies, Newark, USA
ypolyakov@dualitytech.com

Abstract. The Cheon-Kim-Kim-Song (CKKS) homomorphic encryption scheme is currently the most efficient method to perform approximate homomorphic computations over real and complex numbers. Although the CKKS scheme can already be used to achieve practical performance for many advanced applications, e.g., in machine learning, its broader use in practice is hindered by several major usability issues, most of which are brought about by relatively high approximation errors and the complexity of dealing with them.

We present a reduced-error CKKS variant that removes the approximation errors due to the Learning With Errors (LWE) noise in the encryption and key switching operations. We propose and implement its Residue Number System (RNS) instantiation that has a lower error than the original CKKS scheme implementation based on multiprecision integer arithmetic. While formulating the RNS instantiation, we also develop an intermediate RNS variant that has a smaller approximation error than the prior RNS variant of CKKS. The high-level idea of our main RNS-related improvements is to remove the approximate scaling error using a novel procedure that computes level-specific scaling factors. The rescaling operations and scaling factor adjustments in our implementation are done automatically.

We implement both RNS variants in PALISADE and compare their approximation error and efficiency to the prior RNS variant. Our results for uniform ternary secret key distribution, which is the most efficient setting included in the community homomorphic encryption security standard, show that the reduced-error CKKS RNS implementation typically has an approximation error that is 6 to 9 bits smaller for computations with multiplications than the prior RNS variant. The results for the sparse secret setting, which was used for the original CKKS scheme, imply that our reduced-error CKKS RNS implementation has an approximation error up to 12 bits smaller than the prior RNS variant.

1 Introduction

The Cheon-Kim-Kim-Song (CKKS) homomorphic encryption (HE) scheme is currently the most efficient method to perform approximate homomorphic computations over real and complex numbers [14]. The CKKS scheme can already be used

The full version of the paper is available at https://eprint.iacr.org/2020/1118.

to achieve practical performance for many advanced applications, e.g., in machine learning for genomics [5,6,22,23]. Its broader use in practice is hindered by several major usability issues. One of the main challenges is the approximation error inherent to almost every operation in CKKS. A significant error is introduced during encryption and keeps growing as computations are performed. To minimize the growth of approximation error, the original CKKS scheme introduced a rescaling operation [14]. But the rescaling operation brought about several other usability issues, e.g., the need for a user to decide when rescaling should be called to achieve desired precision and optimize the efficiency. Another major challenge is specific to the rescaling approximation error in the Residue Number System (RNS) variants of CKKS, which are preferred in practice for better efficiency [6,11].

Approximation Errors in CKKS. All approximation errors in both multiprecision and RNS CKKS are summarized in Table 1. Here, we briefly describe each approximation error.

Table 1. Approximation errors in the original CKKS and prior RNS CKKS vs our variants of CKKS and RNS CKKS. The errors r_{encode}, e_{fresh}, and e_{ks} in our variants get scaled down by Δ (Δ_ℓ), and hence their contribution becomes negligible. In reduced-error CKKS, the dominant source of approximation error is r_{rs}. The addition of existing error f in unary operations is omitted for brevity.

Algorithm	Errors in CKKS		Errors in RNS CKKS	
	Original CKKS [14]	Ours	Prior RNS CKKS [6,11]	Ours
Encode	r_{encode}, r_{float}	r_{float}	r_{encode}, r_{float}	r_{float}
Encrypt	e_{fresh}	–	e_{fresh}	–
Add	$f_+ = f_1 + f_2$	f_+	f_+	f_+
Mult.	$\frac{f_\times}{\Delta} \approx \frac{m_2 f_1 + m_1 f_2 + e_{ks}}{\Delta}$	$\frac{f_\times}{\Delta}$	$\frac{f_\times}{\Delta_\ell}$	$\frac{f_\times}{\Delta_\ell}$
Automorphism	e_{ks}	–	e_{ks}	–
Rescale	r_{rs}	r_{rs}	r_{rs}, u_Δ	r_{rs}
Decrypt	–	–	–	–
Decode	r_{float}	r_{float}	r_{float}	r_{float}
Scalar Add	$f + r_{encode}, r_{float}$	f, r_{float}	$f + r_{encode}, r_{float}$	f, r_{float}
Scalar Mult.	$f_{\times c}/\Delta \approx \frac{m_c f + m\, r_{encode}}{\Delta}$	$f_{\times c}/\Delta$	$f_{\times c}/\Delta_\ell$	$f_{\times c}/\Delta_\ell$
Crosslevel Add	f_+	f_+	f_+, u_Δ	$f_{1,\times c}/\Delta_\ell + f_2$
Crosslevel Mult.	$f_\times/\Delta$	$f_\times/\Delta$	$f_\times/\Delta_\ell, u_\Delta$	$\approx \frac{m_2 f_{1,\times c} + m_1 f_2 + e_{ks}}{\Delta_\ell}$

The security of the CKKS scheme is based on the Ring Learning With Errors (RLWE) problem, where Gaussian noise is introduced to achieve the desired hardness properties [14]. In the case of CKKS, this LWE noise modifies the least significant bits of the plaintext during encryption, hence resulting in a lossy encryption scheme. If the ciphertext ct encrypts a plaintext m, the decryption of ct outputs a noisy result $\tilde{m} = m + f$. The central problem in CKKS is to keep the error f relatively small to meet the desired precision requirements. We will refer to this type of approximation error caused by LWE noise as an LWE approximation error. The LWE approximation errors are introduced during encryption and key switching, and will be denoted as e_{fresh} and e_{ks}, respectively.

For leveled HE schemes, there is another source of noise related to the integer-division rounding during the modulus switching operation. This noise depends on the norm of the secret key. In CKKS, modulus switching is called rescaling as it effectively rescales the underlying encrypted plaintext and drops a certain number of least significant bits from the message. Due to the lossy nature of CKKS, this rescaling noise brings about an approximation error. We call this error as a rescaling rounding error, and denote it by r_{rs}. There is another related procedure in CKKS called modular reduction, which does modulus switching without scaling the encrypted message (or noise). This operation does not introduce any noise/approximation error, and is not included in Table 1.

Besides LWE and rescaling rounding errors, there are other sources of errors that contribute to the output approximation error in the CKKS scheme. In the encoding and decoding procedures, these sources of error arise from precision limitations, e.g., if using double to represent real numbers. We call these errors as precision errors and will denote them as r_{float}. Precision errors can be reduced by increasing the floating-point precision in computations. The encoding procedure also includes another rounding error caused by converting (rounding) encoded real-number plaintexts to integer plaintexts. We will call this error r_{encode}.

The RNS variants of CKKS introduce another approximation error caused by approximate scaling in the rescale operation. The RNS variants use a chain of small primes q_i that are only approximately close to the scaling factor $\Delta = 2^p$, and the differences between q_i and 2^p bring about this approximation error, which will be denoted as u_Δ. This error is typically few bits higher than the LWE approximation error, and hence the RNS variants have a lower precision than the multiprecision integer instantiation of CKKS.

Addition and multiplication essentially add up approximation errors of both input ciphertexts, resulting in an increased approximation error in the output ciphertext by at most 1 bit (in the worst case of two correlated ciphertexts). There are also somewhat special types of addition/multiplication called scalar and crosslevel addition/multiplication. Their approximation errors are shown in Table 1 and explained in more detail further in the paper.

To better understand the contribution of our work, note that $u_\Delta > \{e_{fresh}, e_{ks}\} > r_{rs}$. We intend to remove u_Δ, e_{fresh}, and e_{ks}, hence effectively reducing the output approximation error to the rescaling rounding error r_{rs} and its accumulation from multiple ciphertexts.

Our Work. The main goal of our work is to modify the CKKS scheme and its RNS variants to systematically remove many of the approximation errors listed in Table 1, achieving a major reduction in the output approximation error and significantly improving the overall usability of the scheme. Before our work, it had been widely believed that CKKS is hard to use in practice because of many sources of approximation errors and the complexity of dealing with them, as illustrated in a recent talk by Yongsoo Song at the Simons Institute [28].

Our first idea is to redefine the multiplication operation in CKKS as

$$\mathsf{ct}_{mult'} = \mathsf{Mult}'(\mathsf{ct}_1, \mathsf{ct}_2) = \mathsf{Mult}\left(\mathsf{Rescale}(\mathsf{ct}_1, \Delta), \mathsf{Rescale}(\mathsf{ct}_2, \Delta)\right).$$

Reordering the rescaling and multiplication operations this way, i.e., reversing the order of multiplication and rescaling in the original CKKS scheme, brings about several benefits. First, if we rescale before the first multiplication, we can remove (scale down) the prior encoding approximation errors, the LWE encryption approximation error, and any addition and key switching approximation errors if these operations are performed before the first multiplication. If we decrypt the ciphertext before the first multiplication, i.e., in computations without multiplications, we will only observe the effect of the floating-point precision error r_{float}, which for the case of double-precision floating-point numbers (52 bits of precision) would typically be about 48–50 bits. Second, delaying the rescaling operation until the following multiplication (in computations with multiplications) enables us to eliminate key-switching approximation errors. The only approximation errors that are left in the non-RNS CKKS are the rescaling rounding error r_{rs}, accumulated error due to additions (after first multiplication) and multiplications, and a relatively small floating-point precision error r_{float}.

Our second idea is to redefine the rescaling operation in RNS by introducing different scaling factors Δ_ℓ at each level to eliminate the approximate scaling error u_Δ. The main algorithmic challenges in the implementation of this idea are related to handling various computation paths, such as adding two ciphertexts that are several levels apart (referred to as *crosslevel* addition), and finding the prime moduli q_i that do not lead to the divergence of the level-specific scaling factor towards zero or infinity for deeper computations. While addressing these challenges, we also restrict (automate) rescaling to being done right before multiplication (following our definition of Mult′). We also redefine the addition operation to include a scalar multiplication and rescaling to bring two ciphertexts to the same scaling factor. We fully automate these procedures in our software implementation, achieving the same practical precision as in the non-RNS CKKS instantiation, as seen in Table 1.

We also provide an efficient implementation of our reduced-error (RE) CKKS variant in RNS along with an intermediate RNS variant that is faster, but at the expense of increasing the output approximation error. Table 2 shows representative results for four different benchmarks: addition of multiple vectors, summation over a vector, binary tree multiplication, and evaluation of a polynomial over a vector. These results suggest that the reduced-error CKKS RNS implementation has an approximation error around 7 bits smaller (we observed values in the range from 6 to 9 bits) for computations with multiplications than the prior RNS variant. For computations without a multiplication, the approximation error can be up to 20 bits lower than in the prior RNS variant. As compared to the original CKKS using multiprecision integer arithmetic, our reduced-error CKKS RNS implementation has an error that is smaller by about 4 and up to 20 bits for computations with multiplications and without multiplications, respectively.

Performance results in Sect. 5 demonstrate that the runtime of our RE-CKKS RNS implementation is 1.2x to 1.9x slower than the prior RNS variant (typically less than 1.5x), which is a relatively small cost paid for the increased precision. This cost can be offset by a decreased ciphertext modulus (lower ring dimension) if the same precision is considered, effectively achieving same or better performance in many practical cases. More concretely, in the case of power-of-two cyclotomics, which all existing implementations work with, the same precision may be achieved using a twice smaller ring dimension due to decreased ciphertext modulus requirements, which improves the runtime by more than 2x. For comparison, the

runtime improvement of RNS-HEEAN over the multiprecision HEAAN implementation was 8.3 times for multiplication [11], and the precision gain of the multiprecision HEAAN implementation over RNS-HEEAN is only half of what we
report in our work.

Table 2. Representative results showing the precision of our RE-CKKS RNS implementation vs original CKKS and prior CKKS RNS variant for the HE-standard-
compliant setting of uniform ternary secrets; $\Delta_i \approx 2^{40}$.

Computation	Prior CKKS RNS [6,11]	CKKS [14]	RE-CKKS RNS (our work)
$\sum_{i=0}^{32} \vec{x}_i$	23.9	23.9	43.8
$\sum_{i=0}^{2048} x_i$	21.1	21.1	40.4
$\prod_{i=1}^{16} \vec{x}_i$	17.8	22.4	26.0
$\sum_{i=0}^{64} \vec{x}^i$	14.9	17.4	21.3

Table 3. Representative results showing the precision of our RE-CKKS RNS implementation vs original CKKS and prior CKKS RNS variant for sparse ternary secrets
(this setting was used in the original CKKS construction [14]); $\Delta_i \approx 2^{40}$.

Computation	Prior CKKS RNS [6,11]	CKKS [14]	RE-CKKS RNS (our work)
$\sum_{i=0}^{32} \vec{x}_i$	24.6	24.6	44.6
$\sum_{i=0}^{2048} x_i$	22.1	22.1	42.0
$\prod_{i=1}^{16} \vec{x}_i$	17.8	23.2	29.7
$\sum_{i=0}^{64} \vec{x}^i$	14.9	18.2	25.0

Although the original CKKS scheme was instantiated for sparse ternary
secrets [14], we use uniform ternary secrets as the main setting in our work because
the sparse secrets are not currently included in the homomorphic encryption security standard [2], and hybrid attacks specific to the sparse setting were recently
devised [16,27]. This choice has a direct effect on the precision gain one gets from
our RE-CKKS variant. Our theoretical estimates suggest that in the sparse setting
the precision gain for a computation with multiplications becomes about 6–8 bits
(higher than 4 bits that we observe for uniform ternary secrets). Some representative experimental results for the sparse setting, which align with our theoretical
estimates, are illustrated in Table 3. Note that the precision gain of our RE-CKKS
RNS implementation gets as high as 12 bits over the prior RNS variant.

We also implemented RE-CKKS in the HEAAN library [13], which uses
multiprecision arithmetic for rescaling, and ran precision experiments there for
selected computations. The observed precision improvement of RE-CKKS over
CKKS [14] was approximately the same (within 0.2 bits) as in our PALISADE
implementation.

Contributions. Our contributions can be summarized as follows.

- We propose a reduced-error variant of CKKS that reduces the approximation error compared to the original CKKS scheme by 4 bits and 6–8 bits for
  uniform and sparse ternary secrets, respectively. The main idea of our modifications is to redefine the multiplication operation by "reversing" the order
  of multiplication and rescaling.

– We adapt this variant to RNS, while keeping the precision roughly the same, by developing a novel procedure that computes different scaling factors for each level and performs rescaling automatically. This procedure required a development of an original algorithm for finding the RNS primes that keep the scaling factor as close to the starting value as possible, thus preventing the divergence of the scaling factor towards zero or infinity for practical numbers of levels. The procedure also required several algorithms for handling ciphertexts at different levels.

– While developing the RNS variant of reduced-error CKKS, we propose an intermediate RNS variant that has a higher approximation error but runs faster. Both of our RNS variants have errors that are lower than the prior RNS variant [6,11].

– We implement both RNS variants in PALISADE and make them publicly available.

Related Work. The CKKS scheme was originally proposed in [14] and implemented in the HEEAN library [13] using a mixture of multiprecision and RNS arithmetic. The main drawback in the original implementation was the use of multiprecision integer arithmetic for rescaling and some other operations, which is in practice less efficient than the so-called RNS variants [3,19]. Then several homomorphic encryption libraries independently developed and implemented RNS variants of CKKS, including RNS-HEAAN [12], PALISADE [1], SEAL [26], and HELib [20]. The typical RNS variant [6,11], which is based on approximate rescaling, works with small primes q_i that are only approximately close to the actual scaling factor, which introduces an approximation error that is higher than the LWE error present in the original CKKS and its HEAAN implementation. The main differences between various RNS variants are primarily in how key switching is done. The documentation of the SEAL library also mentioned the idea of using different scaling factors for each ciphertext but did not provide any (automated) procedure to work with different scaling factors in practice (our paper shows that this can be very challenging and requires the development of new algorithms). A somewhat different approach is implemented in HELib [4]: the noise estimation capability originally written for the Brakersky-Gentry-Vaikuntanathan [9] scheme is used to estimate the current approximation error, the scaling factors are tracked for each ciphertext, and decisions regarding each rescaling are made based on the current values of error estimate and scaling factor, and desired precision. The main drawback of this approach is that encrypted complex values need to be close to one in magnitude for this logic to work properly, limiting the practical use of this method. Bossuat et al. [7] recently proposed a scale-invariant polynomial evaluation method for removing the RNS scaling error in polynomial evaluation, but this method is not general enough to be applied to all CKKS operations, in contrast to the approach proposed in this work. Lee et al. recently proposed two procedures to significantly increase the precision of the CKKS bootstrapping operation [24]: (1) a fast algorithm for deriving the optimal minimax approximation polynomial for modular reduction and (2) a composite-function procedure involving the inverse sine function to reduce the difference between the regular

CKKS and bootstrapping-specific scaling factors. In their implementation, they integrated our CKKS approximation error reduction techniques to achieve high precision for CKKS bootstrapping.

Li and Micciancio recently showed that IND-CPA security may not be sufficient for CKKS in scenarios where decryption results are shared, and demonstrated practical key recovery attacks for these scenarios [25]. To mitigate these attacks, PALISADE has changed its CKKS implementation to add Gaussian noise during decryption, which is proportional to the current approximation noise. All improvements proposed in this work apply to this modified CKKS instantiation to the same extent as to the original CKKS, because they effectively reduce the magnitude of the current approximation noise, which is used as the basis for choosing the standard deviation for the added Gaussian noise.

Cohen et al. explored the idea of reducing the LWE error in CKKS by using fault-tolerant computations over the reals [15]. The high-level idea is to run multiple computations for the same encrypted values and then compute the average. While this is theoretically possible, the practical performance costs would be high enough to make this approach impractical. In contrast, our idea of rescaling before multiplication has a very small performance cost compared to this approach.

2   Preliminaries

All logarithms are base 2 unless otherwise indicated. For complex z, we denote by $\|z\|_2 = \sqrt{z\bar{z}}$ its ℓ_2 norm. For an integer Q, we identify the ring $\mathbb{Z}_Q$ with $(-Q/2, Q/2]$ as a representative interval. For a power-of-two N, we denote cyclotomic rings $\mathcal{R} = \mathbb{Z}[X]/(X^N + 1)$, $\mathcal{S} = \mathbb{R}[X]/(X^N + 1)$, and $\mathcal{R}_Q := \mathcal{R}/Q\mathcal{R}$. Ring elements are in bold, e.g. $\boldsymbol{a}$.

We use $\boldsymbol{a} \leftarrow \chi$ to denote the sampling of $\boldsymbol{a}$ according to a distribution χ. The distribution χ is called *uniform ternary* if all the coefficients of $\boldsymbol{a} \leftarrow \chi$ are selected uniformly from $\{-1, 0, 1\}$. This distribution is commonly used for secret key generation as it is the most efficient option conforming to the HE standard [2]. A *sparse ternary* distribution corresponds to the case when h coefficients are randomly chosen to be non-zero and all others are set to zero, where h is the Hamming weight. The sparse ternary secret distribution was used in the original CKKS scheme [14]. We say that the distribution χ is *discrete Gaussian* with standard deviation σ if all coefficients of $\boldsymbol{a} \leftarrow \chi$ are selected from discrete Gaussian distribution with standard deviation σ. Discrete Gaussian distribution is commonly used to generate error polynomials to meet the desired hardness requirement [2].

For radix base ω and ℓ-level modulus Q_ℓ, let us define the decomposition of $\boldsymbol{a} \in \mathcal{R}_{Q_\ell}$ by $\mathcal{WD}_\ell(\boldsymbol{a})$ and powers of ω, $\mathcal{PW}_\ell(\boldsymbol{a})$. Let $\mathsf{dnum} = \lceil \log_\omega(Q_\ell) \rceil$, then for $\boldsymbol{a} \in \mathcal{R}_{Q_\ell}$:

$$\mathcal{WD}_\ell(\boldsymbol{a}) = \left([\boldsymbol{a}]_\omega, \left[\left\lfloor \frac{\boldsymbol{a}}{\omega} \right\rfloor \right]_\omega, \dots, \left[\left\lfloor \frac{\boldsymbol{a}}{\omega^{\mathsf{dnum}-1}} \right\rfloor \right]_\omega \right) \in \mathcal{R}^{\mathsf{dnum}},$$

$$\mathcal{PW}_\ell(\boldsymbol{a}) = ([\boldsymbol{a}]_{Q_\ell}, [\boldsymbol{a} \cdot \omega]_{Q_\ell}, \dots, [\boldsymbol{a} \cdot \omega^{\mathsf{dnum}-1}]_{Q_\ell}) \in \mathcal{R}_{Q_\ell}^{\mathsf{dnum}}.$$

For any $(\boldsymbol{a}, \boldsymbol{b}) \in \mathcal{R}_\ell^2$, $\mathcal{WD}_\ell$ and $\mathcal{PW}_\ell$ satisfy the following congruence relation:

$$\langle \mathcal{WD}_\ell(\boldsymbol{a}), \mathcal{PW}_\ell(\boldsymbol{b}) \rangle \equiv \boldsymbol{a} \cdot \boldsymbol{b} \pmod{Q_\ell}.$$

The preliminaries for the CKKS scheme and its RNS instantiation are presented in the full version of the paper.

3   Reducing the Approximation Error in the CKKS Scheme

We first describe all approximation errors in the original CKKS scheme (for the case of uniform ternary secrets and hybrid key switching) and then we discuss how many of these errors can be removed. We choose the uniform ternary secret distribution (in contrast to sparse ternary secrets) because sparse ternary secrets are not currently supported by the HE standard [2], and uniform ternary secrets are the most efficient option that is supported by the HE standard. The hybrid key switching [18,21] is selected because it is more efficient than the GHS approach used in the original CKKS scheme and incurs a smaller approximation error than the digit decomposition approach [10] for relatively large digits, which are required for the efficient instantiation of the digit decomposition key switching method.

3.1   Approximation Errors in the CKKS Scheme

Encryption and Decryption. In the original CKKS [14] scheme, to encode the message $\vec{x} \in \mathbb{C}^n$, we apply the inverse embedding transformation $\mu = \tau_n'^{-1}(\vec{x}) \in S$ and then scale μ by a factor $\Delta = 2^p$ and round to obtain the plaintext $m := \lceil \Delta \cdot \mu \rfloor \in \mathcal{R}$. To encrypt m with the public key pk, we sample $v \leftarrow \chi_{\text{enc}}$ and $e_0, e_1 \leftarrow \chi_{\text{err}}$, and output

$$\text{ct} = \text{Enc}(m) = \text{pk} \cdot v + (e_0 + m, e_1) \in \mathcal{R}_Q^2.$$

The full process is $\vec{x} \xrightarrow{\tau_n'^{-1}(\cdot)} \mu \xrightarrow{\lfloor \cdot \times \Delta \rceil} m \xrightarrow{\text{Enc}_{\text{pk}}(\cdot)} \text{ct}$.

To decrypt the ciphertext ct, we need to compute the inner product with sk modulo Q:

$$\tilde{m} = \text{Dec}_{\text{sk}}(\text{ct}(m)) = [\langle \text{ct}, \text{sk} \rangle]_Q = c_0 + c_1 \cdot s \in \mathcal{R}_Q.$$

To decode $\tilde{m}$, we divide it by Δ, i.e., $\tilde{\mu} = \tilde{m}/\Delta$, and apply the embedding transformation $\tilde{\vec{x}} = \tau_n'(\tilde{\mu})$: $\text{ct} \xrightarrow{\text{Dec}_{\text{sk}}(\cdot)} \tilde{m} \xrightarrow{\div \Delta} \tilde{\mu} \xrightarrow{\tau_n'(\cdot)} \tilde{\vec{x}}$.

There are several sources of errors that contribute to the output error $\tilde{\vec{x}} - \vec{x}$. The $\tau_n'^{-1}$ and τ_n' maps are exact in theory, but in practice introduce precision (rounding) errors that depend on the floating-point precision and the value of n. We omit these errors for now, as we can always reduce them by increasing the floating-point precision. The same applies to multiplication $\times \Delta$ and division $\div \Delta$ in the encoding and decoding parts. However, in the encoding procedure, we do not only scale, but also round the scaled value, and the rounding introduces an approximation error r_{encode} with $\|r_{\text{encode}}\|_\infty \leq 1/2$. Public key encryption introduces a fresh encryption (LWE) error e_{fresh}. After encryption, the ciphertext ct satisfies the following relation:

$$c_0 + c_1 \cdot s = m + e_{\text{fresh}} = \Delta \cdot \mu + r_{\text{encode}} + e_{\text{fresh}} = \Delta \cdot \mu + f_{\text{enc}} \in \mathcal{R}_Q.$$

Instead of analyzing f, e, r, it is more natural to analyze the scaled errors $\phi = f/\Delta$, $\epsilon = e/\Delta$, $\rho = r/\Delta$ since the division by the scaling factor is part of the decoding procedure, and the scaled error is the one that is related to the error before applying the τ'_n transformation in the decoding. In what follows, we will mainly refer to ϵ instead of e.

One way to reduce the contribution of f_{enc} is to increase the scaling factor Δ of the scheme. To keep the encryption secure under the RLWE problem, we need to increase the ring dimension in the underlying lattice problem, which may be inefficient in many cases.

We also provide a heuristic bound for fresh encryption noise/approximation error. It will be used for estimating the reduction of approximation error in our CKKS variant.

Lemma 1. *Given a uniform ternary secret key s, we have the following heuristic bound for fresh encryption noise:* $\|f_{enc}\|^{can} \leq \frac{32}{3}\sqrt{6}\sigma N + 6\sigma\sqrt{N}$.

Proof. See the full version of the paper. Note that for the sparse ternary secret setting with Hamming weight h, the bound would be formulated as $\|f_{enc}\|^{can} \leq 8\sqrt{2}\sigma N + 6\sigma\sqrt{N} + 16\sigma\sqrt{hN}$ [14].

Addition. The addition procedure $\mathsf{ct}_{add} = \mathsf{Add}(\mathsf{ct}_1, \mathsf{ct}_2)$ for two ciphertexts at the same level ℓ is done as component-wise addition and leads to the following relation:

$$c_{add,0} + c_{add,1} \cdot s = \Delta \cdot (\mu_1 + \mu_2) + (f_1 + f_2) \in \mathcal{R}_{Q_\ell}.$$

The addition does not introduce any additional errors, but instead adds the errors together, which is exactly what happens in the unencrypted case of adding two approximate numbers together.

Scalar Addition. The scalar addition procedure $\mathsf{ct}_{cadd} = \mathsf{CAdd}(\mathsf{ct}, \mathsf{const})$ leads to the following relation:

$$c_{cadd,0} + c_{cadd,1} \cdot s = \Delta \cdot (\mu + \mu_{const}) + (f + r_{encode}),$$

where $\mathsf{Encode}(\mathsf{const}, \Delta) = \Delta\mu_{const} + r_{encode}$. In addition to the encoding error, the scalar addition also introduces a floating-point precision error. Both errors in the scalar addition are relatively small compared to the ciphertext error.

Key Switching. There are several known key switching procedures

$$\mathsf{ct}_{ks} = \mathsf{KeySwitch}_{swk}(\mathsf{ct}),$$

which switch the ciphertext ct satisfying the relation:

$$c_0 + c_1 \cdot s_1 = \Delta \cdot \mu + f \in \mathcal{R}_{Q_\ell},$$

to the ciphertext ct_{ks} satisfying the relation:

$$c_{ks,0} + c_{ks,0} \cdot s_2 = \Delta \cdot \mu + f + e_{ks} \in \mathcal{R}_{Q_\ell}.$$

The key switching step introduces an LWE-related error e_{ks}.

Lemma 2. *For the hybrid key switching method (see the full version of the paper), we have the following heuristic bound for key switching noise:* $\|e_{ks}\|^{can} \leq \frac{8\sqrt{3}\cdot dnum\cdot\omega\sigma N}{3P} + \sqrt{3N} + \frac{8\sqrt{2N}}{3}$.

Proof. See the full version of the paper. Note that for the sparse ternary secret setting with Hamming weight h, the bound would be formulated as $\|e_{ks}\|^{can} \leq \frac{8\sqrt{3}\cdot dnum\cdot\omega\sigma N}{3P} + \sqrt{3N} + 8\sqrt{\frac{hN}{3}}$.

Multiplication. The multiplication procedure $\mathsf{ct}_{\mathsf{mult}} = \mathsf{Mult}(\mathsf{ct}_1,\mathsf{ct}_2)$ for two ciphertexts at the same level ℓ is done in two steps: tensoring and key switching. The ciphertext after tensoring satisfies the following equation:

$$c_{\mathsf{tensor},0} + c_{\mathsf{tensor},1}\cdot s + c_{\mathsf{tensor},2}\cdot s^2 \equiv (\Delta\cdot\mu_1 + f_1)\cdot(\Delta\cdot\mu_2 + f_2) = \Delta^2\cdot\mu_1\mu_2 + f_\times \in \mathcal{R}_{Q_\ell}.$$

In the tensoring step the error term $f_\times$ is approximate multiplication error of $(\Delta\cdot\mu_i + f_i)$ for the unencrypted case. Hence tensoring does not introduce new approximation errors.

The key switching part switches $\mathsf{ct}' = (0, c_{\mathsf{tensor},2})$ as a ciphertext under the key s^2 to the ciphertext $\mathsf{ct}'' = \mathsf{KeySwitch}_{\mathsf{evk}}(\mathsf{ct}')$ under the key s, and the result is added to $(c_{\mathsf{tensor},0}, c_{\mathsf{tensor},1})$. The ciphertext after the key switching satisfies the following equation:

$$c_{\mathsf{mult},0} + c_{\mathsf{mult},1}\cdot s \equiv \Delta^2\cdot\mu_1\mu_2 + f_\times + e_{ks} = \Delta^2\cdot\mu_1\mu_2 + f_{\mathsf{mult}} \in \mathcal{R}_{Q_\ell},$$

where $f_{\mathsf{mult}} = \Delta\cdot(\mu_1 f_2 + \mu_2 f_1) + f_1 f_2 + e_{ks} = f_\times + e_{ks}$, and since the scaling factor becomes Δ^2 after multiplication, we have the following relation for the scaled error:

$$\phi_{\mathsf{mult}} = \frac{f_{\mathsf{mult}}}{\Delta^2} = \mu_1\phi_2 + \mu_2\phi_1 + \phi_1\phi_2 + \frac{\epsilon_{ks}}{\Delta} = \phi_\times + \frac{\epsilon_{ks}}{\Delta}. \tag{1}$$

In Eq. (1), we see that the scaled switching error ϵ_{ks} is divided by Δ. We can perform the key switching procedure in such a way that the term e_{ks} is much smaller than Δ, which makes the impact of ϕ_{mult} essentially the same as the impact of $\phi_\times$ in an unencrypted case.

Scalar Multiplication. The scalar multiplication procedure $\mathsf{ct}_{\mathsf{cmult}} = \mathsf{CMult}(\mathsf{ct}, \mathsf{const})$ is described using the following relation:

$$c_{\mathsf{cmult},0} + c_{\mathsf{cmult},1}\cdot s = \Delta^2\cdot(\mu\mu_{\mathsf{const}}) + \Delta\cdot(\mu_{\mathsf{const}}f + \mu r_{\mathsf{encode}}) + f r_{\mathsf{encode}}$$
$$= \Delta^2\cdot\mu\mu_{\mathsf{const}} + f_{\mathsf{cmult}} \in \mathcal{R}_{Q_\ell},$$

where $\mathsf{Encode}(x, \Delta) = \Delta\cdot\mu_{\mathsf{const}} + r_{\mathsf{encode}}$, $f_{\mathsf{cmult}} = \Delta\cdot(\mu_{\mathsf{const}}f + \mu r_{\mathsf{encode}}) + f r_{\mathsf{encode}} = f_{\times c}$, and $\phi_{\mathsf{cmult}} = \mu\rho_{\mathsf{encode}} + \mu_{\mathsf{const}}\phi + \phi\rho_{\mathsf{encode}} = \phi_{\times c}$.

Rescaling. In the CKKS scheme the main reason for rescaling is not to manage the noise, as in the case of the Brakerski-Gentry-Vaikuntantanathan (BGV) scheme [9], but to scale down the encrypted message and truncate some least significant bits. The size of the encrypted message increases after multiplication and decreases after rescaling. Other operations, like additions or rotations, do not affect the magnitude of the message. So we should balance multiplications and rescaling operations to control the magnitude of message and its precision. Normally it is advised to perform a rescaling right after each multiplication.

The rescaling procedure $\mathsf{ct}_{\mathsf{rs}} = \mathsf{Rescale}(\mathsf{ct}, \Delta)$ for a ciphertext at level ℓ is done by dividing by the scaling factor and rounding. The procedure is as follows:

$$\mathsf{ct}_{\mathsf{rs}} = \mathsf{Rescale}(\mathsf{ct}, \Delta) = \left(\left\lceil \frac{c_0}{\Delta} \right\rceil, \left\lceil \frac{c_1}{\Delta} \right\rceil \right) = \left(\frac{c_0}{\Delta} + r_0, \frac{c_1}{\Delta} + r_1 \right),$$

where r_0 and r_1 are error terms introduced by rounding, with coefficients in $[-1/2, 1/2]$.

The ciphertext after the multiplication and rescaling procedure $\mathsf{ct}_{\mathsf{mult+rs}} = \mathsf{Rescale}(\mathsf{Mult}(\mathsf{ct}_1, \mathsf{ct}_2), \Delta)$ satisfies the following relation:

$$c_{\mathsf{mult+rs},0} + c_{\mathsf{mult+rs},1} \cdot s \equiv \frac{(\Delta \cdot \mu_1 + f_1) \cdot (\Delta \cdot \mu_2 + f_2) + e_{\mathsf{ks}}}{\Delta} + r_0 + r_1 s$$

$$= \Delta \cdot \mu_1 \mu_2 + f_{\mathsf{mult+rs}} \in \mathcal{R}_{Q_{\ell-1}},$$

where

$$f_{\mathsf{mult+rs}} = \frac{f_\times}{\Delta} + \frac{e_{\mathsf{ks}}}{\Delta} + r_0 + r_1 s = \frac{f_\times}{\Delta} + \frac{e_{\mathsf{ks}}}{\Delta} + r_{\mathsf{rs}}, \quad \phi_{\mathsf{mult+rs}} = \phi_\times + \frac{e_{\mathsf{ks}}}{\Delta} + \rho_{\mathsf{rs}},$$

$r_{\mathsf{rs}} = r_0 + r_1 s$ is the rounding error, and $\rho_{\mathsf{rs}} = r_{\mathsf{rs}}/\Delta$ is the scaled rounding error. Thus after the rescaling procedure, the scaled approximation error $\epsilon_{\mathsf{ks}}/\Delta$ is negligible and gets completely absorbed by the rounding error ρ_{rs}.

Lemma 3. *Given a uniform ternary secret key s, we have the following heuristic bound for the rounding error that is introduced by rescaling:* $\|r_{rs}\|^{can} \leq \sqrt{3N} + \frac{16\sqrt{2N}}{3}$.

Proof. See the full version of the paper. Note that for the sparse ternary secret setting with Hamming weight h, the bound would be formulated as $\|r_{\mathsf{rs}}\|^{can} \leq \sqrt{3N} + 8\sqrt{\frac{hN}{3}}$ [14].

Modulus Reduction. The CKKS scheme also has a modulus reduction procedure that does not change the message or approximation error. This modulus reduction procedure is done simply by evaluating the ciphertext ct at modulus Q_ℓ modulo smaller modulus $Q_{\ell'}$. As $Q_{\ell'} | Q_\ell$, the method does not introduce any additional errors.

Automorphism (Rotation and Conjugation). Similar to the multiplication procedure, the automorphism procedure $\mathsf{ct}_{\mathsf{aut}} = \mathsf{Aut}_{\mathsf{rk}^{(\kappa)}}(\mathsf{ct}, \kappa)$ is done in two steps: automorphism κ and key switching. The ciphertext after automorphism satisfies the following relation:

$$c_0^{(\kappa)} + c_1^{(\kappa)} \cdot s^{(\kappa)} \equiv \Delta \cdot \mu^{(\kappa)} + f^{(\kappa)} \in \mathcal{R}_{Q_\ell}.$$

The key switching part switches $\mathsf{ct}' = (0, c_1^{(\kappa)})$ as a ciphertext under the key $s^{(\kappa)}$ to the ciphertext $\mathsf{ct}'' = \mathsf{KeySwitch}_{\mathsf{rk}^{(\kappa)}}(\mathsf{ct}')$ under the key s, and the result is added to $(c_0^{(\kappa)}, 0)$. The ciphertext after the key switching satisfies the following equation:

$$c_{\mathsf{aut},0} + c_{\mathsf{aut},1} \cdot s \equiv \Delta \cdot (\mu^{(\kappa)}) + f^{(\kappa)} + e_{\mathsf{ks}} = \Delta \cdot \mu^{(\kappa)} + f_{\mathsf{aut}} \in \mathcal{R}_{Q_\ell},$$

where $f_{\mathsf{aut}} = f^{(\kappa)} + e_{\mathsf{ks}}$ and $\phi_{\mathsf{aut}} = \frac{f_{\mathsf{aut}}}{\Delta} = \phi^{(\kappa)} + \epsilon_{\mathsf{ks}}$.

In case of automorphism operations, the key switching error ϵ_{ks} is not negligible anymore compared to $\phi^{(\kappa)}$, as the scaling factor in the case of automorphism is not squared but stays the same.

3.2 Eliminating LWE and Encoding Approximation Errors

One can see that the rescaling operation does not necessarily need to be done right after the multiplication, and instead can be done right before the next multiplication (or before decryption). In other words, we do not rescale after the multiplication and keep the scaling factor as Δ^2. For the first level, we can encrypt the message μ with the scaling factor Δ^2 to make the encryption noise negligible. The ciphertext ct will satisfy the following relation:

$$c_0 + c_1 \cdot s \equiv \lceil \Delta^2 \cdot \mu \rfloor + e_{\mathsf{fresh}} = \Delta^2 \cdot \mu + f' \in \mathcal{R}_{Q_\ell}.$$

All other operations, like additions and automorphisms, are done the same way. The approximation errors will be summed together and in practice will be much smaller than the scaling factor Δ^2. The rescaling operation is done right before the next multiplication so that the scaled LWE and encoding errors are dominated by the rounding error after the rescaling. So we can make all LWE and encoding errors negligible compared to the rounding rescaling errors, starting with the second level.

As the rescaling operation is performed right before the multiplication, we can treat it as part of the multiplication. We can redefine the multiplication Mult' as a combination of rescaling operations and multiplication:

$$\mathsf{ct}_{\mathsf{mult}'} = \mathsf{Mult}'(\mathsf{ct}_1, \mathsf{ct}_2) = \mathsf{Mult}\left(\mathsf{Rescale}(\mathsf{ct}_1, \Delta), \mathsf{Rescale}(\mathsf{ct}_2, \Delta)\right).$$

With this new definition of Mult', we keep the same number of levels while slightly increasing the modulus for the fresh ciphertext from $q_0 \cdot \Delta^L$ to $q_0 \cdot \Delta^{L+1}$. We also ensure that fresh encryption noise and key switching noise, which appear after multiplication or automorphism operations, will be negligible and absorbed by the rescaling rounding error. In other words, we can eliminate all LWE and encoding approximation errors, by making them negligible compared to rescaling rounding errors.

We also reduce the total rounding error when we add ciphertexts. If we perform the rescaling right after multiplication, the rounding error is introduced for each ciphertext and the rescaling errors will be added when we perform addition of the ciphertexts. In the case of the new multiplication Mult', we do rescaling after the additions, and hence we end up only with a single rounding error.

With the modified multiplication, the encryption of a message μ at level ℓ will satisfy the following condition:

$$c_0 + c_1 s \equiv \Delta^2 \cdot \mu + f'.$$

Let $f'/\Delta^2 = \phi'$. After Mult' operation we have:

$$
\begin{aligned}
c_{\text{mult}',0} + c_{\text{mult}',1} s &\equiv \left(\frac{\Delta^2 \cdot \mu_1 + f_1'}{\Delta} + r_{\text{rs},1} \right) \cdot \left(\frac{\Delta^2 \cdot \mu_2 + f_2'}{\Delta} + r_{\text{rs},2} \right) + e_{\text{ks}} \\
&= (\Delta \cdot (\mu_1 + \phi_1') + r_{\text{rs},1}) \cdot (\Delta \cdot (\mu_2 + \phi_2') + r_{\text{rs},2}) + e_{\text{ks}} \\
&= \Delta^2 \cdot \mu_1 \mu_2 + f_{\text{mult}'},
\end{aligned}
$$

where $f_{\text{mult}'} = \Delta^2 \cdot (\mu_1 \phi_2' + \mu_2 \phi_1' + \phi_1' \phi_2') + + \Delta \cdot ((\mu_1 + \phi_1') r_{\text{rs},2} + (\mu_2 + \phi_2') r_{\text{rs},1}) + r_{\text{rs},1} r_{\text{rs},2} + e_{\text{ks}}$, $\phi_{\text{mult}'} = \mu_1 (\phi_2' + \rho_{\text{rs},2}) + \mu_2 (\phi_1' + \rho_{\text{rs},1}) + (\phi_1' + \rho_{\text{rs},1}) (\phi_2' + \rho_{\text{rs},2}) + \frac{e_{\text{ks}}}{\Delta}$.

Remark. We can also substitute Δ^2 in fresh encryption with a tighter scaling factor $\Delta \cdot \Delta'$, where $\Delta' = 2^{p'} < 2^p = \Delta$. We need to choose Δ' in such a way that the sum of all LWE errors during the computations on the level L, including fresh encryption noise, is smaller than Δ'. In this case, in Mult' on the first level we need to do rescaling by Δ' instead of Δ. The modulus Q_L for the fresh ciphertext will be increased by a smaller factor Δ' and become $Q_L = q_0 \cdot \Delta^L \cdot \Delta'$. We use this tighter scaling factor Δ' in our implementation.

3.3   Theoretical Estimates of Error Reduction

Computation without Multiplications. If only additions and automorphism operations are performed, no rescaling errors introduced and the LWE noise is the main source of approximation error. With standard parameters $\sigma = 3.2$, $P = \omega = Q_L^{1/3}$, from Lemma 1 the fresh encryption error is bounded by $\approx 83.6N$, and from Lemma 2 the key switching error is bounded by $\approx 44.3N$. The total number of error bits is $\log(83.6\alpha N + 44.3\beta N)$, where α is the number of fresh ciphertexts used, and β is the number of automorphism operations performed. The extra modulus Δ' in Reduced-Error (RE) CKKS is taken to fully absorb the error: $\Delta' > 83.6\alpha N + 44.3\beta N$. The total error before decryption is bounded by r_{float}, which is in practice only 2–5 bits less than the precision of floating-point arithmetic. This is illustrated by the experimental results presented in Tables 4 and 5 for $\Delta \approx 2^{50}$.

Computation with Multiplications. The extra modulus Δ' used during encryption in RE-CKKS effectively reduces the encryption noise from fresh e_{fresh} to rescaling r_{rs} at the first multiplication step. From Lemmas 1 and 3, we have the following ratio of the upper bounds for fresh encryption and rescaling rounding errors (for the case of uniform ternary secrets):

$$\log \left(\frac{e_{\text{fresh}}}{r_{\text{rs}}} \right) \approx \log \left(\frac{\frac{32}{3} \sqrt{6} \sigma N + 6\sigma \sqrt{N}}{\sqrt{3N} + \frac{8\sqrt{2}N}{3}} \right) \approx \log \left(4\sqrt{3}\sigma \right) \approx 4.5.$$

At the next multiplication, the input error for RE-CKKS can be estimated as

$$f'_{\text{mult+rs}} \approx (\mu_1 r_{\text{rs},2} + \mu_2 r_{\text{rs},1}) + r_{\text{rs}}$$

as compared to

$$f_{\text{mult+rs}} \approx (\mu_1 e_{\text{fresh},2} + \mu_2 e_{\text{fresh},1}) + r_{\text{rs}}$$

for the original CKKS scheme. As $r_{\text{rs},i} \ll e_{\text{fresh},i}$, the rescaling rounding error typically has no effect on multiplications in the original CKKS, while in the case of RE-CKKS, r_{rs} still gives a significant contribution. In practice, this implies there may be a small decline in the precision gain of RE-CKKS over CKKS for subsequent multiplications (typically not more than 0.5 bits), but this decline will become progressively smaller for further multiplications as the rounding errors from prior multiplications accumulate, and the current error will become much larger than the rounding error r_{rs}.

Hence in theory the upper bound of RE-CKKS error is about 4.5 bits smaller than the upper bound of CKKS error after the first multiplication, and it may slighly decline for further multiplications. This is consistent with the implementation results presented in Sect. 5, where the RE-CKKS error is about 4 bits smaller than the CKKS error across different circuits with multiplications, and we also observe a decline of precision gain from 4 (for first multiplication) to 3.5 bits (for deeper multiplications) for a binary tree multiplication benchmark (Table 6).

Note that in the sparse ternary secret key setting with Hamming weight $h = 64$, the precision gain of RE-CKKS over CKKS is higher:

$$\log\left(\frac{e_{\text{fresh}}}{r_{\text{rs}}}\right) \approx \log\left(\frac{8\sqrt{2}\sigma N + 6\sigma\sqrt{N} + 16\sigma\sqrt{hN}}{\sqrt{3N} + 8\sqrt{\frac{hN}{3}}}\right) \approx \log\left(\sqrt{6}\sigma\sqrt{\frac{N}{h}}\right) \approx \frac{1}{2}\log N.$$

For example, for $N = 2^{14}$ the gain of RE-CKKS over CKKS is about 7 bits. But since the sparse setting is not currently supported by the HE standard [2], we implement and examine the uniform ternary secret setting instead.

4   Reducing the Approximation Error in the RNS Instantiation of CKKS

In this section, we describe the procedures needed for eliminating the scaling factor approximation error in RNS and apply the RE-CKKS improvements presented in Sect. 3 to the RNS setting.

4.1   Eliminating the Scaling Factor Approximation Error in RNS CKKS

For the RNS setting, the noise control is more challenging as instead of a suitable ciphertext modulus $Q = 2^{p_0 + p \cdot L} = q_0 \cdot \Delta^L$, we should use a ciphertext modulus $Q = \prod_{i=0}^{L} q_i$ - product of primes q_i. The rescaling operation is done by dividing by q_i, which are no longer powers of two.

The works [6,11] that independently developed RNS variants of CKKS suggested to keep the scaling factor Δ constant, and pick the RNS moduli q_i close to Δ.

Let q_i be such that $\Delta/q_i = 1 + \alpha_i$, where $|\alpha_i|$ is kept as small as possible. Consider again the multiplication procedure with rescaling at some level ℓ:

$$c_{\text{mult+rs},0} + c_{\text{mult+rs},1}s \equiv \frac{(\Delta \cdot \mu_1 + f_1) \cdot (\Delta \cdot \mu_2 + f_2) + e_{\text{ks}}}{q_\ell} + r_{\text{rs}}$$

$$= \Delta \cdot \mu_1\mu_2 + u_\Delta + \frac{f_\times}{q_\ell} + \frac{e_{\text{ks}}}{q_\ell} + r_{\text{rs}} = \Delta \cdot \mu_1\mu_2 + f_{\text{mult+rs}},$$

where $u_\Delta = \alpha_\ell \cdot \Delta \cdot \mu_1\mu_2$, $f_{\text{mult+rs}} = u_\Delta + \frac{f_\times}{q_\ell} + \frac{e_{\text{ks}}}{q_\ell} + r_{\text{rs}}$.

The scaling factor error term u_Δ appears here due to the difference between the scaling factor Δ and prime q_ℓ, and typically is the largest among the summands in the RNS instantiation of CKKS. We can see that u_Δ depends on the distribution of specially chosen prime numbers, and is hence hard to control. We can consider optimizing the prime moduli selection to minimize the scaling factor error at each level. But if we consider operations over ciphertexts at different levels, we would have to deal with different scaling factor errors and the optimal configuration of prime moduli would be different. This implies that we would have to analyze the noise growth and find an optimal configuration of prime moduli for each specific computation circuit separately. A more detailed discussion of this issue is provided in the full version of the paper.

Using a Different Scaling Factor for Each Level. There is a way to eliminate the scaling factor error completely. As moduli q_i are public, we can integrate u_Δ into the scaling factor and adjust the scaling factor after each rescaling. Let the ciphertext ct encrypt μ at some level ℓ with the scaling factor Δ_ℓ. The ciphertext ct satisfies the following relation:

$$c_0 + c_1 \cdot s \equiv \lceil \Delta_\ell \cdot \mu \rfloor + e_{\text{fresh}} = \Delta_\ell \cdot \mu + f_{\text{enc}} \pmod{Q_\ell}.$$

With different scaling factors at different levels, we no longer have the approximate scaling error. However, as the evaluation circuits are often quite complex, we now face different problems. Depending on the order of rescaling operations when evaluating the circuit, we can have different scaling factors for ciphertexts at the same level or different final scaling factors.

A naive solution to resolve these problems is to adjust the scaling factors at the same level by multiplying by corresponding constants. This seems to be highly inefficient and could double the number of levels in the worst case, as we would need to introduce an extra scalar multiplication for many normal operations.

Instead, we enforce the rescaling to be done automatically right after each multiplication of ciphertexts. With this automated rescaling, we ensure that all ciphertexts at the same level have the same scaling factors. The ciphertext after the multiplication procedure with rescaling

$$\mathsf{ct}_{\text{mult+rs}} = \mathsf{Rescale}\left(\mathsf{Mult}\left(\mathsf{ct}_1, \mathsf{ct}_2\right), q_\ell\right),$$

will satisfy the following relation:

$$c_{\mathsf{mult+rs},0} + c_{\mathsf{mult+rs},1}s \equiv \frac{(\Delta_\ell \cdot \mu_1 + f_1) \cdot (\Delta_\ell \cdot \mu_2 + f_2) + e_{\mathsf{ks}}}{q_\ell} + r_{\mathsf{rs}}$$

$$= \Delta_{\ell-1} \cdot \mu_1 \cdot \mu_2 + f_{\mathsf{mult+rs}} \pmod{Q_{\ell-1}},$$

where $f_{\mathsf{mult+rs}} = \frac{f_\times}{q_\ell} + \frac{e_{\mathsf{ks}}}{q_\ell} + r_{\mathsf{rs}}$ and $\Delta_{\ell-1} := \frac{\Delta_\ell^2}{q_\ell}$.

The following table shows how the scaling factors change during the computations depending on the level of the ciphertext:

Level	Fresh Δ_ℓ OR after Mult + Rescale
L	$\Delta_L = q_L$
$L-1$	$\Delta_{L-1} = \Delta_L^2/q_L = q_L$
$L-2$	$\Delta_{L-2} = \Delta_{L-1}^2/q_{L-1} = q_L^2/q_{L-1}$
...	...
ℓ	$\Delta_\ell = \Delta_{\ell+1}^2/q_{\ell+1}$
...	...
0	$\Delta_0 = \Delta_1^2/q_1$

The choice of the initial scaling factor $\Delta_L = q_L$ will become clear from below.

Handling the Operations between Ciphertexts at Different Levels. With the approach of automated rescaling, we always get the same scaling factors for the same level. However, we still have to deal with ciphertexts at different levels, i.e., with different scaling factors. Let us say we have two ciphertexts ct_1, ct_2 with levels $\ell_1 > \ell_2$ and scaling factors Δ_{ℓ_1} and Δ_{ℓ_2}. We have to adjust them to be at level ℓ_2 and to have the scaling factor Δ_{ℓ_2}.

- Adjust (ct_1, ℓ_2). For a ciphertext ct_1 with level ℓ_1 and scaling factor Δ_{ℓ_1}, drop moduli $\{q_{\ell_2+2}, \ldots, q_{\ell_1}\}$, multiply the result by a constant $\left\lceil \frac{\Delta_{\ell_2} \cdot q_{\ell_2+1}}{\Delta_{\ell_1}} \right\rfloor = \frac{\Delta_{\ell_2} \cdot q_{\ell_2+1}}{\Delta_{\ell_1}} + \delta$, with $\delta \in [-1/2, 1/2]$ and finally rescale by q_{ℓ_2+1}.

Let a ciphertext $\mathsf{ct}_1 = (c_0, c_1)$ satisfy the following relation:

$$c_0 + c_1 \cdot s = \Delta_{\ell_1} \cdot \mu + f \pmod{Q_{\ell_1}}.$$

The adjustment procedure $\mathsf{ct}_{\mathsf{adj}} = \mathsf{Adjust}(\mathsf{ct}_1, \ell_2)$ for a ciphertext ct_1 leads to the following relation:

$$c_{\mathsf{adj},0} + c_{\mathsf{adj},1} \cdot s = \frac{1}{q_{\ell_2+1}} \left(\Delta_{\ell_1} \cdot \mu + f \right) \cdot \left(\frac{\Delta_{\ell_2} \cdot q_{\ell_2+1}}{\Delta_{\ell_1}} + \delta \right) + r_{\mathsf{rs}} = \Delta_{\ell_2} \cdot \mu + f_{\mathsf{adj}} \pmod{Q_{\ell_2}},$$

with $f_{\mathsf{adj}} = \frac{\Delta_{\ell_2}}{\Delta_{\ell_1}} \cdot f + \frac{\delta \Delta_{\ell_1} \cdot \mu + \delta f}{q_{\ell_2+1}} + r_{\mathsf{rs}}$, where the second error term is introduced by scalar multiplication and the error r_{rs} is introduced by the rescaling. Consider scaled errors $f/\Delta_\ell = \phi^{(\ell)}$, $r/\Delta_\ell = \rho^{(\ell)}$, $e/\Delta_\ell = \epsilon^{(\ell)}$, then we have

$$\phi_{\mathsf{adj}}^{(\ell_2)} = \phi^{(\ell_1)} + \frac{\delta \Delta_{\ell_1} \cdot \mu}{\Delta_{\ell_2+1}^2} + \frac{\delta \phi^{(\ell_2+1)}}{\Delta_{\ell_2+1}} + \rho_{\mathsf{rs}}^{(\ell_2)}. \tag{2}$$

We now can redefine addition and multiplication operations for ciphertexts at different levels.

- CrossLevelAdd(ct_1, ct_2) If $\ell_1 = \ell_2$, output Add(ct_1, ct_2), else w.l.o.g. $\ell_1 > \ell_2$. We first adjust ct_1 to level ℓ_2, $ct'_1 = $ Adjust(ct_1, ℓ_2), and then output Add(ct'_1, ct_2).
- CrossLevelMult(ct_1, ct_2) If $\ell_1 = \ell_2$, output Mult(ct_1, ct_2), else w.l.o.g. $\ell_1 > \ell_2$. We first adjust ct_1 to level ℓ_2, $ct'_1 = $ Adjust(ct_1, ℓ_2), and then output Mult(ct'_1, ct_2).

In Eq. (2), we want Δ_{ℓ_1} and Δ_{ℓ_2+1} to be close to each other to keep the error $\phi_{\mathsf{adj}}^{(\ell_2)}$ small.

Choosing the Primes to Avoid the Divergence of Scaling Factors. We initially tried to reuse the alternating logic for selecting the prime moduli in the CKKS RNS instantiations [6,11], which was introduced to minimize the approximate scaling error. The algorithm showing this logic is listed in Algorithm 1 of the full version of the paper. However, the scaling factors chosen using this logic diverge after ≈ 20 or ≈ 30 levels (for double-precision floats used in our implementation), as illustrated in Fig. 1. As soon as the scaling factor significantly deviates from 2^p, the scaling factor quickly diverges from 2^p either towards 0 or infinity due to the exponential nature of scaling factor computation (the scaling factor is squared at each level). As this situation is not acceptable, we had to devise alternative algorithms.

To address this problem, we developed two other algorithms (Algorithms 2 and 3 in the full version of the paper) where instead of minimizing the difference between Δ_ℓ and 2^p, we minimize the difference between two subsequent scaling factors. Algorithm 2 directly applies this logic. Algorithm 3 refines this logic by also alternating the selection of moduli w.r.t to the previous scaling factor (first a larger prime modulus is selected, then a smaller modulus, etc.), i.e., it combines Algorithms 1 and 2 to further minimize the error introduced by the deviation of the current scaling factor. Figure 1 shows that the deviation of the scaling factors from 2^p is very small for both Algorithms 2 and 3 up to 50 levels. Eventually both algorithms diverge, but it happened after 200 levels for all ring dimensions N we ran experiments for. As Algorithm 3 has smoother behaviour, we chose it for our implementation.

Note that we chose $\Delta_L = q_L$ to reuse this scaling factor at level $L - 1$, hence getting one level for "free" (without squaring and division).

In our implementation we also added a condition to check that the scaling factor does not diverge much from 2^p. PALISADE throws an exception if the scaling factor is within a factor of 2 of 2^p.

4.2 Applying the Reduced-Error CKKS Modifications

With different scaling factors at different levels, we no longer have the approximate scaling error. Hence now we can apply the RE-CKKS techniques to further reduce the approximation error. For the original CKKS scheme, we considered the idea of modified multiplication where rescaling is done right before the next multiplication. The same idea can be adapted to the RNS instantiation of CKKS to reduce the LWE related noise:

$$\mathsf{ct}_{\mathsf{mult}'} = \mathsf{Mult}'\left(\mathsf{ct}_1, \mathsf{ct}_2\right) = \mathsf{Mult}\left(\mathsf{Rescale}\left(\mathsf{ct}_1, q_\ell\right), \mathsf{Rescale}\left(\mathsf{ct}_2, q_\ell\right)\right).$$

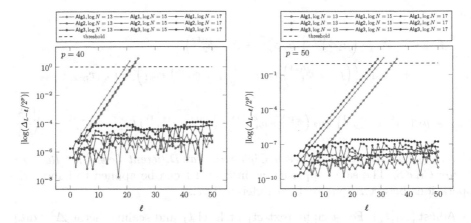

Fig. 1. Deviation of scaling factors from the base value 2^p for $p = 40$ and $p = 50$ and different values of ring dimension N; threshold corresponds to a factor of 2x change.

With the modified multiplication, we also ensure that the ciphertexts at the same level have the same scaling factor, as we do not shuffle Rescale and Mult operations, but just delay the Rescale operation to be done right before next Mult, instead of right after the multiplication. This delay of the Rescale operation has the same effect as eliminating LWE errors in RE-CKKS.

For level L, we add an extra modulus q' satisfying $q' = 1 \pmod{2N}$, such that the sum of all LWE errors during the computations at level L, including fresh encryption noise, is smaller than q'. The following table shows how the scaling factors change during a computation depending on the level of the ciphertext:

Level	Fresh Δ_ℓ OR after Mult$'$
L	$\Delta_L \cdot \Delta' = q_L \cdot q'$
$L-1$	$\Delta_L^2 = q_L^2$
$L-2$	$\Delta_{L-1}^2 = q_L^2$
...	...
$\ell+1$	Δ_ℓ^2
...	...
0	Δ_1^2

With the modified multiplication, the encryption of a message μ at level ℓ will satisfy the following condition (for an encryption with an extra level we need to substitute Δ_ℓ^2 with $\Delta_L \cdot \Delta'$):

$$c_0 + c_1 s \equiv \Delta_\ell^2 \cdot \mu + f'.$$

Let $f'/\Delta_\ell^2 = \phi'^{(\ell)}$. After Mult$'$ operation we have:

$$
\begin{aligned}
c_{\mathsf{mult}',0} + c_{\mathsf{mult}',1} s &\equiv \left(\frac{\Delta_\ell^2 \cdot \mu_1 + f_1'}{q_\ell} + r_{1,\mathsf{rs}} \right) \cdot \left(\frac{\Delta_\ell^2 \cdot \mu_2 + f_2'}{q_\ell} + r_{2,\mathsf{rs}} \right) + e_{\mathsf{ks}} \\
&= \left(\Delta_{\ell-1} \cdot \left(\mu_1 + \phi_1'^{(\ell)} \right) + r_{1,\mathsf{rs}} \right) \cdot \left(\Delta_{\ell-1} \cdot \left(\mu_2 + \phi_2'^{(\ell)} \right) + r_{2,\mathsf{rs}} \right) + e_{\mathsf{ks}} \\
&= \Delta_{\ell-1}^2 \cdot \mu_1 \mu_2 + f_{\mathsf{mult}'},
\end{aligned}
$$

where

$$
f_{\text{mult}'} = \Delta_{\ell-1}^2 \cdot \left(\mu_1 \phi_2'^{(\ell)} + \mu_2 \phi_1'^{(\ell)} + \phi_1'^{(\ell)} \phi_2'^{(\ell)} \right)
$$

$$
+ \Delta_{\ell-1} \cdot \left(\left(\mu_1 + \phi_1'^{(\ell)} \right) r_{\text{rs},2} + \left(\mu_2 + \phi_2'^{(\ell)} \right) r_{\text{rs},1} \right) + r_{\text{rs},1} r_{\text{rs},2} + e_{\text{ks}},
$$

$$
\phi_{\text{mult}'} = \mu_1 \left(\phi_2'^{(\ell)} + \rho_{\text{rs},2}^{(\ell-1)} \right) + \mu_2 \left(\phi_1'^{(\ell)} + \rho_{\text{rs},1}^{(\ell-1)} \right) + \left(\phi_1'^{(\ell)} + \rho_{\text{rs},1}^{(\ell-1)} \right) \left(\phi_2'^{(\ell)} + \rho_{\text{rs},2}^{(\ell-1)} \right) + \frac{\epsilon_{\text{ks}}^{(\ell-1)}}{\Delta_{\ell-1}}.
$$

Handling the Operations Between Ciphertexts at Different Levels for Reduced-Error CKKS. The same approach as in Sect. 4.1 can be applied to handle the operations between ciphertexts at different levels.

– Adjust (ct_1, ℓ_2). For a ciphertext ct_1 at level ℓ_1 and scaling factor $\Delta_{\ell_1}^2$, drop moduli $\{q_{\ell_2+2}, \ldots, q_{\ell_1}\}$, multiply the result by a constant $\lceil \Delta_{\ell_2}^2 \cdot q_{\ell_2+1} / \Delta_{\ell_1}^2 \rfloor = \Delta_{\ell_2}^2 \cdot q_{\ell_2+1} / \Delta_{\ell_1}^2 + \delta$, where $\delta \in [-1/2, 1/2]$, and finally rescale by q_{ℓ_2+1}.

Let a ciphertext $\text{ct}_1 = (c_0, c_1)$ satisfy the following relation:

$$
c_0 + c_1 \cdot s = \Delta_{\ell_1}^2 \cdot \mu + f' \quad (\text{mod } Q_\ell).
$$

The adjustment procedure $\text{ct}_{\text{adj}} = \text{Adjust}(\text{ct}_1, \ell_2)$ for a ciphertext ct_1 leads to the following relation:

$$
c_{\text{adj},0} + c_{\text{adj},1} \cdot s = \frac{\left(\Delta_{\ell_1}^2 \cdot \mu + f' \right)}{q_{\ell_2+1}} \cdot \left(\frac{\Delta_{\ell_2}^2 \cdot q_{\ell_2+1}}{\Delta_{\ell_1}^2} + \delta \right) + r_{\text{rs}} = \Delta_{\ell_2}^2 \cdot \mu + f_{\text{adj}}' \quad (\text{mod } Q_{\ell_2}),
$$

with $f_{\text{adj}}' = \frac{\Delta_{\ell_2}^2}{\Delta_{\ell_1}^2} \cdot f' + \frac{\delta \Delta_{\ell_1}^2 \cdot \mu + \delta f'}{q_{\ell_2+1}} + r_{\text{rs}}$, where the second error term is introduced by scalar multiplication and error r_{rs} is introduced by the rescaling. Then we have

$$
\phi_{\text{adj}}'^{(\ell_2)} = \phi'^{(\ell_1)} + \frac{\delta \Delta_{\ell_1}^2 \cdot \mu}{\Delta_{\ell_2+1}^2 \Delta_{\ell_2}} + \frac{\delta \phi'^{(\ell_2+1)}}{\Delta_{\ell_2}} + \frac{\rho_{\text{rs}}^{(\ell_2)}}{\Delta_{\ell_2}}.
$$

We see that the rescaling part $\frac{\rho_{\text{rs}}^{(\ell_2)}}{\Delta_{\ell_2}}$ becomes negligible.

5   Implementation Details and Results

We implemented both proposed RNS variants of CKKS in PALISADE and evaluated their performance using four representative benchmarks: addition of multiple vectors, summation over a vector, component-wise multiplication of multiple vectors, evaluation of a polynomial over a vector.

We introduce the following notation to distinguish between different RNS variants of CKKS: Reduced-Error CKKS with Delayed Exact (RE-CKKS-DE) rescaling – includes all techniques for reducing the approximation error presented in this work; CKKS with Delayed Exact (CKKS-DE) rescaling – includes only the RNS-specific techniques described in Sect. 4.1 + delayed rescaling; and CKKS with Immediate Approximate (CKKS-IA) rescaling – classical RNS variant, as implemented in RNS-HEAAN and prior versions of PALISADE.

Note that the approximation error of CKKS-DE is approximately the same as the error of the multiprecision CKKS implementation in the HEAAN library. In our comparison of experimentally observed precision for CKKS-DE in PALISADE vs CKKS in the HEAAN library for selected computations (where delayed rescaling in CKKS-DE did not give any advantage to PALISADE over HEAAN), we did not observe differences higher than 0.2 bits, and the differences we saw were not statistically significant.

5.1   Setting the Parameters

The coefficients of error polynomials were sampled using the discrete Gaussian distribution with parameter $\sigma = 3.2$. We used uniform ternary distribution for secrets, which is the most efficient setting that is compliant with the HE standard [2]. We set Q'_L using the logic described in the full version of the paper.

5.2   Software Implementation and Experimental Setup

We implemented all proposed RNS variants of CKKS in PALISADE v1.10. The evaluation environment was a commodity desktop computer system with an Intel(R) Core(TM) i7-9700 CPU @ 3.00 GHz and 64 GB of RAM, running Ubuntu 18.04 LTS. The compiler was g++ 9.3.0. All experiments were executed in the single-threaded mode.

We ran the experiments in the full packing mode, i.e., we packed a vector $\vec{x} \in \mathbb{C}^{N/2}$ of size $N/2$ per ciphertext. The entries x_i were randomly generated from the complex unit circle $\{z \in \mathbb{C} : \|z\|_2 = 1\}$. To estimate the precision after the decryption output $\tilde{\vec{x}}$, we evaluated the average of $\|x_i - \tilde{x}_i\|_2$ and then computed the absolute value of logarithm of it.

5.3   Experimental Results

Addition of Multiple Vectors. Table 4 compares the precision and runtimes for the use case of adding k vectors together for all four RNS variants. This use case does not require any key switching and rescaling operations, and illustrates the pure effect of eliminating fresh LWE encryption noise. The precision of RE-CKKS-DE is about 20 bits higher than for CKKS at $\Delta_i \approx 2^{40}$ for all considered values of k, which implies that $\Delta' = 2^{20}$ gives us a direct improvement in precision. For $\Delta_i \approx 2^{50}$, we get a smaller improvement in precision because of the 52-bit precision of the double-precision floating-point arithmetic used to represent real numbers. The precision is reduced from 52 to roughly 48–49 bits because of the decoding error r_{float}. The runtime slowdown of RE-CKKS-DE vs CKKS-DE for both values of Δ_i is exactly 2x because RE-CKKS-DE works with two RNS limbs (the regular one + the extra modulus Δ'). This slowdown for $\Delta_i \approx 2^{40}$ can be removed by working with a composite modulus $q_0\Delta' \approx 2^{60}$ as it fits a single 64-bit word. But we did not implement this optimization as it only

Table 4. Comparison of precision and runtime when computing $\sum_{i=0}^{k} \vec{x}_i$ for Reduced-Error CKKS with Delayed Exact (RE-CKKS-DE) rescaling, CKKS with Delayed Exact (CKKS-DE) rescaling, and CKKS with Immediate Approximate (CKKS-IA) rescaling RNS variants; CKKS-DE has the same approximation error as the multi-precision CKKS implementation in the HEAAN library and CKKS-IA is equivalent to the RNS implementation in RNS-HEAAN and previous versions of PALISADE; $\Delta_i \approx 2^p, q_0 \approx 2^{60}, \Delta' \approx 2^{20}, K = \lceil \log Q_L \rceil, \lambda > 128$ bits.

		RE-CKKS-DE				CKKS-DE				CKKS-IA	
p	k	$\log N$	K	Prec.	Time	$\log N$	K	Prec.	Time	Prec.	Time
40	2	12	60	45.8	0.04 ms	12	40	25.9	0.02 ms	25.9	0.02 ms
	4	12	60	45.3	0.11 ms	12	40	25.4	0.06 ms	25.4	0.04 ms
	8	12	60	44.9	0.24 ms	12	40	24.9	0.12 ms	24.9	0.08 ms
	16	12	60	44.3	0.51 ms	12	40	24.4	0.25 ms	24.4	0.17 ms
	32	12	60	43.8	1.06 ms	12	40	23.9	0.51 ms	23.9	0.34 ms
	64	12	60	43.3	2.2 ms	12	40	23.4	1.07 ms	23.4	0.74 ms
50	2	13	70	48.1	0.08 ms	13	50	34.9	0.04 ms	34.9	0.03 ms
	4	13	70	48.4	0.22 ms	13	50	34.4	0.11 ms	34.4	0.07 ms
	8	13	70	48.0	0.48 ms	13	50	33.9	0.23 ms	33.9	0.16 ms
	16	13	70	49.6	1.04 ms	13	50	33.4	0.53 ms	33.4	0.34 ms
	32	13	70	48.9	2.16 ms	13	50	32.9	1.1 ms	32.9	0.76 ms
	64	13	70	48.1	4.42 ms	13	50	32.4	2.17 ms	32.4	1.54 ms

works for special cases, and the runtime of about 1 ms is already very small for practical purposes. There is also some performance improvement for CKKS-IA as compared to CCKS-DE, but it is determined by how the code is written (extra memory allocations in the case of CCKS-DE) and has no algorithmic cause.

Table 5. Comparison of precision and runtime when computing $\sum_{i=0}^{N/2} x_i$ for RE-CKKS-DE, CKKS-DE, and CKKS-IA RNS variants (see Table 4 for the definition of RNS variants); $\Delta_i \approx 2^p \approx q_0, \Delta' \approx 2^{20}, K = \lceil \log Q_L \rceil, \lambda > 128$ bits.

	RE-CKKS-DE				CKKS-DE				CKKS-IA	
p	$\log N$	K	Prec.	Time	$\log N$	K	Prec.	Time	Prec.	Time
40	12	60	40.4	17.33 ms	12	40	21.1	8.94 ms	21.1	8.89 ms
50	13	70	47.2	38.67 ms	13	50	28.3	19.79 ms	28.3	19.77 ms

Summation Over a Vector. Table 5 shows the precision and runtimes for the computation adding up all components of a vector. This use case requires key switching but does not need to rescale as there are no multiplications involved. We can see that the precision improvement of RE-CKKS-DE over CKKS-DE is still about 20 bits for $\Delta_i \approx 2^{40}$ and it is slightly smaller for $\Delta_i \approx 2^{50}$ due to the floating-point approximation error. This implies that Δ' removes both encryption and key switching LWE approximation errors, and we only deal with the floating-point precision error here. The runtime slowdown of RE-CKKS-DE compared to all other RNS variants is slightly under 2x. It can be attributed to the extra modulus Δ' and increased computational complexity of hybrid key switching related to this.

Table 6. Comparison of precision and runtime when computing $\prod_{i=1}^{2^k} \bar{x}_i$ for RE-CKKS-DE, CKKS-DE, and CKKS-IA RNS variants (see Table 4 for the definition of RNS variants); $\Delta_i \approx 2^p, q_0 \approx 2^{60}, \Delta' \approx 2^{20}, K = \lceil \log Q_L \rceil, \lambda > 128$ bits.

		RE-CKKS-DE				CKKS-DE			CKKS-IA	
p	k	$\log N$	K	Prec.	Time	$\log N$	K	Prec.	Time	Prec.	Time
40	1	13	120	28.9	5.61 ms	13	100	24.9	3.24 ms	21.8	4.01 ms
	2	14	160	27.1	47.85 ms	14	140	23.4	32.93 ms	20.1	34.25 ms
	3	14	200	26.5	0.14 s	14	180	22.9	99.47 ms	20.7	0.1 s
	4	14	240	26.0	0.38 s	14	220	22.4	0.29 s	17.8	0.29 s
	5	14	280	25.4	0.91 s	14	260	21.9	0.73 s	17.3	0.73 s
	6	14	320	24.9	2.29 s	14	300	21.4	1.79 s	15.9	1.78 s
	7	15	360	23.4	11.27 s	15	340	19.9	8.94 s	14.3	8.86 s
50	1	13	130	38.9	6.22 ms	13	110	34.9	3.17 ms	32.8	4 ms
	2	14	180	37.1	47.83 ms	14	160	33.4	32.77 ms	32.3	34.23 ms
	3	14	230	36.5	0.14 s	14	210	32.9	0.1 s	29.0	0.1 s
	4	14	280	36.0	0.38 s	14	260	32.4	0.29 s	29.5	0.29 s
	5	14	330	35.4	0.97 s	14	310	31.9	0.73 s	27.7	0.73 s
	6	15	380	33.9	4.8 s	15	360	30.4	3.76 s	27.3	3.73 s
	7	15	430	33.4	11.3 s	15	410	29.9	8.94 s	25.9	8.85 s

Binary Tree Multiplication. Table 6 illustrates the precision and runtimes for the case of binary tree multiplication. This use case examines the effect of reduced approximation error for the multiplication operation followed by key switching and rescaling. First, we want to point out that the precision improvement of RE-CKKS-DE over CKKS-DE is about 3.5 to 4 bits (with the highest precision gain after the first multiplication), as theoretically predicted in Sect. 3.3. Second, CKKS-DE gains additional 3 to 6 bits over CKKS-IA. This implies that the RE-CKKS-DE RNS variant can be up to 9 bits more precise than the prior RNS variants. The performance penalty of higher precision varies between 1.2x and 1.6x, which is a relatively small cost.

Evaluation of a Polynomial Over a Vector. Table 7 shows the precision and runtimes for the case of evaluating a polynomial over a vector of real numbers, which is a very common operation in CKKS as a polynomial approximation is often used to approximate "hard", nonlinear functions, such as logistic function, multiplicative inverse, sine wave, etc. This use case examines the combined effect of multiplications and cross-level additions. We can observe that the precision gain of RE-CKKS-DE over CKKS-DE is still 3.5–4 bits. The precision gain of CKKS-DE over CKKS-IA is less pronounced in this case (not higher than 3 bits). The performance penalty is the worst for smaller-degree polynomials (up to 1.9x), but drops to 1.6x for larger-degree polynomials.

Table 7. Comparison of precision and runtime when computing $\sum_{i=0}^{k} \bar{x}^i$ for RE-CKKS-DE, CKKS-DE, and CKKS-IA RNS variants (see Table 4 for the definition of RNS variants); $\Delta_i \approx 2^p, q_0 \approx 2^{60}, \Delta' \approx 2^{20}, K = \lceil \log Q_L \rceil, \lambda > 128$ bits.

		RE-CKKS-DE				CKKS-DE				CKKS-IA	
p	k	$\log N$	K	Prec.	Time	$\log N$	K	Prec.	Time	Prec.	Time
40	2	13	120	28.4	7 ms	13	100	24.3	3.37 ms	21.8	4.14 ms
	4	14	160	26.1	50.88 ms	14	140	22.2	35.63 ms	19.4	29.39 ms
	8	14	200	24.8	0.13 s	14	180	21.0	0.1 s	19.1	75.14 ms
	16	14	240	23.6	0.29 s	14	220	19.8	0.26 s	16.9	0.17 s
	32	14	280	22.4	0.64 s	14	260	18.6	0.58 s	16.3	0.38 s
	48	14	320	21.8	1.12 s	14	300	17.9	1.05 s	15.1	0.67 s
	64	14	320	21.3	1.33 s	14	300	17.4	1.26 s	14.9	0.82 s
50	2	13	130	38.4	7.69 ms	13	110	34.3	3.36 ms	32.8	4.14 ms
	4	14	180	36.0	51.19 ms	14	160	32.1	35.8 ms	29.5	29.48 ms
	8	14	230	34.8	0.13 s	14	210	31.0	0.1 s	28.0	75.42 ms
	16	14	280	33.6	0.29 s	14	260	29.8	0.26 s	27.7	0.17 s
	32	14	330	32.4	0.68 s	14	310	28.6	0.58 s	26.4	0.38 s
	48	15	380	30.8	2.34 s	15	360	26.9	2.21 s	26.1	1.4 s
	64	15	380	30.3	2.78 s	15	360	26.4	2.65 s	25.6	1.72 s

6   Concluding Remarks

Our results suggest that a relatively high precision can be achieved for RE-CKKS in RNS for significantly smaller scaling factors than in the original CKKS scheme and its prior RNS variants. This implies RE-CKKS requires smaller ciphertext moduli (lower ring dimension) to achieve the same precision as the original CKKS or its RNS instantiation, which may also yield certain performance improvements over the prior approach if the same output precision is considered (the ring dimension can be reduced by 2x).

Another benefit of RE-CKKS is that it can be used to increase the CKKS bootstrapping precision in RNS variants of CKKS, which is currently a major practical limitation for the RNS instantiations of CKKS [21]. For example, the extra 6 to 9 bits and 10 to 12 bits for uniform and sparse secrets, respectively, may provide enough room for more accurate polynomial approximations of the modular reduction function. But the precision improvements in CKKS bootstrapping require careful modifications at various stages of the bootstrapping procedure, e.g., in the scaling operations. Hence this problem deserves a separate study and is beyond the scope of our present work.

The main motivation of our study was to improve the usability of the CKKS scheme by eliminating several approximation errors and automating the execution of rescaling. We believe we have achieved this goal, and consider our work as a significant step towards making the CKKS scheme more practical. For instance, all operations related to rescaling or the approximation error management are completely hidden from the application developer in our PALISADE implementation, and the API for CKKS is the same as for integer-arithmetic homomorphic encryption schemes, such as Brakersky-Gentry-Vaikuntanathan [9] and Brakerski/Fan-Vercauteren [8,17] schemes.

References

1. PALISADE Lattice Cryptography Library (release 1.10.3) (2020). https://palisade-crypto.org/
2. Albrecht, M., Chase, M., Chen, H., et al.: Homomorphic encryption security standard. Tech. rep., HomomorphicEncryption.org, Toronto, Canada, November 2018
3. Bajard, J.C., Eynard, J., Hasan, M.A., Zucca, V.: A full RNS variant of FV like somewhat homomorphic encryption schemes. In: SAC 2016, pp. 423–442 (2016)
4. Bergamaschi, F., Halevi, S., Halevi, T.T., Hunt, H.: Homomorphic training of 30, 000 logistic regression models. In: ACNS 2019, pp. 592–611 (2019)
5. Blatt, M., Gusev, A., Polyakov, Y., Goldwasser, S.: Secure large-scale genome-wide association studies using homomorphic encryption. Proc. Natl. Acad. Sci. **117**(21), 11608–11613 (2020)
6. Blatt, M., Gusev, A., Polyakov, Y., Rohloff, K., Vaikuntanathan, V.: Optimized homomorphic encryption solution for secure genome-wide association studies. BMC Med. Genomics **13**(7), 1–13 (2020)
7. Bossuat, J.P., Mouchet, C., Troncoso-Pastoriza, J., Hubaux, J.P.: Efficient bootstrapping for approximate homomorphic encryption with non-sparse keys. Cryptology ePrint Archive, Report 2020/1203 (2020)
8. Brakerski, Z.: Fully homomorphic encryption without modulus switching from classical GapSVP. In: Safavi-Naini, R., Canetti, R. (eds.) CRYPTO 2012. LNCS, vol. 7417, pp. 868–886. Springer, Heidelberg (2012). https://doi.org/10.1007/978-3-642-32009-5_50
9. Brakerski, Z., Gentry, C., Vaikuntanathan, V.: (Leveled) fully homomorphic encryption without bootstrapping. ACM Trans. Comput. Theor. (TOCT) **6**(3), 1–36 (2014)
10. Brakerski, Z., Vaikuntanathan, V.: Fully homomorphic encryption from ring-LWE and security for key dependent messages. In: CRYPTO 2011, pp. 505–524 (2011)
11. Cheon, J.H., Han, K., Kim, A., Kim, M., Song, Y.: A full RNS variant of approximate homomorphic encryption. In: SAC 2018, pp. 347–368 (2018)
12. Cheon, J.H., Han, K., Kim, A., Kim, M., Song, Y.: RNSHEAAN (2018). https://github.com/KyoohyungHan/FullRNS-HEAAN
13. Cheon, J.H., Kim, A., Kim, M., Song, Y.: HEAAN (2016). https://github.com/snucrypto/HEAAN
14. Cheon, J.H., Kim, A., Kim, M., Song, Y.: Homomorphic encryption for arithmetic of approximate numbers. In: ASIACRYPT 2017, pp. 409–437 (2017)
15. Cohen, R., Frankle, J., Goldwasser, S., Shaul, H., Vaikuntanathan, V.: How to trade efficiency and accuracy using fault-tolerant computations over the reals (2019). https://crypto.iacr.org/2019/affevents/ppml/page.html
16. Curtis, B.R., Player, R.: On the feasibility and impact of standardising sparse-secret LWE parameter sets for homomorphic encryption. In: WAHC 2019, pp. 1–10 (2019)
17. Fan, J., Vercauteren, F.: Somewhat practical fully homomorphic encryption. IACR Cryptol. ePrint Arch. **2012**, 144 (2012)

18. Gentry, C., Halevi, S., Smart, N.P.: Homomorphic evaluation of the AES circuit. In: Safavi-Naini, R., Canetti, R. (eds.) CRYPTO 2012. LNCS, vol. 7417, pp. 850–867. Springer, Heidelberg (2012). https://doi.org/10.1007/978-3-642-32009-5_49
19. Halevi, S., Polyakov, Y., Shoup, V.: An improved RNS variant of the BFV homomorphic encryption scheme. In: CT-RSA 2019, pp. 83–105 (2019)
20. Halevi, S., Shoup, V.: HElib (2014). https://github.com/homenc/HElib
21. Han, K., Ki, D.: Better bootstrapping for approximate homomorphic encryption. In: Jarecki, S. (ed.) CT-RSA 2020. LNCS, vol. 12006, pp. 364–390. Springer, Cham (2020). https://doi.org/10.1007/978-3-030-40186-3_16
22. Kim, A., Song, Y., Kim, M., Lee, K., Cheon, J.H.: Logistic regression model training based on the approximate homomorphic encryption. BMC Med. Genomics 11(4), 83 (2018)
23. Kim, M., Song, Y., Li, B., Micciancio, D.: Semi-parallel logistic regression for GWAS on encrypted data. BMC Med. Genomics 13(7), 1–13 (2020)
24. Lee, J.W., Lee, E., Lee, Y., Kim, Y.S., No, J.S.: High-precision bootstrapping of rns-ckks homomorphic encryption using optimal minimax polynomial approximation and inverse sine function. In: EUROCRYPT 2021, pp. 618–647 (2021)
25. Li, B., Micciancio, D.: On the security of homomorphic encryption on approximate numbers. Cryptology ePrint Archive, Report 2020/1533 (2020)
26. Microsoft SEAL (2020). https://github.com/Microsoft/SEAL
27. Son, Y., Cheon, J.H.: Revisiting the hybrid attack on sparse secret LWE and application to HE parameters. In: WAHC 2019, pp. 11–20 (2019)
28. Song, Y.: The CKKS (a.k.a. HEAAN) FHE scheme (2020). https://simons.berkeley.edu/talks/heaan-fhe

Attacks on Pseudo Random Number Generators Hiding a Linear Structure

Florette Martinez[✉]

Sorbonne Université, CNRS, LIP6, 75005 Paris, France
florette.martinez@lip6.fr

Abstract. We introduce lattice-based practical seed-recovery attacks against two efficient number-theoretic pseudo-random number generators: the *fast knapsack generator* and a family of *combined multiple recursive generators*. The fast knapsack generator was introduced in 2009 by von zur Gathen and Shparlinski. It generates pseudo-random numbers very efficiently with strong mathematical guarantees on their statistical properties but its resistance to cryptanalysis was left open since 2009. The given attacks are surprisingly efficient when the truncated bits do not represent a too large proportion of the internal states. Their complexities do not strongly increase with the size of parameters, only with the proportion of discarded bits.

A multiple recursive generator is a pseudo-random number generator based on a constant-recursive sequence. A combined multiple recursive generator is a pseudo-random number generator based on combining two or more multiple recursive generators. L'Écuyer presented the general construction in 1996 and a popular instantiation deemed MRG32k3a in 1999. We use algebraic relations of both pseudo-random generators with underlying algebraic generators to show that they are cryptographically insecure. We provide a theoretical analysis as well as efficient implementations.

Keywords: Pseudo-random number generators · Knapsack problem · Coppersmith methods · Cryptanalysis

1 Introduction

A pseudo-random number generator (PRNG) is an efficient deterministic algorithm that stretches a small random seed into a longer pseudo-random sequence of numbers. These generators can be used to emulate randomness in games, numerical simulations or cryptographic protocols. These different situations call for PRNGs with different properties. A cryptographic application will need a strong PRNG that produces a sequence of bits indistinguishable from "truly" random bits by efficient adversaries while a numerical simulation or a game will ask for a fast and light PRNG.

Analysing the quality of randomness for a PRNG suited for cryptographic applications is natural as a failure in these PRNGs would lead to problematic

S. D. Galbraith (Ed.): CT-RSA 2022, LNCS 13161, pp. 145–168, 2022.
https://doi.org/10.1007/978-3-030-95312-6_7

security breaches. Rueppel and Massey introduced the *knapsack generator* [16] in 1985 for cryptographic purposes. One chooses n secret bits $u_0, \ldots u_{n-1}$ and n secret weights $\omega_0, \ldots, \omega_n$ to form the seed. A linear feedback shift register (LFSR) generates the control bits (u_i) from the n secret bits and a public feedback polynomial of order n. At step i, the generator computes $v_i \equiv \sum_{j=0}^{n-1} u_{i+j} \omega_j$ mod 2^n, discards the least significant bits and outputs the remaining. In 2011, Knellwolf and Meier [11] presented the main attack against this generator. They used a guess-and-determine strategy coupled with lattice-based techniques to recover most of the key in relevant instances of the generator. In order to run said attack, they needed to guess all the n initial control bits. Hence their attack had a time complexity $\Omega(2^n)$. This attack is not fast enough to definitively keep the knapsack generator away from cryptographic applications. In 2009, von zur Gathen and Shparlinski presented a faster and lighter version of the knapsack generator called the *fast knapsack generator* [7]. The main modification was a specialisation of the weights. In their paper, the authors mention that it was not clear if that specialisation had an impact on the security of this generator. Thus it was not known if it was suited for cryptographic purposes. In this article, we notice similarities between the fast knapsack generator and a linear congruential generator (LCG). Because of the specialisation of the weights, the fast knapsack generator tends to act like a LCG one iteration out of four. We present here lattice-based attacks exploiting this new weakness. We first describe three different algorithms to attack the underlying LCG, two using Coppersmith Methods and one based on Stern's attack against the LCG. Then we present how such algorithms can be used to break the fast knapsack generator. These algorithms allow us to completely recover the seed when less than a quarter of the bits are discarded.

Attacking a non-cryptographic PRNG is not irrelevant. Non-cryptographic PRNGs tend to be faster and lighter than their cryptographic counterparts. As they do not pretend to achieve some kind of security, they are less studied by cryptanalysts hence there might not exist any known attack against them. Because of that, one might be tempted to replace a strong but slow cryptographic PRNG with a faster non-cryptographic one. Breaking non-cryptographic PRNGs could deter anyone to use them outside of what they are made for. This had already been done with the PCG64 by Bouillaguet et al. in 2020 [2]. The PCG64 is the default pseudo-random number generator in the popular NumPy [18] scientific computing package for Python.

A combined linear congruential generator (CLCG) is a pseudo-random number generator algorithm based on combining two or more linear-congruential generators. The general construction was proposed in 1982 by Wichmann and Hill in [19]. A multiple recursive generator (MRG) is a pseudo-random generator based on a constant-recursive sequence. Like the LCGs, the MRGs can be combined to obtain CMRGs. In 1999, L'Écuyer presented a family of parameters giving CMRGs with good properties. These PRNGs are fast and pass the "spectral test" evaluating their closeness to the uniform distribution. The more famous of these CMRGs is the MRG32k3a, largely used for producing multiple streams of pseudo random numbers, as seen in [13]. It is one of the PRNGs implanted in Matlab and the native PRNG of the programming language Racket.

This PRNG had already been used once in place of a secure one for the website *Hacker news*. In 2009, Franke [4] managed to hack this website and was able to steal accounts. His attack was not based on breaking the MRG32k3a but on guessing how the seed was generated. In fact the seed was the time (in milliseconds) when the Hacker News software was last started. After crashing the website he had access to the information he needed. In this case, breaking the MRG32k3a could have lead us to an other real life attack against this website. In our paper we will present an attack against CMRGs that output the difference between two MRG of order three. The trick will be to see the two congruential constant-recursive sequences as two projections of a single larger congruential constant-recursive sequence. This attack will cover the particular case of the MRG32k3a. Even if we reduce our study to those specific CMRGs, the same techniques can be used on CMRGs combining more than two MRGs or MRGs of larger orders.

Attacking a non-cryptographic PRNG is not only security-related. As mentioned earlier, PRNGs can be used in numerical simulations and a hidden structure in a PRNG could cause bias in said simulation. In [3], Ferrenberg et al. ran classical Ferromagnetic Ising model Monte-Carlo simulations in specific cases where exact results were known, with different PRNGs. They observed that the choice of the PRNG had a significant impact on the outcome. For example, a given LFSR tented to give energy levels that were too low and a critical temperature that was to high.

In Sect. 2, we will present a simplified version of the Coppersmith method, used in the attacks against both PRNGs. The different attacks on the fast knapsack generator will be discussed in Sects. 3 and 4 while the attack against the CMRGs will be presented in Sect. 5.

2   Coppersmith Method

In this section, we give a short description of a Coppersmith method used to solve a multivariate modular polynomial system of equations over a single modulus. We refer the reader to [8] for proofs.

We consider $P_1(y_0, \ldots, y_n), \ldots, P_s(y_0, \ldots, y_n)$ s irreducible multivariate polynomials defined over $\mathbb{Z}$, having a common small root $(x_0, \ldots, x_n)$ modulo a known integer N. Said root is said small because it must be bounded by known values, namely $|x_0| < X_0, \ldots, |x_n| < X_n$. In order to find this root, we may want to increase the number of polynomials by adding polynomials of the form $y_1^{k_1} \ldots y_n^{k_n} P_i^{k_{n+1}}$. We suppose we have now r polynomials $P_1, \ldots, P_r$ linearly independent but not necessarily irreducible. To each of these polynomials P_i we associate a number k_i that will be the multiplicity of $(x_0, \ldots, x_n)$ as a root of $P_i \bmod N$ (in other terms, k_i is the largest integer such that $P_i(x_0, \ldots, x_n) \equiv 0 \bmod N^{k_i}$). We construct the real matrix $\mathcal{M}$ as follows:

$$
\mathcal{M} =
\begin{pmatrix}
\begin{array}{c|c}
\begin{matrix}
1 & & & \\
 & X_0^{-1} & & \\
 & & \ddots & \\
 & & & X_0^{-a_0} \times \cdots \times X_n^{-a_n}
\end{matrix} &
\begin{matrix}
& P_1 \cdots P_r \\
& \downarrow \cdots \downarrow \\
& \\
\star
\end{matrix} \\
\hline
0 &
\begin{matrix}
N^{k_1} & & \\
 & \ddots & \\
 & & N^{k_r}
\end{matrix}
\end{array}
\end{pmatrix}
\quad
\begin{matrix}
1 \\
y_0 \\
\vdots \\
y_0^{a_0} \times \cdots \times y_n^{a_n}
\end{matrix}
$$

We denote $\mathfrak{M}$ the set of monomials that appear at least in one P_i and $|\mathfrak{M}|$ its cardinality. Each one of the upper rows (between 1 and $|\mathfrak{M}|$) corresponds to one of these monomials and each one of the latest columns (from $|\mathfrak{M}|+1$ to $|\mathfrak{M}|+r$) corresponds to one of the polynomials.

Let i be in $\{1,\ldots,|\mathfrak{M}|\}$, we denote m_i the i-th monomial of $\mathfrak{M}$, $m_i = y_0^{b_0}\ldots y_n^{b_n}$. The value of $\mathcal{M}_{i,i}$ will be the inverse of the bound on m_i, hence $X_0^{-b_0}\ldots X_n^{-b_n}$. For all j between 1 and r, the value of $\mathcal{M}_{i,|\mathfrak{M}|+j}$ will be the coefficient of m_i in P_j. Finally, the value of $\mathcal{M}_{|\mathfrak{M}|+j,|\mathfrak{M}|+j}$ will be k_j as described in the previous paragraph.

We want to show that the smallest vector of the lattice spanned by the rows of $\mathcal{M}$ contains the solution $(x_0,\ldots,x_n)$. We denote by c_i the integer such that $P_i(x_0,\ldots,x_n) = c_i N^{k_i}$. We can construct v:

$$
v = (1, x_0, \ldots, x_0^{a_0}\ldots x_{m-1}^{a_n}, -c_1, \ldots, -c_r) \times \mathcal{M}
$$
$$
= \left(1, \frac{x_0}{X_0}, \ldots, \frac{x_0^{a_0}\ldots x_n^{a_n}}{X_0^{a_0}\ldots X_n^{a_n}}, 0, \ldots, 0\right).
$$

By construction, the vector v is in the lattice. Its first $|\mathfrak{M}|$ coordinates are smaller than one and the remaining ones are null, hence it is a small vector. In general, retrieving the shortest vector of a lattice is a hard problem (called the SVP for Shortest Vector Problem), but if this short vector is abnormally short, it can be far easiest. A common method to find such a vector is applying the LLL algorithm to the lattice. The LLL [12] is a polynomial-time reduction algorithm presented by Lenstra, Lenstra and Lovász in 1982. It takes as input a basis of a lattice and outputs a short and nearly orthogonal basis of the same lattice. The smallest vector of this basis is, as a consequence, a small vector of the lattice. We will thus apply LLL on the matrix $\mathcal{M}$ to obtain the small vector v.

The conditions on the bounds that make this method works are given by the following (simplified) equation:

$$
\prod_{y_0^{a_0}\ldots y_n^{a_n}\in\mathfrak{M}} X_0^{a_0}\ldots X_n^{a_n} < N^{\sum_{i=1}^r k_i}. \tag{1}
$$

For further details see [15].

3 Attacks on the Linear Congruential Generator

A *Linear Congruential Generator* (LCG) is a pseudo-random number generator whose internal states are of the form $v_{i+1} = zv_i + C \bmod N$. The parameter z is called the multiplier, C is the increment and N is the modulus. Those generators have been largely studied in various cases. In 1984, Frieze et al. [6] showed that, provided both the modulus N and the multiplier z, the sequence output by a LCG was completely predictable as long as more than 2/5 of the bits were output. In 1987, Stern [17] presented two algorithms to predict a sequence output by a LCG with $\mathcal{O}(\sqrt{\log(N)})$ outputs. The first algorithm treated the case where only the modulus N was known and the second one treated the case where all the parameters were secret. In 1988, Frieze and al. proposed in [5] a polynomial-time algorithm to retrieve the seed when the multiplier z and the modulus N were known. In 1997, Joux and Stern presented in [9] a polynomial-time algorithm against the LCG to retrieve the parameters z, c and N when they are kept secret.

3.1 Attacks via a Coppersmith Method

In the following, we will study the LCG underlying in the fast knapsack generator. This LCG is particular in the sense that z is unknown, $c = 0$ and $N = 2^n$. We have two options to retrieve the seed of this generator. We can create new attacks specifically against this type of LCG or adapt existing attacks like Stern's. In this subsection we will explore the first option and use our own algorithm based on a Coppersmith method to retrieve z. We also notice that our strategy is easy to adapt to the case where the outputs we have are no longer consecutive.

Let v_0 and z be two n-bits integers. The integer v_0 is the *seed* and z the *multiplier*. We choose z odd (hence coprime to 2^n), otherwise v_1 would be divisible by 2, v_2 by 2^2 and v_k by 2^k. At step $i+1$, our LCG computes $v_{i+1} = z \times v_i \bmod 2^n$ and outputs the $n - \ell$ most significant bits.

For an internal state v_i, we introduce the following notations:

- $H_i = (v_i \ quo \ 2^\ell) \times 2^\ell + 2^{\ell-1}$, where quo denotes the quotient of the Euclidean division (H_i is constructed from the output, hence it is known)
- $\delta_i = v_i - H_i$ (δ_i represents the ℓ discarded bits, it is unknown)

Attack 1: Consecutive outputs. Let v_0, v_1, v_2 be 3 consecutive internal states of the LCG. We have $v_1 = zv_0 \bmod 2^n$ and $v_2 = zv_1 \bmod 2^n$. As z and 2^n are coprime, we obtain:

$$v_1^2 = v_0 v_2 \bmod 2^n.$$

We replace v_i by $H_i + \delta_i$:

$$H_1^2 + 2H_1\delta_1 + \delta_1^2 = H_0 H_2 + H_0 \delta_2 + H_2 \delta_0 + \delta_0 \delta_2 \bmod 2^n,$$

and notice that $(\delta_0, \delta_1, \delta_2)$ is a small root of the polynomial $P \bmod 2^n$ where

$$P(y_0, y_1, y_2) = y_1^2 - y_0 y_2 + 2H_1 y_1 - H_0 y_2 - H_2 y_0 + H_1^2 - H_0 H_2.$$

We will apply the Coppersmith method on P with bounds $X_0 = X_1 = X_2 = 2^\ell$. The set of monomials is $\mathfrak{M} = \{y_0, y_1, y_2, y_1^2, y_0 y_2\}$ hence, by Eq. 1, we should heuristically recover the root if $(2^\ell)^7 = X_0 \times X_1 \times X_2 \times X_1^2 \times X_0 X_2 < 2^n$, that is to say if $\ell/n < 1/7$.

Generalization. Let $v_0, \ldots, v_k$ be $k+1$ consecutive internal states. We will obtain $\binom{k}{2}$ equations of the form $v_j v_{i+1} = v_i v_{j+1} \bmod 2^n$. Hence we will construct $\binom{k}{2}$ polynomials P_i of which $(\delta_0, \ldots, \delta_k)$ is a simple root mod 2^n. The set of appearing monomials will be:

$$\mathfrak{M} = \{y_i | i \in \{0, \ldots, k\}\} \bigcup \{y_i y_{j+1} | i, j \in \{0, \ldots, k-1\}, i \neq j\}.$$

We find that $\prod_{y_i | i \in \{0, \ldots, k\}} X_i \times \prod_{y_i y_{j+1} | i, j \in \{0, \ldots, k-1\}, i \neq j} X_i X_{j+1} = (2^\ell)^{\Gamma(k)}$ where $\Gamma(k) = (k+1) + 2 \times 2\binom{k}{2}$. Thus, by Eq. 1, the attack should work as long as $\ell/n < \binom{k}{2}/\Gamma(k)$. This theoretical bound increases toward $1/4$.

As usual with Coppersmith methods, the theoretical bound is smaller than what we can really achieve.

k	2	3	4	5
ℓ/n (theoretical) $<$	1/7	3/16	6/29	5/23
ℓ/n (experimental) $<$	0.3	0.35	0.38	0.40

We also present the computing times for different n and k.

$n \backslash k$	2	3	4	5
32	$0.002s$	$0.005s$	$0.01s$	$0.04s$
64	$0.003s$	$0.009s$	$0.03s$	$0.1s$
1024	$0.02s$	$0.1s$	$0.7s$	$2s$

These computing times are averages of a hundred instances of the algorithm running on a standard laptop: a Dell Latitude 7400, running on Ubuntu 18.04 with Sagemath version 8.1. The same laptop with the same configuration will be used for the rest of the experiments of this paper.

Remark 1. *As mentioned in Sect. 2, we could try to optimise our Coppersmith method by adding polynomials of the form $y_1^{k_1} \ldots y_n^{k_n} P_i^{k_{n+1}}$, but we refrained for two main reasons. The first one is that without any other polynomial, the size of our lattice remains small and our attack practical. The second reason is that we tried in Appendix B to find a suitable family of polynomials to improve our attack and the results are not encouraging. This will remains true for the next attack.*

Attack 2: Not consecutive outputs. Now we suppose we have two pairs of two consecutive internal states (v_0, v_1) and (v_i, v_{i+1}). Then $(\delta_0, \delta_1, \delta_i, \delta_{i+1})$ is a small root of $P \bmod 2^n$ where

$$P = y_0 y_{i+1} - y_1 y_i + H_0 y_{i+1} + H_{i+1} y_0 - H_1 y_i - H_i y_1 + H_0 H_{i+1} - H_1 H_i.$$

We will apply the Coppersmith method on P with $X_0 = X_1 = X_i = X_{i+1} = 2^\ell$. The set of monomials is $\mathfrak{M} = \{y_0, y_1, y_i, y_{i+1}, y_0 y_{i+1}, y_1 y_i\}$ hence, by Eq. 1, we should heuristically recover the root if $(2^\ell)^8 = X_0 \times X_1 \times X_i \times X_{i+1} \times X_0 X_{i+1} \times X_1 X_i < 2^n$, that is to say if $\ell/n < 1/8$.

Generalisation. Let S be a set of k distinct integers (the larger being i_S) and $\bigcup_{i \in S} \{v_i, v_{i+1}\}$ be at most $2k$ internal states. We will obtain $\binom{k}{2}$ equations of the form $v_j v_{i+1} = v_i v_{j+1} \bmod 2^n$ hence $\binom{k}{2}$ polynomials P_i of which $(\delta_0, \ldots, \delta_{i_S+1})$ is a simple root $\bmod 2^n$. The set of appearing monomials will be:

$$\mathfrak{M} = \{y_i, y_{i+1} | i \in S\} \bigcup \{y_i y_{j+1} | i, j \in S, i \neq j\}.$$

We will have at most $2k$ monomials of degree 1 and $2\binom{k}{2}$ monomials of degree 2. Heuristically, our attack should work if $(2^\ell)^{2k+4\binom{k}{2}} < (2^n)^{\binom{k}{2}}$. In other words, our attack should work if $\ell/n < \frac{k-1}{4k}$. This theoretical bound increases toward $1/4$.

As usual with Coppersmith methods, the theoretical bound is smaller than what we can really achieve.

k	2	3	4	5	6	7	8
ℓ/n (theoretical) <	1/8	1/6	3/16	1/5	5/24	3/14	7/32
ℓ/n (experimental) <	0.16	0.25	0.31	0.34	0.36	0.38	0.4

We also present the computing time for different n and k.

$n\backslash k$	2	3	4	5	6	7	8
32	0.001s	0.003s	0.008s	0.02s	0.04s	0.09s	0.2s
64	0.002s	0.004s	0.02s	0.04s	0.08s	0.2s	0.5s
1024	0.003s	0.2s	0.2s	0.8s	1.6s	5s	13s

These computing times are averages of a hundred instances of the algorithm.

3.2   Attack 3: With Stern's Algorithm

As mentioned earlier, one strategy to attack our simple LCG was to adapt existent attacks to the case where $C = 0$ and $N = 2^n$. Here we are going to describe and adapt Stern's attack against the LCG, presented in [17].

Let us consider a LCG with internal states given by $v_{i+1} = zv_i + C \bmod N$ with v_0, z, C and N secret. To obtain the output y_i, we discard the last ℓ bits of the internal state v_i.

First part of Stern's algorithm. Let K, t and r be three integer parameters to be discussed later, with $r > t$. We consider the vectors:

$$Y_i = \begin{pmatrix} y_{i+1} - y_i \\ y_{i+2} - y_{i+1} \\ \vdots \\ y_{i+t} - y_{i+t-1} \end{pmatrix} \text{ and } V_i = \begin{pmatrix} v_{i+1} - v_i \\ v_{i+2} - v_{i+1} \\ \vdots \\ v_{i+t} - v_{i+t-1} \end{pmatrix}.$$

Then we construct the following matrix:

$$\begin{pmatrix} KY_0 & 1 & & \\ KY_1 & & 1 & \\ \vdots & & & \ddots \\ KY_{r-1} & & & & 1 \end{pmatrix},$$

apply LLL and obtain a small vector $(K\sum_{i=0}^{r-1} \lambda_i Y_i, \lambda_0, \ldots, \lambda_{r-1})$. We will have to choose K big enough to force the λ_i's to satisfy:

$$\sum_{i=0}^{r-1} \lambda_i Y_i = 0.$$

The key point here is that, with t and r well chosen, we can expect:

$$\sum_{i=0}^{r-1} \lambda_i V_i = 0,$$

hence if we consider the polynomial $f(X) = (v_2 - v_1)\sum_{i=1}^{r} \lambda_i X^{i-1}$, it satisfies $f(z) \equiv 0 \bmod N$. In the case where N is prime, the integer parameters K, t, r must satisfy:

$t > n/(n - \ell)$
$r \approx \sqrt{2(n - \ell)t}$
and $K = \lceil \sqrt{r} 2^{(r-1)/2} B \rceil$

where $B = 2^{t((n-\ell)+\log r+1)/(r-t)}$ (see [9,17]).

If we were to use directly this method on our particular LCG (with $C = 0$ and $N = 2^n$) we would face two major inconveniences. The first one is the number of outputs needed. Let suppose $n = 1024$ and $\ell = 128$, then $\ell/n = 1/8$ and we know our algorithm using a Coppersmith method would need 3 outputs to recover z. Here, Stern's algorithm would need a bit more than 60 LCG outputs and we cannot expect the fast knapsack generator to behave like a LCG sixty times in a row. The second inconvenience is the proof of this algorithm. The fact that N is prime (or almost prime) is crucial as it allows us to count the roots of a certain polynomial modulo N. In our case $N = 2^n$ hence we cannot bound the number of roots of a polynomial modulo 2^n any more.

Modified algorithm. As the proof does not hold any more and there is no precise heuristics in the modular case, we will search for good parameters experimentally. But before, we are going to do some modifications. As we know that $C = 0$, we can replace the vectors Y_i and V_i by:

$$Y_i' = \begin{pmatrix} y_i \\ y_{i+1} \\ \vdots \\ y_{i+t-1} \end{pmatrix} \text{ and } V_i' = \begin{pmatrix} v_i \\ v_{i+1} \\ \vdots \\ v_{i+t-1} \end{pmatrix}.$$

Then instead of searching a small vector $(\lambda_0, \ldots, \lambda_{r-1})$ such that:

$$\sum_{i=0}^{r-1} \lambda_i Y_i' = 0,$$

we are going to search for an even smaller vector $(\mu_0, \ldots, \mu_{r-1})$ such that:

$$\sum_{i=0}^{r-1} \mu_i Y_i' = 0 \bmod N$$

(in fact we do not even need this sum to be zero, we just need it to be small). To find such a vector we construct the following matrix:

$$\begin{pmatrix} KY_0' & & & 1 & & & \\ KY_1' & & & & 1 & & \\ \vdots & & & & & \ddots & \\ KY_{r-1}' & & & & & & 1 \\ \hline K2^n & & & & & & \\ & \ddots & & & & & 0 \\ & & K2^n & & & & \end{pmatrix}$$

and apply LLL.

Then if the vector satisfies $\sum_{i=0}^{r-1} \mu_i V_i' = 0 \bmod N$ and v_0 is odd, the polynomial $f(X) = \sum_{i=0}^{r-1} \mu_i X^i$ will satisfiy $f(z) \equiv 0 \bmod N$. When we have this polynomial, we compute its roots modulo 2^n with a lift of Hensel and find a list of hopefully not too many possible values for z.

Experimental Parameters

The parameter K. As said earlier, we need to choose the parameter K big enough such that the small vector $(\mu_0, \ldots, \mu_{r-1})$ satisfies $\sum_{i=0}^{r-1} \mu_i V_i' = 0 \bmod N$. We notice experimentally that the value of K does not influence if our small vector is satisfying the condition or not. At worst, a bigger K seems to reduce the efficiency of our algorithm. For this reason and for simplicity sake, we choose $K = 1$.

The parameters r and t. This attack against a LCG needs $r + t - 1$ consecutive outputs. For a small ℓ, this attack needs more outputs than the one based on a Coppersmith method. But it allows us to recover the multiplier even when $\ell = n/2$. We present in the following table the parameters and computing times to find a polynomial f that satisfies $f(z) \equiv 0 \bmod N$. The experimental values are averages on a hundred instances of the algorithm.

ℓ/n	0.2	0.3	0.4	0.5	0.6
(r, t)	(4,3)	(5,4)	(7,3)	(9,4)	(11,5)
$r + t - 1$	6	8	9	12	15
$n = 32$	0.0007s	0.0008s	0.0008s	0.001s	0.002s
$n = 64$	0.0007s	0.001s	0.001s	0.003s	0.002s
$n = 1024$	0.002s	0.004s	0.004s	0.005s	0.009s

The size of the entries. The parameters K, r and t are chosen and we have constructed a polynomial f satisfying $f(z) \equiv 0 \bmod N$. But finding the polynomial f is only the first part of the algorithm and now we need to compute the roots of f. As $N = 2^n$ is highly composed, the number of roots of f is only bounded by 2^n. Experimentally, it happens quite regularly that f has too many roots and it prevents us to do massive tests or averages as we are easily stuck in bad cases. The following table will resume the different advantages and disadvantages of each attack against the LCG. All the real computing times are averages on ten instances of the algorithm with $n = 1024$.

ℓ/n	0.2	0.3	0.4	0.5
m for attack 1	3	3	6	*none*
m for attack 2	2×3	2×4	2×8	*none*
m for attack 3	6	8	9	12
computing time for attack 1	0.02s	0.02s	2s	*none*
computing time for attack 2	0.2s	0.2s	15s	*none*
computing time for attack 3	1.5s	1.9s	1.4s	1.8s

4 Attacks Against the Fast Knapsack Generator

Let $\omega_0, \ldots, \omega_{n-1}$ be n n-bits integers and let $u_0, u_1, \ldots$ be a sequence of bits generated by a linear feedback shift register (LFSR) over $\mathbb{F}_2$ with an irreducible characteristic polynomial of order n. At step i, the *knapsack generator* computes

$$v_i = \sum_{i=0}^{n-1} u_{i+j} \omega_j \mod 2^n$$

and outputs the leading $n - \ell$ bits of v_i.

This generator is defined by $n^2 + 2n$ bits: n bits for the public feedback polynomial, n bits for the initial control bits and n^2 bits for the weights.

The *fast knapsack generator* is a knapsack generator with special weights introduced by von zur Gathen and Shparlinski in 2009 [7]. We replace the arbitrary weights by $\omega_i = z^{n-i} y$, for y, z two integers of n bits. This new generator is defined by $4n$ bits (as we only need $2n$ bits for the weights) and faster. Instead of computing $v_{i+1} = \sum_{i=0}^{n-1} u_{i+1+j} \omega_j \mod 2^n$, with n additions, we directly compute

$$v_{i+1} = u_i zy + zv_i - u_{n+i} z^{n+1} y \mod 2^n \tag{2}$$

with only three additions. The control bits (u_i) come from a LFSR. Even if the LFSR is not cryptographically secure, as its characteristic polynomial is irreducible, we can assume the (u_i) follow a uniform distribution, at least from a statistical view point [14]. Hence the case where $v_{i+1} = zv_i \mod 2^n$ (i.e. $u_i = u_{n+i} = 0$) appears with probability $\frac{1}{4}$. Then again we will need some notations.

- $H_i = (v_i \text{ } quo \text{ } 2^\ell) \times 2^\ell + 2^{\ell-1}$, where quo denotes the quotient of the Euclidean division (H_i is constructed from the output, hence it is known)
- $\delta_i = v_i - H_i$ (δ_i represents the ℓ discarded bits, it is unknown)
- m is the number of outputs we have.

The trick in this attack is to notice our PRNG behaves like a LCG in one iteration with probability $1/4$. As we have two different algorithms to attack our specific LCG, we will have two different algorithms to attack the fast knapsack generator. These two attacks follow the same scheme: choosing when we are going to assume the PRNG behaves like a LCG, using an attack against the assumed LCG, obtain a z and some complete internal states, using the following outputs to guess the y and finally check the consistency.

4.1 Attack via Coppersmith Method with Consecutive Outputs

Finding z: We choose $k + 1$ consecutive outputs out of m, hence we choose k steps where we assume the PRNG acts as a LCG. On these $k + 1$ outputs H_i's we apply the first algorithm we have against our specific LCG and obtain the δ_i's completing the $k + 1$ chosen outputs (as $v_i = H_i + \delta_i$). If our assumptions is false, the δ_i's returned by our Coppersmith method might not be integers. If it is the case, we start again with other sets of $k + 1$ consecutive outputs until the

δ_i's are integers. Then we can complete our outputs to obtain $k + 1$ complete consecutive internal states. Due to the use of a highly composite modulus 2^n, computing the z is not completely straightforward. If we know v_i and v_{i+1} such that $v_{i+1} = zv_i \bmod 2^n$ we might have to deal with a v_i non-invertible mod 2^n. But usually the exponent of the factor 2 in v_i does not exceed 5 so it is never a problem to do an exhaustive search on the possible values for z.

Finding y: Based on our first assumption, we know z and $k+1$ complete internal states of our PRNG. We call v_i our last known complete internal state and concentrate on v_{i+1} and v_{i+2}. Based on the structure of the PRNG, there is only 16 possibilities for the relations between v_i, v_{i+1} and v_{i+2}. If these relations are part of the 8 following possibilities, we can recover y again with a Coppersmith method using a lattice of dimension 4.

$$\begin{cases} v_{i+1} = zv_i + zy & \bmod 2^n \\ v_{i+2} = zv_{i+1} + zy \bmod 2^n \end{cases} \qquad \begin{cases} v_{i+1} = zv_i - z^{n+1}y & \bmod 2^n \\ v_{i+2} = zv_{i+1} - z^{n+1}y \bmod 2^n \end{cases}$$

$$\begin{cases} v_{i+1} = zv_i + zy & \bmod 2^n \\ v_{i+2} = zv_{i+1} - z^{n+1}y \bmod 2^n \end{cases} \qquad \begin{cases} v_{i+1} = zv_i - z^{n+1}y \bmod 2^n \\ v_{i+2} = zv_{i+1} + zy & \bmod 2^n \end{cases}$$

$$\begin{cases} v_{i+1} = zv_i + zy & \bmod 2^n \\ v_{i+2} = zv_{i+1} + zy - z^{n+1}y \bmod 2^n \end{cases} \qquad \begin{cases} v_{i+1} = zv_i + zy - z^{n+1}y \bmod 2^n \\ v_{i+2} = zv_{i+1} + zy & \bmod 2^n \end{cases}$$

$$\begin{cases} v_{i+1} = zv_i - z^{n+1}y & \bmod 2^n \\ v_{i+2} = zv_{i+1} + zy - z^{n+1}y \bmod 2^n \end{cases} \qquad \begin{cases} v_{i+1} = zv_i + zy - z^{n+1}y \bmod 2^n \\ v_{i+2} = zv_{i+1} - z^{n+1}y & \bmod 2^n \end{cases}$$

For example, we assume we are in the first case, hence

$$\begin{cases} v_{i+1} = zv_i + zy & \bmod 2^n \\ v_{i+2} = zv_{i+1} + zy & \bmod 2^n. \end{cases}$$

Subtracting the first equation to the second and replacing v_{i+1} by $H_{i+1} + \delta_{i+1}$ and v_{i+2} by $H_{i+2} + \delta_{i+2}$, we obtain:

$$H_{i+2} + \delta_{i+2} - H_{i+1} - \delta_{i+1} = zH_{i+1} + z\delta_{i+1} - zv_i \quad \bmod 2^n$$

(we recall that, at this point, v_i and z are assumed to be known). Hence $(\delta_{i+1}, \delta_{i+2})$ is a root of a polynomial in two variables of degree 1 mod 2^n. It can be recovered thanks to a Coppersmith method. Once we have v_{i+1}, computing y is straightforward (once again, if the δ_i are not integers it means either our first assumption is false either the couple (v_{i+1}, v_{i+2}) is not of this form).

Remark 2. *There are several little optimisations/improvements we can do in this step. But it is mostly finding more particular cases so, for the sake of simplicity, we decided to not describe them here.*

Checking consistency: We have made a first assumption: the $k+1$ chosen outputs of our PRNG can be seen as truncated outputs of a LCG. We have made a second assumption: (v_{i+1}, v_{i+2}) is of a chosen form between the eight listed possibilities. If y and z are the correct ones, we should be able to check consistency from one to the next (for example H_{i+3} should be given by one of the four following internal states: zv_{i+2}, $zy + zv_{i+2}$, $zv_{i+2} - z^{n+1}y$ or $zy + zv_{i+2} - z^{n+1}y$). If the consistency is not obtained, it means one of our assumption is false and we must either change our assumption on (v_{i+1}, v_{i+2}) if we did not explore the eight possibilities, either start again from the beginning with a new set of consecutive outputs.

Analysis of the attack. For a given k, we want to know m the number of outputs needed such that the probability of the PRNG acting as a LCG at least k times in a row is greater than $1/2$. We have done the computation and we do not obtain a nice formula for m. The details are given in Appendix A and here we will only give the numerical result for $k = \{2, 3, 4, 5\}$.

Once m is greater than the computed bound, we hope there will be a set of $k + 1$ consecutive outputs acting like a LCG. The two outputs following the last chosen one need to be in eight possibilities out of sixteen. Again it happens with probability $1/2$.

Hence, for a given k, the attack should work with probability greater than $1/4$ if m is greater than what is given in the table and $l/n < \binom{k}{2}/\Gamma(k)$ (as seen in Sect. 3). In this case we will have to run in the worst case $m - k$ instances of LLL on a lattice of dimension $k + 1 + 3\binom{k}{2}$ and $8(m - k)$ instances of LLL on a lattice of dimension 4, each with entries of size n.

k		2	3	4	5
m		15	58	236	944
number of lattices $\leqslant$		13	55	232	939
dimension of lattices		6	13	23	36
ℓ/n (theoretical) $<$		1/7	3/16	6/29	5/23
ℓ/n (experimental) $\leqslant$		0.3	0.35	0.38	0.40
computing time for $n = 32$		0.02s	0.11s	0.9s	10s
computing time for $n = 64$		0.02s	0.15s	2s	28s
computing time for $n = 1024$		0.04s	1.1s	31s	(950s)

The computing time is an average of ten instances of the algorithm. When the algorithm becomes too slow to compute the average we give an estimation. The estimation comes from the execution time for one lattice multiplied by half the number of lattices. These specials cases are between parenthesis.

4.2   Attack via Coppersmith Method Without Consecutive Outputs

Finding z. We choose k outputs H_i out of $m - 1$ outputs (we cannot choose the last one) and consider k pairs of outputs (H_i, H_{i+1}). It does not mean we work with $2k$ outputs as some pairs can overlap. On these k pairs of outputs we apply the second algorithm we have against our specific LCG and obtain δ_i's. If our assumption is false, the δ_i's might not be integers. If it is the case, we start again with other sets of k pairs of outputs until the δ_i's are integers. Then we can complete our outputs (as $v_i = H_i + \delta_i$) to obtain at most $2k$ complete consecutive internal states. Computing the z is not completely straightforward. If we know v_i and v_{i+1} such that $v_{i+1} = zv_i \mod 2^n$ we might have to deal with a v_i non-invertible mod 2^n. But usually the exponent of the factor 2 in v_i does not exceed 5 so it is never a problem to do an exhaustive search on the possible values for z.

The steps of *Finding y* and *Checking consistency* are the same as for the previous attack.

Analysis of the attack. We want our PRNG to act at least k times like a LCG with probability greater than $1/2$. We suppose we clock our PRNG $m - 1$ times (so we obtain m outputs). The probability that the PRNG acts as a LCG on one iteration is $1/4$. Hence we want k to be the unique *median* of a Binomial distribution of parameters $(m - 1, 1/4)$. We consider the following theorem from [10].

Theorem 1. *If X is a $B(n, p)$, the median can be found by rounding off np to k if the following condition holds:*

$$|k - np| \leqslant \min(p, 1 - p)$$

k is the unique median except when $p = 1/2$ and n is odd.

In our case where $p = 1/4$ we see that given a k the smaller number of trials satisfying this inequality is $4k - 1$. Hence we choose $m = 4k$.

Once m is greater than $4k$, we hope our PRNG will act at least k times like a LCG. The two outputs following the last chosen one need to be in eight possibilities out of sixteen. Again it happens with probability $1/2$.

Hence, for a given k, the attack should work with probability greater than $1/4$ if m is greater than $4k$ and $l/n < (k - 1)/4k$ (as seen in Sect. 3). In this case we will have to run in the worst case $\binom{4k}{k}$ instances of LLL on a lattice of dimension at worst $2k + 3\binom{k}{2}$ and $8\binom{4k}{k}$ instances of LLL on a lattice of dimension 4, each with entries of size n.

k	2	3	4	5	6	7	8
m	8	12	16	20	24	28	32
number of lattices $\leq$	21	165	1365	11628	100947	888030	7888725
dimension of lattices $\leq$	7	15	26	40	57	77	100
ℓ/n (theoretical) $<$	1/8	1/6	3/16	1/5	5/24	3/14	7/32
ℓ/n (experimental) $\leqslant$	0.16	0.25	0.31	0.34	0.36	0.38	0.40
computing time for $n = 32$	$0.04s$	$0.6s$	$11s$	$(115s)$	$(2000s)$	$(11h)$	$(219h)$
computing time for $n = 64$	$0.03s$	$0.7s$	$21s$	$(230s)$	$(4000s)$	$(25h)$	$(548h)$
computing time for $n = 1024$	$0.06s$	$4s$	$(130s)$	$(4500s)$	$(22h)$	$(617h)$	$(1.6y)$

Again, the computing time is an average of ten instances of the algorithm running on the same laptop. When the algorithm becomes too slow to compute the average, we give an estimation. The estimation comes from the execution time for one lattice multiplied by half the number of lattices. These specials cases are between parenthesis.

Remark 3. *To compute these probabilities, we assumed we always had two outputs (v_{i+1}, v_{i+2}) following our output v_i. This is not always the case but this problem can be easily solved by choosing either another known v_i or the two preceding values of v_i instead of the following ones.*

Remark 4. *As the number of instances of LLL needed is $\binom{4k}{k}$, the computing time of the algorithm quickly explodes.*

4.3   Attack via Stern's Attack on the LCG

Finding z: We choose $k + 1$ consecutive outputs out of m, hence we choose k steps where we assume the PRNG acts as a LCG. On these $k + 1$ outputs H_i's we apply the modified algorithm we have against our specific LCG and obtain a list of possible values for z. For each of these values, we are going to compute what we assume the internal states are. If we have the right value of z, then the vector of internal states $(v_i, \ldots, v_{i+k})$ is in the lattice spanned by the rows of the following matrix:

$$\begin{pmatrix} 1 & z & \ldots & z^k \\ 0 & 2^n & \ldots & 0 \\ & & \ddots & \\ 0 & 0 & 0 & 2^n \end{pmatrix}.$$

Also, this vector is close to the target vector $(H_i, \ldots, H_{i+k})$. Hence we use a CVP solver on our matrix and the target vector to find our vector of internal states.

Remark 5. *CVP stands for Closest Vector Problem. Given a lattice Λ and an arbitrary target vector T, a CVP solver outputs the closest vector to T which is in the lattice Λ.*

The steps of *Finding y* and *Checking consistency* are the same as for the previous attack.

4.4   Summary of Our Results

These computing times are averages on a hundred instances of the algorithm. As usual between parenthesis are the estimations given by the time for one lattice multiplied by half of the number of lattices.

– Attack via a Coppersmith method with consecutive outputs

ℓ/n	0.2	0.3	0.4	0.5
m	15	15	944	*none*
computing time for $n = 32$	0.02s	0.02s	10s	*none*
computing time for $n = 64$	0.02s	0.02s	28s	*none*
computing time for $n = 1024$	0.04	0.04s	(950s)	*none*

– Attack via a Coppersmith method without consecutive outputs

ℓ/n	0.2	0.3	0.4	0.5
m	12	16	32	*none*
computing time for $n = 32$	0.6s	11s	(219h)	*none*
computing time for $n = 64$	0.7s	21s	(548h)	*none*
computing time for $n = 1024$	4s	(130s)	(1.6y)	*none*

– Attack via Stern's algorithm

ℓ/n	0.2	0.3	0.4	0.5
m	944	15138	60565	3876354
computing time for $n = 32$	3.6s	(53s)	(300s)	(16h)
computing time for $n = 64$	11s	(227s)	(1200s)	(38h)
computing time for $n = 1024$	(700s)	(4h)	(11h)	(970h)

The next generator we are going to analyse is based on constant-recursive sequences. These mathematical objects are completely linear. In the one hand it means they are fairly easy to manipulate. In the other hand it makes them very vulnerable to algebraic attacks. To hides the linear properties of its internal states, the generator uses two different moduli (as the reduction by two different moduli does not commute: $(a + b \bmod m_1) \bmod m_2$ tends to be different from $(a + b \bmod m_2) \bmod m_1$).

5   Combined Multiple Recursive Generators (CMRG)

These PRNGs output a linear operation between two or more congruential constant-recursive sequences over different moduli, pairwise coprime, of the same length. The coefficients of the sequences and the moduli are known, only the initial conditions are secret. We are going to focus on CMRG outputting the difference between two constant-recursive sequences of order three, (x_i) and (y_i) over two different moduli m_1 and m_2 of the same length n.

At step i, the generator computes

$$x_i = a_{11}x_{i-1} + a_{12}x_{i-2} + a_{13}x_{i-3} \mod m_1$$
$$y_i = a_{21}y_{i-1} + a_{22}y_{i-2} + a_{23}y_{i-3} \mod m_2$$
$$z_i = x_i - y_i \mod m_1$$

and outputs z_i.

The values $a_{11}, a_{12}, a_{13}, , a_{21}, a_{22}, a_{23}, m_1$ and m_2 are known. The values x_0, x_1, x_2, y_0, y_1 and y_2 form the seed of the generator.

As m_1 and m_2 are coprime, by the Chinese Reminder Theorem we know that the sequences (x_i) and (y_i) are projections of a lifted constant-recursive sequence modulo $m_1 m_2$ that we will call (X_i). This new sequence will be defined by $X_{i+3} = AX_{i+2} + BX_{i+1} + CX_i \mod m_1 m_2$ where A, B, C are given by:

$$A \equiv a_{11} \bmod m_1 \quad \text{and} \quad A \equiv a_{21} \bmod m_2$$
$$B \equiv a_{12} \bmod m_1 \quad \text{and} \quad B \equiv a_{22} \bmod m_2$$
$$C \equiv a_{13} \bmod m_1 \quad \text{and} \quad C \equiv a_{23} \bmod m_2$$

and the initial conditions X_0, X_1, X_2 in $\{0, \ldots, m_1 m_2 - 1\}$ satisfy:

$$X_0 \equiv x_0 \bmod m_1 \quad \text{and} \quad X_0 \equiv y_0 \bmod m_2$$
$$X_1 \equiv x_1 \bmod m_1 \quad \text{and} \quad X_1 \equiv y_1 \bmod m_2$$
$$X_2 \equiv x_2 \bmod m_1 \quad \text{and} \quad X_2 \equiv y_2 \bmod m_2.$$

The sequences (x_i) and (y_i) are given by $x_i = X_i \bmod m_1$ and $y_i = X_i \bmod m_2$.

5.1   Attack on the MRG32

Notations: We denote by z_i' the integer value $x_i - y_i$ which can be different from $z_i = x_i - y_i \bmod m_1$. As x_i is already in $\{0, \ldots, m_1 - 1\}$ and y_i is already in $\{0, \ldots, m_2 - 1\}$, we have that $z_i' = z_i$ or $z_i' = z_i - m_1$. We also denote by u the inverse of m_1 modulo m_2 ($um_1 \equiv 1 \bmod m_2$).

Proposition 1. *For every $i \geq 0$, $(x_i, x_{i+1}, x_{i+2}, x_{i+3})$ is a root modulo $m_1 m_2$ of*

$$P_i(v_i, v_{i+1}, v_{i+2}, v_{i+3}) = k_{i+3}m_1 + v_{i+3} - A(k_{i+2}m_1 + v_{i+2}) - B(k_{i+1}m_1 + v_{i+1}) - C(k_i m_1 + v_i)$$

where k_i is the only integer in $\{0, \ldots, m_2 - 1\}$ such that $k_i \equiv -z_i' u \bmod m_2$.

Proof. As $X_i \equiv x_i \bmod m_1$, there exists an integer k_i such that $X_i = k_i m_1 + x_i$. For the same reason, there exists an integer $\hat{k}_i$ such that $X_i = \hat{k}_i m_2 + y_i$. Hence

$$z_i' = x_i - y_i = \hat{k}_i m_2 - k_i m_1.$$

Thus $k_i \equiv -z_i' u \bmod m_2$. As X_i is in $\{0, \ldots, m_1 m_2 - 1\}$, then k_i is in $\{0, \ldots, m_2 - 1\}$. To obtain the polynomial P_i we need to remember that $X_{i+3} = AX_{i+2} + BX_{i+1} + CX_i \bmod m_1 m_2$.

We have established that (x_0, x_1, x_2, x_3) is a root modulo $m_1 m_2$ of

$$P_1(v_0, v_1, v_2, v_3) = k_3 m_1 + v_3 - A(k_2 m_1 + v_2) - B(k_1 m_1 + v_1) - C(k_0 m_1 + v_0)$$

and each of its coordinates is bounded by m_1.

If this root is the only small one, we can expect to retrieve it thanks to a Coppersmith method. But it tends not to be the case. We will consider Λ the lattice containing all the differences between two roots of P_1 modulo $m_1 m_2$. If the smallest vector v of Λ has its coordinates smaller than m_1, then the vector $(x_0, x_1, x_2, x_3) - v$ could be a smaller root of $P_1 \bmod m_1 m_2$ and our attack might not work.

The *Gaussian heuristic* "predicts" that if Λ is a full-rank lattice and C is a measurable subset of $\mathbb{R}^d$, then the number of points of $\Lambda \cap C$ is roughly $\mathrm{vol}(C)/\mathrm{vol}(\Lambda)$. In particular, this asserts that the norm of the shortest (non-zero) vector of Λ should be close to $\sqrt{d}\,\mathrm{vol}(\Lambda)^{1/d}$.

If we have two roots (x_0, x_1, x_2) and (x_0', x_1', x_2') then

$$(x_3 - x_3') - A(x_2 - x_2') - B(x_1 - x_1') - C(x_0 - x_0') \equiv 0 \bmod m_1 m_2.$$

Hence the lattice Λ is spanned by the rows of the following matrix:

$$\begin{pmatrix} 1 & 0 & 0 & C \\ 0 & 1 & 0 & B \\ 0 & 0 & 1 & A \\ 0 & 0 & 0 & m_1 m_2 \end{pmatrix}.$$

Following the Gaussian heuristic, we can expect the shortest vector of this lattice to be of norm $\sqrt{4}(m_1 m_2)^{1/4} \approx \sqrt{4} \times 2^{n/2} < \sqrt{4} \times 2^n \approx \sqrt{4} m_1$. Hence it is unlikely that (x_0, x_1, x_2, x_3) is the only root of P_1 modulo $m_1 m_2$ such that each of its coordinates is bounded by m_1. We try to add other polynomials, hoping it will reduce the number of common roots.

If we consider the three polynomials P_1, P_2 and P_3, the lattice containing the difference between two commons roots will be spanned by the rows of the following matrix:

$$\begin{pmatrix} 1 & 0 & 0 & C & AC & BC + A^2C \\ 0 & 1 & 0 & B & C & B^2 + AC \\ 0 & 0 & 1 & A & (B + A^2)C + 2AB + A^3 \\ 0 & 0 & 0 & m_1 m_2 & 0 & 0 \\ 0 & 0 & 0 & 0 & m_1 m_2 & 0 \\ 0 & 0 & 0 & 0 & 0 & m_1 m_2 \end{pmatrix}.$$

Following the Gaussian heuristic, we can expect the shortest vector of this lattice to be of norm $\sqrt{6}(m_1 m_2^3)^{1/6} \approx \sqrt{6} \times 2^n \approx \sqrt{6} m_1$. We are at the limit, we have no clear indication that the smallest vector of Λ is big enough. We cannot say that $(x_0, x_1, x_2, x_3, x_4, x_5)$ is the only common root of P_1, P_2 and P_3 modulo $m_1 m_2$ such that each of its coordinates is bounded by m_1. Adding two polynomials was not enough. But the smallest difference between two common roots is far greater than before. So we keep adding polynomials.

If we consider the four polynomials P_1, P_2, P_3 and P_4, the lattice containing the difference between two commons roots will be spanned by the rows of the following matrix:

$$
\begin{pmatrix}
1 & 0 & 0 & C & AC & BC + A^2C & C^2 + 2ABC + A^3C \\
0 & 1 & 0 & B & C & B^2 + AC & 2BC + AB^2 + A^2C \\
0 & 0 & 1 & A & (B + A^2) & C + 2AB + A^3 & 2AC + B^2 + 2A^2B + A^4 \\
0 & 0 & 0 & m_1 m_2 & 0 & 0 & 0 \\
0 & 0 & 0 & 0 & m_1 m_2 & 0 & 0 \\
0 & 0 & 0 & 0 & 0 & m_1 m_2 & 0 \\
0 & 0 & 0 & 0 & 0 & 0 & m_1 m_2
\end{pmatrix}.
$$

Following the Gaussian heuristic, we can expect the shortest vector of this lattice to be of norm $\sqrt{7}(m_1 m_2^4)^{1/7} \approx \sqrt{7} \times 2^{8n/7} > \sqrt{7} \times 2^n \approx \sqrt{7} m_1$. Hence $(x_0, x_1, x_2, x_3, x_4, x_5, x_6)$ is likely to be the only common root of P_1, P_2, P_3 and P_4 modulo $m_1 m_2$ such that each of its coordinates is bounded by m_1. We could wonder if it is relevant to use the Gaussian heuristic in such specific cases but the parameters given by this reasoning are experimentally recovered.

We can now describe the attack. From a_{11}, a_{12}, a_{13}, , a_{21}, a_{22} and a_{23} we construct A, B and C. Then we consider 7 outputs $z_0, \ldots, z_6$, and from them we guess $z_0', \ldots, z_6'$ (we recall that $z_i' = z_i$ or $z_i' = z_i - m_1$). Now we have all the values we need to construct P_1, P_2, P_3 and P_4 as described in Proposition 1.

We use a Coppersmith method to find the only common root of P_1, P_2, P_3 and P_4 mod $m_1 m_2$ with all of its coordinates bound by m_1. If we have correctly guessed the z_i''s, this root has to be $(x_0, x_1, x_2, x_3, x_4, x_5, x_6)$, hence the initial conditions we were searching for. Finally we check the consistency thanks to an eighth output.

Knowing the z_i's we have 2^7 set of possible values for the z_i's. For each set we run one instance of LLL on a lattice of dimension 12 (8 monomials + 4 polynomials) and entries of size n. So the time complexity is $\mathcal{O}(n^3)$.

5.2   The MRG32k3a by L'Écuyer

For this particular PRNG, the public values are $m_1 = 2^{32} - 209$, $m_2 = 2^{32} - 22853$, $a_{11} = 0$ $a_{12} = 1403580$, $a_{13} = 810728$, $a_{21} = 527612$, $a_{22} = 0$ and $a_{23} = 1370589$.

If we consider the four polynomials P_1, P_2, P_3, P_4 we find that the smallest difference between two common roots modulo $m_1 m_2$ is $(-12600073455, 8717013482, 35458453228, 57149468535, 25239696855, -3505005772, 66309741613)$. We can see that each of its coordinates is greater than $2 \times m_1$, this ensures that $(x_0, x_1, x_2, x_3, x_4, x_5, x_6)$ will be the only small common root of P_1, P_2, P_3 and P_4 modulo $m_1 m_2$. Our algorithm retrieves the initial conditions in 0.01 s with 8 outputs.

A   Bernoulli Trials

We suppose that we have n Bernoulli trials, each with a probability of success of p. We want to compute the probability of having a *run* of at least k consecutive successes. We denote this probability $Pr(n, p, k)$.

As we cannot have more successes than trials, if $k > n$ then $Pr(n, p, k) = 0$. If $k = n$, it means all the trials must be successes, hence $Pr(n, p, k) = p^k$.

If $n > k$ we have two excluding possibilities to have k successes. First possibility, a run of k successes happen in the last $n - 1$ trials. Second possibility, a run of k successes happen in the k first trial an there is *no* run of k successes in the last $n - 1$ trials. It means the first k trials are successes, then the $k + 1$-th trial is a failure and there is no run of k successes in the $n - k - 1$ remaining trials. Hence the probability of having a run of k successes in n trials when $n > k$ is $Pr(n, p, k) = Pr(n - 1, p, k) + p^k \times (1 - p) \times (1 - Pr(n - k - 1, p, k))$

We fix k and p and consider $S[n] = 1 - Pr(n, p, k)$. We notice that $(S[n])_{n \in \mathbb{N}}$ is a constant-recursive sequence:

$$S[n + 1] = S[n] - p^k(1 - p)S[n - k - 1]$$

of order $k+1$ with initial terms being $S[0] = \cdots = S[k-1] = 1$ and $S[k] = 1 - p^k$.

The explicit values of the sequence are given by $S[n] = C_1(r_1)^n + \cdots + C_{k+1}(r_{k+1})^n$ where the r_i are the roots of the characteristic polynomial $x^{k+1} - x^k + p^k(1 - p)$ and the C_i are constants given by the initial terms.

In our case, we have m outputs and we want to know the probability of having $k + 1$ consecutive internal states of the form $v_{i+1} = zv_i \bmod 2^n$. Given a v_i, the probability that $v_{i+1} = zv_i \bmod 2^n$ is $1/4$. So our problem is to compute the probability of having a run of at least k successes in a sequence of $m - 1$ Bernoulli trials, the probability of success of each trial being $1/4$.

In the following table we give the minimal values of m such that the probability of having a run of k successes in $m - 1$ trials is greater than $1/2$.

k	2	3	4	5	6	7	8	11
m	15	58	236	944	3783	15138	60565	3876354

(Warning, these values are given by numerical approximations, they might not be exact.)

B Improvement of Coppersmith?

Let P be the polynomial constructed thanks to the outputs of our LCG. We are searching for a root of P modulo N. In Sect. 2, we saw that we had two possibilities. We could directly construct the matrix used in the Coppersmith method $\mathcal{M}$ with only P or we could build a bigger set of polynomials P_i of the form $f = y_0^{k_0}, \ldots, y_n^{k_n} P^{k_p}$. In Sect. 3, we presented attacks were the set of polynomials was not extended. The goal of this appendix will be to try to find a family of polynomials P_i's such that we can retrieve the root even when more bits are discarded.

For the reader familiar with [1] by Benhamouda et al., we will use the same notations. We denote $\mathcal{P}$ the bigger set constructed from P. The polynomials in $\mathcal{P}$ are of the form $f = y_0^{k_0}, \ldots, y_n^{k_n} P^{k_p}$ and all linearly independent. We denote by $\chi_{\mathcal{P}}(f)$ the multiplicity of our small root as a root of $f \bmod N$: $\chi_{\mathcal{P}}(f) = k_p$. We denote $\mathfrak{M}$ the set of all the monomials appearing in $\mathcal{P}$. If m in $\mathfrak{M}$ is of the form $y_0^{k_0} \ldots y_n^{k_n}$, we denote $\chi_{\mathfrak{M}}(m) = k_0 + \cdots + k_n$. We know by Eq. (1) that the attack is suppose to work as long as

$$\ell/n \le \frac{\sum_{f \in \mathcal{P}} \chi_{\mathcal{P}}(f)}{\sum_{m \in \mathfrak{M}} \chi_{\mathfrak{M}}(m)}$$

where ℓ is the number of discarded bits and n the size of the internal states of our generator.

B.1 Consecutive Outputs

Here our Polynomial is $P = y_1^2 + 2H_1 y_1 + H_1^2 - y_0 y_2 - H_0 y_2 - H_2 y_0 - H_0 H_2$. We fix a parameter T and choose $\mathcal{P}_T$ as following:

$$\mathcal{P}_T = \{y_0^{k_0} y_1^{\epsilon} y_2^{k_2} P^{k_p} | \epsilon \in \{0,1\}, k_0 + \epsilon + k_2 + 2k_p \le T\}$$

All the polynomials in $\mathcal{P}_T$ are linearly independent. Indeed, if we consider the monomial order $y_1 > y_0 > y_2$ then the leading monomial of $y_0^{k_0} y_1^{\epsilon} y_2^{k_2} P^{k_p}$ is $y_1^{2k_p + \epsilon} y_0^{k_0} y_2^{k_2}$ thus all leading monomials are different.

We are not going to precisely compute the set of monomial of $\mathcal{P}_T$ instead we are going to approach it with

$$\mathfrak{M}_T = \{y_0^{k_0} y_1^{k_1} y_2^{k_2} | k_0 + k_1 + k_2 \le T\}.$$

Now we must compute $\sum_{f \in \mathcal{P}_T} \chi_{\mathcal{P}_T}(f)$ and $\sum_{m \in \mathfrak{M}_T} \chi_{\mathfrak{M}_T}(m)$:

$$\sum_{f \in \mathcal{P}_T} \chi_{\mathcal{P}_T}(f) = \sum_{k_0=0}^{T-2} \sum_{\epsilon=0}^{1} \sum_{k_2=0}^{T-2-k_0-\epsilon} \sum_{k_p=1}^{\lfloor \frac{T-k_0-\epsilon-k_2}{2} \rfloor} k_p$$

$$= \lfloor \frac{((T+1)^2 - 1) \times ((T+1)^2 - 3)}{48} \rfloor$$

$$\sum_{m \in \mathfrak{M}_T} \chi_{\mathfrak{M}_T}(m) = \sum_{k_0=0}^{T} \sum_{k_1=0}^{T-k_0} \sum_{k_2=0}^{T-k_0-k_1} k_0 + k_1 + k_2$$

$$= \frac{T(T+1)(T+2)(T+3)}{8}.$$

Thus this new construction should allow us to recover the small root as long as

$$\ell/n \leq \lfloor \frac{((T+1)^2 - 1) \times ((T+1)^2 - 3)}{48} \rfloor \times \frac{8}{T(T+1)(T+2)(T+3)}.$$

This value tends to $1/6$.

To obtain a bound bigger than $1/7$ (our already achieved result), we need $T \geq 13$. But $T = 13$ means our lattice would be of dimension 924, and running the LLL algorithm on a lattice of dimension 900 is hardly doable.

B.2   Not Consecutive Outputs

Here our Polynomial is $P = y_0 y_{i+1} - y_1 y_i + H_{i+1} y_0 + H_0 y_{i+1} - H_i y_1 - H_1 y_i + H_0 H_{i+1} - H_1 H_i$. We fix a parameter T and choose $\mathcal{P}_T$ as following:

$$\mathcal{P}_T = \{y_0^{k_0} y_1^{k_1} y_i^{k_i} P^{k_p} | k_0 + k_1 + k_i + 2k_p \leq T\} \bigcup \{y_1^{k_1} y_i^{k_i} y_{i+1}^{k_{i+1}} P^{k_p} | k_1 + k_i + k_{i+1} + 2k_p \leq T\}.$$

All the polynomials in $\mathcal{P}_T$ are linearly independent.

We are not going to precisely compute the set of monomial of $\mathcal{P}_T$ instead we are going to approach it with

$$\mathfrak{M}_T = \{y_0^{k_0} y_1^{k_1} y_i^{k_i} y_{i+1}^{k_{i+1}} | k_0 + k_1 + k_i + k_{i+1} \leq T\}.$$

Now we must compute $\sum_{f \in \mathcal{P}_T} \chi_{\mathcal{P}_T}(f)$ and $\sum_{m \in \mathfrak{M}_T} \chi_{\mathfrak{M}_T}(m)$:

$$\sum_{f \in \mathcal{P}_T} \chi_{\mathcal{P}_T}(f) = 2 \left(\sum_{k_0=0}^{T-2} \sum_{k_1=0}^{T-2-k_0} \sum_{k_i=0}^{T-2-k_0-k_1} \sum_{k_p=1}^{\lfloor \frac{T-k_0-k_1-k_2}{2} \rfloor} k_p \right)$$

$$= \frac{(T+2)(2T^4 + 16T^3 + 28T^2 - 16T + 15 \times (-1)^T - 15)}{480}$$

$$\sum_{m \in \mathfrak{M}_T} \chi_{\mathfrak{M}_T}(m) = \sum_{k_0=0}^{T} \sum_{k_1=0}^{T-k_0} \sum_{k_i=0}^{T-k_0-k_1} \sum_{k_{i+1}=0}^{T-k_0-k_1-k_i} k_0 + k_1 + k_i + k_{i+1}$$

$$= \frac{T(T+1)(T+2)(T+3)(T+4)}{30}.$$

Thus this new construction should allow us to recover the small root as long as

$$\ell/n \leq \frac{(2T^4 + 16T^3 + 28T^2 - 16T + 15 \times (-1)^T - 15)}{T(T+1)(T+3)(T+4)} \times \frac{30}{480}.$$

This value tends to $1/8$. But our second attack with one polynomial already recover the small root when $\ell/n \leq 1/8$. Hence adding more polynomials in our Coppersmith method does not seem relevant.

References

1. Benhamouda, F., Chevalier, C., Thillard, A., Vergnaud, D.: Easing coppersmith methods using analytic combinatorics: applications to public-key cryptography with weak pseudorandomness. In: Cheng, C.-M., Chung, K.-M., Persiano, G., Yang, B.-Y. (eds.) PKC 2016, Part II. LNCS, vol. 9615, pp. 36–66. Springer, Heidelberg (2016). https://doi.org/10.1007/978-3-662-49387-8_3
2. Bouillaguet, C., Martinez, F., Sauvage, J.: Practical seed-recovery for the PCG pseudo-random number generator. IACR Trans. Symmetric Cryptology **2020**(3), 175–196 (2020)
3. Ferrenberg, A.M., Landau, D.P., Wong, Y.J.: Monte Carlo simulations: hidden errors from "good" random number generators. Phys. Rev. Lett. **69**, 3382–3384 (1992)
4. Franke, D.: How I hacked hacker news (with arc security advisory) (2009). https://news.ycombinator.com/item?id=639976
5. Frieze, A.M., Hastad, J., Kannan, R., Lagarias, J.C., Shamir, A.: Reconstructing truncated integer variables satisfying linear congruences. SIAM J. Comput. **17**(2), 262–280 (1988)
6. Frieze, A.M., Kannan, R., Lagarias, J.C.: Linear congruential generators do not produce random sequences. In: 25th FOCS, pp. 480–484. IEEE Computer Society Press, October 1984. https://doi.org/10.1109/SFCS.1984.715950
7. Von zur Gathen, J., Shparlinski, I.E.: Subset sum pseudorandom numbers: fast generation and distribution. J. Math. Cryptol. **3**(2), 149–163 (2009)
8. Jochemsz, E., May, A.: A strategy for finding roots of multivariate polynomials with new applications in attacking RSA variants. In: Lai, X., Chen, K. (eds.) ASIACRYPT 2006. LNCS, vol. 4284, pp. 267–282. Springer, Heidelberg (2006). https://doi.org/10.1007/11935230_18
9. Joux, A., Stern, J.: Lattice reduction: a toolbox for the cryptanalyst. J. Cryptol. **11**(3), 161–185 (1998). https://doi.org/10.1007/s001459900042
10. Kaas, R., Buhrman, J.: Mean, median and mode in binomial distributions. Stat. Neerl. **34**, 13–18 (1980)
11. Knellwolf, S., Meier, W.: Cryptanalysis of the knapsack generator. In: Joux, A. (ed.) FSE 2011. LNCS, vol. 6733, pp. 188–198. Springer, Heidelberg (2011). https://doi.org/10.1007/978-3-642-21702-9_11
12. Lenstra, A.K., Lenstra, H.W., Lovász, L.: Factoring polynomials with rational coefficients. Mathematische Annalen **261**(Article), 515–534 (1982)
13. L'Écuyer, P.: Random number generation with multiple streams for sequential and parallel computing. In: 2015 Winter Simulation Conference (WSC), pp. 31–44. IEEE (2015)
14. Mitra, A.: On the properties of pseudo noise sequences with a simple proposal of randomness test. Int. J. Electr. Comput. Eng. **3**(3), 164–169 (2008)
15. Ritzenhofen, M.: On efficiently calculationg small solutions of systmes of polynomial equations: lattice-based methods and applications to cryptography. Ph.D. thesis, Verlag nicht ermittelbar (2010)
16. Rueppel, R.A., Massey, J.L.: Knapsack as a nonlinear fonction. In: IEEE International Symposium on Information Theory. IEEE Press, New York (1985)
17. Stern, J.: Secret linear congruential generators are not cryptographically secure. In: 28th FOCS, pp. 421–426. IEEE Computer Society Press, October 1987. https://doi.org/10.1109/SFCS.1987.51

18. Van der Walt, S., Colbert, S.C., Varoquaux, G.: The NumPy array: a structure for efficient numerical computation. Comput. Sci. Eng. **13**(2), 22–30 (2011)
19. Wichmann, B.A., Hill, I.D.: Algorithm as 183: an efficient and portable pseudo-random number generator. J. Roy. Stat. Soc.: Ser. C (Appl. Stat.) **31**(2), 188–190 (1982)

Lattice-Based Fault Attacks
on Deterministic Signature Schemes
of ECDSA and EdDSA

Weiqiong Cao[1,2], Hongsong Shi[2(✉)], Hua Chen[1], Jiazhe Chen[2], Limin Fan[1],
and Wenling Wu[1]

[1] Trusted Computing and Information Assurance Laboratory,
Institute of Software, Chinese Academy of Sciences, South Fourth Street 4#,
ZhongGuanCun, Beijing 100190, China
{caoweiqiong,chenhua}@iscas.ac.cn
[2] China Information Technology Security Evaluation Center, Building 1,
yard 8, Shangdi West Road, Haidian District, Beijing 100085, China

Abstract. The deterministic ECDSA and EdDSA signature schemes
have found plenty of applications since their publication, e.g., block chain
and Internet of Thing, and have been stated in RFC 6979 and RFC 8032
by IETF respectively. Their theoretical security can be guaranteed within
certain well-defined models, and since no randomness is required by the
algorithms anymore their practical risks from the flaw of random number
generators are mitigated. However, the situation is not really optimistic,
since it has been gradually found that delicately designed fault attacks
can threaten the practical security of the schemes.

In this paper, based on the random fault models of intermediate values during signature generation, we propose a lattice-based fault analysis
method to the deterministic ECDSA and EdDSA algorithms. By virtue
of the algebraic structures of the deterministic algorithms, we show that,
when providing with some faulty signatures and an associated correct
signature of the same input message, some instances of SVP or CVP
problems in some lattice can be constructed to recover the signing key.
The allowed faulty bits in the method are close to the size of the signing
key, and obviously bigger than that allowed by the existing differential fault attacks. In addition, the lattice-based approach supports more
alternative targets of fault injection, which further improves its applicability when comparing with the existing approaches.

We perform some experiments to demonstrate the effectiveness of the
key recovery method. In particular, for deterministic ECDSA/EdDSA
algorithm with 256-bit signing key, the key can be recovered efficiently
with significant probability even if the targets are affected by 250/247
faulty bits. However, this is impractical for the existing enumerating
approaches.

Keywords: Side channel attack · Fault attack · Lattice-based attack ·
Deterministic ECDSA · EdDSA

© The Author(s), under exclusive license to Springer Nature Switzerland AG 2022
S. D. Galbraith (Ed.): CT-RSA 2022, LNCS 13161, pp. 169–195, 2022.
https://doi.org/10.1007/978-3-030-95312-6_8

1   Introduction

As a fundamental building block of modern cryptography, digital signature has been widely used in practice. For its efficiency and standardization in FIPS 186 and ANSI X9.62, ECDSA has found various applications since its publication. In spite of the fact that the theoretical security of ECDSA has not been proven finally, it is still believed to be secure and connected with some hard problems in mathematics. However, side channel attacks on various implementations of ECDSA have been continuously discovered during the last decades. Some of the attacks, for example, are induced by the deficiency of the ephemeral random numbers (denoted *nonce* hereinafter) required by the scheme. If the nonce has a few bits leaked or repeated, some lattice-based approaches [12,16,23] can be employed to extract the private key by BDD [19]. This has been demonstrated several times in real IT products with ECDSA implementations [2,6,7,14,21]. Hence, an intuition to improve the security of ECDSA is to remove the randomness requirement from the algorithm. This gave birth to a study of *deterministic signature schemes*. In particular, deterministic ECDSA and EdDSA have received plenty of attention in the research of applied cryptography since recent years. They were respectively standardized in RFC 6979 and RFC 8032 and realized in cryptographic libraries of OpenSSH, Tor, TLS, etc. The deterministic version of ECDSA derives the nonce just from the private key and the input message by means of cryptographic hash or HMAC primitive. In this way, no randomness is required on the implementation platform, and it seems the threat from physical attacks is mitigated.

But the situation is not improved too much, since some new flaws in deterministic signature algorithms have been gradually identified when considering differential fault attacks (DFA) [5,27–29]. DFAs have been proven to be valid for different types of cryptographic schemes [8,9] in the literature. Generally, a DFA adversary manages to disturb the signature generation procedure (by means of voltage glitches, laser or electro-magnetic injection and so on [17]) and make the platform output faulty results, and then exploits them to do key recovery.

The first DFA introduced in [5] shows that if a fault is injected to produce a faulty signature (r', s') during the calculation of the scalar multiplication of deterministic ECDSA or EdDSA, then by the help of the correct signature (r, s) from the same signing key d and input message m, the key d can be recovered by solving some linear equations. Although the approach puts no limitation on the number of allowed faulty bits, it is limited by the possible locations (or rather *targets*) of fault injection (mainly targeting the scalar multiplication). As a relaxation, another approach was introduced in [5], which assumes only limited bits of the target (e.g., the nonce k) would be randomly affected by each fault (hereafter called storage fault). Denote the faulty value by $k' = k + \varepsilon 2^l$, with limited ε and known l to the adversary. Then by constructing a differential distinguisher, the signing key d in deterministic ECDSA can be recovered efficiently by enumerating ε. Both of the approaches have been improved later, especially by those in [27–29], where different fault injection methods and targets are exploited and experimented on different hardware platforms. A recent extension was presented in [1], where more targets of fault injection have been identified and analyzed.

From a common point of view, for the storage fault, the signing key of deterministic schemes can be recovered theoretically by adjusting fault injection actions and enumerating the possible faults. The efficiency of the existing attacks [1,5,27,28] is obviously constrained by the enumeration complexity, thus they are feasible only if the fault injection is controlled and limited bits of the targets are affected. Another limitation of the existing attacks lies in the optional types of targets that can be used for fault injection. Generally, the more targets the attack supports, the more possibility of attack paths it has, and thus the more difficult the attack is to be resisted. In fact, the targets that were considered in the existing attacks are constrained. For example, the first attack in [5] only supports two targets (*i.e.*, the scalar multiplication kG and the nonce k when calculating s during the signature generation), and although some more targets were considered later in [1], it is still far away from covering all the possible attack paths.

A promising solution is to develop lattice-based approaches. It is noticed that lattice-based fault attacks were used in analyzing plain (EC)DSA and qDSA. Targets of fault injection in [10,21,26,30] are usually the nonce itself or the scalar multiplication (with a nonce as the scalar). For those attacks to be effective, the nonce in the plain signature is supposed to be a random number. Hence it is generally thought that deterministic ECDSA is immune to them because of the deterministic nonce generation approach. This conception was later disproved by [15], where a lattice-based attack was devised to compromise deterministic signatures. The attack is specific to lattice-based cryptography, and the lattice constructed for the attack is also specific to the signature scheme. Although it casts a new light on the study of lattice-based fault attacks on more deterministic signature schemes, it is still not known whether the method is effective to deterministic ECDSA or EdDSA (since they have different algebraic structures).

In this paper, we show lattice-based fault attacks can also be applied to deterministic ECDSA and EdDSA schemes. We consider the attacks in a random fault model where a continuous bits block of fault targets is disturbed randomly. Under this model, a corresponding lattice-based key recovery method is proposed. Essentially, by virtue of the special algebraic structures of the signature generation algorithms, the method reduces the key recovery problem to the shortest/closest problems in some lattice, with the instances of the problems being constructed from the collected faulty signatures. Since the problems can be solved within some scale, the signing key can be recovered subsequently (provided that the faulty signatures are valid as per some criteria).

In comparison, some advantages of our lattice-based method over the existing approaches [1,5,27,28] makes it more practical. This is summarized as follows.

- The proposed method allows more choices of target for fault injection. A target of fault injection is denoted by the notation of the interested intermediate and the timing of using it in computation. Since a general representation method of fault is adopted to remove the discrepancies of various targets, a number of possible targets are allowed by our attacks, which relatively covers more possibilities than existing approaches. See Sect. 3.1 for detail. There are 13 and 8 fault targets for deterministic ECDSA and EdDSA respectively, even including the hash functions and the private key itself.

- The proposed method can tolerate more faulty bits. The proposed lattice method is not to enumerate all the faulty patterns, but rather to solve the instances of lattice problems. This makes the tolerable faulty bits can be close to the size of the signing key. For instance, the case of faulty bits up to 250(for 256-bit deterministic ECDSA)/247(for ed25519) has been validated in experiments efficiently. As discussed above, this is infeasible for existing approaches. See Sect. 5 for detail.

The remainder of this paper is organized as follows: Sect. 2 describes the specification of deterministic ECDSA and EdDSA, and refers some results about lattices. Section 3 introduces the fault model and lists all the fault targets. Section 4 illustrates three representative lattice-based attacks based on the described model. Section 5 describes the experimental facets of the validity of the lattice-based key recovery method. The discussion about the corresponding countermeasures is given in Sect. 6. More attacks with other fault targets are presented in Appendix A.

2   Preliminaries

2.1   Notations

We denote the finite field of prime order q by $\mathbb{F}_q$, the field of real numbers by $\mathbb{R}$, and the additive group of integer modulo n by $\mathbb{Z}_n$. Bold lowercase letters such as v denote vectors, while bold uppercase letters such as $\mathbf{M}$ denote matrix. The norm of vector $v = (v_1, \ldots, v_N) \in \mathbb{R}^N$ is denoted by $\|v\| = \sqrt{\sum_{i=1}^{N} v_i^2}$, while the multiplication of v and $\mathbf{M}$ is denoted by $v\mathbf{M}$.

2.2   The Deterministic Signature Algorithms

We recap the deterministic signature generation algorithms below by abstracting from some less important details in the specifications of RFC 6979 and RFC 8032 respectively. As shown in Algorithms 1 and 2, the analysis focuses on Step 6 of Algorithm 1 and Step 4 of Algorithm 2 during the signature generations, where the order n is a prime. Moreover, in EdDSA signature, the two b-bit subkeys d_0 and d_1 are derived by the hash function $H(d) = (h_0, h_1, \ldots, h_{2b-1})$, where d is the private key, $d_0 = 2^{b-2} + \sum_{i=3}^{b-3} 2^i h_i$ and $d_1 = (h_b, \ldots, h_{2b-1})$. The public key P satisfies $P = d_0 G$. The hash functions employed in deterministic ECDSA are generally SHA-1 and SHA-2(e.g., SHA-256 and SHA-512), which all belong to the structure of message digest. For EdDSA, the default hash function(i.e., $H(.)$) is SHA-512. In addition, there still exist other hash functions belonging to the sponge structure, such as SHAKE256(SHA-3) for Ed448. For the sake of simplicity, we just consider the compression function of SHA-2. As shown in Fig. 1, input IV and a group of message(which is extended into $L\ W_i$s), execute L-round compressions and output the final result of compression plus IV as the hash value or the next group of IV.

Algorithm 1. Signature generation of deterministic ECDSA

Require: The definition of a specific elliptic curve $E(\mathbb{F}_q)$, a base point G of the curve with order n, message m, private key d.
Ensure: Signature pair (r, s).
1: $e = H(m)$, where H is a cryptographic hash function;
2: Generate $k = F(d, e) \bmod n$, where $F(d, e)$ denotes the HMAC_DRBG function with d as its input;
3: $Q(x_1, y_1) = kG$;
4: $r = x_1 \bmod n$;
5: **if** $r = 0$ **then** goto step 2;
6: $s = k^{-1}(e + dr) \bmod n$;
7: **if** $s = 0$ **then** goto step 2;
8: **return** (r, s)

Algorithm 2. Signature generation of EdDSA

Require: The definition of a specific elliptic curve $E(\mathbb{F}_q)$, a base point G of the curve with order n, message m, private key (d_0, d_1), and public key $P(P = d_0G)$.
Ensure: Signature pair (R, s).
1: $k = H(d_1, m) \bmod n$, where H is SHA-512 by default;
2: $R(x_1, y_1) = kG$;
3: $r = H(R, P, m) \bmod n$;
4: $s = k + rd_0 \bmod n$;
5: **return** (R, s)

2.3   Problems in Some Lattice

Since the proposed attacks on deterministic signature schemes are related to the construction and computation of some problems in some lattice, we give a basic introduction on the relevant conceptions and results.

In a nutshell, a *lattice* is a discrete subgroup of $\mathbb{R}^m$, generally represented as a spanned vector space of linearly independent row vectors $b_1, b_2, \ldots, b_N \in \mathbb{R}^m$ of matrix $\mathbf{M} \in \mathbb{R}^{N \times m}$, in the form of

$$\mathcal{L} = \mathcal{L}(b_1, b_2, \ldots, b_N) = \{z = \sum_{i=1}^{N} x_i \cdot b_i | x_i \in \mathbb{Z}\}. \tag{1}$$

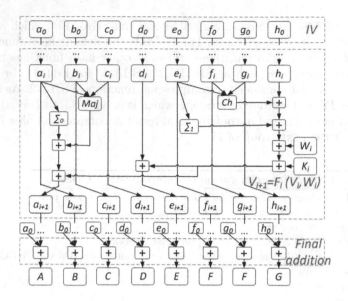

Fig. 1. Compression function of SHA2

The vectors $\boldsymbol{b}_i$s are called a basis of $\mathcal{L}$, and N is the dimension of $\mathcal{L}$. If $m = N$, then $\mathcal{L}$ is full rank. Moreover, if $\boldsymbol{b}_i$ belongs to $\mathbb{Z}^m$ for any $i = 1, ..., N$, $\mathcal{L}$ is called an integer lattice. In this way, it is straightforward to find that for every $\boldsymbol{z} \in \mathcal{L}$, there must exist $\boldsymbol{x} = \{x_1, ..., x_N\} \in \mathbb{Z}^N$ such that $\boldsymbol{z} = \boldsymbol{x}\mathbf{M}$.

In lattice, a few well-known problems have been studied, such as the *shortest vector problem*(SVP) and *closest vector problem*(CVP), which are believed to be hard in computation theoretically.

SVP: given a basis $\boldsymbol{b}_i$s of $\mathcal{L}$, find a nonzero vector $\boldsymbol{v} \in \mathcal{L}$ such that

$$\|\boldsymbol{v}\| = \lambda_1(\mathcal{L}), \tag{2}$$

where $\lambda_1(\mathcal{L})$ means the length of the shortest vector in $\mathcal{L}$.

CVP: given a basis $\boldsymbol{b}_i$s of $\mathcal{L}$ and a target vector $\boldsymbol{u} \in \mathbb{R}^m$, find a nonzero vector $\boldsymbol{v} \in \mathcal{L}$ such that

$$\|\boldsymbol{v} - \boldsymbol{u}\| = \lambda(\mathcal{L}, \boldsymbol{u}), \tag{3}$$

where $\lambda(\mathcal{L}, \boldsymbol{u})$ is the closest distance from vector $\boldsymbol{u}$ to lattice $\mathcal{L}$.

Generally, the best algorithms for solving SVP and CVP are LLL algorithm [18] or BKZ algorithm [31–33] to find their approximate solutions, i.e., solve approximate SVP and CVP. For an N-dimensional approximate SVP, a short lattice vector can be output when the approximate factor is large enough. The approximate factor of the LLL algorithm is given from Lemma 1.

Lemma 1. *[18, 20] Given an integer basis B of N-dimensional lattice $\mathcal{L}$, there exists a polynomial time algorithm to find a nonzero lattice vector x satisfying*

$$\|x\| \leq (2/\sqrt{3})^N \lambda_1 (\mathcal{L}).$$

Hence, the exact SVP and CVP can be approximated within an exponetial factor in polynomial time.

For random lattices with dimension N, Gaussian heuristic [22] expected the shortest length could be defined to be

$$\sigma(\mathcal{L}) = \sqrt{\frac{N}{2\pi e}} \mathrm{vol}(\mathcal{L})^{1/N},$$

where vol denotes the volume or determinant of $\mathcal{L}$.

Actually, the exact shortest vector of N-dimensional random lattices is much easier to be found along with the increment of the gap between the shortest length and $\sigma(\mathcal{L})$. If it is much shorter than $\sigma(\mathcal{L})$, it shall be founded in polynomial time by using LLL and related algorithms. Heuristically, as introduced in [26], assuming the lattice $\mathcal{L}$ behaves like a random lattice, if there exists a lattice vector whose distance from the target is much shorter than $\sigma(\mathcal{L})$, this lattice vector is expected to be the closest vector from the target. Accordingly, this special instance of CVP usually could be solved by Babai algorithm [4] or embedding-based SVP [25].

3 Adversarial Model

In regard to fault attacks on signature schemes, the adversary is allowed to query and at the same time disturb the signing procedure to collect the correct or faulty signatures (in the *fault injection phase*), then employs the collected signatures to recover the private key (in the *key recovery phase*). The difference between various fault attacks lies in the approaches used for both fault injection and key recovery. The following describes the adversarial model for these two phases.

3.1 Fault Injection Model

During the fault injection phase, we assume the adversary is capable of inducing *transient* faults to some specific intermediates in computation. That is, during the invocation of signature generation, faults can be injected to the data when it is transmitted over the physical circuit (such as buses), or stored in the memory cells or CPU registers. Then, after the invocation, the computation device will restore to a normal state and the faults will not be passed on to the next invocation. In this way, the computation may be temporarily tampered to produce available faulty results for the adversary.

The fault model assumes that a random fault is induced to a specific intermediate $v \in \mathbb{Z}_n$ and thereby there are (at most) w bits of v disturbed randomly, which is formalized as an addition with a (bounded) random value $\varepsilon \in \mathbb{Z}$ in the form of $v + \varepsilon 2^l \bmod n$, where $-2^w < \varepsilon < 2^w$, l is a random integer in interval $[0, l_v - w]$ and l_v is the maximum bit length of v (which is usually equal to the bit length of n). That means, there are continuous w bits of v (starting from l-th bit) disturbed randomly. It is noted that we do not use modulo-2 addition as in [13] (e.g., $v \oplus \beta 2^l \bmod n$ and β is a w-bit random number) but rather the equivalent group addition in $\mathbb{Z}_n$ to represent the effect of a fault to an intermediate. In addition, although it is hard to determine the concrete bit index l of the faulty starting location and number w of the faulty bits for each faulty signature generation, we can conservatively estimate the maximum number w of faulty bits starting from highest or least significant bit to determine l for all the faulty signature generations. For example, if we estimate there are at most w continuous faulty bits starting from the highest (or least) significant bit of v, then $l = l_v - w$ (or $l = 0$). Hence, in the following analysis, w is the pre-set maximum number of faulty bits and $l (= l_v - w$ or $0)$ is known.

To facilitate the description, the specific intermediates which may suffer from faults are called (potential) *targets* of fault injection in this paper. All the potential targets that can be exploited by the proposed attacks are listed in Table 1, in which there are 13 and 8 targets for deterministic ECDSA and EdDSA respectively. It is noted that a target is determined by two factors, i.e., *the notation of the variant* (corresponding to the intermediate), and *the timing for fault injection*. For example, the two items "k before the calculation of scalar multiplication kG" and "k during the calculation of s" are recognized as two different targets in this paper. In comparison, although some of the identified targets in Table 1 have also been considered in [1], not all of them can be exploited to do key recovery in their method, especially when the target is affected by lots of faulty bits.

On the other hand, different targets may be equivalent if considering the final effect of fault injection. For example, the targets on hash function in deterministic ECDSA: "registers before outputting the hash value $F(d, e)$", "last modular additions before outputting the hash value $F(d, e)$" and "hash value $F(d, e)$ during the reduction of k" are equivalent to the target "k before the calculation of kG", since the fault injection to the four targets will produce a same type of faulty k to construct the same key recovery model. Therefore, we define 'k before the calculation of kG" as the *representative* target of the four targets, and indicate it in **bold** type in the table. Similarly, other representative targets are also indicated in Table 1 in the same way. In addition, it is noted that all the hash functions in the targets refer to SHA-2 hash function (see Sect. 2.2).

In each of the proposed attack, the adversary is required to pre-determine at most one target and then fix the choice throughout the signature queries. Note that we don't consider the possibility that more than one target is chosen in a query, since the key recovery model doesn't support this case. Hence, there is no guarantee that the key can be recovered successfully. A set of faulty signatures are called *valid* if they are computed with the same message as input and the same equivalent target for fault injection.

Table 1. The fault targets and solved problem in our attacks on deterministic ECDSA and EdDSA.

Algorithm	Target of fault injection	Related problem
Deterministic ECDSA	r during the calculation of s	SVP
	k^{-1} during the calculation of s	SVP
	k during the calculation of s	SVP
	d during the calculation of s	SVP
	e during the calculation of s	SVP
	–Registers before outputting hash value $H(m)$	
	–Last modular additions before outputting $H(m)$	
	rd during the calculation of s	SVP
	$e + rd$ during the calculation of s	SVP
	k before the calculation of kG	CVP
	–Registers before outputting hash value $F(d, e)$	
	–Last modular additions before outputting $F(d, e)$	
	–Hash value $F(d, e)$ during the reduction of k	
EdDSA	**r during the calculation of s**	SVP
	–Registers before outputting hash value $H(R, P, m)$	
	–Last modular additions before outputting $H(R, P, m)$	
	–Hash value $H(R, P, m)$ during the reduction of r	
	k before the calculation of kG	CVP
	–Registers before outputting hash value $H(d_1, m)$	
	–Last modular additions before outputting $H(d_1, m)$	
	–Hash value $H(d_1, m)$ during the reduction of k	

It is noted that, since the paper aims to examine the conception that some deterministic signature schemes may be threatened by lattice-based fault attacks, we don't consider the so-called instruction skipping attacks (where the execution flow is disturbed such that some instructions are skipped without being executed) and persistent faults (i.e., permanently modifying data in the memory), although the model may be somehow extended to cover these cases.

3.2 Key Recovery by Solving Problems in Some Lattice

When enough faulty results are collected, the adversary manages to recover the signing key. This section is devoted to describe the fundamental idea behind the attacks, the instantiation is left to be described in Sect. 4.

Intuitively, the proposed attacks in this paper exploit some special algebraic structures of the signature generation algorithm of deterministic ECDSA and EdDSA, which are discovered by the following observations.

We found the lattice-based attacks on plain (EC)DSA [12] have demonstrated that when there are small partial bits fixed between the random nonces, for instance, the nonces k_i and k_j for any i and j ($i \neq j$) satisfy $k_i = c2^l + b_i$ and $k_j = c2^l + b_j$ (where $b_i \neq b_j$ and c is the fixed bits of the nonces), an instance of CVP in some lattice can be constructed to recover the private key. Heuristically, although our fault models (there are many partial bits disturbed randomly) are different from that in [12], the same type of faulty nonces (consisting of fixed partial bits and random partial bits) can be derived and thereby the similar instance of CVP can be constructed to recover the private key. Moreover, our fault models are more feasible than that in [12], since many of the bits can be changed randomly except several fixed bits. Furthermore, due to the particularity of deterministic signature, our attack not only targets the nonce to construct an instance of CVP, but also targets the signature result r, the hash value e, the private key and so on to construct some instances of SVP (see Table 1). The following universal representation of faults and key recovery can be extracted from all the fault models (i.e., $v+\varepsilon 2^l \bmod n$), targets in Table 1 and the algebraic structures (i.e., step 6 in Algorithm 1 and step 4 in Algorithm 2).

a) **Representation of faults.** Firstly, due to the special structure of the deterministic ECDSA and EdDSA, when gathering a correct signature and $N-1$ faulty results for a common message, the adversary can construct one of the following two relations(corresponding to SVP and CVP) for the random faulty values $\{\varepsilon_i\}_{i=1}^{N-1} \in \mathbb{Z}$ (corresponding to the faulty signatures):

$$\varepsilon_i = A_i D + h_i n, \tag{4}$$

$$\varepsilon_i = A_i D + h_i n - B_i \tag{5}$$

with $-2^w < \varepsilon_i < 2^w < n$, where A_i, B_i, w, n are known values (with prime n being the order of base point G), and D, ε_i, h_i are unknown values.

In detail, $D \in \mathbb{Z}_n$ is a function of the private key, the input message and some known variables. Then it is important to notice that when the input message is known, D is reversible and subsequently the key can be recovered. This is true when the input message is not affected by the injected faults, and by the fact that the input message is chosen and known to the adversary before the attack. Thus the goal of the proposed attacks is translated to recover D.

b) **Key recovery using lattice.** Based on the above observation, we can construct a lattice $\mathcal{L}$ with a basis being the row vectors of a matrix $\mathbf{M}$ as

$$\mathbf{M} = \begin{pmatrix} n & 0 & \cdots & & 0 \\ 0 & \ddots & & & \vdots \\ \vdots & & n & & 0 \\ A_1 & \cdots & A_{N-1} & 2^w/n \end{pmatrix}.$$

It is noted that, under the random models of faults injection, $\mathcal{L}$ behaves like a random lattice. Then, a target vector $v \in \mathcal{L}$ can be constructed from the coordinate vector $\boldsymbol{x} = (h_1, \ldots, h_{N-1}, D) \in \mathbb{Z}^N$ as

$$v = \boldsymbol{x}\mathbf{M} = (A_1 D + h_1 n, \ldots, A_{N-1}D + h_{N-1}n, D2^w/n).$$

The given volume of $\mathcal{L}$ meets $\mathrm{vol}(\mathcal{L}) = \det(\mathbf{M}) = n^{N-2}2^w$, where $\det(\mathbf{M})$ denotes the determinant of $\mathbf{M}$. Under the condition of $|\varepsilon_i| < 2^w$, supposing $f = \lceil \log n \rceil$, $w < f - \log \sqrt{2\pi e}$ and $N \gg 1 + \frac{f+\log \sqrt{2\pi e}}{f-w-\log \sqrt{2\pi e}}$, one of the following relations will hold:

(i) when the faulty value is represented by Eq. (4), we have

$$\|\boldsymbol{v}\| < \sqrt{N}2^w \ll \sqrt{\frac{N}{2\pi e}} \text{vol}(\mathcal{L})^{\frac{1}{N}}; \tag{6}$$

(ii) when the faulty value is represented by Eq. (5), then for vector $\boldsymbol{u} = (B_1, \ldots, B_{N-1}, 0) \in \mathbb{Z}^N \notin \mathcal{L}$, we have

$$\|\boldsymbol{v} - \boldsymbol{u}\| < \sqrt{N}2^w \ll \sqrt{\frac{N}{2\pi e}} \text{vol}(\mathcal{L})^{\frac{1}{N}}. \tag{7}$$

Then, heuristically we expect that the vector $\boldsymbol{v}$ in inequalities (6) is the shortest vector in $\mathcal{L}$ and the $\boldsymbol{v}$ in inequalities (7) is the closest vector to $\boldsymbol{u}$ in $\mathcal{L}$ as introduced in [26]. By the discussion in Sect. 2.3, when N is bounded, vector $\boldsymbol{v}$ can be found efficiently by solving the SVP or CVP with LLL or other related algorithm, and then the value of D can be recovered, which immediately leaks the private key d in deterministic ECDSA or d_0 in EdDSA. To have a complete view about the proposed attacks, Table 1 relates the targets with the relevant problems in some lattice.

4   Concrete Lattice-Based Fault Attacks on Deterministic ECDSA and EdDSA Algorithms

In this section, we instantiate the idea of the attacks discussed in Sect. 3. The key point is to show that Eqs. (4) and (5) can be constructed when concrete targets are selected. Then, the lattice-based approach described in Sect. 3.2 can be followed to do key recovery. Since most of the attacks presented in this paper are of similar structure in description, to simplify presentation, only three representative attacks are described in this section, while other attacks, with targets shown in Table 1, are gathered in Appendix A.

4.1   Fault Attacks with Target r During the Calculation of s

Suppose the adversary decides to inject a fault against r before using it to calculate s. Then after getting a correct signature for a message m (chosen by the adversary in advance), the adversary manages to get $N-1$ faulty signatures with the same message m as input, and r as the target of fault injection.

4.1.1   Attacks on Deterministic ECDSA
Step 1: inject fault to r during the calculation of s
During the calculation of s, if injected with a fault, r can be represented as $r_i = r + \varepsilon_i 2^{l_i}$ for $i = 1, \ldots, N-1$, where ε_i is a random number satisfying $-2^w < \varepsilon_i < 2^w < n$ (by the random fault model) and the known $l_i \in \mathbb{N}$ satisfies

$l_i = f - w$ or 0 (see Sect. 3.1, $f = \lceil \log n \rceil$). The correct signature (r, s_0) and $N - 1$ faulty results (r_i, s_i) for the same input message m can be represented as

$$\begin{cases} s_0 = k^{-1}(e + rd) \bmod n \\ s_i = k^{-1}(e + (r + \varepsilon_i 2^{l_i})d) \bmod n \text{ (for } i = 1, ..., N - 1). \end{cases} \tag{8}$$

Step 2: recover the private key d by solving SVP

After reduction, Eq. (8) can be transformed as

$$\varepsilon_i = (s_i - s_0) 2^{-l_i} d^{-1} k \bmod n. \tag{9}$$

Let $A_i = (s_i - s_0)2^{-l_i} \bmod n$ and $D = d^{-1}k \bmod n$. There must exist $h_i \in \mathbb{Z}$ for $i = 1, ..., N - 1$ such that

$$\varepsilon_i = A_i D + h_i n, \tag{10}$$

where D is a fixed value due to the same input message m for all the signature queries.

It is clear that Eq. (10) is exactly Eq. (4). Then following the strategy described in Sect. 3.2, if $w < f - \log \sqrt{2\pi e}$ and $N \gg 1 + \frac{f + \log \sqrt{2\pi e}}{f - w - \log \sqrt{2\pi e}}$ ($N \approx 1 + \frac{f + \log \sqrt{2\pi e}}{f - w - \log \sqrt{2\pi e}}$ in practice), D can be recovered by solving SVP and subsequently the private key d can be recovered by virtue of the equation

$$d = (Ds_0 - r)^{-1} e \bmod n.$$

4.1.2 Attacks on EdDSA

Before we proceed, it should be noted that the existing DFAs against EdDSA [1, 5, 27–29] do not recover the private key d, but rather recover the sub-keys d_0 or d_1. This is still a real risk to the security of EdDSA since knowing a partial key d_0 or d_1 suffices to forge signatures [28].

Just like in the case of deterministic ECDSA, if the target r during the calculation of s is chosen, the correct and faulty signatures can be expressed as

$$\begin{cases} s_0 = k + rd_0 \bmod n \\ s_i = k + (r + \varepsilon_i 2^{l_i})d_0 \bmod n \, (i = 1, ..., N - 1). \end{cases} \tag{11}$$

After reduction, there must exist $h_i \in \mathbb{Z}$ for $i = 1, ..., N - 1$ such that Eq. (11) can be transformed as

$$\varepsilon_i = A_i D + h_i n, \tag{12}$$

where $A_i = (s_i - s_0)2^{-l_i} \bmod n$, and $D = d_0^{-1} \bmod n$.

Equation (12) is exactly Eq. (4). Analogously, by applying the general strategy described in Sect. 3.2, D can be found by solving SVP and subsequently the signing key d_0 can be obtained.

4.2 Fault Attacks with Target k Before the Calculation of kG

Suppose the adversary decides to inject a fault to k before using it to calculate kG. Then after getting a correct signature for a message m (chosen by the adversary also), the adversary can manage to get $N - 1$ faulty signatures with the same message m as input, and k as the target.

4.2.1 Attacks on Deterministic ECDSA
Step 1: inject fault to k before the calculation of kG
When k is injected with a fault, we have $k_i = k + \varepsilon_i 2^{l_i}$ for $i = 1, ..., N - 1$, where ε_i satisfying $-2^w < \varepsilon_i < 2^w$ is a random number and $l_i = f - w$ or 0 (see Sect. 3.1). The correct signature (r_0, s_0) and $N - 1$ faulty ones (r_i, s_i) for the same message m can be represented as

$$\begin{cases} k = s_0^{-1}(e + r_0 d) \bmod n \\ k + \varepsilon_i 2^{l_i} = s_i^{-1}(e + r_i d) \bmod n\, (i = 1, ..., N - 1). \end{cases} \tag{13}$$

Step 2: recover the private key d by solving CVP
After reduction, Eq. (13) can be transformed as

$$\varepsilon_i = \left(s_i^{-1} r_i - s_0^{-1} r_0\right) 2^{-l_i} d - \left(s_0^{-1} - s_i^{-1}\right) 2^{-l_i} e \bmod n. \tag{14}$$

Let $A_i = \left(s_i^{-1} r_i - s_0^{-1} r_0\right) 2^{-l_i} \bmod n$, $B_i = (s_0^{-1} - s_i^{-1}) 2^{-l_i} e \bmod n$ and $D = d \bmod n$. Then there must exist $h_i \in \mathbb{Z}$ for $i = 1, ..., N - 1$ such that

$$\varepsilon_i = A_i D + h_i n - B_i. \tag{15}$$

Equation (15) is exactly Eq. (5). Analogously, by applying the general strategy described in Sect. 3.2, if $w < f - \log \sqrt{2\pi e}$ and $N \gg 1 + \frac{f + \log \sqrt{2\pi e}}{f - w - \log \sqrt{2\pi e}}$, D, i.e., the private key d can be obtained in polynomial time in N.

4.2.2 Attacks on EdDSA
Just like in the case of deterministic ECDSA, if the target k before the calculation of kG is chosen, the correct and faulty signatures can be expressed as

$$\begin{cases} s_0 = k + r_0 d_0 \bmod n \\ s_i = k + \varepsilon_i 2^{l_i} + r_i d_0 \bmod n\, (i = 1, ..., N - 1). \end{cases} \tag{16}$$

After reduction, there must exist $h_i \in \mathbb{Z}$ for $i = 1, ..., N - 1$ such that Eq. (16) can be transformed as

$$\varepsilon_i = A_i D + h_i n - B_i, \tag{17}$$

where $A_i = (r_0 - r_i) 2^{-l_i} \bmod n$, $D = d_0 \bmod n$ and $B_i = (s_0 - s_i) 2^{-l_i} \bmod n$.
Equation (17) is exactly Eq. (5). Analogously, by applying the strategy described in Sect. 3.2, d_0 can be obtained in polynomial time in N.

4.3   Fault Attacks with the Targets During the Calculation of k

As described in Sect. 4.2, if injecting a fault into the target "k before the calculation of kG" to obtain some faulty k_is satisfying $k_i = k + \varepsilon_i 2^{l_i}(-2^w < \varepsilon_i < 2^w, w < f - \log\sqrt{2\pi e}$ and $i = 1, ..., N-1)$, then Eq. (5) can be constructed to recover the private key in deterministic ECDSA or EdDSA. As in Table 1, besides the target "k before the calculation of kG", we found some other fault targets during the calculation of k also can generate the same type of faulty k_is, including "registers before outputting hash value $F(d, e)$ (or $H(d_1, m)$)", "last modular additions before outputting hash value $F(d, e)$ (or $H(d_1, m)$)" and "hash value $F(d, e)$ (or $H(d_1, m)$) during the reduction of k".

The following will introduce the three targets and the fault models whose *final purpose* is to generate some faulty signatures satisfying $k_i = k + \varepsilon_i 2^{l_i}(-2^w < \varepsilon_i < 2^w$ and $w < f - \log\sqrt{2\pi e})$. For simplicity, we just consider the case when $l_i = 0$ for $i = 1, ..., N-1$(i.e., the continuous w bits of k starting from the least significant bit are disturbed randomly) and the hash function is SHA-2, to which the other cases are similar.

4.3.1   Hash Function Generating k

Although different SHA2-based derived functions are employed for generating k in deterministic ECDSA and EdDSA (for example, HMAC_DRBG_SHA256 $F(d, e)$ is utilized in deterministic ECDSA and hash algorithm SHA512 $H(d_1, m)$ is utilized in EdDSA by default), they all have the similar final computational steps before outputting the hash value to generate k (as shown Fig. 1). As shown in Figs. 2 and 3, after the L-round compression, the modular additions (mod 2^t, t is bit length of register) of the registers $(a_{L-1}, ..., g_{L-1}) \in [0, 2^t)$ and $(a_0, ..., h_0) \in [0, 2^t)$ are calculated and the results are assigned to the registers $(a_L, ..., h_L) \in [0, 2^t)$ as the hash value. Hence, once a fault is injected into these registers, the calculation of the additions or the hash value during the following reduction, k will be affected by the fault.

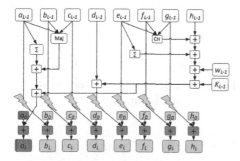 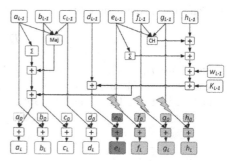

Fig. 2. Fault targets in the hash function of deterministic ECDSA

Fig. 3. Fault targets in the hash function of EdDSA

Table 2. The targets of fault injection during the calculation of k.

target	algorithm	concrete location of fault injection
registers before	deterministic ECDSA	(partial bits of a_0, a_L), $(b_0, ..., h_0)$,
		$(b_L, ..., h_L)$, $(a_{L-1}, ..., g_{L-1})$
outputting hash values	EdDSA	(partial bits of e_0, e_L), (f_0, g_0, h_0),
		(f_L, g_L, h_L), $(e_{L-1}, f_{L-1}, g_{L-1})$
modular additions before	deterministic ECDSA	all the modulo-2^t additions
outputting hash values	EdDSA	modulo-2^t additions in the right half
hash value during	deterministic ECDSA	the value of $F(d, e)$
the reduction of k	EdDSA	the value of $H(d_1, m)$

Table 2 gives an overview of all the fault targets before outputting the hash value and during the reduction of k for deterministic ECDSA and EdDSA respectively. The following sections will describe the detailed attack process with the targets in Table 2.

4.3.2 Fault Attacks with Target: Registers Before Outputting Hash Value

Attacks on deterministic ECDSA

For the HMAC_DRBG_SHA256 during signature generation of deterministic ECDSA, the final output registers $(a_L, \ldots, h_L)$ can be reduced into a big number $k = T2^{8t} + a_L 2^{7t} + \ldots + g_L 2^t + h_L \bmod n$, where T is the concatenation of the previous u-times HMAC values, i.e., $T = HMAC_0 || HMAC_1 || \ldots || HMAC_{u-1}$ ($T = 0$ in 256-bit deterministic ECDSA), and t is the bit length of register.

As shown in Fig. 2, assuming that all or arbitrary one of the registers $(a_0, \ldots, h_0)$, $(a_{L-1}, \ldots, g_{L-1})$ before the last additions and $(a_L, \ldots, h_L)$ before outputting the hash value are affected with a fault, the consequent k can be represented as $k_i = T2^{8t} + (a_L 2^{7t} + b_L 2^{6t} + \ldots + g_L 2^t + h_L + \varepsilon_i) \bmod n$ for $i = 1, \ldots, N - 1$, with a random faulty value ε_i satisfying $-2^w < \varepsilon_i < 2^w$ and $w < f - \log \sqrt{2\pi e} \le 8t - \log \sqrt{2\pi e}$ ($8t = f$ for 256-bit deterministic ECDSA). That is, k_i, which is derived from the faulty hash value and is to participate in the next calculation of kG, is equal to $k + \varepsilon_i \bmod n$.

Similar to the key recovery with target "k before the calculation of kG", Eq. (5) can be constructed. Then following the general strategy described in Sect. 3.2, the private key d can be recovered by solving the instance of CVP in lattice.

Note that in 256-bit deterministic ECDSA, to make sure $w < f - \log \sqrt{2\pi e}$, the register h_{L-1} can not be viewed as target, and as listed in Table 2, more than $\lceil \log \sqrt{2\pi e} \rceil$ most significant bits of the registers a_0 and a_L can not be disturbed when a fault is injected into them. Except this, all the fault injections against the other registers are arbitrary and uncontrolled.

Attacks on EdDSA

In the hash algorithm SHA512 $H(d_1, m)$ of EdDSA, the final output 512-bit registers $(a_L, \ldots, h_L)$ as the hash value must be reduced into the nonce $k =$

$a_L 2^{7t} + \ldots + g_L 2^t + h_L \bmod n$, where t as the bit length of register equals to 64 in SHA512. For 256-bit EdDSA, e.g., Ed25519, the modular reduction will reduce the 512-bit hash value into a 253-bit nonce k. Hence, in order to obtain available faulty signatures, fault injection here will take the four registers in the right half as the targets.

As shown in Fig. 3, when all or arbitrary one of the registers $(e_0, \ldots, h_0)$, $(e_{L-1}, \ldots, g_{L-1})$ before the last additions and $(e_L, \ldots, h_L)$ before outputting hash value are injected with a fault, the consequent k can be represented as $k_i = a_L 2^{7t} + \ldots + d_L 2^{4t} + (e_L 2^{3t} + \ldots + h_L + \varepsilon_i) \bmod n$ for $i = 1, \ldots, N-1$, with a random faulty value ε_i satisfying $-2^w < \varepsilon_i < 2^w$ and $w < f - \log \sqrt{2\pi e} \leq 4t - \log \sqrt{2\pi e}$ ($f \approx 4t$ for 256-bit EdDSA). That is, $k_i = k + \varepsilon_i \bmod n$. Similar to the key recovery with target "k before the calculation of kG", Eq. (5) can be constructed. Then according to the general strategy described in Sect. 3.2, the private key d_0 can be recovered by solving the instance of CVP in lattice.

Note that in 256-bit EdDSA, to make sure $w < f - \log \sqrt{2\pi e}$, only the right half of the registers are viewed as targets, and as listed in Table 2, at least $4t - f + \lceil \log \sqrt{2\pi e} \rceil$ most significant bits of the registers e_0 and e_L can not be disturbed when a fault is injected into them. Except this, the fault injection to the remaining three registers is arbitrary and uncontrolled. In addition, if the registers in the left half are disturbed, then $k_i = k + \varepsilon_i 2^{4t} \bmod n$. Similarly, we also can construct an instance of CVP in lattice to recover the private key.

4.3.3 Fault Attacks with Target: Last Modular Additions Before Outputting Hash Value

As described in Sect. 4.3.1 and 4.3.2, if the last modulo-2^t additions are disturbed by a fault to generate a group of faulty hash value $\{a_L, ..., h_L\}$, then the nonce k derived by the hash value has w bits disturbed, by which Eq. (5) can be constructed to recover the private key d.

For 256-bit deterministic ECDSA, as shown in Fig. 2, all or arbitrary one of the last modulo-2^t additions could be affected with a fault. Moreover, it is noted that the fault injection towards the first addition on the left must ensure more than $\lceil \log \sqrt{2\pi e} \rceil$ most significant bits of a_L undisturbed.

Similarly, for 256-bit EdDSA, as shown in Fig. 3, all or arbitrary one of the last modulo-2^t additions in the right half could be affected with a fault. Moreover, the fault injection towards the first addition in the right half must ensure more than $4t - f + \lceil \log \sqrt{2\pi e} \rceil$ most significant bits of e_L undisturbed. In addition, similarly, if the additions in the left half are disturbed, we also can construct an instance of CVP in lattice to recover the key.

4.3.4 Fault Attacks with Target: Hash Value During the Reduction of k

After calculating the last modular additions in the hash function, the final registers are combined into a big number $E(E = F(d, e)$ in deterministic ECDSA or $E = H(d_1, m)$ in EdDSA), and E must be reduced into nonce k, That is, $k = E \bmod n$. Assuming that a fault is injected into E during the reduction, the reduction $k = E \bmod n$ is changed into $k_i = E + \varepsilon_i 2^{l_i} \bmod n$ for $i = 1, \ldots, N-1$. Hence, as long as the random number ε_i satisfying $-2^w < \varepsilon_i < 2^w$ and $w < f - \log \sqrt{2\pi e}$, Eq. (5) can be constructed. Thereby, the private key can be recovered by solving an instance of CVP in lattice.

To sum up, the three fault targets above during the calculation of k are equivalent to the *representative* target "k before the calculation of kG", and thereby Eq. (5) can be constructed to recover the private key d in deterministic ECDSA and d_0 in EdDSA. The other attacks targeting the hash functions generating e and r have the similar procedures, which are specified in Appendix A.5 and A.6.

5   Experiment and Complexity Discussion

The validity of the proposed attacks lies in two aspects, namely, the validity of fault injection and the validity of key recovery. Section 3 presents the conditions and allowed adversarial actions for fault injection, and it is reasonable to believe that suitable faults can be induced during the signature generation process since our adversarial model is not completely new compared with the models in [13, 27–29]. Thus, we do not conduct concrete experiments to demonstrate the applicability of these fault injections. On the other hand, experiments are performed to check the validity of lattice-based key recovery algorithms. This is helpful to understand the relations between the allowed faulty bits(w), the required number of faulty signatures (N), and the success rate (γ) of the presented key recovery.

The experiments are conducted in a computer with 2.4 GHz CPU, 8 GB memory and Windows7 OS. The BKZ algorithm with block size of 20 implemented in NTL library [34] is employed to solve the instances of SVP/CVP. The experimental results for 256-bit deterministic ECDSA(based on NIST P-256) and EdDSA (based on curve25519, i.e., Ed25519) under some specific elliptic curve parameterized, are listed in Table 3 and Table 4 respectively.

Table 3. Success rate when attacking 256-bit deterministic ECDSA ($f = 256$)

target of fault injection	$w = 250$		$w = 245$		$w = 192$		$w = 160$		$w = 128$	
	N	γ	N	γ	N	γ	N	γ	N	γ
r during the calculation of s	80	100%	29	100%	6	96%	4	85%	3	70%
k^{-1} during the calculation of s	80	100%	29	100%	6	96%	4	89%	3	65%
k during the calculation of s	80	100%	29	100%	6	97%	4	87%	3	82%
$e, rd, e + rd$ during the calculation of s	80	100%	27	100%	6	97%	4	87%	3	67%
d during the calculation of s	80	100%	26	100%	6	95%	4	85%	3	67%
k before the calculation of kG	80	74%	30	100%	6	100%	4	100%	3	55%

Table 4. Success rate when attacking 256-bit EdDSA $(f = 253)$

target of fault injection	$w = 247$		$w = 245$		$w = 192$		$w = 160$		$w = 128$	
	N	γ	N	γ	N	γ	N	γ	N	γ
r during the calculation of s	80	100%	45	98%	6	97%	4	84%	3	23%
k before the calculation of kG	110	13%	29	100%	6	100%	4	100%	3	12%

Before proceeding to describe the experiment results some points should be clarified. First, to simplify the experiments, we only conduct key recovery experiments for representative targets (defined in Sect. 3.1). Similarly, due to the similarity of key recovery for targets $e, rd, e + rd$ during the calculation of s, we just conduct key recovery experiments with the target e.

Then, for each experiment of key recovery, we use a pseudo-random generator to generate the input message m and $N - 1$ groups of w-bit random numbers β_is. For simplicity, the chosen target v is set to be $v \oplus \beta_i$ for $i = 1, \ldots, N - 1$, which is equivalent to $v + \varepsilon_i$ mod n (where $l_i = 0$ and ε_i is also random with bound $-2^w < \varepsilon_i < 2^w$). Then the simulated faulty signatures are used to do key recovery. If the signing key can be recovered finally, the experiment is marked *successful*, otherwise *failed*. A such-designed experiment could fail because the short (or close) vector derived by LLL algorithm could be not the shortest (or closest) one if the selected N is not big enough, or the constructed lattice basis is not nice due to the oversize w and so on. For simplicity, we record the success rate of the experiments as $\gamma = \frac{\text{number of successful experiments}}{\text{total number of experiments}}$. In addition, when $l_i \neq 0$, e.g., $l_i = f - w$, the experiments are similar and will not be detailed here.

Third, for each selected fault target (corresponding to each row of Table 3 and Table 4), we illustrate the validity of attacks in five groups, each of them corresponding to a specific value of parameter (w, N). Note that when n is fixed, the range of w and N can be determined from the relations $w < f - \log \sqrt{2\pi e}$ and $N \gg 1 + \frac{f + \log \sqrt{2\pi e}}{f - w - \log \sqrt{2\pi e}}$ respectively. Hence, when $f = \lceil \log n \rceil = 256$(or $f = 253$ in Ed25519), the tolerant bound of w can be up to 253(or 250) in theory. Then, for each pair (w, N), a number of experiments are conducted to validate the effectiveness of key recovery.

Regarding the experiment number of each case, when $w \leq 245$, we conduct 1000 experiments to derive each success rate γ; when $w = 250$ or 247, only 100 experiments is conducted since our experiment platform cannot afford the significant computational cost of BKZ algorithm. The maximal w in our experiments is considered as 250(or 247), which is slightly less than the tolerable bound(i.e., 253 or 250) in theory. It is hopeful that if some other improved lattice reduction algorithms, such as BKZ 2.0 [11] with some optimum parameters, are utilized in the experiments, the theoretical bounds (i.e., 253 and 250) could be achieved. Moreover, as the previous lattice reduction, the needed N is approximate to $1 + \frac{f + \log \sqrt{2\pi e}}{f - w - \log \sqrt{2\pi e}}$ in experiments, which is obviously better than the N needed in theory. In addition, the success rate γ is tightly related to the parameters w and N. When w is set to be closed to 245, 30 and 45 faulty signatures suffice to recover the key with absolute success rate for deterministic ECDSA and Ed25519 respectively. However, when w is significantly less than the bound, a few faulty signatures suffice to recover the key. For example, when $w = 128$, 1 correct signature and 2 faulty signatures suffice to recover the key with success rate over 12% in experimental time $2 \sim 3$ms (with block size of 20). As a comparison (without considering the number of fault injections), it is impractical for the existing DFAs [1,5,27,28] to break the deterministic signature when $w \geq 64$, since exponential complexity $O(2^w)$ is required to enumerate the faulty patterns. In addition, as introduced in Sect. 3.1, since w is unknown and required to preset in practice, a conservative way is to set w as the (practical) maximum tolerable bound such that the key recovery can succeed.

Table 5. Comparison of attack complexity on 256-bit deterministic ECDSA or EdDSA

Scheme Item	Our attacks	Previous DFAs [1, 5, 27, 28]
tolerable bound of faulty bits (in w)	250 or 247	≈ 64
asymptotic time complexity	$O(N^5(N + \log A)\log A)^*$	$O(2^w)$
time cost in experiments ($w = 128$)	$2 \sim 3$ ms ($N = 3$)	impractical

$^* N \approx 1 + \frac{f + \log \sqrt{2\pi e}}{f - w - \log \sqrt{2\pi e}}$.

To have a more complete view about the computational complexity of the proposed key recovery algorithms, we compare them with the existing attacks in Table 5. In our experiments, the block size of BKZ algorithm is set as 20, and thus the LLL-based reduction with asymptotic complexity $O(N^5(N + \log A)\log A)$ [24] consumes the main time, where A is the maximum length in the original lattice vectors. When N is chosen as a polynomial of (f, w) (where f is a fixed value in a concrete algorithm), the computational complexity is thus polynomial in w, which is obviously less than the exponential complexity required by the existing approaches [1,5,27,28].

As a conclusion, our approach has obvious advantages over the mentioned existing approaches in terms of the tolerance of faulty bits (characterized by w) and time complexity, which also means the proposed attacks are of higher applicability when comparing with those approaches.

6   Countermeasures

In this section, we discuss the effectiveness of some possible countermeasures.

-**Randomization.** As introduced above, the proposed attacks take advantage of the fact that k is determined by the input message and the private key, and remains unchanged during the process of signature queries. Intuitively the condition can be removed by reintroducing randomness to the derivation of k.

This is the exact idea of hedged signature schemes, where the input message, secret key and a nonce are input to generate the per-signature random k. The security of hedged signature schemes against fault attacks has recently been proven under some limited models [3]. This strategy can theoretically defeat our attacks but it remains unclear whether it can be used to resist all fault attacks.

-**Data integrity protection.** Integrity protection is a natural choice for fault attacks resistance. It is a fact that the security of data transmission and storage can be consolidated by adopting error detection (or correction) code in the circuit level. However, limited by the computing power and cost factors, it is usually impossible to adopt strong integrity protection in the smart card like products. Thus the usually implemented Parity check and Cyclic Redundancy Code will leave rooms for fault injection. Namely, though they can be used to resist our attacks to some extent, more considerations are required to validate the real effectiveness of the mechanism. In addition, though the strategy that checking whether the input and output points are on the original elliptic curve can be used to resist the attacks in [1], our attacks are still effective in this case.

-**Signature verification before outputting.** Note the signature result of the two targeted deterministic algorithms is the form of (r, s). If k is tampered before the calculation of kG, the result (r, s) is derived by the faulty k. Hence, verifying the signature before outputting cannot detect the fault. This means the attack selecting k before the calculation of kG as the *representative* target can survive, but the other proposed attacks can be prevented.

-**Consistency check of repeated computations.** In this strategy, the signature calculation on an input message is repeated for two or more times, and the signature result will be output only when all the computation results are consistent. This can be effective to resist all the proposed attacks since there is no guarantee that the fault induced each time will be the same under the random fault model. But this countermeasure may not be efficient, since in this case two scalar multiplications have to be computed, which is unaffordable for some devices (such as IoT devices) whose computing power is very limited.

-**Infective computation.** This strategy is graceful in that the adversary in this case cannot distinguish whether the faulty signature is valid or not, thus the key recovery can be defeated. We propose two infective countermeasures to resist the proposed attacks to a considerable extent, where the hash function is SHA-2 (Figure 1) by default.

(i) For EdDSA, the *final* 8-*round compressions* in the hash function $H(d_1, m)$ generating k are calculated twice to obtain two identical nonces k_1 and k_2, and *the final* 8-*round compressions* in the hash function $H(R, P, m)$ generating r are calculated twice to obtain two identical r_1 and r_2; moreover, a random infective factor β is introduced, which has the same bit length with k, and is regenerated per signature. Then compute $s = (1 + \beta)(k_1 + d_0 r_1) - \beta(k_2 + d_0 r_2) \bmod n$.

(ii) For deterministic ECDSA, the *final* 8-*round compressions* in the hash function $F(d, e)$ generating k are calculated twice to obtain two identical nonces k_1 and k_2. The *final* 8-*round compressions* in the hash function $H(m)$ generating e are calculated twice to obtain two identical e_1 and e_2. The *reduction*(i.e., $r = x_1$

mod n) generating r is calculated twice to obtain two identical r_1 and r_2. The private key d defined as d_1 and d_2 is invoked twice during the calculation of s, respectively. Then compute $s = (1+\beta)k_1^{-1}(e_1+d_1r_1) - \beta k_2^{-1}(e_2+d_2r_2) \bmod n$.

7 Conclusion

We present a new fault analysis method to deterministic ECDSA and EdDSA. In the new model, the faulty intermediate can be characterized as an addition of the original intermediate with a random value of left-shifted l bits. The range of the random value is determined by and close to the size of the signing key. This makes the method much more practical than the existing enumerating approaches [1,5,27,28] in terms of tolerance of faulty bits.

The advantage is guaranteed by the lattice-based key recovery method. By noticing the algebraic structures of the deterministic algorithms, we show that, when providing with some faulty signatures and an associated correct signature of the same input message, some instances of lattice problems can be constructed to recover the signing key. Moreover, the lattice-based approach supports much more alternative targets of fault injection than the existing approaches, which further improves the applicability of the approach.

Experiments are performed to validate the effectiveness of the key recovery method. It is demonstrated that, for 256-bit deterministic ECDSA and EdDSA, the signing key can be recovered efficiently with high probability even if the intermediates are affected by 250 and 247 faulty bits respectively. This is, however, impractical for the existing faulty pattern enumerating approaches to achieve the same objective.

Acknowledgment. We thank the anonymous reviewers for their careful reading and insightful comments. This work is supported by the National Natural Science Foundation of China (No. 62172395) and the National Key Research and Development Program of China (No. U1936209).

A Appendix

This appendix will introduce the attacks with the remaining targets listed in Table 1 to deterministic ECDSA and EdDSA, including the attacks with targets k, k^{-1}, e, rd, $e+rd$ and d during the calculation of s and the attacks taking the hash functions generating e and r as fault targets.

A.1 Fault Attacks with Target k During the Calculation of s to Deterministic ECDSA

Suppose the adversary decides to inject a fault to k before using it during the calculation of s. Then after getting a correct signature for a message m (chosen by the adversary in advance), the adversary can try to get $N-1$ faulty signatures with the same message m as input, and k as the target.

Step 1: inject fault to k during the calculation of s

When k is injected with a fault, we have $k_i = k + \varepsilon_i 2^{l_i}$ for $i = 1, ..., N - 1$, where ε_i satisfying $-2^w < \varepsilon_i < 2^w < n$ is a random number and $l_i = f - w$ or 0 (see Sect. 3.1). The correct signature (r, s_0) and $N - 1$ faulty ones (r, s_i) for the same input message m can be represented as

$$\begin{cases} k = s_0^{-1} (e + rd) \bmod n \\ k + \varepsilon_i 2^{l_i} = s_i^{-1} (e + rd) \bmod n (i = 1, ..., N - 1) \end{cases}. \tag{18}$$

Step 2: recover the private key d by solving SVP

After reduction, Eq. (18) can be transformed as

$$\varepsilon_i = \left(s_i^{-1} - s_0^{-1}\right) 2^{-l_i} (e + rd) \bmod n. \tag{19}$$

Let $A_i = (s_i^{-1} - s_0^{-1})2^{-l_i} \bmod n$ and $D = e + rd \bmod n$. There must exist $h_i \in \mathbb{Z}$ for $i = 1, ..., N - 1$ such that

$$\varepsilon_i = A_i D + h_i n, \tag{20}$$

where D is a fixed value due to the same input message m for all the signature queries.

Equation (20) is exactly Eq. (4). Then following the general strategy described in Sect. 3.2, if $w < f - \log \sqrt{2\pi e}$ and $N \gg 1 + \frac{f + \log \sqrt{2\pi e}}{f - w - \log \sqrt{2\pi e}}$, D can be found by solving an instance of SVP and subsequently the private key d can be recovered by virtue of the equation

$$d = r^{-1}(D - e) \bmod n.$$

A.2 Fault Attacks with Target $k^{-1} \bmod n$ During the Calculation of s to Deterministic ECDSA

Suppose the adversary decides to inject a fault to $k^{-1} \bmod n$ (after being generated by modular inversion of k) before using it during the calculation of s. Then after getting a correct signature for a message m, the adversary can try to get $N - 1$ faulty signatures with the same message m as input, and k^{-1} as the target.

Step 1: inject fault to $k^{-1} \bmod n$ during the calculation of s

When $k^{-1} \bmod n$ derived by k is injected with a fault, we have $k_i^{-1} = k^{-1} + \varepsilon_i 2^{l_i} \bmod n$ for $i = 1, ..., N - 1$, where ε_i satisfying $-2^w < \varepsilon_i < 2^w$ is a random number, w is a preset value and $l_i = f - w$ or 0 (see Sect. 3.1). The correct signature (r, s_0) and $N - 1$ groups of faulty (r, s_i) for the same input message m can be represented as

$$\begin{cases} s_0 = k^{-1} (e + rd) \bmod n \\ s_i = \left(k^{-1} + \varepsilon_i 2^{l_i}\right) (e + rd) \bmod n (i = 1, ..., N - 1). \end{cases} \tag{21}$$

Step 2: recover the private key d by solving SVP

After reduction, Eq. (21) can be transformed as

$$\varepsilon_i = (e + rd)^{-1} (s_i - s_0) \, 2^{-l_i} \bmod n. \tag{22}$$

Let $A_i = (s_i - s_0) 2^{-l_i} \bmod n$ and $D = (e + rd)^{-1} \bmod n$. There must exist $h_i \in \mathbb{Z}$ for $i = 1, ..., N - 1$ such that

$$\varepsilon_i = A_i D + h_i n, \tag{23}$$

where D is a fixed value due to the same input message m for all the signature queries.

Equation (23) is exactly Eq. (4). Then following the general strategy described in Sect. 3.2, if $w < f - \log \sqrt{2\pi e}$ and $N \gg 1 + \frac{f + \log \sqrt{2\pi e}}{f - w - \log \sqrt{2\pi e}}$, D can be found by solving an instance of SVP and subsequently the private key d can be recovered by virtue of the equation

$$d = r^{-1}(D^{-1} - e) \bmod n.$$

A.3 Fault Attacks with Target d During the Calculation of s to Deterministic ECDSA

Suppose the adversary decides to inject a fault to d before using it during the calculation of s. Then after getting a correct signature for a message m, the adversary can try to get $N - 1$ faulty signatures with the same message m as input, and d as the target.

Step 1: inject fault to d during the calculation of s

When d is injected with a fault, we have $d_i = d + \varepsilon_i 2^{l_i}$ for $i = 1, ..., N - 1$, where ε_i satisfying $-2^w < \varepsilon_i < 2^w$ is a random number, w is a preset value and $l_i = f - w$ or 0 (see Sect. 3.1). The correct signature (r, s_0) and $N - 1$ groups of faulty (r, s_i) for the same input message m can be represented as

$$\begin{cases} s_0 = k^{-1} (e + rd) \bmod n \\ s_i = k^{-1} \left(e + r(d + \varepsilon_i 2^{l_i}) \right) \bmod n (i = 1, ..., N - 1). \end{cases} \tag{24}$$

Step 2: recover the private key d by solving SVP

After reduction, Eq. (24) can be transformed as

$$\varepsilon_i = (s_i - s_0) \, 2^{-l_i} r^{-1} k \bmod n. \tag{25}$$

Let $A_i = (s_i - s_0) r^{-1} 2^{-l_i} \bmod n$ and $D = k \bmod n$. There must exist $h_i \in \mathbb{Z}$ for $i = 1, ..., N - 1$ such that

$$\varepsilon_i = A_i D + h_i n, \tag{26}$$

where D is a fixed value due to the same input message m for all the signature queries.

Equation (26) is exactly Eq. (4). Then following the general strategy described in Sect. 3.2, if $w < f - \log \sqrt{2\pi e}$ and $N \gg 1 + \frac{f + \log \sqrt{2\pi e}}{f - w - \log \sqrt{2\pi e}}$, D can be found by solving an instance of SVP and subsequently the private key d can be recovered by virtue of the equation

$$d = r^{-1} (Ds_0 - e) \bmod n.$$

A.4   Fault Attacks with Targets e, rd and $e + rd$ During the Calculation of s to Deterministic ECDSA

If the targets e, rd and $e + rd$ targets are disturbed by fault injection, a same model of key recovery can be constructed. Therefore, for simplicity, we define mv as any one of the three targets, that is, mv could be e, rd or $e + rd$. Suppose the adversary decides to inject a fault to mv before using it during the calculation of s. Then after getting a correct signature for a message m, the adversary can try to get $N - 1$ faulty signatures with the same message m as input, and mv as the target.

Step 1: inject fault to mv during the calculation of s

When mv is injected with a fault, we have $mv_i = mv + \varepsilon_i 2^{l_i}$ for $i = 1, ..., N-1$, where ε_i satisfying $-2^w < \varepsilon_i < 2^w$ is a random number, w is a preset value and $l_i = f - w$ or 0 (see Sect. 3.1). The correct signature (r, s_0) and $N - 1$ faulty ones (r, s_i) for the same input message m can be represented as

$$\begin{cases} s_0 = k^{-1} (e + rd) \bmod n \\ s_i = k^{-1} (e + rd + \varepsilon_i 2^{l_i}) \bmod n (i = 1, ..., N - 1). \end{cases} \tag{27}$$

Step 2: recover the private key d by solving SVP

After reduction, Eq. (27) can be transformed as

$$\varepsilon_i = (s_i - s_0) 2^{-l_i} k \bmod n. \tag{28}$$

Let $A_i = (s_i - s_0) 2^{-l_i} \bmod n$ and $D = k \bmod n$. There must exist $h_i \in \mathbb{Z}$ for $i = 1, ..., N - 1$ such that

$$\varepsilon_i = A_i D + h_i n, \tag{29}$$

where D is a fixed value due to the same input message m for all the signature queries.

Equation (29) is exactly Eq. (4). Then following the general strategy described in Sect. 3.2, if $w < f - \log \sqrt{2\pi e}$ and $N \gg 1 + \frac{f + \log \sqrt{2\pi e}}{f - w - \log \sqrt{2\pi e}}$, D can be found by solving an instance of SVP. Naturally, as mentioned above, the private key d can be recovered by virtue of D.

A.5   Fault Attacks with Targets During the Calculation of e to Deterministic ECDSA

As introduced in Appendix A.4, if injecting a fault into e before using it during the calculation of s to obtain some valid e_is satisfying $e_i = e + \varepsilon_i 2^{l_i}$ ($-2^w < \varepsilon_i < 2^w$ and $l_i = f - w$ or 0), then Eq. (4) can be constructed to recover the private key in deterministic ECDSA.

Similarly, besides directly injecting fault into the target "e during the calculation of s", there still exist two other fault targets during the calculation of e which can generate some valid faulty e_is for key recovery, including "registers before outputting the hash value $H(m)$" and "last modular additions before outputting the hash value $H(m)$". The models of fault injection with these two targets are similar to the ones introduced in Sects. 4.3.2 and 4.3.3, and thereby Eq. (4) which is similar to that with target "e during the calculation of s", can be constructed to recover the private key in deterministic ECDSA.

A.6   Fault Attacks with targets During the Calculation of r to EdDSA

As introduced in Sect. 4.1.2, if injecting a fault into r before using it during the calculation of s to obtain some valid r_is satisfying $r_i = r + \varepsilon_i 2^{l_i}$ ($-2^w < \varepsilon_i < 2^w$, $w < f - \log\sqrt{2\pi e}$ and $l_i + w \le f$), Eq. (4) can be constructed to recover the private key in EdDSA.

Similarly, besides directly injecting fault into the target "r during the calculation of s", there still exist another three fault targets during the calculation of r which can generate some valid faulty r_is for key recovery, including "registers before outputting hash value $H(R, P, m)$", "last modular additions before outputting hash value $H(R, P, m)$" and "hash value $H(R, P, m)$ during the reduction of r". The models of fault injection with these three targets are similar to the ones in Sects. 4.3.2, 4.3.3 and 4.3.4, and thereby Eq. (4) which is similar to that with target "r during the calculation of s", can be constructed to recover the private key in EdDSA.

References

1. Ambrose, C., Bos, J.W., Fay, B., Joye, M., Lochter, M., Murray, B.: Differential attacks on deterministic signatures. In: Smart, N.P. (ed.) CT-RSA 2018. LNCS, vol. 10808, pp. 339–353. Springer, Cham (2018). https://doi.org/10.1007/978-3-319-76953-0_18
2. Aranha, D.F., Novaes, F.R., Takahashi, A., Tibouchi, M., Yarom, Y.: LadderLeak: breaking ECDSA with less than one bit of nonce leakage. In: Proceedings of the 2020 ACM SIGSAC Conference on Computer and Communications Security, pp. 225–242 (2020)
3. Aranha, D.F., Orlandi, C., Takahashi, A., Zaverucha, G.: Security of hedged Fiat–Shamir signatures under fault attacks. In: Canteaut, A., Ishai, Y. (eds.) EUROCRYPT 2020. LNCS, vol. 12105, pp. 644–674. Springer, Cham (2020). https://doi.org/10.1007/978-3-030-45721-1_23

4. Babai, L.: On Lovászlattice reduction and the nearest lattice point problem. Combinatorica **6**(1), 1–13 (1986)
5. Barenghi, A., Pelosi, G.: A note on fault attacks against deterministic signature schemes. In: Ogawa, K., Yoshioka, K. (eds.) IWSEC 2016. LNCS, vol. 9836, pp. 182–192. Springer, Cham (2016). https://doi.org/10.1007/978-3-319-44524-3_11
6. Belgarric, P., Fouque, P.-A., Macario-Rat, G., Tibouchi, M.: Side-channel analysis of Weierstrass and Koblitz curve ECDSA on android smartphones. In: Sako, K. (ed.) CT-RSA 2016. LNCS, vol. 9610, pp. 236–252. Springer, Cham (2016). https://doi.org/10.1007/978-3-319-29485-8_14
7. Benger, N., van de Pol, J., Smart, N.P., Yarom, Y.: "Ooh Aah... Just a Little Bit": a small amount of side channel can go a long way. In: Batina, L., Robshaw, M. (eds.) CHES 2014. LNCS, vol. 8731, pp. 75–92. Springer, Heidelberg (2014). https://doi.org/10.1007/978-3-662-44709-3_5
8. Biehl, I., Meyer, B., Müller, V.: Differential fault attacks on elliptic curve cryptosystems. In: Bellare, M. (ed.) CRYPTO 2000. LNCS, vol. 1880, pp. 131–146. Springer, Heidelberg (2000). https://doi.org/10.1007/3-540-44598-6_8
9. Boneh, D., DeMillo, R.A., Lipton, R.J.: On the importance of checking cryptographic protocols for faults. In: Fumy, W. (ed.) EUROCRYPT 1997. LNCS, vol. 1233, pp. 37–51. Springer, Heidelberg (1997). https://doi.org/10.1007/3-540-69053-0_4
10. Cao, W., et al.: Two lattice-based differential fault attacks against ECDSA with wNAF algorithm. In: Kwon, S., Yun, A. (eds.) ICISC 2015. LNCS, vol. 9558, pp. 297–313. Springer, Cham (2016). https://doi.org/10.1007/978-3-319-30840-1_19
11. Chen, Y., Nguyen, P.Q.: BKZ 2.0: better lattice security estimates. In: Lee, D.H., Wang, X. (eds.) ASIACRYPT 2011. LNCS, vol. 7073, pp. 1–20. Springer, Heidelberg (2011). https://doi.org/10.1007/978-3-642-25385-0_1
12. Faugère, J.-C., Goyet, C., Renault, G.: Attacking (EC)DSA given only an implicit hint. In: Knudsen, L.R., Wu, H. (eds.) SAC 2012. LNCS, vol. 7707, pp. 252–274. Springer, Heidelberg (2013). https://doi.org/10.1007/978-3-642-35999-6_17
13. Fischlin, M., Günther, F.: Modeling Memory faults in signature and authenticated encryption schemes. In: Jarecki, S. (ed.) CT-RSA 2020. LNCS, vol. 12006, pp. 56–84. Springer, Cham (2020). https://doi.org/10.1007/978-3-030-40186-3_4
14. Genkin, D., Pachmanov, L., Pipman, I., Tromer, E., Yarom, Y.: ECDSA key extraction from mobile devices via nonintrusive physical side channels. In: Proceedings of the 2016 ACM SIGSAC Conference on Computer and Communications Security, pp. 1626–1638 (2016)
15. Groot Bruinderink, L., Pessl, P.: Differential fault attacks on deterministic lattice signatures. IACR Trans. Cryptographic Hardware Embed. Syst. **2018**, 21–43 (2018)
16. Howgrave-Graham, N.A., Smart, N.P.: Lattice attacks on digital signature schemes. Des. Codes Crypt. **23**(3), 283–290 (2001)
17. Karaklajić, D., Schmidt, J.M., Verbauwhede, I.: Hardware designer's guide to fault attacks. IEEE Trans. Very Large Scale Integr. (VLSI) Syst. **21**(12), 2295–2306 (2013)
18. Lenstra, A.K., Lenstra, H.W., Lovász, L.: Factoring polynomials with rational coefficients. Math. Ann. **261**(4), 515–534 (1982)
19. Liu, M., Nguyen, P.Q.: Solving BDD by enumeration: an update. In: Dawson, E. (ed.) CT-RSA 2013. LNCS, vol. 7779, pp. 293–309. Springer, Heidelberg (2013). https://doi.org/10.1007/978-3-642-36095-4_19

20. Micciancio, D., Goldwasser, S.: Complexity of Lattice Problems: A Cryptographic Perspective, vol. 671. Springer, Boston (2002). https://doi.org/10.1007/978-1-4615-0897-7
21. Naccache, D., Nguyên, P.Q., Tunstall, M., Whelan, C.: Experimenting with faults, lattices and the DSA. In: Vaudenay, S. (ed.) PKC 2005. LNCS, vol. 3386, pp. 16–28. Springer, Heidelberg (2005). https://doi.org/10.1007/978-3-540-30580-4_3
22. Nguyen, P.Q.: Hermite's constant and lattice algorithms. In: Nguyen, P., Vallée, B. (eds.) The LLL Algorithm. Information Security and Cryptography, pp. 19–69. Springer, Heidelberg (2010). https://doi.org/10.1007/978-3-642-02295-1_2
23. Nguyen, P.Q., Shparlinski, I.E.: The insecurity of the elliptic curve digital signature algorithm with partially known nonces. Des. Codes Crypt. **30**(2), 201–217 (2003)
24. Nguên, P.Q., Stehlé, D.: Floating-point LLL revisited. In: Cramer, R. (ed.) EUROCRYPT 2005. LNCS, vol. 3494, pp. 215–233. Springer, Heidelberg (2005). https://doi.org/10.1007/11426639_13
25. Nguyen, P.Q., Stern, J.: Lattice reduction in cryptology: an update. In: Bosma, W. (ed.) ANTS 2000. LNCS, vol. 1838, pp. 85–112. Springer, Heidelberg (2000). https://doi.org/10.1007/10722028_4
26. Nguyen, P.Q., Tibouchi, M.: Lattice-based fault attacks on signatures. In: Joye, M., Tunstall, M. (eds.) Fault Analysis in Cryptography, pp. 201–220. Springer, Heidelberg (2012). https://doi.org/10.1007/978-3-642-29656-7_12
27. Poddebniak, D., Somorovsky, J., Schinzel, S., Lochter, M., Rösler, P.: Attacking deterministic signature schemes using fault attacks. In: IEEE European Symposium on Security and Privacy (Euro S&P), pp. 338–352. IEEE (2018)
28. Romailler, Y., Pelissier, S.: Practical fault attack against the Ed25519 and EdDSA signature schemes. In: Workshop on Fault Diagnosis and Tolerance in Cryptography (FDTC), pp. 17–24 (2017)
29. Samwel, N., Batina, L.: Practical fault injection on deterministic signatures: the case of EdDSA. In: Joux, A., Nitaj, A., Rachidi, T. (eds.) AFRICACRYPT 2018. LNCS, vol. 10831, pp. 306–321. Springer, Cham (2018). https://doi.org/10.1007/978-3-319-89339-6_17
30. Schmidt, J.M., Medwed, M.: A fault attack on ECDSA. In: Workshop on Fault Diagnosis and Tolerance in Cryptography (FDTC), pp. 93–99. IEEE (2009)
31. Schnorr, C.P., Euchner, M.: Lattice basis reduction: improved practical algorithms and solving subset sum problems. Math. Program. **66**(1–3), 181–199 (1994)
32. Schnorr, C.P., Hörner, H.H.: Attacking the Chor-Rivest cryptosystem by improved lattice reduction. In: Guillou, L.C., Quisquater, J.-J. (eds.) EUROCRYPT 1995. LNCS, vol. 921, pp. 1–12. Springer, Heidelberg (1995). https://doi.org/10.1007/3-540-49264-X_1
33. Schnorr, C.: A hierarchy of polynomial time lattice basis reduction algorithms. Theoret. Comput. Sci. **53**(2), 201–224 (1987)
34. Shoup, V.: Number Theory C++ Library (NTL) version 9.6.4 (2016). http://www.shoup.net/ntl/

More Accurate Geometric Analysis on the Impact of Successful Decryptions for IND-CCA Secure Ring/Mod-LWE/LWR Based Schemes

Han Wu[1,2] and Guangwu Xu[1,2]($\boxtimes$)

[1] School of Cyber Science and Technology, Shandong University,
Qingdao 266237, Shandong, China
hanwu97@mail.sdu.edu.cn
[2] Key Laboratory of Cryptologic Technology and Information Security of Ministry
of Education, Shandong University, Qingdao 266237, Shandong, China
gxu4sdq@sdu.edu.cn

Abstract. Majority of lattice-based encryption schemes allow the possibility of decryption failures. It is now understood that this property makes such encryption systems susceptible to the so-called decryption failure attack. In such an attack, an adversary can use a large number of ciphertexts that cause decryption failures to help to recover a private key. In PQC2020, Bindel and Schanck observed that successful decryptions also imply some information about the secret as the secret vector must be away from certain spherical caps. In this paper, we revisit this problem by exploring certain geometric properties in lattice based schemes. We are able to produce more tools for crypt-analysis and operations of these schemes and provide a more accurate interpretation of the information brought from successful decryptions to enhance the failure boosting. By using (recent) precise formulas, we develop some techniques to accurately characterize relationships between a private key and successful queries to the decryption oracle. A finer estimation of the valid proportion of key candidates that can be excluded from successful queries is given. The decryption failure probability is also more accurately analysed. Our discussion addresses and corrects previous errors and our experimental data is usable in assessing the IND-CCA security of (R/M)-LWE/LWR based systems.

Keywords: Lattice-based cryptography · Decryption oracle · Failure boosting · Crypt-analysis

1 Introduction

Lattice-based cryptography has been an important field for research and applications. Over the past decades, many new ideas have been developed and new

Supported by National Key Research and Development Program of China (Grant No. 2018YFA0704702) and Department of Science and Technology of Shandong Province of China (Grant No. 2019JZZY010133).

designs have been proposed. It is believed that several fundamental lattice problems are resistant to quantum attacks, public key systems using lattice construction have been a major option for new post-quantum cryptosystems.

The environment for setting up lattice-based encryption systems seems to be much more complicated than that for the classical public key encryption systems such as RSA and Elgamal (finite fields version and elliptic curve version). Because of the involvements of adding errors and rounding operations, the decryption is not a deterministic one. Given a valid pair of ciphertext and private key, one can only assert that such a system recovers the correct plaintext with overwhelming probability.

In 2018, the impact of decryption failures was studied for measuring the chosen-ciphertext security of (Ring/Module)-Learning With Errors/Rounding ((R/M)-LWE/LWR)-based primitives by D'Anvers etc. in [10,11]. Their results show that such an impact could be significant. Especially when the failure probability is relatively high, the security of (R/M)-LWE/LWR-based schemes could be reduced. On the other hand, since NIST poses some limits on the number of available oracle queries, the NIST post-quantum standardization candidates could be immune to this kind of attack. The authors of [10,11] have developed failure boosting technique to increase the failure rate in the above work. It is noted that more ways of achieving failure boosting have been proposed more recently [9,12–16].

In 2020, Bindel and Schanck [5] considered the problem from a new angle by arguing that for an imperfectly correct lattice-based public-key encryption scheme, information about their private key can be leaked even when the answers for decryption queries are successful. In their refinement of the D'Anvers-Guo-Johansson-Nilsson-Vercauteren-Verbauwhede failure boosting attack, through a geometric formulation of the problem, partial information about the private key can be obtained by calculating (a low order approximation of) a union of spherical caps. It should be pointed out that the discussion in [5] contains an error which also affects the correctness of bounds and corresponding experiments.

In this paper, we revisit the problem of using the information brought from successful queries to enhance the failure boosting. Combining with some recent mathematical tools, we develop some techniques to characterize the information about private key more accurately, given that decryption queries all succeed. Our discussion corrects previous errors and our experimental data is usable in assessing the security of (R/M)-LWE/LWR-based systems. More specifically, our contributions are

- We characterize the compression errors (rounding errors) that are used by several important lattice-based schemes. For the cases of practical interest, we are able to obtain their precise distributional behavior.
- The information inferred by a successful answer from querying the decryption oracle is correctly characterized. More precise geometric formulas are used to calculate the valid proportion of private key candidates that can be excluded in the decryption failure attack.

- By refining the (recently confirmed) orthogonality hypothesis, the effect of more queries and their overlaps are investigated and better estimations are obtained.
- Using the information of the success of previous queries, a more accurate posterior decryption failure probability is given according to Bayes' theorem.

The paper is organized into 6 sections. Necessary terminologies and notations are introduced in Sect. 2. We discuss the distributional behaviors of compression errors in Sect. 3. Section 4 reformulates the problem of extracting private key information from successful queries with more concise formulas. The content of dealing with general case by using the second-order approximation is included in Sect. 5 where the overlaps among queries are treated in detail and a more accurate way of estimating posterior decryption failure probability is given. Finally, experiments of our framework for some NIST post-quantum candidates are conducted in Sect. 6.

2   Preliminaries

We shall introduce necessary terminologies and notations for (R/M-) LWE/LWR-based encryption schemes.

2.1   (R/M-)LWE/LWR-Based Public-Key Encryption Scheme

First let us fix some notations. Let q be a positive integer. In lattice-based cryptography, one uses the minimum absolute residue system modulo q, with the notation "x mods q" denoting the remainder in the range $\left[-\frac{q}{2}, \frac{q}{2}\right)$ of x dividing by q (remainder with sign). By choosing the representatives accordingly, we may write

$$\mathbb{Z}_q = \mathbb{Z} \cap \left[-\frac{q}{2}, \frac{q}{2}\right).$$

Let n be another positive integer. We will mainly work on the rings $R = \mathbb{Z}[x]/(x^n + 1)$ and $R_q = \mathbb{Z}_q[x]/(x^n + 1)$. The ℓ_2-norm and ℓ_∞-norm are written as $\| \cdot \|$ and $\| \cdot \|_\infty$ respectively. More precisely, for $a = (a_0\ a_1\ \cdots a_{n-1})^T \in \mathbb{Z}_q^n$ or $a = a_0 + a_1 x + \cdots + a_{n-1} x^{n-1} \in R_q$,

$$\|a\| = \sqrt{\sum_{i=0}^{n-1} a_i^2}, \quad \|a\|_\infty = \max_{0 \leq i \leq n-1} |a_i|.$$

As for $\alpha = (\alpha_1, \cdots, \alpha_k)^T \in R_q^k$, its norms are respectively $\|\alpha\| = \sqrt{\sum_{j=1}^{k} \|\alpha_j\|^2}$ and $\|\alpha\|_\infty = \max_{1 \leq j \leq k} \|\alpha_j\|_\infty$.

For integers $p, q > 0$, we write $x_{q \to p} = \left\lceil \frac{px}{q} \right\rfloor$ where $\lceil \cdot \rfloor$ is the usual rounding to the nearest integer. We use $a \leftarrow \chi(X)$ to denote the sampling $a \in X$ according to the distribution χ, and X can be omitted when there is no ambiguity.

Table 1. A summary of some security parameters for NIST post-quantum schemes.

PKE.KeyGen()	PKE.Enc($pk = (b, seed_A)$)	PKE.Dec ($sk = s, c = (v', b')$)
$seed_A \leftarrow \mathcal{U}(\{0,1\}^{256})$	$A = \text{gen}(seed_A) \in R_q^{k \times k}$	$b_r' = \lceil b' \rfloor_{p \to q}$
$A = \text{gen}(seed_A) \in R_q^{k \times k}$	$s' \leftarrow \chi_{s'}(R_q^k), \ e' \leftarrow \chi_{e'}(R_q^k), \ e'' \leftarrow \chi_{e''}(R_q)$	$v_r' = \lceil v' \rfloor_{t \to q}$
$s \leftarrow \chi_s(R_q^k), \ e \leftarrow \chi_e(R_q^k)$	$b_r = \lceil b \rfloor_{p \to q}$	$v = b_r'^T s$
$b = \lceil As + e \rfloor_{q \to p}$	$b' = \lceil A^T s' + e' \rfloor_{q \to p}$	$m' = \text{dec}(v_r' - v)$
	$v' = \lceil b_r^T s' + e'' + \text{enc}(m) \rfloor_{q \to t}$	
return ($pk := (b, seed_A), sk := s$)	return $c = (v', b')$	return m'

The general model we discuss in this paper is the one that unifies the essential ideas of several (R/M-)LWE/LWR-based schemes. Here is the description:

The condition for a decryption failure of the (R/M-)LWE/LWR-based public-key encryption scheme described in the above model was extensively considered in [10,11]. To explain that, we first define u, u', u'' as the errors introduced by the rounding and reconstruction operations:

$$\begin{cases} u = As + e - b_r \\ u' = A^T s' + e' - b_r' \\ u'' = b_r^T s' + e'' + \text{enc}(m) - v_r'. \end{cases}$$

Then, we form $S = \begin{pmatrix} -s \\ e - u \end{pmatrix}, C = \begin{pmatrix} e' + u' \\ s' \end{pmatrix}$ and $G = e'' - u''$. The following lemma gives the precise condition for a decryption failure of the scheme.

Lemma 1 [10]. *For a fixed triple (S, C, G), the decryption failure occurs if and only if $\|S^T C + G\|_\infty > \frac{q}{4}$.*

A more convenient way of writing the failure condition just in terms of vectors with components in $\mathbb{Z}_q$ was described in [12]. Let $\alpha = (\alpha_1, \cdots, \alpha_k)^T \in R_q^k$ be a vector of polynomials, we write $\overline{\alpha} \in \mathbb{Z}_q^{kn}$ to be the concatenation of coefficient vectors of polynomials $\alpha_1, \cdots, \alpha_k$, namely

$$\overline{\alpha} = (a_{10}, a_{11}, \cdots, a_{1,n-1}, \cdots, a_{k0}, a_{k1}, \cdots, a_{k,n-1})^T$$

where $\alpha_j = a_{j0} + a_{j1}x + \cdots + a_{j,n-1}x^{n-1}$.

Fix a positive integer r, an r-rotation of a polynomial vector $\alpha = (\alpha_1, \cdots, \alpha_k)^T$ in R_q^k is

$$\alpha^{(r)} = \left(x^r \cdot \alpha_1(x^{-1}) \pmod{x^n + 1}, \cdots, x^r \cdot \alpha_k(x^{-1}) \pmod{x^n + 1} \right)^T \in R_q^k.$$

The following properties of rotations are evident.

1. For any polynomial vector $\alpha \in R_q^k$ and $r \in \mathbb{Z}$, we have $\alpha^{(n+r)} = -\alpha^{(r)}$ and $\alpha^{(2n+r)} = \alpha^{(r)}$.
2. For $a = \sum_{i=0}^{n-1} a_i x^i \in R_q$, the coefficients of $a^{(r)}$ satisfy

$$a_j^{(r)} = \begin{cases} a_{r-j} & 0 \leq j \leq r \\ -a_{n+r-j} & r+1 \leq j \leq n-1 \end{cases} \quad r, j = 0, 1, \cdots, n-1.$$

3. For any polynomial vectors $\alpha, \beta \in R_q^k$, we have $\alpha^T \beta = \sum_{j=0}^{n-1} \overline{\alpha^T \beta^{(j)}} x^j$.

Thus, the failure condition of Lemma 1 can also be written as:

$$\exists r \in [0, 2n-1], \text{ such that } \left| \overline{S}^T \overline{C^{(r)}} + G_r \right| > \frac{q}{4}.$$

where G_i is the i-th degree coefficient of $G, i = 0, 1, \cdots, n-1$.

In our setting, the IND-CCA security for PKE schemes is considered. The adversary has no control on the random variables such as s', e', e'' as they are the results of hash function calls. This means that s', e', e'' can actually be seen as being extracted from particular distributions. As shown in Table 1, one treats $s' \leftarrow \chi_{s'}(R_q^k)$, $e' \leftarrow \chi_{e'}(R_q^k)$ and $e'' \leftarrow \chi_{e''}(R_q)$.

However, the adversary can pick a message and then get the values of s', e', e''. In a failure boosting attack, the adversary improves his odds of triggering a decryption failure by searching for s', e', e'' with large norms. The adversary needs to balance the cost of searching randomness that meet the length condition with the success rate of finding decryption failures. He only sends ciphertexts generated by such randomness to the decryption oracle as these ciphertexts have a failure probability greater than a certain value.

In this paper, we will focus on the case where the attacker only uses values of s', e' with a greater-than-average length (see Sect. 4.1). It is noticed that our discussion also applies to other cases.

The coefficients of s, s', e, e', e'' are always small. Let $\eta > 0$ be a positive integer. Recall that the centered binomial distribution β_η is the probability distribution defined on the set $X = \{-\eta, -\eta + 1, \cdots, -1, 0, 1, \cdots, \eta\}$ with the probability assignment at $k \in X$ to be

$$\beta_\eta(k) = \binom{2\eta}{k + \eta} \frac{1}{2^{2\eta}}.$$

This distribution has variance $\frac{\eta}{2}$. To sample according to β_η, one sample $(a_1, \cdots, a_\eta, b_1, \cdots, b_\eta) \leftarrow \{0, 1\}^{2\eta}$ and output $\sum_{i=1}^{\eta} (a_i - b_i)$.

When we write that a polynomial $f \in R_q$ or a vector of such polynomials is sampled from β_η, we mean that each coefficient of it is sampled from β_η. In practice, the number η is much smaller than q.

2.2   Spherical Cap

Let d be a positive integer. For vectors $u, v \in \mathbb{R}^d$, the angle between u, v is

$$\theta(u, v) = \arccos \left(\frac{< u, v >}{\|u\| \cdot \|v\|} \right).$$

This is a useful notation to describe the difference between two vectors and is known as "angular distance". It is an important tool in our analysis throughout this paper. We will focus more on the directions and the angles instead of the length of vectors. In [5], the *spherical cap* is introduced to characterize the information available from each successful query.

Definition 1. *Let $\mathcal{S}_d$ be the unit hypersphere in $\mathbb{R}^d$. For any $u \in \mathcal{S}_d$, the spherical cap of angle θ about u is*

$$\mathcal{C}(d, u, \theta) = \{v \in \mathcal{S}_d : \theta(u, v) \leq \theta\}.$$

It is proved in [5] that each successful decryption can rule out key candidates in the corresponding spherical caps. Thus, the size of the surface area of caps is closely related to the number of excluded key candidates. Let σ_{d-1} denote the usual surface measure on $\mathcal{S}_d$, the following heuristic from [5] is useful in applying surface area of spherical caps to measure points of interest and will be assumed in our later discussion.

Heuristic 1. *For a fixed $u \in \mathcal{S}_d$, let v be a uniformly random point on $\mathcal{S}_d$. The probability of $\theta(u, v) \leq \theta$ is*

$$\sigma_{d-1}\left(\mathcal{C}(d, u, \theta)\right).$$

We shall perform some explicit calculation for the surface area of a spherical cap. In [19], a concise area formula for such a cap is derived in closed form. This formula involves with the so called *incomplete beta function* defined by

$$B(x, \nu, \mu) = \int_0^x t^{\nu-1}(1-t)^{\mu-1}dt, \ 0 \leq x \leq 1.$$

Note that $B(1, \nu, \mu)$ is the usual beta function $B(\nu, \mu) = \int_0^1 t^{\nu-1}(1-t)^{\mu-1}dt = \frac{\Gamma(\nu)\Gamma(\mu)}{\Gamma(\nu+\mu)}$. We normalize the incomplete beta function and denote it by

$$I_x(\nu, \mu) = \frac{B(x, \nu, \mu)}{B(\nu, \mu)}.$$

The formula for the cap surface area of $\mathcal{C}(d, u, \theta)$ given in [19] is

$$A_d^{cap}(\theta) = \frac{1}{2}A_d I_{\sin^2(\theta)}\left(\frac{d-1}{2}, \frac{1}{2}\right),$$

where $A_d = \frac{2\pi^{\frac{d}{2}}}{\Gamma(\frac{d}{2})}$ is the surface area of $\mathcal{S}_d$.

As for the surface area of the intersection of two spherical caps, some concise formulas are given in [18]. Let $A_d\left(\theta, \theta(u_1, u_2)\right)$[1] be the intersection area of $\mathcal{C}(d, u_1, \theta)$ and $\mathcal{C}(d, u_2, \theta)$. The following two cases are of greatest concern to us:

1. When $\theta(u_1, u_2) \geq 2\theta$, $A_d\left(\theta, \theta(u_1, u_2)\right) = 0$.

---

[1] The surface area of the intersection does not depend on u_1 or u_2. It is only related to the angle between them.

2. When $\theta < \theta(u_1, u_2) < 2\theta < 2\pi - \theta(u_1, u_2)$,

$$A_d\left(\theta, \theta(u_1, u_2)\right) = \frac{\pi^{\frac{d-1}{2}}}{\Gamma\left(\frac{d-1}{2}\right)} \cdot \left(J_d\left(\widetilde{\theta}, \theta\right) + J_d\left(\theta(u_1, u_2) - \widetilde{\theta}, \theta\right)\right), \text{ where}$$

$$\begin{cases} \widetilde{\theta} = \arctan\left(\frac{1}{\sin(\theta(u_1, u_2))} - \frac{1}{\tan(\theta(u_1, u_2))}\right) \\ J_d(\theta_1, \theta_2) = \int_{\theta_1}^{\theta_2} \sin(\phi)^{d-2} I_{1-\left(\frac{\tan(\theta_1)}{\tan(\phi)}\right)^2}\left(\frac{d}{2} - 1, \frac{1}{2}\right) d\phi \end{cases}$$

The formulas for $A_d\left(\theta, \theta(u_1, u_2)\right)$ for other cases can be found in [18].

3   Compression Errors

As mentioned earlier, there are compression errors u, u', u'' in the (R/M-)LWE/LWR-based schemes. In practice, many schemes based on (R/M-)LWE also have a step for ciphertext compression, such as Kyber and Newhope, so there are also compression errors in these schemes. According to our experiments in Sect. 6, the compression error is sometimes as large as the LWE error when they both are present. Therefore, it is desirable to consider both errors. However, many previous works on schemes based on (R/M-)LWE only considered the LWE error and ignored the compression error. The purpose of this section is to characterize compression error more precisely by proving that it is essentially a uniform distribution on certain set. This will be useful in analyzing the distributions of S, C, G as well as decryption failure later.

Definition 2. *Fix two positive integers $p < q$, the compression error function $CD_{p,q} : \mathbb{Z} \to \mathbb{Z}$ is defined as*

$$CD_{p,q}(y) = y - \left\lceil \frac{q}{p} \left\lceil \frac{p}{q} y \right\rceil \right\rceil.$$

This function measures the difference caused by the rounding and reconstruction operations. It can be easily extended to the cases of vectors of integers and polynomials with integer coefficients, by working in a component-wise manner.

Now let us consider the characterization of the distribution of $CD_{p,q}(y)$. In practice, the only cases of interest are $\gcd(p, q) = 1$ and $p|q$, so we shall simply deal with these two cases. But we would like to remark that the discussion also applies to the general case of $\gcd(p, q) > 1$. The following theorem states the results whose proof is given in Appendix A.

Theorem 1. *For positive integers $p < q$, characterizations of $CD_{p,q}$ for the following two cases are:*

1. *If $(p, q) = 1$, then $CD_{p,q}(y) = \left\lceil \frac{b}{p} \right\rceil$ where $b = py$ mods q. Furthermore, if y is uniformly random chosen from $\mathbb{Z}$ or $\mathbb{Z}_q$, b is uniformly random in $\mathbb{Z}_q$, $CD_{p,q}(y)$ belongs to $\left\{-\left\lceil \frac{q}{2p} \right\rceil, \cdots, \left\lceil \frac{q}{2p} \right\rceil\right\}$ and has the same probability at all of the integer points except $-\left\lceil \frac{q}{2p} \right\rceil$ and $\left\lceil \frac{q}{2p} \right\rceil$.*

2. If $p|q$, then with $m = \frac{q}{p}$, $CD_{p,q}(y) = d$ where $d = y$ mods m. Furthermore, if y is uniformly random chosen from $\mathbb{Z}$ or $\mathbb{Z}_q$, $CD_{p,q}(y)$ is uniformly random in $\mathbb{Z}_m$.

With this theorem, we are able to analyze the distributions of u, u' and u''.

Under the difficulty hypothesis of LWE, $As + e$, $A^T s' + e'$, $b_r^T s' + e' + enc(m)$ are computationally indistinguishable from uniform distributions on R_q^k, R_q^k and R_q respectively. Therefore, when $\gcd(p,q) = \gcd(t,q) = 1$, each coefficient of u, u' belongs to $\left\{-\left\lceil\frac{q}{2p}\right\rceil, \cdots, \left\lceil\frac{q}{2p}\right\rceil\right\}$ and has the same probability at all integer points inside except $\pm\left\lceil\frac{q}{2p}\right\rceil$, each coefficient of u'' belongs to $\left\{-\left\lceil\frac{q}{2t}\right\rceil, \cdots, \left\lceil\frac{q}{2t}\right\rceil\right\}$ and has the same probability at all integer points inside except $\pm\left\lceil\frac{q}{2t}\right\rceil$.

While if $t|p|q$, each coefficient of u, u' is computationally indistinguishable from a uniform random point in $\mathbb{Z}_{\frac{q}{p}}$, each coefficient of u'' is computationally indistinguishable from a uniform random point in $\mathbb{Z}_{\frac{q}{t}}$.

We use $\psi_{p,q}^k$ to denote the *compression error distribution* for sampling a vector of k polynomials of degree $n - 1$ in the following steps

1. choose $y \leftarrow \mathcal{U}(R^k)$ where $\mathcal{U}$ denotes the uniform distribution;
2. return $CD_{p,q}(y)$ mods q.

This distribution will be used in our later discussion of the concrete schemes of Kyber and Newhope.

4   The Information Inferred by Successful Decryptions

In [5], the authors show that a successful decryption implies that the secret $\overline{S}$ (after normalization) stays away from one (or two) spherical caps.[2] It is noted that [5] contains some ideas for rotations of polynomials, but did not use it in a full extent. In addition, some formulas and experiment settings in [5] do not seem to be consistent. In this section, we will consider excluding caps corresponding to each rotation of a polynomial vector. A more accurate and precise calculation is given using the results in Sect. 3 and some formulas in [19].

4.1   The Relationship Between Successful Decryptions and Caps

We are considering CCA security for schemes where both C and G are obtained by hash function calls. We can view a pair of (C, G) as a query to the decryption oracle. Our setting will restrict to the reaction attack, namely, the adversary only cares if the query succeeds, not what it returns if the decryption fails.

Let $\overline{\overline{S}}$, $\overline{\overline{C}}$ be the normalization of $\overline{S}, \overline{C}$, namely, $\overline{\overline{S}} = \frac{\overline{S}}{\|\overline{S}\|}$, $\overline{\overline{C}} = \frac{\overline{C}}{\|\overline{C}\|}$. It has been proven in [5] that the success of query C is related to the fact whether $\overline{\overline{S}}$

---

[2] Two caps are considered at the end of page 8 of [5], but the definition of efficacy on page 9 contains only one cap.

belongs to some spherical caps about $\overline{\overline{C}}$. Combined with the analysis of the distributions of u, u', u'' given in Sect. 3, a finer description of the angle information obtained by a successful decryption can be obtained.

To this end, we know that for each pair of (C, G), the success of the decryption implies that

$$\left| \overline{S}^T \overline{C^{(r)}} + G_r \right| \leq \frac{q}{4}$$

holds true for all $r = 0, 1, \cdots, n - 1$. Recall that $G = e'' - u''$. The distribution of the coefficients of u'' has been discussed in Sect. 3, while the distribution of the coefficients of e'' depends on the specific algorithm (and e'' is available to be selected by the adversary). So one can find a constant γ such that $\gamma \geq |G_r|$, $r = 0, 1, \cdots, n - 1$. γ should be as small as possible. Therefore, for every successful query, the information that the attacker can definitely obtain is[3]

$$\left| \overline{S}^T \overline{C^{(r)}} \right| \leq \frac{q}{4} + \gamma, r = 0, 1, \cdots, n - 1.$$

Let θ_r be the angle between $\overline{S}$ and $\overline{C^{(r)}}$ (which is also the angle between $\overline{\overline{S}}$ and $\overline{\overline{C^{(r)}}}$). We denote the distribution that the user uses to pick S by χ_S, and the distribution that the attacker uses to pick C by χ_C. Let $\mathfrak{S}, \mathfrak{C}$ be two random variables with $\mathfrak{S} \leftarrow \chi_S, \mathfrak{C} \leftarrow \chi_C$. Suppose that the attacker only selects those C such that $\|C\| \geq E[\|\mathfrak{C}\|]$ to query. The attack model assumes that S satisfies

$$\|S\| \geq E[\|\mathfrak{S}\|].$$

This means that some private key candidates cannot be treated in the present setting. However, as we will comment later that this condition can be weakened to cover a bigger set of private keys with some efficiency trade-off. With the assumption of $\|S\| \geq E[\|\mathfrak{S}\|]$, we see that

$$|\cos(\theta_r)| = \left| \frac{\langle \overline{S}, \overline{C^{(r)}} \rangle}{\|\overline{S}\| \cdot \|\overline{C^{(r)}}\|} \right| = \frac{\left| \overline{S}^T \overline{C^{(r)}} \right|}{\|\overline{S}\| \cdot \|\overline{C^{(r)}}\|} \leq \frac{\frac{q}{4} + \gamma}{\|\overline{S}\| \cdot \|\overline{C^{(r)}}\|} \leq \frac{\frac{q}{4} + \gamma}{E[\|\mathfrak{S}\|] \cdot E[\|\mathfrak{C}\|]}.$$

Let us denote $\theta^* \in \left[0, \frac{\pi}{2} \right)$ to be the angle that satisfies $\cos \theta^* = \frac{\frac{q}{4} + \gamma}{E[\|\mathfrak{S}\|] \cdot E[\|\mathfrak{C}\|]}$. If $\cos(\theta_r) \geq 0$, we have $\theta_r \geq \theta^*$, this implies that $\overline{\overline{S}} \notin \mathcal{C}\left(2kn, \overline{\overline{C^{(r)}}}, \theta^* \right)$. Similarly, if $\cos(\theta_r) < 0$, we have $\overline{\overline{S}} \notin \mathcal{C}\left(2kn, -\overline{\overline{C^{(r)}}}, \theta^* \right)$. In summary, for each successful C, we can exclude key candidates in $2n$ spherical caps, in the sense that

$$\overline{\overline{S}} \notin \mathcal{C}\left(2kn, \pm \overline{\overline{C^{(r)}}}, \theta^* \right), \ r = 0, 1, \cdots, n - 1.$$

---

[3] $\frac{q}{4} - \gamma$ was used to bound the LHS in [5], the experiments were performed accordingly. Corrections are necessary.

In the above analysis, the attacker just deals with the set of S such that $\|S\| \geq E[\|\mathbb{S}\|]$ since the exact value of $\|S\|$ is unknown.[4] This condition can be relaxed. For any $\beta > 0$, he can suppose that $\|S\| \geq \beta \cdot E[\|\mathbb{S}\|]$ and the information he can get is $|\cos(\theta_r)| \leq \frac{\frac{q}{4}+\gamma}{\beta \cdot E[\|\mathbb{S}\|] \cdot E[\|\mathbb{C}\|]}$. (When $\beta \leq \frac{\frac{q}{4}+\gamma}{E[\|\mathbb{S}\|] \cdot E[\|\mathbb{C}\|]}$, nothing is available.) It is easy to see that, the larger β is, the larger θ^* is, the more information he can obtain, but the less likely S is to satisfy this condition. Moreover, we assume that the attacker only uses C that satisfies $\|C\| \geq E[\|\mathbb{C}\|]$. That is, given a ciphertext C, if $\|C\| < E[\|\mathbb{C}\|]$, he will discard it and regenerate another ciphertext for attack. Similarly, he can also choose to use only longer queries, but the cost of finding such ciphertexts will increase significantly. In this paper, we only consider the case where $\|S\| \geq E[\|\mathbb{S}\|]$ and all queries used by the attacker have a length at least $E[\|\mathbb{C}\|]$. In this way, we can always use the same θ^* for different queries. It is noticed that our discussion also applies to other cases.

4.2   The Range of the Proportion of Excluded Key Candidates

Recall that we use θ_r to denote the angle between $\overline{\overline{S}}$ and $\overline{\overline{C^{(r)}}}$. The following lemma from [5] is useful in numerical characterization of the proportion of key candidates.

Lemma 2. *For a fixed S and $C \leftarrow \chi_C$, for any $r \in [0, 2n-1]$, the probability that $\theta_r < \theta^*$ is $\sigma_{2kn-1}\left(\mathcal{C}\left(2kn, \overline{\overline{C^{(r)}}}, \theta^*\right)\right)$.*

This lemma says that the proportion of key candidates in $\mathcal{C}\left(2kn, \overline{\overline{C^{(r)}}}, \theta^*\right)$ is exactly $\sigma_{2kn-1}\left(\mathcal{C}\left(2kn, \overline{\overline{C^{(r)}}}, \theta^*\right)\right)$. In other words, candidates with a ratio of $\sigma_{2kn-1}\left(\mathcal{C}\left(2kn, \overline{\overline{C^{(r)}}}, \theta^*\right)\right)$ can be eliminated by each cap.

By the formula we mentioned in Sect. 2 (from [19]), we give an exact and effective[5] way of calculating of $\sigma_{2kn-1}\left(\mathcal{C}\left(2kn, \overline{\overline{C^{(r)}}}, \theta^*\right)\right)$ using the explicit expression of the surface area of a cap. That is

$$\sigma_{2kn-1}\left(\mathcal{C}\left(2kn, \overline{\overline{C^{(r)}}}, \theta^*\right)\right) = \frac{A_{2kn}^{cap}(\theta^*)}{A_{2kn}} = \frac{1}{2}I_{\sin^2(\theta^*)}\left(kn - \frac{1}{2}, \frac{1}{2}\right).$$

As mentioned earlier, each successful decryption can help with excluding key candidates in $2n$ spherical caps. However, the overlaps among them is not certain.

---

[4] In fact, the adversary might know what $\|S\|$ is. In some schemes, s, e are sampled according to the centered binomial distribution with fixed Hamming weight, such as LAC. In this case, $\|S\|$ is fixed and the attacker can just use the value of $\|S\|$. However, there are also some schemes that use a discrete Gaussian or centered binomial distribution to sample s, e, such as Kyber and Saber. Some restrictions on $\|S\|$ are necessary.

[5] The normal incomplete beta function can be effectively calculated using software such as Matlab.

It is easy to see that $C\left(2kn, \overline{\overline{C^{(r)}}}, \theta^*\right) \cap C\left(2kn, -\overline{\overline{C^{(r)}}}, \theta^*\right) = \emptyset, r = 0, 1,$
$\cdots, n-1,$ but different $C\left(2kn, \overline{\overline{C^{(r)}}}, \theta^*\right)$ may intersect with each other. So the proportion of key candidates that can be excluded by a successful decryption belongs to

$$\left[I_{\sin^2(\theta^*)}\left(kn - \frac{1}{2}, \frac{1}{2}\right), nI_{\sin^2(\theta^*)}\left(kn - \frac{1}{2}, \frac{1}{2}\right)\right].$$

Then the proportion of key candidates that can be excluded by m successful decryptions belongs to

$$\left[I_{\sin^2(\theta^*)}\left(kn - \frac{1}{2}, \frac{1}{2}\right), mnI_{\sin^2(\theta^*)}\left(kn - \frac{1}{2}, \frac{1}{2}\right)\right].$$

We summarize the above analysis as the following proportion.

Proposition 1. *Suppose that an adversary has made some successful queries to the decryption oracle, then the proportion of key candidates that can be excluded is at least $I_{\sin^2(\theta^*)}\left(kn - \frac{1}{2}, \frac{1}{2}\right)$.*

In this section, we only give a rough range of the proportion of the excluded key candidates after m successful queries. It is noticed that, if the attacker has made m successful queries, this proportion could even be $mnI_{\sin_{\theta^*}^2}\left(kn - \frac{1}{2}, \frac{1}{2}\right)$ when certain conditions are met. In the next section, we shall specify such conditions in terms of overlap reduction by quantifying the overlaps among queries. Some exact formulas for the overlaps among queries are presented and a finer range of the proportion is given.

5   The Overlaps Among Queries and the Effect of Successful Decryptions on the Failure Probability

In Sect. 4, a more accurate calculation of the proportion of key candidates contained in each spherical cap has been developed. However, when considering several caps corresponding to one or more queries, the intersections of them will directly affect the attack efficiency. In [5], the notion of *efficacy* of a query set is defined to measure the information available from it, and the use of the principle of inclusion-exclusion to calculate the efficacy is proposed. Due to the complexity of the high-order inclusion-exclusion principle, a first-order approximation to the efficacy is used in [5].

However, it is noticed that the first-order approximation leads to an overestimate of the information available to the attacker, so it can not be used to calculate the number of queries needed for finding a decryption failure. In this section, we use a second-order approximation to measure the information from successful queries to get a lower bound. These two approximations result a fine range of the proportion of excluded key candidates together.

Let W_C denote the set of $2n$ spherical caps according to the query C, i.e.

$$W_C = \left\{C\left(2kn, \pm\overline{\overline{C^{(r)}}}, \theta^*\right) : r = 0, 1, \cdots, n - 1\right\}.$$

Suppose the attacker has made m successful queries $C_1, \cdots, C_m$. Not only the overlaps among the caps in each W_{C_i}, but also the overlaps among $W_{C_1}, \cdots, W_{C_m}$ should be considered. The former was considered in [5] as they only calculated one of the $2n$ caps in each W_{C_i}, but the latter was left untreated.[6]

In this section, we consider both of the overlapping situations. We give the conditions and probability of the first-order approximation. The second-order approximation is obtained with more precise formulas to quantify the overlaps. Meanwhile, we come up with some suggestions on how to make the overlaps smaller.

We shall start by dealing with the simplest case – the overlap between two spherical caps.

5.1   The Overlap Between Two Spherical Caps

First of all, we need the one-to-one correspondences between angle and inner product, distance respectively. Two useful relationships are given in the following proposition and the proofs are given in Appendix B.

Proposition 2. *For* $\overline{\overline{C_1}}, \overline{\overline{C_2}} \in \mathcal{S}_d$, *let* $\theta_{1,2} = \theta\left(\overline{\overline{C_1}}, \overline{\overline{C_2}}\right)$, $d_{1,2} = \left\|\overline{\overline{C_1}} - \overline{\overline{C_2}}\right\|$ *and* $ip_{1,2} = \langle \overline{\overline{C_1}}, \overline{\overline{C_2}} \rangle$, *then*

1. $\theta_{1,2} = \arccos\left(ip_{1,2}\right),\ ip_{1,2} = \cos(\theta_{1,2}).$
2. $\theta_{1,2} = 2\arcsin\left(\frac{1}{2}d_{1,2}\right),\ d_{1,2} = 2\sin\left(\frac{1}{2}\theta_{1,2}\right).$

Let us consider the overlap between two caps $\mathcal{C}\left(2kn, \overline{\overline{C_1}}, \theta^*\right)$ and $\mathcal{C}\left(2kn, \overline{\overline{C_2}}, \theta^*\right)$. We denote $\mathcal{C}_{1,2} = \mathcal{C}\left(2kn, \overline{\overline{C_1}}, 0^*\right) \cap \mathcal{C}\left(2kn, \overline{\overline{C_2}}, \theta^*\right)$. We will show that the disjointness of these two caps can be characterized by the inner product, angle, and distance of $\overline{\overline{C_1}}, \overline{\overline{C_2}}$ respectively. The following theorem is given and its proof is in Appendix C.

Theorem 2. *Let* $\overline{\overline{C_1}}, \overline{\overline{C_2}}$ *be two points on* $\mathcal{S}_d$, *then the following are equivalent:*

1. $\mathcal{C}_{1,2} = \emptyset.$
2. $\theta_{1,2} > 2\theta^*.$
3. $ip_{1,2} < \cos\left(2\theta^*\right).$
4. $d_{1,2} > 2\sin\theta^*.$

The above theorem give strategies for selecting completely disjoint spherical caps. The adversary can choose one of the angle condition, the distance condition and the inner product condition to check the disjointness. However, sometimes it may be impractical to choose completely non-overlapping queries for reasons such as efficiency. Therefore, the situation where those caps intersect is of interest. The following proposition is a direct consequence of formulas in [18]. It can be used to calculate the proportion of key candidates in $\mathcal{C}_{1,2}$.

---

[6] In other words, they assumed that the first order approximation is true.

Proposition 3. *Let $\overline{\overline{C_1}}$, $\overline{\overline{C_2}}$ be two points on S_{2kn}. Let $\theta_{1,2}$ be as in Proposition 2 and $J_d(\theta_1, \theta_2)$ be as in Sect. 2.2. Then, if $\theta_{1,2} \geq 2\theta^*$, $\sigma_{2kn-1}(C_{1,2}) = 0$. If $\theta^* < \theta_{1,2} < 2\theta^*$, we have[7]*

$$\sigma_{2kn-1}(C_{1,2}) = \frac{A_{2kn}(\theta^*, \theta_{1,2})}{A_{2kn}} = \frac{1}{2\sqrt{\pi}} \frac{\Gamma(kn)}{\Gamma\left(kn - \frac{1}{2}\right)} \cdot \left(J_{2kn}\left(\widetilde{\theta}_{1,2}, \theta^*\right) + J_{2kn}\left(\theta_{1,2} - \widetilde{\theta}_{1,2}, \theta^*\right)\right),$$

where $\widetilde{\theta}_{1,2} = \arctan\left(\frac{1}{\sin(\theta_{1,2})} - \frac{1}{\tan(\theta_{1,2})}\right)$. In particular, if kn is even, we have

$$\sigma_{2kn-1}(C_{1,2}) = \frac{1}{2\pi} \cdot \frac{(2kn-2)!!}{(2kn-3)!!} \cdot \left(J_{2kn}\left(\widetilde{\theta}_{1,2}, \theta^*\right) + J_{2kn}\left(\theta_{1,2} - \widetilde{\theta}_{1,2}, \theta^*\right)\right).$$

The above proposition gives an efficient[8] way of calculating the total proportion of the keys candidates inside two intersecting caps by the following relation:

$$\sigma\left(\mathcal{C}\left(2kn, \overline{\overline{C_1}}, \theta^*\right) \cup \mathcal{C}\left(2kn, \overline{\overline{C_2}}, \theta^*\right)\right) = \sigma\left(\mathcal{C}\left(2kn, \overline{\overline{C_1}}, \theta^*\right)\right) + \sigma\left(\mathcal{C}\left(2kn, \overline{\overline{C_2}}, \theta^*\right)\right) - \sigma(C_{1,2}).$$

From this, we can raise the lower bound in Proposition 1.

As we can see, $\theta_{1,2}$ is an important indicator for characterizing $C_{1,2}$. However, because of the tedium of calculating the angles between each pair of queries one by one, an estimation of $\theta_{1,2}$ is needed. Since we are considering the CCA setting where queries are the results of hash function calls, we can view each query $\overline{C}$ (after normalization) as a uniform random point on S_{2kn}. Then $\theta_{1,2}$ can be regarded as an angle in random packing on the sphere. To proceed further, we need some technical argument on this kind of random angles.

The dimension of (R/M-)LWE/LWR-based public-key encryption schemes is usually very high. There is a folklore conjecture that random vectors in high dimensional spaces are almost nearly orthogonal. This is also referred to as the orthogonality hypothesis. Recently, Cai et al. [7] presented a precise formulation and gave the proof of the orthogonality hypothesis.

Lemma 3 [7]. *Let u, v be two random points on S_d, then*

$$Pr\left(\left|\theta(u, v) - \frac{\pi}{2}\right| \geq \epsilon\right) \leq K\sqrt{d}\left(\cos\epsilon\right)^{d-2}$$

for any $d \geq 2$ and $\epsilon \in \left(0, \frac{\pi}{2}\right)$, where K is a universal constant.

As indicated in [7], any number K satisfies $K \geq \sqrt{\frac{\pi}{d}}\frac{\Gamma\left(\frac{d}{2}\right)}{\Gamma\left(\frac{d-1}{2}\right)}$ would be sufficient.

It is remarked that a tighter estimation of K is of great interest in practice. To this end, we use some results for Wallis type inequalities. Let $P_d = \frac{(2d-1)!!}{(2d)!!}$ and $P_{d+\frac{1}{2}} = \frac{(2d)!!}{(2d+1)!!}$, then it has been proven in [8,17] that

$$\frac{1}{\sqrt{\pi(d + 4/\pi - 1)}} \leq P_d < \frac{1}{\sqrt{\pi(d + 1/4)}}, \quad \frac{\sqrt{\pi}}{2\sqrt{d + 9\pi/16 - 1}} \leq P_{d+\frac{1}{2}} < \frac{\sqrt{\pi}}{2\sqrt{d + 3/4}}.$$

---

[7] The conditions chosen here are satisfied in all of the schemes in our experiments. The result can be generalized to the case where $\theta_{1,2} < \theta^*$ by using formulas in [18].

[8] The code for computing $J_d(\theta_1, \theta_2)$ is given in [18]. Since we have made a slight change in the definition of $J_d(\theta_1, \theta_2)$, a small adjustment to the code is required.

From these, we can derive a better bound for $\sqrt{\frac{\pi}{d}}\frac{\Gamma(\frac{d}{2})}{\Gamma(\frac{d-1}{2})}$, namely

$$\sqrt{\frac{\pi}{d}}\frac{\Gamma(\frac{d}{2})}{\Gamma(\frac{d-1}{2})} \leq \begin{cases} \sqrt{\frac{\pi}{2} - \frac{2\pi - 4}{d}} & \text{if } d \text{ is even} \\ \sqrt{\frac{\pi}{2} - \frac{\frac{5}{2}\pi - \frac{9}{16}\pi^2}{d}} & \text{if } d \text{ is odd.} \end{cases}$$

Normally, one can simply set $K = \sqrt{\frac{\pi}{2}}$. When considering specific schemes, the dimension $d = 2kn$ is even, so we get the following result about the distribution of $\theta_{1,2}$ with a better bound:

Corollary 1. *Let* $\overline{\overline{C_1}}$, $\overline{\overline{C_2}}$ *be two points on* S_{2kn}, *let* $\theta_{1,2}$ *be as in Proposition 2. For any* $\epsilon \in \left(0, \frac{\pi}{2}\right)$, *we have*

$$Pr\left(\left|\theta_{1,2} - \frac{\pi}{2}\right| \geq \epsilon\right) \leq \sqrt{\pi kn + 4 - 2\pi}\,(\cos\epsilon)^{2kn-2}.$$

Let $M > 0$ be some security parameter and set $\epsilon(M) = \arccos\left(\frac{2^M - 1}{2^M\sqrt{\pi kn + 4 - 2\pi}}\right)^{\frac{1}{2kn-2}}$. Then it can be verified that

$$\epsilon(M) = \min_{\epsilon\in\left(0,\frac{\pi}{2}\right)}\left\{\sqrt{\pi kn + 4 - 2\pi}\,(\cos\epsilon)^{2kn-2} \geq 1 - \frac{1}{2^M}\right\}.$$

From this, an estimate of the range of $\theta_{1,2}$ is given.

Theorem 3. *Let* $\overline{\overline{C_1}}$, $\overline{\overline{C_2}}$ *be two points on* S_{2kn}. *For any given security parameter* M, *we have*

$$\frac{\pi}{2} - \epsilon(M) \leq \theta_{1,2} \leq \frac{\pi}{2} + \epsilon(M)$$

with a probability no less than $1 - \frac{1}{2^M}$.

Together with Theorem 2, we know that if $2\theta^* < \frac{\pi}{2} - \epsilon(M)$, the probability of $C_{1,2} = \emptyset$ is bigger than $1 - \frac{1}{2^M}$. On the other hand, if $2\theta^* > \frac{\pi}{2} + \epsilon(M)$, the probability of $C_{1,2} = \emptyset$ is less than $\frac{1}{2^M}$. It is worth noting that, from our experiments in Sect. 6, θ^* is greater than $\frac{\pi}{4}$ in most schemes. Hence, $C_{1,2} = \emptyset$ is almost not true and Proposition 3 is useful in measuring the surface area of the intersections.

5.2   The Overlaps Among Queries

Suppose that the attacker is making m queries. Just like [Equation (9), [5]], we only consider one cap for each query C_i, for example, $\mathcal{C}\left(2kn, \overline{\overline{C_i^{(0)}}}, \theta^*\right)$. The reason is that we want to consider the overlaps among the caps of different queries. This will not make much difference to the result as $m \gg n$ in practice. For convenience, for each C_i, we write $C_i = \mathcal{C}\left(2kn, \overline{\overline{C_i^{(r_i)}}}, \theta^*\right), 0 \leq r_i \leq n - 1$ to be the cap used by the attacker.

It is noted that $\overline{C_i^{(r_i)}}(i = 1, 2, \cdots, m)$ can be seen as m uniformly random points on $\mathcal{S}_{2kn}$. Let $\theta_{i,j}$ ($1 \leq i < j \leq m$) be the angles between $\overline{C_i^{(r_i)}}$ and $\overline{C_j^{(r_j)}}$. We assume that these angles are independent and identically distributed and are likely in the range described in Theorem 3 in the sense that

$$\frac{\pi}{2} - \epsilon(M) \leq \theta_{i,j} \leq \frac{\pi}{2} + \epsilon(M) \text{ with a probability no less than } 1 - \frac{1}{2^M}.$$

We use a second-order approximation to estimate the proportion of key candidates that can be excluded after m successful queries to get a lower bound, that is

$$\sigma\left(\bigcup_{i=1}^m \mathcal{C}_i\right) \geq \sum_{i=1}^m \sigma\left(\mathcal{C}_i\right) - \sum_{1 \leq i < j \leq m} \sigma\left(\mathcal{C}_{i,j}\right),$$

where $\mathcal{C}_{i,j}$ is the intersection of $\mathcal{C}_i$ and $\mathcal{C}_j$.

Consequently, we can get a range of the proportion of excluded key candidates, that is

$$\sigma\left(\bigcup_{i=1}^m \mathcal{C}_i\right) \in \left[\sum_{i=1}^m \sigma\left(\mathcal{C}_i\right) - \sum_{1 \leq i < j \leq m} \sigma\left(\mathcal{C}_{i,j}\right), \sum_{i=1}^m \sigma\left(\mathcal{C}_i\right)\right]$$

Now we give a more specific description. It is noted that if $2\theta^* \geq \frac{\pi}{2} - \epsilon(M)$, the spherical caps may intersect. From Proposition 3, if $\theta_{i,j} \geq 2\theta^*$, we have $\sigma\left(\mathcal{C}_{i,j}\right) = 0$. Otherwise, if $\theta_{i,j} < 2\theta^*$, we have (n is assumed to be even, which is always true in practice)

$$\sigma\left(\mathcal{C}_{i,j}\right) = \frac{J_{2kn}\left(\tilde{\theta}_{i,j}, \theta^*\right) + J_{2kn}\left(\theta_{i,j} - \tilde{\theta}_{i,j}, \theta^*\right)}{2\pi P_{kn-1}},$$

where $\tilde{\theta}_{i,j} = \arctan\left(\frac{1}{\sin(\theta_{i,j})} - \frac{1}{\tan(\theta_{i,j})}\right), 1 \leq i < j \leq m$. Hence,

$$\sigma\left(\bigcup_{i=1}^m \mathcal{C}_i\right) \geq \frac{m}{2} I_{\sin^2 \theta^*}\left(kn - \frac{1}{2}, \frac{1}{2}\right) - \sum_{1 \leq i < j \leq m} \frac{J_{2kn}\left(\tilde{\theta}_{i,j}, \theta^*\right) + J_{2kn}\left(\theta_{i,j} - \tilde{\theta}_{i,j}, \theta^*\right)}{2\pi P_{kn-1}}.$$

We denote the right-hand side of the above inequality by $\Omega(m)$, which represents the second-order approximation of the proportion of key candidates that can be excluded by m successful decryption. It can be calculated efficiently using the codes in [18].

On the other hand, if $2\theta^* < \frac{\pi}{2} - \epsilon(M)$, the probability that $\sigma\left(\mathcal{C}_{i,j}\right) = 0$ is at least $1 - \frac{1}{2^M}$ for each pair of (i, j). Hence, one can take M to be a large integer, then the following

$$\sigma\left(\bigcup_{i=1}^m \mathcal{C}_i\right) = \frac{m}{2} I_{\sin^2 \theta^*}\left(kn - \frac{1}{2}, \frac{1}{2}\right)$$

holds with a probability no less than $\left(1 - \frac{1}{2^M}\right)^{\frac{m(m-1)}{2}}$.

There is a little trick for picking a suitable M. Since $\lim_{x\to\infty}\left(1 - \frac{1}{x}\right)^x = \frac{1}{e}$, the attacker can take $M = \left\lceil \log_2\left(\frac{m(m-1)}{2}\right)\right\rceil$ to make sure the probability is no less than $\frac{1}{e}$.

In fact, in the case where $2\theta^* < \frac{\pi}{2} - \epsilon(M)$, we can refine our results slightly. Since $\theta\left(\overline{C_i^{(r_i)}}, \overline{C_j^{(r_j)}}\right) = \pi - \theta\left(\overline{C_i^{(r_i)}}, -\overline{C_j^{(r_j)}}\right)$, $\theta\left(\overline{C_i^{(r_i)}}, -\overline{C_j^{(r_j)}}\right)$ also belongs to $\left[\frac{\pi}{2} - \epsilon(M), \frac{\pi}{2} + \epsilon(M)\right]$ when $\theta_{i,j} \in \left[\frac{\pi}{2} - \epsilon(M), \frac{\pi}{2} + \epsilon(M)\right]$. So in this case, if we consider two caps associated with each query, the result can be improved to:

$$\sigma\left(\bigcup_{i=1}^{m} \mathcal{C}\left(2kn, \pm\overline{\overline{C_i^{(r_i)}}}, \theta^*\right)\right) = m I_{\sin^2\theta^*}\left(kn - \frac{1}{2}, \frac{1}{2}\right) \text{ with a probability no}$$

less than $\left(1 - \frac{1}{2^M}\right)^{\frac{m(m-1)}{2}}$.

Then, Proposition 1 can be further extended to the following theorem.

Theorem 4. *Suppose that an adversary has made m successful queries to the decryption oracle. The proportion of excluded key candidates is greater than $\Omega(m)$. Moreover, for a positive integer M, if $2\theta^* < \frac{\pi}{2} - \epsilon(M)$, this proportion is at least $m I_{\sin^2\theta^*}\left(kn - \frac{1}{2}, \frac{1}{2}\right)$ with a probability no less than $\left(1 - \frac{1}{2^M}\right)^{\frac{m(m-1)}{2}}$.*

The experimental data in Sect. 6 shows that, the results of the first-order and the second-order approximations are usually very close. Therefore, we can always get a finer range of the proportion of key candidates that can be excluded.

In the analysis above, we only consider one (or two) of the caps for each query because of the strong correlation between two different rotations of the same query. Theorem 3 does not apply in this case.[9] Moreover, we also give some results on the overlaps among different caps of the same query in Appendix D.

5.3 The Decryption Failure Probability

In this paper, we have been using the relationship between the fact that C fails to be correctly decrypted and the event that $\overline{\overline{S}}$ belongs to some spherical caps about C. However, how much are the two different? In this subsection, we discuss the relationship between their probabilities.

For each query C_i, we write F_i to denote the event that "C_i fails", S_i to denote the event "C_i succeeds". We denote $P[F_i]$ to be the unconditional failure probability of C_i (i.e., the probability is independent of the status of the previous decryptions). $P[F_i]$ is estimated in [10] for the first time, and is further improved by [9]. The main idea for calculating $P[F_i]$ is that, the longer C_i is, the more likely it is to fail.

---

[9] It is noted that, from our experiments, the coefficient vectors of different rotations of the same query are always nearly orthogonal in practice, so the actual situation of the attack may be better than that stated in Theorem 4.

Recall that $C_i = \mathcal{C}\left(2kn, \overline{\overline{C_i^{(r_i)}}}, \theta^*\right), i = 1, 2, \cdots, m$. Now let us describe the relationship between $P[F_i]$ and $\sigma(\mathcal{C}_i)$. Because the failure of C_i is a necessary condition for $\overline{\overline{S}} \in \mathcal{C}_i$, the probability of $\overline{\overline{S}} \in \mathcal{C}_i$ should not be greater than that of F_i, in the sense that

$$P[F_i] \geq Pr\left[\overline{\overline{S}} \in \mathcal{C}_i\right] = \sigma(\mathcal{C}_i).$$

It should be noted that, since we have scaled up some conditions in the derivation in Sect. 4.1 and Sect. 5.2, $P[F_i]$ is very unlikely to be $\sigma(\mathcal{C}_i)$.[10]

Moreover, besides excluding wrong key candidates, the information obtained by successful decryptions can also give us a more accurate description of the failure probability of each query. For simplicity, let us take the case of two queries C_1 and C_2. We suppose that C_1 has been successful, then the posterior decryption failure probability of C_2 will be influenced by C_1. According to Bayes' theorem,

$$P[F_2|S_1] = \frac{P[S_1|F_2]}{P[S_1]} \cdot P[F_2] = \frac{P[S_1|F_2]}{1 - P[F_1]} \cdot P[F_2] = \frac{1 - P[F_1|F_2]}{1 - P[F_1]} \cdot P[F_2].$$

As previously mentioned, $P[F_1]$ and $P[F_2]$ can be estimated according to [9, 10]. Furthermore, how to estimate the failure probabilities of subsequent queries after one or more failed queries is exactly what failure boosting studied. The way of calculating $P[F_1|F_2]$ is proposed in [12] and improved in [9]. Hence, a more accurate characterization of the failure probability of C_2 can be obtained.

In summary, the method used for calculating the failure probability in failure boosting can be applied in a similar way to the case where the decryptions are successful. By using the information obtained by successful decryptions, a more accurate way of estimating the posterior decryption failure probability is obtained.

6   (R/M-)LWE-Based Public-Key Encryption Schemes

In the previous sections, by using (recent) precise geometric formulas, we get some finer numerical indication about the proportion of key candidates that can be excluded when an adversary makes successful queries to the decryption oracle. The decryption failure probability of (R/M-)LWE/LWR-based schemes has been analyzed in terms of more accurate formulations.

In this section, we use our analysis to specific encryption schemes including Kyber [3,6], Saber [4], Frodo [20], and Newhope [1]. We adopt $m = 2^{64}$ (the largest number of queries allowed by NIST) and $M = \log_2\left(\frac{m(m-1)}{2}\right)$ in

---

[10] An experiment in [Table 2, [5]] shows that $P[F_i]$ and $\sigma(\mathcal{C}_i)$ are approximately equal. This result is due to the incorrect use of $\frac{q}{4} - \gamma$, resulting in an overestimate of $\sigma(\mathcal{C}_i)$. In fact, from our experiments in Sect. 6, these two values will be very different in all schemes.

the following experiments. Given the failure probability δ (available from each parameter set of each individual scheme), we calculate the following values and display them in Table 2:

- $\epsilon(M)$, the maximum difference between the angles among queries and $\frac{\pi}{2}$, in the sense that, each angle will belong to $\left[\frac{\pi}{2} - \epsilon(M), \frac{\pi}{2} + \epsilon(M)\right]$ with a probability at least $1 - \frac{1}{2^M}$.
- θ^*, the angle that an attacker can obtain.
- $\frac{1}{2}I_{\sin^2\theta^*}\left(kn - \frac{1}{2}, \frac{1}{2}\right)$, the proportion of key candidates in each spherical cap.
- $J_{2kn}\left(\frac{\pi}{4}, \theta^*\right)$, a quantity characterizing the overlaps. The larger $J_{2kn}\left(\frac{\pi}{4}, \theta^*\right)$ is, the bigger the overlaps are.
- $\widetilde{\Omega}(m)$, an estimate of $\Omega(m)$, to be exact, an estimate of the second-order approximation of the proportion of key candidates that can be excluded by m successful decryption.

The estimation $\widetilde{\Omega}(m)$ of $\Omega(m)$ is derived by the following process. Since $\left|\theta_{i,j} - \frac{\pi}{2}\right| \le \epsilon(M)$ with a probability no less than $1 - \frac{1}{2^M}$, and $\epsilon(M)$ is always a very small angle in practice, we have

$$\theta_{i,j} \approx \frac{\pi}{2} \quad \text{and} \quad \widetilde{\theta}_{i,j} \approx \arctan(1) = \frac{\pi}{4}.$$

From the fact that $\sqrt{\pi d + \frac{\pi}{4}} < \frac{1}{P_d} \le \sqrt{\pi d + 4 - \pi}$ for any positive integer d, an estimate of $\Omega(m)$ is obtained:

$$\widetilde{\Omega}(m) := \frac{m}{2}I_{\sin^2\theta^*}\left(kn - \frac{1}{2}, \frac{1}{2}\right) - \frac{m^2 J_{2kn}\left(\frac{\pi}{4}, \theta^*\right) \cdot \sqrt{\pi(kn-1)}}{2\pi}.$$

Table 2. A summary of some security parameters for NIST post-quantum schemes.

schemes	δ	$\epsilon(M)$	θ^*	$\frac{1}{2}I_{\sin^2\theta^*}\left(kn - \frac{1}{2}, \frac{1}{2}\right)$	$J_{2kn}\left(\frac{\pi}{4}\right)$	$\widetilde{\Omega}(m)$
Kyber512	2^{-139}	4.87°	55.15°	2^{-297}	2^{-796}	2^{-233}
Kyber768	2^{-164}	4.08°	59.68°	2^{-331}	2^{-805}	2^{-267}
Kyber1024	2^{-174}	3.60°	66.65°	2^{-258}	2^{-572}	2^{-194}
LightSaber	2^{-120}	4.87°	56.20°	2^{-278}	2^{-727}	2^{-215}
Saber	2^{-136}	4.08°	65.90°	2^{-207}	2^{-464}	2^{-143}
FireSaber	2^{-165}	3.60°	69.54°	2^{-198}	2^{-429}	2^{-134}
Newhope512	2^{-213}	4.87°	20.03°	$<2^{-1000}$	\	\
Newhope1024	2^{-216}	3.60°	61.98°	2^{-374}	2^{-876}	2^{-310}
Frodo640	2^{-139}	4.42°	66.10°	2^{-171}	2^{-382}	2^{-107}

As can be seen from Table 2, all schemes except Newhope512 satisfy $2\theta^* > \frac{\pi}{2} + \epsilon(M)$, so there are overlaps in these cases. However, as the fact that $J_{2kn}\left(\frac{\pi}{4}\right) \ll I_{\sin^2\theta^*}\left(kn - \frac{1}{2}, \frac{1}{2}\right)$ in all schemes, the surface area of the overlap between two spherical caps is much smaller than that of these two caps. Therefore, for these schemes, the effect of overlaps is far from significant and $\widetilde{\Omega}(m)$ is a sufficiently accurate estimation of the proportion of key candidates that can be excluded by m successful decryption. As for Newhope512, since it satisfies $2\theta^* < \frac{\pi}{2} - \epsilon(M)$, the proportion of excluded key candidates is no less than $mI_{\sin^2\theta^*}\left(kn - \frac{1}{2}, \frac{1}{2}\right)$ with overwhelming probability. It is noted that because θ^* is small in Newhope512, $I_{\sin^2\theta^*}\left(kn - \frac{1}{2}, \frac{1}{2}\right)$ is too small to be calculated.

Recall that $\frac{1}{2}I_{\sin^2\theta^*}\left(kn - \frac{1}{2}, \frac{1}{2}\right)$ is the proportion of key candidates in a single spherical cap. We can see that $\delta \gg \frac{1}{2}I_{\sin^2\theta^*}\left(kn - \frac{1}{2}, \frac{1}{2}\right)$ in all schemes as mentioned earlier in Sect. 5.3. Such proportion of key candidates was calculated in [Table 1 (Adversary $\mathcal{B}$), [5]] using the approximation $Q_\alpha(\chi_e(2), \chi_e(2))$. It is pointed out that such an approximation is based on an erroneous interpretation of θ^* (i.e., incorrect use of $\frac{q}{2} - \gamma$). From the comparisons in Table 3, we can see that the values given in [5] are significantly bigger than the ones obtained after correction and by using accurate formulas. It is remarked that experimental data also shows that the security of those schemes in our discussion is not affected by knowing the key candidates are excluded from those spherical caps.

Table 3. Comparison with [5]

schemes	$2Q_\alpha(\chi_e(2), \chi_e(2))$ in [5]	$I_{\sin^2\theta^*}\left(kn - \frac{1}{2}, \frac{1}{2}\right)$ in this paper
Kyber512	2^{-187}	2^{-296}
Kyber768	2^{-169}	2^{-330}
Kyber1024	2^{-178}	2^{-257}
LightSaber	2^{-123}	2^{-278}
Saber	2^{-139}	2^{-206}
FireSaber	2^{-170}	2^{-197}
Frodo640	2^{-146}	2^{-170}

In the next subsection, we give the detailed calculation of each parameter of specific example of Saber. The calculations of other schemes can be seen in Appendix E.

6.1   Saber

Saber is a MLWR-based lattice scheme, and a third round candidate in NIST's post-quantum standardization effort. Its key generation, encryption, decryption algorithms as well as its common parameter set are given in [4]. The error term of Saber is the following

$$\omega = s'^T u - u'^T s + e_r,$$

where $s, s' \leftarrow \beta_\mu$, u and u' is the compression error of As and $A^T s'$ respectively. $e_r \in R_q$ is a polynomial with uniformly distributed coefficients in the range $\left[-\frac{p}{2t}, \frac{p}{2t}\right]$. Using the previous notation, we write

$$S = \begin{pmatrix} -s \\ u \end{pmatrix}, \; C = \begin{pmatrix} u' \\ s' \end{pmatrix} \text{ and } G = e_r.$$

In Saber, $k = 3, n = 256, q = 2^{13}, p = 2^{10}, t = 2^4, \mu = 4, \delta = 2^{-136}$. Since $\frac{q}{p} = 8$, then from Theorem 1, each coefficient of each polynomial of u, u' is uniformly random in $\mathbb{Z}_8$. Let $\mathcal{E}_u$ be the expected values of $\|u\|$. Meanwhile, $\mathcal{E}_{u'}, \mathcal{E}_s, \mathcal{E}_{s'}$ and so on are defined in the same way. Then it can be calculated that $\mathcal{E}_u = \mathcal{E}_{u'} = \sqrt{4224}$.

As for the norm of s and s', since each coefficient of each polynomial of s, s' follows β_4, which is centered and has a variance of 2, we have $\mathcal{E}_s = \mathcal{E}_{s'} = \sqrt{1536}$.

As mentioned in [5], due to the difference in size between the coefficients of u' and s', we need to isotropize C. Let $w = \sqrt{\frac{\mathcal{E}_{s'}}{\mathcal{E}_{u'}}}$, we denote $\widetilde{S} = \begin{pmatrix} -\frac{s}{w} \\ u \cdot w \end{pmatrix}$ and $\widetilde{C} = \begin{pmatrix} u' \cdot w \\ \frac{s'}{w} \end{pmatrix}$. It is noted that $\langle \widetilde{S}, \widetilde{C} \rangle = \langle S, C \rangle$ and the expected values of $\|u' \cdot w\|, \left\| \frac{s'}{w} \right\|$ are both $\sqrt{\mathcal{E}_{u'} \cdot \mathcal{E}_{s'}}$. According to the above, we have

$$\mathcal{E}_{\widetilde{S}} = \mathcal{E}_{\widetilde{C}} = \sqrt{2 \times \mathcal{E}_{u'} \cdot \mathcal{E}_{s'}} \approx 84.88.$$

It's easy to see that $\gamma = \frac{p}{2t} = 32$, then

$$\theta^*_{Saber} = \arccos \left(\frac{\frac{q}{4} + \gamma}{\mathcal{E}_{\widetilde{C}} \cdot \mathcal{E}_{\widetilde{S}}} \right) \approx 65.90° \text{ and } I_{\sin^2(\theta^*_{Saber})} \left(kn - \frac{1}{2}, \frac{1}{2} \right) \approx 2^{-206}.$$

Finally, as $J_{2kn} \left(\frac{\pi}{4}, \theta^*_{Saber} \right) \approx 2^{-464} \ll 2^{-206} \approx I_{\sin^2(\theta^*_{Saber})} \left(kn - \frac{1}{2}, \frac{1}{2} \right)$, the impact of the overlaps is negligible. Hence, the proportion of excluded key candidates after m successful queries is about

$$\widetilde{\Omega}(m) = \frac{m}{2} I_{\sin^2 \theta^*_{Saber}} \left(kn - \frac{1}{2}, \frac{1}{2} \right) - \frac{m^2 J_{2kn} \left(\frac{\pi}{4}, \theta^*_{Saber} \right) \cdot \sqrt{\pi(kn - 1)}}{2\pi} \approx 2^{-143}.$$

A   The Proof of Theorem 1

Let us consider the distribution of $CD_{p,q}(y)$. First of all, we start with a special case where $p = 1$, then

$$CD_{1,q}(y) = y - \left[q \left[\frac{1}{q} y \right] \right].$$

Let $y = aq + b$ with b being the minimum absolute residue, i.e., $b = y \text{ mods } q$, then

$$CD_{1,q}(y) = y - \left[q \left[\frac{1}{q} y \right] \right] = y - q \cdot \left[\frac{aq + b}{q} \right] = y - aq = b.$$

In addition, when y is uniformly random in $\mathbb{Z}$ or $\mathbb{Z}_q$, $CD_{1,q}(y)$ is uniformly random in $\mathbb{Z}_q$.

Now we consider the general case. We decompose py into $py = aq + b$ in a similar manner, where $b = py \bmod s \, q$, then

$$y - \left\lceil \frac{q}{p} \left\lceil \frac{p}{q} y \right\rceil \right\rceil = y - \left\lceil \frac{1}{p} \cdot q \left\lceil \frac{1}{q}(py) \right\rceil \right\rceil = y - \left\lceil \frac{1}{p} \cdot (py - b) \right\rceil = y - \left\lceil y - \frac{b}{p} \right\rceil = \left\lceil \frac{b}{p} \right\rceil.$$

In this case, the value of $CD_{p,q}(y)$ entirely depends on b. The following two situations are of interest in practice.

1. $\gcd(p, q) = 1$

   In this case, when y is uniformly random in $\mathbb{Z}$ or $\mathbb{Z}_q$, $b = py \bmod s \, q$ is also uniformly random in $\mathbb{Z}_q$, then $CD_{p,q}(y)$ is uniformly random in $\left\lceil \frac{\mathbb{Z}_q}{p} \right\rceil$. In other words, $CD_{p,q}(y)$ belongs to $\left\{ -\left\lceil \frac{q}{2p} \right\rceil, \cdots, \left\lceil \frac{q}{2p} \right\rceil \right\}$ and has the same probability at all integer points inside except $-\left\lfloor \frac{q}{2p} \right\rfloor$ and $\left\lceil \frac{q}{2p} \right\rceil$.

   In particular, when $\frac{q}{2} \gg p$, we can roughly think that $CD_{p,q}(y)$ is uniformly random in $\left\{ -\left\lceil \frac{q}{2p} \right\rceil, \cdots, \left\lceil \frac{q}{2p} \right\rceil \right\}$.

2. $p | q$

   We denote $m = \frac{q}{p}$, then

   $$CD_{p,q}(y) = y - \left\lceil \frac{q}{p} \left\lceil \frac{p}{q} y \right\rceil \right\rceil = y - \left\lceil m \left\lceil \frac{1}{m} y \right\rceil \right\rceil = CD_{1,m}(y).$$

   We decompose y into $y = cm + d$, where $d = y \bmod s \, m$, then we have

   $$CD_{p,q}(y) = CD_{1,m}(y) = d.$$

   Thus, when y is uniformly random in $\mathbb{Z}$ or $\mathbb{Z}_q$, $CD_{p,q}(y)$ is uniformly random in $\mathbb{Z}_m$.

B   The Proof of Proposition 2

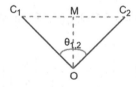

Fig. 1. The construction of C'.

As shown in Fig. 1, let O be the center of $\mathcal{S}_d$. Since $\overline{\overline{C_1}}, \overline{\overline{C_2}} \in \mathcal{S}_d$, then $O\overline{\overline{C_1}} = O\overline{\overline{C_2}} = 1$ and

$$ip_{1,2} = \langle \overline{\overline{C_1}}, \overline{\overline{C_2}} \rangle = \left\| \overline{\overline{C_1}} \right\| \cdot \left\| \overline{\overline{C_2}} \right\| \cdot \cos(\theta_{1,2}) = \cos(\theta_{1,2})$$

We denote M to be the midpoint of $\overline{\overline{C_1 C_2}}$. According to the properties of isosceles triangles, we know that

$$\theta\left(O\overline{\overline{C_1}}, OM\right) = \frac{1}{2}\theta_{1,2} \text{ and } \overline{\overline{C_1}}M \perp OM$$

Hence,

$$\frac{1}{2}d_{1,2} = \left|M\overline{\overline{C_1}}\right| = \frac{\left|M\overline{\overline{C_1}}\right|}{\left|O\overline{\overline{C_1}}\right|} = \sin\left(\theta\left(O\overline{\overline{C_1}}, OM\right)\right) = \sin\left(\frac{1}{2}\theta_{1,2}\right)$$

C The Proof of Theorem 2

For $\overline{\overline{C_1}}$, $\overline{\overline{C_2}} \in S_{2kn}$, let $\theta_{1,2}, d_{1,2}, ip_{1,2}$ and $\mathcal{C}_{1,2}$ be as in Sect. 5, then

$$\mathcal{C}_{1,2} \neq \emptyset \iff \exists x \in S_{2kn}, \text{ such that } x \in C\left(2kn, \overline{\overline{C_1}}, \theta^*\right) \text{ and } x \in C\left(2kn, \overline{\overline{C_2}}, \theta^*\right)$$

$$\iff \exists x \in S_{2kn}, \text{ such that } \theta\left(x, \overline{\overline{C_1}}\right) < \theta^* \text{ and } \theta\left(x, \overline{\overline{C_2}}\right) < \theta^*.$$

From the analysis above, to make $\mathcal{C}_{1,2} = \emptyset$ true, we need the event that at most one of $\theta\left(x, \overline{\overline{C_1}}\right) \leq \theta^*, \theta\left(x, \overline{\overline{C_2}}\right) \leq \theta^*$ is true for any $x \in S_{2kn}$. It is easy to find that $\theta_{1,2} > 2\theta^*$ is a sufficient condition for $\mathcal{C}_{1,2} = \emptyset$. Because when it is true, for any $x \in S_{2kn}$, $\theta\left(x, \overline{\overline{C_1}}\right) + \theta\left(x, \overline{\overline{C_2}}\right) \geq \theta_{1,2} > 2\theta^*$.

Now let us prove that $\theta_{1,2} > 2\theta^*$ is a necessary condition $\mathcal{C}_{1,2} = \emptyset$. Using Proposition 2, we can easily give its equivalent representations, namely, the disjoint condition about inner product $(ip_{1,2} < \cos(2\theta^*))$ and about distance $(d_{1,2} > 2\sin(\theta^*))$. In the following, we take $d_{1,2} > 2\sin(\theta^*)$ as an example to prove that they are all necessary conditions for $\mathcal{C}_{1,2} = \emptyset$. Because these three conditions are equivalent, this will prove that each of them is a sufficient and necessary condition for $\mathcal{C}_{1,2} = \emptyset$ respectively.

Assume that $d_{1,2} \leq 2\sin(\theta^*)$, we will show that in this case we can always find a $C' \in S_{2kn}$, such that $\theta\left(C', \overline{\overline{C_1}}\right) \leq \theta^*$ and $\theta\left(C', \overline{\overline{C_2}}\right) \leq \theta^*$.

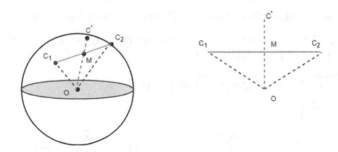

Fig. 2. The construction of C'.

Actually, as shown in Fig. 2, we denote the midpoint of $\overline{\overline{C_1}}$ and $\overline{\overline{C_2}}$ by M, and suppose that the line OM and $\mathcal{S}_{2kn}$ intersect at point C', then C' is the point we are looking for.

Since $O\overline{\overline{C_1}} = O\overline{\overline{C_2}} = 1$, the triangle $O\overline{\overline{C_1}}\overline{\overline{C_2}}$ is an isosceles triangle. Hence, $\theta\left(C', \overline{\overline{C_1}}\right) = \theta\left(C', \overline{\overline{C_2}}\right) = \frac{1}{2}\theta_{1,2}$. Then we have

$$\sin\left(\theta\left(C', \overline{\overline{C_1}}\right)\right) = \frac{\left|M\overline{\overline{C_1}}\right|}{\left|O\overline{\overline{C_1}}\right|} = \frac{1}{2}d_{1,2} < \sin(\theta^*).$$

Since $\theta^* < \frac{\pi}{2}$ and $\theta\left(C', \overline{\overline{C_1}}\right) = \frac{1}{2}\theta_{1,2} \leq \frac{\pi}{2}$, we have

$$\theta\left(C', \overline{\overline{C_1}}\right) < \theta^*.$$

We can prove that $\theta\left(C', \overline{\overline{C_2}}\right) < \theta^*$ in a similar way, then we know that $\mathcal{C}_{1,2} \neq \emptyset$, since $C' \in \mathcal{C}_{1,2}$.

D   Some Results about the Overlaps among Different Caps of the Same Query

Let C be a query. Now let us consider the two rotations $C^{(r_1)}, C^{(r_2)}$ $(0 \leq r_1 < r_2 \leq n-1)$ of C. Although the angle between $\overline{C^{(r_1)}}$ and $\overline{C^{(r_2)}}$ cannot be accurately described, we can instead use their inner product to analyze the overlap, achieving exactly the same effect. According to Theorem 2, the overlap between $\mathcal{C}\left(2kn, \overline{C^{(r_1)}}, \theta^*\right)$ and $\mathcal{C}\left(2kn, \overline{C^{(r_2)}}, \theta^*\right)$ depends entirely on $\langle C^{(r_1)}, C^{(r_2)} \rangle$.

It is mentioned in Sect. 2.1 that $\langle C^{(r_1)}, C^{(r_2)} \rangle$ is the r_2-th degree coefficient of $\langle C^{(r_1)}, C \rangle$, so we can get $\langle C^{(r_1)}, C^{(r_2)} \rangle$ by calculating $\langle C^{(r_1)}, C \rangle$. Let $C_{i,u}(i = 1, 2, \cdots, k; u = 0, 1, \cdots n-1)$ be the coefficient of the u-th degree coefficient of the i-th polynomial of C. From the properties of rotations given in Sect. 2.1, $\langle C^{(r_1)}, C^{(r_2)} \rangle$ can be represented by

$$\sum_{i=1}^{k}\left(\sum_{u=0}^{r_1} C_{i,r_1-u}C_{i,r_2-u} - \sum_{u=r_1+1}^{r_2} C_{i,n+r_1-u}C_{i,r_2-u} + \sum_{u=r_2+1}^{n-1} C_{i,n+r_1-u}C_{i,n+r_2-u}\right).$$

The following corollaries can be derived directly from Theorem 2.

Corollary 2. *For a given C and its two rotations $C^{(r_1)}, C^{(r_2)}$ $(0 \leq r_1 < r_2 \leq n-1)$. The following are equivalent:*

1. $\mathcal{C}\left(2kn, \overline{C^{(r_1)}}, \theta^*\right) \cap \mathcal{C}\left(2kn, \overline{C^{(r_2)}}, \theta^*\right) = \emptyset.$

2. $\theta\left(\overline{C^{(r_1)}}, \overline{C^{(r_2)}}\right) > 2\theta^*.$

3. $\sum_{i=1}^{k}\left(\sum_{u=0}^{r_1} C_{i,r_1-u}C_{i,r_2-u} - \sum_{u=r_1+1}^{r_2} C_{i,n+r_1-u}C_{i,r_2-u} + \sum_{u=r_2+1}^{n-1} C_{i,n+r_1-u}C_{i,n+r_2-u}\right)$
$$< \cos\left(2\theta^*\right)\|C\|^2.$$

Corollary 3. *For a given C, the following are equivalent:*

1. *all the caps $C\left(2kn, \pm\overline{\overline{C^{(r)}}}, \theta^*\right), r = 0, 1, \cdots, n-1$ do not intersect each other.*

2. *$2\theta^* < \theta\left(\overline{\overline{C^{(r_1)}}}, \overline{\overline{C^{(r_2)}}}\right) < \pi - 2\theta^*$, for any $0 \le r_1 < r_2 \le n-1$.*

3. *$\left|\sum_{i=1}^{k}\left(\sum_{u=0}^{r_1} C_{i,r_1-u}C_{i,r_2-u} - \sum_{u=r_1+1}^{r_2} C_{i,n+r_1-u}C_{i,r_2-u} + \sum_{u=r_2+1}^{n-1} C_{i,n+r_1-u}C_{i,n+r_2-u}\right)\right|$*
$< \cos\left(2\theta^*\right)\|C\|^2$, *for any $0 \le r_1 < r_2 \le n-1$.*

The above corollary deals with the overlaps among $2n$ spherical caps in W_C, and gives the conditions for a query C to achieve the best query effect. This may provide advice to the attacker on how to choose queries.

E   (R/M-)LWE-Based Public-Key Encryption Schemes

E.1   Kyber

Kyber is a MLWE-based lattice scheme, and a third round candidate in NIST's post-quantum standardization effort. [3] introduces the key generation, encryption, decryption algorithm of Kyber, and gives its common parameter set. [6] proves that the error term of Kyber is

$$\omega = e^T r + e_2 + c_v - s^T e_1 - s^T c_u,$$

where $e, s, r, e_1 \leftarrow \beta_{\eta_1}, e_2 \leftarrow \beta_{\eta_2}, c_u \leftarrow \psi_{2^{d_u},q}^k, c_v \leftarrow \psi_{2^{d_v},q}^k$. Using the previous notation, we write

$$S = \begin{pmatrix} -s \\ e \end{pmatrix}, \quad C = \begin{pmatrix} e_1 + c_u \\ r \end{pmatrix} \text{ and } G = e_2 + c_v.$$

Since all parameter sets of Kyber have $q = 3329$, then $\gcd(2^{d_u}, q) = 1$, $\gcd(2^{d_v}, q) = 1$. We denote the j-th degree coefficient of the i-th polynomial of c_u and c_v by $(c_u)_{i,j}$ and $(c_v)_{i,j}$ respectively, then from Theorem 4.1, $(c_u)_{i,j} = \left\lceil \frac{(b_u)_{i,j}}{2^{d_u}} \right\rfloor$, where $(b_u)_{i,j}, i = 1, \cdots, k, j = 0, 1, \cdots, n-1$ are independent and all uniformly random in $\mathbb{Z}_q$. $(c_v)_{i,j} = \left\lceil \frac{(b_v)_{i,j}}{2^{d_v}} \right\rfloor$, where $(b_v)_{i,j}, i = 1, \cdots, k, j = 0, 1, \cdots, n-1$ are independent and all uniformly random in $\mathbb{Z}_q$.

Let us take Kyber768 as an example, then $d_u = 10, d_v = 4, \eta_1 = \eta_2 = 2, \delta = 2^{-164}$. It can be prove that the expected value of $|(c_u)_{i,j}|$ is about $\sqrt{\frac{13}{14}}$. As for the value of $(c_v)_{i,j}$, since $q >> 2^{d_v}$ and $\frac{q/2}{2^4} \approx 104$, we can approximately think that $(c_v)_{i,j}$ is uniformly random in $[-104, 104]$.

As for the values of other parameters, since $\|G\|_\infty \le \|e_2\|_\infty + \|c_v\|_\infty \approx \eta_2 + 104 = 106$, we can take $\gamma = 106$. Taking $M = \log_2\left(\frac{m(m-1)}{2}\right)$, we have $\epsilon(M) \approx 4.08°$. As $s, e, r, e_1, e_2 \sim \beta_2$, and the variance of β_2 is 1, we have $\mathcal{E}_s = \mathcal{E}_e = \mathcal{E}_r = \mathcal{E}_{e_1} = \sqrt{768}$. Since e_1, c_u are independent, we have $D\left[(c_u + e_1)_{i,j}\right] = D\left[(c_u)_{i,j}\right] + D\left[(e_1)_{i,j}\right] = \frac{27}{14}$, then $\mathcal{E}_{e_1+c_u} \approx \sqrt{1481}$.

Just like before, due to the difference in size between the coefficients of $e_1 + c_u$ and r, we need to isotropize C. Let $w = \sqrt{\frac{\mathcal{E}_r}{\mathcal{E}_{e_1+c_u}}}$, then we form $\widetilde{S} = \begin{pmatrix} -\frac{s}{w} \\ e \cdot w \end{pmatrix}$ and $C = \begin{pmatrix} (e_1 + c_u) \cdot w \\ \frac{r}{w} \end{pmatrix}$. It is noted that $\langle \widetilde{S}, \widetilde{C} \rangle = \langle S, C \rangle$ and the expected values of $\|(e_1 + c_u) \cdot w\|, \|\frac{r}{w}\|$ are both $\sqrt{\mathcal{E}_{e_1+c_u} \cdot \mathcal{E}_r}$. According to the above, we have

$$\mathcal{E}_{\widetilde{S}} \approx 40.24 \text{ and } \mathcal{E}_{\widetilde{C}} \approx 46.19.$$

Then the angle that the attacker can obtain is $\theta^*_{Kyber768} = \arccos\left(\frac{\frac{q}{4}+\gamma}{\mathcal{E}_{\widetilde{S}} \cdot \mathcal{E}_{\widetilde{C}}}\right) \approx 59.68°$, the proportion is $I_{\sin^2(\theta^*_{Kyber768})}\left(kn - \frac{1}{2}, \frac{1}{2}\right) \approx 2^{-330}$. Finally, it can be calculated that $J_{2kn}\left(\frac{\pi}{4}, \theta^*_{Kyber768}\right) \approx 2^{-805}$ and $\widetilde{\Omega}(m) \approx 2^{-267}$.

E.2   Newhope

Newhope is a RLWE-based lattice scheme, which is proposed by Alkim et al. [2] in 2016. [1] describes in detail the key generation, encryption and decryption algorithm of Newhope. The error term of Newhope is

$$\omega = es' - e's + e'' + c_v,$$

where $e, s, s', e', e'' \leftarrow \beta_\mu, c_v \leftarrow \psi_{8,q}$. Using the previous notation, we write

$$S = \begin{pmatrix} -s \\ e \end{pmatrix}, \quad C = \begin{pmatrix} e' \\ s' \end{pmatrix} \text{ and } G = e'' + c_v.$$

Let us take Newhope1024 as an example, then $n = 1024, q = 12289, \mu = 8, \delta = 2^{-216}$. From Theorem 1, since $\frac{q/2}{8} \approx 768$, we can approximately think that $(c_v)_{i,j}$ is uniformly random in $[-768, 768]$.

Now let us calculate the values of other parameters. Taking $M = \log_2\left(\frac{m(m-1)}{2}\right)$, we have $\epsilon(M) \approx 3.60°$. Since $\|G\|_\infty \leq \|e''\|_\infty + \|c_v\|_\infty \leq 8 + 768 = 776$, we can take $\gamma = 776$. As $S, C \sim \beta_8$, and the variance of β_8 is 4, we have $\mathcal{E}_S = \mathcal{E}_C = \sqrt{8192}$. Then the angle is $\theta^*_{Newhope1024} = \arccos\left(\frac{\frac{q}{4}+\gamma}{\mathcal{E}_S \cdot \mathcal{E}_C}\right) \approx 61.98°$ and the proportion is $I_{\sin^2(\theta^*_{Newhope1024})}\left(n - \frac{1}{2}, \frac{1}{2}\right) \approx 2^{-372.89}$. Finally, it can be calculated that $J_{2n}\left(\frac{\pi}{4}, \theta^*_{Newhope1024}\right) \approx 2^{-876}$ and $\widetilde{\Omega}(m) \approx 2^{-310}$.

E.3   Frodo

Frodo is a LWE-based lattice scheme, and a second round candidate in NIST's post-quantum standardization effort. [20] introduces the basic information about Frodo. The success condition is

$$\|E'''\|_\infty < \frac{q}{2^{B+1}},$$

where $E''' = S'E - E'S + E''$, $S, E \in \mathbb{Z}_q^{n \times \overline{n}}$, $S', E' \in \mathbb{Z}_q^{\overline{m} \times n}$, $E'' \in \mathbb{Z}_q^{\overline{m} \times \overline{n}}$, and each of their elements is sampled from the distribution χ (an approximation to the discrete Gaussian distribution).

Let us take Frodo640 as an example, then $q = 2^{15}$, $n = 640$, $\gamma = 12$, $\overline{m} = \overline{n} = 8$, $B = 2$ and $\delta = 2^{-139}$. It can be calculated that $\epsilon(M) \approx 4.42°$. [20] gives the probability distribution function of χ. For any $a \leftarrow \chi$, the expected value of a^2 is $\frac{64895}{2^{13}} \approx 7.92$.

As S, S', E, E', E'' are all matrices, the angles are uncomputable. Some transformation is needed. We write $S = (s_1 \; s_2 \; \cdots s_{\overline{n}})$, $E = (e_1 \; e_2 \; \cdots e_{\overline{n}})$ where $s_i, e_i, i = 1, 2, \cdots, \overline{n}$ are all column vectors. We write $S' = \begin{pmatrix} s'_1 \\ \vdots \\ s'_{\overline{m}} \end{pmatrix}$, $E' = \begin{pmatrix} e'_1 \\ \vdots \\ e'_{\overline{m}} \end{pmatrix}$

where $s'_j, e'_j, j = 1, 2, \cdots, \overline{m}$ are all row vectors. Then the success condition can be further expressed as

$$|s'_j e_i - e'_j s_i + e''_{ij}| < \frac{q}{8}, i, j = 1, 2, \cdots, 8.$$

Just like [5], we consider each entry of E''' respectively. For each pair of (i, j), the angle that an attacker can obtain is $\theta^*_{Frodo640} = \arccos\left(\frac{\frac{q}{8} + \gamma}{\sqrt{2 \times n \times 7.92} \times \sqrt{2 \times n \times 7.92}}\right) \approx 66.10°$, and the proportion is $I_{\sin^2(\theta^*_{Frodo640})}$ $(n - \frac{1}{2}, \frac{1}{2}) \approx 2^{-169.6}$. Finally, it can be calculated that $J_{2n}\left(\frac{\pi}{4}, \theta^*_{Frodo640}\right) \approx 2^{-381.6}$ and $\widetilde{\Omega}(m) \approx 2^{-106.6}$.

References

1. Alkim, E., et al.: NewHope algorithm specifications and supporting documentation. NIST PQC Round **2**, 4–11 (2019)
2. Alkim, E., Ducas, L., Pöppelmann, T., Schwabe, P.: Post-quantum key exchange: a new hope. In: Proceedings of the 25th USENIX Conference on Security Symposium, pp. 327–343 (2016)
3. Avanzi, R., et al.: CRYSTALS-Kyber algorithm specifications and supporting documentation. NIST PQC Round **2**, 4 (2019)
4. Basso, A., et al.: SABER: mod-LWR based KEM (round 3 submission) (2020)
5. Bindel, N., Schanck, J.M.: Decryption failure is more likely after success. In: International Conference on Post-Quantum Cryptography, pp. 206–225 (2020)
6. Bos, J., et al.: CRYSTALS-Kyber: a CCA-secure module-lattice-based KEM. In: European Symposium on Security and Privacy, pp. 353–367 (2018)
7. Cai, T.T., Fan, J., Jiang, T.: Distributions of angles in random packing on spheres. J. Mach. Learn. Res. **14**, 1837 (2013)
8. Cao, J., Niu, D.W., Qi, F.: A Wallis type inequality and a double inequality for probability integral. Aust. J. Math. Anal. Appl. **4**, 6 (2007). Art. 3
9. D'Anvers, J.P., Batsleer, S.: Multitarget decryption failure attacks and their application to saber and kyber. Cryptology ePrint Archive, Report 2021/193 (2021)
10. D'Anvers, J.P., Vercauteren, F., Verbauwhede, I.: On the impact of decryption failures on the security of LWE/LWR based schemes. Cryptology ePrint Archive, Report 2018/1089 (2018)

11. D'Anvers, J.P., Guo, Q., Johansson, T., Nilsson, A., Vercauteren, F., Verbauwhede, I.: Decryption failure attacks on IND-CCA secure lattice-based schemes. In: Public-Key Cryptography - PKC 2019, pp. 565–598 (2019)
12. D'Anvers, J.P., Rossi, M., Virdia, F.: (One) failure is not an option: bootstrapping the search for failures in lattice-based encryption schemes. In: Advances in Cryptology - EUROCRYPT 2020, pp. 3–33. Springer, Cham (2020). https://doi.org/10.1007/978-3-030-45727-3_1
13. D'Anvers, J.-P., Vercauteren, F., Verbauwhede, I.: The impact of error dependencies on Ring/Mod-LWE/LWR based schemes. In: Ding, J., Steinwandt, R. (eds.) PQCrypto 2019. LNCS, vol. 11505, pp. 103–115. Springer, Cham (2019). https://doi.org/10.1007/978-3-030-25510-7_6
14. Guo, Q., Johansson, T.: A new decryption failure attack against HQC. In: Moriai, S., Wang, H. (eds.) ASIACRYPT 2020. LNCS, vol. 12491, pp. 353–382. Springer, Cham (2020). https://doi.org/10.1007/978-3-030-64837-4_12
15. Guo, Q., Johansson, T., Nilsson, A.: A generic attack on lattice based schemes using decryption errors. Cryptology ePrint Archive, Report 2019/043 (2019)
16. Guo, Q., Johansson, T., Yang, J.: A novel CCA attack using decryption errors against LAC. In: Galbraith, S.D., Moriai, S. (eds.) ASIACRYPT 2019. LNCS, vol. 11921, pp. 82–111. Springer, Cham (2019). https://doi.org/10.1007/978-3-030-34578-5_4
17. Koumandos, S.: Remarks on a paper by Chao-Ping Chen and Feng Qi. Proc. Am. Math. Soc. **134**(5), 1365–1367 (2006)
18. Lee, Y., Kim, W.C.: Concise formulas for the surface area of the intersection of two hyperspherical caps. KAIST Technical Report (2014)
19. Li, S.: Concise formulas for the area and volume of a hyperspherical cap. Asian J. Math. Stat. **4**, 66–70 (2011)
20. Naehrig, M., et al.: FrodoKEM: learning with errors key encapsulation-algorithm specifications and supporting documentation. NIST Technical Report (2019)

Integral Attacks on Pyjamask-96 and Round-Reduced Pyjamask-128

Jiamin Cui[1,2], Kai Hu[1,2], Qingju Wang[3], and Meiqin Wang[1,2](✉)

[1] School of Cyber Science and Technology, Shandong University, Qingdao 266237, Shandong, China
{cuijiamin,hukai}@mail.sdu.edu.cn, mqwang@sdu.edu.cn
[2] Key Laboratory of Cryptologic Technology and Information Security, Ministry of Education, Shandong University, Qingdao, Shandong, China
[3] SnT, University of Luxembourg, Esch-sur-Alzette, Luxembourg
qingju.wang@uni.lu

Abstract. In order to provide benefits in the areas of fully homomorphic encryption (FHE), multi-party computation (MPC), post-quantum signature schemes, or efficient masked implementations for side-channel resistance, reducing the number of multiplications has become a quite popular trend for the symmetric cryptographic primitive designs. With an aggressive design strategy exploiting the extremely simple and low-degree S-box and low number of rounds, Pyjamask, the fundamental block cipher of the AEAD with the same name, has the smallest number of AND gates per bit among all the existing block ciphers (except LowMC or Rasta which work on unconventional plaintext/key sizes). Thus, although the AEAD Pyjamask stuck at the second round of the NIST lightweight cryptography standardization process, the block cipher Pyjamask itself still attracts a lot of attention. Not very unexpectedly, the low degree and the low number of rounds are the biggest weakness of Pyjamask. At FSE 2020, Dobraunig et al. successfully mounted an algebraic and higher-order differential attack on full Pyjamask-96, one member of the Pyjamask block cipher family. However, the drawback of this attack is that it has to use the full codebook, which makes the attack less appealing. In this paper, we take integral attacks as our weapon, which are also sensitive to the low degree. Based on a new 11-round integral distinguisher found by state-of-the-art detection techniques, and combined with the relationship between round keys that reduces the involved keys, we give the key recovery attack on the full Pyjamask-96 without the full codebook for the first time. Further, the algebraic and higher-order differential technique does not work for Pyjamask-128, the other member of the Pyjamask block cipher family. To better understand the security margin of Pyjamask-128, we present the first third-party cryptanalysis on Pyjamask-128 up to 11 out of 14 rounds.

Keywords: Pyjamask · Lightweight cipher · Integral attack · Division property · Monomial prediction

© The Author(s), under exclusive license to Springer Nature Switzerland AG 2022
S. D. Galbraith (Ed.): CT-RSA 2022, LNCS 13161, pp. 223–246, 2022.
https://doi.org/10.1007/978-3-030-95312-6_10

1   Introduction

Recently, block ciphers implemented in resource-constrained environments have received a lot of attention with the increasing deployments of small computing devices. To meet such trend, NIST initiated a lightweight cryptography (LWC) competition for developing a standard of lightweight cryptographic algorithms.

Pyjamask, as an authenticated encryption with associated data (AEAD) scheme which targets at side-channel resistance [12], has been selected as one of the second round candidates for NIST LWC competition. The mode of operation chosen by the authors is OCB AEAD [17]. The underlying block ciphers contain two versions: Pyjamask-96 and Pyjamask-128, named according to the block size. To allow efficient masked implementations, especially for high-order masking, the S-box layer aggressively minimizes costs in terms of AND gates, which also leads to relatively slow growth in algebraic degree. At FSE 2020, Dobraunig et al. [10] noticed this vulnerability and presented an 11.5-round[1] higher-order differential distinguisher. Combined with the solution of linearized systems for monomials and the guess-and-determine strategy, they proposed a chosen-ciphertext attack for the full-round Pyjamask-96 using the whole codebook. Later, Tian and Hu [22] found a 10-round integral distinguisher based on the division property [23,26] that leads to an 11-round attack of Pyjamask-96 with time complexity $2^{93.8}$. So far, there is no third-party analysis for Pyjamask-128.

The integral attack was firstly proposed by Daemen et al. [7] to evaluate the security of the block cipher Square, and later formalized by Knudsen and Wagner [16]. It mainly has two steps: the construction of an integral distinguisher followed by a key recovery step. In order to construct an integral distinguisher, a structure of plaintexts is chosen firstly and encrypted for a few rounds. If the corresponding state has an integral property, an integral distinguisher is obtained, which can be used to perform the key recovery attack with many techniques.

Detecting integral distinguishers. Currently, the division property, proposed as a generalized integral property by Todo at EUROCRYPT 2015 [24], is the most efficient and accurate method of detecting the integral distinguishers. It can better exploit the algebraic degree information and identify balanced output bits. Its powerfulness was undoubtedly demonstrated by the break of full MISTY1 [23]. However, the original division property is word-oriented, i.e., it only exploits the algebraic degree of the non-linear exponents, and could not utilize the internal structure of ciphers in a fine-grained way. So Todo and Morii introduced the bit-based division property at FSE 2016 [26], including the conventional bit-based division property and the three-subset bit-based division

---

[1] This 11.5-round distinguisher works under the chosen-ciphertext scenario, so the last MixRows can be removed naturally, i.e., without the MixRows operation, the distinguisher is actually 11 full rounds. Our 11-round distinguisher (introduced later) works under the chosen-plaintext setting, so we cannot remove the MixRows operation for the distinguisher. However, equivalently, in the key-recovery phase, we can ignore the last MixRows operation also.

property. In [29], Wang et al. showed that the three-subset bit-based division property could be used to recover the exact superpoly in the cube attack. This observation was soon refined by Hao et al. in [13] as the three-subset bit-based division property without unknown subsets (3SDPwoU). Recently, Hebborn et al. pointed out that the idea behind the 3SDPwoU from the perspective of the parity set [5] is that the 3SDPwoU actually determined the existence or absence of a certain monomial in the polynomial of the cipher output. At ASIACRYPT 2020, Hu et al. [15] proposed the concept of the monomial prediction, which is another language for the division properties from the viewpoint of the polynomial directly. By counting the so-called monomial trails, they are able to determine if a monomial of the plaintext or IV appears in the polynomial of the cipher output. Indeed, the monomial prediction and the 3SDPwoU were proved to be equivalent [15].

In practice, searching for the division properties or the monomial trails is time and memory consuming where the complexity is usually the exponential function of the block size. At ASIACRYPT 2016 [30], Xiang et al. introduced the Mixed Integral Linear Programming (MILP) models for the conventional division properties and thereafter the MILP models have been the dominant tool in this area. Later, the integral attacks on dozens of symmetric primitives are then improved [6,8,18,27,28].

Techniques used in the key recovery attacks. When mounting the key recovery attack, we guess some involved round keys, partially decrypt the corresponding ciphertexts backwards to the tail of the integral distinguishers and check whether the summation of the statements is zero. Since the presentation of the integral attack, many refined key-recovery techniques are presented. The partial sum technique was one of the most important tools, which was introduced by Ferguson et al. in [11] to improve the time complexity of integral attacks. The statement after the distinguisher, the ciphertexts and the involved round keys can be separated into several parts and considered independently. Thus, we can reuse some derived partial sum and optimize the time complexity. The original attack target was AES. They dramatically reduced the complexity of the 6-round attacks on AES by a factor of 2^{28}. Recently, this powerful method has lead to a significant reduction in the time complexity of the integral attack on the full MISTY1 [4,23].

Motivation. In order to provide benefits in the areas of fully homomorphic encryption (FHE), multi-party computation (MPC), or post-quantum signature schemes, reducing the number of multiplications has become a quite popular trend for the symmetric cryptographic primitive designs. Unlike earlier designs such as LowMC [3], or Rasta [9] and many others that follow an unconventional design approach, e.g., incomplete non-linear layer, Pyjamask follows a classical design approach to benefit from the mature cryptanalysis methods and security arguments. Within this design space, it aggressively reduces the number of rounds of the internal block ciphers and makes Pyjamask one of the existing members with the smallest number of AND gates per bit processed. Moreover, the low number of nonlinear building blocks of Pyjamask allows side-channel countermeasures. Although the AEAD Pyjamask was not selected as the finalists of the NIST LWC competition, the block cipher Pyjamask still attracts a lot of attention because of its low multiplication complexity characteristic. The most important side effect of the low number of multiplicative operations is the slow growth of algebraic degree, which makes it vulnerable to the attacks such as the higher-order differential attacks [10] and the integral attacks [22]. However, the only attack on the full Pyjamask-96 has to take the whole codebook. We are naturally interested in whether we can improve the attacks without using the whole codebook. The algebraic degree of Pyjamask-128 grows much faster than Pyjamask-96, which the technique in [10] heavily relies on. As a result, their technique fails when applied to Pyjamask-128. On the other hand, block ciphers with 128-bit block size are more popular since almost all protocols support 128-bit block ciphers (for the compatibility with AES) rather than 96-bit ones. Thus, it is of special significance to study the security margin of this 128-bit version of Pyjamask. Thanks to the development of the division properties recently, we have more powerful tools to detect the integral distinguishers for Pyjamask. Thus the security of Pyjamask can be better evaluated by more refined integral attacks.

Our contributions. In this paper, we take state-of-the-art techniques for detecting division properties to give a more fine-grained study of the security strength of Pyjamask-96 and Pyjamask-128 against the integral attacks. To find more integral properties, we construct the MILP models for the encryption algorithm considering the effect of the round keys for Pyjamask simultaneously. 11- and 9-round integral distinguishers are established for Pyjamask-96 and Pyjamask-128, respectively. Based on the new 11-round integral distinguisher for Pyjamask-96, capturing the relationship between the round keys that dramatically reduces the number of involved subkey bits in the key recovery phase from 165 to 121 bits, we manage to attack the full Pyjamask-96 without the full codebook for the first time. Equipped with the partial sum and equivalent key skills, the complexities for some fewer rounds of Pyjamask-96 are also improved. We also give the first third-party cryptanalysis on Pyjamask-128 up to 11 (out of 14) rounds, which helps to better understand its security margin. All the results are summarized in Table 1. The full version of the paper can be found in [1].

Outline. The rest of this paper is organized as follows. In Sect. 2, we introduce some background knowledge needed in this paper. The technique of obtaining the integral distinguishers is described in Sect. 3. In Sect. 4, we mainly describe the key recovery attack on 13-round and 14-round Pyjamask-96. The attack on Pyjamask-128 is present in Sect. 5. Finally, the paper is concluded in Sect. 6.

2   Preliminaries

2.1   Pyjamask Block Cipher Family

Pyjamask is a family of the block ciphers used by the AEAD Pyjamask, one of the second-round candidates of the NIST LWC competition. In the remaining sections, Pyjamask is always the name of the block ciphers without ambiguity.

Table 1. Comparisons of attack results for Pyjamask-96 and Pyjamask-128

Instance	Approach	#Round	Data	Time	Reference
Pyjamask-96	Higher-order	9/14	2^{71} CC	2^{67}	[10]
	Integral	**9/14**	$\mathbf{2^{66}}$ **CP**	$\mathbf{2^{66}}$	**Sect. 4**
	Higher-order	10/14	2^{87} CC	2^{83}	[10]
	Integral	**10/14**	$\mathbf{2^{81}}$ **CP**	$\mathbf{2^{81}}$	**Sect. 4**
	Higher-order	11/14	2^{95} CC	2^{91}	[10]
	Integral	11/14	2^{93} CP	$2^{93.8}$	[22]
	Integral	**11/14**	$\mathbf{2^{90}}$ **CP**	$\mathbf{2^{90}}$	**Sect. 4**
	Higher-order	12/14	2^{96} CC	2^{96}	[10]
	Integral	**12/14**	$\mathbf{2^{93}}$ **CP**	$\mathbf{2^{93}}$	**Sect. 4**
	Higher-order	13/14	2^{96} CC	2^{99}	[10]
	Higher-order	13/14	2^{94} CC	2^{125}	[10]
	Integral	**13/14**	$\mathbf{2^{95}}$ **CP**	$\mathbf{2^{95.2}}$	**Sect. 4.1**
	Higher-order	14/14	2^{96} CC	2^{115}	[10]
	Integral	**14/14**	$\mathbf{2^{95}}$ **CP**	$\mathbf{2^{122.6}}$	**Sect. 4.2**
Pyjamask-128	**Integral**	**5/14**	$\mathbf{2^{20}}$ **CP**	$\mathbf{2^{23}}$	**Sect. 5**
	Integral	**6/14**	$\mathbf{2^{52}}$ **CP**	$\mathbf{2^{54}}$	**Sect. 5**
	Integral	**7/14**	$\mathbf{2^{90}}$ **CP**	$\mathbf{2^{91.5}}$	**Sect. 5**
	Integral	**8/14**	$\mathbf{2^{90}}$ **CP**	$\mathbf{2^{107.8}}$	**Sect. 5**
	Integral	**9/14**	$\mathbf{2^{112}}$ **CP**	$\mathbf{2^{112}}$	**Sect. 5**
	Integral	**10/14**	$\mathbf{2^{122}}$ **CP**	$\mathbf{2^{122}}$	**Sect. 5**
	Integral	**11/14**	$\mathbf{2^{127}}$ **CP**	$\mathbf{2^{127}}$	**Sect. 5**

CC – chosen ciphertext; CP – chosen plaintext

Pyjamask includes two members Pyjamask-96 and Pyjamask-128 named according to the block sizes. Both versions take the same 128-bit length key and have the same 14 rounds. The internal states are represented as rectangles with t rows and 32 columns, where $t = 3$ for Pyjamask-96 and $t = 4$ for Pyjamask-128.

In the specification [12], the round function of Pyjamask consists of three steps: AddRoundKey, SubBytes and MixRows. After 14 rounds of iterations, one additional AddRoundKey is appended at last. In this paper, we equivalently regard SubBytes, MixRows and AddRoundKey as one full round (see Fig.1) and thus there is a whitening AddRoundKey before the first round function. The operations in one round are described as follows,

– SubBytes. The same t-bit S-box is applied to each of the 32 columns of the internal state in parallel ($t = 3$ for Pyjamask-96 and $t = 4$ for Pyjamask-128). For SubBytes^{-1}, the inverse of the S-box is applied. S_3 and S_4 used in Pyjamask-96 and Pyjamask-128 respectively are given by the following table.

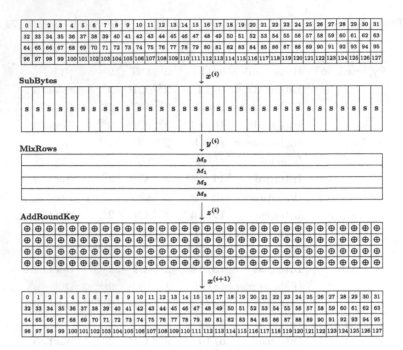

Fig. 1. The round function of Pyjamask-128

x	0	1	2	3	4	5	6	7	8	9	A	B	C	D	E	F
$S_3(x)$	1	3	6	5	2	4	7	0	-	-	-	-	-	-	-	-
$S_4(x)$	2	D	3	9	7	B	A	6	E	0	F	4	8	5	1	C

- MixRows. For each row R_i of the internal state where $0 \le i < 4$, the updated state can be calculated by $M_i \cdot R_i^T$. The binary matrices M_i used in the MixRows layer are 32×32 circulant matrices defined as follows:

$$M_0 = \mathrm{cir}([1, 1, 0, 1, 0, 0, 0, 0, 1, 0, 0, 0, 0, 1, 0, 0, 0, 0, 1, 1, 0, 0, 0, 0, 1, 1, 1, 0, 0, 0, 1, 0]),$$
$$M_1 = \mathrm{cir}([0, 1, 0, 0, 0, 0, 1, 0, 0, 0, 0, 0, 0, 1, 1, 1, 0, 1, 0, 0, 0, 0, 0, 1, 0, 1, 1, 0, 0, 0, 1, 1]),$$
$$M_2 = \mathrm{cir}([0, 0, 0, 0, 0, 0, 0, 0, 1, 0, 1, 0, 0, 1, 1, 1, 1, 0, 0, 1, 1, 0, 1, 0, 0, 1, 0, 0, 1, 0, 1, 1]),$$
$$M_3 = \mathrm{cir}([0, 1, 1, 0, 0, 1, 0, 0, 0, 0, 0, 0, 1, 0, 0, 1, 0, 1, 0, 1, 0, 0, 1, 0, 1, 0, 0, 0, 1, 0, 0, 1]),$$

where M_0, M_1, M_2 are used for both Pyjamask-96 and Pyjamask-128, and M_3 is only used in Pyjamask-128. The function cir generates a matrix where the ith row equals the input vector rotated by i positions to the right. The hamming weight of each row is 11 for M_0, M_1, M_3 and 13 for M_2. For MixRows^{-1}, the matrices are also circulant and the Hamming weight of each row is 11, 13, 11, 15 for M_0^{-1}, M_1^{-1}, M_2^{-1}, M_3^{-1}, respectively.

- AddRoundKey. An n-bit round key $k^{(i)}$ for the ith round is extracted from the key schedule and XORed to the internal state, where $0 \le i \le 13$ and

$n = 96, 128$. The pre-whitening key (which is also the master key as shown later) is denoted by $k^{(-1)}$.

Key schedule. Pyjamask-96 and Pyjamask-128 share a similar key schedule, where only the sizes of the subkeys differ due to the extra row in Pyjamask-128. Let $k^{(-1)}$ be the master key. The same round function is operated on $k^{(-1)}$ for 14 times, and the round keys $k^{(i)}$ for $0 \leq i \leq 13$ are generated. Note that the key state in each round is loaded into the 128-bit key state in the same ordering as the internal state of the encryption.

- **MixColumns.** Update each column of the key state by the same matrix M, where

$$M = \begin{pmatrix} 0 & 1 & 1 & 1 \\ 1 & 0 & 1 & 1 \\ 1 & 1 & 0 & 1 \\ 1 & 1 & 1 & 0 \end{pmatrix}$$

and $M = M^{-1}$.
- **MixAndRotateRows.** Update the first row of the key state R_0 by $M_k \cdot R_0^T$. The circular matrix M_k is defined as:

$M_k = \mathtt{cir}([1, 0, 1, 0, 1, 0, 0, 1, 1, 1, 0, 0, 1, 1, 1, 0, 1, 1, 0, 0, 0, 0, 0, 0, 1, 0, 0, 0, 1, 1, 1, 0])$.

The hamming weight of each row is 15 for M_k and 11 for M_k^{-1}. R_1, R_2, R_3 are left-rotated by 8, 15 and 18 positions. Namely, they are replaced by $R_1 \lll 8$, $R_2 \lll 15$ and $R_3 \lll 18$, respectively.
- **AddConstant.** Four-byte constants are added bitwisely to different bytes in the key state. The first 28-bit constant is denoted in hexadecimal notation as 0x243f6a8 while the extra 4-bit constant is the binary representation of the round index i.

2.2 Notations

In this paper, the state matrix of Pyjamask at the beginning of round i is denoted by $x^{(i)}$ where $0 \leq i \leq 13$. The state matrix after the SubBytes and the MixRows operations of round i are denoted by $y^{(i)}$ and $z^{(i)}$, respectively. Bits of every state are labeled by $0, 1, 2, \ldots, 95$ for Pyjamask-96 and $0, 1, \ldots, 127$ for Pyjamask-128, illustrated in Fig. 1. The jth row vector of the binary matrix M_i is denoted by $M_i[j]$, $0 \leq j < 32$. We denote the subkey of round i by $k^{(i)}$, and the first (pre-whitening) key by $k^{(-1)}$. In the key-recovery process, we are interested in swapping the order of the MixRows operation and the AddRoundKey. As these operations are linear or affine they can be interchanged, by first XORing the data with an equivalent subkey and then applying the MixRows operation. We denote the equivalent subkey for the altered version by $u^{(i)}$, i.e., $u^{(i)} = \mathtt{MixRows}^{-1}(k^{(i)})$. When we interchange the order of the MixRows operation of round i and the AddRoundKey, we denote the state right after the AddRoundKey (and just before the MixRows operation) by $\bar{z}^{(i)}$.

2.3   Monomial Prediction

The monomial prediction is a new technique proposed by Hu et al. in [15] to determine whether a monomial appears in any product of the coordinate functions of a vectorial boolean function f. It provides a new perspective from the polynomial for the division properties [13, 26]. Let $f : \mathbb{F}_2^{n_0} \to \mathbb{F}_2^{n_r}, y = f(x)$ be a composite vectorial Boolean function of a sequence of smaller vectorial Boolean functions $f^{(i)} : \mathbb{F}_2^{n_i} \to \mathbb{F}_2^{n_{i+1}}, x^{(i+1)} = f^{(i)}(x^{(i)}), 0 \le i \le r - 1$, i.e.,

$$f = f^{(r-1)} \circ f^{(r-2)} \circ \ldots \circ f^{(0)}.$$

We use the notation $\pi_{u^{(i)}}(x^{(i)})$ to represent a monomial of $x^{(i)}$ related to $u^{(i)}$, where $\pi_u(x)$ stands for $\prod x_i^{u_i}$ and x_i, u_i is the ith coordinate of the vector x, u, respectively. Note that $\pi_{u^{(i)}}(x^{(i)})$ is also a Boolean function of the $x^{(j)}$ for $j < i$. If the ANF of $f^{(i)}$ is available and relatively simple, we can tell whether the polynomial of $\pi_{u^{(i+1)}}(x^{(i+1)})$ contains the term $\pi_{u^{(i)}}(x^{(i)})$ for any $u^{(i)}$ and $u^{(i+1)}$. $\pi_{u^{(i)}}(x^{(i)}) \to \pi_{u^{(i+1)}}(x^{(i+1)})$ denotes $\pi_{u^{(i+1)}}(x^{(i+1)})$ contains $\pi_{u^{(i)}}(x^{(i)})$ according to [15]. Then we introduce the definition of the monomial trail [15].

Definition 1 (Monomial Trail [15]). *Let $x^{(i+1)} = f^{(i)}(x^{(i)})$ for $0 \le i < r$. We call a sequence of monomials $(\pi_{u^{(0)}}(x^{(0)}), \pi_{u^{(1)}}(x^{(1)}), \ldots, \pi_{u^{(r)}}(x^{(r)}))$ an r-round monomial trail connecting $\pi_{u^{(0)}}(x^{(0)})$ and $\pi_{u^{(r)}}(x^{(r)})$ with respect to the composite function $f = f^{(r-1)} \circ f^{(r-2)} \circ \cdots \circ f^{(0)}$ if*

$$\pi_{u^{(0)}}(x^{(0)}) \to \cdots \to \pi_{u^{(i)}}(x^{(i)}) \to \cdots \to \pi_{u^{(r)}}(x^{(r)}).$$

If there is at least one monomial trail connecting $\pi_{u^{(0)}}(x^{(0)})$ and $\pi_{u^{(r)}}(x^{(r)})$, we write $\pi_{u^{(0)}}(x^{(0)}) \rightsquigarrow \pi_{u^{(r)}}(x^{(r)})$. Otherwise, $\pi_{u^{(0)}}(x^{(0)}) \not\rightsquigarrow \pi_{u^{(r)}}(x^{(r)})$.

The monomial prediction is another language for the division property from the polynomial viewpoint. The paper [15] has shown the equivalence between 3SDPwoU and the monomial prediction. In theory, they are perfectly accurate in detecting the integral distinguishers by counting the number of monomial trails. However, counting trails are time and memory consuming in most cases especially for the block ciphers, then some trade-off between the accuracy and the efficiency is necessary. The previous division properties (except the 3SDPwoU) can be regarded as the compromised algorithms of the monomial prediction. In this paper, we mainly take the fact in Lemma 1 to search for the integral distinguishers for Pyjamask.

Lemma 1 ([15]). *$\pi_{u^{(0)}}(x^{(0)}) \rightsquigarrow \pi_{u^{(r)}}(x^{(r)})$ if $\pi_{u^{(0)}}(x^{(0)}) \to \pi_{u^{(r)}}(x^{(r)})$, and thus $\pi_{u^{(0)}}(x^{(0)}) \not\rightsquigarrow \pi_{u^{(r)}}(x^{(r)})$ implies $\pi_{u^{(0)}}(x^{(0)}) \not\to \pi_{u^{(r)}}(x^{(r)})$.*

2.4   MILP Modeling for the Monomial Prediction

In this subsection, we denote by $x \in \mathbb{F}_2^n, k \in \mathbb{F}_2^m$ the vectors for the plaintext and the master key, respectively. Let c be a certain output bit of the targeted cipher, then c is a function of $\boldsymbol{x}$ and $\boldsymbol{k}$ written as $c = f(\boldsymbol{x}, \boldsymbol{k})$. For a fix constant $\boldsymbol{u} \in \mathbb{F}_2^n$, we consider the encryption of the following structure of plaintexts

$$\mathbb{X} = \{\boldsymbol{x} \preceq \boldsymbol{u} : \boldsymbol{x} \in \mathbb{F}_2^n\}.$$

Then whether c has the integral property is decided by whether $\bigoplus_{\boldsymbol{x} \in \mathbb{X}} c = \bigoplus_{\boldsymbol{x} \in \mathbb{X}} f(\boldsymbol{x}, \boldsymbol{k})$ is a constant (0 or 1), which is further decided by whether for all possible $\boldsymbol{v} \in \mathbb{F}_2^m \setminus \{\boldsymbol{0}\}$, $\pi_{\boldsymbol{v}}(\boldsymbol{k}) \cdot \pi_{\boldsymbol{u}}(\boldsymbol{x})$ does not appear in the ANF of $c = f(\boldsymbol{x}, \boldsymbol{k})$. According to Lemma 1, if for all possible $\boldsymbol{v} \in \mathbb{F}_2^m \setminus \{\boldsymbol{0}\}$, $\pi_{\boldsymbol{v}}(\boldsymbol{k}) \cdot \pi_{\boldsymbol{u}}(\boldsymbol{x})$ does not have the monomial trails connecting $c = f(\boldsymbol{x}, \boldsymbol{k})$, then $\bigoplus_{\boldsymbol{x} \in \mathbb{X}} c$ is a constant, and c is key-independent.

In [26], Todo and Morri proposed the bit-based division properties, but the time and memory complexities of the corresponding algorithm are $\mathcal{O}(2^n)$ where n is the block size. To search for the division properties efficiently, Xiang et al. introduced the Mixed Integral Linear Programming (MILP) models in [30]. Since then, the MILP model has been the most common tool in the area about the division properties [6,8,18,27,28].

In the monomial prediction, we take a similar method to construct the MILP model by modeling the propagation of the monomial trails. Considering a monomial trail

$$(\pi_{\boldsymbol{u}^{(0)}}(\boldsymbol{x}^{(0)}), \pi_{\boldsymbol{u}^{(1)}}(\boldsymbol{x}^{(1)}), \dots, \pi_{\boldsymbol{u}^{(r)}}(\boldsymbol{x}^{(r)})),$$

it is enough to only model the vectors of $\boldsymbol{u}^{(i)}$ since the $\boldsymbol{x}^{(i)}$ are only symbolic variables. Then we only need to model the transitions of $(\boldsymbol{u}^{(0)}, \boldsymbol{u}^{(1)}, \dots, \boldsymbol{u}^{(r)})$. For any Boolean function $\boldsymbol{y} = \boldsymbol{f}(\boldsymbol{x})$, every pair of $(\boldsymbol{u}, \boldsymbol{v})$ is a valid monomial trail through $\boldsymbol{f}$ if and only if $\boldsymbol{x}^u \rightarrow \boldsymbol{y}^v$. Then we add constraints on $(\boldsymbol{u}, \boldsymbol{v})$ to force them be the valid transitions. Since every block cipher can be decomposed into some smaller components such as XOR, COPY, S-box and the linear layer, we introduce the MILP models for these functions.

Model 1 (COPY [13]). *Let $(a) \xrightarrow{COPY} (b_1, b_2, \dots, b_m)$ denote the monomial trail through the COPY function, where one bit is copied to m bits. Then, it can be depicted using the following MILP constraints:*

$$\begin{cases} b_1 + b_2 + \dots + b_m \geq a; \\ a \geq b_i, \ for \ all \ i \in \{1, 2, \dots, m\}; \\ a, b_1, b_2, \dots, b_m \ are \ binary \ variables. \end{cases}$$

Model 2 (XOR [13]). *Let $(a_1, a_2, \dots, a_m) \xrightarrow{XOR} (b)$ denote monomial trail through an XOR function, where m bits are compressed to one bit using an XOR operation. Then, it can be depicted using the following MILP constraints:*

$$\begin{cases} a_1 + a_2 + \dots + a_m - b = 0; \\ a_1, a_2, \dots, a_m, b \ are \ binary \ variables. \end{cases}$$

Model for S-box [29,30]. Given an S-box sending an n-bit vector to an m-bit vector, the monomial trails through the S-box can be represented as a set of

$(n+m)$-dimensional binary vectors which has a convex hull. With the help of `inequality_generator()` function in Sagemath [2] set of linear inequalities can be derived to describe the H-Representation of this convex hull. Then we use the greedy algorithm [21] to simplify them.

Model for the linear layer [20]. In [20], Sun et al. explained how to deduce a MILP model of the linear layers for the two-subset bit-based division properties. Here we slightly modify it for the monomial trails. Let M be a $n \times n$ matrix over $\mathbb{F}_2$, which can be represented at the bit level and denote

$$M = \begin{pmatrix} m_{0,0} & m_{0,1} & \cdots & m_{0,n-1} \\ m_{1,0} & m_{1,1} & \cdots & m_{1,n-1} \\ \vdots & \vdots & \ddots & \vdots \\ m_{n-1,0} & m_{n-1,1} & \cdots & m_{n-1,n-1} \end{pmatrix}$$

where $m_{i,j} \in \{0,1\}$. To represent the monomial trails through the linear layer, we introduce a set of auxiliary binary variables $t_{i,j} (0 \le i, j \le n-1)$ to decompose the binary matrix into XOR and COPY operations. Denote $(x_0, x_1, ..., x_{n-1}) \rightarrow (y_0, y_1, ..., y_{n-1})$ as a monomial trail of M, then we can construct linear inequality system as $x_j \xrightarrow{COPY} (t_{0,j}, t_{1,j}, ..., t_{n-1,j})$ and $(t_{i,0}, t_{i,1}, ..., t_{i,n-1}) \xrightarrow{XOR} y_i$, where the inequalities for COPY and XOR are from Model 1 and Model 2.

3   Automatic Search Model for Pyjamask and Integral Distinguishers

3.1   MILP Model for Pyjamask-96 and Pyjamask-128

The works in [13,15] have implied that the 3SDPwoU and the monomial prediction can be used to detect the integral properties for ciphers considering the key schedule. In this paper, we regard all the round keys are independent input variables, and the whole model we consider is illustrated in Fig. 2. Inspired by [14], we describe both encryption algorithm and the round keys into the MILP model. Suppose the length of the block size and the round key is n ($n = 96$ for

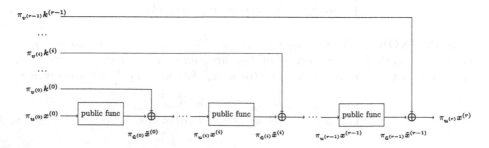

Fig. 2. General structure of our MILP model

Pyjamask-96 while $n = 128$ for Pyjamask-128). For $0 \leq i < r$, let $\pi_{u^{(i)}}(x^{(i)})$ and $\pi_{\tilde{u}^{(i)}}(\tilde{x}^{(i)})$ denote the monomials of the input and output statements of the ith round function, respectively. $\pi_{u^{(r)}}(x^{(r)})$ denotes a monomial of the ciphertext we are interested in. Practically, $u^{(r)}$ is set as a unit vector to study a certain bit of the ciphertext. $\pi_{v^{(i)}}(k^{(i)})$ denotes the monomial of the ith round key. We use inequalities to add constraints for variables $u^{(i)}, \tilde{u}^{(i)}$ and $v^{(i)}$ according to the functions between them (recall $x^{(i)}, \tilde{x}^{(i)}$ and $k^{(i)}$ are only symbolic variables). The whole process is very similar to [30] except,

1. Besides the encryption, the round keys are also considered. The monomials $\pi_{v^{(i)}}(k^{(i)})$ are treated equivalently as $\pi_{u^{(i)}}(x^{(i)})$ when we add constraints.
2. The monomial trails through public functions are described in the models introduced in Sect. 2.4 rather than the constraints for the two-subset bit-based division properties.

Initial constraints on $(u^{(0)}, v^{(0)}, \ldots, v^{(r-1)})$. Given a structure of plaintexts that all the active bits are a subset $I \subset \{0, 1, \ldots, n-1\}$, then we use

$$\begin{cases} u_i^{(0)} = 1, \text{ if } i \in I; \\ u_i^{(0)} = 0, \text{ if } i \notin I. \end{cases}$$

to add the initial constraints on $u^{(0)}$. Note we do not add any constraints on $(v^{(0)}, \ldots, v^{(r-1)})$ to allow $(v^{(0)}, \ldots, v^{(r-1)})$ to be free variables over $\mathbb{F}_2^{m \times r}$.

Stopping constraints on $u^{(r)}$. If we consider the integral property of the i'th ciphertext bit, then we use

$$\begin{cases} u_i^{(r)} = 1, \text{ if } i = i'; \\ u_i^{(r)} = 0, \text{ if } i \neq i'. \end{cases}$$

to add the stopping constraints on $u^{(r)}$.

Once we obtain the whole MILP model, we then call the MILP solver to solve the model. If the model is not feasible, for any $(v^{(0)}, \ldots, v^{(r-1)}) \in \mathbb{F}_2^{m \times r}$, $\pi_{v^{(0)}, \ldots, v^{(r-1)}}(k^{(0)}, \ldots, k^{(r-1)}) \cdot \pi_{u^{(0)}}(x^{(0)})$ has no trails connecting to $\pi_{u^{(r)}}(x^{(r)})$, i.e.,

$$\pi_{v^{(0)}, \ldots, v^{(r-1)}}(k^{(0)}, \ldots, k^{(r-1)}) \cdot \pi_{u^{(0)}}(x^{(0)}) \not\rightsquigarrow \pi_{u^{(r)}}(x^{(r)}), \forall (v^{(0)}, \ldots, v^{(r-1)}) \in \mathbb{F}_2^{m \times r}.$$

According to Lemma 1, $\pi_{v^{(0)}, \ldots, v^{(r-1)}}(k^{(0)}, \ldots, k^{(r-1)}) \cdot \pi_{u^{(0)}}(x^{(0)})$ does not appear in $\pi_{u^{(r)}}(x^{(r)})$ for any $(v^{(0)}, \ldots, v^{(r-1)}) \in \mathbb{F}_2^{m \times r}$. Consequently, $\pi_{u^{(r)}}(x^{(r)})$ is zero-sum.

Optional Extra Constraint to Obtain More Integral Property. In the integral attacks, not only the zero-sum ciphertext bits but also the one-sum ciphertext bits are useful. So we add an extra constraint to exclude the case that $\pi_{u^{(0)}}(x^{(0)}) \rightsquigarrow \pi_{u^{(r)}}(x^{(r)})$ as follows,

$$\mathcal{M} \leftarrow \sum_{0 \leq i < r,\, 0 \leq j < m} v_j^{(i)} \geq 1. \tag{1}$$

In this case, if the model is not feasible, then

$$\pi_{\boldsymbol{v}^{(0)},\ldots,\boldsymbol{v}^{(r-1)}}(\boldsymbol{k}^{(0)},\ldots,\boldsymbol{k}^{(r-1)})\cdot\pi_{\boldsymbol{u}^{(0)}}(\boldsymbol{x}^{(0)})\not\succ\pi_{\boldsymbol{u}^{(r)}}(\boldsymbol{x}^{(r)}),\forall(\boldsymbol{v}^{(0)},\ldots,\boldsymbol{v}^{(r-1)})\in\mathbb{F}_2^{m\times r}\setminus\{\boldsymbol{0}\}.$$

According to Lemma 1, $\pi_{\boldsymbol{v}^{(0)},\ldots,\boldsymbol{v}^{(r-1)}}(\boldsymbol{k}^{(0)},\ldots,\boldsymbol{k}^{(r-1)})\cdot\pi_{\boldsymbol{u}^{(0)}}(\boldsymbol{x}^{(0)})$ does not appear in $\pi_{\boldsymbol{u}^{(r)}}(\boldsymbol{x}^{(r)})$ for any $(\boldsymbol{v}^{(0)},\ldots,\boldsymbol{v}^{(r-1)})\in\mathbb{F}_2^{m\times r}\setminus\{\boldsymbol{0}\}$. Consequently, the ith bit of $\boldsymbol{x}^{(r)}$ is key-independent, i.e., zero-sum or one-sum (the concrete property can be determined by an additional experiment). All the source codes are avaliable at https://github.com/iljido/MILP_pyjamask. We refer the readers to our codes for more details of the MILP model.

3.2 Integral Distinguishers of Pyjamask-96 and Pyjamask-128

Since the goal for the first step is to obtain the longest distinguisher, e.g., for Pyjamask-96, we set the 95 bit of the input to active and one bit to constant to find r-round distinguisher. Then the 96 positions of the constant bits are traversed. If there are some balanced bits, we increase the round to $r+1$ and repeat the search process until no balanced bits are available. Then we found a 10.5-round distinguisher for Pyjamask-96 with 96 balanced bits, which can be naturelly extended to 11 rounds since the MixRows is linear. Then, we try to reduce the data complexity by minimizing the number of the active bits of the input as described in [19]. The reduced-round distinguishers can be obtained in the similar way.

For Pyjamask-96, we found distinguishers up to 11 rounds as follows, where $\mathcal{A},\mathcal{C}$ represent ACTIVE, CONSTANT bits respectively. And $\mathcal{B}$ denotes the zero-sum property while $\mathcal{B}_c$ represents the key-independent bits. Note that only for finding the 11-round distinguisher, we use the extra constraint in Eq. (1). Comparing to the results without the constraint, we find 32 more key-independent bits (the middle 32 bits denoted by $\mathcal{B}_c^{32}$), which helps to reduce the complexity of the key recovery attack on 14-round Pyjamask-96.

$$(\mathcal{C}^{32},\mathcal{C}^{32},\mathcal{A}^9\mathcal{C}^{23})\xrightarrow{5R}(\mathcal{B}^{32},\mathcal{B}^{32},\mathcal{B}^{32})$$

$$(\mathcal{C}^{32},\mathcal{C}^{32},\mathcal{A}^{17}\mathcal{C}^{15})\xrightarrow{6R}(\mathcal{B}^{32},\mathcal{B}^{32},\mathcal{B}^{32})$$

$$(\mathcal{C}^{10}\mathcal{A}^{22},\mathcal{C}^{10}\mathcal{A}^{22},\mathcal{C}^{10}\mathcal{A}^{22})\xrightarrow{7R}(\mathcal{B}^{32},\mathcal{B}^{32},\mathcal{B}^{32})$$

$$(\mathcal{C}^5\mathcal{A}^{27},\mathcal{C}^5\mathcal{A}^{27},\mathcal{C}^5\mathcal{A}^{27})\xrightarrow{8R}(\mathcal{B}^{32},\mathcal{B}^{32},\mathcal{B}^{32})$$

$$(\mathcal{C}^2\mathcal{A}^{30},\mathcal{C}^2\mathcal{A}^{30},\mathcal{C}^2\mathcal{A}^{30})\xrightarrow{9R}(\mathcal{B}^{32},\mathcal{B}^{32},\mathcal{B}^{32})$$

$$(\mathcal{C}^1\mathcal{A}^{31},\mathcal{C}^1\mathcal{A}^{31},\mathcal{C}^1\mathcal{A}^{31})\xrightarrow{10R}(\mathcal{B}^{32},\mathcal{B}^{32},\mathcal{B}^{32})$$

$$(\mathcal{C}^1\mathcal{A}^{31},\mathcal{A}^{32},\mathcal{A}^{32})\xrightarrow{11R}(\mathcal{B}^{32},\mathcal{B}_c^{32},\mathcal{B}^{32})$$

For Pyjamask-128, distinguishers up to 9 rounds are available.

$$(\mathcal{A}^5\mathcal{C}^{27}, \mathcal{A}^5\mathcal{C}^{27}, \mathcal{A}^5\mathcal{C}^{27}, \mathcal{A}^5\mathcal{C}^{27}) \xrightarrow{4R} (\mathcal{B}^{32}, \mathcal{B}^{32}, \mathcal{B}^{32}, \mathcal{B}^{32})$$

$$(\mathcal{A}^{13}\mathcal{C}^{19}, \mathcal{A}^{13}\mathcal{C}^{19}, \mathcal{A}^{13}\mathcal{C}^{19}, \mathcal{A}^{13}\mathcal{C}^{19}) \xrightarrow{5R} (\mathcal{B}^{32}, \mathcal{B}^{32}, \mathcal{B}^{32}, \mathcal{B}^{32})$$

$$(\mathcal{A}^{23}\mathcal{C}^9, \mathcal{A}^{22}\mathcal{C}^{10}, \mathcal{A}^{23}\mathcal{C}^9, \mathcal{A}^{22}\mathcal{C}^{10}) \xrightarrow{6R} (\mathcal{B}^{32}, \mathcal{U}^{32}, \mathcal{B}^{32}, \mathcal{U}^{32})$$

$$(\mathcal{A}^{28}\mathcal{C}^4, \mathcal{A}^{28}\mathcal{C}^4, \mathcal{A}^{28}\mathcal{C}^4, \mathcal{A}^{28}\mathcal{C}^4) \xrightarrow{7R} (\mathcal{B}^{32}, \mathcal{U}^{32}, \mathcal{U}^{32}, \mathcal{U}^{32})$$

$$(\mathcal{A}^{31}\mathcal{C}^1, \mathcal{A}^{30}\mathcal{C}^2, \mathcal{A}^{31}\mathcal{C}^1, \mathcal{A}^{30}\mathcal{C}^2) \xrightarrow{8R} (\mathcal{B}^{32}, \mathcal{U}^{32}, \mathcal{B}^{32}, \mathcal{U}^{32})$$

$$(\mathcal{A}^{32}, \mathcal{C}^1\mathcal{A}^{31}, \mathcal{A}^{32}, \mathcal{A}^{32}) \xrightarrow{9R} (\mathcal{B}^{32}, \mathcal{U}^{32}, \mathcal{B}^{32}, \mathcal{U}^{32})$$

4 Key Recovery Attack on Pyjamask-96

In this section, we present the key-recovery attacks for up to 14 rounds of Pyjamask-96. Since the attacks on rounds less than 13 is simple, here we only give the details of the attacks on 13- and 14-round Pyjamask-96 based on the same 11-round distinguisher available in Sect. 3. For a set of 2^{95} plaintexts denoted by $\mathbb{P}$ with the form of $(\mathcal{C}^1\mathcal{A}^{31}, \mathcal{A}^{32}, \mathcal{A}^{32})$, the intermediate state after 11 rounds (say, $x^{(11)}$) has the form of $(\mathcal{B}^{32}, \mathcal{B}^{32}, \mathcal{B}^{32})$. Taking a pre-computation with 2^{95} chosen plaintexts, the integral property (zero-sum or one-sum) of the middle 32-bit ciphertext can be determined. Since the complexities of our attack on 14-round Pyjamask-96 are significantly larger than 2^{95} (see Table 1), so the pre-computation is negligible. For the 13-round attack, we only use the 64 bits with zero-sum property.

As is well known, once an integral characteristic is found, we can take it to mount a key-recovery attack. If we denote by f the Boolean function that represents the mapping from the ciphertext of Pyjamask-96 to one of the balanced intermediate bit of $x^{(11)}$ (the output of the integral distinguisher), then we are interested in the following equation

$$\sum_{p\in\mathbb{P}} x^{(11)}[i] = \sum_{c\in\mathbb{C}} f(c) = 0 \tag{2}$$

where $x^{(11)}[i]$ is any one balanced bit and $\mathbb{C}$ is the corresponding ciphertext sets encrypted from $\mathbb{P}$. In the process of evaluating Eq. (2), we guess the involved subkey bits used in f, and check whether Eq. (2) holds. Those subkey values which violate Eq. (2) will be filtered out and discarded, and the remaining are the candidates of the correct subkeys.

4.1 Attack on 13-Round Pyjamask-96

By appending two rounds after the distinguisher, we can get a 13-round key recovery attack on Pyjamask-96. Note that we have changed the order of the MixRows and AddRoundKey, so the last operation of the 13-round Pyjamask is the MixRows that can be ignored and then the ciphertext is actually $\bar{z}^{(12)}$. Firstly, we try to write out explicitly the mapping f from $\bar{z}^{(12)}$ to any one balanced bit of $x^{(11)}$. Without loss of generality, here we take $x^{(11)}[0]$ as an example.

Since the Boolean function of f is too complicated, we split it into two steps and in each step, we make clear the subkey bits we need to guess.

Step 1: Express $x^{(11)}[0]$ by $\bar{z}^{(11)}$. We first express $x^{(11)}[0]$ in a polynomial of $\bar{z}^{(11)}$, according to the ANF of the inverse of S_3

$$
\begin{aligned}
x^{(11)}[0] &= y^{(11)}[0] \cdot y^{(11)}[32] + y^{(11)}[64] + 1 \\
&= (\bar{z}^{(11)}[0] + u^{(11)}[0])(\bar{z}^{(11)}[32] + u^{(11)}[32]) + (\bar{z}^{(11)}[64] + u^{(11)}[64]) + 1.
\end{aligned}
$$

If we have known $\bar{z}^{(11)}[0], \bar{z}^{(11)}[32]$ and $\bar{z}^{(11)}[64]$, through guessing $u^{(11)}[0], u^{(11)}[32]$ and $u^{(11)}[64]$ we can compute $x^{(11)}[0]$.

Step 2: Express respectively $\bar{z}^{(11)}[0], \bar{z}^{(11)}[32], \bar{z}^{(11)}[64]$ by $\bar{z}^{(12)}$. We first express $\bar{z}^{(11)}[64]$ in a polynomial of $\bar{z}^{(12)}$ as an example, the processes for $\bar{z}^{(11)}[0]$ and $\bar{z}^{(11)}[32]$ are similar.

$$
\begin{aligned}
\bar{z}^{(11)}[64] &= M_2^{-1}[0] \cdot (x^{(12)}[64], x^{(12)}[65], \ldots, x^{(12)}[95])^T \\
&= \sum_{i \in I_2} x^{(12)}[i] \\
&= \sum_{i \in I_2} (y^{(12)}[i - 64] \cdot y^{(12)}[i] + y^{(12)}[i - 32] + y^{(12)}[i] + 1) \qquad (3) \\
&= \sum_{i \in I_2} ((\bar{z}^{(12)}[i - 64] + u^{(12)}[i - 64]) \cdot (\bar{z}^{(12)}[i] + u^{(12)}[i]) \\
&\qquad + (\bar{z}^{(12)}[i - 32] + u^{(12)}[i - 32]) + (\bar{z}^{(12)}[i] + u^{(12)}[i]) + 1)
\end{aligned}
$$

where I_2 is a set of indices corresponding to the coefficient of $M_2^{-1}[0]$ (recall that $M_i[j]$ is the jth row of M_i). For $\bar{z}^{(11)}[0]$ and $\bar{z}^{(11)}[32]$, the index sets are I_0 and I_1, which corresponds to $M_0^{-1}[0]$ and $M_1^{-1}[0]$ respectively. At first glance, to calculate $\bar{z}^{(11)}[64]$, we need to guess $u^{(12)}[i - 64], u^{(12)}[i - 32]$ and $u^{(12)}[i]$ for each $i \in I_2$, totally $3 \times |I_2|$ subkey bits. However, Eq. (3) can be rewritten as

$$
\begin{aligned}
\bar{z}^{(11)}[64] &= \sum_{i \in I_2} \bar{z}^{(12)}[i - 64]\bar{z}^{(12)}[i] + \sum_{i \in I_2} u^{(12)}[i]\bar{z}^{(12)}[i - 64] \\
&\quad + \sum_{i \in I_2} \bar{z}^{(12)}[i]u^{(12)}[i - 64] + \sum_{i \in I_2} u^{(12)}[i - 64]u^{(12)}[i] \\
&\quad + \sum_{i \in I_2} \bar{z}^{(12)}[i - 32] + \sum_{i \in I_2} \bar{z}^{(12)}[i] \qquad (4) \\
&\quad + \sum_{i \in I_2} u^{(12)}[i - 32] + \sum_{i \in I_2} u^{(12)}[i] + 1.
\end{aligned}
$$

The subkey bits in the underlined term $\sum_{i \in I_2} u^{(12)}[i - 32]$ are independent of other subkey or intermediate state bits, so we can regard the whole as one equivalent subkey bit. Consequently, we now need to guess much less (equivalent) subkey bits, totally $2 \times |I_2| + 1$ bits. For $\bar{z}^{(11)}[0]$ and $\bar{z}^{(11)}[32]$, we need $2 \times |I_0| + 1$ and $2 \times |I_1| + 1$ subkey bits respectively. By removing the 11 reusable subkey bits $u^{(12)}[10]$, $u^{(12)}[20]$, $u^{(12)}[24]$, $u^{(12)}[32]$, $u^{(12)}[39]$, $u^{(12)}[44]$, $u^{(12)}[55]$, $u^{(12)}[65]$, $u^{(12)}[73]$, $u^{(12)}[86]$ and $u^{(12)}[94]$, we need 55 subkey bits in $u^{(12)}$ and 3 equivalent subkey bits $\sum_{i \in I_0} u^{(12)}[i+64]$, $\sum_{i \in I_1} u^{(12)}[i-32]$, $\sum_{i \in I_2} u^{(12)}[i-32]$ to compute $\bar{z}^{(11)}[0], \bar{z}^{(11)}[32]$ and $\bar{z}^{(11)}[64]$.

The relevant data bits can be compressed similarly as above. To calculate $\bar{z}^{(11)}[64]$, $3 \times |I_2|$ bits in $\bar{z}^{(12)}$ are required. For $\bar{z}^{(11)}[0]$ and $\bar{z}^{(11)}[32]$, we need $3 \times |I_0|$ and $3 \times |I_1|$ bits in $\bar{z}^{(12)}$, respectively. By removing the reusable bits, totally 66 data bits in $\bar{z}^{(12)}$ are required, which are highlighted gray in Fig. 3. However, the underwaved term $\sum_{i \in I_2} \bar{z}^{(12)}[i-32]$ are also independent from other subkey or intermediate state bits. So we can pre-compute the whole as one equivalent data bit for each ciphertext. Then, some of the $u^{(12)}[i]$ make no contribution to the further calculation and can be removed. For $\bar{z}^{(11)}[64]$, we need $2 \times |I_2|$ data bits in $\bar{z}^{(12)}$ and one equivalent data bit $c_2 = \sum_{i \in I_2} \bar{z}^{(12)}[i-32]$. It is the same for $\bar{z}^{(11)}[0]$ and $\bar{z}^{(11)}[32]$. The equivalent data bits are $c_0 = \sum_{i \in I_0} \bar{z}^{(12)}[i+64]$ and $c_1 = \sum_{i \in I_1} \bar{z}^{(12)}[i-32]$, respectively. Consequently, 11 bits in $\bar{z}^{(12)}$ are reduced in total (indicated by a cross in Fig. 3). We now need 58 data bits in $\bar{z}^{(12)}$ for the calculation of $x^{(11)}[0]$, including 3 equivalent data bits c_0, c_1 and c_2.

Furthermore, the 3 bit equivalent subkey bit $\sum_{i \in I_0} u^{(12)}[i+64]$, $\sum_{i \in I_1} u^{(12)}[i-32]$, $\sum_{i \in I_2} u^{(12)}[i-32]$ can be merged into the corresponding subkey bits $u^{(11)}[0]$, $u^{(11)}[32]$, $u^{(11)}[64]$ and consider together. Consequently, only 58 (equivalent) key bits are required to calculate $\sum_{p \in \mathbb{P}} x^{(11)}[0]$, including 55 bits in $u^{(12)}$ and 3 bits in $u^{(11)}$.

Partial Sum. An additional technique to reduce the complexity of the attack is the partial sum technique described in [11]. It observes that the small S-boxes are applied separately and the output of the MixRows is a linear combination of several input bits. Then, the relevant subkey bits are divided into relatively independent parts and guessed one after another. When a part of the subkey is guessed, the corresponding ciphertext can be compressed with the information and stored in a counter for further calculation. Meanwhile, the complexity can also be influenced by the order of guessing. So the trade-off between the increase of the guessed subkey bits and the decrease in the size of the counters deserves consideration. We first consider columns in $\bar{z}^{(12)}$ which correspond to only 2 equivalent subkey bits and then the columns related to 3-bit equivalent subkey.

Key Recovery Procedure. We give the process of the 13-round attack with the observations described before in this section. The attack consists of three phases.

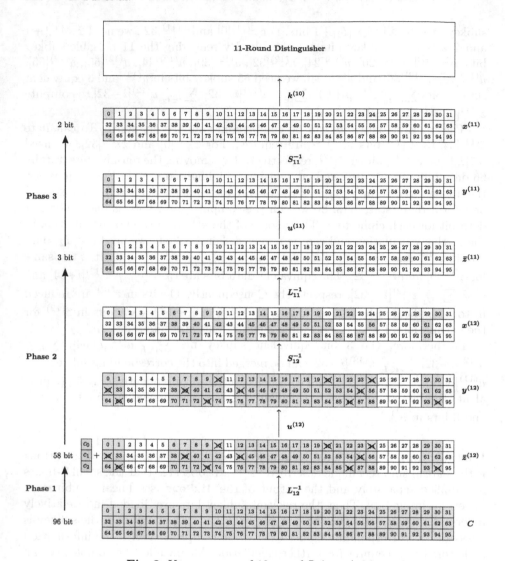

Fig. 3. Key-recovery of 13-round Pyjamask-96

1. **Preparing for the counters:**

   1.1 Choose a set of 2^{95} plaintexts $\mathbb{P}$ of the form $(\mathcal{C}^1\mathcal{A}^{31}, \mathcal{A}^{32}, \mathcal{A}^{32})$, $0 \leq i < 2^{95}$.

   1.2 Allocate a counter $\boldsymbol{T}_0$ of size 2^{66} containing 1-bit values and initialized by 0. For each $P_i \in \mathbb{P}$, call 13-round Pyjamask-96 (without the last MixRows) to encrypt P_i and obtain the corresponding ciphertext $\bar{z}^{(12)}$. Take the cascaded value of the 66-bit value $\bar{z}^{(12)}[0 - 1]$, $\bar{z}^{(12)}[6 - 10]$, $\bar{z}^{(12)}[12 - 24]$, $\bar{z}^{(12)}[29 - 30]$, $\bar{z}^{(12)}[32 - 33]$, $\bar{z}^{(12)}[38 - 42]$, $\bar{z}^{(12)}[44 - 56]$, $\bar{z}^{(12)}[61 - 62]$, $\bar{z}^{(12)}[64 - 65]$, $\bar{z}^{(12)}[70 - 74]$, $\bar{z}^{(12)}[76 - 88]$, $\bar{z}^{(12)}[93 - 94]$ as an index (denoted by i_0) and update $\boldsymbol{T}_0$ by $\boldsymbol{T}_0[i_0] = \boldsymbol{T}_0[i_0] + 1 \pmod 2$.

1.3 Allocate another counter T_1 of size 2^{58} containing 1-bit values and initialized by 0. For each T_0, calculate the 58-bit index i_1 of T_1.

(a) The first 55-bit index of T_1 can be calculated by taking out the 11-bit value $\bar{z}^{(12)}[10]$, $\bar{z}^{(12)}[20]$, $\bar{z}^{(12)}[24]$, $\bar{z}^{(12)}[32]$, $\bar{z}^{(12)}[39]$, $\bar{z}^{(12)}[44]$, $\bar{z}^{(12)}[55]$, $\bar{z}^{(12)}[65]$, $\bar{z}^{(12)}[73]$, $\bar{z}^{(12)}[86]$, $\bar{z}^{(12)}[94]$ and cascading the rest bits in order.

(b) The last 3 bits are derived according to $\sum_{i \in I_0} \bar{z}^{(12)}[i + 64]$, $\sum_{i \in I_1} \bar{z}^{(12)}[i - 32]$ and $\sum_{i \in I_2} \bar{z}^{(12)}[i - 32]$.

(c) Update T_1 by $T_1[i_1] = T_1[i_1] + 1 \pmod 2$.

2. **Guessing subkeys in $u^{(12)}$:** Based on the 58-bit counter T_1 derived, we now guess the 55-bit equivalent subkey in $u^{(12)}$.

2.1 The relevant subkey bits of the column 0, 1, 7, 9, 10, 12, 20, 22, 23, 24, 30 in $\bar{z}^{(12)}$ are guessed separately first. For each 2-bit guess, decrypt through S_3 and calculate the contribution to the corresponding $\bar{z}^{(11)}[i]$, $i = 0, 32, 64$. We treat the cost of the operation at once as 2 times 3-bit S-box computations. In total, 22 subkey bits are guessed in this step and the complexity is around $2^{60} \times 11 \times 2$ 3-bit S-box computations.

2.2 The relevant subkey bits of the remaining 11 columns in $\bar{z}^{(12)}$ are guessed separately. For each 3-bit guess, decrypt through S_3 and calculate the contribution to the corresponding $\bar{z}^{(11)}[i]$, $i = 0, 32, 64$. 33 subkey bits are guessed in this step and the complexity of this step is around $2^{61} \times 11 \times 2$ 3-bit S-box computations.

3. **Guessing subkeys in $u^{(11)}$:** The 3 bits equivalent key in $u^{(11)}$ are guessed in this step. For each guess, decrypt $\bar{z}^{(11)}[0]$, $\bar{z}^{(11)}[32]$, $\bar{z}^{(11)}[64]$ through the 3-bit S-box. Keep the subkey where $(x^{(11)}[0], x^{(11)}[64]) = (0, 0)$. The complexity of this step is around $2^{55+3+3} \times 2$ 3-bit S-box computations.

4. **Exhaustive search the rest of the key:** The key space is reduced by a factor of 2^{-2} for the 58-bit guess. By altering the position of the balanced bit and repeating the above steps, the key space can be further reduced. We choose 18 balanced columns and find the remaining subkey bits by an exhaustive search of 2^{92} possible combinations.

Complexity of the attack. In Phase 1.1 and 1.2, the complexity is calculated as 2^{95} 13-round Pyjamask-96 calls and 2^{95} times MixRows operations. The cost of Phase 1.3, Phase 2 and Phase 3 is calculated as

$$(2^{60} \times 11 \times 2 + 2^{61} \times 11 \times 2 + 2^{55+3+3} \times 2)/32 \approx 2^{61}$$

times SubBytes operations and $2^{66} \times 3/96 = 2^{61}$ times MixRows operations. For Phase 4, the same operations repeat for 18 times. The complexity is given as $18 \times 2^{61} + 2^{92}$ 13-round Pyjamask-96 calls. If we regard both SubBytes and MixRows as half a round of Pyjamask-96, the time complexity is calculated as

$$2^{95} + 2^{95}/2/13 + 18 \times 2^{61}/13 + 2^{92} \approx 2^{95.2}$$

times 13-round Pyjamask-96 calls. The data complexity is 2^{95} plaintexts. As the counters T_0 for the 18 positions can be prepared together in Phase 1, the memory complexity is $2^{66} \times 18 \approx 2^{70}$ bits, which is around 2^{67} bytes.

4.2   Attack on Full-Round Pyjamask-96

In this section, we extend one more round to get the full-round attack on Pyjamask-96. The order of MixRows and AddRoundKey has been changed, so the ciphertext is actually $\bar{z}^{(13)}$. Before going any further, we would like to briefly discuss the Fast Fourier Transform (FFT) key recovery technique. Following by the approach in [25], the key recovery process of 13-round attack can be expressed as $\sum_{i=1}^{N} F_{2,K'}(c_i' \oplus K_r') = 0$, where K_r' and K' denotes the 66-bit $u^{(12)}$ and the 3-bit $u^{(11)}$, respectively. The time complexity is $O(2^3 \times 66 \times 2^{66})$ for one balanced bit. So we believe that the FFT technique can achieve similar performance to our 13-round attack on Pyjamask-96 and the description can be simplified. However, for the full-round attack, this technique fails since we could not truncate K_r' from the 96-bit $u^{(13)}$.

As is seen in the attack on the 13-round case, the critical point of reducing the complexity is to reduce the subkey bits we need to guess and the relevant state bits. However, due to the strong diffusion from the additional round, we need 165 subkey bits to express one balanced bit of $x^{(11)}$, which exceeds the size of master key. To express one balanced bit of $x^{(11)}$, we need 3 bits in $\bar{z}^{(11)}$. Since for one bit in $\bar{z}^{(11)}$ we still need 96 bits in $u^{(13)}$ and at least 33 bits in $u^{(12)}$, we try to split one bit of $\bar{z}^{(11)}$ into small expressions. Here we take $x^{(11)}[0]$ as an example. To express $x^{(11)}[0]$, we need $\bar{z}^{(11)}[0]$, $\bar{z}^{(11)}[32]$, $\bar{z}^{(11)}[64]$, which can be rewritten as $\sum_{i \in I_0} x^{(12)}[i]$, $\sum_{i \in I_1} x^{(12)}[i]$, $\sum_{i \in I_2} x^{(12)}[i]$ respectively. We then split each $I_j, 0 \le j \le 2$ into two disjoint sets $I_{j,0}$ and $I_{j,1}$ and make clear the subkey we need to guess for each set. Without loss of generality, we take $\sum_{i \in I_{1,0}} x^{(12)}[i]$ as an example, where $I_{1,0} = \{38, 40, 42, 45, 46, 47, 48\}$.

According to Eq. (3) and Eq. (4), we can express $\sum_{i \in I_{1,j}} x^{(12)}[i]$ by $u^{(12)}$ and $\bar{z}^{(12)}$, and reduce the relevant subkey bits and data bits. In total, we need $2 \times |I_{1,0}|$ data bits in $\bar{z}^{(12)}$ and one equivalent data bit $\sum_{i \in I_{1,0}} \bar{z}^{(12)}[i - 32]$. The relevant key bits are $2 \times |I_{1,0}|$ bits in $u^{(12)}$ (the equivalent key bit $\sum_{i \in I_{1,0}} u^{(12)}[i - 32]$ can be merged into the relevant subkey bit in $u^{(11)}$ and guessed together).

Next, we show how to take the relationship between the round keys to further reduce the $2 \times |I_{1,0}|$ bits in $u^{(12)}$ to $|I_{1,0}|$ bits. In the key schedule, each 128 bit output of the ith round function is composed of the 96-bit round key $k^{(i)} = (k^{(i)}[0], k^{(i)}[1], \ldots, k^{(i)}[95])$ and an additional 32-bit value $\bar{k}^{(i)} = (\bar{k}^{(i)}[96], \bar{k}^{(i)}[97], \ldots, \bar{k}^{(i)}[127])$. In the key recovery phase, we are interested in the relationship between the 128-bit output $(k^{(12)}, \bar{k}^{(12)})$ and $(k^{(13)}, \bar{k}^{(13)})$, So we introduce a new 128-bit transform $\overline{\text{MixRows}}$ consisting of 4 matrices M_0, M_1, M_2 and E , where M_0, M_1, M_2 are the three matrices used in MixRows and E is a 32×32 identity matrix. Moreover, it is easy to check that $\overline{\text{MixRows}}^{-1}$ consists of $M_0^{-1}, M_1^{-1}, M_2^{-1}$ and E.

According to the key schedule, let $g : \mathbb{F}_2^{128} \to \mathbb{F}_2^{128}$ be a linear transform and $k^{(12)}[i] = g(k^{(13)}, \bar{k}^{(13)})[i], 0 \le i < 96$. The relationship between $u^{(12)}$ and $u^{(13)}$ is as follows,

$$u^{(12)}[i] = \text{MixRows}^{-1}(k^{(12)})[i]$$
$$= \overline{\text{MixRows}}^{-1} \circ g(k^{(13)}, \bar{k}^{(13)})[i]$$
$$= \overline{\text{MixRows}}^{-1} \circ g \circ \overline{\text{MixRows}}(u^{(13)}, \bar{k}^{(13)})[i]$$
$$= g(\dot{u}^{(13)}, \bar{k}^{(13)})[i]$$

Therefore, $u^{(12)}$ is a linear function of $u^{(13)}$ and $\bar{k}^{(13)}$. Considering the expression of $u^{(12)}[32]$ and suppose $v^{(i)}$ and $w^{(i)}$ are the output of Mixcolumns (recall a 4×4 matrix M is used in Mixcolumns) and MixAndRotateRows of the ith round, respectively, we have

$$u^{(12)}[32] = M^{-1}[1] \cdot (v^{(13)}[0], v^{(13)}[32], v^{(13)}[64], v^{(13)}[96])$$
$$= v^{(13)}[0] + v^{(13)}[64] + v^{(13)}[96]$$
$$= \sum_{i \in I_k} w^{(13)}[i] + w^{(13)}[81] + w^{(13)}[110] \tag{5}$$
$$= \underline{\sum_{i \in I_k} u^{(13)}[i] + u^{(13)}[81]} + \bar{k}^{(13)}[110] + 1$$

where I_k is a set of indices corresponding to the coefficient of $M_k^{-1}[0]$. So $u^{(12)}[32]$ relates to only one bit in $\bar{k}^{(13)}$. For other bits in $u^{(12)}$, things is similar. Moreover, bits in every column of $u^{(12)}$ correspond to the same bit in $\bar{k}^{(13)}$ e.g., $u^{(12)}[0], u^{(12)}[32], u^{(12)}[96]$ all relate to $\bar{k}^{(13)}[110]$. Once we guess the full $u^{(13)}$, we can compute $u^{(12)}$ by the above Eq. (5) with the additional knowledge of one corresponding bit in $\bar{k}^{(13)}$. Since the partial value of $u^{(12)}$ related to $u^{(13)}$ (e.g., the underlined part of Eq. (5)) can be computed beforehand, for one bit in $\bar{k}^{(13)}$ guessed, we derive the value of three bits in $u^{(12)}$ with only 3 XORs.

We then give the process of the calculation for $\sum_{i \in I_{1,0}} x^{(12)}[i]$, $I_{1,0} = \{38, 40, 42, 45, 46, 47, 48\}$.

1. **Preparing for the counters:**
   1.1 Choose a set of 2^{95} plaintexts $\mathbb{P}$ with the form of $(C^1 A^{31}, A^{32}, A^{32})$, $0 \leq i < 2^{95}$.
   1.2 Allocate a counter T_0 of size 2^{96} containing 1-bit values and initialized by 0. For each $P_i \in \mathbb{P}$, call 14-round Pyjamask-96 (without the last MixRows) to encrypt P_i and obtain the corresponding ciphertext $\bar{z}^{(13)}$ as an index (denoted by i_0). Update T_0 by $T_0[i_0] = T_0[i_0] + 1 \pmod 2$.
2. **Guessing then 96 bits in $u^{(13)}$:**
   2.1 Partially decrypt through the 15-bit subkey bits $u^{(13)}[0 - 4]$, $u^{(13)}[32 - 36]$, $u^{(13)}[64 - 68]$. For each 3-bit guess, partially decrypt the ciphertext through S_3. We treat the cost of each above operation as 2 times 3-bit S-box computations, then the complexity is around $2 \times (2^{3+96} + 2^{6+96} + 2^{9+96} + 2^{12+96} + 2^{15+96}) \approx 2^{112.2}$ times 3-bits S-box computation.

2.2 After all 15-bit subkey bits have been guessed, calculate the contribution of the 15 bits in $x^{(13)}$ to the 15 bits in $\bar{z}^{(12)}$. Keep the new 96-bit as the index of the counter. We treat the cost of each above operation as $7/32$ times MixRows operations, then the complexity is $2^{96+15} \times 7/32 \approx 2^{108.9}$ times MixRows operations.

2.3 The remaining 81 bits in $u^{(13)}$ are guessed separately. For each 3-bit guess, partially decrypt the ciphertext through S_3 and calculate the contribution to the 15 bits in $\bar{z}^{(12)}$. We treat the cost of each above operation as 2 times 3-bit S-box computations and $7/(32 \times 11)$ times MixRows operations. The complexity of this step is bounded by $2^{15+96+3} \times 27 \times 2 \approx 2^{119.8}$ times 3-bit S-box computations and $2^{15+96+3} \times 27 \times 7/(32 \times 11) \approx 2^{113.2}$ times MixRows operations.

3. **Guessing the 7 bits in $\bar{k}^{(13)}$:** Up to now, we have guessed the 96 bit in $u^{(13)}$. For each 96-bit guess:

3.1 Calculate the 14 expression of $u^{(12)}[i]$ according to the 96 bits in $u^{(13)}$, $i \in I_{1,0}$. The complexity of this step is 2^{96} times one round inverse key schedule.

3.2 Guess 7 bits in $\bar{k}^{(13)}$. For each 1-bit guess, derive the relevant 3-bit $u^{(12)}$ and calculate the contribution to $\sum_{i \in I_{1,0}} x^{(12)}[i]$. The complexity is around $2 \times (2^{96+1+15} + 2^{96+2+13} + 2^{96+3+11} + 2^{96+4+9} + 2^{96+5+7} + 2^{96+6+5} + 2^{96+7+3}) \approx 2^{114}$ times 3-bit S-box computations.

After that, we derive the corresponding value of $\sum_{i \in I_{1,0}} x^{(12)}[i]$ for each 103-bit subkey guess and store them in a table. The complexity is dominated by $(2^{112.2} + 2^{119.8} + 2^{114})/32 \approx 2^{114.9}$ times SubBytes operations and $2^{108.9} + 2^{113.2} \approx 2^{113.3}$ times MixRows operations. Then the total complexity is bounded by $2^{110.6}$ times 14-round Pyjamask-96.

Then we calculate the table for the other 5 sets. The total complexity is bounded by $2^{110.6} + 2^{108.6} \times 3 + 2^{106.6} \times 2 \approx 2^{111.4}$ times 14-round Pyjamask-96.

After all 6 tables have been established, we then go through the relevant 118-bit $(u^{(13)}, \bar{k}^{(13)})$. For each 118-bit key guess, we search for the corresponding $\bar{z}^{11}[0]$, $\bar{z}^{11}[32]$, $\bar{z}^{11}[64]$. Then we guess the corresponding 3-bit subkey in $u^{(11)}$ and keep the subkey where $x^{(11)}[0]$, $x^{(11)}[32]$, $x^{(11)}[64]$ satisfying the tail of 11-round distinguisher (calculated by 2^{95} 11-round encryption). We treat the cost for searching table as one time 14-round Pyjamask-96 encryption. The time complexity for this step is $2^{118} \times 6 + 2^{118+3} \times 2/(32 \times 2 \times 14) \approx 2^{120.6}$ Pyjamask-96 calls. So the total complexity is

$$2^{95} + 2^{95}/(2 \times 14) + 2^{95} \times 11/14 + 2^{110.6} + 2^{120.6} \approx 2^{120.7}$$

times 14-round Pyjamask-96. The key space is reduced by $1/2^3$ each time. We choose 3 balanced columns and find the remaining key by 2^{119} exhaustive search. The time complexity is $2^{120.7} \times 3 + 2^{120} \approx 2^{122.6}$ times 14-round Pyjamask-96. The memory complexity is around $(2^{103} + 3 \times 2^{102} + 2 \times 2^{101})/2^3 = 2^{101.6}$ bytes.

5   Integral Attacks on Round-Reduced Pyjamask-128

In this section we present the attack on Pyjamask-128 with the distinguishers shown in Sect. 3. The attack results are summarized in Table 1.

The 11-round attack on Pyjamask-128 is by appending two rounds after the 9-round distinguisher. For a set of 2^{127} plaintexts of the form $(\mathcal{A}^{32}, \mathcal{C}^1 \mathcal{A}^{31}, \mathcal{A}^{32}, \mathcal{A}^{32})$, the intermediate state after 9 rounds has the form of $(\mathcal{B}^{32}, \mathcal{U}^{32}, \mathcal{B}^{32}, \mathcal{U}^{32})$. The order of MixRows and AddRoundKey has been exchanged like 13-round attack of Pyjamask-96. So the ciphertext is actually $\bar{z}^{(10)}$.

To express one bit in $x^{(9)}$, for example $x^{(9)}[0]$, we need 4 bits in $\bar{z}^{(9)}$ and 4 bits in $u^{(9)}$. Using the same method as Eq. (3), we can compress the relevant data bits by the equivalent data bits $c_1 = \sum_{i \in I_1} \bar{z}^{(10)}[i - 32]$ and $c_2 = \sum_{i \in I_2} \bar{z}^{(10)}[i - 32] + \bar{z}^{(10)}[i + 32]$. By removing the reusable bits and redundant bits, we need 99 bits in $\bar{z}^{(10)}$ and 2 equivalent data bits. The equivalent key is utilized similarly, and the involved key bits are 99 bits in $u^{(10)}$ and 4 equivalent bits in $u^{(9)}$. Then we guess the subkey bits partially and compress the ciphertext.

For each 101-bit equivalent $\bar{z}^{(10)}$, we guess the 99-bit $u^{(10)}$ partially. Each time, we decrypt the ciphertext through the 4-bit S-box and calculate the contribution to $\bar{z}^{(9)}[0]$, $\bar{z}^{(9)}[32]$, $\bar{z}^{(9)}[64]$, $\bar{z}^{(9)}[96]$. If we treat the cost of each above operation as 2 times 4-bit S-box computation, the complexity of this phase is $(2^{107} \times 21 + 2^{106} \times 3 + 2^{105} \times 2 + 2^{103}) \times 2/32 \approx 2^{107.6}$ times SubBytes operation.

Then we guess the 4 bits in $u^{(9)}$ and compare them with the tail of the distinguisher. The complexity for this phase is $2^{99+4+4} \times 2/32 = 2^{103}$ times SubBytes. The key space is reduced by $1/2^2$ each time. We choose 3 balanced columns and find the remaining key bits by an exhaustive search of 2^{122} possible combinations. The time complexity is dominated by the 2^{127} times encryption and the memory complexity is dominated by $2^{108} \times 3/2^3 \approx 2^{106.5}$ bytes.

For Pyjamask-128 of round r $(r = 7, 8, 9)$, we append 2 rounds after the $(r-2)$-round distinguisher. The process is similar. The time complexity is dominated by the encryption of plaintext for 10- and 9-round attacks, which are 2^{122} times 10-round Pyjamask-128 and 2^{112} times 9-round Pyjamask-128. For 8-round attack, each time when the key space is reduced by $1/2^2$, we need around $2^{107.6}/(2 \times 8) = 2^{103.6}$ times 8-round Pyjamask-128. We repeat the process for 12 times and the total complexity is $12 \times 2^{103.6} + 2^{106} \approx 2^{107.8}$ times 8-round Pyjamask-128.

For Pyjamask-128 of round r, $r = 5, 6, 7$, we append 1 round after the $(r-1)$-round distinguisher. Then we partially guess 4-bit subkey, decrypt the ciphertexts through S_4 and compare with the tail of the distinguisher. For 7-round Pyjamask-128, the time complexity is $2^{90+4} \times 2/(32 \times 2 \times 7) \approx 2^{86.2}$ times 7-round Pyjamask-128 for each 4-bit guess. We choose 20 balanced columns and the total complexity is $2^{90} + 2^{90}/(2 \times 7) + 20 \times 2^{86.2} + 2^{88} \approx 2^{91.5}$ times 7-round Pyjamask-128. For 6-round Pyjamask-128, the time complexity is composed by 2^{52} times 6-round Pyjamask-128, 2^{52} times MixRows^{-1} and $20 \times 2^{52+4} \times 2/(32 \times 2 \times 6) + 2^{128-4 \times 20} \approx 2^{52.8}$ times 6-round Pyjamask-128, which is bounded by 2^{54} times 6-round Pyjamask-128. For 5-round Pyjamask-128, the time complexity is composed by 2^{20} times 5-round Pyjamask-128, 2^{20}

times $\texttt{MixRows}^{-1}$ and $32 \times 2^{20+4} \times 2/(32 \times 2 \times 5) \approx 2^{21.7}$ times 5-round Pyjamask-128, which is bounded by 2^{23} times 5-round Pyjamask-128.

6 Conclusion

This paper studies the security strength of the block ciphers Pyjamask-96 and Pyjamask-128 against the integral attacks. With a new MILP model for the division property considering the encryption function and the round keys simultaneously, we detect efficient integral distinguishers for both Pyjamask-96 and Pyjamask-128. For Pyjamask-96, we utilize the 11-round integral distinguisher, combined with a novel property of the key schedule, to mount a key recovery attack for full Pyjamask-96 without the full codebook for the first time. The results for fewer rounds, e.g., 13-round Pyjamask-96 are also improved. What's more, we give the first third-party cryptanalysis on the Pyjamask-128, which sheds more light on its security margin. The integral attacks on both versions of Pyjamask are significant to understand the low degree property of block ciphers.

Acknowledgements. We thank the anonymous reviewers for their valuable comments. This work is supported by the National Natural Science Foundation of China (Grant No. 62032014), the National Key Research and Development Program of China (Grant No. 2018YFA0704702), the Major Basic Research Project of Natural Science Foundation of Shandong Province, China (Grant No. ZR202010220025). Qingju Wang is funded by Huawei Technologies Co., Ltd (Agreement No.: YBN2020035184).

References

1. https://eprint.iacr.org/2021/1572.pdf
2. https://www.sagemath.org/
3. Albrecht, M.R., Rechberger, C., Schneider, T., Tiessen, T., Zohner, M.: Ciphers for MPC and FHE. In: Oswald, E., Fischlin, M. (eds.) EUROCRYPT 2015, Part I. LNCS, vol. 9056, pp. 430–454. Springer, Heidelberg (2015). https://doi.org/10.1007/978-3-662-46800-5_17
4. Bar-On, A., Keller, N.: A 2^{70} attack on the full MISTY1. In: Robshaw, M., Katz, J. (eds.) CRYPTO 2016, Part I. LNCS, vol. 9814, pp. 435–456. Springer, Heidelberg (2016). https://doi.org/10.1007/978-3-662-53018-4_16
5. Boura, C., Canteaut, A.: Another view of the division property. In: Robshaw, M., Katz, J. (eds.) CRYPTO 2016, Part I. LNCS, vol. 9814, pp. 654–682. Springer, Heidelberg (2016). https://doi.org/10.1007/978-3-662-53018-4_24
6. Boura, C., Coggia, D.: Efficient MILP modelings for sboxes and linear layers of SPN ciphers. IACR Trans. Symmetric Cryptol. **2020**(3), 327–361 (2020)
7. Daemen, J., Knudsen, L., Rijmen, V.: The block cipher square. In: Biham, E. (ed.) FSE 1997. LNCS, vol. 1267, pp. 149–165. Springer, Heidelberg (1997). https://doi.org/10.1007/BFb0052343
8. Derbez, P., Fouque, P.-A.: Increasing precision of division property. IACR Trans. Symmetric Cryptol. **2020**(4), 173–194 (2020)
9. Dobraunig, C., et al.: Rasta: a cipher with low ANDdepth and few ANDs per bit. In: Shacham, H., Boldyreva, A. (eds.) CRYPTO 2018, Part I. LNCS, vol. 10991, pp. 662–692. Springer, Cham (2018). https://doi.org/10.1007/978-3-319-96884-1_22

10. Dobraunig, C., Rotella, Y., Schoone, J.: Algebraic and higher-order differential cryptanalysis of pyjamask-96. IACR Trans. Symmetric Cryptol. **2020**(1), 289–312 (2020)
11. Ferguson, N., et al.: Improved cryptanalysis of rijndael. In: Goos, G., Hartmanis, J., van Leeuwen, J., Schneier, B. (eds.) FSE 2000. LNCS, vol. 1978, pp. 213–230. Springer, Heidelberg (2001). https://doi.org/10.1007/3-540-44706-7_15
12. Goudarzi, D., et al.: Pyjamask: block cipher and authenticated encryption with highly efficient masked implementation. IACR Trans. Symmetric Cryptol. **2020**(S1), 31–59 (2020)
13. Hao, Y., Leander, G., Meier, W., Todo, Y., Wang, Q.: Modeling for three-subset division property without unknown subset. In: Canteaut, A., Ishai, Y. (eds.) EUROCRYPT 2020, Part I. LNCS, vol. 12105, pp. 466–495. Springer, Cham (2020). https://doi.org/10.1007/978-3-030-45721-1_17
14. Hebborn, P., Lambin, B., Leander, G., Todo, Y.: Lower bounds on the degree of block ciphers. In: Moriai, S., Wang, H. (eds.) ASIACRYPT 2020, Part I. LNCS, vol. 12491, pp. 537–566. Springer, Cham (2020). https://doi.org/10.1007/978-3-030-64837-4_18
15. Hu, K., Sun, S., Wang, M., Wang, Q.: An algebraic formulation of the division property: revisiting degree evaluations, cube attacks, and key-independent sums. In: Moriai, S., Wang, H. (eds.) ASIACRYPT 2020, Part I. LNCS, vol. 12491, pp. 446–476. Springer, Cham (2020). https://doi.org/10.1007/978-3-030-64837-4_15
16. Knudsen, L.R., Wagner, D.A.: Integral cryptanalysis. In: Daemen, J., Rijmen, V. (eds.) FSE 2002. LNCS, vol. 2365, pp. 112–127. Springer, Heidelberg (2002). https://doi.org/10.1007/3-540-45661-9_9
17. Krovetz, T., Rogaway, P.: The OCB authenticated-encryption algorithm. RFC **7253**, 1–19 (2014)
18. Lambin, B., Derbez, P., Fouque, P.-A.: Linearly equivalent s-boxes and the division property. Des. Codes Cryptogr. **88**(10), 2207–2231 (2020)
19. Sun, L., Wang, W., Wang, M.: Automatic search of bit-based division property for ARX ciphers and word-based division property. In: Takagi, T., Peyrin, T. (eds.) ASIACRYPT 2017, Part I. LNCS, vol. 10624, pp. 128–157. Springer, Cham (2017). https://doi.org/10.1007/978-3-319-70694-8_5
20. Sun, L., Wang, W., Wang, M.: Milp-aided bit-based division property for primitives with non-bit-permutation linear layers. IET Inf. Secur. **14**(1), 12–20 (2020)
21. Sun, S., Hu, L., Wang, P., Qiao, K., Ma, X., Song, L.: Automatic security evaluation and (related-key) differential characteristic search: application to SIMON, PRESENT, LBlock, DES(L) and other bit-oriented block ciphers. In: Sarkar, P., Iwata, T. (eds.) ASIACRYPT 2014, Part I. LNCS, vol. 8873, pp. 158–178. Springer, Heidelberg (2014). https://doi.org/10.1007/978-3-662-45611-8_9
22. Tian, W., Bin, H.: Integral cryptanalysis on two block ciphers pyjamask and uBlock. IET Inf. Secur. **14**(5), 572–579 (2020)
23. Todo, Y.: Integral cryptanalysis on full MISTY1. In: Gennaro, R., Robshaw, M. (eds.) CRYPTO 2015, Part I. LNCS, vol. 9215, pp. 413–432. Springer, Heidelberg (2015). https://doi.org/10.1007/978-3-662-47989-6_20
24. Todo, Y.: Structural evaluation by generalized integral property. In: Oswald, E., Fischlin, M. (eds.) EUROCRYPT 2015, Part I. LNCS, vol. 9056, pp. 287–314. Springer, Heidelberg (2015). https://doi.org/10.1007/978-3-662-46800-5_12
25. Todo, Y., Aoki, K.: FFT key recovery for integral attack. In: Gritzalis, D., Kiayias, A., Askoxylakis, I. (eds.) CANS 2014. LNCS, vol. 8813, pp. 64–81. Springer, Cham (2014). https://doi.org/10.1007/978-3-319-12280-9_5

26. Todo, Y., Morii, M.: Bit-based division property and application to SIMON family. In: Peyrin, T. (ed.) FSE 2016. LNCS, vol. 9783, pp. 357–377. Springer, Heidelberg (2016). https://doi.org/10.1007/978-3-662-52993-5_18
27. Wang, Q., Grassi, L., Rechberger, C.: Zero-sum partitions of PHOTON permutations. In: Smart, N.P. (ed.) CT-RSA 2018. LNCS, vol. 10808, pp. 279–299. Springer, Cham (2018). https://doi.org/10.1007/978-3-319-76953-0_15
28. Wang, Q., Hao, Y., Todo, Y., Li, C., Isobe, T., Meier, W.: Improved division property based cube attacks exploiting algebraic properties of superpoly. In: Shacham, H., Boldyreva, A. (eds.) CRYPTO 2018, Part I. LNCS, vol. 10991, pp. 275–305. Springer, Cham (2018). https://doi.org/10.1007/978-3-319-96884-1_10
29. Wang, S., Hu, B., Guan, J., Zhang, K., Shi, T.: MILP-aided method of searching division property using three subsets and applications. In: Galbraith, S.D., Moriai, S. (eds.) ASIACRYPT 2019, Part III. LNCS, vol. 11923, pp. 398–427. Springer, Cham (2019). https://doi.org/10.1007/978-3-030-34618-8_14
30. Xiang, Z., Zhang, W., Bao, Z., Lin, D.: Applying MILP method to searching integral distinguishers based on division property for 6 lightweight block ciphers. In: Cheon, J.H., Takagi, T. (eds.) ASIACRYPT 2016, Part I. LNCS, vol. 10031, pp. 648–678. Springer, Heidelberg (2016). https://doi.org/10.1007/978-3-662-53887-6_24

Related-Tweakey Impossible Differential Attack on Reduced-Round SKINNY-AEAD M1/M3

Yanhong Fan[1,2], Muzhou Li[1,2], Chao Niu[1,2], Zhenyu Lu[1,2], and Meiqin Wang[1,2(✉)]

[1] School of Cyber Science and Technology, Shandong University, Qingdao 266237, Shandong, China
{fanyh,muzhouli,niuchao,luzhenyu}@mail.sdu.edu.cn, mqwang@sdu.edu.cn
[2] Key Laboratory of Cryptologic Technology and Information Security of Ministry of Education, Shandong University, Qingdao 266237, Shandong, China

Abstract. SKINNY-AEAD is one of the second-round candidates of the Lightweight Cryptography Standardization project held by NIST. SKINNY-AEAD M1 is the primary member of six SKINNY-AEAD schemes, while SKINNY-AEAD M3 is another member with a small tag. In the design document, only security analyses of their underlying primitive SKINNY-128-384 are provided. Besides, there are no valid third-party analyses on SKINNY-AEAD M1/M3 according to our knowledge. Therefore, this paper focuses on constructing the first third-party security analyses on them under a nonce-respecting scenario. By taking the encryption mode of SKINNY-AEAD into consideration and exploiting several properties of SKINNY, we can deduce some necessary constraints on the input and tweakey differences of related-tweakey impossible differential distinguishers. Under these constraints, we can find distinguishers suitable for mounting powerful tweakey recovery attacks. With the help of the automatic searching algorithms based on STP, we find some 14-round distinguishers. Based on one of these distinguishers, we mount a 20-round and an 18-round tweakey recovery attack on SKINNY-AEAD M1/M3. To the best of our knowledge, all these attacks are the best ones so far.

Keywords: Related-tweakey · Impossible differential cryptanalysis · SKINNY-AEAD M1/M3 · Tweakey recovery · SKINNY-128-384

1 Introduction

SKINNY-AEAD schemes are proposed by Beierle *et al.* [5] and accepted as one of the second-round candidates of the NIST Lightweight Cryptography (LWC) Standardization project[1]. There are six schemes for SKINNY-AEAD and SKINNY-AEAD M1 is the primary member. SKINNY-AEAD M3 is the same as M1 except

---

[1] https://csrc.nist.gov/Projects/lightweight-cryptography/round-2-candidates.

© The Author(s), under exclusive license to Springer Nature Switzerland AG 2022
S. D. Galbraith (Ed.): CT-RSA 2022, LNCS 13161, pp. 247–271, 2022.
https://doi.org/10.1007/978-3-030-95312-6_11

that M3 has smaller length of tag than M1. These two authenticated encryption schemes M1/M3 use a mode following the ΘCB3 framework [13] and adopts SKINNY-128-384 [4] as their internal tweakable block cipher. For M1/M3, only security analyses of their underlying primitive SKINNY-128-384 are introduced in the design document [5]. As for M1/M3 themselves, no cryptanalytic results are presented there.

SKINNY-128-384 belongs to the well-known SKINNY family designed by Beierle *et al.* [4]. It adopts 128-bit plaintexts and 384-bit tweakeys. Since its proposal, many cryptanalytic results have been proposed [9,15,20–22]. Among all of them, the best attack so far was provided by [9], where a 30-round related-tweakey rectangle attack was mounted with time complexity $2^{361.38}$. As for impossible differential attacks, Liu *et al.* gave a 27-round attack in related-tweakey setting [15] with time complexity 2^{378}, while a 22-round attack in single-tweakey setting was proposed by Tolba *et al.* in [21] with time complexity $2^{373.48}$. Besides, there is a 22-round Demirci-Selçuk meet-in-the-middle attack provided in [20] with time complexity $2^{382.46}$.

From above security analyses of SKINNY-128-384, we can see that there are no constraints on the value or difference of the tweakey. However, when it comes to SKINNY-AEAD, some constraints should be considered in the attack procedure because of the encryption mode, the nonce-respecting scenario and complex tweakey initialization. In [5], the designers depict that SKINNY-AEAD M1/M3 apply a 384-bit tweakey but a 128-bit key, and claim full 128-bit security for key recovery in the nonce-respecting scenario. Thus, only attacks on SKINNY-128-384 with time complexity less than 2^{128} is valid for SKINNY-AEAD M1/M3. Due to this constraints on time complexity, above attacks [9,15,20–22] cannot be directly applied to SKINNY-AEAD M1/M3. Zhao *et al.* [22] gave a related-tweakey rectangle attack on SKINNY-AEAD M1. However, the second-round status update document of SKINNY-AEAD [1] pointed that the attack of [22] on SKINNY-AEAD M1 is invalid. To the best of our knowledge, there is no valid third-party analysis of SKINNY-AEAD M1/M3 up to now. This motivates us to evaluate their security considering these restrictions.

In this paper, we mount tweakey recovery attacks by searching for the related-tweakey impossible differential distinguishers. As one of the most popular cryptanalytic methods, the impossible differential attack was proposed in [7]. Biham [6] firstly proposed the related-key attack, where only the relations between pairs of related keys are chosen by the attacker, who does not know the keys themselves. Jakimoski *et al.* [10] proposed the related-key impossible differential attack firstly combining the two aforementioned attacks. In recent years, the related-key/tweakey impossible differential attacks [2,15,19] gave some better cryptanalysis results in block ciphers.

Our Contributions. The main contribution of our work is providing the third-party cryptanalytic results on SKINNY-AEAD M1/M3 by utilizing related-tweakey impossible differentials. All these distinguishers are found with the automatic solver STP after setting several constraints on the input and tweakey differences.

1) **Automatically Searching for Distinguishers of SKINNY-AEAD M1/M3.**
   Unlike finding distinguishers of SKINNY-128-384 itself, distinguishers exploited
   here should fulfill several conditions due to the encryption mode of SKINNY-
   AEAD M1/M3, as well as the complex tweakey initialization. By combining
   these restrictions with several properties of SKINNY cipher, we can deduce
   some constraints on the input and tweakey differences of the target related-
   tweakey impossible differential distinguishers. Based on the method of searching for related-tweakey impossible differentials [15,19], we find some 14-round
   distinguishers with only one active input and output state differences with
   the help of STP.
2) **Tweakey Recovery Attacks for SKINNY-AEAD M1/M3.** Based on one 14-
   round distinguisher, we mount a 20-round and an 18-round tweakey recovery
   attack under nonce-respecting scenario. All the attacks are applicable to M1
   and M3. Our attack results along with [22] are illustrated in Table 1. To
   our knowledge, they are the best tweakey recovery attacks on SKINNY-AEAD
   M1/M3 so far.

Table 1. Summary of attack results on SKINNY-AEAD M1/M3

Attack	Cipher	Rounds	Data	Time	Memory	Ref.
RTID	M1/M3	20	$2^{121.6}$ CP	$2^{127.1}$	$2^{124.8}$ bits	Sect. 4
		18	$2^{121.6}$ CP	$2^{125.9}$	$2^{52.8}$ bits	Sect. 5
RTR$^+$	M1	24	$2^{123.0}$ CP	$2^{123.0}$	$2^{121.0}$	[22]

Note: RTID: Related-Tweakey Impossible Differential. CP:
Chosen PlaintextS.
RTR: Related-Tweakey Rectangle. $^+$: This attack is invalid, as
pointed out in [1].

Outline. In Sect. 2, we give the brief description of SKINNY-AEAD M1/M3,
SKINNY-128-384 and properties of SKINNY, and then introduce some notations
used in the paper. Section 3 gives the 14-round related-tweakey impossible differential distinguishers that are found by an automatic search algorithm with
STP. Based on one of these 14-round distinguishers, Sect. 4 and 5 discuss a
20-round and an 18-round tweakey recovery attack, respectively. In Sect. 6, we
summarize and conclude our work.

2   Preliminaries

2.1   Description of SKINNY-AEAD M1/M3

In this section, we briefly give some specifications for SKINNY-AEAD M1/M3. The
input parameters of SKINNY-AEAD M1/M3 might contain an associated data A, a
message M and a nonce N. In our attack scenario, A is set to be empty, and then
the message block is handled directly, which can reduce the time complexity of

the tweakey recovery attack. The output parameters of M1/M3 are a ciphertext with the same length as the plaintext and a tag. The tag length of M1 and M3 are 128 and 64 bits, respectively. Figure 1 illustrates the message encryption part of SKINNY-AEAD M1/M3 without padding.

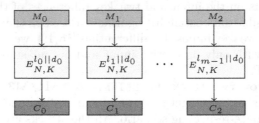

Fig. 1. The message encryption part of SKINNY-AEAD M1/M3 with SKINNY-128-384 without padding. E refers to SKINNY-128-384. For simplicity, we denote the block counter by $l_0, \ldots, l_{m-1}$ but actually refer to the state of the LFSRs serving as a block counter.

Messages are encrypted with SKINNY-128-384 under the 384-bit tweakey $i.e.$, $\mathrm{rev}_{64}(\mathrm{LSFR})||0^{56}||d_0||N||K$. The 384-bit tweakey states can be seen as a group of three 128-bit data that are denoted as $TK1, TK2$, and $TK3$, where $TK_1 \leftarrow \mathrm{rev}_{64}(\mathrm{LSFR})||0^{56}||d_0, TK2 \leftarrow N$, and $TK3 \leftarrow K$. In SKINNY-AEAD M1/M3, TK_1, TK_2 and TK_3 store information corresponding to block counter l_i, nonce N and a 128-bit key, respectively. $\mathrm{rev}_{64}(\mathrm{LSFR})$ stores 8-byte values from a 64-bit LFSR. d_0 is a domain separation value and denotes encryption of a full message block without padding, where $d_0 = \texttt{0x00}$ for M1, $d_0 = \texttt{0x08}$ for M3. $\mathrm{rev}_{64}(\mathrm{LSFR})$ can be updated in a series of blocks in the following way.

The 64-bit state of the LFSR can be expressed as: $x_{63}||x_{62}||\ldots||x_1||x_0$ and initialized to $\mathrm{LSFR}_0 = 0^{63}||1$. The LFSR is updated by the function upd_{64} ($i.e.$, $\mathrm{LSFR}_{t+1} = \mathrm{upd}_{64}(\mathrm{LSFR}_t)$), where upd_{64} is defined as

$$\mathrm{upd}_{64} : x_{63}||x_{62}||\ldots||x_1||x_0 \to y_{63}||y_{62}||\ldots||y_1||y_0$$

with

$$y_i \leftarrow x_{i-1} \text{ for } i \in \{63, 62, \ldots, 1\}\backslash\{4, 3, 1\},$$
$$y_4 \leftarrow x_3 \oplus x_{63}, \quad y_3 \leftarrow x_2 \oplus x_{63},$$
$$y_1 \leftarrow x_0 \oplus x_{63}, \quad y_0 \leftarrow x_{63}.$$

Before loaded into the tweakey state, the order of the bytes of the LFSR state should be first reversed by rev_{64} function, where rev_{64} is defined as

$$\mathrm{rev}_{64} : S_7||S_6||S_5||S_4||S_3||S_2||S_1||S_0 \mapsto S_0||S_1||S_2||S_3||S_4||S_5||S_6||S_7,$$

where S_i is an 8-bit value, $0 \le i \le 7$.

2.2   Specification of the Underlying Primitive of SKINNY-AEAD M1/M3

In the SKINNY-AEAD M1/M3, 56-round SKINNY-128-384 is adopted as their underlying tweakable block cipher. The SKINNY family ciphers follow the TWEAKEY framework from [11] and therefore take a tweakey input. Here, we provide a brief specification of SKINNY-128-384 that is relevant to our related-tweakey impossible differential attacks. For more details about SKINNY, please refer to [4].

Initialization. SKINNY-128-384 has 128-bit internal states and 384-bit tweakey. 128-bit internal states are represented as 4×4 array of cells with each cell being a byte. The tweakey states can be seen as a group of three 4×4 arrays (*i.e.*, $TK1$, $TK2$ and $TK3$). Note that the internal states and tweakey states are loaded row-wise as shown in Fig. 2.

0	1	2	3
4	5	6	7
8	9	10	11
12	13	14	15

Fig. 2. Cell number of the states in the 4×4 array

Round Function. One encryption round of SKINNY-128-384 contains five operations in the following order: SubCells, AddConstants, AddRoundTweakey, ShiftRows and MixColumns, as shown in Fig. 3 (a).

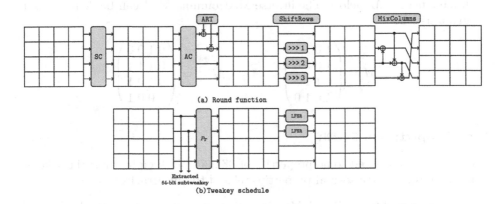

(a) Round function

(b) Tweakey schedule

Fig. 3. Round function and tweakey schedule of SKINNY-128-384

1) **SubCells** (*SC*). An 8-bit S-box is applied to each cell of the internal states. It is a non-linear operation in the round function.

2) **AddConstants** (AC). Three round constants (*i.e.*, c_0, c_1 and c_2) are XORed to the first three cells of the first column of an internal state. c_0 and c_1 are generated by a 6-bit affine LFSR, and $c_2 = \text{0x02}$.

3) **AddRoundTweakey** (ART). Only the first two rows of round tweakey are XORed with the first two rows of the corresponding internal state. The round tweakey (tk_i) in the i-th round is defined as $tk_i = TK1_i \oplus TK2_i \oplus TK3_i$. The tweakey arrays are updated by permutation and LFSR operations in the tweakey schedule algorithm as shown in Fig. 3 (b). In the permutation phase, a permutation $P_T = [9, 15, 8, 13, 10, 14, 12, 11, 0, 1, 2, 3, 4, 5, 6, 7]$ on cell positions is applied to $TK1, TK2$ and $TK3$, respectively. In the LFSR update phase, each cell of the first two rows of $TK2$ and $TK3$ are individually updated using an 8-bit LFSR, while there is no LFSR updating on $TK1$. The LFSRs are given in Table 2.

Table 2. The LFSRs used in SKINNY-128-384 to generate round tweakeys

TK	LFSR
$TK2$	$(x_7\|\|x_6\|\|x_5\|\|x_4\|\|x_3\|\|x_2\|\|x_1\|\|x_0) \rightarrow (x_6\|\|x_5\|\|x_4\|\|x_3\|\|x_2\|\|x_1\|\|x_0\|\|x_7 \oplus x_5)$
$TK3$	$(x_7\|\|x_6\|\|x_5\|\|x_4\|\|x_3\|\|x_2\|\|x_1\|\|x_0) \rightarrow (x_0 \oplus x_6\|\|x_7\|\|x_6\|\|x_5\|\|x_4\|\|x_3\|\|x_2\|\|x_1)$

Note: x_7 (resp. x_0) is the MSB (resp. LSB) bit of the cell.

4) **ShiftRow** (SR). The second, third and fourth rows are rotated by 1, 2 and 3 cell positions to the right, respectively.

5) **MixColumns** (MC). Every column of the internal state is multiplied by a binary matrix M below. The inverse MixColumns M^{-1} can be deduced and given as follows.

$$M = \begin{pmatrix} 1 & 0 & 1 & 1 \\ 1 & 0 & 0 & 0 \\ 0 & 1 & 1 & 0 \\ 1 & 0 & 1 & 0 \end{pmatrix} \qquad M^{-1} = \begin{pmatrix} 0 & 1 & 0 & 0 \\ 0 & 1 & 1 & 1 \\ 0 & 1 & 0 & 1 \\ 1 & 0 & 0 & 1 \end{pmatrix}$$

2.3   Properties of SKINNY

Liu *et al.* [15] proposed some properties of SKINNY block cipher. For the sake of completeness, we give several properties related to our attacks below.

1) The order of ART, SR and MC operations in any round can be changed by first using SR and MC, and then xoring the internal state with an equivalent round tweakey. The equivalent tweakey denoted as tk^{eq} can be computed by $tk^{eq} = MC(SR(tk))$ as given in Fig. 4.

2) Tweakey schedule of SKINNY is linear. Thus, if the differential value injected in the master tweakey is known, we can determine the exact differences in all the other subtweakeys.

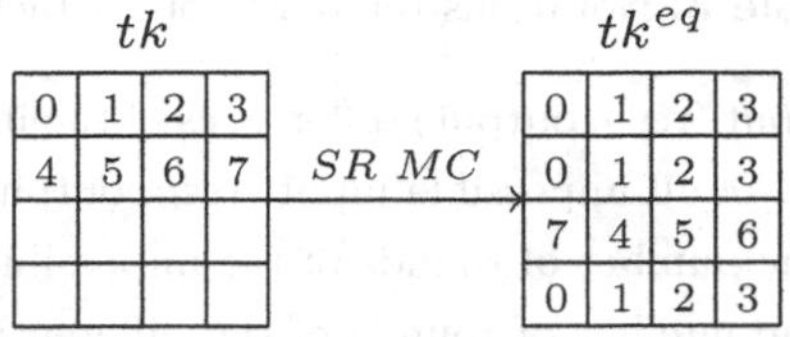

$$tk \qquad\qquad\qquad tk^{eq}$$

0	1	2	3
4	5	6	7

$SR\ MC$
→

0	1	2	3
0	1	2	3
7	4	5	6
0	1	2	3

Fig. 4. Obtain tk^{eq} by changing the order of ART, SR and MC

3) Subtweakey difference cancellation. In our attack scenario, a single cell of $TK1$ and $TK2$ is active and the active cell position is in the first and second rows. There is no difference for $TK3$. Hence, we take $TK2$ as an example. As noticed in [4], for a given active tweakey cell, there is only one subtweakey difference cancellation every 30 rounds for $TK2$. Let α_1 and α_2 be nonzero differences of the active cells for $TK1$ and $TK2$, respectively. In the first round, the subtweakey difference is $\alpha_1 \oplus \alpha_2$ for the active cell. For the $(2i+1)$-th round, the subtweakey difference is $\alpha_1 \oplus \text{LFSR}_2^i(\alpha_2)$ by ignoring the permutation P_T, where LFSR_2 has a cycle of 15. Thus one subtweakey cancellation (*i.e.*, $\alpha_1 \oplus \text{LFSR}_2{}^i(\alpha_2) = 0$) can occur every 30 rounds. In SKINNY-128-384, only the first two rows of the round tweakey tk_i are XORed with the internal state in i-th round. Moreover, according to the permutation P_T, the subtweakey cells involved in the i-th round will next appear in $(i+2)$-th round. Therefore, we can deduce that there are three rounds of fully inactive internal states for $TK2$.

2.4 Notations

We give the following notations (see Table 3) which are used in this paper. Some of them follow [8,15].

3 Related-Tweakey Impossible Differential Distinguisher

Due to the encryption mode, nonce-respecting scenario and complex tweakey initialization, the attacks on SKINNY-AEAD M1/M3 should fulfill some constraints. In this section, based on these constraints and several properties of SKINNY cipher, we search for the related-tweakey impossible differential distinguishers. Here, we first give the descriptions of constraints for distinguishers in SKINNY-AEAD M1/M3.

3.1 Constraints of Searching for Distinguishers in SKINNY-AEAD M1/M3

To facilitate the description, we use $\Delta \mathcal{T}\mathcal{K}_1^1$, $\Delta \mathcal{T}\mathcal{K}_1^2$ and $\Delta \mathcal{T}\mathcal{K}_1^3$ to denote tweakey differences of the distinguisher corresponding to $TK1$, $TK2$ and $TK3$ in the

Table 3. Notations related to our attacks

Δ_{X} (resp. Δ_{Y})	Input (resp. output) differences of the impossible differential
Δ_{in} (resp. Δ_{out})	Set of all impossible input (resp. output) differences
r_Δ	The number of rounds of the impossible differential
r_{in} (resp. r_{out})	The number of rounds of the differential $\Delta_{\mathrm{X}} \to \Delta_{in}$ (resp. $\Delta_{\mathrm{Y}} \to \Delta_{out}$)
c_{in} (resp. c_{out})	The number of bit-conditions that have to be verified from Δ_{in} to Δ_{X} (resp. from Δ_{out} to Δ_{Y})
K_{in} (resp. K_{out})	The subset of subtweakey bits involved in the first r_{in} rounds (resp. the last r_{out} rounds)
X_i (resp. Y_i)	The state before SC (resp. AC, ART) in the i-th round
Z_i (resp. W_i)	The state before SR (resp. MC) in the i-th round
tk_i	The round tweakey of i-th round
$\mathrm{col}(k)$	The k-th column, where $1 \le k \le 4$
$\Delta X/Y/Z/W,$	The difference of the state $X/Y/Z/W$
$\Delta X_i[n]$	The n-th cell difference value of state X in i-th round, where $0 \le n \le 15$
$\Delta X_i[k,\dots,l]$	The k-th, ..., l-th cell difference value of state X in i-th round, where $0 \le k, l \le 15$

first round, respectively. ΔSC_1 represents the internal state difference after SC in the first round of the distinguisher. Usually, to achieve powerful impossible differential tweakey recovery attacks, the number of active cells of input/output differences in the distinguisher is constrained to be as small as possible. Besides, to obtain longer distinguishers for SKINNY-128-384, two strategies are often used, as shown in [15,19]: (1) using the subtweakey difference $(\Delta \mathcal{TK}_1^1 \oplus \Delta \mathcal{TK}_1^2 \oplus \Delta \mathcal{TK}_1^3)$ to cancel ΔSC_1; and (2) applying the subtweakey difference cancellation property (i.e., $\mathrm{LFSR}(\Delta \mathcal{TK}_1^2[p]) = \Delta \mathcal{TK}_1^1[p]$), which ensure that there is no active tweakey cell for 3 consecutive rounds (i.e., second, third and fourth round of the distinguisher).

Recall the composition of tweakey used in SKINNY-AEAD M1/M3 in Sect. 2.1. The highest 64 bits of $\mathcal{TK}_1^1$ serve as a block counter l_i. To reduce the time complexity of tweakey recovery attacks, we set $|A| = 0^2$ and $\Delta \mathcal{TK}_1^1[p] = \text{0x03}^3$, where p ($0 \le p \le 7$) is the position of the active cell. $\mathcal{TK}_1^3$ stores the 128-bit key. To make our attack more practical, we set $\Delta \mathcal{TK}_1^3 = 0$, and then we can mount our attacks after obtaining only one encryption oracle. $\mathcal{TK}_1^2$ stores nonce

---

[2] $|A|$ denotes the bit length of associated data A. When $|A| = 0$, there is no encryption of associated data in the tweakey recovery attack.

[3] Taking a 20-round tweakey recovery attack as an example, we explain why $\Delta \mathcal{TK}_1^1[p] = \text{0x03}$. In the tweakey recovery attacks, if $\Delta \mathcal{TK}_1^1[p] = \text{0x03}$, we will utilize plaintext-ciphertext pairs in the i-th and $(i + 1)$-th block of encryptions in SKINNY-AEAD M1/M3, where $i = 8 \cdot ((P_T^{-1}) \circ (P_T^{-1}(p))) + 1$, which needs less time complexity than other values once p is fixed.

N. Since we mount attacks under a nonce-respecting scenario and $\Delta \mathcal{T}\mathcal{K}_1^3 = 0$, $\Delta \mathcal{T}\mathcal{K}_1^2 \neq 0$.

Combining all the above constraints on the tweakey differences, we can get $\Delta \mathcal{T}\mathcal{K}_1^2[p] = \text{0x81}$, $\Delta \mathcal{SC}_1[p] = \text{0x82}$ under $\Delta \mathcal{T}\mathcal{K}_1^1[p] = \text{0x03}$, where the p-th cell is the only active one in the corresponding difference of the first round of distinguishers.

3.2 Searching for Related-Tweakey Impossible Differential Distinguisher with STP

In recent years, some works [12,14,16,18] use the Boolean Satisfiability Problem (SAT) [17]/Satisfiability Modulo Theories (SMT) problem [3] solver STP[4] (Simple Theorem Prover) to search for distinguishers of some ciphers. The application of STP for cryptanalysis is a decision problem to confirm whether there is a solution to a set of equations. To search for related-tweakey impossible differential distinguishers, we should use some equations to describe the differential propagation properties of basic operations in the round function and tweakey schedule. To make it clear, we present all relevant equations for basic operations as follows.

Equations for Basic Operations. In the round function and tweakey schedule of SKINNY-128-384, basic operations consist of XOR, three-branch, Substitution and confusion layer. We give the following properties describing the differential propagation equations.

Property 1 (XOR [14]). Let Δ_{in1} and Δ_{in2} represent two input differences and Δ_{out} denote the output difference for the XOR operation. Then the corresponding equation can be expressed as $\Delta_{out} = \Delta_{in1} \oplus \Delta_{in2}$.

Property 2 (Three-Branch [14]). Let Δ_{in} denote the input difference of this operation, two output differences are represented as Δ_{out1} and Δ_{out2}. Then the relation between them is $\Delta_{out1} = \Delta_{out2} = \Delta_{in}$.

Property 3 (Substitution). Let S be an S-box used in the round function of SKINNY cipher. Define X_{in} as the input value of S. Let Δ_{in} and Δ_{out} represent input and output differences, respectively. Denote v as a flag variable indicating the validity of difference propagation. Then their relations are

$$v = \begin{cases} 0 \text{ (invalid)}, & \text{if } S(X_{in}) \oplus S(X_{in} \oplus \Delta_{in}) \neq \Delta_{out}, \\ 1 \text{ (valid)}, & \text{if } S(X_{in}) \oplus S(X_{in} \oplus \Delta_{in}) = \Delta_{out}, \end{cases}$$

where $v = 1$ represents that there is a value X_{in} that makes the difference propagation $\Delta_{in} \to \Delta_{out}$ valid.

---

[4] https://github.com/stp/stp.

Property 4 (Confusion Layer). Denote M as the confusion matrix. $\overrightarrow{\Delta C_{in}}$ and $\overrightarrow{\Delta C_{out}}$ represent the column-wise input and output difference, respectively. Then the equation is $\overrightarrow{\Delta C_{out}} = M \cdot \overrightarrow{\Delta C_{in}}$.

In this section, we utilize a similar method used in [15,19] to search for related-tweakey impossible differential distinguishers with STP. Firstly, according to the round function and tweakey schedule, we use Property 1~4 to construct some equations to express the bit-level differential propagation properties between input and output differences. In addition, we should construct some equations representing the constraints on tweakey and state differences. Finally, we can confirm whether an expected impossible differential distinguisher exists through the result returned by the solver STP. If the solver STP returns *Invalid* for the specific input and output active cell positions, it shows that this differential distinguisher is impossible.

Note that, only the active input difference values are fixed as mentioned earlier (*i.e.*, $\Delta \mathcal{TK}_1^1[p] = $ 0x03, $\Delta \mathcal{TK}_1^2[p] = $ 0x81 and $\Delta \mathcal{SC}_1[p] = $ 0x82), but to determine the value of p, we have to traverse all the values of cell position p and active cell positions of output differences as shown in Algorithm 1.

Algorithm 1: Seaching Related-Tweakey Impossible Distinguishers

---

Input: R: The number of rounds covered by the expected distinguisher.

Output: R-round related-tweakey impossible differential distinguisher or "*No solution*".

1 ▷ p_i: Active cell position of input differences of the distinguisher.

2 ▷ p_o: Active cell position of output differences of the distinguisher.

3 **for** $p_i \leftarrow 0$ *to* 7 **do**

4   **for** $p_o \leftarrow 0$ *to* 15 **do**

5   ▷ (1) Construct equations to describe differential propagation.

6   **for** $r \leftarrow 1$ *to* $R+1$ **do**

7   Use the Property 1~4 to construct equations for the round function and tweakey schedule of r-th round.

8   ▷ (2) Construct equations to represent the distinguisher's restrictive conditions.

9   Construct equations to describe the difference values for the active cells of the internal state after SC and tweakey in the first round (*i.e.*, $\Delta \mathcal{SC}_1[p_i] = $ 0x82, $\Delta \mathcal{TK}_1^1[p_i] = $ 0x03 and $\Delta \mathcal{TK}_1^2[p_i] = $ 0x81) and the differential value of the active cell in the output difference of the distinguisher (*i.e.*, $\Delta \mathcal{SC}_{R+1}[p_o] \neq$ 0x00).

10   Input all the equations (1) and (2) into STP solver and solve them.

11   **if** *STP return "Invalid"* **then**

12   Return the active cell position (p_i, p_o) of the R-round relate-tweakey impossible differential distinguisher.

---

13 Return "*No solution*"

3.3   14-Round Related-Tweakey Impossible Differential Distinguishers

Utilizing Algorithm 1, we find some 14-round distinguishers. Under the related-tweakey model, our impossible differential distinguishers start with one active cell in internal state after SC of the first round and end with one active cell after SC of the 15-th round. Thus, they can be seen as complete 14-round distinguishers for the underlying primitive SKINNY-128-384 in SKINNY-AEAD M1/M3. In the tweakey recovery phase, we select the related-tweakey impossible differential distinguisher with $(p_i, p_o) = (2, 10)^5$, which can obtain a lower attack complexity for both 20-round and 18-round attacks. This distinguisher is illustrated in Fig. 5. The 14-round related-tweakey impossible differential is: $(00\alpha0|0000|0000|0000) \xrightarrow{14r} (0000|0000|00*0|0000)$, where $\alpha = $ 0x82 and $*$ denotes any non-zero difference. An 8.5-round related-tweakey differential in the forward direction (having probability 1) starting at Y_1 (after SC in the first round) is concatenated to a 5.5-round related-tweakey differential (having probability 1) starting from Y_{15} (before the AC and ART in the 15-th round) in the backward direction. The contradiction takes place at X_{10} in the 10-th round.

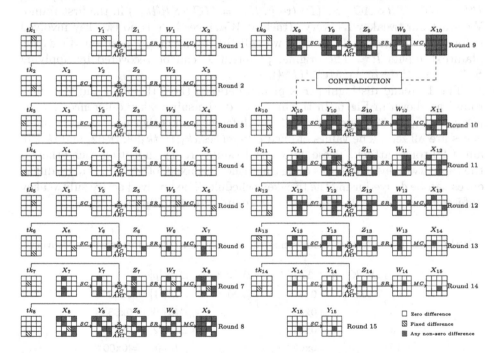

Fig. 5. 14-round related-tweakey impossible differential distinguisher for the underlying primitive SKINNY-128-384 in SKINNY-AEAD M1/M3

---

[5] p_i and p_o denote the active cell positions corresponding to the input and out differences of the distinguisher, respectively.

4   Tweakey Recovery Attack on 20-Round SKINNY-AEAD M1/M3

In this section, we propose a 20-round related-tweakey impossible differential attack on SKINNY-AEAD M1/M3. The whole attack contains two phases (i.e., distinguisher construction phase in Sect. 3 and tweakey recovery phase in this section). In the distinguisher construction phase, we find some 14-round impossible differential distinguishers under some constraints for the underlying primitive SKINNY-128-384. As a result, we select one distinguisher with $(p_i, p_o) = (2, 10)$ to mount our tweakey recovery attack to achieve a lower attack complexity. In the tweakey recovery phase, we construct a 20-round related tweakey recovery attack to derive the right tweakey by filtering out the wrong candidates suggested by the impossible differential distinguisher.

Figure 6 presents a 20-round tweakey recovery attack on SKINNY-AEAD M1/M3 based on the 14-round related-tweakey impossible differential distinguisher. We extend the distinguisher 4 rounds on the top and 2 rounds at the bottom to cover 6 rounds in the tweakey recovery phase. As discussed in Sect. 2.3, we can obtain the equivalent plaintext P^{eq} (resp. equivalent tweakey tk_1^{eq}) by applying $P^{eq} = MC \circ SR \circ AC \circ SC(P)$ (resp. $tk_1^{eq} = MC \circ SR(tk_1)$) in the first round. We start our tweakey recovery attack at W_1 since there is no tweakey involved before W_1. In the rest of section, we call the inputs at the position W_1 as the plaintext inputs P^{eq}. The original plaintext P can be recovered by applying $SC^{-1} \circ AC^{-1} \circ SR^{-1} \circ MC^{-1}(P^{eq})$.

The 14-round distinguisher is placed between the 5-th round and the 19-th round as shown in Fig. 6. In the first round, the subtweakey difference $\Delta tk_1[1]$ (*i.e.*, $\Delta tk_1^{eq}[1, 5, 13]$) is a nonzero fixed difference, the other cell-position differences are all zero. The values of fixed differences $tk_1[1]$, $tk_3[0]$, $tk_5[2]$ and $tk_{19}[0]$ affect 20-round attack. These differential values are dependent on each other. If the input tweakey differences of distinguisher are fixed, other subtweakey differences can be derived using the tweakey schedule. The involved active subtweakey differences in the whole attack procedure are shown in Table 4.

Table 4. Active subtweakey difference values related to 20-round tweakey recovery

r	$\Delta TK1_r[p]$	$\Delta TK2_r[p]$	$\Delta TK3_r[p]$	$\Delta tk_r[p]$
1	0x03	0xE0	0x00	$\Delta tk_1[1] = $ 0xE3
3		0xC0		$\Delta tk_3[0] = $ 0xC3
5		0x81		$\Delta tk_5[2] = $ 0x82
19		0xC3		$\Delta tk_{19}[0] = $ 0xC0

Note: $\Delta tk_r[p] = \Delta TK1_r[p] \oplus \Delta TK2_r[p] \oplus \Delta TK3_r[p]$. r and p denote the number of round and active cell position, respectively.

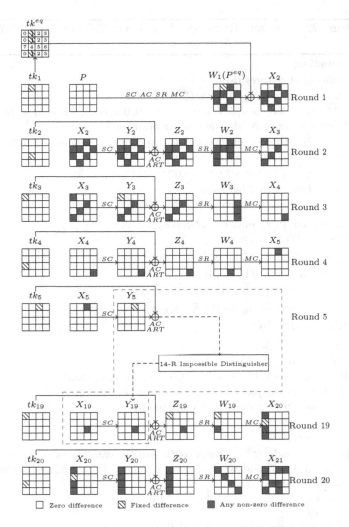

Fig. 6. 20-round tweakey recovery attack for SKINNY-AEAD M1/M3

In the 20-round attack, $r_\Delta = 14$, $r_{in} = 4$, $r_{out} = 2$, $c_{in} = 48$, $|\Delta_{in}| = 56$, $c_{out} = 56$, $|\Delta_{out}| = 64$ and $|K_{in} \cup K_{out}| = 13 \times 8 + 2 \times 8 = 120$. The attack procedure is briefly described in Algorithm 2. Detailed steps of 20-round cryptanalysis are given as follows.

Data Collection. The adversary should construct 2^N pairs of structures S_1 and S_2 at W_1, where each structure contains $2^{|\Delta_{in}|} = 2^{56}$ equivalent plaintexts. For each equivalent plaintext pair $P^{eq} \in S_1$ and $\overline{P^{eq}} \in S_2$, its difference is $P^{eq} \oplus \overline{P^{eq}} = (0, \alpha, *, 0, *, *, 0, *, *, 0, *, 0, 0, *, 0, 0)$, where $\alpha = \Delta tk_1[1] = \text{0xE3}$ and $*$ denotes any nonzero byte value. Using $2^N \cdot (2 \cdot 2^{|\Delta_{in}|}) = 2^{N+|\Delta_{in}|+1}$ equivalent plaintexts, we can generate $2^{N+2|\Delta_{in}|}$ plaintext pairs

---

Algorithm 2: Tweakey Recovery Attack on 20-Round SKINNY-AEAD M1/M3

---

1 ▷ Data collection;
2 **for** 2^N pairs of structures **do**
3   **for** $2^{|\Delta_{in}|}$ equivalent plaintext P_i^{eq} in S_1 **do**
4          $\overline{P_i^{eq}} = P_i^{eq} \oplus (0, \alpha, *, 0, *, *, 0, *, *, 0, *, 0, 0, *, 0, 0)$, where $\alpha = $ 0xE3;
5   Choose a nonce N_i that has never been used;
6          $\overline{N_i} = N_i \oplus (0, \gamma, 0, 0, 0, 0, 0, 0, 0, 0, 0, 0, 0, 0, 0, 0)$, where $\gamma = $ 0xE0;
7          $P_i = SC^{-1} \circ AC^{-1} \circ SR^{-1} \circ MC^{-1}(P_i^{eq})$;
8          $\overline{P_i} = SC^{-1} \circ AC^{-1} \circ SR^{-1} \circ MC^{-1}(\overline{P_i^{eq}})$;
9   **for** m from 0 to 7 by 1 **do**
10             $C \leftarrow$ encrypt P_i under (l_m, N_i, Key);
11          $C_i \leftarrow$ encrypt P_i under (l_8, N_i, Key);
12          $W_{20_i} \leftarrow MC^{-1}(C_i)$;
13   **for** $2^{|\Delta_{in}|}$ plaintext $\overline{P_i}$ in S_2 **do**
14   **for** n from 0 to 8 by 1 **do**
15             $\overline{C} \leftarrow$ encrypt $\overline{P_i}$ under $(l_n, \overline{N_i}, Key)$;
16          $\overline{C_i} \leftarrow$ encrypt $\overline{P_i}$ under $(l_9, \overline{N_i}, Key)$;
17          $\overline{W_{20_i}} \leftarrow MC^{-1}(\overline{C_i})$;
18   **for** $2^{2|\Delta_{in}|}$ pairs **do**
19          $\Delta W_{20} \leftarrow W_{20_i} \oplus \overline{W_{20_i}}$;
20   **if** $\Delta W_{20} = (*, 0, 0, 0, 0, *, 0, 0, 0, 0, *, 0, 0, 0, 0, *)$ **then**
21   Remain the pair of (P_i, N_i, C_i) and $(\overline{P_i}, \overline{N_i}, \overline{C_i})$;
22   ▷Seive 2^{N+16} remaining pairs finally;

23 ▷ Subkey recovery;
24 Call Algorithm 3 under 2^{N+16} pairs to discard the candidates of $tk_1[0, 1, 2, 3, 4, 5, 6, 7]$, $tk_2[0, 3, 4, 5, 7]$ and $tk_{20}[0, 4]$, and obtain $2^\rho |K_{in} \cup K_{out}|$-bit remaining subtweakey candidates tk_{rem};
25 ▷ Brute force;
26 **for** 2^ρ tk_{rem} **do**
27   **for** 2^8 remaining master key $MK[12]$ **do**
28   Compute the master key MK from tk_{rem} and $MK[12]$ using the tweakey schedule;
29   Get a random new pair of (P, C) with a nonce value N and a number related to the first block counter l_0;
30          $C' \leftarrow$ encrypt P under (l_0, N, MK);
31   **if** $C' = C$ **then**
32   Return the MK as the right tweakey.

$(P, \overline{P})$. In the 20-round tweakey recovery attack, we define the two related-tweakey inputs as $(TK1||TK2||TK3)$ and $(\overline{TK1}||\overline{TK2}||\overline{TK3})$. Encrypt the plaintexts P (resp. $\overline{P}$) under $TK1||TK2||TK3$ (resp. $\overline{TK1}||\overline{TK2}||\overline{TK3}$) to obtain the corresponding ciphertexts C (resp. $\overline{C}$). In the 20-round attack of SKINNY-AEAD M1/M3, $(TK1,TK2,TK3)$ (resp. $(\overline{TK1},\overline{TK2},\overline{TK3})$) is expressed as (l_8, N, Key) (resp. $(l_9, \overline{N}, Key)$), where l_8 (resp. l_9) represents the first 128-bit tweakey value in the 9-th (resp. 10-th) block message encryption, N and $\overline{N}$ denote different nonce values, and Key means the 128-bit key. Note that $l_8 \oplus l_9 = (0, \beta, 0, 0, 0, 0, 0, 0, 0, 0, 0, 0, 0, 0, 0, 0)$ and $N \oplus \overline{N} = (0, \gamma, 0, 0, 0, 0, 0, 0, 0, 0, 0, 0, 0, 0, 0, 0)$, where $\beta = $ 0x03 and $\gamma = $ 0xE0 (see the case of $r = 1$ in Table 4).

After obtaining ciphertexts C and $\overline{C}$, we can get W_{20} and $\overline{W_{20}}$ directly respectively, as shown in line[12] and line[17] of Algorithm 2. For each ciphertext pair, check whether the condition in line[20] is satisfied and remain it if true. In total, $2^{N+2|\Delta_{in}|-(128-|\Delta_{out}|)-32} = 2^{N+16}$ plaintext-ciphertext pairs are remained in the phase of data collection. Time complexity of this phase is $(2^N \cdot (2^{|\Delta_{in}|} \cdot (2 \cdot \frac{1}{20} + 9 + \frac{1}{2} \cdot \frac{1}{20} + 10 + \frac{1}{2} \cdot \frac{1}{20}))) \approx 2^{N+60.3}$ times of 20-round encryptions, and the memory complexity is

$$\mathcal{M}_{col} = 2^{|\Delta_{in}|} \cdot (2 \cdot 128) + 2 \cdot 2^{|\Delta_{in}|} \cdot (3 \cdot 128) + 2 \cdot 2^{N+16} \cdot (3 \cdot 128)$$

$$= (2^{|\Delta_{in}|-0.59} + 2^{|\Delta_{in}|+1} + 2^{N+17}) \cdot (3 \cdot 128) \text{ bits.}$$

Tweakey Recovery. The tweakey recovery procedure of the 20-round attack is briefly described in Algorithm 3. We will show the detailed attack procedure as follows. In the attack process of SKINNY-AEAD M1/M3, the value of $(l_8, l_9, N, \overline{N})$ is known, in the following section, we focus on guessing the value of subtweakey tk_i $(i \in \{1, 2, 20\})$ to deduce the master tweakey corresponding to Key[6].

1) Line[1, 2, 3] in Algorithm 3. Guess $tk_{20}[4]$ and compute $\Delta X_{20}[4]$ under 2^{N+16} remaining pairs. According to Fig. 6, get $\Delta X_{20}[4] = SC^{-1}(Z_{20}[4] \oplus tk_{20}[4] \oplus c_{20}^1) \oplus SC^{-1}(\overline{Z_{20}[4]} \oplus tk_{20}[4] \oplus c_{20}^1)$, where $c_{20}^1 = $ 0x02 is the 20-th round constant corresponding to c_1. Checking if $\Delta X_{20}[4] = \Delta tk_{19}[0] = $ 0xC0 will lead to an 8-bit filter and generally sieve $2^{N+16-8} = 2^{N+8}$ plaintext-ciphertext pairs. The time complexity of this step is $2^8 \cdot 2 \cdot 2^{N+16} \cdot \frac{1}{16} \cdot \frac{1}{20} \approx 2^{N+16.7}$ 20-round encryptions.

2) Line[4, 5, 6] in Algorithm 3. Guess $tk_{20}[0]$ and compute $\Delta X_{20}[0, 4, 8, 12]$ under 2^{N+8} remaining pairs from the previous step. According to Fig. 6, compute $\Delta X_{20}[0] = SC^{-1}(Z_{20}[0] \oplus tk_{20}[0] \oplus c_{20}^0) \oplus SC^{-1}(\overline{Z_{20}[0]} \oplus tk_{20}[0] \oplus c_{20}^0)$, $\Delta X_{20}[4] = SC^{-1}(Z_{20}[4] \oplus tk_{20}[4] \oplus c_{20}^1) \oplus SC^{-1}(\overline{Z_{20}[4]} \oplus tk_{20}[4] \oplus c_{20}^1)$, $\Delta X_{20}[8] = SC^{-1}(Z_{20}[8] \oplus c_{20}^2) \oplus SC^{-1}(\overline{Z_{20}[8]} \oplus c_{20}^2)$ and $\Delta X_{20}[12] = SC^{-1}(Z_{20}[12]) \oplus SC^{-1}(\overline{Z_{20}[12]})$, where $c_{20}^0 = $ 0x0B, $c_{20}^1 = $ 0x02, and $c_{20}^2 = $ 0x02 are the 20-th round constants corresponding to c_0, c_1 and c_2, respectively. Based on the properties of MC operations on col(1) of W_{19}, we have the conditions $\Delta X_{20}[0] = \Delta X_{20}[12]$ and $\Delta X_{20}[4] \oplus \Delta X_{20}[8] = \Delta X_{20}[12]$. Check whether the conditions are satisfied or not, which can act as a 16-bit filter to choose $2^{N+8-16} = 2^{N-8}$ remaining pairs. In this step, the time complexity is $2^{16} \cdot 2 \cdot 2^{N+8} \cdot \frac{4}{16} \cdot \frac{1}{20} \approx 2^{N+18.7}$ 20-round encryptions.

---

[6] We define the master tweakey corresponding to Key as master key MK.

Algorithm 3: Subtweakey Recovery Procedure of the 20-Round Attack

---

1 **for** 2^8 $tk_{20}[4]$ **do**
2   **for** 2^{N+16} remaining pairs **do**
3   Compute $\Delta X_{20}[4]$ and use the condition (*i.e.*, $\Delta X_{20}[4]$ is a fixed
     difference) to get $2^{N+16-8} = 2^{N+8}$ remaining pairs;
4   **for** 2^8 $tk_{20}[0]$ **do**
5   **for** 2^{N+8} remaining pairs **do**
6   Compute $\Delta X_{20}[0, 4, 8, 12]$ and use the conditions
      $\Delta X_{20}[0] = \Delta X_{20}[12]$ and $\Delta X_{20}[4] \oplus \Delta X_{20}[8] = \Delta X_{20}[12]$ to obtain
      $2^{N+8-16} = 2^{N-8}$ remaining pairs;
7   **for** 2^{16} $tk_1[3, 5]$ **do**
8   **for** 2^{N-8} remaining pairs **do**
9   Compute $\Delta W_2[4, 8]$ and use the condition $\Delta W_2[4] = \Delta W_2[8]$ to
       choose $2^{N-8-8} = 2^{N-16}$ remaining pairs;
10   **for** 2^{24} $tk_1[1, 2, 7]$ **do**
11   **for** 2^{N-16} remaining pairs **do**
12   Compute $\Delta W_2[2, 6, 10]$ and use the conditions
        $\Delta W_2[6] = \Delta W_2[10]$ and $\Delta W_2[2] = \Delta W_2[10]$ to sieve
        $2^{N-16-16} = 2^{N-32}$ remaining pairs;
13   **for** 2^{16} $tk_1[0]$ $tk_2[0]$ **do**
14   **for** 2^{N-32} remaining pairs **do**
15   Compute $\Delta Y_3[0]$ and use the condition (*i.e.*, $\Delta Y_3[0]$ is a
         fixed difference) to get $2^{N-32-8} = 2^{N-40}$ remaining
         pairs;
16   **for** 2^{16} $tk_1[6]$ $tk_2[4]$ **do**
17   **for** 2^{N-40} remaining pairs **do**
18   Compute $\Delta W_3[7, 11, 15]$ and use the conditions
          $\Delta W_3[7] = \Delta W_3[11]$ and $\Delta W_3[11] = \Delta W_3[15]$ to
          obtain $2^{N-40-16} = 2^{N-56}$ remaining pairs;
19   **for** 2^{32} $tk_1[4]$ $tk_2[3, 5, 7]$ **do**
20   **for** 2^{N-56} remaining pairs **do**
21   Compute $\Delta Y_5[2]$ and use the condition (*i.e.*,
           $\Delta Y_5[2]$ is a fixed difference) to filter out the
           wrong subkeys.

---

3) Line[7, 8, 9] in Algorithm 3. Guess $tk_1[3, 5]$ and compute $\Delta W_2[4, 8]$ under 2^{N-8} remaining pairs from step 2). Base on $tk^{eq}[7] = tk_1[3]$ and $tk^{eq}[10] = tk_1[5]$, we can compute $\Delta W_2[4] = SC(P^{eq}[7] \oplus tk_1[3]) \oplus SC(\overline{P^{eq}[7]} \oplus tk_1[3])$ and $\Delta W_2[8] = SC(P^{eq}[10] \oplus tk_1[5]) \oplus SC(\overline{P^{eq}[10]} \oplus tk_1[5])$. According to the properties of MC^{-1} operations on col(1) of X_3, we have $\Delta W_2[4] = \Delta W_2[8]$. Checking if $\Delta W_2[4] = \Delta W_2[8]$ will lead to an 8-bit filter and select $2^{N-8-8} = 2^{N-16}$ remaining pairs. In this step, the time complexity is $2^{32} \cdot 2 \cdot 2^{N-8} \cdot \frac{2}{16} \cdot \frac{1}{20} \approx 2^{N+17.7}$ 20-round encryptions.

4) Line[10, 11, 12] in Algorithm 3. Guess $tk_1[1, 2, 7]$ and compute $\Delta W_2[2, 6, 10]$ under 2^{N-16} remaining pairs from the previous step. Base on $tk^{eq}[2] = tk_1[2]$, $tk^{eq}[5] = tk_1[1]$ and $tk^{eq}[8] = tk_1[7]$, we can compute $\Delta W_2[2] = SC(P^{eq}[2] \oplus tk_1[2]) \oplus SC(\overline{P^{eq}[2]} \oplus tk_1[2])$, $\Delta W_2[6] = SC(P^{eq}[5] \oplus tk_1[1]) \oplus SC(\overline{P^{eq}[5]} \oplus tk_1[1] \oplus \Delta tk_1[1])$ and $\Delta W_2[10] = SC(P^{eq}[8] \oplus tk_1[7]) \oplus SC(\overline{P^{eq}[8]} \oplus tk_1[7])$. In the light of the properties of MC^{-1} operations on col(3) of X_3, we have the conditions $\Delta W_2[2] = \Delta W_2[10]$ and $\Delta W_2[6] = \Delta W_2[10]$. Checking whether the conditions are satisfied or not will act as a 16-bit filter and sieve $2^{N-16-16} = 2^{N-32}$ remaining pairs. The time complexity of this step is $2^{56} \cdot 2 \cdot 2^{N-16} \cdot \frac{3}{16} \cdot \frac{1}{20} \approx 2^{N+34.3}$ 20-round encryptions.

5) Line[13, 14, 15] in Algorithm 3. Guess $tk_1[0]$, $tk_2[0]$ and compute $\Delta Y_3[0]$ under 2^{N-32} remaining pairs from step 4). Base on $tk^{eq}[0] = tk_1[0]$, we can compute $\Delta Y_3[1] = (SC((SC(P^{eq}[0] \oplus tk_1[0]) \oplus tk_2[0] \oplus c_2^0) \oplus SC(P^{eq}[10] \oplus tk_1[5]) \oplus SC(P^{eq}[13] \oplus tk_1[1]))) \oplus (SC((SC(\overline{P^{eq}[0]} \oplus tk_1[0]) \oplus tk_2[0] \oplus c_2^0) \oplus SC(\overline{P^{eq}[10]} \oplus tk_1[5]) \oplus SC(\overline{P^{eq}[13]} \oplus tk_1[1] \oplus \Delta tk_1[1])))$, where $c_2^0 = $ 0x03 is the second round constant corresponding to c_0. As shown in Fig. 6, $\Delta Y_3[0] = \Delta tk_3[0]$ is a fixed difference that is 0xC3. Checking if $\Delta Y_3[0] = $ 0xC3 will act as an 8-bit filter and sieve $2^{N-32-8} = 2^{N-40}$ remaining pairs. In this step, the time complexity is $2^{72} \cdot (2 \cdot 2^{N-32}) \cdot (\frac{3}{16} + \frac{1}{16} \cdot \frac{1}{2}) \cdot \frac{1}{20} \approx 2^{N+34.5}$ 20-round encryptions.

6) Line[16, 17, 18] in Algorithm 3. Guess $tk_1[6]$, $tk_2[4]$ and compute $\Delta W_3[7, 11, 15]$ under 2^{N-40} remaining pairs from the step 5). Based on $tk_1[0, 2, 5]$, $tk_2[0]$ determined by steps 3) to 5) and $tk_2[2]$ derived from $tk_{20}[4]$, we can compute $\Delta W_3[7] = (SC(SC(P^{eq}[2] \oplus tk_1[2]) \oplus tk_2[2])) \oplus (SC(SC(\overline{P^{eq}[2]} \oplus tk_1[2]) \oplus tk_2[2]))$, $\Delta W_3[11] = SC((SC(P^{eq}[4] \oplus tk_1[0]) \oplus tk_2[4]) \oplus SC(P^{eq}[11] \oplus tk_1[6])) \oplus SC((SC(\overline{P^{eq}[4]} \oplus tk_1[0]) \oplus tk_2[4]) \oplus SC(\overline{P^{eq}[11]} \oplus tk_1[6]))$ and $\Delta W_3[15] = SC((SC(P^{eq}[0] \oplus tk_1[0]) \oplus tk_2[0]) \oplus SC(P^{eq}[10] \oplus tk_1[5])) \oplus SC((SC(\overline{P^{eq}[0]} \oplus tk_1[0]) \oplus tk_2[0]) \oplus SC(\overline{P^{eq}[10]} \oplus tk_1[5]))$. Based on the properties of MC^{-1} operations on col(4) of X_4, we have the conditions $\Delta W_3[7] = \Delta W_3[11]$ and $\Delta W_3[11] = \Delta W_3[15]$. Checking whether the conditions are satisfied or not will act as a 16-bit filter and sieve $2^{N-40-16} = 2^{N-56}$ remaining pairs. The time complexity of this step is $2^{88} \cdot (2 \cdot 2^{N-40}) \cdot (\frac{5}{16} + \frac{3}{16}) \cdot \frac{1}{20} \approx 2^{N+43.7}$ 20-round encryptions.

7) Line[19, 20, 21] in Algorithm 3. Guess $tk_1[4]$, $tk_2[3, 5, 7]$ and compute $\Delta Y_5[2]$ under 2^{N-56} remaining pairs from step 6). As shown in Fig. 6, $\Delta Y_5[2]$ is a fixed difference that equals to $\Delta tk_5[2] = $ 0x82. Checking if $\Delta Y_5[2] = \Delta tk_5[2] = $ 0x82 can act as an 8-bit filter and discard the wrong subtweakeys. The time complexity of this step is $2^{120} \cdot (2 \cdot 2^{N-56}) \cdot (\frac{11}{16} + \frac{7}{16} + \frac{3}{16} + \frac{1}{16}) \cdot \frac{1}{20} \approx 2^{N+61.1}$ 20-round encryptions.

In step 7), the number of the wrong subtweakeys $tk_1[0, 1, 2, 3, 4, 5, 6, 7]$, $tk_2[0, 3, 4, 5, 7]$ and $tk_{20}[0, 4]$ left is

$$2^\rho = (2^{|K_{in} \cup K_{out}|} - 1) \times (1 - 2^{-8})^{2^{N-56}} = (2^{120} - 1) \times (1 - 2^{-8})^{2^{N-56}},$$

where we set $N = 64.6$ and $\rho = 117.8$.

Brute Force. The values of master key $MK[0, 1, 2, 3, \ 4, 5, 6, 7, \ 8, 9, 10, \ 11,$ $13, 14, 15]$ can be derived from tk_{rem} using the tweakey schedule. For the remaining master key $MK[12]$, we traverse 2^8 candidate values. For each guessed value of $MK[12]$, we verify the master key by one plaintext-ciphertext pair under a number related to the first block counter l_0, given nonce value N and $MK[0, 1, 2, 3, 4, 5, 6, 7, 8, 9, 10, 11, 13, 14, 15]$. In this step, the time complexity is $2^\rho \times 2^8 = 2^{\rho+8}$ 20-round encryptions.

Complexity Computation. The 20-round attack above on SKINNY-AEAD M1/M3 requires a data complexity of

$$\mathcal{D} = 2^N \cdot (2^{|\Delta_{in}|} + 2^{|\Delta_{in}|}) = 2^{N+57} = 2^{64.6+57} = 2^{121.6}$$

chosen plaintexts. The total time complexity is the summation of the time consumption in all the steps. When $N = 64.6$ and $\rho = 117.8$, the total time complexity is

$$\mathcal{T} = 2^{N+60.3} + 2^{N+16.7} + 2^{N+18.7} + 2^{N+17.7} + 2^{N+34.3} + 2^{N+34.5}$$
$$+ 2^{N+43.7} + 2^{N+61.1} + 2^{\rho+8} \approx 2^{127.1}$$

20-round encryptions. In the attack procedure, we should store the wrong candidates of guessing tweakey and the pairs of equivalent plaintext, ciphertext and nonce. The total memory complexity is

$$\mathcal{M} = \mathcal{M}_{col} + 2 \cdot (2^{N+8} + 2^{N-8} + 2^{N-16} + 2^{N-32} + 2^{N-40} + 2^{N-56}) \cdot (3 \cdot 128)$$
$$+ 2^\rho \cdot 128 = 2^{90.2} + 2^{82.2} + 2^{124.8} \approx 2^{124.8} \text{ bits.}$$

5   Tweakey Recovery Attack on 18-Round SKINNY-AEAD M1/M3

We propose an 18-round related-tweakey impossible differential attack on SKINNY-AEAD M1/M3 in this section. The 14-round distinguisher with $(p_i, p_o) = (2, 10)$ is placed between the third round and 17-th round. Based on the 14-round related-tweakey impossible differential distinguisher, an 18-round attack on SKINNY-AEAD M1/M3 is shown in Fig. 7 of Appendix A. We extend the distinguisher 2 rounds on the top and 2 rounds at the bottom to cover 4 rounds in the tweakey recovery phase. In the first round, the subtweakey difference $\Delta tk_1[0]$ (*i.e.*, $\Delta tk_1^{eq}[0, 4, 12]$) is a nonzero fixed difference, the other cell-position differences are all zero. The involved active subtweakey differences (*i.e.*, the values of $\Delta tk_1[0]$, $\Delta tk_3[2]$ and $\Delta tk_{17}[0]$) in the attack procedure are given in Table 5.

Table 5. Active subtweakey difference values related to 18-round tweakey recovery

r	$\Delta TK1_r[p]$	$\Delta TK2_r[p]$	$\Delta TK3_r[p]$	$\Delta tk_r[p]$
1	0x03	0xC0	0x00	$\Delta tk_1[0] = \text{0xC3}$
3		0x81		$\Delta tk_3[2] = \text{0x82}$
17		0xC3		$\Delta tk_{17}[0] = \text{0xC0}$

Note: $\Delta tk_r[p] = \Delta TK1_r[p] \oplus \Delta TK2_r[p] \oplus \Delta TK3_r[p]$. r and p denote the number of round and active cell position, respectively.

In the 18-round attack, $r_\Delta = 14$, $r_{in} = 2$, $r_{out} = 2$, $c_{in} = 0$, $|\Delta_{in}| = 8$, $c_{out} = 56$, $|\Delta_{out}| = 64$, and $|K_{in} \cup K_{out}| = 4 \times 8 + 2 \times 8 = 48$. Algorithm 4 briefly describes the 18-round attack process. We will give the detailed attack steps as follows.

Data Collection. 2^N pairs of structures S_1 and S_2 at W_1 should be constructed, where each structure contains $2^{|\Delta_{in}|} = 2^8$ equivalent plaintexts. For each equivalent plaintext pair $P^{eq} \in S_1$ and $\overline{P^{eq}} \in S_2$, its difference is $P^{eq} \oplus \overline{P^{eq}} = (\alpha, 0, 0, 0, \alpha, 0, 0, 0, 0, 0, 0, 0, \alpha, 0, 0, *)$, where $\alpha = \Delta tk_1[0] = \text{0xC3}$ and $*$ denotes any nonzero difference. We use $2^N \cdot (2 \cdot 2^{|\Delta_{in}|}) = 2^{N+|\Delta_{in}|+1}$ equivalent plaintexts to construct $2^{N+2|\Delta_{in}|}$ plaintext pairs $(P, \overline{P})$. Under (l_0, N, Key) and $(l_1, \overline{N}, Key)$, we use the line[10] and line[14] in Algorithm 4 to compute W_{18} and $\overline{W_{18}}$, respectively. Note that $l_0 \oplus l_1 = (\beta, 0, 0, 0, 0, 0, 0, 0, 0, 0, 0, 0, 0, 0, 0, 0)$ and $N \oplus \overline{N} = (\gamma, 0, 0, 0, 0, 0, 0, 0, 0, 0, 0, 0, 0, 0, 0, 0)$, where $\beta = \text{0x03}$ and $\gamma = \text{0xC0}$ (see the case of $r = 1$ in Table 5). For each ciphertext pair, check whether the condition in line[17] is satisfied and remain it if true. In total, $2^{N+2|\Delta_{in}|-(128-|\Delta_{out}|)-32} = 2^{N-80}$ plaintext-ciphertext pairs are remained in the step of data collection. The time complexity of this step is $(2^N \cdot (2^{|\Delta_{in}|} \cdot (2 \cdot \frac{1}{18} + 1 + \frac{1}{2} \cdot \frac{1}{18} + 2 + \frac{1}{2} \cdot \frac{1}{18}))) \approx 2^{N+9.7}$ times of 18-round encryptions, and the memory complexity is

$$\mathcal{M}_{col} = 2^{|\Delta_{in}|} \cdot (2 \cdot 128) + 2 \cdot 2^{|\Delta_{in}|} \cdot (3 \cdot 128) + 2 \cdot 2^{N-80} \cdot (3 \cdot 128)$$

$$= (2^{|\Delta_{in}|-0.59} + 2^{|\Delta_{in}|+1} + 2^{N-79}) \cdot (3 \cdot 128) \text{ bits.}$$

Algorithm 4: Tweakey Recovery Attack on 18-Round SKINNY-AEAD M1/M3

---

1 ▷ Data collection;
2 **for** 2^N pairs of structures **do**
3   **for** $2^{|\Delta_{in}|}$ equivalent plaintext P_i^{eq} in S_1 **do**
4         $\overline{P_i^{eq}} = P_i^{eq} \oplus (\alpha,0,0,0,\alpha,0,0,0,0,0,0,0,\alpha,0,0,*)$, where $\alpha = $ 0xC3;
5   Choose a nonce N_i that has never been used;
6         $\overline{N_i} = N_i \oplus (\gamma,0,0,0,0,0,0,0,0,0,0,0,0,0,0,0)$, where $\gamma = $ 0xC0;
7         $P_i = SC^{-1} \circ AC^{-1} \circ SR^{-1} \circ MC^{-1}(P_i^{eq})$;
8         $\overline{P_i} = SC^{-1} \circ AC^{-1} \circ SR^{-1} \circ MC^{-1}(\overline{P_i^{eq}})$;
9         $C_i \leftarrow$ encrypt P_i under (l_0, N_i, Key);
10         $W_{18_i} \leftarrow MC^{-1}(C_i)$;
11   **for** $2^{|\Delta_{in}|}$ plaintext $\overline{P_i}$ in S_2 **do**
12         $\overline{C} \leftarrow$ encrypt $\overline{P_i}$ under $(l_0, \overline{N_i}, Key)$;
13         $\overline{C_i} \leftarrow$ encrypt $\overline{P_i}$ under $(l_1, \overline{N_i}, Key)$;
14         $\overline{W_{18_i}} \leftarrow MC^{-1}(\overline{C_i})$;
15   **for** $2^{2|\Delta_{in}|}$ pairs **do**
16         $\Delta W_{18} \leftarrow W_{18_i} \oplus \overline{W_{18_i}}$;
17   **if** $\Delta W_{18} = (*,0,0,0,0,*,0,0,0,0,*,0,0,0,0,*)$ **then**
18   Remain the pair of (P_i, N_i, C_i) and $(\overline{P_i}, \overline{N_i}, \overline{C_i})$;
19   ▷Seive 2^{N-80} remaining pairs finally;

20 ▷ Subkey recovery;
21 **for** 2^8 $tk_{18}[4]$ **do**
22   **for** 2^{N-80} remaining pairs **do**
23   Compute $\Delta X_{18}[4]$ and use the condition (*i.e.*, $\Delta X_{18}[4]$ is a fixed difference) to get $2^{N-80-8} = 2^{N-88}$ remaining pairs;
24   **for** 2^8 $tk_{18}[0]$ **do**
25   **for** 2^{N-88} remaining pairs **do**
26   Compute $\Delta X_{18}[0,4,8,12]$ and use the conditions $\Delta X_{18}[0] = \Delta X_{18}[12]$ and $\Delta X_{18}[4] \oplus \Delta X_{18}[8] = \Delta X_{18}[12]$ to obtain $2^{N-88-16} = 2^{N-104}$ remaining pairs;
27   **for** 2^{32} $tk_1[2,3,7]$ $tk_2[2]$ **do**
28   **for** 2^{N-104} remaining pairs **do**
29   Compute $\Delta Y_3[2]$ and use the condition (*i.e.*, $\Delta Y_3[2]$ is a fixed difference) to filter out the wrong subkeys. Finally, 2^ρ $|K_{in} \cup K_{out}|$-bit subtweakey candidates tk_{rem} have been left;

30 ▷ Brute force;
31 **for** 2^ρ tk_{rem} **do**
32   **for** 2^{80} remaining master key $MK[0,1,4,5,6,11,12,13,14,15]$ **do**
33   Compute the master key MK from tk_{rem} and $MK[0,1,4,5,6,11,12,13,14,15]$ using the tweakey schedule algorithm;
34   Get a random new pair of (P,C) with a nonce value N and a number related to the first block counter l_0;
35         $C' \leftarrow$ encrypt P under (l_0, N, MK) ;
36   **if** $C' = C$ **then**
37   Return the MK as the right key.

Tweakey Recovery. In the attack process of SKINNY-AEAD M1/M3, we are concerned about guessing the value of subtweakey tk_i ($i \in \{1,2,18\}$) to deduce the master tweakey corresponding to Key.

1) Line[21, 22, 23] in Algorithm 4. Guess $tk_{18}[4]$ and compute $\Delta X_{18}[4]$ under 2^{N-80} remaining pairs, where $\Delta X_{18}[4] = SC^{-1}(Z_{18}[4] \oplus tk_{18}[4] \oplus c_1) \oplus SC^{-1}(\overline{Z_{18}[4]} \oplus tk_{18}[4] \oplus c_{18}^1)$ as shown in Fig. 7 , where $c_{18}^1 = $ 0x03 is the 18-th round constant corresponding to c_1. Checking if $\Delta X_{18}[4] = \Delta tk_{17}[0] = $ 0xC0 will lead to an 8-bit filter and generally sieve $2^{N-80-8} = 2^{N-88}$ plaintext-ciphertext pairs. The time complexity of this step is $2^8 \cdot 2 \cdot 2^{N-80} \cdot \frac{1}{16} \cdot \frac{1}{18} \approx 2^{N-79.2}$ times of 18-round encryptions.

2) Line[24, 25, 26] in Algorithm 4. Guess $tk_{18}[0]$ and compute $\Delta X_{18}[0,4,8,12]$ under 2^{N-88} remaining pairs from the previous step. According to Fig. 7, compute $\Delta X_{18}[0] = SC^{-1}(Z_{18}[0] \oplus tk_{18}[0] \oplus c_{18}^0) \oplus SC^{-1}(\overline{Z_{18}[0]} \oplus tk_{18}[0] \oplus c_{18}^0)$, $\Delta X_{18}[4] = SC^{-1}(Z_{18}[4] \oplus tk_{18}[4] \oplus c_{18}^1) \oplus SC^{-1}(\overline{Z_{18}[4]} \oplus tk_{18}[4] \oplus c_{18}^1)$, $\Delta X_{18}[8] = SC^{-1}(Z_{18}[8] \oplus c_{18}^2) \oplus SC^{-1}(\overline{Z_{18}[8]} \oplus c_{18}^2)$, and $\Delta X_{18}[12] = SC^{-1}(Z_{18}[12]) \oplus SC^{-1}(\overline{Z_{18}[12]})$, where $c_{18}^0 = $ 0x0A, $c_{18}^1 = $ 0x03, and $c_{18}^2 = $ 0x02 are the 18-th round constants corresponding to c_0, c_1, and c_2, respectively. Based on the properties of MC operations on col(1) of W_{17}, we have the conditions $\Delta X_{18}[0] = \Delta X_{18}[12]$ and $\Delta X_{18}[4] \oplus \Delta X_{18}[8] = \Delta X_{18}[12]$. Check whether the conditions are satisfied or not, which can act as a 16-bit filter to choose $2^{N-88-16} = 2^{N-104}$ remaining pairs. In this step, the time complexity is $2^{16} \cdot 2 \cdot 2^{N-88} \cdot \frac{4}{16} \cdot \frac{1}{18} \approx 2^{N-77.2}$ 18-round encryptions.

3) Line[27, 28, 29] in Algorithm 4. Guess $tk_1[2,3,7]$, $tk_2[2]$ and compute $\Delta Y_3[2]$ under 2^{N-104} remaining pairs from step 2). As shown in Fig. 7, $\Delta Y_3[2]$ is a fixed difference that equals to $\Delta tk_3[2] = $ 0x82. Checking if $\Delta Y_3[2] = $ 0x82 can act as an 8-bit filter and discard the wrong subtweakeys. The time complexity of this step is $2^{48} \cdot (2 \cdot 2^{N-104}) \cdot (\frac{3}{16} + \frac{1}{16}) \cdot \frac{1}{18} \approx 2^{N-61.2}$ 18-round encryptions.

In step 3), the number of the wrong subtweakeys $tk_1[2,3,7]$, $tk_2[2]$ and $tk_{20}[0,4]$ left is

$$2^\rho = (2^{|K_{in} \cup K_{out}|} - 1) \times (1 - 2^{-8})^{2^{N-104}} = (2^{48} - 1) \times (1 - 2^{-8})^{2^{N-104}},$$

where we set $N = 112.6$ and $\rho = 45.8$.

Brute Force. The values of master key $MK[2,3,7,8,9,10]$ can be derived from tk_{rem} using the tweakey schedule. For the remaining master key $MK[0,1,4,5,6,11,12,13,14,15]$, we exhaustively traverse 2^{80} candidate values. We verify the master key by one plaintext-ciphertext pair under (l_0, N, MK). In this step, the time complexity is $2^\rho \times 2^{80} = 2^{\rho+80}$ 18-round encryptions.

Complexity Computation. For the 18-round attack on SKINNY-AEAD M1/M3, the data complexity is:

$$\mathcal{D} = 2^N \cdot (2^{|\Delta_{in}|} + 2^{|\Delta_{in}|}) = 2^N \cdot 2 \cdot 2^{|\Delta_{in}|} = 2^{N+9} = 2^{112.6+9} = 2^{121.6}$$

chosen plaintexts, the time complexity is:

$$\mathcal{T}_{cal} = 2^{N+9.7} + 2^{N-79.2} + 2^{N-77.2} + 2^{N-61.2} + 2^{\rho+80} \approx 2^{125.9}$$

18-round encryptions, and the memory complexity is:

$$\mathcal{M} = \mathcal{M}_{col} + 2 \cdot (2^{N-88} + 2^{N-104}) \cdot (3 \cdot 128) + 2^{\rho} \cdot 128$$
$$= 2^{42.2} + 2^{34.2} + 2^{52.8} \approx 2^{52.8} \text{ bits.}$$

6 Conclusion

In this paper, we analyze the security of SKINNY-AEAD M1/M3 using the related-tweakey impossible differential attack. Firstly, based on the encryption mode, nonce-respecting scenario and complex tweakey initialization of M1/M3, we propose some constraints to search for longer distinguishers and mount tweakey recovery attacks with less time complexity. Then, according to the constraints given in Sect. 3.1, we search for the related-tweakey impossible differential distinguishers with the help of automatic searching algorithm based on STP. As a result, we find some 14-round distinguishers. Finally, based on one of these distinguishers, 20-round and 18-round tweakey recovery attacks are conducted under a nonce-respecting scenario. To our knowledge, all the attacks are the best tweakey recovery attacks on these two ciphers so far.

The underlying primitive SKINNY-128-384 of SKINNY-AEAD M1/M3 have 128-bit security, while the block cipher SKINNY-128-384 has 384-bit security. Previous attack results (related-tweakey impossible differential, meet-in-the-middle, related-tweakey rectangle) cannot directly be used in SKINNY-AEAD M1/M3. This paper only investigates the related-tweakey impossible differential attacks on M1/M3. The security of SKINNY-AEAD M1/M3 against other attacks deserves further analysis.

Acknowledgements. This work has been supported by the National Natural Science Foundation of China (Grant No. 62032014 and Grant No. 62002204), the National Key Research and Development Program of China (Grant No. 2018YFA0704702), the Major Basic Research Project of Natural Science Foundation of Shandong Province, China (Grant No. ZR202010220025).

A   18-Round Related-Tweakey Impossible Differential Attack for SKINNY-AEAD M1/M3

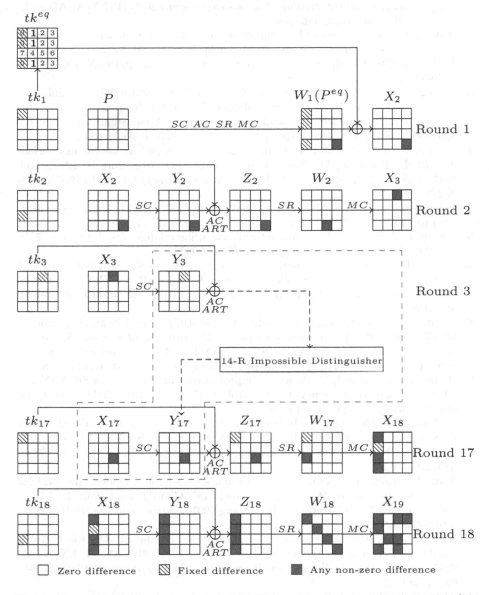

Fig. 7. 18-round related-tweakey impossible differential attack for SKINNY-AEAD M1/M3

References

1. SKINNY-AEAD and SKINNY-Hash: NIST LWC second-round candidate status update (2020). https://csrc.nist.gov/CSRC/media/Projects/lightweight-cryptography/documents/round-2/status-update-sep2020/SKINNY-AEAD_and_SKINNY-Hash_status_update.pdf
2. Ankele, R., et al.: Related-key impossible-differential attack on reduced-round SKINNY. In: Gollmann, D., Miyaji, A., Kikuchi, H. (eds.) ACNS 2017. LNCS, vol. 10355, pp. 208–228. Springer, Cham (2017). https://doi.org/10.1007/978-3-319-61204-1_11
3. Barrett, C.W., Sebastiani, R., Seshia, S.A., Tinelli, C.: Satisfiability modulo theories. In: Biere, A., Heule, M., van Maaren, H., Walsh, T. (eds.) Handbook of Satisfiability, Frontiers in Artificial Intelligence and Applications, vol. 185, pp. 825–885. IOS Press (2009). https://doi.org/10.3233/978-1-58603-929-5-825
4. Beierle, C., et al.: The SKINNY family of block ciphers and its low-latency variant MANTIS. In: Robshaw, M., Katz, J. (eds.) CRYPTO 2016, Part II. LNCS, vol. 9815, pp. 123–153. Springer, Heidelberg (2016). https://doi.org/10.1007/978-3-662-53008-5_5
5. Beierle, C., et al.: SKINNY-AEAD and skinny-hash. IACR Trans. Symmetric Cryptol. 2020(S1), 88–131 (2020). https://doi.org/10.13154/tosc.v2020.iS1.88-131
6. Biham, E.: New types of cryptanalytic attacks using related keys. J. Cryptol. 7(4), 229–246 (1994). https://doi.org/10.1007/BF00203965
7. Biham, E., Biryukov, A., Shamir, A.: Cryptanalysis of skipjack reduced to 31 rounds using impossible differentials. In: Stern, J. (ed.) EUROCRYPT 1999. LNCS, vol. 1592, pp. 12–23. Springer, Heidelberg (1999). https://doi.org/10.1007/3-540-48910-X_2
8. Boura, C., Naya-Plasencia, M., Suder, V.: Scrutinizing and improving impossible differential attacks: applications to CLEFIA, camellia, LBlock and SIMON. In: Sarkar, P., Iwata, T. (eds.) ASIACRYPT 2014, Part I. LNCS, vol. 8873, pp. 179–199. Springer, Heidelberg (2014). https://doi.org/10.1007/978-3-662-45611-8_10
9. Hadipour, H., Bagheri, N., Song, L.: Improved rectangle attacks on SKINNY and CRAFT. IACR Trans. Symmetric Cryptol. 2021(2), 140–198 (2021). https://doi.org/10.46586/tosc.v2021.i2.140-198
10. Jakimoski, G., Desmedt, Y.: Related-key differential cryptanalysis of 192-bit key AES variants. In: Matsui, M., Zuccherato, R.J. (eds.) SAC 2003. LNCS, vol. 3006, pp. 208–221. Springer, Heidelberg (2004). https://doi.org/10.1007/978-3-540-24654-1_15
11. Jean, J., Nikolić, I., Peyrin, T.: Tweaks and keys for block ciphers: the TWEAKEY framework. In: Sarkar, P., Iwata, T. (eds.) ASIACRYPT 2014, Part II. LNCS, vol. 8874, pp. 274–288. Springer, Heidelberg (2014). https://doi.org/10.1007/978-3-662-45608-8_15
12. Kölbl, S., Leander, G., Tiessen, T.: Observations on the SIMON block cipher family. In: Gennaro, R., Robshaw, M. (eds.) CRYPTO 2015, Part I. LNCS, vol. 9215, pp. 161–185. Springer, Heidelberg (2015). https://doi.org/10.1007/978-3-662-47989-6_8
13. Krovetz, T., Rogaway, P.: The software performance of authenticated-encryption modes. In: Joux, A. (ed.) FSE 2011. LNCS, vol. 6733, pp. 306–327. Springer, Heidelberg (2011). https://doi.org/10.1007/978-3-642-21702-9_18
14. Li, M., Hu, K., Wang, M.: Related-tweak statistical saturation cryptanalysis and its application on QARMA. IACR Trans. Symmetric Cryptol. 2019(1), 236–263 (2019). https://doi.org/10.13154/tosc.v2019.i1.236-263

15. Liu, G., Ghosh, M., Song, L.: Security analysis of SKINNY under related-tweakey settings (long paper). IACR Trans. Symmetric Cryptol. **2017**(3), 37–72 (2017). https://doi.org/10.13154/tosc.v2017.i3.37-72
16. Liu, Y., Wang, Q., Rijmen, V.: Automatic search of linear trails in ARX with applications to SPECK and chaskey. In: Manulis, M., Sadeghi, A.-R., Schneider, S. (eds.) ACNS 2016. LNCS, vol. 9696, pp. 485–499. Springer, Cham (2016). https://doi.org/10.1007/978-3-319-39555-5_26
17. Longo, G., Zilli, M.V.: Complexity of theorem-proving procedures: some general properties. RAIRO Theor. Informatics Appl. **8**(3), 5–18 (1974). https://doi.org/10.1051/ita/197408R300051
18. Niu, C., Li, M., Sun, S., Wang, M.: Zero-correlation linear cryptanalysis with equal treatment for plaintexts and tweakeys. In: Paterson, K.G. (ed.) CT-RSA 2021. LNCS, vol. 12704, pp. 126–147. Springer, Cham (2021). https://doi.org/10.1007/978-3-030-75539-3_6
19. Sadeghi, S., Mohammadi, T., Bagheri, N.: Cryptanalysis of reduced round SKINNY block cipher. IACR Trans. Symmetric Cryptol. **2018**(3), 124–162 (2018). https://doi.org/10.13154/tosc.v2018.i3.124-162
20. Shi, D., Sun, S., Derbez, P., Todo, Y., Sun, B., Hu, L.: Programming the Demirci-Selçuk meet-in-the-middle attack with constraints. In: Peyrin, T., Galbraith, S. (eds.) ASIACRYPT 2018, Part II. LNCS, vol. 11273, pp. 3–34. Springer, Cham (2018). https://doi.org/10.1007/978-3-030-03329-3_1
21. Tolba, M., Abdelkhalek, A., Youssef, A.M.: Impossible differential cryptanalysis of reduced-round SKINNY. In: Joye, M., Nitaj, A. (eds.) AFRICACRYPT 2017. LNCS, vol. 10239, pp. 117–134. Springer, Cham (2017). https://doi.org/10.1007/978-3-319-57339-7_7
22. Zhao, B., Dong, X., Meier, W., Jia, K., Wang, G.: Generalized related-key rectangle attacks on block ciphers with linear key schedule: applications to SKINNY and GIFT. Des. Codes Crypt. **88**(6), 1103–1126 (2020). https://doi.org/10.1007/s10623-020-00730-1

Side-Channeling the Kalyna Key Expansion

Chitchanok Chuengsatiansup[1]([✉]), Daniel Genkin[2], Yuval Yarom[1],
and Zhiyuan Zhang[1]

[1] University of Adelaide, Adelaide, Australia
chitchanok.chuengsatiansup@adelaide.edu.au
[2] Georgia Institute of Technology, Atlanta, USA

Abstract. In 2015, the block cipher Kalyna has been approved as the
new encryption standard of Ukraine. The cipher is a substitution-permutation network, whose design is based on AES, but includes several different features. Most notably, the key expansion in Kalyna is designed to
resist recovering the master key from the round keys.

In this paper we present a cache attack on the Kalyna key expansion
algorithm. Our attack observes the cache access pattern during key expansion, and uses the obtained information together with one round key to
completely recover the master key. We analyze all five parameter sets of
Kalyna. Our attack significantly reduces the attack cost and is practical
for the Kalyna-128/128 variant, where it is successful for over 97% of the
keys and has a complexity of only $2^{43.58}$. To the best of our knowledge,
this is the first attack on the Kalyna key expansion algorithm.

To show that the attack is feasible, we run the cache attack on the
reference implementation of Kalyna-128/128, demonstrating that we can
obtain the required side-channel information. We further perform the key-
recovery step on our university's high-performance compute cluster. We
find the correct key within 37 hours and note that the attack requires 50K
CPU hours for enumerating all key candidates.

As a secondary contribution we observe that the additive key whitening used in Kalyna facilitates first round cache attacks. Specifically, we
design an attack that can recover the full first round key with only seven
adaptively chosen plaintexts.

1 Introduction

Since the seminal work of Kocher [32], side-channel attacks have become a major
threat to the security of virtually any cryptographic primitive. While side channels come in many forms and exploitation techniques [33,40,67], a particular
recent concern is microarchitectural side channels [21], which extract secret information by exploiting variations in instruction timing due to contention on CPU
resources. Since the introduction of cache attacks [47,48], it appears that nearly
every microarchitectural feature in modern CPUs can be used to attack cryptographic primitives across hardware-backed security boundaries [1,2,12,14,47,66].

S. D. Galbraith (Ed.): CT-RSA 2022, LNCS 13161, pp. 272–296, 2022.
https://doi.org/10.1007/978-3-030-95312-6_12

With respect to targeted cryptographic protocols, most research attention have been given to Western standards such as AES [8,29,30,42,47], RSA [7,13,37,64], elliptic-curve cryptography [4,49], presumably due to their wide spread adoption, readily-available standardization documents, and acceptability of reference implementations. Much less attention in comparison has been given to national cipher standards of former Eastern Bloc countries, which often deploy their own cryptography standards [6,34,45,54]. While modern symmetric Eastern Bloc designs are often based on AES, these often include variations in features such as round function and key expansion, due to different trade-offs between security and performance made by local standardization agencies while adapting the cipher to local use. As side-channel attacks are by their very nature implementation specific, it is unclear how such local adaptations impact the cipher's side-channel resistance.

1.1 Our Contribution

Tackling this issue, in this work we investigate the Ukrainian cipher Kalyna [45] as a case study of an Eastern Bloc cipher. At a high level, Kalyna is modeled after AES, but has some important differences. First, Kalyna's key expansion algorithm is considered to be non-reversible [3,20]. Thus, a side-channel adversary that wishes to attack Kalyna needs to retrieve all of the round keys. Moreover, Kalyna uses an arithmetic addition operation, which is non-linear in $GF(2)$, for pre- and post-whitening. This is known to hinder cryptanalysis [35,43].

Despite these changes, we present the first cache attack against the Kalyna key expansion algorithm, which significantly reduces the attack complexity in all five variants (see Table 1). We also show that an attacker can practically extract the secret key from Kalyna-128/128's reference implementation with a 97% success probability and an expected complexity of $2^{43.58}$. We demonstrate that Kalyna's computation of the round keys from the master key propagates differences between internal values in a way that allows using them for recovering the master key. To the best of our knowledge, this is the first attack that recovers the master key of Kalyna.

We further demonstrate that the additive key whitening used in Kalyna is more vulnerable to cache attacks than the more common Boolean whitening. The main cause is that due to carry ripples during addition, an attacker can use a simple binary search to find the key. The attack requires only seven (chosen) plaintexts to completely recover the key.

Table 1. Attack cost

Variant	Block size	Key length	Rounds	Columns	Attack cost
Kalyna-128/128	128	128	10	2	$2^{43.58}$
Kalyna-128/256	128	256	14	2	$2^{80.47}$
Kalyna-256/256	256	256	14	4	$2^{168.60}$
Kalyna-256/512	256	512	18	4	$2^{173.45}$
Kalyna-512/512	512	512	18	8	$2^{363.27}$

1.2   Paper Outline

The rest of this paper is organized as follows. Section 3 presents an overview of the attack and describes the information obtained through the side channel. The details of the attack on Kalyna-128/128 is described in Sect. 4, followed by a description of the attacks on other variants of Kalyna in Sect. 5. In Sect. 6 we describe our implementations of proof-of-concept attacks, showing that both the cache side-channel attack and key recovery are feasible.

2   Background

In this section we present background on the Kalyna cipher and the notation we use to describe it, cache attacks, and the related work.

2.1   Kalyna

Kalyna is a substitution-permutation network whose design is based on AES. It was one of the proposals for the Ukrainian National Public Cryptographic Competition which was held between 2007 and 2010. In 2015, the cipher was approved as the national standard of Ukraine.

Kalyna has five variants offering different key and block sizes as summarized in Table 1. We mainly focus on the Kalyna-128/128 variant. For further details and for other variants, see [45].

Bytes. The basic unit of information that Kalyna uses is a byte, which, following standard convention, is a sequence of eight bits each having the value zero or one. We use subscripts to refer to specific bits of a byte. Thus, a byte b consists of the bits $b_0, \ldots, b_7$. Depending on context, a byte represents one of three entities: a sequence of bits, a number in the range $[0, \ldots, 255]$ where the byte b represents $\sum b_i 2^i$, or an element in the field of polynomials modulo $x^8 + x^4 + x^3 + x^2 + 1$ over $GF(2^8)$.

We use the $+$ and $\cdot$ operations for addition and multiplication of numbers. Symbol $\oplus$ is used for polynomial addition and also doubles as bitwise XOR (exclusive or). We denote the bitwise **and** operation with $\&$.

Matrices. Kalyna represents most of its data as matrices of bytes. These matrices have eight rows. The number of columns varies, but most matrices in Kalyna-128/128 have two columns. For a matrix M we use $M[i]$ to refer to the ith byte, in column-first order, i.e. $M[0]$ is the first byte of the first column, $M[1]$ is the second byte of the first column, and $M[8]$ is the first byte of the second column. We use $M[i, \ldots, j]$ to denote a subsequence of bytes in a matrix. Columns can be interpreted both as sequences of bytes and as numbers modulo 2^{64}, where $M[8i, \ldots, 8i + 7]$ represents the number $\sum_{j=0}^{7} 256^j M[8i + j]$. Given a set of indices Q, the projection of a matrix M over Q, denoted by $M|_Q$ is the matrix M where all indices not in Q are zeroed. That is:

$$M|_Q[i] = \begin{cases} M[i] & i \in Q \\ 0 & i \notin Q \end{cases}$$

We sometimes use a graphical notation to better highlight the indices selected by the set of indices. Specifically, we draw a matrix, with filled rectangles representing the selected indices. Thus $M_{\blacksquare}$ selects the even indices of M, i.e. $M|_{\{2i|0 \leq i < 8\}}$, and $M_{\blacksquare} = M|_{\{5,7,9,11\}}$.

Kalyna supports two addition operations on matrices. Matrix (bitwise) addition, denoted with $\oplus$, designates the conventional operation over the polynomial field. Matrix column addition modulo 2^{64}, denoted by $\boxplus$, produces an output matrix by adding columns. Specifically, the operator treats each column of the input matrices as a 64-bit number. To produce a column of the output matrix, the operator adds the two corresponding input columns (modulo 2^{64}) and interprets the result of the sum as a matrix column. Crucially, unlike regular addition, in column addition modulo 2^{64} carries propagate between the cells of same matrix column.

More formally, let $M[8i, \ldots, 8i+7] = \sum_{j=0}^{7} 256^j M[8i+j]$ and $N[8i, \ldots, 8i+7] = \sum_{j=0}^{7} 256^j N[8i+j]$, for matrices M and N we have:

$$(M \boxplus N)[8i, \ldots, 8i+7] = M[8i, \ldots, 8i+7] + N[8i, \ldots, 8i+7]$$

$$= \left(\sum_{j=0}^{7} 256^j M[8i+j] + \sum_{j=0}^{7} 256^j N[8i+j] \right) \bmod 2^{64}.$$

Moreover, we use $\boxminus$ to denote the matrix column subtraction modulo 2^{64}. Finally, we use $\Sigma(M)$ to denote the sum of the columns of the matrix M modulo 2^{64}. That is, $\Sigma(M) = \sum_i M[8i, \ldots, 8i+7] = \sum_i \sum_{j=0}^{7} 256^j M[8i+j] \bmod 2^{64}$.

Cipher Structure. Kalyna follows the design of AES with multiple rounds. Each round consists of four operations: SubBytes, ShiftRows, MixColumns, and AddRoundKey. Like AES, Kalyna also includes an initial plaintext whitening operation. Encryption starts by setting the initial *state* to the plaintext. The cipher then applies the operations to the state. The resulting state is the ciphertext. Decryption applies the operations in the reverse order.

SubBytes. Kalyna specifies four *substitution boxes* (S-Boxes), which provide the non-linear substitution step of each round. Each S-Box consists of 256 entries. Given a state S, the SubBytes step applies one of the S-Boxes to each of the state's byte. Specifically,

$$SB(S)[i] = SB_{i \bmod 4}[S[i]]$$

ShiftRows. As in AES, the ShiftRows moves bytes across rows in the state matrix. The transformation depends on the state size and thus varies with the different variants of the cipher. For Kalyna-128/128, the transform (see Fig. 1) is defined as:

$$SR(S)[i] = \begin{cases} S[i] & i < 4 \\ S[i+8] & i \geq 4 \end{cases}$$

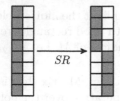

$$\begin{pmatrix} 1 & 1 & 5 & 1 & 8 & 6 & 7 & 4 \\ 4 & 1 & 1 & 5 & 1 & 8 & 6 & 7 \\ 7 & 4 & 1 & 1 & 5 & 1 & 8 & 6 \\ 6 & 7 & 4 & 1 & 1 & 5 & 1 & 8 \\ 8 & 6 & 7 & 4 & 1 & 1 & 5 & 1 \\ 1 & 8 & 6 & 7 & 4 & 1 & 1 & 5 \\ 5 & 1 & 8 & 6 & 7 & 4 & 1 & 1 \\ 1 & 5 & 1 & 8 & 6 & 7 & 4 & 1 \end{pmatrix}$$

Fig. 1. The ShiftRows in Kalyna-128/128.　　　**Fig. 2.** The MixColumns matrix.

MixColumns. The MixColumns transformation computes a linear function that mixes the values along the columns of the state. For Kalyna, MixColumns operates by multiplying the state matrix with the pre-defined 8-by-8 matrix (see Fig. 2). An important property of the matrix is that it is maximum distance separable [38]. Consequently, given a total of eight out of sixteen known bytes in the inputs and outputs of the transformation, we can recover the missing eight bytes.

AddRoundKey. The AddRoundKey operation mixes key material into the state. Kalyna expands the master key K to multiple *round keys*, where round key RK_i is used in the ith round. In each of the first nine rounds in Kalyna-128/128, AddRoundKey uses matrix addition, i.e. $ARK(S, RK_i) = S \oplus RK_i$. The 10th round (last round) uses column addition modulo 2^{64}, i.e. $ARK(S, RK_{10}) = S \boxplus RK_{10}$. Furthermore, Kalyna has a key whitening step before the first round, where it uses column addition modulo 2^{64} to mix additional round key, RK_0, with the plaintext.

Key Expansion. Unlike AES, Kalyna uses a complex, non-reversible procedure for generating the round keys. The procedure first generates an intermediate key K_σ. This K_σ is then combined with the master key K to generate the *even* round keys. Figure 3 shows the process.

Generating K_σ. As the left side of Fig. 3 shows, to generate the intermediate key K_σ, Kalyna performs three sets of SubBytes, ShiftRows and MixColumns operations. The inputs of this process are the master key K and a constant C that depends on the Kalyna variant. Kalyna-128/128 uses the constant 5, i.e. a matrix having all bytes zero except for the least significant byte whose value is 5.

Generating RK_i. Generating the round keys RK_i follows a similar procedure, but with two sets of SubBytes, ShiftRows and MixColumns operations, see Fig. 3 (right). For Kalyna-128/128, one of the input is K_i which is either the master key K, if $i \bmod 4$ is 0 or 1, or the master key with the two columns swapped, if $i \bmod 4$ is 2 or 3. More formally, we have:

$$K_i[j] = \begin{cases} K[j] & \text{if } \lfloor i/2 \rfloor \text{ is even} \\ K[j \oplus 8] & \text{if } \lfloor i/2 \rfloor \text{ is odd} \end{cases}$$

Another input is the intermediate key K_σ modified by column addition modulo 2^{64} with a round constant C_i. The round constant for round i is a matrix with the value 0 in odd indices, and $2^{\lfloor i/2 \rfloor}$ in even indices.

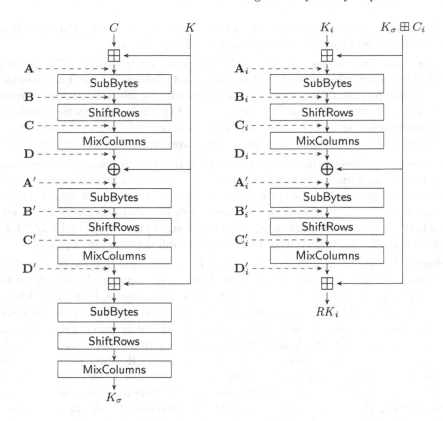

Fig. 3. The Kalyna-128/128 key expansion. Notations such as $\mathbf{A}, \mathbf{A}', \mathbf{A}_i, \mathbf{A}'_i$ are used as explicit reference to internal values computed during the key expansion.

Notation. To facilitate referencing the intermediate states during the generation of the round keys, Fig. 3 also contains explicit names of various intermediate states. For instance, State $\mathbf{A}_0$ is the result of column addition modulo 2^{64} of K_0 and $K_\sigma \boxplus C_0$, i.e. $\mathbf{A}_0 = K_0 \boxplus K_\sigma \boxplus C_0$, $\mathbf{B}_0$ is the result of applying SubBytes to $\mathbf{A}_0$. Hence, $\mathbf{B}_0 = SB(K_0 \boxplus K_\sigma \boxplus C_0)$.

2.2   Cache Attacks

Caches. Caches are small and fast banks of memory that bridge the speed gap between the fast processor and the slower memory by exploiting the temporal and spatial locality that software exhibits. More specifically, the entire memory space is divided into fixed-size *lines*, typically of size 64 bytes. When the processor needs to access memory, it first checks if the required line resides in the cache. In case of *cache hit*, when the required line is in the cache, the memory access request is served from the cache. Conversely, in a *cache miss*, when the required line is not in the cache, the processor is forced to retrieve the line from the slower main memory, storing a copy in the cache for potential future use. Typically, due to the limited size of the cache, the processor needs to *evict* another line from the cache to make room for storing the retrieved cache line.

Set-associative caches. Modern caches are often *set-associative*. The cache is divided into multiple *sets*, each containing a fixed number of *ways*. Each memory block is mapped to a single cache set and can only be stored in the set it maps to. Vendors do not always publish the details of the mapping function; however past research has shown that the function can be reverse engineered, allowing a user to determine the cache set that stores a given memory block [27,28,41,65].

Cache-based side-channels. Because caches are typically shared between multiple programs, a malicious program that monitors the cache can learn information on the execution of other programs. This can be used to leak sensitive information across security-domain boundaries. Over the years, many cache attacks have been designed, demonstrating retrieval of encryption keys [13,15,17,22,23, 26,31,37,42,47,50,64] as well as other sensitive information [24,25,55,62].

Prime+Probe. Prime+Probe [37,47] is a cache attack technique that exploits the set-associative structure of the cache. In the *Prime* phase, the attacker completely fills one or more cache sets with its data. The attacker then waits, letting the victim execute for a certain duration. As the cache is already full, any memory access performed by the victim during its execution must cause eviction of the attacker's data back into the machine's main memory. Finally, in the *Probe* phase, the attacker measures the time to access the data previously used in the prime phase to fill the machine's cache. A short access time indicates that the data is still cached, whereas long access time indicates that data has been evicted. Thus, the attacker learns which cache sets the victim has accessed between the prime and the probe phases, exploiting the mapping between cache sets and address bits to recover which address the victim has accessed.

Temporal resolution. The time to execute one round of Prime+Probe depends on the specific cache and the number of cache sets monitored, ranging from a few thousands of cycles [37] and up to millions [55]. Past research has demonstrated several techniques for improving the temporal resolution of observed events. These include exploiting the OS scheduler to frequently interrupt the victim [14, 26,31], degrading the performance of the victim by contending on resources the victim requires [4,7,11,50,51], and exploiting elevated privileges [9,10,17,42,56].

2.3   Related Work

A few side-channel attacks on Kalyna have been published. Fernbandes Medeiros et al. [20] propose a correlation power analysis on Kalyna-128/128 where the attack recovers all round keys with the success rate of 96% using 250 measured values. Later on, Duman and Youssef [19] propose fault attacks on Kalyna. They employ differential fault analysis and ineffective fault analysis to recover round keys. Their attack works by reducing the number possible candidates then brute-force to find the correct ones. To the best of our knowledge, no cache attacks on Kalyna have been published.

There also exist differential cryptanalysis on reduced-round Kalyna where most of the focus is on the variants whose key length is double the block size. Akshima et al. [3] use meet-in-the-middle attack to recover subkeys for 9-round Kalyna-128/256 and Kalyna-256/512. In [5], the authors recover all round keys using parameters matching. Later on, [59] improve the attack on Kalyna-128/256 by using more optimal differential paths. Similarly, [36] propose a chosen plaintext, reduced-round Kalyna attack on Kalyna-128/256 and Kalyna-256/512 where the attack recovers the round keys.

In addition to differential cryptanalysis attack, the recent work [35] employs an impossible differential attack, i.e. analysing input difference which never results in a particular output difference, on all variants of Kalyna. Nevertheless, with the reduced-round attacks, the complexity is still relatively high. For example, the attack on 4-round Kalyna-128/128 requires 2^{103} time complexity.

Note that all those attacks, only recover the round keys. Kalyna's key expansion prevents using information from one or more round keys to derive the missing keys or the master key. Hence, those attacks are forced to recover all of the (reduced) round keys to be able to encrypt/decrypt messages. No published attacks have recovered the master key.

Twofish [52,53] is a block cipher that also uses a non-reversible key expansion procedure. Ortiz and Compton [46] demonstrate a power analysis attack on the key schedule of Twofish. Specifically, they target an 80-bit implementation of Twofish for a smartcard and show that the key can be recovered from the power traces even in the presence of errors. Attack on key schedules have also been demonstrated on DES [57,58], AES [18,39,60], and Serpent [16]. We note that the key schedule of these ciphers is not designed to deter recovery of the master key from the round keys.

3   Cryptanalysis Overview

Due to the complex key expansion algorithm in Kalyna, knowing one or even all of the round keys does not reveal the master key. Consequently, prior attacks on Kalyna focus on recovering the round keys. Instead, in this work we focus on recovering the master key in the presence of side-channel leakage from the key expansion algorithm. Specifically, we assume a side-channel oracle that reveals the two most significant bits (MSBs) of each S-Box access. More formally, given a byte b, the oracle $O(b)$ returns $64 \cdot \lfloor b/64 \rfloor$. In Sect. 6 we show how we realize such an oracle using the Prime+Probe [37,47] attack on the S-Box access.

Side-channel oracles tend to provide partial information on the observed state. To find the missing information, prior cache attacks on block ciphers combine the information observed over multiple inputs, which are typically assumed to be randomly chosen. In our attack, we do not have this option since we target the key expansion which is executed once (as opposed to the encryption which goes into multiple rounds) and the inputs used for key expansion are fixed and are not under attacker's control. Instead, our attack exploits the differences

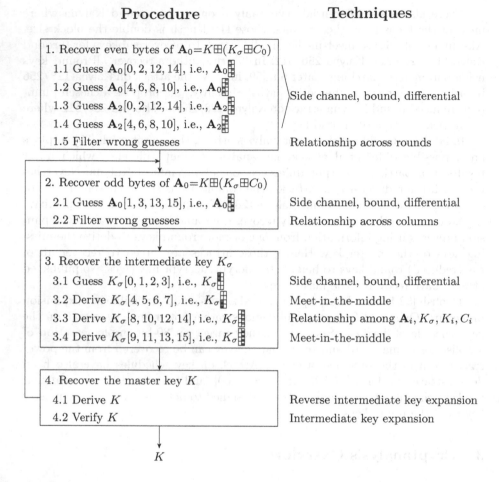

Fig. 4. Steps of our attacks and techniques used.

between the inputs used for generating the different round keys and relationships between key parts to allow a more efficient search in the potential key space.

Our attack consists of four main steps as illustrate in Fig. 4 for Kalyna-128/128. We first use the structure of the key schedule algorithm to guess the value of $\mathbf{A}_0$, we then use a meet-in-the-middle attack to find the value of K_σ, which allows us to recover K.

4   Attacking Kalyna-128/128

In this section, we present the attack on the smallest variant of the cipher, Kalyna-128/128. Section 5 presents an outline of the differences due to the increase in the block size or the key in other variants of the cipher.

4.1   Recover Even Bytes of $\mathbf{A}_0$

The first step in recovering the master key K is to recover the even byte of $\mathbf{A}_0 = K \boxplus (K_\sigma \boxplus C_0)$. Naively, there are 2^{64} possible candidates for the even bytes of $\mathbf{A}_0$. This section explain how we reduce the search space and narrow down to only 1.4 candidates on average. The main tool is the side-channel information from the oracle revealing the two MSBs of each SubBytes access. This enables us to set the bound of the search and verify the correctness of the guesses.

According to the description of the Kalyna cipher [45], we observe that $K_0 = K_4 = K_8$ and $K_2 = K_6 = K_{10}$. Consequently, we have $\mathbf{A}_4 = \mathbf{A}_0 \boxplus (C_4 \boxminus C_0)$ where $C_4 \boxminus C_0$ is a known constant with the value 3 for even bytes and 0 for odd bytes. Depending on the value of the LSBs of $\mathbf{A}_0[0]$, adding 3 may or may not cause a change in the two MSBs, i.e. the value returned from the side-channel oracle $O(\cdot)$. For example, $O(\mathbf{A}_0[0]) \neq O(\mathbf{A}_4[0])$ indicates that the value in the six LSBs of $\mathbf{A}_0[0]$ is between 61 and 63. Otherwise, it is below 61. By comparing $O(\mathbf{A}_0)$ to $O(\mathbf{A}_4)$ we can tighten the bounds on possible values of the six LSBs of $\mathbf{A}_0$. This also applies to $\mathbf{A}_2$ by considering $O(\mathbf{A}_2), O(\mathbf{A}_6)$ and $O(\mathbf{A}_{10})$. Table 2 shows the bounds for the six LSBs of even bytes of $\mathbf{A}_0$ and $\mathbf{A}_2$ in Kalyna-128/128. Note that the table ignores carries from odd to even bytes because they are rare. They only make minor changes to the bounds and even make the attack easier since they reveal a significant amount of information about the key.

Table 2. Bounds on LSBs of even bytes of $\mathbf{A}_0$ and $\mathbf{A}_2$ in Kalyna-128/128.

Condition	Range for $\mathbf{A}_0[j]$	Range for $\mathbf{A}_2[j]$
$O(\mathbf{A}_i[j]) = O(\mathbf{A}_{i+8}[j])$	0–48	0–33
$O(\mathbf{A}_{i+4}[j]) \neq O(\mathbf{A}_{i+8}[j])$	49–60	34–57
$O(\mathbf{A}_i[j]) \neq O(\mathbf{A}_{i+4}[j])$	61–63	58–63

Recall that with a high probability, there is only a small difference in the even bytes of $\mathbf{A}_0$, $\mathbf{A}_4$, and $\mathbf{A}_8$ (resp. $\mathbf{A}_2$, $\mathbf{A}_6$, and $\mathbf{A}_{10}$) while the odd bytes are identical. We initially observe the propagated differences among round key expansions at $\mathbf{A}_0'$, $\mathbf{A}_4'$, and $\mathbf{A}_8'$ under two simplifying assumptions.

Assumption 1. Overflows of even bytes when adding C_i to $K_i \boxplus K_\sigma$ do not depend on i. This implies that for odd j, $\mathbf{A}_i[j] = \mathbf{A}_{i+4}[j]$, i.e. $\mathbf{A}_0\boxplus = \mathbf{A}_4\boxplus = \mathbf{A}_8\boxplus$ and $\mathbf{A}_2\boxplus = \mathbf{A}_6\boxplus = \mathbf{A}_{10}\boxplus$.

Assumption 2. When adding C_i to K_σ, the carry from bit five to bit six of even bytes does not depend on i. This implies that $O((K_\sigma \boxplus C_i)[j]) = O((K_\sigma \boxplus C_{i+4})[j])$ for all $0 \leq j < 16$. We omit the index j when we refer to all the 16 bytes.

We can guess some of the even bytes of $\mathbf{A}_0$, determining the corresponding bytes in $\mathbf{A}_4$ and $\mathbf{A}_8$. We can then track how the differences between the bytes propagate through the first round of the round-key generation step to see how they affect $\mathbf{A}_i'$ and compare with the side-channel information we obtain on $\mathbf{A}_i'$.

We now look at the difference between oracle observations for $\mathbf{A}'_i$ and $\mathbf{A}'_{i+4}$.

$$O\left(\mathbf{A}'_i\right) \oplus O\left(\mathbf{A}'_{i+4}\right) = O\left(\mathbf{A}'_i \oplus \mathbf{A}'_{i+4}\right)$$
$$= O\left(\mathbf{D}_i \oplus (K_\sigma \boxplus C_i) \oplus \mathbf{D}_{i+4} \oplus (K_\sigma \boxplus C_{i+4})\right)$$
$$= O\left(\mathbf{D}_i \oplus \mathbf{D}_{i+4}\right) \oplus O\left((K_\sigma \boxplus C_i) \oplus (K_\sigma \boxplus C_{i+4})\right) \quad (1)$$

Let Δ_i be the oracle difference between $K_\sigma \boxplus C_i$ and $K_\sigma \boxplus C_{i+4}$. That is,

$$\Delta_i = O\left((K_\sigma \boxplus C_i) \oplus (K_\sigma \boxplus C_{i+4})\right) = O\left(\mathbf{A}'_i\right) \oplus O\left(\mathbf{A}'_{i+4}\right) \oplus O\left(\mathbf{D}_i \oplus \mathbf{D}_{i+4}\right)$$

By Assumption 2, we have $\Delta_i = 0$. Hence,

$$O\left(\mathbf{A}'_i\right) \oplus O\left(\mathbf{A}'_{i+4}\right) = O\left(\mathbf{D}_i \oplus \mathbf{D}_{i+4}\right) \quad (2)$$

We now look at each column of $\mathbf{A}'_i$ separately. For the first column, we have:

$$\mathbf{D}_i \boxminus \oplus \mathbf{D}_{i+4} \boxminus = MC(\mathbf{C}_i \boxminus) \oplus MC(\mathbf{C}_{i+4} \boxminus) = MC(SR(\mathbf{B}_i \boxminus)) \oplus MC(SR(\mathbf{B}_{i+4} \boxminus))$$
$$= MC(SR(\mathbf{B}_i \boxminus \oplus \mathbf{B}_i \boxminus)) \oplus MC(SR(\mathbf{B}_{i+4} \boxminus \oplus \mathbf{B}_{i+4} \boxminus))$$
$$= MC(SR(SB(\mathbf{A}_i \boxminus) \oplus SB(\mathbf{A}_{i+4} \boxminus))) \oplus MC(SR(SB(\mathbf{A}_i \boxminus) \oplus SB(\mathbf{A}_{i+4} \boxminus))) \quad (3)$$

By Assumption 1 we have $SB(\mathbf{A}_i \boxminus) = SB(\mathbf{A}_{i+4} \boxminus)$. Hence,

$$O(\mathbf{A}'_i) \oplus O(\mathbf{A}'_{i+4}) = O(MC(SR(SB(\mathbf{A}_i \boxminus) \oplus SB(\mathbf{A}_{i+4} \boxminus)))) \quad (4)$$

The side-channel observation provides the oracle values for the left-hand side of Eq. 4. We can now guess $\widetilde{\mathbf{A}}_0$, the values of the four even bytes of $\mathbf{A}_0 \boxminus$, and calculate the corresponding $\widetilde{\mathbf{A}}_4 = \widetilde{\mathbf{A}}_0 \boxplus (C_4 \boxminus C_0)$, $\widetilde{\mathbf{D}}_0 = (MC(SR(SB(\widetilde{\mathbf{A}}_0))))$, and $\widetilde{\mathbf{D}}_4 = (MC(SR(SB(\widetilde{\mathbf{A}}_4))))$. If the guess is correct, i.e. when $\widetilde{\mathbf{A}}_0 = \mathbf{A}_0 \boxminus$, we will get

$$O\left(\mathbf{A}'_0\right) \boxminus \oplus O\left(\mathbf{A}'_4\right) \boxminus = O\left(\widetilde{\mathbf{D}}_0 \oplus \widetilde{\mathbf{D}}_4\right) \boxminus \quad (5)$$

If the guess is incorrect, the probability of a match is 2^{-16}. To see this, there is only one correct pattern of the 16 bits (two MSBs per byte of eight bytes). Similarly, for $\widetilde{\mathbf{A}}_8 = \widetilde{\mathbf{A}}_0 \boxplus (C_8 \boxminus C_0)$, $\widetilde{\mathbf{D}}_8 = (MC(SR(SB(\widetilde{\mathbf{A}}_8))))$ we have

$$O\left(\mathbf{A}'_0\right) \boxminus \oplus O\left(\mathbf{A}'_8\right) \boxminus = O\left(\widetilde{\mathbf{D}}_0 \oplus \widetilde{\mathbf{D}}_8\right) \boxminus \quad (6)$$

with a probability 2^{-16} unless $\widetilde{\mathbf{A}}_0 = \mathbf{A}_0 \boxminus$.

With each byte having at most 49 possible values (c.f. Table 2), we need to examine $49^4 \approx 2^{22.5}$ possible combinations of values. The probability that the wrong guess matches both Eq. 5 and Eq. 6 is 2^{-32}. Hence, we expect that only the correct guess will match both.

Repeating the process for the right column of $\mathbf{A}'_0$ and for both columns of $\mathbf{A}'_2$, we can recover the even bytes of $\mathbf{A}_0$ and $\mathbf{A}_2$, at a complexity of less than $2^{22.5} \cdot 4 = 2^{24.5}$.

Handling Overflows in $K_\sigma \boxplus C_i$. The discussion so far makes two simplifying assumptions We now remove Assumption 2 and account for the possibility of carries from bit five to bit six of even bytes of $K_\sigma \boxplus C_i$. The main consequence is that Δ_i is not always zero and we need to accept some candidates when Eqs. 5 or 6 are not satisfied.

We now investigate the possible values in Δ_i. When an overflow occurs in an even byte $2j'$ for $0 \le j' < 8$, we have $O(K_\sigma \boxplus C_i)[2j'] = O(K_\sigma \boxplus C_{i+4})[2j'] + 64$ (mod 256). Hence, $\Delta_i[2j'] \in \{0x40, 0xc0\}$.

Under rare conditions, the overflow can percolate and affect the oracle of the following odd byte. Specifically, this can happen when an overflow occurs in byte $2j'$, the top two bits of the byte (before the overflow) are both set, and the six least significant bits of byte $2j' + 1$ are also set. The probability of an overflow is less than $1/2$, hence the probability of a change in the oracle of a given odd byte is lower than 2^{-9}, and the probability that this happens in any of the eight odd bytes of K_σ is less than 2%.

Thus, every byte of Δ_i can have three potential values: 0x00, 0x40, and 0xc0. However, if we naively accept all possible guesses where the oracle matches any of these values, we will accept incorrect guesses with a probability $2^{-3.32}$, which would leave a rather long list of candidates.[1] However, we observe that an overflow to an odd byte $2j' + 1$ can only occur if $\Delta_i[2j'] = 0xc0$ and that at most one of $\Delta_i[2j']$ and $\Delta_{i+4}[2j']$ can be non-zero. Thus, there are only nine possible value assignments for the tuple

$$\tau_{j'} = (\Delta_i[2j'], \Delta_i[2j' + 1], \Delta_{i+4}[2j'], \Delta_{i+4}[2j' + 1]). \tag{7}$$

The probability that an incorrect guess results in a possible combination of values, therefore, is $(9/256)^4 \approx 2^{-19.3}$. Hence, with an initial list of $2^{22.5}$ candidates, we expect that $2^{3.2} \approx 9$ incorrect guesses will remain.

Another strategy an attacker can adopt is to assume that overflows to odd bytes do not occur. This reduces the expected number of incorrect guesses to about 1, but also means that the attack will fail on some percentage of the keys.

Handling Overflows to Odd Bytes. We now handle the case that Assumption 1 does not hold. That is, when an odd byte $2j' + 1$ changes between $\mathbf{A}_i$ and $\mathbf{A}_{i+4}$. This happens when the addition of C_i to $K_i \boxplus K_\sigma$ does not overflow byte $2j'$ whereas adding C_{i+4} does overflow the byte. We can detect such overflows by observing the oracle of $\mathbf{A}_i$ and $\mathbf{A}_{i+4}$. In the case of an overflow, we will have $O(\mathbf{A}_i)[2j'] = 0xc0$ and $O(\mathbf{A}_{i+4})[2j'] = 0x00$. This is in contrast with the case of the overflows of $K_\sigma \boxplus C_i$ discussed in the previous subsection, where we cannot observe overflows and need to guess them.

The main implication of overflows is that we can no longer split the even and odd bytes as in Sect. 4.1 and expect the part with the odd bytes to cancel out. To overcome this issue, we also guess odd bytes that we know change between key rounds, and adapt the split accordingly. For example, if we know that $\mathbf{A}_0[3] \ne \mathbf{A}_4[3]$, we get

$$\mathbf{D}_0 \boxminus \oplus \mathbf{D}_4 \boxminus = MC(SR(SB(\mathbf{A}_0 \boxminus) \oplus SB(\mathbf{A}_4 \boxminus))) \oplus MC(SR(SB(\mathbf{A}_0 \boxminus) \oplus SB(\mathbf{A}_4 \boxminus)))$$

---

[1] For each byte, the probability of accepting is $3/4$. For eight bytes, it is $(3/4)^8 \approx 2^{-3.32}$.

Having to guess odd bytes increases the number of guesses, affecting both the complexity of the step and the length of the list of potential guesses. In the worst case, when all the odd bytes in $\mathbf{A}_6^{\boxed{}}$ differ from the corresponding bytes of $\mathbf{A}_{10}^{\boxed{}}$, we need to guess four odd bytes at a complexity of 63^4 as well as four even bytes at a complexity of 24^4, giving a total complexity of $2^{42.3}$ (see Table 2). Note also that if the six LSBs of an odd byte $2j' + 1$ are all set, we will observe that $O(\mathbf{A}_6[2j' + 1]) \neq O(\mathbf{A}_{10}[2j' + 1])$.

We can reduce the complexity of this case by first filtering the guesses based on $O(\mathbf{A}_2') \oplus O(\mathbf{A}_6')$ and only guess odd bytes for the surviving guesses. There is a total of $24^4 \approx 2^{18.3}$ guesses of even bytes. By the argument above, there are only five possible assignments for $\tau_{j'}$ (see Eq. 7). Hence, the expected number of surviving guesses is $24^4 \cdot (5/16)^4 \approx 2^{11.6}$. Only for these surviving guesses we need to guess values of odd bytes, reducing the overall complexity to $63^4 \cdot 24^4 \cdot (5/16)^4 \approx 2^{35.5}$. While this approach reduces the search space, it does not reduce the expected number of guesses that survives the process, which remains at $63^4 \cdot 24^4 \cdot (9/256)^4 \approx 2^{22.9}$.

Another issue is that the subsequent steps of the attack make no use of the values of odd bytes of $\mathbf{A}_2$ and only limited use of odd bytes of $\mathbf{A}_0$. Consequently, when we need to guess more than two odd bytes in a column, the attack becomes significantly harder. In such a case, the maximum number of guesses for the two odd bytes is 63^2, for the two corresponding even bytes the number of guesses is no more than 24^2, and for the other two even bytes is up to 34^2. Thus, the total number of guesses is less than $63^2 \cdot 24^2 \cdot 34^2 \approx 2^{31.3}$. After filtering, we expect to remain with approximately 2^{12} valid guesses for the even bytes in a column.

The probability that we need to guess more than two odd bytes in at least one of the columns of the key is less than 2%. Thus, for over 98% of the keys, we have an effective attack.

Relationship Across Rounds. So far, we have created independent lists of even bytes for each of the halves of $\mathbf{A}_0$ and $\mathbf{A}_2$. As calculated above, for some keys we can expect these list to consist of up to 2^{12} candidates. Because these lists are independent, combining the guesses of the two halves can yield several millions of possible candidates. To further trim these lists, we exploit the known relationship between $\mathbf{A}_0$ and $\mathbf{A}_2$.

Recall that $\mathbf{A}_i = K_i \boxplus (K_\sigma \boxplus C_i)$ and that K_2 is just K_0 with the columns swapped, i.e. $K_0[0, \ldots, 7] = K_2[8, \ldots 15]$ and $K_0[8, \ldots 15] = K_2[0, \ldots, 7]$, hence the sum of the columns of the two is the same, i.e. $\Sigma(K_0) = \Sigma(K_2)$. Moreover, $C_0[0, \ldots, 7] = C_0[8, \ldots, 15] = \text{0x0001000100010001}$, and $C_2 = C_0 \boxplus C_0$, hence $\Sigma(C_0) = \Sigma(C_2) - \Sigma(C_0) = \text{0x0002000200020002}$. Thus,

$$\Sigma(\mathbf{A}_0) = \Sigma(K_0 \boxplus K_\sigma \boxplus C_0) = \Sigma(K_0) + \Sigma(K_\sigma) + \Sigma(C_0)$$
$$= \Sigma(K_2) + \Sigma(K_\sigma) + \Sigma(C_2) - \Sigma(C_0) = \Sigma(\mathbf{A}_2) - \Sigma(C_0) \qquad (8)$$

Recall that we have four lists of guesses, one for each of $\mathbf{A}_0^{\boxed{}}$, $\mathbf{A}_0^{\boxed{}}$, $\mathbf{A}_2^{\boxed{}}$, and $\mathbf{A}_2^{\boxed{}}$. Selecting one guess from each of the lists provides us with guesses of the even bytes $\widetilde{\mathbf{A}}_0^{\boxed{}}$ and $\widetilde{\mathbf{A}}_2^{\boxed{}}$. We can now calculate $\widetilde{S}_0 = \widetilde{\mathbf{A}}_0^{\boxed{}} + \widetilde{\mathbf{A}}_0^{\boxed{}} + \Sigma(C_0)$

and $\widetilde{S}_2 = \widetilde{\mathbf{A}}_2\boxplus + \widetilde{\mathbf{A}}_2\boxplus$ where we abuse the notation to mean adding one column of the matrix to the other. By Sect. 4.1, if our guesses are correct, we expect the even bytes of $\widetilde{S}_0$ and $\widetilde{S}_2$ to have similar values. Specifically, we expect the corresponding least significant bytes to be identical. Because we may miss carries from odd bytes, we expect a difference of up to 1 between other corresponding even bytes. For incorrect guesses, the probability of identical bytes is $1/256$ and for a difference of up to 1 between a pair of bytes is $3/256$. Hence, the probability of accepting a wrong guess is $2^{-27.2}$.

We verify experimentally that after this step, for 80% of the key only one candidate survives and for 15% two candidates survive. Based on a sample of 1000 random keys, the expected number of candidates is 1.4.

4.2   Recovering Odd Bytes of $\mathbf{A}_0$

So far, we have focused on the even bytes of $\mathbf{A}_0$, showing that the expected number of candidates for those is 1.4. We now discuss guessing the odd bytes we require for the meet-in-the-middle attack.

In total, we need to guess bytes $\mathbf{A}_0\boxplus$, which together with the even bytes will give us a guess of $\mathbf{A}_0\boxplus$. From the side-channel oracle, we learn the two MSBs of each of those bytes, hence a naive approach would be to guess the remaining six bits of each byte, arriving at a complexity of 2^{24}.

However, using side-channel information we can reduce the number of combinations to roughly 2^{16}. Specifically, we note that on the one hand, $K_\sigma \boxplus C_0 = \mathbf{A}_0 \boxminus K_0 = \mathbf{A}_0 \boxminus K$, while on the other, $K_\sigma \boxplus C_0 = \mathbf{A}'_0 \oplus \mathbf{D}_0$. We have side-channel information on $O(\mathbf{A}) = O(K \boxplus 5) \approx O(K)$ from the generation for K_σ, and on $O(\mathbf{A}'_0)$ from the expansion of RK_0. Moreover, given a guess of $\mathbf{A}_0\boxplus$, we can find $\mathbf{D}_0\boxplus$. We can therefore compute two approximations of $O(K_\sigma \boxplus C_0)$, and eliminate guesses in case of a mismatch.

4.3   Recovering K_σ

To recover K_σ we first split it into four parts of four bytes each. We guess one of these parts and exploit the structure of the cipher for a meet-in-the-middle attack to derive the remaining parts.

Guess $K_\sigma[0, 1, 2, 3]$. We first guess $K_\sigma\boxplus$. Note that we only need to guess the six LSBs since the two MSBs are derived from $\mathbf{D}_0 \oplus O(\mathbf{A}'_0)$, where $\mathbf{D}_0$ is known from the previous step and $O(\mathbf{A}'_0)$ is obtained from the side-channel oracle.

Derive $K_\sigma[4, 5, 6, 7]$. Once we know $K_\sigma\boxplus$, we use the meet-in-the-middle attack to derive $K_\sigma\boxplus$. As Fig. 5 shows, we assume that we have a guess of $\mathbf{A}_0\boxplus$, which determines $\mathbf{D}_0\boxplus$. Together with a guess of $K_\sigma\boxplus$, these determine the value of $\mathbf{A}'_0\boxplus$ which determines $\mathbf{C}'_0\boxplus$. From the other end, the (assumed known) value of RK_0 together with the guess of $K_\sigma\boxplus$ allow us to determine $\mathbf{D}'_0\boxplus$. Thus, with a guess of four bytes of a column of K_σ, we can determine four bytes in the input of the MixColumns transformation as well as four bytes in its output.

Using the MDS property of MixColumns, we can now determine the missing bytes, specifically, the value of $\mathbf{D}_0'\hspace{-0.3em}\begin{smallmatrix}\blacksquare\end{smallmatrix}$. Combining this with RK_0, allows us to determine the missing bytes of $K_\sigma\hspace{-0.3em}\begin{smallmatrix}\blacksquare\end{smallmatrix}$. We note that the information we have on the MSBs of $K_\sigma \boxplus C_0$ allows us to eliminate wrong guesses with a probability of $1 - 2^{-8}$. (Two bits for each of four bytes.)

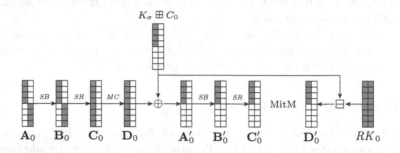

$$K_\sigma \boxplus C_0$$

Fig. 5. Meet-in-the-middle attack recovering $K_\sigma[0,\ldots,7]$.

Derive $K_\sigma[8, 10, 12, 14]$. In contrast to previous step, this time we consider the relationship among $\mathbf{A}_i$, K, K_σ and C_i. The first relationship that we use is

$$\mathbf{A}_0\begin{smallmatrix}\blacksquare\end{smallmatrix} = K\begin{smallmatrix}\blacksquare\end{smallmatrix} \boxplus (K_\sigma \boxplus C_0)\begin{smallmatrix}\blacksquare\end{smallmatrix} \tag{9}$$

Recall that we know $\mathbf{A}_0\begin{smallmatrix}\blacksquare\end{smallmatrix}$ and $(K_\sigma \boxplus C_0)\begin{smallmatrix}\blacksquare\end{smallmatrix}$. Through subtraction, we obtain $K\begin{smallmatrix}\blacksquare\end{smallmatrix}$ as illustrated in Fig. 6a. The obtained value in byte $K[6]$ may not be exact due to a possible borrow from the unknown byte $\mathbf{A}_0[5]$. Hence, $K[6]$ could be $(\mathbf{A}_0 \boxminus (K_\sigma \boxplus C_0))[6] \pm 1$ due to carry or borrow.

To recover the four target bytes $K_\sigma\begin{smallmatrix}\blacksquare\end{smallmatrix}$, we relate the obtained $K\begin{smallmatrix}\blacksquare\end{smallmatrix}$ to the known constant C_2 and the already known $\mathbf{A}_0\begin{smallmatrix}\blacksquare\end{smallmatrix}$ through the following relationship

$$\mathbf{A}_2\begin{smallmatrix}\blacksquare\end{smallmatrix} = K\begin{smallmatrix}\blacksquare\end{smallmatrix} \boxplus (K_\sigma \boxplus C_2)\begin{smallmatrix}\blacksquare\end{smallmatrix} \tag{10}$$

where we abuse the notation to mean operations are performed as a single column on the colored columns. As illustrated in Fig. 6b, $K_\sigma\begin{smallmatrix}\blacksquare\end{smallmatrix}$ can be recovered by subtracting $(K\begin{smallmatrix}\blacksquare\end{smallmatrix} \boxplus C_2\begin{smallmatrix}\blacksquare\end{smallmatrix})$ from $\mathbf{A}_2\begin{smallmatrix}\blacksquare\end{smallmatrix}$. Note that similar remark as when recovering $K[6]$ also applies here, namely, carries and/or borrows can affect the value of bytes $K_\sigma[2, 4, 6]$.

Obtain $K_\sigma[9, 11, 13, 15]$. Since we now know half a column of $K_\sigma\begin{smallmatrix}\blacksquare\end{smallmatrix}$ which also allows us to compute the corresponding half a column of $\mathbf{D}_0'\begin{smallmatrix}\blacksquare\end{smallmatrix}$, we wish to apply a similar meet-in-the-middle technique as for recovering $K_\sigma\begin{smallmatrix}\blacksquare\end{smallmatrix}$. To do so, another piece of information that we need is half a corresponding column of $\mathbf{C}_0'$.

Recall that we start the K_σ recovery process by guessing $(K_\sigma \boxplus C_0)\begin{smallmatrix}\blacksquare\end{smallmatrix}$. This allows us to obtain $\mathbf{A}_0'\begin{smallmatrix}\blacksquare\end{smallmatrix}$. Now, with the extra information of $K_\sigma\begin{smallmatrix}\blacksquare\end{smallmatrix}$ obtained

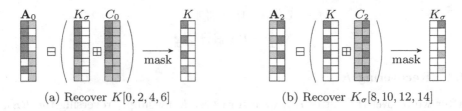

(a) Recover $K[0, 2, 4, 6]$ (b) Recover $K_\sigma[8, 10, 12, 14]$

Fig. 6. Relationships among $\mathbf{A}_i$, K, K_σ and C_i to derive K_σ. The gray shade highlights bytes whose values are known but not used in this recovery. The blue shade highlights bytes whose values are known and used in this recovery. The lighter blue shade denotes bytes with uncertainly. Note that here we abuse the notation to mean performing operations as a single column of the matrix.

in Sect. 4.3, we can compute $(K_\sigma \boxplus C_0)\textstyle\substack{\boxminus}$ by adding the known constant C_0 which allows us to compute $\mathbf{A}_0'\textstyle\substack{\boxminus}$. Then, following the sequence of SubBytes and ShiftRows provides us $\mathbf{C}_0'\textstyle\substack{\boxminus}$. That is, we compute:

$$\mathbf{A}_0'\textstyle\substack{\boxminus} \leftarrow \mathbf{D}_0\textstyle\substack{\boxminus} \oplus (K_\sigma \boxplus C_0)\textstyle\substack{\boxminus}$$
$$\mathbf{B}_0'\textstyle\substack{\boxminus} \leftarrow SB(\mathbf{A}_0'\textstyle\substack{\boxminus})$$
$$\mathbf{C}_0'\textstyle\substack{\boxminus} \leftarrow SR(\mathbf{B}_0'\textstyle\substack{\boxminus})$$

At this stage, we know $\mathbf{C}_0'\textstyle\substack{\boxminus}$, i.e. half-column input to MixColumns and $\mathbf{D}_0'\textstyle\substack{\boxminus}$, i.e. its corresponding half-column output. We can proceed with splitting the input of MixColumns and solving for the unknown input half $\mathbf{C}_0'\textstyle\substack{\boxminus}$ as illustrate in Fig. 7. Even though the four MixColumns output bytes that we know are not consecutive, this does not affect our technique since both $MC(\mathbf{C}_0'\textstyle\substack{\boxminus})$ and $MC(\mathbf{C}_0'\textstyle\substack{\boxminus})$ contribute to $\mathbf{D}_0'\textstyle\substack{\boxminus}$. Therefore, we can simply construct a system of linear equations focusing on the four bytes $\mathbf{C}_0'\textstyle\substack{\boxminus}$ and $\mathbf{D}_0'\textstyle\substack{\boxminus}$ that we know and solve for the four unknown bytes $\mathbf{C}_0'\textstyle\substack{\boxminus}$.

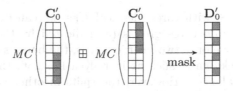

Fig. 7. Recover $\mathbf{C}_0'[8, 9, 10, 11]$

Once we know the full-column $\mathbf{C}_0'\textstyle\substack{\boxminus}$, performing MixColumns allows us to recover the full-column $\mathbf{D}_0'\textstyle\substack{\boxminus}$. Then, $K_\sigma\textstyle\substack{\boxminus}$ can be recovered by subtracting $\mathbf{D}_0'\textstyle\substack{\boxminus}$ from $RK_0\textstyle\substack{\boxminus}$. That is, we compute:

$$\mathbf{D}'_0\mathord{\text{▯}} \leftarrow MC(\mathbf{C}'_0\mathord{\text{▯}})$$
$$K_\sigma\mathord{\text{▯}} \leftarrow RK_0\mathord{\text{▯}} \boxminus \mathbf{D}'_0\mathord{\text{▯}}$$

4.4   Recovering K

After we recover the entire K_σ, we can recover K by simply reversing the RK_0 expansion. For the Kalyna-l/k variants where the block size l is the same as the key length k, i.e. $l = k$, we compute the following steps:

$$\mathbf{A}'_0 \leftarrow SB^{-1}(SR^{-1}(MC^{-1}(RK_0 \boxminus (K_\sigma \boxplus C_0))))$$
$$\mathbf{A}_0 \leftarrow SB^{-1}(SR^{-1}(MC^{-1}(\mathbf{A}'_0 \oplus (K_\sigma \boxplus C_0))))$$
$$K \leftarrow \mathbf{A}_0 \boxminus (K_\sigma \boxplus C_0)$$

Once we obtain K, we can verify by computing the K_σ expansion and check against our recovered K_σ. If both match, this guarantees that we successfully recover the correct K. In other words, if our guess of either the odd bytes of $(K \boxplus (K_\sigma \boxplus C_0))\mathord{\text{▯}}$ or $(K_\sigma \boxplus C_0)\mathord{\text{▯}}$ was not correct, we would detect at this step. If that is the case, we try different candidates until we recover the correct K.

5   Attacks on Other Kalyna Variants

Most of the techniques described in Sect. 4 also apply to other variants of Kalyna, which have larger block size (l) and/or key length (k). This section discusses the hurdles that increasing the sizes adds and explains how we tackle them to recover the master key.

5.1   Relationship of K_i

Recall that K_i is one of the inputs to RK_i expansion. With an increase in the key length k (regardless whether the block size l also increases), the variations of K_i key part also increase. As a consequence, there are fewer K_i's that are identical to K_0.

As shown in Fig. 8, with three identical K_i's, we can divide the bounds on the six LSBs of $\mathbf{A}_0$ into three groups (as indicated by the number lines). In contrast, when we have only two identical K_i's, the bounds can be divided into two groups. In a lucky case, such as in Kalyna-128/256, the size of those two groups are nearly balanced. However, the splits in other variants may not be well balanced, which results in less tight bound in a larger group. This implies an increase in the cost of guessing $\mathbf{A}_i$.

Another impact of having many variations of K_i is that it is more difficult to apply the relationship across columns. Recall that in Kalyna-128/128 there are only two variations of K_i whose difference in the column-wise sum is a known

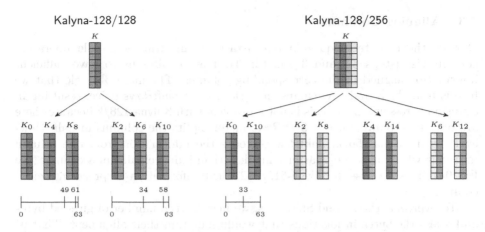

Fig. 8. The relationship between the full master key K and K_i key part used for RK_i expansion in Kalyna-128/k. The effect on the bounds of the 6 LSBs of $\mathbf{A}_i$ is presented using number lines.

constant. Therefore, the cost of applying the column-wise sum is equivalence to guessing $\mathbf{A}_i$ of those two K_i variations. For other variants of Kalyna, it requires significantly more guesses to be able to apply the column-wise sum. Take Kalyna-128/256 as an example (see Fig. 8). We need to guess all four K_i variations so that the column-wise sum of, for example, K_0 and K_2 is equivalent (up to a known constant) to that of K_4 and K_6. Therefore, we opt for guessing relevant bytes of $\mathbf{A}_0$ instead of guessing $\mathbf{A}_0, \mathbf{A}_2, \mathbf{A}_4$ and $\mathbf{A}_6$.

Observe that not being able to use the relationship across column affects our attacks in two ways. First, we lose an extra filter to eliminate wrong $\mathbf{A}_i$ guesses (step 2.2 in Fig. 4) thus resulting in having more candidates for subsequent steps. Second, we can no longer derive a different column of K_σ from a known column (step 3.3 in Fig. 4). This forces us to guess more bits of K_σ to be able to derive the full key K.

5.2   Large Constant C_i

Each RK_i expansion uses a known constant C_i which is defined as a value 0x00010001...0001 shifted by the round key index $i/2$. The length of C_i is the same as the block size l. Observe that if $0 \leq i < 16$, all even bytes of C_i are non-zero while all odd bytes of C_i are zero, which is the case for Kalyna-l/128 and Kalyna-l/256. However, in Kalyna-l/512, i can be as high as 18, which means that in rounds 16 and 18 the even bytes are zero while the odd bytes are non-zero. Therefore, we can no longer assume that the odd bytes from different round keys (but with the same K_i) are identical (step 1 in Fig. 4). Thus, we need to guess odd bytes in addition to even bytes, increasing the complexity of our attacks.

5.3 Aligning Columns

One of the core techniques in our attacks is meet-in-the-middle operating column-wise (steps 3.2 and 3.4 in Fig. 4). This requires us to have sufficient information aligned in the corresponding columns. The main obstacle that we face is that the round key expansion performs the ShiftRows twice, resulting in diffusion across columns. This is not a problem with Kalyna-128/k because there are only two columns where ShiftRows merely splits the columns in half. However, with Kalyna-256/k, ShiftRows spreads the information from one column into four where only one quarter (thus less than half) remains in a column (see Fig. 9a). This is worse in Kalyna-512/512 where information is spread into eight columns.

To overcome the second ShiftRows, we increase the number of guessed bytes and guess the bytes in locations that would maintain their alignment. That is, instead of attempting to align a single column, we align multiple columns. We guess bytes in an alternating pattern (see Fig. 9b). This pattern applies to both guessing A_i and K_σ.

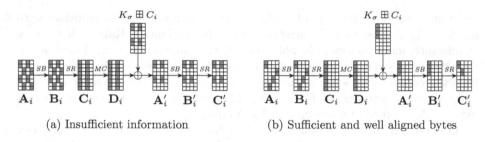

(a) Insufficient information   (b) Sufficient and well aligned bytes

Fig. 9. Propagation and alignment of known bytes from initial guessed bytes to perform meet-in-the-middle attack in Kalyna-256/k.

6 The Practical Attack

We now proceed to empirically validate the assumptions made for the analysis. We implement a cache-based side-channel attack against the key expansion algorithm in the reference implementation of Kalyna [44] and demonstrate that we can instantiate the required oracle. We also describe how we exploit the additive key whitening used in Kalyna to efficiently recover the first round key RK_0.

6.1 Instantiating the Oracle

Experimental Setup. We implement the attack on a Dell Vostro 5581, featuring Intel Core i5-8265U CPU, with four cores and a 6 MB last-level cache, running Ubuntu-18.04.5. We use the Prime+Probe attack as implemented

in the Mastik toolkit [63]. To achieve a high temporal resolution, we use
SGX-Step [56]. We note that other approaches for achieving high temporal resolution exist [4,11,14,26,31]. Thus the attack is feasible outside SGX.

Victim. The victim is an SGX enclave that runs the reference implementation
of Kalyna [44]. The implementation uses four S-Boxes, each 256-bytes long, occu-
pying four consecutive cache lines each, to a total of 16 consecutive cache lines.
The cache attack identifies the cache line accessed. Hence, with four cache lines
per S-Box, the attack recovers the two most significant bits of the index.

Attack. As in past works, before the attack we disable frequency scaling, automatic power management, and Intel Turbo Boost. We further isolate the core
that runs the victim and disable the cache prefetcher. We use a controlled-
channel attack [61] to stop enclave execution at the start of key expansion. That
is, we mark the page containing the S-Boxes as not existing, forcing an interrupt
when the enclave executes the first SubBytes operation. We then use SGX-Step
to single-step the enclave. We use Mastik to prime the cache sets that hold the
S-Boxes and mark the page that contains the S-Boxes as not-accessed prior to
each single step. After stepping, if the page has been access, we probe the cache
sets of the S-Boxes and record the results. We stop after 240 S-Box accesses.

Results. Similar to prior works [26,31,42], we find that even though we only
execute a single instruction, we can observe multiple accesses to the S-Boxes.
After filtering the accesses, we can correctly identify 96.55% of the memory
accesses, with the only failures being on Byte 7 of the state. In cases of failures, we
have two or three options for the oracle of Byte 7, depending on the subsequent
accesses to S-Box 3.

Summary. The attack takes several seconds and retrieves S-Box accesses with a
high success rate. Thus, it can be used as the oracle for our key-recovery attack.

6.2   Recovering the First Round Key

In Sect. 4.3 we use RK_0 as part of recovering the master key. We now show how
we can exploit the additive key whitening of Kalyna to easily recover RK_0.

   In AES and in many similar ciphers, the first operation during encryption
is to apply Boolean whitening to the plaintext, i.e. to XOR it with a key. In
contrast, Kalyna uses additive whitening. Specifically, it computes $P \boxplus RK_0$
where P denotes a plaintext, and uses the result as the input to the first round.
Because (arithmetic) addition is not a linear operation in $GF(2)$, additive key
whitening hinders cryptanalysis [35,43].

   We observe, however, the additive masking is inferior when it comes to protection against cache attacks. The reason is that cache attacks observe specific
bits of the data. For example, the oracle we use observes the two MSBs of the
input to an S-Box. When Boolean whitening is used, changes in the plaintext
remain local, i.e. a change in the plaintext only affects the changed bit but not
other bits and cannot, therefore, expose more information to the attacker.

   In contrast, with additive whitening, a change of a bit can change the pattern
of ripples of the carries, resulting in changes in other bits, which can reveal more

information. To exploit this property, we first encrypt an all-zero plaintext and use our attack to recover the oracle for the SubBytes operation of the first round. Because $P = 0$, we have $P \boxplus RK_0 = RK_0$, and the oracle reveals the two MSBs of each byte of RK_0.

We now encrypt a plaintext where all the bytes have the value 32. We note that if bit five of a key byte is zero, adding 32 will not change the values of bits six or seven of the sum. Consequently, the oracle reading will be the same as for the all-zero plaintext. If, however, bit five of the key byte is set, adding 32 will cause a carry to bit six and the oracle reading will be different. Thus with the value 32 we learn the value of bit five of each byte in RK_0.

In the next step we repeat the process, this time with a value of 16 for bytes where bit five of the key is set and a value of 48 where it is clear. Using the same argument, we now learn bit four of the key. We note that this is, basically, a binary search that exploits carry ripples to recover the next bit. Hence, using only seven adaptively chosen plaintexts, we can completely recover RK_0.

6.3   Recover the Master Key K of Kalyna-128/128

Experimental Setup. To validate our cryptanalysis, we performed a practical attack on recovering the master key K of Kalyna-128/128 on a compute cluster. We spawn a task for each 16 guesses of the odd bytes of $\mathbf{A_0}$. During the experiment, we record the task execution time and the execution time of testing a single candidate.

Practical Attack. To prove that the attack is practical, we picked a random secret key ensuring no overflows in $K_\sigma \boxplus C_i$ when recovering the K_σ. We note that overflows facilitate the attack, hence this choice represent a conservative estimate. For the selected key, there are 69,249 candidates for odd bytes of $\mathbf{A_0}$. We spawn 4,329 tasks, each of which tests 16 candidates. (The last task only tests one candidate.) We then let the cluster schedule the tasks according to its scheduling policies.

Results. To determine the worst-case execution time we run all 4,329 tasks to completion. The key was found after 37 hours, but full completion took 49 hours. Testing a wrong guess takes on average about 44 minutes. The full attack takes about 50 K CPU hours.

Acknowledgements. We would like to thank all reviewers for the insightful feedback, which has improved the paper.

This work was supported by the ARC Discovery Early Career Researcher Award (project number DE200101577); the ARC Discovery Project (project number DP210102670); the Air Force Office of Scientific Research (AFOSR) under award number FA9550-20-1-0425; The Blavatnik ICRC at Tel-Aviv University; the National Science Foundation under grant CNS-1954712; the Phoenix HPC service at the University of Adelaide; and gifts from AMD, Google, and Intel.

References

1. Acıiçmez, O.: Yet another microarchitectural attack: exploiting I-cache. In: CSAW (2007)
2. Acıiçmez, O., Koç, Ç.K., Seifert, J.: Predicting secret keys via branch prediction. In: CT-RSA (2007)
3. Akshima, D.C., Ghosh, M., Goel, A., Sanadhya, S.K.: Single key recovery attacks on 9-round Kalyna-128/256 and Kalyna-256/512. In: ICISC (2015)
4. Allan, T., Brumley, B.B., Falkner, K.E., van de Pol, J., Yarom, Y.: Amplifying side channels through performance degradation. In: ACSAC (2016)
5. AlTawy, R., Abdelkhalek, A., Youssef, A.M.: A meet-in-the-middle attack on reduced-round Kalyna-b/2b. IEICE Trans. Inf. Syst. **99-D**(4), 1246–1250 (2016)
6. Belarus Standard STB 34.101.31-2011: Information technology and security data encryption and integrity algorithms (2011). http://apmi.bsu.by/assets/files/std/belt-spec27.pdf
7. Bernstein, D.J., Breitner, J., Genkin, D., Groot Bruinderink, L., Heninger, N., Lange, T., van Vredendaal, C., Yarom, Y.: Sliding right into disaster: left-to-right sliding windows leak. In: CHES (2017)
8. Bonneau, J., Mironov, I.: Cache-collision timing attacks against AES. In: Goubin, L., Matsui, M. (eds.) CHES 2006. LNCS, vol. 4249, pp. 201–215. Springer, Heidelberg (2006). https://doi.org/10.1007/11894063_16
9. Brasser, F., Müller, U., Dmitrienko, A., Kostiainen, K., Capkun, S., Sadeghi, A.: Software grand exposure: SGX cache attacks are practical. In: WOOT (2017)
10. Van Bulck, J., Piessens, F., Strackx, R.: Nemesis: Studying microarchitectural timing leaks in rudimentary CPU interrupt logic. In: CCS (2018)
11. Cabrera Aldaya, A., Brumley, B.B.: HyperDegrade: from GHz to MHz effective CPU frequencies. arXiv:2101.01077 (2021)
12. Cabrera Aldaya, A., Brumley, B.B., ul Hassan, S., Pereida García, C., Tuveri, N.: Port contention for fun and profit. In: IEEE SP (2019)
13. Cabrera Aldaya, A., García, C.P., Tapia, L.M.A., Brumley, B.B.: Cache-timing attacks on RSA key generation. TCHES **2019**(4), 213–242 (2019)
14. Chakraborty, A., Bhattacharya, S., Alam, M., Patranabis, S., Mukhopadhyay, D.: RASSLE: return address stack based side-channel leakage. TCHES **2021**(2), 275–303 (2021)
15. Chuengsatiansup, C., Feutrill, A., Sim, R.Q., Yarom, Y.: RSA key recovery from digit equivalence information. In: ACNS (2022)
16. Compton, K.J., Timm, B., VanLaven, J.: A simple power analysis attack on the Serpent key schedule. ePrint Archive 2009/473 (2009)
17. Dall, F., De Micheli, G., Eisenbarth, T., Genkin, D., Heninger, N., Moghimi, A., Yarom, Y.: CacheQuote: efficiently recovering long-term secrets of SGX EPID via cache attacks. TCHES **2018**(2), 171–191 (2018)
18. Dassance, F., Venelli, A.: Combined fault and side-channel attacks on the AES key schedule. In: FDTC (2012)
19. Duman, O., Youssef, A.M.: Fault analysis on Kalyna. Inf. Secur. J. A Glob. Perspect. **26**(5), 249–265 (2017)
20. Fernandes Medeiros, S., Gérard, F., Veshchikov, N., Lerman, L., Markowitch, O.: Breaking Kalyna 128/128 with power attacks. In: SPACE (2016)
21. Ge, Q., Yarom, Y., Cock, D., Heiser, G.: A survey of microarchitectural timing attacks and countermeasures on contemporary hardware. J. Cryptogr. Eng. **8**(1), 1–27 (2016). https://doi.org/10.1007/s13389-016-0141-6

22. Genkin, D., Pachmanov, L., Tromer, E., Yarom, Y.: Drive-by key-extraction cache attacks from portable code. In: ACNS (2018)
23. Genkin, D., Poussier, R., Sim, R.Q., Yarom, Y., Zhao, Y.: Cache vs. key-dependency: side channeling an implementation of Pilsung. TCHES **2020**(1), 231–255 (2020)
24. Gras, B., Razavi, K., Bosman, E., Bos, H., Giuffrida, C.: ASLR on the line: practical cache attacks on the MMU. In: NDSS (2017)
25. Gruss, D., Spreitzer, R., Mangard, S.: Cache template attacks: automating attacks on inclusive last-level caches. In: USENIX Security (2015)
26. Gullasch, D., Bangerter, E., Krenn, S.: Cache games - bringing access-based cache attacks on AES to practice. In: IEEE SP (2011)
27. Hund, R., Willems, C., Holz, T.: Practical timing side channel attacks against kernel space ASLR. In: IEEE SP (2013)
28. Irazoqui, G., Eisenbarth, T., Sunar, B.: Systematic reverse engineering of cache slice selection in Intel processors. In: DSD (2015)
29. Irazoqui Apecechea, G., Eisenbarth, T., Sunar, B.: S$A: a shared cache attack that works across cores and defies VM sandboxing - and its application to AES. In: IEEE SP (2015)
30. Irazoqui Apecechea, G., Inci, M.S., Eisenbarth, T., Sunar, B.: Wait a minute! A fast, cross-VM attack on AES. In: RAID (2014)
31. Kayaalp, M., Abu-Ghazaleh, N.B., Ponomarev, D.V., Jaleel, A.: A high-resolution side-channel attack on last-level cache. In: DAC (2016)
32. Kocher, P.C.: Timing attacks on implementations of Diffie-Hellman, RSA, DSS, and other systems. In: Koblitz, N. (ed.) CRYPTO 1996. LNCS, vol. 1109, pp. 104–113. Springer, Heidelberg (1996). https://doi.org/10.1007/3-540-68697-5_9
33. Kocher, P.C., Jaffe, J., Jun, B.: Differential Power Analysis. In: Power Analysis Attacks, pp. 119–165. Springer, Boston, MA (2007). https://doi.org/10.1007/978-0-387-38162-6_6
34. Kryptos Logic: A brief look at North Korean cryptography, July 2018. https://www.kryptoslogic.com/blog/2018/07/a-brief-look-at-north-korean-cryptography/
35. Kumar Gupta, S., Ghosh, M., Mohanty, S.K.: Cryptanalysis of Kalyna block cipher using impossible differential technique. In: Giri, D., Buyya, R., Ponnusamy, S., De, D., Adamatzky, A., Abawajy, J.H. (eds.) Proceedings of the Sixth International Conference on Mathematics and Computing. AISC, vol. 1262, pp. 125–141. Springer, Singapore (2021). https://doi.org/10.1007/978-981-15-8061-1_11
36. Lin, L., Wu, W.: Improved meet-in-the-middle attacks on reduced-round Kalyna-128/256 and Kalyna-256/512. Des. Codes Crypt. **86**(4), 721–741 (2017). https://doi.org/10.1007/s10623-017-0353-5
37. Liu, F., Yarom, Y., Ge, Q., Heiser, G., Lee, R.B.: Last-level cache side-channel attacks are practical. In: IEEE SP (2015)
38. MacWilliams, F.J., Sloane, N.: The Theory of Error-Correcting Codes. North-Holland Publishing Company, Amsterdam (1977)
39. Mangard, S.: A simple power-analysis (SPA) attack on implementations of the AES key expansion. In: Lee, P.J., Lim, C.H. (eds.) ICISC 2002. LNCS, vol. 2587, pp. 343–358. Springer, Heidelberg (2003). https://doi.org/10.1007/3-540-36552-4_24
40. Mangard, S., Oswald, E., Popp, T.: Power Analysis Attacks. Springer, Boston, MA (2007). https://doi.org/10.1007/978-0-387-38162-6
41. Maurice, C., Le Scouarnec, N., Neumann, C., Heen, O., Francillon, A.: Reverse engineering Intel last-level cache complex addressing using performance counters. In: RAID (2015)

42. Moghimi, A., Irazoqui, G., Eisenbarth, T.: CacheZoom: how SGX amplifies the power of cache attacks. In: CHES (2017)
43. Mukhopadhyay, D., Chowdhury, D.R.: Key mixing in block ciphers through addition modulo 2^n. ePrint Archive 2005/383 (2005)
44. Oliynykov, R.: Kalyna block cipher reference implementation. https://github.com/Roman-Oliynykov/Kalyna-reference (2015). Accessed 6 Dec 2021
45. Oliynykov, R., Gorbenko, I., Kazymyrov, O., Ruzhentsev, V., Kuznetsov, O., Gorbenko, Y., Dyrda, O., Dolgov, V., Pushkaryov, A., Mordvinov, R., Kaidalov, D.: A new encryption standard of Ukraine: The Kalyna block cipher. ePrint Archive 2015/650 (2015)
46. Ortiz, J.J.G., Compton, K.J.: A simple power analysis attack on the twofish key schedule. CoRR abs/1611.07109 (2016)
47. Osvik, D.A., Shamir, A., Tromer, E.: Cache attacks and countermeasures: the case of AES. In: Pointcheval, D. (ed.) CT-RSA 2006. LNCS, vol. 3860, pp. 1–20. Springer, Heidelberg (2006). https://doi.org/10.1007/11605805_1
48. Percival, C.: Cache missing for fun and profit. In: Proceedings of BSDCan (2005). https://www.daemonology.net/papers/htt.pdf
49. Pereida García, C., Brumley, B.B.: Constant-time callees with variable-time callers. In: USENIX Security (2017)
50. Pereida García, C., Brumley, B.B., Yarom, Y.: Make sure DSA signing exponentiations really are constant-time. In: CCS (2016)
51. Pessl, P., Groot Bruinderink, L., Yarom, Y.: To BLISS-B or not to be: attacking strongSwan's implementation of post-quantum signatures. In: CCS (2017)
52. Schneier, B., Kelsey, J., Whiting, D., Ferguson, N., Wagner, D., Hall, C.: Twofish: a 128-bit block cipher. In: First AES Conference (1998)
53. Schneier, B., Kelsey, J., Whiting, D., Wagner, D., Hall, C., Ferguson, N.: On the Twofish key schedule. In: Tavares, S., Meijer, H. (eds.) SAC 1998. LNCS, vol. 1556, pp. 27–42. Springer, Heidelberg (1999). https://doi.org/10.1007/3-540-48892-8_3
54. Shishkin, V., Dygin, D., Lavrikov, I., Marshalko, G., Rudskoy, V., Trifonov, D.: Low-weight and hi-end: draft Russian encryption standard. In: Current Trends in Cryptology (CTCrypt) (2014)
55. Shusterman, A., Kang, L., Haskal, Y., Meltser, Y., Mittal, P., Oren, Y., Yarom, Y.: Robust website fingerprinting through the cache occupancy channel. In: USENIX Security (2019)
56. Van Bulck, J., Piessens, F., Strackx, R.: SGX-step: a practical attack framework for precise enclave execution control. In: SysTex (2017)
57. Wagner, M., Heyse, S.: Single-trace template attack on the DES round keys of a recent smart card. ePrint Archive 2017/57 (2017)
58. Wagner, M., Heyse, S.: Improved brute-force search strategies for single-trace and few-traces template attacks on the DES round keys. ePrint Archive 2018/937 (2018)
59. Wang, G., Zhu, C.: Single key recovery attacks on reduced AES-192 and Kalyna-128/256. Sci. China Inf. Sci. **60**(9), 1–3 (2016). https://doi.org/10.1007/s11432-016-0417-7
60. Wichelmann, J., Moghimi, A., Eisenbarth, T., Sunar, B.: MicroWalk: a framework for finding side channels in binaries. In: ACSAC (2018)
61. Xu, Y., Cui, W., Peinado, M.: Controlled-channel attacks: deterministic side channels for untrusted operating systems. In: IEEE SP (2015)
62. Yan, M., Fletcher, C.W., Torrellas, J.: Cache telepathy: leveraging shared resource attacks to learn DNN architectures. In: USENIX Security (2020)

63. Yarom, Y.: Mastik: a micro-architectural side-channel toolkit (2016). https://cs. adelaide.edu.au/~yval/Mastik
64. Yarom, Y., Falkner, K.: Flush+Reload: a high resolution, low noise, L3 cache side-channel attack. In: USENIX Security (2014)
65. Yarom, Y., Ge, Q., Liu, F., Lee, R.B., Heiser, G.: Mapping the Intel last-level cache. ePrint Archive 2015/905 (2015)
66. Yarom, Y., Genkin, D., Heninger, N.: CacheBleed: a timing attack on OpenSSL constant-time RSA. J. Cryptogr. Eng. **7**(2), 99–112 (2017). https://doi.org/10. 1007/s13389-017-0152-y
67. Yuce, B., Schaumont, P., Witteman, M.: Fault attacks on secure embedded software: threats, design, and evaluation. J. Hardw. Syst. Secur. **2**(2), 111–130 (2018)

Fake It Till You Make It: Data Augmentation Using Generative Adversarial Networks for All the Crypto You Need on Small Devices

Naila Mukhtar[1]($\boxtimes$) (iD), Lejla Batina[2], Stjepan Picek[3,4] (iD), and Yinan Kong[1]

[1] Macquarie University, Sydney, Australia
naila.mukhtar@ieee.org, yinan.kong@mq.edu.au
[2] Radboud University, Nijmegen, The Netherlands
[3] Radboud University, Nijmegen, Nijmegen, The Netherlands
lejla@cs.ru.nl
[4] Delft University of Technology, Delft, The Netherlands

Abstract. Deep learning-based side-channel analysis performance heavily depends on the dataset size and the number of instances in each target class. Both small and imbalanced datasets might lead to unsuccessful side-channel attacks. The attack performance can be improved by generating traces synthetically from the obtained data instances instead of collecting them from the target device, but this is a cumbersome and challenging task.

We propose a novel data augmentation approach based on conditional Generative Adversarial Networks (cGAN) and Siamese networks, enhancing the attack capability. We also present a quantitative comparative deep learning-based side-channel analysis between a real raw signal leakage dataset and an artificially augmented leakage dataset. The analysis is performed on the leakage datasets for both symmetric and public-key cryptographic implementations. We investigate non-convergent networks' effect on the generation of fake leakage signals using two cGAN based deep learning models.

The analysis shows that the proposed data augmentation model results in a well-converged network that generates realistic leakage traces, which can be used to mount deep learning-based side-channel analysis successfully even when the dataset available from the device is not optimal. Our results show that the datasets enhanced with "faked" leakage traces are breakable (while not without augmentation), which might change how we perform deep learning-based side-channel analysis.

Keywords: Deep learning-based side-channel attacks · ASCAD · Elliptic curve cryptography · GANs · Data augmentation · Signal processing

S. D. Galbraith (Ed.): CT-RSA 2022, LNCS 13161, pp. 297–321, 2022.
https://doi.org/10.1007/978-3-030-95312-6_13

1   Introduction

Profiling side-channel attacks (SCAs) are the class of attacks in which the adversary is assumed to have access to the target device's open copy. Then, the attacker uses that copy of a device to build a strong profiling model. In the second phase of the attack, the attacker infers the secret information, e.g., the secret key from the target device based on the profiling model and measurements of some physical activity of the target device while cryptographic implementation is running on it. Recently, deep learning-based attacks have been extensively studied for improving the profiling SCA, see, e.g. [1–3]. The deep learning model's performance can suffer if enough data is not provided during the training phase. What is more, using deep learning may not even make sense if not enough data is available. This lack of availability could be a consequence of implemented countermeasure prohibiting collecting a large number of traces or due to the evaluation setup [4]. Additionally, it is common to use side-channel leakage models like the Hamming weight or Hamming distance, which will result in an imbalanced class scenario [5].

Deep learning is data-hungry. Not providing enough data can mean that either we do not reach the full potential of a certain method or, in more extreme cases, that the method shows very poor performance. One common reason for it is overfitting, where the deep learning model learns how to model the noise, making it difficult to generalize to the previously unseen examples. To fight against it, researchers commonly use techniques like 1) hyperparameter tuning - to find architectures that are better tuned for the task and thus have less tendency to overfit, 2) regularization - to lower the complexity of a neural network model during training, and thus prevent the overfitting, and 3) data augmentation - to provide additional (synthetic) examples, utilizing the capacity of a model better, but also regularize the model with noise inherent to the synthetic examples. Each of those techniques has its advantages and drawbacks, and they are also successfully applied to the side-channel domain. Interestingly, while hyperparameter tuning and regularization (e.g., dropout, L2 regularization) are commonly used in SCA, data augmentation received less attention, despite very good preliminary results. One possible reason lies in the difficulty of clearly visualizing how a successful synthetic side-channel measurement should look (something much simpler in, e.g., image classification domain).

Cagli et al. proposed the first data augmentation setup for deep learning-based SCA to counter the effects of clock jitter countermeasure [6]. Still, the authors do not consider scenarios where the number of measurements is significantly limited. Picek et al. presented the results with "traditional" machine learning data augmentation techniques and concluded that Synthetic Minority Over-sampling Technique (SMOTE) could aid in data generation, resulting in improved attack performance [5]. Differing from us, the authors used the Hamming weight leakage model, resulting in an imbalanced dataset. In our work, we used intermediate values resulting in more classes and more challenging analyses. Luo et al. used a mixup data augmentation technique where new synthetic examples are based on randomly selected combinations of existing examples [7].

The authors conducted experiments for several datasets and leakage models and obtained mostly similar behavior for the original and mixup traces. Generative Adversarial Networks (GAN) is another popular data augmentation technique that is widely used in the image processing domain for generating fake images [8], which significantly improves the machine learning model's performance [9]. Only one existing study presents the realization of using GAN-generated fake signals as leakage signals for deep learning-based side-channel analysis [10]. However, the authors use more profiling traces and the Hamming weight leakage model (which will result in fewer classes), making their work significantly different from ours. What is more, this work misses providing a detailed analysis of the GAN network before using it for the fake data generation.

GAN's performance for generating fake images/signals depends on the generator's progressive learning based on the discriminator's response. The design and selection of a GAN play an important role in generating realistic leakage signals. A well-convergent GAN network will generate traces carrying relevant/significant features similar to the original data samples. Designing a GAN-based model with optimum convergence or equilibrium point is one of the greatest challenges for generating fake signals [11] that contain the characteristics of real leakage traces. Several techniques, presented for fake image generation, can help achieve convergence, including feature matching [12], conditional GAN (cGAN) [13], and semi-supervised learning [12].

In our work, we generated 50% traces for each class ($256 \times 150 \times 2$ real and fake traces for AES and $16 \times 150 \times 2$ real traces for ECC), making the setting very challenging.

Our approach is inspired by the fake image generation presented in [14]. Our presented generic model can generate fake data for various leakage datasets, including symmetric and public-key algorithm implementations. We provide a comparative analysis with the existing simple dense layer-based GAN used for leakage generation.

Specifically, we list our contributions as follows:

- We present a layered approach for generating the 1-dimensional fake signals for deep learning-based side-channel analysis (DL-SCA). Our approach combines Siamese network and conditional GAN (cGAN) characteristics with an extra model loss monitoring layer introduced to detect the model convergence. The visual representation of the loss function of the proposed data augmentation technique helps analyze the well-converged GAN model. A well-converged network helps in generating indistinguishable fake traces that will give the same insights to the data as that of the original signals. With this, we showcase the relevance of "real vs. fake" data and exhibit successful attacks with synthetic data that could impact various real-world use cases and security applications.
- We provide a comparative analysis exhibiting the fake leakage trace datasets' effect on the side-channel model training performance. These fake leakage traces are generated from various converging points during the proposed Siamese-cGAN model training, which helps to analyze the importance of the well-converged models.

- The proposed Siamese-cGAN model can be generalized to any leakage dataset (from varying cryptographic algorithm implementations). To demonstrate this, we trained our proposed model on datasets containing either symmetric or public-key algorithm implementations, using two different neural networks for generator and discriminator. Best performing neural networks are further selected for analysis. While several results show the benefits of data augmentation for symmetric-key implementations, data augmentation is significantly less explored in the context of attacks on public-key implementations (we are aware of only one work [15]).
- We provide a comparative analysis of our proposed Siamese-cGAN model with the existing used cGAN model [10] (named as $cGANModelA$ in this study) for generating fake leakage traces.[1]
- The performance of the Siamese-cGAN data augmentation model is evaluated by applying the actual deep learning-based side-channel attack on the generated leakage traces using four different neural network architectures (one multilayer perceptron (MLP) and two Convolutional Neural Networks (CNNs) for symmetric algorithm implementation leakages and one CNN for public-key implementation leakages). Our results show that the fake data samples generated from the well-convergent model combined with 50% real data successfully recovered the secret with similar efficiency as real data traces alone. What is more, for the ASCAD dataset case (AES measurements), the key rank suggests even improved results for the dataset consisting of real and fake traces. We emphasize that the goal of our approach is not only to improve the attack performance in scenarios where there are enough real measurements for a successful attack. Rather, we envision it for constrained settings where more measurements than available are needed to break the target. We think here of implementations that randomize the secret (key) after a number of algorithm's execution such that the adversary can collect only a limited number of traces for the analysis.

2   Preliminaries

2.1   Profiled Side-Channel Attacks

The profiled attack represents the most powerful side-channel attack where the adversary has access to the target device's open copy. There are two phases of the attack: the profiling phase and the attack phase. In the profiling phase, the adversary creates a profile of the device with all the possibilities for the data leakages and then uses that profile (template in the case of template attack [16] or machine learning model) in the attack phase to distinguish/predict the unknown secret information [17].

Commonly, profiled attacks are divided into classical ones like template attacks [16] and stochastic model [18], and machine learning-based attacks [1,19].

---

[1] We note that the provided details were not sufficient to ensure the reproducibility of the results, so we did our best to infer the used architecture from the description.

Machine learning-based side-channel attacks (ML-SCA) follow the same steps as the classical profiling attacks. More precisely, they have two phases: training phases (profiling phase) and test phase (attack phase). The adversary can train the model with the leakage examples collected from the identical copy of a target device and then evaluate the trained model using previously unseen examples. When using deep learning instead of other machine learning techniques, we denote such attacks as deep learning-based side-channel attacks (DL-SCA).

2.2 Generative Adversarial Networks (GANs)

The Generative Adversarial Networks were first introduced by Goodfellow et al. in 2014 [9]. Since then, many variations of GAN have been proposed, including conditional GAN (cGAN), Deep Convolutional GAN (DC-GAN), Information Maximizing (InfoGAN), and Stacked GAN (StackGAN) [13,20–23].

A Generative Adversarial Network (GAN) is a neural network architecture for training a generative model, which can generate plausible data. It consists of two neural networks adversarial models, discriminator D and generator G. Real data is labeled as '1' and artificially generated (fake) data is labeled '0'. Generator G network generates the fake data with random noise input z, and discriminator D network discriminates between real and fake data.

GANs are based on the concept of a zero-sum non-cooperative game where one network (discriminator) is trying to minimize the loss, and the other network (generator) is trying to maximize the loss (this min-max problem as given by Eq. (1), where x and z represent the real and fake generated trace, respectively).

The discriminator's task is to distinguish the real and generated data instances, whereas the generator's task is to improve the model based on the feedback from the discriminator. However, the generator is trying to generate data traces that are alike. This makes it hard to find a good convergence point. GAN converges when both D and G reach a Nash equilibrium, meaning that one (D/G) will not change its actions anymore, no matter what opponent (D/G) does. This is the optimal point that adversarial loss in GANs aims to optimize.

$$E_x[log(D(x))] + E_z[log(1 - D(G(z)))]. \tag{1}$$

2.3 Conditional Generative Adversarial Networks (cGANs)

GANs help generate plausible data, but there is no way to control what random data they will generate. GAN can be conditioned with extra data to control the generated information to handle that issue. GAN with an extra condition is called conditional Generative Adversarial Network (cGAN). The extra data in cGANs is the class label of the data samples. Using class labels for cGAN training has two main advantages: firstly, it helps in improving the GAN performance, and secondly, it helps in generating the specific target class samples.

In the training process of the cGAN model, the generator network generates data based on the label and the random input and tries to replicate the actual distribution in the real data samples. The generated samples are of the same structure as the input labeled data. In the next step, the real and the generated/fake data are given as input to the discriminator. The discriminator is first trained with the original/real labeled data samples and is then trained with the fake generated data samples. Similar to GANs, the discriminator's task is to separate the fake from real data samples, which helps the generator generate better (realistic) samples [13].

2.4   Data Augmentation

Data augmentation is an umbrella term representing various techniques used to increase the amount of data by adding (slightly) modified copies of already existing examples or newly created synthetic examples from existing data. Data augmentation can act as a regularization technique and will help reduce overfitting. While data augmentation can be applied to any domain, most of the results and techniques were developed for data augmentation in image classification [24].

2.5   Deep Learning Algorithms

Based on the deep learning-based side-channel attacks (DL-SCA) performance on various cryptographic algorithms [6,25,26], we tested our newly generated datasets using two state-of-the-art deep learning approaches: multilayer perceptron (MLP) and Convolutional Neural Network (CNN). MLP and two variations of CNN [3,27] are used to evaluate the AES dataset, and one CNN architecture [25] is used to evaluate the ECC dataset.

2.6   Siamese Neural Network

Siamese neural network (also called twin/identical neural network) is an artificial neural network architecture consisting of two similar neural networks (with the same weights and network parameters). It is capable of processing two different input vectors to produce comparable output vectors [28]. The two neural networks are feedforward multilayer perceptrons that work in tandem and are trained in a backpropagation manner. The idea behind the Siamese neural network is not to learn to classify the labels but to discriminate between the input vectors. Hence a special loss function, contrastive loss, or Triplet Loss is used for the training of the network [29]. For training the network, the input vector pairs (x_i, x_j) are prepared; a few pairs consist of similar vectors, and a few pairs consist of dissimilar vectors. The similar vector pair is labeled as $y =$ '1', whereas the dissimilar pair is labeled as $y =$ '0'. Each pair is fed to the Siamese network, and distance is computed to check the similarity. The output vectors from each network are compared using cosine or Euclidean distance and can be considered as a semantic similarity between projected representation of the input vectors [30].

2.7   Cryptographic Algorithms Under Evaluation

For our analysis, we investigate the performance of our proposed model on two publicly available datasets. One dataset corresponds to the implementation of

Advanced Encryption Standard (AES) and the other to the Elliptic Curve Cryptography (ECC) implementation.

- The ASCAD dataset [27] is the first dataset that acts as a basis for comparative analysis of deep learning-based side-channel analysis (DL-SCA). The traces are collected from the masked AES-128 bit implementation on an 8-bit AVR microcontroller (ATmega8515). The leakage model is first-round S-box (Sbox$[P(i)_3 \oplus k^*]$) where the third byte is exploited (as that is the first masked byte). There are 60 000 total traces along with the metadata (plaintext/ciphertext/key). These traces are further split into two datasets, one for training (profiling) consisting of 50 000 and the other for the test (attack), consisting of 10 000 traces. Each trace consists of 700 features. The labels are stored in a separate file.
- The publicly available ECC dataset [25,31] consists of power consumption traces collected from a Pinata development board (developed by Riscure). The board is equipped with a 32-bit STM32F4 microcontroller (with an ARM-based architecture), running at the clock frequency of 168 MHz and having Ed25519 implementation of WolfSSL 3.10.2. The target is profiling a single EC scalar multiplication operation with the ephemeral key with the base point of curve Ed25519. The 256-bit scalar/ephemeral key is interpreted as slices of four nibbles. Hence, there are 16 classes/labels in the dataset. The dataset has a similar format as ASCAD. The database consists of two groups of traces; profiling traces and attack traces. Each group further consists of "TRACES" and "LABELS". Each raw trace consists of 1 000 features, representing the nibble information used during the encryption. Profiling and attack traces groups consist of n_p and n_a tuples, with a corresponding label for each trace. In total, there are 6 400 traces, out of which 80/20 are used for profiling ($n_p = 5\,120$) and attacking ($n_a = 1\,280$).

The profiling traces from both datasets are used to train the cGAN models. Half of the real traces per class are kept in the final dataset, along with the generated data samples. The attacking traces are used for evaluating the performance of the DL-SCA model trained with the new dataset.

It should be noted that the purpose of this research is to analyze the effect of artificially generated features in data traces for environments where the adversary has an additional constraint on collecting leakage traces to form a dataset. The presented methodology can be extended to produce and test the fake leakage traces for any other cryptographic algorithms.

3 Related Works

Data augmentation represents a set of techniques to reduce overfitting and improve the supervised machine learning task (commonly, classification). Data augmentation is a well-researched topic, mostly framed in the context of image data augmentation [24]. While there are multiple ways to divide the data augmentation techniques, a common one is on 1) techniques transforming the input, 2) deep learning techniques (where our work also belongs), and 3) meta-learning.

Data augmentation in SCA is used to improve side-channel attack performance and can be put in the same general direction as, e.g., works exploring how to improve hyperparameter tuning. As data augmentation increases the amount of data, it is commonly considered in the deep learning perspective as there, very large datasets are beneficial. There are significantly more works considering symmetric-key cryptography and deep learning-based SCA than public-key cryptography.

The first investigation that uses convolutional neural networks for side-channel attacks on AES is conducted by Maghrebi et al. [1]. This work represents a significant milestone for the SCA community as it demonstrated how deep learning could be used without feature engineering and efficiently break various targets.[2]

Cagli et al. investigated how deep learning could break implementations protected with jitter countermeasures [6]. This work is highly relevant as it introduced data augmentation to the SCA domain. The authors used two data augmentation techniques: shifting (simulating a random delay) and add-remove (simulating a clock jitter). Picek et al. investigated how reliable are machine learning metrics in the context of side-channel analysis. Their results showed that machine learning metrics could not be used as sound indicators of side-channel performance [5]. Additionally, as the authors used the Hamming weight leakage model that results in class imbalance, they utilized a well-known data balancing technique called SMOTE, showing that the attack performance can be significantly improved. Kim et al. explored how to design deep learning architectures capable of breaking different datasets [2]. Additionally, they used Gaussian noise at the input to serve as a regularization factor to prevent overfitting. Luo et al. investigated how mixup data augmentation can improve CPA and deep learning-based side-channel attacks [7].

Next, several works aimed at improving neural network performance by providing a systematic approach for tuning neural network architectures. Zaid et al. were the first to propose a methodology to tune the hyperparameters related to the convolutional neural network size (number of learnable parameters, i.e., weights and biases) [3]. Wouters et al. [32] further improved upon the work from Zaid et al. [3] by showing how to reach similar attack performance with even smaller neural network architectures. Rijsdijk et al. used reinforcement learning to provide an automated way to construct small convolutional neural networks that perform well [33]. Following a different approach to improving the attack performance, Wu and Picek showed how denoising autoencoder could be used to reduce the effect of countermeasures [34]. The first work that considers the usage of GANs (more specifically, cGANs) for the SCA domain is made by Wang et al. [10]. While this work shows the potential of GANs in SCA, the results indicate that a large profiling set is required to construct useful synthetic data.

---

[2] We note earlier works are also using neural networks like multilayer perceptron, but the results were in line with other machine learning techniques, and researchers commonly used feature engineering to prepare the traces.

There are several works using template attack (and its variants) to attack public-key cryptography, see, e.g., [35–40]. Lerman et al. used a template attack and several machine learning techniques to attack an unprotected RSA implementation [19]. Carbone et al. used deep learning to attack a secure implementation of RSA [41]. The authors showed that deep learning could reach strong performance against secure implementations of RSA. Weissbart et al. showed a deep learning attack on EdDSA using the curve Curve25519 as implemented in WolfSSL, where their results indicate it is possible to break the implementation with a single attack trace [25]. Weissbart et al. considered deep learning-based attacks on elliptic curve Curve25519 implementation protected with countermeasures and showed that even protected implementations could be efficiently broken [42]. Perin et al. used a deep learning approach to remove noise stemming from the wrong choice of labels after a horizontal attack [15]. The authors showed that protected implementations having an accuracy of around 52% after a horizontal attack could reach 100% after deep learning noise removal (note that the authors also used data augmentation to reach 100% accuracy). Zaid et al. introduced a new loss function called ensembling loss, generating an ensemble model that increases the diversity [43]. The authors attacked RSA and ECC secure implementations and showed improved attack performance.

4 Proposed Approach

4.1 Data Splitting

The leakage data traces L are collected from the device while AES or ECC algorithms encryptions E are performed using the secret key K or scalar/ephemeral key K, respectively. The labeled collected traces are then divided into two sets: Training ($D_{Training}$) and Testing ($D_{Testing}$). The training set is used to train the Siamese-cGAN model, which produces fake traces. The newly generated dataset (real+fake traces) is used to train the DL-SCA model, and the test set is used to evaluate the SCA model's performance. For a fair evaluation of the trained Siamese-cGAN model, the test set is never shown to the network during the Siamese-cGAN model training process.

For the rest of the paper, "cGAN models" or "Siamese-cGAN models" refer to the model used for generating data. However, "DL-SCA models" refer to the deep learning models, which are used to evaluate the performance of the generated data by applying profiling side-channel attacks.

4.2 Siamese-cGAN Model for Data Augmentation

In contrast to the standard GANs, conditional GANs (cGANs) perform conditional generation of the fake data based on the class label rather than generating signals blindly. The labels c of the data traces/instances are used to train GANs in a zero-sum or adversarial manner to improve the learning of the generator (G). As mentioned before, the generator's G task is to generate the leakage signals that carry similar properties as the original traces using the random noise z and the latent space input ls. The discriminator's D task is to distinguish real and fake signals. In the cGAN training process, first, the discriminator D is trained with the labeled real data traces T_{real}, and then the discriminator D is trained with the fake generated signals $G(z)$ or T_{Gen}. The objective function for cGAN is given by Eq. (2).

$$E_{x \sim T_{Real}}[log(D(x|c))] + E_z[log(1 - D(G(z|c)))]. \tag{2}$$

In our proposed design of the Siamese-conditional Generative Adversarial Network ($Siamese - cGAN$), we combine cGAN with the Siamese network concept. Siamese network is an architecture in which two identical/twin networks carrying the same weights are trained with two different inputs. In the proposed model, two generators $G1$ and $G2$ take two random input noise vectors $z1$ and $z2$, generating fake signals $G(z1)$ and $G(z2)$, respectively, in a Siamese fashion. Both the generators share the same network weights, and only the input is different. The discriminator D is first trained with the labeled real data T_{Real} and then with the fake data T_{Gen}, originating from the two twin generator networks $G1$ and $G2$.

As mentioned before, convergence is a challenging issue in training GANs. In some cases, the model converges and then starts diverging again; that is, it forgets its learned examples. Several techniques include memory-based learning, to handle such scenarios [44]. Training the model simultaneously, in a Siamese setting, with the random noise from two sources can help obtain a better-converged model in fewer epochs by combining output from both. Moreover, to analyze the impact of convergence, we introduced another layer in the two-step cGAN model. This layer monitors the real traces loss L_{Real}, generated traces loss L_{Gen}, and GAN model Loss L_{GAN}.

Let $D_{GAN \to R}$ represent the loss difference between L_{GAN} and L_{Real}, and $DGAN \to G$ represent the loss difference between L_{GAN} and L_{Gen}, then the average of loss differences over last t iterations will be given by:

$$\frac{1}{t} \sum_{i=1}^{t} (|D_{GAN \to R(i)}| + |D_{GAN \to G(i)}|). \tag{3}$$

The Siamese-cGAN model stops training when the average model loss $Loss_{Avg}$ over the last t iteration is less than the average loss over the last $t * 2$ iterations. The trained Siamese-cGAN model is then used to generate the n_g fake traces T_{Gen}, containing features similar to the original signals. T_{Gen} and T_{Real}, having n_g and n_r instances respectively, are combined together to form a resultant dataset T_{GAN}. This dataset is then used to train the deep learning model to analyze the generated dataset's performance with DL-SCA. A test set is set aside for a fair evaluation before adding the generated traces into the training dataset. The test set is never shown to the neural network during training. The proposed Siamese-cGAN specific for DL-SCA is shown in Fig. 1.

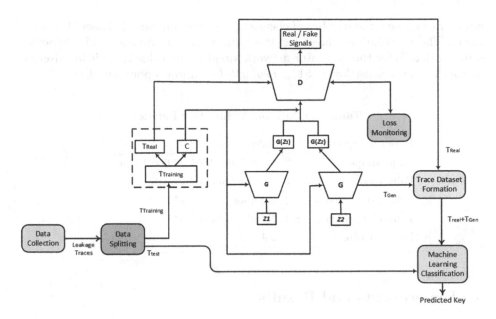

Fig. 1. Proposed Siamese-cGAN architecture for ML-SCA.

4.3 cGAN Models for Discriminator and Generator

In the proposed Siamese-cGAN model, the selection of generator and discriminator plays a vital role. The authors in [10] recommended using a generator and discriminator with fully connected dense layers only, without any complex layers. However, in this study, we explore the possibility of using fully connected dense layers and the convolutional layers in discriminator. The reason for evaluating CNN layer-based network is that it has provided better fake images generation in image processing [20]. Hence, for evaluating the trained Siamese-cGAN model performance, two different networks are used for the generator and discriminator. These networks are denoted as *Model A* and *Model B*. *Model A* is based on two fully connected layers for the generator and the discriminator. However, *Model B* (CNN-based) has a more complex architecture with four fully connected and one convolutional layer. Batch normalization, *LeakyRelu*, and dropout are introduced, which help achieve a more stable model that avoids overfitting. Additionally, we tested both *Model A* and *Model B* generators and discriminators with and without Siamese settings to analyze the improvements introduced by using the Siamese configuration.

Figures 8 and 9, given in Appendix A, show the structure of both the models. We use the same generator and discriminator model architectures to generate symmetric and public-key leakages data samples. The only parameter that needs to be changed is the size of dense layers, which changes based on the number of classes per target dataset. The size in each subsequent layer is doubled from the previous layer. That is, layer 1, layer 2, and layer 3 have a size equal to the number of classes, the number of classes*2, and the number of classes*4, respectively. The convolutional layer has the *tanh* activation function. The hyperparameter details for the generator network are given in Table 1, while for discriminator, we use a dense layer (512), *LeakyReLU*, and dropout set at 0.4.

Table 1. Generator Architecture Details

Hyper-parameter	Value
Input shape	(700,1) for AES, (1 000,1) for ECC
Fully Connected layer 1	Number of classes
Fully Connected layer 2	Number of classes*2
Fully Connected layer 3	Number of classes*4
Dropout rate	0.4

5   Experiments and Results

5.1   DL-SCA Evaluation Model Architectures

As mentioned in Sect. 2.5, we use MLP and CNN architectures to evaluate the performance of the newly generated datasets using the cGAN model. The state-of-the-art DL-SCA model architectures for evaluating the original publicly available datasets [3,25,27] are used in the same setting except for the batch size and epochs, which are varied between 50–200 to see the impact on the results.

For evaluating the ASCAD dataset, the first architecture is an MLP-based network from [27]. The first CNN architecture is denoted as ASCAD-CNN1 [27], while the second one is denoted as ASCAD-CNN2 [3]. For evaluating the ECC dataset performance, we use the deep learning architecture presented in [25]. We use the existing state-of-the-art DL-SCA model architectures to allow fair comparison. What is more, the goal of this work is not to find new deep learning architectures but to enhance the performance of the existing architectures.

The performance of the DL-SCA trained models with the newly generated datasets is evaluated using two commonly used evaluation metrics: key rank and accuracy. Accuracy represents the number of correctly classified examples divided by the number of examples. Key rank is the position of the correct key guess in the key guessing vector. More precisely, this vector contains the key candidates in decreasing order of probability, and finding the position of the correct key indicates the effort required by the attacker to break the target.

5.2   Experimental Setup

The proposed GAN models have been developed and trained using Keras and Tensorflow libraries for our experiments. The models are trained to generate the fake data on a common computer equipped with 32 Gb RAM, i7-4770 CPU with

3.40 GHz, and Nvidia GTX 1080 Ti. The time required for fake data generation will vary depending on the number of classes and generated fake traces per class. The $Siamese-cGANModels$ training took less than 5 min to train and less than 5 min to generate 150 fake traces for 256 classes in total. For training a GAN model, real data traces are given as an input in the batches of 30 data traces, and the model is trained for 1 000 epochs.

We divide our experimental analysis into two sections.

- Analysis-1: first, in Sect. 5.3, we provide the visual representation of the trained cGAN models over 1 000 epochs. Visual representation helps identify the convergent model, which is then further selected for analysis in the second phase of analysis. We trained four cGAN models, out of which two are existing and two are newly proposed, based on the generator and discriminator as explained in Sect. 4.3. Details of the cGAN models are given in Table 2. We also provide the model convergence-based comparison of our proposed Siamese-cGAN-based model with the existing cGAN models [10].
- Analysis-2: second, in Sect. 5.4, we provide the deep learning-based side-channel analysis of two datasets; dataset containing real leakage signals only and the dataset consisting of both real and fake leakages, by training with two neural networks (MLP and CNN). We also compare generating leakage signals from the non-converging and converging networks for this analysis. To achieve this, we generated fake signals from various points while training the Siamese-cGAN network. More precisely, we generated the signals when the model converged the best and generated the signals when the model was the least convergent (initial epochs). Converging details of each model are given in the respective sections. This comparison is performed to highlight that not any cGAN can be selected blindly. *Only a well-convergent network will generate traces that are more alike in characteristics to that of original real traces.*

Table 2. cGAN Model Details

Model Name	Description
cGAN Model A	Model without CNN and Siamese network
cGAN Model B	Model with CNN but without Siamese network
Siamese − cGAN Model A	Model without CNN but with Siamese network
Siamese − cGAN Model B	Model with CNN and with Siamese network

5.3   Analysis-1: Existing and Proposed GAN-based Approaches

This section presents a convergence-based comparative analysis of our approach with the existing cGAN models. The existing cGAN networks (without layered Siamese-cGAN setting) are denoted as *CGAN Model A/B*, whereas our proposed models are denoted as $Siamese - cGAN\ Model\ A/B$. For this analysis, all four cGAN networks are trained with the $D_{Training}$ dataset and the GAN model loss for both AES and ECC, as shown in Figs. 2 and 3, respectively. Figure 2 a and b presents the real, fake, and GAN loss for training with $cGAN\ Model\ A$ and $cGAN\ Model\ B$ without Siamese settings, respectively. Next, Fig. 2 c and d presents the real, fake, and GAN loss for training with $Siamese - cGAN\ Model\ A$ and $Siamese - cGAN\ Model\ B$ with the Siamese setting. Similarly, Fig. 3 presents all four cGAN training models' loss for the ECC dataset.

$Siamese - cGAN$ and $cGAN$ models, for the ASCAD and ECC dataset analysis, are trained for 1 000 epochs, and history is recorded every ten epoch. Hence x-axis is scaled by 10. It can be seen that the proposed $Siamese - cGAN\ Model\ B$ architecture (based on CNN) provides the best loss convergence of real, fake, and GAN models as the models converge around 100–150 epochs and 700–1 000 epochs for AES and ECC datasets, respectively.

This shows that the generator started generating traces similar to the real traces at this convergence point, making it harder for the discriminator to discriminate between real and fake. Existing $cGAN\ Model\ A$ and $cGAN\ Model\ B$ without Siamese configuration did not converge well in 1 000 epochs. Moreover, for $Siamese - cGAN\ Model\ B$, GAN loss is high and quickly decreases in initial epochs. Hence, the proposed $Siamese - cGAN\ Model\ B$ is the robust solution for generating artificial/fake leakage signals for both algorithms as it converges better and faster than other cGAN models. Interestingly, $Siamese - cGAN\ Model\ A$ performs relatively poorly, indicating that the more powerful neural network architecture was required for this task. In conclusion, from this analysis, $Siamese - cGAN\ Model\ B$ is further selected to generate fake data in analysis phase 2.

5.4   Analysis-2: Analysis of the Proposed Siamese-CGAN for DL-SCA

Based on the results from the previous analysis, $Siamese - cGAN\ Model\ B$ is selected for further experiments in this section. Now, we perform DL-SCA (using MLP, ASCAD-CNN1, and ASCAD-CNN2) on the newly generated T_{GAN} (real+fake traces) datasets, generated using $Siamese - cGAN\ Model\ B$. However, we also analyzed the real dataset (with reduced traces per class). Hence, two datasets are formed: one with real traces only and the other (T_{GAN}) with both real and fake traces. For T_{GAN} datasets, two further datasets are formed, one for the fake data generated from the well-converged model and the second from the non-convergent model. Finally, we analyze how all these different settings impact the key rank of a side-channel attack.

Analysis on Real Traces. In our experiments, we reduced the size of the ASCAD and ECC leakage datasets intentionally to analyze the effect of the artificially generated traces on the small-size datasets. We selected $n_r = 150$ (for

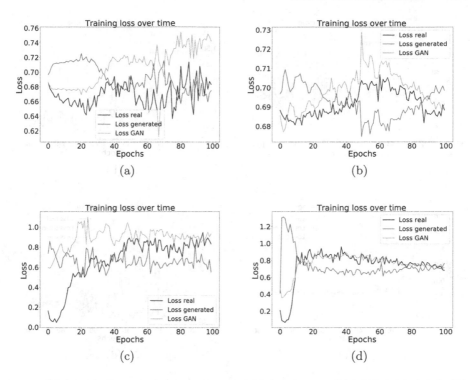

Fig. 2. CGAN Model Training Loss for the ASCAD dataset (a) *cGAN Model A*, (b) *cGAN Model B*, (c) *Siamese − cGAN Model A*, (d) *Siamese − cGAN Model B*

each class) leakage traces from the ASCAD and ECC datasets. The reason for selecting precisely 150 traces per class is because we wanted an equal number of real traces for all the classes. In the ASCAD dataset, class 213 has a minimum number of traces (154 traces); hence 150 is selected. No artificial/fake traces are included in the training dataset, so $n_g = 0$. Hence, total number of traces in AES and ECC datasets are 38 400 (150 traces × 256 classes) and 24 00 (150 traces × 16 classes), respectively. For deep learning-based attacks, we used the previously successful DL-SCA models for AES and ECC in respective studies [3, 25, 27].

The purpose of using the same deep learning-based models is to show that the artificially generated traces produce the same results as the real traces with the same model architectures. When considering the ASCAD-CNN1 architecture, everything stays the same as in previous studies' analysis except that we perform normalization on the training and test data. For normalization, each input variable feature is scaled in the range $[-1, 1]$ by using MinMaxScaler from the Sklearn library. For MLP, 10-fold cross-validation is performed. For ASCAD-CNN2 analysis, in addition to applying normalization, a standardization is added as per the proposed architecture in [3], and data is standardized around mean with a unit standard deviation (between 0 and 1) [45,46]. For ECC, the same model is used for training and test as proposed in [25].

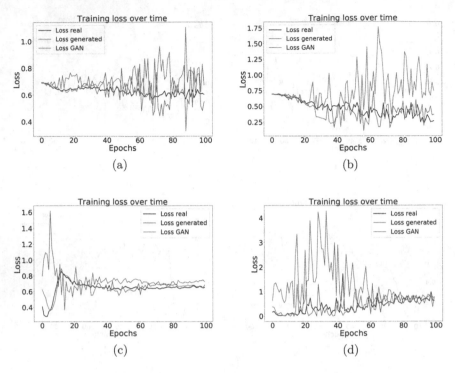

Fig. 3. cGAN Model Training Loss for the ECC dataset (a) *cGAN Model A*, (b) *cGAN Model B*, (c) *Siamese − cGAN Model A*, (d) *Siamese − cGAN Model B*

Figure 4 (a) shows the key rank for the real traces (38 400) dataset for the ASCAD dataset analysis using MLP and 10-fold cross-validation. We compare our results of reduced, original traces with the results of MLP_{best} reported in [27], which is plotted for the trained model on 50 000 traces. We can see a slight deviation though both figures are for the trained model on real traces. Figure 4 (b) shows the key rank on reduced ASCAD dataset trained using ASCAD-CNN2. It shows key rank not approaching zero in the first 1 000 traces. This confirms that the reduced dataset did not perform as expected with the existing models.

Figure 5 shows the accuracy for the real traces dataset for ECC dataset analysis using CNN architecture [3]. Raw, real data traces analysis for ECC shows that the private key can be recovered with 100% accuracy using CNN. It should be noted that preprocessing and alignment have not been applied to these datasets.

Analysis on Real and Generated Traces Dataset with the Maximum and Minimum Convergence. We introduce the terms maximum and minimum convergence for our analysis. Maximum convergence refers to the point (epochs) when a stable GAN model is achieved. Minimum convergence simply refers to the epochs when the GAN model is not stable, mostly in start epochs and often towards the end epochs as well. In certain failure modes or mode

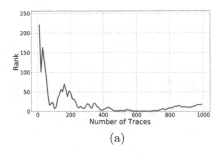 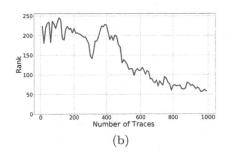

(a)   (b)

Fig. 4. Results for (a) Key rank for the ASCAD dataset having 38 400 profiling traces trained using MLP, and (b) Key rank for the ASCAD dataset having 38 400 profiling traces trained using ASCAD-CNN2

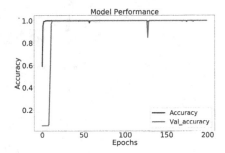

Fig. 5. Results for training and validation accuracy for the ECC dataset having 2 400 profiling traces

collapse scenarios, the GAN model stabilizes initially and might become unstable after a few epochs when the generator trains itself that it is hard to distinguish between the traces of different classes (meaning traces for all the classes look similar). The purpose of using these two types of analysis is to demonstrate that, in contrast to the non-convergent GAN model, the traces generated with the well convergent GAN model only produces traces similar in characteristics to the traces of the same class but different from the traces of the other classes.

For the GAN analysis, the training dataset consists of an equal proportion of the real traces and the artificially generated fake traces, that is, $n_r = 150$ and $n_g = 150$ per class, which means that in total, $300 \times 256 = 76\,800$ traces are in the dataset. Fake leakage signals are generated for the epochs during which the cGAN-Siamese model achieves maximum convergence. For the minimum convergence analysis, we combined the real traces with the artificially generated traces in equal proportion, the same as the maximum convergence case. However, traces are collected for the epochs during which the GAN model showed the minimum convergence.

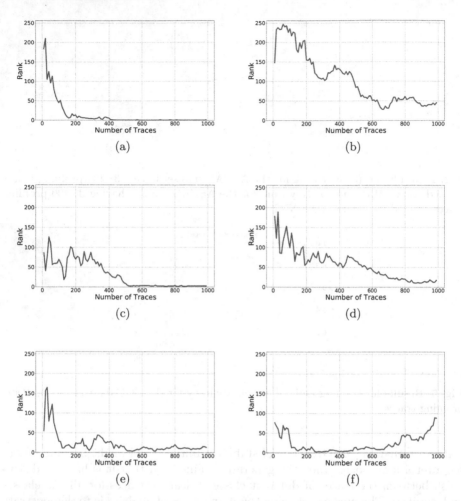

Fig. 6. Key rank for the ASCAD dataset for (a) Maximum convergence $cGAN - Siamese\ Model\ B$ using MLP, (b) Minimum convergence $cGAN - Siamese\ Model\ B$ using MLP, (c) Maximum convergence $cGAN - Siamese\ Model\ B$ using ASCAD-CNN1, (d) Minimum convergence $cGAN - Siamese\ Model\ B$ using ASCAD-CNN1, (e) Maximum convergence $cGAN - Siamese\ Model\ B$ using ASCAD-CNN2, (f) Minimum convergence $cGAN - Siamese\ Model\ B$ using ASCAD-CNN2

Figure 6 shows the key rank for both maximum and minimum convergence for all three DL-SCA models and the ASCAD dataset. We notice that generating fake traces from the maximum convergence point significantly impacts key rank. The maximum convergence is achieved around 100–150 epochs for $Siamese - cGAN\ Model\ B$. Hence, data traces are generated around those epochs for analysis. It is observed that with the generated traces, all models (MLP, ASCAD-CNN1, and ASCAD-CNN2) gave the best performance, and the secret key can be obtained efficiently. *Thus, we can conclude that the artificially generated traces contain significant information that improved the ML-SCA performance.*

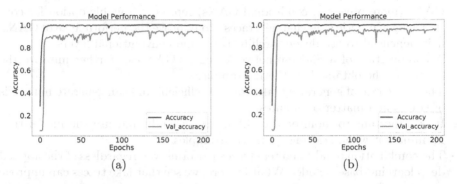

Fig. 7. Training and validation accuracy on the ECC dataset collected from (a) Maximum convergence point, (b) Minimum convergence point

The minimum convergence is observed around initial epochs, so artificial 150 traces per class are generated around this point and are combined with the real 150 traces to train the DL-SCA model. Observe that with minimum convergence, the DL-SCA attack model shows key rank is not stable, as it reaches zero in certain cases and starts increasing again as can be seen from Figs. 6b and 6f. However, for Fig. 6d (trained with ASCAD-CNN1), it appears to reach a key rank of zero near 1 000 traces, so more investigation is required to assess this case properly.

Figure 3 shows the GAN convergence curve for the ECC dataset. The model trained with the proposed *Siamese − cGAN Model B* shows a better convergence than the other three cGAN models' losses. The traces with the maximum convergence analysis are generated around epoch 700–1 000 (70–100 scaled in Fig. 3), and traces for the minimum convergence are generated around 20–30 epochs. The performance accuracy is high after adding artificial traces. The trained model with the artificial traces generated with the convergent model (Fig. 7a) shows accuracy greater than 97% using CNN, which is nearly the same accuracy as achieved on the real traces. However, the trained model with artificial traces, with the least convergent model, shows around 90% accuracy. While this performance is still good, we note that it cannot be compared with the performance on the real dataset. *Hence, the maximum convergent model generates the artificial traces that are more alike in characteristics to the real leakage traces and helps in training an efficient model for profiling side-channel analysis.*

5.5   Discussion

Based on the conducted experiments, we draw some general observations:

- GANs (more precisely, conditional GANs) represent a viable option for constructing synthetic side-channel traces. To improve the performance of GANs, it is beneficial to use deeper architectures and convolutional layers.
- A combination of a Siamese network and a cGAN can further improve the quality of the obtained synthetic examples.
- The procedure of generating fake traces is efficient and can generate hundreds of traces in a matter of minutes.
- It is important to monitor the GAN loss carefully and use the model that minimizes it when crafting synthetic examples.
- The combination of fake and real traces performs well regardless of the applied deep learning-based model. What is more, we see that fake traces can improve attack performance.
- It is possible to construct synthetic examples for various cryptographic implementations with similar success, i.e., this technique is not limited to a specific cryptographic implementation.

6   Conclusions and Future Work

A dataset of leakage traces with insufficient traces can pose a significant problem for accurate attack modeling using deep learning-based side-channel analysis. Data augmentation using a Generative Adversarial Network (GAN) can be useful for such scenarios. This work proposed a layered architecture (Siamese-cGAN) based on cGAN and Siamese network that presents a well-convergent model to generate artificial traces similar to real traces. We performed two sets of analyses. In the first set of analyses, we run the experiments and present a visual comparative analysis between the performance of the proposed model and the existing cGAN based models for leakage signal generation. For this analysis, two neural network-based models (MLP and CNN) have been used for modeling the generator and the discriminator networks. The best model is selected based on the comparative analysis. The second set of analyses evaluated the generated fake dataset by applying the DL-SCA on the leakage datasets from the exiting AES and ECC algorithm implementations. Four state-of-the-art neural network architectures (one MLP and three CNNs) are used for this evaluation. We also provided a comparative analysis of the dataset's performance consisting of data generated from the well-convergent network and data generated from the non-convergent network.

The proposed Siamese-cGAN model performed better than the existing simple cGAN models for both existing symmetric and public-key datasets. The quantitative analysis results show that the well-converged Siamese-cGAN network produces fake leakage traces similar to the collected traces. Hence, they enable a better deep learning-based model for side-channel attacks. We also observed that the CNN-trained models performed better than MLP for the key recovery. We conclude that leakage traces/instances with significant contributing features can be efficiently generated. However, selecting a fully converging model might vary for each cryptographic algorithm.

As future work, we plan to explore the limits of our approach from the perspective of the number of synthetic traces. Indeed, while our results indicate that 150 traces per class are more than sufficient to construct convincing synthetic data, understanding the minimum required number of traces would allow a proper evaluation of the method's viability. Furthermore, we used only the intermediate value leakage model, which results in more classes and balanced measurements per class. We plan to evaluate different leakage models like the Hamming weight model, resulting in imbalanced data and fewer classes. Finally, it would be interesting to explore if the GAN-based approach could generate measurements that would help reduce the effect of portability for deep learning-based SCA [47].

A   Appendix

A.1   Siamese-cGAN Model Architectures

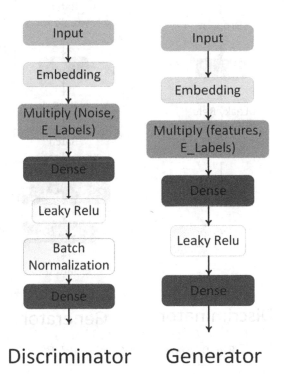

Fig. 8. *Siamese − cGAN Model A*

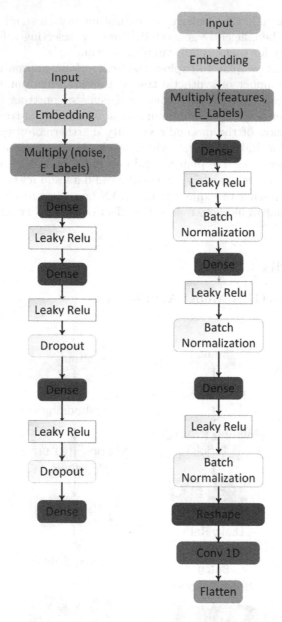

Discriminator   Generator

Fig. 9. *Siamese − cGAN Model B*

References

1. Maghrebi, H., Portigliatti, T., Prouff, E.: Breaking cryptographic implementations using deep learning techniques. In: Carlet, C., Hasan, M.A., Saraswat, V. (eds.) SPACE 2016. LNCS, vol. 10076, pp. 3–26. Springer, Cham (2016). https://doi.org/10.1007/978-3-319-49445-6_1

2. Kim, J., Picek, S., Heuser, A., Bhasin, S., Hanjalic, A.: Make some noise. Unleashing the power of convolutional neural networks for profiled side-channel analysis. IACR Trans. Cryptogr. Hardw. Embed. Syst. **2019**, 148–179 (2019)

3. Zaid, G., Bossuet, L., Habrard, A., Venelli, A.: Methodology for efficient CNN architectures in profiling attacks. IACR Trans. Cryptogr. Hardw. Embed. Syst. **2020**(1), 1–36 (2019)

4. Picek, S., Heuser, A., Guilley, S.: Profiling side-channel analysis in the restricted attacker framework. IACR Cryptology ePrint Archive **2019**, 168 (2019)

5. Picek, S., Heuser, A., Jovic, A., Bhasin, S., Regazzoni, F.: The curse of class imbalance and conflicting metrics with machine learning for side-channel evaluations. IACR Trans. Cryptogr. Hardw. Embed. Syst. **2019**(1), 209–237 (2018)

6. Cagli, E., Dumas, C., Prouff, E.: Convolutional neural networks with data augmentation against jitter-based countermeasures. In: Fischer, W., Homma, N. (eds.) CHES 2017. LNCS, vol. 10529, pp. 45–68. Springer, Cham (2017). https://doi.org/10.1007/978-3-319-66787-4_3

7. Luo, Z., Zheng, M., Wang, P., Jin, M., Zhang, J., Hu, H.: Towards strengthening deep learning-based side channel attacks with mixup. Cryptology ePrint Archive, Report 2021/312 (2021). https://eprint.iacr.org/2021/312

8. Liu, M.-Y., Huang, X., Yu, J., Wang, T.-C., Mallya, A.: Generative adversarial networks for image and video synthesis: algorithms and applications. CoRR, abs/2008.02793 (2020)

9. Goodfellow, I.J., et al.: Generative adversarial nets. In: Proceedings of the 27th International Conference on Neural Information Processing Systems - Volume 2, NIPS 2014, pp. 2672–2680. MIT Press, Cambridge (2014)

10. Wang, P., et al.: Enhancing the performance of practical profiling side-channel attacks using conditional generative adversarial networks (2020)

11. Kodali, N., Abernethy, J., Hays, J., Kira, Z.: On convergence and stability of GANs (2017)

12. Salimans, T., Goodfellow, I.J., Zaremba, W., Cheung, V., Radford, A., Chen, X.: Improved techniques for training GANs. CoRR, abs/1606.03498 (2016)

13. Mirza, M., Osindero, S.: Conditional generative adversarial nets. CoRR, abs/1411.1784 (2014)

14. Hsu, C.-C., Lin, C.-W., Su, W.-T., Cheung, G.: SiGAN: siamese generative adversarial network for identity-preserving face hallucination. CoRR, abs/1807.08370 (2018)

15. Perin, G., Chmielewski, L., Batina, L., Picek, S.: Keep it unsupervised: horizontal attacks meet deep learning. IACR Trans. Cryptogr. Hardw. Embed. Syst. **2021**(1), 343–372 (2021)

16. Chari, S., Rao, J.R., Rohatgi, P.: Template attacks. In: Kaliski, B.S., Koç, K., Paar, C. (eds.) CHES 2002. LNCS, vol. 2523, pp. 13–28. Springer, Heidelberg (2003). https://doi.org/10.1007/3-540-36400-5_3

17. Whitnall, C., Oswald, E., Standaert, F.-X.: The myth of generic DPA...and the magic of learning. In: Benaloh, J. (ed.) CT-RSA 2014. LNCS, vol. 8366, pp. 183–205. Springer, Cham (2014). https://doi.org/10.1007/978-3-319-04852-9_10

18. Schindler, W., Lemke, K., Paar, C.: A stochastic model for differential side channel cryptanalysis. In: Rao, J.R., Sunar, B. (eds.) CHES 2005. LNCS, vol. 3659, pp. 30–46. Springer, Heidelberg (2005). https://doi.org/10.1007/11545262_3

19. Lerman, L., Bontempi, G., Markowitch, O.: Power analysis attack: an approach based on machine learning. Int. J. Appl. Cryptol. **3**(2), 97–115 (2014)

20. Radford, A., Metz, L., Chintala, S.: Unsupervised representation learning with deep convolutional generative adversarial networks. In: Bengio, Y., LeCun, Y. (eds.) 4th International Conference on Learning Representations, ICLR 2016, San Juan, Puerto Rico, 2–4 May 2016, Conference Track Proceedings (2016)

21. Chen, X., Duan, Y., Houthooft, R., Schulman, J., Sutskever, I., Abbeel, P.: InfoGAN: interpretable representation learning by information maximizing generative adversarial nets. In: Lee, D.D., Sugiyama, M., Luxburg, U.V., Guyon, I., Garnett, R. (eds.) Advances in Neural Information Processing Systems, vol. 29, pp. 2172–2180. Curran Associates Inc. (2016)

22. Zhang, H., et al.: StackGAN: text to photo-realistic image synthesis with stacked generative adversarial networks. In: 2017 IEEE International Conference on Computer Vision (ICCV), pp. 5908–5916 (2017)

23. Brock, A., Donahue, J., Simonyan, K.: Large scale GAN training for high fidelity natural image synthesis. CoRR, abs/1809.11096 (2018)

24. Shorten, C., Khoshgoftaar, T.M.: A survey on image data augmentation for deep learning. J. Big Data **6**(1), 60 (2019)

25. Weissbart, L., Picek, S., Batina, L.: One trace is all it takes: machine learning-based side-channel attack on EdDSA. In: Bhasin, S., Mendelson, A., Nandi, M. (eds.) SPACE 2019. LNCS, vol. 11947, pp. 86–105. Springer, Cham (2019). https://doi.org/10.1007/978-3-030-35869-3_8

26. Mukhtar, N., Mehrabi, A., Kong, Y., Anjum, A.: Machine-learning-based side-channel evaluation of elliptic-curve cryptographic FPGA processor. Appl. Sci. **9**, 64 (2018)

27. Benadjila, R., Prouff, E., Strullu, R., Cagli, E., Dumas, C.: Deep learning for side-channel analysis and introduction to ASCAD database. J. Cryptogr. Eng. **10**(2), 163–188 (2019). https://doi.org/10.1007/s13389-019-00220-8

28. Koch, G., Zemel, R., Salakhutdinov, R.: Siamese neural networks for one-shot image recognition (2015)

29. Leyva-Vallina, M., Strisciuglio, N., Petkov, N.: Generalized contrastive optimization of Siamese networks for place recognition. CoRR, abs/2103.06638 (2021)

30. Chicco, D.: Siamese neural networks: an overview. In: Cartwright, H. (ed.) Artificial Neural Networks. MMB, vol. 2190, pp. 73–94. Springer, New York (2021). https://doi.org/10.1007/978-1-0716-0826-5_3

31. Database for EdDSA (2019). https://github.com/leoweissbart/MachineLearningBasedSideChannelAttackonEdDSA

32. Wouters, L., Arribas, V., Gierlichs, B., Preneel, B.: Revisiting a methodology for efficient CNN architectures in profiling attacks. IACR Trans. Cryptogr. Hardw. Embed. Syst. **2020**(3), 147–168 (2020)

33. Rijsdijk, J., Lichao, W., Perin, G., Picek, S.: Reinforcement learning for hyperparameter tuning in deep learning-based side-channel analysis. IACR Trans. Cryptogr. Hardw. Embed. Syst. **2021**(3), 677–707 (2021)

34. Lichao, W., Picek, S.: Remove some noise: on pre-processing of side-channel measurements with autoencoders. IACR Trans. Cryptogr. Hardw. Embed. Syst. **2020**(4), 389–415 (2020)

35. Medwed, M., Oswald, E.: Template attacks on ECDSA. In: Chung, K.-I., Sohn, K., Yung, M. (eds.) WISA 2008. LNCS, vol. 5379, pp. 14–27. Springer, Heidelberg (2009). https://doi.org/10.1007/978-3-642-00306-6_2

36. Heyszl, J., Mangard, S., Heinz, B., Stumpf, F., Sigl, G.: Localized electromagnetic analysis of cryptographic implementations. In: Dunkelman, O. (ed.) CT-RSA 2012. LNCS, vol. 7178, pp. 231–244. Springer, Heidelberg (2012). https://doi.org/10.1007/978-3-642-27954-6_15

37. Batina, L., Chmielewski, Ł., Papachristodoulou, L., Schwabe, P., Tunstall, M.: Online template attacks. In: Meier, W., Mukhopadhyay, D. (eds.) INDOCRYPT 2014. LNCS, vol. 8885, pp. 21–36. Springer, Cham (2014). https://doi.org/10.1007/978-3-319-13039-2_2

38. Batina, L., Chmielewski, Ł., Papachristodoulou, L., Schwabe, P., Tunstall, M.: Online template attacks. J. Cryptogr. Eng. 9(1), 21–36 (2019)

39. Özgen, E., Papachristodoulou, L., Batina, L.: Classification algorithms for template matching. In: IEEE International Symposium on Hardware Oriented Security and Trust, HOST 2016, McLean, VA, USA (2016)

40. Roelofs, N., Samwel, N., Batina, L., Daemen, J.: Online template attack on ECDSA: In: Nitaj, A., Youssef, A. (eds.) AFRICACRYPT 2020. LNCS, vol. 12174, pp. 323–336. Springer, Cham (2020). https://doi.org/10.1007/978-3-030-51938-4_16

41. Carbone, M., et al.: Deep learning to evaluate secure RSA implementations. IACR Trans. Cryptogr. Hardw. Embed. Syst. 2019(2), 132–161 (2019)

42. Weissbart, L., Chmielewski, Ł., Picek, S., Batina, L.: Systematic side-channel analysis of curve25519 with machine learning. J. Hardware Syst. Secur. 4(4), 314–328 (2020)

43. Zaid, G., Bossuet, L., Habrard, A., Venelli, A.: Efficiency through diversity in ensemble models applied to side-channel attacks: - a case study on public-key algorithms -. IACR Trans. Cryptogr. Hardw. Embed. Syst. 2021(3), 60–96 (2021)

44. Wu, C., Herranz, L., Liu, X., Wang, Y., van de Weijer, J., Raducanu, B.: Memory replay GANs: learning to generate images from new categories without forgetting (2019)

45. Goodfellow, I., Bengio, Y., Courville, A.: Deep Learning. MIT Press (2016). http://www.deeplearningbook.org

46. LeCun, Y.A., Bottou, L., Orr, G.B., Müller, K.-R.: Efficient BackProp. In: Montavon, G., Orr, G.B., Müller, K.-R. (eds.) Neural Networks: Tricks of the Trade. LNCS, vol. 7700, pp. 9–48. Springer, Heidelberg (2012). https://doi.org/10.1007/978-3-642-35289-8_3

47. Bhasin, S., Chattopadhyay, A., Heuser, A., Jap, D., Picek, S., Shrivastwa, R.R.: Mind the portability: a warriors guide through realistic profiled side-channel analysis. In: 27th Annual Network and Distributed System Security Symposium, NDSS 2020, San Diego, California, USA, 23–26 February 2020. The Internet Society (2020)

A New Adaptive Attack on SIDH

Tako Boris Fouotsa[1]([⊠]) and Christophe Petit[2,3]([⊠])

[1] Università Degli Studi Roma Tre, Rome, Italy
takoboris.fouotsa@uniroma3.it
[2] Université Libre de Bruxelles, Brussels, Belgium
christophe.petit@ulb.be
[3] School of Computer Science, University of Birmingham, Birmingham, UK

Abstract. The SIDH key exchange is the main building block of SIKE, the only isogeny based scheme involved in the NIST standardization process. In 2016, Galbraith et al. presented an adaptive attack on SIDH. In this attack, a malicious party manipulates the torsion points in his public key in order to recover an honest party's static secret key, when having access to a key exchange oracle. In 2017, Petit designed a passive attack (which was improved by de Quehen et al. in 2020) that exploits the torsion point information available in SIDH public key to recover the secret isogeny when the endomorphism ring of the starting curve is known.

In this paper, firstly, we generalize the torsion point attacks by de Quehen et al. Secondly, we introduce a new adaptive attack vector on SIDH-type schemes. Our attack uses the access to a key exchange oracle to recover the action of the secret isogeny on larger subgroups. This leads to an unbalanced SIDH instance for which the secret isogeny can be recovered in polynomial time using the generalized torsion point attacks. Our attack is different from the GPST adaptive attack and constitutes a new cryptanalytic tool for isogeny based cryptography. This result proves that the torsion point attacks are relevant to SIDH (Disclaimer: this result is applicable to SIDH-type schemes only, not to SIKE.) parameters in an adaptive attack setting. We suggest attack parameters for some SIDH primes and discuss some countermeasures.

Keywords: Post-quantum cryptography · Cryptanalysis · Adaptive attacks · SIDH

1 Introduction

The first isogeny-based cryptographic schemes are the CGL (Charles-Goren-Lauter) hash function [5] and the CRS (Couveignes-Rostovtsev-Stolbunov) key exchange [10,30]. The CRS scheme is a Diffie-Hellman type key exchange scheme using ordinary isogenies of elliptic curves. It is vulnerable to a sub-exponential quantum hidden shift like attack [6] and is not practically efficient.

In 2011, Jao and De Feo proposed SIDH [15,23] that uses isogenies of super-singular elliptic curves. SIDH is efficient and it is not vulnerable to the sub-exponential quantum attack presented in [6]. Nevertheless, a recent paper by

© The Author(s), under exclusive license to Springer Nature Switzerland AG 2022
S. D. Galbraith (Ed.): CT-RSA 2022, LNCS 13161, pp. 322–344, 2022.
https://doi.org/10.1007/978-3-030-95312-6_14

Kutas et al. [25] proves that hidden shift like attacks apply to variants of SIDH with considerably overstretched parameters. The problem of computing isogenies between given supersingular elliptic curves is somehow new in cryptography. Its relation with the supersingular endomorphism ring computation problem have been studied in [12,29]. A rigorous proof of the equivalence between the two problems was recently proposed by Wesolowski [37].

Contrarily to the ordinary case where isogenies commute, supersingular isogenies do not commute in general. In order to solve this issue in SIDH, the images of some well-chosen torsion points trough the secret isogeny are computed and included in the public keys. This implies that the hard problem underlying the security of SIDH is different from the general supersingular isogeny problem. Moreover, this torsion points have been used in designing adaptive and passive attacks on SIDH and/or its (unbalanced) variants.

The most relevant adaptive attack (excluding side channel attacks) on SIDH is due to Galbraith, Petit, Shani and Ti (GPST) [19]. They suppose that one honest party Alice uses a static secret key, and the other malicious party Bob performs multiple key exchanges with Alice. The main idea of the attack is that Bob replaces the images of the torsion points in his public key by malicious ones and obtains some information on Alice's static secret isogeny when looking at the obtained shared secret. Repeating this process a polynomial number of times, Bob totally recovers Alice's private key. The pairing-based key validation method present in SIDH does not detect the GPST adaptive attack. In SIKE [22] (Supersingular Isogeny Key Encapsulation), the GPST adaptive attack is avoided by leveraging SIDH with a variant [21] of the Fujisaki-Okamoto transform [17].

The first passive torsion points attacks are due to Petit [28] and were recently improved by de Quehen et al. [11]. These attacks combine the availability of the endomorphism ring of the starting curve E_0 in SIDH and the torsion point information available in SIDH public keys, to compute a suitable endomorphism of Alice's public curve E_A. The secret isogeny is then recovered using the later endomorphism. For sufficiently unbalanced SIDH parameters (the degrees of the secret isogenies of the parties are of different size), the latest version of the attack [11] is more efficient compared to the generic meet in the middle and the van-Oorschot - Wiener (vOW) attack [35]. For balanced parameters (the degrees of the secret isogenies of both parties are approximately of the same size), the quantum version of the attack is as efficient as the best known quantum attacks [11, Figure 1]. Other passive attacks exploiting the availability of torsion points in the public key are described in [16,25].

The improved torsion points attacks do not apply to SIKE and BSIDH [7] parameters since these parameters are balanced. Therefore, one may argue that they are not relevant to SIDH, BSIDH or any other SIDH like schemes using balanced isogenies degrees.

Contributions. The contribution of this paper is twofold.

First, we revisit the torsion point attacks. The torsion point attacks are used to recover a secret isogeny $\phi : E_0 \rightarrow E$ of degree N_A when the images of torsion points of order N_B in E_0 are provided. We prove that one can tweak the algorithm in such a way that it recovers ϕ when only the images of three cyclic disjoint groups $G_1, G_3, G_3 \subset E_0[N_B]$ of order N_B are provided. This constitutes a generalisation of the torsion point attacks and will be useful in the design of our adaptive attack.

Secondly, we design a new adaptive attack on SIDH-types schemes, including BSIDH. Our attack uses torsion point attacks as a subroutine.

Let $\phi_A : E_0 \to E_A$ be Alice's secret static isogeny in an SIDH instance. Let N_A and N_B be the isogeny degrees of Alice and Bob respectively. Our attack actively recovers the images through ϕ_A of three cyclic disjoint groups $G_1, G_3, G_3 \subset E_0[NN_B]$ of order $N_B N$ where N is a well chosen integer coprime to N_A. This leads to an unbalanced SIDH instance for which the torsion point attacks can be used to recover the secret isogeny in polynomial time.

Our attack differs from the GPST adaptive attack as follows. In the GPST adaptive attack, the malicious Bob computes isogenies of correct degrees N_B and manipulates torsion point images. Our attack consists of computing isogenies of degrees larger than N_B and scaling the torsion point images by a suitable scalar to make the public key pass the pairing-based key validation method in SIDH. One then utilises the torsion point attack to recover the secret.

We prove that our attack runs in polynomial time. We provide specific attack parameters for SIDH primes $IDHp182, $IDHp217, SIDHp377, SIDHp434, SIDHp503 and SIDHp546. For these SIDH primes, the attack fully recovers Bob's secret isogeny querying a few tens of thousand times the key exchange key exchange oracle. Determining specific attack parameters for BSIDH primes is computationally intensive. We only give an example of generic attack parameters for the smallest BSIDH prime. We suggest countermeasures among which the Fujisaki-Okamoto transform (as used in SIKE), using SIDH proof of isogeny knowledge as recently proposed in [14] or setting the starting curve in SIDH to be a random supersingular curve with unknown endomorphism ring.

The torsion point attacks do not apply to SIDH parameters [11, §1.1 Fig. 1] since they do not (yet) outperform generic passive attacks such as the meet in the middle on SIDH parameters. This attack comes as an ice breaker. This result, despite being less efficient when compared to the GPST adaptive attack, it proves that the torsion point attacks become relevant to SIDH and BSIDH parameters in an adaptive attack setting. Moreover, this attack vector is the first of its kind. It exploits the fact that in an SIDH instance, the pairing check does not suffices to convince Alice that Bob effectively computed an isogeny of degree N_B. We believe this attack fosters the understanding of SIDH and is a new cryptanalytic tool for isogeny based cryptography.

Outline. The remaining of this paper is organized as follows: in Sect. 2, we recall some generalities about elliptic curves and isogenies. We briefly present SIDH and the GPST adaptive attack. In Sect. 3, we present the torsion point attacks and describe our generalisation. In Sect. 4 we present an overview of our attack and describe the active phase. We also discuss the computation of the attack parameters and summarize the attack. In Sect. 5, we suggest attack parameters for some SIDH primes and we briefly describe some countermeasures. We conclude the paper in Sect. 6.

2 Preliminaries

2.1 Elliptic Curves and Isogenies

An elliptic curve is a rational smooth curve of genus one with a distinguished point at infinity. Elliptic curves can be seen as commutative groups with respect to a group addition having the point at infinity as neutral element. When an elliptic curve E is defined over a finite field $\mathbb{F}_q$, the set of $\mathbb{F}_q$-rational points $E(\mathbb{F}_q)$ of E is a subgroup of E. For every integer N coprime with q, the N-torsion subgroup $E[N]$ of E is isomorphic to $\mathbb{Z}_N \oplus \mathbb{Z}_N$.

An isogeny from E to E' is a rational map from E to E' which is also a group morphism. The kernel of an isogeny is always finite and entirely defines the isogeny up to powers of the Frobenius. Given a finite subgroup G of E, there exists a Frobenius free isogeny of domain E having kernel G, called a separable isogeny. Its degree is equal to the size of its kernel. The co-domain of this isogeny is denoted by E/G. The isogeny and the co-domain E/G can be computed from the knowledge of the kernel using Vélu's formulas [33] whose efficiency depends on the smoothness of the isogeny degree.

An endomorphism of an elliptic curve E is an isogeny from E to E. The structure of E is closely related to that of its endomorphism ring. When E is defined over a finite field, the endomorphism ring of E is either an order in a quadratic field, in which case we say E is ordinary, or a maximal order in a quaternion algebra in which case we say E is supersingular. The generic isogeny problem is harder to solve for supersingular curves (for which the best attacks are exponential) than ordinary curves (for which there exists a sub-exponential attack [3]). SIDH is based on supersingular isogenies.

We refer to the book of Washington [36] and the book of Silverman [32] for more background on elliptic curves and isogenies. For a quick introduction to isogeny-based cryptography, we recommend these notes [13] from De Feo.

2.2 SIDH: Supersingular Isogeny Diffie-Hellman

The SIDH scheme is defined as follows.

Setup. Let $p = \ell_A^{e_A} \ell_B^{e_B} - 1$ be a prime such that $\ell_A^{e_A} \approx \ell_B^{e_B} \approx \sqrt{p}$. Let E_0 be a supersingular curve defined over $\mathbb{F}_{p^2}$. Set $E_0[\ell_A^{e_A}] = \langle P_A, Q_A \rangle$ and $E_0[\ell_B^{e_B}] = \langle P_B, Q_B \rangle$. The public parameters are E_0, p, ℓ_A, ℓ_B, e_A, e_B, P_A, Q_A, P_B, Q_B.

KeyGeneration. The secret key sk_A of Alice is a uniformly random integer α sampled from $\mathbb{Z}_{\ell_A^{e_A}}$. Compute the cyclic isogeny $\phi_A : E_0 \to E_A = E_0/\langle P_A + [\alpha]Q_A \rangle$. The public key of Alice is the tuple $\mathsf{pk}_A = (E_A, \phi_A(P_B), \phi_A(Q_B))$. Analogously, Bob's secret key sk_B is a uniformly random integer β sampled from $\mathbb{Z}_{\ell_B^{e_B}}$ and his public key is $\mathsf{pk}_B = (E_B, \phi_B(P_A), \phi_B(Q_A))$ where $\phi_B : E_0 \to E_B = E_0/\langle P_B + [\beta]Q_B \rangle$.

KeyExchange. Upon receiving Bob's public key (E_B, R_a, S_a), Alice checks[1] that $e(R_a, S_a) = e(P_A, Q_A)^{\ell_B^{e_B}}$, if not she aborts. She computes the isogeny $\phi_A' : E_B \rightarrow E_{BA} = E_B/\langle R_a + [\alpha]S_a\rangle$. Her shared key is $j(E_{BA})$. Similarly, upon receiving (E_A, R_b, S_b), Bob checks that $e(R_b, S_b) = e(P_B, Q_B)^{\ell_A^{e_A}}$, if not he aborts. He computes the isogeny $\phi_B' : E_A \rightarrow E_{AB} = E_A/\langle R_b + [\beta]S_b\rangle$. His shared key is $j(E_{AB})$.

The correctness of the key exchange follows from the fact that

$$E_A/\langle \phi_A(P_B) + [\beta]\phi_A(Q_B)\rangle \simeq E_0/\langle P_A + [\alpha]Q_A, P_B + [\beta]Q_B\rangle \simeq E_B/\langle \phi_B(P_A) + [\alpha]\phi_B(Q_A)\rangle.$$

The scheme is summarized in Fig. 1.

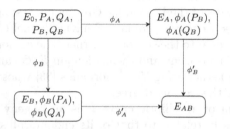

Fig. 1. SIDH key exchange

The security of the SIDH key exchange protocol against shared key recovery relies on Problem 1. Furthermore, Problem 2 states that it is difficult to distinguish the shared secret from a random supersingular elliptic curve.

Problem 1 (Supersingular Isogeny Computational Diffie-Hellman). Given E_0, P_A, Q_A, P_B, Q_B, E_A, $\phi_A(P_B)$, $\phi_A(Q_B)$, E_B, $\phi_B(P_A)$, $\phi_B(Q_A)$ (defined as in SIDH), compute E_{AB}.

Problem 2 (Supersingular Isogeny Decisional Diffie-Hellman). Given E_0, P_A, Q_A, P_B, Q_B, E_A, $\phi_A(P_B)$, $\phi_A(Q_B)$, E_B, $\phi_B(P_A)$, $\phi_B(Q_A)$ (defined as in SIDH) and a random supersingular curve E, distinguish between $E = E_{AB}$ and $E \neq E_{AB}$.

In the rest of this paper, we denote by N_A and N_B the degree of Alice's and Bob's isogeny respectively.

2.3   GPST Adaptive Attack

In SIDH [15] one does a pairing-based check on the torsion points $\phi_B(P_A)$ and $\phi_B(Q_A)$ returned by a potentially malicious Bob. Let E be a supersingular elliptic curve, let N be an integer and let μ_N be the group of N-roots of unity.

---

[1] Note that in the original SIDH [23], this pairing check is not part of the scheme. But, as precised in [9] and [19], one includes the check to discard some malformed public keys.

Let $e_N : E[N] \times E[N] \to \mu_N$ be the Weil pairing [18]. Let $\phi : E \to E'$ be an isogeny of degree M, then for $P, Q \in E[N]$,

$$e_N(\phi(P), \phi(Q)) = e_N(P, Q)^M$$

where the first pairing is computed on E' and the second one on E.

In SIDH, given (E_B, R_a, S_a) returned by Bob as public key, Alice checks if

$$e_{\ell_A^{e_A}}(R_a, S_a) = e_{\ell_A^{e_A}}(P_A, Q_A)^{\ell_B^{e_B}}.$$

As we will see below, this verification does not assure that the points R, S were honestly generated. More precisely, the pairing verification does not capture the GPST adaptive attack.

The GPST Adaptive Attack. The main idea of the Galbraith et al. adaptive attack [19] is that if Bob manipulates the torsion points $\phi_B(P_A)$ and $\phi_B(Q_A)$ conveniently, then he can get some information about Alice's private key α given that he knows if the secret curve computed by Alice is equal to E_{AB} or not. Hence in the attack scenario, Bob needs to have access to the later information. This access is provided to Bob through a key exchange oracle:

$O(E, R, S, E')$ which returns 1 if $j(E') = j(E/\langle R + [\alpha]S \rangle)$ and 0 otherwise

If one supposes that $\ell_A = 2$ and $e_A = n$, then after each query, Bob recovers one bit of
$$\alpha = \alpha_0 + 2^1 \alpha_1 + 2^2 \alpha_2 + \cdots + 2^{n-1} \alpha_{n-1}.$$

Concretely, let us suppose that Bob has successfully recovered the first i bits of α, say $K_i = \alpha_0 + 2^1 \alpha_1 + \cdots + 2^{i-1} \alpha_{i-1}$ so that

$$\alpha = K_i + 2^i \alpha_i + 2^{i+1} \alpha'$$

He generates $(E_B, \phi_B(P_A), \phi_B(Q_A))$ and computes the resulting key E_{AB}. To recover α_i, he chooses suitable integers a, b, c, d and queries the oracle O on (E_B, R, S, E_{AB}) where $R = [a]\phi_B(P_A) + [b]\phi_B(Q_A)$ and $S = [c]\phi_B(P_A) + [d]\phi_B(Q_A)$. The integers a, b, c and d are chosen to satisfy the following conditions:

1. if $\alpha_i = 1$, $\langle R + [\alpha]S \rangle = \langle \phi_B(P_A) + [\alpha]\phi_B(Q_A) \rangle$;
2. if $\alpha_i = 0$, $\langle R + [\alpha]S \rangle \neq \langle \phi_B(P_A) + [\alpha]\phi_B(Q_A) \rangle$;
3. the Weil paring $e_{2^n}(R, S)$ must be equal to $e_{2^n}(\phi_B(P_A), \phi_B(Q_A))$

The first two conditions help to distinguish the bit α_i. The third one prevents the attack from being detected by the pairing-based check presented in Sect. 2.3. When attacking the ith bit of alpha where $1 \leq i \leq n - 2$, the attack uses the integers

$$a = \theta, \quad b = -\theta 2^{n-i-1} K_i, \quad c = 0, \quad d = \theta(1 + K_i 2^{n-i-1})$$

where $\theta = \sqrt{(1 + 2^{n-i-1})-1}$. The attack recovers the first $n - 2$ bits of α using $n - 2$ oracle queries, and it recovers the two remaining bits by brute force. We refer to [19] for more details.

The GPST adaptive attack exploits the fact that the pairing check does not convince Alice that the torsion points returned by Bob were honestly computed. In the rest of this paper, we will design a new adaptive attack that exploits the fact that the pairing check does not convince Alice that Bob effectively computed an isogeny of degree N_B.

3 Generalizing Torsion Points Attacks

In this section, we revisit the torsion point attacks. Firstly, we describe the torsion point attacks. Next, we provide a generalisation of these attacks that can be used to solve weaker version of the key recovery problem in SIDH (Problem 3, described below).

3.1 Torsion Points Attacks on SIDH

The direct key recovery attack (attacking one party's secret key) in SIDH translates into solving the following *Computational Supersingular Isogeny Problem.*

Problem 3. Let N_A and N_B be two smooth[2] integers such that $\gcd(N_A, N_B) = 1$. Let E_0 be a supersingular elliptic curve defined over $\mathbb{F}_{p^2}$. Set $E_0[N_B] = \langle P, Q \rangle$ and let $\phi : E_0 \to E$ be a random isogeny of degree N_A. Given E_0, E, P, Q, $\phi(P)$ and $\phi(Q)$, compute ϕ.

The difference between Problem 3 and the general isogeny problem is the fact that the action of ϕ on the group $E_0[N_B]$ is revealed. In 2017, Petit [28] exploited these torsion point images and the knowledge of the endomorphism ring of the starting curve E_0 to design an algorithm that solves Problem 3 for a certain choice of unbalanced ($N_A \ll N_B$) parameters. Petit's attack has recently been considerably improved by de Quehen et al. [11].

The idea of the torsion points attacks is to find a trace 0 endomorphism $\theta \in \text{End}(E_0)$ that can be efficiently evaluated on $E_0[N_B]$, an integer d and a small smooth integer e such that

$$N_A^2 \deg \theta + d^2 = N_B^2 e. \tag{1}$$

Writing Eq. 1 in terms of isogenies we get

$$\phi \circ \theta \circ \widehat{\phi} + [d] = \psi_2 \circ \psi_e \circ \psi_1 \tag{2}$$

where ψ_1 and ψ_2 are isogenies of degree N_B, ψ_e is an isogeny of degree e. The torsion point information $\phi(P)$, $\phi(Q)$ is used to evaluate $\tau = \phi \circ \theta \circ \widehat{\phi} + [d]$ on

---

[2] In all this paper, an integer is said to be smooth if it is b-smooth for some integer $b \approx O(\log p)$ where p is the characteristic of the base field considered.

$E[N_B]$. Knowing τ on $E_0[N_B]$, the kernels of the isogenies $\psi_1 : E \to E_1$ and $\widehat{\psi_2} : E \to E_2$ can be recovered efficiently. The isogeny $\psi_e : E_1 \to E_2$ is recovered by brute force or meet in the middle. We refer to [11, § 4.1] for technical details.

Having computed $\psi_2 \circ \psi_e \circ \psi_1$, one recovers

$$\ker \widehat{\phi} = \ker (\psi_2 \circ \psi_e \circ \psi_1 - [d]) \cap E[N_A].$$

Figure 2 illustrates the attack.

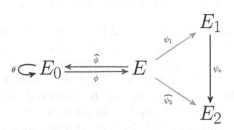

Fig. 2. Improved torsion points attack.

The efficiency of torsion point attacks mostly depends on the imbalance between the isogeny degree N_A and the order N_B of the torsion points images.

de Quehen et al. [11] show that under some heuristics, when $j(E_0) = 1728$, Problem 3 can be solved in:

1. Polynomial time when: $N_B > pN_A$ and $p > N_A$;
2. Superpolynomial time but asymptotically more efficient than meet-in-the-middle on a classical computer when: $N_B > \sqrt{p}N_A$;
3. Superpolynomial time but asymptotically more efficient than quantum claw-finding [24] when: $N_B > \max\{N_A, \sqrt{p}\}$.

More concretely, if $N_A \approx p^\alpha$ and $N_B \approx N_A p^\eta$, then the improved torsion points attack runs in time $\tilde{O}\left(N_A^{\frac{1+2(\alpha-\eta)}{4\alpha}}\right)$ and $\tilde{O}\left(N_A^{\frac{1+2(\alpha-\eta)}{8\alpha}}\right)$ on a classical computer and a quantum computer respectively [11, §6.2 Proposition 27]. In the special case where $\alpha = \frac{1}{2}$, we get the following corollary.

Corollary 1. *Suppose that $N_A \approx p^{\frac{1}{2}}$ and $N_B \approx p^{\frac{1}{2}+\eta}$ where $1 \leq \eta$. Under some heuristics, [11, Algorithm 7] solves Problem 3 in polynomial time when $j(E_0) = 1728$.*

Remark 1. SIKE parameters (for which E_0 is close to a curve having j-invariant 1728 and $N_A \approx N_B \approx \sqrt{p}$) are not affected by these improved torsion points attacks. Also, the attack does not affect any SIDH-type scheme in which the starting curve E_0 is a random supersingular curve with unknown endomorphism ring.

In our attack setting, we will not be provided with the images of torsion points through isogenies, but with the images of cyclic torsion groups. In the next section, we generalize the torsion point attacks such that they directly apply to our setting.

3.2 Generalized Torsion Points Attacks

We consider the following problem.

Problem 4. Let N_A and N_B be two integers such that $\gcd(N_A, N_B) = 1$. Let E_0 be a supersingular elliptic curve defined over $\mathbb{F}_{p^2}$. Let G_1, G_2, G_3 be three cyclic groups of E_0 of order N_B such that $G_1 \cap G_2 = G_1 \cap G_3 = G_2 \cap G_3 = \{0\}$. Let $\phi : E_0 \to E$ be a random isogeny of degree N_A.
  Given $E_0, G_1, G_2, G_3, E, \phi(G_1), \phi(G_2)$ and $\phi(G_3)$, compute ϕ.

The difference between Problem 4 and Problem 3 is the way the torsion point information is provided. In Problem 3, image points of a basis of the N_B-torsion group are given, while in Problem 4, only the images of three cyclic disjoint groups of order N_B are provided. This a priori represents less information, but as we show below, this is sufficient to run the improved torsion point attacks.
  Let θ, d and e be such that Eq. 1 is satisfied, set $\tau = \phi \circ \theta \circ \hat{\phi} + [d]$. Let G_1, G_2 and G_3 be as in Problem 4. In the improved torsion point attacks, the torsion point information $(\phi(P), \phi(Q))$ is solely used to recover the action of τ on $E[N_B]$ as explained in Sect. 3.1. Hence we only need to prove that the knowledge of $\phi(G_1)$, $\phi(G_2)$ and $\phi(G_3)$ is sufficient to evaluate τ on $E[N_B]$.
  First we prove that from the action of ϕ on 3 cyclic disjoint groups of order N_B, we can recover the image of a basis of $E_0[N_B]$ through $[\lambda] \circ \phi$ for some integer λ coprime to N_B. Concretely, we have the following lemma.

Lemma 1. *Let $\phi : E_0 \to E$ an isogeny of degree N_A and let N_B be a smooth integer coprime to N_A. Let $G_1 = \langle P_1 \rangle$, $G_2 = \langle P_2 \rangle$, $G_3 = \langle P_3 \rangle$ be three cyclic groups of E_0 of order N_B such that $G_1 \cap G_2 = G_1 \cap G_3 = G_2 \cap G_3 = \{0\}$. Given $H_1 = \langle Q_1 \rangle$, $H_2 = \langle Q_2 \rangle$, $H_3 = \langle Q_3 \rangle$ such that $\phi(G_i) = H_i$ for $i = 1, 2, 3$; there exists an integer $\lambda \in (\mathbb{Z}/N_B\mathbb{Z})^\times$ such that we can compute λ^2 and $[\lambda] \circ \phi(P)$ for any $P \in E_0[N_B]$.*

The result in Lemma 1 partially available in [2, Lemma 1 §3.2] where Basso et al. prove that from the action of ϕ on 3 well chosen cyclic groups of smooth order N_B, one can recover the action of ϕ on any group of order N_B. Our Lemma goes a bit further and proves that we can evaluate $[\lambda] \circ \phi$ on the N_B torsion for some $\lambda \in (\mathbb{Z}/N_B\mathbb{Z})^\times$ such that λ^2 is known. Note that knowing λ^2 does not always enable us to compute λ, since when N_B is not a prime power, the equation $x^2 \equiv a^2 \mod N_B$ may have more than two solutions.

Proof (of Lemma 1). For $i = 1, 2, 3$, set $\phi(P_i) = [\lambda_i]Q_i$ where $\lambda_i \in (\mathbb{Z}/N_B\mathbb{Z})^\times$. Since $G_1 \cap G_2 = \{0\}$, then $\{P_1, P_2\}$ is a basis of $E_0[N_B]$ and $\{Q_1, Q_2\}$ is a basis of $E[N_B]$. Write $P_3 = [v_1]P_1 + [v_2]P_2$ and $Q_3 = [u_1]Q_1 + [u_2]Q_2$. Then, we get

$$[\lambda_3 u_1]Q_1 + [\lambda_3 u_2]Q_2 = [\lambda_3]Q_3 = \phi(P_3) = [v_1]\phi(P_1) + [v_2]\phi(P_2) = [v_1 \lambda_1]Q_1 + [v_2 \lambda_2]Q_2.$$

Hence $\lambda_3 u_1 = v_1 \lambda_1$, $\lambda_3 u_2 = v_2 \lambda_2$ and $\lambda_i / \lambda_3 = u_i / v_i$ for $i = 1, 2$. Since $G_1 \cap G_3 = G_2 \cap G_3 = \{0\}$ and N_A is coprime to N_B, then $H_1 \cap H_3 = H_2 \cap H_3 = \{0\}$ and

$u_1, u_2, v_1, v_2 \in (\mathbb{Z}/N_B\mathbb{Z})^\times$. Thus $\lambda_1 v_1/u_1 = \lambda_3 = \lambda_2 v_2/u_2$, and $\phi(P_1) = [\lambda_3]Q'_1$, $\phi(P_2) = [\lambda_3]Q'_2$ where $Q'_1 = [v_1/u_1]Q_1$ and $Q'_2 = [v_2/u_2]Q_2$.

We have

$$e_{N_B}(P_1, P_2)^{\deg \phi} = e_{N_B}(\phi(P_1), \phi(P_2)) = e_{N_B}([\lambda_3]Q'_1, [\lambda_3]Q'_2) = e_N(Q'_1, Q'_2)^{\lambda_3^2}.$$

We recover λ_3^2 by solving the following discrete logarithm

$$\lambda_3^2 = DLP\left(e_{N_B}(P_1, P_2)^{\deg \phi}, e_{N_B}(Q'_1, Q'_2)\right).$$

For any $S = [\alpha]P_1 + [\beta]P_2 \in E_0[N_B]$ we have $[\lambda_3] \circ \phi(S) = [\alpha]Q'_1 + [\beta]Q'_2$. $\square$

Now that we can evaluate $[\lambda] \circ \phi$ point wise on $E_0[N_B]$ for some $\lambda \in (\mathbb{Z}/N_B\mathbb{Z})^\times$ such that λ^2 is provided, we show how to evaluate τ on $E[N_B]$.

Since we can evaluate $\phi_\lambda = [\lambda] \circ \phi$ on $E_0[N_B]$, then we can evaluate $\widehat{\phi_\lambda}$ on $E[N_B]$ as well. Therefore we can evaluate $\phi_\lambda \circ \theta \circ \widehat{\phi_\lambda}$ on $E[N_B]$. Meanwhile, we have

$$\phi_\lambda \circ \theta \circ \widehat{\phi_\lambda} = ([\lambda] \circ \phi) \circ \theta \circ ([\lambda] \circ \widehat{\phi}) = [\lambda^2] \circ \phi \circ \theta \circ \widehat{\phi}.$$

Since $\lambda^2 \in (\mathbb{Z}/N_B\mathbb{Z})^\times$ is provided, then we get

$$\phi \circ \theta \circ \widehat{\phi} = [\lambda^{-2}] \circ \phi_\lambda \circ \theta \circ \widehat{\phi_\lambda}$$

on $E[N_B]$. Hence $\tau = \phi \circ \theta \circ \widehat{\phi} + [d]$ can be efficiently evaluated on $E[N_B]$. This concludes our discussion.

From now on, we can translate the solutions in [11] computing θ, d, e, and using the torsion point attacks to solve Problem 3 into solutions that compute θ, d, e, and solve Problem 4 in the same time and memory complexity, ignoring polylogarithmic factors.

Theorem 1 (Generalized Torsion Point Attacks). *Suppose we are given an instance of Problem 4 where N_A has $O(\log \log p)$ distinct prime factors. Assume we are given the restriction of a trace-zero endomorphism $\theta \in End(E_0)$ to $E_0[N_B]$, an integer d coprime to N_B, and a smooth integer e such that*

$$\deg\left(\phi \circ \theta \circ \widehat{\phi} + [d]\right) = N_B^2 e \quad or \quad \deg\left(\phi \circ \theta \circ \widehat{\phi} + [d]\right) = N_B^2 p e.$$

Then we can compute ϕ in time $\tilde{O}(\sqrt{e})$.

Proof. Follows from the previous discussion, [11, Theorem 3] and [11, Theorem 5].

We have the following Corollary.

Corollary 2. *Suppose that $N_A \approx p^{\frac{1}{2}}$ and $N_B \approx p^{\frac{1}{2}+\eta}$ where $1 \leq \eta$. Under some heuristics, Problem 4 can be solved in polynomial time when $j(E_0) = 1728$.*

In the following section, we use the generalized torsion point attacks to design a new adaptive attack on SIDH.

4   A New Adaptive Attack on SIDH

In this section, we present our attack. First we present an overview, next we describe the active phase of our attack.

4.1   Overview

In our attack, we suppose that one party is using a static secret/public key pair, and the other party runs multiple key exchanges with the honest party. He is provided with a the same oracle $O(E, R, S, E')$ described in Sect. 2.3.

The main idea of the attack is to use a key exchange oracle to recover the action of Alice's secret isogeny on a larger torsion point group. Doing so leads to an unbalanced SIDH. The malicious Bob then uses the revisited torsion point attacks, which in this case run in polynomial time, to recover Alice's secret key. Hence our attack has two phases.

Let N_A and N_B be the isogeny degrees of Alice and Bob respectively. In general, we have $N_A N_B | p + 1$ in the case of SIDH schemes, $N_A | p + 1$, $N_B | p - 1$ or $N_B | p + 1$, $N_A | p - 1$ for BSIDH. Let $E_0 = E(1728)$ be the starting curve, $E_0[N_B] = \langle P_B, Q_B \rangle$, and let $(E_A, \phi_A(P_B), \phi_A(Q_B))$ be Alice's public key where her static secret key is an isogeny $\phi_A : E_0 \to E_A$ of degree N_A. Moreover, suppose that you are given some "suitable" smooth integer N coprime to N_A such that $E_0[N_B N] \subset E_0(\mathbb{F}_{p^{2k}})$ for some integer k (we will provide the requirements on N as we describe the attack in the following sections).

The two phases of the attack can be summarized as follows.

- **The active phase.** Bob uses the access to a key exchange oracle $O(E, R, S, E')$ to secretly transform Alice's static public key $(E_A, \phi_A(P_B), \phi_A(Q_B))$ into a tuple $(E_A, \phi_A(G_1), \phi_A(G_2), \phi_A(G_3))$ where $G_1 = \langle P \rangle$, $G_2 = \langle Q \rangle$, $G_3 = \langle R \rangle$ are cyclic subgroups of maximal order in $E_0[N_B N]$, such that $G_1 \cap G_2 = G_1 \cap G_3 = G_2 \cap G_3 = \{0\}$.
- **The passive phase.** Having $(E_A, \phi_A(G_1), \phi_A(G_2), \phi_A(G_3))$, Bob applies the revisited torsion point attacks to recover Alice's secret.

The passive phase is nothing else than the revisited torsion point attacks described in Sect. 3.2. In the rest of this section, we provide a full description of the active phase.

4.2   Explicit Description of the Active Phase

Let p be the base prime. Let $N = \ell_1^{v_1} \cdots \ell_n^{v_n}$ be a smooth integer coprime to N_A such that $E_0[\ell_i^{v_i}] \subset E(\mathbb{F}_{p^{2k_i}})$ and for each prime ℓ_i which is not a square modulo N_A, v_i is even. Let G_1, G_2, G_3 be cyclic subgroups of $E_0[N_B N]$ or order $N_B N$ such that $G_1 \cap G_2 = G_1 \cap G_3 = G_2 \cap G_3 = \{0\}$. The active phase of the attack consists in recovering $\phi_A(G_j)$ for $j = 1, 2, 3$.

For $j = 1, 2, 3$, we can represent G_j as $G_j = \sum_{i=1}^r G_{ji}$ where G_{ji} is a group of order $N_B \ell_i^{v_i}$. The action of ϕ_A on G_j is recovered by computing $\phi_A(G_{ji})$ for $i =$

$1, \cdots, n$. Storing $\phi_A(G_j)$ in this form enables us to perform all computations in extension fields of degree $k_1, \cdots, k_n$, instead of $LCM(k_1, \cdots, k_n)$ the full group G_j is considered. This is because all supersingular isogenies are $\mathbb{F}_{p^2}$-rational. Hence we never go to extension fields with degree beyond $\max\{k_i, i = 1, \cdots, r\}$. Let us describe how we compute $\phi_A(G_{ji})$ for $j = 1, 2, 3$ and $i = 1, \cdots, n$.

Let G be a cyclic subgroup of $E_0[N_B \ell^v]$ of order $N_B \ell^v$. Let us suppose that $\ell \equiv \mu^2 \mod N_A$ is a square modulo N_A and that $v = 1$. Note that $\phi_A([\ell]G)$ is readily provided in Alice's public key since this group has order N_B. To compute the action of ϕ_A on G of order $N_B \ell$, Bob computes the isogeny $\phi_G : E_0 \to E_G$ having kernel G together with $R = [\mu^{-1}]\phi_G(P_A)$, $S = [\mu^{-1}]\phi_G(Q_A)$. Let H be a random cyclic subgroup of $E_A[N_B \ell]$ of order $N_B \ell$ containing $\phi_A([\ell]G)$. Let $\phi_H : E_A \to E_H$ be the isogeny of kernel H and $\phi'_A : E_G \to E_G/\phi_G(\ker(\phi_A))$ be the isogeny of kernel $\phi_G(\ker(\phi_A))$. Then if H is the image of the group G through ϕ_A then the diagram in Fig. 3 commutes and $O(E_G, R, S, E_H) = 1$. In the other case, when $H \neq \phi_A(G)$, Lemma 2 shows that the oracle returns 1 with negligible probability.

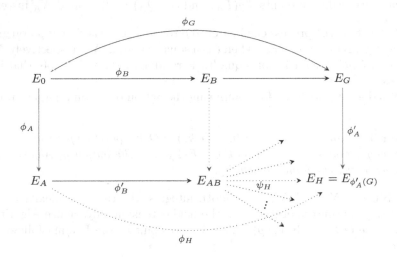

Fig. 3. Computing the action of ϕ_A on G.

Lemma 2. *Suppose that $\ell \approx O(\log p)$ and $N_A N_B \approx p$ (or $N_A N_B > p$), and let G, H, E_H and $E_G/\phi_G(\ker(\phi_A))$ be defined as above. If $H \neq \phi_A(G)$ then $E_H = E_G/\phi_G(\ker(\phi_A))$ with negligible probability.*

Proof. Suppose that $E_H = E_G/\phi_G(\ker(phi_A))$ and let $H' = \phi_A(G)$. Let $H' = \phi_A(G)$. By construction, we get $[\ell]H = [\ell]\phi_A(G) = [\ell]H'$, and we can decompose ϕ_H and ϕ'_H as $\phi_H = \psi_H \circ \phi'_B$ and $\phi_{H'} = \psi_{H'} \circ \phi'_B$ where ϕ_H and $\phi_{H'}$ are isogenies of degree ℓ from E_{AB} to $E_G/\phi_G(\ker(\phi_A))$. Since $H \neq H'$, then $\widehat{\psi_{H'}} \neq \pm\psi_H$ and $\widehat{\psi_{H'}} \circ \psi_H$ is a non scalar endomorphism of E_{AB} of degree ℓ^2. Therefore, the curve E_{AB} is an ℓ^2-small curve as defined in [27].

On the other hand, since $N_A N_B \approx p$, then E_{AB} is statistically a random supersingular curve [20]. Moreover, the number of ℓ^2-small curves is roughly ℓ^3 [27]. Considering the fact that the number of supersingular curves defined over $\mathbb{F}_{p^2}$ is $\frac{p}{12}$, then the probability that E_{AB} is an ℓ^2-small curve is at roughly $\frac{12\ell^3}{p}$, which is negligible since $\ell \approx O(\log p)$. $\qquad\square$

Remark 2. We scale $\phi_G(P_A)$ and $\phi_G(Q_A)$ by μ^{-1} in order to avoid the detection by pairing computation. When scaled by μ^{-1}, we have

$$
\begin{aligned}
e_{N_A}(R, S) &= e_{N_A}([\mu^{-1}]\phi_G(P_A), [\mu^{-1}]\phi_G(Q_A)) \\
&= e_{N_A}(P_A, Q_A)^{\mu^{-2} \deg \phi_G} \\
&= e_{N_A}(P_A, Q_A)^{N_B}.
\end{aligned}
$$

The above equation also justifies the requirement that ℓ should be a quadratic residue modulo N_A. When ℓ is not a quadratic residue modulo N_A and ℓ^2 divides N, we set the group G to have order $N_B \ell^2$ and we proceed the same way. In the later case, we scale the points $\phi_G(P_A)$ and $\phi_G(Q_A)$ by $\ell^{-1} \mod N_A$ instead.

If $1 < v$, then the process can be iterated to recover the action of ϕ_A on groups of order $N_B \ell, N_B \ell^2, \cdots, N_B \ell^v$ when ℓ is a square modulo N_A, respectively $N_B \ell^2$, $N_B \ell^4, \cdots, N_B \ell^v$ when ℓ is not a quadratic residue modulo N_A. Note that in the later case, v is even.

We deduce Algorithm 1 for computing the action of ϕ_A on a larger group G.

Lemma 3. *Algorithm 1 runs in time $\tilde{O}(k_v) = O(k_v \cdot \text{poly}(\log p))$ time whenever ℓ is of polynomial size and $E_0[N_B \ell^v] \subset E(\mathbb{F}_{p^{2k_v}})$. The output of Algorithm 1 is $\phi_A(G)$ with overwhelming probability.*

Proof. Since ℓ, N_A and N_B are smooth integers, the time complexity of Algorithm 1 depends on the degree k_v of the field extension only. Hence Algorithm 1 runs in time $O(k_v \cdot \text{poly}(\log p))$. The second point of the Lemma follows from Lemma 2. $\qquad\square$

Recall that $E_0[N_B \ell_i^{v_i}] \subset E(\mathbb{F}_{p^{2k_i}})$. Set $k^* = \max\{k_i\}$. Algorithm 2 fully describes the active phase our attack.

Lemma 4. *Algorithm 2 runs in time $\tilde{O}(\max\{k^*\})$ whenever ℓ_i for $i = 1, \cdots, n$, N_A, N_B are smooth integers.*

Proof. Follows from the Lemma 3. $\qquad\square$

This concludes our description of the active phase. In the next section, we discuss the computation of the integer N.

Algorithm 1 Evaluating the action of ϕ_A on a larger group G of order $N_B \ell^v$ using $O(E, R, S, E')$.

Require: E_0, P_A, Q_A, P_B, Q_B, E_A, $\phi_A(P_B)$, $\phi_A(Q_B)$, G.
Ensure: $\phi_A(G)$.
1: Set $G_0 = [\ell^v]G$;
2: **if** ℓ is a square modulo N_A **then**
3:     Compute $\mu = \sqrt{\ell} \bmod N_A$;
4:     **for** $i = 1, \cdots, v$ **do**
5:         $G_i = [\ell^{v-i}]G$
6:         Compute $\phi_{G_i} : E_0 \to E_{G_i}$ of degree $N_B \ell^i$ and of kernel G_i, together
            with $R = [\mu^{-i}]\phi_{G_i}(P_A)$ and $S = [\mu^{-i}]\phi_{G_i}(Q_A)$;
7:         **for** H cyclic group of E_A of order $N_B \ell^i$ containing $\phi_A(G_{i-1})$ **do**
8:             Compute $\phi_H : E_A \to E_H$ of kernel H;
9:             **if** $O(E_{G_i}, R, S, E_H) = 1$ **then**
10:                 Set $\phi_A(G_i) = H$;
11:     $G' = \phi_A(G_v)$;
12: **else**
13:     **for** $i = 1, \cdots, v/2$ **do**
14:         $G_i = [\ell^{v-2i}]G$
15:         Compute $\phi_{G_i} : E_0 \to E_{G_i}$ of degree $N_B \ell^{2i}$ and of kernel G_i, together
            with $R = [\ell^{-i}]\phi_{G_i}(P_A)$ and $S = [\ell^{-i}]\phi_{G_i}(Q_A)$;
16:         **for** H cyclic group of E_A of order $N_B \ell^{2i}$ containing $\phi_A(G_{i-1})$ **do**
17:             Compute $\phi_H : E_A \to E_H$ of kernel H;
18:             **if** $O(E_{G_i}, R, S, E_H) = 1$ **then**
19:                 Set $\phi_A(G_i) = H$;
20:     $G' = \phi_A(G_{v/2})$;
21: **return** G'.

Algorithm 2 Recovering the action of ϕ_A on cyclic disjoint groups G_1, G_2, G_3 of order $N_B N$ using the oracle $O(E, R, S, E')$

Require: E_0, P_A, Q_A, P_B, Q_B, E_A, $\phi_A(P_B)$, $\phi_A(Q_B)$, N_A, N_B, $N = \ell_1^{v_1} \cdots \ell_n^{v_n}$, G_{ji}
    for $j = 1, 2, 3$ and $i = 1, \cdots, n$.
Ensure: $\phi_A(G_{ji})$ for $j = 1, 2, 3$ and $i = 1, \cdots, r$.
1: **for** $i = 1, \cdots, n$ **do**
2:     **for** $j = 1, 2, 3$ **do**
3:         Compute $\phi_A(G_{ji})$ using Algorithm 1;
4: **return** $\phi_A(G_{ji})$ for $j = 1, 2, 3$ and $i = 1, \cdots, n$.

4.3 Computing the Integer N

We address the existence and the computation of the integer N. We would like to compute a smooth integer $N = \ell_1^{v_1} \cdots \ell_n^{v_n}$ coprime to N_A such that $E_0[N_B \ell_i^{v_i}] \subset E(\mathbb{F}_{p^{2k_i}})$ and for each prime ℓ_i which is not a square modulo N_A, v_i is even. Recall that by Corollary 2, the torsion point attacks run in polynomial time when $p < N$.

We start by the following Lemma which describes the group structure of supersingular curves over extension fields.

Lemma 5. *Let $E/\mathbb{F}_{p^2}$ be a supersingular elliptic curve such that $E(\mathbb{F}_{p^2}) \simeq (\mathbb{Z}_{p-\epsilon})^2$ where $\epsilon = \pm 1$ corresponds to the sign of the trace of Frobenius $t = 2\epsilon p$ of E over $\mathbb{F}_{p^2}$.*
Then for every natural number k, the group structure of E over $\mathbb{F}_{p^{2k}}$ is given by

$$E(\mathbb{F}_{p^{2k}}) \simeq (\mathbb{Z}_{p^k - \epsilon^k})^2 \tag{3}$$

Proof. Let k be natural number and let t_k be the trace of Frobenius of E over $\mathbb{F}_{p^{2k}}$. Then by Hasse Theorem (theorem V.1.1 of [33]),

$$|E(\mathbb{F}_{p^{2k}})| = p^{2k} + 1 - t_k.$$

Over $\mathbb{F}_{p^2}$, the characteristic equation of Frobenius is given by

$$X^2 - 2\epsilon p X + p^2 = (X - \epsilon p)^2$$

By Theorem 4.12 of [36]
$$t_k = 2(\epsilon p)^k = 2\epsilon^k p^k$$
where ϵ^k is the sign of t_k. Hence $t_k^2 = 4p^{2k}$ and by lemma 4.8 of [31]

$$E(\mathbb{F}_{p^{2k}}) \simeq (\mathbb{Z}_{\sqrt{p^{2k}} - \epsilon^k})^2 \simeq (\mathbb{Z}_{p^k - \epsilon^k})^2.$$

$\square$

From Eq. 3, we have that $E_0[N_B \ell_i^{v_i}] \subset E_0(\mathbb{F}_{p^{2k_i}})$ if and only if $N_B \ell_i^{v_i} | p^{k_i} - \epsilon^{k_i}$ where ϵ is the sign of the trace of Frobenius of E_0 as described in the proof of Lemma 5.

Let ℓ be a small prime. Then $\ell^v | p^{2k} - 1$ for some $k \leq \ell^v$. This means that for each prime ℓ_i dividing N, $k_i \leq \ell_i^{v_i}$. This heals a easy way to compute N : choose the smallest primes ℓ_i coprime to $N_A N_B$, such that $p < N = \prod \ell_i^2$. Then the largest ℓ_i is in $O(\log p)$. Moreover we have k_i at most ℓ_i^2.

To moderate the fields extension degrees, we also include in N primes ℓ that are squares modulo N_A. For this primes, we only require ℓ to divide $p^{2k} - 1$, hence obtaining a smaller field extension.

We describe the full process in Algorithm 3. The algorithm returns the list P of prime power factors of N with the list D of the corresponding extension field degrees.

Lemma 6. *Algorithm 3 runs in polynomial time and for each prime ℓ_i dividing N, $k_i \leq \ell_i^2 \approx O(\log^2 p)$.*

Proof. Follows from the previous discussion. $\square$

Algorithm 3 Computing N

Require: p, N_A, N_B.
Ensure: P, D.
1: Create the lists P and D, set $N = 1$, set $\ell = 1$;
2: **while** $N < p$ **do**
3:     choose the next prime ℓ coprime to $N_A N_B$;
4:     **if** ℓ is a square modulo N_A **then**
5:         Compute the smallest integer k such that $\ell | p^{2k} - 1$.
6:         Append ℓ to the list P and $2k$ to the list D;
7:         $N = N * \ell$;
8:     **else**
9:         Compute the smallest integer k such that $\ell^2 | p^{2k} - 1$.
10:       Append ℓ^2 to the list P and $2k$ to the list D;
11:       $N = N * \ell^2$;
12: **return** P, D;

Remark 3. In all this section, we were attacking Alice's secret isogeny. To attack Bob's secret isogeny instead, one interchanges the roles of N_A and N_B. Mostly, the quadratic residuosity condition on N will depend on N_B.

Remark 4. In practice, on may set a bound a bound on the extension degrees and slightly increase the size of the primes ℓ_i. This will be the case in the attack parameters we will present in Sect. 5.

4.4 Attack Summary

The full attack can is summarised in Algorithm 4.

Algorithm 4 New Adaptive attack on SIDH

Require: E_0, P_A, Q_A, P_B, Q_B, E_A, $\phi_A(P_B)$, $\phi_A(Q_B)$, N_A, N_B.
Ensure: $\ker(\phi_A)$.
1: Compute a suitable smooth integer N using Algorithm 3.
2: Let G_1, G_2, G_3 cyclic disjoint subgroups of $E_0[N_B N]$ of order $N_B N$.
3: Compute $\phi_A(G_1)$, $\phi_A(G_2)$, $\phi_A(G_3)$ using the oracle $O(E, R, S, E')$ and Algorithm 2.
4: Compute ϕ_A using the revisited torsion point attacks of Theorem 1.
5: **return** $\ker(\phi_A)$.

Now we evaluate the number of oracle queries. Since $N = \ell_1^{v_1} \cdots \ell_n^{v_n}$ where for each prime ℓ_i which is not a square modulo N_A, v_i is even, then we can write $N = \ell_1^{2v_1} \cdots \ell_n^{2v_n} \ell_{n+1}^{u_1} \cdots \ell_{n+m}^{u_m}$ where the primes ℓ_{n+j} for $j = 1, \cdots, m$ are squares modulo N_A. From Algorithm 1, for each prime factor ℓ_i $(1 \le i \le n)$ of N, the maximum number of queries to the oracle (E, R, S, E') is equal to the number of cyclic subgroups of $(\mathbb{Z}/\ell_i^2 \mathbb{Z})^2$ order ℓ_i^2, which is $\ell_i(\ell_i + 1)$. Note that if the first $\ell_i(\ell_i+1)-1$ queries fail, then there is no need to perform the last query since it will succeed. Also, for each prime factor ℓ_{n+j} $(1 \leq j \leq m)$ of N, the maximum number of queries to the oracle (E, R, S, E') is equal to the number of cyclic subgroups of $(\mathbb{Z}/\ell_i\mathbb{Z})^2$ order ℓ_i, which is $\ell_i + 1$. Here also, there is no need to perform the last query when the first ℓ_i queries failed. Therefore, the maximum number of oracle queries in the attack is

$$O_q = \sum_{i=1}^{n} v_i \left[\ell_i(\ell_i+1) - 1\right] + \sum_{j=1}^{m} u_j \ell_{n+j}.$$

Now we can state the main result of this paper.

Theorem 2. *Let p, E_0, $N_A < p$, $N_B < p$, P_A, Q_A, P_B, Q_B, E_A, $\phi_A(P_B)$, $\phi_A(Q_B)$ be the public parameters and the public key of an SIDH type scheme.*

Provided a key exchange oracle $O(E, R, S, E')$, Algorithm 4 recovers ϕ_A in polynomial time.

Furthermore, Algorithm 4 performs at most

$$O_q = \sum_{i=1}^{n} v_i \left[\ell_i(\ell_i+1) - 1\right] + \sum_{j=1}^{m} u_j \ell_{n+j}$$

queries to the key exchange oracle where $N = \ell_1^{2v_1} \cdots \ell_n^{2v_n} \ell_{n+1}^{u_1} \cdots \ell_{n+m}^{u_m}$ is the integer computed in Step 1.

Proof. By Lemma 3, Step 1 outputs a smooth integer N such that $\max\{k_i\} \approx O(\log^2 p)$. Hence by Lemma 3, Step 3 runs in time $\tilde{O}(\log^2 p) = \tilde{O}(1)$. Step 4 runs in polynomial time since $p < N$. The number of oracle queries follows from the discussion preceding Theorem 2. $\qquad\square$

Remark 5. In our attack, the malicious Bob computes isogenies of degree $N_B\ell^2$ or $N_B\ell$ depending on the quadratic residuosity of ℓ modulo N_A. In Appendix A, we suggest a variant of the attack where isogenies Bob computes isogenies of degree ℓ^2 or ℓ instead. Nevertheless, this variant can be easily detected.

5   Relevance and Countermeasures

In this section, we suggest some attack parameters for \$IDH and SIDH primes. We discuss possible countermeasures to the attack.

5.1   Attack Parameters for Some SIDH Primes

We propose attack parameters for the two (non cryptographic size) primes suggested for the \$IKE challenge [8, §10], the SIDH primes SIDHp377 and SIDHp546 suggested by Longa et al. [26], SIDHp434 and SIDHp503 as specified in SIKE [22].

As attack parameters, we provide the prime factorisation of N, the maximum field extension degree $k^* = \max\{k_i\}$, $\eta \approx N/p$ and the number O_q of oracle queries. We also precise which party is attacked: B stands for Bob and A stands for Alice.

The outcome of our investigations on the above mentioned $IDH primes and SIDH primes is summarised in Table 1 and Table 2 respectively.

Table 1. Attack parameters for the two $IDH primes.

Party	k^*	η	O_q	N
\$IDHp182 prime: $p = 2^{91}3^{57} - 1$				
B	96	$\frac{185}{182}$	7251	$5^2 * 7 * 11^2 * 13 * 19 * 31 * 37 * 43 * 47^2 * 61 * 67 * 73 * 79 * 97 * 103 *$ $109 * 127 * 139 * 157 * 181 * 241 * 277 * 421 * 433 * 541 * 661 * 919$
\$IDHp217 prime: $p = 2^{110}3^{67} - 1$				
B	96	$\frac{222}{217}$	9349	$5^2 * 7 * 13 * 19 * 31 * 37 * 43 * 61 * 67 * 73 * 79 * 97 * 109 * 157 *$ $163 * 181 * 193 * 199 * 211 * 223 * 229 * 271 * 277 * 307 * 337 *$ $571 * 631 * 1009 * 1093 * 1249 * 1381$

When it comes to BSIDH instances, generating specific attack parameters is less trivial. We believe this may be because BSIDH primes[3] are twin primes. Using the generic attack parameters computation described in Algorithm 3, the degree of the field extensions are relatively larger compared to those used when running the attack on SIDH. For example, let us consider the smallest BSIDH prime (prime in example 6 of [7])

$$p = 2 \cdot (2^3 \cdot 3^4 \cdot 17 \cdot 19 \cdot 31 \cdot 37 \cdot 53^2)^6 - 1.$$

Set $N_A = p + 1$ and $N_B = p - 1$. Then we get

$$N = 5^2 \cdot 11^2 \cdot 23^2 \cdot 29^2 \cdot 41^2 \cdot 47^2 \cdot 59^2 \cdot 61^2 \cdot 67^2 \cdot 71^2 \cdot 79^2 \cdot$$
$$83^2 \cdot 89^2 \cdot 97^2 \cdot 101^2 \cdot 107^2 \cdot 109^2 \cdot 113^2 \cdot 127^2 \cdot 131^2 \cdot 137^2$$

and the ℓ_i^2 torsion points for ℓ_i dividing N are defined over extension fields of $\mathbb{F}_{p^2}$ of degree

$$20, 55, 253, 406, 820, 23, 3422, 15, 402, 2485, 3081, 3403, 1958,$$
$$9312, 2020, 5671, 11772, 12656, 8001, 1310, 2329,$$

the order is the same as in the prime factorisation of N. The number of oracle queries is $O_q = 152523$. Note that here, one will be working with extension fields of degree up to 12656. One may prefer to compute a different integer N for which the maximum extension field degree is relatively small, but as we mentioned before, this requires intensive computations which we could not do on a personal computer.

---

[3] Primes p such that both $p + 1$ and $p - 1$ are smooth.

Table 2. Attack parameters for some SIDH primes.

Party	k	η	O_q	N
SIDHp377 prime: $p = 2^{191}3^{117} - 1$				
B	120	$\frac{377}{377}$	40728	$5^2 * 7 * 11^2 * 13 * 19 * 31 * 37 * 43 * 61 * 67 * 73 * 79 * 97 * 103 * 109 * 157 * 181 * 193 * 199 * 229 * 241 * 271 * 277 * 307 * 313 * 331 * 337 * 433 * 487 * 571 * 631 * 661 * 739 * 1009 * 1021 * 1051 * 1093 * 1249 * 1993 * 2161 * 2707 * 3433 * 3529 * 4003 * 4603 * 5419$
SIDHp434 prime: $p = 2^{216}3^{137} - 1$				
B	152	$\frac{438}{434}$	66169	$5^2 * 7 * 11^2 * 13 * 17^2 * 19 * 31 * 37 * 43 * 61 * 67 * 71^2 * 73 * 79 * 97 * 103 * 109 * 127 * 139 * 151 * 181 * 193 * 211 * 277 * 373 * 409 * 421 * 433 * 457 * 547 * 601 * 613 * 739 * 751 * 757 * 1123 * 1171 * 1231 * 1489 * 1741 * 1873 * 2311 * 2593 * 2887 * 3037 * 3061 * 4357 * 5227 * 6091 * 6661 * 7621$
SIDHp503 prime: $p = 2^{250}3^{159} - 1$				
B	158	$\frac{512}{503}$	81049	$5^2 * 7 * 11^2 * 13 * 19 * 31 * 37 * 43 * 61 * 67 * 73 * 79 * 97 * 103 * 109 * 127 * 139 * 151 * 157 * 163 * 181 * 193 * 199 * 211 * 229 * 241 * 277 * 409 * 421 * 433 * 439 * 457 * 463 * 571 * 577 * 601 * 859 * 967 * 1093 * 1153 * 1171 * 1201 * 1303 * 1327 * 1741 * 2131 * 2179 * 2269 * 2371 * 2377 * 2689 * 3037 * 3169 * 4663 * 6151 * 6469 * 6529 * 8893 * 9769$
SIDHp546 prime: $p = 2^{273}3^{172} - 1$				
B	152	$\frac{551}{546}$	112441	$5^2 * 7 * 11^2 * 13 * 19 * 31 * 37 * 43 * 61 * 67 * 73 * 79 * 83^2 * 97 * 103 * 109 * 127 * 139 * 151 * 157 * 163 * 181 * 193 * 223 * 277 * 307 * 379 * 409 * 421 * 433 * 457 * 613 * 631 * 661 * 691 * 751 * 1117 * 1153 * 1249 * 1321 * 1621 * 1741 * 1753 * 1801 * 1933 * 1999 * 2053 * 2137 * 2281 * 3571 * 3823 * 5059 * 5281 * 5563 * 6373 * 6397 * 6481 * 7549 * 7639 * 8161 * 9151$

Remark 6. Our attack applies to eSIDH [4] as well. It can be easily adapted to k-SIDH [1] and it's variant by Jao and Urbanik [34]. In the later case, the number of oracle queries is exponential in k.

5.2   Countermeasures to the Attack

A straightforward countermeasure of the attack is to use a variant of the Fujisaki-Okamoto transform [17,21] as in SIKE. This transform obliges Bob to disclose his secret key to Alice who will recompute Bob's public to verify its correctness. Recomputing Bob's public key will enable Alice to detect Bob's maliciousness.

A second countermeasure is that Bob uses the SIDH proof of Knowledge as recently suggested in [14]. In this proof of knowledge, Bob proves that there exists an isogeny of degree N_B between E_0 and E_B and that the provided torsion points were not maliciously computed. Nevertheless, this countermeasure is very costly, since the proof of isogeny knowledge is nothing else than the SIDH based signature scheme, which is relatively slow and has large signatures.

Another less costly countermeasure is to set the curves E_0 to be a random supersingular elliptic curve with unknown endomorphism ring. This counters the improved torsion points attack. Hence Bob will not be able to recover Alice's secret isogeny after recovering its action on a larger torsion group. Nevertheless, one should keep in mind that this later countermeasure does not counter the GPST adaptive attack.

6   Conclusion

In this paper, we generalized the torsion point attacks in such a way that they can be used to recover a secret isogeny provided its action on three disjoint cyclic subgroup of relatively large order. We then used this generalized torsion point attacks to design a new adaptive attack on SIDH type schemes. The attack consists of maliciously computing isogenies of larger degrees than expected in SIDH, then using an access to the key exchange oracle to recover the action of the honest party's secret isogeny on a larger torsion groups. Afterwards, one obtains an unbalanced SIDH instance on which one applies the generalized torsion points attack to recover the honest party's secret isogeny. Our attack runs in polynomial time.

We provide concrete attack parameters for SIDH instances instantiated with the SIDH primes \$IDHp182, \$IDHp217, SIDHp377, SIDHp434, SIDHp546 and SIDHp503. A search of attack parameters on BSIDH primes is ongoing. We finally suggest countermeasures among which the Fujisaki-Okamoto transform (as used in SIKE), using a proof of isogeny knowledge as recently proposed in [14] or setting the starting curve in SIDH to be a random supersingular curve with unknown endomorphism ring.

This result proves that torsion point attacks, which do not yet apply to SIDH, become relevant to SIDH parameters in an adaptive attack setting. Moreover, it introduces a new cryptanalytic tool for isogeny based cryptography.

Acknowledgements. We would like to thank the anonymous reviewers for their valuable comments and feedback.

A   A Simpler, But Detectable Variant of the Attack

We present a simpler variant of our attack, but which can be easily detected. In Sect. 4.2, we use Algorithm 1 to recover the action of ϕ_A on groups of order $N_B \ell^v$. In the case where ℓ is coprime to N_B, there is no need to consider groups of order $N_B \ell^v$ since we already know the action of ϕ_A on the N_B-torsion points. Therefore, we can directly recover the action of ϕ_A on groups of order ℓ^v.

Let d be the smallest divisor of N_B such that $N_B = dN_B'$ and N_B' is a square modulo N_A, say $N_B' \equiv \gamma^2 \mod N_A$. To recover the action of ϕ_A on a cyclic group G_1 of order ℓ where $\ell \equiv \mu^2 \mod N_A$, Bob chooses a cyclic group G_0 of order d and sets $G = G_0 + G_1$, which is a group of order $d\ell$. He computes the isogeny $\phi_G : E_0 \rightarrow E_G = E_0/G$ together with $R = [\gamma\mu^{-1}]\phi_G(P_A)$ $S = [\gamma\mu^{-1}]\phi_G(Q_A)$. For each cyclic group $H \subset E_A[d\ell]$ containing $\phi_A(G_0)$, Bob computes $E_H = E_A/H$ and queries the oracle (E_G, R, S, E_H). Note that

$$
\begin{aligned}
e_{N_A}(R, S) &= e_{N_A}([\gamma\mu^{-1}]\phi_G(P_A), [\gamma\mu^{-1}]\phi_G(Q_A)) \\
&= e_{N_A}(P_A, Q_A)^{\gamma^2\mu^{-2}\deg\phi_G} \\
&= e_{N_A}(P_A, Q_A)^{N'_B\ell^{-1}d\ell} \\
&= e_{N_A}(P_A, Q_A)^{N_B},
\end{aligned}
$$

Hence the pairing check does not detect the attack. Nevertheless, when N_B is a very smooth integer (like in SIDH where $N_B = 3^b$ and $d \in \{1, \ell\}$), d is small. Hence Alice can easily check if the curves E_0 and E_G are $d\ell$-isogenous to discard such malicious public keys.

References

1. Azarderakhsh, R., Jao, D., Leonardi, C.: Post-quantum static-static key agreement using multiple protocol instances. In: Adams, C., Camenisch, J. (eds.) SAC 2017. LNCS, vol. 10719, pp. 45–63. Springer, Cham (2018). https://doi.org/10.1007/978-3-319-72565-9_3

2. Basso, A., Kutas, P., Merz, S.P., Petit, C., Sanso, A.: Cryptanalysis of an oblivious PRF from supersingular isogenies. Cryptology ePrint Archive, Report 2021/706, 2021. https://ia.cr/2021/706

3. Biasse, J.F., Jao, D., Sankar, A.: A quantum algorithm for computing isogenies between supersingular elliptic curves. In: Meier, W., Mukhopadhyay, D. (eds.) INDOCRYPT 2014. LNCS, vol. 8885, pp. 428–442. Springer, Cham (2014). https://doi.org/10.1007/978-3-319-13039-2_25

4. Cervantes-Vázquez, D., Ochoa-Jiménez, E., Rodríguez-Henríquez, F.: eSIDH: the revenge of the SIDH. Cryptology ePrint Archive, Report 2020/021 (2020). https://ia.cr/2020/021

5. Charles, D.X., Lauter, K.E., Goren, E.Z.: Cryptographic hash functions from expander graphs. J. Cryptol. **22**(1), 93–113 (2009)

6. Childs, A., Jao, D., Soukharev, V.: Constructing elliptic curve isogenies in quantum subexponential time. J. Math. Cryptol. **8**(1), 1–29 (2014)

7. Costello, C.: B-SIDH: supersingular isogeny diffie-hellman using twisted torsion. In: Moriai, S., Wang, Hu. (eds.) ASIACRYPT 2020. LNCS, vol. 12492, pp. 440–463. Springer, Cham (2020). https://doi.org/10.1007/978-3-030-64834-3_15

8. Costello, C.: The case for SIKE: a decade of the supersingular isogeny problem. Cryptology ePrint Archive, Report 2021/543 (2021). https://ia.cr/2021/543

9. Costello, C., Longa, P., Naehrig, M.: Efficient algorithms for supersingular isogeny diffie-hellman. In: Robshaw, M., Katz, J. (eds.) CRYPTO 2016. LNCS, vol. 9814, pp. 572–601. Springer, Heidelberg (2016). https://doi.org/10.1007/978-3-662-53018-4_21

10. Couveignes, J.M.: Hard homogeneous spaces. Cryptology ePrint Archive, Report 2006/291 (2006). https://eprint.iacr.org/2006/291

11. de Quehen, V., et al.: Improved torsion point attacks on SIDH variants. Cryptology ePrint Archive, Report 2020/633 (2020). https://eprint.iacr.org/2020/633

12. Eisenträger, K., Hallgren, S., Lauter, K., Morrison, T., Petit, C.: Supersingular isogeny graphs and endomorphism rings: reductions and solutions. In: Nielsen, J.B., Rijmen, V. (eds.) EUROCRYPT 2018. LNCS, vol. 10822, pp. 329–368. Springer, Cham (2018). https://doi.org/10.1007/978-3-319-78372-7_11
13. De Feo, L.: Mathematics of isogeny based cryptography. CoRR, abs/1711.04062 (2017)
14. De Feo, L., Dobson, S., Galbraith, S.D., Zobernig, L.: SIDH Proof of Knowledge. Cryptology ePrint Archive, Report 2021/1023 (2021). https://ia.cr/2021/1023
15. De Feo, L., Jao, D., Plût, J.: Towards quantum-resistant cryptosystems from supersingular elliptic curve isogenies, pp. 209–247 (2014)
16. Tako, B.F., Kutas, P., Merz, S.P.: On the isogeny problem with torsion point information. Cryptology ePrint Archive, Report 2021/153 (2021). https://eprint.iacr.org/2021/153
17. Fujisaki, E., Okamoto, T.: Secure integration of asymmetric and symmetric encryption schemes. In: Wiener, M. (ed.) CRYPTO 1999. LNCS, vol. 1666, pp. 537–554. Springer, Heidelberg (1999). https://doi.org/10.1007/3-540-48405-1_34
18. Steven, D.: Galbraith. Mathematics of Public Key Cryptography, Cambridge University Press, Cambridge (2012)
19. Galbraith, S.D., Petit, C., Shani, B., Ti, Y.B.: On the security of supersingular isogeny cryptosystems. In: Cheon, J.H., Takagi, T. (eds.) ASIACRYPT 2016. LNCS, vol. 10031, pp. 63–91. Springer, Heidelberg (2016). https://doi.org/10.1007/978-3-662-53887-6_3
20. Galbraith, S.D., Petit, C., Silva, J.: Identification protocols and signature schemes based on supersingular isogeny problems. In: Takagi, T., Peyrin, T. (eds.) ASIACRYPT 2017. LNCS, vol. 10624, pp. 3–33. Springer, Cham (2017). https://doi.org/10.1007/978-3-319-70694-8_1
21. Hofheinz, D., Hövelmanns, K., Kiltz, E.: A modular analysis of the fujisaki-okamoto transformation. In: Kalai, Y., Reyzin, L. (eds.) TCC 2017. LNCS, vol. 10677, pp. 341–371. Springer, Cham (2017). https://doi.org/10.1007/978-3-319-70500-2_12
22. Jao, D., et al.: Supersingular isogeny key encapsulation, 1, October 2020. https://sike.org/files/SIDH-spec.pdf
23. Jao, D., De Feo, L.: Towards quantum-resistant cryptosystems from supersingular elliptic curve isogenies. In: Yang, B.Y. (ed.) PQCrypto 2011. LNCS, vol. 7071, pp. 19–34. Springer, Heidelberg (2011). https://doi.org/10.1007/978-3-642-25405-5_2
24. Jaques, S., Schrottenloher, A.: Low-gate quantum golden collision finding. Cryptology ePrint Archive, Report 2020/424 (2020). https://eprint.iacr.org/2020/424
25. Kutas, P., Merz, S.P., Petit, C., Weitkämper, C.: One-way functions and malleability oracles: hidden shift attacks on isogeny-based protocols. IACR Cryptol. ePrint Arch., 2021:282 (2021)
26. Longa, P., Wang, W., Szefer, J.: The cost to break SIKE: a comparative hardware-based analysis with AES and SHA-3. Cryptology ePrint Archive, Report 2020/1457 (2020). https://ia.cr/2020/1457
27. Love, J., Boneh, D.: Supersingular curves with small non-integer endomorphisms. ArXiv, abs/1910.03180 (2019)
28. Petit, C.: Faster algorithms for isogeny problems using torsion point images. In: Takagi, T., Peyrin, T. (eds.) ASIACRYPT 2017. LNCS, vol. 10625, pp. 330–353. Springer, Cham (2017). https://doi.org/10.1007/978-3-319-70697-9_12
29. Petit, C., Lauter, K.E.: Hard and easy problems for supersingular isogeny graphs. Cryptology ePrint Archive, Report 2017/962 (2017). https://eprint.iacr.org/2017/962

30. Rostovtsev, A., Stolbunov, A.: Public-key cryptosystem based on isogenies. IACR Cryptol. ePrint Arch. 2006, 145 (2006)
31. Schoof, R.: Nonsingular cubic curves over finite fields, November 1987. http://www.mat.uniroma2.it/~schoof/cubiccurves.pdf
32. Silverman, J.H.: Advanced Topics in the Arithmetic of Elliptic Curves. Graduate Texts in Mathematics, vol. 151. Springer-Verlag, New-York (1994)
33. Silverman, J.H.: The Arithmetic of Elliptic Curves, vol. 106. Springer Science & Business Media, Heidelberg (2009)
34. Urbanik, D., Jao, D.: New techniques for SIDH-based NIKE. J. Math. Cryptol. **14**(1), 120–128 (2020)
35. Van Oorschot, P.C., Wiener, M.J.: Parallel collision search with cryptanalytic applications. J. Cryptol. **12**(1), 1–28 (1999)
36. Lawrence, C.: Elliptic Curves: Number Theory and Cryptography, 2 edn. Chapman & Hall/CRC, Washington (2008)
37. Wesolowski, B.: The supersingular isogeny path and endomorphism ring problems are equivalent. Cryptology ePrint Archive, Report 2021/919 (2021). https://ia.cr/2021/919

On Fingerprinting Attacks
and Length-Hiding Encryption

Kai Gellert[✉], Tibor Jager[✉], Lin Lyu[✉], and Tom Neuschulten[✉]

Bergische Universität Wuppertal, Wuppertal, Germany
{kai.gellert,tibor.jager,lin.lyu,tom.neuschulten}@uni-wuppertal.de

Abstract. It is well known that already the *length* of encrypted messages may reveal sensitive information about encrypted data. *Fingerprinting attacks* enable an adversary to determine web pages visited by a user and even the language and phrases spoken in voice-over-IP conversations.

Prior research has established the general perspective that a length-hiding padding which is long enough to improve security significantly incurs an unfeasibly large bandwidth overhead. We argue that this perspective is a consequence of the choice of the security models considered in prior works, which are based on classical indistinguishability of *two* messages, and that this does not reflect the attacker model of typical fingerprinting attacks well.

Therefore we propose a new perspective on length-hiding encryption, which aims to capture security against fingerprinting attacks more accurately. This makes it possible to concretely quantify the security provided by length-hiding padding against fingerprinting attacks, depending on the real message distribution of an application. We find that for many real-world applications (such as webservers with static content, DNS requests, Google search terms, or Wikipedia page visits) and their *specific* message distributions, even length-hiding padding with relatively small bandwidth overhead of only 2–5% can already significantly improve security against fingerprinting attacks. This gives rise to a new perspective on length-hiding encryption, which helps understanding how and under what conditions length-hiding encryption can be used to improve security.

Supported by the European Research Council (ERC) under the European Union's Horizon 2020 research and innovation programme, grant agreement 802823. We thank Hans-Jörg Bauer and Michael Simon, ZIM of University of Wuppertal, for their assistance with determining a real-world DNS host name distribution and the anonymous reviewers of CT-RSA 2022 for helpful comments.

S. D. Galbraith (Ed.): CT-RSA 2022, LNCS 13161, pp. 345–369, 2022.
https://doi.org/10.1007/978-3-030-95312-6_15

1   Introduction

"Secure encryption" is today a very well-understood concept. However, standard cryptographic security definitions for encryption schemes (symmetric and asymmetric alike) consider a security experiment where an adversary chooses two plaintext messages m_0 and m_1, receives back an encryption of a randomly chosen message $m^* \in \{m_0, m_1\}$, and then has to determine which of the two messages was encrypted. A common, crucial restriction of such security definitions is that the two messages must have *equal length*. Otherwise it may be trivial to determine the encrypted message based on the length of the given ciphertext, such that security in this sense is impossible to achieve.

There are other standard security notions, such as "real-or-random" definitions, where an adversary has to distinguish between an encryption of a chosen message m and a random string of equal length or simulation-based semantic security, which requires the existence of an efficient simulator that produces the same output as the adversary given only the length of a ciphertext (e.g., [1,2,18,19]). All these definitions have in common that they do not provide security against attacks that are based on the length of messages.

Due to their simplicity and generality, these definitions have been extremely useful for building a general theory of secure encryption. However, assuming that only messages of equal length are encrypted is a necessary theoretical idealization and unrealistic from a practical perspective. In most real-world applications already the length of messages may reveal sensitive information.

The real-world relevance of hiding message lengths. Well-known examples of attacks leveraging message lengths consider a passive adversary that merely observes the encrypted network traffic and can identify web pages visited by a user [10,16,21,23,30], or the language and even phrases spoken in an encrypted voice-over-IP conversation [32,33], all this without breaking the expected security of the underlying encryption scheme. Even revealing the length of user passwords makes it possible to identify individual users in TLS-encrypted sessions and provides an advantage in password guessing attacks [13], in particular when passwords are re-used across different services. Hence, it is a desirable goal to hide the length of transmitted messages in practice.

Impossibility of hiding message lengths in cryptographic theory. Tezcan and Vaudenay [29] considered the *asymptotic* setting commonly used in theoretical cryptography and showed essentially that efficiently hiding the length of messages is impossible for arbitrary message distributions. Concretely, an exponential-sized padding is necessary, if the adversary in a standard security experiment is allowed to choose arbitrary messages of different lengths, and one aims at achieving a *negligible* distinguishing advantage. This suggests that *in theory* it is impossible to hide plaintext length efficiently, which supports the common belief that a considerable bandwidth overhead incurred by length-hiding padding is inevitable.

Dependence of encrypted messages and length-hiding padding. In order to overcome this impossibility, Paterson, Ristenpart, and Shrimpton introduce the notion of length-hiding encryption (LHE) [24]. Essentially, LHE augments the encryption algorithm with an additional *length-hiding parameter* ℓ, which is specified by an application calling the encryption algorithm. The length-hiding parameter determines the amount of length-hiding padding used for a particular message. Secure LHE in the sense of [24] essentially guarantees security for plaintexts of different lengths, provided that the length-hiding parameter ensures that the corresponding ciphertexts have equal size. However, [24] does not yet explain how ℓ can be chosen in order to obtain any security guarantees for realistic message distributions.

Furthermore, this work considers a classical "two-message indistinguishability" security model, where an adversary outputs two challenge messages m_0 and m_1 whose length difference must be *bounded* by some Δ, i.e., it holds that $0 \leq \left| |m_0| - |m_1| \right| \leq \Delta$. Here, Δ depends on ℓ. Note that this requires the messages in the security experiment to be chosen depending on the length-hiding parameter used by the underlying encryption scheme.

We argue that in order to determine suitable length-hiding padding to protect against fingerprinting attacks on a given application layer protocol, such as HTTP, DNS, etc., we do not want to make the distribution of application-layer messages dependent on the used padding scheme, but rather the other way around. That is, we want to determine a suitable length-hiding parameter for the given message distribution of the application. Therefore we propose a security definition which does not mandate any *a priori* length difference Δ of messages, but rather quantifies the security of a certain padding length for a given message distribution (or an approximation thereof).

Quantifying the security of length-hiding encryption. There is currently no methodology that makes it possible to concretely assess and *quantify* the security of a given length-hiding padding scheme against fingerprinting attacks. In order to understand under which circumstances length-hiding schemes can reduce the effectivity of fingerprinting attacks *without* very large performance penalty, we have to analyze which *concrete* security guarantees can be obtained by length-hiding schemes with reasonable (i.e., non-exponential-sized) length-hiding parameters.

We know that suitable choice of a padding length must depend on the message distribution of an application (more precisely, on the distribution of the lengths of encrypted messages), as otherwise security is known to be not achievable [29]. In order to determine a suitable padding length for a given application in practice, it is therefore necessary to determine the message distribution of the given application. This can be achieved, for instance, by implementing a server-side monitoring algorithm that records (an approximation of) the distribution. This algorithm could run in set intervals and update the length-hiding parameter on the fly, if the distribution changes over time (e.g., due to changed web site contents or access patterns).

Our Contributions. We develop a methodology that makes it possible to *concretely quantify* the effect of LHE on the security of a given application. To this end, we introduce a new cryptographic security model, which aims to preserve the simplicity and generality of classical models, while capturing security against fingerprinting attacks in order to reflect such security requirements of applications. Based on this definition, we describe a methodology to concretely quantify the effect of LHE for a given application.

In a next step, we demonstrate the feasibility of our approach by applying it to different types of fingerprinting attacks. Each of these scenarios cover multiple application-based aspects such as which block mode (e.g., CBC, CTR) is used for encryption, or whether compression for transmitted data is enabled. Note that due to attacks such as CRIME [6], compression in TLS is usually disabled in practice; Qualys SSL Labs finds the percentage of websites using compression among the Alexa's lists of most popular websites in the world to be 0.1% in November 2021[1] We further remark that we intentionally compare length-padding-after-compression to no-length-padding-no-compression. This allows us to emphasize that in some cases enabling compression might increase security. Since the security impact of such aspects are often very subtle, we provide a more detailed explanation in the full version of this work [8]. We summarize our results as follows:

Simple webpage fingerprinting. As a first example, we consider a website consisting of many static HTML pages, a user that visits one page, and an adversary that tries to determine the visited page based on the size of encrypted data. Since we want to base our analysis on a publicly-available web site with static contents, we used the IACR Cryptology ePrint archive at https://eprint.iacr.org/2020/.[2]

We find that switching from counter mode to block mode encryption already decreases the advantage of the adversary from 0.74 to 0.14 (where an advantage of 1 means that the adversary can uniquely determine a web page, while 0 means that the size of the transmitted data reveals no information about the visited page). This makes fingerprinting much less effective, without noticeable bandwidth overhead.

Reducing the advantage to 0 costs about 95% bandwidth overhead *without* compression, however, by additionally using compression and advantage to 0 can even be achieved *without* any overhead, by slightly reducing the amount of data transmitted by 0.3%. Hence, from a website fingerprinting perspective, it seems to make sense to enable LHE, possibly in combination with compression, on this server.

Web page fingerprinting with patterns. In order to analyze more complex fingerprinting attacks, we again consider the IACR Cryptology ePrint Archive

---

[1] https://www.ssllabs.com/ssl-pulse/.

[2] We also considered basing this analysis on other web sites, such as Wikipedia and a user that accesses a certain Wikipedia page. However, the IACR ePrint server also enables us to easily consider a natural extension to more complex access pattern, see below.

and an adversary that tries to determine the visited page based on the size of encrypted data. This time, we consider a user that first visits the web page of a random paper from the year 2020, and then downloads the corresponding paper (a pdf file). Note that this yields a much more distinguishable pattern, in particular due to the highly varying size of pdf documents, and the fact that pdf files are not as easily compressible as text-based web pages.

We find that the advantage in counter mode is 1, that is, all papers are *uniquely* identifiable, such that the encryption provides no security at all against such attacks. This can be reduced to 0.12 by applying length-hiding padding with a bandwidth overhead of only about 2.4%. Hence, LHE can significantly improve security against fingerprinting at negligible overhead, which refutes the common belief that a significant overhead is necessary in order to achieve a considerable security improvement.

Google search term fingerprinting. Here we consider the scenario that one user is searching some term in a search engine. A passive adversary observes the encrypted traffic and tries to determine which search term the user is searching for. We used 503 most popular search terms from the daily search trends published by Google at https://trends.google.com/trends/ in a time period of one month in Spring 2021.

We find that without LHE an adversary achieves very high advantage of almost 1. LHE with only 2% bandwidth overhead can reduce this very significantly to only 0.07. In combination with compression, the advantage can be reduced to 0.006, while *reducing* the amount of transmitted data by 50%.

Simple Wikipedia fingerprinting. All the three application examples above consider a uniform message distribution, which does not necessarily capture the message distribution in the real-world applications. Obtaining real-world message distributions, e.g. by capturing Internet traffic, is difficult (for practical reasons, as well as due to privacy concerns). However, the Wikimedia Foundation publishes statistics of the Wikipedia website since May 2015, which provides us with the real distribution of visited webpages of the Wikipedia website. To better demonstrate the feasibility of our approach with respect to *real-world message distributions*, we carry out a webpage fingerprinting analysis for the Wikipedia webpages in simple English language, based on the real webpage visit distribution of May 2021.

We find that without LHE an adversary achieves very high trivial advantage (0.875). LHE with only 2% bandwidth overhead can reduce this to 0.13. In combination with compression, the advantage can be reduced to 0.0058, while *reducing* the amount of transmitted data by 50%.

DNS fingerprinting. Here we consider the *Domain Name System* (DNS) protocol and DNS request/response pairs. This setting is particularly interesting because there is an increasing trend to encrypt DNS protocol messages to hide the requested domain names. However, it turns out that the length of DNS requests/response pairs exhibit a very distinctive pattern, which make it easy to determine the requested domain name from the ciphertext length. We consider two different settings:

1. A user that issues a DNS request for a randomly chosen host name from 1,000 most popular hosts according to the *Majestic Million* list.
2. In collaboration with the IT department of a medium-sized university (with 23k students and 3.5k staff members), we collected the host names of DNS requests performed by staff and students within a 24 h time interval in July 2021. The data collection was carried out under supervision of the university data privacy officer and in accordance with applicable data protection laws. In particular, only the hostnames and their frequency were collected, but not the requesting IP addresses or any other personal data. This provides us with a real-world message distribution that makes it possible to determine the security and appropriate padding sizes for this particular DNS service.

In both cases, the adversary that tries to determine the requested host name based on the size of request and response.

In the *Majestic Million* case, we find that the advantage of an adversary can be reduced from 0.644 (in counter mode without compression) down to 0.01 with a bandwidth overhead of about 79% without compression, or 57% with. For the university DNS case, the advantage of an adversary can be reduced from 0.551 (in counter mode without compression) to below 0.01 with a bandwidth overhead of about 54% without compression.

In summary, we find that LHE can, contrary to the common belief, improve security against fingerprinting attacks very significantly, often with minor bandwidth overhead. This also confirms the recent tendency to switch from block-mode to counter-mode encryption indeed makes fingerprinting attacks much more effective.

We support our theoretical model and calculations with a proof-of-concept implementation in form of an Apache module. Our implementation consists of two parts. One part is a server-side monitoring algorithm that records (an approximation of) the message distribution and computes a suitable length-hiding parameter. The other part applies the length-hiding parameter as input to the encryption procedure of server responses. We used this proof-of-concept implementation to validate the results of our theoretical analysis.

Application of our results. Some standards and implementations of cryptographic protocols already provide means to conceal the length of plaintexts, in order to prevent fingerprinting attacks or reduce their effectivity. One such example is the TLS 1.3 standard [25], which directly supports the use of length-hiding padding and functions as basis of our implementation.

Another example of an Internet standard that supports length-hiding padding is DNS. RFC 8467 [22] describes *block-length padding*, which recommends to pad all DNS requests to a multiple of 128 bytes and all DNS responses to a multiple of 468 bytes (as originally proposed in [9]). We remark that these numbers are derived from an empirical analysis conducted specifically for DNS, and that we do not yet have a clear methodology to quantify to which degree they improve security concretely.

Related Works. The work of Boldyreva *et al.* [3] focuses on hiding message boundaries in a ciphertext stream with fragmented message transmission. This work is similar in spirit to ours in the sense that it tries to find a balance between the conflicting aims of keeping the generality and simplicity of traditional security definitions on the one hand, and developing an approach that can be used to provide meaningful provable security analyses of practical schemes on the other hand.

A very recent work on length-hiding encryption is due to Degabriele [5], which will appear at ACM CCS 2021. We compare our approach with the one in [5] in the full version [8] of our work.

Fingerprinting attacks have been intensively studied in the context of web page fingerprinting, deanonymization of Tor private channels, and other applications such as LTE/4G. Early approaches were based on the length of encrypted messages, as well as their direction and the frequency of messages [15,16,21]. More recent approaches use additional features advanced analysis techniques based on machine learning [14,20,28]. Also active attacks have been considered [20,27]. Countermeasures to fingerprinting attacks were proposed [31,34], but could be broken with refined analysis methods [7,28]. Cai *et al.* [4] give a systematic analysis of attacks and defenses to understand what features convey the most information.

We note that many works on the feasibility of fingerprinting attacks make use of side-channels beyond message lengths and we discuss this in the full version of our work [8].

Outline of this Paper. In Sect. 2 we describe a new perspective on LHE, which is more suitable for our approach, and conveniently yields schemes that follow the *standard* syntax of symmetric encryption schemes. Furthermore, we establish a definitional framework to analyze and quantify the concrete effect of LHE. Section 3 contains the results of an empirical analysis of different real-world message distributions. In Sect. 4 we present our implementation of LHE and compare its performance with our empirical results.

2   A New Perspective on Length-Hiding Encryption

Now we can describe our new perspective on length-hiding encryption (LHE), which makes it possible to concretely quantify the effect of length-hiding padding on security. We first introduce a new syntactical notion of LHE in Sect. 2.1 and a corresponding security experiment in Sect. 2.2. Based on these foundations, we can then define the *trivial success probability* and the *trivial advantage* to concretely quantify the security of an encryption scheme with respect to different length-hiding parameters.

In the full version of our work [8], we also discuss k-anonymity as an alternative approach and explain why we consider it as not suitable for our purposes.

2.1   A New Syntactical Definition

We first recap the formal definition of symmetric-key encryption.

Definition 1 (Symmetric-key encryption). *A symmetric-key encryption scheme* SE *consists of two algorithms* E *and* D. *The (possibly) randomized encryption algorithm* E *takes input a secret key* sk *and a plaintext* $m \in \{0,1\}^*$, *and outputs a ciphertext* ct. *The deterministic decryption algorithm* D *takes input a secret key* sk *and a ciphertext* ct *then outputs a plaintext* m *or a symbol* $\perp$. *The correctness of* SE *requires that* $D_{sk}(E_{sk}(m)) = m$ *for all* $sk \in \{0,1\}^k$ *and* $m \in \{0,1\}^*$.

Note that, in the above definition, the ciphertext length is implicitly defined by the encryption algorithm and cannot be altered or controlled outside the algorithm. Paterson *et al.* introduced the concept of *length-hiding encryption* in [24], which makes it possible to control the ciphertext length outside the encryption algorithm. In this paper we will work with a slightly different perspective, which we consider as more practical.

Recall that in [24] the length-hiding parameter ℓ is the total *ciphertext length* and it is an explicit input to the encryption algorithm. The parameter can be controlled by the adversary in the security experiment, the only restriction is that it must be at least as large as the largest of the two messages submitted by the adversary in the indistinguishability security experiment. We believe this does not capture real-world attacks based on ciphertext lengths very well, because it considers only the indistinguishability of two messages that are encrypted with respect to the same ciphertext length ℓ.

To protect against such attacks, we find it more practical to view the length hiding parameter as a fixed system parameter and to make the ciphertexts length dependent on both ℓ and the size of encrypted messages. More precisely, the global parameter ℓ (of a symmetric-key encryption scheme) defines a fixed *function* which maps plaintext length to certain ciphertext length.

Now, for any symmetric-key encryption scheme SE, we formalize a new symmetric-key encryption scheme $SE^{(\ell)}$ as the scheme SE instantiated with length hiding parameter ℓ as follows.

Definition 2 (Symmetric-key encryption with length-hiding parameter ℓ). *Let* $SE = (E, D)$ *be a symmetric encryption scheme. Let* $pad(m, \ell)$ *be a function that pads a plaintext* m *such that*

$$|pad(m, \ell)| = \left\lceil \frac{|m|}{\ell} \right\rceil \cdot \ell.$$

That is, pad *applies length-hiding padding to the plaintext* m *such that the length of* $pad(m, \ell)$ *is an integer multiple of* ℓ. *Let* pad^{-1} *be the function that removes the padding, that is,* $pad^{-1}(pad(m, \ell)) = m$ *for all* m *and* $pad^{-1}(\perp) = \perp$. *We call* ℓ *the* length-hiding *parameter and define the length-hiding encryption scheme* $SE^{(\ell)} = (E^{(\ell)}, D^{(\ell)})$ *as*

$$E_{sk}^{(\ell)}(m) := E_{sk}(pad(m, \ell)) \quad and \quad D_{sk}^{(\ell)}(m) := pad^{-1}(D_{sk}(m)).$$

Note that in particular we have $\mathsf{SE}^{(1)} = \mathsf{SE}$.

Padding a message to a multiple of some parameter ℓ is a generalization of the *block-length padding* scheme proposed in [9] and recommended for encrypted DNS requests in RFC 8467 [22].

Note that this scheme allows to capture "perfect" length-hiding padding, where the length-hiding parameter ℓ is at least as large as the largest possible message in an application, such that all ciphertexts have identical length and no information is leaked through the length. However, if ℓ is smaller, then we will get weaker security guarantees. We will show that this is very useful to achieve a trade-off between improved resilience to attacks based on message length and bandwidth overhead of the length-hiding padding. Furthermore, we will analyze the concrete impact of different length-hiding parameters on the security and bandwidth requirements of an application.

Security notions for symmetric-key encryption schemes. Since $\mathsf{SE}^{(\ell)}$ follows the standard syntax of encryption schemes for all $\ell \in \mathbb{N}$, standard security definitions (without considering length leakage) for symmetric-key encryption apply to it. There are many different ways to define security for symmetric-key encryption schemes. In this paper we will consider two flavors of standard IND-CCA security, the IND-M-CCA security and the IND-C-CCA security. Both provide protection for message privacy but none of them provides protection against length leakage. However, they serve as an important tool in our approach to capture the effectiveness of length-hiding encryption.

IND-M-CCA security. The first notion is the indistinguishability of encryptions of chosen *messages* from encryptions of random strings. It is equivalent to the classical "left-or-right" definition where an adversary outputs two messages m_0 and m_1, receives back an encryption of message m_b for a random $b \xleftarrow{\$} \{0,1\}$, and has to determine b.

Definition 3 (IND-M-CCA security). *A symmetric-key encryption scheme* $\mathsf{SE} = (\mathsf{E}, \mathsf{D})$ *is* IND-M-CCA *secure if for any PPT adversary* $\mathcal{A}$, *the advantage*

$$\mathsf{Adv}^{\mathsf{SE},\mathcal{A}}_{\mathsf{IND}\text{-}\mathsf{M}\text{-}\mathsf{CCA}}(1^k) := \left| 2 \cdot \Pr\left[\mathsf{IND}\text{-}\mathsf{M}\text{-}\mathsf{CCA}^{\mathsf{SE},\mathcal{A}}(1^k) = 1 \right] - 1 \right|$$

is negligible, where game $\mathsf{IND}\text{-}\mathsf{M}\text{-}\mathsf{CCA}^{\mathsf{SE}}$ *is defined in Fig. 1.*

IND-C-CCA security. The second notion we consider is indistinguishability of *ciphertexts* from random strings (the "IND" notion in [18]), which is commonly used in recent works, such as [11,12]. This security considers the "ciphertext pseudorandomness" of the symmetric-key encryption scheme.

Definition 4 (IND-C-CCA security). *A symmetric-key encryption scheme* $\mathsf{SE} = (\mathsf{E}, \mathsf{D})$ *is* IND-C-CCA *secure if for any PPT adversary* $\mathcal{A}$, *the advantage*

$$\mathsf{Adv}^{\mathsf{SE},\mathcal{A}}_{\mathsf{IND}\text{-}\mathsf{C}\text{-}\mathsf{CCA}}(1^k) := \left| 2 \cdot \Pr\left[\mathsf{IND}\text{-}\mathsf{C}\text{-}\mathsf{CCA}^{\mathsf{SE},\mathcal{A}}(1^k) = 1 \right] - 1 \right|$$

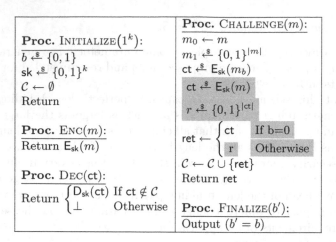

Fig. 1. The security game IND-M-CCA^{SE} and the security game IND-C-CCA^{SE}. The gray background codes only applies to game IND-C-CCA^{SE}.

is negligible, where game IND-C-CCA^{SE} is defined in Fig. 1.

Since the length-hiding parameter ℓ is a global system parameter and known to the adversary (the adversary does not have to break the scheme or make any encryption or decryption queries to know this parameter), we point out that the length-hiding property is orthogonal to the exact oracle query ability of the adversary. Our choice to consider security against chosen-ciphertext attacks should merely serve as a concrete example. For instance, CPA security is easily obtained by removing the decryption oracle, passive eavesdropping by additionally removing the encryption oracle. It is also possible to consider advanced security notions, such as misuse-resistant encryption [26], where the adversary is able to specify the nonce used by an encryption algorithm. Furthermore, it can be considered in both the symmetric-key and the public-key setting. We chose security against chosen-ciphertext attacks in order to demonstrate that the approach works also with this rather strong standard security definition.

2.2   New Security Model

Our objective is to define a model that is independent of a particular application, but capable of capturing complex application settings where multiple messages of varying lengths are encrypted using multiple keys and the adversary wants to deduce information about these messages from the ciphertexts. Therefore we parametrize our security model as follows:

Message distribution. Note that the information an adversary can deduce from the size of observed ciphertexts depends inherently on the message distribution of a given application, and possibly other application-specific properties, such as observable patterns of messages, for instance. Since we want to preserve as much of the simplicity and generality of classical security models as possible, our new security definition is parametrized by a *message distribution* M of a given application.

For instance, in the web page fingerprinting setting, the distribution M would assign probabilities to different web pages on a server. If a client performs a search with an Internet search engine, then $m^* \xleftarrow{\$} $ M would correspond to the messages exchanged between a client and the search engine. Note that, in this case, the message distribution M is defined by the client and the server may not know this distribution M beforehand. However, we consider strong adversaries that know M so that it obtains some a prior knowledge about this search term.

Specification of data to-be-protected. We introduce a function $\mathcal{P}$ which specifies the information that an adversary wants to learn about the encrypted data. For instance, if a client performs a search with an Internet search engine and the adversary wants to learn the search term, then the data exchanged between client and search engine would be $m^* \xleftarrow{\$} $ M, and the goal of the adversary would be to determine the search term $\mathcal{P}(m^*)$.

Multiple symmetric keys. We want to be able to consider complex fingerprinting attacks on applications transmitting encrypted data. For instance, in the context of Internet search engines a client might first connect to a search engine and to perform a search, then connect to a DNS server to make a DNS request for the first search result, and then connect to the server hosting the corresponding web site. We will consider a setting where all three connections are encrypted, such that this involves three different encrypted sessions with three different, independent symmetric keys.[3] In order to reflect this accurately, we need to define a security model which involves d symmetric keys.

Adversarial model. Finally, we need to specify the capabilities that we grant the attacker. We will consider *chosen-ciphertext attacks* (CCA), as already discussed in Sect. 2.1.

In Sect. 3, we will show how to define M, $\mathcal{P}$, and d for a particular given applications to obtain concrete security statements for this application. In most practical cases, $\mathcal{P}$ will be efficiently computable, but we do not have to demand this.

Security Experiment. Motivated by this discussion, we define the $(\mathsf{SE}, \mathsf{M}, \mathcal{P}, d)$-CCA security experiment based on the game described in Fig. 2. In this game, we consider an encryption scheme SE with $d \geq 1$ independent secret keys and a message distribution M that outputs $t \geq 1$ messages where $t = t_1 + \ldots + t_d$ for some $t_1, \ldots, t_d \in \mathbb{N}$. We model M as a probabilistic algorithm defining a message distribution over $(\{0,1\}^*)^t$. In the sequel it will be convenient to view the output of M as a tuple of tuples of messages $m = ((m_{1j})_{j \in [t_1]}, \ldots, (m_{dj})_{j \in [t_d]}) \xleftarrow{\$} $ M. Here

---

[3] In practice the TLS protocol would be used for these three connections, where different keys are used for sending and receiving data, but we view these keys as a single symmetric key.

$(m_{ij})_{j \in [t_i]}$ is the tuple of messages encrypted under the i-th symmetric key sk_i. The function $\mathcal{P}$ maps $\mathcal{P} : (\{0,1\}^*)^t \to \{0,1\}^*$.

Proc. INITIALIZE(1^k):	**Proc. CHALLENGE():**
$\mathsf{sk}_1, \cdots, \mathsf{sk}_d \xleftarrow{\$} \{0,1\}^k$	If challenged = True return $\perp$
challenged $\leftarrow$ False	challenged $\leftarrow$ True
$\mathcal{C} \leftarrow \emptyset$	$\underbrace{((m^*_{1j})_{j \in [t_1]}, \cdots, (m^*_{dj})_{j \in [t_d]})}_{\boldsymbol{m}^*} \xleftarrow{\$} \mathsf{M}$
Return $(\mathsf{M}, \mathcal{P})$	
	For $i \in [d], j \in [t_i]$:
Proc. ENC(i, m):	$\quad \mathsf{ct}^*_{ij} \xleftarrow{\$} \mathsf{E}_{\mathsf{sk}_i}(m^*_{ij})$
Return $\mathsf{E}_{\mathsf{sk}_i}(m)$	$\quad \mathcal{C} \leftarrow \mathcal{C} \cup \{(i, \mathsf{ct}^*_{ij})\}$
	Return $(\mathsf{ct}^*_{ij})_{i \in [d], j \in [t_i]}$
Proc. DEC(i, ct):	
If $(i, \mathsf{ct}) \in \mathcal{C}$:	**Proc. FINALIZE(p):**
$\quad$ Return $\perp$	Output $(\mathcal{P}(\boldsymbol{m}^*) = p)$
Return $\mathsf{D}_{\mathsf{sk}_i}(\mathsf{ct})$	

Fig. 2. The $(\mathsf{SE}, \mathsf{M}, \mathcal{P}, d)$-CCA security game with respect to encryption scheme SE, message distribution M, property $\mathcal{P}$ and number of secret key d.

Definition 5. *For any adversary $\mathcal{A}$, define the success probability of $\mathcal{A}$ in game $(\mathsf{SE}, \mathsf{M}, \mathcal{P}, d)$-CCA as the probability that $\mathcal{A}$ is able to determine $\mathcal{P}(\boldsymbol{m}^*)$. Formally:*

$$\mathsf{RealSucc}(\mathsf{SE}, \mathsf{M}, \mathcal{P}, d, \mathcal{A}) := \Pr\left[(\mathsf{SE}, \mathsf{M}, \mathcal{P}, d)\text{-CCA}^{\mathcal{A}}(1^k) = 1\right].$$

Our security model is restricted in the sense that 1) it only considers the single-challenge setting and 2) the message distribution is fixed and not adaptively chosen by the adversary. Our security notion could be generalized to capture both aspects; however, this seems not to provide any non-trivial additional insight to the impact of length-hiding encryption and therefore we chose not to do this.

Non-triviality of M *and* $\mathcal{P}$. In the sequel we will only consider M and $\mathcal{P}$ such that there exist $\boldsymbol{m}$ and $\boldsymbol{m}'$ such that $\Pr[\boldsymbol{m} \xleftarrow{\$} \mathsf{M}] > 0$, $\Pr[\boldsymbol{m}' \xleftarrow{\$} \mathsf{M}] > 0$, and $\mathcal{P}(\boldsymbol{m}) \neq \mathcal{P}(\boldsymbol{m}')$. This is necessary for technical reasons, but also sufficient because we would otherwise not get a meaningful notion of security (because otherwise it would be trivial to predict $\mathcal{P}$ with respect to M with success probability 1, even without seeing any ciphertexts).

Our security definition implies non-adaptive IND-M-CCA security where messages are chosen non-adaptively. We discuss this in the full version of our work [8].

2.3   Trivial Success Probability and Advantage

Trivial success probability. We introduce the *trivial success probability* of an adversary, which captures the success probability that an adversary trivially obtains from the *length* of ciphertexts, without "breaking" the underlying encryption scheme SE. Note that this depends on the degree to which SE hides the size of plaintexts, the message distribution M, and the function $\mathcal{P}$.

Definition 6. *The* trivial success probability *with respect to* $(\mathsf{SE}, \mathsf{M}, \mathcal{P})$ *is defined as the largest possible probability of guessing* $\mathcal{P}(\boldsymbol{m}^*)$, *given* M, $\mathcal{P}$, *and the size of the ciphertexts* $(|\mathsf{ct}^*_{ij}|)_{i \in [d], j \in [t_i]}$, *but not the ciphertexts themselves. More formally,*

$$\mathsf{TrivSucc}(\mathsf{SE}, \mathsf{M}, \mathcal{P}) := \max_{\mathcal{S}} \Pr\left[\mathcal{S}(\mathsf{M}, \mathcal{P}, (|\mathsf{ct}^*_i|)_{i \in [t]}) = \mathcal{P}(\boldsymbol{m}^*)\right]$$

where $\boldsymbol{m}^* = \left((m^*_{1j})_{j \in [t_1]}, \cdots, (m^*_{dj})_{j \in [t_d]}\right) \xleftarrow{\$} \mathsf{M}$, $\mathsf{sk}_1, \cdots, \mathsf{sk}_d \xleftarrow{\$} \{0, 1\}^k$ *and* $\mathsf{ct}^*_{ij} \xleftarrow{\$} \mathsf{E}_{\mathsf{sk}_i}(m^*_{ij})$ *for* $i \in [d], j \in [t_i]$ *and where the maximum is taken over all algorithms* $\mathcal{S}$.

The following property is necessary to avoid contrived and unnatural examples of encryption schemes, where the length of ciphertexts depends not only on the size of the message, but also on the secret key. To our best knowledge, this property is met by any concrete symmetric encryption schemes, except for contrived counterexamples.

Definition 7. *We say an encryption scheme* $\mathsf{SE} = (\mathsf{E}, \mathsf{D})$ *has* secret key oblivious ciphertext length distribution *if for any* $m \in \{0, 1\}^*$, *any* $\mathsf{sk}, \mathsf{sk}' \in \{0, 1\}^k$, $|\mathsf{E}_{\mathsf{sk}}(m)|$ *distributes identically to* $|\mathsf{E}_{\mathsf{sk}'}(m)|$.

If we would restrict to settings with deterministic padding length, then we could instead require $|\mathsf{E}_{\mathsf{sk}}(m)| = |\mathsf{E}_{\mathsf{sk}'}(m)|$. However, we will also consider randomized padding, so that it is necessary to require identical *distribution* of ciphertext lengths.

Relation between trivial and real success probability. We will now prove that $\mathcal{A}$'s real success probability $\mathsf{RealSucc}(\mathsf{SE}, \mathsf{M}, \mathcal{P}, d, \mathcal{A})$ cannot exceed the trivial success probability $\mathsf{TrivSucc}(\mathsf{SE}, \mathsf{M}, \mathcal{P})$ significantly, provided that SE is IND-C-CCA secure in the sense of Definition 4 and satisfies Definition 7. This establishes that in order to minimize $\mathsf{RealSucc}(\mathsf{SE}, \mathsf{M}, \mathcal{P}, d, \mathcal{A})$ it suffices to minimize $\mathsf{TrivSucc}(\mathsf{SE}, \mathsf{M}, \mathcal{P})$.

Theorem 8. *For any encryption scheme* SE *that has secret key oblivious ciphertext length distribution in the sense of Definition 7, any message distribution* M, *any property* $\mathcal{P}$ *and any adversary* $\mathcal{A}$, *we can construct an adversary* $\mathcal{B}$ *such that*

$$\mathsf{RealSucc}(\mathsf{SE}, \mathsf{M}, \mathcal{P}, d, \mathcal{A}) \leq d \cdot \mathsf{Adv}^{\mathsf{SE}, \mathcal{B}}_{\mathsf{IND\text{-}C\text{-}CCA}}(1^k) + \mathsf{TrivSucc}(\mathsf{SE}, \mathsf{M}, \mathcal{P}).$$

The running time of $\mathcal{B}$ *is* $T(\mathcal{B}) \approx T(\mathcal{A}) + T(\mathsf{M}) + T(\mathcal{P}) + (t + q_e) \cdot T(\mathsf{E}) + q_d \cdot T(\mathsf{D})$, *where* $T(\mathsf{M})$ *is the time to sample messages from distribution* M, $T(\mathcal{P})$ *is the time to evaluate* $\mathcal{P}$, $T(\mathsf{E})$ *is the time to execute the encryption algorithm once,* $T(\mathsf{D})$ *is the time to execute the decryption algorithm once,* q_e *is the number of* ENC *queries made by* $\mathcal{A}$ *and* q_d *is the number of* DEC *queries made by* $\mathcal{A}$.

Due to space limitations, we defer the proof to the full version of our work [8].

Theorem 8 provides an upper bound of the adversary's success probability in our practical "real world" security model and this bound is a sum of the CCA advantage with the trivial success probability. So if the encryption scheme itself is secure in the standard sense (i.e., the IND-C-CCA advantage of any adversary is negligible, which is provided by the IND-C-CCA security of the scheme) then the sum is close to the trivial advantage. In this way, we can focus on reducing the trivial success probability by choosing a proper length-hiding encryption scheme to reduce the information that is leaked through ciphertext length.

In the following, we show a methodology of evaluating the "effectiveness" of length-hiding encryption in reducing the trivial success probability. Intuitively speaking, we first define the "most likely probability" to capture prior information leaked by the distribution M known to the adversary. And this probability provides a lower bound for the trivial success probability. For any concrete encryption scheme, we compare its trivial success probability with this lower bound to evaluate its "effectiveness" in hiding the length information. And we further quantify it by providing a new definition of *trivial advantage*.

Trivial advantage. Based on the trivial success probability, we define the *trivial advantage* with respect to encryption scheme SE, message distribution M, and property $\mathcal{P}$ as follows.

Definition 9. *For message distribution* M *and property* $\mathcal{P}$, *let*

$$\mathsf{PrMostLikely}(\mathsf{M}, \mathcal{P}) := \max_{\mathcal{S}} \Pr\left[\mathcal{S}(\mathsf{M}, \mathcal{P}) = \mathcal{P}(\boldsymbol{m}^*)\right]$$

denote the probability of the most likely output of $\mathcal{P}$ *on input* $\boldsymbol{m}^*$, *where* $\boldsymbol{m}^* = \left((m^*_{1j})_{j \in [t_1]}, \cdots, (m^*_{dj})_{j \in [t_d]}\right) \xleftarrow{\$} \mathsf{M}$. *The* trivial advantage *with respect to* (SE, $\mathsf{M}, \mathcal{P}$) *is defined as difference between the trivial success probability and* PrMostLikely($\mathsf{M}, \mathcal{P}$), *scaled to an number that ranges from 0 to 1 for any* M *and* $\mathcal{P}$:

$$\mathsf{TrivAdv}(\mathsf{SE}, \mathsf{M}, \mathcal{P}) := \frac{\mathsf{TrivSucc}(\mathsf{SE}, \mathsf{M}, \mathcal{P}) - \mathsf{PrMostLikely}(\mathsf{M}, \mathcal{P})}{1 - \mathsf{PrMostLikely}(\mathsf{M}, \mathcal{P})}.$$

Recall that we consider M and $\mathcal{P}$ such that there exist $\boldsymbol{m}$ and $\boldsymbol{m}'$ such that $\Pr[\boldsymbol{m}^* = \boldsymbol{m}] > 0$, $\Pr[\boldsymbol{m}^* = \boldsymbol{m}'] > 0$, and $\mathcal{P}(\boldsymbol{m}) \neq \mathcal{P}(\boldsymbol{m}')$, as otherwise it is trivial to predict $\mathcal{P}$ with respect to M with success probability 1. Therefore we have PrMostLikely($\mathsf{M}, \mathcal{P}$) < 1.

3   Analysis of Real-World Message Distributions

In this section, we will consider different types of attacks, where an adversary observes encrypted communication and wants to determine the plaintext based on the communication pattern. As a concrete example we consider counter mode encryption (with AES-GCM, for instance) where the adversary is able to determine the size of the encrypted message precisely, as well as block mode encryption (using AES-CBC as an example) where the adversary is able to determine the size of the encrypted message up to the minimal message padding required for this mode. We apply our methodology to concretely calculate the trivial advantage for the considered message distribution M and function $\mathcal{P}$ that we define for each application. Then we compare the results to the same schemes, but using length-hiding encryption with different length-hiding parameters. This makes it possible to quantify the security gained by length-hiding encryption and compression precisely. Most interestingly, we will show that relatively small length-hiding parameters are able to significantly reduce the effectivity of fingerprinting attacks.

In all the subsequent parts of this work, we will use different units for the length-hiding parameter for counter mode and block mode encryption. The reason for this is that counter mode ciphers (like AES-GCM) usually encrypt messages *byte-wise*, therefore the size of ciphertexts and the length-hiding parameter ℓ are measured in bytes. Block ciphers (like AES-CBC) encrypts messages *block-wise*, so we will measure the size of ciphertexts and ℓ in blocks, where one block corresponds to the block size of the underlying block cipher (16 bytes in case of AES).

Due to space limitations, we only include two examples in the body, which we deemed most simple (i.e., simple website fingerprinting and simple Wikipedia fingerprinting). However, we also consider more complex examples (i.e., webpage fingerprinting with patterns, Google search term fingerprinting, and DNS fingerprinting) in the full version of this work [8].

3.1   Simple Website Fingerprinting

Adversarial model. We consider an adversary performing a *website fingerprinting* attack against the IACR ePrint archive[4] at https://eprint.iacr.org/2020/, based on the size of encrypted data. The ePrint page for the year 2020 links to 1620 different subpages, one for each archived research papers. We chose the year 2020 because it is the most recent year where the number of archived research papers was fixed at the time this paper is written, which makes the analysis more easily reproducible. Each subpage contains the title, list of authors, abstract, and some other metadata for one archived research paper.

Let $\mathcal{M} := \{m_1, \ldots, m_{1620}\}$ be the set of the 1620 different web pages. We assume that a user Alice picks one out of these 1620 subpages uniformly at

---

[4] We use this server since URLs from the IACR ePrint archive are particularly easy to parse and analyse.

random and then visits the corresponding page. Hence, the message distribution M_e that we consider here is the uniform distribution over $\mathcal{M}$. The adversary tries to guess the subpage visited by Alice. Hence, the adversary outputs an index $i \in \{1, \ldots, 1620\}$, such that we define function $\mathcal{P}$ as $\mathcal{P} : \mathcal{M} \to [1, 1620]$ for $m_i \mapsto i$.

Considered encryption schemes. The IACR ePrint server uses TLS 1.2 and allows the client and the server to negotiate one out of two different symmetric ciphers for the encryption of payload data:

Counter mode. The first option is AES-GCM, which is essentially a stream cipher and we refer it as $\mathsf{SE}_{\mathrm{CTR}}^{(\ell)}$. Note that in this case the attacker learns the size of the underlying plaintext *exactly* (in case of TLS the attacker merely has to subtract a known constant from the ciphertext size), provided that no length-hiding padding is used ($\ell = 1$).

Block mode. The second option is AES-CBC and we refer it as $\mathsf{SE}_{\mathrm{BLK}}^{(\ell)}$. Due to the padding required by CBC-mode encryption, the attacker learns only that the plaintext lies within a certain (small) range even if no length-hiding padding is used ($\ell = 1$). Since the block size of AES is 16 bytes, AES-CBC uses a padding of length between 1 and 16 bytes, this holds also for AES-CBC in TLS 1.2.

We decided to use these two algorithms as the basis of our analysis, since they cover both a stream cipher and a block mode cipher, and are very widely used in practice. We consider a length-hiding padding with length-hiding parameter $\ell \in \mathbb{N}$. Ciphertexts are padded to a multiple of ℓ *bytes* for $\mathsf{SE}_{\mathrm{CTR}}^{(\ell)}$, and ℓ *blocks* for $\mathsf{SE}_{\mathrm{BLK}}^{(\ell)}$. Thus, if $\ell = 1$, then no additional length-hiding padding is used.

We also consider enabled compression where the full plaintext message is compressed using the `gzip` algorithm, which implements DEFLATE compression (a combination of the LZ77 algorithm and Huffman coding). This is the algorithm standardized for use in TLS versions up to 1.2 [17], and therefore seems to be a reasonable choice for an analysis of real-world algorithms.

In order to indicate whether compression is used, we will refer to the encryption algorithm as $\mathsf{SE}_{\mathrm{M,C}}^{(\ell)}$ where $\mathrm{M} \in \{\mathrm{CTR}, \mathrm{BLK}\}$ represents its mode and $\mathrm{C} \in \{\mathrm{True}, \mathrm{False}\}$ represents whether compression is applied before encryption.

Empirical Data Generation. We implemented a simple script that downloaded all subpages of https://eprint.iacr.org/2020/ and determined the size of the page in both uncompressed and compressed form. These sizes are stored in a database and enable us to compute the size[5] of counter- and block-mode ciphertexts that encrypt the pages in compressed or uncompressed form, with and without length-hiding encryption, and with respect to different length-hiding parameters.

---

[5] To make our calculation more realistic, we consider the ciphertext is split across TLS fragments with a maximum payload of 2^{14} bytes per fragment, whereby each fragment needs an additional 22 bytes reserved for the fragment header. The length for all the TLS headers is also considered and summed to the ciphertext length.

Calculating the trivial advantage $\mathsf{TrivAdv}(\mathsf{SE}_{\mathsf{M},\mathsf{C}}^{(\ell)}, \mathsf{M_e})$. We determined the number $|U|$ of uniquely identifiable web pages, the size $|S_{\mathsf{max}}|$ of the largest set of pages of identical size, the number $|S|$ of different possible ciphertext lengths, and the trivial advantage $\mathsf{TrivAdv}(\mathsf{SE}_{\mathsf{M},\mathsf{C}}^{(\ell)}, \mathsf{M_e})$ for both counter mode and block mode encryption, with and without compression, and with respect to different length-hiding parameters, and with respect to the uniform distribution $\mathsf{M_e}$ over the ePrint 2020 webpages.

Recall that the trivial success probability is defined as

$$\mathsf{TrivSucc}(\mathsf{SE}_{\mathsf{M},\mathsf{C}}^{(\ell)}, \mathsf{M_e}, \mathcal{P}) := \max_S \Pr\left[\mathcal{S}(\mathsf{M_e}, \mathcal{P}, |\mathsf{ct}^*|) = \mathcal{P}(m^*)\right]$$

where the probability is over the random choice $m^* \xleftarrow{\$} \mathsf{M_e}$ and ct^* is the encryption of m^*. Since $\mathsf{M_e}$ is the uniform distribution, the trivial success probability for a given ciphertext length λ is equal to the number of messages $m^* \in \mathcal{M}$ that encrypt to a ciphertext of the given length $\lambda = |\mathsf{ct}^*|$. Hence, defining $\mathcal{M}_\lambda := \{m \in \mathcal{M} : |\mathsf{E_{sk}}(m)| = \lambda\}$ as the set of messages that encrypt to a ciphertext of size λ, we have

$$\mathsf{TrivSucc}(\mathsf{SE}_{\mathsf{M},\mathsf{C}}^{(\ell)}, \mathsf{M_e}, \mathcal{P}) = \sum_{\lambda \in S} \frac{|\mathcal{M}_\lambda|}{|\mathcal{M}|} \cdot \frac{1}{|\mathcal{M}_\lambda|} = \frac{|S|}{|\mathcal{M}|} = \frac{|S|}{1620}.$$

Hence, the trivial advantage is $\mathsf{TrivAdv}(\mathsf{SE}_{\mathsf{M},\mathsf{C}}^{(\ell)}, \mathsf{M_e}, \mathcal{P})$

$$= \frac{\mathsf{TrivSucc}(\mathsf{SE}_{\mathsf{M},\mathsf{C}}^{(\ell)}, \mathsf{M_e}, \mathcal{P}) - \mathsf{PrMostLikely}(\mathsf{M_e}, \mathcal{P})}{1 - \mathsf{PrMostLikely}(\mathsf{M_e}, \mathcal{P})}$$

$$= \left(\frac{|S|}{1620} - \frac{1}{1620}\right) \div \left(1 - \frac{1}{1620}\right) = \frac{|S| - 1}{1619}.$$

We consider length-hiding block mode ciphertexts with $\ell \in \{1, 5, 10, 25\}$ and counter mode ciphertexts with $\ell \in \{1, 80, 160, 400\}$. Table 1 summarizes the results of this analysis.

Achieving a Trivial Advantage of 0. Note that according to Table 1 an increasing length-hiding parameter ℓ reduces the trivial advantage significantly, but not to 0. This may be sufficient to make traffic analysis attacks significantly less effective, but for some applications a trivial advantage of 0 may be desirable.

Rows 9, 10, 19 and 20 of Table 1 give the minimal length-hiding parameter ℓ that is necessary to reduce the trivial advantage to 0.

Conclusions. For the message distribution considered in this section, we come to the following conclusions:

- A block mode of operation improves the indistinguishability of the considered web pages, compared to a counter mode when $\ell = 1$. In combination with length-hiding encryption and compression, the adversary's trivial advantage can be reduced from 0.7400 (in counter mode without compression) down to 0.0037 (in block mode with compression and length-hiding parameter $\ell = 25$), together with a reduction in traffic by 45.278%.

Table 1. Analysis of simple website fingerprinting attacks. "CTR" refers to AES-GCM, "BLK" to AES-CBC. "Comp." indicates whether compression is enabled, ℓ is the length-hiding parameter. Recall that plaintexts are padded to a multiple of ℓ *bytes* for counter mode and ℓ *blocks* for block mode encryption, thus, if $\ell = 1$, then no additional length-hiding padding is used. $|U|$ is the number of uniquely identifiable pages, $|S_{max}|$ is the size of the largest set of pages of identical size, $|\mathcal{S}|$ is the number of different ciphertext lengths that are possible for the considered message distribution. "TrivAdv" is the trivial advantage $\mathsf{TrivAdv}(\mathsf{SE}_{M,C}^{(\ell)}, \mathsf{M_e})$. The column "Total data" lists the total amount of data transferred from the server to the client when each of the 1620 web pages is accessed exactly once, "Overhead" the traffic overhead incurred by LHE when compared to the same encryption mode with $\ell = 1$ and without compression.

	Mode	ℓ	Comp.	$|U|$	$|S_{max}|$	$|\mathcal{S}|$	TrivAdv	Total data	Overhead
1	CTR	1	False	868	4	1199	0.7400	5.39 MB	—
2	CTR	1	True	400	8	822	0.5071	2.65 MB	−50.888%
3	CTR	80	False	8	85	54	0.0327	5.45 MB	1.158%
4	CTR	80	True	3	205	24	0.0142	2.71 MB	−49.745%
5	CTR	160	False	6	166	30	0.0179	5.52 MB	2.311%
6	CTR	160	True	3	404	14	0.0080	2.77 MB	−48.610%
7	CTR	400	False	1	409	14	0.0080	5.70 MB	5.677%
8	CTR	400	True	2	826	7	0.0037	2.96 MB	−45.159%
9	CTR	8995	False	0	1620	1	0.0000	13.93 MB	158.346%
10	CTR	3458	True	0	1620	1	0.0000	5.38 MB	−0.294%
11	BLK	1	False	40	23	213	0.1309	5.40 MB	—
12	BLK	1	True	17	46	100	0.0611	2.66 MB	−50.777%
13	BLK	5	False	8	85	54	0.0327	5.45 MB	0.938%
14	BLK	5	True	3	205	24	0.0142	2.71 MB	−49.854%
15	BLK	10	False	6	166	30	0.0179	5.52 MB	2.089%
16	BLK	10	True	3	404	14	0.0080	2.77 MB	−48.722%
17	BLK	25	False	1	409	14	0.0080	5.70 MB	5.448%
18	BLK	25	True	2	826	7	0.0037	2.96 MB	−45.278%
19	BLK	563	False	0	1620	1	0.0000	13.95 MB	158.157%
20	BLK	217	True	0	1620	1	0.0000	5.40 MB	−0.111%

- In most cases compression reduces the trivial advantage of the adversary by a factor of about 2 or better. The only exception is counter mode without length-hiding padding, where the reduction is still by a significant factor of about 1.5.
- Compression significantly reduces the number $|U|$ of uniquely identifiable web pages in all cases by a factor of 2 or better, and increases the size $|S_{max}|$ of the largest set of pages of identical size.

– To analyze the impact of different length-hiding parameters and compression on communication complexity, we also measured the total amount of data transferred from the server to the client when each of the 1620 web pages is accessed exactly once. Note that compression not only reduces the adversary's advantage by a factor around 2, but also reduces the communication complexity by a factor around 2.

– Without compression, even for a relatively large LHE parameter ℓ, such as $400 = 25 \cdot 16$ for counter mode or 25 for block mode encryption, the added communication complexity is relatively small, in particular when compared to the corresponding reduction in the adversary's trivial advantage.

– Achieving a trivial advantage of 0 costs a traffic overhead 159% without compression and even reduces traffic with compression.

We also consider a more powerful fingerprinting attack on the IACR ePrint archive website based on *user patterns* and another fingerprinting attack on the Google search engine. Due to space limitations, these two sections can be found in the full version of our work [8].

3.2   Simple Wikipedia Fingerprinting

Adversarial model. We consider webpage fingerprinting attack on the Wikipedia website. In this model, a user visits the Wikipedia website. A passive adversary observes the encrypted traffic and tries to determine the visited page.

Considered algorithms. Same as in Sect. 3.1.

Empirical data generation. The Wikimedia Foundation publishes *pageview statistics* of the Wikipedia website since May 2015. The pageview statistics contain the number of requests for each webpage in Wikipedia, which provides us with a real world message distribution of Wikipedia pages. We used the pageview data of May 2021 from https://dumps.wikimedia.org/other/pageviews/readme. html. We considered the data for 164270 webpages written in *simple English* and used a script issuing an HTTP HEAD-request for every webpage to determine the size, in uncompressed and in compressed form. These values are stored in a database and used to compute the size of counter- and block-mode ciphertexts for these schemes that encrypt the web page in either compressed or uncompressed form, with or without length-hiding encryption, and with respect to different length-hiding parameters. We note that the Simple Wikipedia project has a total number of 260478 webpages, as of May 2021, but not all webpages were accessed at least once during this period. Therefore we consider only the subset of webpages that were accessed in the considered time period (thus, the message distribution implicitly assigns a probability of zero to other pages).

Let $\mathcal{M} := \{m_1, \ldots, m_{164270}\}$ be the set of different Simple Wikipedia webpages accessed in May 2021. We assume that the user picks one out of the 164270 webpages according to the distribution (denoted by $\mathsf{M_{Wiki}}$) based on the pageview statistics and then gets the corresponding encrypted webpage. The

Table 2. Analysis of Simple Wikipedia article fingerprinting. "CTR" refers to AES-GCM, "BLK" to AES-CBC. "Comp." indicates whether compression is enabled, ℓ is the length-hiding parameter. Ciphertexts are padded to a multiple of ℓ bytes for counter mode, and ℓ blocks for block mode encryption, $\ell = 1$ means that no additional length-hiding padding is used. $|U|$ is the number of uniquely identifiable pages, $|S_{max}|$ is the size of the largest set of pages of identical size, $|S|$ is the number of different ciphertext lengths that are possible for the considered message distribution. "TrivAdv" is the trivial advantage $\mathsf{TrivAdv}(\mathsf{SE}_{M,C}^{(\ell)}, \mathsf{M}_{\mathsf{Wiki}})$. The column "Total data" contains the total amount of data transferred from the sever to the client when each of the 164270 web pages exactly once, "Overhead" the overhead incurred by LHE when compared to the same encryption mode with $\ell = 1$ and without compression.

	Mode	ℓ	Comp.	$|U|$	$|S_{max}|$	$|S|$	TrivAdv	Total data	Overhead
1	CTR	1	False	26597	232	62524	0.8750	400.24 GB	0.000%
2	CTR	1	True	12908	81757	25689	0.5635	72.93 GB	−81.780%
3	CTR	400	False	293	2251	1081	0.2775	401.14 GB	0.226%
4	CTR	400	True	132	81757	507	0.1557	73.82 GB	−81.556%
5	CTR	4000	False	27	21876	193	0.1354	409.24 GB	2.248%
6	CTR	4000	True	26	81757	100	0.0701	81.76 GB	−79.573%
7	CTR	40000	False	4	75284	34	0.0499	493.69 GB	23.349%
8	CTR	40000	True	6	158278	20	0.0058	199.47 GB	−50.162%
9	CTR	160000	False	2	160609	11	0.0091	828.22 GB	106.930%
10	CTR	160000	True	2	164063	7	0.0012	728.39 GB	81.987%
11	CTR	2290976	False	0	164270	1	0.0000	10.14 TB	2493.687%
12	CTR	1331408	True	0	164270	1	0.0000	5.89 TB	1407.331%
13	BLK	1	False	3283	238	10540	0.6023	401.35 GB	0.000%
14	BLK	1	True	1457	81757	4901	0.3763	74.40 GB	−81.462%
15	BLK	25	False	293	2251	1081	0.2775	402.22 GB	0.217%
16	BLK	25	True	132	81757	507	0.1557	75.26 GB	−81.250%
17	BLK	250	False	27	21876	193	0.1354	410.31 GB	2.232%
18	BLK	250	True	26	81757	100	0.0701	83.19 GB	−79.272%
19	BLK	2500	False	4	75284	34	0.0499	494.67 GB	23.251%
20	BLK	2500	True	6	158278	20	0.0058	200.75 GB	−49.983%
21	BLK	10000	False	2	160609	11	0.0091	828.85 GB	106.514%
22	BLK	10000	True	2	164063	7	0.0012	728.99 GB	81.632%
23	BLK	143186	False	0	164270	1	0.0000	10.14 TB	2486.567%
24	BLK	83213	True	0	164270	1	0.0000	5.89 TB	1403.497%

adversary tries to guess the webpage. Hence, the adversary outputs an index $i \in \{1, \ldots, 164270\}$, such that we define function $\mathcal{P}$ as $\mathcal{P} : \mathcal{M} \to [1, 164270]$, for $m_i \mapsto i$.

Calculating the trivial advantage. Table 2 summarizes the results of the analysis. We calculate $\mathsf{TrivAdv}(\mathsf{SE}^{(\ell)}_{\mathsf{M,C}}, \mathsf{M_{Wiki}})$ for $\mathsf{M} \in \{\mathsf{CTR}, \mathsf{BLK}\}$, $\mathsf{C} \in \{\mathsf{True}, \mathsf{False}\}$ and different length-hiding parameter ℓ.

Conclusions. Table 2 allows us to make the following observations:

- The adversary achieves very high trivial advantage (0.875) when $\ell = 1$. This indicates that the adversary could successfully identify the webpage with high probability only from the ciphertext length.
- Compression reduces the overhead incurred by length-hiding encryption, and also reduces the trivial advantage.
- A length-hiding parameter of 40K in the CTR mode (resp. 2.5K in the BLK mode) reduces the trivial advantage to 0.01 and increases the total data by about 23% without compression, but reduces about 50% total data with compression.

We believe that the example of Wikipedia webpage fingerprinting illustrates very well that length-hiding encryption with proper length-hiding parameter together with compression provides us with both security and bandwidth reduction for real-world message distributions.

Beyond the above analyses, we have conducted two more analyses on DNS fingerprinting (one using random host names from the *Majestic Million* list, the other using real-world DNS data collected in cooperation with a medium-sized university), which can be found in the full version of our work [8].

4 Implementation and Analysis

We have implemented our new approach as an Apache module, based on the most recent versions of an Apache HTTP server (Apache/2.4.38) and the OpenSSL library (version 1.1.1d) for Debian 10. The implementation is currently experimental, we plan to make a more stable version publicly available.

The implementation consists of two components. The first component monitors the server's requests and responses. It stores the block-length and number of occurrences of requests to static URLs and the corresponding responses in a database. This database then provides an approximation of the server's message distribution, which will be used by the second component to determine an appropriate length-hiding parameter ℓ. Furthermore, this component applies length-hiding padding to plaintext messages. Since OpenSSL currently does not support length-hiding padding beyond the last fragment of a plaintext, even though this is possible according to the TLS 1.3 standard, our experimental implementation currently simulates padding beyond frame bounds by appending NULL-bytes to the plaintext.[6]

---

[6] As we will discuss below, we aim to extend OpenSSL to allow for length-hiding padding beyond the TLS fragment boundary, by appending further TLS fragments, if necessary.

The second component of our implementation computes the length-hiding parameter ℓ, based on the request-response database and a given upper bound on the desired trivial advantage. It computes the smallest ℓ that satisfies this trivial advantage for the message distribution defined by the database. Currently, the computation proceeds iteratively, that is, at first it tests whether the parameter $\ell = 1$ satisfies the trivial advantage bound. If it does not, ℓ is incremented and the process repeated until an optimal value ℓ is found. Since the trivial advantage does not necessarily decrease monotonously for a given message distributions[7], this approach yields the smallest possible value ℓ. The resulting parameter ℓ is then used to define the size of length-hiding padding in the first component. Note that the second component can run in the background at predefined times (e.g., once per hour or once per day).

4.1   Validation of Pencil-and-Paper Analysis

To validate the theoretical pencil-and-paper analysis from Sect. 3 we configured the webserver as a proxy for the IACR ePrint server (resp. Google search engine). Then we requested each of the webpages (resp. search terms) once, to establish the same message distribution that was considered in Sect. 3. We used our implementation to record the message distribution, determine the LHE parameter ℓ, and then again accessed every web page once. We considered both AES-GCM and AES-CBC cipher suites. In all cases, we were able to accurately reproduce our results.

So far we have considered only the case without compression, for the following reason. The plaintext data is accessible from within an Apache module by accessing an appropriate "data bucket" of the Apache processing filter chain. This enabled us to circumvent the fact that OpenSSL currently does not support length-hiding padding beyond the last fragment of a plaintext, by padding the plaintext directly with NULL bytes. However, in order to apply the same approach to *compressed* plaintext data, we would need access to a bucket that contains the plaintext *after* compression, but *before* encryption. This seems not possible from an Apache module, and therefore we could not yet validate the pencil-and-paper analysis of compress-then-encrypt.

In future work we aim to perform further experiments, on a public web server with real-world message distributions and with compression. To this end, we have to extend OpenSSL to allow for length-hiding padding beyond the TLS fragment boundary, by appending further TLS fragments, if necessary. Such low-level modifications to OpenSSL and experiments on a public web server in production require significant additional care. Therefore we view this as out of scope of the present paper and leave this for future work.

---

[7] For example, if we have only two messages with length 12 and 17, a block length of 10 would perfectly hide everything, while a block length of 15 would not.

5 Conclusions

Fingerprinting attacks are a very powerful technique to extract information from an encrypted channel, which are known to be very difficult to defend against. We have introduced a methodology that makes it possible to concretely quantify the security gained by length-hiding encryption. Our goal is to go beyond the assumption that the length of a ciphertext does reveal sensitive information, which is typically made implicitly in theoretical security models. In this sense, understanding security in presence of messages of different lengths contributes to our understanding of "secure encryption" in general.

We find that a surprisingly small amount of padding that incurs only a minor bandwidth overhead of a few percent can already reduce the advantage of an adversary very significantly. Even only the use of *block mode* encryption schemes, whose padding provides some very simple form of length-hiding encryption, may already reduce the concrete advantage of fingerprinting attacks very significantly. We also observe that the general recommendation to disable compression before encryption in all applications seems overgeneralized. While useful and necessary in some applications (when active attacks are feasible), in some other cases (e.g., "big brother" attacks) it may be harmful to security. It is therefore necessary to consider the security requirements of the application at hand with a more detailed analysis.

References

1. Bellare, M., Desai, A., Jokipii, E., Rogaway, P.: A concrete security treatment of symmetric encryption. In: 38th FOCS, pp. 394–403. IEEE Computer Society Press (1997)
2. Bellare, M., Namprempre, C.: Authenticated encryption: relations among notions and analysis of the generic composition paradigm. J. Cryptol. **21**(4), 469–491 (2008)
3. Boldyreva, A., Degabriele, J.P., Paterson, K.G., Stam, M.: Security of symmetric encryption in the presence of ciphertext fragmentation. In: Pointcheval, D., Johansson, T. (eds.) EUROCRYPT 2012. LNCS, vol. 7237, pp. 682–699. Springer, Heidelberg (2012). https://doi.org/10.1007/978-3-642-29011-4_40
4. Cai, X., Nithyanand, R., Wang, T., Johnson, R., Goldberg, I.: A systematic approach to developing and evaluating website fingerprinting defenses. In: ACM CCS 2014, pp. 227–238. ACM Press (2014)
5. Degabriele, J.P.: Hiding the lengths of encrypted messages via Gaussian padding. In: ACM CCS 2021 (2021, to appear). Preliminary copy directly obtained from the author
6. Duong, T., Rizzo, J.: The CRIME attack (2012). http://www.ekoparty.org/archive/2012/CRIME_ekoparty2012.pdf
7. Dyer, K.P., Coull, S.E., Ristenpart, T., Shrimpton, T.: Peek-a-boo, i still see you: why efficient traffic analysis countermeasures fail. In: 2012 IEEE Symposium on Security and Privacy, pp. 332–346. IEEE Computer Society Press (2012)
8. Gellert, K., Jager, T., Lyu, L., Neuschulten, T.: On fingerprinting attacks and length-hiding encryption. Cryptology ePrint Archive, Report 2021/1027 (2021). https://eprint.iacr.org/2021/1027

9. Gillmor, D.K.: Empirical DNS padding policy (2017). https://dns.cmrg.net/ndss2017-dprive-empirical-DNS-traffic-size.pdf

10. Gong, X., Borisov, N., Kiyavash, N., Schear, N.: Website detection using remote traffic analysis. In: Fischer-Hübner, S., Wright, M. (eds.) PETS 2012. LNCS, vol. 7384, pp. 58–78. Springer, Heidelberg (2012). https://doi.org/10.1007/978-3-642-31680-7_4

11. Gueron, S., Lindell, Y.: GCM-SIV: full nonce misuse-resistant authenticated encryption at under one cycle per byte. In: ACM CCS 2015, pp. 109–119. ACM Press (2015)

12. Gueron, S., Lindell, Y.: Simpleenc and simpleencsmall - an authenticated encryption mode for the lightweight setting. Cryptology ePrint Archive, Report 2019/712 (2019). https://eprint.iacr.org/2019/712

13. Harsha, B., Morton, R., Blocki, J., Springer, J., Dark, M.: Bicycle attacks considered harmful: Quantifying the damage of widespread password length leakage (2020)

14. Hayes, J., Danezis, G.: k-fingerprinting: a robust scalable website fingerprinting technique. In: USENIX Security 2016, pp. 1187–1203. USENIX Association (2016)

15. Herrmann, D., Wendolsky, R., Federrath, H.: Website fingerprinting: attacking popular privacy enhancing technologies with the multinomial Naïve-Bayes classifier. In: CCSW, pp. 31–42. ACM (2009)

16. Hintz, A.: Fingerprinting websites using traffic analysis. In: Dingledine, R., Syverson, P. (eds.) PET 2002. LNCS, vol. 2482, pp. 171–178. Springer, Heidelberg (2003). https://doi.org/10.1007/3-540-36467-6_13

17. Hollenbeck, S.: Transport Layer Security Protocol Compression Methods. RFC 3749 (2004). https://doi.org/10.17487/RFC3749, https://rfc-editor.org/rfc/rfc3749.txt

18. Jager, T., Stam, M., Stanley-Oakes, R., Warinschi, B.: Multi-key authenticated encryption with corruptions: reductions are lossy. In: Kalai, Y., Reyzin, L. (eds.) TCC 2017. LNCS, vol. 10677, pp. 409–441. Springer, Cham (2017). https://doi.org/10.1007/978-3-319-70500-2_14

19. Katz, J., Yung, M.: Characterization of security notions for probabilistic private-key encryption. J. Cryptol. **19**(1), 67–95 (2006)

20. Kohls, K., Rupprecht, D., Holz, T., Pöpper, C.: Lost traffic encryption: fingerprinting LTE/4G traffic on layer two. In: WiSec, pp. 249–260. ACM (2019)

21. Liberatore, M., Levine, B.N.: Inferring the source of encrypted HTTP connections. In: ACM CCS 2006, pp. 255–263. ACM Press (2006)

22. Mayrhofer, A.: Padding policies for extension mechanisms for DNS (EDNS(0)). RFC 8467 (2018). https://doi.org/10.17487/RFC8467, https://rfc-editor.org/rfc/rfc8467.txt

23. Miller, B., Huang, L., Joseph, A.D., Tygar, J.D.: I know why you went to the clinic: risks and realization of HTTPS traffic analysis. In: De Cristofaro, E., Murdoch, S.J. (eds.) PETS 2014. LNCS, vol. 8555, pp. 143–163. Springer, Cham (2014). https://doi.org/10.1007/978-3-319-08506-7_8

24. Paterson, K.G., Ristenpart, T., Shrimpton, T.: Tag size *does* matter: attacks and proofs for the TLS record protocol. In: Lee, D.H., Wang, X. (eds.) ASIACRYPT 2011. LNCS, vol. 7073, pp. 372–389. Springer, Heidelberg (2011). https://doi.org/10.1007/978-3-642-25385-0_20

25. Rescorla, E.: The Transport Layer Security (TLS) protocol Version 1.3. RFC 8446 (2018). https://doi.org/10.17487/RFC8446, https://rfc-editor.org/rfc/rfc8446.txt

26. Rogaway, P., Shrimpton, T.: A provable-security treatment of the key-wrap problem. In: Vaudenay, S. (ed.) EUROCRYPT 2006. LNCS, vol. 4004, pp. 373–390. Springer, Heidelberg (2006). https://doi.org/10.1007/11761679_23

27. Shusterman, A., et al.: Robust website fingerprinting through the cache occupancy channel. In: USENIX Security 2019, pp. 639–656. USENIX Association (2019)

28. Sirinam, P., Imani, M., Juárez, M., Wright, M.: Deep fingerprinting: undermining website fingerprinting defenses with deep learning. In: ACM CCS 2018, pp. 1928–1943. ACM Press (2018)

29. Tezcan, C., Vaudenay, S.: On hiding a plaintext length by Preencryption. In: Lopez, J., Tsudik, G. (eds.) ACNS 2011. LNCS, vol. 6715, pp. 345–358. Springer, Heidelberg (2011). https://doi.org/10.1007/978-3-642-21554-4_20

30. Wang, T., Goldberg, I.: On realistically attacking tor with website fingerprinting. PoPETs **2016**(4), 21–36 (2016)

31. Wang, T., Goldberg, I.: Walkie-talkie: an efficient defense against passive website fingerprinting attacks. In: USENIX Security 2017, pp. 1375–1390. USENIX Association (2017)

32. Wright, C.V., Ballard, L., Coull, S.E., Monrose, F., Masson, G.M.: Spot me if you can: Uncovering spoken phrases in encrypted VoIP conversations. In: 2008 IEEE Symposium on Security and Privacy. pp. 35–49. IEEE Computer Society Press, 2008

33. Wright, C.V., Ballard, L., Monrose, F., Masson, G.M.: Language identification of encrypted VoIP traffic: Alejandra y roberto or alice and bob? In: USENIX Security 2007. USENIX Association, 2007

34. Wright, C.V., Coull, S.E., Monrose, F.: Traffic morphing: An efficient defense against statistical traffic analysis. In: NDSS 2009. The Internet Society, 2009

CCA Secure *A Posteriori* Openable Encryption in the Standard Model

Xavier Bultel[✉][iD]

INSA Centre Val de Loire, Laboratoire d'informatique fondamentale d'Orléans,
Bourges, France
xavier.bultel@insa-cvl.fr

Abstract. *A Posteriori* Openable Public Key Encryptions (APOPKE) allow any user to generate a constant-size key that decrypts the messages they have sent over a chosen period of time. As an important feature, the period can be dynamically chosen after the messages have been sent. This primitive was introduced in 2016 by Bultel and Lafourcade. They also defined the Chosen-Plaintext Attack (CPA) security for APOPKE, and designed a scheme called GAPO, which is CPA secure in the random oracle model. In this paper, we formalize the Chosen-Ciphertext Attack (CCA) security for APOPKE, then we design a scheme called CHAPO (for *CHosen-ciphetext attack resistant A Posteriori Openable encryption*), and we prove its CCA security in the standard model. CHAPO is approximately twice as efficient as GAPO and is more generic. We also give news applications, and discuss the practical impact of its CCA security.

1 Introduction

Over the past decade, the development of smartphones has made instant messaging increasingly accessible and popular with the general public. The security of such applications has become a crucial issue since Edward Snowden's revelations in 2013, which made people aware of the importance of protecting their personal data on the Internet. Today, there are many encrypted messaging protocols that allow anyone to protect their private conversations from hackers and mass surveillance, such as Signal, Telegram, Whatsapp, Wire, Keybase, or Line. However, because they are within everyone's reach, these tools are also used by criminals. The example of the terrorist group Daesh, which uses Telegram to communicate, is a good illustration of this. For that reason, encrypting the communications can be seen as a suspicious act, and can harm a user during a legal case, especially if the judicial authority requests the assistance of the user's Internet service provider to use lawful interception: if a user encrypts his communications, then lawful interception will only intercept unintelligible data. In such a scenario, the authorities requisition the smartphone and the user has to reveal his access codes and secret keys so that the investigators exculpate him. However, the investigators get unlimited access to the user's data, and can get to know private data that does not concern the investigation.

© The Author(s), under exclusive license to Springer Nature Switzerland AG 2022
S. D. Galbraith (Ed.): CT-RSA 2022, LNCS 13161, pp. 370–394, 2022.
https://doi.org/10.1007/978-3-030-95312-6_16

A Posteriori Openable Public Key Encryption (APOPKE), introduced by Bultel and Lafourcade in [6], offers a practical solution to this problem. In addition to the standard features of public key encryptions, an APOPKE scheme implements a mechanism that allows a user to generate a special key called *interval key* from any pair of indexes i and j, which allows a user called *the opener* to decrypt the messages sent by the user (potentially from several different devices) from the ith to the jth. The interval can be chosen *a posteriori*, *i.e.* after the user has sent the messages. In addition, since the resources of user's device(s) are potentially limited, the interval key must be generated in constant time using a single secret key, and must be of constant size: this prevents the user from storing too much data, from having to perform a large number of operations on data spread over several devices, or from having to send very large data to the opener growing with the size of the interval. Moreover, the complexity of the encryption algorithm and the size of the ciphertexts should not depend on the size of the interval for similar efficiency reasons. Note that the interval key allows to decrypt any message sent between the indexes i and j, regardless of the public key of the recipient of the message. Let us consider that an instant messaging uses an APOKPE scheme, and that each encrypted message is dated and stored on the server of the application. If a user wants to reveal his conversations over a given time period to a judge during an investigation, then he can generate an interval key with the indexes of the first and last messages sent during this period. The judge can then decrypt and view the messages stored on the server for the time period.

In [6], the authors define a security model for the *Chosen-Plaintext Attack* (CPA) security and for the *integrity* of APOPKE. The integrity property ensures that the messages decrypted by the opener with the interval keys are the same as the one decrypted by the recipients of the messages. The authors also design a scheme that is proven CPA secure and has the integrity property in the so-called Random Oracle Model (ROM). They leave as an open problem the design of a scheme secure against the Chosen-Ciphertext Attacks (CCA), and the design of a scheme proven secure in the standard model. In this paper, we solve these two problems. We also show that CPA security is insufficient in practice for the application of this primitive in secure messaging, but also in the applications proposed in [6].

Our Contribution. In this paper, we extend the security model proposed by Bultel and Lafourcade in order to capture the CCA security of the APOPKE. We instantiate our model with a new scheme called CHAPO, then we present some applications for the (CCA secure) APOPKE on encrypted messaging and voice calls. As in [6], we distinguish two CCA security notions: *Indistinguishability Against Chosen Ciphertext Attack* security (IND-CCA), and *Indistinguishability Against Chosen Set of Ciphertext Attack* (IND-CSCA) security.

IND-CCA: This property is an extension of the IND-CCA property for PKE. The adversary is a malicious opener who tries to guess which message has been encrypted by the challenger between two chosen messages. This adversary has access to oracles that encrypt, decrypt, and generate an interval key using the secrets of some honest users. In order to avoid trivial attacks, the challenge ciphertext cannot be decrypted by the oracles, and cannot be decrypted by the queried interval key.

IND-CSCA: Since the opening mechanism of an APOPKE can be viewed as an alternate decryption algorithm for the opener (where the ciphertext is the association of the interval key with the set of the ciphertexts in the interval), our CCA model must consider the attacks where the adversary has access to an oracle that decrypts a set of ciphertexts using the opening algorithm. The IND-CSCA property considers a collusion of dishonest users who receives the interval keys of an honest opener. These users try to learn some information about the messages encrypted for the honest users, and can query some oracles that encrypt, decrypt, generate interval keys, and open intervals, using the secrets of the honest users and the honest opener.

Note that the two properties IND-CCA and IND-CSCA are complementary. They capture two different adversary models, *i.e.* a collusion between the opener and some users trying to attack a ciphertext outside the interval, and a collusion of users attacking the ciphertexts in the interval without the help of the opener. Neither of the two involves the other. Our second contribution is a new APOPKE scheme called CHAPO, that have the following features:

Security: We prove that CHAPO is IND-CCA and IND-CSCA secure in the standard model. Moreover we prove its integrity according to the definition given in [6].

Genericity: Our scheme is based on standard cryptographic tools: it requires a Pseudorandom Function (PRF), a Message Authentication Code scheme (MAC), a Symmetric Key Encryption scheme (SKE) and a Public Key Encryption scheme (PKE). We stress that unlike GAPO, there is no restriction in the choice of the PKE, making CHAPO more generic. For instance, CHAPO can be instantiated with the CPA variant of the McEliece cryptosystem [21] (for a CPA secure instantiation), which is not possible for GAPO since it is not *random coin decryptable* (according to a definition given in [6]), *i.e.* the random coin used by the encryption algorithm cannot be used as an alternative secret key to decrypt the corresponding ciphertext.

Efficiency. The dominating operations in CHAPO are the encryptions and decryptions of the PKE. The encryption/decryption of a message requires one PKE encryption/decryption, and the opening algorithm on a set of n ciphertexts requires n PKE encryptions. In comparison, the GAPO encryption/decryption of a message requires 2 PKE encryptions/decryptions, and the opening algorithm of GAPO on a set of n ciphertexts requires $2 \cdot n$ PKE encryptions and $2 \cdot n$ PKE decryptions by random-coin. Finally, instantiated with a CPA secure

PKE, CHAPO is approximately twice as efficient as GAPO for any instantiation that yields the same level of security (CPA).

As in [6], our model considers only a single dishonest opener (or several openers who do not collude) who receives only one interval key. Actually, we relax this constraint a bit compared to [6] since we allow the opener to receive keys for several intervals as long as the index of the challenge is not between the lowest and the greatest index of the queried intervals. We let the design of a secure scheme that allows multiple disjoint (constant-size) interval keys as an open problem.

Related Works. Some encryption primitives have time-dependent decryption properties, and are therefore related to our work. Time-Release Encryption (TRE) [7,20] allows to produce ciphertexts that cannot be decrypted before a given date. Some schemes implement a pre-open mechanism that allows to decrypt the ciphertexts before the date [15]. In this case, both decryption methods must return the same message; this property, called *binding property*, is similar to the APOPKE integrity property. Time-Specific Encryption (TSE) [22] extends the TRE concept: the encryption algorithm produces ciphertexts that can be decrypted in a pre-defined time interval only. Even if this line of research is close to ours, the goals of TSE differ significantly from APOPKE: in TSE, the time is bounded by a max value T, and the time interval is chosen *a priori* in $[0, T-1]$, *i.e.* before than the message is encrypted. TSE constructions are less generic than CHAPO [16,17], and there is no scheme that ensures that both ciphertexts and keys are of constant size [16]. Key-Insulated Encryption (KIE) [9] deals with the problem of storing secret keys on insecure device. The keys are refreshed periodically by a secure server using a master secret key. The encryption algorithm encrypts the messages from a time period tag and a public key that remains unchanged over time. In [9] the authors show that KIE can be used to delegate the decryption on a time interval by sending the keys that match the interval. However, the periods are fixed, which avoids the fine-grained management of the opener decryption capabilities if the interval does not perfectly match the periods, and the opener decryption key grows linearly with the number of periods. Moreover, this solution allows the opener to decrypt messages received by the user, whereas APOPKE allows the opener to decrypt messages sent by the user (potentially with different public keys), which constitutes an important conceptual break between these two primitives. Delegatable/constraint pseudorandom functions [4,18] allow to delegate the computation of a pseudorandom function over an interval of inputs. By using such a function to generate the encryption keys of successive ciphertexts, a user can delegate the generation of decryption keys over a given interval, and thus obtain features similar to APOPKE. However, using [4,18] the total number of ciphertexts is bounded and the interval key is logarithmic in this bound, whereas an APOPKE must allow the generation of an unlimited number of ciphertexts while ensuring a constant size interval key.

On the application side, Key-Escrow (KE) and Key-Recovery (KR) [14,19, 24,25] schemes deal with the capability of an authority to decrypt the messages exchanged between two users by recovering their secret key. Some works deal with KR mechanisms for lawful interception [1,14,25], where a set of authorities has to collude to open an encrypted phone conversation between two users. As in APOPKE, the security model ensures that the recovered conversation is the same as the exchanged one. However, the motivations of such schemes differ from ours since the authorities recover the keys one by one, contrary to APOPKE where a single key makes it possible to open all the messages between two dates. In this paper, we discuss the advantage of using our solution in the voice call lawful interception context.

Finally, to the best of our knowledge, with the exception of [6], there are no encryption schemes with features similar to CHAPO. Note that such a scheme could be obtained with generic primitives such as functional encryption [11], by considering the set of ciphertexts as the blocks of a single large ciphertext, and by considering a function that returns the plaintexts of an interval on the blocks. However, such a solution would be inefficient and would limit the number of possible ciphertexts. We could also use attribute-based encryption [13], and give the judge a key to decrypt on the attributes used during the time interval, but to the best of our knowledge, no attribute-based encryption scheme offers both constant-size ciphertexts and keys, and the limit on the number of attributes would limit the number of possible messages.

2   Cryptographic Tools

Notation. In this paper, $y \leftarrow \mathsf{Alg}(x)$ denotes that the output of the deterministic algorithm Alg running on the input x is assigned to y. Moreover, $\mathsf{Alg}(x; r)$ denotes that the probabilistic algorithm Alg uses the random coin r to generate its randomness. If the context is clear, we omit to mention the random coin in the description of some algorithms, especially for adversaries (denoted $\mathcal{A}$) and key generators (denoted Gen). $x \leftarrow y$ denotes the assignment of the value of y to the variable x, and $x \xleftarrow{\$} X$ denotes the random sample of x in the uniform distribution on X. We assume that any variable has the value $\bot$ by default, which means that it is not defined, or not instantiated. For any security property denoted Prop defined in this paper, any cryptographic scheme P, and any Probabilistic Polynomial Time (PPT) algorithm $\mathcal{A}$, we define an advantage denoted $\mathbf{Adv}_{P,\mathcal{A}}^{\mathsf{Prop}}(\lambda)$, where λ is a security parameter. We say that P is Prop-secure when the following function, called the Prop-advantage of P, is negligible:
$$\mathbf{Adv}_P^{\mathsf{Prop}}(\lambda) = \max_{\mathcal{A} \in \mathrm{POLY}(\lambda)} \left\{ \mathbf{Adv}_{P,\mathcal{A}}^{\mathsf{Prop}}(\lambda) \right\}.$$

Definition 1 (PRF [10]**).** *Let λ be a security parameter, $\mathcal{K}_\lambda$ be a set, and (α, β) be two integers. A* Pseudorandom Function *(PRF) is a function* $\mathsf{PRF} : \mathcal{K}_\lambda \times \{0,1\}^\alpha \rightarrow \{0,1\}^\beta$.
For any PPT algorithm $\mathcal{A}$, and for $\mathcal{F} = \{f : \{0,1\}^\alpha \rightarrow \{0,1\}^\beta\}$, the advantage of $\mathcal{A}$ on the pseudorandomness of PRF *is defined by the function:* $\mathbf{Adv}_{\mathsf{PRF},\mathcal{A}}^{\mathsf{PR}}(\lambda) =$
$$\left| \Pr\left[f \xleftarrow{\$} \mathcal{F} : 1 \leftarrow \mathcal{A}^{f(\cdot)}(\lambda) \right] - \Pr\left[\begin{matrix} \mathsf{rk} \xleftarrow{\$} \mathcal{K}_\lambda; \\ f(.) \leftarrow \mathsf{PRF}(\mathsf{rk}, \cdot); \end{matrix} : 1 \leftarrow \mathcal{A}^{f(\cdot)}(\lambda) \right] \right|.$$

Definition 2 (MAC [2]**).** *Let λ be a security parameter. A* Message Authentication Code scheme *(MAC) is defined by a tuple $(\mathcal{K}_\lambda, \mathsf{Mac}, \mathsf{Ver})$ such that $\mathcal{K}_\lambda$ is a set, and the (deterministic) algorithms Mac and Ver are defined by:*

$\mathsf{Mac}(\mathsf{mk}, m)$**:** *On input a key $\mathsf{mk} \in \mathcal{K}_\lambda$, and a message m. return a tag t.*

$\mathsf{Ver}(\mathsf{mk}, t, m)$**:** *On input a key $\mathsf{mk} \in \mathcal{K}_\lambda$, a tag t, and a message $m \in \{0, 1\}^*$. Return a bit b.*

Let P be a MAC scheme, and let $\mathcal{A}$ be a PPT algorithm. The Existential UnForgeability against Chosen Message Attack *(EUF-CMA) security experiment for P is defined by:*
$$\mathbf{Exp}_{P,\mathcal{A}}^{\mathsf{EUF\text{-}CMA}}(\lambda):$$

$\quad\quad \mathcal{S} \leftarrow \emptyset; \mathsf{mk}_* \xleftarrow{\$} \mathcal{K}_\lambda;$

$\quad\quad (t_*, m_*) \leftarrow \mathcal{A}^{\mathsf{Mac}(\mathsf{mk}_*, \cdot), \mathsf{Ver}(\mathsf{mk}_*, \cdot, \cdot)}(\lambda);$

$\quad\quad$ *If* $1 = \mathsf{Ver}(\mathsf{mk}_*, t_*, m_*)$ *and* $(t_*, m_*) \notin \mathcal{S}$,

$\quad\quad\quad$ *then return 1, else 0;*

where the oracle $\mathsf{Mac}(\mathsf{mk}_*, \cdot)$ takes a message m as input, runs $t \leftarrow \mathsf{Mac}(\mathsf{mk}_*, m)$, updates $\mathcal{S} \leftarrow \mathcal{S} \cup \{(t, m)\}$ and returns t, and the oracle $\mathsf{Ver}(\mathsf{mk}_*, \cdot, \cdot)$ takes (t, m) as input, runs $b \leftarrow \mathsf{Ver}(\mathsf{mk}_*, t, m)$ and returns b. The EUF-CMA-advantage of $\mathcal{A}$ is defined by $\mathbf{Adv}_{P,\mathcal{A}}^{\mathsf{EUF\text{-}CMA}}(\lambda) = \Pr[\mathbf{Exp}_{P,\mathcal{A}}^{\mathsf{EUF\text{-}CMA}}(\lambda) = 1]$.

Definition 3 (SKE [3]**).** *Let λ be a security parameter. A* Symmetric Key Encryption scheme *(SKE) is defined by a tuple $(\mathcal{K}_\lambda, \mathcal{R}_\lambda, \mathsf{SEnc}, \mathsf{SDec})$ such that $\mathcal{K}_\lambda$, and $\mathcal{R}_\lambda$ are two sets, and the algorithms SEnc and SDec are defined by:*

$\mathsf{PEnc}(\mathsf{ek}, m; r)$**:** *On input a key $\mathsf{ek} \in \mathcal{K}_\lambda$, a message $m \in \{0, 1\}^*$, and a random coin $r \in \mathcal{R}_\lambda$, return a ciphertext c.*

$\mathsf{PDec}(\mathsf{ek}, c)$**:** *On input a key $\mathsf{ek} \in \mathcal{K}_\lambda$, and a ciphertext c, return a message m.*

Let P be a SKE, and let $\mathcal{A} = (\mathcal{A}_0, \mathcal{A}_1)$ be a pair of PPT algorithms. The Indistinguishability against Chosen Ciphertexts Attacks security *(IND-CCA) security experiment for P is defined by:*
$$\mathbf{Exp}_{b,P,\mathcal{A}}^{\mathsf{IND\text{-}CCA}}(\lambda):$$

$\quad\quad \mathsf{ek}_* \xleftarrow{\$} \mathcal{K}_\lambda;$

$\quad\quad (m_0, m_1, \mathsf{st}) \leftarrow \mathcal{A}_1^{\mathsf{SEnc}(\mathsf{ek}_*, \cdot), \mathsf{SDec}(\mathsf{ek}_*, \cdot)}(\lambda);$

$\quad\quad$ *If $|m_0| \neq |m_1|$, then return a random bit;*

$\quad\quad r \xleftarrow{\$} \mathcal{R}_\lambda; c_* \leftarrow \mathsf{Enc}(\mathsf{ek}_*, m_b; r);$

$\quad\quad b_* \leftarrow \mathcal{A}_2^{\mathsf{SEnc}(\mathsf{ek}_*, \cdot), \mathsf{SDec}(\mathsf{ek}_*, \cdot)}(\lambda, \mathsf{st}, c_*);$

$\quad\quad$ *If $b = b_*$, then return 1, else 0;*

where the oracle $\mathsf{SEnc}(\mathsf{ek}_*, \cdot)$ takes a message m as input, picks a random coin $r \xleftarrow{\$} \mathcal{R}_\lambda$, and returns $\mathsf{PEnc}(\mathsf{ek}_*, m; r)$, and the oracle $\mathsf{SDec}(\mathsf{ek}_*, \cdot)$ takes a ciphertext c as input, and returns $\mathsf{SDec}(\mathsf{ek}_*, c)$, except if $c = c_*$ during the second phase. The IND-CCA-advantage of $\mathcal{A}$ is defined by $\mathbf{Adv}_{P,\mathcal{A}}^{\mathsf{IND\text{-}CCA}}(\lambda) = |\Pr[b \xleftarrow{\$} \{0, 1\} : 1 \leftarrow \mathbf{Exp}_{b,P,\mathcal{A}}^{\mathsf{IND\text{-}CCA}}(\lambda)] - 1/2|$.

Definition 4 (PKE [12]**).** *Let λ be a security parameter. A* Public Key Encryption scheme *(PKE) is defined by a tuple $P = (\mathcal{R}_\lambda, \mathcal{M}_\lambda, \mathsf{PGen}, \mathsf{PEnc}, \mathsf{PDec})$ such that $\mathcal{R}_\lambda$ is a set, and the algorithms $\mathsf{PGen}, \mathsf{PEnc}$, and PDec are defined by:*

$\mathsf{PGen}(1^\lambda)$: *Return a pair of public/secret keys* $(\mathsf{pk}, \mathsf{sk})$.

$\overline{\mathsf{PEnc}(\mathsf{pk}, m; r)}$: *On input a public key* pk, *a message* $m \in \mathcal{M}_\lambda$, *and a random coin* $r \in \mathcal{R}_\lambda$, *return a ciphertext* c.

$\mathsf{PDec}(\mathsf{sk}, c)$: *On input a secret key* sk *and a ciphertext* c, *return a message* m.

P *is said to be correct if for any* $(\mathsf{pk}, \mathsf{sk}) \leftarrow \mathsf{PGen}(1^\lambda)$, *any* $m \in \mathcal{M}_\lambda$ *and any* $r \in \mathcal{R}_\lambda$ *it holds that* $m = \mathsf{PDec}(\mathsf{sk}, \mathsf{PEnc}(\mathsf{pk}, m; r))$.

Let $\mathcal{A} = (\mathcal{A}_0, \mathcal{A}_1)$ *be a pair of PPT algorithms. The* Indistinguishability against Chosen-Ciphertext attack *(IND-CCA) security experiment for* P *is defined by:*

$$\mathbf{Exp}_{b,P,\mathcal{A}}^{\mathsf{IND\text{-}CCA}}(\lambda):$$

$$(\mathsf{pk}_*, \mathsf{sk}_*) \leftarrow \mathsf{PGen}(1^\lambda);$$

$$(m_0, m_1, \mathsf{st}) \leftarrow \mathcal{A}_1^{\mathsf{PDec}(\mathsf{sk}_*, \cdot)}(\lambda, \mathsf{pk}_*);$$

$$r \xleftarrow{\$} \mathcal{R}_\lambda; c_* \leftarrow \mathsf{PEnc}(\mathsf{pk}_*, m_b; r);$$

$$b_* \leftarrow \mathcal{A}_2^{\mathsf{PDec}(\mathsf{sk}_*, \cdot)}(\lambda, \mathsf{pk}_*, \mathsf{st}, c_*);$$

$$\textit{If } b = b_*, \textit{ then return } 1, \textit{ else } 0;$$

where the oracle $\mathsf{PDec}(\mathsf{sk}_*, \cdot)$ *takes a ciphertext* c *as input, and returns* $\mathsf{PDec}(\mathsf{sk}_*, c)$, *except if* $c = c_*$ *during the second phase. The* IND-CCA-*advantage of* $\mathcal{A}$ *is defined by* $\mathbf{Adv}_{P,\mathcal{A}}^{\mathsf{IND\text{-}CCA}}(\lambda) = |\Pr[b \xleftarrow{\$} \{0,1\} :\leftarrow \mathbf{Exp}_{b,P,\mathcal{A}}^{\mathsf{IND\text{-}CCA}}(\lambda)] - 1/2|$.

Finally, we recall the notion of *Verifiable Key* defined in [6].

Definition 5 (Verifiable key generator). *A public/private keys pair generation algorithm* PGen *is verifiable if there exists a deterministic polynomial-time algorithm* KVer *such that, for any security parameter* λ, *it holds that:* $\mathsf{KVer}(\mathsf{pk}_*, \mathsf{sk}_*) = 1 \Leftrightarrow (\mathsf{pk}_*, \mathsf{sk}_*) \in \{(\mathsf{pk}, \mathsf{sk}) : (\mathsf{pk}, \mathsf{sk}) \leftarrow \mathsf{PGen}(1^\lambda)\}$.

We show a simple trick to turn any key generator PGen into a verifiable key generator PGen'. In what follows we explicit the use of the random coin (denoted r) by the key generator: $(\mathsf{pk}, \mathsf{sk}) \leftarrow \mathsf{PGen}(1^\lambda; r)$. We define a new key generator PGen' that runs $(\mathsf{pk}, \mathsf{sk}) \leftarrow \mathsf{PGen}(1^\lambda; r)$ and returns $(\mathsf{pk}', \mathsf{sk}') = (\mathsf{pk}, (\mathsf{sk}, r))$. The generator PGen' can be used to replace PGen because it outputs the same public key as the one returned by PGen, and it returns a secret key sk' that contains the secret key sk outputted by PGen. Moreover, PGen' is verifiable because $\mathsf{KVer}(\mathsf{pk}_*, \mathsf{sk}_*)$ can be instantiated by the following algorithm: parse sk_* as (sk, r), run $(\mathsf{pk}', \mathsf{sk}') \leftarrow \mathsf{PGen}(1^\lambda; r)$, if $\mathsf{pk}_* = \mathsf{pk}'$ and $\mathsf{sk}_* = (\mathsf{sk}', r)$, then return 1, else return 0. Thus, in this paper, we will implicitly consider that any key generator is verifiable.

3   Formal Definitions

An APOPKE is defined by a *public/private key pair generator*, an *encryption key generator* that generates an encryption key for each user, an *encryption algorithm* that encrypts a message from its index, the user encryption key, and the recipient public key, a *decryption algorithm* that decrypts a ciphertext from the secret key of the recipient, an *extractor algorithm* that generates an interval key for an opener from two indexes (i, j), the user encryption key and the opener public key, and an *opening algorithm* that allows the opener to decrypt each message labelled by an index in $[\![i, j]\!]$ using his interval key and his secret key.

Definition 6 (APOPKE). *Let λ be a security parameter. An APOPKE scheme is defined by a tuple $(\mathcal{R}_\lambda, \mathcal{M}_\lambda, \mathsf{Gen}, \mathsf{EGen}, \mathsf{Enc}, \mathsf{Dec}, \mathsf{Ext}, \mathsf{Open})$ such that $\mathcal{R}_\lambda$ and $\mathcal{M}_\lambda$ are two sets, and are defined by:*

$\underline{\mathsf{Gen}(1^\lambda)}$: *Return a pair of public/secret keys $(\mathsf{pk}, \mathsf{sk})$. The same algorithm is used to generate the keys of the users and the opener. In what follows, we will use the notation $(\mathsf{pko}, \mathsf{sko})$ to designate the opener keys.*

$\underline{\mathsf{EGen}(1^\lambda)}$: *Return an encryption secret key k.*

$\underline{\mathsf{Enc}(\mathsf{pk}_l, \mathsf{k}, m_l, l; r_l)}$: *On input a receiver public key pk_l, a sender secret encrytion key k, a message $m_l \in \mathcal{M}_\lambda$, an index $l \in \mathbb{N}$, and a random coin $r_l \in \mathcal{R}_\lambda$, return a ciphertext c_l.*

$\underline{\mathsf{Dec}(\mathsf{sk}_l, c_l)}$: *On input a receiver secret key sk_l and a ciphertext c_l, return a message m_l.*

$\underline{\mathsf{Ext}(\mathsf{pko}, \mathsf{k}, i, j; r)}$: *On input an opener public key pko, a sender secret encrytion key k, two indexes i and j, and a random coin $r \in \mathcal{R}_\lambda$. Return an interval key $\mathsf{ik}_{i \to j}$.*

$\underline{\mathsf{Open}(\mathsf{sko}, i, j, \mathsf{ik}_{i \to j}, (c_l, \mathsf{pk}_l)_{i \le l \le j})}$: *On input an opener secret key sko, two indexes i and j, an interval key $\mathsf{ik}_{i \to j}$, and a vector of ciphertexts couped with their respective public keys $(c_l, \mathsf{pk}_l)_{i \le l \le j}$. Return messages $(m_l)_{i \le l \le j}$.*

The IND-CCA experiment features an adversary who knows the public key of an honest user, chooses two messages, receives the encryption of one of them as challenge, and tries to guess which one has been encrypted with that public key. The adversary has access to an encryption oracle that encrypts chosen messages using an index n incremented by the experiment after each encryption and the (secret) encryption key of the honest user, as well as a decryption oracle that decrypts any chosen ciphertext except the challenge. At the beginning of the experiment, n is initialized to 1. Note that the experiment simulates an honest user encrypting several successive messages. Allowing forks in the ciphertext sequence would introduce trivial and unrealistic attacks to deal with (in practice the attacked user would have no interest in using non-successive indices) artificially complicating the model and the proofs. In addition, the adversary has access to an extraction oracle that generates interval keys for chosen intervals. However, the adversary cannot query the oracle for intervals (i_k, j_k) such that the index of the challenge is between $\min_k(i_k)$ and $\max_k(j_k)$.

Definition 7 (IND-CCA experiment). *Let $P = (\mathcal{R}_\lambda, \mathcal{M}_\lambda, \mathsf{Gen}, \mathsf{EGen}, \mathsf{Enc}, \mathsf{Dec}, \mathsf{Ext}, \mathsf{Open})$ be an APOPKE, let λ be a security parameter, and let $\mathcal{A} = (\mathcal{A}_0, \mathcal{A}_1)$ be a pair of PPT algorithms. The Indistinguishability against Chosen Ciphertext Attack (IND-CCA) security experiment for P is defined by:*

$\mathbf{Exp}_{b,P,\mathcal{A}}^{\text{IND-CCA}}(\lambda)$:

$\quad n \leftarrow 1; (i_*, j_*) \leftarrow (0,0);$

$\quad (\mathsf{pk}_*, \mathsf{sk}_*) \leftarrow \mathsf{Gen}(1^\lambda); \mathsf{k}_* \leftarrow \mathsf{EGen}(1^\lambda);$

$\quad \mathcal{O} \leftarrow \left\{ \begin{array}{l} \mathsf{Enc}(\cdot, \mathsf{k}_*, \cdot, n); \mathsf{Dec}(\mathsf{sk}_*, \cdot); \\ \mathsf{Ext}(\cdot, \mathsf{k}_*, \cdot, \cdot); \end{array} \right\};$

$\quad (m_{(*,0)}, m_{(*,1)}, \mathsf{st}) \leftarrow \mathcal{A}_1^{\mathcal{O}}(\lambda, \mathsf{pk}_*);$

$\quad l_* \leftarrow n; r_* \xleftarrow{\$} \mathcal{R}_\lambda; n \leftarrow n+1;$

$\quad c_{l_*} \leftarrow \mathsf{Enc}(\mathsf{pk}_*, \mathsf{k}_*, m_{(*,b)}, l_*; r_*);$

$\quad b_* \leftarrow \mathcal{A}_2^{\mathcal{O}}(\lambda, \mathsf{pk}_*, \mathsf{st}, c_{l_*});$

$\quad$ If $l_* \in [\![i_*, j_*]\!]$, then return a random bit;

$\quad$ If $b = b_*$, then return 1, else 0;

where the oracles are defined by:

$\underline{\mathsf{Enc}(\cdot, \mathsf{k}_*, \cdot, n)}$: On input (pk_n, m_n), pick $r_n \xleftarrow{\$} \mathcal{R}_\lambda$, run $c_n \leftarrow \mathsf{Enc}(\mathsf{pk}_n, \mathsf{k}_*, m_n, n; r_n)$ and increment $n \leftarrow (n+1)$, then return c_n.

$\underline{\mathsf{Dec}(\mathsf{sk}_*, \cdot)}$: On input c, during the second phase if $c_{l_*} = c$, then return $\perp$. Finally, run $m \leftarrow \mathsf{Dec}(\mathsf{sk}_*, c)$ and return m.

$\underline{\mathsf{Ext}(\cdot, \mathsf{k}_*, \cdot, \cdot)}$: On input (pko, i, j), if $i \leq 0$ or $j \leq 0$ or $i \geq j$ or $j \geq n$, then return $\perp$. if $i_* = j_* = 0$, then set $(i_*, j_*) \leftarrow (i, j)$. If $i < i_*$, then $i_* \leftarrow i$. If $j > j_*$, then $j_* \leftarrow j$. Finally, pick $r \xleftarrow{\$} \mathcal{R}_\lambda$, run $\mathsf{ik}_{i \to j} \leftarrow \mathsf{Ext}(\mathsf{pko}, \mathsf{k}_*, i, j; r)$ and return $\mathsf{ik}_{i \to j}$.

The IND-CCA-advantage of $\mathcal{A}$ is defined by: $\mathbf{Adv}_{P,\mathcal{A}}^{\text{IND-CCA}}(\lambda) = \left| \Pr[b \xleftarrow{\$} \{0,1\} : 1 \leftarrow \mathbf{Exp}_{b,P,\mathcal{A}}^{\text{IND-CCA}}(\lambda)] - 1/2 \right|.$

The IND-CSCA experiment features an adversary who knows the public keys of a set of honest users and the public key of an honest opener. The adversary chooses two vectors of messages and a vector of public keys (of same size), then the experiment picks one of the two vectors and generates a vector of ciphertexts by encrypting each message using the corresponding public key and the encryption key of a designated honest user. For each encryption, if the public key belongs to an honest user, then the experiment encrypts the message of the picked vector, else it encrypts the message of the first vector (this disables the trivial attacks where the adversary receives messages of the picked vector encrypted with his own keys). The experiment also generates an interval key for the vector of ciphertexts using the opener public key and the designated user encryption key. The adversary receives the vector of ciphertexts and the interval key as challenge and tries to guess which vector has been encrypted.

The adversary has access to an encryption oracle that encrypts chosen messages using an index n incremented by the experiment after each encryption and the encryption key of the designated user, as well as a decryption oracle that decrypts any chosen ciphertext with the secret key of an honest user except the ciphertexts in the challenge. At the beginning of the experiment, the index n is initialized to 1, then n is incremented at each call to the encryption oracle, and at each encryption performed by the experiment in order to build the challenge. The adversary has access to an extraction oracle that generates interval keys for chosen intervals using the designated user encryption key and the public key of the honest opener, except for the intervals that contain the index of one of the ciphertexts of the challenge. Note that without the secret key of the honest opener, the interval keys are supposed to be unusable by the adversary. Finally the adversary has access to an opening oracle that decrypts the ciphertexts on a chosen interval using a chosen vector of ciphertexts, a chosen interval key, and the secret key of the honest opener as the opening algorithm, except if the query exactly matches the challenge. The role of this oracle is more subtle than that of the decryption oracle: it allows the IND-CSCA security to prevent not only attacks where the adversary opens some modified ciphertexts from the challenge, but also attacks where the adversary adds or removes ciphertexts from the challenge, or reorders them before sending it to the opening oracle.

Definition 8 (μ-IND-CSCA experiment). *Let $P = (\mathcal{R}_\lambda, \mathcal{M}_\lambda, \mathsf{Gen}, \mathsf{EGen},$ $\mathsf{Enc}, \mathsf{Dec}, \mathsf{Ext}, \mathsf{Open})$ be an APOPKE, let λ be a security parameter and μ be an integer, and let $\mathcal{A} = (\mathcal{A}_0, \mathcal{A}_1)$ be a pair of PPT algorithms. The μ-Indistinguishability Against Chosen Set of Ciphertexts security (IND-CSCA) experiment for P is defined by:*

$\mathbf{Exp}_{b,P,\mathcal{A}}^{\mu\text{-IND-CSCA}}(\lambda)$:

   $n \leftarrow 1$;
   $(\mathsf{pko}_*, \mathsf{sko}_*) \leftarrow \mathsf{Gen}(1^\lambda)$;
   $\forall l \in [\![1, \mu]\!], (\mathsf{pk}_{(*,l)}, \mathsf{sk}_{(*,l)}) \leftarrow \mathsf{Gen}(1^\lambda)$;
   $k_* \leftarrow \mathsf{EGen}(1^\lambda)$;
   $\mathcal{O} \leftarrow \left\{ \begin{array}{l} \mathsf{Enc}(\cdot, k_*, \cdot, n); \mathsf{Dec}(\cdot, \cdot); \\ \mathsf{Ext}(\mathsf{pko}_*, k_*, \cdot, \cdot); \mathsf{Open}(\mathsf{sko}_*, \cdot, \cdot, \cdot, \cdot); \end{array} \right\}$;
   $(j_*, (m_{(0,l)}, m_{(1,l)}, \bar{\mathsf{pk}}_l)_{n \leq l \leq j_*}, \mathsf{st}_*) \leftarrow \mathcal{A}_1^{\mathcal{O}}(\lambda, \mathsf{pko}_*, (\mathsf{pk}_{(*,l)})_{1 \leq l \leq \mu})$;
   $i_* \leftarrow n$;
   $\forall\, l \in [\![i_*, j_*]\!]: r_{(*,l)} \xleftarrow{\$} \mathcal{R}_\lambda$;
      If $\exists\, q, \mathsf{pk}_{(*,q)} = \bar{\mathsf{pk}}_l$, then $c_{(*,l)} \leftarrow \mathsf{Enc}(\bar{\mathsf{pk}}_l, k_*, m_{(b,l)}, l)$;
      Else $c_{(*,l)} \leftarrow \mathsf{Enc}(\bar{\mathsf{pk}}_l, k_*, m_{(0,l)}, l)$;
   $n \leftarrow j_* + 1$;
   $r_* \xleftarrow{\$} \mathcal{R}_\lambda$; $\mathsf{ik}_{i_* \rightarrow j_*} \leftarrow \mathsf{Ext}(\mathsf{pko}_*, k_*, i_*, j_*; r_*)$;
   $b_* \leftarrow \mathcal{A}_2^{\mathcal{O}}(\lambda, \mathsf{pko}_*, (\mathsf{pk}_{(*,l)})_{1 \leq l \leq \mu}, \mathsf{st}, \mathsf{ik}_{i_* \rightarrow j_*}, (c_{(*,l)})_{i_* \leq l \leq j_*})$;
   If $b = b_*$, then return 1, else 0;
where the oracles are defined by:

$\underline{\mathsf{Enc}(\cdot, k_*, \cdot, n)}$: *On input* (pk_n, m_n), *pick* $r_n \xleftarrow{\$} \mathcal{R}_\lambda$, *run* $c_n \leftarrow \mathsf{Enc}(\mathsf{pk}_n, k_*,$ $m_n, n; r_n)$ *and increment* $n \leftarrow (n + 1)$, *then return* c_n.

$\underline{\mathsf{Dec}(\cdot, \cdot)}$: *On input* (q, c), *if* $q \leq 0$ *or* $q > \mu$ *then return* $\bot$. *During the second phase if* $\exists\, l$ *such that* $\mathsf{pk}_{(*,q)} = \bar{\mathsf{pk}}_l$ *and* $c_{(*,l)} = c$, *then return* $\bot$. *Finally, run* $m \leftarrow \mathsf{Dec}(\mathsf{sk}_{(*,q)}, c)$ *and return* m.

$\underline{\mathsf{Ext}(\mathsf{pko}_*, k_*, \cdot, \cdot)}$: *On input* (i, j), *if* $i \leq 0$ *or* $i \geq j$ *or* $j \geq n$, *then return* $\bot$. *During the second phase, if* $[\![i, j]\!] \cap [\![i_*, j_*]\!] \neq \emptyset$, *then return* $\bot$. *Finally, pick* $r \xleftarrow{\$} \mathcal{R}_\lambda$, *run* $\mathsf{ik}_{i \rightarrow j} \leftarrow \mathsf{Ext}(\mathsf{pko}_*, k_*, i, j; r)$ *and return* $\mathsf{ik}_{i \rightarrow j}$.

$\underline{\mathsf{Open}(\mathsf{sko}_*, \cdot, \cdot, \cdot, \cdot)}$: *On input* $(i, j, \mathsf{ik}_{i \rightarrow j}, (c_l, \mathsf{pk}_l)_{i \leq l \leq j})$, *if* $i \leq 0$ *or* $i \geq j$ *or* $j \geq n$, *then return* $\bot$. *During the second phase, if* $(\mathsf{ik}_{i \rightarrow j}, (c_l, \mathsf{pk}_l)_{i \leq l \leq j}) = (\mathsf{ik}_{i_* \rightarrow j_*}, (c_{(*,l)}, \bar{\mathsf{pk}}_l)_{i_* \leq l \leq j_*})$, *then return* $\bot$. *Finally, run* $(m_l)_{i \leq l \leq j} \leftarrow \mathsf{Open}(\mathsf{sko}_*, i, j, \mathsf{ik}_{i \rightarrow j}, (c_l, \mathsf{pk}_l)_{i \leq l \leq j})$ *and return* $(m_l)_{i \leq l \leq j}$.

The μ-IND-CSCA-advantage of $\mathcal{A}$ is defined by:

$$\mathbf{Adv}_{P,\mathcal{A}}^{\mu\text{-IND-CSCA}}(\lambda) = \left| \Pr[b \xleftarrow{\$} \{0,1\} : 1 \leftarrow \mathbf{Exp}_{b,P,\mathcal{A}}^{\mu\text{-IND-CSCA}}(\lambda)] - 1/2 \right|.$$

Finally, we recall the *integrity* experiment of [6]. This property ensures that for the same ciphertext produced by an adversary, an honest receiver and an honest opener do not decrypt different plaintexts. This property should not be confused with the correctness, which ensures that a ciphertext will be decrypted correctly by the decryption algorithms only if it is generated by an honest user.

Definition 9 (Integrity experiment). *Let $P = (\mathcal{R}_\lambda, \mathcal{M}_\lambda, \mathsf{Gen}, \mathsf{EGen}, \mathsf{Enc}, \mathsf{Dec}, \mathsf{Ext}, \mathsf{Open})$ be an APOPKE, let λ be a security parameter, and let $\mathcal{A}$ be a PPT algorithm. We define the integrity (Integrity) experiment for P as follows:*

$\mathbf{Exp}_{P,\mathcal{A}}^{\mathsf{Integrity}}(\lambda)$:

   $(\mathsf{pko}_*, \mathsf{sko}_*) \leftarrow \mathsf{Gen}(1^\lambda)$;
   $(i, j, (c_l, \mathsf{pk}_l)_{i \leq l \leq j}, x, \mathsf{sk}_x, \mathsf{ik}_{i \to j}) \leftarrow \mathcal{A}(\lambda, \mathsf{pko}_*)$;
   $(m_l)_{i \leq l \leq j} \leftarrow \mathsf{Open}(\mathsf{sko}_*, i, j, \mathsf{ik}_{i \to j}, (c_l, \mathsf{pk}_l)_{i \leq l \leq j})$;
   $m_x' \leftarrow \mathsf{Dec}(\mathsf{sk}_x, c_x)$;
   If $m_x \neq \perp$ and $m_x' \neq \perp$ and $m_x \neq m_x'$ and $1 = \mathsf{KVer}(\mathsf{pk}_x, \mathsf{sk}_x)$,
   then return 1, else 0;

The Integrity-advantage is defined by $\mathbf{Adv}_{P,\mathcal{A}}^{\mathsf{Integrity}}(\lambda) = \Pr[\mathbf{Exp}_{P,\mathcal{A}}^{\mathsf{Integrity}}(\lambda) = 1].$

4   Our Scheme: CHAPO

Designing APOPKE schemes. CHAPO is based on the opening technique introduced in GAPO [6]: each message m_l is split in two parts $\widehat{m}_l$ and $\widetilde{m}_l$ such that $m_l = \widehat{m}_l \oplus \widetilde{m}_l$. The encryption algorithm uses four indexed keys denoted $\widehat{\mathsf{ek}}_l$, $\widehat{\mathsf{ek}}_{l-1}$, $\widetilde{\mathsf{ek}}_l$ and $\widetilde{\mathsf{ek}}_{l+1}$, and encrypts the message m_l in two blocs $\widehat{C}_l$ and $\widetilde{C}_l$ such that the part $\widehat{C}_l$ encrypts $\widehat{m}_l$ and $\widehat{\mathsf{ek}}_{l-1}$, and can be decrypted by the key $\widehat{\mathsf{ek}}_l$, and the part $\widetilde{C}_l$ encrypts $\widetilde{m}_l$ and $\widetilde{\mathsf{ek}}_{l+1}$, and can be decrypted by the key $\widetilde{\mathsf{ek}}_l$. The interval key for the interval $[i, j]$ is generated by encrypting the pair of keys $(\widetilde{\mathsf{ek}}_i, \widehat{\mathsf{ek}}_j)$ for the opener. Using $\widehat{\mathsf{ek}}_j$, the opener decrypts $\widehat{C}_j$ and obtains $\widehat{m}_j$ and $\widehat{\mathsf{ek}}_{j-1}$, then he uses $\widehat{\mathsf{ek}}_{j-1}$ to decrypt $\widehat{C}_{j-1}$ and repeats this operation recursively until he gets $(\widehat{m}_l)_{i \leq l \leq j}$. On the other hand, using $\widetilde{\mathsf{ek}}_i$, the opener decrypts $\widetilde{C}_i$ and obtains $\widetilde{m}_i$ and $\widetilde{\mathsf{ek}}_{i+1}$, then it uses $\widetilde{\mathsf{ek}}_{i+1}$ to decrypt $\widetilde{C}_{i+1}$ and repeats this operation recursively until he gets $(\widetilde{m}_l)_{i \leq l \leq j}$. Finally, he computes $(m_l)_{i \leq l \leq j} = (\widehat{m}_l \oplus \widetilde{m}_l)_{i \leq l \leq j}$.

We stress that the opener cannot decrypt the ciphertexts $\widetilde{C}_l$ for $l < i$ and $\widehat{C}_l$ for $l > j$, hence he is missing one share of each message m_l such that $l \notin [i, j]$, so he cannot rebuild these messages. The Fig. 1 illustrates this mechanism for the interval $[2, 4]$. Note that this mechanism does not protect the messages between two openable intervals. However, it is possible to enlarge the interval over which the opener can decrypt the messages without altering the security of the scheme.

CHAPO overview. CHAPO uses a PRF, a MAC, a SKE and a PKE. The public/private keys $(\mathsf{pk}, \mathsf{sk})$ generation algorithm is defined as in the PKE scheme. The encryption key generator returns a secret pair $(\mathsf{rk}, \mathsf{mk})$ where rk is a PRF key and mk is a MAC key. For each index l, the keys $\widehat{\mathsf{ek}}_l$ and $\widetilde{\mathsf{ek}}_l$ are the outputs of the PRF on the (secret) key rk and the index l. Our scheme also requires a MAC key mk_l for each index l, that is also generated from the PRF on rk and l.

X. Bultel

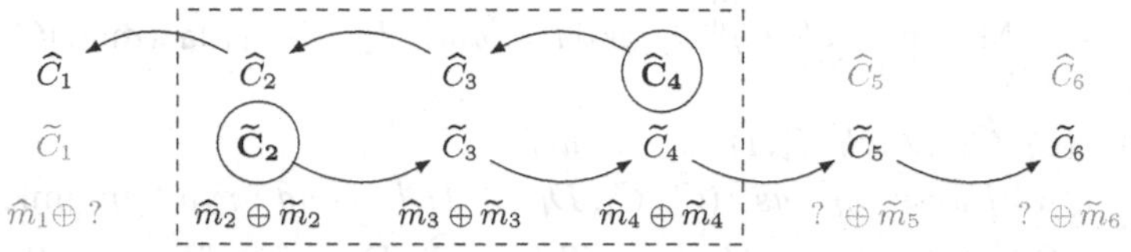

Fig. 1. Opening mechanism for the interval $[2, 4]$

The encryption algorithm takes as input the encryption key $(\mathsf{rk}, \mathsf{mk})$ of the user, the message m_l and the public key pk of the message recipient. The algorithm first generates the ciphertext D_l by encrypting $[m_l \| \mathsf{mk}_l \| l]$ using the public key pk and a random coin denoted by v_l, then it splits m_l, mk_l, and v_l in two parts $(\widehat{m}_l, \widetilde{m}_l)$, $(\widehat{\mathsf{mk}}_l, \widetilde{\mathsf{mk}}_l)$, and $(\widehat{v}_l, \widetilde{v}_l)$, such that $m_l = \widehat{m}_l \oplus \widetilde{m}_l$, $\mathsf{mk}_l = \widehat{\mathsf{mk}}_l \oplus \widetilde{\mathsf{mk}}_l$, and $v_l = \widehat{v}_l \oplus \widetilde{v}_l$. The algorithm generates $\widetilde{C}_l$ by encrypting $[\widehat{\mathsf{ek}}_{l+1} \| \widetilde{m}_l \| \widetilde{\mathsf{mk}}_l \| \widetilde{v}_l \| \mathsf{pk} \| l]$ with the key $\widetilde{\mathsf{ek}}_l$ using the SKE, and $\widehat{C}_l$ by encrypting $[\widetilde{\mathsf{ek}}_{l-1} \| \widehat{m}_l \| \widehat{\mathsf{mk}}_l \| \widehat{v}_l \| \mathsf{pk} \| l]$ with the key $\widehat{\mathsf{ek}}_l$ using the SKE. Finally, the algorithm generates the MAC tag S_l using the key mk on $[\widetilde{C}_l \| \widehat{C}_l \| D_l \| \mathsf{pk} \| l]$ and the MAC tag T_l using mk_l on $[\widetilde{C}_l \| \widehat{C}_l \| D_l \| S_l \| \mathsf{pk} \| l]$. The ciphertext is the tuple $(\widetilde{C}_l, \widehat{C}_l, D_l, S_l, T_l, l)$.

The recipient of $(\widetilde{C}_l, \widehat{C}_l, D_l, S_l, T_l, l)$ decrypts D_l using sk in order to obtain the message m_l and the key mk_l, then it checks the MAC tag T_l using mk_l. The interval key extraction algorithm on the interval $[i, j]$ returns mk, $\widehat{\mathsf{ek}}_i$, and $\widetilde{\mathsf{ek}}_j$ encrypted with the public key of the opener. Using these keys, the opener recovers the messages $(m_l)_{i \leq l \leq j}$ by running the algorithm described above on the parts $\widetilde{C}_l$ and $\widehat{C}_l$ of each ciphertext. The opener also verifies the tags S_l, and verifies the correctness of D_l ans T_l by regenerating them.

Definition 10 (CHAPO). *Let λ be a security parameter.* CHAPO $=$ $(\mathcal{R}_\lambda, \mathcal{M}_\lambda, \mathsf{Gen}, \mathsf{EGen}, \mathsf{Enc}, \mathsf{Dec}, \mathsf{Ext}, \mathsf{Open})$ *is an APOPKE scheme instantiated by a set $\mathcal{M}_\lambda$, an (unforgeable) message authentication code scheme* MAC $=$ $(\mathcal{K}_\lambda^m, \mathsf{Mac}, \mathsf{Ver})$, *an (IND-CCA secure) symmetric encryption scheme* SKE $=$ $(\mathcal{K}_\lambda^s, \mathcal{R}_\lambda^s, \mathsf{SEnc}, \mathsf{SDec})$, *a pseudorandom function* PRF : $\mathcal{K}_\lambda^r \times \{0,1\}^{\lambda+1} \rightarrow$ $\mathcal{K}_\lambda^s$, *and an (IND-CCA secure) public key encryption scheme* PKE $=$ $(\mathcal{R}_\lambda^p, \mathcal{M}_\lambda^p, \mathsf{PGen}, \mathsf{PEnc}, \mathsf{PDec})$. CHAPO *is defined by:*

$\mathsf{Gen}(1^\lambda)$: *Run $(\mathsf{pk}, \mathsf{sk}) \leftarrow \mathsf{PGen}(1^\lambda)$ and return $(\mathsf{pk}, \mathsf{sk})$.*

$\underline{\mathsf{EGen}(1^\lambda)}$: *Pick* $(\mathsf{rk},\mathsf{mk}) \overset{\$}{\leftarrow} \mathcal{K}^r_\lambda \times \mathcal{K}^m_\lambda$, *set* $\mathsf{k} \leftarrow (\mathsf{rk},\mathsf{mk})$ *and return* k.

$\underline{\mathsf{Enc}(\mathsf{pk}_l,\mathsf{k},m_l,l;r_l)}$: *Parse* k *as* $(\mathsf{rk},\mathsf{mk})$. *Using the random coin* r_l, *pick at random* $(\widehat{u}_l,\widetilde{u}_l) \overset{\$}{\leftarrow} (\mathcal{R}^s_\lambda)^2$, $v_l \overset{\$}{\leftarrow} \mathcal{R}^p_\lambda$, $\mathsf{mk}_l \overset{\$}{\leftarrow} \mathcal{K}^m_\lambda$, $\widehat{\mathsf{mk}}_l \overset{\$}{\leftarrow} \{0,1\}^{|\mathsf{mk}_l|}$, $\widehat{v}_l \overset{\$}{\leftarrow} \{0,1\}^{|v_l|}$, *and* $\widehat{m}_l \overset{\$}{\leftarrow} \{0,1\}^{|m_l|}$.

Set $\widetilde{\mathsf{mk}}_l \leftarrow \widehat{\mathsf{mk}}_l \oplus \mathsf{mk}_l$, $\widetilde{v}_l \leftarrow \widehat{v}_l \oplus v_l$, *and* $\widetilde{m}_l \leftarrow \widehat{m}_l \oplus m_l$.

$\forall\, h \in \{l-1,l,l+1\}$, *run* $\widehat{\mathsf{ek}}_h \leftarrow \mathsf{PRF}(\mathsf{k},0\|h)$ *and* $\widetilde{\mathsf{ek}}_h \leftarrow \mathsf{PRF}(\mathsf{k},1\|h)$. *Set:*

- $\widetilde{C}_l \leftarrow \mathsf{SEnc}(\widetilde{\mathsf{ek}}_l,[\widetilde{\mathsf{ek}}_{i+1}\|\widetilde{m}_l\|\widetilde{\mathsf{mk}}_l\|\widetilde{v}_l\|\mathsf{pk}_l\|l];\widetilde{u}_l)$ *and* $\widehat{C}_l \leftarrow \mathsf{SEnc}(\widehat{\mathsf{ek}}_l,[\widehat{\mathsf{ek}}_{i-1}\|\widehat{m}_l\|\widehat{\mathsf{mk}}_l\|\widehat{v}_l\|\mathsf{pk}_l\|l];\widehat{u}_l)$

- $D_l \leftarrow \mathsf{PEnc}(\mathsf{pk}_l,[m_l\|\mathsf{mk}_l\|l];v_l)$

- $S_l \leftarrow \mathsf{Mac}(\mathsf{mk},[\widetilde{C}_l\|\widehat{C}_l\|D_l\|\mathsf{pk}_l\|l])$ *and* $T_l \leftarrow \mathsf{Mac}(\mathsf{mk}_l,[\widetilde{C}_l\|\widehat{C}_l\|D_l\|S_l\|\mathsf{pk}_l\|l])$

Set $c_l \leftarrow (\widetilde{C}_l,\widehat{C}_l,D_l,S_l,T_l,i)$ *and return* c_l.

$\underline{\mathsf{Dec}(\mathsf{sk}_l,c_l)}$: *Parse* c_l *as* $(\widetilde{C}_l,\widehat{C}_l,D_l,S_l,T_l,l)$ *and run* $[m_l\|\mathsf{mk}_l\|l'] \leftarrow \mathsf{PDec}(\mathsf{sk}_l,D_l)$. *If* $l = l'$ *and* $\mathsf{Ver}(\mathsf{mk}_l,T_l,[\widetilde{C}_l\|\widehat{C}_l\|D_l\|S_l\|\mathsf{pk}_l\|l]) = 1$, *then return* m_l, *else return* $\perp$.

$\underline{\mathsf{Ext}(\mathsf{pko},\mathsf{k},i,j;r)}$: *Parse* k *as* $(\mathsf{rk},\mathsf{mk})$. *Using the random coin* r, *pick at random* $u \overset{\$}{\leftarrow} \mathcal{R}^p_\lambda$ *Run* $\widehat{\mathsf{ek}}_j \leftarrow \mathsf{PRF}(\mathsf{rk},0\|j)$ *and* $\widetilde{\mathsf{ek}}_i \leftarrow \mathsf{PRF}(\mathsf{rk},1\|i)$, *then run* $X_{i\to j} \leftarrow \mathsf{PEnc}(\mathsf{pko},[\widetilde{\mathsf{ek}}_i\|\widehat{\mathsf{ek}}_j\|\mathsf{mk}];u)$ *and* $Y_{i\to j} \leftarrow \mathsf{Mac}(\mathsf{mk},[i\|j\|X_{i\to j}])$. *Set* $\mathsf{ik}_{i\to j} \leftarrow (X_{i\to j},Y_{i\to j},i,j)$ *and return* $\mathsf{ik}_{i\to j}$.

$\underline{\mathsf{Open}(\mathsf{sko},i,j,\mathsf{ik}_{i\to j},(c_l,\mathsf{pk}_l)_{i\le l\le j})}$: *Parse* $\mathsf{ik}_{i\to j}$ *as* $(X_{i\to j},Y_{i\to j},i',j')$, *run* $[\widetilde{\mathsf{ek}}_i\|\widehat{\mathsf{ek}}_j\|\mathsf{mk}] \leftarrow \mathsf{PDec}(\mathsf{sko},X_{i\to j})$. *If* $1 \ne \mathsf{Ver}(\mathsf{mk},Y_{i\to j},[i\|j\|X_{i\to j}])$ *or* $(i,j) \ne (i',j')$, *then abort and return* $\perp$.

$\forall\, l \in [\![i,j]\!]$, *from* i *to* j, *parse* c_l *as* $(\widetilde{C}_l,\widehat{C}_l,D_l,S_l,T_l,l)$ *and run* $[\widetilde{\mathsf{ek}}_{l+1}\|\widetilde{m}_l\|\widetilde{\mathsf{mk}}_l\|\widetilde{v}_l\|\widetilde{\mathsf{pk}}_l\|\widetilde{l}] \leftarrow \mathsf{SDec}(\widetilde{\mathsf{ek}}_l,\widetilde{C}_l)$.

$\forall\, l \in [\![i,j]\!]$, *from* j *to* i, *run* $[\widehat{\mathsf{ek}}_{l-1}\|\widehat{m}_l\|\widehat{\mathsf{mk}}_l\|\widehat{v}_l\|\widehat{\mathsf{pk}}_l\|\widehat{l}] \leftarrow \mathsf{SDec}(\widehat{\mathsf{ek}}_l,\widehat{C}_l)$. *If:*

- $\widetilde{\mathsf{pk}}_l \ne \mathsf{pk}_l$ *or* $\widetilde{l} \ne l$ *or* $\widehat{\mathsf{pk}}_l \ne \mathsf{pk}_l$ *or* $\widehat{l} \ne l$, *or*

- $D_l \ne \mathsf{PEnc}(\mathsf{pk}_l,[\widetilde{m}_l \oplus \widehat{m}_l\|\widetilde{\mathsf{mk}}_l \oplus \widehat{\mathsf{mk}}_l\|l];(\widetilde{v}_l \oplus \widehat{v}_l))$, *or*

- $T_l \ne \mathsf{Mac}((\widetilde{\mathsf{mk}}_l \oplus \widehat{\mathsf{mk}}_l),[\widetilde{C}_l\|\widehat{C}_l\|D_l\|S_l\|\mathsf{pk}_l\|l])$, *or*

- $1 \ne \mathsf{Ver}(\mathsf{mk},S_l,[\widetilde{C}_l\|\widehat{C}_l\|D_l\|\mathsf{pk}_l\|l])$,

then return $\perp$.

Finally, return $(\widetilde{m}_l \oplus \widehat{m}_l)_{i\le l\le j}$.

Moreover, let le *be a function such that for any set* S, $\mathsf{le}(S) = \max_{x\in S}(|x|)$, *the set* $\mathcal{R}_\lambda$ *is defined by* $\mathcal{R}_\lambda = (\mathcal{R}^s_\lambda)^2 \times \mathcal{R}^p_\lambda \times \mathcal{K}^m_\lambda \times \{0,1\}^{\mathsf{le}(\mathcal{K}^m_\lambda)} \times \{0,1\}^{\mathsf{le}(\mathcal{R}^s_\lambda)} \times \{0,1\}^{\mathsf{le}(\mathcal{R}^s_\lambda)} \times \{0,1\}^{\mathsf{le}(\mathcal{M}_\lambda)}$, *and the set* $\mathcal{M}^p_\lambda$ *verifies* $\{0,1\}^{(\mathsf{le}(\mathcal{M}_\lambda)+\mathsf{le}(\mathcal{K}^m_\lambda)+\lambda)} \subseteq \mathcal{M}^p_\lambda$.

Security of CHAPO. The CCA security is achieved when the decryption oracles give no advantage to the adversary. The idea being that the decryption oracles will reject the ciphertexts that have not been produced by the experiment, or that have not been encrypted correctly by the adversary. In particular, the decryption oracles should reject any alteration of the challenge.

In the IND-CCA scenario, if the adversary alters the challenge c_{l_*}, then the tag T_{l_*} is no longer valid, and should be refreshed by the adversary. Hence, the adversary should recover the corresponding MAC key mk_{l_*}. This key is encrypted in $\widetilde{C}_{l_*}$ and $\widehat{C}_{l_*}$, however the adversary can decrypt only one of these two ciphertexts. Indeed, the challenge cannot be in the interval that the adversary can decrypt using his interval keys, according to the winning conditions of the IND-CCA experiment. In this case, one of the shares of mk_{l_*} remains encrypted by the SKE. mk_{l_*} is also encrypted in D_{l_*}, but since SKE and PKE are IND-CCA, the adversary cannot recover mk_{l_*} from $\widetilde{C}_{l_*}$ and $\widehat{C}_{l_*}$, or from D_{l_*}. Moreover, since the adversary does not know the key rk, he cannot generate mk_{l_*} from the PRF. Finally, the adversary cannot alter the challenge c_{l_*}.

In the IND-CSCA scenario, if the adversary alters a ciphertext c in the challenge, then the tag T is no longer valid for the key mk, and should be refreshed by the adversary. Otherwise, the opening oracle will fail on any vector of ciphertexts that contains the alteration of c. However, the adversary has not the key mk. To recover it, the adversary would have to decrypt one of the interval keys without the secret key sko of the honest opener, which is not possible since the PKE scheme is IND-CCA secure. Similarly, the opening oracle rejects any query that contains new ciphertexts created by the adversary because he cannot generate the corresponding MAC tags. On the other hand, the adversary could try to use the opening oracle on a vector that contains the ciphertexts of the challenge in a new order. However, since the MAC tags authenticate the indexes of the ciphertexts, the opening oracle will always fail on such a query. Note that since there is only one opener in our model, using a single MAC key mk for all the ciphertexts produced by the same user does not lead to security problem: the key mk can be seen as an authentication key shared between the user who encrypts the messages and the opener.

Finally, when the opener decrypts the ciphertext $c_l = (\widetilde{C}_l, \widehat{C}_l, D_l, S_l, T_l, l)$ encrypted with a key pk_l in some interval, he recovers the message m_l and learns the values mk_l and v_l, then he checks that $D_l = \mathsf{PEnc}(\mathsf{pk}_l, [m_l \| \mathsf{mk}_l \| l]; v_l)$, which ensures that $[m_l \| \mathsf{mk}_l \| l] = \mathsf{PDec}(\mathsf{sk}_l, D_l)$. This implies that the decryption algorithm returns the same message m_l as the opening algorithm, which shows that CHAPO has the integrity property.

Comparaison with GAPO. CHAPO is based on the same approach as GAPO. However, the design of GAPO does not achieve the functionality required by CHAPO, and the two schemes differ in several points. First, the extraction algorithm of GAPO takes as input the first and last ciphertexts of the interval instead of using the corresponding indices, and the encryption algorithm uses a *secret state* that is updated with each encryption. This implies that the user must have access to all the ciphertexts they sent, and that their devices must synchronize to share the secret state in a secure way, which limits the practicality of GAPO.

GAPO uses a PKE family called *Random Coin Decryptable* (RCD) PKE, which means that the ciphertext can be decrypted with its random coin in addition to the standard decryption via the secret key. A GAPO ciphertext consists of two RCD ciphertexts. The first one contains half of the message, and the (symmetric) encryption of the seed of the random coin and the (symmetric) key used for the next encryption, and the second one contains the other half of the message, and the (symmetric) encryption of the seed of the random coin and the (symmetric) key used by the previous encryption. This method makes it very easy to achieve integrity because the opener and the receiver decrypt the same ciphertext. On the other hand, it is slightly less generic since it uses a specific family of encryption, and it requires two public key encryptions, doubling the encryption time of GAPO compared to CHAPO. Moreover, the random coins are obtained by hashing the seeds, and the hash function must be modeled by a random oracle so that the coins are *truly random*. This makes GAPO's security highly relying on the random oracle. Finally, GAPO is not CCA secure by design. To achieve this security, CHAPO uses messages authentication codes, as explained in the previous paragraph.

Security proofs. We prove each theorem by using a sequence of games between a *challenger* and an *adversary* where the adversary plays an experiment run by the challenger. Due to page limitation, we only give the sequences of games, but we omit the reductions between the games. The full proofs are given in the full version of this paper [5].

Theorem 1. *If* PRF *is pseudorandom,* MAC *is* EUF-CMA, SKE *is* IND-CCA, *and* PKE *is correct and* IND-CCA, *then* CHAPO *is* IND-CSCA. *Moreover, the following holds, where* q_n *(resp.* q_x*) denotes the number of queries to the oracle* Enc *(resp.* Ext*) during the experiment, and* q_* *is an upper bound on* $j_* - i_*$*:*

$$\mathbf{Adv}_{\mathsf{CHAPO}}^{\mathsf{IND\text{-}CSCA}}(\lambda) \leq 2 \cdot \left(q_x + q_* \cdot \mu \cdot (1 + (q_n + q_*)^2)\right) \cdot \mathbf{Adv}_{\mathsf{PKE}}^{\mathsf{IND\text{-}CCA}}(\lambda)$$
$$+ (2 + (q_n + q_*)^2 \cdot q_*) \cdot \mathbf{Adv}_{\mathsf{MAC}}^{\mathsf{EUF\text{-}CMA}}(\lambda) + 4 \cdot (q_n + q_*) \cdot \mathbf{Adv}_{\mathsf{SKE}}^{\mathsf{IND\text{-}CCA}}(\lambda)$$
$$+ \mathbf{Adv}_{\mathsf{PRF}}^{\mathsf{PR}}(\lambda).$$

Proof (sketch). Let $\mathcal{A}$ be a PPT algorithm, we use the following sequence of games:

Game G_0: This game is the original IND-CSCA experiment.

Game G_1: This game is similar to G_0, but the challenger replaces each output of the PRF by a random value picked at random in $\mathcal{K}_\lambda^s$. We prove by reduction that:

$$|\Pr\left[\mathcal{A} \text{ wins } G_0\right] - \Pr\left[\mathcal{A} \text{ wins } G_1\right]| \leq \mathbf{Adv}_{\mathsf{PRF}}^{\mathsf{PR}}(\lambda).$$

Game G_2: Let q_x be the number of queries sent to the oracle $\mathsf{Ext}(\mathsf{pko}_*, \mathsf{k}_*, \cdot, \cdot)$. This game is similar to G_1, but the challenger replaces the elements encrypted in the interval keys by random values:

- At the beginning of the experiment, the challenger initializes an empty list $\mathcal{L}_X[\,]$.
- Each time that the oracle $\mathsf{Ext}(\mathsf{pko}_*, \mathsf{k}_*, \cdot, \cdot)$ receives a query (i, j), the challenger parses k_* as $(\mathsf{rk}_*, \mathsf{mk}_*)$. If $i \leq 0$, or $i \geq j$, or $j \geq n$, or $[\![i, j]\!] \cap [\![i_*, j_*]\!] \neq \emptyset$, then it returns $\bot$ according to the definition of the oracle Ext. It then picks $r \xleftarrow{\$} \mathcal{R}_\lambda^p$ and $\mathsf{rnd} \xleftarrow{\$} \{0,1\}^{|\widetilde{\mathsf{ek}}_i\|\widehat{\mathsf{ek}}_j\|\mathsf{mk}_*|}$, runs $X_{i \to j} \leftarrow \mathsf{PEnc}(\mathsf{pko}_*, \mathsf{rnd}; r)$, sets $\mathcal{L}_{\mathsf{Ext}}[X_{i \to j}] \leftarrow [i\|j]$, runs $Y_{i \to j} \leftarrow \mathsf{Mac}(\mathsf{mk}_*, [i\|j\|X_{i \to j}])$, sets $\mathsf{ik}_{i \to j} \leftarrow (X_{i \to j}, Y_{i \to j}, i, j)$ and returns $\mathsf{ik}_{i \to j}$.

– Each time that the challenger runs $\mathsf{Open}(\mathsf{sko}_*, i, j, \mathsf{ik}_{i\to j}, (c_l, \mathsf{pk}_l)_{i\le l\le j})$ such that, parsing $\mathsf{ik}_{i\to j}$ as $(X_{i\to j}, Y_{i\to j}, i, j)$, $\mathcal{L}_X[X_{i\to j}] \ne \perp$, it replaces the instruction $[\widetilde{\mathsf{ek}}'_i\|\widehat{\mathsf{ek}}'_j\|\mathsf{mk}'] \leftarrow \mathsf{PDec}(\mathsf{sko}_*, X_{i\to j})$ by the instructions $[i'\|j'] \leftarrow \mathcal{L}_X[X_{i\to j}]$; $\widetilde{\mathsf{ek}}'_i \leftarrow \widetilde{\mathsf{ek}}_{i'}$; $\widehat{\mathsf{ek}}'_j \leftarrow \widehat{\mathsf{ek}}_{j'}$; $\mathsf{mk}' \leftarrow \mathsf{mk}_*$.

We prove by reduction that:

$$|\Pr\left[\mathcal{A} \text{ wins } G_1\right] - \Pr\left[\mathcal{A} \text{ wins } G_2\right]| \le 2 \cdot q_x \cdot \mathbf{Adv}_{\mathsf{PKE}}^{\mathsf{IND\text{-}CCA}}(\lambda).$$

We stress that from this game, **the key mk_* is never used by the challenger except to generate/verify the message authentication codes.**

Game G_3: In this game, the challenger aborts and returns a random bit if the adversary sends a valid query with a fresh interval key $\mathsf{ik}_{i\to j}$ to the oracle Open, *i.e.* an interval key that has not been generated by the experiment and that does not abort the oracle. More precisely, this game is similar to G_2, but:

– At the beginning, the challenger initializes an empty set $\mathcal{S}_{\mathsf{ik}}$.
– Each time that the challenger generates an interval key $\mathsf{ik}_{i\to j}$, the challenger sets $\mathcal{S}_{\mathsf{ik}} \leftarrow \mathcal{S}_{\mathsf{ik}} \cup \{\mathsf{ik}_{i\to j}\}$.
– Each time that the oracle $\mathsf{Open}(\mathsf{sko}_*, \cdot, \cdot, \cdot, \cdot)$ receives a query $(i, j, \mathsf{ik}_{i\to j}, (c_l, \mathsf{pk}_l)_{i\le l\le j})$ such that the oracle does not returns $\perp$, if parsing $\mathsf{ik}_{i\to j}$ as $(X_{i\to i}, Y_{i\to i}, i, j)$ it holds that $\mathsf{ik}_{i\to j} \notin \mathcal{S}_{\mathsf{ik}}$ and $1 = \mathsf{Ver}(\mathsf{mk}_*, Y_{i\to j}, [i\|j\|X_{i\to i}])$, then the challenger sets $\mathsf{Abort}_3 \leftarrow 1$, aborts the experiment and returns a random bit.

We claim that:

$$|\Pr\left[\mathcal{A} \text{ wins } G_2\right] - \Pr\left[\mathcal{A} \text{ wins } G_3\right]| \le \mathbf{Adv}_{\mathsf{MAC}}^{\mathsf{EUF\text{-}CMA}}(\lambda).$$

We have that $|\Pr\left[\mathcal{A} \text{ wins } G_2\right] - \Pr\left[\mathcal{A} \text{ wins } G_3\right]| \le \Pr[\mathsf{Abort}_3 = 1]$. We prove this claim by showing that $\Pr[\mathsf{Abort}_3 = 1] \le \mathbf{Adv}_{\mathsf{MAC}}^{\mathsf{EUF\text{-}CMA}}(\lambda)$.

Game G_4: In this game, the challenger aborts and returns a random bit if the adversary sends a valid query with a fresh ciphertext c_l to the oracle Open, *i.e.* a ciphertext that has not been generated by the experiment and that does not abort the oracle. More precisely, this game is similar to G_3, but:

– At the beginning of the experiment, the challenger initializes an empty set $\mathcal{S}_{\mathsf{Enc}}$.
– Each time that the challenger runs the encryption algorithm $c \leftarrow \mathsf{Enc}(\mathsf{pk}_{(*,q)}, \mathsf{k}_*, m, l; r)$ for any input m and l, and any key index q, the challenger sets $\mathcal{S}_{\mathsf{Enc}} \leftarrow \mathcal{S}_{\mathsf{Enc}} \cup \{(\mathsf{pk}_{(*,q)}, c)\}$.
– Each time that the oracle $\mathsf{Open}(\mathsf{sko}_*, \cdot, \cdot, \cdot, \cdot)$ receives a query $(i, j, \mathsf{ik}_{i\to j}, (c_l, \mathsf{pk}_l)_{i\le l\le j})$ such that $\exists\, l$ such that parsing c_l as $(\widetilde{C}_l, \widehat{C}_l, D_l, S_l, T_l, l)$, it holds that $(\mathsf{pk}_l, c_l) \notin \mathcal{S}_{\mathsf{Enc}}$ and $1 = \mathsf{Ver}(\mathsf{mk}_*, S_l, [\widetilde{C}_l\|\widehat{C}_l\|D_l\|\mathsf{pk}_l\|l])$, and such that the oracle do not return $\perp$, the challenger sets $\mathsf{Abort}_4 \leftarrow 1$, aborts the experiment and returns a random bit.

We claim that:

$$|\Pr\left[\mathcal{A} \text{ wins } G_3\right] - \Pr\left[\mathcal{A} \text{ wins } G_4\right]| \leq \mathbf{Adv}_{\mathsf{MAC}}^{\mathsf{EUF\text{-}CMA}}(\lambda).$$

We have that $|\Pr\left[\mathcal{A} \text{ wins } G_3\right] - \Pr\left[\mathcal{A} \text{ wins } G_4\right]| \leq \Pr[\mathsf{Abort}_4 = 1]$. We prove this claim by showing that $\Pr[\mathsf{Abort}_4 = 1] \leq \mathbf{Adv}_{\mathsf{MAC}}^{\mathsf{EUF\text{-}CMA}}(\lambda)$.

Game G_5: In what follows, c_l denotes the encryption of the lth message m_l by the experiment, and $\bar{\mathsf{pk}}_l$ denotes the corresponding public key. Moreover, for any pair of indexes (i,j), $\mathsf{ik}_{i \to j}^h$ denotes the hth interval key returned by the oracle $\mathsf{Ext}(\mathsf{pko}_*, \mathsf{k}_*, \cdot, \cdot)$ on the input (i,j). This game is the same as G_5 but the oracle $\mathsf{Open}(\mathsf{sko}_*, \cdot, \cdot, \cdot, \cdot)$ is re-defined by:

- On input $(i, j, \mathsf{ik}_{i \to j}', (c_l', \mathsf{pk}_l')_{i \leq l \leq j})$, if $i \leq 0$ or $i \geq j$ or $j \geq n$, then return $\bot$. During the second phase, if $(\mathsf{ik}_{i \to j}', (c_l', \mathsf{pk}_l')_{i \leq l \leq j}) = (\mathsf{ik}_{i_* \to j_*}, (c_{(*,l)}, \bar{\mathsf{pk}}_l)_{i_* \leq l \leq j_*})$, then return $\bot$.
- If $(c_l', \mathsf{pk}_l')_{i \leq l \leq j} = (c_l, \mathsf{pk}_l)_{i \leq l \leq j}$ and $\exists\, h$ such that $\mathsf{ik}_{i \to j}' = \mathsf{ik}_{i \to j}^h$, then return $(m_l)_{i \leq l \leq j}$, else return $\bot$.

From the properties of G_4 given above, we deduce that:

$$\Pr\left[\mathcal{A} \text{ wins } G_4\right] = \Pr\left[\mathcal{A} \text{ wins } G_5\right].$$

We stress that from this game, **the challenger no longer use the algorithm SDec during the experiment**.

Game G_6: In this game, the challenger replaces the message encrypted in each ciphertext $\widetilde{C}_l$ by a random value. More precisely, this game is similar to G_5, but each time that the encryption algorithm $c_n \leftarrow \mathsf{Enc}(\mathsf{pk}_n, \mathsf{k}_*, m_n, n; r_n)$ is run by the Enc oracle or by the experiment during the generation of the challenge, the challenger replaces the instruction $\widetilde{C}_n \leftarrow \mathsf{SEnc}(\widetilde{\mathsf{ek}}_n, [\bar{\mathsf{ek}}_{n+1}\|\widetilde{m}_n\|\widetilde{\mathsf{mk}}_n\|\widetilde{v}_n\|\mathsf{pk}_n\|n]; \widetilde{u}_n)$ by the sequence of instructions $\mathsf{str}_n \leftarrow [\bar{\mathsf{ek}}_{n+1}\|\widetilde{m}_n\|\widetilde{\mathsf{mk}}_n\|\widetilde{v}_n\|\mathsf{pk}_n\|n]$; $\mathsf{rnd}_n \xleftarrow{\$} \{0,1\}^{|\mathsf{str}_n|}$; $\widetilde{C}_n \leftarrow \mathsf{SEnc}(\widetilde{\mathsf{ek}}_n, \mathsf{rnd}_n; \widetilde{u}_n)$;

Let q_* be an upper bound on the number of ciphertexts sending by the adversary $\mathcal{A}_1$, i.e. $j_* - i_* \leq q_*$. We claim that:

$$|\Pr\left[\mathcal{A} \text{ wins } G_5\right] - \Pr\left[\mathcal{A} \text{ wins } G_6\right]| \leq 2 \cdot (q_n + q_*) \cdot \mathbf{Adv}_{\mathsf{SKE}}^{\mathsf{IND\text{-}CCA}}(\lambda).$$

We prove this claim by using an hybrid argument. We define an hybrid game $G_{6,h}$ as follows:

Game $G_{6,h}$: In this game, the challenger replaces the messages encrypted in the h first ciphertexts $\widetilde{C}_l$ by random values. More precisely, If $h = 0$, then $G_{6,h} = G_5$, else if $1 \leq h \leq (q_n + q_*)$, then the game $G_{6,h}$ is the same as $G_{6,h-1}$, but when the encryption algorithm $c_n \leftarrow \mathsf{Enc}(\mathsf{pk}_n, \mathsf{k}_*, m_n, n; r_n)$ is run for $n = h$ by the Enc oracle or by the experiment during the generation of the challenge, the challenger replaces the instructions $\widetilde{C}_n \leftarrow \mathsf{SEnc}(\widetilde{\mathsf{ek}}_n, [\bar{\mathsf{ek}}_{n+1}\|\widetilde{m}_n\|\widetilde{\mathsf{mk}}_n\|\widetilde{v}_n\|\mathsf{pk}_n\|n]; \widetilde{u}_n)$ by the instructions $\mathsf{str}_n \leftarrow$

$[\widetilde{\mathrm{ek}}_{n+1}\|\widetilde{m}_n\|\widetilde{\mathrm{mk}}_n\|\widetilde{v}_n\|\mathrm{pk}_n\|n]$; $\mathrm{rnd}_n \xleftarrow{\$} \{0,1\}^{|\mathrm{str}_n|}$; $\widetilde{C}_n \leftarrow \mathsf{SEnc}(\widetilde{\mathrm{ek}}_n, \mathrm{rnd}_n; \widetilde{u}_n)$. We prove by reduction that, for all $h \in [\![1, q_n + q_*]\!]$:

$$|\Pr[\mathcal{A} \text{ wins } G_{6,h-1}] - \Pr[\mathcal{A} \text{ wins } G_{6,h}]| \leq 2 \cdot \mathbf{Adv}_{\mathsf{SKE}}^{\mathsf{IND\text{-}CCA}}(\lambda).$$

Game G_7: In this game, the challenger replaces the message encrypted in each ciphertext $\widehat{C}_l$ by a random value. More precisely, this game is similar to G_6, but when the encryption algorithm $c_n \leftarrow \mathsf{Enc}(\mathrm{pk}_n, \mathrm{k}_*, m_n, n; r_n)$ is run for $n = h$ by the Enc oracle or by the experiment during the generation of the challenge, the challenger replaces the instructions $\widehat{C}_n \leftarrow \mathsf{SEnc}(\widehat{\mathrm{ek}}_n, [\widehat{\mathrm{ek}}_{n-1}\|\widehat{m}_n\|\widehat{\mathrm{mk}}_n\|\widehat{v}_n\|\mathrm{pk}_n\|n]; \widehat{u}_n)$ by the sequence $\mathrm{str}_n \leftarrow [\widehat{\mathrm{ek}}_{n-1}\|\widehat{m}_n\|\widehat{\mathrm{mk}}_n\|\widehat{v}_n\|\mathrm{pk}_n\|n]$; $\mathrm{rnd}_n \xleftarrow{\$} \{0,1\}^{|\mathrm{str}_n|}$; $\widehat{C}_n \leftarrow \mathsf{SEnc}(\widehat{\mathrm{ek}}_n, \mathrm{rnd}_n; \widehat{u}_n)$. Let q_* be an upper bound on the number of ciphertexts sending by the adversary $\mathcal{A}_1$, i.e. $j_* - i_* \leq q_*$. We claim that:

$$|\Pr[\mathcal{A} \text{ wins } G_6] - \Pr[\mathcal{A} \text{ wins } G_7]| \leq 2 \cdot (q_n + q_*) \cdot \mathbf{Adv}_{\mathsf{SKE}}^{\mathsf{IND\text{-}CCA}}(\lambda).$$

This claim can be proved using the following hybrid argument: We define an hybrid game $G_{7,h}$ as follows:

Game $G_{7,h}$: In this game, the challenger replaces the messages encrypted in the $(q_n + q_* + 1 - h)$ last ciphertexts $\widehat{C}_l$ by random values. More precisely, if $h = q_n + q_* + 1$, then $G_{7,h} = G_6$, else if $1 \leq h \leq (q_n + q_*)$, then the game $G_{7,h}$ is the same as $G_{7,h+1}$, but each time the challenger runs the encryption algorithm $c_n \leftarrow \mathsf{Enc}(\mathrm{pk}_n, \mathrm{k}_*, m_n, n; r_n)$ during the Enc oracle or during the challenge generation such that $n = h$, it replaces the instruction $\widehat{C}_n \leftarrow \mathsf{SEnc}(\widehat{\mathrm{ek}}_n, [\widehat{\mathrm{ek}}_{n-1}\|\widehat{m}_n\|\widehat{\mathrm{mk}}_n\|\widehat{v}_n\|\mathrm{pk}_n\|n]; \widehat{u}_n)$ by the sequence $\mathrm{str}_n \leftarrow [\widehat{\mathrm{ek}}_{n-1}\|\widehat{m}_n\|\widehat{\mathrm{mk}}_n\|\widehat{v}_n\|\mathrm{pk}_n\|n]$; $\mathrm{rnd}_n \xleftarrow{\$} \{0,1\}^{|\mathrm{str}_n|}$; $\widehat{C}_n \leftarrow \mathsf{SEnc}(\widehat{\mathrm{ek}}_n, \mathrm{rnd}_n; \widehat{u}_n)$. We prove by reduction that, for all $h \in [\![1, q_n + q_*]\!]$:

$$|\Pr[\mathcal{A} \text{ wins } G_{7,h+1}] - \Pr[\mathcal{A} \text{ wins } G_{7,h}]| \leq 2 \cdot \mathbf{Adv}_{\mathsf{SKE}}^{\mathsf{IND\text{-}CCA}}(\lambda).$$

Game G_8: In what follows, we parse the lth ciphertext $c_{(*,l)}$ of the challenge by $(\widetilde{C}_{(*,l)}, \widehat{C}_{(*,l)}, D_{(*,l)}, S_{(*,l)}, T_{(*,l)}, l)$. In this game, the challenger replaces the keys mk_l for all l in $[\![i_*, j_*]\!]$ encrypted by a public key generated by the challenger (*i.e.* in $\{\mathrm{pk}_{(*,q)}\}_{1 \leq q \leq \mu}$) in each ciphertext $D_{(*,l)}$ by a random value. More precisely, this game is similar to G_7, except that when the challenger build the challenge $(\mathrm{ik}_{i_* \to j_*}, (c_{(*,l)})_{i_* \leq l \leq j_*})$, $\forall\, l \in [\![i_*, j_*]\!]$ such that $\exists\, q, \mathrm{pk}_{(*,q)} = \bar{\mathrm{pk}}_l$:

the challenger picks $\mathrm{mk}'_l \xleftarrow{\$} \mathcal{K}_\lambda^m$,
when the challenger runs $c_{(*,l)} \leftarrow \mathsf{Enc}(\bar{\mathrm{pk}}_l, \mathrm{k}_*, m_{(b,l)}, l)$, it replaces the instruction $D_{(*,l)} \leftarrow \mathsf{PEnc}(\mathrm{pk}_{(*,q)}, [m_{(b,l)}\|\mathrm{mk}_l\|l]; v_l)$ by $D_{(*,l)} \leftarrow \mathsf{PEnc}(\mathrm{pk}_{(*,q)}, [m_{(b,l)}\|\mathrm{mk}'_l\|l]; v_l)$.
For each query (p, c) (where we parse c as $(\widetilde{C}, \widehat{C}, D, S, T, l')$) sending to the oracle $\mathsf{Dec}(\cdot, \cdot)$ such that $p = q$, $c \neq c_{(*,l)}$ and $D = D_{(*,l)}$, the challenger runs $\mathsf{Dec}(\mathrm{sk}_{(*,q)}, c)$ as in the real experiment except that it replaces the instruction $[m\|\mathrm{mk}\|l''] \leftarrow \mathsf{PDec}(\mathrm{sk}_{(*,q)}, D)$ by $[m\|\mathrm{mk}\|l''] \leftarrow [m_{(b,l)}\|\mathrm{mk}_l\|l]$.

We prove by reduction that:

$$|\Pr\left[\mathcal{A} \text{ wins } G_7\right] - \Pr\left[\mathcal{A} \text{ wins } G_8\right]| \leq 2 \cdot q_* \cdot \mu \cdot \mathbf{Adv}_{\mathsf{PKE}}^{\mathsf{IND\text{-}CCA}}(\lambda).$$

We stress that from this game, for each index l in $[\![i_*, j_*]\!]$ such that $\bar{\mathsf{pk}}_l \in \{\mathsf{pk}_{(*,q)}\}_{1 \leq q \leq \mu}$, **the key mk_l is only used to produced the MAC tag $T_{(*,l)}$. Especially, mk_l is never encrypted in a ciphertext known by the adversary.**

Game G_9: In this game, the challenger tries to guess the indexes i_* and j_*, and aborts in case of failure. More precisely, this game is similar to G_8, but the challenger picks $(i'_*, j'_*) \leftarrow [\![1, q_n + q_*]\!]^2$ at the beginning of the experiment. At the end of the experiment, if $i'_* \neq j_*$ or $i'_* \neq j_*$, then the challenger returns a random bit. The adversary increases its winning advantage by a factor equalling the probability of guessing correctly i_* and j_*:

$$|\Pr\left[\mathcal{A} \text{ wins } G_8\right] - 1/2| = (q_n + q_*)^2 \cdot |\Pr\left[\mathcal{A} \text{ wins } G_9\right] - 1/2|$$

We stress that n is incremented $(q_n + q_*)$ times during the experiment: q_n times by the oracle $\mathsf{Enc}(\cdot, \mathsf{k}_*, \cdot, n)$ and q_* times after the generation of $(c_{(*,l)})_{i_* \leq l \leq j_*}$.

Game G_{10}: We parse the challenge $(c_{(*,l)})_{i_* \leq l \leq j_*}$ as $(\widetilde{C}_{(*,l)}, \widehat{C}_{(*,l)}, D_{(*,l)}, S_{(*,l)}, T_{(*,l)}, l)_{i_* \leq l \leq j_*}$. In this game, the challenger aborts if the adversary tries to reuse the element $D_{(*,l)}$ in a ciphertext $c \neq c_{(*,l)}$ sending to the decryption oracle for all l in $[\![i_*, j_*]\!]$ such that $\bar{\mathsf{pk}}_l \in \{\mathsf{pk}_{(*,q)}\}_{1 \leq q \leq \mu}$. More concretely, this game is similar to G_9, but if the adversary sends a query (p, c) (where we parse c as $(\widetilde{C}, \widehat{C}, D, S, T, l)$) to the oracle $\mathsf{Dec}(\cdot, \cdot)$ such that, $\mathsf{pk}_{(*,q)} = \bar{\mathsf{pk}}_l$ and $D = D_{(*,l)}$ and $c \neq c_{(*,l)}$ and $\mathsf{Ver}(\mathsf{mk}_l, T, [\widetilde{C}\|\widehat{C}\|D\|S\|\mathsf{pk}_{(*,q)}\|l]) = 1$, then the challenger set $\mathsf{Abort}_{10} \leftarrow 1$, aborts the game G_{10} and returns a random bit. We claim that:

$$|\Pr\left[\mathcal{A} \text{ wins } G_9\right] - \Pr\left[\mathcal{A} \text{ wins } G_{10}\right]| \leq q_* \cdot \mathbf{Adv}_{\mathsf{MAC}}^{\mathsf{EUF\text{-}CMA}}(\lambda).$$

We prove this claim by using an hybrid argument. We define the game $G_{10,h}$ as follows:

Game $G_{10,h}$: We define $G_{10,0}$ as G_9, and for all $1 \leq h \leq q_*$, we define $G_{10,h}$ as $G_{10,h-1}$ but the challenger aborts if (i) $\bar{\mathsf{pk}}_{(*,i'_*+h)} \in \{\mathsf{pk}_{(*,q)}\}_{1 \leq q \leq \mu}$, and (ii) the adversary tries to reuse the element $D_{(*,i'_*+h)}$ in a ciphertext $c \neq c_{(*,i'_*+h)}$ sending to the decryption oracle. More concretely, we define $G_{10,h}$ as the same game as $G_{10,h-1}$ except that parsing the challenge $(c_{(*,l)})_{i_* \leq l \leq j_*}$ as $(\widetilde{C}_{(*,l)}, \widehat{C}_{(*,l)}, D_{(*,l)}, S_{(*,l)}, T_{(*,l)})_{i_* \leq l \leq j_*}$, if the adversary sends a query (p, c) to the oracle $\mathsf{Dec}(\cdot, \cdot)$ such that, parsing c as $(\widetilde{C}, \widehat{C}, D, S, T, l)$, it holds that $\mathsf{pk}_{(*,q)} = \bar{\mathsf{pk}}_{i'_*+h}$ and $D = D_{(*,i'_*+h)}$ and $c \neq c_{(*,i'_*+h)}$ and $\mathsf{Ver}(\mathsf{mk}_{i'_*+h}, T, [\widetilde{C}\|\widehat{C}\|D\|S\|\mathsf{pk}_{(*,q)}\|l]) = 1$, then the challenger set $\mathsf{Abort}_{10,h} \leftarrow 1$, aborts the game $G_{10,h}$ and returns a random bit. We note that $G_{10,q_*} = G_{10}$. We prove by reduction that:

$$|\Pr\left[\mathcal{A} \text{ wins } G_{10,h-1}\right] - \Pr\left[\mathcal{A} \text{ wins } G_{10,h}\right]| \leq \mathbf{Adv}_{\mathsf{MAC}}^{\mathsf{EUF\text{-}CMA}}(\lambda).$$

Game G_{11}: This game is similar to G_{10}, but the challenger substitutes each message that depends on b by a random message of same length. More formally, for each $l \in [\![i'_*, j'_*]\!]$ such that $\bar{pk}_l \in \{pk_{(*,q)}\}_{1 \leq q \leq \mu}$ it replaces the message $m_{(b,l)}$ encrypted in $c_{(*,l)}$ by the public key $\bar{pk}_l$ by a message $m_{(*,l)} \xleftarrow{\$} \{0,1\}^{|m_{(b,l)}|}$ chosen at random. We prove by reduction that:

$$|\mathrm{Pr}[\mathcal{A} \text{ wins } G_{10}] - \mathrm{Pr}[\mathcal{A} \text{ wins } G_{11}]| = 2 \cdot q_* \cdot \mu \cdot \mathbf{Adv}_{\mathsf{PKE}}^{\mathsf{IND\text{-}CCA}}(\lambda).$$

By composing the winning probabilities of $\mathcal{A}$ in all games, we obtain the upper bound on $\mathbf{Adv}_{\mathsf{CHAPO}}^{\mathsf{IND\text{-}CSCA}}(\lambda)$ given in the theorem, which concludes the proof. $\square$

Theorem 2. *If* PRF *is pseudorandom,* MAC *is* EUF-CMA, SKE *and* PKE *are correct and* IND-CCA, *then* CHAPO *is* IND-CCA. *Moreover, the following holds, where q_n denotes the number of queries to the oracle* Enc *during the experiment:*

$$\mathbf{Adv}_{\mathsf{CHAPO}}^{\mathsf{IND\text{-}CCA}}(\lambda) \leq 2 \cdot \mathbf{Adv}_{\mathsf{PRF}}^{\mathsf{PR}}(\lambda) + 4 \cdot (q_n + 1) \cdot \mathbf{Adv}_{\mathsf{SKE}}^{\mathsf{IND\text{-}CCA}}(\lambda)$$
$$+ 8 \cdot (q_n + 1) \cdot \mathbf{Adv}_{\mathsf{PKE}}^{\mathsf{IND\text{-}CCA}}(\lambda) + 2 \cdot (q_n + 1) \cdot \mathbf{Adv}_{\mathsf{MAC}}^{\mathsf{EUF\text{-}CMA}}(\lambda).$$

Proof (sketch). We recall that in order to win the IND-CCA experiment with a non negligible advantage, the following must hold: $l_* \notin [\![i_*, j_*]\!]$. We separate our proof in two distinct cases: $l_* < i_*$ and $l_* > j_*$. More concretely, we define two variants of the IND-CCA experiment: the IND-CCA$_0$ (resp. IND-CCA$_1$) experiment denotes the same experiment as IND-CCA except that if $l_* < i_*$ (resp. $l_* > j_*$), then the challenger returns a random bit. We have that:

$$\mathbf{Adv}_{\mathsf{CHAPO},\mathcal{A}}^{\mathsf{IND\text{-}CCA}}(\lambda) \leq \mathbf{Adv}_{\mathsf{CHAPO},\mathcal{A}}^{\mathsf{IND\text{-}CCA}_0}(\lambda) + \mathbf{Adv}_{\mathsf{CHAPO},\mathcal{A}}^{\mathsf{IND\text{-}CCA}_1}(\lambda).$$

Case IND-CCA$_0$ (*i.e. $l_* < i_*$*): We use the following sequence of games. Let $\mathcal{A}$ be a PPT algorithm:

Game G_0: This game is the original IND-CCA$_0$ experiment.

Game G_1: This game is similar to G_0, but the challenger replaces each output of the PRF by a random value picked in $\mathcal{K}_\lambda^s$. We prove by reduction that:

$$|\mathrm{Pr}[\mathcal{A} \text{ wins } G_0] - \mathrm{Pr}[\mathcal{A} \text{ wins } G_1]| \leq \mathbf{Adv}_{\mathsf{PRF}}^{\mathsf{PR}}(\lambda).$$

Game G_2: In this game, the challenger tries to guess the index i_* and aborts in case of failure. Let q_n be the number of calls to the oracle $\mathsf{Enc}(\cdot, k_*, \cdot, n)$. This game is similar to G_1, but the challenger picks $i'_* \leftarrow [\![1, q_n + 1]\!]$ at the beginning of the experiment. At the end of the experiment, if $i'_* \neq i_*$, then the challenger returns a random bit. The adversary increases its winning advantage by a factor equalling the probability of guessing correctly i_*:

$$|\mathrm{Pr}[\mathcal{A} \text{ wins } G_1] - 1/2| = (q_n + 1) \cdot |\mathrm{Pr}[\mathcal{A} \text{ wins } G_2] - 1/2|.$$

Note that n is incremented $(q_n + 1)$ times during the experiment: q_n times by the oracle $\mathsf{Enc}(\cdot, k_*, \cdot, n)$ and one time after the generation of c_{l_*}.

Game G_3: In this game, for all $n \leq i_*$, the challenger replaces the part $\widetilde{C}_n$ of the ciphertext c_n by the encryption of a random message, which includes the challenge c_{l_*} if $l_* \leq i_*$ (otherwise, the challenger returns a random bit by definition of the IND-CCA$_0$ experiment). This game is similar to G_2, but while $n < i'_*$, each time the oracle $\mathsf{Enc}(\cdot, \mathsf{k}_*, \cdot, n)$ is called on a query (pk_n, m_n) and runs $c_n \leftarrow \mathsf{Enc}(\mathsf{pk}_n, \mathsf{k}_*, m_n, n; r_n)$, it replaces the instruction $\widetilde{C}_n \leftarrow \mathsf{SEnc}(\widetilde{\mathsf{ek}}_n, [\widetilde{\mathsf{ek}}_{n+1}\|\widetilde{m}_n\|\widetilde{\mathsf{mk}}_n\|\widetilde{v}_n\|\mathsf{pk}_n\|n]; \widetilde{u}_n)$ by the sequence of instructions $\mathsf{str}_n \leftarrow [\widetilde{\mathsf{ek}}_{n+1}\|\widetilde{m}_n\|\widetilde{\mathsf{mk}}_n\|\widetilde{v}_n\|\mathsf{pk}_n\|n]$; $\mathsf{rnd}_n \xleftarrow{\$} \{0,1\}^{|\mathsf{str}_n|}$; $\widetilde{C}_n \leftarrow \mathsf{SEnc}(\widetilde{\mathsf{ek}}_n, \mathsf{rnd}_n; \widetilde{u}_n)$. Moreover, when it computes the challenge $c_{l_*} \leftarrow \mathsf{Enc}(\mathsf{pk}_*, \mathsf{k}_*, m_{(*,0)}, l_*; r_*)$, the challenger replaces the instruction $\widetilde{C}_{l_*} \leftarrow \mathsf{SEnc}(\widetilde{\mathsf{ek}}_{l_*}, [\widetilde{\mathsf{ek}}_{l_*+1}\|\widetilde{m}_{(*,b)}\|\widetilde{\mathsf{mk}}_{l_*}\|\widetilde{v}_{l_*}\|\mathsf{pk}_*\|l_*]; \widetilde{u}_{l_*})$; by the sequence $\mathsf{str}_{l_*} \leftarrow [\widetilde{\mathsf{ek}}_{l_*+1}\|\widetilde{m}_{(*,b)}\|\widetilde{\mathsf{mk}}_{l_*}\|\widetilde{v}_{l_*}\|\mathsf{pk}_*\|l_*]$; $\mathsf{rnd}_{l_*} \xleftarrow{\$} \{0,1\}^{|\mathsf{str}_{l_*}|}$; $\widetilde{C}_{l_*} \leftarrow \mathsf{SEnc}(\widetilde{\mathsf{ek}}_{l_*}, \mathsf{rnd}_{l_*}; \widetilde{u}_{l_*})$. We claim that:

$$|\Pr[\mathcal{A} \text{ wins } G_2] - \Pr[\mathcal{A} \text{ wins } G_3]| \leq 2 \cdot (q_n + 1) \cdot \mathbf{Adv}_{\mathsf{SKE}}^{\mathsf{IND\text{-}CCA}}(\lambda).$$

We prove this claim by using an hybrid argument. We define the hybrid game $G_{3,i}$ as follows:

Game $G_{3,i}$: If $i = 0$, then $G_{3,0} = G_2$, else for all $n \leq i$, if $i \leq i'_*$, then the challenger replaces the part $\widetilde{C}_n$ of the ciphertext c_n by the encryption of a random message. More concretely, if $1 \leq i \leq (q_n + 1)$, then the game $G_{3,i}$ is the same as $G_{3,i-1}$, but if $i < i'_*$ and $l_* \neq i$, then when the oracle $\mathsf{Enc}(\cdot, \mathsf{k}_*, \cdot, i)$ is called on a query (pk_i, m_i) and runs $c_i \leftarrow \mathsf{Enc}(\mathsf{pk}_i, \mathsf{k}_*, m_i, i; r_i)$, it replaces the instruction $\widetilde{C}_i \leftarrow \mathsf{SEnc}(\widetilde{\mathsf{ek}}_i, [\widetilde{\mathsf{ek}}_{i+1}\|\widetilde{m}_i\|\widetilde{\mathsf{mk}}_i\|\widetilde{v}_i\|\mathsf{pk}_i\|i]; \widetilde{u}_i)$ by the sequence of instructions $\mathsf{str}_i[\widetilde{\mathsf{ek}}_{i+1}\|\widetilde{m}_i\|\widetilde{\mathsf{mk}}_i\|\widetilde{v}_i\|\mathsf{pk}_i\|i]$; $\mathsf{rnd}_i \xleftarrow{\$} \{0,1\}^{|\mathsf{str}_i|}$; $\widetilde{C}_i \leftarrow \mathsf{SEnc}(\widetilde{\mathsf{ek}}_i, \mathsf{rnd}_i; \widetilde{u}_i)$. Moreover, if $l_* = i$, then when it computes the challenge $c_{l_*} \leftarrow \mathsf{Enc}(\mathsf{pk}_*, \mathsf{k}_*, m_{(*,0)}, l_*; r_*)$, the challenger replaces the instruction $\widetilde{C}_{l_*} \leftarrow \mathsf{SEnc}(\widetilde{\mathsf{ek}}_{l_*}, [\widetilde{\mathsf{ek}}_{l_*+1}\|\widetilde{m}_{(*,b)}\|\widetilde{\mathsf{mk}}_{l_*}\|\widetilde{v}_{l_*}\|\mathsf{pk}_*\|l_*]; \widetilde{u}_{l_*})$ by $\mathsf{str}_{l_*} \leftarrow [\widetilde{\mathsf{ek}}_{l_*+1}\|\widetilde{m}_{(*,b)}\|\widetilde{\mathsf{mk}}_{l_*}\|\widetilde{v}_{l_*}\|\mathsf{pk}_*\|l_*]$; $\mathsf{rnd}_{l_*} \xleftarrow{\$} \{0,1\}^{|\mathsf{str}_{l_*}|}$; $\widetilde{C}_{l_*} \leftarrow \mathsf{SEnc}(\widetilde{\mathsf{ek}}_{l_*}, \mathsf{rnd}_{l_*}; \widetilde{u}_{l_*})$. We prove by reduction that, for all $i \in [\![1, q_n + 1]\!]$:

$$|\Pr[\mathcal{A} \text{ wins } G_{3,i-1}] - \Pr[\mathcal{A} \text{ wins } G_{3,i}]| \leq 2 \cdot \mathbf{Adv}_{\mathsf{SKE}}^{\mathsf{IND\text{-}CCA}}(\lambda).$$

Game G_4: This is the same game as G_3, but $\widehat{m}_{(*,b)}$, $\widehat{\mathsf{mk}}_{l_*}$ and $\widehat{v}_{l_*}$ are substituted by random bit-strings of same length. At this step, since $\widetilde{m}_{(*,b)}$ is replaced by a random bit string in $\widetilde{C}_{l_*}$ and $\widehat{m}_{(*,b)} = m_{(*,b)} \oplus \widetilde{m}_{(*,b)}$, then $\widehat{m}_{(*,b)}$ is indistinguishable from a random bit string, so it no longer depends on b, and can be substituted by a random bit-string without any influence on the adversary advantage. Using a similar argument, we have that $\widehat{\mathsf{mk}}_{l_*}$ and $\widehat{v}_{l_*}$ can also be substituted by random bit-strings. We deduce that:

$$\Pr[\mathcal{A} \text{ wins } G_3] = \Pr[\mathcal{A} \text{ wins } G_4].$$

Game G_5: In this game, the challenger replaces the MAC key mk_{l_*} by a random value in the part D_{l_*} (encrypted by PKE) of the ciphertext challenge c_{l_*}. More concretely, This game is similar to G_5, except that:

- when it computes the challenge by running $c_{l_*} \leftarrow \mathsf{Enc}(\mathsf{pk}_*, \mathsf{k}_*, m_{(*,b)}, l_*; r_*)$, it replaces the instruction $D_{l_*} \leftarrow \mathsf{PEnc}(\mathsf{pk}_*, [m_{(*,b)}\|\mathsf{mk}_{l_*}\|l_*]; v_{l_*})$ by the sequence of instructions $\mathsf{mk}'_{l_*} \xleftarrow{\$} \mathcal{K}^m_\lambda$; $D_{l_*} \leftarrow \mathsf{PEnc}(\mathsf{pk}_*, [m_{(*,b)}\|\mathsf{mk}'_{l_*}\|l_*]; v_{l_*})$,

- For each query $c = (\widetilde{C}, \widehat{C}, D, S, T, l)$ sending to the oracle $\mathsf{Dec}(\mathsf{sk}_*, \cdot)$ such that $c \neq c_{l_*}$ and $D = D_{l_*}$, the challenger runs $\mathsf{Dec}(\mathsf{sk}_*, c)$ as in the real experiment except that it replaces the instruction $[m\|\mathsf{mk}\|l] \leftarrow \mathsf{PDec}(\mathsf{sk}_*, D)$ by $[m\|\mathsf{mk}\|l] \leftarrow [m_{(*,b)}\|\mathsf{mk}_{l_*}\|l_*]$.

We prove by reduction that:

$$|\Pr[\mathcal{A} \text{ wins } G_4] - \Pr[\mathcal{A} \text{ wins } G_5]| \leq 2 \cdot \mathbf{Adv}_{\mathsf{PKE}}^{\mathsf{IND\text{-}CCA}}(\lambda).$$

Game G_6: In what follows, we parse the challenge c_{l_*} as $(\widetilde{C}_{l_*}, \widehat{C}_{l_*}, D_{l_*}, S_{l_*}, T_{l_*})$. In this game, the challenger aborts if the adversary tries to reuse D_{l_*} in a ciphertext $c \neq c_{l_*}$ sending to the decryption oracle. More concretely, this game is similar to G_5, but if the adversary sends a query $c = (\widetilde{C}, \widehat{C}, D, S, T, l)$ to the oracle $\mathsf{Dec}(\mathsf{sk}_*, \cdot)$ such that $D = D_{l_*}$, $c \neq c_{l_*}$ and $\mathsf{Ver}(\mathsf{mk}_{l_*}, T, [\widetilde{C}\|\widehat{C}\|D\|S\|\mathsf{pk}_*\|l]) = 1$, then the challenger set $\mathsf{Abort}_6 \leftarrow 1$, aborts the game G_6 and returns a random bit. We prove by reduction that:

$$|\Pr[\mathcal{A} \text{ wins } G_5] - \Pr[\mathcal{A} \text{ wins } G_6]| \leq \mathbf{Adv}_{\mathsf{MAC}}^{\mathsf{EUF\text{-}CMA}}(\lambda).$$

Game G_7: This game is similar to G_6, but the challenger substitutes the message $m_{(*,b)}$ by a random message $m_* \xleftarrow{\$} \{0,1\}^{|m_{(*,b)}|}$. We prove by reduction that:

$$|\Pr[\mathcal{A} \text{ wins } G_6] - \Pr[\mathcal{A} \text{ wins } G_7]| = 2 \cdot \mathbf{Adv}_{\mathsf{PKE}}^{\mathsf{IND\text{-}CCA}}(\lambda).$$

At this step, the parts $\widehat{C}_{l_*}$, $\widetilde{C}_{l_*}$, and D_{l_*} of the challenge c_{l_*} encrypts random values instead of the messages $\widehat{m}_{(*,b)}$, $\widetilde{m}_{(*,b)}$, and $m_{(*,b)}$, which implies that the game G_7 do not depend on the challenge bit b. We deduce that $\Pr[\mathcal{A} \text{ wins } G_7] = 1/2$. Case $\mathsf{IND\text{-}CCA}_1$ $(l_* > j_*)$ is similar to case $\mathsf{IND\text{-}CCA}_0$. By composing the winning probabilities of $\mathcal{A}$ in all games, we obtain the upper bound on $\mathbf{Adv}_{\mathsf{CHAPO}}^{\mathsf{IND\text{-}CCA}}(\lambda)$ given in the theorem, which concludes the proof. $\qquad\square$

Theorem 3. *If* PKE *is correct and key verifiable, then* CHAPO *is Integrity-secure. Moreover, it holds that* $\mathbf{Adv}_{\mathsf{CHAPO}}^{\mathsf{Integrity}}(\lambda) = 0$.

Proof. We prove this theorem by negation. Assume that the adversary returns $(i, j, (c_l, \mathsf{pk}_l)_{i \leq l \leq j}, x, \mathsf{sk}_x, \mathsf{ik}_{i \to j})$ to the challenger such that running $(m_l)_{i \leq l \leq j} \leftarrow \mathsf{Open}(\mathsf{sko}_*, i, j, \mathsf{ik}_{i \to j}, (c_l, \mathsf{pk}_l)_{i \leq l \leq j})$ and $m'_x \leftarrow \mathsf{Dec}(\mathsf{sk}_x, c_x)$, it holds that $m_x \neq \bot$ and $m'_x \neq \bot$ and $m_x \neq m'_x$ and $1 = \mathsf{KVer}(\mathsf{pk}_x, \mathsf{sk}_x)$. We show that this implies the following contradiction: $m'_x = m_x$.

We parse c_x as $(\widetilde{C}_x, \widehat{C}_x, D_x, S_x, T_x, x)$. According to the algorithm Open, if $m_x \neq \bot$, then during the run of $\mathsf{Open}(\mathsf{sko}_*, i, j, \mathsf{ik}_{i \to j}, (c_l, \mathsf{pk}_l)_{i \leq l \leq j})$, the challenger computes two values mk_x and v_x such that $D_x = \mathsf{PEnc}(\mathsf{pk}_x, [m_x\|\mathsf{mk}_x\|x]; v_l)$. We have that $1 = \mathsf{KVer}(\mathsf{pk}_x, \mathsf{sk}_x)$, so $(\mathsf{pk}_x, \mathsf{sk}_x) \in \{(\mathsf{pk}, \mathsf{sk}) : (\mathsf{pk}, \mathsf{sk}) \leftarrow \mathsf{KVer}(1^\lambda)\}$. Moreover, since PKE is correct, then we have that for any $(\mathsf{pk}, \mathsf{sk}) \leftarrow \mathsf{KVer}(1^\lambda)$, any message m and any random coin r, it holds that $m = \mathsf{PDec}(\mathsf{sk}, \mathsf{PEnc}(\mathsf{pk}, m; r))$. We deduce that $[m_x\|\mathsf{mk}_x\|x] = \mathsf{PDec}(\mathsf{sk}_x, D_x)$.

On the other hand, According to the algorithm Dec, $m'_x \leftarrow \mathsf{Dec}(\mathsf{sk}_x, c_x)$ implies that there exists a values mk'_x such that $[m'_x\|\mathsf{mk}'_x\|x] = \mathsf{PDec}(\mathsf{sk}_x, D_x)$. We deduce that $m'_x = m_x$, which concludes the proof. $\qquad\square$

5   Applications

Chosen ciphertext security in practice. Our CCA security model provides several properties that are essential for practical applications: the IND-CCA security ensures that the ciphertexts are not malleable, and the IND-CSCA ensures that if an adversary modifies, drops, adds or rearranges the encrypted messages in the open interval, the open algorithm fails. In what follows, we show several applications of APOPKE, and we discuss the practical impact of the CCA security.

Encrypted invoices during tax audit. Bultel and Lafourcade give the following application for their APOPKE scheme. A company sends invoices to its customers by encrypted e-mail. One day, the company has to pass a tax audit, and the court asks the company's mail server to provide the invoices sent over a given period of time. The company does not want to reveal the invoices of its customers that were not sent over the period of the tax audit. It therefore uses an APOPKE to reveal only the invoices sent over the time period. The CPA security only takes into account the cases where the server is passive: a dishonest server could discredit the company in court by adding or removing invoices, or changing their amounts in an undetectable way. The dishonest server can also modify the invoices before the clients receive them. Our CCA security fixes this drawback by preventing this kind of attacks.

Interception of secure messaging and vocal chat. In the introduction, we have already mentioned the use of APOPKE to reveal his textual conversations during a given period of time in a court of law, in order to prove his honesty. Again, a dishonest server might want to alter the user's conversations, so the CCA security is necessary. Often messaging applications also implement voice calls. In this case, encrypting the conversation with a public key encryption becomes infeasible for the sake of effectiveness. However, it is possible to use an APOPKE to encapsulate a session key used throughout the call to encrypts the packets with an authenticated encryption scheme [23]. To open the conversations over the interval, the opener will decrypt each session key using his interval key, then use each session key to decrypt the packets from the corresponding conversation. From a security point of view, the CCA security prevents the server from altering the session key, and the authenticated encryption ensures the integrity of the conversations decrypted with the session key.

Bypass the limitations. The main limitation of CHAPO is that the user cannot securely generate keys for two disjoint intervals. This limitation can be bypassed in practice by refreshing the user's encryption key from time to time. In this case, the refresh rate must be chosen so as to obtain the best tradeoff between the number of encryption keys and the number of ciphertexts in the period covered by each key. To take the example of the instant messaging, we can consider that the user must refresh his encryption key every year. On the one hand, he is unlikely to accumulate several court cases for different periods during a year, and on the other hand, even if he uses the instant messaging all his life, he will only need to store less than one hundred keys. The user will have to send as many interval keys as there are years in the selected period to the opener, which seems reasonable in practice.

6 Conclusion

In this paper, we revisited the *a posteriori* openable encryption schemes introduced by Bultel and Lafourcade in [6]. We gave a security model for the chosen-ciphertext attack security of this primitive, and we proposed a new scheme called CHAPO which improves four points of the scheme given in [6]: it is more secure (CCA security), more generic, more efficient, and it does not require the random oracle model. We also presented new applications for this primitive. In the future, we would like to put these applications into practice. Moreover, it would be interesting to adapt the *a posteriori* openable encryptions to the secure messaging based on the double ratchet algorithm [8], such as Signal or Whatsapp.

Acknowledgements. The author would like to thank Angèle Bossuat and David Gérault for their helpful comments and suggestions.

References

1. Arfaoui, G., et al.: How to (Legally) keep secrets from mobile operators. In: Bertino, E., Shulman, H., Waidner, M. (eds.) ESORICS 2021. LNCS, vol. 12972, pp. 23–43. Springer, Cham (2021). https://doi.org/10.1007/978-3-030-88418-5_2
2. Bellare, M., Canetti, R., Krawczyk, H.: Keying hash functions for message authentication. In: Koblitz, N. (ed.) CRYPTO 1996. LNCS, vol. 1109, pp. 1–15. Springer, Heidelberg (1996). https://doi.org/10.1007/3-540-68697-5_1
3. Bellare, M., Desai, A., Jokipii, E., Rogaway, P.: A concrete security treatment of symmetric encryption. In FOCS. IEEE (1997)
4. Bost, R., Minaud, B., Ohrimenko, O.: Forward and backward private searchable encryption from constrained cryptographic primitives. In: ACM CCS. ACM (2017)
5. Bultel, X.: CCA secure a posteriori openable encryption in the standard model. Cryptology ePrint Archive, Report 2021/1504 (2021). https://ia.cr/2021/1504
6. Bultel, X., Lafourcade, P.: A posteriori openable public key encryption. In: Hoepman, J.-H., Katzenbeisser, S. (eds.) SEC 2016. IAICT, vol. 471, pp. 17–31. Springer, Cham (2016). https://doi.org/10.1007/978-3-319-33630-5_2
7. Choi, G., Vaudenay, S.: Timed-release encryption with master time bound key. In: You, I. (ed.) WISA 2019. LNCS, vol. 11897, pp. 167–179. Springer, Cham (2020). https://doi.org/10.1007/978-3-030-39303-8_13
8. Cohn-Gordon, K., Cremers, C., Dowling, B., Garratt, L., Stebila, D.: A formal security analysis of the signal messaging protocol. In: EuroS&P 2017 (2017)
9. Dodis, Y., Katz, J., Xu, S., Yung, M.: Key-insulated public key cryptosystems. In: Knudsen, L.R. (ed.) EUROCRYPT 2002. LNCS, vol. 2332, pp. 65–82. Springer, Heidelberg (2002). https://doi.org/10.1007/3-540-46035-7_5
10. Goldreich, O., Goldwasser, S., Micali, S.: How to construct random functions. J. ACM **33**(4), 792–807 (1986)
11. Goldwasser, S., Kalai, Y.T., Popa, R.A., Vaikuntanathan, V., Zeldovich, N.: Reusable garbled circuits and succinct functional encryption. In: 45th ACM STOC. ACM Press (2013)

12. Goldwasser, S., Micali, S.: Probabilistic encryption. J. Comput. Syst. Sci. **28**(2), 270–299 (1984)
13. Goyal, V., Pandey, O., Sahai, A., Waters, B.: Attribute-based encryption for fine-grained access control of encrypted data. In: CCS 206. ACM (2006)
14. Han, K., Yeun, C.Y., Shon, T., Park, J.H., Kim, K.: A scalable and efficient key escrow model for lawful interception of IDBC-based secure communication. Int. J. Commun. Syst. **24**(4), 461–472 (2011)
15. Hwang, Y.H., Yum, D.H., Lee, P.J.: Timed-release encryption with pre-open capability and its application to certified E-mail system. In: Zhou, J., Lopez, J., Deng, R.H., Bao, F. (eds.) ISC 2005. LNCS, vol. 3650, pp. 344–358. Springer, Heidelberg (2005). https://doi.org/10.1007/11556992_25
16. Ishizaka, M., Kiyomoto, S.: Time-specific encryption with constant-size secret-keys secure under standard assumption. Cryptology ePrint Archive, Report 2020/595 (2020). https://eprint.iacr.org/2020/595
17. Kasamatsu, K., Matsuda, T., Emura, K., Attrapadung, N., Hanaoka, G., Imai, H.: Time-specific encryption from forward-secure encryption: generic and direct constructions. Int. J. Inf. Secur. **15**(5), 549–571 (2015). https://doi.org/10.1007/s10207-015-0304-y
18. Kiayias, A., Papadopoulos, S., Triandopoulos, N., Zacharias, T.: Delegatable pseudorandom functions and applications. In: ACM CCS. ACM (2013)
19. Martin, K.M.: Increasing efficiency of International key escrow in mutually mistrusting domains. In: Darnell, M. (ed.) Cryptography and Coding 1997. LNCS, vol. 1355, pp. 221–232. Springer, Heidelberg (1997). https://doi.org/10.1007/BFb0024467
20. May, T.: Time-release crypto. Manuscript (1993)
21. Nojima, R., Imai, H., Kobara, K., Morozov, K.: Semantic security for the McEliece cryptosystem without random oracles. Des Codes Crypt. **49**, 289–305 (2008)
22. Paterson, K.G., Quaglia, E.A.: Time-specific encryption. In: Garay, J.A., De Prisco, R. (eds.) SCN 2010. LNCS, vol. 6280, pp. 1–16. Springer, Heidelberg (2010). https://doi.org/10.1007/978-3-642-15317-4_1
23. Rogaway, P.: Authenticated-encryption with associated-data. In: CCS. ACM (2002)
24. Shamir, A.: Partial key escrow: a new approach to software key escrow. In: Presented at Key Escrow Conference (1995)
25. Wang, Z., Ma, Z., Luo, S., Gao, H.: Key escrow protocol based on a tripartite authenticated key agreement and threshold cryptography. IEEE Access **7**, 149080–149096 (2019)

Dynamic Universal Accumulator with Batch Update over Bilinear Groups

Giuseppe Vitto[✉] and Alex Biryukov

DCS&SnT, University of Luxembourg, Esch-sur-Alzette, Luxembourg
{giuseppe.vitto,alex.biryukov}@uni.lu

Abstract. We propose a Dynamic Universal Accumulator in the Accumulator Manager setting for bilinear groups which extends Nguyen's positive accumulator and Au et al. [4] and Damgård and Triandopoulos non-membership proof mechanism [20]. The new features include support for batch addition and deletion operations as well as a privacy-friendly batch witness update protocol, where the witness update information is the same for all users. Together with a non-interactive zero-knowledge protocol, these make the proposed scheme suitable as an efficient and scalable Anonymous Credential System, accessible even by low-resource users. We show security of the proposed protocol in the Generic Group Model under a (new) generalized version of the t-SDH assumption and we demonstrate its practical relevance by providing and discussing an implementation realized using state-of-the-art libraries.

Keywords: Acumulator · Universal · Dynamic · Batch update · Privacy-preserving KYC · Anonymous credentials

1 Introduction

A cryptographic accumulator allows to aggregate many different values from a finite set into a fixed-length digest called *accumulator value*. Differently than hash functions, accumulators permit to further verify if an element is either accumulated or not in a given accumulator value by using the so-called *membership* and *non-membership witnesses*, respectively. Accumulator schemes which support membership witnesses are referred to as *positive* accumulators, the ones that support non-membership witnesses are called *negative*, while the ones that support both are called *universal* accumulators. A common requirement for the accumulator schemes is the ability to change the set of accumulated elements, hence permitting *accumulator updates*: when the accumulator allows to dynamically *add* and *delete* elements, it is said to be a *dynamic accumulator*.

Whenever addition or deletion operations occur for one or several elements (in the latter case these are called *batch additions and deletions*), already issued

---

This work is supported by the Luxembourg National Research Fund (FNR) project FinCrypt (C17/IS/11684537).

witnesses should be updated to be consistent with the new accumulator value. Ideally this should be done using a short amount of *witness update data* (i.e. whose cost/size is not dependent on the number of elements involved) and with only publicly available information (i.e. without knowledge of any *secret* accumulator parameters). While there are many constructions that satisfy the public update condition, as regards to the update cost, Camacho and Hevia showed in [15] an impossibility result to have *batch witness updates* whose update data size is independent from the number of elements involved. More precisely, they showed that for an accumulator state which accumulates n elements, the witness update data size for a batch delete operation involving m elements cannot be less than $\Omega(m \log \frac{n}{m})$, thus requiring at least $\Omega(m)$ operations to update.

Our Contributions. In this paper we propose a Dynamic Universal Accumulator in the Accumulator Manager setting which supports batch operations and public batch witness updates as well as privacy preserving zero-knowledge proof of knowledge for membership and non-membership witnesses. Its features are manifold:

- **Support for Batch Operations:** Starting from Nguyen's positive accumulator and Au *et al.* [4] and Damgård and Triandopoulos non-membership proof mechanism [20], we state a Dynamic Universal Accumulator for bilinear groups in the *Accumulator Manager* setting (i.e. it is managed by a central authority who knows the accumulator trapdoor) and we extend it to fully support batch addition and deletion operations, as well as membership and non-membership batch witness updates.
- **Optimal Batch Update:** the number of operations needed to batch update witnesses equals the lower bound given by Camacho and Hevia [15] in the case of a batch deletion operation. The same complexity holds in the case of either a batch addition operation and a batch addition & deletion operation, where m new elements are added and other m elements are deleted, namely $\mathcal{O}(m)$ update time for a batch witness update information size of $m \log pq$ bits, where p is the size of the underlying bilinear group and q is the bit-size of group elements representations.
- **Batch Witness Update Protocol:** we designed a batch witness update protocol where the batch witness update information published by the Accumulator Manager after a batch operation is the same for all users. This information can be pre-processed by third-party servers in order to allow users to update their witnesses in a constant number of elementary operations, even in the case many batch operations occurred from their last update. This allows the accumulator to be used even when only limited-resource devices (ex. smartphones) are available to users.
- **Security:** we introduce a weaker definition for collision resistance and a new more general definition of $t-$SDH assumption for which we provide in the Generic Group Model a lower bound complexity of a generic algorithm that solves the corresponding hardness problem. We show that our scheme along with its public batch update protocol and published information is secure under this more general security assumption and we address the relevant

recent attacks found in [8] by showing that with a proper initialization of the accumulator value, a generic algorithm has negligible probability to compute elements belonging to a certain reference string $\mathcal{RS}$, whose knowledge would allow to issue arbitrary witnesses.

– **Zero-Knowledge Friendly:** zero-knowledge protocols are supported for any operation involving witnesses: we detail an efficient non-interactive zero-knowledge protocol to show ownership of a valid witness.
– **Implementation:** to show efficiency and its practical relevance, we implemented and benchmarked the proposed accumulator using state-of-the-art libraries for pairing-friendly elliptic curves. Following feedback received from the community, we briefly report benchmarks of third-party implementations of our scheme which are already employed in production applications.

It follows that our accumulator is well suited to be the building block of an *Anonymous Credential System*, which originally motivated this work. In these systems only the users which were previously authorized by a central authority (the Accumulator Manager) can use the issued credentials to authenticate to the third-party verifier (ex. some financial service provider, like bank or an exchange). They do so by proving in zero-knowledge ownership of a valid membership or non-membership witnesses, depending if the accumulator is used as a white- or black-list. Furthermore, doing so anonymously and unlinkably, even if the verifier colludes with the accumulator manager. This could be crucial in many applications given current societal challenges of protecting user privacy on the one hand and government-imposed know-your-customer regulations on the other hand.

Limitations. Our protocol assumes a trusted Accumulator Manager that, by knowing the secret accumulator parameter α, can forge membership and non-membership witnesses at will. In practice, the secret α can be secret-shared among multiple managers, but the construction and security analysis of such scheme is left as future work. In case of a batch addition and deletion operation where m elements are added and/or deleted, the batch update data has $O(m)$ size, as in the case for non-batch operations: this is indeed a theoretical lower bound that cannot be improved, although our construction provides better constants, detailed at the end of Sect. 5.1, than the non-batch approach. We note, however, that our protocol support a delegation technique (not possible for non-batch operations) which allows users to safely update witnesses in constant time, if third-party servers process, on their behalf, the $O(m)$-sized public witness batch update data published by the Accumulator Manager.

Related Works. The first accumulator scheme was formalized by Benaloh and De Mare [7] in 1993 as a time-stamping protocol. Since then, many other accumulator schemes have been proposed. Currently, three main families of accumulators can be distinguished in literature: schemes designed in groups of unknown order [5–7, 11, 18, 26, 27, 31], others designed in groups of known order [4, 17, 20, 30] and hash-based constructions [12–14, 16, 28]. Relevant to this paper are the schemes belonging to the second family, where the considered group is a prime order bilinear group.

Nguyen in [30] proposed a dynamic positive accumulator for symmetric bilinear groups, where up to t elements can be accumulated assuming that the t–Strong Diffie-Hellman assumption holds in the underlying group. Damgård and Triandopoulos [20] extended Nguyen's scheme, under the same security assumptions, to support non-membership proofs, thus defining a *universal* accumulator based on bilinear pairings. Soon after this work, Au *et al.* [4] extended Nguyen's scheme to a universal accumulator by proposing two possible variants: the more efficient α-based construction best suitable when a central authority –the Accumulator Manager– keeps the accumulator updated, and the alternative more decentralized but less efficient reference string-based construction. We note that non-membership witness definition provided in the latter construction is equivalent to Damgård and Triandopoulos' one.

Recently, Biryukov, Udovenko and Vitto [8] cryptanalized both Au *et al.* variants and found different attacks able to either recover the accumulator secret parameter or issue arbitrary witnesses. While they consider the α-based construction insecure, they conclude that in presence of an Accumulator Manager, it is possible to safely use the witness defining equations provided in the reference string-based construction (or equivalently, the Damgård and Triandopoulos' construction) by properly initializing the accumulator value.

The Dynamic Universal Accumulator obtained by combining Nguyen's positive accumulator and Au *et al.* and Damgård and Triandopoulos' non-membership witness mechanism, will be the starting point of our dynamic universal accumulator scheme, which we will further extend to support batch operations and a public batch witness update protocol.

Another approach on how to build a dynamic positive accumulator based on bilinear groups is given by Camenisch *et al.* in [17] where, alternatively to Nguyen's construction, a scheme relying on the t–DHE assumption is proposed.

2   Notation

Following the notation of [22], an efficiently computable non-degenerate bilinear map $e : G_1 \times G_2 \to G_T$ is said to be a Type-I pairing if $G_1 = G_2$, while it's called Type-III pairing if $G_1 \neq G_2$ and there are no efficiently computable isomorphisms between G_1 and G_2. We will denote with uppercase Roman letters (e.g. P, V) elements belonging to G_1 and with uppercase Roman letters with a tilde above (e.g. $\tilde{P}, \tilde{Q}$) elements in G_2. The identity points of G_1 and G_2 are denoted with O and $\tilde{O}$, respectively.

Sets are denoted with uppercase letters in calligraphic fonts (e.g. $\mathcal{ACC}, \mathcal{Y}$) while accumulator elements are denoted with (eventually indexed) lowercase Roman letters: y usually denotes the *reference element*, that is the one we take as an example to perform operations, while y_S denotes an element in the set S. Exceptions are the membership and non-membership witness, denoted respectively with w and $\bar{w}$, and the partial non-membership witness d.

Vectors are denoted with capital Greek letters (e.g. Υ, Ω). The vector operation $\langle \Phi, \Psi \rangle$ is the dot product, that is the sum of the products of the corresponding entries of Φ and Ψ, while $a \circ \Phi$ denotes the usual scalar-vector multiplication where each entry of Φ is multiplied by a.

We also use a convention that sum and the product of a sequence of terms with starting index greater than the ending one are assumed to be equal to $\sum_i^j a_i = 0$ and $\prod_i^j b_i = 1$ when $i > j$.

3 Preliminaries: A Dynamic Universal Accumulator for Bilinear Groups

We now summarize Nguyen's positive accumulator scheme [30] (i.e. *Membership Witness, Update and Verification*) extended with the non-membership proof system of Au *et al.* [4] and Damgård and Triandopoulos [20] (i.e. *Non-membership Witness, Update and Verification*).

Due to recent progresses in discrete logarithm computations [1,25], which weaken the security of efficient implementable elliptic curves provided with a Type-I pairing, we restate their definitions into a Type-III setting, making it best suitable for efficient and more secure pairing-friendly elliptic curves. In light of this, we will often refer, with a bit abuse of notation, to elements belonging in the defining groups of the working bilinear group as *points*, thus stressing the fact that in concrete efficient implementations they will, in fact, correspond to elliptic curve points.

In addition, we introduce new concepts (e.g. *Accumulator States, Epochs*) and parameters (e.g. `batchMax`), to make the accumulator definition coherent with the batch operations and the batch witness update protocol we will describe starting from Sect. 4.

Bilinear Group Generation.[1] Given a security parameter 1^λ, generate a bilinear group $\mathbb{G} = (p, G_1, G_2, G_T, P, \tilde{P}, e)$ where:

- $e : G_1 \times G_2 \to G_T$ is an efficiently computable non-degenerate bilinear map;
- $(G_1, +)$ is an additive group generated by P with identity element $\mathcal{O}$;
- $(G_2, +)$ is an additive group generated by $\tilde{P}$ with identity element $\tilde{\mathcal{O}}$;
- $(G_T, \cdot)$ is an multiplicative group generated by $e(P, \tilde{P})$;
- $|G_1| = |G_2| = |G_T| = p$ is prime;

Accumulator Parameters. Uniformly sample an $\alpha \in (\mathbb{Z}/p\mathbb{Z})^*$ and consider $\mathcal{ACC} = (\mathbb{Z}/p\mathbb{Z})^* \setminus \{-\alpha\}$ as the domain of accumulatable elements. Moreover, set a bound `batchMax` to the maximum number of batch additions and/or deletions possible in each epoch (See Sect. 4).

The bilinear group $\mathbb{G}$, the bound `batchMax` and the point $\tilde{Q} = \alpha\tilde{P}$ are the accumulator *public parameters* and are available to all accumulator users, while α is the accumulator *secret parameter* and is known only to the Accumulator Manager.

---

[1] We refer, for example, to [3] for more technical details on how these bilinear groups can be efficiently generated and implemented.

Accumulator Initialization. Select a set $\mathcal{Y}_{V_0} \subset \mathcal{ACC}$ and let the initial accumulator value to be equal to $V_0 = \left(\prod_{y \in \mathcal{Y}_{V_0}} (y + \alpha) \right) P$. The set $\mathcal{Y}_{V_0}$ is kept secret and its elements are never removed from the accumulator.[2]

Accumulator States and Epochs. An accumulator state is a pair $(V, \mathcal{Y}_V)$ where $V \in G_1$ is the corresponding accumulator value and $\mathcal{Y}_V \subseteq \mathcal{ACC}$ denotes the set of elements accumulated into V (initialization elements excluded). We call *epoch* the period of time during which an accumulator state remains unchanged.

Given an accumulator state $(V, \mathcal{Y}_V)$, the accumulator value V is equal to $V = \left(\prod_{y \in \mathcal{Y}_V} (y + \alpha) \right) V_0 = \left(\prod_{y \in \mathcal{Y}_V \cup \mathcal{Y}_{V_0}} (y + \alpha) \right) P$ and can be computed from $\mathcal{Y}_V$ and V_0 if the secret parameter α is known.

Accumulator Update. The accumulator state $(V, \mathcal{Y}_V)$ changes when one or more elements are added or removed from the accumulator. This can be done using the following single element Addition or Deletion operations.

– **Addition:** if $y \in \mathcal{ACC} \setminus \mathcal{Y}_V$, the element y is added into the accumulator when the accumulator value is updated from V to V' as $V' = (y + \alpha)V$ It follows that $\mathcal{Y}_{V'} = \mathcal{Y}_V \cup \{y\}$.
– **Deletion:** if $y \in \mathcal{Y}_V$, the element y is deleted from the accumulator when the accumulator state is updated from V to V' as $V' = \frac{1}{y+\alpha}V$ It follows that $\mathcal{Y}_{V'} = \mathcal{Y}_V \setminus \{y\}$.

Membership Witness. Let $(V, \mathcal{Y}_V)$ be an accumulator state and y an element in $\mathcal{ACC}$. Then $w_{y,V}$ is a *membership witness for y with respect to the accumulator value V* if $C = \frac{1}{y+\alpha}V$ and $w_{y,V} = C$. The Accumulator Manager issues the membership witness $w_{y,V}$ to a user associated to the element y, in order to permit him to prove that y *is* accumulated into V.[3]

Non-Membership Witness. Let $(V, \mathcal{Y}_V)$ be an accumulator state and y an element in $\mathcal{ACC}$. Then $\bar{w}_{y,V}$ is a *non-membership witness for y with respect to the accumulator state V* if, by letting $f_V(x) = \prod_{y_i \in \mathcal{Y}_V \cup \mathcal{Y}_{V_0}} (y_i + x) \in \mathbb{Z}/p\mathbb{Z}[x]$, it holds $d = f_V(-y) \mod p$ with $d \neq 0$, $C = \frac{f_V(\alpha)-d}{y+\alpha}P$ and $\bar{w}_{y,V} = (C, d)$. The Accumulator Manager issues the non-membership witness $\bar{w}_{y,V}$ to a user associated to the element y, in order to permit him to prove that y *is not* accumulated into the accumulator value V.

Witness Update. When accumulator state changes happen, users whose elements are not involved in the corresponding Addition or Deletion operations,

---

[2] The security of the scheme strongly depends on how the elements in $\mathcal{Y}_{V_0}$ are chosen. See Sect. 7 for a complete discussion.

[3] When the accumulator is employed as an authentication mechanism, single additions in place of batch operations lack users' privacy and expose to impersonation attacks since the membership witness C would be equal to the previous accumulator state value, while y can be deduced from the public witness update information.

have to update their witnesses with respect to the new accumulator state to continue being able to prove statements about their associated elements.

After an accumulator state change, users' membership and non-membership witnesses are updated according to the following operations:

- **On Addition**: suppose the accumulator state changes from $(V, \mathcal{Y}_V)$ to $(V', \mathcal{Y}_{V'})$ as a result of an Addition operation. Hence, for a certain $y' \in \mathcal{ACC} \setminus \mathcal{Y}_V$, $V' = (y' + \alpha)V$ and $\mathcal{Y}_{V'} = \mathcal{Y}_V \cup \{y'\}$.

  Then, for any $y \in \mathcal{Y}_V$ the membership witness $w_{y,V} = C$ is updated with respect to the accumulator state $(V', \mathcal{Y}_{V'})$ by computing $C' = (y' - y)C + V$ and letting $w_{y,V'} = C'$, while for any $y \notin \mathcal{Y}_V$, the non-membership witness $\bar{w}_{y,V} = (C, d)$ is updated, if issued, with respect to $(V', \mathcal{Y}_{V'})$ by computing $C' = (y' - y)C + V$, $d' = d \cdot (y' - y)$ and letting $\bar{w}_{y,V'} = (C', d')$.

- **On Deletion**: suppose the accumulator state changes from $(V, \mathcal{Y}_V)$ to $(V', \mathcal{Y}_{V'})$ as a result of a Deletion operation. Hence, for a certain $y' \in \mathcal{Y}_V$, $V' = \frac{1}{y' + \alpha}V$ and $\mathcal{Y}_{V'} = \mathcal{Y}_V \setminus \{y'\}$.

  Then, for any $y \in \mathcal{Y}_{V'}$, the membership witness $w_{y,V} = C$ is updated with respect to the accumulator state $(V', \mathcal{Y}_{V'})$ by computing $C' = \frac{1}{y'-y}C - \frac{1}{y'-y}V'$ and letting $w_{y,V'} = C'$, while for any $y \notin \mathcal{Y}_{V'}$, the non-membership witness $\bar{w}_{y,V} = (C, d)$ is updated, if issued, with respect to $(V', \mathcal{Y}_{V'})$ by computing $C' = \frac{1}{y'-y}C - \frac{1}{y'-y}V'$, $d' = d \cdot \frac{1}{y'-y}$ and letting $\bar{w}_{y,V'} = (C', d')$.

Witness Verification. A membership witness $w_y = C$ for an element $y \in \mathcal{ACC}$ is *valid* for the accumulator state $(V, \mathcal{Y}_V)$ if and only if $e(C, y\tilde{P} + \tilde{Q}) = e(V, \tilde{P})$. When w_y is a valid membership witness for the state $(V, \mathcal{Y}_V)$ we assume that $y \in \mathcal{Y}_V$ and hence $w_y = w_{y,V}$.

A non-membership witness $\bar{w}_y = (C, d)$ for an element $y \in \mathcal{ACC}$ is *valid* for the accumulator state $(V, \mathcal{Y}_V)$ if $d \neq 0$ and $e(C, y\tilde{P} + \tilde{Q})e(P, \tilde{P})^d = e(V, \tilde{P})$. When $\bar{w}_y$ is a valid non-membership witness for the state $(V, \mathcal{Y}_V)$ we assume that $y \notin \mathcal{Y}_V$ and hence $\bar{w}_y = \bar{w}_{y,V}$.

4   Adding Support for Batch Operations

We now describe how the Dynamic Universal Accumulator defined in previous Section can be further extended to coherently support batch addition and deletions operations both for accumulator and users' witnesses update.

We start by defining a family of polynomials which will help us show in a compact way correctness of our batch operations with respect to the underlying accumulator scheme.

Batch Polynomials. Given the secret accumulator parameter α and two disjoint sets $\mathcal{A}, \mathcal{D} \subseteq \mathbb{Z}/p\mathbb{Z}$ where $\mathcal{A} = \{y_{\mathcal{A},1}, \ldots, y_{\mathcal{A},n}\}$ and $\mathcal{D} = \{y_{\mathcal{D},1}, \ldots, y_{\mathcal{D},m}\}$, we define the following polynomials in $\mathbb{Z}/p\mathbb{Z}$:

$$v_{\mathcal{A}}(x) \doteq \sum_{s=1}^{n} \left(\prod_{i=1}^{s-1}(y_{\mathcal{A},i} + \alpha) \prod_{j=s+1}^{n} (y_{\mathcal{A},j} - x) \right)$$

$$v_{\mathcal{D}}(x) \doteq \sum_{s=1}^{m} \left(\prod_{i=1}^{s} (y_{\mathcal{D},i} + \alpha)^{-1} \prod_{j=1}^{s-1} (y_{\mathcal{D},j} - x) \right)$$

$$v_{\mathcal{A},\mathcal{D}}(x) \doteq v_{\mathcal{A}}(x) - v_{\mathcal{D}}(x) \cdot \prod_{i=1}^{n} (y_{\mathcal{A},i} + \alpha)$$

$$d_{\mathcal{A}}(x) \doteq \prod_{t=1}^{n} (y_{\mathcal{A},t} - x), \quad d_{\mathcal{D}}(x) \doteq \prod_{t=1}^{m} (y_{\mathcal{D},t} - x)$$

Accumulator Batch Update. Several elements are added into or removed from the accumulator using the following Batch Addition and Batch Deletion operations.

- **Batch Addition:** if $\mathcal{A} = \{y_{\mathcal{A},1}, \ldots, y_{\mathcal{A},n}\} \subseteq \mathcal{ACC} \setminus \mathcal{Y}_V$, the elements in $\mathcal{A}$ are *batch added* into the accumulator when the accumulator value is updated from V to V' as $V' = d_{\mathcal{A}}(-\alpha) \cdot V$. It follows that $\mathcal{Y}_{V'} = \mathcal{Y}_V \cup \mathcal{A}$.

- **Batch Deletion:** if $\mathcal{D} = \{y_{\mathcal{D},1}, \ldots, y_{\mathcal{D},m}\} \subseteq \mathcal{Y}_V$, the elements in $\mathcal{D}$ are *batch deleted* from the accumulator when the accumulator state is updated from V to V' as $V' = \frac{1}{d_{\mathcal{D}}(-\alpha)} \cdot V$. It follows that $\mathcal{Y}_{V'} = \mathcal{Y}_V \setminus \mathcal{D}$.

- **Batch Addition & Deletion:** if $\mathcal{A} = \{y_{\mathcal{A},1}, \ldots, y_{\mathcal{A},n}\} \subseteq \mathcal{ACC} \setminus \mathcal{Y}_V$, $\mathcal{D} = \{y_{\mathcal{D},1}, \ldots, y_{\mathcal{D},m}\} \subseteq \mathcal{Y}_V$ and $\mathcal{A} \cap \mathcal{D} = \emptyset$, the elements in $\mathcal{A}$ are batch added into the accumulator and the elements in $\mathcal{D}$ are batch deleted from the accumulator when the accumulator state is updated from V to V'' as $V'' = \frac{d_{\mathcal{A}}(-\alpha)}{d_{\mathcal{D}}(-\alpha)} \cdot V$. It follows that $\mathcal{Y}_{V''} = \mathcal{Y}_V \cup \mathcal{A} \setminus \mathcal{D}$.

Batch Witness Update. When a batch addition or deletion changes the accumulator state, users' membership and non-membership witnesses are updated according to the following operation.

- **On Batch Addition:** suppose the accumulator state changes from $(V, \mathcal{Y}_V)$ to $(V', \mathcal{Y}_{V'})$ as a result of an Batch Addition operation. Hence, for certain $\mathcal{A} = \{y_{\mathcal{A},1}, \ldots, y_{\mathcal{A},n}\} \subseteq \mathcal{ACC} \setminus \mathcal{Y}_V$, we have $V' = d_{\mathcal{A}}(-\alpha) \cdot V$ and $\mathcal{Y}_{V'} = \mathcal{Y}_V \cup \mathcal{A}$. Then, for any $y \in \mathcal{Y}_V$, the membership witness $w_{y,V} = C$ is updated with respect to the accumulator state $(V', \mathcal{Y}_{V'})$ computing $C' = d_{\mathcal{A}}(y) \cdot C + v_{\mathcal{A}}(y) \cdot V$ and letting $w_{y,V'} = C'$. While for any $y \notin \mathcal{Y}_V$, the non-membership witness $\bar{w}_{y,V} = (C, d)$ is updated with respect to $(V', \mathcal{Y}_{V'})$ by computing $C' = d_{\mathcal{A}}(y) \cdot C + v_{\mathcal{A}}(y) \cdot V$, $d' = d \cdot d_{\mathcal{A}}(y)$ and letting $\bar{w}_{y,V'} = (C', d')$.

Proof. For the ease of notation, we will denote the elements $y_{\mathcal{A},i}$ with y_i, the accumulator value corresponding to $\left(\prod_{i=1}^{j} (y_i + \alpha) \right) V$ with V_j and, for any $y \in \mathcal{Y}_V$, the intermediate membership witnesses w_{y,V_j} with C_j.

We prove the formula by induction on n, the number of batch added elements:

$\boxed{n = 1}$ We get $C_1 = V + (y_1 - y)C$, the same formula defined for the membership witness update after a single addition operation.

$\boxed{n - 1 \to n}$ Let $b_s = \prod_{i=1}^{s-1}(y_i + \alpha) \prod_{j=s+1}^{n}(y_j - y)$. Using the inductive hypothesis for C_{n-1}, we have

$$C_n = (y_n - y)C_{n-1} + V_{n-1} = \left(\prod_{t=1}^{n}(y_t - y) \right) C + \left(\sum_{s=1}^{n-1} b_s + \prod_{t=1}^{n-1}(y_t + \alpha) \right) V$$

which is equal to $\left(\prod_{t=1}^{n}(y_t - y) \right) C + \left(\sum_{s=1}^{n} b_s \right) V$ as required. The induction on d' in the case of non-membership witnesses is straightforward.   □

– **On Batch Deletion**: suppose the accumulator state changes from $(V, \mathcal{Y}_V)$ to $(V', \mathcal{Y}_{V'})$ as a result of a Batch Deletion operation. Hence, for certain $\mathcal{D} = \{y_{\mathcal{D},1}, \ldots, y_{\mathcal{D},m}\} \subseteq \mathcal{Y}_V$, we have $V' = \frac{1}{d_{\mathcal{D}}(-\alpha)}V$.

  Then, for any $y \in \mathcal{Y}_{V'}$, the witness $w_{y,V} = C$ is updated with respect to the accumulator state $(V', \mathcal{Y}_{V'})$ computing $C' = \frac{1}{d_{\mathcal{D}}(y)}C - \frac{v_{\mathcal{D}}(y)}{d_{\mathcal{D}}(y)}V$ and letting $w_{y,V'} = C'$. While for any $y \notin \mathcal{Y}_{V'}$, the non-membership witness $\bar{w}_{y,V} = C$ is updated with respect to $(V', \mathcal{Y}_{V'})$ by computing $C' = \frac{1}{d_{\mathcal{D}}(y)} \cdot C - \frac{v_{\mathcal{D}}(y)}{d_{\mathcal{D}}(y)} \cdot V$, $d' = d \cdot \frac{1}{d_{\mathcal{D}}(y)}$ and letting $\bar{w}_{y,V'} = (C', d')$.

Proof. Similarly as before, we will denote the elements $y_{\mathcal{D},i}$ with y_i, the accumulator value corresponding to $\left(\prod_{i=1}^{j}(y_i + \alpha)^{-1} \right) V$ with V_j and, for any $y \in \mathcal{Y}_{V'}$, the intermediate membership witnesses w_{y,V_j} with C_j. We prove the formula by induction on m, the number of batch deleted elements:

$\boxed{m = 1}$ We get $C_1 = \frac{1}{y_1 - y}C - \frac{1}{(y_1 - y)(y_1 + \alpha)}V = \frac{1}{y_1 - y}(C - V_1)$, the same formula defined for the membership witness update after a single deletion operation.

$\boxed{m - 1 \to m}$ Let $b_s = \prod_{i=1}^{s}(y_i + \alpha)^{-1} \prod_{j=1}^{s-1}(y_j - y)$. Then

$$C_m = \frac{1}{y_m - y}(C_{m-1} - V_m)$$

$$= \frac{1}{d_{\mathcal{D}}(y)}C - \frac{1}{d_{\mathcal{D}}(y)} \cdot \left(\sum_{s=1}^{m-1} b_s \right) V - \left((y_m - y)^{-1} \prod_{i=1}^{m}(y_i + \alpha)^{-1} \right) V$$

which is equal to $\frac{1}{d_{\mathcal{D}}(y)}C - \frac{1}{d_{\mathcal{D}}(y)} \cdot \left(\sum_{s=1}^{m} b_s \right) V$ as required. The induction on d' in the case of non-membership witnesses is straightforward.   □

– **On Batch Addition & Deletion:** suppose the accumulator state changes from $(V, \mathcal{Y}_V)$ to $(V'', \mathcal{Y}_{V'})$ as a result of a Batch Addition & Deletion operation. Hence for certain disjoint sets $\mathcal{A} = \{y_{\mathcal{A},1}, \ldots, y_{\mathcal{A},n}\} \subseteq ACC \setminus \mathcal{Y}_V$ and $\mathcal{D} = \{y_{\mathcal{D},1}, \ldots, y_{\mathcal{D},m}\} \subseteq \mathcal{Y}_V$ we have $V'' = \frac{d_{\mathcal{A}}(-\alpha)}{d_{\mathcal{D}}(-\alpha)} \cdot V$.

  Then, for any $y \in \mathcal{Y}_V$, the witness $w_{y,V} = C$ is updated with respect to the accumulator state $(V', \mathcal{Y}_{V'})$ computing $C' = \frac{d_{\mathcal{A}}(y)}{d_{\mathcal{D}}(y)} \cdot C + \frac{v_{\mathcal{A},\mathcal{D}}(y)}{d_{\mathcal{D}}(y)} \cdot V$ and letting

$w_{y,V'} = C'$. While for any $y \notin \mathcal{Y}_V$, the non-membership witness $\bar{w}_{y,V} = (C, d)$ is updated with respect to the accumulator state $(V', \mathcal{Y}_{V'})$ by computing $C' = \frac{d_{\mathcal{A}}(y)}{d_{\mathcal{D}}(y)} \cdot C + \frac{\nu_{\mathcal{A},\mathcal{D}}(y)}{d_{\mathcal{D}}(y)} \cdot V$, $d' = d \cdot \frac{d_{\mathcal{A}}(y)}{d_{\mathcal{D}}(y)}$ and letting $\bar{w}_{y,V'} = (C', d')$.

Proof. Performing a batch addition and then a batch deletion, the membership witness $w_{y,V} = C$ for y with respect to the accumulator value V is iteratively updated to $\bar{w}_{y,V''} = (C'', d'')$ with respect to the updated accumulator value $V'' = \left(\frac{\prod_{i=1}^{n}(y_{\mathcal{A},i}+\alpha)}{\prod_{i=1}^{m}(y_{\mathcal{D},i}+\alpha)} \right) V$ as follows

$$C \xrightarrow{\text{Add}} C' = d_{\mathcal{A}}(y)C + v_{\mathcal{A}}(y)V \xrightarrow{\text{Delete}}$$

$$C'' = \frac{1}{d_{\mathcal{D}}(y)}C' - \frac{v_{\mathcal{D}}(y)}{d_{\mathcal{D}}(y)}V' = \frac{d_{\mathcal{A}}(y)}{d_{\mathcal{D}}(y)}C + \left(\frac{v_{\mathcal{A}}(y)}{d_{\mathcal{D}}(y)} - \frac{v_{\mathcal{D}}(y)}{d_{\mathcal{D}}(y)} \cdot \prod_{i=1}^{n}(y_{\mathcal{A},i}+\alpha) \right) V$$

where $V' = \prod_{i=1}^{n}(y_{\mathcal{A},i}+\alpha) \cdot V$. The induction on d' in the case of non-membership witnesses is straightforward. □

5   The Batch Witness Update Protocol

Users cannot batch update their witnesses directly using the formula defined in previous section, since they would need the secret parameter α. However, starting from their definition, the Accumulator Manager can efficiently compute and publish some update information (more precisely, the polynomials $d_{\mathcal{A}}(x), d_{\mathcal{D}}(x)$ and a *points vector*) so that users are able to update their witnesses without requiring or leaking (see Sect. 5.1) any information related to α. This will allow us to define a batch membership and non-membership witness update protocol for the proposed accumulator scheme.

5.1   The Batch Witness Update Information

From now on, we will focus on the Batch Witness Update Addition & Deletion polynomial $v_{\mathcal{A},\mathcal{D}}(x)$ only: indeed, the polynomials $v_{\mathcal{A}}(x)$ and $v_{\mathcal{D}}(x)$ are special cases of this more general one.

We recall that our main goal is to allow users possessing a witness (C, d) for an element y with respect to the accumulator value V to compute the quantities

$$C' = \frac{d_{\mathcal{A}}(y)}{d_{\mathcal{D}}(y)} \cdot C + \frac{\nu_{\mathcal{A},\mathcal{D}}(y)}{d_{\mathcal{D}}(y)} \cdot V , \qquad d' = d \cdot \frac{d_{\mathcal{A}}(y)}{d_{\mathcal{D}}(y)}$$

We note that the Accumulator Manager cannot publish all the polynomials $d_{\mathcal{A}}(x), d_{\mathcal{D}}(x)$ and $v_{\mathcal{A},\mathcal{D}}(x)$, because their coefficients can leak some information related to the secret accumulator parameter α. To give an example, suppose that after a batch addition operation, the Accumulator Manager publishes the polynomials $v_{\mathcal{A}}(x)$ and $d_{\mathcal{A}}(x)$, defined as above, with $|\mathcal{A}| > 1$. Doing simple algebra, we find that the coefficient of the $(|\mathcal{A}| - 2)-$degree monomial of $v_{\mathcal{A}}(x)$

is equal to $\alpha + \sum_{y_A \in \mathcal{A}} y_A$: extracting the roots of $d_{\mathcal{A}}(x)$ in $\mathbb{Z}/p\mathbb{Z}$ we obtain all the elements in $\mathcal{A}$ and hence the secret parameter α.

Leakages about α can be prevented by requiring the Accumulator Manager to publish in place of $v_{\mathcal{A},\mathcal{D}}(x)$, the vector of points

$$\Omega = \Omega_{\mathcal{A},\mathcal{D},V} = (\ c_0 V,\ c_1 V,\ \dots,\ c_{\texttt{batchMax}} V\ )$$

where $v_{\mathcal{A},\mathcal{D}}(x) = \sum_{i=0}^{\texttt{batchMax}} c_i x^i$ and $c_i = 0$ if $i > max(|\mathcal{A}|, |\mathcal{D}|)$.

Users can then update their membership witness $w_{y,V} = C$ to $w_{y,V'} = C'$ by first evaluating the two polynomials $d_{\mathcal{A}}(x)$ and $d_{\mathcal{D}}(x)$ in the element y and then computing

$$C' = \frac{d_{\mathcal{A}}(y)}{d_{\mathcal{D}}(y)} \cdot C + \frac{1}{d_{\mathcal{D}}(y)} \cdot \langle \Upsilon_y, \Omega \rangle$$

where $\Upsilon_y = (1, y, y^2, ..., y^{\texttt{batchMax}})$ and $\langle \cdot, \cdot \rangle$ denotes the dot product.

Similarly, a non-membership witness $\bar{w}_{y,V} = (C, d)$ is updated to $\bar{w}_{y,V'} = (C', d')$ by computing

$$C' = \frac{d_{\mathcal{A}}(y)}{d_{\mathcal{D}}(y)} \cdot C + \frac{1}{d_{\mathcal{D}}(y)} \cdot \langle \Upsilon_y, \Omega \rangle\ , \qquad d' = d \cdot \frac{d_{\mathcal{A}}(y)}{d_{\mathcal{D}}(y)}$$

In this scenario, assuming the Discrete Logarithm Problem to be hard in G_1 (a weaker assumption with respect to the $t-$SDH assumption under which accumulator collision resistance is shown), from the published Ω, $d_{\mathcal{A}}(x)$ and $d_{\mathcal{D}}(x)$ it is only possible, performing roots extraction on the polynomials, to compute the respective sets $\mathcal{A}$ and $\mathcal{D}$ of batch added and batch deleted elements.

It follows that witness update operations can be performed either autonomously by users or by delegating to third-party servers the computation of (some of) the values $\langle \Upsilon_y, \Omega \rangle, d_{\mathcal{A}}(y), d_{\mathcal{D}}(y)$. Indeed, since the required updating values are decoupled from users' previous witnesses, third-party servers which are asked to compute such values with respect to an element y, cannot impersonate the corresponding user, since they don't know any previous valid witness for y.

When the computation of the elements $\langle \Upsilon_y, \Omega \rangle, d_{\mathcal{A}}(y), d_{\mathcal{D}}(y)$ is delegated, users are then able to update witnesses in a constant number of elementary operations, i.e., 2 scalar-point multiplication and 1 point addition[4]. Delegation thus allows even resource-constrained devices to be able to keep users' witnesses updated.

As a side note, if third-party servers are *untrusted* (e.g. we want to prevent linkability attacks from subsequent evaluation requests for the same element y), it is possible to use Oblivious Polynomial Evaluation techniques such as [29], [24] and [19] to delegate the computation of the point $\langle \Upsilon_y, \Omega \rangle = v_{\mathcal{A},\mathcal{D}}(y) \cdot V$

---

[4] We note that this is not against the impossibility result of Camacho and Hevia to have batch witness update data size independent from the number of elements added/deleted, since the provided values $\langle \Upsilon_y, \Omega \rangle, d_{\mathcal{A}}(y), d_{\mathcal{D}}(y)$ are *per* user and not for *all* users, similarly as any constant-sized (updated) witness is.

and of the values $d_\mathcal{A}(y)$ and $d_\mathcal{D}(y)$, in a way that third-parties will not learn anything about y. We note however that such protocols have time complexity at least proportional to the degree of the polynomials involved and thus allow users to just save data rather than time, i.e., users are not required to download the public batch witness update data (available instead to third-party servers) and can oblivious evaluate $v_{\mathcal{A},\mathcal{D}}(y) \cdot V$, $d_\mathcal{A}(y)$ and $d_\mathcal{D}(y)$ with time complexities comparable to standard polynomial evaluations.

Improvements with Respect to Non-Batch Operations. Due to the lower bound showed by Camacho and Hevia in [15], in case of a batch addition and deletion operation where m elements are added and/or deleted, the batch update data cannot have size less than $O(m)$ (and thus witnesses cannot be updated in time less than $O(m)$), as in the case for non-batch operations. Our protocol, that reaches this optimal lower bound, provides, however, better constants with respect to the naive approach of iteratively adding and/or deleting each involved element at a time.

In particular, for m added and deleted elements, the public batch witness information in our protocol would have size $|\Omega| + |d_\mathcal{A}(x)| + |d_\mathcal{D}(x)|$, i.e. $m \cdot (\log q + 2\log p)$, while the naive approach consisting in executing m addition operations followed by m deletion operations requires[5] $2m \cdot (\log q + \log p)$ data. Furthermore, as regards time complexities to update witnesses, our protocol requires $m + 2$ scalar-point multiplications, 1 point addition and 2 degree-m polynomials evaluations (possible in $2m$ multiplications and $2m$ additions), while the naive approach requires $2m$ scalar-point multiplications, $2m$ point additions and $2m$ multiplications.

To summarise, with respect to the naive approach our protocol provides, approximately, the following improvements:

- 1/4 reduction in witness update data communication;
- 1/2 reduction in running time in order to update witnesses.

5.2   Batch Witness Update Among Epochs

We now show how the adoption of the points vector $\Omega = \Omega_{\mathcal{A},\mathcal{D},V}$ not only permits the users to batch update their (non-)membership witnesses from the previous accumulator state, but also enables them to directly update from the accumulator state of any older epoch. This feature doesn't force users to permanently keep their witnesses updated to the latest accumulator state, enabling them to update their witnesses just right before they want to prove statements about the associated element y.

Before showing how this is possible, we extend our notation to associate accumulator and batch witness update data to a specific epoch. Given an epoch $i > 0$, we denote with $(V_i, \mathcal{Y}_{V_i})$ the corresponding accumulator state, where $\mathcal{Y}_{V_1} = \mathcal{A}_1 \setminus \mathcal{D}_1$ and $\mathcal{Y}_{V_i} = \mathcal{Y}_{V_{i-1}} \cup \mathcal{A}_i \setminus \mathcal{D}_i$ for $i > 1$, with $d_{\mathcal{A}_i}(x)$ and $d_{\mathcal{D}_i}(x)$ the

---

[5] Each of these operations send users the element added/deleted and the corresponding updated accumulator value, i.e. $\log q + \log p$ data.

Table 1. Data published by the Accumulator Manager in each epoch.

Epoch	Accumulator state	Witness update information		
0	$(V_0, \emptyset)$			
1	$(V_1, \mathcal{Y}_{V_1})$	Ω_1	$d_{\mathcal{A}_1}(x)$	$d_{\mathcal{D}_1}(x)$
$\vdots$	$\vdots$		$\vdots$	
i	$(V_i, \mathcal{Y}_{V_i})$	Ω_i	$d_{\mathcal{A}_i}(x)$	$d_{\mathcal{D}_i}(x)$

addition and deletion batch witness update polynomials, respectively, and with $\Omega_i = \Omega_{\mathcal{A}_i, \mathcal{D}_i, V_i}$. An overview of the data published by the Accumulator Manager is given in Table 1.

We further denote a membership witness w_{y, V_i} for an element y with respect to the accumulator value V_i as $w_{y, V_i} = C_i$ and, similarly, a non-membership witness $\bar{w}_{y, V_i}$ as $\bar{w}_{y, V_i} = (C_i, d_i)$.

Epoch Witnesses Batch Update. A user who owns a valid non-membership witness $\bar{w}_{y, V_i} = (C_i, d_i)$ (resp. a valid membership witness $w_{y, V_i} = C_i$) with respect to the accumulator state $(V_i, \mathcal{Y}_{V_i})$ can update it to $\bar{w}_{y, V_j} = (C_j, d_j)$ (resp. $w_{y, V_j} = C_j$), for any $j > i$, as

$$C_j = \frac{d_{\mathcal{A}_{i \to j}}(y)}{d_{\mathcal{D}_{i \to j}}(y)} \cdot C_i + \frac{1}{d_{\mathcal{D}_{i \to j}}(y)} \cdot \langle\, \Upsilon_y \;,\; \Omega_{i \to j}(y) \,\rangle \,, \qquad d_j = d_i \cdot \frac{d_{\mathcal{A}_{i \to j}}(y)}{d_{\mathcal{D}_{i \to j}}(y)}$$

where

$$d_{\mathcal{A}_{a \to b}}(x) = \prod_{s=a+1}^{b} d_{\mathcal{A}_s}(x) \qquad d_{\mathcal{D}_{a \to b}}(x) = \prod_{s=a+1}^{b} d_{\mathcal{D}_s}(x)$$

$$\Omega_{i \to j}(y) = \sum_{t=i+1}^{j} \left(d_{\mathcal{D}_{i \to t-1}}(y) \cdot d_{\mathcal{A}_{t \to j}}(y) \right) \circ \Omega_t$$

Proof. We prove the result by induction on $j > i$.

$\boxed{j = i+1}$ A witness $\bar{w}_{y, V_i} = (C_i, d_i)$ is updated to $\bar{w}_{y, V_{i+1}} = (C_{i+1}, d_{i+1})$ as

$$C_{i+1} = \frac{d_{\mathcal{A}_{i+1}}(y)}{d_{\mathcal{D}_{i+1}}(y)} \cdot C_i + \frac{1}{d_{\mathcal{D}_{i+1}}(y)} \cdot \langle\, \Upsilon_y \,,\, \Omega_{i+1} \,\rangle \,, \qquad d_{i+1} = d_i \cdot \frac{d_{\mathcal{A}_{i+1}}(y)}{d_{\mathcal{D}_{i+1}}(y)}$$

obtaining the same result we get by using the formula for non-membership witnesses batch update.

$\boxed{j \Rightarrow j+1}$ By inductive hypothesis, we assume the formula holds for C_j. Then

$$
\begin{aligned}
C_{j+1} &= \frac{d_{\mathcal{A}_{j+1}}(y)}{d_{\mathcal{D}_{j+1}}(y)} \cdot C_j + \frac{1}{d_{\mathcal{D}_{j+1}}(y)} \cdot \langle \Upsilon_y, \Omega_{j+1} \rangle \\
&= \frac{d_{\mathcal{A}_{i \to j+1}}(y)}{d_{\mathcal{D}_{i \to j+1}}(y)} \cdot C_i + \frac{1}{d_{\mathcal{D}_{i \to j+1}}(y)} \cdot \langle \Upsilon_y, d_{\mathcal{A}_{j+1}}(y) \circ \Omega_{i \to j} \rangle \\
&\quad + \frac{1}{d_{\mathcal{D}_{i \to j+1}}(y)} \cdot \langle \Upsilon_y, d_{\mathcal{D}_{i \to j}}(y) \circ \Omega_{j+1} \rangle \\
&= \frac{d_{\mathcal{A}_{i \to j+1}}(y)}{d_{\mathcal{D}_{i \to j+1}}(y)} \cdot C_i + \frac{1}{d_{\mathcal{D}_{i \to j+1}}(y)} \cdot \langle \Upsilon_y, \Omega_{i \to j+1} \rangle
\end{aligned}
$$

as required, since

$$
\begin{aligned}
\Omega_{i \to j+1} &= \sum_{t=i+1}^{j+1} \left(\prod_{h=i+1}^{t-1} d_{\mathcal{D}_h}(y) \prod_{k=t+1}^{j+1} d_{\mathcal{A}_k}(y) \right) \circ \Omega_t \\
&= \left(\sum_{t=i+1}^{j} \left(\prod_{h=i+1}^{t-1} d_{\mathcal{D}_h}(y) \prod_{k=t+1}^{j+1} d_{\mathcal{A}_k}(y) \right) \circ \Omega_t \right) + \left(\prod_{h=i+1}^{j} d_{\mathcal{D}_h}(y) \right) \circ \Omega_{j+1} \\
&= d_{\mathcal{A}_{j+1}}(y) \circ \Omega_{i \to j} + d_{\mathcal{D}_{i \to j}}(y) \circ \Omega_{j+1}
\end{aligned}
$$

The proof on d_j is straightforward. $\square$

6   Security Proofs for the Proposed Protocol

Security of accumulator schemes is usually intended as *collision resistance*: for universal accumulators, this property requires that an adversary forges with negligible probability in the security parameter λ a valid membership witness for a not-accumulated element and, respectively, a non-membership witness for an accumulated element.

Since the outlined Dynamic Universal Accumulator is built on top of Nguyen's positive dynamic accumulator [30] and Au *et al.* [4] and Damgård and Triandopoulos' non-membership proof system [20], we might be tempted to generalize the security proofs provided in [20,30] to show security of our scheme under the standard $t-$Strong Diffie-Hellman assumption.

However, there are some technicalities which prevent us to do so straightforwardly: i) in the proposed protocol, the attacker doesn't necessarily have access to the $\mathcal{RS} = \{P, \alpha P, \ldots, \alpha^t P\}$ (needed in [4,20,30] security reductions, see Theorem 4 in Appendix A), while he has access to the batch witness update information and valid witnesses, as regular users do; ii) differently than [4,20,30], we allow the accumulator Manager to initialize the accumulator value to V_0 by accumulating a certain number of secret values.

To show security of our proposed accumulator scheme we then need to provide two slightly more general definitions, tailored to the data our attacker would be able to access. We propose the followings.

Definition 1. (Collision Resistance) *Let $\mathcal{A}$ be a probabilistic polynomial time adversary that has access to an oracle $\mathcal{O}$ which replies to:*

- *"Batch Addition and/or Deletion" queries that batch add non-accumulated and/or delete accumulated elements into/from the accumulator (which is initialized to V_0) and return the resulting updated accumulator value and the corresponding public batch witness update data;*
- *"Issue Witness" queries that return, for any input element y, its membership witness if y is accumulated, or, if not, its non-membership witness with respect to the latest accumulator value.*

Then, the proposed Dynamic Universal Accumulator is collision resistant if the probability

$$\mathbb{P}\left(\begin{array}{cc} (\mathbb{G}, \alpha, \mathcal{Y}_{V_0}, \tilde{Q}) \leftarrow Gen(1^\lambda)\,, & f(x) = \prod_{y_i \in \mathcal{Y}_{V_0}} (y_i + x), \\ V_0 = f(\alpha) \cdot P, & (y, w_y, \bar{w}_y, \mathcal{Y}) \leftarrow \mathcal{A}^\mathcal{O}(V_0, \mathbb{G}, \tilde{Q}) \ : \\ \mathcal{Y} \subseteq (\mathbb{Z}/p\mathbb{Z})^* \quad \wedge & V = \left(\prod_{y_i \in \mathcal{Y}} (y_i + \alpha)\right) \cdot V_0 \quad \wedge \\ \Omega(y, w_y, V, membership) = 1 \quad \wedge & \Omega(y, \bar{w}_y, V, non\text{-}membership) = 1 \end{array}\right)$$

is a negligible function in the security parameter λ, where w_y, $\bar{w}_y$ denote a membership and non-membership witness for y, respectively, and $\Omega(y, w, V, type) = 1$ if and only if w is a valid type witness for y with respect to V.

Proposition 1. *Collision Resistance of Definition 1 is weaker than Au et al. Collision resistance (Definition 3 - Appendix A) when $\deg f > 0$, while it is equivalent if $\deg f = 0$.*

Proof. In Lemma 1 we proved that the oracle $\mathcal{O}$ of Definition 3 gives the attacker access to the $\mathcal{RS}_t$ for some $t > 0$. By using Extended Euclidean Algorithm, the set $\mathcal{RS}_t$ further allows the attacker to issue valid membership witnesses for accumulated elements and valid non-membership witnesses for any non-accumulated element, as originally reported in [4]. In other words, if an attacker successfully breaks collision resistance of Definition 3, he can output in polynomial time using the $\mathcal{RS}_t$ a valid membership witness if forged a non-membership witness for an accumulated element y, or, similarly, the valid non-membership witness if he forged a membership witness for a non-accumulated element y. In fact, the two probabilities of Definition 3 can be combined, by equivalently requiring that

$$\mathbb{P}\left(\begin{array}{cc} (\mathbb{G}, \alpha, \tilde{Q}) \leftarrow Gen(1^\lambda), & (y, w_y, \bar{w}_y, \mathcal{Y}) \leftarrow \mathcal{A}^\mathcal{O}(\mathbb{G}, \tilde{Q}) \ : \\ \mathcal{Y} \subseteq (\mathbb{Z}/p\mathbb{Z})^* \quad \wedge & V = \left(\prod_{y_i \in \mathcal{Y}} (y_i + \alpha)\right) \cdot P \quad \wedge \\ \Omega(y, w_y, V, membership) = 1 \quad \wedge & \Omega(y, \bar{w}_y, V, non\text{-}membership) = 1 \end{array}\right)$$

is negligible in the security parameter λ.

Since the public batch update information can be computed in polynomial time from the $\mathcal{RS}_t$ (we can compute any element of the form $h(\alpha)P$, where $h(x) \in \mathbb{Z}/p\mathbb{Z}$ has degree $\leq t$), it immediately follows that Definition 1 is equivalent to Definition 3 if $\deg f = 0$, i.e. $f = 1$ and thus $V_0 = P$.

If instead deg $f > 0$, an attacker that breaks collision resistance of Definition 1 by outputting a tuple $(y, w_y, \bar{w}_y, \mathcal{Y})$, can, before terminating, query in polynomial time the corresponding oracle $\mathcal{O}$ to get $|\mathcal{Y}_{V_0}| + 1$ valid non-membership witnesses for (random) non-accumulated elements and use Lagrange interpolation to recover from the d-values the polynomial $f(x) \in \mathbb{Z}/p\mathbb{Z}$, similarly as done at the beginning of the Witness Forgery Attack outlined in [8] and briefly discussed in Sect. 7. Once the attacker obtains the polynomial $f(x)$, he recovers the set $\mathcal{Y}_{V_0}$ by computing its roots and can then use the tuple $(y, w_y, \bar{w}_y, \mathcal{Y} \cup \mathcal{Y}_{V_0})$ to break collision resistance of Definition 3.   □

Definition 2. (Generalized t–Strong Diffie-Hellman Assumption) *Let $\mathcal{G}$ be a probabilistic polynomial time algorithm that, given a security parameter 1^λ, outputs a bilinear group $\mathbb{G} = (p, G_1, G_2, G_T, P, \tilde{P}, e)$. We say that the generalized t–Strong Diffie-Hellman Assumption holds for $\mathcal{G}$ with respect to a uniformly sampled $\alpha \leftarrow (\mathbb{Z}/p\mathbb{Z})^*$ and a non-zero $f(x) \in \mathbb{Z}/p\mathbb{Z}[x]$ if, for any probabilistic polynomial time adversary $\mathcal{A}$ and for every polynomially bounded function $t :$ $\mathbb{Z} \to \mathbb{Z}$, the probability*

$$\mathbb{P}\left(\mathcal{A}(P, \alpha f(\alpha)P, \alpha^2 f(\alpha)P, ..., \alpha^{t(\lambda)} f(\alpha)P, \tilde{P}, \alpha\tilde{P}) = \left(y, \frac{1}{y+\alpha}P\right)\right)$$

is a negligible function in λ for any freely chosen value $y \in \mathbb{Z}/p\mathbb{Z} \setminus \{-\alpha\}$.

To give confidence in this more general security assumption, we prove the following Theorem which gives a lower bound on the complexity of a generic algorithm that solves the Generalized t–SDH Assumption in the Generic Group Model [33].

We briefly recall that in the Generic Group Model [33] elements in the three groups G_1, G_2, G_T are represented with strings given by (random) unique *encoding* functions $\xi_i : G_i \to \{0,1\}^*$. Operations with groups elements (additions, pairings, isomorphism computations $\psi : G_2 \to G_1$) are performed by querying different oracles which communicates with the external word only by using ξ_i–encoding of group elements. In other words, an adversary who interacts with these oracles can only test equality among received encodings to understand relations between group elements.

Theorem 1. *Let $\mathcal{A}$ be an algorithm that solves the corresponding generalized t–SDH problem in the Generic Group Model, making a total of at most q_G queries to the oracles computing the group action in G_1, G_2, G_T, the oracle computing the isomorphism $\psi : G_2 \to G_1$ and the oracle computing the bilinear pairing e. If $\alpha \in \mathbb{Z}/p\mathbb{Z}^*$ and the encoding functions ξ_1, ξ_2, ξ_T are chosen at random, then the probability ϵ that*

$$\mathcal{A}\left(p, \xi_1(1), \xi_1(f(\alpha)), \xi_1(\alpha \cdot f(\alpha)), \ldots, \xi_1(\alpha^t \cdot f(\alpha)), \xi_2(1), \xi_2(\alpha)\right)$$

outputs $\left(y, \xi_1\left(\frac{1}{y+\alpha}\right)\right)$ with $y \in \mathbb{Z}/p\mathbb{Z}^*$ is bounded by

$$\epsilon \leq \frac{(\deg f + t) \cdot (q_G + t + 4)^2 + 1}{p}$$

Proof. We will essentially go through the original proof of Boneh and Boyen [9] of the generic security of the standard t–SDH assumption, by slightly readapting it to the definition of the generalized t–SDH assumption. The following game setting and query definitions are due to Boneh and Boyen [9] as well.

Let $\mathcal{B}$ be an algorithm that maintains three lists of pairs

$$L_j = \{(F_{j,i}, \xi_{j,i}) : i = 0, \ldots, \tau_j - 1\} \text{ with } j = 1, 2, T$$

where $F_{1,i}$, $F_{2,i}$ and $F_{T,i}$ are polynomials in $\mathbb{Z}/p\mathbb{Z}[x]$ verifying $\deg F_{1,i} \leq \deg f + t$, $\deg F_{2,i} \leq t$ and $\deg F_{T,i} \leq 2t$ and such that at step τ of the game $\tau_1 + \tau_2 + \tau_T = \tau + t + 3$. The lists are initialized at step $\tau = 0$ by taking $\tau_1 = t + 1$, $\tau_2 = 2$, $\tau_T = 0$ and letting $F_{1,0} = 1$, $F_{1,i} = x^i \cdot f(x)$ for $0 \leq i \leq t$ and $F_{2,i} = x^i$ with $i = 0, 1$. The corresponding $\xi_{j,i}$ encodings are set to arbitrary distinct strings in $\{0, 1\}^*$. $\mathcal{B}$ then starts a game by providing $\mathcal{A}$ the $q + 3$ encodings $\xi_{1,0}, \ldots, \xi_{1,q}, \xi_{2,0}, \xi_{2,1}$ and $\mathcal{A}$'s queries go as follows:

- *Group actions*: given an add (resp. subtract) query and two operands $\xi_{1,i}, \xi_{1,j}$ with $0 \leq i, j < \tau_1$, $\mathcal{B}$ computes $F_{1,\tau_1} \leftarrow F_{1,i} + F_{1,j}$ (resp. $F_{1,i} - F_{1,j}$). If $F_{1,\tau_1} = F_{1,l}$ for some $l < \tau_1$ then $\mathcal{B}$ sets $\xi_{1,\tau_1} = \xi_{1,l}$, otherwise sets ξ_{1,τ_1} to a new distinct string in $\{0, 1\}^*$. The pair $(F_{1,\tau_1}, \xi_{1,\tau_1})$ is added in L_1, τ_1 is incremented by 1 and ξ_{1,τ_1} is returned to $\mathcal{A}$. Operations in G_2, G_T are treated similarly.
- *Isomorphism*: given an encoding $\xi_{2,i}$ with $0 \leq i < \tau_2$, $\mathcal{B}$ sets $F_{1,\tau_1} \leftarrow F_{2,i}$. If $F_{1,\tau_1} = F_{1,l}$ for some $l < \tau_1$, then $\mathcal{B}$ sets $\xi_{1,\tau_1} \leftarrow \xi_{1,l}$, otherwise sets ξ_{1,τ_1} to a new distinct string in $\{0, 1\}^*$. The pair $(F_{1,\tau_1}, \xi_{1,\tau_1})$ is added in L_1, τ_1 is incremented by 1 and ξ_{1,τ_1} is returned to $\mathcal{A}$.
- *Pairing*: given two operands $\xi_{1,i}, \xi_{2,j}$ with $0 \leq i < \tau_1$ and $0 \leq j < \tau_2$, $\mathcal{B}$ computes the product $F_{T,\tau_T} \rightarrow F_{1,i} \cdot F_{2,j} \in \mathbb{Z}/p\mathbb{Z}[x]$. If $F_{T,\tau_T} = F_{T,l}$ for some $l < \tau_T$, then $\mathcal{B}$ sets $\xi_{T,\tau_T} \leftarrow \xi_{T,l}$, otherwise sets ξ_{T,τ_T} to a new distinct string in $\{0, 1\}^*$. The pair $(F_{T,\tau_T}, \xi_{T,\tau_T})$ is added in L_T, τ_T is incremented by 1 and ξ_{T,τ_T} is returned to $\mathcal{A}$.

$\mathcal{A}$ terminates and returns to $\mathcal{B}$ a pair $(y, \xi_{1,l})$ with $0 \leq l < \tau_1$. To show correctness of $\mathcal{A}$'s answer, $\mathcal{B}$ considers the corresponding polynomial $F_{1,l}$ in L_1 and computes the polynomial

$$F_{T,*}(x) = F_{1,l} \cdot (F_{2,1} + y F_{2,0}) = F_{1,l} \cdot (x + y) = f(x) \cdot g(x) \cdot (x + y)$$

for a certain polynomial $g(x) \in \mathbb{Z}/p\mathbb{Z}[x]$ of degree $\leq t$. If $\mathcal{A}$'s answer is correct, then $F_{T,*}(x) = 1$ (which corresponds to check in the current framework that it results to be a correct DDH pair when representing $\xi_{1,l}$ with an element of G_1). Now, unless $\deg F_{T,*} \geq p - 2$ (due to Fermat's Little Theorem), the equation $F_{T,*}(x) - 1 = 0$ admits at most $\deg f + t + 1$ roots in $\mathbb{Z}/p\mathbb{Z}$.

At this point, $\mathcal{B}$ chooses a random $x^* \in \mathbb{Z}/p\mathbb{Z}$ and his simulation is perfect unless $x^* \leftarrow x$ creates equality relations between simulated elements not revealed to $\mathcal{A}$. Thus the success probability of $\mathcal{A}$ is bounded by the probability that any of the following conditions holds:

1. $F_{1,i}(x^*) - F_{1,j}(x^*) = 0$ for some i,j so that $F_{1,i} \neq F_{1,j}$
2. $F_{2,i}(x^*) - F_{2,j}(x^*) = 0$ for some i,j so that $F_{2,i} \neq F_{2,j}$
3. $F_{T,i}(x^*) - F_{T,j}(x^*) = 0$ for some i,j so that $F_{T,i} \neq F_{T,j}$
4. $f(x^*)g(x^*)(x^* + y) - 1 = 0$

Now since, for some fixed i,j, the polynomial $F_{1,i} - F_{1,j}$ has degree at most $\deg f + t$ while $F_{2,i} - F_{2,j}$ has degree at most t, they vanishes at x^* with probability $(\deg f + t)/p$ and t/p, respectively. Similarly, $F_{T,i} - F_{T,j}$ being a polynomial of degree at most $2t$, vanishes at x^* with probability $2t/p$. As regards $f(x^*)g(x^*)(x^* + y) - 1$, it vanishes at x^* with probability $(\deg f + t + 1)/p$. Hence, by summing these probabilities over all valid pairs (i,j) for the first three cases, $\mathcal{A}$ wins the game with probability

$$\epsilon \leq \binom{\tau_1}{2} \frac{\deg f + t}{p} + \binom{\tau_2}{2} \frac{t}{p} + \binom{\tau_T}{2} \frac{2t}{p} + \frac{\deg f + t + 1}{p}$$

Given that $\tau_1 + \tau_2 + \tau_T \leq q_G + t + 3$, we obtain $\epsilon \leq \frac{(\deg f + t) \cdot (q_G + t + 4)^2 + 1}{p}$ $\quad\square$

We're now ready to prove that breaking collision resistance of our accumulator scheme in the Generic Group Model cannot be easier than breaking the generalized t-SDH assumption:

Theorem 2. *Consider a Generic Group Model instance of the Dynamic Universal Accumulator outlined in Sect. 3 equipped with the public Batch Witness Update protocol detailed in Sect. 5. If $|\mathcal{Y}_{V_0}|$ elements are accumulated to initialize the accumulator value, then the probability ϵ that an attacker $\mathcal{A}$ breaks collision resistance of Definition 1 in q_G queries to the group oracles, is bounded by*

$$\epsilon \leq \frac{(|\mathcal{Y}_{V_0}| + t) \cdot (q_G + t + 4)^2 + 1}{p}$$

where t is the maximum number of elements allowed to be accumulated simultaneously.

Proof. We refer to the proof of Theorem 1 for the definition of the game setting between $\mathcal{A}$ and the Accumulator Manager and the corresponding notation.

Since $\mathcal{Y}_{V_0}$ contains distinct elements from $\mathbb{Z}/p\mathbb{Z}$, then at any epoch all elements in the batch witness update information Upd sent from the Accumulator manager to $\mathcal{A}$ are of the form $\xi_1(g(x) \cdot f(x))$ where $f(x) = \prod_{y \in \mathcal{Y}_{V_0}}(y + x)$ and $g(x) \in \mathbb{Z}/p\mathbb{Z}[x]$ has degree $\leq t$.

Since any such polynomial $g(x) \cdot f(x)$ can be represented uniquely in the base $\{f(x), xf(x), \ldots, x^t f(x)\}$, we can assume $\mathcal{A}$ to be slightly more powerful by having initial access to all the following encodings:

$$\xi_1(1), \xi_1(f(\alpha)), \xi_1(\alpha \cdot f(\alpha)), \ldots, \xi_1(\alpha^t \cdot f(\alpha)), \xi_2(1), \xi_2(\alpha)$$

We note that accumulator values at different epochs can be obtained in polynomial time with queries to the group action oracle from the remaining update information, i.e. the elements added and deleted. All in all, this corresponds to the information the attacker would have access to under the hypothesis of Theorem 1.

Now, suppose that after q_G queries, $\mathcal{A}$ terminates and returns the tuple $(y, w_y, \bar{w}_y, \mathcal{Y})$ with $w_y = (\xi_{1,i}, 0)$ and $\bar{w}_y = (\xi_{1,j}, d)$. If the answer is correct and breaks the collision resistance property of the accumulator scheme, then the corresponding polynomials $F_{1,i}(x)$, $F_{1,j}(x)$ will satisfy

$$F_{1,i}(x) \cdot (x + y) = F_{1,j}(x) \cdot (x + y) + d$$

Note, that $\mathcal{A}$ can transform the tuple $(y, \xi_{1,i}, \xi_{1,j}, d)$ to the pair $(y, d^{-1}(\xi_{1,i} - \xi_{1,j}))$ by querying the oracles in polynomial time. This pair, if correct, would then solve the generalized t-SDH problem since, by letting $F_{T,*} = d^{-1}(F_{1,i} - F_{1,j})$, it holds $F_{T,*}(x) \cdot (x + y) - 1 = 0$ for all $x \in \mathbb{Z}/p\mathbb{Z}$. Hence $\mathcal{A}$ would win in q_G queries the game instantiated in the proof of Theorem 2 and, as was shown, this cannot be done with probability greater than $\frac{(|\mathcal{Y}_{V_0}| + t) \cdot (q_G + t + 4)^2 + 1}{p}$. $\qquad\square$

Relation with Previous Security Assumptions and Proofs. The proposed Generalized t-Strong Diffie-Hellman assumption straightforwardly reduces to the standard t-SDH assumption in the case when $\deg f = 0$, similarly as happens in Proposition 1 for our definition of Collision Resistance (Definition 1) and Au *et al.* one (Definition 3).

Thus, when $\deg f = 0$ (without loss of generality, $f(x) = 1$), collision resistance of the scheme can be shown directly under the standard t-SDH assumption of Definition 4 without requiring the Generic Group Model and similarly as done in [4,20]: a summary of all relevant definitions and a proof showing standard collision resistance under t-SDH assumption can be found in Appendix A.

Generalizing definitions and security proofs to allow for $\deg f > 0$, will ultimately permit us to address accumulator initialization, which (surprisingly) has a direct connection to the attacker ability to have access to (any element in) the $\mathcal{RS}_t$ (which can be (ab)used to compute witnesses and update the accumulator value), a circumstance that would be against our will to design an accumulator scheme suited also for authentication purposes, where only the accumulator manager can update and issue witnesses and whose construction will be finalized in next Section.

7 Accumulator Initialization

Depending on which would be the final application of the proposed accumulator scheme, it might be necessary to prevent the possibility to forge non-membership witnesses for *"never authorized"* non-accumulated elements, i.e. elements for which the Accumulator Manager did not issue witnesses.[6] This is relevant, for

---

[6] Membership witnesses for new elements would require an accumulator value update, an operation that we could assume to be executed by the Accumulator Manager that has exclusive access to the public register containing the current accumulator value. When issuing non-membership witnesses, instead, the accumulator value remains unchanged.

example, in the cases when the accumulator is used as an authentication mechanism and accumulated elements represents either white-listed or black-listed users which authenticate with respect to the accumulator value by showing possession of a valid membership or non-membership witness.

Forging witnesseses in the case when the Accumulator Manager should be the only authorized entity to do so is, in fact, what the *Witness Forgery Attack* outlined by Biryukov, Udovenko and Vitto in [8] does: a set of colluding users who share their non-membership witnesses can recover the (secret) *reference-string* sets $\mathcal{RS}_s = \{P, \alpha P, ..., \alpha^s P\}_{s>0}$, which enable them to compute membership and non-membership witnesses with respect to the latest accumulator value. Indeed, the knowledge of the set $\mathcal{RS} = \mathcal{RS}_t$ results to be functionally equivalent to the knowledge of α: it is possible to either update the accumulator value (see Lemma 1) or issue valid membership and non membership witnesses (see the reference string $\mathcal{RS}$-based construction in [4,8]).

The Witness Forgery Attack is possible as long as the number of colluding users is equal or greater to the number of elements added to initialize the accumulator value. In fact, the countermeasure proposed in [8] is to set an upper limit NMWitnessesMax to the total number of issuable non-membership witnesses and initialize the accumulator by adding at least NMWitnessesMax+1 secret elements.

This will clearly prevent the reconstruction of the sets $\mathcal{RS}_s$, but in our protocol the attackers have access in each epoch to the witness update information (see Table 1), which in principle could help circumventing the fact that they will not be able to collect and share enough non-membership witnesses or can be used to directly compute some elements in $\mathcal{RS}_s$.

We will show that this is indeed possible, but we will prove that a generic algorithm in the Generic Group Model would compute any element in $\mathcal{RS}_t$ with negligible probability just by carefully choosing few of the elements added to initialize the accumulator value.

We start by introducing some theoretical result. The purpose of the following Proposition is to show some properties on elements that have particular multiplicative orders in the group $(\mathbb{Z}/p\mathbb{Z})^*$. These properties will be useful to prove the subsequent Theorem 3, which will give us sufficient conditions on the elements we need to add to prevent the reconstruction of the $\mathcal{RS}$ from the publicly available information. Thus, initializing the accumulator with NMWitnessesMax + 1 random elements where some of them satisfies the hypothesis of Theorem 3 will ultimately prevent any, even partial, successful execution of the Witness Forgery Attack [8].

Proposition 2. *Let $p \in \mathbb{N}$ be a prime such that $p - 1 = p_1^{e_1} \cdot ... \cdot p_n^{e_n}$ factorizes as the product of $n > 1$ powers of distinct primes $p_i \in \mathbb{N}$. Let $f(x) \in \mathbb{Z}/p\mathbb{Z}[x]$ be a polynomial with $n \leq m < p - 1$ distinct non-zero roots $x_1, \ldots, x_m \in \mathbb{Z}/p\mathbb{Z}$ such that the multiplicative order in $(\mathbb{Z}/p\mathbb{Z})^*$ of x_i, for $1 \leq i \leq n$, is $p_i^{e_i}$. Then*

- i. *The least $k > 0$ for which there exists $z \in \mathbb{Z}/p\mathbb{Z}$ and $g(x) \in \mathbb{Z}/p\mathbb{Z}[x]$ such that $g(x)f(x) \equiv x^k - z \mod p$ is $k = p - 1$.*
- ii. *The degree of the minimal-degree non-constant monomial of $f(x)$ is s with $0 < s < m$.*

Proof. Suppose there exists $z \in \mathbb{Z}/p\mathbb{Z}$ and $g(x) \in \mathbb{Z}/p\mathbb{Z}[x]$ such that

$$g(x)f(x) \equiv x^k - z \mod p$$

Then, each root $x_1, \ldots, x_m$ of $f(x)$ must be a root for $x^k - z$ in $\mathbb{Z}/p\mathbb{Z}$, that is

$$x_1^k \equiv \cdots \equiv x_t^k \equiv z \mod p \tag{1}$$

Since, by hypothesis $(\mathbb{Z}/p\mathbb{Z})^* \simeq \mathbb{Z}/(p-1)\mathbb{Z} \simeq \langle x_1 \rangle \times \cdots \times \langle x_n \rangle$ with $n > 1$ we have $z \in \bigcap_{i=1}^m \langle x_i \rangle \leq \bigcap_{i=1}^n \langle x_i \rangle = \langle 1 \rangle$. Hence a solution to (1) exists only if $z \equiv 1$ and the least k for which it holds is $k = lcm(\mathrm{ord}(x_1), \ldots, \mathrm{ord}(x_m)) \geq lcm(\mathrm{ord}(x_1), \ldots, \mathrm{ord}(x_n)) = p - 1$. Since $k \leq p - 1$, we have $k = p - 1$.

It follows that as long as $m < p - 1$, there are no $z \in \mathbb{Z}/p\mathbb{Z}$ such that $f(x) \equiv x^t - z \mod p$. Hence the degree of the minimal-degree non-constant monomial of $f(x)$ is s with $0 < s < m$. □

Theorem 3. *Let $p \in \mathbb{N}$ be a prime such that $p - 1 = p_1^{e_1} \cdot \ldots \cdot p_n^{e_n}$ factorizes as the product of $n > 1$ powers of distinct primes $p_i \in \mathbb{N}$. Let $f(x) \in \mathbb{Z}/p\mathbb{Z}[x]$ be a polynomial with $n \leq m < p - 1$ distinct non-zero roots $x_1, \ldots, x_t \in \mathbb{Z}/p\mathbb{Z}$ such that the multiplicative order in $(\mathbb{Z}/p\mathbb{Z})^*$ of x_i, for $1 \leq i \leq n$, is $p_i^{e_i}$.*

Let $(\mathcal{V}, +)$ be the vector space of polynomials with degree lower equal $p - 2$ and $\mathcal{B} = \{1, x, \ldots, x^{p-2}\}$ its $(p-1)$-dimensional canonical basis. Then, for every $1 \leq k < p - 1$

$$rank \left(\begin{bmatrix} 1 \\ f(x) \\ xf(x) \\ \vdots \\ x^{p-m-2}f(x) \\ x^k \end{bmatrix}_{\mathcal{B}} \right) = p - m + 1$$

Proof. The rank is maximum when the row vectors are linearly independent in $\mathcal{V}$, that is for any $a_0, \ldots, a_{p-m-2}, b, c \in \mathbb{Z}/p\mathbb{Z}$ such that

$$\left(\sum_{j=0}^{p-m-2} a_j x^j f(x) \right) + bx^k + c = 0 \tag{2}$$

we have $a_0 \equiv \cdots \equiv a_{p-m-2} \equiv b \equiv c \equiv 0$.

We will prove the statement by exhaustion on the values of k.

$\boxed{1 \leq k < m}$ The dependence relation (2) can be rewritten as $g(x)f(x) = -bx^k - c$ where $g(x) = \sum_{j=0}^{p-m-2} a_j x^j$. By hypothesis $f(x)$ has m different roots, while $-bx^k - c$ can have at most $k < m$ distinct roots. The equation then holds only if both sides are equal to the 0 polynomial, that is $-bx^i - c = 0$ and $g(x) = 0$. This implies $a_0 \equiv \cdots \equiv a_{p-m-2} \equiv 0$ and $b \equiv c \equiv 0$ because the elements $\{1, x, \ldots, x^{p-m-2}\}$ are linearly independent vectors of $\mathcal{V}$.

$\boxed{k = m}$ In this case the dependence relation (2) can be rewritten as $g(x)f(x) = -bx^m - c$ with $g(x)$ defined as in the previous case. By hypothesis $f(x)$ has m distinct roots, while the right side can have at most m distinct roots. This implies that $g(x) = g(0) = a_0$ is a constant polynomial or, equivalently, that $a_1 \equiv \cdots \equiv a_{p-m-2} \equiv 0$. Suppose by contradiction that $a_0 \neq 0$, then $f(x) = -a_0^{-1}bx^m - a_0^{-1}c$ is a contradiction since, by Proposition 2, the degree of the minimal-degree non-constant monomial of $f(x)$ is s with $s \neq m$ and $s > 0$. Hence $a_0 \equiv 0$, and then $-bx^m - c = 0$ which implies $b \equiv c \equiv 0$.

$\boxed{m < k < p - 1}$ Let $k = m + k'$ with $1 \leq k' \leq p - m - 2$. From $g(x)f(x) = -bx^{m+k'} - c$ it follows that $deg(g) \leq k'$ and then, if $k' < p - m - 2$, we have $a_{k'+1} \equiv \cdots \equiv a_{p-m-2} \equiv 0$.

Assume, by contradiction, $b \neq 0$ and $c \equiv 0$. In this case the dependence relation becomes $g(x)f(x) = -bx^{m+k'}$, but the right side has only 0 as root while the left side has, by hypothesis, at least t non-zero distinct roots. This implies, similarly as before, that $g(x) = 0$ and $b \equiv 0$, a contradiction.

Let us therefore assume $b \neq 0$ and $c \neq 0$. In this case the dependence relation can be rewritten as $g'(x)f(x) = x^{m+k'} - z$ where $g'(x) = (-b)^{-1}g(x)$ and $z = (-b)^{-1}c \neq 0$.

If, by contradiction, $g'(x) \neq 0$, then, by Proposition 2, the least value for $m + k'$ such that the dependence relation holds is $m + k' = p - 1$, that is $k' = p - m - 1$, a contradiction to $1 \leq k' \leq p - m - 2$. Hence $g'(x) = 0$, which in turn implies $b \equiv c \equiv 0$, a contradiction to our assumption $b \neq 0$.

It follows that $b \equiv 0$ and then $g(x)f(x) = -c$. Since by hypothesis f has m distinct roots, this equation holds only if $c = 0$ and $g(x) = 0$, which, similarly as before, implies $a_0 \equiv \cdots \equiv a_{k'} \equiv b \equiv c \equiv 0$. $\square$

Corollary 1. *Let $f(x) \in \mathbb{Z}/p\mathbb{Z}[x]$ be a polynomial satisfying the hypothesis of Theorem 3 and consider a Generic Group Model instance of the proposed Dynamic Universal Accumulator equipped with the public Batch Witness Update protocol. If the accumulator value is initialized by adding all the roots in $\mathbb{Z}/p\mathbb{Z}$ of $f(x)$, then the probability ϵ that an attacker $\mathcal{A}$ outputs in q_G queries to the group oracles the value $\xi_1\left(\alpha^k\right)$ for any $1 \leq k < p - 1$ is bounded by*

$$\epsilon \leq \frac{(\deg f + t) \cdot (q_G + t + 3)^2}{p}$$

where t is the maximum number of elements allowed to be accumulated simultaneously.

Proof. The proof proceeds similarly as done in the proof of Theorem 2. The only difference is the condition checked by the Accumulator Manager to ensure correctness of $\mathcal{A}$'s output value $(\xi_{1,l})$. This new check corresponds to verifying the polynomial equation $F_{1,l} - x^k = 0$ where $F_{1,l} = g(x) \cdot f(x)$ with $\deg g \leq t$. The Accumulator Manager then chooses a random value $x^* \in \mathbb{Z}/p\mathbb{Z}$: by Theorem 3 the equation $F_{1,l} - x^k = 0$ vanishes in x^* with probability 0 for any $1 \leq k < p-1$, thus $\mathcal{A}$ wins the game with non-zero probability only if some of the following conditions holds:

1. $F_{1,i}(x^*) - F_{1,j}(x^*) = 0$ for some i, j so that $F_{1,i} \neq F_{1,j}$
2. $F_{2,i}(x^*) - F_{2,j}(x^*) = 0$ for some i, j so that $F_{2,i} \neq F_{2,j}$
3. $F_{T,i}(x^*) - F_{T,j}(x^*) = 0$ for some i, j so that $F_{T,i} \neq F_{T,j}$

From this we conclude, in a similar way as done at the end of the proof of Theorem 2, that $\mathcal{A}$ wins the game with the Accumulator Manager with a probability $\epsilon \leq \frac{(\deg f + t) \cdot (q_G + t + 3)^2}{p}$. $\qquad\square$

We are now ready to explicitly define the Accumulator Initialization procedure for our protocol:

Accumulator Initialization. Set an upper limit NMWitnessesMax to the total number of issuable non-membership witnesses. Assume p is such that $p - 1 = p_1^{e_1} \cdot \ldots \cdot p_n^{e_n}$ factorizes as the product of $n > 1$ powers of distinct primes p_i and consider n elements $x_1, \ldots, x_n \in \mathbb{Z}/p\mathbb{Z}$ such that the multiplicative order in $(\mathbb{Z}/p\mathbb{Z})^*$ of x_i is $p_i^{e_i}$, for $1 \leq i \leq n$. Then, the Accumulator Manager sets

$$\mathcal{Y}_{V_0} = \{x_1, \ldots, x_n\} \cup \{\texttt{NMWitnessesMax} - n + 1 \text{ random elements in } \mathcal{ACC}\}$$

so that $|\mathcal{Y}_{V_0}| = \texttt{NMWitnessesMax} + 1$ and defines the corresponding initialization polynomial as $f_0(x) = \prod_{x_i \in \mathcal{Y}_{V_0}} (x - x_i)$, where $V_0 = f_0(\alpha)P$. He then publishes $(V_0, \emptyset)$, the accumulator state at epoch 0, and keeps secret and never deletes the elements in $\mathcal{Y}_{V_0}$.

We note that as soon as an epoch changes, the Accumulator Manager publishes the corresponding Batch Witnesses Update information: at epoch 1, for example, this corresponds to the new state $(V_1, \mathcal{Y}_{V_1})$, the updating vector Ω_1 and the polynomials $d_{\mathcal{A}_1}(x)$ and $d_{\mathcal{D}_1}(x)$. At this point, the polynomial

$$f_{V_1}(x) = f_0(x) \cdot f_1(x) = \prod_{y_i \in \mathcal{Y}_{V_0}} (y_i + x) \cdot \prod_{y_j \in \mathcal{Y}_{V_1}} (y_j + x)$$

has $|\mathcal{Y}_{V_0}| + |\mathcal{Y}_{V_1}|$ distinct non-zero roots, n of which are $x_1, \ldots, x_n$, and is such that $V_1 = f_{V_1}(\alpha)P$. Even if it is possible to obtain from Ω_1, $\mathcal{A}_1$ and $\mathcal{D}_1$ all the values $\alpha^k V_1$ for $1 \leq k < p - |\mathcal{Y}_{V_0}| - 1$ (we relax the condition $k \leq \texttt{batchMax}$) we still are under the hypothesis of Theorem 3 and Corollary 1, which assure us the infeasibility to obtain any element of the $\mathcal{RS}$. This reasoning can be easily generalized to any subsequent epoch.

One last question arises with regard to all these considerations: is it possible to obtain some elements in the $\mathcal{RS}$ combining the vectors Ω_i coming from different epochs? When the accumulator is initialized as described in Theorem 3, the answer is *no*. To show this, consider, without loss of generality, the m vectors $\Omega_1, \ldots, \Omega_m$, where the j-entry of any Ω_i is of the form $c_j V_i$. Hence a linear combination with coefficients $a_{i,j} \in \mathbb{Z}/p\mathbb{Z}$ of entries of these vectors can be written as

$$\sum_{i=1}^{m} \sum_{j=0}^{|\texttt{batchMax}|} a_{i,j} c_j V_i = \left(\sum_{i=1}^{m} \sum_{j=0}^{|\texttt{batchMax}|} a_{i,j} c_j f_i(\alpha) \right) \cdot f_0(\alpha) P = g(\alpha) \cdot V_0$$

where $g(x) = \sum_{i=1}^{m} \sum_{j=0}^{\text{batchMax}} a_{i,j} c_j f_i(x)$. In other words, in the luckiest situation, what we can obtain combining all these vectors is a *"basis"* made of elements of the form $\alpha^k f_0(\alpha) P = \alpha^k V_0$ with $1 \leq k \leq$ batchMax which, as we already discussed, does not permit to obtain any element in $\mathcal{RS}$.

8   Zero-Knowledge Proof of Knowledge

We now explicitly show how an interactive zero-knowledge protocol can be instantiated between a Prover and a Verifier to prove the ownership of a valid non-membership witness $\bar{w}_{y,V}$ for y with respect to the accumulator state $(V, \mathcal{Y}_V)$ (the corresponding protocol to show ownership of a valid membership witness $w_{y,V}$ is similar and will not be discussed). Although different NIZK protocols for bilinear equations verification can be adopted for this purpose (e.g. Groth-Sahai [23]), we chose to detail a construction which doesn't need a trusted setup (to avoid extra storage needs on users' side) and that can be easily implemented in order to provide a reference for our benchmarks.

To this end, we will then extend the zero-knowledge proof of knowledge protocol defined by Boneh *et al.* in [9], which proves under the Decision Linear Diffie-Hellman assumption the knowledge of a pair (y, C) such that $(y+\alpha)C = V$, in order to support tuples (y, C, d) which verify $(y + \alpha)C + dP = V$.

However, for non-membership witnesses we need to further ensure that $d \neq 0$ or, equivalently in G_1, that has a multiplicative inverse. In this regard we will then consider, for a random generator $K \in G_1$ and random $a, b \in \mathbb{Z}/p\mathbb{Z}$, the Pedersen commitments $E_d = dP + aK$ and $E_{d^{-1}} = d^{-1}P + bK$ for d and d^{-1}, respectively. Noticing that $P = dE_{d^{-1}} - dbK$, we then extend the protocol applying EQ-composition to the factor d among the values E_d and P, thus showing that $E_{d^{-1}}$ is a Pedersen commitment to the multiplicative inverse of the committed value in E_d.

Under the Random Oracle Model, we can make such proof of knowledge non-interactive and full zero-knowledge by applying Fiat-Shamir heuristic [21]. We will do so by using an heuristic variant adopted by Boneh *et al.* in [9] in order to reduce Prover's proof size. We assume that calls to the random oracle can be concretely realized through evaluations to a cryptographic hash function $H : \{0,1\}^* \rightarrow \mathbb{Z}/p\mathbb{Z}$.

Security proofs. By reporting the relative security proofs, we will substantially replicate the original results of the respective authors: we therefore refer to [9] and [32, Ex. 5.3.4] for the completeness, soundness and (special) honest-verifier zero-knowledgeness security proofs of Boneh *et al.* protocol and EQ-composition for multiplicative-inverse relation, respectively.

The resulting protocol is the following.

Setup The Prover and Verifier agree on the public values $P, X, Y, Z, K \in G_1$ and $\tilde{P}, \tilde{Q} \in G_2$, where X, Y, Z, K are distinct random generators of G_1.

Proof of Knowledge The Prover randomly selects $\sigma, \rho, \tau, \pi \in \mathbb{Z}/p\mathbb{Z}$ and computes

$$E_C = C + (\sigma + \rho)Z, \qquad E_d = dP + \tau K, \qquad E_{d^{-1}} = d^{-1}P + \pi K,$$

$$T_\sigma = \sigma X, \qquad T_\rho = \rho Y, \qquad \delta_\sigma = y\sigma, \qquad \delta_\rho = y\rho$$

A non-interactive zero knowledge Proof of Knowledge of values $(y, d, \sigma, \rho, \tau, \pi, \delta_\sigma, \delta_\rho)$ satisfying

$$P = dE_{d^{-1}} - d\pi K, \qquad E_d = dP + \tau K,$$

$$\sigma X = T_\sigma, \qquad \rho Y = T_\rho, \qquad yT_\sigma - \delta_\sigma X = O, \qquad yT_\rho - \delta_\rho Y = O,$$

$$e(E_C, \tilde{P})^y e(Z, \tilde{P})^{-\delta_\sigma - \delta_\rho} e(Z, \tilde{Q})^{-\sigma - \rho} e(K, \tilde{P})^{-\tau} = \frac{e(V, \tilde{P})}{e(E_C, \tilde{Q}) e(E_d, \tilde{P})}$$

is undertaken between Prover and Verifier as follows:

Blinding (P) The Prover randomly picks $r_y, r_u, r_v, r_w, r_\sigma, r_\rho, r_{\delta_\sigma}, r_{\delta_\rho} \in \mathbb{Z}/p\mathbb{Z}$, computes

$$R_A = r_u P + r_v K, \qquad R_B = r_u E_{d^{-1}} + r_w K,$$

$$R_E = e(E_C, \tilde{P})^{r_v} e(Z, \tilde{P})^{-r_{\delta_\sigma} - r_{\delta_\rho}} e(Z, \tilde{Q})^{-r_\sigma - r_\rho} e(K, \tilde{P})^{-r_v},$$

$$R_\sigma = r_\sigma X, \qquad R_\rho = r_\rho Y, \qquad R_{\delta_\sigma} = r_y T_\sigma - r_{\delta_\sigma} X, \qquad R_{\delta_\rho} = r_y T_\rho - r_{\delta_\rho} Y$$

Challenge (P) The Prover sets the challenge $c \in \mathbb{Z}/p\mathbb{Z}$ to

$$c = H(V, E_C, E_d, E_{d^{-1}}, T_\sigma, T_\rho, R_A, R_B, R_E, R_\sigma, R_\rho, R_{\delta_\sigma}, R_{\delta_\rho})$$

Response (P) The Prover computes

$$s_y = r_y + cy, \qquad s_u = r_u + cd, \qquad s_v = r_v + c\tau, \qquad s_w = r_w - cd\pi,$$

$$s_\sigma = r_\sigma + c\sigma, \qquad s_\rho = r_\rho + c\rho, \qquad s_{\delta_\sigma} = r_{\delta_\sigma} + c\delta_\sigma, \qquad s_{\delta_\rho} = r_{\delta_\rho} + c\delta_\rho$$

and sends $(E_C, E_d, E_{d^{-1}}, T_\sigma, T_\rho, c, s_y, s_u, s_v, s_w, s_\sigma, s_\rho, s_{\delta_\sigma}, s_{\delta_\rho})$ to the Verifier.

Verify (V) The Verifier computes

$$R_A = s_u P + s_v K - cE_d, \qquad R_B = s_w K + s_u E_{d^{-1}} - cP,$$

$$R_\sigma = s_\sigma X - cT_\sigma, \qquad R_\rho = s_\rho Y - cT_\rho, \qquad R_{\delta_\sigma} = s_y T_\sigma - s_{\delta_\sigma} X, \qquad R_{\delta_\rho} = s_y T_\rho - s_{\delta_\rho} Y,$$

$$R_E = e(E_C, \tilde{P})^{s_y} \cdot e(Z, \tilde{P})^{-s_{\delta_\sigma} - s_{\delta_\rho}} \cdot e(Z, \tilde{Q})^{-s_\sigma - s_\rho} \cdot e(K, \tilde{P})^{-s_v} \cdot \left(\frac{e(V, \tilde{P})}{e(E_C, \tilde{Q}) e(E_d, \tilde{P})} \right)^{-c}$$

and accepts if $c = H(V, E_C, E_d, E_{d^{-1}}, T_\sigma, T_\rho, R_A, R_B, R_E, R_\sigma, R_\rho, R_{\delta_\sigma}, R_{\delta_\rho})$.

8.1 Complexity Analysis

Within this protocol, zero-knowledge proofs for valid non-membership witnesses consists of 5 elements in G_1 and 11 elements in $\mathbb{F}_p$, while they consists of 3 elements in G_1 and 6 elements in $\mathbb{F}_p$ in the case of membership witnesses. Thus, if elliptic curves are used to concretely implement the underlying bilinear group (in particular, we assume elements in G_1 are elliptic curve points over $\mathbb{F}_q$) and elliptic curve points compression is used, zero-knowledge non-membership and membership proofs can be represented with $5(\log q + 1) + 9 \log p$ bits and $3(\log q + 1) + 6 \log p$ bits, respectively. In our concrete instance (see Sect. 9) this translates to 4926 bits $\approx$ 616 bytes proofs for non-membership witnesses and 3135 bits $\approx$ 392 bytes proofs for membership witnesses.

As regards computational costs, if the quantities $e(Z, \tilde{P})$, $e(Z, \tilde{Q})$, $e(K, \tilde{P})$ and $e(V, \tilde{P})$ are pre-computed and stored by both Prover and Verifier, zero-knowledge proofs of knowledge for non-membership witnesses are computed with 15 scalar-point multiplications in G_1, 7 point additions in G_1, 4 exponentiation in G_T and 1 pairing. We note that the Prover can reduce the cost of evaluating $e(E_C, \tilde{P})$ by computing and storing the value $e(C, \tilde{P})$. Thus, with just 1 pairing per-epoch, the Prover can compute each $e(E_C, \tilde{P})$ as $e(Z, \tilde{P})^{\sigma + \rho} \cdot e(C, \tilde{P})$ with 1 exponentiation and 1 multiplication in G_T. Using this optimization, the cost to compute a proof of knowledge of a membership witness boils down to a total of 9 scalar-point multiplications in G_1, 3 point additions in G_1, 5 exponentiation in G_T and 1 multiplication in G_T.

Similarly, the Verifier needs 16 scalar-point multiplications in G_1, 9 point additions in G_1, 4 exponentiation in G_T and 2 pairings (if computes the product $e(E_C, \tilde{P})^{s_y} e(E_C, c\tilde{Q})$ as $e(E_C, s_y\tilde{P} + c\tilde{Q})$) to verify a non-membership witness zero-knowledge proof, while he needs 10 scalar-point multiplications in G_1, 5 point additions in G_1, 3 exponentiation in G_T and 1 pairing to verify a zero-knowledge proof of knowledge for a membership witness.

9 Implementation Results

To show efficiency and its practical relevance, we implemented the proposed accumulator scheme by using the RELIC library [2]. In order to guarantee a security level of 128-bits, we selected the available pairing-friendly Type-III prime curve $B12\text{-}P446$. We then benchmarked the main features of the proposed accumulator, obtaining the following average results:

- **Accumulator Updates**: 0.75 s to add $1,000,000$ elements (random elements generation requires 1.46 s); 0.48 s to delete $1,000,000$ elements.
- **Witness Issuing**: 1.9 ms to issue a membership witness; 229.5 ms for a non-membership witness ($1,000,000$ elements accumulated).
- **Witness Verification**: 2.2 ms to verify a membership witness; 3.2 ms to verify a non-membership witness.
- **Public Batch Witness Update**: 37.9 s to generate batch update data corresponding to a $10,000$ elements batch addition operation; 27.1 s for a $10,000$ elements batch deletion operation.

- **Batch Witness Update**: 2.1 s to update a membership or non-membership witness after a batch addition or deletion operation of 10, 000 elements.
- **Non-Batch Witness Update**: 4.4 s to update a membership or non-membership witness after a batch addition or deletion operation of 10, 000 elements.
- **Zero-Knowledge Proof Creation**: 5.2 ms to create a zero knowledge proof of knowledge of a membership witness; 7.4 ms to create a proof for a non-membership witness.
- **Zero-Knowledge Proof Verification**: 6.5 ms to verify a zero knowledge proof of knowledge of a membership witness; 11.2 ms to verify a proof for a non-membership witness.

These benchmarks came from running our implementation on a standard Intel(R) Core(TM) i7-3770 CPU @ 3.40 GHz desktop provided with 8.00 GB of RAM and running Ubuntu 18.04 x64. No parallelization was used.

Our implementation can be found on GitHub at:

$$\text{https://github.com/cryptolu/accumulator/}$$

Feedback from the Community. We were contacted by a company that implemented our accumulator (including the Public Batch Witness Update and Zero-Knowledge protocols) as a revocation mechanism for verifiable credentials. Their implementation, public on GitHub[7], is used already in production applications where 10–20 millions entries remain accumulated at any given time and 1000/600 elements are added/deleted, respectively, per day. They reported to us that in their implementation (i) witness update data generation takes 17 s and 99 KB/day; (ii) users' witness update after 1 year offline requires 80 s and 36 MB of update data; (iii) witness updates work on IoT; (iv) using the pairing-friendly elliptic curve BLS12-381, RAM requirements are few megabytes. They added that our scheme "solves their scaling problem" compared to Hyperledger-Indy[8] implementation of [17], which would take hours/day and larger proof sizes.

10   Conclusions

We presented a Dynamic Universal Accumulator in the Accumulator Manager setting over bilinear groups, which supports batch operations and batch membership and non-membership public witness updates.

The proposed accumulator extends a combination of previous schemes by adding batch operations, enabling users to update witnesses in optimal time. Furthermore, since batch update data is designed to be decoupled from users' witnesses, our protocol permits (privacy-preserving) witness updates delegation, thus enabling lightweight users to keep their witnesses updated with a constant number of elementary operations.

---

[7] https://github.com/mikelodder7/accumulator-rs.
[8] https://www.hyperledger.org/use/hyperledger-indy.

We showed in the Generic Group Model its security in terms of collision resistance by introducing a more general version of the t−SDH assumption for which we give an upper bound complexity for a generic algorithm that solves the corresponding problem. We further showed how to initialize the accumulator in order to be safe from an attack which would allow to forge witnesses for non-authorized elements, an essential requirement in the case the accumulator scheme is used as an authentication mechanism under the Accumulator Manager authority.

We then described how to instantiate a zero-knowledge proof of ownership of a valid witness for a given accumulator state and we implemented the accumulator logic along with batch operations, the public witness update protocol and the zero-knowledge proof mechanism in order to show its practical relevance as an efficient and scalable privacy-preserving authentication mechanism.

A   Collision Resistance of Au *et al.* Accumulator

We here report both Au *et al.* definition of collision resistance (slightly restated) and Boneh and Boyen definition of t−SDH assumption.

Definition 3. (Collision Resistance [4]) *The Dynamic Universal Accumulator outlined in Sect. 3 is collision resistant if, for any probabilistic polynomial time adversary $\mathcal{A}$ that has access to an oracle $\mathcal{O}$ which returns the accumulator value resulting from the accumulation of the elements of any given input subset of $(\mathbb{Z}/p\mathbb{Z})^*$, the following probabilities*

$$\mathbb{P}\left(\begin{array}{cc} (\mathbb{G}, \alpha, \tilde{Q}) \leftarrow Gen(1^\lambda)\,, & (y, w_y, \mathcal{Y}) \leftarrow \mathcal{A}^{\mathcal{O}}(\mathbb{G}, \tilde{Q}) \qquad : \\ \mathcal{Y} \subset (\mathbb{Z}/p\mathbb{Z})^* & \wedge \quad V = \left(\prod_{y_i \in \mathcal{Y}}(y_i + \alpha)\right) \cdot P \quad \wedge \\ y \in (\mathbb{Z}/p\mathbb{Z})^* \setminus \mathcal{Y} & \wedge \quad \Omega(y, w_y, V, \textbf{membership}) = 1 \end{array} \right)$$

$$\mathbb{P}\left(\begin{array}{cc} (\mathbb{G}, \alpha, \tilde{Q}) \leftarrow Gen(1^\lambda)\,, & (y, \bar{w}_y, \mathcal{Y}) \leftarrow \mathcal{A}^{\mathcal{O}}(\mathbb{G}, \tilde{Q}) \qquad : \\ \mathcal{Y} \subset (\mathbb{Z}/p\mathbb{Z})^* & \wedge \quad V = \left(\prod_{y_i \in \mathcal{Y}}(y_i + \alpha)\right) \cdot P \quad \wedge \\ y \in \mathcal{Y} & \wedge \quad \Omega(y, \bar{w}_y, V, \textbf{non-membership}) = 1 \end{array} \right)$$

*are both negligible functions in the security parameter λ, where w_y, $\bar{w}_y$ denote a membership and non-membership witness for y, respectively, and $\Omega(y, w, V, \textbf{type})$ is equal to 1 if and only if w is a valid **type** witness for y with respect to V.*

Definition 4. (t−Strong Diffie-Hellman Assumption [10]) *Let $\mathcal{G}$ be a probabilistic polynomial time algorithm that, given a security parameter 1^λ, outputs a bilinear group $\mathbb{G} = (p, G_1, G_2, G_T, P, \tilde{P}, e)$. We say that the t−Strong Diffie-Hellman Assumption holds for $\mathcal{G}$ with respect to an $\alpha \leftarrow (\mathbb{Z}/p\mathbb{Z})^*$ if, for any probabilistic polynomial time adversary $\mathcal{A}$ and for every polynomially bounded function $t : \mathbb{Z} \rightarrow \mathbb{Z}$, the probability $\mathbb{P}\left(\mathcal{A}(P, \alpha P, \alpha^2 P, ..., \alpha^{t(\lambda)} P, \tilde{P}, \alpha\tilde{P}) = \left(y, \frac{1}{y+\alpha}P\right)\right)$ is a negligible function in λ for any freely chosen value $y \in \mathbb{Z}/p\mathbb{Z} \setminus \{-\alpha\}$.*

We can see that in Definition 3, the adversary has access to an oracle $\mathcal{O}$ that outputs the accumulator value $V = \left(\prod_{y \in \mathcal{Y}_V} (y + \alpha) \right) P$ for any chosen input set $\mathcal{Y}_V$. Its purpose is to model the information the adversary can eventually get by looking at the published accumulator states, although in practice the adversary has no control over the values accumulated by the Accumulator Manager. This oracle doesn't make their attacker more powerful when compared to the requirements of the Boneh and Boyen $t-$SDH assumption (where the $\mathcal{RS}$ is directly given to the attacker) due to the following:

Lemma 1. *Having access to the oracle $\mathcal{O}$ of Definition 3 where sets of size at most t can be queried is equivalent to the knowledge of the set $\mathcal{RS} = \{P, \alpha P, ..., \alpha^t P\}$.*

Proof. $\boxed{\Rightarrow}$ Let y be a generator of $(\mathbb{Z}/p\mathbb{Z})^*$. Then the polynomials $\{1, (y + x), (y + x) \cdot (y^2 + x), \ldots, \prod_{i=1}^{t} (y^i + x)\}$ form a basis for the additive vector space of polynomials in $\mathbb{Z}/p\mathbb{Z}[x]$ with degree lower equal t and, hence, for any given $1 \leq i \leq t$, there exists a linear combination of these polynomials that sums up to x^i. It follows that, iteratively calling $\mathcal{O}$ on the set $\mathcal{Y}_i = \{y, y^2, \ldots, y^i\}$, it is possible to write a linear combination of the $V_{\mathcal{Y}_i}$ values returned which is equal to $\alpha^i P$.

$\boxed{\Leftarrow}$ Suppose the set $\mathcal{RS}$ is known. Then, for any given $\mathcal{Y}_V \subset (\mathbb{Z}/p\mathbb{Z})^*$ with $|\mathcal{Y}_V| \leq t$, using the $\mathcal{RS}$, it is possible to compute $V = \left(\prod_{y_i \in \mathcal{Y}_V} (y_i + \alpha) \right) P = \sum_{i=0}^{|\mathcal{Y}|} c_i \cdot (\alpha^i P)$. $\square$

Theorem 4. *Let $\mathcal{G}$ be a probabilistic polynomial time algorithm that, given a security parameter 1^λ, outputs a bilinear group $\mathbb{G} = (p, G_1, G_2, G_T, P, \tilde{P}, e)$ and consider an instantiation of the Dynamic Universal Accumulator obtained using $\mathcal{G}$ for the bilinear group generation and $\alpha \in (\mathbb{Z}/p\mathbb{Z})^*$ as the secret accumulator parameter. Then, the accumulator is collision resistant (Definition 3) if the $t-$Strong Diffie-Hellman Assumption (Definition 4) holds for $\mathcal{G}$ with respect to α.*

Proof. We note that a solution (y, C, d) for the pairing equation $e(C, y\tilde{P} + \tilde{Q})e(P, \tilde{P})^d = e(V, \tilde{P})$ is also a solution for the elliptic curve points equation $(y + \alpha)C + dP = V$. We will then prove the Theorem considering this last equation only, distinguishing between membership and non-membership witnesses.

Membership Witnesses. By contradiction, suppose there exists a probabilistic polynomial time adversary $\mathcal{A}$ that with respect to an (non-trivial) accumulator state $(V, \mathcal{Y}_V)$ outputs with a non-negligible probability a membership witness $C \in G_1$ for an element $y \in (\mathbb{Z}/p\mathbb{Z})^* \setminus \mathcal{Y}_V$. It follows that $(y+\alpha)C = V = f_V(\alpha)P$ where $f_V(x) = \prod_{y_i \in \mathcal{Y}_V} (y_i + x)$. Since $y \notin \mathcal{Y}_V$, we have that $(y + \alpha) \nmid f_V(x)$. Using the polynomial extended Euclidean algorithm, $\mathcal{A}$ computes $g(x) \in \mathbb{Z}/p\mathbb{Z}[x]$ of degree $|\mathcal{Y}_V| - 1$ and $r \in (\mathbb{Z}/p\mathbb{Z})^*$ such that $f_V(x) = g(x) \cdot (y + x) + r$. Therefore, $C = g(\alpha)P + \frac{r}{y+\alpha}P$ and using the $\mathcal{RS} = \{P, \alpha P, \alpha^2 P, ..., \alpha^{q(\lambda)}\}$, with $|\mathcal{Y}_V| \leq q(\lambda)$, can compute $g(x)P$ and hence $\frac{1}{y+\alpha}P = r^{-1}(C - g(\alpha)P)$, contradicting the $t-$SDH assumption.

Non-membership Witnesses. Suppose there exists a probabilistic polynomial time adversary $\mathcal{A}$ that with respect to an (non-trivial) accumulator state $(V, \mathcal{Y}_V)$ outputs with a non-negligible probability a non-membership witness $(C, d) \in G_1 \times (\mathbb{Z}/p\mathbb{Z})^*$ for an element $y \in \mathcal{Y}_V$. Then $(y + \alpha)C = f_V(\alpha)P - dP$. Now, since $(y + x)|f_V(x)$ we have that $(y + x) \nmid f_V(x) - d$ for any $d \neq 0$. Thus, similarly as done before, $\mathcal{A}$ uses the polynomial extended Euclidean algorithm to compute $g(x) \in \mathbb{Z}/p\mathbb{Z}[x]$ of degree $|\mathcal{Y}_V| - 1$ and $r \in (\mathbb{Z}/p\mathbb{Z})^*$ such that $f_V(x) - d = g(x) \cdot (y + x) + r$. Therefore, $C = g(\alpha)P + \frac{r}{y+\alpha}P$ and, using the $\mathcal{RS}$, $\mathcal{A}$ can compute $\frac{1}{y+\alpha}P = r^{-1}(C - g(\alpha)P)$, contradicting the $t-$SDH assumption.

$\square$

References

1. Adj, G., Menezes, A., Oliveira, T., Rodríguez-Henríquez, F.: Computing discrete logarithms in $\mathbb{F}_{3^{6 \cdot 137}}$ and $\mathbb{F}_{3^{6 \cdot 163}}$ using magma. In: Koç, Ç.K., Mesnager, S., Savaş, E. (eds.) Arithmetic of Finite Fields, pp. 3–22. Springer International Publishing, Cham (2015)

2. Aranha, D.F., Gouvêa, C.P.L., Markmann, T., Wahby, R.S., Liao, K.: RELIC is an Efficient LIbrary for Cryptography. https://github.com/relic-toolkit/relic

3. Aranha, D.F., Fuentes-Castañeda, L., Knapp, E., Menezes, A., Rodríguez-Henríquez, F.: Implementing pairings at the 192-bit security level. In: Abdalla, M., Lange, T. (eds.) Pairing 2012. LNCS, vol. 7708, pp. 177–195. Springer, Heidelberg (2013). https://doi.org/10.1007/978-3-642-36334-4_11

4. Au, M.H., Tsang, P.P., Susilo, W., Mu, Y.: Dynamic universal accumulators for DDH groups and their application to attribute-based anonymous credential systems. In: Fischlin, M. (ed.) CT-RSA 2009. LNCS, vol. 5473, pp. 295–308. Springer, Heidelberg (2009). https://doi.org/10.1007/978-3-642-00862-7_20

5. Baldimtsi, F., et al.: Accumulators with applications to anonymity-preserving revocation. In: 2017 IEEE European Symposium on Security and Privacy, EuroS&P 2017, Paris, France, 26–28 April 2017, pp. 301–315. IEEE (2017). https://doi.org/10.1109/EuroSP.2017.13

6. Barić, N., Pfitzmann, B.: Collision-free accumulators and fail-stop signature schemes without trees. In: Fumy, W. (ed.) EUROCRYPT 1997. LNCS, vol. 1233, pp. 480–494. Springer, Heidelberg (1997). https://doi.org/10.1007/3-540-69053-0_33

7. Benaloh, J., de Mare, M.: One-way accumulators: a decentralized alternative to digital signatures. In: Helleseth, T. (ed.) EUROCRYPT 1993. LNCS, vol. 765, pp. 274–285. Springer, Heidelberg (1994). https://doi.org/10.1007/3-540-48285-7_24

8. Biryukov, A., Udovenko, A., Vitto, G.: Cryptanalysis of a dynamic universal accumulator over bilinear groups. In: Paterson, K.G. (ed.) CT-RSA 2021. LNCS, vol. 12704, pp. 276–298. Springer, Cham (2021). https://doi.org/10.1007/978-3-030-75539-3_12

9. Boneh, D., Boyen, X.: Short signatures without random Oracles. In: Cachin, C., Camenisch, J.L. (eds.) EUROCRYPT 2004. LNCS, vol. 3027, pp. 56–73. Springer, Heidelberg (2004). https://doi.org/10.1007/978-3-540-24676-3_4

10. Boneh, D., Boyen, X.: Short signatures without random Oracles and the SDH assumption in bilinear groups. J. Cryptol. **21**(2), 149–177 (2007). https://doi.org/10.1007/s00145-007-9005-7

11. Boneh, D., Bünz, B., Fisch, B.: Batching techniques for accumulators with applications to IOPs and stateless blockchains. In: Boldyreva, A., Micciancio, D. (eds.) CRYPTO 2019. LNCS, vol. 11692, pp. 561–586. Springer, Cham (2019). https://doi.org/10.1007/978-3-030-26948-7_20

12. Boneh, D., Corrigan-Gibbs, H.: Bivariate polynomials modulo composites and their applications. In: Sarkar, P., Iwata, T. (eds.) ASIACRYPT 2014. LNCS, vol. 8873, pp. 42–62. Springer, Heidelberg (2014). https://doi.org/10.1007/978-3-662-45611-8_3

13. Buldas, A., Laud, P., Lipmaa, H.: Accountable certificate management using undeniable attestations. In: Gritzalis, D., Jajodia, S., Samarati, P. (eds.) ACM CCS 2000, pp. 9–17. ACM Press, Athens, Greece, 1–4 November 2000. https://doi.org/10.1145/352600.352604

14. Buldas, A., Laud, P., Lipmaa, H.: Eliminating counterevidence with applications to accountable certificate management. J. Comput. Secur. **10**(3), 273–296 (2002)

15. Camacho, P., Hevia, A.: On the impossibility of batch update for cryptographic accumulators. In: Abdalla, M., Barreto, P.S.L.M. (eds.) LATINCRYPT 2010. LNCS, vol. 6212, pp. 178–188. Springer, Heidelberg (2010). https://doi.org/10.1007/978-3-642-14712-8_11

16. Camacho, P., Hevia, A., Kiwi, M., Opazo, R.: Strong accumulators from collision-resistant hashing. In: Wu, T.-C., Lei, C.-L., Rijmen, V., Lee, D.-T. (eds.) ISC 2008. LNCS, vol. 5222, pp. 471–486. Springer, Heidelberg (2008). https://doi.org/10.1007/978-3-540-85886-7_32

17. Camenisch, J., Kohlweiss, M., Soriente, C.: An accumulator based on bilinear maps and efficient revocation for anonymous credentials. In: Jarecki, S., Tsudik, G. (eds.) PKC 2009. LNCS, vol. 5443, pp. 481–500. Springer, Heidelberg (2009). https://doi.org/10.1007/978-3-642-00468-1_27

18. Camenisch, J., Lysyanskaya, A.: Dynamic accumulators and application to efficient revocation of anonymous credentials. In: Yung, M. (ed.) CRYPTO 2002. LNCS, vol. 2442, pp. 61–76. Springer, Heidelberg (2002). https://doi.org/10.1007/3-540-45708-9_5

19. Chang, Y.-C., Lu, C.-J.: Oblivious polynomial evaluation and oblivious neural learning. In: Boyd, C. (ed.) ASIACRYPT 2001. LNCS, vol. 2248, pp. 369–384. Springer, Heidelberg (2001). https://doi.org/10.1007/3-540-45682-1_22

20. Damgård, I., Triandopoulos, N.: Supporting non-membership proofs with bilinear-map accumulators. Cryptology ePrint Archive, Report 2008/538 (2008). https://eprint.iacr.org/2008/538

21. Fiat, A., Shamir, A.: How To prove yourself: practical solutions to identification and signature problems. In: Odlyzko, A.M. (ed.) CRYPTO 1986. LNCS, vol. 263, pp. 186–194. Springer, Heidelberg (1987). https://doi.org/10.1007/3-540-47721-7_12

22. Galbraith, S.D., Paterson, K.G., Smart, N.P.: Pairings for cryptographers. Discrete Appl. Math. **156**(16), 3113–3121 (2008). https://doi.org/10.1016/j.dam.2007.12.010

23. Groth, J., Sahai, A.: Efficient non-interactive proof systems for bilinear groups. In: Smart, N. (ed.) EUROCRYPT 2008. LNCS, vol. 4965, pp. 415–432. Springer, Heidelberg (2008). https://doi.org/10.1007/978-3-540-78967-3_24

24. Hazay, C.: Oblivious polynomial evaluation and secure set-intersection from algebraic PRFs. In: Dodis, Y., Nielsen, J.B. (eds.) TCC 2015. LNCS, vol. 9015, pp. 90–120. Springer, Heidelberg (2015). https://doi.org/10.1007/978-3-662-46497-7_4

25. Kleinjung, T., Wesolowski, B.: Discrete logarithms in quasi-polynomial time in finite fields of fixed characteristic. J. Am. Math. Soc. 44 (2021). https://doi.org/10.1090/jams/985

26. Li, J., Li, N., Xue, R.: Universal accumulators with efficient Nonmembership proofs. In: Katz, J., Yung, M. (eds.) ACNS 2007. LNCS, vol. 4521, pp. 253–269. Springer, Heidelberg (2007). https://doi.org/10.1007/978-3-540-72738-5_17

27. Lipmaa, H.: Secure accumulators from Euclidean rings without trusted setup. In: Bao, F., Samarati, P., Zhou, J. (eds.) ACNS 2012. LNCS, vol. 7341, pp. 224–240. Springer, Heidelberg (2012). https://doi.org/10.1007/978-3-642-31284-7_14

28. Merkle, R.C.: A certified digital signature. In: Brassard, G. (ed.) CRYPTO 1989. LNCS, vol. 435, pp. 218–238. Springer, New York (1990). https://doi.org/10.1007/0-387-34805-0_21

29. Naor, M., Pinkas, B.: Oblivious polynomial evaluation. SIAM J. Comput. **35**(5), 1254–1281 (2006). https://doi.org/10.1137/S0097539704383633

30. Nguyen, L.: Accumulators from bilinear pairings and applications. In: Menezes, A. (ed.) CT-RSA 2005. LNCS, vol. 3376, pp. 275–292. Springer, Heidelberg (2005). https://doi.org/10.1007/978-3-540-30574-3_19

31. Sander, T.: Efficient accumulators without trapdoor extended abstract. In: Varadharajan, V., Mu, Y. (eds.) ICICS 1999. LNCS, vol. 1726, pp. 252–262. Springer, Heidelberg (1999). https://doi.org/10.1007/978-3-540-47942-0_21

32. Schoenmakers, B.: Lecture notes cryptographic protocols (2020). https://www.win.tue.nl/~berry/CryptographicProtocols/LectureNotes.pdf

33. Shoup, V.: Lower bounds for discrete logarithms and related problems. In: Fumy, W. (ed.) EUROCRYPT 1997. LNCS, vol. 1233, pp. 256–266. Springer, Heidelberg (1997). https://doi.org/10.1007/3-540-69053-0_18

Adaptively Secure Laconic Function Evaluation for $\mathbf{NC}^1$

Răzvan Roşie[(✉)]

JAO, Luxembourg, Luxembourg
rosie@jao.eu

Abstract. Laconic Function Evaluation (LFE) protocols, introduced by Quach *et al.* in FOCS'18, allow two parties to evaluate functions *laconically*, in the following manner: first, Alice sends a compressed "digest" of some function – say $\mathscr{C}$ – to Bob. Second, Bob constructs a ciphertext for his input M given the digest. Third, Alice, after getting the ciphertext from Bob and in full knowledge of her circuit, can recover $\mathscr{C}(M)$ and (ideally) nothing more about Bob's message. The protocol is said to be *laconic* if the sizes of the digest, common reference string (crs) and ciphertext are much smaller than the circuit size $|\mathscr{C}|$.

Quach *et al.* put forward a construction of laconic function evaluation for general circuits under the learning with errors (LWE) assumption (with sub-exponential approximation factors), where all parameters grow polynomially with the depth but not the size of the circuit. Under LWE, their construction achieves the restricted notion of *selective* security where Bob's input M must be chosen non-adaptively before even the crs is known.

In this work, we provide the first construction of LFE for NC^1, which satisfies *adaptive* security from the ring learning with errors assumption (with polynomial approximation factors). The construction is based on the functional encryption scheme by Agrawal and Rosen (TCC 2017).

Keywords: Functional encryption · Laconic function evaluation · Laconic oblivious transfer

1 Introduction

Laconic Function Evaluation (LFE) is a novel primitive that was introduced in a recent work by Quach *et al.* [14]. Intuitively, the notion proposes a setting where two parties want to evaluate a function $\mathscr{C}$ in the following manner: Alice computes a "digest" of the circuit representation of $\mathscr{C}$ and sends this digest to Bob; Bob computes a ciphertext CT for his input M using the received digest and sends this back to Alice; finally Alice is able to compute the value $\mathscr{C}(M)$ in the clear without learning anything else about Bob's input. Put differently, an LFE protocol is a type of secure multi-party computation[4,9,11] that is Bob-optimized.

© The Author(s), under exclusive license to Springer Nature Switzerland AG 2022
S. D. Galbraith (Ed.): CT-RSA 2022, LNCS 13161, pp. 427–450, 2022.
https://doi.org/10.1007/978-3-030-95312-6_18

The work of [14] provided an elegant construction of laconic function evaluation for all circuits from LWE. In their construction, the size of the digest, the complexity of the encryption algorithm and the size of the ciphertext only scale with the depth but not the size of the circuit. However, under LWE, their construction only achieves the restricted notion of *selective* security where Bob's input M must be chosen non-adaptively before even the crs is known. Moreover they must rely on LWE with sub-exponential modulus to noise ratio, which implies that the underlying lattice problem must be hard for sub-exponential approximation factors. Achieving adaptive security from LWE was left as an explicit open problem in their work.

In this work, we provide a new construction of LFE for NC^1 circuits that achieves adaptive security. Our construction relies on the ring learning with errors (RLWE) assumption with polynomial modulus to noise ratio. We start with the construction by Agrawal and Rosen for functional encryption for NC^1 circuits [3] and *simplify* it to achieve LFE. To achieve a laconic digest, we make use of the *laconic* oblivious transfer (LOT) primitive [8,15]. Our main result may be summarized as follows.

Theorem 1 (LFE for NC^1 – Informal). *Assuming the hardness of RLWE with polynomial approximation factors, there exists an adaptively-secure LFE protocol for NC^1.*

The authors of [14] also studied the relations between LFE and other primitives, and in particular showed that LFE implies succinct functional encryption (FE) [6,13]. Functional encryption is a generalisation of public key encryption in which the secret key corresponds to a function, say f, rather than a user. The ciphertext corresponds to an input $\mathbf{x}$ from the domain of f. Decryption allows to recover $f(\mathbf{x})$ and nothing else. Succinctness means that the size of the ciphertext in the scheme depends only on the depth of the supported circuit rather than on its size [1,3,10]. One can apply, as well, the LFE to FE compiler of [14] to our new, adaptively secure LFE for NC^1, and obtain an alternative variant of adaptively secure, succinct FE for NC^1.

Technical Overview. The techniques that we use exploit the algebraic structure in the construction by Agrawal and Rosen [3]. Say that the plaintext $M \in \{0,1\}^k$. If the encryption algorithm obtains a ciphertext $\mathsf{CT} := \{C_1, \ldots, C_k\}$ where each C_i encrypts a single bit M_i of plaintext, in isolation from all different M_j, we say that the ciphertext is decomposable.

The construction supports circuits of depth d and uses a tower of moduli $p_0 < p_1 < \cdots < p_d$. Building upon a particular levelled fully homomorphic encryption scheme (FHE) [7], it encrypts each bit of the plaintext, independently, as follows:

– first multiplication level – the ciphertext consists of a "Regev encoding":

$$C^1 \leftarrow a \cdot s + p_0 \cdot e + M_i \ \in \mathcal{R}_{p_1}$$

where $M_i \in \mathcal{R}_{p_0}$ and $s \leftarrow_\$ \mathcal{R}_{p_1}$ is a fixed secret term; $a \leftarrow_\$ \mathcal{R}_{p_1}$ is provided through public parameters, while $e \leftarrow_\chi \mathcal{R}_{p_1}$ is the noise;

- next multiplication level – two ciphertexts are provided under the same s:

$$a' \cdot s + p_1 \cdot e' + C^1 \in \mathcal{R}_{p_2} \quad \text{and} \quad a'' \cdot s + p_1 \cdot e'' + (C^1 \cdot s) \in \mathcal{R}_{p_2}.$$

The computational pattern is repeated recursively up to d multiplication levels, and then for every bit of the input.

- an addition layer is interleaved between any two multiplication layers C^i and C^{i+1}: essentially it "replicates" ciphertexts in C^i and uses its modulus p_i.
- the public key (the "$\vec{a}$"s) corresponding to the last layer are also the master public key mpk of a linear functional encryption scheme Lin-FE [2].
- the decryption algorithm computes $\mathcal{C}$ obliviously over the ciphertext, layer by layer, finally obtaining:

$$\mathsf{CT}_{\mathcal{C}(M)} \leftarrow \mathcal{C}(M) + \mathsf{Noise} + \mathsf{PK}_{\mathcal{C}} \cdot s \tag{1}$$

where $\mathsf{PK}_{\mathcal{C}}$ is a "functional public key" that depends only on the public key and the circuit $\mathcal{C}$, and can be viewed as a succinct representation of $\mathcal{C}$. The term $\mathsf{PK}_{\mathcal{C}} \cdot s$ occurring in (1) will be cancelled using the functional key $\mathsf{sk}_{\mathcal{C}}$, in order to recover $\mathcal{C}(M)$ plus noise (which can be modded out).

Our Technique. The crux idea when building an LFE is to set the ciphertext to be essentially the data-dependent part of the FE ciphertext, while the digest to be $\mathsf{PK}_{\mathcal{C}}$. Concretely, the mpk will form the crs. Whenever a circuit $\mathcal{C}$ is to be compressed, a circuit-dependent public value – denoted $\mathsf{PK}_{\mathcal{C}}$ – is returned as *digest*. The receiver of $\mathsf{PK}_{\mathcal{C}}$ samples its own secret s and computes recursively the Regev encodings (seen above) as well as $\mathsf{PK}_{\mathcal{C}} \cdot s + \mathsf{Noise}'$ (the $\mathsf{sk}_{\mathcal{C}}$-dependent term). These terms suffice to recover $\mathcal{C}(M)$ from (1) on the sender's side.

Our construction departs significantly from the approach in [14]. In short, the original work makes use of generic transforms for obtaining attribute-based LFEs (AB-LFEs), obtaining AB-LFEs supporting multi-bit outputs, using ideas behind the transform of [10] to hide the "attribute" in AB-LFE and compressing the digests via laconic oblivious transfer [8]. On the other hand, we do not need to go via AB-LFE, making our transformation conceptually simpler. Moreover, by relying on the adaptive security of the underlying FE scheme that we use, we obtain adaptive security.

Towards Short Digests. As per [14], we use the *laconic oblivious transfer* protocol in the following way: after getting the digest in the form of $\mathsf{PK}_{\mathcal{C}}$, we apply a second compression round, which yields:

$$(\mathsf{digest}_{\mathsf{LOT}}, \hat{\mathbf{D}}) \leftarrow \mathsf{LOT}.\mathsf{Compress}(\mathsf{crs}_{\mathsf{LOT}}, \mathsf{PK}_{\mathcal{C}}) .$$

We stress that both compression methods used are deterministic. Put differently, at any point in time, the sender, in full knowledge of her circuit representation, can recreate the digest. On the receiver's side, instead of following the technique proposed in [14] – garbling an entire FHE decryption circuit and encrypting under an ABE the homomorphic ciphertext and the labels – we garble only the circuit that provides

$$\mathsf{PK}_{\mathscr{C}} \cdot s + p_{d-1} \cdot \mathsf{Noise} \ ,$$

while leaving the actual ciphertext intact. The advantage of such an approach resides into its conceptual simplicity, as the size of the *core* ciphertext Bob sends back to Alice remains manageable for simple $\mathscr{C}$, and is not suppressed by the size of the garbling scheme.

Roadmap. Section 2 puts forth the algorithmic and mathematical conventions to be adopted throughout this work, as well as the definitions of primitives we use herein. In Sect. 3 we review the decomposable FE scheme proposed by Agrawal and Rosen in [3]. In Sect. 4, we introduce a new LFE scheme for NC^1 circuits, and show in Sect. 5 how to combine it with laconic oblivious transfer in order to achieve a scheme with laconic digests.

2   Background

Algorithmic and Mathematical Notation. We denote the security parameter by $\lambda \in \mathbb{N}^*$ and we assume it is implicitly given to all algorithms in the unary representation 1^λ. An algorithm is equivalent to a Turing machine. Algorithms are assumed to be randomized unless stated otherwise; PPT stands for "probabilistic polynomial-time" in the security parameter (rather than the total length of its inputs). Given a randomized algorithm $\mathcal{A}$ we write the action of running $\mathcal{A}$ on input(s) $(1^\lambda, x_1, \dots)$ with uniform random coins r and assigning the output(s) to $(y_1, \dots)$ by $(y_1, \dots) \leftarrow_{\$} \mathcal{A}(1^\lambda, x_1, \dots ; r)$. When $\mathcal{A}$ is given oracle access to some procedure $\mathcal{O}$, we write $\mathcal{A}^{\mathcal{O}}$. For a finite set S, we denote its cardinality by $|S|$ and the action of sampling an element x uniformly at random from X by $x \leftarrow_{\$} X$. We let bold variables such as $\mathbf{w}$ represent column vectors. Similarly, bold capitals stand for matrices (e.g. $\mathbf{A}$). A subscript $\mathbf{A}_{i,j}$ indicates an entry in the matrix. We overload notation for the power function and write α^u to denote that variable α is associated to some level u in a levelled construction. For any variable $k \in \mathbb{N}^*$, we define $[k] := \{1, \dots, k\}$. A real-valued function $\mathrm{NEGL}(\lambda)$ is negligible if $\mathrm{NEGL}(\lambda) \in \mathcal{O}(\lambda^{-\omega(1)})$. We denote the set of all negligible functions by NEGL. Throughout the paper $\perp$ stands for a special error symbol. We use $||$ to denote concatenation. For completeness, we recall standard algorithmic and cryptographic primitives to be used.

Circuit Representation. We consider circuits as the main model of computation for representing (abstract) functions. Unless stated otherwise, we use k to denote the input length of the circuit and d for its depth. As we assume that circuits have a tree like structure we denote as *subcircuits* the corresponding subtrees.

2.1   Computational Hardness Assumptions

The Learning With Errors (LWE) search problem [16] asks to find the secret vector **s** over $\mathbb{F}_q^\ell$ given a polynomial-size set of tuples $(\mathbf{A}, \mathbf{A} \cdot \mathbf{s} + \mathbf{e})$, where $\mathbf{A}$ stands for a randomly sampled matrix over $\mathbb{F}_q^{k \times \ell}$, while $\mathbf{e} \in \mathbb{F}^k$ represents a small error vector sampled from an appropriate distribution χ. In rough terms, the decisional version of the LWE problems, asks any PPT adversary to distinguish between the uniform distribution and one induced by the LWE tuples.

Definition 1 (Learning With Errors). *Let $\mathcal{A}$ stand for a PPT adversary. The advantage of $\mathcal{A}$ in distinguishing between the following two distributions is negligible:*

$$\mathsf{Adv}_{\mathcal{A}}^{\mathsf{LWE}}(\lambda) := \left| \Pr[1 \leftarrow \mathcal{A}(1^\lambda, \mathbf{A}, \mathbf{u})] - \Pr[1 \leftarrow \mathcal{A}(1^\lambda, \mathbf{A}, \mathbf{A} \cdot \mathbf{s} + \mathbf{e})] \right| \in \mathrm{NEGL}(\lambda)$$

where $\mathbf{s} \leftarrow_\$ \mathbb{Z}_q^\ell$, $\mathbf{A} \leftarrow_\$ \mathbb{Z}_q^{k \times \ell}$, $\mathbf{e} \leftarrow_\chi \mathbb{Z}_q^k$ *and* $\mathbf{u} \leftarrow_\$ \mathbb{Z}_q^k$.

Later, Lyubashevsky, Peikert and Regev [12] proposed a ring version. Let $\mathcal{R} := \mathbb{Z}[X]/(X^n + 1)$ for n a power of 2, while $\mathcal{R}_q := \mathcal{R}/q\mathcal{R}$ for a safe prime q satisfying $q \equiv 1 \bmod 2n$.

Definition 2 (Ring LWE). *For $s \leftarrow_\$ \mathcal{R}_q$, given a polynomial number of samples that are either: (1) all of the form $(a, a \cdot s + e)$ for some $a \leftarrow_\$ \mathcal{R}_q$ and $e \leftarrow_\chi \mathcal{R}_q$ or (2) all uniformly sampled over $\mathcal{R}_q^2$; the (decision) $\mathsf{RLWE}_{q,\phi,\chi}$ states that a PPT-bounded adversary can distinguish between the two settings only with negligible advantage.*

2.2   Garbling Schemes

Garbling schemes were introduced by Yao in its pioneering work [18,19], to solve the famous "Millionaires' Problem". Since then, garbled circuits became a standard building-block for many cryptographic primitives. Their definition follows.

Definition 3 (Garbling Scheme). *Let $\{\mathscr{C}_k\}_\lambda$ be a family of circuits taking as input k bits. A garbling scheme is a tuple of PPT algorithms $(\mathsf{Garble}, \mathsf{Enc}, \mathsf{Eval})$ such that:*

- *$(\Gamma, \mathsf{sk}) \leftarrow_\$ \mathsf{Garble}(1^\lambda, \mathscr{C})$: takes as input the unary representation of the security parameter λ and a circuit $\mathscr{C} \in \{\mathscr{C}_k\}_\lambda$; outputs a garbled circuit Γ and a secret key sk.*
- *$c \leftarrow_\$ \mathsf{Enc}(\mathsf{sk}, x)$: $x \in \{0,1\}^k$ is given as input, as well as the secret key sk; the encoding procedure returns an encoding c.*
- *$\mathscr{C}(x) \leftarrow \mathsf{Eval}(\Gamma, c)$: the evaluation procedure receives as inputs a garbled circuit and an encoding of x, returning $\mathscr{C}(x)$.*

*We say that a garbling scheme Γ is **correct** if for all $\mathscr{C} : \{0,1\}^k \to \{0,1\}^l$ and for all $x \in \{0,1\}^k$ we have that:*

$$\Pr \left[\mathscr{C}(x) = y \; \middle| \; \begin{matrix} (\Gamma, \mathsf{sk}) \leftarrow_\$ \mathsf{GS.Garble}(1^\lambda, \mathscr{C}) \wedge \\ y \leftarrow \mathsf{GS.Eval}(\Gamma, \mathsf{GS.Enc}(\mathsf{sk}, x)) \end{matrix} \right] = 1 \ .$$

Yao's Garbled Circuit [18]. One of the most pre-eminent types of garbling schemes is represented by the original proposal of Yao, which considers a family of circuits of n input wires and outputting a single bit. In his proposal, a circuit's secret key can be viewed as two labels (L_i^0, L_i^1) for each input wire, where $i \in [n]$. The evaluation of the circuit at point x corresponds to an evaluation of $\mathsf{Eval}(\Gamma, (L_1^{x_1}, \ldots, L_n^{x_n}))$, where x_i is the ith bit of x,—thus the encoding $c :=$ $(L_1^{x_1}, \ldots, L_n^{x_n})$.

2.3   Functional Encryption Scheme - Public-Key Setting

We define the notion of functional encryption[6] in the public key-settings and provide a simulation-based security definition. Roughly speaking, the semantic security of the functional encryption scheme guarantees the adversary cannot learn more on M as by knowing only $\mathscr{C}(M)$.

Definition 4 (Functional Encryption - Public Key Setting). *Let $\mathcal{F} = \{\mathcal{F}_\lambda\}_{\lambda \in N}$ be an ensemble, where $\mathcal{F}_\lambda$ is a finite collections of functions $\mathscr{C} : \mathcal{M}_\lambda \to Y_\lambda$. A functional encryption scheme FE in the public-key setting consists of a tuple of PPT algorithms $(\mathsf{Setup}, \mathsf{KeyGen}, \mathsf{Enc}, \mathsf{Dec})$ such that:*

- *$(\mathsf{msk}, \mathsf{mpk}) \leftarrow_\$ \mathsf{FE.Setup}(1^\lambda)$: takes as input the unary representation of the security parameter λ and outputs a pair of master secret/public keys.*
- *$\mathsf{sk}_\mathscr{C} \leftarrow_\$ \mathsf{FE.KeyGen}(\mathsf{msk}, \mathscr{C})$: given the master secret key and a function $\mathscr{C}$, the (randomized) key-generation procedure outputs a corresponding $\mathsf{sk}_\mathscr{C}$.*
- *$\mathsf{CT} \leftarrow_\$ \mathsf{FE.Enc}(\mathsf{mpk}, \mathsf{M})$: the randomized encryption procedure encrypts the plaintext M with respect to mpk.*
- *$\mathsf{FE.Dec}(\mathsf{CT}, \mathsf{sk}_\mathscr{C})$: decrypts the ciphertext CT using the functional key $\mathsf{sk}_\mathscr{C}$ in order to learn a valid message $\mathscr{C}(\mathsf{M})$ or a special symbol $\perp$, in case the decryption procedure fails.*

We say that FE satisfies correctness if for all $\mathscr{C} : \mathcal{M}_\lambda \to Y_\lambda$ we have that:

$$\Pr\left[y = \mathscr{C}(M) \;\middle|\; \begin{array}{l} (\mathsf{msk}, \mathsf{mpk}) \leftarrow_\$ \mathsf{FE.Setup}(1^\lambda) \wedge \\ \mathsf{sk}_\mathscr{C} \leftarrow_\$ \mathsf{FE.KeyGen}(\mathsf{msk}, \mathscr{C}) \wedge \\ \mathsf{CT} \leftarrow_\$ \mathsf{FE.Enc}(\mathsf{mpk}, \mathsf{M}) \wedge \\ y \leftarrow \mathsf{FE.Dec}(\mathsf{CT}, \mathsf{sk}_\mathscr{C}) \end{array}\right] = 1 \; .$$

A public-key functional encryption scheme FE is semantically secure if there exists a stateful PPT simulator $\mathcal{S}$ such that for any PPT adversary $\mathcal{A}$,

$$\mathsf{Adv}_{\mathcal{A}, \mathsf{FE}}^{\mathsf{FULL\text{-}SIM\text{-}FE}}(\lambda) := \left| \Pr[\mathsf{FULL\text{-}SIM\text{-}FE}_{\mathsf{FE}}^{\mathcal{A}}(\lambda) = 1] - \frac{1}{2} \right|$$

is negligible, where the $\mathsf{FULL\text{-}SIM\text{-}FE}$ experiment is described in Fig. 1 (left).

FULL-SIM-FE$_{\mathsf{FE}}^{\mathcal{A}}(\lambda)$:	FULL-SIM-LFE$_{\mathsf{LFE}}^{\mathcal{A}}(\lambda)$:
$b \leftarrow_\$ \{0, 1\}$	$b \leftarrow_\$ \{0, 1\}$
$(\mathsf{msk}, \mathsf{mpk}) \leftarrow_\$ \mathsf{FE.Setup}(1^\lambda)$	$(1^k, 1^d) \leftarrow_\$ \mathcal{A}(1^\lambda)$
$\mathscr{C} \leftarrow \mathcal{A}(\mathsf{mpk})$	$\mathsf{crs} \leftarrow_\$ \mathsf{LFE.crsGen}(1^\lambda, 1^k, 1^d)$
$\mathsf{sk}_{\mathscr{C}} \leftarrow \mathsf{FE.KeyGen}(\mathsf{msk}, \mathscr{C})$	$(M^*, \mathscr{C}) \leftarrow_\$ \mathcal{A}(\mathsf{crs})$
$M^* \leftarrow \mathcal{A}(\mathsf{mpk}, \mathsf{sk}_{\mathscr{C}})$	$\mathsf{digest}_{\mathscr{C}} \leftarrow_\$ \mathsf{LFE.Compress}(\mathsf{crs}, \mathscr{C})$
if $b = 0$:	if $b = 0$:
$\quad$ CT$^* \leftarrow_\$ \mathsf{FE.Enc}(\mathsf{mpk}, M^*)$	$\quad$ CT$^* \leftarrow_\$ \mathsf{LFE.Enc}(\mathsf{crs}, \mathsf{digest}_{\mathscr{C}}, M^*)$
else:	else
$\quad$ CT$^* \leftarrow \mathcal{S}(\mathsf{mpk}, \mathsf{sk}_{\mathscr{C}}, \mathscr{C}, \mathscr{C}(M^*))$	$\quad$ CT$^* \leftarrow_\$ \mathcal{S}(\mathsf{crs}, \mathscr{C}, \mathsf{digest}_{\mathscr{C}}, \mathscr{C}(M^*))$
$b' \leftarrow_\$ \mathcal{A}(\mathsf{CT}^*)$	$b' \leftarrow_\$ \mathcal{A}(\mathsf{CT}^*)$
return $b' = b$	return $b = b'$

Fig. 1. Left: FULL-SIM-FE-security defined for a functional encryption scheme in the public-key setting. Right: the simulation security experiment FULL-SIM-LFE defined for a laconic function evaluation scheme LFE.

2.4   Laconic Oblivious Transfer

Definition 5 (LOT). *A Laconic Oblivious Transfer (LOT) scheme consists of a tuple of* PPT *algorithms* (crsGen, Compress, Enc, Dec) *with the following functionality:*

- crs $\leftarrow_\$$ crsGen(1^λ): *takes as input the security parameter λ in unary and outputs a common reference string* crs.
- (digest, $\hat{\mathbf{D}}$) $\leftarrow_\$$ Compress(crs, $\mathbf{D}$): *given a database $\mathbf{D}$ and the* crs, *outputs a digest of the circuit* digest *as well as a state of the database $\hat{\mathbf{D}}$.*
- CT $\leftarrow_\$$ Enc(crs, digest, ℓ, M_0, M_1): *the randomized encryption algorithm takes as input the common reference string* crs, *the digest* digest, *an index position ℓ, and two messages; it returns a ciphertext* CT.
- $M \leftarrow$ Dec(crs, digest, $\hat{\mathbf{D}}$, CT, ℓ): *the decryption algorithm takes as input $\hat{\mathbf{D}}$, an index location ℓ the digest* digest *and the common reference string* crs *and outputs a message M.*

We require an LOT *to satisfy the following properties:*

- **Correctness:** *for all $(M_0, M_1) \in \mathcal{M} \times \mathcal{M}$, for all $\mathbf{D} \in \{0, 1\}^k$ and for any index $\ell \in [k]$ we have:*

$$
\Pr \left[M = M_{\mathbf{D}[\ell]} \ \middle| \ \begin{array}{l} \mathsf{crs} \leftarrow_\$ \mathsf{LOT.crsGen}(1^\lambda, 1^k) \wedge \\ (\mathsf{digest}, \hat{\mathbf{D}}) \leftarrow_\$ \mathsf{LOT.Compress}(\mathsf{crs}, \mathbf{D}) \wedge \\ \mathsf{CT} \leftarrow_\$ \mathsf{LOT.Enc}(\mathsf{crs}, \mathsf{digest}, \ell, M_0, M_1) \wedge \\ M \leftarrow \mathsf{LOT.Dec}(\mathsf{crs}, \mathsf{digest}, \hat{\mathbf{D}}, \mathsf{CT}, \ell) \end{array} \right] = 1 \ .
$$

- **Laconic Digest:** *the length of the digest is a fixed polynomial in the security parameter λ, independent of the size of the database $\mathbf{D}$.*

– **Sender Privacy against Semi-Honest Adversaries:** *there exists a* PPT *simulator* S *such that for a correctly generated* crs *the following two distributions are computationally indistinguishable:*

$$\Big| \Pr\left[\mathcal{A}(\text{crs}, \text{Enc}(\text{crs}, \text{digest}, \ell, M_0, M_1))\right] - \Pr\left[\mathcal{A}(\text{crs}, S(\text{crs}, \mathbf{D}, \ell, M_{\mathbf{D}[\ell]}))\right] \Big| \in \text{Negl}(\lambda)$$

2.5   Laconic Function Evaluation

We described the motivation behind LFE in Sect. 1. We proceed with its definition from [14].

Definition 6 (Laconic Function Evaluation [14]). *A laconic function evaluation scheme* LFE *for a class of circuits* $\mathfrak{C}_\lambda$ *consists of four algorithms* (crsGen, Compress, Enc, Dec)*:*

– crs←$ LFE.crsGen($1^\lambda, 1^k, 1^d$): *assuming the input size and the depth of the circuit in the given class are k and d, a common reference string* crs *of appropriate length is generated. We assume that* crs *is implicitly given to all algorithms.*
– digest$_\mathscr{C}$ ← LFE.Compress(crs, $\mathscr{C}$): *the compression algorithm takes a description of the circuit $\mathscr{C}$ and produces a digest* digest$_\mathscr{C}$.
– CT←$ LFE.Enc(crs, digest$_\mathscr{C}$, M): *takes as input the message M as well as the digest of $\mathscr{C}$ and produces a ciphertext* CT.
– LFE.Dec(crs, CT, $\mathscr{C}$): *if the parameters are correctly generated, the decryption procedure recovers $\mathscr{C}(M)$, given the ciphertext encrypting M and circuit $\mathscr{C}$ or a special symbol $\perp$, in case the decryption procedure fails.*

We require the LFE *scheme to achieve the following properties:*

– **Correctness** - *for all $\mathscr{C} : \{0,1\}^k \to \{0,1\}^\ell$ of depth d and for all $M \in \{0,1\}^k$ we have:*

$$\Pr\left[y = \mathscr{C}(M) \,\middle|\, \begin{array}{l} \text{crs}\leftarrow\!\!{\scriptstyle\$}\, \mathsf{LFE.crsGen}(1^\lambda, 1^k, 1^d) \wedge \\ \text{digest}_\mathscr{C} \leftarrow \mathsf{LFE.Compress}(\text{crs}, \mathscr{C}) \wedge \\ \text{CT}\leftarrow\!\!{\scriptstyle\$}\, \mathsf{LFE.Enc}(\text{crs}, \text{digest}_\mathscr{C}, M) \wedge \\ y \leftarrow \mathsf{LFE.Dec}(\text{crs}, \mathscr{C}, \text{CT}) \end{array} \right] = 1 \ .$$

– **Security:** *there exists a* PPT *simulator S such that for any stateful* PPT *adversary $\mathcal{A}$ we have:*

$$\mathsf{Adv}^{\mathsf{FULL\text{-}SIM\text{-}LFE}}_{\mathcal{A},\mathsf{LFE}}(\lambda) := \left| \Pr[\mathsf{FULL\text{-}SIM\text{-}LFE}^{\mathcal{A}}_{\mathsf{LFE}}(\lambda) = 1] - \frac{1}{2} \right|$$

is negligible, where FULL-SIM-LFE *is defined in Fig. 1 (right side).*

– **Laconic outputs:** *As per [14, p 13–14], we require the size of digest to be laconic (|digest$_\mathscr{C}$| $\in O(poly(\lambda))$) and we impose succinctness constraints for the sizes of the ciphertext, encryption runtime and common reference string.*

3   Background on the AR17 FE Scheme

Overview. In this section, we recall a construction of functional encryption for circuits with logarithmic depth d in input length [3].

3.1   The AR17 Construction for NC^1

In [3], the authors provided a functional encryption scheme supporting general circuits and a bounded number of functional keys. The first distinctive feature is represented by the supported class of functions, which are now described by arithmetic, rather than Boolean circuits. This is beneficial, as arithmetic circuits natively support multiple output bits. Second, the (input-dependent) ciphertext's size in their construction is succinct [3, Appendix E], as it grows with the depth of the circuit, rather than its size. Third, the ciphertext enjoys decomposability: assuming a plaintext is represented as a vector, each of its k elements gets encrypted independently. We describe the scheme for NC^1 below.

Regev Encodings. We commence by recalling a simple symmetric encryption scheme due to Brakerski and Vaikuntanathan [7]. Let "s" stand for an RLWE secret acting as a secret key, while a and e are the random mask and noise:

$$\begin{aligned} c_1 &\leftarrow a && \in \mathcal{R}_p \\ c_2 &\leftarrow a \cdot s + 2 \cdot e + M && \in \mathcal{R}_p \end{aligned} \tag{2}$$

Recovering the message M (a bit, in this case) is done by subtracting $c_1 \cdot s$ from c_2 and then removing the noise through the "mod 2" operator. This plain scheme comes up with powerful homomorphic properties, and is generalized in [3] to recursively support levels of encodings. Henceforth, we use the name "Regev encoding" for the following map between rings $\mathcal{E}^i : \mathcal{R}_{p_{i-1}} \to \mathcal{R}_{p_i}$, where:

$$\mathcal{E}^i(M) = a^i \cdot s + p_{i-1} \cdot e^i + M \quad \in \mathcal{R}_{p_i} . \tag{3}$$

As a general notation and unless stated, we write as a *superscript* of a variable the *level* to which it is associated.

The NC^1 Construction. To be self-contained in the forthcoming parts, we give an informal specification of AR17's procedures.

Encryption. The encryption procedure samples a RLWE secret s, and computes a Regev encoding for each input $M_i \in \mathcal{R}_{p_0}$ independently. This step produces the following set $\{\mathcal{E}^1(M_i) | \ M_i \in \mathcal{R}_{p_0} \wedge i \in [k]\}$, where $\mathcal{E}^1$ is the encoding mapping $\mathcal{E}^1 : \mathcal{R}_{p_0} \to \mathcal{R}_{p_1}$ defined in Eq. (3). This represents the *Level 1* encoding of M_i. Next, the construction proceeds recursively; the encoding of M_i corresponding to *Level 2* takes the parent node P (in this case P is $\mathcal{E}^1(M_i)$), and obtains on the left branch:

$$\mathcal{E}^2(P) = \mathcal{E}^2(\mathcal{E}^1(M_i)) = a_{1,i}^2 \cdot s + p_1 \cdot e_{1,i}^2 + \left((a_{1,i}^1 \cdot s + p_0 \cdot e_{1,i}^1 + M_i) \cdot s \right) ,$$

while for the right branch:

$$\mathcal{E}^2(P \cdot s) = \mathcal{E}^2(\mathcal{E}^1(M_i) \cdot s) = a_{2,i}^2 \cdot s + p_1 \cdot e_{2,i}^2 + \left((a_{1,i}^1 \cdot s + p_0 \cdot e_{1,i}^1 + M_i) \cdot s \right) ,$$

where $(a_{1,i}^2, a_{2,i}^2) \leftarrow_\$ \mathcal{R}_{p_2}^2$ and noise terms are sampled from a Gaussian distribution: $(e_{1,i}^2, e_{2,i}^2) \leftarrow_\chi \chi_{p_2}^2$. This procedure is executed recursively up to a number of levels – denoted as d – as presented in Fig. 2.

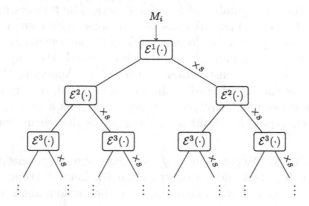

Fig. 2. The tree encoding M_i in a recursive manner corresponds to ciphertext CT_i.

Between any two successive multiplication layers, an *addition* layer is interleaved. This layer replicates the ciphertext in the previous multiplication layer (and uses its modulus). As it brings no new information, we ignore additive layers from our overview. The encoding procedure is applied for each $M_1, \ldots, M_k$. In addition, Level 1 also contains $\mathcal{E}^1(s)$, while Level i (for $2 \le i \le d$) also contains $\mathcal{E}^i(s \cdot s)$. Hitherto, the technique used by the scheme resembles to the ones used in levelled fully homomorphic encryption. We also remind that encodings at Level i are denoted as CT^i and are included in the ciphertext. The high level idea is to compute the function $\mathscr{C}$ obliviously with the help of the encodings.

However, as we are in the FE setting, the ciphertext also contains additional information on s. This is achieved by using a linear functional encryption scheme Lin-FE. Namely, an extra component of the form:

$$\mathbf{d} \leftarrow \mathbf{w} \cdot s + p_{d-1} \cdot \eta \tag{4}$$

is provided as an independent part of the ciphertext, also denoted as $\mathsf{CT}_{\mathsf{ind}}$, where $\eta \leftarrow_\chi \mathcal{R}_{p_d}$ stands for a noisy term and $\mathbf{w}$ is part of mpk. $\mathbf{d}$ is computed once, at top level d.

The **master secret key** of the NC^1 construction is set to be the msk for Lin-FE. The **master public key** consists of the Lin-FE.mpk (the vector $\mathbf{w}$ appended to $\mathbf{a}^d$) as well as of the set of vectors $\{\mathbf{a}^1, \mathbf{a}^2, \ldots, \mathbf{a}^{d-1}\}$ that will be used by each $\mathcal{E}^i$. Once again, we *emphasize* that the vector $\mathbf{a}^d$ from Lin-FE.mpk coincides with the public labelling used by the mapping $\mathcal{E}^d$. It can be easily observed that the dimension of $\mathbf{a}^{i+1}$ follows from a first-order recurrence:

$$|\mathbf{a}^{i+1}| = 2 \cdot |\mathbf{a}^i| + 1 \tag{5}$$

where the initial term (the length of $\mathbf{a}^1$) is set to the length of the input. The extra 1, which is added per each layer is generated by the supplemental encodings of the key-dependent messages $\mathsf{CT}_s := \{\mathcal{E}^1(s), \mathcal{E}^2(s^2), \ldots, \mathcal{E}^d(s^2)\}$, where $s^2 := s \cdot s$, as opposed to a level superscript.

A **functional-key** $\mathsf{sk}_\mathscr{C}$ is issued through the $\mathsf{Lin}\text{-}\mathsf{FE.KGen}$ procedure in the following way: (1) using the circuit representation $\mathscr{C}$ of the considered function as well as the public set of $\{\mathbf{a}^1, \mathbf{a}^2, \ldots, \mathbf{a}^d\}$, a publicly computable value $\mathsf{PK}_\mathscr{C} \leftarrow \mathsf{Eval}_\mathsf{PK}(\mathsf{mpk}, \mathscr{C})$ is obtained by performing $\mathscr{C}$-dependent arithmetic combinations of the values in $\{\mathbf{a}^1, \mathbf{a}^2, \ldots, \mathbf{a}^d\}$. Then, a functional key $\mathsf{sk}_\mathscr{C}$ is issued for $\mathsf{PK}_\mathscr{C}$. The $\mathsf{Eval}_\mathsf{PK}(\mathsf{mpk}, \mathscr{C})$ procedure uses mpk to compute $\mathsf{PK}_\mathscr{C}$.

Similarly, $\mathsf{Eval}_\mathsf{CT}(\mathsf{mpk}, \mathsf{CT}, \mathscr{C})$ computes the value of the function $\mathscr{C}$ obliviously on the ciphertext. Both procedures are defined recursively; that is, to compute $\mathsf{PK}_\mathscr{C}^i$ and $\mathsf{CT}_{\mathscr{C}(\mathbf{x})}^i$ at level i, $\mathsf{PK}_\mathscr{C}^{i-1}$ and $\mathsf{CT}_{\mathscr{C}(\mathbf{x})}^{i-1}$ are needed. For a better understanding of the procedures, we will denote the encoding of $\mathscr{C}^i(\mathbf{x})$[1] by c^i, i.e. $c^i = \mathcal{E}^i(\mathscr{C}^i(\mathbf{x}))$ and the public key or label of an encoding $\mathcal{E}^i(\cdot)$ by $\mathsf{PK}(\mathcal{E}^i(\cdot))$. Due to space constraints, we defer the *full* description of the evaluation algorithms and refer the reader to [3], but provide a *summary* after presenting decryption.

Decryption works by evaluating the circuit of $\mathscr{C}$ (known in plain by the decryptor) over the Regev encodings forming the ciphertext. At level d, the ciphertext obtained via $\mathsf{Eval}_\mathsf{CT}$ has the following structure:

$$\mathsf{CT}_{\mathscr{C}(\mathbf{x})} \leftarrow \mathsf{PK}_\mathscr{C} \cdot s + p_{d-1} \cdot \eta^d + p_{d-2} \cdot \eta^{d-1} + \ldots + p_0 \cdot \eta^1 + \mathscr{C}(\mathbf{x}) . \tag{6}$$

Next, based on the independent ciphertext $\mathbf{d} \leftarrow \mathbf{w} \cdot s + p_{d-1} \cdot \eta$ and on the functional key, the decryptor recovers

$$\mathsf{PK}_\mathscr{C} \cdot s + p_{d-1} \cdot \eta' \in \mathcal{R}_{p_d} . \tag{7}$$

Finally, $\mathscr{C}(\mathbf{x})$ is obtained by subtracting (7) from (6) and repeatedly applying the *mod* operator to eliminate the noise terms: (mod p_{d-1}) ... (mod p_0). We note that correctness should follow from the description of these algorithms.

Ciphertext and Public-Key Evaluation Algorithms Let $\mathscr{C}^n$ be the circuit $\mathscr{C}$ restricted to some level n. For a better understanding of the procedures, we will denote the encoding of $\mathscr{C}^n(\mathbf{x})$ at some gate ℓ by c_ℓ^n, and the public key (or label) of an encoding $\mathcal{E}^n(\cdot)$ by $\mathsf{PK}(\mathcal{E}^n(\cdot))$. Furthermore, C^n are a set of level n encodings provided by the encryptor as part of the ciphertext, that enable the decryptor to compute c^n.

---

[1] Here, by $\mathscr{C}^i$ we denote the restriction of the circuit $\mathscr{C}$ computing f to level i.

$\mathsf{Eval}^n_{\mathsf{PK}}(\cup_{t\in[n]}\mathsf{PK}(C^t),\ell)$ computes the label for the ℓth wire in the n level circuit, from the ith and j^{th} wires of $n-1$ level:

1. Addition Level:
    - If $n=1$ (base case), define $\mathsf{PK}(c_\ell^1):=\mathsf{PK}(a_\ell^1\cdot s+p_0\cdot\eta_\ell^1+M_\ell):=a_\ell^1$.
    - Otherwise, let $u_i^{n-1}\leftarrow\mathsf{Eval}^{n-1}_{\mathsf{PK}}(\cup_{t\in[n-1]}\mathsf{PK}(C^t),i)$ and
      $u_j^{n-1}\leftarrow\mathsf{Eval}^{n-1}_{\mathsf{PK}}(\cup_{t\in[n-1]}\mathsf{PK}(C^t),j)$. Set $\mathsf{PK}(c_\ell^n):=u_i^{n-1}+u_j^{n-1}$.
2. Multiplication Level:
    - If $n=2$ (base case), then compute
      $\mathsf{PK}(c_\ell^2):=a_i^1\cdot a_j^1\cdot\mathsf{PK}(\mathcal{E}^2(s^2))-a_j^1\cdot\mathsf{PK}(\mathcal{E}^2(c_i^1\cdot s))-a_i^1\cdot\mathsf{PK}(\mathcal{E}^2(c_j^1\cdot s))$.
    - Otherwise, let $u_i^{n-1}\leftarrow\mathsf{Eval}^{n-1}_{\mathsf{PK}}(\cup_{t\in[n-1]}\mathsf{PK}(C^t),i)$ and
      $u_j^{n-1}\leftarrow\mathsf{Eval}^{n-1}_{\mathsf{PK}}(\cup_{t\in[n-1]}\mathsf{PK}(C^t),j)$. Set

$$\mathsf{PK}(c_\ell^n):=u_i^{n-1}\cdot u_j^{n-1}\cdot\mathsf{PK}(\mathcal{E}^n(s^2))-u_i^{n-1}\cdot\mathsf{PK}(\mathcal{E}^n(c_i^{n-1}\cdot s))$$
$$-u_i^{n-1}\cdot\mathsf{PK}(\mathcal{E}^n(c_j^{n-1}\cdot s))\ .$$

$\mathsf{Eval}^n_{\mathsf{CT}}(\cup_{t\in[n]}C^t,\ell)$ computes the encoding of the ℓth wire in the n level circuit, from the ith and j^{th} wires of $n-1$ level:

1. Addition Level:
    - If $n=1$ (base case), then, set $c_\ell^1:=\mathcal{E}^1(M_\ell)$.
    - Otherwise, let $c_i^{n-1}\leftarrow\mathsf{Eval}^{n-1}_{\mathsf{CT}}(\cup_{t\in[n-1]}C^t,i)$ and
      $c_j^{n-1}\leftarrow\mathsf{Eval}^{n-1}_{\mathsf{CT}}(\cup_{t\in[n-1]}C^t,j)$. Set $c_\ell^n\leftarrow c_i^{n-1}+c_j^{n-1}$.
2. Multiplication Level:
    - If $n=2$ (base case), then set
      $$c_\ell^2:=c_i^1\cdot c_j^1\cdot\mathcal{E}^2(s^2)-u_j^1\cdot\mathcal{E}^2(c_i^1\cdot s)-u_i^1\cdot\mathcal{E}^2(c_j^1\cdot s)\ .$$
    - Else: $c_i^{n-1}\leftarrow\mathsf{Eval}^{n-1}_{\mathsf{CT}}(\cup_{t\in[n-1]}C^t,i),c_j^{n-1}\leftarrow\mathsf{Eval}^{n-1}_{\mathsf{CT}}(\cup_{t\in[n-1]}C^t,j)$,
      $u_i^{n-1}\leftarrow\mathsf{Eval}^{n-1}_{\mathsf{PK}}(\cup_{t\in[n-1]}\mathsf{PK}(C^t),i),u_j^{n-1}\leftarrow\mathsf{Eval}^{n-1}_{\mathsf{PK}}(\cup_{t\in[n-1]}\mathsf{PK}(C^t),j)$.
      Set $\mathsf{CT}_\ell^n:=c_i^{n-1}\cdot c_j^{n-1}+u_i^{n-1}\cdot u_j^{n-1}\cdot\mathcal{E}^n(s^2)-u_j^{n-1}\cdot\mathcal{E}^n(c_i^{n-1}\cdot s)-u_i^{n-1}\cdot$
      $\mathsf{PK}(\mathcal{E}^n(c_j^{n-1}\cdot s))$.

4 Laconic Function Evaluation for $\mathbf{NC^1}$ Circuits

We show how to instantiate an LFE protocol starting from the AR17 scheme described above. Furthermore, we show our construction achieves adaptive security (Definition 6) under RLWE (Definition 2) with polynomial approximation factors. Finally, we compare its efficiency to the scheme for general circuits proposed in [14] in Sect. 4.2.

4.1 LFE for $\mathbf{NC^1}$ Circuits

The core idea behind our proposal is rooted in the design of the AR17 construction. Specifically, the mpk in AR17 acts as the crs for the LFE scheme. The *compression* procedure generates a new digest by running $\mathsf{Eval}_{\mathsf{PK}}$ on the fly, given an algorithmic description of the circuit $\mathscr{C}$ (the circuit computing the desired function). As shown in [3], the public-key evaluation algorithm can be successfully executed having knowledge of only mpk and the gate-representation of the circuit. After performing the computation, the procedure sets:

$$\text{digest}_{\mathscr{C}} \leftarrow \text{PK}_{\mathscr{C}} .$$

The digest is then handed in to the other party (say Bob).

Bob, having acquired the digest of $\mathscr{C}$ in the form of $\text{PK}_{\mathscr{C}}$, encrypts his message M using the FE encryption procedure in the following way: first, a secret s is sampled from the "d-level" ring $\mathcal{R}_{p_d}$; s is used to recursively encrypt each element up to level d, thus generating a tree structure, as explained in Sect. 3.1. Note that Bob does not need to access the ciphertext-independent part (the vector $\mathbf{w}$ from Sect. 3.1) in any way. This is a noteworthy difference from the AR17 construction: an FE ciphertext is intended to be decrypted at a latter point, by (possibly) multiple functional keys. However, this constitutes an overkill when it comes to *laconic function evaluation*, as there is need to support a *single* function (for which the ciphertext is specifically created).

As a second difference from the way the ciphertext is obtained in [3], we emphasize that in our LFE protocol Bob computes directly:

$$\text{PK}_{\mathscr{C}} \cdot s + p_{d-1} \cdot \eta^d ,$$

where $\text{PK}_{\mathscr{C}}$ is the digest Alice sent. Thus, there is no need to generate a genuine functional key and to obtain the ciphertext component that depends on $\mathbf{w}$. Directly, the two former elements constitute the ciphertext, which is sent back to Alice. Finally, the LFE *decryption* step follows immediately. Alice, after computing the *auxiliary* ciphertext in (6) "on the fly" and having knowledge of the term in (7), is able to recover $\mathscr{C}(M)$.

Formally, the construction can be defined as follows:

Definition 7 (LFE for NC^1 Circuits from [3]). *Let* FE *denote the functional encryption scheme for* NC^1 *circuits proposed in [3].*

- crs $\leftarrow_\$ $ crsGen($1^\lambda, 1^k, 1^d$): *the* crs *is instantiated by first running[2]* FE.Setup

$$(\text{mpk}, \text{msk}) \leftarrow_\$ \text{FE.Setup}(1^\lambda, 1^k, 1^d) .$$

As described, mpk *has the following elements:*

$$\{\mathbf{a}^1, \ldots, \mathbf{a}^{d-1}, (\mathbf{a}^d, \mathbf{w})\}$$

with $(\mathbf{a}^d, \mathbf{w})$ *coming from the* mpk$_{\text{Lin-FE}}$ *and* msk $\leftarrow$ msk$_{\text{Lin-FE}}$.
Set crs $\leftarrow \{\mathbf{a}^1, \ldots, \mathbf{a}^d\}$ *and return it.*
- digest$_{\mathscr{C}}$ $\leftarrow$ Compress(crs, $\mathscr{C}$): *the compression function, given a circuit description of some function* $\mathscr{C} : \{0,1\}^k \rightarrow \{0,1\}$ *and the* crs, *computes* $\text{PK}_{\mathscr{C}} \leftarrow \text{Eval}_{\text{PK}}(\mathbf{a}^1, \ldots, \mathbf{a}^d, \mathscr{C})$ *and then returns:*

$$\text{digest}_{\mathscr{C}} \leftarrow \text{PK}_{\mathscr{C}} .$$

---

[2] Note that we need only a part of the mpk generated by FE.Setup, but for simplicity we call this procedure and drop the unneeded part.

- $\mathsf{CT} \leftarrow_\$ \mathsf{Enc}(\mathsf{crs}, \mathsf{digest}_\mathscr{C}, M)$: *the encryption algorithm first samples* $s \leftarrow_\$ \mathcal{R}_{p_d}$, *randomness R and computes recursively the Regev encodings[3] of each bit:*

$$(\mathsf{CT}_1, \ldots, \mathsf{CT}_k, \mathsf{CT}_s, \mathsf{CT}_{\mathsf{ind}}) \leftarrow \mathsf{FE.Enc}((\mathbf{a}^1, \ldots, \mathbf{a}^d), (M_1, \ldots, M_k); s, R)$$

Moreover, a noise η^d is also sampled from the appropriate distribution χ and

$$\mathsf{PK}_\mathscr{C} \cdot s + p_{d-1} \cdot \eta^d \tag{8}$$

is obtained. The ciphertext CT that is returned consists of the tuple:

$$\left(\underbrace{\mathsf{PK}_\mathscr{C} \cdot s + p_{d-1} \cdot \eta^d}_{\mathsf{CT}_a}, \ \underbrace{\mathsf{CT}_1, \ldots, \mathsf{CT}_k, \mathsf{CT}_s}_{\mathsf{CT}_b} \right) . \tag{9}$$

- $\mathsf{Dec}(\mathsf{crs}, \mathscr{C}, \mathsf{CT})$: *first, the ciphertext evaluation is applied and $\mathsf{CT}_\mathscr{C}$ is obtained:*

$$\mathsf{CT}_\mathscr{C} \leftarrow \mathsf{Eval}_{\mathsf{CT}}(\mathsf{mpk}, \mathscr{C}, \mathsf{CT}) . \tag{10}$$

Then $\mathscr{C}(M)$ is obtained via the following step:

$$(\mathsf{CT}_\mathscr{C} - \mathsf{CT}_a) \mod p_{d-1} \ldots \mod p_0 .$$

Proposition 1 (Correctness). *The LFE scheme in Definition 7 enjoys correctness.*

Proof. By the correctness of $\mathsf{Eval}_{\mathsf{CT}}$, the structure of the resulting ciphertext at level d is the following:

$$\mathsf{PK}_\mathscr{C} \cdot s + p_{d-1} \cdot \eta^d + \ldots + p_0 \cdot \eta^1 + \mathscr{C}(M) . \tag{11}$$

Given the structure of the evaluated ciphertext in (11) as well as the first part of the ciphertext described by (9), the decryptor obtains $\mathscr{C}(M)$ as per the decryption procedure. □

Lemma 1 (Security). *Let FE denote the $\mathsf{FULL\text{-}SIM\text{-}FE}$-secure functional encryption scheme for NC^1 circuits described in [3]. The LFE scheme described in Definition 7 enjoys $\mathsf{FULL\text{-}SIM\text{-}LFE}$ security against any PPT adversary $\mathcal{A}$ such that:*

$$\mathsf{Adv}^{\mathsf{FULL\text{-}SIM\text{-}LFE}}_{\mathcal{A}, \mathsf{LFE}}(\lambda) \leq d \cdot \mathsf{Adv}^{\mathsf{RLWE}}_{\mathcal{A}'}(\lambda) .$$

Proof (Lemma 1). First, we describe the internal working of our simulator. Then we show how the ciphertext can be simulated via a hybrid argument, by describing the hybrid games and their code. Third, we prove the transition between each consecutive pair of hybrids.

---

[3] Note that we only need the Regev encodings, but for simplicity of notation, we call the $\mathsf{FE.Enc}$ procedure and drop the unneeded part within the FE ciphertext.

The Simulator. Given the digest $\mathsf{digest}_\mathscr{C}$, the circuit $\mathscr{C}$, the value of $\mathscr{C}(M^*)$ and the crs, our simulator $\mathcal{S}_{\mathsf{LFE}}$ proceeds as follows:

- Samples all Regev encodings forming CT_b in Eq. (9) uniformly at random.
- Replaces the functional-key surrogate value $\mathsf{PK}_\mathscr{C} \cdot s + p_{d-1} \cdot \eta^d$ with $\mathsf{Eval}_{\mathsf{CT}} - \eta^* - \mathscr{C}(M^*)$. Observe this is equivalent to running $\mathsf{Eval}_{\mathsf{CT}}$ with respect to random Regev encodings, and subtracting a lower noise term and $\mathscr{C}(M^*)$.

The Hybrids. The way the simulator is built follows from a hybrid argument. Note that we only change the parts that represent the outputs of the intermediate simulators.

Game_0: Real game, corresponding to the setting $b = 0$ in the FULL-SIM-LFE experiment.

Game_1: We switch from $\mathsf{PK}_\mathscr{C} \cdot s + p_{d-1} \cdot \eta^d$ to $\mathsf{Eval}_{\mathsf{CT}}(\mathsf{CT}_b) - \eta^* - \mathscr{C}(M^*)$, such that during decryption one recovers $\eta^* + \mathscr{C}(M^*)$. The transition to the previous game is possible as we can sample the noise η^* such that:

$$\mathsf{SD}\Big(\mathsf{PK}_\mathscr{C} \cdot s + p_{d-1} \cdot \eta^d, \mathsf{Eval}_{\mathsf{CT}}(\mathsf{CT}_b) - \eta^* - \mathscr{C}(M^*)\Big) \in \mathrm{NEGL}(\lambda) .$$

This game is identical to $\mathsf{Game}_{2,0}$.

$\mathsf{Game}_{2,i}$: We rely on the security of RLWE in order to switch all encodings on level $d - i$ with randomly sampled elements over the corresponding rings $\mathcal{R}_{p_{d+1-i}}$. Note that top levels are replaced before the bottom ones; the index $i \in \{0, 1, \ldots, d - 1\}$.

$\mathsf{Game}_{2,d}$: This setting corresponds to $b = 1$ in the FULL-SIM-LFE experiment.

We now prove the transitions between the hybrid games.

Claim (Distance between Game_0 and Game_1). There exists a PPT simulator $\mathcal{S}_1$ such that for any stateful PPT adversary $\mathcal{A}$ we have:

$$\mathsf{Adv}_\mathcal{A}^{\mathsf{Game}_0 \to \mathsf{Game}_1}(\lambda) := \Big| \Pr[\mathsf{Game}_0^\mathcal{A}(\lambda) \Rightarrow 1] - \Pr[\mathsf{Game}_1^\mathcal{A}(\lambda) \Rightarrow 1] \Big|$$

is statistically close to 0.

Proof Let $\mathcal{D}_0$ (respectively $\mathcal{D}_1$) be the distribution out of which CT_a is sampled in Game_0 (respectively Game_1). The statistical distance between $\mathcal{D}_0$ and $\mathcal{D}_1$ is negligible:

$$\mathsf{SD}(\mathcal{D}_0, \mathcal{D}_1) = \frac{1}{2} \cdot \sum_{v \in \mathcal{R}_{p_d}} \Big| \Pr[v = \mathsf{PK}_{\mathscr{C}} \cdot s + p_{d-1} \cdot \eta^d]$$

$$- \Pr[v = \mathsf{Eval}_{\mathsf{CT}}(\mathsf{CT}_b) - \eta^* - \mathscr{C}(M^*)] \Big|$$

$$= \frac{1}{2} \cdot \sum_{v \in \mathcal{R}_{p_d}} \Big| \Pr[v = \mathsf{PK}_{\mathscr{C}} \cdot s + p_{d-1} \cdot \eta^d]$$

$$- \Pr[v = \mathsf{PK}_{\mathscr{C}} \cdot s + \sum_{i=0}^{d-1} p_i \cdot \mu^{i+1} + \mathscr{C}(M^*) - \eta^* - \mathscr{C}(M^*)] \Big|$$

$$= \frac{1}{2} \cdot \sum_{v \in \mathcal{R}_{p_d}} \Big| \Pr[v = \mathsf{PK}_{\mathscr{C}} \cdot s + p_{d-1} \cdot \eta^d]$$

$$- \Pr[v = \mathsf{PK}_{\mathscr{C}} \cdot s + \sum_{i=0}^{d-1} p_i \cdot \mu^{i+1} - \eta^*] \Big|$$

We can apply the result in [3, p. 27]: we sample the noise term η^* such that

$$\mathsf{SD}(\eta^*, \sum_{i=0}^{d-2} p_i \cdot \mu^{i+1}) \leq \epsilon .$$

Thus, the advantage of any adversary in distinguishing between Game_0 and Game_1 is statistically close to 0.   □

Games 1 and 2.0 are identical.

Claim (Distance between $\mathsf{Game}_{2.i}$ and $\mathsf{Game}_{2.i+1}$). There exists a PPT simulator $\mathcal{S}_1$ such that for any stateful PPT adversary $\mathcal{A}$ we have:

$$\mathsf{Adv}_{\mathcal{A}}^{\mathsf{Game}_{2.i} \to \mathsf{Game}_{2.i+1}}(\lambda) := \Big| \Pr[\mathsf{Game}_{2.i}^{\mathcal{A}}(\lambda) \Rightarrow 1] - \Pr[\mathsf{Game}_{2.i+1}^{\mathcal{A}}(\lambda) \Rightarrow 1] \Big|$$

$$\leq \mathsf{Adv}_{\mathcal{B}}^{\mathsf{RLWE}}(\lambda) .$$

Proof. The reduction $\mathcal{B}$ is given as input a sufficiently large set of elements which are either: RLWE samples of the form $a \cdot s^{(d-i)} + p_{d-1-i} \cdot \eta^{(d-i)}$ or u where $u \leftarrow_{\$} \mathcal{R}_{p_{d-i}}$.

$\mathcal{B}$ constructs CT_b as follows: for upper levels $j > d - i$, $\mathcal{B}$ samples elements uniformly at random over $\mathcal{R}_{p_j}$. For each lower levels $j < d - i$, $\mathcal{R}$ samples independent secrets s^j and builds the lower level encodings correctly, as stated in Fig. 2.

For challenge level $d-i$, $\mathcal{B}$ takes the challenge values of the RLWE experiment – say z – and produces the level $d-i$ encodings from the level $d-1-i$ encodings as follows:

- for each encoding $\mathcal{E}^{d-1-i}$ in level $d - i - 1$, produce a left encoding in level $d - i$:

$$z_1^{d-i} + \mathcal{E}^{d-1-i} .$$

– for each encoding $\mathcal{E}^{d-1-i}$ in level $d - i - 1$, produce a right encoding in level $d - i$:

$$z_2^{d-i} + \mathcal{E}^{d-1-i} \cdot s^{d-1-i} .$$

Note that s^{d-1-i} is known in plain by $\mathcal{B}$.

Considering level 1 as a special case, the (input) message bits themselves are encrypted, as opposed to encodings from lower levels.

The first component of the ciphertext – CT_a – is computed by getting $v \leftarrow \mathsf{Eval_{CT}}(\mathscr{C}, \{C^i\}_{i \in [d]})$ over the encodings, and then subtracting the noise and the value $\mathscr{C}(M^*)$.

The adversary is provided with the simulated ciphertext. The analysis of the reduction is immediate: the winning probability in the case of $\mathcal{B}$ is identical to that of the adversary distinguishing.   □

Finally, we apply the union bound and conclude with: $\mathsf{Adv}_{\mathcal{A},\mathsf{LFE}}^{\mathsf{FULL\text{-}SIM\text{-}LFE}}(\lambda) \leq d \cdot \mathsf{Adv}_{\mathcal{A}'}^{\mathsf{RLWE}}(\lambda)$.   □

In Sect. 5, we show how the digest can be further compressed.

4.2 Efficiency Analysis

A main benefit of the LFE scheme in Definition 7 is the simplicity of the common reference string, digest and ciphertext structures. These are essentially elements over known quotient rings of polynomial rings. The representation size of elements within rings $\mathcal{R}_{p_i}$ are decided by the prime factors $p_0, p_1, \ldots, p_d$. As stated in [3, Appendix E] $p_d \in O(B_1^{2^d})$ where B_1 denotes the magnitude of the noise used for Level-1 encodings and being bounded by $p_1/4$ in order to ensure correct decryption[4]. However, we observe that a tighter bound may have the following form: $p_d \in O(B_1^{2^{d_{\mathsf{Mul}}}})$, where d_{Mul} denotes the number of multiplicative levels in the circuit.

From the point of view of space complexity, we rely on the original analysis of [3] that provides guidelines for the size of the primes $p_0, p_1, \ldots, p_d$. We are only interested in the case stipulating that $|p_d|$ belongs to $\mathsf{poly}(\lambda)$. The aforementioned constraint can be achieved by imposing further restrictions on the multiplicative depth of the circuit, namely

$$d_{\mathsf{Mul}} \in O(\log(\mathsf{poly}(\lambda))),$$

meaning that the digest is short enough whenever the circuit belongs to the NC^1 class. Once we obtained a succinctness constraint for the size of elements in the fields $\mathbb{F}_{p_i}$ over which the coefficients of quotient ring elements are going to be sampled, we can proceed with an asymptotic analysis of the sizes of digest, common reference string and ciphertext.

digest$_\mathscr{C}$ **size:** consists of n elements, each belonging to $O(B_1^{2^{d_{\mathsf{Mul}}}})$, where n denotes the degree of the quotient polynomial in the RLWE definition (Definition 2). Henceforth, digest$_\mathscr{C} \in \mathsf{poly}(\lambda)$ given the analysis above on the size of p_d.

---

[4] Our scheme is intended to support Boolean circuits, thus p_0 is set to 2.

CT **size:** consists of k "tree-like" structures (Fig. 2), k standing for input length; each tree is a perfect binary tree having of $2^d - 1$ ring elements. Therefore, the ciphertext's size is upper bounded $k \cdot 2^d \cdot (n \cdot \mathsf{poly}(\lambda))$ and fulfils succinctness requirements whenever $d_{\mathsf{Mul}} \in O(\log(\mathsf{poly}(\lambda)))$.

Enc **runtime:** the encryption runtime is essentially proportional to the size of the ciphertext, up to a constant factor needed to perform inner operations when each node of the tree is built.

crs **size:** the crs has the size identical to the size of the ciphertext, and inherits similar succinctness properties.

Handling multiple bits of output. Regarding the ability to support multiple output bits (say ℓ), this is inherent by using an arithmetic circuit and setting $\lfloor \log_2(p_0) \rfloor = \ell$. If binary circuits are needed, then ℓ public evaluation can be obtained through $\mathsf{Eval}_{\mathsf{PK}}$, and the scheme modified by having the garbling circuit producing ℓ outputs.

Remark 1. Another potentially beneficial point is the ability of the scheme in Definition 7 (and also Definition 8) to support a bounded number of circuits without changing the data-dependent ciphertext. This happens when the second party involved is stateful: given two functions f, g represented through circuits $\mathscr{C}_f, \mathscr{C}_g$, and assuming the receiver stores s (it is stateful), the Enc algorithm may simply recompute $\mathsf{PK}_g \cdot s + p_{d-1} \cdot \mu^d$ in the same manner it has already computed $\mathsf{PK}_\mathscr{C} \cdot s + p_{d-1} \cdot \eta^d$.

Comparison with [14]. Reflecting on the construction presented by Quach *et al.*, one can note that its core stems from the attribute-based encryption[17] scheme in [5], and the post-processing steps of their attribute-based LFE rely on techniques from [10]; Quach *et al.* provide a comparison between their AB-LFE and the underlying ABE; the size of their crs consists of k LWE matrices, where k is the input length, each entry belonging to $\mathbb{Z}/q\mathbb{Z}$. The size of q can be tracked by inspecting $\mathsf{Eval}_{\mathsf{PK}}$ ([14, Claim 2.4] and [5, p. 6, 23]): as the noise grows exponentially with the depth of the circuit, q has to grow accordingly: $q \approx 2^{\mathsf{poly}(\lambda, d)}$; in [3] the size of p_d grows exponentially with the multiplicative depth of the circuit, which limits the circuit class our scheme can support.

5   Further Compression for Digest

In this part, we put forth an LFE scheme with a digest independent by the size of the input, starting from the LFE construction in Sect. 4.1. The main idea consists in using a laconic oblivious transfer (Definition 5) in order to generate a small digest.

The bulk of the idea is to observe that the encryption algorithm in Sect. 4.1 outputs a ciphertext having two components: the first one consists of the AR17 ciphertext; the second component is literally $\mathsf{PK}_\mathscr{C} \cdot s + p_{d-1} \cdot \eta^d$. We create an auxiliary circuit $\mathscr{C}_{aux}$ that takes as input $\mathsf{PK}_\mathscr{C}$ and outputs $\mathsf{PK}_\mathscr{C} \cdot s + p_{d-1} \cdot \eta^d$. We garble $\mathscr{C}_{aux}$ using Yao's garbling scheme [18] and use LOT to encrypt the garbling labels. Thus, instead of garbling a circuit that produces the entire ciphertext (i.e. following the template proposed by [14]) we garble $\mathscr{C}_{aux}$. Such an approach is advantageous, as the complexity of the latter circuit, essentially performing a multiplication of two elements over a ring, is in general low when compared to a circuit that reconstructs the entire ciphertext. We present our construction below:

Definition 8 (LFE for NC^1 with Laconic Digest). *Let* LFE *denote the laconic function evaluation scheme for* NC^1 *circuits presented in Sect. 4.1,* LOT *stand for a laconic oblivious transfer protocol and* GS *denote Yao's garbling scheme.* $\overline{\text{LFE}}$ *stands for a laconic function evaluation scheme for* NC^1 *with digest of size* $O(\lambda)$:

- $\overline{\text{crs}} \leftarrow_{\$} \overline{\text{LFE}}.\text{crsGen}(1^\lambda, 1^k, 1^d)$: *the* $\overline{\text{crs}}$ *is instantiated by running the* LFE.Setup

$$\text{crs} \leftarrow_{\$} \text{LFE.Setup}(1^\lambda, 1^k, 1^d) .$$

  Let crs_{LOT} *stand for the common reference string of the* LOT *scheme. Set* $\overline{\text{crs}} \leftarrow (\text{crs}, \text{crs}_{\text{LOT}})$ *and return it.*
- $\text{digest}_{\mathscr{C}} \leftarrow \overline{\text{LFE}}.\text{Compress}(\overline{\text{crs}}, \mathscr{C})$: *the compression function, given a circuit description of some function* $\mathscr{C} : \{0,1\}^k \rightarrow \{0,1\}$ *and the* $\overline{\text{crs}} \leftarrow (\text{crs}, \text{crs}_{\text{LOT}})$, *computes* $\text{PK}_{\mathscr{C}} \leftarrow \text{LFE.Compress}(\text{crs}, \mathscr{C})$ *and then returns:*

$$\text{digest}_{\mathscr{C}} \leftarrow \text{PK}_{\mathscr{C}} .$$

  Then, using crs_{LOT}, *a new digest/database pair is obtained as:*

$$(\overline{\text{digest}_{\mathscr{C}}}, \hat{\mathbf{D}}) \leftarrow \text{LOT.Compress}(\text{crs}_{\text{LOT}}, \text{digest}_{\mathscr{C}}) .$$

  Finally, $\overline{\text{digest}_{\mathscr{C}}}$ *is returned.*
- $\text{CT} \leftarrow_{\$} \overline{\text{LFE}}.\text{Enc}(\overline{\text{crs}}, \overline{\text{digest}_{\mathscr{C}}}, M)$: *after parsing the* $\overline{\text{crs}}$ *as* $(\text{crs}_{\text{LOT}}, \text{crs})^5$, *the encryption algorithm first samples* $s \leftarrow_{\$} \mathcal{R}_{p_d}$, *randomness* R *and computes recursively the Regev encodings of each bit:*

$$\text{CT}_{\text{LFE}} \leftarrow \text{LFE.Enc}(\text{crs}, (M_1, \ldots, M_k); s, R)$$

  Moreover, a noise η^{d-1} *is also sampled from the appropriate distribution* χ *and an auxiliary circuit* $\mathscr{C}_{aux}$ *that returns*

$$\text{PK}_{\mathscr{C}} \cdot s + p_{d-1} \cdot \eta^d \tag{12}$$

  is obtained, where $\text{PK}_{\mathscr{C}}$ *constitutes the input and* $s, p_{d-1} \cdot \eta^d$ *are hardwired.*

  Then, $\mathscr{C}_{aux}$ *is garbled by Yao's garbling scheme:*

$$(\Gamma, \{L_i^0, L_i^1\}_{i=1}^t) \leftarrow_{\$} \text{GS.Garble}(\mathscr{C}_{aux})$$

---

[5] Even if we omit that explicitly, note that crs includes the bulk of mpk in [3], consistently with the execution of the subroutine LFE.Setup.

and the labels are encrypted under LOT:

$$\overline{L}_i \leftarrow_\$ \mathsf{LOT.Enc}(\mathsf{crs}_{\mathsf{LOT}}, \overline{\mathsf{digest}_{\mathscr{C}}}, i, L_i^0, L_i^1), \forall\, i \in [t] \ .$$

The ciphertext CT is set to be the tuple $(\mathsf{CT}_{\mathsf{LFE}}, \Gamma, \overline{L}_1, \ldots, \overline{L}_t)$.

- $\overline{\mathsf{LFE}}.\mathsf{Dec}(\overline{\mathsf{crs}}, \mathscr{C}, \mathsf{CT})$: First, the labels L_i corresponding to the binary decomposition of $\mathsf{PK}_{\mathscr{C}}$ are obtained:

$$L_i^{\mathsf{PK}_{\mathscr{C}}[i]} \leftarrow \mathsf{LOT.Dec}(\mathsf{crs}_{\mathsf{LOT}}, \mathsf{digest}_{\mathscr{C}}, i, \overline{L}_i)$$

When feeding Γ with L_i, the decryptor recovers $\mathsf{PK}_{\mathscr{C}} \cdot s + p_{d-1} \cdot \eta^{d-1}$.

Then, the ciphertext evaluation is applied and $\mathsf{CT}_{\mathscr{C}}$ is obtained:

$$\mathsf{CT}_{\mathscr{C}} \leftarrow \mathsf{Eval}_{\mathsf{CT}}(\mathsf{mpk}, \mathscr{C}, \mathsf{CT}) \ . \tag{13}$$

Then $\mathscr{C}(M)$ is obtained via the following step:

$$\left(\mathsf{CT}_{\mathscr{C}} - (\mathsf{PK}_{\mathscr{C}} \cdot s + p_{d-1} \cdot \eta^d)\right) \quad \mathrm{mod}\ p_{d-1} \ \ldots \ \mathrm{mod}\ p_0$$

Proposition 2 (Correctness). *The laconic function evaluation scheme in Definition 8 is correct.*

Proof. By the correctness of the LOT scheme, the correct labels corresponding to the value of $\mathsf{PK}_{\mathscr{C}}$ are recovered. By the correctness of the garbling scheme, when fed with the correct labels, the value of $\mathsf{PK}_{\mathscr{C}} \cdot s + p_{d-1} \cdot \eta^d$ is obtained. Finally, by the correctness of LFE, we recover $\mathscr{C}(M)$. □

In the remaining part, we prove the scheme above achieves simulation security, assuming the same security level from the underlying primitive.

Theorem 2 (Security). *Let $\mathfrak{C}_\lambda$ stand for a class of circuits and let $\overline{\mathsf{LFE}}$ denote the laconic function evaluation scheme put forth in Definition 8. Let GS and LOT denote the underlying garbling scheme, respectively laconic oblivious transfer scheme. The advantage of any probabilistic polynomial time adversary $\mathcal{A}$ against the adaptive simulation security of the $\overline{\mathsf{LFE}}$ scheme is bounded by:*

$$\mathsf{Adv}_{\overline{\mathsf{LFE}},\mathcal{A}}^{\mathsf{FULL\text{-}SIM\text{-}LFE}}(\lambda) \leq \mathsf{Adv}_{\mathsf{GS},\mathcal{B}_1}^{\mathsf{FULL\text{-}SIM\text{-}GS}}(\lambda) + \mathsf{Adv}_{\mathsf{LOT},\mathcal{B}_2}^{\mathsf{FULL\text{-}SIM\text{-}LOT}}(\lambda) + \mathsf{Adv}_{\mathsf{LFE},\mathcal{B}_3}^{\mathsf{FULL\text{-}SIM\text{-}LFE}}(\lambda) \ .$$

Proof. (Theorem 2). We prove the scheme enjoys adaptive security. Our proof makes use of the LFE simulator, and of the simulation security of the garbling protocol and of the LOT scheme.

Simulator. Our simulator $\mathcal{S}_{\overline{\mathsf{LFE}}}$ is obtained in the following manner: first, we run the simulator of the underlying LFE scheme that will provide the bulk of the ciphertext. Independently, we run the simulator of the garbled circuit $\mathcal{S}_{\mathsf{GS}}$. In the end, we employ the simulator of the LOT scheme ($\mathcal{S}_{\mathsf{LOT}}$) on the labels obtained from the $\mathcal{S}_{\mathsf{GS}}$.

The proof presented herein follows from a hybrid argument. The games are described below, and the game hops are motivated afterwards:

Game$_0$: corresponds to the FULL-SIM-LFE experiment, having the b is set to 0.

Game$_1$: in this game, we use the simulator $\mathcal{S}_{\text{LOT}}$ to simulate the corresponding component of the ciphertext (i.e. $\overline{L_i}$) . The distance to the previous game is bounded by the simulation security of the LOT protocol.

Game$_2$: in this game, we proceed with the following change: we employ the garbled scheme simulator GS for generating the labels corresponding to the second component contained within the ciphertext. The game distance to the previous one is bounded by the simulation security of the garbling scheme.

Game$_3$: we switch the main part of ciphertext to one provided by the $\mathcal{S}_{\text{LFE}}$ simulator, the distance to the previous hybrid being bounded by the advantage in Lemma 1.

Claim (Transition between Game$_0$ *and* Game$_1$*).* The advantage of any PPT adversary to distinguish between Game$_0$ and Game$_1$ is bounded as follows:

$$\mathsf{Adv}_{\mathcal{A}_1}^{\mathsf{Game}_0 \to \mathsf{Game}_1}(\lambda) \leq \mathsf{Adv}_{\mathsf{LOT},\mathcal{B}_1}^{\mathsf{FULL\text{-}SIM\text{-}LOT}}(\lambda) .$$

*Proof (*Game$_0$ $\to$ Game$_1$*).* We provide a reduction to the LOT security experiment, which initially samples and publishes crs$_{\text{LOT}}$. Let $\mathcal{B}_1$ denote the reduction. $\mathcal{B}_1$ simulates the LFE game in front of the PPT bounded adversary $\mathcal{A}_1$: (1) First, it samples crs$_{\text{LFE}}$, and publishes (crs$_{\text{LFE}}$, crs$_{\text{LOT}}$); (2) Next, $\mathcal{B}_1$ receives from the LFE adversary $\mathcal{A}_1$ the tuple $(\mathscr{C}, \mathscr{C}(M^*))$; (3) computes the digest digest$_{\mathscr{C}}$, the underlying LFE ciphertext, and the garbled circuits with the associated labels.

Next, $\mathcal{B}_1$ impersonates an adversary against the LOT security game, by submitting the tuple $\left(\mathsf{PK}_{\mathscr{C}} \cdot s + p_{d-1} \cdot \eta^d, \{L_{i,i0}, L_{i,1}\}_{i \in |\text{digest}_{\mathscr{C}}|}\right)$.

The LOT game picks a random $b \in \{0, 1\}$ and provides the adversary with either a correctly generated LOT ciphertext encrypting the labels L_i^0, L_i^1 under position i, or by a simulated ciphertext. The latter ciphertext is generated by $\mathcal{S}_{\text{LOT}}$.

Thus $\mathcal{B}_1$ obtains the entire $\overline{\text{LFE}}$ ciphertext, which is passed to $\mathcal{A}_1$. $\mathcal{A}_1$ returns a bit, indicating its current setting. It is clear that any PPT adversary able to distinguish between the two settings breaks the LOT security of the underlying LOT scheme. $\square$

Claim (Transition between Game$_1$ *and* Game$_2$*).* The advantage of any PPT adversary to distinguish between Game$_1$ and Game$_2$ is bounded by:

$$\mathsf{Adv}_{\mathcal{A}_2}^{\mathsf{Game}_1 \to \mathsf{Game}_2}(\lambda) \leq \mathsf{Adv}_{\mathsf{GS},\mathcal{B}_2}^{\mathsf{FULL\text{-}SIM\text{-}GS}}(\lambda) .$$

*Proof (*Game$_1$ $\to$ Game$_2$*).* By the input and circuit privacy of the garbling scheme, there exists $\mathcal{S}_{\text{GS}}$ that produces a tuple $(\tilde{\Gamma}, \{\tilde{L}_i^0, \tilde{L}_i^1\}_{i \in [t]})$.

Let $\mathcal{B}_2$ denote the reduction, and let $\mathcal{A}_2$ denote the adversary against the $\overline{\text{LFE}}$ game. As for the previous game, $\mathcal{B}_2$ samples and publishes crs$_{\overline{\text{LFE}}}$, $\mathcal{A}_2$ provides $(\mathscr{C}, \mathscr{C}(M^*))$. $\mathcal{B}_2$ builds the LFE ciphertext.

Next, $\mathcal{B}_2$ impersonates an adversary against the GS security experiment. $\mathcal{B}_2$ provides the GS game with $(\mathscr{C}_{aux}, \mathsf{PK}_{\mathscr{C}} \cdot s + p_{d-1} \cdot \eta^d)$, and receives either correctly generated garbled circuit and labels or a simulated garbled circuit and the simulated labels.

Thus, if $\mathcal{A}_2$ distinguishes between the two games, $\mathcal{B}_2$ distinguishes between the two distributions of labels in the GS experiment.   □

Claim (Transition between Game$_2$ *and* Game$_3$*).* The advantage of any PPT adversary to distinguish between Game$_2$ and Game$_3$ is bounded by:

$$\mathsf{Adv}_{\mathcal{A}_3}^{\mathsf{Game}_2 \to \mathsf{Game}_3}(\lambda) \leq \mathsf{Adv}_{\mathsf{LFE},\mathcal{B}_3}^{\mathsf{FULL\text{-}SIM\text{-}LFE}}(\lambda) .$$

*Proof (*Game$_2 \to$ Game$_3$*).* During the last hop, we rely on the security of the LFE component for changing elements of the first component of the ciphertext to simulated ones. It is easy to see that the advantage any adversary has in distinguishing the transition is bounded by the advantage of winning the FULL-SIM-LFE security experiment against the underlying LFE.

The FULL-SIM-LFE experiment generates crs$_\mathsf{LFE}$. $\mathcal{B}_3$ samples crs$_\mathsf{LOT}$ and provides the resulting $\overline{\mathsf{crs}}$ to $\mathcal{A}_3$. The adversary returns $(\mathscr{C}, \mathscr{C}(M^*))$, which are forwarded to FULL-SIM-LFE. The experiment generates the ciphertext either correctly or using $\mathcal{S}_\mathsf{LFE}$.

Then $\mathcal{B}_3$ employs $\mathcal{S}_\mathsf{GS}$ and $\mathcal{S}_\mathsf{LOT}$ to obtain the remaining $\overline{\mathsf{LFE}}$ ciphertext components and runs $\mathcal{A}_3$ on the full ciphertext. $\mathcal{B}_3$ returns the corresponding output to the setting indicated by $\mathcal{A}_3$.

Finally, we remark that this setting simulates exactly the FULL-SIM-LFE experiment with $b = 1$.   □

This completes the proof of Theorem 2.   □

6   Concluding Remarks

As for the concluding remarks, we note that our work introduces new constructions of laconic function evaluation for the NC^1 class. The schemes we propose follow from the FE scheme in [3] and exploit standard cryptographic tools, such as laconic oblivious transfer and garbled circuits in order to further reduce the size of digest.

As open questions, apart from having adaptive security for general circuits, we would like to see a candidate having a short common reference string, as our parameters are impractical for high-depth circuits. Another fruitful research direction would investigate if schemes fulfilling the syntax of special homomorphic encodings with succinct ciphertexts can be generically converted into LFEs.

Acknowledgements. The author is grateful to Shweta Agrawal for numerous valuable comments and improvement suggestions on this work. Most work was done while the author was affiliated with the University of Luxembourg. The author was supported in part by the ERC grant CLOUDMAP 787390.

References

1. Agrawal, S.: Stronger security for reusable garbled circuits, general definitions and attacks. In: Katz, J., Shacham, H. (eds.) CRYPTO 2017. Part I. LNCS, vol. 10401, pp. 3–35. Springer, Cham (2017). https://doi.org/10.1007/978-3-319-63688-7_1

2. Agrawal, S., Libert, B., Stehlé, D.: Fully secure functional encryption for inner products, from standard assumptions. In: Robshaw, M., Katz, J. (eds.) CRYPTO 2016. Part III. LNCS, vol. 9816, pp. 333–362. Springer, Heidelberg (2016). https://doi.org/10.1007/978-3-662-53015-3_12

3. Agrawal, S., Rosen, A.: Functional encryption for bounded collusions, revisited. In: Kalai, Y., Reyzin, L. (eds.) TCC 2017. Part I. LNCS, vol. 10677, pp. 173–205. Springer, Cham (2017). https://doi.org/10.1007/978-3-319-70500-2_7

4. Badrinarayanan, S., Jain, A., Ostrovsky, R., Visconti, I.: UC-secure multiparty computation from one-way functions using stateless tokens. In: Galbraith, S.D., Moriai, S. (eds.) ASIACRYPT 2019. Part II. LNCS, vol. 11922, pp. 577–605. Springer, Cham (2019). https://doi.org/10.1007/978-3-030-34621-8_21

5. Boneh, D., et al.: Fully key-homomorphic encryption, arithmetic circuit ABE and compact garbled circuits. In: Nguyen, P.Q., Oswald, E. (eds.) EUROCRYPT 2014. LNCS, vol. 8441, pp. 533–556. Springer, Heidelberg (2014). https://doi.org/10.1007/978-3-642-55220-5_30

6. Boneh, D., Sahai, A., Waters, B.: Functional encryption: definitions and challenges. In: Ishai, Y. (ed.) TCC 2011. LNCS, vol. 6597, pp. 253–273. Springer, Heidelberg (2011). https://doi.org/10.1007/978-3-642-19571-6_16

7. Brakerski, Z., Vaikuntanathan, V.: Fully homomorphic encryption from ring-LWE and security for key dependent messages. In: Rogaway, P. (ed.) CRYPTO 2011. LNCS, vol. 6841, pp. 505–524. Springer, Heidelberg (2011). https://doi.org/10.1007/978-3-642-22792-9_29

8. Cho, C., Döttling, N., Garg, S., Gupta, D., Miao, P., Polychroniadou, A.: Laconic oblivious transfer and its applications. In: Katz, J., Shacham, H. (eds.) CRYPTO 2017. Part II. LNCS, vol. 10402, pp. 33–65. Springer, Cham (2017). https://doi.org/10.1007/978-3-319-63715-0_2

9. Goldreich, O., Micali, S., Wigderson, A.: How to play any mental game or a completeness theorem for protocols with honest majority. In: Aho, A. (ed.) 19th Annual ACM Symposium on Theory of Computing, 25–27 May, pp. 218–229. ACM Press, New York (1987)

10. Goldwasser, S., Tauman Kalai, Y., Popa, R.A., Vaikuntanathan, V., Zeldovich, N.: Reusable garbled circuits and succinct functional encryption. In: Boneh, D., Roughgarden, T., Feigenbaum, J. (eds.) 45th Annual ACM Symposium on Theory of Computing, Palo Alto, CA, USA, 1–4 June 2013, pp. 555–564. ACM Press (2013)

11. Halevi, S., Hazay, C., Polychroniadou, A., Venkitasubramaniam, M.: Round-optimal secure multi-party computation. In: Shacham, H., Boldyreva, A. (eds.) CRYPTO 2018. Part II. LNCS, vol. 10992, pp. 488–520. Springer, Cham (2018). https://doi.org/10.1007/978-3-319-96881-0_17

12. Lyubashevsky, V., Peikert, C., Regev, O.: On ideal lattices and learning with errors over rings. In: Gilbert, H. (ed.) EUROCRYPT 2010. LNCS, vol. 6110, pp. 1–23. Springer, Heidelberg (2010). https://doi.org/10.1007/978-3-642-13190-5_1

13. O'Neill, A.: Deterministic public-key encryption revisited. Cryptology ePrint Archive, Report 2010/533 (2010). http://eprint.iacr.org/2010/533

14. Quach, W., Wee, H., Wichs, D.: Laconic function evaluation and applications. In: Thorup, M. (ed.) 59th Annual Symposium on Foundations of Computer Science, Paris, France, 7–9 October 2018, pp. 859–870. IEEE Computer Society Press (2018)

15. Rabin, M.O.: How to exchange secrets with oblivious transfer. Cryptology ePrint Archive, Report 2005/187 (2005). http://eprint.iacr.org/2005/187

16. Regev, O.: On lattices, learning with errors, random linear codes, and cryptography. In: Gabow, H.N., Fagin, R. (eds.) 37th Annual ACM Symposium on Theory of Computing, Baltimore, MA, USA, 22–24 May 2005, pp. 84–93. ACM Press (2005)

17. Waters, B.: Ciphertext-policy attribute-based encryption: an expressive, efficient, and provably secure realization. In: Catalano, D., Fazio, N., Gennaro, R., Nicolosi, A. (eds.) PKC 2011. LNCS, vol. 6571, pp. 53–70. Springer, Heidelberg (2011). https://doi.org/10.1007/978-3-642-19379-8_4
18. Yao, A.C.: Protocols for secure computations (extended abstract). In: 23rd Annual Symposium on Foundations of Computer Science, Chicago, Illinois, 3–5 November 1982, pp. 160–164. IEEE Computer Society Press (1982)
19. Yao, A.C.: How to generate and exchange secrets (extended abstract). In: 27th Annual Symposium on Foundations of Computer Science, Toronto, Ontario, Canada, 27–29 October 1986, pp. 162–167. IEEE Computer Society Press (1986)

FASTA – A Stream Cipher for Fast FHE Evaluation

Carlos Cid[1,2] , John Petter Indrøy[2], and Håvard Raddum[2(✉)]

[1] Royal Holloway University of London, Egham, UK
carlos.cid@rhul.ac.uk
[2] Simula UiB, Bergen, Norway
{johnpetter,haavardr}@simula.no

Abstract. In this paper we propose FASTA, a stream cipher design optimised for implementation over popular fully homomorphic encryption schemes. A number of symmetric encryption ciphers have been recently proposed for FHE applications, e.g. the block cipher LowMC, and the stream ciphers Rasta (and variants), FLIP and Kreyvium. The main design criterion employed in these ciphers has typically been to minimise the multiplicative complexity of the algorithm. However, other aspects affecting their efficient evaluation over common FHE libraries are often overlooked, compromising their real-world performance. Whilst FASTA may also be considered as a variant of Rasta, it has its parameters and linear layer especially chosen to allow efficient implementation over the BGV scheme, particularly as implemented in the HElib library. This results in a speedup by a factor of 25 compared to the most efficient publicly available implementation of Rasta. FASTA's target is BGV, as implemented in HElib. However the design ideas introduced in the cipher could also be potentially employed to achieve improvements in the homomorphic evaluation in other popular FHE schemes/libraries. We do consider such alternatives in this paper (e.g. BFV and BGVrns, as implemented in SEAL and PALISADE), but argue that, unlike BGV in HElib, it is more challenging to make use of their parallelism in a Rasta-like stream cipher design.

Keywords: Stream ciphers · Homomorphic encryption · Hybrid encryption

1 Introduction

Fully homomorphic encryption (FHE) is a relatively new and active research area in cryptography. FHE schemes allow arbitrary operations to be performed on ciphertexts, to produce some encrypted result, which when decrypted results in data that would be obtained if we had decrypted the ciphertexts first and then performed the operations on the plaintexts.

FHE opens up for new and exciting secure applications, in particular in cloud computing. The party doing the operations on the ciphertexts does not need to

© The Author(s), under exclusive license to Springer Nature Switzerland AG 2022
S. D. Galbraith (Ed.): CT-RSA 2022, LNCS 13161, pp. 451–483, 2022.
https://doi.org/10.1007/978-3-030-95312-6_19

have the decryption key. One can therefore upload FHE-encrypted ciphertexts to the cloud and have the cloud provider perform the necessary operations on the ciphertexts. Since the cloud does not need the decryption key, there is no need to place any trust in the cloud provider. This gives a higher level of security as the cloud provider does not have the ability to read the plaintext information.

The main drawback of FHE is that it is very computationally demanding. Since Gentry demonstrated the first FHE scheme [Gen09] in 2009 many improvements in efficiency have been made [CIM16, DM15, CHK20], but the most useful applications still struggle with being practical. This impracticality comes not least because clients of a cloud need to perform FHE encryptions themselves. One notices however that the computing power of a cloud is much higher than that of a typical client, so research has gone into finding ways to transfer most of the burden of doing FHE encryptions from the clients to the cloud.

A solution for achieving this goal is to let the client encrypt its data using a symmetric cipher, which is computationally very cheap, and upload the symmetrically encrypted ciphertexts to the cloud. The cloud also receives the key used for the symmetric encryption, but only as a ciphertext encrypted under the FHE scheme. The cloud is then in a position to *homomorphically* remove the symmetric encryption and end up with the FHE encryption of the client's data.

A number of symmetric ciphers designed for use together with FHE have been proposed, e.g. the block cipher LowMC [ARS+15], and the stream ciphers Kreyvium [CCF+16], FLIP [MJSC16], and Rasta [DEG+18] (and variants [HL20, HKC+20, DGH+21b]). Their main design criterion has been to minimise the multiplicative complexity of the algorithms since homomorphic multiplications are the most expensive operations in FHE. However, as a rule they have mostly overlooked an important aspect for their application target: how suitable they are for their homomorphic evaluation over existing FHE schemes, as implemented in the main libraries. For example, the HElib and PALISADE libraries [HS20, PAL] implement the BGV scheme [BGV12], which offers a good degree of parallelism by utilising *slots* in BGV ciphertexts. The BFV scheme, implemented in PALISADE and SEAL [SEA20], also offer the same kind of parallelism. Since these are some of the most popular FHE implementations, one may argue that a symmetric encryption design should – in addition to minimising multiplicative complexity – also select its components and parameters to take advantage of the libraries' features to allow their efficient homomorphic evaluation.

In this paper we propose FASTA, a stream cipher design optimised for implementation over HElib. FASTA may be considered as a variant of Rasta, but has its parameters and linear layers especially chosen to allow efficient implementation over the BGV scheme. The selected parameters utilise the parallelism offered by BGV, where the slots in ciphertexts are packed to achieve full parallelisation when evaluating the non-linear layer. However the packing is inefficient when the linear layer consists of random matrices (as with Rasta). Thus FASTA also features a new BGV-friendly linear layer. These changes result in FASTA running more than 6 times faster than a corresponding (modified) Rasta instance, and 25 times faster than the original Rasta, when evaluated homomorphically.

Whilst FASTA's target is BGV, as implemented in the HElib library, we also look into the BFV scheme implemented in PALISADE and SEAL, and the variant of BGV called BGVrns that is implemented in PALISADE. We consider the implementation features in these libraries and explain why it is more challenging to make good use of their parallelism in Rasta-like stream ciphers.

The paper is organised as follows. In Sect. 2 we give an overview of the main concepts and schemes discussed in the paper. Section 3 focuses on the design of symmetric key linear layers for efficient FHE evaluation. We specify the FASTA stream cipher in Sect. 4, and provide a security analysis in Sect. 5. We describe the homomorphic implementation of FASTA in Sect. 6, and close with our conclusions in Sect. 7.

2   Preliminaries

In this section we briefly recall a main use case for using symmetric ciphers with homomorphic encryption schemes. We also review the Rasta stream cipher and the BGV scheme, in particular how the latter is implemented in popular FHE libraries.

2.1   FHE Hybrid Encryption: Combining Symmetric Ciphers with Fully Homomorphic Encryption

The concept of Fully Homomorphic Encryption (FHE) was first described in [RAD78]. However no actual FHE schemes were found before Gentry proposed a construction in 2009 [Gen09]. Since then much work has been invested in this field, not least because FHE gives strong solutions to privacy problems related to cloud computing. The problem that FHE faces today concerns computational efficiency. Significant improvements have been made in recent years, but efficiency is still a bottleneck for deploying practical and useful FHE applications.

One approach to address the efficiency issue is to combine FHE schemes with symmetric ciphers as shown in Fig. 1. This is often referred to as *FHE hybrid encryption*. The idea is that clients in a cloud system, who typically have much less computational power than the cloud provider, rather than homomorphically encrypting a (potentially large) plaintext P, will instead encrypt P using a symmetric cipher $\mathcal{E}$ under a secret key K, and then only homomorphically encrypt K under the FHE scheme HE using a public key pk. Both the ciphertext $C = \mathcal{E}_K(P)$ and the FHE-encrypted key K^* are uploaded to the cloud.[1] The cloud will now encrypt the bits in C using HE under the public key pk, and homomorphically run the decryption circuit of $\mathcal{E}$ on the inputs $C^* = HE(C, pk)$

---

[1] To avoid confusion between symmetric and FHE ciphertexts, we will normally use an asterisk "*" as a superscript on any literal denoting a FHE ciphertext.

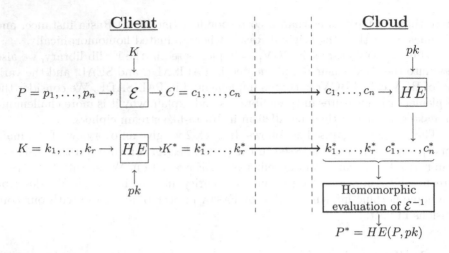

Fig. 1. FHE hybrid encryption: the client only needs to encrypt the key K with an FHE scheme HE; the plaintext P is encrypted with symmetric algorithm $\mathcal{E}$. The cloud gets the bits of K encrypted under HE, it encrypts the ciphertext bits c_i with HE, and homomorphically evaluates the decryption circuit of $\mathcal{E}$ to obtain $HE(P, pk)$.

and $K^* = HE(K, pk)$. The homomorphic properties of HE ensure that the output from doing this is $HE(P, pk)$.[2] In other words, the effect of the symmetric cipher can be removed, and the cloud is now left with a pure FHE encryption of P, which may then be used for further processing. The benefit of this construction is that the client side only needs to encrypt K using HE – in fact it needs not be the same device that encrypts the plaintext P with $\mathcal{E}$, and K with HE. All other homomorphic encryptions and evaluations are done by the cloud.

The basic homomorphic operations performed in a circuit are additions and multiplications, corresponding to the bit-wise XOR and AND operations when the plaintext space is $\mathbb{F}_2$. Both of these operations have a cost in terms of the growth of *noise*, and multiplication is by far the most expensive. Thus, to support such FHE hybrid encryption construction, there has been much research effort in designing symmetric ciphers that minimise the multiplicative complexity – the number of bit-wise AND-gates, both in the total number and in a critical path (i.e. the AND-depth) – of their decryption circuit. Examples include LowMC [ARS+15], FLIP [MJSC16], Kreyvium [CCF+16], and Rasta and its variants Dasta, Masta and Pasta [DEG+18, HL20, HKC+20, DGH+21b].

2.2   The Rasta Stream Cipher

Rasta is a family of stream ciphers proposed by Dobraunig *et al.* [DEG+18]. The target application for the ciphers is the use as a component in secure computation constructions based on MPC and FHE schemes, particularly the latter. In

---

[2] Strictly speaking, the result will be in fact a ciphertext which will decrypt to P under the FHE private key sk.

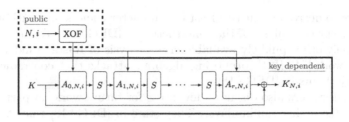

Fig. 2. The r-round Rasta keystream generator construction (from [DEG+18]).

these applications, symmetric key algorithm designs will seek to minimise multiplications as much as possible. In the Rasta construction, the designers aimed to minimise two multiplicative metrics of interest: AND-depth and ANDs per encrypted bit. Rasta uses a cryptographic permutation based on a public and fixed substitution layer, and variable affine layers (which are derived from public information), iterated for d rounds. The construction achieves AND-depth d, while requiring only d ANDs per encrypted bit.

In more detail, the Rasta keystream generator is based on a n-bit permutation featuring the $A(SA)^d$ structure, where S is the χ-transformation (prominently also used in KECCAK [BDPA11]), and the jth-round affine layers $A_{j,N,i}$ are generated pseudorandomly based on a nonce N and a counter i. To produce the keystream, it applies the permutation in feed-forward mode, with the n-bit secret key K as input. Figure 2 shows a diagrammatic representation of the Rasta keystream generator.

The generation procedure for the affine layers $A_{j,N,i}$ results in pseudorandomly generated $n \times n$ invertible binary matrices and n-bit round constants, which since they are based on unique (N, i), are unlikely to be re-used during encryption under the same key. To ensure S is invertible, we require n to be odd. If the permutation has d rounds, it is straightforward to show that the Rasta construction achieves AND-depth d and requires d ANDs per encrypted bit.

In [DEG+18], the authors suggest several parameter sets for 80-, 128- and 256-bit security. For example, Rasta with a 6-round permutation with block/key size of 219 bits should provide 80 bits of security. Same for a 4-round permutation with 327-bit block/key. On the other hand, Rasta based on a 6-round permutation with block/key size 351 bits is expected to provide 128 bits of security (see Table 1 of [DEG+18] for other proposed parameters). In general, the authors suggest the number of rounds to be between 4 and 6, while the key size will typically be at least three times larger than the security level. However they also propose a more "aggressive" version of the cipher (Agrasta), for which the block size coincides with the security level (plus one, to ensure n is odd). For example, Agrasta based on an 81-bit, 4-round permutation, claims 80 bits of security.

In order to derive and justify Rasta's parameter choices, the authors provide a detailed security analysis of the construction in [DEG+18]. To our best knowledge, the only other publicly available cryptanalysis of Rasta[3] (and variants) is the recent work [LSMI21], proposing algebraic attacks that contradict some of the security claims in [DEG+18].

Rasta's designers also discuss a few areas for future work, in particular how to improve the cipher's affine layer. They state in [DEG+18] that "[n]ew ideas for linear-layer design are needed which impose structure in one way or another which on one hand allows for significantly more efficient implementations while at the same time still resist attacks and allows for arguments against such attacks." A variant of Rasta, called Dasta [HL20] was later proposed, considering a particular efficiency aspect: it features a more efficient generation procedure for the linear layer, which does not make use of a XOF algorithm. In this paper we consider another implementation efficiency aspect: the evaluation of Rasta-like ciphers over popular FHE schemes and libraries.

We note that, in [DEG+18], the designers did describe a few experiments for the main use case for Rasta – namely, the homomorphic evaluation of the cipher in a hybrid symmetric/FHE construction. However these experiments, using BGV as implemented in HElib, appeared to have been carried out mainly to "validate" the Rasta design approach, as well as a means to compare it with other prominent ciphers, e.g. FLIP, Kreyvium and LowMC. In particular, there appeared to be no efforts to take advantage of features of BGV/HElib in a more efficient implementation, which in turn might have fed into more efficient design choices for the cipher (beyond simply minimising AND-depth and AND per bit). More recent variants of Rasta [HKC+20, DGH+21b] do take into account FHE schemes' features in their design, and come accompanied by comprehensive experiments. However they feature more distinctive structures, e.g. they are defined over fields of prime characteristic $p > 2$. In contrast, in this paper we propose FASTA as a closer variant of Rasta, also defined over the binary field, in which however we carefully consider the features of BGV in the design of its keystream generator.

2.3 The BGV Scheme

The BGV homomorphic encryption scheme [BGV12] was proposed by Brakerski, Gentry and Vaikuntanathan in 2012 and is implemented in the HElib and PALISADE libraries. BGV is a levelled FHE scheme, which means that the multiplicative depth of the circuit one wants to evaluate must be known at the time the parameters of the cipher are chosen.

The starting point for the BGV scheme is the m-th cyclotomic polynomial over the integers $\Phi_m(X)$. Plaintexts in BGV can be seen as elements of the quotient ring $\mathbb{Z}_{p^r}[X]/(\overline{\Phi}_m(X))$, where p is a prime and $\overline{\Phi}_m(X)$ is the image

---

[3] The designers also mention in [DEG+18] the technical report "Algebraic cryptanalysis of RASTA", by Bile, Perret and Faugère. However we were unable to publicly locate this work.

of $\Phi_m(X)$ in $\mathbb{Z}_{p^r}[X]$. In this paper we are only interested in encrypting bits as plaintext, i.e. $p = 2$ and $r = 1$, and so in fact our plaintexts can be seen as polynomials over $\mathbb{F}_2$ of degree less than $\phi(m)$, where $\phi(\cdot)$ is Euler's totient function. A very useful feature of BGV is that one ciphertext may encrypt several plaintext bits. The notion is that one ciphertext contains multiple *slots*. The number of slots in a ciphertext is denoted by s, which is understood differently in HElib and PALISADE. In HElib the number of slots is given as $s = \phi(m)/d$, where d is the multiplicative order of the size of the plaintext space (in our case, 2) modulo m. In PALISADE the number of slots is given as $s = \phi(m)$. In both cases we use the notation

$$c^* = \{(b_1, b_2, \ldots, b_s)\}$$

to indicate that the ciphertext c^* encrypts the plaintext bits $b_1, \ldots, b_s$.

The homomorphic properties of BGV apply slot-wise. If $c_a^* = \{(a_1, \ldots, a_s)\}$ and $c_b^* = \{(b_1, \ldots, b_s)\}$ are two ciphertexts, then

$$c_a^* + c_b^* = \{(a_1 \oplus b_1, \ldots, a_s \oplus b_s)\},$$
$$c_a^* \times c_b^* = \{(a_1 \cdot b_1, \ldots, a_s \cdot b_s)\},$$

where $\oplus$ and $\cdot$ denote the bit-wise XOR and AND operations, respectively.

BGV in HElib. If we have $\phi(m) = s \cdot d$ as above, it follows from the structure of the ring $\mathbb{F}_2[X]/(\overline{\Phi}_m(X))$ that the plaintext space in HElib can be understood to be instead in $\mathbb{F}_{2^d}$, and multiplications and additions work homomorphically in this field (see [HS20]). As $\mathbb{F}_2 \subset \mathbb{F}_{2^d}$, we can use HElib for our purpose, and ciphertexts will encrypt s plaintext bits.

HElib contains functions to manipulate the slots in a ciphertext, and two of these will be important to us. The first is $\mathsf{mul}(c^*, M)$, where c^* is a ciphertext and M is a binary $s \times s$ matrix. The function[4] returns a ciphertext that encrypts the slots in c^* multiplied with M, and so when $c^* = \{(b_1, \ldots, b_s)\}$, we have

$$\mathsf{mul}(c^*, M) = \{((b_1, \ldots, b_s) \cdot M)\}.$$

The second function we would like to highlight is $\mathsf{rotate}(c^*, a)$. This function returns a ciphertext that encrypts the slots of c^* cyclically rotated by a positions to the right. We also use the notation $(c^* >> a)$ for the rotate operation, so for $c^* = \{(b_1, \ldots, b_s)\}$ we have

$$\mathsf{rotate}(c^*, a) = (c^* >> a) = \{(b_{s-a+1}, \ldots, b_s, b_1, \ldots, b_{s-a})\}.$$

We note that both rotate and additions of ciphertexts are computationally very cheap to do, while mul is not.

---

[4] The mul function was optimised in HElib in March 2018, the earlier name for the same function was matMul [HS18].

BGV in PALISADE. PALISADE implements the BGV scheme using residue number systems, and works in a different fashion from HElib. This particular scheme is denoted by BGVrns.[5] As noted above, the number of slots in PALISADE is $s = \phi(m)$, and will therefore always be an even number. In PALISADE v.1.11.4 (the latest version at the time of writing [PRRC21]), the plaintext space of BGVrns can only be integers modulo a chosen plaintext modulus p. Addition and multiplication in the slots will be performed as integer additions and multiplications modulo p. As we are only interested in doing operations in $\mathbb{F}_2$ and not in any extension field, this is again sufficient for our purpose. In BGVrns the plaintext modulus needs to be odd, but by selecting p to be high enough that our computation never reaches it, the computations will simply be done over the integers. After decryption we then only need to reduce the plaintext returned by PALISADE modulo 2 to get the desired result.

PALISADE does not yet implement a function similar to HElib's mul. It does however have a function that cyclically rotates a ciphertext by a given number of positions, called evalAtIndex. Like HElib, both evalAtIndex and additions are computationally cheap to do in BGVrns, but the number of slots in PALISADE's BGVrns is much higher.

3   Linear Layers in Symmetric Ciphers for FHE Hybrid Encryption

The purpose of the linear layer in a symmetric cipher is to provide "diffusion". The concept of diffusion is often not precisely formalised, but intuitively we would like a linear layer to provide an *avalanche effect*, i.e. that any single bit of the cipher state at a particular point of the encryption process quickly influences as many bits in the cipher state as possible after a few rounds. Deploying linear layers with good diffusion – together with good non-linear layers – in iterated constructions should ensure that, for the entire cipher, the output bits are described via complex expressions in all input bits.

The notion of *optimal diffusion* for symmetric encryption linear layers was introduced in [Dae95, RDP+96], together with a metric to quantify the diffusion of a linear layer L. The *branch number* of L is defined as the minimum of the sums of the weights of inputs and corresponding outputs of L. For matrices of dimension n over $\mathbb{F}_{2^r}$ ($r > 1$), it was shown how maximum distance separable (MDS) codes of length $2n$ and dimension n can be used to construct invertible linear transformations providing optimal diffusion.

In this work we are interested in large, invertible linear transformations over $\mathbb{F}_2$, which can offer good diffusion. Given our parameters, the use of the MDS construction is not possible, and measuring the branch number of individual matrices seems infeasible. Similar to the approach in [ARS+15, DEG+18], we will instead define a family of linear transformations which we will argue offer good diffusion properties. FASTA's iterated construction will then use linear layers that

---

[5] See [HPS18] for a discussion on the very similar BFVrns scheme.

are pseudorandomly generated from this family. We claim that the construction should then provide strong diffusion after just a few rounds.

Most existing work on quantifying diffusion have focused on features of one particular linear transformation used multiple times in a cipher. Our case is different: we will make use of a *family* of linear transformations, from which we will draw transformations to be used only once during encryption. We therefore introduce the notion of "balanced diffusion" which we will use in our construction.

Definition 1. *Let $\mathcal{L}$ be a family of invertible $n \times n$ matrices over $\mathbb{F}_2$, where $|\mathcal{L}|$ is a large even number. Let $\mathbf{e}_0, \ldots, \mathbf{e}_{n-1}$ be the canonical basis of $(\mathbb{F}_2)^n$. Then we say that $\mathcal{L}$ offers balanced diffusion if, for all $0 \leq i, j \leq n - 1$, we have*

$$\Pr_{L \in \mathcal{L}}[\langle \mathbf{e}_i L, \mathbf{e}_j \rangle = 1] = 1/2.$$

Intuitively it means that if L is a member of a family of matrices offering balanced diffusion, then if $\mathbf{w} = \mathbf{v} \cdot L$, we expect that every bit of $\mathbf{v}$ influences each bit of $\mathbf{w}$ with probability $1/2$. In cryptographic applications, we expect that the iteration of randomly generated members of $\mathcal{L}$ should maximise the diffusion of the entire construction.

Some designers of FHE-friendly symmetric ciphers, e.g. in [ARS+15, DEG+18], have adopted a similar approach, using $\mathcal{L} = GL(n, \mathbb{F}_2)$ the family of all invertible $n \times n$ binary matrices. The ciphers' round linear transformations are then randomly generated from $\mathcal{L}$. This seems in principle to make sense: designers mainly focused on minimising the number of AND gates and the AND-depth of the decryption circuit, under the argument that linear operations on FHE ciphertexts are almost for free compared to multiplications. Moreover, with no particular structure in the linear layer that a cryptanalyst can exploit in an attack, this approach also simplifies the arguments in the security analysis. However this approach seems also to indicate that little attention was paid to how the structure of the linear layer may affect the performance of the ciphers' homomorphic evaluation in practice.

While it is true that addition of homomorphic ciphertexts is cheap compared to multiplication, a tacit assumption is that ciphertexts only encrypt a single bit each. As discussed in Sect. 2.3, popular FHE libraries have the ability to pack multiple plaintext bits into a single FHE ciphertext, and operate on all bits encrypted into each ciphertext in parallel. Packing the full state of a symmetric cipher into a few, or perhaps only one, FHE ciphertexts can give big speed-ups when processing the non-linear layer of a symmetric cipher. For example, an S-box layer of LowMC that covers $3/4$ of the state can be processed with only three FHE multiplications, while the χ transformation used in Rasta (Sect. 2.2) can be performed with only one homomorphic multiplication.

However, when packing the state of a symmetric cipher into few FHE ciphertexts, the additions carried out in a linear layer will now fall into two categories:

1. additions of elements in the same slot positions from two FHE ciphertexts;

2. additions of elements from two FHE ciphertexts in different slots, or addition of elements from different slots inside a single FHE ciphertext.

The first type is in fact the addition of two FHE ciphertexts, and is therefore quick and easy to perform. The second type is however slower and more involved, as it mixes elements inside a single FHE ciphertext, or moves elements inside a ciphertext to make them line up in the same slot. Type 2 additions are thus not homomorphic additions per se. For a randomly generated linear layer, most additions will be of type 2; that in turn will outweigh much of the gains that packed ciphertexts give in the non-linear layer. A natural question is then to investigate whether we can find another family of linear transformations, which only uses additions of type 1, but is still expected to offer balanced diffusion.

We now describe the design of a family of linear layers that only use rotations and additions of type 1, which we employ in FASTA. Of course, linear transformations drawn from this family are no longer *random*, and some structure may be found in them. Nevertheless, we aim to construct linear transformations that are still expected to provide balanced diffusion, as per Definition 1, and which in respect to the diffusion at least, behave as randomly generated binary matrices.

3.1 Rotation-Based Linear Layers

In FASTA, we follow the principle introduced in Rasta to (pseudorandomly) draw linear transformations from a large family $\mathcal{L}$, to be used only once in a particular instantiation of the cipher. Below we describe a general method for constructing a family of FHE-friendly linear transformations, with the aim of providing balanced diffusion. In Sect. 4 we use this method to construct the specific class of linear transformations used in FASTA. In the following explanation we use the notation $v[i]$ to indicate bit number i in a bit-string v, and $v[i,j], i < j$ to indicate the sequence of bits from position i up to and including position j in v.

The linear transformations we produce are based on *column parity mixers* [SD18]. Let the cipher state consist of bs bits, split into b words $w_0, \ldots, w_{b-1}$ of s bits each. A column parity mixer works by first computing $u = w_0 \oplus \ldots \oplus w_{b-1}$ and then applying a simple linear transformation Θ to the sum to compute $v = \Theta(u)$. The word v is added back onto the input words to form the output words w_i' of the column parity mixer, as $w_i' = w_i + v$. See Fig. 3 for a schematic description. In the following we also refer to one application of the column parity mixer as an *iteration*.

We are concerned with constructing a class of linear transformations $\mathcal{L}$ of dimension bs over $\mathbb{F}_2$ that provides close to balanced diffusion. Let $x_0, \ldots, x_{b-1}$ be the input words to any $L \in \mathcal{L}$, and $y_0, \ldots, y_{b-1}$ be the output words. For any $0 \le i, k < b$ and $0 \le j, l < s$, we want $x_i[j]$ to appear in the linear expression for $y_k[l]$ for approximately half of the linear transformations in $\mathcal{L}$. As we will only use rotations of words and the column parity mixer construction, we can without loss of generality focus on $x_0[0]$ and ensure this bit will appear in approximately half of the linear combinations giving output bits $y_k[l]$. We say that a bit in any word w_i during the computation of the linear transformation is *affected* if it has

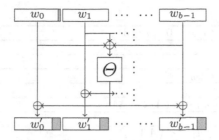

Fig. 3. One iteration of a column parity mixer used to construct rotation-based linear layers (Step 1). Gray areas indicate affected bits.

a non-zero probability of depending on $x_0[0]$. We propose the following general strategy for constructing a family of rotation-based linear layers:

1. Define a column parity mixer based on a transformation Θ that uses rotations of low amounts compared to s, in such a way that all bits in a small neighbourhood of $w_0[0]$ will be affected in all words output from the column parity mixer (see Fig. 6 in Sect. 4 for an example of such Θ, as used in FASTA).
2. Rotate the words w_i between applications of the column parity mixer such that the affected parts are spread to larger portions of the cipher state.
3. Iterate applications of column parity mixers interleaved with word rotations as many times as required until the whole cipher state is affected.

We note that if b is even the column parity mixer (step 1 above) is an involution; if b is odd, the column parity mixer operation is invertible iff $(\Theta + \mathbf{I})$ is invertible [SD18]. Moreover, let $w'_0, \ldots, w'_{b-1}$ be the cipher state after the application of the column parity mixer. Then Θ should be designed such that $w'_i[0, a-1]$ is affected for all $0 \le i < b$ and some value of a relatively small compared to s. This is shown in Fig. 3.

After the first iteration the a least significant bits of each output word w'_i will be affected. More generally, assume that in the output of any one iteration of the column parity mixer, the A least significant bits of each output word are affected, for some $A \ge a$. Here we will denote these words as w_i, as the input to the word rotation operation (step 2). For these rotations, we choose to have the word w_0 left unchanged, while w_i for $1 \le i < b$ are rotated as follows: every word w_i is rotated by $i \cdot A/2 + r_i$ positions, where $r_i \in [0, A/2 - 1]$. The output of step 2 is denoted as $w'_0, \ldots, w'_{b-1}$. See Fig. 4 for an illustration of how each word is rotated.

These rotation amounts ensure three properties. First, the affected parts of w_{i-1} and w_i will overlap in at least one bit when added together in the next iteration, for $i = 1, \ldots, b - 1$. So there cannot be any "gap" where some bit in a word will not be affected. Second, after rotations the least significant bit

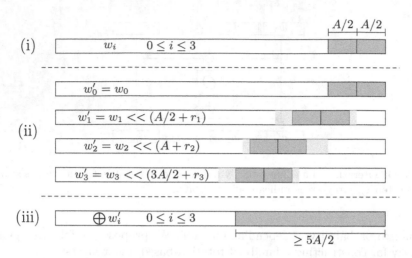

Fig. 4. Word rotation operation (step 2), applied between two iterations of the column parity mixer, acting on states with $b = 4$ words. The output words of the previous the column parity mixer, each with A least significant bits affected, are represented in region (i). The word rotation operation itself is shown in region (ii). Region (iii) represents the initial sum operation in the next iteration of the column parity mixer, with at least $5A/2$ affected bits in the input to next iteration's Θ. The block of affected bits can be anywhere in the light grey areas, depending on the values of r_i.

of the affected part of w_{i-1} cannot overlap with the affected part of w_i, for $i = 1, \ldots, b-1$. In other words, the affected parts of w_i and w_j may not overlap exactly when $i \neq j$, for any choice of r_i and r_j. Two neighboring w_i-words may therefore not cancel out when added together in the input to the next iteration. Third, the input to Θ in the next iteration will then be affected in (at least) all bits in positions $0, \ldots, (b+1)A/2$. Hence the size of the block of affected bits will increase by a factor of at least $(b+1)/2$ from one iteration to the next.

Using this strategy, the number of affected bits in $w_0, \ldots, w_{b-1}$ will grow exponentially with the number of iterations, and after $\lceil \log_{(b+1)/2}(s) \rceil$ iterations we are guaranteed the whole cipher state will be affected.

3.2   The Structure in Rotation-Based Linear Layers

One can imagine many other ways of designing a linear transformation acting on a state consisting of s-bit words, using only rotations within the words and XOR additions of whole words. We show below that any linear transformation within these constraints will have a particular structure.

Assume that the state consists of $w_0, \ldots, w_{b-1}$, where each w_i is a word of s bits. We let the state block w be a binary vector of length bs, given as the concatenation of the words: $w = (w_0 || \ldots || w_{b-1})$. Let M be the $bs \times bs$ matrix over $\mathbb{F}_2$ that realises a rotation-based linear transformation L, such that the output of L is given as $L(\boldsymbol{w}) = \boldsymbol{w}M$.

Proposition 1. *The matrix M can be decomposed into b^2 sub-matrices $M_{i,j}$ for $0 \leq i, j \leq b-1$ of size $s \times s$ each. Let $M_{i,j}[r]$ be row r in $M_{i,j}$, for $0 \leq r \leq s-1$. Then $M_{i,j}[r] = M_{i,j}[0] << r$.*

Proof. Let the state $\boldsymbol{e}_i$ be given as the state where bit number i in $\boldsymbol{e}_i$ is 1, and all others are 0, for $0 \leq i \leq bs - 1$. Then the top row of M is given as $L(\boldsymbol{e}_0)$. Whatever bits are set in $L(\boldsymbol{e}_0)$, they are all a result of the single 1-bit in $\boldsymbol{e}_0$ being added multiple times onto the words, with rotations of the words in between.

The second row of M is given as $L(\boldsymbol{e}_1)$. The exact same additions and rotations that produced $L(\boldsymbol{e}_0)$ from the single set input bit will also produce $L(\boldsymbol{e}_1)$, except everything happens shifted by one position to the left, modulo s. Hence every word in $L(\boldsymbol{e}_1)$ will be equal to the same word in $L(\boldsymbol{e}_0)$, but shifted by one position. This repeats for every row of M, so $M_{0,j}[r] = M_{0,j}[r-1] << 1$.

Row s of M is produced as $L(\boldsymbol{e}_s)$. The single set bit in the input then jumps from appearing in w_0 of the state to w_1. The word w_1 is rotated independently of w_0, so the cancellations and additions from the single set bit in $\boldsymbol{e}_s$ that occurs when producing $L(\boldsymbol{e}_s)$ are different from those that produced $L(\boldsymbol{e}_{s-1})$. Hence row s of M, and the top row of each $M_{1,j}$, will be unrelated to row $s-1$ of M. However, each row $M_{1,j}[r]$ will be rotations of $M_{1,j}[0]$ by the same reason given above. This argument repeats every time the single set bit in $\boldsymbol{e}_i$ jumps from one word to the next, and the result follows.

Proposition 1 essentially states that M can be decomposed into b^2 circulant matrices. This can also be observed by noticing that M may be considered as the binary representation of a linear transformation over the module $\mathcal{R}^b$, where $\mathcal{R}$ is the ring $\mathbb{F}_2[X]/(X^s + 1)$. We provide more details in Appendix A. Also in the Appendix, Fig. 9 gives an example of a matrix realising a rotation-based linear layer with $b = 5$ and $s = 329$ (as used in FASTA). For comparison, it also shows a matrix realising five parallel applications of Rasta (with same parameters). The block structure is clearly visible in the rotation-based linear transformation, whilst the comparable matrix for Rasta is a block diagonal matrix with random blocks.

4   Specification of FASTA

In this section we define FASTA, a stream cipher whose circuit for generating the keystream has been designed to be efficiently evaluated homomorphically. As the name suggests, FASTA is based on *Rasta* and is *fast* to execute when implemented in HElib using the BGV levelled homomorphic encryption scheme (see Sect. 2.3). We define a single instantiation of FASTA, with parameters selected to give 128 bits of security, both as a stand-alone symmetric cipher and when used in tandem with a specific instantiation of the BGV scheme it is designed for. It is of course possible to make variants of FASTA with higher or lower security claims, but one should then also find instances of FHE schemes with the same security level and with a number of slots that matches the given variant of FASTA. Finding matching combinations of FHE parameters and symmetric designs is a study in itself, so we limit ourselves to focus on only one particular variant here. We follow Rasta's approach for setting the data limit, that at most $2^{64}/1645$ calls to FASTA with the same key can be made.[6]

Fig. 5. High-level description of FASTA.

4.1   High-Level Overview

FASTA takes a 329-bit secret key K and produces 1645 bits of keystream at each call. The cipher state consists of five words $w_0, \ldots, w_4$ of 329 bits each that are initialised as $w_i = (K << i)$, for the secret key K. The choice of word length (329 bits) follows a search for values of m as an instantiation of BGV, that provided 128 bits of security (as FHE scheme) and gave a large, odd number of slots s. The value selected was the prime $m = 30269$, so that $\phi(m) = 30268 = 329 \times 92$, giving $s = 329$ slots (see Sect. 2.3). The number of state words (five) provided a good trade-off between the size of the state and the number of iterations required to generate invertible rotation-based linear layers which are expected to offer balanced diffusion.

---

[6] Since FASTA has a 1645-bit state, this sets the maximum length of the keystream generated under the same key to 2^{64} bits.

Each application of FASTA takes in $7 \cdot (63 + 1645) = 11956$ pseudo-random bits for specifying the particular permutation that produces a keystream block. These bits are labelled $\alpha = (\alpha_0, \ldots, \alpha_6)$, where each α_j is a 1708-bit value. In the same way as Rasta, the contents of α are pseudorandomly generated based on a counter and a nonce N which are fed into a XOF (see Fig. 2).

The keystream generation applies a round function 6 times. The round function consists of an affine layer A_{α_j}, indexed by α_j for $0 \le j \le 5$, followed by a non-linear transformation of the cipher state. The keystream generation ends with a final affine layer A_{α_6} and a feed-forward of the secret key XORed onto each of the words. The resulting output is taken as 1645 bits of keystream. The cipher is shown in Fig. 5.

4.2   The Non-linear Layer

The non-linear layer uses the χ-function proposed in [Dae95], which is also used in Rasta and KECCAK. It is applied on each of the five words of the state in parallel as shown in Fig. 5. If we label the input bits to χ as $x_0, \ldots, x_{328}$, the output bits y_i are given by

$$y_i = x_{i+1}x_{i+2} + x_i + x_{i+2},$$

where all indices are computed modulo 329.

4.3   The Affine Layer

Affine layers in FASTA consist of a rotation-based $\mathbb{F}_2$-linear transformation, followed by the addition of a round constant. The linear transformation is constructed as described in Sect. 3.1, with $b = 5$ and $s = 329$, and will consist of four iterations. A guiding principle in Rasta, which we also follow in FASTA, is that every linear transformation is pseudorandomly generated from a large family of transformations and is used only once in an instantiation of FASTA. The affine transformation we use is parameterised by a 1708-bit value α_j, which will select instances from the class of linear mappings from Sect. 3.1, as well as selecting the constant to be added after the linear transformation.

The Θ-function in each iteration is shown in Fig. 6. It ensures that the number of affected bits in the output is increased by 9 from the number of affected bits in the input. Moreover, as b is odd, the possible choices for rotation values ensure that the resulting column parity mixer operation, and therefore the entire affine layer, is invertible.

Recall that the affected part of each word at any point is defined as the bits that may depend on the bit $x_0[0]$ at the input of the linear transformation. After the first iteration, the number of affected bits in each word will be 10. The rotations before the next iteration are therefore given as:

$$\begin{aligned} w_1 &= (w_1 << 5 + i_1), & w_3 &= (w_3 << 15 + i_3) \\ w_2 &= (w_2 << 10 + i_2), & w_4 &= (w_4 << 20 + i_4) \end{aligned}, \text{ where } 0 \le i_* \le 4.$$

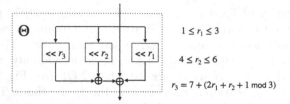

Fig. 6. The Θ-function used in FASTA's linear layer. The values of r_1 and r_2 are generated randomly from the nonce N, and the value given for r_3 ensures invertibility of the resulting column parity mixer operation.

The number of affected bits in the block going into the second Θ will therefore be at least $20 + 10 = 30$, and the number of affected bits in each word after the second iteration will be at least 39. The words $w_1, \ldots, w_4$ are then rotated by

$$w_1 = (w_1 << 19 + j_1), w_3 = (w_3 << 57 + j_3)$$
$$w_2 = (w_2 << 38 + j_2), w_4 = (w_4 << 76 + j_4), \text{ where } 0 \leq j_* \leq 18.$$

The affected part of the word going into Θ in the third iteration will then cover at least the $39 + 76 = 115$ least significant bits, and the output will have at least 124 affected bits. The output is added onto every word, so the 124 least significant bits of every w_i will be affected. The words $w_1, \ldots, w_4$ are then rotated by the following amounts before going into the fourth and last iteration:

$$w_1 = (w_1 << 62 + l_1), w_3 = (w_3 << 186 + l_3)$$
$$w_2 = (w_2 << 124 + l_2), w_4 = (w_4 << 248 + l_4), \text{ where } 0 \leq l_* \leq 61.$$

Note that the most significant bits of the affected part of the word w_4 (located in positions $123, 122, \ldots$) wraps around when rotated by 248 positions, as the words have length 329. This means that the entire input block to Θ in the last iteration will be affected, and after adding the output of Θ onto each w_i the entire cipher state is affected. The complete linear transformation is depicted in Fig. 7.

Pseudorandomly generating the rotation-based affine layers A_{α_j}. The rotation values of the linear transformations and the constant part of the affine layers A_{α_j} are defined based on 1708-bit values α_j generated pseudorandomly (using a XOF). We take 1645 bits from α_j to define the constants value. The remaining 63 bits are used to define 24 rotation values (three used in each of the four instances of Θ and four in each of the three word rotations between Θ-iterations). Details on how this is done are given in Appendix B.

4.4   Comparing FASTA with Other Ciphers for Hybrid Encryption

Rasta is a family of stream ciphers, with the benefit of having a low and constant multiplicative depth regardless of how much keystream is produced (Sect. 2.2).

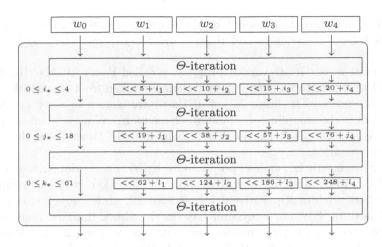

Fig. 7. The linear transformation of FASTA. The exact rotation amounts i_*, j_*, l_* and in the Θ-iterations are determined by α_j.

As discussed, FASTA is a variant of Rasta with a dedicated design for the efficient evaluation over FHE schemes. In fact, as shown in Fig. 5, FASTA could be seen as five parallel calls of Rasta (with block size $s = 329$ and 6 rounds), but with one main difference. In the 5-parallel Rasta calls, the combined affine transformations A_i would be represented by a block diagonal matrix, with each 329×329 block being generated pseudorandomly. On the other hand, in FASTA the A_i are 1645×1645 rotation-based transformations, essentially tying the transformations of the five blocks together. Motivation for the choices for the value of s and the structure of A_i were given early in this section. As shown in Sect. 6, this structure and parameter choices will allow FASTA to be homomorphically evaluated much more efficiently in BGV/HElib, when compared to five parallel calls of Rasta.

Another drawback from Rasta is the inefficiency of requiring many random linear transformations, which need to be generated and stored. Other variants have also been proposed to address this feature. Dasta [HL20] simplifies the generation of the linear layers, by using a single fixed matrix composed with a permutation of the bits in the cipher block. These permutations are constructed by cyclically rotating smaller bit sequences that are part of the cipher block. This means much less randomness is needed from the XOF. However, rotating only part of a cipher block is difficult to achieve in a packed FHE implementation of Dasta. Thus FASTA presents the same advantages when evaluated homomorphically compared to Dasta.

Masta [HKC+20] abandons $\mathbb{F}_2^s$ as the native plaintext space, and can be seen as a Rasta variant with plaintext elements in $\mathbb{F}_p$ for a prime $p > 2$. The linear transformations of Masta are then simply chosen as a multiplication with an element chosen pseudo-randomly from $\mathbb{F}_{p^s}$, where s is the number of slots in the FHE ciphertext. The designers state that this speeds up the homomorphic evaluation of the cipher by a factor of more than 3000 compared to Rasta.

However, this comparison should be done with caution as Masta is tailored to computations on integers and Rasta (and FASTA) was designed for binary circuits.

The most recent Rasta variant proposal is called Pasta [DGH+21b]. In contrast to FASTA, Pasta has the plaintext elements taken from the field $\mathbb{F}_p$, where p is a large prime. The linear layers in Pasta are chosen in a structured way, requiring only the sampling of s random elements from $\mathbb{F}_p$ to generate an $s \times s$ matrix. All together, this leads to Pasta being up to 6 times faster than Masta in certain scenarios.

Other symmetric key ciphers proposed for hybrid encryption include LowMC [ARS+15], FLIP [MJSC16] and Kreyvium [CCF+16]. LowMC is a family of block ciphers, with multiplicative depth at least 12, while Kreyvium is a stream cipher based on Trivium. Kreyvium has the drawback that the multiplicative depth for producing keystream increases with the output length. For comparison with FASTA, producing 1645 bits of keystream with Kreyvium requires multiplicative depth of at least 17 (compared to 6 for FASTA). FLIP is also a stream cipher, with the benefit that the multiplicative depth for producing the keystream is held constant at 4. However, FLIP requires a much larger number of AND operations per bit; moreover, the successful cryptanalysis of its original version [DLR16] called for the selection of more conservative parameters. Finally, we also mention Ciminion [DGGK21], a recent proposal oriented around a large field $\mathbb{F}_q$, which aims to minimise the number of field multiplications in its design. However, while the total number of field multiplications in Ciminion might arguably be small (at least 56), they all appear sequentially. This leads to a multiplicative depth of Ciminion of at least 56, making it very unsuitable for hybrid encryption in the FHE setting.

Overall, among the ecosystem of FHE-friendly stream ciphers, FASTA has been specifically designed to improve on the efficiency of both Rasta and Dasta, while keeping the original plaintext elements as bits in $\mathbb{F}_2$.

5   Security Analysis

FASTA is a Rasta variant, which introduces a new idea for a FHE-friendly linear-layer design. Like Rasta, it also uses the $A(SA)^d$ structure, with the non-linear layer S based on the χ-transformation, and affine round transformations drawn from a large family of affine mappings. Moreover, as discussed above, FASTA can be seen as five parallel calls of a particular Rasta instance, however under the operation of different enlarged linear layers – FASTA's composed of a rotation-based transformation and the 5-parallel Rasta a block diagonal matrix, in both cases pseudo-randomly generated. As a result of these design choices, we claim that we can leverage most of the analysis originally performed for Rasta in [DEG+18] to assess the security of FASTA. For example, like Rasta we also disallow related-key attacks, and thus differential-type attacks should likewise not apply to FASTA. In this section we will therefore only discuss a subset of attacks considered in [DEG+18], indicating when required how to adapt the original discussion to FASTA's setting. We first consider the properties of the rotation-based linear transformations introduced earlier, and used in FASTA. We also discuss the feasibility of attacks based on the algebraic structure of the cipher, and of linear approximation based attacks, again leveraging the corresponding discussions from [DEG+18].

5.1   On the Structure of FASTA's Linear Transformation

Balanced diffusion of FASTA's family of linear transformations. The Θ function used FASTA's linear layer has the property that every input bit in position i, for $0 \le i \le 328$, will affect the output bits in positions $i, \ldots, i + 9$ mod 329. As explained in Sect. 4.3, the influence of $x_0[0]$ will spread to the entire cipher state after applying the linear transformation once. By rotational symmetry, this applies to every bit in the input words, so every bit in the output of the linear transformation may have any of the input bits in its linear expression.

When adding words together at the start of every iteration, some of the affected parts of the input words will overlap. As an input bit to Θ is spread to approximately half of the bits in its neighbourhood of the output, this makes approximately half of the affected part of the cipher state depend on approximately half of the input bits it depends on. In total, we therefore expect balanced diffusion for the linear layers in our family.

To confirm this, we have generated 10000 matrices appearing as linear transformations in FASTA, and considered their statistics compared to rotation-based random matrices. Fig. 8a shows the distribution of the percentage of set bits in these matrices. The distribution is well approximated by a normal distribution with mean 50%, but have a slightly higher variance of set bits than random invertible rotation-based matrices.

In Fig. 8b we have measured how well a sample of 10000 matrices satisfies balanced diffusion according to Definition 1. More precisely, for a given pair of numbers (i, j), $0 \le i, j \le 1644$ we measured $Pr[\langle \mathbf{e}_i L, \mathbf{e}_j \rangle = 1]$ across the 10000 matrices. We did this for all $1645 \times 1645 = 2706025$ different pairs (i, j), and counted the frequencies of probabilities seen. The plot is shown in Fig. 8b, and compared against the same experiment for random invertible rotation-based matrices. As we can see, all probabilities are normally distributed around 0.5, and there is no significant difference between the matrices used in FASTA and those generated at random.

Pairwise dependence/independence of entries in the linear transformation. The FASTA state consists of 5 words with 329 bits each. Proposition 1 decomposes the linear transformation matrix M into 25 submatrices, each of size 329×329. Each of these 25 submatrices are defined in terms of their respective top row. Looking at each submatrix in isolation, each of its rows is a cyclic rotation by 1 of the row above. Let D be a submatrix of M, and $D_{i,j}$ be an entry

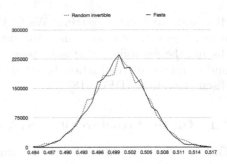

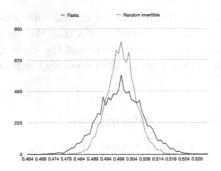

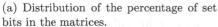

(a) Distribution of the percentage of set bits in the matrices.

(b) Distribution of measured values of $Pr[\langle e_i L, e_j \rangle]$ across the matrices, for all $0 \le i, j \le 1644$.

Fig. 8. Statistics for 10000 matrices used in FASTA and 10000 rotation-based invertible matrices with 5×5 blocks and random top row in each block.

in D. It follows from the row rotation property that $D_{i+1,j+1} = D_{i,j}$, which generalizes to $D_{0,j} = D_{a,j+a}$, for $0 \le a, j \le 328$ and where indices are computed modulo 329.

As M displays random behaviour and is expected to provide balanced diffusion, we will make the reasonable assumption that pairwise entries are independent, for any of the 25 submatrices in M. Furthermore, two entries from different submatrices are also treated as independent.

5.2   Algebraic Attacks

Given the keystream $Z = (z_0, \ldots, z_{1644})$ produced on a call to FASTA's keystream generator for an unknown key $K = (k_0, \ldots, k_{328})$, it is possible to express the keystream bits as polynomials in $k_0, \ldots, k_{328}$ to get a set of polynomial equations over $\mathbb{F}_2$:

$$
\begin{aligned}
f_0(k_0, \ldots, k_{328}) + z_0 &= 0 \\
f_1(k_0, \ldots, k_{328}) + z_1 &= 0 \\
&\vdots \\
f_{1644}(k_0, \ldots, k_{328}) + z_{1644} &= 0
\end{aligned}
\tag{1}
$$

The attacker may repeat calls to the keystream generator to gather more such equations. The fact that new linear layers will be applied for each repetition means that new functions f_i will be used to define these fresh equations, up to 2^{64} due to the cipher's data limit. We therefore consider algebraic attacks to be the most promising cryptanalytical technique against FASTA, and consider its feasibility below.

Standard linearization-based attack. The equation system (1) forms the foundation of the standard linearization attack. In such an attack, given a system of non-linear multivariate polynomial equations, all monomials are substituted with a new "variable", and the resulting set is considered as a system of linear equations over these variables. To fully solve this system, an attacker needs to collect as many equations as there are variables, which then allows for a unique solution to be found through Gaussian elimination. Thus, the complexity of solving such a system based on this method is directly dependent on the number of monomials in the original system.

The maximum number of different monomials we can get is dependent on the algebraic degree of each f_i. For FASTA, the algebraic degree of f_i is upper bounded by $2^6 = 64$, since the degree doubles with every application of χ and FASTA has six rounds. Thus the size of the linearized system will be at most $\sum_{i=0}^{64} \binom{329}{i} \approx 2^{535}$.

This value is computed by only considering χ in the forward direction. It is well known that the inverse of χ has high degree, but through careful study of the relationships between input and output bits to the χ operation, the authors of [LSMI21] derived further equations arising in the last round of Rasta, Dasta, and in fact FASTA. There are two important consequences of this result. Firstly, $5 \times 1645 = 8225$ equations can be derived per application of FASTA, instead of only 1645. Secondly, the last round can effectively be peeled off since the equations describing χ in the last round do not multiply inputs together, only inputs and outputs. The outputs of χ in the last round can be described as linear polynomials in $k_0, \dots, k_{328}$, and the inputs will be polynomials of degree 32. So the number of monomials in the generated equations is reduced to at most

$$U = \sum_{i=0}^{33} \binom{329}{i} \approx 329^{33} \approx 2^{276}. \tag{2}$$

Under the assumption that all U monomials of degree up to 33 over the 329 variables are present in the system of equations, the complexity of such attack (solving a system of linear equations of size $\approx 2^{276}$) is way higher than the security level claimed for FASTA (128 bits of security). This is the behaviour we may expect for large random systems. However, for FASTA (and Rasta) we are not guaranteed that U is the number of monomials which will actually occur in the system. We explore this question in Appendix C, and conclude that the expected number of monomials appearing in the algebraic equations linking the unknowns $k_0, \dots, k_{328}$ to the keystream bits is indeed approximated by U. Thus, similar to Rasta, linearization-based attacks are not a threat to FASTA.

Other algebraic approaches. The maximum number U of monomials could be reduced by guessing g key bits, at the cost of increasing the complexity of the linearization attack by a factor of 2^g. This implies a cut-off for guessing bits at $g = 128$, where the complexity increase alone will equal the claimed security level.

Even when guessing 128 of the bits in K, we are still left with $U = \sum_{i=0}^{33} \binom{201}{i} \approx 2^{252}$ monomials to linearise. As the data complexity is limited to

$2^{64}/1645 \approx 2^{54}$ calls to FASTA for a given key K, the maximum number of equations we can generate, taking [LSMI21] into account, is $5 \cdot 1645 \cdot 2^{64}/1645 \approx 2^{66.3}$. We can therefore conclude that an attacker will not be able to generate enough equations for a linearization attack to succeed.

A more advanced form of algebraic attacks is based on Gröbner basis algorithms. In this case, the cipher's non-linear system is considered in its original form, and attempted to be solved using, e.g. Faugère's F5 algorithm [Fau02]. The complexity of Gröbner basis algorithms is not fully understood for systems arising from cryptographic algorithms. Although they have been applied successfully in cryptanalysis, given the sizes involved in the FASTA system, we do not consider GB-based attacks a threat to FASTA.

5.3   Attacks Based on Linear Approximations

To assess the feasibility of attacks based on linear approximations against FASTA, we refer to the discussion in [DEG+18, Section 3.2]. There, the authors of Rasta derive upper bounds for the correlation of linear approximations after $d = 2r$ rounds based on the properties of the χ transformation. This is done by estimating the number of active bits in the input/output of applications of χ, under the assumption the linear layers are randomly generated. For example, they conclude that Rasta with block $n = 351$ and $d = 6$ rounds is not susceptible to attacks based on linear approximations.

For FASTA, the transformations in the linear layer are not random, but rather pseudo-randomly generated among the rotation-based matrices defined in Sect. 3. More importantly however, the non-linear layer in FASTA consists of five parallel applications of the χ transformation. Given the diffusion properties that the linear layer is expected to feature, we expect that any linear trail over two rounds of FASTA will have a correlation of much lower magnitude than for Rasta (which would consist of six applications of χ, compared to $5 \times 6 = 30$ for FASTA). Our conclusion is therefore that, as with Rasta, attacks based on linear approximations are not feasible against the parameters chosen for FASTA.

5.4   Other Classical Attacks

Differential attacks, higher-order differential attacks, cube attacks, and integral attacks all try to exploit the structure of a cipher in one way or another. A differential attack looks for advantageous characteristics present in the structure, before attempting to find pairs of plaintexts which satisfy these characteristics. Higher-order attacks and cube attacks exploit the algebraic degree of the output bits of a primitive, while integral attacks make use of curated sets of plaintexts. They all have in common a need to evaluate the cryptographic primitive more than once and with different inputs. With FASTA, the circuit generating a block of keystream is only used once. Furthermore, the attacker does not have the freedom to choose different inputs to FASTA's keystream generation function, as it is always the secret key. We therefore conclude that these attacks are infeasible to execute against FASTA.

6   Homomorphic Implementation of FASTA

Software libraries implementing FHE or levelled homomorphic encryption (LHE) schemes have gone through extensive development over the last years. They now appear as quite robust, well documented, and user friendly. The libraries and schemes we have considered during the design of FASTA were: HElib and PALISADE with their implementations of the BGV scheme; SEAL and PALISADE with the BFV scheme; TFHE with the torus-based FHE scheme; and PALISADE's FHEW scheme. HElib, PALISADE, and SEAL also implement the CKKS scheme, but as CKKS is an approximate LHE scheme with real numbers as the plaintext space, it is not suitable for implementing Boolean circuits.

We have designed FASTA to be fast when evaluated homomorphically, while also being based on a dedicated symmetric cipher for FHE, namely Rasta. In order to ensure fast evaluation, the parallelism offered by multiple slots in the FHE scheme is used to pack many bits of the cipher state into one FHE ciphertext. The TFHE library does not yet support such parallelism, and has therefore not been a target for the design of FASTA.

Both the BFV and BGV schemes provide ciphertexts with multiple slots, but BFV needs the number of slots to be a power of 2. Also, the BGVrns scheme will always have an even number of slots. As we use the χ-transformation in FASTA's non-linear layer, this makes BFV and BGVrns less suitable since χ is only invertible when the cipher state words going through χ have an odd number of bits. Implementing FASTA (or Rasta for that matter) in BFV using packing will then have to use *dummy slots*, i.e. slots in the FHE ciphertext that are not used, but still need to be accounted for when doing rotations, as discussed below. A symmetric cipher suitable for the BFV scheme should be designed differently, and use a set of small S-boxes in a bit-sliced fashion instead of χ as the non-linear transformation.

As the number of slots in BFV and BGVrns is much higher than 329, typically in the range 2^{13} to 2^{16} for parameters giving 128-bit security, we will only use the 329 first slots of a ciphertext $c^* = \{(c_1, c_2, \ldots, c_{329}, 0, 0, \ldots, 0)\}$, and need to do cyclic rotations over only these slots. A natural way to rotate c by a positions in the 329 first slots is to first rotate c by a positions to the right, $c_r^* = (c^* >> a)$, then by $329 - a$ positions to the left, $c_l^* = (c^* << (329 - a))$, and add the two ciphertexts:

$$c_r^* = \{(\overbrace{0, \ldots, 0, c_1, c_2, \ldots, c_{329-a}}^{329 \text{ first slots}}, c_{329-a+1}, \ldots, c_{329}, 0, \ldots, 0)\}$$

$$c_l^* = \{(\overbrace{c_{329-a+1}, \ldots, c_{329}, 0, \ldots, 0}^{329 \text{ first slots}}, 0, 0, \ldots, 0, c_1, \ldots, c_{329-a})\}$$

$$c_l^* + c_r^* = \{(\overbrace{c_{329-a+1}, \ldots, c_{329}, c_1, \ldots, c_{329-a}}^{329 \text{ first slots}}, c_{329-a+1}, \ldots, c_{329}, 0, \ldots, 0, c_1, \ldots, c_{329-a})\}$$

This effectively does a cyclic rotation of the first 329 slots, but leaves non-zero plaintext values in the dummy slots, which need to be zeroed out to prevent them from being shifted back in on subsequent rotations. This can be done by *masking*, multiplying with a plaintext that is 1 in the 329 first slots and zero elsewhere. Unfortunately, a plaintext-ciphertext multiplication is only somewhat cheaper in terms of noise growth than a ciphertext-ciphertext multiplication, so making a customized rotation in BFV or BGVrns to accommodate for dummy slots is simply too costly in a practical implementation.

On the other hand, the BGV scheme as implemented in HElib have instances with an odd number of slots in each ciphertext. We have therefore designed FASTA to take advantage of these features, and thus enable particularly efficient homomorphic evaluation with BGV in HElib. The basis for the BGV scheme is the cyclotomic polynomial Φ_m, where m is chosen by the user. The parameter m decides the number of slots, and together with the noise budget in fresh ciphertexts, a parameter denoted by bits in HElib, also decides the estimated security level for the instance of BGV. Searching for suitable values of m we found that $m = 30269$ gives 329 slots in HElib and a security level of just over 128 bits when bits = 500 (if bits is lower, the security level increases). Hence we designed FASTA to give 128-bit security in itself, and to be used with the particular instance of BGV where $m = 30269$. Running FASTA in HElib with $m = 30269$ consumes approximately 260 bits , leaving up to 240 bits more for further computations in an actual use case.

Implementing FASTA in HElib starts by encrypting the 329-bit key K five times into five different HElib ciphertexts $w_0^*, \ldots, w_4^*$ with 329 slots each. Five copies of w_i^* are then made for the feed-forward of the key at the end of FASTA. The initial rotations are done by setting $w_i^* = (w_i^* << i)$, before the first affine layer is executed using only rotations and additions of the five ciphertexts. The χ-transformation works on each w_i^* individually, and is done by making two copies of w_i^* that are rotated by 1 and 2 positions respectively: $u_1^* = (w_i^* << 1)$ and $u_2^* = (w_i^* << 2)$. The output of χ is then computed as $u_1^* \times u_2^* + w_i^* + u_2^*$, using only a single ciphertext-ciphertext multiplication. The rest of FASTA is executed homomorphically in the same way, using only rotations, additions and a single multiplication for each word in the non-linear layer of each round. Finally the initial copies of w_i^* are added to the five ciphertexts in the end to produce a block of 1645 bits of key stream encrypted under FHE.

6.1   Timings of Implementations

We have made both packed and bit-sliced implementations of FASTA and Rasta in some of the libraries, and timed the execution times. The code is available at https://github.com/Simula-UiB/Fasta. The packed version of Rasta used mul when multiplying with random matrices in the linear layer, and the block size was modified from 351 to 329 to make the block fit exactly in the BGV ciphertext (we denote this version as Rasta* in Table 1). In addition we also ran 6-round Rasta implementations published at [DGH+21a]. Parameters in the BFV and BGV schemes used were chosen to give roughly 500 bits in noise budget, for equal comparison. The timings were done on a MacBook Pro with a 2.3 GHz Intel Core i5 processor and 16 GB RAM. The results are given in Table 1.

Table 1. Amortized time (in seconds) to produce one bit of key stream when executing homomorphic implementations of Rasta and FASTA. (Rasta* denotes the cipher with a 329-bit block.)

	Library(Scheme)	Cipher	FHE encoding	time χ	time lin. trans	time total
Implementations from [DGH+21a]	TFHE	Rasta (6 r.)	bit-sliced	0.3640	13.902	14.266
	HElib(BGV)	Rasta (6 r.)	bit-sliced	3.079	0.510	3.589
	SEAL(BFV)	Rasta (6 r.)	bit-sliced	0.6122	0.1918	0.8040
	HElib(BGV)	Rasta (6 r.)	packed	0.0956	1.0083	1.1039
Our own implementations	PALISADE (FHEW)	Rasta (6 r.)	bit-sliced	15.73	1197.8	1213.6
	TFHE	Rasta (6 r.)	bit-sliced	0.2296	11.331	11.56
	HElib(BGV)	Rasta* (6 r.)	packed	0.0166	0.2670	0.2836
	HElib(BGV)	FASTA (6 r.)	packed	0.0166	0.0260	0.0427

Unsurprisingly, the packed implementations are faster than the bit-sliced ones encrypting only a single bit in each ciphertext. The bit-sliced implementations were all optimized with "the method of the four russians" in the matrix multiplication. In the user manual of PALISADE [PRRC21, Sec. 9.3] it is noted that both the XOR and AND gates take the same amount of time in that library's implementation of FHEW. Hence the very large number of XOR gates in the matrix multiplication of Rasta explains the extremely high execution time. Note that the packed implementation from [DGH+21a] uses the 351-bit block size specified for Rasta, and therefore needs to use masking in its operations. This explains the faster run times we have for Rasta with 329-bit block.

For the packed versions, we find that FASTA is 25 times faster than Rasta, and more than 6 times faster than the "optimized" version of Rasta where the block size fits the FHE ciphertext. The difference in runtimes for Rasta with 329-bit block and FASTA is entirely due to the linear layer of FASTA having been designed for fast execution in HElib.

7 Conclusions

The design of symmetric ciphers for use with FHE has so far focused primarily on minimising multiplicative complexity. However the libraries implementing various FHE schemes have matured over the last years, with some attractive implementation features, and are now more robust and user friendly than the early versions. This motivated us to study the implementation and homomorphic evaluation of a prominent family of FHE-friendly ciphers, Rasta, on the most well-known FHE libraries.

We found that the parameters of Rasta make it difficult to efficiently use the parallelism offered by some of the FHE schemes, namely BGV and BFV. The reason for this is that these schemes are quite inflexible when it comes to the number of slots available in a single FHE ciphertext. In the case of BFV and BGVrns, the number of slots becomes much larger than we need when these schemes are instantiated with parameters giving 128-bit security. On the other hand, for BGV in HElib the number of slots in a single ciphertext is more in line with the block size of a symmetric cipher, but it is still determined by the m-parameter and cannot be chosen freely by the user. This led us to propose FASTA.

Our research showed that when packing the bits of the symmetric cipher state into single FHE ciphertexts, only two operations are cheap to perform: additions of full FHE ciphertexts, and cyclic rotations. Multiplications, both between two ciphertexts and between plaintext and ciphertext, are expensive and should be kept to a minimum. Moreover we also found that for efficient implementations, it is important to fit the cipher block exactly into FHE ciphertexts. Otherwise, excessive slots need to be zeroed out after rotations, which invokes multiplications with a plaintext mask.

Typical FHE-friendly symmetric designs, focusing primarily on low multiplicative complexity, appear to assume bit-sliced implementations of the cipher, where we only encrypt a single bit into each FHE ciphertext and do not need to worry about slots. They are indeed easy to implement, but these choices lead to a high run-time when evaluated homomorphically. As computational complexity is the major bottleneck for FHE it is crucial that implementations can take advantage of packing features in the main FHE libraries. Our proposal FASTA demonstrates that by taking into account the features of FHE libraries and schemes in the design process we may achieve a secure and efficient FHE-friendly symmetric cipher.

Acknowledgements. We wish to thank Joan Daemen for helpful advice and discussions on column parity mixers in the early stage of this work.

A   Matrix Structure of Rotation-Based Linear Transformations

To observe and study the structure of rotation-based linear transformation matrices introduced in Sect. 3.1, we recall the steps for constructing a rotation-based linear transformation acting on b s-bit words $w_0, \ldots, w_{b-1}$.

1. Define a column parity mixer based on a Θ operation using rotations of low amounts (compared to the word length s; see Fig. 3).
2. Apply rotations to the words w_i between applications of the column parity mixer.
3. Iterate applications of column parity mixers with rotations in between, as much as needed until the entire cipher state is affected.

To describe the structure of (binary) matrices defined as above, it is helpful to consider rotation-based linear transformations as operations over the module $\mathcal{R}^b$, where $\mathcal{R}$ is the ring $\mathbb{F}_2[X]/(X^s + 1)$. In this case, each w_i can be considered as a polynomial $w_i(X) = a_{s-1}X^{s-1} + \ldots + a_2X^2 + a_1X + 1$, where $a_j \in \mathbb{F}_2$. Note that the XOR operation of two words w_i, w_j corresponds to addition in $\mathcal{R}$, while the rotation operation $w_i << r$ corresponds to the multiplication of $w_i(X)$ by X^r.

Then let $\boldsymbol{w} = (w_0, \ldots, w_{b-1}) \in \mathcal{R}^b$ be the input of a rotation-based linear transformation L defined as above. The application of a column parity mixer based on a Θ operation using rotations/XORs (step 1) corresponds to:

(i) $(w_0, \ldots, w_{b-1}) \mapsto (w_0 + \ldots + w_{b-1}) = w \in \mathcal{R}$
(ii) $w \mapsto w \cdot p_\Theta$, where $p_\Theta \in \mathcal{R}$ is a polynomial defined by the rotations and XOR operations in Θ.
(iii) $w \cdot p_\Theta \mapsto (w_0 + w \cdot p_\Theta, \ldots, w_{b-1} + w \cdot p_\Theta) \in \mathcal{R}^b$.

Thus application of a column parity mixer operation on $\boldsymbol{w} = (w_0, \ldots, w_{b-1}) \in \mathcal{R}^b$ can be represented as a matrix over $\mathcal{R}$ given by

$$P_\Theta = \begin{pmatrix} p_\Theta + 1 & p_\Theta & \cdots & p_\Theta \\ p_\Theta & p_\Theta + 1 & \cdots & p_\Theta \\ \cdots & \cdots & \cdots & \cdots \\ p_\Theta & p_\Theta & \cdots & p_\Theta + 1 \end{pmatrix}$$

Likewise, the application of rotations $<< r_i$ to the individual words w_i of the state (step 2) can be represented as a matrix

$$R_v = \begin{pmatrix} X^{r_0} & 0 & \cdots & 0 \\ 0 & X^{r_1} & \cdots & 0 \\ \cdots & \cdots & \cdots & \cdots \\ 0 & 0 & \cdots & X^{r_{b-1}} \end{pmatrix},$$

where $v = (r_0, r_1, \ldots, r_{b-1})$. These two operations are then iterated n times, using different Θ_i and word rotations $v_i = (r_0, \ldots r_{b-1})$ (step 3). It follows that the matrix M representing a rotation-based linear transformation over $\mathcal{R}^b$ can be defined as

$$M = P_{\Theta_1} \cdot R_{v_1} \cdot P_{\Theta_2} \cdot R_{v_2} \cdot \ldots \cdot R_{v_{n-1}} \cdot P_{\Theta_n}$$

Every entry of M is a univariate polynomial of degree at most $s - 1$. Note that the multiplication of $w_i \in \mathcal{R}$ by a polynomial $p \in \mathcal{R}$, when considered as a $\mathbb{F}_2$-linear transformation, can be represented as a binary circulant matrix. It follows that, when considered as a $\mathbb{F}_2$-linear transformation acting on the state block $\boldsymbol{w} \in (\mathbb{F}_2)^{bs}$, the $bs \times bs$ matrix M realising a rotation-based linear transformation L, with $L(\boldsymbol{w}) = \boldsymbol{w}M$, can be decomposed into b^2 sub-matrices as described in Proposition 1.

For example in FASTA, we have $b = 5$ and $s = 329$. Moreover, Θ can be realised by multiplication by the polynomial $p_\Theta = X^{r_3} + X^{r_2} + X^{r_1} + 1$ (where $1 \leq r_1 \leq 3$, $4 \leq r_2 \leq 6$, and $7 \leq r_3 \leq 9$; refer to Fig. 6), and the word rotation operations R_v are defined as given in Fig. 7. Four iterations are required to generate the matrix M. As discussed in Sect. 4, these choices ensure that the matrices P_Θ, R_v, and as consequence M, are invertible. An example of such a matrix M generated following this method can be seen in Fig. 9a. Each of the 25 blocks is a 329×329 circulant matrix over $\mathbb{F}_2$.

For the purpose of comparison, we also include the matrix for a linear transformation realising five parallel calls to Rasta with same parameters (Fig. 9b).

In this case, the resulting linear transformation can be represented as a block diagonal matrix, with random 329×329 sub-matrices in the diagonal, and all zero matrices elsewhere.

(a) Matrix realising a rotation-based linear transformation with 5 words of length 329.

(b) Matrix for linear layer tying five parallel applications of Rasta together.

Fig. 9. Structure of matrices for FASTA and five parallel calls to Rasta. Black pixels indicate 1-bits and blue pixels are 0-bits.

B   Mapping α_j to Rotation Values and Round Constants

Let $r_1^{(t)}$, $r_2^{(t)}$ and $r_3^{(t)}$ be the rotation amounts used in Θ in iteration t, for $1 \le t \le 4$. There are then 24 rotation amounts that need to be decided from α_j. The $r_1^{(t)}$ and $r_2^{(t)}$ can take 3 values each, and $r_3^{(t)}$ is computed from these, for a total of nine different instances of Θ. Each of the four i_*, j_*, l_* can take 5, 19, and 62 values each, respectively. There are therefore $T = 3^8 \cdot 5^4 \cdot 19^4 \cdot 62^4 \approx 2^{62.78}$ different instances in the class $\mathcal{L}$ of rotation-based linear transformations we have defined.

We split α_j into $\alpha_j = (\alpha_j^r, \alpha_j^c)$, where α_j^r is 63 bits and α_j^c is 1645 bits. The 24 rotation values are computed from α_j^r, as in Algorithm 1. Apart from the $r_3^{(t)}$ values, what we are essentially doing is first computing $B = \alpha_j^r \mod T$, and then writing B in a mixed base: the eight least significant digits in base 3, the next four digits in base 5, the next four in base 19, and the four most significant digits in base 62. Keeping in mind that $r_1^{(t)}$ and $r_2^{(t)}$ will have 1 and 4 added to them, the rotation amounts can then be read out as the digits of B, written in this mixed base:

$$B = k_3 \cdot 62^3 \cdot 19^4 \cdot 5^4 \cdot 3^8 + k_2 \cdot 62^2 \cdot 19^4 \cdot 5^4 \cdot 3^8 + \dots$$
$$+ r_2^{(2)} \cdot 3^5 + r_2^{(1)} \cdot 3^4 + r_1^{(4)} \cdot 3^3 + r_1^{(3)} \cdot 3^2 + r_1^{(2)} \cdot 3 + r_1^{(1)}.$$

After applying the linear transformation, the 1645-bit value α_j^c is XORed onto the state to produce the affine layer output.

Algorithm 1: Determining rotation amounts from α_j^r.

Result: Rotation amounts for linear transformation are fixed.

$B \leftarrow \alpha_j^r \bmod T$

for $t = 1$ to 4 **do**

   $r_1^{(t)} \leftarrow 1 + (B \bmod 3)$

   $B \leftarrow \lfloor B/3 \rfloor$

end for

for $t = 1$ to 4 **do**

   $r_2^{(t)} \leftarrow 4 + (B \bmod 3)$

   $r_3^{(t)} \leftarrow 7 + (2r_1^{(t)} + r_2^{(t)} + 1 \bmod 3)$

   $B \leftarrow \lfloor B/3 \rfloor$

end for

for $t = 1$ to 4 **do**

   $i_t \leftarrow B \bmod 5$

   $B \leftarrow \lfloor B/5 \rfloor$

end for

for $t = 1$ to 4 **do**

   $j_t \leftarrow B \bmod 19$

   $B \leftarrow \lfloor B/19 \rfloor$

end for

for $t = 1$ to 4 **do**

   $l_t \leftarrow B \bmod 62$

   $B \leftarrow \lfloor B/62 \rfloor$

end for

C Standard Linearization-Based Attack Against FASTA

We examine the question of the number of monomials actually occurring in an algebraic description of FASTA, following a similar discussion from [DEG+18].

Let M be the matrix over $\mathbb{F}_2$ that realises one of FASTA's rotation-based linear transformations, let $x = (x_0, \ldots, x_{1644})$ be the input state and $A(x) = M \cdot x + c$. From the description of χ in the non-linear layer S, one round $S \circ A(x)$ of FASTA can be described by the following equations (from [DEG+18]):

$$S \circ A(x)_i = \sum_{j=0}^{k-1} \sum_{l=j+1}^{k-1} a_{j,l}^i \cdot x_j \cdot x_l + \sum_{j=0}^{k-1} b_j^i \cdot x_j + g^i, \qquad (3)$$

where i denotes the polynomial representing the i-th bit in the cipher block after $S \circ A(x)$. As the word size is 329, $i + 1$ and $i + 2$ "wrap around", i.e. they are calculated as $i - 328$ and $i - 327$ when $i \bmod 329 = 328$ and 327. The coefficients of $S \circ A(x)_i$ are given by

$$a_{j,l}^i = M_{i+1,j} \cdot M_{i+2,l} + M_{i+2,j} \cdot M_{i+1,l},$$

$$b_j^i = M_{i,j} + c_{i+2} \cdot M_{i+1,j} + (1 + c_{i+1}) \cdot M_{i+2,j},$$

$$g^i = c_i + c_{i+2} + c_{i+1} \cdot c_{i+2}.$$

We can see that the term containing the coefficient $a^i_{j,l}$ contains the only multiplication, meaning it is the only place where the algebraic degree may increase. We only need $a^i_{j,l} = 1$ for at least one i for the corresponding monomial to be present in the output. We first find the probability that each coefficient $a^i_{j,l}$ is 0. From the above equations we get

$$
\begin{aligned}
P[a^i_{j,l} = 0] = {}& P[M_{i+1,j}M_{i+2,l} = M_{i+2,j}M_{i+1,l} = 0] \\
& + P[M_{i+1,j}M_{i+2,l} = M_{i+2,j}M_{i+1,l} = 1]
\end{aligned}
\tag{4}
$$

In Sect. 5.1, we found when two entries in M are equal with certainty, due to the rotational structure in M, and when they are considered independent. Put into context of Eq. 4, we have that two entries $M_{i+1,j}$ and $M_{i+2,l}$ are equal when

$$
l = \begin{cases} j+1 & \text{for } j \neq 328 \mod 329 \\ j - 328 & \text{for } j = 328 \mod 329 \end{cases}
$$

Otherwise, $M_{i+1,j}$ and $M_{i+2,l}$ are considered as independent in our analysis.

The equal entries are split into two cases, depending on whether j or l are crossing from one sub matrix to another or not, i.e., to handle "wrap-around" of sub-matrices.

We expect each entry in M to be present with probability one half, following the discussion in Sect. 5.1. This allows us to calculate $P[a^i_{j,l} = 0]$. We begin with the case where the two entries from M are equal, i.e., in general when $l = j+1$:

$$
\begin{aligned}
P[a^i_{j,j+1} = 0] = {}& P[M_{i+1,j}M_{i+2,j+1} = M_{i+2,j}M_{i+1,j+1} = 0] \\
& + P[M_{i+1,j}M_{i+2,j+1} = M_{i+2,j}M_{i+1,j+1} = 1] \\
= {}& \frac{1}{2} \cdot \frac{3}{4} + \frac{1}{2} \cdot \frac{1}{4} = \frac{1}{2}.
\end{aligned}
$$

For all independent entries, we get instead:

$$
P[a^i_{j,l} = 0] = \left(\frac{3}{4}\right)^2 + \left(\frac{1}{4}\right)^2 = \frac{5}{8}.
$$

This last result is the same as expected for any two entries in a random matrix. It follows that the probability that all the coefficients for the product $x_j \cdot x_l$ are equal to 0 can be estimated as

$$
P[a^i_{j,l} = 0, \; \forall i = 0, \ldots, 328] \leq \left(\frac{5}{8}\right)^{329}.
$$

In other words, at least one of these coefficients are 1 with probability at least $1 - \left(\frac{5}{8}\right)^{329}$.

If we consider the monomials of degree 2, it follows that we can expect an average number of monomials in each word w_i of degree 2 to be at least

$$\binom{329}{2} \cdot \left(1 - \left(\frac{5}{8}\right)^{329}\right) \simeq \binom{329}{2}.$$

We can use the same reasoning we used for monomials of degree 1, resulting in an expected number of these monomials to be $329 \cdot (1 - 2^{-329}) \approx 329$. This argument can also be applied for monomials of higher degrees. We therefore conclude that the expected number of monomials appearing in the algebraic equations linking the unknowns $k_0, \ldots, k_{328}$ to the keystream bits is approximated by U, the maximum possible number of monomials.

References

[ARS+15]   Albrecht, M.R., Rechberger, C., Schneider, T., Tiessen, T., Zohner, M.: Ciphers for MPC and FHE. In: Oswald, E., Fischlin, M. (eds.) EURO-CRYPT 2015. LNCS, vol. 9056, pp. 430–454. Springer, Heidelberg (2015). https://doi.org/10.1007/978-3-662-46800-5_17

[BDPA11]   Bertoni, G., Daemen, J., Peeters, M., Van Assche, G.: The Keccak reference, version 3.0, January 2011. https://keccak.team/files/Keccak-reference-3.0.pdf

[BGV12]   Brakerski, Z., Gentry, C., Vaikuntanathan, V.: (Leveled) fully homomorphic encryption without bootstrapping. In: Proceedings of the 3rd Innovations in Theoretical Computer Science Conference, ITCS'12, pp. 309–325. ACM, New York (2012)

[CCF+16]   Canteaut, A., et al.: Stream ciphers: a practical solution for efficient homomorphic-ciphertext compression. In: Peyrin, T. (ed.) FSE 2016. LNCS, vol. 9783, pp. 313–333. Springer, Heidelberg (2016). https://doi.org/10.1007/978-3-662-52993-5_16

[CHK20]   Cheon, J.H., Han, K., Kim, D.: Faster bootstrapping of FHE over the integers. In: Seo, J.H. (ed.) ICISC 2019. LNCS, vol. 11975, pp. 242–259. Springer, Cham (2020). https://doi.org/10.1007/978-3-030-40921-0_15

[CIM16]   Chillotti, I., Gama, N., Georgieva, M., Izabachène, M.: Faster fully homomorphic encryption: bootstrapping in less than 0.1 seconds. In: Cheon, J.H., Takagi, T. (eds.) ASIACRYPT 2016. LNCS, vol. 10031, pp. 3–33. Springer, Heidelberg (2016). https://doi.org/10.1007/978-3-662-53887-6_1

[Dae95]   Daemen, J.: Cipher and hash function design, strategies based on linear and differential cryptanalysis. Ph.D. thesis. K.U. Leuven (1995). http://jda.noekeon.org/

[DEG+18]   Dobraunig, C., et al.: Rasta: a cipher with low ANDdepth and few ANDs per bit. In: Shacham, H., Boldyreva, A. (eds.) CRYPTO 2018. LNCS, vol. 10991, pp. 662–692. Springer, Cham (2018). https://doi.org/10.1007/978-3-319-96884-1_22

[DGGK21]   Dobraunig, C., Grassi, L., Guinet, A., Kuijsters, D.: CIMINION: symmetric encryption based on Toffoli-gates over large finite fields. Cryptology ePrint Archive, Report 2021/267 (2021). https://ia.cr/2021/267

[DGH+21a] Dobraunig, C., Grassi, L., Helminger, L., Rechberger, C., Schofnegger, M., Walch, R.: Framework for hybrid homomorphic encryption (2021). https://github.com/IAIK/hybrid-HE-framework

[DGH+21b] Dobraunig, C., Grassi, L., Helminger, L., Rechberger, C., Schofnegger, M., Walch, R.: Pasta: a case for hybrid homomorphic encryption. Cryptology ePrint Archive, Report 2021/731 (2021). https://ia.cr/2021/731

[DLR16] Duval, S., Lallemand, V., Rotella, Y.: Cryptanalysis of the FLIP family of stream ciphers. In: Robshaw, M., Katz, J. (eds.) CRYPTO 2016. LNCS, vol. 9814, pp. 457–475. Springer, Heidelberg (2016). https://doi.org/10.1007/978-3-662-53018-4_17

[DM15] Ducas, L., Micciancio, D.: FHEW: bootstrapping homomorphic encryption in less than a second. In: Oswald, E., Fischlin, M. (eds.) EUROCRYPT 2015. LNCS, vol. 9056, pp. 617–640. Springer, Heidelberg (2015). https://doi.org/10.1007/978-3-662-46800-5_24

[Fau02] Faugère, J.C.: A new efficient algorithm for computing gröbner bases without reduction to zero (f5). In: ISSAC'02: Proceedings of the 2002 International Symposium on Symbolic and Algebraic Computation, pp. 75–83, July 2002

[Gen09] Gentry, C.: Fully homomorphic encryption using ideal lattices. In: Proceedings of the Forty-first Annual ACM Symposium on Theory of Computing, STOC'09, pp. 169–178. ACM, New York (2009)

[HKC+20] Ha, J., et al.: Masta: an HE-friendly cipher using modular arithmetic. IEEE Access 8, 194741–194751 (2020)

[HL20] Hebborn, P., Leander, G.: Dasta - alternative linear layer for Rasta. IACR Trans. Symmetric Cryptol. 2020(3), 46–86 (2020)

[HPS18] Halevi, S., Polyakov, Y., Shoup, V.: An improved RNS variant of the BFV homomorphic encryption scheme. Cryptology ePrint Archive, Report 2018/117 (2018). https://eprint.iacr.org/2018/117

[HS18] Halevi, S., Shoup, V.: Faster homomorphic linear transformations in HElib. Cryptology ePrint Archive, Report 2018/244 (2018). https://eprint.iacr.org/2018/244

[HS20] Halevi, S., Shoup, V.: Design and implementation of HElib: a homomorphic encryption library. Cryptology ePrint Archive, Report 2020/1481 (2020). https://eprint.iacr.org/2020/1481

[LSMI21] Liu, F., Sarkar, S., Meier, W., Isobe, T.: Algebraic attacks on Rasta and Dasta using low-degree equations. Cryptology ePrint Archive, Report 2021/474 (2021). https://eprint.iacr.org/2021/474

[MJSC16] Méaux, P., Journault, A., Standaert, F.-X., Carlet, C.: Towards stream ciphers for efficient FHE with low-noise ciphertexts. In: Fischlin, M., Coron, J.-S. (eds.) EUROCRYPT 2016. LNCS, vol. 9665, pp. 311–343. Springer, Heidelberg (2016). https://doi.org/10.1007/978-3-662-49890-3_13

[PAL] PALISADE - An Open-Source Lattice Crypto Software Library. https://palisade-crypto.org/

[PRRC21] Polyakov, Y., Rohloff, K., Ryan, G.W., Cousins, D.: PALISADE Lattice Cryptography Library User Manual (v1.11.2) (2021). https://eprint.iacr.org/2018/117

[RAD78] Rivest, R.L., Adleman, L., Dertouzos, M.L.: On Data Banks and Privacy Homomorphisms. Foundations of Secure Computation, pp. 169–179. Academia Press (1978)

[RDP+96] Rijmen, V., Daemen, J., Preneel, B., Bosselaers, A., De Win, E.: The cipher SHARK. In: Gollmann, D. (ed.) FSE 1996. LNCS, vol. 1039, pp. 99–111. Springer, Heidelberg (1996). https://doi.org/10.1007/3-540-60865-6_47

[SD18] Stoffelen, K., Daemen, J.: Column parity mixers. IACR Trans. Symmetric Cryptol. **2018**(1), 126–159 (2018)

[SEA20] Microsoft SEAL (release 3.6). Microsoft Research, Redmond, November 2020. https://github.com/Microsoft/SEAL

New Attacks from Old Distinguishers
Improved Attacks on Serpent

Marek Broll[1], Federico Canale[1(✉)], Nicolas David[2], Antonio Flórez-Gutiérrez[2], Gregor Leander[1], María Naya-Plasencia[2], and Yosuke Todo[3]

[1] Horst Görtz Institute for IT Security, Ruhr University Bochum, Bochum, Germany
{marek.broll,federico.canale,gregor.leander}@rub.de
[2] Inria, Paris, France
{nicolas.david,antonio.florez-gutierrez,maria.naya_plasencia}@inria.fr
[3] NTT Social Informatics Laboratories, Tokyo, Japan
yosuke.todo.xt@hco.ntt.co.jp

Abstract. Serpent was originally proposed in 1998 and is one of the most studied block ciphers. In this paper we improve knowledge of its security by providing the current best attack on this cipher, which is a 12-round differential-linear attack with lower data, time and memory complexities than the best previous attacks. Our improvements are based on an improved conditional key guessing technique that exploits the properties of the Sboxes.

Keywords: Differential-linear cryptanalysis · Key-recovery · Serpent · Conditional differential · Conditional linear

1 Introduction

Symmetric primitives play a vital role in today's secure communication. In a nutshell, their success is certainly based on their outstanding performance on the one hand and the trust in their security on the other hand. The block cipher Serpent [3] is an excellent example of the successful interplay between security and performance considerations. Serpent was a finalist in the Advanced Encryption Standard competition organized by NIST, and – unofficially – ranked second. Its design greatly contributed to our understanding of performance block ciphers by being consequently designed with a bit-sliced implementation in mind. It has also been the target of an impressively large amount of cryptanalysis like [4,5,7,8,14–17,19,21,23,24] over the years.

All of those attacks are based on variants or generalizations of differential [10] and linear [22] cryptanalysis, which are two of the fundamental families of attacks on symmetric primitives. Differential cryptanalysis is based on differences between pairs of plaintexts which propagate through the cipher with high probability, while linear cryptanalysis is based on linear approximations which exhibit high correlation. In both cases the aim is to distinguish the cipher from a random permutation by collecting enough plaintext-ciphertext pairs. In [20] a

S. D. Galbraith (Ed.): CT-RSA 2022, LNCS 13161, pp. 484–510, 2022.
https://doi.org/10.1007/978-3-030-95312-6_20

Table 1. Summary of working 12-round attacks on Serpent. The adjustment of some of the complexities and attacks with flaws is discussed in the text.

Target	Rounds	Source	Attack type	Complexity		
				Time	Data	Memory
	12	[23,24]	Multidimensional linear	$2^{253.8}$	$2^{125.8}$	$2^{125.8}$
	12	[23,24]	Multidimensional linear	2^{242}	$2^{125.8}$	2^{236}
Serpent	12	[21] [a]	Differential-linear	2^{251}	2^{127}	2^{127}
(256-bit)	12	Sect. 5.3	Differential-linear	$2^{233.55}$	$2^{127.92}$	$2^{127.92}$
	12	Sect. 5.3	Differential-linear	$2^{236.91}$	$2^{125.74}$	$2^{125.74}$
	12	Sect. 5.3	Differential-linear	$2^{242.93}$	$2^{118.40}$	$2^{118.40}$

[a] This attack starts from round 4 instead of round 0.

combination of both types of distinguishers was introduced. It is shown that a probability 1 differential and a linear approximation can be combined to obtain a distinguisher that covers more rounds. The technique was extended in [6] to allow for probabilities different from 1 in the differential part.

In this paper we make use of two main observations to construct the best attack on Serpent. We start by extending some ideas presented in [2] for differential-linear attacks on ARX constructions to SPN networks.

In addition, and this is the technically most important part, we use some ideas for improving the key recovery part of these attacks. The idea is to minimize the parts of the key that need to be guessed by closely investigating the involved Sboxes. As we will see, in the case of the coordinate functions of the Serpent Sboxes (and its derivatives) it is possible to deduce information on its output given only partial information on its input. Here, and this allows a significantly more fine-grained approach, we consider not only reductions that are possible for the entire input space, but rather split the input space (repeatedly) into halves by considering linear conditions on the input.

By using these techniques we are able to propose the best known attacks on Serpent, as summarized in Table 1. While the first and third attack yield the best time and data/memory complexity, respectively, the second attack shows that we can get a much better time complexity than the best previously known attacks and better data and memory complexity.

Related Work
Serpent has been the target of multiple reduced-round cryptanalysis efforts ever since it was first introduced. These include linear [4,16], multiple and multi-dimensional linear [14,15,24], nonlinear [23], boomerang [7,19], rectangle [4,6], and differential-linear [8,17,21] attacks. We will next discuss the best known attacks. All those claim to attack 12 rounds and consider the Serpent version using a 256-bit key.

Flawed Complexity Estimates. Before doing so, we would like to point out that unfortunately, quite some previous attacks turned out to be flawed. In some cases flaws were not describe previously. In all those cases, the overly optimistic complexity estimates were confirmed by the authors of the corresponding papers.

First published 12-round attack. Some differential-linear attacks on 11 and 12-round Serpent were proposed in [17]. However, we have found that the 12-round attack is incorrect (also pointed out in [21] and acknowledged by the authors). Indeed, the attack consists of a 112 keybit guess in the first round, which should allow the attacker to perform the 11-round variant of the attack on the rest of the rounds. This assumption is incorrect, as although the difference in the state after the first round is determined, the input values of the active Sboxes in the second round are unknown, which are required by the 11-round attack as they are part of the plaintext. Any evident workaround would either increase the data complexity beyond the whole codebook or the time complexity over the exhaustive search. The attacks which are presented in this paper are amended versions of this 12-round attack, as they are based on the same distinguisher.

Multidimensional-linear 12-round attacks. A family of multidimensional linear attacks on up to 12 rounds are presented in [24]. The complexity estimates for these attacks were found to be overly optimistic in [23], where new estimates were provided. The original estimates in [24] rely on an overestimated capacity, mistaken time complexity conversion to full encryptions, and very small advantage and success probability. Of the two proposed variants of the 12-round attack, the complexities of the first were corrected to $2^{125.8}$ data complexity, a time complexity of 2^{242} memory accesses, and 2^{108} memory complexity, while the second variant was found to be invalid and no valid corrected version was presented given for it. We have found, however, that the memory complexity for the first attack is also incorrect. The attack consists of 2^{128} repetitions of the 11-round attack, once for each guess of the last round subkey. We can choose between a memory complexity of $2^{125.813}$ to store the data but with a larger time complexity of $2^{253.813}$, or a large memory complexity of 2^{236} with the same time complexity.[1] The values given in Table 1 correspond to the corrected complexities.

Differential-Linear. In a recent work which is independent from ours [21], a new 12-round differential-linear attack on Serpent is proposed that tries to improve the distinguisher bias and the key recovery complexity simultaneously with an algebraic approach. The complexities of their attack can be seen in Table 1, where we have corrected the memory complexity for the sake of comparison: while in the original paper the authors claimed a memory of 2^{99}, they have confirmed to us that they did not take into account the cost of storing the data (as each plaintext-ciphertext pair has to be accessed multiple times), and agree with this comparison. In their paper the authors also indicate the problems with the attack from [17], and state that they were not able to fix these problems without increasing the complexity beyond that of exhaustive search.

　　This shows how powerful our new key-recovery techniques are, as they allow to bring the time complexity of this attack below 2^{256}. Even more, we are able

---

[1] We contacted the authors with respect to this, but they were unable to provide any further information. We also contacted the authors of [21] and they agreed in a personal communication, which is why these results are not cited in [21].

to provide the best known 12-round attack on Serpent, as can be seen in Table 1. The time complexity of [21], as can be seen in Table 1 is quite higher than ours even in the version where we have also better data and memory. As a side note our attack is also the only known differential-linear attack on 12 rounds that starts from the first round of Serpent.

Finally, our attack shares some basics with [12]. Indeed, as the authors from [12] point out, our original ideas used specifically for Serpent have inspired that paper's generalized framework used for other ciphers and other attacks than differential-linear ones.

Outline

The paper is structured as follows: Sect. 2 provides the specifications of Serpent as well as a short introduction to differential-linear attacks. Section 3 provides a first "fixed" version of the 12-round attack which was introduced in [17] whose corrected time complexity is very close to exhaustive search. Section 4 focuses on some useful properties of the Serpent Sboxes, as well as discussing how similar properties should be exploitable in all small Sboxes. Finally, in Sect. 5 we use these properties in an improved version of the attack which reduces the time complexity by a factor of around 2^{22}.

2 Preliminaries

2.1 Description of the Serpent Cipher

Serpent is a block cipher which was introduced in [3] by Anderson, Biham and Knudsen. Its design consists of a substitution-permutation network (SPN) with an internal state of 128 bits. It admits 128, 192 or 256 bit keys. The encryption map consists of a round function which is iterated 32 times. The round function consists of three steps: first the state is XORed with key material, then a layer of 4-bit Sboxes is applied, and the round ends with a linear transformation. The cipher makes use of the following 8 Sboxes, which were constructed in a pseudo random way to fulfil several cryptographic criteria:

x	0	1	2	3	4	5	6	7	8	9	A	B	C	D	E	F
$S_0(x)$	3	8	F	1	A	6	5	B	E	D	4	2	7	0	9	C
$S_1(x)$	F	C	2	7	9	0	5	A	1	B	E	8	6	D	3	4
$S_2(x)$	8	6	7	9	3	C	A	F	D	1	E	4	0	B	5	2
$S_3(x)$	0	F	B	8	C	9	6	3	D	1	2	4	A	7	5	E
$S_4(x)$	1	F	8	3	C	0	B	6	2	5	4	A	9	E	7	D
$S_5(x)$	F	5	2	B	4	A	9	C	0	3	E	8	D	6	7	1
$S_6(x)$	7	2	C	5	8	4	6	B	E	9	1	F	D	3	A	0
$S_7(x)$	1	D	F	0	E	8	2	B	7	4	C	A	9	3	5	6

We now provide a precise description of the round function, which will be given using the bitsliced notation of [3]. The 128-bit internal state X is represented by four 32-bit words which are denoted X_0, X_1, X_2 and X_3, with $X_j[i]$ being the i-th leftmost bit of word j. The 32 rounds are numbered 0 to 31. Each round consists of the following four steps:

- **Key mixing.** A 128 bit subkey is XORed to the internal state. The subkey at round i will be denoted by $\widehat{K}_i$.
- **Sbox Layer.** Different Sboxes are used depending on the round, in particular $S_{(i \bmod 8)}$ is used at round i. The Sbox Layer operation consists of the application of 32 copies of the Sbox to the internal state. For each $i \in \{0, \ldots, 31\}$ we perform the appropriate Sbox transformation to the 4-bit string $(X_0[i], X_1[i], X_2[i], X_3[i])$. The parallel application of the Sbox in round i will be denoted $\widehat{S}_i$.
- **Linear transformation.** The linear operation is denoted by LT and consists of the following steps:

$$X_0 \leftarrow X_0 \lll 13; \quad X_2 \leftarrow X_2 \lll 3$$
$$X_1 \leftarrow X_1 \oplus X_0 \oplus X_2; \quad X_3 \leftarrow X_3 \oplus X_2 \oplus (X_0 \ll 3)$$
$$X_1 \leftarrow X_1 \lll 1; \quad X_3 \leftarrow X_3 \lll 7$$
$$X_0 \leftarrow X_0 \oplus X_1 \oplus X_3; \quad X_2 \leftarrow X_2 \oplus X_3 \oplus (X_1 \ll 7)$$
$$X_0 \leftarrow X_0 \lll 5; \quad X_2 \leftarrow X_2 \lll 22$$

Here $\ll j$ denotes a j-bit left shift and $\lll j$ denotes a j-bit left rotation. In round 31 this linear transformation is omitted and an additional subkey $\widehat{K}_{32}$ is XORed to the state instead.

If we denote by $\widehat{B}_i$ the 128-bit value at round i, the cipher operates as follows:

$$\widehat{B}_0 \leftarrow IP(P)$$
$$\widehat{B}_{i+1} \leftarrow R_i(\widehat{B}_i)$$
$$C \leftarrow IP^{-1}(\widehat{B}_{32})$$

where

$$IP \text{ is an initial permutation}$$
$$R_i(X) = LT(\widehat{S}_i(X \oplus \widehat{K}_i)) \text{ for } i = 0, \ldots, 30$$
$$R_i(X) = \widehat{S}_i(X \oplus \widehat{K}_i) \oplus \widehat{K}_{32} \text{ for } i = 31$$

Key schedule. The key schedule described in [3] turns the 256-bit user key K into 33 128-bit round subkeys, that is, 132 32-bits words of key material. The user key is first written as 8 32-bit words $K = w_{-8}w_{-7}\cdots w_{-1}$. This prekey sequence is extended using the recurrence relation

$$w_i = (w_{i-8} \oplus w_{i-5} \oplus w_{i-1} \oplus \phi \oplus i) \lll 11,$$

where $\phi = \mathtt{0x9e3779b9}$. We then build the sequence k_i from w_i using the Sboxes:

$$\{k_0, k_{33}, k_{66}, k_{99}\} = S_3(w_0, w_{33}, w_{66}, w_{99})$$
$$\{k_1, k_{34}, k_{67}, k_{100}\} = S_2(w_1, w_{34}, w_{67}, w_{100})$$
$$\cdots$$
$$\{k_{31}, k_{64}, k_{97}, k_{130}\} = S_4(w_{31}, w_{64}, w_{97}, w_{130})$$
$$\{k_{32}, k_{65}, k_{98}, k_{131}\} = S_3(w_{32}, w_{65}, w_{98}, w_{131})$$

We then distribute the 32-bit words k_j to build the 128-bit subkeys K_i:

$$K_i = \{k_{4i}, k_{4i+1}, k_{4i+2}, k_{4i+3}\}$$

The round key $\widehat{K_i}$ is the result of the application of the fixed initial permutation IP to K_i, hence $\widehat{K_i} = IP(K_i)$.

2.2 Differential-Linear Cryptanalysis

We consider a cipher E_K decomposed in two parts F_K and G_K, thus $E_K = G_K \circ F_K$. The ideas developed in [6,20] allow to combine differential properties of F_K and linear properties of G_K to build a more global property on E_K. Let $\delta \longrightarrow \Delta$ be a differential with probability p for F_K. In other words,

$$\mathrm{Prob}_{x,K}\left(F_K(x+\delta) = F_K(x) + \Delta\right) = p.$$

Let $\langle \alpha, y \rangle \oplus \langle \beta, z \rangle$ be a linear approximation of G_K with correlation q:

$$\mathrm{Prob}_{x,K}\left(\langle \alpha, y \rangle \oplus \langle \beta, G_K(y) \rangle = 0\right) - \mathrm{Prob}_{x,K}\left(\langle \alpha, y \rangle \oplus \langle \beta, G_K(y) \rangle = 1\right) = q.$$

In [6,20] it is shown that

$$\mathrm{Corr}_{x,K}\left(\langle \beta, E_K(x) \rangle \oplus \langle \beta, E_K(x \oplus \delta) \rangle\right) = pq^2$$

under certain independence assumptions. This means that E_K can be distinguished from a random permutation with $O\left(p^2 q^4\right)$ chosen plaintext-ciphertext pairs. It suffices to generate plaintext pairs $(x, x \oplus \delta)$ and compute the correlation of $\langle \beta, E_K(x) \rangle \oplus \langle \beta, E_K(x \oplus \delta) \rangle$. Note that the presence of truncated differentials and linear hulls will influence the correlation of a differential-linear distinguisher. Furthermore, the independence assumption is not always satisfied, so the transition between the differential and the linear part may have an unexpected correlation. To overcome this issue, several approaches, such as the differential-linear connectivity table (DLCT) [1] have been introduced. One of the most commonly-used techniques is to remove a small number of transition rounds from the differential and the linear paths and estimate their correlation r experimentally, and consider the correlation of the full distinguisher is prq^2. This approach is of course limited to sufficiently large correlations r.

Another improvement we use is the idea introduced in [2] of generating many pairs which verify the differential part of the distinguisher from a single pair. In the paper, it is noted that flipping certain bits in the input will not change the fact that a pair fulfils the differential part of the differential-linear distingusher. In the best case, this reduced the data complexity by a factor of $1/p$.

A differential-linear distinguisher can be used to mount a key-recovery attack by extending it at the top and/or at the bottom with key guesses. We can guess some key material which determines the input difference of the distinguisher from the plaintext and some key material which determines the output parity bit from the ciphertext. By computing the correlation of the differential-linear distinguisher for each guess of the key, we can separate the correct key guess from all the wrong ones. In order to determine the advantage and success probability of our attacks, we will use the models introduced for linear cryptanalysis in [11].

3   First Version of the Attack

In this section we present a corrected version of the flawed 12-round attack from [17] by considering the correct diffusion on the key recovery rounds along with the idea introduced in [2] of generating multiple good differential pairs.

3.1   Differential-Linear Distinguisher

Our attack is based on the same differential-linear distinguisher that was used in the flawed 12-round attack in [17]. We start from a "central" distinguisher which starts with a fixed difference at the beginning of round 2, progresses through a three-round truncated differential with probability $p = 2^{-6}$, and then ends with a five-round linear approximation with correlation $q = 2^{-21}$ (we remove the last round of the original distinguisher). The expected correlation for the differential-linear distinguisher is thus $pq^2 = 2^{-48}$. However, experiments with the correlation of the transition rounds between the differential and the linear trail suggest that the actual correlation should be at least $2^{-46.75}$. Our aim for the twelve-round attack is to effectively extend this distinguisher by two rounds at the top and two rounds at the bottom.

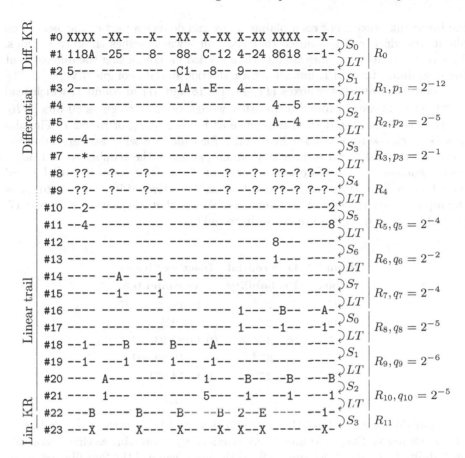

Fig. 1. The basic differential-linear attack on 12-round Serpent obtained by simple extension of the distinguisher, which requires more data than the whole codebook. The hyphen – represents a zero difference/mask in the nibble to improve readability. The nibble difference * is undetermined but is zero in the rightmost bit.

If we consider (one of) the best differential transition(s) for each active round 1 Sbox and the best linear approximation for each active Sbox in round 10 (in other words, if we extend the distinguisher to these rounds without any key recovery), the data needed for a reasonable probability of success would be more than $2^{2 \cdot (48.75+12+2.5)} = 2^{141.5}$, which surpasses the size of the codebook. This version of the attack is illustrated in Fig. 1.

3.2 Improving the First Rounds

Our first improvement is inspired by the ideas proposed in [2] in the context of ARX, which we adapt to SPN constructions. The idea is to make sure that some of the differential transitions in round 1 hold for all the data by guessing all the keybits required to know the input values to these Sboxes, instead of only the input differences. For each plaintext, we can deduce a part of the associated plaintexts which will guarantee that the pair always verifies these transitions. This requires guessing more keybits than needed for computing the difference at the beginning of round 1, but allows a reduction in data complexity.

There are five active Sboxes (11, 14, 17, 18 and 31) in round 1, which lead to 20 active Sboxes in round 0. In other words, we have to guess 80 bits of $\widehat{K}_0$ in order to obtain the desired difference at the beginning of round 1. The aim now is to choose some Sboxes in round 1 for which we will also determine the input values, and to do so in a way which optimizes the number of additional keybit guesses. We therefore look at each of the active Sboxes in round 1 and see which additional Sboxes in round 0 would be activated if we decide to guess the input values as well as the differences. We see that in the case of Sboxes 17, 18 and 31, not all Sboxes are active in round 0.

Round 1 Sbox	Differential Probability	Inactive Sboxes in round 0
11	2^{-2}	$\{3, 16, 19, 22, 23, 27\}$
14	2^{-2}	$\{19, 20, 22\}$
17	2^{-3}	$\{0, 14, 22, 23, 27\}$
18	2^{-2}	$\{2, 10, 19, 23, 24\}$
31	2^{-3}	$\{0, 10, 14, 23\}$

From this table we infer that our efforts should be directed towards Sboxes 11, 17, 18 and 31. Sboxes 31 and 17 are particularly interesting as their transition probability is smaller. If we simply fixed the input value of the four Sboxes to one which satisfies the transition with the input difference indicated in the figure, the amount of available data for each key guess would be reduced by a factor of 2^{10}. Instead we consider that the input differences to these Sboxes are variable, as we just need the correct output difference to be satisfied. This also means that the target output difference for round 0 is variable.

Giving this treatment to the four Sboxes would make all Sboxes except for 23 active in round 1. In order to reduce the number of keybit guesses, we will only choose 3 out of these 4 Sboxes, and we will impose some conditions in the input differences in order to obtain the best data complexity: the best choice are Sboxes 31, 18 and 17. Let us point out that at the end of Sect. 5.3 another variant is proposed by considering the four Sboxes that provides the best data complexity. We have chosen two conditions that provide the best trade-off between the reduction of available data and the reduction of keybits to guess. We first impose a 1-bit condition to the difference in state #2 by requiring the difference in bit x_3 in column 17 to be 0. This rejects half of the plaintext pairs, but reduces the number of active bits in the previous round. This condition is compatible with the original difference, which was 1. Additionally, in column 31 we only consider differences in which the difference in x_0 is zero. This condition is not compatible with the original difference of 5 and rejects $3/4$ of the plaintexts, but makes column 29 in the previous round inactive. In the end we keep 2^{-3} of the plaintext pairs, which means we can generate up to 2^{124} differential pairs for each key guess from the whole codebook. This new path is represented in Fig. 2.

In addition to the 76 keybits[2] corresponding to the difference, computing the input values to these three Sboxes requires guessing all the other keybits except for Sboxes 23 and 29, which are inactive. This implies a 120 bit key guess in round 0 plus 12 bits in the round 1 for the three active Sboxes in #2 whose input values are required. In the end the amount of pairs required by the attack is reduced by a factor of $2^{2\cdot(3+3+2)-3} = 2^{13}$ with respect to the previous version.

We can summarise the differential pair generation as follows:

- Pick a random plaintext x.
- Guess 120 bits of $\widehat{K}_0$ and 12 bits of $\widehat{K}_1$. With these we can compute the outputs of S_1 in columns 17, 18 and 31, $y[17], y[18]$ and $y[31]$, respectively.
- With these we can compute $\Delta[17] = S_1^{-1}(y[17]) + S_1^{-1}(y[17] + \mathtt{A})$, $\Delta[18] = S_1^{-1}(y[18]) + S_1^{-1}(y[18] + 1)$ and $\Delta[31] = S_1^{-1}(y[31]) + S_1^{-1}(y[31] + 2)$, which are the input differences to these Sboxes. If $\Delta[17]_3 = 1$ or $\Delta[31]_0 = 1$, we reject the plaintext for this key guess.
- Together with the fixed $\Delta[11] = 9, \Delta[14] = 8$, we have obtained the appropriate input difference for round 1, Δ.
- The associated plaintext is $x' = S_0^{-1}(S_0(x+\widehat{K}_0)+LT^{-1}(\Delta))+\widehat{K}_0$, and (x, x') is a candidate differential pair.

3.3 Last Rounds

As before, we want to reduce the data complexity by making some changes to round 10. For each of the five active Sboxes (0, 5, 10, 15, 27), we determine which bits are required to compute the full output values as opposed to a single parity bit. In other words, for each of these Sboxes we compute which Sboxes would remain inactive in round 11 if we determine the full output value:

Round 10 Sbox	Correlation	Inactive Sboxes in round 11
0	2^{-1}	$\{2, 4, 6, 9, 10, 12, 14, 15, 16, 17, 19, 20, 21, 24, 26, 27, 29, 30, 31\}$
5	2^{-1}	$\{0, 3, 4, 9, 14, 15, 16, 17, 19, 20, 21, 22, 24, 25, 26, 29, 31\}$
10	2^{-1}	$\{2, 4, 5, 9, 14, 16, 19, 20, 21, 22, 24, 25, 26, 27, 29, 30, 31\}$
15	2^{-1}	$\{0, 2, 3, 4, 6, 7, 9, 10, 14, 19, 21, 24, 25, 26, 27, 29, 30, 31\}$
27	2^{-1}	$\{3, 4, 5, 6, 7, 9, 10, 12, 14, 15, 16, 19, 21, 22, 25, 26, 31\}$

We will use a linear output mask spread between the inputs and the outputs of the S_2 layer in round 10. If we determine the full output (instead of just the

---

[2] There are 4 less bits to guess as column 29 is now inactive.

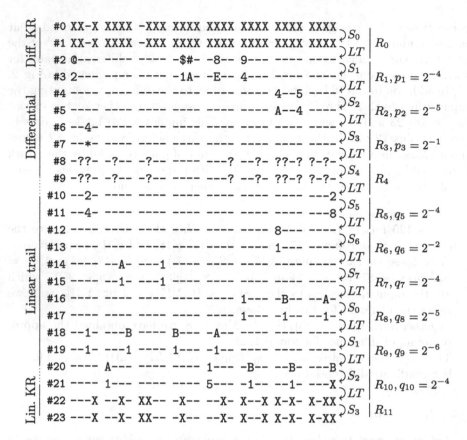

Fig. 2. The slightly improved differential-linear attack on 12-round Serpent with staggered key-recovery. The nibble difference \$ is undetermined but is one in the leftmost bit x_3 because of the differential properties of S_1. The nibble difference * is undetermined but is zero in the rightmost bit x_0. The nibble difference @ is undetermined but is zero in the rightmost bit x_0. The nibble difference # is undetermined but is zero in the leftmost bit x_3.

desired parity bit) of Sbox 0, there are 13 active Sboxes in the last round. The other four active Sboxes in round 10 are part of the differential-linear distinguisher. We thus need to guess $4 \cdot 13 = 52$ keybits of $\widehat{K}_{12}$, and 4 bits of $\widehat{K}_{11}$.

The key recovery in the linear part can be performed efficiently by using the FFT algorithm for multiple rounds which was introduced in [18], with a cost of $2 \cdot 52 \cdot 2^{2 \cdot 52}$ additions/subtractions and $2^{2 \cdot 52}$ products for each guess of the key in the top and each of the 2^4 key guesses in round 10.

3.4 Complexity Analysis

In order to properly evaluate the time complexity, we need to compare the cost of the basic operations of the attack against 12-round Serpent encryptions. We first focus on the distillation phase of the FFT algorithm For each generated plaintext: we perform a two round encryption at the beginning and a one round decryption at the end. However, the partial encryption can be performed for one plaintext x and the result can be reused for all input values of the two inactive Sboxes in round 0. The filtering requires us to process 2^3 plaintexts to find one which satisfies the desired conditions. The cost of processing each plaintext is thus $(2^{-8} \cdot 2^3 \cdot 2/12 + 1/12) = 2^{-3.50}$ encryptions.

For the comparison of a 12-round encryption with one of the arithmetic operations, we note that we can consider $128 \cdot 3 \cdot 12 = 4608$ as a lower bound for the number of bit operations in a 12-round Serpent encryption. On the other hand, a 128 bit addition can be performed with 256 bit operations and a 128 bit product with $128 \cdot \log_2(128) \simeq 961$ bit operations. We thus get a worst-case $2^{-4.17}$ conversion factor for the additions and $2^{-2.26}$ for the products.

Given the distinguisher's correlation of $2^{-48.75-4-2.4} = 2^{-60.75}$, and using the model from [11], we obtain that with $2^{123.96}$ pairs, ($2^{127.96}$ data before sieving), an advantage of 15 bits is obtained with probability 0.1.

The time complexity of the attack is as follows:

$$\underbrace{2^{120} \cdot 2^{12}}_{\text{Top key guess}} \cdot \left(2^{123.96} \cdot 2^{-3.5} + \underbrace{2^4 \cdot \left(104 \cdot 2^{-4.17} + 2^{-2.26}\right) \cdot 2^{104}}_{\text{Bottom key guess}}\right) + 2^{256-15} \simeq 2^{252.46}$$

encryptions. We need $2^{127.96}$ registers for the data, as well as 2^{104} for the distillation tables of the FFT. The overall memory complexity is thus around $2^{127.96}$.

4 Sbox Conditions

The purpose of the present Section is to illustrate some conditional properties of the Serpent Sboxes which can improve the differential part of the attack, as well as studying the presence of similar properties in small (4-bit) Sboxes.

4.1 Conditions on the Serpent Sboxes

We consider the first Serpent Sbox, S_0, which is used in round 0. If we denote its input by $x = (x_3, x_2, x_1, x_0)$ and the output by $y = (y_3, y_2, y_1, y_0)$ then the following set of conditional relations always holds:

$$x_2 \oplus x_1 \oplus x_0 = 1 \Rightarrow y_0 = x_3 \oplus x_2 \oplus x_0 \oplus 1$$
$$x_3 \oplus x_2 \oplus x_1 = 0 \Rightarrow y_1 = x_3 \oplus x_2 \oplus x_0 \oplus 1$$
$$x_2 = 1 \Rightarrow y_2 = x_3 \oplus x_1 \oplus x_0$$
$$x_3 = 0 \Rightarrow y_3 = x_2 \oplus x_1 \oplus x_0$$
$$x_3 = 1 \Rightarrow y_3 = x_3 \oplus x_2 \oplus x_1$$

Thanks to these relations, we can compute output bit y_3 without querying the full input. We first query x_3. Depending on this bit, we query either $x_2 \oplus x_1 \oplus x_0$ or $x_3 \oplus x_2 \oplus x_1$ to obtain y_3. This decreases the amount of key material that needs to be guessed in an attack, as in the end we only have to consider four different guesses of the key as opposed to the usual sixteen. More specifically, if $x_i = m_i \oplus k_i$ where (m_0, m_1, m_2, m_3) is the known state before adding the key guess (k_0, k_1, k_2, k_3), then in order to compute the output bit y_3 of S_0, we first guess k_3 and determine the input bit $x_3 = m_3 \oplus k_3$. If $x_3 = 0$, we guess the bit $k_2 \oplus k_1 \oplus k_0$ and, thanks to the above conditions, we have that

$$y_3 = x_2 \oplus x_1 \oplus x_0 = (m_2 \oplus m_1 \oplus m_0) \oplus (k_2 \oplus k_1 \oplus k_0).$$

Otherwise, when $x_3 = 1$ we guess $k_3 \oplus k_2 \oplus k_1$ and determine

$$y_3 = x_3 \oplus x_2 \oplus x_1 = (m_3 \oplus m_2 \oplus m_1) \oplus (k_3 \oplus k_2 \oplus k_1).$$

We can find some similar relations which determine y_0, y_1 and y_2 in the cases which were not covered by the previous set of relations:

$$x_2 \oplus x_1 \oplus x_0 = 0 \text{ and } x_2 = 0 \Rightarrow y_0 = x_3 \oplus 1$$
$$x_2 \oplus x_1 \oplus x_0 = 0 \text{ and } x_2 = 1 \Rightarrow y_0 = x_0 \oplus 1$$
$$x_3 \oplus x_2 \oplus x_1 = 1 \text{ and } x_2 = 0 \Rightarrow y_1 = x_0 \oplus 1$$
$$x_3 \oplus x_2 \oplus x_1 = 1 \text{ and } x_2 = 1 \Rightarrow y_1 = x_3 \oplus 1$$
$$x_2 = 0 \text{ and } x_1 = 0 \Rightarrow y_2 = x_3$$
$$x_2 = 0 \text{ and } x_1 = 1 \Rightarrow y_2 = x_0 \oplus 1$$

With these relations we can determine any one bit of the output of the Sbox with either four (output bit y_3) or six different guesses of key-bits on average. We can construct analogous conditional relations which determine more than one output bit at the same time. A more convenient representation of these conditions can be given with binary trees, as it is explained in the appendix.

The same technique can be applied to reduce the guesses necessary to determine whether a pair $(x, x') = (m \oplus k, m' \oplus k)$ satisfies a certain output difference Δ, i.e., if $S_0(x) \oplus S_0(x') = \Delta$. We consider the function

$$F_\Delta(x) = S_0^{-1}(S_0(x) \oplus \Delta) \oplus x,$$

and we search for conditional relationships which allow us to find a good pair (x, x') by guessing k only partially. The reason is that, if (x, x') is a good pair,

$$F_\Delta(x) = x' \oplus x = m' \oplus m,$$

and knowing $F_\Delta(x)$ and m is therefore enough to recover m'.

We give a partial example for $\Delta = 4$. From the relations of F_4 represented as a tree in Fig. 6a, we derive the following (partial) conditions for the case $x_0 = 0$:

$$x_0 = 0 \text{ and } x_1 = 0 \Rightarrow F_4(x) = \mathsf{C}$$
$$x_0 = 0 \text{ and } x_1 = 1 \Rightarrow F_4(x) = 5 \oplus x_3 2$$

Therefore, in order to guess $F_4(x)$, we have first to guess bit k_0. If $x_0 = m_0 \oplus k_0 = 0$, then we guess k_1 and find that $F_4(x) = m' \oplus m = \texttt{C}$ if $x_1 = k_1 \oplus m_1 = 1$, i.e. $m' = m \oplus \texttt{C}$. Otherwise, if $x_1 = k_1 \oplus m_1 = 0$, we guess k_3 and find out that

$$m' = \begin{cases} m \oplus 5 & \text{if } x_3 = k_3 \oplus m_3 = 0 \\ m \oplus 7 & \text{if } x_3 = k_3 \oplus m_3 = 1. \end{cases}$$

The case for which $x_0 = 0$ can be treated in a similar way. Thanks to this gradual way of guessing k, we obtain the desired information by doing only an average of six guesses instead of sixteen.

4.2   Conditions on General 4-Bit Sboxes

We will now show that the presence of linear conditions like the ones we have shown for S_0 is unavoidable if the number of bits of the Sbox is small compared to the number of (linear) restrictions in the input.

Lemma 1. *Let $f : \mathbb{F}_2^n \to \mathbb{F}_2^n$ be a permutation (Sbox). If $2^k - k \leq n$, then there exist a subspace U of dimension k of $\mathbb{F}_2^n$ and a vector $u \in \mathbb{F}_2^n$ such that $f|_{U+u}$ has maximum linearity, that is, there exist nonzero linear masks $\alpha \in U + u$, $\beta \in \mathbb{F}_2^n$ for which $\alpha \cdot x + \beta \cdot f(x)$ is constant in $U + u$.*

Proof. Pick any subspace $V \subseteq \mathbb{F}_2^n$ of dimension $n - k$ and set $U = V^\perp$. Let L_V be an $n - k \times n$ matrix whose row subspace is V and let M_U be a $2^k \times n$ matrix whose rows are all the elements of U. Note that $x \in U$ if and only if $L_V x = 0$. We denote by $f(M_U)$ the matrix which is generated by applying f to every row of M_U. We can also define $M_U + u$ in the same way for an arbitrary vector $u \in \mathbb{F}_2^n$.

For an arbitrary vector u, $[\alpha, \beta] \in \mathbb{F}_2^{2n}$ is a correlation 1 mask in $U + u$ if

$$\underbrace{\begin{bmatrix} L_V & 0 \\ M_U + u & f(M_U + u) \end{bmatrix}}_{W} \begin{bmatrix} \alpha \\ \beta \end{bmatrix} = \begin{bmatrix} L_V \alpha \\ c \\ \vdots \\ c \end{bmatrix} \tag{1}$$

for some $c \in \{0, 1\}$. We are only interested in solutions where $\alpha \in U + u$. We set $u = 0$ for convenience, in which case $L_V \alpha$ must be equal to zero.

The matrix W has $2n$ columns and $n - k + 2^k$ rows, so if $n - k + 2^k < 2n$, the system is necessarily under-determined, the kernel of W is nonempty, and all its elements are masks with correlation 1. If $n - k + 2^k = 2n$ and the kernel contains only the trivial mask (that is, if W is a full rank square matrix), then $W^{-1}[0, 1, \ldots, 1]^t$ is a non-trivial mask with correlation 1.

With this lemma we can justify the existence of linear relations in several cases for small Sboxes:

n	1		2			3				4				
k	0	1	0	1	2	0	1	2	3	0	1	2	3	4
$n-2^k+k$	0	0	1	1	0	2	2	1	-2	3	3	2	-1	-8
Relation?	✓	✓	✓	✓	✓	✓	✓	✓	✗	✓	✓	✓	?	✗

It is quite clear that in the cases $n = k = 3$ and $n = k = 4$ it is impossible to find such a relation unless the map f is linear, however, in the case $n = 4, k = 3$ we can still prove the existence of these relations:

Lemma 2. *For every permutation $f : \mathbb{F}_2^4 \to \mathbb{F}_2^4$ there exist a subspace U of dimension 3 and a vector $u \in \mathbb{F}_2^4$ such that $f|_{U+u}$ has linearity 8.*

Proof. Without loss of generality we assume that $f(0) = 0$, via affine equivalence. We remove the corresponding row from W and we consider $c = 0$, as for $c = 1$ would get a contradiction. We again set $u = 0$. We pick V at random as above but in such a way that U contains certain vectors a, b, c, d.

W is then a square matrix which either has $\mathrm{rank}(W) < 8$, in which case the kernel of W contains at least one non-trivial solution and we are done, or has rank 8. In the latter case the only solution to the equation is the trivial one. We will now show that it is impossible for the matrix W to have rank 8 if we choose a, b, c, d appropriately.

Since $n = 4$, f cannot be an APN permutation, and it must have a vanishing 2-flat (Theorem 5 in [13]). There exist distinct a, b, c, d for which

$$a + b + c + d = 0 = f(a) + f(b) + f(c) + f(d). \tag{2}$$

This provides a nontrivial relationship between the rows of W which can be used to obtain an equivalent matrix of rank 7 or lower.

4.3 A Conditional Linear Property of S_2

Another improvement we will apply is based on the framework for conditional linear cryptanalysis which was presented in [9]. We consider the Sbox S_2 (which is used in round 10 in the attack) and the linear approximation $\langle B, x \rangle \oplus \langle 1, S_2(x) \rangle$:

	$(y_2, y_0) \neq (1,1)$												$y_2 = y_0 = 1$			
x	0	1	3	4	5	6	9	A	B	C	D	F	2	7	8	E
$S_2(x)$	8	6	9	3	C	A	1	E	4	0	B	2	7	F	D	5
$\langle B, x \rangle \oplus \langle 1, S_2(x) \rangle$	0	1	1	1	1	1	1	0	1	1	0	1	0	1	0	1

If we consider the whole domain, the correlation is $\frac{4-12}{16} = -\frac{1}{2}$. However, under the condition $(y_2, y_0) \neq (1,1)$ the correlation increases to $\frac{2-10}{12} = -\frac{2}{3}$. We will use this condition to improve the correlation of the linear part of the distinguisher.

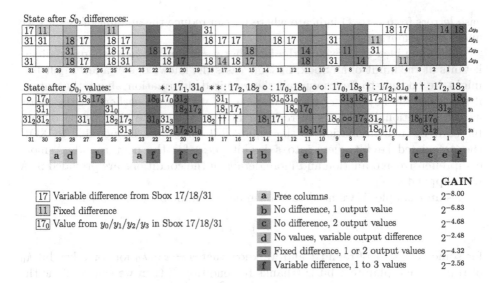

Fig. 3. Reducing the required keybit guesses in the first round.

5 Improved 12-Round Attack Using Sbox Properties

In this section, we apply some of the Sbox properties we have discussed in Sect. 4 to the 12-round attack of Sect. 3, whose complexity was only barely lower than that of an exhaustive key search. The reduction in time complexity is achieved by a careful analysis of the key recovery in the first two rounds, as well as a small improvement to the linear approximation of round 10 by using conditional linear cryptanalysis [9].

5.1 Improving the Differential Key Recovery

We start by looking at the configuration of required differences and values at the output of S_0 in the first round, which is represented in detail in Fig. 3. The figure contains both the differences (top half) and the values (bottom half) which are required at the output of the S_0 layer (state #1). On the top half, if a number is written in a cell, then the bit difference on this cell will influence the difference in the column indicated by the number written inside at the input of S_1 in state #2 (more differences might affect it but it is not important and for a better readability of the drawing we just write one here). The color of the background of such a cell indicates whether the difference is fixed (grey) or variable (white). On the bottom half, if an indexed number a_b is written inside a cell, then the bit associated to this cell will influence the value of bit b of the input of Sbox a in the S_1 layer. For space reasons, symbols are used when more than one bit is influenced. We only need the values associated to columns $31, 18$ and 17 as the other two Sboxes are part of the differential and thus only knowledge of the input difference is required. The colors of the columns (also indexed with lower case letters from a to f) indicate where we can reduce the amount of keybits we guess below four.

The main idea is to exploit the fact that we might not need to guess all the keybits at the input of an Sbox: in some cases the knowledge of a few input bits might be enough to determine all the required information about the output if we guess the key in an orderly manner, as we showed earlier. Furthermore, as the conditional relations introduced in Sect. 4 describe the desired output bit as a linear combination of the inputs it'll sometimes be possible to XOR the associated keybit guess into a keybit guess for the next round. A more comprehensive explanation and more details in the conditions are provided in A from appendix.

As an example, if we need to determine the input bit of State #2

$$z = y \oplus \widehat{k}_1$$

for some keybit $\widehat{k}_1$ of round 1 and we know that $y = x \oplus \widehat{k}_0$ for some key-bit $\widehat{k}_0$ of round 0 and plaintext bit x (thanks to conditions), then we can combine the two key guesses into one, as $z = x \oplus \widehat{k}_1 \oplus \widehat{k}_0$. This can only be done once for each input bit of S_1 (it is impossible to merge one bit of $\widehat{K}_1$ with several bits of $\widehat{K}_0$ at the same time).

We have considered all the active Sboxes of the state immediately after the application of S_0, as shown in Fig. 3. We consider six categories of columns "of interest" depending on the outputs which are required for the attack. For each of this, we are going to compute the multiplicative time factor that we gain with respect to guessing naively, as was done in the previous attack.

Columns of type a (yellow). There are 2 Sboxes (23,29) which are inactive and need no key guessing at all (the same as in the previous attack). These provide gain factor of 2^{-8} with respect to a full subkey guess.

Columns of type b (orange). In columns 10, 14 and 26 we require no output differences, but we need to determine a single output bit from each. Instead of guessing sixteen keybits, we can make use of the properties of S_0:

- Column 26: we only need y_0, which we can determine as follows:
  - If $x_2 \oplus x_1 \oplus x_0 = 0$ then:
    - If $x_1 \oplus x_0 = 0$ then $y_0 = x_3 \oplus 1$.
    - If $x_1 \oplus x_0 = 1$ then $y_0 = x_0 \oplus 1$.
  - If $x_2 \oplus x_1 \oplus x_0 = 1$ then $y_0 = x_3 \oplus x_2 \oplus x_0 \oplus 1$.

  For a given plaintext, we consider six possible guesses of the key instead of sixteen on each column, thus resulting in a 6/16 gain factor for each.
- Column 14: we only need y_2, which can be determined as follows with a gain factor of 6/16:
  - If $x_2 = 0$ then:
    - If $x_1 = 0$ then $y_2 = x_3$.
    - If $x_1 = 1$ then $y_2 = x_0 \oplus 1$.
  - If $x_2 = 1$ then $y_2 = x_3 \oplus x_1 \oplus x_0 \oplus 1$.

- Column 10: we only need y_3 which can be determined as follows with a gain of 4/16:
  - If $x_3 = 0$ then $y_3 = x_2 \oplus x_1 \oplus x_0$.
  - If $x_3 = 1$ then $y_3 = x_3 \oplus x_2 \oplus x_1$.

We obtain a gain factor of $\frac{6}{16} \cdot \frac{6}{16} \cdot \frac{4}{16} \simeq 2^{-4.83}$. In addition, we can absorb the last bit guess for some of the columns into the next round. As bit x_3 of column 17 in S_1 is associated to both Sboxes 10 and 26 in S_0, we can only do this a total of two times (round 1 input bits x_3 in column 17 and x_1 in column 18). The overall gain factor with respect to a full subkey guess is $2^{-4.83} \cdot 2^{-2} = 2^{-6.83}$. The trees associated to these conditions can be seen in Fig. 4 from the appendix.

Columns of type c (red). In columns 2, 3 and 19, we require no output difference but two output bits are needed. We proceed as in the previous case, but considering both bits at the same time.

- Column 19: We need y_1 and y_3. Using the trees from Fig. 5c in the appendix we can see that determining both bits y_3 and y_1 requires three bits in total. We are also able to absorb one keybit into the next round (x_2 from column 17), but the other bit has to be guessed. The gain for this column is thus $\frac{2 \times 2^3}{2^6} = 2^{-2}$.
- Column 3: We need y_0 and y_2. We can obtain an average guessing cost of 10 as seen in the corresponding tree from Fig. 5b, which gives a gain factor of $2^{-0.68}$.
- Column 2: This column (Fig. 5a) has the same complexity as 19, as both their trees have the same number of leaves, and also contains two new keybits that might be absorbed: we need 3 input bits to determine the two desired output bits. We can absorb also one keybit in the last linear relation, that can be the keybit from x_0 of column 17 or from x_2 of column 31. We thus also obtain a gain factor of 2^{-2}.

Combining the gains from these Sboxes we obtain a total factor of $2^{-4.68}$.

Columns of type d (pink). Columns 15 and 28 only require no output difference, but this difference is not fixed. There are four possible differences in column 28: 0, 4, A or E (as both Δx_1 and Δx_3 come from difference Δx_2 in column 18 from the next round), which appear with probability 1/4 (this can be deduced from the DDT of S_1 and the output differences for columns 18 and 31).

We first guess the parts of the first round subkey which determine the values at the inputs of columns 18 and 31, so that we know which difference we want at the output of column 28. This is only possible because we only need the output differences from these two columns, and no actual bit values.

We will use the trees built with function F_Δ mentioned in Sect. 4.1 that are detailed in Fig. 6 in the appendix. As an example, if we compute the cost when the desired output difference in column 28 is 4 on average there are 6 possible guesses. The costs for the other non-zero differences are obtained in a similar way and are 2^3 for both. The overall cost becomes:

$$\frac{1}{4}6 + \frac{1}{4}2^3 + \frac{1}{4}2^3 + \frac{1}{4} \cdot 1 \simeq 2^{2.52}$$

instead of 2^4, and implies a gain factor of $2^{-1.48}$.

For column 15 we have two possible output differences: 4 and C (as input Δx_3 in column 18 is always 1). For difference 4 the average cost is 6, and for C the average cost is 10, which gives a total gain factor of $\frac{6/2+10/2}{16} = 2^{-1}$.

Both gain factors multiply to $2^{-2.48}$.

Columns of type e (turquoise). In columns 1, 7, 8 and 11 we have a fixed difference and we also need to determine some output values. We will also use the conditions given by functions F_Δ mentioned in Sect. 4.1, but now we have also to look at the values of the inputs and outputs to satisfy the conditions. Let us illustrate the example for column 1.

In column 1 we have a fixed output difference of $\Delta = 1$ and we want to determine bit y_1. If we consider function F_1, we can see that there are 8 possible input differences δ: 3, 6, 9, C, B, A, E or F. In order to determine whether a pair $(x, x \oplus \delta)$ leads indeed to the desired output difference 1, we always need to guess three key bits: this is because for any fixed δ the set $\{x : S_0(x) \oplus S_0(x \oplus \delta) = 1\}$ is an affine space (of dimension 1) and therefore can be described by three linear conditions, i.e. three key bits are needed in order to verify them. In each of these cases, the three bits needed to guess whether a pair is a good pair are enough to determine y_1. Column 1 has therefore a gain factor of 2^{-1}.

We can do the same thing with columns 7, 8 and 11. In the case of columns 7, some of the possible input differences define an affine space $\{x : S_0(x) \oplus S_0(x \oplus \delta) = 8\}$ of dimension 2, that means only 2 keybits are needed for guessing a good pair with this particular input difference. Taking into account that a further guess is sometimes needed for then determining the desired output values, the number of needed known key bits can be reduced from the full guess and we obtain a gain factor of $2^{-1.13}$. For column 8 we have the output difference that affects one of the needed values, so we will need to guess the four input bits, but we can always absorb the bit x_3 of column 31, so the gain factor is still 2^{-1}. For column 11 all four input bits need to be guessed for each considered input difference, but for two input differences that represent half of the cases (B and 2) two of the guesses independently determine the values of the two needed values. That means that bit y_3, that corresponds to bit x_3, of column 18 can always be absorbed, as it wasn't done before; and that bit y_1, corresponding to bit x_0 of column 17 that was absorbed half of the times in column 2, can now be absorbed the other half of the time. For the other half of the cases only y_3 can be absorbed. The overall gain factor for column 11 is $2^{-1.19}$.

In total these columns generate a gain factor of $2^{-4.32}$.

Columns of type f (purple). We have three columns of this type: variable difference and some values needed. Depending on the value of the difference, we will find some of the cases previously studied.

For half of the cases of column 22, when the difference is zero, we can just use the same tree from Fig. 5b, which gives a factor of $10/16$, while in the other half of the cases, when the difference is 4, the case is similar as for the e column 8, and we obtain a gain factor of $1/2$ absorbing the bit 31_0, which gives $1/2 \cdot \frac{10}{16} + 1/2 \cdot 2^{-1} = 2^{-0.83}$. For column 20, the desired bits are y_0, y_1 and y_3. When the difference is 0, an optimal tree for simultaneously determining these bits is given in Fig. 7. From this we obtain a gain factor for this columns of $1/2 \cdot 2^{-0.42} + 1/2 = 2^{-0.19}$.

Column 0 is exactly the case of column 26 when the difference is zero. We can even absorb bit x_0 of column 18 as it hasn't been absorbed before. When the difference is 1, we recover a similar case as for columns of type e, having in this case a gain factor of $1/2$. The gain factor of this column is therefore $1/2 \cdot \frac{6}{16} \cdot 1/2 + 1/4 = 2^{-1.54}$.

This gives a total gain factor for these columns of:

$$2^{-0.83} \cdot 2^{-0.19} \cdot 2^{-1.54} = 2^{-2.56}.$$

5.2 Conditional Linear Cryptanalysis

In the case of the linear key-recovery for the last rounds, even though similar properties exist for S_3 to the ones we have used for S_0, exploiting them is much more complicated than in the differential part, as we are performing the last round key recovery with the FFT. Nevertheless, we can apply conditional properties in the Sbox S_2 of the previous round, round 10, using the framework which was established in [9].

If we look at the linear approximation of Sbox 10, if we impose the condition that its outputs y_0 and y_2 are not both 1 at the same time, then the correlation goes from $-1/2$ to $-2/3$. This would improve the overall correlation by a factor $(2/3 \times (1/2)^{-1})^4 = 2^{1.66}$. As we have to discard the ciphertext pairs which do not verify the condition, we only keep a proportion of $(3/4)^2 = 2^{-0.83}$. With this we can reduce the data complexity to $2^{0.83-1.66}$, resulting in $2^{123.13} \times 2^4 = 2^{127.13}$. However, since the bottleneck of the previous attack was the exhaustive search, we instead keep a similar data complexity of $2^{123.92} \times 2^4 = 2^{127.92}$, so that the advantage increases to 23.

We still have to see how this affects the the key recovery in the final round: with respect to the previous attack, we require output bit y_2 of Sbox 10 in round 10. This additional bit only activates column 6 in the next round. The number of active keybits in the last round is thus 56.

5.3 Complexity and Trade-Offs

We now compute the time complexity of this improved version of the attack. The data and memory complexities are $2^{127.92}$. If we consider all the gain factors we have accumulated, the cost of the key recovery part is

$$2^{140-8-6.83-4.68-2.48-4.32-2.56} \cdot \left(2^{123.92-3.5} + 2^4 \cdot 112 \cdot 2^{112} \cdot 2^{-4.17}\right) \simeq 2^{231.91}$$

equivalent encryptions, while the exhaustive search has cost 2^{256-23}. The total time complexity is thus around $2^{233.55}$ 12-round encryptions.

Trade-offs between data and time. We can reduce the data and memory complexities by relaxing one of the conditions in the first rounds, though this increases the time complexity. We remove the condition on the difference in bit x_0 in column 31 of state #2. This reduces the data complexity by a factor 2^2. This changes the differences in columns 29, 26 and 13 from Fig. 3: column 29 becomes a column of type e, column 26 becomes a column of type f, and column 13 won't impact the complexity as it was not exploited in the attack.

Column 29. Its previous gain factor was 2^{-4}. For the 3/4 of the cases where the previous bit condition in column 31 no longer holds, we want an output difference of 8 (Fig. 6e). The new cost for this column is

$$1/4 \times 1 + 3/4 \times 10 = 2^{2.954},$$

which results in a more modest gain factor of $2^{2.954-4} = 2^{-1.04}$.

Column 26. Its previous gain factor was $6/16 = 2^{-1.415}$. However, this will now only apply to 1/4 of the data, which is when the bit condition in column 31 holds. For the other 3/4, the guessing cost is 12/16, results in the cost

$$1/4 \times 6 + 3/4 \times 12 = 2^{3.39},$$

and a new gain factor of $2^{-0.6}$.

Time complexity for a data complexity of $2^{125.74}$. By considering the new gain factors and choosing a different amount of data and advantage, we obtain:

$$2^{140-4-1.04-5.40-0.6-4.68-2.48-4.32-2.56} \cdot \left(2^{123.74-3.5} + 2^4 \cdot 112 \cdot 2^{112} \cdot 2^{-4.17}\right)$$

equivalent encryptions for the key recovery and 2^{256-21} encryptions for the exhaustive search, which result in an overall time complexity of $2^{236.31}$. This time the data and memory complexities are $2^{123.74} \times 2^2 = 2^{125.74}$.

Attack with the best data complexity. As we have discussed in Sect. 3.2, in order to improve the correlation of the distinguisher, we chose to determine three of the five Sboxes active in round 1. We now show how to also determine the fourth one that was considered interesting, allowing to make the data complexity smaller.

In this case there will then be no conditions imposed in the differences of state #2. We can proceed as in the previous attack, and we will obtain one column of type a (23), three columns of type c (2,3 and 19), three columns of type e (0, 7 and 8), and four columns of type f (12, 22, 26 and 29). We compute the gain factor the same way as before, and we obtain for column 29: $2^{-1.607}$, column 26: $2^{-1.192}$, column 23: 2^{-4}, column 22: $2^{-1.35}$, column 19: $2^{1.41}$, column 12: 2^{-1}, column 8: $2^{-1.678}$, column 7: $2^{1.41}$, column 3: $2^{-0.415}$, column 2: $2^{-0.415}$ and column 0: $2^{-1.54}$.

This gives a total gain factor of $2^{-16.023}$.

We will not consider the conditional linear property in the output as otherwise the term related to the FFT would be the bottleneck, and this implies that for a data and memory complexity of $2^{118.40}$, which gives an advantage of 16 bits, we have a time complexity of:

$$2^{128+16-16.023} \cdot \left(2^{118.40-3.5} + 2^4 \cdot 104 \cdot 2^{104} \cdot 2^{-4.17}\right) + 2^{256-16} = 2^{242.93}$$

12-round encryptions.

6 Conclusion

In this paper we improved upon the best known attacks on Serpent. Our improved differential-linear attack has *simultaneously* lower time, data, and memory complexities than the best previous attacks. We would like to stress that our improvements do not modify the underlying distinguisher at all, and only focus on the data selection and, most importantly, the key-guessing procedure. We find it remarkable that by focusing solely on this part, we are able to significantly improve (and thereby actually fix) previous results.

While our approach in this paper is highly specific to Serpent and the differential-linear distinguishers we used, its ideas can be applied more generally, both to other attacks as well as to other ciphers. Indeed, as mentioned above, our work here is the predecessor of the general framework of [12]. Our work also serves as an application of these ideas to differential-linear cryptanalysis, an example of which was not present in [12].

Acknowledgment. This work was partially funded by the DFG, (German Research Foundation) under Germany's Excellence Strategy - EXC 2092 CASA - 390781972. This project has received funding from the European Research Council (ERC) under the European Union's Horizon 2020 research and innovation programme (grant agreement no. 714294 - acronym QUASYModo).

A   Connection to the Tree-Based Key-Recovery of [12] and Conditions used in Sect. 5

The conditions used in the attack of Sect. 5 and Sect. 4.1 can be expressed in terms of a special type of binary decision trees (called affine decision trees in [12] and parity decision trees elsewhere when the bit-length of the output is one). The authors of [12] examine those trees formally.

An affine decision tree is a regular binary tree for which the inner nodes represent the decision rule for evaluation and the leaves represent the function values of all inputs arriving there.

Given a tree for a (non-constant) function f and undetermined (resp. partially determined, key-dependent) input x which has to be evaluated in the key guessing phase, one needs to guess the bit $b = \langle \alpha, x \rangle$ indicated by the root and then follow the appropriate edge to the sub-tree representing the function $f|_{\langle \alpha,x \rangle = b}$ (here: the left sub-tree represents $f|_{\langle \alpha,x \rangle = 0}$ and the right $f|_{\langle \alpha,x \rangle = 1}$). Each leaf represents an affine subspace on which the function is constant and whose codimension is the depth of the corresponding leaf.

Let the tree for f have k leaves with corresponding affine spaces $A_1, \ldots, A_k$ (which we identify with the leaves) and depths $d_1, \ldots, d_k$. When we arrive in a leaf A_i, we have made at most d_i additional guesses during the key guessing phase. The size of each space is $|A_i| = 2^{n-d_i}$. That means that the total cost incurred is

$$\sum_{i=1}^{k} 2^{d_i} 2^{-d_i} = k$$

since 2^{d_i} is the cost of guessing d_i bits and we will end up in A_i for a proportion of 2^{-d_i} inputs. Put differently, the multiplicative gain over guessing all n bits of input is

$$\frac{k}{2^n}.$$

As noted in [12], the goal in most attack scenarios is therefore to minimize the number of leaves (the *size* of the tree).

In the following, we write selection patterns α as hexadecimal numbers, whose binary representation is regarded as an element of $\mathbb{F}_2^4$. The bold numbers refer to leaves, and depending on the number of output bits m, is a hexadecimal number between 0 and $2^m - 1$.

In the following, we give the trees used in the attack of Sect. 5.

Columns of type b. Let us first look at the set of relations for Sbox S_0 given in Sect. 4.1. Those relations make up size-minimal trees for coordinate functions of S_0:

$$y_i(x) = \langle 2^i, S(x) \rangle.$$

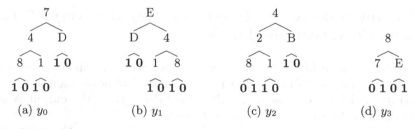

Fig. 4. Trees for $\langle 2^i, S_0(x) \rangle$

In the attack for columns of type b we use the trees from Figs. 4a, 4c and 4d.

Columns of type c. For column 19 (type c) one can derive from the conditions given in Sect. 4.1 that only three bits are necessary to determine both y_1 and y_3 using the tree from Fig. 5c. The resulting gain (8/16) is optimal. One additional bit can be absorbed by adding the corresponding keybit from the next round to the final linear relation. The same happens for column 2, giving each of these two columns a gain factor of 2^{-2}. Column 3 has a smaller gain of $2^{-0.68}$.

The trees for columns of type c can be found in Fig. 5.

Columns of type d (and e). For columns of type d we have to determine good pairs (x, x') whose output difference $\Delta = S_0(x) + S_0(x')$ belongs to a fixed subset, like for example $\Delta = 4$: Given x, we look at the function F_Δ mentioned in Sect. 4.1. Its corresponding tree is given in Fig. 6a. It has size 6 and therefore a gain factor of 6/16.

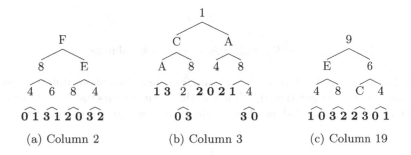

(a) Column 2   (b) Column 3   (c) Column 19

Fig. 5. Trees for columns of type c

When the expected output difference is 0, so must be the input difference. Therefore instead of guessing 4 bits, we need not guess any. Hence we gain a factor of 1/16 in this case. The corresponding tree has one leaf only.

The size-minimal trees for the other three possible differences C (for column 15) and A and E (for column 28) can be found in Fig. 6, as well as the tree for the difference 8 of column 29 used for the better memory trade-off.

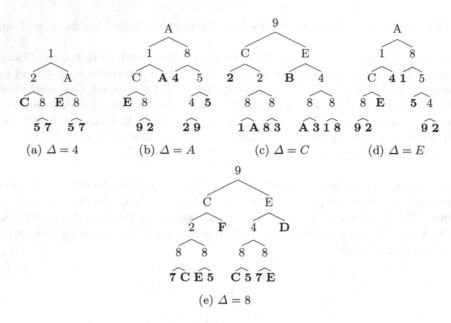

Fig. 6. Trees for $F_\Delta = S_0^{-1}(S_0(x) + \Delta) + x$, columns of type d

A tree for column 20 of type f. For column 20, when the output difference is zero the right input pairs are trivial, while the three output bits must be determined. The tree shown in Fig. 7 shows how to do an optimal guess in order to do that.

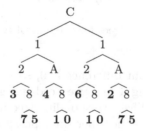

Fig. 7. Tree for column 20, to determine output bits y_0, y_1 and y_3

References

1. Bar-On, A., Dunkelman, O., Keller, N., Weizman, A.: DLCT: a new tool for differential-linear cryptanalysis. In: Ishai, Y., Rijmen, V. (eds.) EUROCRYPT 2019, Part I. LNCS, vol. 11476, pp. 313–342. Springer, Cham (2019). https://doi.org/10.1007/978-3-030-17653-2_11
2. Beierle, C., Leander, G., Todo, Y.: Improved differential-linear attacks with applications to ARX ciphers. In: Micciancio, D., Ristenpart, T. (eds.) CRYPTO 2020, Part III. LNCS, vol. 12172, pp. 329–358. Springer, Cham (2020). https://doi.org/10.1007/978-3-030-56877-1_12

3. Biham, E., Anderson, R., Knudsen, L.: Serpent: a new block cipher proposal. In: Vaudenay, S. (ed.) FSE 1998. LNCS, vol. 1372, pp. 222–238. Springer, Heidelberg (1998). https://doi.org/10.1007/3-540-69710-1_15
4. Biham, E., Dunkelman, O., Keller, N.: Linear cryptanalysis of reduced round serpent. In: Matsui, M. (ed.) FSE 2001. LNCS, vol. 2355, pp. 16–27. Springer, Heidelberg (2002). https://doi.org/10.1007/3-540-45473-X_2
5. Biham, E., Dunkelman, O., Keller, N.: The rectangle attack — rectangling the serpent. In: Pfitzmann, B. (ed.) EUROCRYPT 2001. LNCS, vol. 2045, pp. 340–357. Springer, Heidelberg (2001). https://doi.org/10.1007/3-540-44987-6_21
6. Biham, E., Dunkelman, O., Keller, N.: Enhancing differential-linear cryptanalysis. In: Zheng, Y. (ed.) ASIACRYPT 2002. LNCS, vol. 2501, pp. 254–266. Springer, Heidelberg (2002). https://doi.org/10.1007/3-540-36178-2_16
7. Biham, E., Dunkelman, O., Keller, N.: New results on boomerang and rectangle attacks. In: Daemen, J., Rijmen, V. (eds.) FSE 2002. LNCS, vol. 2365, pp. 1–16. Springer, Heidelberg (2002). https://doi.org/10.1007/3-540-45661-9_1
8. Biham, E., Dunkelman, O., Keller, N.: Differential-linear cryptanalysis of serpent. In: Johansson, T. (ed.) FSE 2003. LNCS, vol. 2887, pp. 9–21. Springer, Heidelberg (2003). https://doi.org/10.1007/978-3-540-39887-5_2
9. Biham, E., Perle, S.: Conditional linear cryptanalysis - cryptanalysis of DES with less than 2^{42} complexity. IACR Trans. Symmetric Cryptol. **2018**(3), 215–264 (2018). https://doi.org/10.13154/tosc.v2018.i3.215-264
10. Biham, E., Shamir, A.: Differential cryptanalysis of DES-like cryptosystems. In: Menezes, A.J., Vanstone, S.A. (eds.) CRYPTO 1990. LNCS, vol. 537, pp. 2–21. Springer, Heidelberg (1991). https://doi.org/10.1007/3-540-38424-3_1
11. Blondeau, C., Nyberg, K.: Improved parameter estimates for correlation and capacity deviates in linear cryptanalysis. IACR Trans. Symmetric Cryptol. **2016**(2), 162–191 (2016). https://doi.org/10.13154/tosc.v2016.i2.162-191
12. Broll, M., Canale, F., Florez-Gutierrez, A., Leander, G., Naya-Plasencia, M.: Generic framework for key-guessing improvements. In: Advances in Cryptology - ASIACRYPT 2021, 27th International Conference on the Theory and Application of Cryptology and Information Security, Singapore, 5–9 December 2021. Springer, Cham (2021). https://doi.org/10.1007/978-3-030-92062-3_16
13. Carlet, C., Charpin, P., Zinoviev, V.A.: Codes, bent functions and permutations suitable for DES-like cryptosystems. Des. Codes Cryptogr. **15**(2), 125–156 (1998). https://doi.org/10.1023/A:1008344232130
14. Cho, J.Y., Hermelin, M., Nyberg, K.: A new technique for multidimensional linear cryptanalysis with applications on reduced round serpent. In: Lee, P.J., Cheon, J.H. (eds.) ICISC 2008. LNCS, vol. 5461, pp. 383–398. Springer, Heidelberg (2009). https://doi.org/10.1007/978-3-642-00730-9_24
15. Collard, B., Standaert, F.-X., Quisquater, J.-J.: Improved and multiple linear cryptanalysis of reduced round serpent. In: Pei, D., Yung, M., Lin, D., Wu, C. (eds.) Inscrypt 2007. LNCS, vol. 4990, pp. 51–65. Springer, Heidelberg (2008). https://doi.org/10.1007/978-3-540-79499-8_6
16. Collard, B., Standaert, F.-X., Quisquater, J.-J.: Improving the time complexity of Matsui's linear cryptanalysis. In: Nam, K.-H., Rhee, G. (eds.) ICISC 2007. LNCS, vol. 4817, pp. 77–88. Springer, Heidelberg (2007). https://doi.org/10.1007/978-3-540-76788-6_7
17. Dunkelman, O., Indesteege, S., Keller, N.: A differential-linear attack on 12-round serpent. In: Chowdhury, D.R., Rijmen, V., Das, A. (eds.) INDOCRYPT 2008. LNCS, vol. 5365, pp. 308–321. Springer, Heidelberg (2008). https://doi.org/10.1007/978-3-540-89754-5_24

18. Flórez-Gutiérrez, A., Naya-Plasencia, M.: Improving key-recovery in linear attacks: application to 28-round PRESENT. In: Canteaut, A., Ishai, Y. (eds.) EURO-CRYPT 2020, Part I. LNCS, vol. 12105, pp. 221–249. Springer, Cham (2020). https://doi.org/10.1007/978-3-030-45721-1_9
19. Kelsey, J., Kohno, T., Schneier, B.: Amplified boomerang attacks against reduced-round MARS and serpent. In: Goos, G., Hartmanis, J., van Leeuwen, J., Schneier, B. (eds.) FSE 2000. LNCS, vol. 1978, pp. 75–93. Springer, Heidelberg (2001). https://doi.org/10.1007/3-540-44706-7_6
20. Langford, S.K., Hellman, M.E.: Differential-linear cryptanalysis. In: Desmedt, Y.G. (ed.) CRYPTO 1994. LNCS, vol. 839, pp. 17–25. Springer, Heidelberg (1994). https://doi.org/10.1007/3-540-48658-5_3
21. Liu, M., Lu, X., Lin, D.: Differential-linear cryptanalysis from an algebraic perspective. In: Malkin, T., Peikert, C. (eds.) CRYPTO 2021, Part III. LNCS, vol. 12827, pp. 247–277. Springer, Cham (2021). https://doi.org/10.1007/978-3-030-84252-9_9
22. Matsui, M.: Linear cryptanalysis method for DES cipher. In: Helleseth, T. (ed.) EUROCRYPT 1993. LNCS, vol. 765, pp. 386–397. Springer, Heidelberg (1994). https://doi.org/10.1007/3-540-48285-7_33
23. McLaughlin, J., Clark, J.A.: Filtered nonlinear cryptanalysis of reduced-round serpent, and the wrong-key randomization hypothesis. In: Stam, M. (ed.) IMACC 2013. LNCS, vol. 8308, pp. 120–140. Springer, Heidelberg (2013). https://doi.org/10.1007/978-3-642-45239-0_8
24. Nguyen, P.H., Wu, H., Wang, H.: Improving the algorithm 2 in multidimensional linear cryptanalysis. In: Parampalli, U., Hawkes, P. (eds.) ACISP 2011. LNCS, vol. 6812, pp. 61–74. Springer, Heidelberg (2011). https://doi.org/10.1007/978-3-642-22497-3_5

Pholkos – Efficient Large-State Tweakable Block Ciphers from the **AES** Round Function

Jannis Bossert[✉], Eik List, Stefan Lucks, and Sebastian Schmitz

Bauhaus-Universität Weimar, Weimar, Germany
{jannis.bossert,eik.list,stefan.lucks,sebastian.schmitz}@uni-weimar.de

Abstract. This paper proposes Pholkos, a family of heavyweight tweakable block ciphers with state and key sizes of ≥ 256 and tweaks of either 128 or 256 bits. When encrypting large chunks of data under the same key, modes with Pholkos do not require "beyond-birthday security" since it provides "bigger birthday security". This also makes it a good choice for quantum-secure authenticated encryption modes like QCB. Pholkos runs at 1–2 cycles per byte on Intel 6-th generation and more recent, following design principles from Haraka, AESQ, and the TWEAKEY framework. Building on the AES round function not only boosts software performance but also improves security, employing knowledge from two decades of cryptanalysis of the AES.

Keywords: AES · Tweakable block cipher · Bigger birthday security

1 Introduction

Large-State Block Ciphers. Many schemes and modes for n-bit block-cipher-based authentication, encryption, or authenticated encryption are only secure up to the birthday bound ($O(2^{n/2})$ calls to the internal primitive). This is a practical issue when state sizes are as small as 64 bits (cf. [10]), yet even $n = 128$ bits can be insufficient for future-proof high-end applications or post-quantum security.

While modes of operation secure beyond the birthday bound are one way to address this issue, such modes are usually more complicated than modes with birthday-only security (CTR, CBC, GCM [63], OCB [72], ...). Another idea would be to instantiate modes with heavyweight block primitives (cf. [9]) for "bigger" birthday security. In the same spirit, 128-bit keys can be considered sufficiently secure for most applications at the moment. Though, for u users with respective secret keys, the security against adversaries that aim to recover any of them decreases linearly in u. Thus, for high birthday-bound and multi-user security, keys of at least 256 bits are recommended.

A similar argument can be formulated for post-quantum applications. While Shor's seminal algorithm [79] is less applicable to analyze symmetric-key algorithms, Grover's algorithm [46] can reduce the exhaustive key search to $O(2^{n/2})$

S. D. Galbraith (Ed.): CT-RSA 2022, LNCS 13161, pp. 511–536, 2022.
https://doi.org/10.1007/978-3-030-95312-6_21

operations, cf. [1].[1] Thus, at least 256-bit keys are recommended for 128-bit security [1,28]. Kaplan et al. [57] introduced two models to formalize quantum-computing-aided adversaries: in the Q1 model, the adversary can use a quantum computer only for offline computations; in the Q2 model, it can also ask superposition queries – giving quantum algorithms a quadratic speedup not only for exhaustive key search but also certain attacks. Moreover, quantum adversaries may profit further if the key size exceeds the state size and some classical modes break in the Q2 model, including OCB [56].

Modes of operation can benefit from a tweakable block cipher (TBC) by increased security, simplified domain separation in proofs [30,51,68], or the ability to process additional inputs. Moreover, Bhaumik et al. [11] showed that the use of a dedicated TBC yields a quantum-secure mode QCB.

Two design concepts have been shown promising for the construction of TBCs: using the AES [65] as a base, and the TWEAKEY concept and the STK schedule [54]. Building on the AES round function allows for applying decades of cryptanalysis of it, and higher performance due to widespread performant hardware instruction sets. Intel even announced to integrate the _mm512_aesenc_epi128 instruction with almost fourfold throughput compared to the existing 128-bit instruction from 10th-generation Core-i models on [39]. The TWEAKEY design is a well-established principle for turning a block cipher into a TBC while minimizing the risk of the additional input space.

Research Questions. The aspects above form the interesting research question to design an efficient family of (tweakable) block ciphers that provides:

(1) Sufficiently long keys against quantum-computing cryptanalysis,
(2) Sufficiently long blocks for greater birthday bounds,
(3) Tweaks to support classical and Q2-secure modes with high security and high performance, and
(4) An AES-round-based design to benefit from hardware instructions.

We aim at keys of 256, blocks of at least 256, and tweaks of at least 128 bits.

Design Strategies. Peyrin outlined three high-level strategies for TBC designs [67]: (1) minimal area, (2) low energy consumption and lightweightness, and (3) high authentication/encryption performance. Our focus will be on Use Case (3). Peyrin suggested using larger tweaks since the tweak-update function can be lighter than that of the plaintext input.

Few large-state block ciphers exist in literature, e.g. ThreeFish [42] with 256, 512, and 1024-bit state or the recent 256-bit Trax [8], both with 128-bit tweaks. Both are ARX-based (additions, XORs, and rotations) constructions optimized for 32-bit microcontrollers. Kalyna [66] is a recent Rijndael-like substitution-permutation network (SPN) with state and key lengths of 128, 256, and 512 bits and a dedicated S-box. Saturnin is a 256-bit SPN with a cubic structure and a lightweight S-box whose purpose is a small footprint.

---

[1] Though, Grover's algorithm does not parallelize well: when running q quantum cores, it still needs $O(2^{n/2}/\sqrt{q})$ operations.

Table 1. Comparison and versions.

(a) Parameters of **Pholkos**. Std. = standard model, RT = related-tweak, RTK = related-tweakey.

Version (bits)			#Steps	Security (bits)		
n	k	t	s	Std.	RT	RTK
256	256	128	8	256	256	256
256	256	256	8	256	256	256
512	256	128	10	256	256	256
1024	256	128	12	256	256	256

(b) Large-state block ciphers and permutations based on the AES-round function.

Construction	Size variants $(n/k/t)$		
Block ciphers			
3D [55]	256/256/–	512/512/–	–
LANE [48]	256/256/–	512/512/–	–
Kalyna [66]	128/128/–	256/256/–	512/512/–
Tweakable block ciphers			
Saturnin [26]	256/256/4		
ThreeFish [42]	256/256/128	512/512/128	1024/1024/128
Trax [8]	256/256/128		
AES-round-based Permutations			
AESQ [17]	512/–/–		
Haraka v2 [60]	256/–/–	512/–/–	

Several constructions already transformed larger states based on the AES round function. 3D [55] was an early attempt to design a larger block cipher based on the AES round function, but was not tweakable and extended the complex AES key schedule. Moreover, it needs additional instructions in optimized x86 implementations since it employed the involutive MDS matrix of Anubis [71].

The SHA-3 candidate LANE was a hash function that used two (LANE-224 and -256) or four (LANE-384 and -512) AES substates. In contrast to 3D, which used byte-wise mixing in each round, LANE shuffled the 32-bit words between the 128-bit states after the MixColumns operation. The authenticated encryption scheme PAEQ [17,18] is built on the 512-bit permutation AESQ that transformed four AES-states in parallel with a claimed security level of 256 bits. In contrast to 3D or LANE, AESQ was the first such construction that mixed parts (32-bit words) among individual substates only after two rounds for faster diffusion.

The hash function family Haraka (v1) [59] and v2 [60] adopted this approach from AESQ. Due to invariant substates in the initial proposal, the designers changed the round constants; we focus on v2 hereafter. Haraka also uses 256- and 512-bit variants and employs a permutation that consists of five steps, following an AESQ-like design of mixing the 32-bit words after each step, i.e., after every second round. Since the designers focused on 256-bit (second-)preimage security for short-input hashing, they could reduce the number of steps to five. Bao et al. [4] challenged this assumption with recent MITM preimage attacks, which are less relevant for this work since we use considerably more steps.

Several works considered the construction of (authenticated) keystream generators from the AES round function with excellent performance, e.g. Tiaoxin [64], AEGIS [87], or the proposals from [53], all aiming at 128 bits of security under nonce-respecting adversaries. Rocca [76] is a recent nonce-based AE scheme with 256-bit security. In contrast, Pholkos' security is independent of a mode or nonce.

Contribution. In this work, we propose Pholkos, a family of large-state tweakable block ciphers based on the AES round function and the design strategy of two-round steps from Haraka v2 and AESQ. Pholkos has two major variants with

256- and 512-bit state, 256-bit key, and 128-bit tweak. Thus, they combine block sizes for post-quantum applications, with 256-bit keys that provide a sufficient level of security, and long tweaks for high-security modes.

We propose two further variants: For use cases where a larger tweak is beneficial, e.g. in modes such as ZMAC, we add a variant with 256-bit state, key, and tweak. While a similar step would appear beneficial for the variant with a 512-bit state, we refrained from it in this work only since the analysis would have become infeasible. For use cases benefiting from large blocks, we include a variant with 1024-bit state, 256-bit key, and 128-bit tweak. For all instances, we claim 256-bit security in classical and 128-bit in the single-key post-quantum model.

In contrast to AESQ, Haraka, 3D, and LANE, our proposal is tweakable, which allows its usage in modes with high security guarantees. Our design differs from 3D and LANE by adopting the approach of mixing the words between substate for higher performance from AESQ and Haraka. Compared to Trax, our proposal can exploit the performance and security results from the AES. As a major difference to AEGIS, Tiaoxin346 or [53], Pholkos targets higher security guarantees and is not only a scheme but a versatile primitive.

We show the security in the standard, related-tweak, and related-tweakey model against differential, linear, and integral distinguishers, and provide initial security arguments concerning zero-correlation, boomerang, yoyo, mixture, and meet-in-the-middle attacks. On Intel Skylake, Pholkos can encrypt at about 1.5 cycles per byte, depending on the version. We propose the instantiation of QCB with Pholkos for quantum-secure authenticated encryption. Due to the larger tweaks, it provides higher security bounds than QCB-Saturnin.

While it is based on many existing works, Pholkos distinguishes itself by being a highly performant block cipher with 256-bit security, offering larger bounds for modes against birthday bound attacks, providing large tweaks that enable its use in many modes including QCB, and processing larger chunks of data, reducing the number of required key changes.

Overview. We provide notations in Sect. 2, before specifying Pholkos in Sect. 3. Section 4 will give a design rationale. We report on the software performance of Pholkos in Sect. 5, and provide an initial security analysis in Sect. 6. Section 7 concludes. We provide details of our analysis in the supplementary material that we plan to publish in a full version alongside this work.

2   Preliminaries

We denote by $\mathbb{F}_2$ the finite field of characteristic two. We write functions and variables by uppercase, indices by lowercase, and sets by calligraphic characters. $\{0,1\}^n$ is the set of all n-bit strings and $\{0,1\}^*$ the set of bit strings of arbitrary length. Let $X, Y \in \mathbb{F}_2^n$; we index bits as $X = (X_{n-1} \ldots X_1 X_0)$ where X_{n-1} is the most significant and X_0 the least significant bit of X. For $t \leq n$, $\mathsf{msb}_t(X)$ returns the t most significant bits of X. For a set $\mathcal{X}$, $\mathsf{Perm}(\mathcal{X})$ denotes the set of all permutations over $\mathcal{X}$. For a bit string X, we write $(X_0, \ldots, X_{w-1}) \xleftarrow{n} X$

Table 2. The word-wise permutations π used in Pholkos.

i	0	1	2	3	4	5	6	7	8	9	10	11	12	13	14	15	16	17	18	19	20	21	22	23	24	25	26	27	28	29	30	31
$\pi_{256}(i)$	0	5	2	7	4	1	6	3																								
$\pi_{512}(i)$	0	5	10	15	4	9	14	3	8	13	2	7	12	1	6	11																
$\pi_{1024,0}(i)$	0	9	18	27	4	13	22	31	8	17	26	3	12	21	30	7	16	25	2	11	20	29	6	15	24	1	10	19	28	5	14	23
$\pi_{1024,1}(i)$	0	5	2	7	4	9	6	11	8	13	10	15	12	17	14	19	16	21	18	23	20	25	22	27	24	29	26	31	28	1	30	3

Table 3. The byte-wise permutation for the Tweakey schedule.

i	0	1	2	3	4	5	6	7	8	9	10	11	12	13	14	15
$\pi_\tau(i)$	11	12	1	2	15	0	5	6	3	4	9	10	7	8	13	14

for the unique splitting of X into n-bit parts s. t. $|X_i| = n$ for $0 \le i < w - 1$, $|X_{w-1}| \le n$, and $(X_0 \| \dots \| X_{w-1}) = X$.

The AES-128 [33] is an SPN that transforms 128-bit inputs through ten rounds of SubBytes (SB), ShiftRows (SR), MixColumns (MC), and the addition (AK) with a round key K^i. Before the first round, a whitening key K^0 is XORed to the state; the final round omits MixColumns. S^i denotes the state after Round i, and $S^i[j]$ for the j-th byte, for $0 \le i \le 10$ and $0 \le j \le 15$. So, the byte order is columnwise from top to bottom and left to right. We write $\mathsf{R}[K^i] \stackrel{\text{def}}{=} \mathsf{AK}[K^i] \circ \mathsf{MC} \circ \mathsf{SR} \circ \mathsf{SB}$ for one call to the round function and $\widehat{\mathsf{R}}[K^i] \stackrel{\text{def}}{=} \mathsf{AK}[K^i] \circ \mathsf{SR} \circ \mathsf{SB}$ for a call to the round function without MC. $S^{r,\mathsf{SB}}$, $S^{r,\mathsf{SR}}$, and $S^{r,\mathsf{MC}}$ denote the states in the r-th round directly after the application of SB, SR, and MC, respectively. We use $\mathbf{M}$ for the MixColumns matrix. MixColumns interprets each input byte as element in $\mathbb{F}_{2^8}$ with the irreducible polynomial $p(\mathbf{x}) = \mathbf{x}^8 + \mathbf{x}^4 + \mathbf{x}^3 + \mathbf{x} + 1$.

3 Specification

This section specifies the family of Pholkos-n, or more precisely, Pholkos-n-k-t. It takes an n-bit plaintext M, a $k = 256$-bit key K, and a t-bit tweak T. Algorithm 1 defines the en- and decryption procedures as well as the tweakey schedule. We propose two major versions, Pholkos-256 and Pholkos-512, with 256-bit key and 128-bit tweak each. Moreover, we propose two minor versions, Pholkos-1024-256-128 for use cases that can benefit from longer blocks, and Pholkos-256-256 as a fourth version for applications that can benefit from a larger tweak.

3.1 Encryption

An n-bit plaintext is split into 128-bit substates of four 32-bit words each. Before the first round, the round tweakey RTK^0 is XORed to the plaintext (Fig. 2).

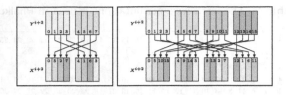

Fig. 1. The permutations of Pholkos-256 (left) and Pholkos-512 (right).

The Step Function. In a step, each substate is encrypted individually by two consecutive AES rounds. Each round, except for the final one, consists of the operations SubBytes (SB), ShiftRows (SR), MixColumns (MC), and AddRound-Tweakey (ATK), the addition of the round tweakey RTK^i. Thereupon, a word permutation π_n permutes all 32-bit words of all substates to mix the substates. This sequence of two rounds and the application of the word permutation is called a step. The final step omits the final word permutation at the end; the final AES round omits the MixColumns operation as in the AES. We write

- s for the number of steps, $r_s = 2$ for the fixed number of rounds per step, and $r = s \cdot r_s$ rounds in total, counted from $1..r$. Table 1a summarizes the numbers of proposed steps for the instances.
- X^i for the n-bit state after Round i. X^0 is initialized with the plaintext M.
- Y^i, for even $i > 0$, for the state directly after the i-th round and before π is applied. X^i is the state directly after the words of Y^i were permuted by π.
- X^i_j, for $j \in [0..w-1]$ for 32-bit words of the state X^i. Thus, each state $X^i = (X^i_0, \ldots, X^i_{w-1})$ is a list of w 32-bit words.
- $m = 32$ for the length of each word in bits.
- $X^{i,j}$ for $j \in [0..v-1]$ for the 128-bit substates, where $v = w/4 = n/128$.
- $X^i[j]$ for a *cell*, i.e., a byte. We index cells as in the AES, but in sequence throughout the state, i.e., $X^i[16]$ is the first byte in the second substate.
- RTK^i for the round tweakey used at the end of Round i. Its words and bytes are indexed as those of states as $RTK^i = (RTK^i_0, \ldots, RTK^i_{w-1})$. We write RTK^0 for the initial tweakey.

The Permutation. The word permutation $\pi \in \mathsf{Perm}(\mathbb{Z}_w)$ shuffles the words across the substates. Each instantiation of Pholkos employs a different permutation. It also differs from those used in Haraka, AESQ, 3D, and LANE. For Pholkos-256 and Pholkos-512, we denote the corresponding permutations as π_n according to the state size n. Pholkos-1024 applies two permutations $\pi_{1024,0}$ and $\pi_{1024,1}$ alternatingly, starting with $\pi_{1024,0}$ after the first step. Each permutation π_n maps the word at index $\pi(j)$ to index j: $X^i_j \leftarrow Y^i_{\pi(j)}$, as given in Table 2.

3.2   The Tweakey Schedule

Key Expansion. If $n > k$, the 256-bit secret key SK is first expanded by a function $\varphi : \mathbb{F}_2^k \to \mathbb{F}_2^n$. The leftmost 256 bits of the generated key employ K. All

Algorithm 1. Definition of Pholkos-n.

```
11: function Encrypt $_K^T(M)$                          52: function Decrypt $_K^T(C)$
12:    $RTK \leftarrow$ Schedule$(K, T)$                 53:    $RTK \leftarrow$ Schedule$(K, T)$
13:    $X^0 \leftarrow M \oplus RTK^0$                   54:    $Y^{2 \cdot s} \leftarrow C$
14:    for $i \leftarrow 1..s - 1$ do                    55:    $X^{2 \cdot (s-1)} \leftarrow$ Step$^{-1}(Y^{2 \cdot s})$
15:       $Y^{2 \cdot i} \leftarrow$ Step$(X^{2 \cdot (i-1)})$  56:    for $i \leftarrow s - 1$ down to 1 do
16:       $P \leftarrow$ getPerm$(i)$                    57:       $P \leftarrow$ getPerm$(i)$
17:       $X^{2 \cdot i} \leftarrow$ PermWords$(P, Y^{2 \cdot i})$  58:       $Y^{2 \cdot i} \leftarrow$ PermWords$(P^{-1}, X^{2 \cdot i})$
18:    $Y^{2 \cdot s} \leftarrow$ Step$(X^{2 \cdot (s-1)})$  59:       $X^{2 \cdot (i-1)} \leftarrow$ Step$^{-1}(Y^{2 \cdot i})$
19:    return $Y^{2 \cdot s}$                            60:    return $X^0 \oplus RTK^0$

20: function Step$(X^i)$                                 61: function Step$^{-1}(Y^i)$
21:    $(X_0^i, \ldots, X_{w-1}^i) \leftarrow X^i$       62:    $(X_0^i, \ldots, X_{w-1}^i) \leftarrow Y^i$
22:    for $\ell \leftarrow 1..2$ do                     63:    for $\ell \leftarrow 1..2$ do
23:       for $j \leftarrow 0..v - 1$ do                 64:       for $j \leftarrow 0..w - 1$ do
24:          if $i + \ell < r$ then      ▷ Substates     65:          if $i + \ell < r$ then      ▷ Substates
25:             $X^{i+\ell,j} \leftarrow$ R$[RTK^{i+\ell,j}](X^{i+\ell,j})$  66:             $X^{i-\ell,j} \leftarrow$ R$[RTK^{i+1-\ell,j}]^{-1}(X^{i+1-\ell,j})$
26:          else          ▷ Substates, final round      67:          else          ▷ Substates, final round
27:             $X^{i+\ell,j} \leftarrow \widehat{R}[RTK^{i+\ell,j}](X^{i+\ell,j})$  68:             $X^{i-\ell,j} \leftarrow \widehat{R}[RTK^{i+1-\ell,j}]^{-1}(X^{i+1-\ell,j})$
28:    return $X^{i+2}$                                  69:    return $X^{i-2}$

30: function R$[RTK](X)$                                 71: function R$[RTK]^{-1}(X)$
31:    return $RTK \oplus$ MC(SR(SB($X$)))               72:    return SB$^{-1}$(SR$^{-1}$(MC$^{-1}$($RTK \oplus X$)))

32: function $\widehat{R}[RTK](X)$                       73: function $\widehat{R}[RTK]^{-1}(X)$
33:    return $RTK \oplus$ SR(SB($X$))                   74:    return SB$^{-1}$(SR$^{-1}$($RTK \oplus X$))

34: function PermWords$(P, Y^i)$                         75: function $\kappa(\alpha, \pi, K^{i-1})$
35:    for $j \leftarrow 0..w - 1$ do $X_j^i \leftarrow Y_{P(j)}^i$  ▷ Words  76:    for $j \leftarrow 0..w - 1$ do
36:    return $X^i$                                      77:       $K_j^i \leftarrow K_{\pi(j)}^{i-1}$      ▷ Words
                                                         78:    for $j \leftarrow 0..v - 1$ do
37: function getPerm$(i)$                                79:       $K^{i,j} \leftarrow \tau(K^{i,j})$      ▷ Substates
38:    if $n = 1024$ then return $\pi_{1024,(i-1) \bmod 2}$  80:       for $b \leftarrow 0..15$ do
39:    else return $\pi_n$                               81:          $K_j^i[b] \leftarrow \alpha \cdot K_j^i[b]$      ▷ Cells
                                                         82:    return $(K_0^i, \ldots, K_{w-1}^i)$
40: function Schedule$(K, T)$
41:    $K^0 \leftarrow \varphi(K)$                       82: function $\theta(\pi, T^{i-1})$
42:    $T^0 \leftarrow T$                                83:    if $|T^{i-1}| > 128$ then return $\kappa(1, \pi, T^{i-1})$
43:    $RTK^0 \leftarrow \gamma(RC^0, K^0, T^0)$          84:    return $\tau(T^{i-1})$
44:    for $i \leftarrow 1..r$ do
45:       $T^i \leftarrow \theta(\pi, T^{i-1})$           85: function $\tau(X)$
46:       $K^i \leftarrow \kappa(2, \pi, K^{i-1})$        86:    for $b \leftarrow 0..15$ do $Z[b] \leftarrow X[\pi_\tau(b)]$  ▷ Cells
47:       $RTK^i \leftarrow \gamma(RC^i, K^i, T^i)$       87:    return $Z$
48:    return $(RTK^0, \ldots, RTK^r)$
                                                         88: function $\gamma(RC^i, K^i, T^i)$
49: function $\varphi(K)$                                89:    for $j \leftarrow 0..w - 1$ do      ▷ Words
50:    if $|K| \geq n$ then return $K$                    90:       $RTK_j^i \leftarrow K_j^i \oplus T_{j \bmod 4}^i$
51:    return msb$_n(K \| M_A \cdot K \| M_B \cdot K \| M_C \cdot K)$  91:       if $j \leq 3$ then $RTK_j^i \leftarrow RTK_j^i \oplus RC_j^i$
                                                         92:    return $(RTK_0^i, \ldots, RTK_{w-1}^i)$
```

subsequent 256-bit chunks are generated by multiplying K with binary circular matrices $\in (\mathbb{F}_{2^{32}})^{8 \times 8}$ with branch numbers of four:

$$\mathbf{M}_A \stackrel{\text{def}}{=} \text{circ}(11001000), \quad \mathbf{M}_B \stackrel{\text{def}}{=} \text{circ}(10101000), \quad \text{and} \quad \mathbf{M}_C \stackrel{\text{def}}{=} \text{circ}(10011000).$$

$\mathbf{K} = (K_0, \ldots, K_7)$ denotes the eight key words. The expanded key words are computed as $(K_8, \ldots, K_{15}) =^{\text{def}} \mathbf{M}_A \cdot \mathbf{K}^\top$. For the 1024-bit variant, more words are derived as $(K_{16}, \ldots, K_{23}) =^{\text{def}} \mathbf{M}_B \cdot \mathbf{K}^\top$ and $(K_{24}, \ldots, K_{31}) =^{\text{def}} \mathbf{M}_C \cdot \mathbf{K}^\top$.

Generation of Round Tweakeys. The tweakey schedule generates round tweakeys from the tweak T^0 and the (expanded) secret key K^0. For Pholkos with s steps,

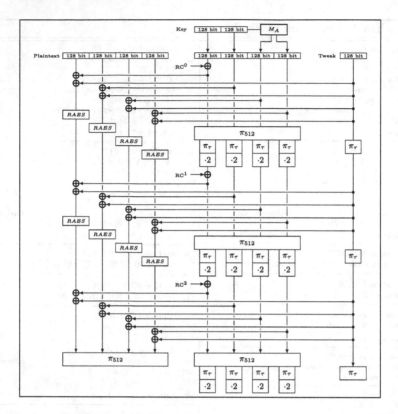

Fig. 2. The first step of Pholkos-512-256-128 including the initial key whitening. It shows also how the key is expanded, and how the 128-bit tweak is added to the 256-bit key. R_{AES} means the AES-round without the key addition.

$2s + 1$ round tweakeys are needed during en- or decryption, RTK^0 to RTK^{2s}. In general, the tweakey schedule of Pholkos follows the route from the STK [54] construction, our proposal keeps the words for the tweak and the key separated, which are processed in parallel as depicted in Fig. 3a. The tweakey schedule initializes a key state K^0 from the expanded secret key and an initial tweak state from the user-supplied tweak $T^0 \leftarrow T$. It applies

- a function $\kappa : \mathcal{K} \to \mathcal{K}$ to compute $K^i \leftarrow \kappa(K^{i-1})$.
- a function $\theta : \mathcal{T} \to \mathcal{T}$ to compute $T^i \leftarrow \theta(T^{i-1})$ and
- a function γ which combines T^i and K^i to derive the round tweakey as $RTK^i \leftarrow \gamma(K^i, T^i, RC^i)$, where RC^i is the round constant of Round i.

κ transforms each 128-bit substate of the key by (1) the word-wise permutation π_n, (2) a layer τ that applies a byte-wise permutation π_τ to each substate, and (3) a cell-wise doubling in $\mathbb{F}_{2^8}$ (Fig. 2).

The function θ depends on the tweak length. For versions, where the tweak is smaller than the original key, θ simply applies τ. For Pholkos-256-256-256, both

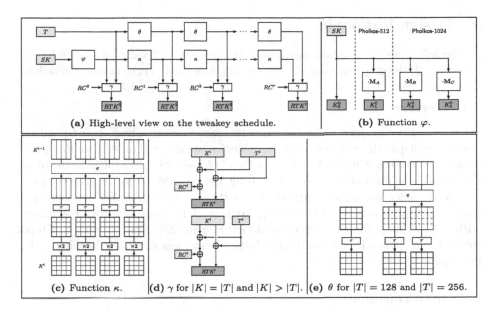

Fig. 3. Components of the tweakey schedule of Pholkos.

key and tweak are processed almost equally, but the tweak cells are not doubled in $\mathbb{F}_{2^8}$ to prevent iterative related-tweakey differentials. Thus

$$\theta(T^{i-1}) \stackrel{\text{def}}{=} \begin{cases} \tau(\pi(T^{i-1})) & \text{if } |T| = |K| = 256 \\ \tau(T^{i-1}) & \text{otherwise.} \end{cases}$$

RTK^0 is derived from K^0 and T^0 with γ before any call to the update functions κ and θ. If $|T| = 128$, γ XORs T^i to every 128-bit substate of K^i. The round tweakey word is computed as $RTK_j^i \leftarrow K_j^i \oplus T_{j \bmod 4}^i$; if $j = 0$, the round constant RC^i is further XORed to it (see Fig. 3). The tweak-update function τ uses the permutation π_τ from Table 3 for mixing the tweakey cells. The key-update function κ permutes the words of the round key RK^i with π_n from the step permutation. In Pholkos-1024, the i-th invocation of κ applies $\pi_{1024,(i-1) \bmod 2}$ and then τ to each substate; finally, each cell of the round key is doubled in $\mathbb{F}_{2^8}$.

Round Constants. As Haraka v2 [60], we derived the round constants from the initial digits of the number π as "nothing-up-my-sleeve" numbers. They are listed explicitly in the full version of this work.

Security Claims. For all variants of Pholkos, we claim 256-bit security in the standard, related-tweak, and related-tweakey model against known attacks. We claim 128-bit security in the standard secret-key Q1 model. We do **not** claim security in quantum related-tweak(ey) models.

4   Design Rationale

In the following, we explain our design decisions for Pholkos. We consider (1) versions, (2) the step function, (3) the mixing layer, and (4) the tweakey schedule.

4.1   Versions

We consider two major and two minor variants of Pholkos. The former to address our research questions of long keys, long blocks, tweaks, and an AES-round-based design are Pholkos-256-256-128 and Pholkos-512-256-128. They differ in the block size to address individual use cases. 256-bit keys should suffice in all settings.

We consider two minor variants for particular use cases. For settings that may benefit from very large blocks, e.g. large-block hashing, we provide a variant with a 1024-bit state. Moreover, we added Pholkos-256-256-256 with a 256-bit tweak for use cases that benefit from large tweaks, again e.g. for hashing or for processing associated data.

4.2   Step Function

The AES round function allows us to derive security bounds efficiently and to profit from hardware instructions that boost the performance of the AES round function [49,50]. While the AES round function provides confusion and diffusion inside the individual substates, the core question considers how to mix the words across substate boundaries. In particular, the detail questions are (1) after how many rounds and (2) how should the bytes or words be mixed.

How Many Rounds Per Step? 3D and LANE added a mixing operation after every single round. In contrast, PAEQ [18] and Haraka [59] exploited the fact that, 1.5 AES rounds can be viewed as the application of four parallel 32-bit Super-boxes [32], followed by ShiftRows and MixColumns, which mix the outputs of the Super-Box. The branch number in terms of active columns (words) is maximal for a Super-box, i.e., a single active column maps to four active columns after two rounds. The permutation of AESQ transfers exactly one word from each substate to each substate (as ShiftRows does for the AES). Thus, they employ two rounds per step, before a mixing layer takes place. Hence, using more than two rounds per step would slow down diffusion, which is why Pholkos too uses two rounds per step. Shiba et al. [78] considered whether one or two rounds would be optimal in detail and also showed that mixing after two rounds provided faster diffusion than mixing after a single round. The question of how to mix will be addressed separately. Since our focus lies on processors with at least AVX2 and AES-NI instructions, where we consider Intel 6-th generation iCore processors and above. We briefly compare the relevant AVX2 instructions before.

4.3   AVX2 Instructions for Efficient Implementations

Three useful up-to-date approaches exist for implementing a permutation layer on platforms with support for AVX2 or higher: shuffles, packings, or blend

	Icelake		Skylake		Haswell		
	L	T^{-1}	L	T^{-1}	L	T^{-1}	Ports
aesenc	3	1	4	1	6	1	0
pblendd	1	0.33	1	0.33	1	0.33	0,5
pshufd	1	0.5	1	1	1	1	5
punpckhdq	1	1	1	1	1	1	5
punpckldq	1	–	1	1	1	1	5

(a) Instructions.

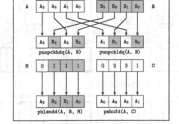

(b) punpck{h,l}dq, pblendd, and pshufd.

Fig. 4. Relevant instructions and their characteristics. L = latency, T^{-1} means inverse throughput, in cycles per instruction each.

instructions. Those are illustrated in Fig. 4b. All three instructions operate on 128-bit words; the AVX variants with v-prefix process 256-bit registers but operate on the 128-bit halves of the parameters in an isolated fashion.

pshufd shuffles 32-bit words, pshufb even 8-bit bytes in a register according to a mask of indices. Despite its flexibility, the instruction induces a cycle of latency. punpckhdq interleaves the 32-bit dwords from the most significant (higher) half of two registers and stores them into the first register; punpckldq performs a similar interleaving on the lower halves. vpblendd chooses the i-th word from either input A or B and stores it into another register of the same size, where the i-th bit of the provided mask indicates the input to choose from.

pblendd preserves the relative positions of 32-bit words in the register. To break these indices without the addition of round constants, one would have to use additional instructions such as pshufd, or use the punpck{l,h}dq instructions. Both strategies would need either more (e.g. additional shuffles) or slower (i.e., punpck{l,h}dq) instructions. Table 4a compares the throughput and the cycles per instruction (cpi) of the instructions (cf. [50]). Note that CISC instructions may consist of several micro-operations, each of which has specific ports that can execute it. Latency is the number of cycles an instruction needs in total, inverse throughput is the number of cycles until another instruction of the same kind can be started. The latter may be lower than a cycle when multiple ports can execute multiple of the considered micro-operations in parallel.

4.4 Mixing-Layer Approaches

We see three potential mixing-layer approaches.

- (M1) A SPARX-like mixing-layer [36], that adds the linearly transformed first half of the state to the second half, and then swaps them;
- (M2) A byte-wise shuffle;
- (M3) A word-wise permutation of different word sizes. Here, we refined our search to permutations over (2a) 16-, (2b) 32-, and (2c) 64-bit words.

Approach (M1) needed considerably more rounds to yield the same security as the one we found optimal. The second approach (M2) means to shuffle not only

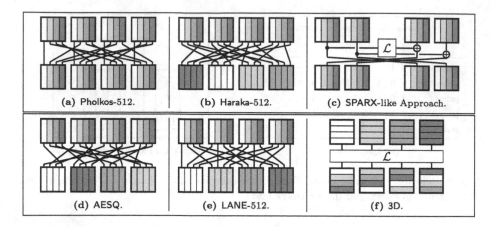

Fig. 5. The word permutations for Pholkos-512 and similar constructions.

words across substates but also cells across word boundaries, which would need at least eight `pshufb` instructions per round. This provides sufficient diffusion and an equivalent number of operations but is slower than our third approach.

Concerning approach (M3), we found that implementations with 16-bit words were painfully slower; 64-bit word permutations prolonged the diffusion. Thus, the use of 32-bit word permutations had the highest performance of our studied options. Therefore, our subsequent search focused on 32-bit word-wise permutations with higher security or performance than those of Haraka and AESQ which ensured 150 active S-Boxes over six steps for 512-bit states. In the following, we provide our rationale for the word permutation of Pholkos-512.

4.5   The Permutations π

Permutation of Pholkos-512. For Pholkos-512, the state consists of four sub-states of four words each. For fast diffusion, each substate should receive one word from every substate, which yields $(4!)^8 \simeq 2^{36.68}$ permutation candidates. Our interest lied in the subset of permutations that preserve the relative indices of words within substates (see the left side of Fig. 5) can be implemented with only `pblendd` instructions. Permutations that change the relative index of a word within the substate either need `punpck{h,l}dq` or additional `pshufd` instructions, which decreases the performance and led us to exclude such permutations. Those permutations yield the same lower bound on active S-Boxes for differential attacks if we disregard related-tweakey attacks, as we show in the full version of this work. Thus, we chose a permutation from the 864 permutations of this subset that was easy to analyze and implement. The difference to earlier similar designs is easy to see from Fig. 5. The permutations of Haraka, AESQ, and LANE try to cluster 32-bit words from the same positions of substates. This is visualized by the single color in their substates after the permutation. Therefore, they could not be implemented with `pblendd` instructions alone.

Permutations of Pholkos-256 **and** -1024. The permutations of Pholkos-256 and Pholkos-1024 were chosen with the same aspects in mind as the choice for π_{512}: to achieve full diffusion as fast as possible, to be efficiently implementable with pblendd instructions, and to provide the maximal number of active S-boxes, which was 43 over seven rounds of Pholkos-256. For Pholkos-1024, similar rules applied. A single permutation could achieve full diffusion in the same number of steps but would have needed to change the relative word-indices within a substate. Thus, we chose to alternate two permutations $\pi_{1024,0}$ and $\pi_{1024,1}$.

Comparison of Implementations We evaluated the theoretical performance of the mixing layers when they are implemented with pblendd or punpck{l,h}dq instructions. They can be found in the extended version. Table 4a also lists results of our experiments when the word-wise permutations π_n are implemented with punpck{l,h}dq instructions. For Pholkos-256, punpck{l,h}dq instructions can be slightly faster. However, our permutations can be implemented with them as well as pblendd, whereas the permutations of Haraka or AESQ cannot use the latter. The advantage of permutations that can employ pblendd instructions becomes clearer when considering larger states.

4.6   Tweakey Schedule

STK Schedule. A TWEAKEY schedule unifies the generation of round tweaks and round keys in an STK-like manner [54]. STK processes multiple words of the block length and iteratively generates the subtweakeys STK^i for Round i. A function h' is applied to each cell to prevent subsequent cancellations of differences between words. STK provides three security properties: (1) all words have equal sizes, (2) each tweak cell is XORed with the same key cell in each schedule round, and (3) each word is multiplied with a different factor in each round so that subsequent rounds cannot cancel differences between words. Pholkos employs an STK-like schedule, but treats key and tweak words slightly differently.

128-bit Tweaks. We propose 128-bit tweaks for three variants of Pholkos since this size suffices for many practical purposes like domain separation. It employs the same permutation π_n as in the mixing layer, which preserves the relative cell positions within the substate. Since the cell substitution τ is applied to each subkey and the tweak, each tweak cell gets XORed to the same key cell in every round. The schedule multiplies each cell of the key bytes by 2 in $\mathbb{F}_{2^8}$, but not the tweak bytes to prevent iterative differentials from cancellations among key and tweak cells. We multiply only the key cells since they are usually updated less frequently than the tweak. Thus, Pholkos fulfills the security properties needed by STK. As an instantiation of π_τ, the permutation by [58] proved resistant against differential and MitM distinguishers in our analysis, as shown in Sect. 6. Moreover, since our tweakey schedule is efficiently invertible, it is incompatible with backdoors studied in [69].

Table 4. Benchmarks for Pholkos on x86 with AVX2 and AES-NI support on Intel Skylake and permutation experiments with `pblendd` and `punpck{l,h}dq` instructions. cpb = cycles/byte.

(a) Parallel encryption.

| Version (bit) | | | CTR mode | | Permutations | |
| | | | | | blend | unpck |
n	k	t	#Blocks	(cpb)	(cpb)	(cpb)
256	256	128	1	**1.36**	1.31	1.24
256	256	256	1	**1.35**	–	–
256	256	128	2	**1.27**	1.32	1.25
256	256	128	4	**1.05**	1.06	1.05
512	256	128	1	**1.91**	1.83	2.07
512	256	128	2	**1.43**	1.49	1.91
1024	256	128	1	**1.78**	2.09	2.41

(b) En-/decryption for retweaking and rekeying.

| Version (bit) | | | Retweak | | Rekey | |
n	k	t	Enc	Dec	Enc	Dec
256	256	128	2.36	1.34	3.92	4.38
256	256	256	2.12	3.74	3.93	4.38
512	256	128	1.43	1.44	4.49	5.36
1024	256	128	1.94	1.93	6.17	6.90

256-bit Tweaks. Larger tweaks can increase the throughput in hashing modes, e.g. in ZMAC [51] or associated-data processing in ZOCB/ZOTR [5]. Though, they provide the adversary with more capabilities. We provided a 256-bit tweak only for the version with a 256-bit state size since the analysis of the versions with a larger state size and a 256-bit tweak were too costly for our hardware, even for only a few rounds.

Key Expansion. We extend the 256-bit key to 512 or 1024 bits by using one or three matrix multiplications with matrices $\mathbf{M}_A$, $\mathbf{M}_B$, and $\mathbf{M}_C$, chosen so that each generated keyword is a different combination of the original key. Furthermore, each state word influences the same number of output words. The main goal for the matrices is that they can be implemented more efficiently than MDS codes. Although they possess a branch number of only four, their diffusion is sufficient to thwart related-key differential and linear attacks for our concerned versions of Pholkos, similar to the codes by [27].

5   Software Implementation

All instances of Pholkos have been implemented in C with AVX2 instructions.[2] Table 4a presents the performance of the variants of Pholkos. Table 4b lists that of the retweaking and rekeying processes for en- and decryption. All benchmarks were conducted on an Intel(R) Core(TM) i5-6200U CPU at 2.30 GHz (Skylake), with TurboBoost, HyperThreading, and SpeedBoost disabled. The results are medians of 1024 means over 1024 encryptions each. It also lists compares them with implementations of the word-wise permutations π_n via `punpck{l,h}dq` instructions, which have been benchmarked in the same setting as Pholkos.

---

[2] The code is freely available at https://gitlab.com/elist/pholkos.

Table 5. Existing distinguishers. $r = $ #rounds, Mem. $=$ memory, $p_{\mathsf{succ}} = $ success probability, Ref. $=$ reference, n/a $=$ not available.

(a) On the AESQ Permutation.

		Complexity			
r	Attack Type	Time	Mem.	p_{succ}	Ref.
8	CICO	2^{32}	n/a	n/a	[17]
8	Yoyo	1	negl.	n/a	[75]
12	Impossible Yoyo	2^{126}	negl.	0.84	[75]
12	Rebound	2^{256}	2^{256}	0.61	[75]
12	Rebound	2^{128}	negl.	0.83	[2]
12	TMTO	$2^{102.4}$	$2^{102.4}$	0.83	[2]
12	TMTO	$2^{128-x/4}$	2^x	n/a	[2]
16	Rebound	2^{192}	2^{128}	0.83	[2]
16	Limited birthday	2^{188}	2^{128}	0.83	[2]
16	TMTO	2^{192+x}	2^{128-x}	n/a	[2]
16	Impossible Yoyo	2^{126}	negl.	0.84	[75]

(b) On PAEQ and Haraka.

			Complexity		
Constr.	r	Attack type	Time	Mem.	Ref.
PAEQ	8	Guess-and-determine	2^{34}	n/a	[74]
PAEQ	8	Guess-and-determine	2^{66}	n/a	[74]
PAEQ	8	Guess-and-determine	2^{98}	n/a	[74]
Haraka v2					
256-256	7	Preimage	2^{248}	2^8	[60]
512-256	8	Preimage	2^{504}	2^8	[60]
512-256	10	Preimage	2^{504}	2^8	[3]

For comparison, the designers of Saturnin claimed up to 3.5 cpb in parallel modes [26]. Saturnin targets lightweight platforms and provides only a minimal tweak, while Pholkos is a dedicated heavyweight TBC. We do not expect large block sizes to be used on lightweight devices but rather on servers and consumer PCs. Another example would be Simpira [47], which achieves 1.19 cycles for 1024-bit blocks on the same hardware and measurement setup used for benchmarking Pholkos. Though, Simpira aims at "only" 128-bit security against classical adversaries that is a considerably lower security goal than that of Pholkos.

6 Security Analysis

First, we consider linear and differential cryptanalysis before we view boomerang, integral, impossible-differential attacks, as well as adapted versions of recent attacks on the AES. We end this chapter with an intuition regarding the quantum security of Pholkos. Some attacks that do not break Pholkos consider probabilities $\ll 2^{-256}$ but are direct adaptions of attacks on similar primitives.

Existing Attacks. Several works have analyzed AESQ, its mode PAEQ/PPAE [17], or Haraka v1 [60] and Haraka v2 [59]. From the structural similarity, all distinguishers on AESQ apply similarly to Pholkos-512 when used as a permutation. Plus, attacks in the secret-key model on r-round AES-128 may apply in adapted form also to r-step Pholkos-512. Those are summarized in Table 5.

Differential Cryptanalysis [16] studies the propagation of differences $\Delta X = X \oplus X'$ between inputs $X, X' \in \mathbb{F}_2^n$ and the difference $\Delta Y = Y \oplus Y'$ of their corresponding outputs $Y, Y' \in \mathbb{F}_2^n$ through a map F. The resistance of AES-like ciphers against differential and linear cryptanalysis is commonly analyzed

Table 6. Minimum #active S-boxes for differential characteristics over 1–10 steps. gray = derived, underlined = uses tweak differences.

$n-t$	Standard										Related tweak										Related tweakey									
	1	2	3	4	5	6	7	8	9	10	1	2	3	4	5	6	7	8	9	10	1	2	3	4	5	6	7	8	9	10
256-128	5	25	35	60	80	100	110	135	140	160	2	20	35	40	55	70	75	90	105	110	0	8	22	22	30	44	44	52	66	66
256-256	5	25	35	60	80	100	110	135	140	160	1	10	22	32	45	54	55	67	77	90	0	4	17	26	26	34	43	52	52	60
512	5	25	45	80	130	150	170	205	210	230	4	25	45	80	84	104	125	160	164	185	0	24	45	48	69	90	93	114	135	138
1024	5	25	35	70	105	165	240	245	265	275	5	25	35	70	87	95	112	140	157	174	0	10	35	35	45	70	70	80	105	105

by lower bounding the minimal number of active S-boxes for any differential characteristic – assuming that the transform is an iterated Markov cipher. For the AES S-box, it is well-known that the maximal differential probability is 2^{-6}.

Linear Cryptanalysis [62] exploits biases in linear relations between input and output bits. Kranz et al. [61] studied the effect of linear key schedules and tweaks on linear cryptanalysis. They found that (1) linear key schedules do not enhance attacks considerably and (2) no new linear characteristics are introduced from a linear tweak schedule. Our analysis benefits from the symmetries in the AES substates among different columns. The lower bounds on the number of active S-boxes apply to differential as well as to linear cryptanalysis. For the AES S-box, the maximal correlation is 2^{-3} [33]. Thus, for an AES-like SPN even with a linear tweak schedule, the success of linear distinguishers is closely related to the maximum probability of differential characteristics in the secret-key model.

MILP Model. We used a MILP-aided approach with Gurobi to find lower bounds on the numbers of active S-boxes for Pholkos in the standard, related-tweak, and related-tweakey model. The source code is publicly available alongside the reference implementation of Pholkos. Since the complexities of the MILP models grow significantly in terms of variables and constraints, several models could be solved only for a reduced number of steps. Table 6 summarizes the minimal numbers of active S-boxes of our analysis. For 256-bit security against basic differential and linear cryptanalysis under the Markov-cipher assumption, at least 43 S-boxes must be active, which is the case after at most four steps for all instances in the standard model. Under related tweaks, Pholkos-256 reaches 43 active S-boxes after five steps, Pholkos-512 after three steps, and the largest instance after four steps. We could determine lower bounds for up to three steps in the related-tweakey model. We derived the bounds for more steps from those results, which leads to pessimistic lower bounds, with security only after six, seven, four, and five steps, respectively, for the individual variants since the diffusion is highly likely to increase over more steps. Table 6 shows the desired maximal probabilities of differential characteristics of 2^{-256} is reached after six, four and five steps for Pholkos-256, Pholkos-512, and Pholkos-1024, respectively.

Table 7. Maximal #full steps covered by boomerang distinguishers.

	Model		
Instance	Standard	RT	RTK
Pholkos-256	2	3	4
Pholkos-256-256	2	4	5
Pholkos-512	2	2	3
Pholkos-1024	2	2	3

Table 8. Maximal #rounds (not steps) covered by integral distinguishers.

	#Iterated bits					
Primitive	128	255	256	511	512	1 023
Pholkos-256	7	7	–	–	–	–
Pholkos-512	7	–	7	7	–	–
Pholkos-1024	7	–	9	–	11	11

Boomerangs and Rectangles [14,15,84] split the primitive E into parts $E = E_2 \circ E_1 \circ E_0$ to combine two differential trails over E_0 and E_2; E_1 represents the (potentially empty) middle phase. Let $\alpha \to \beta$ be a differential trail with probability p through E_0, and $\gamma \to \delta$ a trail with probability q through E_2. A boomerang encrypts pairs (P, P') with difference α to a ciphertext pair (C, C'), derives a second pair (D, D') from adding δ to both ciphertexts, decrypts it back to (Q, Q'), and checks if $Q \oplus Q' = \alpha$. If the trails have probabilities p and q and a probability r through E_1, the boomerang probability is $O(p^2 q^2 r)$.

In theory, resistance against boomerangs can be derived from the best differential characteristics. Yet, determining the probability through the middle is sophisticated [29,80]. Truncated differentials can lead to better results than differential characteristics, e.g., see [20,77], which is not provided in our tables. From the bounds on the number of active S-boxes in Table 6, we derived the maximal number of steps, where the sum of active S-boxes in p and q surpasses 21.5. In the standard model, boomerang distinguishers can exist on up to two steps for all instances, as every differential p or q that covers at least 2 steps would have at least 25 active S-boxes already. With related tweaks, boomerang distinguishers can exist on up to three-step Pholkos-256 and on two-step Pholkos-512 and Pholkos-1024. In the related-tweakey model, there may exist boomerang attacks on at most five full steps. Our analyses exclude distinguishers on half-steps and assume an empty middle phase. Thanks to the considerable security margins of Pholkos in all settings, we assume that a non-empty middle phase, as well as truncated differentials, will not yield boomerang attacks. Though, we leave it as a research topic for future work. The use of differentials that cover half-steps could extend the boomerang distinguisher by at most one step (one half-step per differential). Boomerang attacks with a non-empty middle phase can be extended by at most 1.5 steps. Our results are given in Table 7.

Integral Cryptanalysis [21,31] is a structural attack that exploits a degree below n of a component function. When interpreting the transform as a (vector) Boolean function, its maximal algebraic degree d allows excluding distinguishers that iterate over 2^{d+1} values and necessarily must sum to zero. Todo [83] generalized integrals with the division property. They were refined e.g. by [25] and shown to evolve as the evolution of the algebraic degree [19]. Thus, distinguishers are bounded by the number of rounds whereafter the algebraic normal form of each component function reaches degree $n - 1$. Table 8 lists our results of the propagation of the degree through Pholkos. Since the division property propagates equally as the degree, integral distinguishers exist over at most seven rounds of Pholkos-256 and -512, and at most 11 rounds of Pholkos-1024. Note that the distinguisher on Pholkos-512 is similar to the higher-order integral distinguisher on four-round AES.

Impossible-differential [13] **and Zero-correlation Attacks** [24] exploit differentials with probability and approximations with correlation zero, respectively. Since zero-correlation distinguishers imply integral distinguishers [82], our upper bounds on the numbers of steps for integrals also yield upper bounds for zero-correlation trails. The implication relation between integrals and impossible-differential distinguishers is more complex. Though, longer impossible differentials are unlikely in the standard model. The longest impossible differentials with zero tweak differences we found cover seven rounds for Pholkos-256 when starting from a full step, and eight rounds when starting from a round inside a step. No longer distinguishers from a single active cell are possible. An example for an eight-round distinguisher, covering e.g. Rounds 2–9, is given in Fig. 6. At the input side, the structures can be combined from pairs over four active diagonals, i.e., 2^{128} texts can yield 2^{255} pairs. At the output side, the probability is $2 \cdot 2^{-128}$ since two patterns are possible. Thus, a structure of 2^{64} texts can produce one pair with the desired output difference.

We can use a similar argument for Pholkos-512. The longest impossible-differential distinguishers with zero tweak differences cover seven rounds for Pholkos-512 when starting from a full step, and eight when starting from inside a step. Moreover, the structural similarity to the AES allows us to adopt the security arguments from it for Pholkos-512. There exist no impossible differentials over five rounds of the AES structure [81,85,86]. Thus, such distinguishers cover less than five full steps of Pholkos-512 without tweak differences.

With tweak differences, we can argue similarly as in the analysis of Kiasu-BC [37,38]: the tweak difference can cancel out the state difference on both sides. Since Pholkos-512 adds tweaks after each round, the length of impossible differentials of Pholkos-512 exceeds that without tweaks by at most two, yielding at most ten rounds. With related tweakeys, a third free round can be added where the differences in key and tweak words cancel to cover up to 11 rounds.

For Pholkos-1024, there exist impossible differentials for up to 12 rounds with output probability 2^{-512}. While we did not find longer distinguishers from tweak differences, it might be possible to extend them to 14 rounds with related tweaks and by three rounds to 15 rounds under related tweakeys.

Slide Attacks [22,23,40] exploit that round functions and the key schedule produce equal states after different rounds. The tweak addition will allow canceling the difference between states in at most one round. However, there are no reported slide attacks on the AES. And while invariant-subspace attacks have been a threat to Haraka v1 [52], the round constants of Haraka v2 - that Pholkos

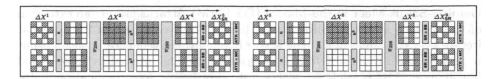

Fig. 6. Impossible-differential distinguisher for eight-round Pholkos-256.

Table 9. Distinguishers and key-recovery attacks (†) in the standard secret-key model; r = #rounds, imp. = impossible, diff. = differential, mem. = memory, p_{succ} = success probability.

r	Type	Complexity			p_{succ}	r	Type	Complexity			p_{succ}
		Time	Mem.	Data				Time	Mem.	Data	
Pholkos-256						**Pholkos-512**					
6	DS-MitM	2^{216}	negl.	2^{216} CP	$\simeq 1$	7	DS-MitM	2^{456}	negl.	2^{456} CP	$\simeq 1$
8	Imp.-diff. Yoyo	2^{127}	negl.	2^{128} ACC	0.84	8	Imp.-diff. Yoyo	2^{127}	negl.	2^{128} ACC	0.84
8	Imp.-diff.	2^{64}	negl.	2^{64} CP	0.63	8	Imp.-diff.	2^{127}	negl.	2^{128} ACC	0.84
Pholkos-1024						10	Boomerang	2^{260}	2^{32}	2^{260} ACC	0.63
10	DS-MitM	2^{904}	2^{32}	2^{904} CP	$\simeq 1$	10	Boomeyong† [70]	$2^{188.8}$	$2^{189.8}$	2^{122} ACC	0.78
12	Imp.-diff.	$2^{256.5}$	negl.	$2^{256.5}$ CP	0.63	12	Mixture-diff.	2^{394}	negl.	2^{394} CP	n/a
15	Mixture-diff.	2^{625}	negl.	2^{625} CP	n/a						

adopts - have been tweaked to thwart such attacks. We consider the round constants to effectively prevent slide attacks and their extensions.

Yoyo Attacks are variants of boomerangs [12]. On AESQ, the distinguisher by Saha et al. [75] started from an eight-round yoyo through rounds 2–9. From that base, they added a second, mirrored yoyo, which started from the middle after Round 9 back to Round 2, where they derived the mixed second pair, re-encrypted it, mixed the ciphertexts, decrypted the results back to the middle, and checked for the property. If one would try to construct a keyless permutation from Pholkos, it should consider similar attacks. For Pholkos, the attacks by Rønjom et al. [7,73] apply. Moreover, Rahman et al. [70] proposed boomeyongs, i.e., boomerangs that integrated a yoyo distinguisher. In particular, they combined a yoyo at the top with a variant of the boomerang at the bottom, showing key-recovery attacks on up to 10-round Pholkos-512.

Mixture-differential Cryptanalysis has been proposed by Grassi [44] in deterministic form, and extended probabilistically by follow-up works [6,7,45]. We applied a variant of Bardeh and Rønjom's [7] AES distinguisher to Pholkos-512, covering six steps. Details are given in the extended version of this work. For Pholkos-1024, a similar distinguisher can cover up to 15 rounds (7.5 steps).

Demirci-Selçuk Meet-in-the-Middle (DS-MitM) Attacks [34] are an extension of the collision attack by Gilbert and Minier [43]: given a δ-set of 2^8 texts that iterate over the values of a single active byte only, the sequence in each output byte after three rounds of AES is determined by nine internal bytes only and has at most $(2^8)^9$ possible sequences instead of $(2^8)^{256}$ for a random permutation. This distinguisher was wrapped by two key-recovery phases. While the data complexity is low, those attacks required many precomputations. Demirci and Selçuk extended the distinguisher to four rounds. Dunkelman et al. and Derbez et al. [35,41] proposed new trade-offs, but could not extend the distinguisher for AES-128 beyond four rounds. Since Pholkos-512 is structurally similar to the AES, an r-step distinguisher on Pholkos-512 without tweak differences yields an r-round distinguisher for the AES. Thus, distinguishers on more than four full subsequent steps are unlikely, but distinguishers with tweak differences could cover more rounds. For Pholkos-256, the best such distinguishers we found covered five rounds without and seven rounds with tweak differences.

Quantum Attacks are a long-term threat. The claimed 256-bit security in the classical setting reduces to 128 bits in the presence of quantum adversaries. This assumption is based on the speed-up of exhaustive key search with Grover's algorithm and the results of [57]. Though, there are still uncertainties. While Kaplan et al. [57] did not investigate the influence of a tweak, they studied the cases where the key size equaled or exceeded the state size. For Pholkos, the key is smaller than the state in two instances. This should not benefit a quantum adversary since it should not increase the number of key bits depending on a single state-bit within a small number of rounds (as is typically the case when the key size is larger). Yet, this setting is worth further investigation. We claim only 128-bit post-quantum security in the secret-key setting. While we can imagine that the presence of the public tweak will not help a quantum-computing-aided adversary further, post-quantum cryptanalysis of tweakable block ciphers is still open research. Conservatively, we do not claim security in the post-quantum related-tweak and related-tweakey model.

7   Conclusion

This work introduced the family of tweakable block ciphers Pholkos. With 256 to 1024 bits, its instances provide an efficient large-state keyed primitive with high security guarantees also in post-quantum applications. Furthermore, its tweak allows for using it in many modes, including the post-quantum secure QCB, further distinguishing it from other large state block ciphers. Its analysis benefits from existing results on AESQ and Haraka. Moreover, the analysis of the 512-bit instance simplifies due to its structural similarity to that of the AES. Thus, our analysis not only covers the most general attack vectors but can also apply lessons learned from very recent results on the AES or AESQ as well as constants chosen for the absence of subspace trails in Haraka. Yet, we would like to motivate third-party cryptanalysis to shed more light on the security of Pholkos, which would be particularly interesting since any novel result on the untweaked variant of Pholkos-512 might also yield insights to the AES. Moreover, the security in the post-quantum related-tweak and the post-quantum related-tweakey models pose interesting research questions, as these models are still relatively new and not investigated thoroughly.

Acknowledgments. We are highly thankful for the fruitful discussions with Maria Eichlseder, Lorenzo Grassi, Reinhard Lüftenegger, Christian Rechberger, and Markus Schofnegger and that from the comments by the anonymous reviewers of SAC 2021 and CT-RSA 2022. Parts of the research leading to these results was made possible by DFG Grant LU 608/9-1.

References

1. Augot, D., et al.: Initial recommendations of long-term secure post-quantum systems. Revision 1. Technical report (2015)
2. Bagheri, N., Mendel, F., Sasaki, Yu.: Improved rebound attacks on AESQ: core permutation of CAESAR candidate PAEQ. In: Liu, J.K., Steinfeld, R. (eds.) ACISP 2016, Part II. LNCS, vol. 9723, pp. 301–316. Springer, Cham (2016). https://doi.org/10.1007/978-3-319-40367-0_19
3. Bao, Z., Ding, L., Guo, J., Wang, H., Zhang, W.: Improved meet-in-the-middle preimage attacks against AES hashing modes. IACR Trans. Symmetric Cryptol. **2019**(4), 318–347 (2019)
4. Bao, Z., et al.: Automatic search of meet-in-the-middle preimage attacks on AES-like hashing. In: Canteaut, A., Standaert, F.-X. (eds.) EUROCRYPT 2021, Part I. LNCS, vol. 12696, pp. 771–804. Springer, Cham (2021). https://doi.org/10.1007/978-3-030-77870-5_27
5. Bao, Z., Guo, J., Iwata, T., Minematsu, K.: ZOCB and ZOTR: tweakable blockcipher modes for authenticated encryption with full absorption. ToSC **2019**(2), 1–54 (2019)
6. Bardeh, N.G., Rønjom, S.: Practical attacks on reduced-round AES. In: Buchmann, J., Nitaj, A., Rachidi, T. (eds.) AFRICACRYPT 2019. LNCS, vol. 11627, pp. 297–310. Springer, Cham (2019). https://doi.org/10.1007/978-3-030-23696-0_15
7. Bardeh, N.G., Rønjom, S.: The exchange attack: *how to distinguish six rounds of AES with $2^{88.2}$ chosen plaintexts*. In: Galbraith, S.D., Moriai, S. (eds.) ASIACRYPT 2019, Part III. LNCS, vol. 11923, pp. 347–370. Springer, Cham (2019). https://doi.org/10.1007/978-3-030-34618-8_12
8. Beierle, C., et al.: Alzette: a 64-bit ARX-box. In: Micciancio, D., Ristenpart, T. (eds.) CRYPTO 2020, Part III. LNCS, vol. 12172, pp. 419–448. Springer, Cham (2020). https://doi.org/10.1007/978-3-030-56877-1_15
9. Daniel, J.: Bernstein. Some Challenges in Heavyweight Cipher Design, Technical report (2016)
10. Bhargavan, K., Leurent, G.: On the practical (In-)security of 64-bit block ciphers: collision attacks on HTTP over TLS and OpenVPN. In: ACM CCS, pp. 456–467 (2016)
11. Bhaumik, R., et al.: QCB: efficient quantum-secure authenticated encryption. In: Tibouchi, M., Wang, H. (eds.) ASIACRYPT 2021. LNCS, vol. 13090. Springer, CHam (2021). https://doi.org/10.1007/978-3-030-92062-3_23

12. Biham, E., Biryukov, A., Dunkelman, O., Richardson, E., Shamir, A.: Initial observations on skipjack: cryptanalysis of Skipjack-3XOR. In: Tavares, S., Meijer, H. (eds.) SAC 1998. LNCS, vol. 1556, pp. 362–375. Springer, Heidelberg (1999). https://doi.org/10.1007/3-540-48892-8_27

13. Biham, E., Biryukov, A., Shamir, A.: Cryptanalysis of Skipjack reduced to 31 rounds using impossible differentials. In: Stern, J. (ed.) EUROCRYPT 1999. LNCS, vol. 1592, pp. 12–23. Springer, Heidelberg (1999). https://doi.org/10.1007/3-540-48910-X_2

14. Biham, E., Dunkelman, O., Keller, N.: The rectangle attack—rectangling the Serpent. In: Pfitzmann, B. (ed.) EUROCRYPT 2001. LNCS, vol. 2045, pp. 340–357. Springer, Heidelberg (2001). https://doi.org/10.1007/3-540-44987-6_21

15. Biham, E., Dunkelman, O., Keller, N.: New results on boomerang and rectangle attacks. In: Daemen, J., Rijmen, V. (eds.) FSE 2002. LNCS, vol. 2365, pp. 1–16. Springer, Heidelberg (2002). https://doi.org/10.1007/3-540-45661-9_1

16. Biham, E., Shamir, A.: Differential cryptanalysis of DES-like cryptosystems. In: Menezes, A.J., Vanstone, S.A. (eds.) CRYPTO 1990. LNCS, vol. 537, pp. 2–21. Springer, Heidelberg (1991). https://doi.org/10.1007/3-540-38424-3_1

17. Biryukov, A., Khovratovich, D.: PAEQ: parallelizable permutation-based authenticated encryption. In: Chow, S.S.M., Camenisch, J., Hui, L.C.K., Yiu, S.M. (eds.) ISC 2014. LNCS, vol. 8783, pp. 72–89. Springer, Cham (2014). https://doi.org/10.1007/978-3-319-13257-0_5

18. Biryukov, A., Khovratovich. D.: PAEQ v1. Technical report, 2nd-round Submission to the CAESAR competition (2014)

19. Biryukov, A., Khovratovich, D., Perrin, L.: Multiset-algebraic cryptanalysis of reduced Kuznyechik, Khazad, and secret SPNs. ToSC 2016(2), 226–247 (2016)

20. Biryukov, A., Nikolić, I.: Automatic search for related-key differential characteristics in byte-oriented block ciphers: application to AES, Camellia, Khazad and Others. In: Gilbert, H. (ed.) EUROCRYPT 2010. LNCS, vol. 6110, pp. 322–344. Springer, Heidelberg (2010). https://doi.org/10.1007/978-3-642-13190-5_17

21. Biryukov, A., Shamir, A.: Structural cryptanalysis of SASAS. In: Pfitzmann, B. (ed.) EUROCRYPT 2001. LNCS, vol. 2045, pp. 395–405. Springer, Heidelberg (2001). https://doi.org/10.1007/3-540-44987-6_24

22. Biryukov, A., Wagner, D.: Slide attacks. In: Knudsen, L. (ed.) FSE 1999. LNCS, vol. 1636, pp. 245–259. Springer, Heidelberg (1999). https://doi.org/10.1007/3-540-48519-8_18

23. Biryukov, A., Wagner, D.: Advanced slide attacks. In: Preneel, B. (ed.) EUROCRYPT 2000. LNCS, vol. 1807, pp. 589–606. Springer, Heidelberg (2000). https://doi.org/10.1007/3-540-45539-6_41

24. Bogdanov, A., Rijmen, V.: Linear hulls with correlation zero and linear cryptanalysis of block ciphers. Des. Codes Crypt. 70(3), 369–383 (2012). https://doi.org/10.1007/s10623-012-9697-z

25. Boura, C., Canteaut, A.: Another view of the division property. In: Robshaw, M., Katz, J. (eds.) CRYPTO 2016, Part I. LNCS, vol. 9814, pp. 654–682. Springer, Heidelberg (2016). https://doi.org/10.1007/978-3-662-53018-4_24

26. Canteaut, A., et al.: Saturnin: a suite of lightweight symmetric algorithms for post-quantum security. ToSC 2020(S1), 160–207 (2020)

27. Chakraborti, A., Datta, N., Jha, A., Mancillas-López, C., Nandi, M., Sasaki, Yu.: Elastic-Tweak: A Framework for Short Tweak Tweakable Block Cipher. IACR ePrint 2019/440 (2019)

28. Chen, L., et al.: Report on Post-Quantum Cryptography. NISTIR, 8105 (2016)

29. Cid, C., Huang, T., Peyrin, T., Sasaki, Yu., Song, L.: Boomerang connectivity table: a new cryptanalysis tool. In: Nielsen, J.B., Rijmen, V. (eds.) EUROCRYPT 2018, Part II. LNCS, vol. 10821, pp. 683–714. Springer, Cham (2018). https://doi.org/10.1007/978-3-319-78375-8_22

30. Cogliati, B., Lee, J., Seurin, Y.: New constructions of MACs from (tweakable) block ciphers. ToSC **2**, 27/2017-58 (2017)

31. Daemen, J., Knudsen, L., Rijmen, V.: The block cipher square. In: Biham, E. (ed.) FSE 1997. LNCS, vol. 1267, pp. 149–165. Springer, Heidelberg (1997). https://doi.org/10.1007/BFb0052343

32. Daemen, J., Lamberger, M., Pramstaller, N., Rijmen, V., Vercauteren, F.: Computational aspects of the expected differential probability of 4-round AES and AES-like ciphers. Computing **85**(1–2), 85–104 (2009). https://doi.org/10.1007/s00607-009-0034-y

33. Daemen, J., Rijmen, V.: The Design of Rijndael: AES - The Advanced Encryption Standard (2002)

34. Demirci, H., Selçuk, A.A.: A meet-in-the-middle attack on 8-round AES. In: Nyberg, K. (ed.) FSE 2008. LNCS, vol. 5086, pp. 116–126. Springer, Heidelberg (2008). https://doi.org/10.1007/978-3-540-71039-4_7

35. Derbez, P., Fouque, P.-A., Jean, J.: Improved key recovery attacks on reduced-round, in the single-key setting. In: Johansson, T., Nguyen, P.Q. (eds.) EUROCRYPT 2013. LNCS, vol. 7881, pp. 371–387. Springer, Heidelberg (2013). https://doi.org/10.1007/978-3-642-38348-9_23

36. Dinu, D., Perrin, L., Udovenko, A., Velichkov, V., Großschädl, J., Biryukov, A.: Design strategies for ARX with provable bounds: SPARX and LAX. In: Cheon, J.H., Takagi, T. (eds.) ASIACRYPT 2016, Part I. LNCS, vol. 10031, pp. 484–513. Springer, Heidelberg (2016). https://doi.org/10.1007/978-3-662-53887-6_18

37. Dobraunig, C., Eichlseder, M., Mendel, F.: Square attack on 7-round Kiasu-BC. In: Manulis, M., Sadeghi, A.-R., Schneider, S. (eds.) ACNS 2016. LNCS, vol. 9696, pp. 500–517. Springer, Cham (2016). https://doi.org/10.1007/978-3-319-39555-5_27

38. Dobraunig, C., List, E.: Impossible-differential and Boomerang cryptanalysis of round-reduced Kiasu-BC. In: Handschuh, H. (ed.) CT-RSA 2017. LNCS, vol. 10159, pp. 207–222. Springer, Cham (2017). https://doi.org/10.1007/978-3-319-52153-4_12

39. Drucker, N., Gueron, S., Krasnov, V.: Making AES great again: the forthcoming vectorized AES instruction. In: Latifi, S. (ed.) 16th International Conference on Information Technology-New Generations (ITNG 2019). AISC, vol. 800, pp. 37–41. Springer, Cham (2019). https://doi.org/10.1007/978-3-030-14070-0_6

40. Dunkelman, O., Keller, N., Lasry, N., Shamir, A.: New Slide Attacks on Almost Self-Similar Ciphers. IACR ePrint 2019/509 (2019)

41. Dunkelman, O., Keller, N., Shamir, A.: Improved single-key attacks on 8-round AES-192 and AES-256. In: Abe, M. (ed.) ASIACRYPT 2010. LNCS, vol. 6477, pp. 158–176. Springer, Heidelberg (2010). https://doi.org/10.1007/978-3-642-17373-8_10

42. Ferguson, N., et al.: The Skein hash function family. 3rd-round submission to the NIST SHA-3 competition, p. 100 (2010)

43. Gilbert, H., Minier, M.: A collision attack on 7 rounds of Rijndael. In: The Third AES Candidate Conference, pp. 230–241 (2000)

44. Grassi, L.: Mixture differential cryptanalysis: a new approach to distinguishers and attacks on round-reduced AES. ToSC **2018**(2), 133–160 (2018)

45. Grassi, L.: Probabilistic mixture differential cryptanalysis on round-reduced AES. In: Paterson, K.G., Stebila, D. (eds.) SAC 2019. LNCS, vol. 11959, pp. 53–84. Springer, Cham (2020). https://doi.org/10.1007/978-3-030-38471-5_3

46. Grover, LK.: A fast quantum mechanical algorithm for database search. In: STOC, pp. 212–219 (1996)

47. Gueron, S., Mouha, N.: Simpira v2: a family of efficient permutations using the AES round function. In: Cheon, J.H., Takagi, T. (eds.) ASIACRYPT 2016, Part I. LNCS, vol. 10031, pp. 95–125. Springer, Heidelberg (2016). https://doi.org/10.1007/978-3-662-53887-6_4

48. Indesteege, S., et al.: The LANE hash function. In: Handschuh, H., Lucks, S., Preneel, B., Rogaway, P. (eds.) Symmetric Cryptography, 11 January – 16 January 2009, Dagstuhl Seminar Proceedings, vol. 09031 (2009)

49. Intel. Intel architecture instruction set extensions programming reference (2017). https://software.intel.com/sites/default/files/managed/c5/15/architecture-instruction-set-extensions-programming-reference.pdf

50. Intel. Intrinsics guide (2019). https://software.intel.com/sites/landingpage/IntrinsicsGuide

51. Iwata, T., Minematsu, K., Peyrin, T., Seurin, Y.: ZMAC: a fast tweakable block cipher mode for highly secure message authentication. In: Katz, J., Shacham, H. (eds.) CRYPTO 2017, Part III. LNCS, vol. 10403, pp. 34–65. Springer, Cham (2017). https://doi.org/10.1007/978-3-319-63697-9_2

52. Jean, J.: Cryptanalysis of Haraka. ToSC **2016**(1), 1–12 (2016)

53. Jean, J., Nikolić, I.: Efficient design strategies based on the AES round function. In: Peyrin, T. (ed.) FSE 2016. LNCS, vol. 9783, pp. 334–353. Springer, Heidelberg (2016). https://doi.org/10.1007/978-3-662-52993-5_17

54. Jean, J., Nikolić, I., Peyrin, T.: Tweaks and keys for block ciphers: the TWEAKEY framework. In: Sarkar, P., Iwata, T. (eds.) ASIACRYPT 2014, Part II. LNCS, vol. 8874, pp. 274–288. Springer, Heidelberg (2014). https://doi.org/10.1007/978-3-662-45608-8_15

55. Nakahara, J.: 3D: a three-dimensional block cipher. In: Franklin, M.K., Hui, L.C.K., Wong, D.S. (eds.) CANS 2008. LNCS, vol. 5339, pp. 252–267. Springer, Heidelberg (2008). https://doi.org/10.1007/978-3-540-89641-8_18

56. Kaplan, M., Leurent, G., Leverrier, A., Naya-Plasencia, M.: Breaking symmetric cryptosystems using quantum period finding. In: Robshaw, M., Katz, J. (eds.) CRYPTO 2016, Part II. LNCS, vol. 9815, pp. 207–237. Springer, Heidelberg (2016). https://doi.org/10.1007/978-3-662-53008-5_8

57. Kaplan, M., Leurent, G., Leverrier, A., Naya-Plasencia, M.: Quantum differential and linear cryptanalysis. ToSC **2016**(1), 71–94 (2016)

58. Khoo, K., Lee, E., Peyrin, T., Sim, S.M.: Human-readable proof of the related-key security of AES-128. ToSC **2017**(2), 59–83 (2017)

59. Kölbl, S., Lauridsen, M.M., Mendel, F., Rechberger, C.: Haraka - Efficient Short-Input Hashing for Post-Quantum Applications. IACR ePrint 2016/98 (2016)

60. Kölbl, S., Lauridsen, M.M., Mendel, F., Rechberger, C.: Haraka v2 - efficient short-input hashing for post-quantum applications. ToSC **2016**(2), 1–29 (2016)

61. Kranz, T., Leander, G., Wiemer, F.: Linear cryptanalysis: key schedules and tweakable block ciphers. ToSC **2017**(1), 474–505 (2017)

62. Matsui, M.: Linear cryptanalysis method for DES cipher. In: Helleseth, T. (ed.) EUROCRYPT 1993. LNCS, vol. 765, pp. 386–397. Springer, Heidelberg (1994). https://doi.org/10.1007/3-540-48285-7_33

63. McGrew, D.A., Viega, J.: The security and performance of the Galois/counter mode (GCM) of operation. In: Canteaut, A., Viswanathan, K. (eds.) INDOCRYPT 2004. LNCS, vol. 3348, pp. 343–355. Springer, Heidelberg (2004). https://doi.org/10.1007/978-3-540-30556-9_27
64. Nikolić, I.: Tiaoxin - 346. 3rd-round Submission to the CAESAR competition (2016)
65. NIST. Advanced Encryption Standard (AES). Federal Information Processing Standards (FIPS) Publication 197 (2001)
66. Oliynykov, R., Gorbenko, I., Kazymyrov, O., Ruzhentsev, V., et al.: A New Encryption Standard of Ukraine: The Kalyna Block Cipher. IACR ePrint 2015/650 (2015)
67. Peyrin, T.: Tweakable Block Cipher-Based Cryptography (2020)
68. Peyrin, T., Seurin, Y.: Counter-in-tweak: authenticated encryption modes for tweakable block ciphers. In: Robshaw, M., Katz, J. (eds.) CRYPTO 2016, Part I. LNCS, vol. 9814, pp. 33–63. Springer, Heidelberg (2016). https://doi.org/10.1007/978-3-662-53018-4_2
69. Peyrin, T., Wang, H.: The MALICIOUS framework: embedding backdoors into tweakable block ciphers. In: Micciancio, D., Ristenpart, T. (eds.) CRYPTO 2020, Part III. LNCS, vol. 12172, pp. 249–278. Springer, Cham (2020). https://doi.org/10.1007/978-3-030-56877-1_9
70. Rahman, M., Saha, D., Paul, G.: Boomeyong: embedding Yoyo within Boomerang and its applications to key recovery attacks on AES and Pholkos. IACR Trans. Symmetric Cryptol. 2021(3), 137–169 (2021)
71. Rijmen, V., Barreto, P.S.L.M.: The Anubis block cipher. Submission to NESSIE (2000)
72. Rogaway, P., Bellare, M., Black, J.: OCB: A block-cipher mode of operation for efficient authenticated encryption. TISSEC 6(3), 365–403 (2003)
73. Rønjom, S., Bardeh, N.G., Helleseth, T.: Yoyo tricks with AES. In: Takagi, T., Peyrin, T. (eds.) ASIACRYPT 2017, Part I. LNCS, vol. 10624, pp. 217–243. Springer, Cham (2017). https://doi.org/10.1007/978-3-319-70694-8_8
74. Saha, D., Kakarla, S., Mandava, S., Chowdhury, D.R.: Gain: practical key-recovery attacks on round-reduced PAEQ. J. Hardw. Syst. Secur. 1(3), 282–296 (2017)
75. Saha, D., Rahman, M., Paul, G.: New Yoyo tricks with AES-based permutations. ToSC 2018(4), 102–127 (2018)
76. Sakamoto, K., Liu, F., Nakano, Y., Kiyomoto, S., Isobe, T.: Rocca: an efficient AES-based encryption scheme for beyond 5G. IACR Trans. Symmetric Cryptol. 2021(2), 1–30 (2021)
77. Sasaki, Yu.: Improved related-Tweakey Boomerang attacks on Deoxys-BC. In: Joux, A., Nitaj, A., Rachidi, T. (eds.) AFRICACRYPT 2018. LNCS, vol. 10831, pp. 87–106. Springer, Cham (2018). https://doi.org/10.1007/978-3-319-89339-6_6
78. Shiba, R., Sakamoto, K., Isobe, T.: Efficient constructions for large-state block ciphers based on AES New Instructions. IET Inf. Secur. 2021, 1–16 (2021). https://doi.org/10.1049/ise2.12053
79. Shor, P.W.: Polynomial-time algorithms for prime factorization and discrete logarithms on a quantum computer. SIAM J. Comput. 26(5), 1484–1509 (1997)
80. Song, L., Qin, X., Lei, H.: Boomerang connectivity table revisited. Appl. SKINNY AES. ToSC 2019(1), 118–141 (2019)
81. Sun, B., Liu, M., Guo, J., Rijmen, V., Li, R.: Provable security evaluation of structures against impossible differential and zero correlation linear cryptanalysis. In: Fischlin, M., Coron, J.-S. (eds.) EUROCRYPT 2016, Part I. LNCS, vol. 9665, pp. 196–213. Springer, Heidelberg (2016). https://doi.org/10.1007/978-3-662-49890-3_8

82. Sun, B., et al.: Links among impossible differential, integral and zero correlation linear cryptanalysis. In: Gennaro, R., Robshaw, M. (eds.) CRYPTO 2015, Part I. LNCS, vol. 9215, pp. 95–115. Springer, Heidelberg (2015). https://doi.org/10.1007/978-3-662-47989-6_5

83. Todo, Y.: Structural evaluation by generalized integral property. In: Oswald, E., Fischlin, M. (eds.) EUROCRYPT 2015, Part I. LNCS, vol. 9056, pp. 287–314. Springer, Heidelberg (2015). https://doi.org/10.1007/978-3-662-46800-5_12

84. Wagner, D.: The Boomerang attack. In: Knudsen, L. (ed.) FSE 1999. LNCS, vol. 1636, pp. 156–170. Springer, Heidelberg (1999). https://doi.org/10.1007/3-540-48519-8_12

85. Wang, Q., Jin, C.: Upper bound of the length of truncated impossible differentials for AES. Des. Codes Crypt. **86**(7), 1541–1552 (2017). https://doi.org/10.1007/s10623-017-0411-z

86. Wang, Q., Jin, C.: More accurate results on the provable security of AES against impossible differential cryptanalysis. Des. Codes Crypt. **87**(12), 3001–3018 (2019). https://doi.org/10.1007/s10623-019-00660-7

87. Wu, H., Preneel, B.: AEGIS: A Fast Authenticated Encryption Algorithm (v1.1). 3rd-round submission to the CAESAR competition (2015)

Robust Subgroup Multi-signatures for Consensus

David Galindo[2,3]($\boxtimes$) [iD] and Jia Liu[1]

[1] Fetch.ai, Cambridge, UK
[2] University of Birmingham, Birmingham, UK
d.galindo@bham.ac.uk
[3] Valory, Zug, Switzerland

Abstract. Multi-signatures are used to attest that a given collection of n parties, indexed by their respective public keys, have all signed a given message. A recent popular application of multi-signatures is to be found in consensus protocols to attest that a qualified subset of a global set of n validators have reached agreement. In this paper, we point out that the traditional security model for multi-signatures is insufficient for this new application, as it assumes that every party in the set *participates* in every multi-signature computation and that *is honest*. None of these assumptions hold in the typical adversarial scenarios in consensus protocols (aka. byzantine agreement), where malicious players can launch a denial-of-service attack by injecting malformed individual signatures and cause liveness to halt. We address this by introducing a new multi-signature variant called *robust subgroup multi-signatures*, whereby any eligible subgroup of signers from the global set can produce a multi-signature on behalf of the group, in the presence of a byzantine adversary. We provide syntax and security definitions thereof and argue that existing unforgeability security proofs for multi-signatures do not carry over to the consensus setting; a consequence of this observation is that many multi-signature based consensus protocols are left lacking a rigorous security proof for correctness. To remediate this we propose several constructions which we prove secure under widely held cryptographic assumptions using our newly introduced formal definitions and also improve upon multi-signature computation time. Finally, we report on benchmarks from a proof-of-concept implementation.

1 Introduction

A multi-signature protocol[1] enables n entities indexed by their respective public keys $\{pk_i\}_{i=1}^n$ to sign a message m and produce n individual signatures $\{s_i\}_{i=1}^n$ which are later compressed into a multi-signature σ. Recently there has been a renewed interest in multi-signatures for securing distributed ledgers, e.g., [14, 16, 23]. Multi-signatures can be used to build secure ledgers more efficiently, namely

---

[1] We also use the term *scheme*.

S. D. Galbraith (Ed.): CT-RSA 2022, LNCS 13161, pp. 537–561, 2022.
https://doi.org/10.1007/978-3-030-95312-6_22

they can help reduce block storage and/or block correctness verification time or reduce the time to validate that consensus on a block has been reached [8,14].

A multi-signature can be trivially obtained from any unforgeable signature scheme by concatenating every individuals' signature on m, while verification simply checks that each atomic signature passes the individual signature verification test. Often designs that improve on that trivial construction in terms of the final signature length or the performance of the verification process are preferred. It is expected that multi-signature designs achieve compactness [8], that is, the length of the final multi-signature is independent of the number of signers. The verification of the short multi-signature σ should convince a verifier that all the n entities signed the message m. Multi-signatures can be constructed, for example, from Schnorr signatures e.g. [23], and from BLS signatures [6,8,9]. Schnorr-based multi-signatures involve multiple rounds of communication, while pairing-based multi-signature schemes can be non-interactive. The latter is highly desirable for applications in distributed settings where the potential participants are unknown upfront and the network nodes are sparsely connected. The focus on this paper is therefore on non-interactive multi-signature protocols.

Despite the recent popularity gained by multi-signatures for the specific purpose of recording blockchain consensus, both in the literature [8,14,16,23] and in actual platforms [1,10,15,20,28], the existing multi-signatures formal models fail to address the particularities of consensus protocols. Indeed, existing multi-signatures formal models apply in scenarios where the signing entities are controlled by a single party or where they are highly coordinated, so that the incoming individual signatures are assumed to be valid before being combined in a single multi-signature. Such is the case for instance in a scenario where a user owns multiple wallets that can transfer funds by generating a multi-signature that if correct shows every wallet sign the corresponding transfer (this actually constitutes their main usage so far in the cryptocurrency space).

Thus, existing (non-interactive) multi-signature schemes mechanics do not explicitly address the verification and selection of *valid* individual signatures before running the multi-signature creation process. However, in the context of signaling block agreement amongst a group of validators in Proof-of-Stake consensus protocols, it is not reasonable to assume that the individual signatures coming from consensus nodes are valid by default. This applies likewise in the case of aggregating transaction signatures. Therefore individual signatures need to be verified before being aggregated into a multi-signature, as we simply cannot assume they are valid when the combining party runs the combining process. To reflect this, we introduce a notion of *robustness* for multi-signatures which is a form of correctness but allowing the adversary to submit signatures to the signature combination algorithm.

A variant of multi-signatures that can be particularly useful for consensus applications is subgroup multi-signatures [6,24]. Subgroup multi-signatures allow any eligible subgroup of signers from a global set to produce a multi-signature on behalf of the global group, as the right solution to recording consensus. This concept is most useful in scenarios where the group of entities that will participate in the signing process of a given message belong to a fixed set but is not fully determined. For example that is the case in t-out-of-n multi-signatures, where a combined multi-signature is valid if any t members out of a given n-member set have signed.

The current practice of using BLS-based multi-signatures with bitmaps as subgroup multi-signatures for blockchain consensus, for example [12, 15, 16, 20] is, however, not necessarily provably secure in a subgroup model. Elrond [15] uses a modified version of the multi-signature scheme MSP proposed in [8] for subgroup multi-signature. However, no security analysis is provided for their modified scheme. The unforgeability of the original MSP scheme [8] is proven based on a condition that each signer has a prior knowledge of all other entities that will definitely sign, which makes MSP unsuitable to be used as a subgroup multi-signatures. Technically this condition is crucial for defending against the notorious rogue-key attacks [27] and is guaranteed by hashing all the signers in the coefficients $a_i = H_1(\mathsf{pk}_i, \{\mathsf{pk}_1, \cdots, \mathsf{pk}_n\})$ during the signing process. In the security reduction of unforgeability, these coefficients enable the generalised forking lemma to output two different multi-signatures signed by the same set of signers after rewinding to the point where a_i is chosen in order to extract the underlying secret key of the challenging signer. Elrond's modified version breaks this condition by using the coefficients $a_i = H_1(\mathsf{pk}_i)$ instead which can no longer guarantee the signers are the same when using the generalised forking lemma, thus it cannot be proven secure using the techniques in [8]. Other consensus projects like [12, 16, 20] implement proof-of-possession (PoP) based multi-signatures MSP-pop originally proposed in [27], but MSP-pop has not yet been formalised and proven secure in a subgroup model.

Our contributions. We introduce *robust subgroup multi-signature* protocols, a multi-signature variant specially designed for consensus. We define *robustness* for multi-signatures, and present a rigorous definition of *existential unforgeability* for subgroup multi-signature protocols. The former evaluates the correctness of the signature combination algorithm in the presence of an adversary that may control a subset of the signers. As a side benefit of explicitly capturing the signature combination function, we are able to optimise the validation of individual signatures by using zero-knowledge proofs instead of time-consuming pairing operations, which improves upon the efficiency of signature combination algorithms of several existing multi-signatures. Regarding existential unforgeability, we point out that the previous syntax and security definitions for subgroup multi-signatures in [6] are incomplete and somewhat informal. This is undesirable from a scientific point of view, and in fact this lack of formality may explain why [6] presents a security proof for their construction while it is known to be insecure [8]. We believe that robust subgroup multi-signatures capture the variant of multi-signatures that best suits consensus applications.

We shall present four constructions of robust subgroup multi-signatures, i.e., RSMSP, RSMSP-zk, RSMS-pop and RSMS-pop-zk respectively. While RSMS-pop is a natural adaption of MSP-pop scheme [27] to our subgroup model, the other three constructions RSMSP, RSMSP-zk and RSMS-pop-zk are new. Our RSMSP scheme is a twist to the MSP scheme [8]: the determination of the actual co-signers is deferred to the signature combination phase thanks to our explicit combine function, and we include the set of identities I of the co-signers in the hash values $a_i = H_2(\mathsf{pk}_i, I, \{\mathsf{pk}_1, \mathsf{pk}_2, \cdots, \mathsf{pk}_n\})$. This trick enables us to remove the restriction that the co-signers have to be fixed from the beginning. It also enables us to use the Generalised Forking Lemma to rewind the adversary to the point a_i is generated and produce another multi-signature with the same set of cosigners I in order to prove existential unforgeability. The variants RSMSP-zk (resp. RSMS-pop-zk) optimise the combination of individual signatures in RSMSP (resp. RSMS-pop) by introducing NIZKs to validate individual signatures. Note that the combine function does not use any secret information and can be run by any entity, making it still a non-interactive process. Our experiments show that this optimisation makes the combination process 2x faster. Last but not least, by proving secure the construction RSMS-pop using our refined subgroup multi-signature model, we provide the missing evidence that the multi-signatures protocols for consensus in [12, 16, 20] are indeed sound.

Related work. Sequential aggregate multi-signatures are studied in [7, 21, 22] where each signer modifies the aggregate signature in turn. Such signatures are suitable for applications like secure route attestation and ceritificate chains. Pixel [14] is a complex multi-signature scheme based on hierarchical identity-based encryption (HIBE), which involves a key update method in order to provide forward security. Plumo [16] implements a SNARK based validation for checking aggregated BLS signatures. Adhoc Threshold Multisignatures [17] extend pop-based multi-signatures with a Merkle tree commitment to validate the membership of the individual public keys.

Accountable-subgroup multi-signatures [8, 24] allow any subgroups to produce a multi-signature for a message in a provably secure way but involve an interactive key setup. This is mainly due to the requirement of not involving individual public keys for multi-signature verification. While this setting can be useful for some applications (e.g., multisig wallets with 2 or 3 addresses [2]), it is neither optimal nor flexible in general consensus setting. Indeed that would require validator nodes to run a joint setup phase which is expensive. In the decentralised consensus application, validator groups are formed ad hoc by the network nodes which are sparsely connected. An interactive key setup requires synchronisation among n participating nodes which is the top challenge for implementation of decentralised applications, especially when n is big, for example, Ethereum 2.0 requires a minimum of 128 validators for each committee. Moreover, the expensive interactive setup makes it difficult for nodes to join or leave dynamically. Therefore, we focus on non-interactive multi-signature schemes in this paper. The individual public keys are used in the verification of our multi-signatures but they are only stored in the blockchain once when nodes register themselves as validators.

2   Preliminaries

In this section we briefly recall some building blocks needed in the rest of the paper, such as the computational assumptions under which our constructions are proven secure, the equality of discrete logarithms proof system and the generalised forking lemma.

2.1 Bilinear Groups

Definition 1 (Asymmetric Pairing Groups). *Let* $\mathbb{G}_1 = \langle g_1 \rangle, \mathbb{G}_2 = \langle g_2 \rangle$ *and* $\mathbb{G}_T$ *be (cyclic) groups of prime order* q. *A map* $\mathbf{e} : \mathbb{G}_1 \times \mathbb{G}_2 \to \mathbb{G}_T$ *to a group* $\mathbb{G}_T$ *is called a* bilinear *map, if it satisfies the following three properties:*

- *Bilinearity:* $\mathbf{e}(g_1^x, g_2^y) = \mathbf{e}(g_1, g_2)^{xy}$ *for all* $x, y \in \mathbb{Z}_p$.
- *Non-Degenerate:* $\mathbf{e}(g_1, g_2) \neq 1$.
- *Computable:* $\mathbf{e}(g_1, g_2)$ *can be efficiently computed.*

We assume there exists an efficient bilinear pairing generator algorithm $\mathcal{IG}$ *that on input a security parameter* 1^λ *outputs the description of* $\langle \mathbf{e}(\cdot, \cdot), \mathbb{G}_1, \mathbb{G}_2, \mathbb{G}_T, q \rangle$.

Asymmetric pairing groups can be efficiently generated [18]. Pairing group exponentiations and pairing operations can also be efficiently computed [13].

2.2 Computational Assumptions

Definition 2 (Computational co-CDH assumption [8]). *Let* $X \leftarrow (\mathbb{G}_1, \mathbb{G}_2, q, g_1, g_2, g_1^\alpha, g_1^\beta, g_2^\alpha)$ *where* $\mathbb{G}_1 = \langle g_1 \rangle$ *and* $\mathbb{G}_2 = \langle g_2 \rangle$ *are cyclic groups of prime order* q, *and* $\alpha, \beta \xleftarrow{\$} \mathbb{Z}_q^*$. *We define the advantage* $\mathbf{Adv}_{\mathcal{A}}^{\text{co-CDH}}$ *of an adversary* $\mathcal{A}$ *as*

$$\mathbf{Adv}_{\mathcal{A}}^{\text{co-CDH}} := \Pr\left[\mathcal{A}(X) = g_1^{\alpha\beta}\right]$$

We say $\mathcal{A}$ (τ, ϵ)-*breaks the co-CDH problem if it runs in time at most* τ *and* $\mathbf{Adv}_{\mathcal{A}}^{\text{co-CDH}} \geq \epsilon$. *co-CDH is* (τ, ϵ)-*hard if no such adversary exists.*

Definition 3 (Computational ψ-co-CDH assumption [8]). *Let* $X \leftarrow (\mathbb{G}_1, \mathbb{G}_2, q, g_1, g_2, g_1^\alpha, g_1^\beta, g_2^\alpha)$ *where* $\mathbb{G}_1 = \langle g_1 \rangle$ *and* $\mathbb{G}_2 = \langle g_2 \rangle$ *are cyclic groups of prime order* q, *and* $\alpha, \beta \xleftarrow{\$} \mathbb{Z}_q^*$. *Let* $\mathcal{O}^\psi(\cdot)$ *be an oracle that on input* $g_2^\alpha \in \mathbb{G}_2$ *returns* $g_1^\alpha \in \mathbb{G}_1$. *We define the advantage* $\mathbf{Adv}_{\mathcal{A}}^{\psi\text{-co-CDH}}$ *of an adversary* $\mathcal{A}$ *as*

$$\mathbf{Adv}_{\mathcal{A}}^{\psi\text{-co-CDH}} := \Pr\left[\mathcal{A}^{\mathcal{O}^\psi(\cdot)}(X) = g_1^{\alpha\beta}\right]$$

We say $\mathcal{A}$ (τ, ϵ)-*breaks the ψ-co-CDH problem if it runs in time at most* τ *and* $\mathbf{Adv}_{\mathcal{A}}^{\psi\text{-co-CDH}} \geq \epsilon$. ψ-*co-CDH is* (τ, ϵ)-*hard if no such adversary exists.*

2.3 Equality of Discrete Logarithms

We need NIZK proof systems as an ingredient to our construction, namely the *Equality of Discrete Logarithms* proof system. Formally, given a cyclic group $\mathbb{G}$ of order q and $g, h \in \mathbb{G}$, the NIZK proof $(\mathsf{PrEq}_H, \mathsf{VerEq}_H)$ to show $k = \log_g x = \log_h y$ for $x, y \in \mathbb{G}$, $k \in \mathbb{Z}_q$ is described as below [11]:

- $\mathsf{PrEq}_H(g, h, x, y, k)$: choose $r \xleftarrow{\$} \mathbb{Z}_q$, compute $R_1 = g^r, R_2 = h^r$ and set $c \leftarrow H(g, h, x, y, R_1, R_2)$. Output is $(c, s = r + k \cdot c)$.
- $\mathsf{VerEq}_H(g, h, x, y, (c, s))$: compute $R_1 \leftarrow g^s / x^c$ and $R_2 \leftarrow h^s / y^c$ and output $c \overset{?}{=} H(g, h, x, y, R_1, R_2)$.

The security of the above NIZK is random oracle (RO) based, rather than common reference string (CRS) based. CRS-based model assumes a trusted setup which embeds a secret trapdoor. The trapdoor, if known by any party, can be used to subvert the security of the system, which poses a challenge for decentralised applications. In contrast, our construction does not involve the generation of any trusted parameters. Moreover, the security of multi-signatures is based on RO-model, so it is natural to use RO-based model for NIZKs in our case.

2.4   Generalized Forking Lemma

The forking lemma [26] for proving the security of schemes based on Schnorr signatures was generalised to a wider class of schemes [3,4]. Below we describe the version due to [3].

Consider an algorithm $\mathcal{A}$ that on input in interacts with a random oracle $H : \{0,1\}^* \mapsto \mathbb{Z}_q$. Let $f = (\rho, h_1, \ldots, h_{q_H})$ be the randomness involved in an execution of $\mathcal{A}$, where ρ is $\mathcal{A}$'s random tape, h_i is the response to $\mathcal{A}$'s i-th query to H, and q_H is its maximal number of random-oracle queries. Let Ω be the space of all such vectors f and let $f|_i = (\rho, h_1, \ldots, h_{i-1})$. We consider an execution of $\mathcal{A}$ on input in and randomness f, denoted by $\mathcal{A}(in, f)$, as successful if it outputs a pair $(J, \{out_j\}_{j \in J})$, where J is a multi-set that is a non-empty subset of $\{1, \ldots, q_H\}$ and $\{out_j\}_{j \in J}$ is multi-set of side outputs. We say that $\mathcal{A}$ failed if it outputs $J = \emptyset$. Let p be the probability that $\mathcal{A}(in, f)$ is successful for fresh randomness $f \xleftarrow{\$} \Omega$ and for an input $in \xleftarrow{\$} \mathcal{IG}$ generated an input generator $\mathcal{IG}$.

For a given input in, the generalised forking algorithm $\mathcal{GF}$ is defined as shown in Fig. 1. We say that $\mathcal{GF}_\mathcal{A}$ succeeds if it doesn't output `fail`.

Lemma 1 (Generalised Forking Lemma [3]). *Let $\mathcal{IG}$ be a randomised algorithm and $\mathcal{A}$ be a randomised algorithm running in time τ making at most q_H random-oracle queries that succeeds with probability ϵ. If $q > 8nq_H / \epsilon$, then $\mathcal{GF}_\mathcal{A}(in)$ runs in time at most $\tau \cdot 8n^2 q_H / \epsilon \cdot \ln(8n/\epsilon)$ and succeeds with probability at least $\epsilon/8$, where the probability is over the choice of $in \xleftarrow{\$} \mathcal{IG}$ and over the coins of $\mathcal{GF}_\mathcal{A}$.*

3   Definitions of Robust Subgroup Multi-signatures

We now introduce syntax and security definitions for our robust subgroup multi-signatures. We describe a notion of *robustness*, a generalised notion of correctness, by allowing adversaries to participate in the signature combination process. Then we define unforgeability in a subgroup model where the adversary outputs

$$\underline{\mathcal{GF}_{\mathcal{A}}(in)}:$$

$f = (\rho, h_1, \ldots, h_{q_H}) \xleftarrow{\$} \omega$

$(J, \{out_j\}_{j \in J}) \leftarrow \mathcal{A}(in, f)$

If $J = \emptyset$ then output **fail**

Let $J = \{j_1, \ldots, j_n\}$ such that $j_1 \leq \cdots \leq j_n$

For $i = 1, \ldots, n$ do

$\quad succ_i \leftarrow 0; k_i \leftarrow 0; k_{\max} \leftarrow 8nq_H/\epsilon \cdot \ln(8n/\epsilon)$

$\quad$ Repeat until $succ_i = 1$ or $k_i > k_{\max}$

$\qquad f'' \xleftarrow{\$} \Omega$ such that $f'|_{j_i} = f|_{j_i}$

$\qquad$ Let $f'' = (\rho, h_1, \ldots, h_{j_i-1}, h''_{j_i}, \ldots, h''_{q_H})$

$\qquad (J'', \{out''_j\}_{j \in J''}) \leftarrow \mathcal{A}(in, f'')$

$\qquad$ If $h''_{j_i} \neq h_{j_i}$ and $J'' \neq \emptyset$ and $j_i \in J''$ then

$\qquad\quad out'_{j_i} \leftarrow out''_{j_i}; succ_i \leftarrow 1$

If $succ_i = 1$ for all $i = 1, \ldots, n$

$\quad$ Then output $(J, \{out_j\}_{j \in J}, \{out'_j\}_{j \in J})$

$\quad$ Else output **fail**

Fig. 1. Algorithm $\mathcal{GF}$

a forgery (J, σ^*) where J is a subset of indices of signers from a group $\mathcal{PK}$ chosen by the adversary and σ^* is a multi-signature.

Definition 4. *A robust subgroup multi-signature scheme (RSMS)* Π = (KeyGen, KeyAgg, GroupSet, Sign, Combine, VerifyMul) *consists of the following algorithms:*

KeyGen(1^λ): *this algorithm is used by each entity locally to output, on input a security parameter* λ, *their own key pair* (sk, pk).

GroupSet($\mathcal{PK}$): *on input a set of public keys* $\mathcal{PK}$, *the algorithm forms a group and outputs a group public key* gpk = (gtag, $\mathcal{PK}$), *where gtag is a group tag that depends on the context where the subgroup multi-signature is used[2]. When the algorithm fails to form the group,* gpk = $\perp$.

Sign($m, \mathsf{sk}_i, \mathsf{pk}_i, \mathsf{gtag}$): *on input a message* m, *a secret key* sk_i, *a public key* pk_i, *a group tag* gtag, *the algorithm outputs an individual signature* s_i.

Combine($m, \mathcal{E}, \mathsf{gpk}$): *on input a message, a set of individual signatures* $\mathcal{E} = \{s_i\}_i$ *created by* $|\mathcal{E}|$ *different signers, a group public key* gpk, *the algorithm identifies an index set* J *of valid individual signatures and combines them into a single multi-signature* σ *and outputs* (J, σ). *When the algorithm fails to combine the individual signatures,* $(J, \sigma) = (\emptyset, \perp)$.

VerifyMul($m, J, \sigma, \mathsf{gpk}$): *on input a message* m, *an index set* J, *a group public key* gpk, *the algorithm outputs 1 if* σ *is a valid multi-signature and outputs 0 otherwise.*

---

[2] In order to simplify the notation we choose this contextual information to be implicit.

Sometimes we make use of the following auxiliary algorithm when describing particular instances:

KeyAgg($J, \mathcal{PK}$): on input an index set J and a set of public keys $\mathcal{PK}$, this algorithm aggregates $\mathcal{PK}$ into a single aggregate public key apk. Output apk.

Definition 5 (Robustness). *The* robustness *of a RSMS scheme* Π = (KeyGen, GroupSet, Sign, Combine, VerifyMul) *is defined by a three-stage game:*

Setup. *The challenger generates the system parameters* pp *and a challenge entity with key tuple* $(\mathsf{sk}^\star, \mathsf{pk}^\star) \leftarrow$ KeyGen(1^λ). *It gives* $(\mathsf{pk}^\star, \mathsf{pp})$ *to the adversary.*

Signature queries. $\mathcal{A}$ *is allowed to make signature queries on any message* m *for any* gtag, *meaning that it has access to oracle* $\mathcal{O}^{\mathsf{Sign}(\cdot, \mathsf{sk}^\star, \mathsf{pk}^\star, \cdot)}$ *that simulates the honest signer signing a message* m.

Output. *Finally, the challenger receives from the adversary a message* $m^\star$ *and a group public key* gpk = (gtag, $\mathcal{PK} = \{\mathsf{pk}_i\}_{i \in U}$), *and a set of individual signatures* $\mathcal{E} = \{s_i\}_{i \in I}$ *from* $|I|$ *different entities such that* $I \subseteq U$. *The adversary wins if*

  1. $\mathsf{pk}^\star = \mathsf{pk}_k$ *for some* $k \in U$ *and* $k \notin I$
  2. gpk $\neq \perp$ *and* gpk = GroupSet($\mathcal{PK}$)
  3. VerifyMul($m^\star, J, \sigma^\star,$ gpk) = 0, *where* $s^\star \leftarrow$ Sign($m^\star, \mathsf{sk}^\star, \mathsf{pk}^\star,$ gtag) *and* $(J, \sigma^\star) \leftarrow$ Combine($m^\star, \mathcal{E} \cup \{s^\star\},$ gpk).

We say $\mathcal{A}$ $(\tau, q_S, q_H, \epsilon)$-*breaks the robustness of* RSMS *if* $\mathcal{A}$ *runs in time at most* τ, *makes at most* q_S *signing queries and at most* q_H *random oracle queries, and the above game outputs 1 with probability at least* ϵ. RSMS *is* $(\tau, q_S, q_H, \epsilon)$-*robust if no such adversary exists.*

In the above definition, the challenger controls an honest signer $(\mathsf{sk}^\star, \mathsf{pk}^\star)$, while the adversary controls all other signers and is given access to the signing oracle for $\mathsf{sk}^\star$ to maximise its attacking capabilities. In the Output phase, the adversary forms and submits a group $\mathcal{PK}$ which consists of the honest signer $\mathsf{pk}^\star$ generated by the challenger and other signers generated by the adversary. The signatures $\mathcal{E}$ created by the adversary are combined with the signature $s^\star$ from the honest signer. Robustness demands that the output of the Combine function is a valid multi-signature in the presence of the adversary's inputs.

Definition 6 (Unforgeability). *The* unforgeability *of a RSMS scheme* Π = (KeyGen, GroupSet, Sign, Combine, VerifyMul) *is defined by a three-stage game:*

Setup. *The challenger generates the system parameters* pp *and a challenge key pair* $(\mathsf{sk}^\star, \mathsf{pk}^\star) \leftarrow$ KeyGen(1^λ). *It gives* $(\mathsf{pk}^\star, \mathsf{pp})$ *to the adversary.*

Signature queries. $\mathcal{A}$ *is allowed to make signature queries on any message* m *for any group tag* gtag, *meaning that it has access to oracle* $\mathcal{O}^{\mathsf{Sign}(\cdot, \mathsf{sk}^\star, \mathsf{pk}^\star, \cdot)}$ *that simulates the honest signer signing a message* m.

Output. *Finally, the adversary outputs a multi-signature forgery* $(J, \sigma^\star)$, *a message* $m^\star$, *a group public key* gpk = (gtag$^\star, \mathcal{PK} = \{\mathsf{pk}_i\}_{i \in U}$). *The adversary wins if*

1. gpk $\neq \perp$ *and* gpk = GroupSet($\mathcal{PK}$)
2. pk* = pk$_k$ *for some* $k \in U \cap J$
3. $\mathcal{A}$ *made no signing queries on* $(m^\star, \mathsf{gtag}^\star)$ *and* VerifyMul$(m^\star, J, \sigma^\star, \mathsf{gpk}) = 1$

We say $\mathcal{A}$ *is a* $(\tau, q_S, q_H, \epsilon)$-*forger for* RSMS *if* $\mathcal{A}$ *runs in time at most* τ, *makes at most* q_S *signing queries and at most* q_H *random oracle queries, and wins the above game with probability at least* ϵ. RSMS *is* $(\tau, q_S, q_H, \epsilon)$-*unforgeable if no such adversary exists.*

Remark 1 (On including an explicit tag gtag *when signing).* Our unforgeability definition lets the adversary query the signing oracle $\mathcal{O}^{\mathsf{Sign}(\cdot, \mathsf{sk}^\star, \mathsf{pk}^\star, \cdot)}$ on the forged message $m^\star$ as long as it is queried on tags gtag $\neq$ gtag*. We think that given the current trend of multi-chain frameworks, where the same signing key pair (pk, sk) may be used to validate consensus simultaneously in different chains, embedding contextual information in the form of a tag gtag when signing, is of material importance given security issues with rogue key attacks and aggregation in a multi-chain setting are potentially more likely.

4 Our Pairing-Based Robust-Subgroup Multi-signature Scheme

Generally speaking, the major technical problem in constructing a secure multi-signature scheme is to prevent the rogue-key attack [23,27] which enables an adversary to use a specially crafted public key to deprive all other entities of their signing right. We consider two ways to prevent rogue-key attacks for our robust subgroup multi-signatures: one is using techniques proposed in [8,23] to combine individual signatures with hash values derived from the related public keys; the other way is called the proof-of-possession [8,27] which introduces an additional public key $H(\mathsf{pk}_i)^{\mathsf{sk}_i}$ to show the knowledge of the secret key sk_i. Moreover, we optimise the Combine process by introducing NIZKs to validate individual signatures to replace the checking based on time-consuming pairing equations. This optimisation can make the signature combination process x2 faster.

In this section, we present four constructions of robust-subgroup multi-signatures: RSMSP and its optimised version RSMSP-zk, and RSMS-pop and its optimised version RSMS-pop-zk.

4.1 Construction of RSMSP

Our RSMSP is constructed based on MSP scheme proposed in [8]. As mentioned in the introduction, MSP in [8] cannot be used as a subgroup multi-signature scheme in the provably secure sense. Here we propose a twist to MSP in order to construct a secure robust-subgroup multi-signature: we defer the determination of the actual co-signers to the combine phase thanks to the explicit introduction of the Combine function in our robust subgroup multi-signature scheme, and we include the identities of the subset of co-signers in the hash values $H_2(\mathsf{pk}_j, J, \mathcal{PK})$ generated for each co-signer j. In the security proof, this twist allows us to determine the co-signers at the moment when the hash value $c_{j_f} = H_2(\mathsf{pk}^\star, J, \mathcal{PK})$ is generated so that we can use the generalised forking lemma to rewind the adversary to this point and produce another multi-signature with the same set of cosigners J in order to extract the underlying secret key $\mathsf{sk}^\star$ of $\mathsf{pk}^\star$. Note that the Combine function does not use any secret information and can be run by any entity, making it still a non-interactive process.

Construction of RSMSP. Let $(q, \mathbb{G}_1, \mathbb{G}_2, \mathbb{G}_T, e, g_1, g_2)$ be a bilinear group with prime order q and $g_1 \in \mathbb{G}_1, g_2 \in \mathbb{G}_2$. Assume hash functions $H_1 : \{0,1\}^* \mapsto \mathbb{Z}_q$, $H_2 : \{0,1\}^* \mapsto \mathbb{G}_1$ and $H_3 : \{0,1\}^* \mapsto \mathbb{G}_1$.

$\mathsf{KeyGen}(1^\lambda)$: Choose $\mathsf{sk} \xleftarrow{\$} \mathbb{Z}_q$, compute $\mathsf{pk} = g_2^{\mathsf{sk}}$, and output $(\mathsf{sk}, \mathsf{pk})$. The public key pk is made public.

$\mathsf{GroupSet}(\mathcal{PK})$: Compute $\mathsf{gtag} = H_1(\mathcal{PK})$. Output $\mathsf{gpk} = (\mathsf{gtag}, \mathcal{PK})$.

$\mathsf{KeyAgg}(J, \mathcal{PK})$: Parse $\mathcal{PK} = \{\mathsf{pk}_i\}_{i \in I}$. Output $\perp$ if $J \not\subseteq I$. Compute $a_j = H_2(\mathsf{pk}_j, J, \mathcal{PK})$ for each $j \in J$. Output $\mathsf{apk} = \prod_{j \in J} \mathsf{pk}_j^{a_j}$.

$\mathsf{Sign}(m, \mathsf{sk}_i, \mathsf{gtag})$: Output an individual signature $s_i = H_3(\mathsf{gtag}, m)^{\mathsf{sk}_i}$.

$\mathsf{Combine}(m, \mathcal{E}, \mathsf{gpk})$: Parse $\mathcal{E} = \{s_i\}_{i \in I}$ of individual signatures originating from $|I|$ different entities, and $\mathsf{gpk} = (\mathsf{gtag}, \mathcal{PK})$. The combiner verifies each signature by checking $e(s_i, g_2) = e(H_3(\mathsf{gtag}, m), \mathsf{pk}_i)$. Assume the index set of valid signatures is $J \subseteq I$. The combiner computes the multi-signature as $\sigma = \prod_{j \in J} s_j^{a_j}$ with $a_j = H_2(\mathsf{pk}_j, J, \mathcal{PK})$ for $j \in J$. Output (J, σ).

$\mathsf{VerifyMul}(m, J, \sigma, \mathsf{gpk})$: Parse $\mathsf{gpk} = (\mathsf{gtag}, \{\mathsf{pk}_i\}_{i \in I})$. If $J = \emptyset$ or $J \not\subseteq I$, then output 0. Otherwise, compute $\mathsf{apk} \leftarrow \mathsf{KeyAgg}(J, \mathcal{PK})$. Output 1 if $e(\sigma, g_2) = e(H_3(\mathsf{gtag}, m), \mathsf{apk})$; else output 0.

Remark 2. Note that when hashing the message m in the signing algorithm, it is a good practice to include the unique group tag gtag in the hash function $H_1(\mathsf{gtag}, m)$ since the same node may be able to join different committee groups at the same time using the same public key (e.g., [19]). In this way, in the security definition of unforgeability, the adversary is allowed to issue signing query on different combinations $(m^\star, \cdot)$ and $(\cdot, \mathsf{gtag}^\star)$ of the challenge message and the challenge group tag as long as it does not query $(m^\star, \mathsf{gtag}^\star)$.

Batch verification. As usual, n multi-signatures on n-distinct pairs of (gtag, m) can be verified as a batch faster than verifying them one by one:

- Compute an aggregate multi-signature $\Sigma = \sigma_1 \cdots \sigma_n \in \mathbb{G}_1$
- Accept all n multisignatures as valid iff

$$e(\Sigma_n, g_2) = \prod_{1 \leq i \leq n} e(H_3(\mathsf{gtag}_i, m_i), \mathsf{apk}_i)$$

Theorem 1. RSMSP *is robust.*

Proof. Suppose there exists an adversary $\mathcal{A}$ that $(\tau, q_S, q_H, \epsilon)$-breaks robustness of RSMSP. We will show that this leads to a contradiction. At the end of the robustness game, the adversary outputs $(m^\star, \mathsf{gpk} = (\mathsf{gtag}^\star, \mathcal{PK} = \{\mathsf{pk}_i\}_{i\in U}), \mathcal{E} = \{s_i\}_{i\in I})$ with $\mathsf{pk}^\star = \mathsf{pk}_k$ for some $k \in U$. When the challenger outputs 1, we know that $e(\sigma^\star, g_2) \neq e(H_3(\mathsf{gtag}^\star, m^\star), \mathsf{apk})$ where $s \leftarrow \mathsf{Sign}(m^\star, \mathsf{sk}^\star, \mathsf{pk}^\star, \mathsf{gtag}^\star)$, $(J, \sigma^\star) \leftarrow \mathsf{Combine}(m^\star, \mathcal{E} \cup \{s\}, \mathsf{gpk})$ and $\mathsf{apk} \leftarrow \mathsf{KeyAgg}(J, \mathcal{PK})$. Thus there exists $j \in J$ such that $e(s_j, g_2) \neq e(H_3(\mathsf{gtag}^\star, m^\star), \mathsf{pk}_j)$. We consider two cases. If $j = k$, then this is impossible because $s_j = H_3(\mathsf{gtag}^\star, m^\star)^{\mathsf{sk}^\star}$ and $\mathsf{pk}_j = g_2^{\mathsf{sk}^\star}$. If $j \neq k$, this directly contradicts to the verification $e(s_j, g_2) = e(H_3(\mathsf{gtag}^\star, m^\star), \mathsf{pk}_j)$ performed in the Combine process. This completes the proof.

Theorem 2. RSMSP *is unforgeable under the computational co-CDH assumption in the random oracle model. Formally,* RSMSP *is* $(\tau, q_S, q_H, \epsilon)$-*unforgeable if* $q > 8q_H/\epsilon$ *and co-CDH is* $((\tau + (q_H + q_S)) \cdot \tau_{\exp_1} + \ell \cdot \tau_{\exp_2}) \cdot 8q_H^2/\epsilon \cdot \ln(8q_H/\epsilon), \epsilon/(8q_H))$-*hard where* ℓ *is the maximum number of signers involved in a single multi-signature and* $\tau_{\exp_1}$ *is the time required to compute one exponentiation in* $\mathbb{G}_1$.

Proof. Suppose $\mathcal{A}$ is a $(\tau, q_S, q_H, \epsilon)$ forger against RSMSP. We shall first construct an adversary $\mathcal{B}$ using $\mathcal{A}$ as a subroutine and then construct another adversary $\mathcal{F}$ to run $\mathcal{GF}_{\mathcal{B}}$ to derive a solution to the co-CDH instance.

Given a co-CDH instance $(e, \mathbb{G}_1, \mathbb{G}_2, \mathbb{G}_T, q, g_1, g_2, g_1^\alpha, g_1^\beta, g_2^\beta)$ with $g_1 \in \mathbb{G}_1, g_2 \in \mathbb{G}_2, \alpha, \beta \xleftarrow{\$} \mathbb{Z}_q$. The goal is to find the solution $g_1^{\alpha\beta}$ to the instance. We first construct $\mathcal{B}$ to run $\mathcal{A}$ as follows:

1. Give to $\mathcal{A}$ the public parameters $(e, \mathbb{G}_1, \mathbb{G}_2, \mathbb{G}_T, q, g_1, g_2)$ and the challenge public key $\mathsf{pk}^\star = g_2^\beta$ as input. $\mathcal{B}$ runs $\mathcal{A}$ on randomness $f = (\rho, c_1, \cdots, c_{q_H})$.
2. The random oracle H_1 is answered as follows: initialise a list $\mathcal{L}_{H_1} = \emptyset$. For a query on y, if there exists $(y, c) \in \mathcal{L}_{H_1}$ then output c; otherwise choose a random $c \xleftarrow{\$} \mathbb{Z}_q$, update $\mathcal{L}_{H_1} = \mathcal{L}_{H_1} \cup \{(y, c)\}$ and output c.
3. The random oracle H_2 is programmed as follows: Define a list $\mathcal{L}_{H_2} = \emptyset$. For a query on y, if there exists $(y, c) \in \mathcal{L}_{H_2}$, then output c; otherwise
   (a) If $y = (\mathsf{pk}, J, \mathcal{PK})$ with $\mathsf{pk} \in \mathcal{PK}$ and $\mathsf{pk}^\star \in \mathcal{PK}$, assume this is the i-th query to H_2. For each $j \in J$ and $\mathsf{pk}_j \neq \mathsf{pk}^\star$, choose a random value $d_j \xleftarrow{\$} \mathbb{Z}_q$ and set $H_2(\mathsf{pk}_j, J, \mathcal{PK}) = d_j$. For $(\mathsf{pk}^\star, J, \mathcal{PK})$, it fixes $H_2(\mathsf{pk}^\star, J, \mathcal{PK}) = c_i$. Output $H_2(y)$.
   (b) Else choose a random $d \xleftarrow{\$} \mathbb{Z}_q$ and set $H_2(y) = d$. Output d.
4. The random oracle H_3 is answered as follows: initialise $\mathcal{L}_{H_3} = \emptyset$. Let q_H be the total number of distinct random oracle queries asked in this game. Choose an index $\eta^\star \xleftarrow{\$} [q_H]$ uniformly at random.
   - If there exists a tuple $(x, r, h) \in \mathcal{L}_{H_3}$, output h.
   - Otherwise,
     - If this is the $\eta^\star$-th distinct call, set $r = \perp$ and $h = g_1^\alpha$ where g_1^α is from the co-CDH problem.

- Else choose a random $r \xleftarrow{\$} \mathbb{Z}_q$ and set $h = g_1^r$.
- Update $\mathcal{L}_{H_3} = \mathcal{L}_{H_3} \cup (x, r, h)$ and output h.

5. To answer the sign query $\mathsf{Sign}(\cdot, \mathsf{sk}^\star, \mathsf{pk}^\star, \cdot)$ on a message x, call the H_3 oracle to obtain $(x, r, h) \in \mathcal{L}_{H_3}$,
   - If $r = \bot$, return $\bot$
   - Else output $g_1^{\beta \cdot r}$

Finally $\mathcal{A}$ outputs a forgery $(J, \sigma^\star)$, a message $m^\star$, a group public key $\mathsf{gpk} = (\mathsf{gtag}^\star, \mathcal{PK})$. If $(\mathsf{gtag}^\star, m^\star)$ is not the $\eta^\star$-th query to H_3, then $\mathcal{B}$ aborts. Since $\eta^\star$ is randomly chosen, the probability that $\mathcal{B}$ does not abort is $1/q_H$. Let's assume $\mathcal{B}$ does not abort. Parse $\mathcal{PK} = \{\mathsf{pk}_1, \ldots, \mathsf{pk}_n\}$. Suppose $\mathsf{pk}^\star = \mathsf{pk}_k$ for some $1 \le k \le n$. Let j_f be the index such that $H_1(\mathsf{pk}^\star, J, \mathcal{PK}) = c_{j_f}$. Let $\mathsf{apk} \leftarrow \mathsf{KeyAgg}(J, \mathcal{PK})$ and $a_j = H_2(\mathsf{pk}_j, J, \mathcal{PK})$ for each $j \in J$. $\mathcal{B}$ outputs $(\{j_f\}, \{(\sigma^\star, \mathcal{PK}, J, \mathsf{apk}, \{a_j\}_{j \in J})\})$.

The running time of $\mathcal{B}$ is that of $\mathcal{A}$ plus the additional computations that $\mathcal{B}$ makes. Let $\tau_{\exp_1}$ (resp. $\tau_{\exp_2}$) be the time required to compute one exponentiation in $\mathbb{G}_1$ (resp. $\mathbb{G}_2$). Let q_H be the combined number of random oracle queries to H_1, H_2, H_3. To answer q_H random oracle queries, $\mathcal{B}$ spends at most $q_H \cdot \tau_{\exp_1}$ time. To answer the signing queries, $\mathcal{B}$ spends at most $q_S \cdot \tau_{\exp_1}$ time. To construct apk, it takes $\ell \cdot \tau_{\exp_2}$ time where ℓ is the maximum number of signers involved in a single multi-signature. In total, $\mathcal{B}$'s running time is therefore $\tau + (q_H + q_S) \cdot \tau_{\exp_1} + \ell \cdot \tau_{\exp_2}$. $\mathcal{B}$'s success rate $\epsilon_{\mathcal{B}}$ is the probability that $\mathcal{A}$ succeeds and that $\mathcal{B}$ correctly guesses the hash index of $\mathcal{A}$'s forgery, thus $\epsilon_{\mathcal{B}} = \epsilon/q_H$.

Now we construct another adversary $\mathcal{F}$ that on input a co-CDH instance and a forger $\mathcal{A}$, outputs a solution to the co-CDH instance. $\mathcal{F}$ runs the generalised forking lemma $\mathcal{GF}_{\mathcal{B}}$ with algorithm $\mathcal{B}$ constructed above. If $\mathcal{GF}_{\mathcal{B}}$ outputs $(\{j_f\}, \{out\}, \{out'\})$, then $\mathcal{B}$ proceeds as follows. $\mathcal{B}$ parses $out = (\sigma, \mathcal{PK}, J, \mathsf{apk}, \{a_j\}_{j \in J})$ and $out' = (\sigma', \mathcal{PK}', J', \mathsf{apk}', \{a'_j\}_{j \in J'})$. Let K be the index of $\mathsf{pk}^\star$ in $\mathcal{PK}$. Then we know $a_k = c_{j_f}$ and $a'_k = c'_{j_f}$ and $a_k \ne a'_k$. Since out, out' are obtained from two executions of $\mathcal{B}$ with randomness f, f' such that $f \mid_{j_f} = f' \mid_{j_f}$, we can derive that $\mathcal{PK} = \mathcal{PK}', J = J'$ and $a_j = a'_j$ for $j \in J \setminus \{k\}$. Therefore we have $\mathsf{apk}/\mathsf{apk}' = g_2^{\beta(a_k - a'_k)}$. Since $\mathcal{B}$'s output satisfies $e(\sigma, g_2) = e(g_1^\alpha, \mathsf{apk})$ and $e(\sigma', g_2) = e(g_1^\alpha, \mathsf{apk}')$, we can compute $(\sigma/\sigma')^{1/(a_k - a'_k)}$ as a solution to the co-CDH instance.

Using the generalised forking lemma, if $q > 8q_H/\epsilon$, $\mathcal{F}$ runs in time at most $(\tau + (q_H + q_S) \cdot \tau_{\exp_1} + \ell \cdot \tau_{\exp_2}) \cdot 8q_H^2/\epsilon \cdot \ln(8q_H/\epsilon)$ and succeeds with probability at least $\epsilon/(8q_H)$.

4.2 Optimising RSMSP with NIZKs

We can use NIZKs validate individual signatures in order to speed up the verification of individual signatures in the Combine function in RSMSP. We call this optimised scheme RSMSP-zk.

Construction of RSMSP-zk. The algorithms KeyGen, GroupSet, KeyAgg and VerifyMul are implemented exactly the same as RSMSP, but the algorithms Sign and Combine are optimised as below:

$\mathsf{Sign}(m, \mathsf{sk}_i, \mathsf{gtag})$: Output $s_i = (v_i, \pi_i)$ where $v_i = H_3(\mathsf{gtag}, m)^{\mathsf{sk}_i}$ and $\pi_i \leftarrow$
$\mathsf{PreEq}_{H_4}(g_2, H_3(\mathsf{gtag}, m), \mathsf{pk}_i, v_i; r)$ for randomness $r \xleftarrow{\$} \mathbb{Z}_q$.

$\mathsf{Combine}(m, \mathcal{E}, \mathsf{gpk})$: Parse $\mathcal{E} = \{(v_i, \pi_i)\}_{i \in I}$ of individual signatures originating
from $|I|$ different entities, and $\mathsf{gpk} = (\mathsf{gtag}, \mathcal{PK})$. The combiner verifies each
signature by checking $\mathsf{VerEq}_{H_4}((g_2, H_3(\mathsf{gtag}, m), \mathsf{pk}_i, v_i, \pi_i) = 1$. Assume the
index set of valid signatures is $J \subseteq I$. The combiner computes the multi-
signature as $\sigma = \prod_{j \in J} v_j^{a_j}$ with $a_j = H_2(\mathsf{pk}_j, J, \mathcal{PK})$ for $j \in J$. Output (J, σ).

Theorem 3. RSMSP-zk *is robust in the random oracle model.*

Theorem 4. RSMSP-zk *is unforgeable under the computational co-CDH*
assumption in the random oracle model. Formally, RSMSP-zk *is* $(\tau, q_S, q_H, \epsilon)$-
unforgeable if $q > 8q_H/\epsilon$ *and co-CDH is* $(\tau + (q_H + 3q_S) \cdot \tau_{\exp_1} + (2q_S + \ell) \cdot$
$\tau_{\exp_2}) \cdot 8q_H^2/\epsilon \cdot \ln(8q_H/\epsilon), \epsilon/(8q_H))$-*hard where* ℓ *is the maximum number of sign-*
ers involved in a single multi-signature and $\tau_{\exp_1}$ *(resp.* $\tau_{\exp_2}$*) is the time required*
to compute one exponentiation in $\mathbb{G}_1$ *(resp.* $\mathbb{G}_2$*).*

Proof. The analysis is similar to Theorem 2 except that the Sign queries are
answered with simulated NIZKs generated by an additional random oracle $H_4 :$
$\{0, 1\}^* \mapsto \mathbb{Z}_q$:

- The random oracle H_4 is programmed as follows: Define a list $\mathcal{L}_{H_4} = \emptyset$. For
  a query on y, if $(y, c) \in \mathcal{L}_{H_4}$, then output c. Otherwise choose a random
  $c \xleftarrow{\$} \mathbb{Z}_q$, update the list $\mathcal{L}_{H_4} = \mathcal{L}_{H_4} \cup (y, c)$ and output c.
- To answer the sign query $\mathsf{Sign}(\cdot, \mathsf{sk}^\star, \mathsf{pk}^\star, \cdot)$ on a message x, call the H_3 oracle
  to obtain $(x, r, h) \in \mathcal{L}_{H_3}$,
  - If $r = \bot$, return $\bot$
  - Else output $g_1^{\beta \cdot r}$ and a simulated NIZK proof π using the random oracle
    H_4

To compute a simulated NIZK proof, it costs $\mathcal{B}$ $2(\tau_{\exp_1} + \tau_{\exp_2})$ time. Adding the
time $\tau_{\exp_1}$ for computing each signature, $\mathcal{B}$ spends at most $q_S \cdot (3\tau_{\exp_1} + 2\tau_{\exp_2})$
time to answer all the signing queries. In total $\mathcal{B}$'s running time is at most
$\tau + (q_H + 3q_S) \cdot \tau_{\exp_1} + (2q_S + \ell) \cdot \tau_{\exp_2}$ and success rate is ϵ/q_H. The running
time of the adversary $\mathcal{F}$ that runs $\mathcal{GF}_\mathcal{B}$ is $(\tau + (q_H + 3q_S) \cdot \tau_{\exp_1} + (2q_S + \ell) \cdot$
$\tau_{\exp_2}) \cdot 8q_H^2/\epsilon \cdot \ln(8q_H/\epsilon)$ and succeeds with probability at least $\epsilon/(8q_H)$.

4.3 Construction of RSMS-pop from Proof-of-possession

In proof-of-possession (PoP) based multi-signatures, an additional public key is
generated as a proof of knowledge of the secret key. Obviously the disadvan-
tage of using PoPs is the extra storage and computation overhead introduced
by the PoPs. However, PoPs offer a few competitive advantages as well. The
aggregation of signatures and public keys in PoPs are simply multiplications
without any exponentiation. The security argument of PoPs does not require
the generalised forking lemma which gives much tighter reductions. Constructing secure robust-subgroup multi-signatures from PoPs [8,27] turns out to be

quite straightforward, since security reductions of PoPs do not require to fix the set of co-signers. For the completeness of this work, we describe the construction of RSMS-pop and give security proofs below.

Construction of RSMS-pop. Let $(q, \mathbb{G}_1, \mathbb{G}_2, \mathbb{G}_T, e, g_1, g_2)$ be a bilinear group with prime order q and $g_1 \in \mathbb{G}_1, g_2 \in \mathbb{G}_2$. Assume hash functions $H_1 : \mathbb{G}_2 \mapsto \mathbb{G}_1$, $H_2 : \{0,1\}^* \mapsto \mathbb{Z}_q$, $H_3 : \{0,1\}^* \mapsto \mathbb{G}_1$.

KeyGen(1^λ): Choose sk $\stackrel{\$}{\leftarrow} \mathbb{Z}_q$, compute pk $= (pk, pop)$ with $pk = g_2^{\mathsf{sk}}$ and $pop = H_1(pk)^{\mathsf{sk}}$, and output (sk, pk). The public key pk is made public and its validity can be checked by $e(pop, g_2) = e(H_1(pk), pk)$.

GroupSet($\mathcal{PK}$): Parse $\mathcal{PK} = \{(pk_i, pop_i)\}_{i \in I}$. For each $i \in I$, check if $e(pop_i, g_2) = e(H_1(pk_i), pk_i)$. If all successful, compute gtag $= H_2(\mathcal{PK})$ and output gpk $= (\mathsf{gtag}, \mathcal{PK})$; else output $\perp$.

KeyAgg($J, \mathcal{PK}$): Parse $\mathcal{PK} = \{(pk_i, pop_i)\}_{i \in I}$. If $J \not\subseteq I$, then output $\perp$. Compute and output apk $= \prod_{j \in J} pk_j$.

Sign($m, \mathsf{sk}_i, \mathsf{pk}_i, \mathsf{gtag}$): Output signature $s_i = H_3(\mathsf{gtag}, m)^{\mathsf{sk}_i}$.

Combine($m, \mathcal{E}, \mathsf{gpk}$): Parse gpk $= (\mathsf{gtag}, \{\mathsf{pk}_i\}_{i \in U})$ and the set $\mathcal{E} = \{s_i\}_{i \in I}$ of individual signatures originating from $|I|$ different entities such that $I \subseteq U$. The combiner verifies each signature in $\mathcal{E}$ by checking $e(s_i, g_2) = e(H_3(\mathsf{gtag}, m), pk_i)$ where $\mathsf{pk}_i = (pk_i, pop)$. Assume the index set of valid signatures is $J \subseteq I$. The combiner computes the multi-signature as $\sigma = \prod_{j \in J} \sigma_j$ and outputs (J, σ).

VerifyMul($m, J, \sigma, \mathsf{gpk}$): Parse gpk $= (\mathsf{gtag}, \mathcal{PK} = \{\mathsf{pk}_i\}_{i \in I})$. If $J = \emptyset$ or $J \not\subseteq I$, then output 0. Otherwise, compute apk $\leftarrow$ KeyAgg($J, \mathcal{PK}$). Output 1 if $e(\sigma, g_2) = e(H_3(\mathsf{gtag}, m), \mathsf{apk})$; else output 0.

Theorem 5. RSMS-pop *is robust.*

Proof. Suppose there exists an adversary $\mathcal{A}$ $(\tau, q_S, q_H, \epsilon)$-breaks robustness. We will show that this leads to a contradiction. At the end of the robustness game, the adversary outputs $(m^\star, \mathsf{gpk} = (\mathsf{gtag}^\star, \mathcal{PK} = \{\mathsf{pk}_i\}_{i \in U}), \mathcal{E} = \{s_i\}_{i \in I})$ with $\mathsf{pk}_i = (pk_i, pop_i)$ for each $i \in U$ and $\mathsf{pk}^\star = \mathsf{pk}_k$ for some $k \in U$. When the challenger outputs 1, we know $e(\sigma^\star, g_2) \neq e(H_3(\mathsf{gtag}^\star, m^\star), \prod_{j \in J \cup \{k\}} pk_j)$ where $s \leftarrow$ Sign($m^\star, \mathsf{sk}^\star, \mathsf{pk}^\star, \mathsf{gtag}^\star$), $(J, \sigma^\star) \leftarrow$ Combine($m^\star, \mathcal{E} \cup \{s\}, \mathsf{gpk}^\star$). This means there exists $j \in J$ such that $e(s_j, g_2) \neq e(H_3(\mathsf{gtag}^\star, m^\star), pk_j)$ and $\mathsf{pk}_j = (pk_j, pop_j)$. This contradicts to the fact that all the individual signatures with indices included in $J^\star$ satisfy $e(s_j, g_2) = e(H_3(\mathsf{gtag}^\star, m^\star), pk_j)$ for $j \in J$. $\qquad\qquad\square$

Theorem 6. RSMS-pop *is unforgeable under the computational co-CDH assumption in the random oracle model. Formally,* RSMS-pop *is $(\tau, q_S, q_H, \epsilon)$-unforgeable if co-CDH is $(\tau + (q_H + q_S + \ell) \cdot \tau_{\exp_1}, \epsilon/q_H)$-hard where ℓ is the maximum number of signers involved in a single multi-signature and $\tau_{\exp_1}$ is the time required to compute one exponentiation in $\mathbb{G}_1$.*

Proof. Given a co-CDH problem $(e, \mathbb{G}_1, \mathbb{G}_2, \mathbb{G}_T, q, g_1, g_2, g_1^\alpha, g_1^\beta, g_2^\beta)$ with $g_1 \in \mathbb{G}_1, g_2 \in \mathbb{G}_2, \alpha, \beta \stackrel{\$}{\leftarrow} \mathbb{Z}_q$. $\mathcal{B}$'s goal is to output $g_1^{\alpha\beta}$:

1. Give to $\mathcal{A}$ the public parameters $(e, \mathbb{G}_1, \mathbb{G}_2, \mathbb{G}_T, q, g_1, g_2)$, the challenge public key $\mathsf{pk}^\star = (pk^\star, pop^\star)$ where $pk^\star = g_2^\beta$ and $pop^\star = g_1^{\beta \cdot r^\star}$ with $r^\star \xleftarrow{\$} \mathbb{Z}_p$.
2. The random oracle H_1 is answered as follows: initialise a list $\mathcal{L}_{H_1} = \emptyset$.
   - If there exists a tuple $(x, r, h) \in \mathcal{L}_{H_1}$, output h.
   - Otherwise,
     - If $x = pk^\star$, set $h = g_1^{r^\star}$ and update $\mathcal{L}_{H_1} = \mathcal{L}_{H_1} \cup (x, r^\star, h)$ and output h.
     - Else choose a random $r \xleftarrow{\$} \mathbb{Z}_q$ and set $h = g_1^{\alpha \cdot r}$ where g_1^α is from the co-CDH problem, update $\mathcal{L}_{H_1} = \mathcal{L}_{H_1} \cup (x, r, h)$ and output h.
3. The random oracle H_2 is programmed as follows: Define a list $\mathcal{L}_{H_2} = \emptyset$. For a query on y, if $(y, c) \in \mathcal{L}_{H_2}$, then output c. Otherwise choose a random $c \xleftarrow{\$} \mathbb{Z}_q$, update the list $\mathcal{L}_{H_2} = \mathcal{L}_{H_2} \cup (y, c)$ and output c.
4. The random oracle H_3 is answered as follows: initialise $\mathcal{L}_{H_3} = \emptyset$. Let q_{H_3} be the total number of distinct random oracle queries asked in this game. Choose an index $\eta^\star \xleftarrow{\$} [q_{H_3}]$ uniformly at random.
   - If there exists a tuple $(x, r, h) \in \mathcal{L}_{H_3}$, output h.
   - Otherwise,
     - If this is the $\eta^\star$-th distinct call, set $r = \bot$ and $h = g_1^\alpha$ where g_1^α is from the co-CDH problem.
     - Else choose a random $r \xleftarrow{\$} \mathbb{Z}_q$ and set $h = g_1^r$.
     - Update $\mathcal{L}_{H_3} = \mathcal{L}_{H_3} \cup (x, r, h)$ and output h.
5. To answer the sign query $\mathsf{Sign}(\cdot, \mathsf{sk}^\star, \mathsf{pk}^\star, \cdot)$ on a message x, call the H_3 oracle to obtain $(x, r, h) \in \mathcal{L}_{H_3}$,
   - If $r = \bot$, return $\bot$
   - Else output $g_1^{\beta \cdot r}$

Finally $\mathcal{A}$ outputs a forgery $(J, \sigma^\star)$, a message $m^\star$, a group public key $\mathsf{gpk}^\star = (\mathsf{gtag}^\star, \mathcal{PK})$. If $(m^\star, \mathsf{gtag}^\star)$ is not the $\eta^\star$-th query to H_3, then $\mathcal{B}$ aborts. Since $\eta^\star$ is randomly chosen, the probability that $\mathcal{B}$ does not abort is $1/q_{H_3}$. Let's assume $\mathcal{B}$ does not abort. Parse $\mathcal{PK} = \{\mathsf{pk}_i\}_{i \in U}$ with each $\mathsf{pk}_i = (pk_i, pop_i)$. Suppose $\mathsf{pk}^\star = \mathsf{pk}_k$ for some $k \in U$. Based on the construction of H_1, we have $H_1(pk_i) = g_1^{\alpha \cdot r_i}$ for each $i \in U \setminus \{k\}$. Combing with $e(H_1(pk_i), pk_i) = e(pop_i, g_2)$ obtained from Condition 1 in Definition 6, we have $e(g_1^\alpha, pk_i) = e(pop_i^{r_i^{-1}}, g_2)$ for each $i \in U \setminus \{k\}$. Because $e(\sigma^\star, g_2) = e(H_3(\mathsf{gtag}^\star, m^\star), \prod_{i \in J} pk_i)$ by the Condition 3 in Definition 6, we can derive $e(\sigma^\star, g_2) = e(g_1^\alpha, g_2^\beta \cdot \prod_{i \in J}^{i \neq k} pk_i) = e(g_1^\alpha, g_2^\beta) \cdot e(g_1^\alpha, \prod_{i \in J}^{i \neq k} pk_i) = e(g_1^\alpha, g_2^\beta) \cdot e(\prod_{i \in J}^{i \neq k} pop_i^{r_i^{-1}}, g_2)$. Let $\delta = \sigma^\star \cdot \prod_{i \in J}^{i \neq k} pop_i^{-r_i^{-1}}$. Then we have $e(\delta, g_2) = e(\sigma^\star \cdot \prod_{i \in J}^{i \neq k} pop_i^{-r_i^{-1}}, g_2) = e(\sigma^\star, g_2)/e(\prod_{i \in J}^{i \neq k} pop_i^{r_i^{-1}}, g_2) = e(g_1^\alpha, g_2^\beta)$. Therefore, $\mathcal{B}$ can return δ as a solution to the co-CDH problem with a success probability at least ϵ/q_H.

The running time of $\mathcal{B}$ is that of $\mathcal{A}$ plus the additional computations that $\mathcal{B}$ makes. Let $\tau_{\exp_1}$ be the time required to compute one exponentiation in $\mathbb{G}_1$. The setup of the challenge verification key costs $\tau_{\exp_1}$. Let q_H be the combined number of random oracle queries to H_1, H_2, H_3, H_4. To answer q_H random oracle queries, $\mathcal{B}$ spends at most $(q_H - 1) \cdot \tau_{\exp_1}$ time. $\mathcal{B}$ spends at most $q_S \cdot \tau_{\exp_1}$ to answer all the signing queries. To construct the solution δ, it takes at most $\ell \cdot \tau_{\exp_1}$ time where ℓ is the maximum number of signers involved in a single multi-signature. In total, $\mathcal{B}$'s running time is $\tau + (q_H + q_S + \ell) \cdot \tau_{\exp_1}$.

Remark 3. Theorems 5 and 6 validate the correctness of using the multi-signatures protocols for achieving consensus in [12, 16, 20].

In the next subsection, we shall discuss how to optimise RSMS-pop with NIZKs to obtain a more efficient scheme RSMS-pop-zk. The performance evaluation given in Sect. 6 will show our construction RSMS-pop-zk is 2x faster than RSMS-pop in terms of combination of individual signatures.

4.4   Optimising **RSMS-pop** with NIZKs

Construction of RSMS-pop-zk. The KeyGen, KeyAgg, GroupSet, VerifyMul algorithms are instantiated in the same way as RSMS-pop, but the algorithms Sign and Combine now use NIZKs to validate individual signatures:

Sign(m, sk$_i$, pk$_i$, gtag): Parse pk$_i$ = (pk_i, pop_i). Compute $v_i = H_3(\text{gtag}, m)^{\text{sk}_i}$ and $\pi_i \leftarrow \text{PrEq}_{H_4}(H_1(pk_i), H_3(\text{gtag}, m), pop_i, v_i; r)$ for randomness $r \overset{\$}{\leftarrow} \mathbb{Z}_q$. Output $s_i = (v_i, \pi_i)$.

Combine($m, \mathcal{E}$, gpk): Parse gpk = $(\text{gtag}, \{(pk_i, pop_i)\}_{i \in U})$ and $\mathcal{E} = \{(v_i, \pi_i)\}_{i \in I}$ the set of individual signatures originating from $|I|$ different entities such that $I \subseteq U$. The combiner verifies each signature in $\mathcal{E}$ by checking

$$\text{VerEq}_{H_4}(H_1(pk_i), pop_i, H_3(\text{gtag}, m), v_i, \pi_i) = 1.$$

Assume the index set of valid signatures is $J \subseteq I$. The combiner computes the multi-signature as $\sigma = \prod_{j \in J} v_j$ and outputs (J, σ).

Theorem 7. *Our* RSMS-pop-zk *scheme is robust in the random oracle model.*

Theorem 8. RSMS-pop-zk *is unforgeable under the computational co-CDH assumption in the random oracle model. Formally,* RSMS-pop-zk *is* $(\tau, q_S, q_H, \epsilon)$-*unforgeable if co-CDH is* $(\tau + (q_H + 5q_S + \ell) \cdot \tau_{\exp_1}, \epsilon/q_H)$-*hard where* ℓ *is the maximum number of signers involved in a single multi-signature and* $\tau_{\exp_1}$ *is the time required to compute one exponentiation in* $\mathbb{G}_1$.

Proof. The analysis is the same as Theorem 6 except that Sign queries are answered with simulated NIZKs generated by an additional random oracle $H_4 : \{0, 1\}^* \mapsto \mathbb{Z}_q$:

-   The random oracle H_4 is programmed as follows: Define a list $\mathcal{L}_{H_4} = \emptyset$. For a query on y, if $(y, c) \in \mathcal{L}_{H_4}$, then output c. Otherwise choose a random $c \overset{\$}{\leftarrow} \mathbb{Z}_q$, update the list $\mathcal{L}_{H_4} = \mathcal{L}_{H_4} \cup (y, c)$ and output c.
-   To answer the sign query Sign($\cdot$, sk*, pk*, $\cdot$) on a message x, call the H_3 oracle to obtain $(x, r, h) \in \mathcal{L}_{H_3}$,
    -   If $r = \bot$, return $\bot$.

- Else output $g_1^{\beta \cdot r}$ and a simulated NIZK proof π using the random oracle H_4

For each Sign query, $\mathcal{B}$ needs to generate a simulated NIZK proof which takes $4\tau_{\exp_1}$ time for each proof. Adding the time $\tau_{\exp_1}$ for computing each signature, $\mathcal{B}$ spends at most $q_S \cdot 5\tau_{\exp_1}$ to answer all the signing queries. Therefore, $\mathcal{B}$'s total running time is at most $\tau + (q_H + 5q_S + \ell) \cdot \tau_{\exp_1}$ and $\mathcal{B}$'s success probability is ϵ / q_H.

5 Extensions

In this section, we extend our robust subgroup multi-signatures with two useful functions: compression and aggregation. We give formal definitions and security analysis for the extended multi-signatures.

5.1 Compressing Two Multi-signatures on the Same Message

It is possible to *compress* two multi-signatures on the same message if signed by disjoint subgroups. In practice, this enables any entity to start the signature combination process without the need of waiting until the entity gets all the individual signatures. It is a type of incremental aggregation mentioned in [14] but was never formalised. Below we shall extend our definition of robust subgroup multi-signature scheme RSMS with an additional algorithm called Compress:

Compress($m, J_1, \sigma_1, J_2, \sigma_2, \mathsf{gpk}$): on input a message m, two multi-signatures $(J_1, \sigma_1), (J_2, \sigma_2)$, and a group public key gpk, the algorithm compress two multi-signatures into a single multi-signature and outputs (J, σ) with $J = J_1 \cup J_2$. When the algorithm fails to compress the multi-signatures, output $(J, \sigma) = (\emptyset, \perp)$.

Robustness. We extend the robustness in Definition 5 to include *compressibility*: for any $m, J_1, J_2, \sigma_1, \sigma_2, \mathsf{gpk}$ such that $J_1 \cap J_2 = \emptyset$ and $J_1, J_2 \neq \emptyset$, if VerifyMul($m, J_b, \sigma_b, \mathsf{gpk}$) = 1 for $b = 1, 2$, then VerifyMul($m, J, \sigma, \mathsf{gpk}$) = 1 where $(J, \sigma) \leftarrow$ Compress($m, J_1, \sigma_1, J_2, \sigma_2, \mathsf{gpk}$).

Unforgeability. The definition of unforgeability does not change since Compress does not involve any secret information and the adversary can run this algorithm by itself.

Instantiations. Unfortunately, RSMSP and RSMSP-zk are not compressible, because two multi-signatures $\sigma_b = \prod_{i \in J_b} s_i^{a_{i,b}}$ with coefficients $a_{i,b} = H_2(\mathsf{pk}_i, J_b, \mathcal{PK})$ and $b = 0, 1$, cannot be compressed into $\sigma = \prod_{i \in J_1 \cup J_2} s_i^{a_i}$ with coefficients $a_i = H_2(\mathsf{pk}_i, J_1 \cup J_2, \mathcal{PK})$. In comparison, the PoP-based schemes RSMS-pop and RSMS-pop-zk can be extended with Compress as follows:

Compress($m, J_1, \sigma_1, J_2, \sigma_2, \mathsf{gpk}$): Check if $J_1 \cap J_2 = \emptyset$, VerifyMul($m, J_b, \sigma_b, \mathsf{gpk}$) = 1 for $b = 0, 1$. If successful, output $(J_1 \cup J_2, \sigma_1 \cdot \sigma_2)$. Otherwise output $(\emptyset, \perp)$.

Theorem 9. *The extended* RSMS-pop *and* RSMS-pop-zk *are robust in the random oracle model.*

Proof. We only need to show the compressibility defined above. Since $e(\sigma_i, g_2) = e(H_2(\text{gtag}, m), \text{apk}_i)$ for $i = 1, 2$, we know that $e(\sigma, g_2) = e(H_2(\text{gtag}, m), \text{apk})$ where $\sigma = \sigma_1 \cdot \sigma_2$ and $\text{apk} = \text{apk}_1 \cdot \text{apk}_2$.

Theorem 10. *The extended* RSMS-pop *and* RSMS-pop-zk *are unforgeable under the computational co-CDH problem in the random oracle model.*

Proof. As mentioned above, adding Compress algorithm does not change the definition of unforgeability since the adversary can run Compress himself. The proofs of unforgeability of RSMS-pop (resp. RSMS-pop-zk) are therefore the same as Theorem 6 (resp. 8) and are omitted.

5.2   Aggregating Multi-signatures on Different Messages

Multi-signatures on different messages can be further aggregated into a single aggregate signature, e.g., [8]. In this section, we show that the multi-signatures on different messages signed by different groups in our robust-subgroup multi-signature schemes can also be aggregated, and we call this extension *aggregate robust-subgroup multi-signatures* (ARSMS).

Definition 7 (Aggregate Robust-Subgroup Multi-signature). *An aggregate robust-subgroup multi-signature (ARSMS) scheme consists of the following algorithms* $\Pi = $ (KeyGen, GroupSet, Sign, Combine, VerifyMul, Aggregate, VerifyAgg), *where algorithms* KeyGen, GroupSet, Sign, Combine *and* VerifyMul *are exactly the same as* RSMS *in Definition 4, and*

Aggregate($\{(m_i, J_i, \sigma_i, \text{gpk}_i)\}_{i \in I}$): *on input a set of tuples of message, multi-signature and group public key, the algorithm identifies an index set $K \subseteq I$ of valid multi-signatures and aggregates them into a single aggregate signature Σ and outputs* $(\{J_i\}_{i \in K}, \Sigma)$. *When the algorithm fails to aggregate signatures, output $\perp$.*

VerifyAgg($\{(m_i, J_i, \text{gpk}_i)\}_{i \in K}, \Sigma$): *on input tuples of messages, indices and group public keys, and an aggregate signature Σ, the algorithm outputs 1 if Σ is a valid aggregate signature and outputs 0 otherwise.*

Robustness of ARSMS. We define robustness for an ARSMS scheme by extending Definition 5 with the robustness for aggregate signatures: if VerifyMul($m_i, J_i, \sigma_i, \text{gpk}_i$) = 1 for each $i \in I$, and $\Sigma \leftarrow$ Aggregate($\{(m_i, J_i, \sigma_i, \text{gpk}_i)\}_{i \in I}$), then VerifyAgg($\{(m_i, J_i, \text{gpk}_i)\}_{i \in I}, \Sigma$) = 1.

Definition 8 (Unforgeability of ARSMS). *The* unforgeability *of an* ARSMS *scheme* $\Pi = $ (KeyGen, GroupSet, Sign, Combine, VerifyMul, Aggregate, VerifyAgg) *is defined by a three-stage game:*

Setup. *The challenger generates the system parameters* pp *and a challenge key pair* $(\mathsf{sk}^\star, \mathsf{pk}^\star) \leftarrow \mathsf{KeyGen}(1^\lambda)$. *It gives* $(\mathsf{pk}^\star, \mathsf{pp})$ *to the adversary.*

Signature queries. $\mathcal{A}$ *is allowed to make signature queries on any message* m *for any group tag* gtag, *meaning that it has access to oracle* $\mathcal{O}^{\mathsf{Sign}(\cdot, \mathsf{sk}^\star, \mathsf{pk}^\star, \cdot)}$ *that simulates the honest signer signing a message* m.

Output. *Finally, the adversary outputs an aggregate signature forgery* $(\{m_i, J_i, \mathsf{gpk}_i = (\mathsf{gtag}_i, \mathcal{PK}_i)\}_{i \in K}, \Sigma^\star)$. *The adversary wins if*

1. *For each* $i \in K$, $\mathsf{gpk}_i \neq \perp$ *and* $\mathsf{gpk}_i = \mathsf{GroupSet}(\mathcal{PK}_i)$
2. *For each* $i \in K$, *let* $\mathcal{PK}_i = \{\mathsf{pk}_{i,j}\}_{j \in I_i}$, *then* $J_i \subseteq I_i$. $\mathsf{pk}^\star = \mathsf{pk}_{k^\star, j^\star}$ *for some* $k^\star \in K$ *and* $j^\star \in J_{k^\star}$.
3. *The pairs* (gtag_i, m_i) *with* $i \in K$ *are pairwise-distinct.* $\mathcal{A}$ *made no signing queries on* $(m_{k^\star}, \mathsf{gtag}_{k^\star})$.
4. $\mathsf{VerifyAgg}(\{(m_i, J_i, \mathsf{gpk}_i)\}_{i \in K}, \Sigma^\star) = 1$.

We say $\mathcal{A}$ *is a* $(\tau, q_S, q_H, \epsilon)$-*forger for* ARSMS *if* $\mathcal{A}$ *runs in time at most* τ, *makes at most* q_S *signing queries and at most* q_H *random oracle queries, and wins the above game with probability at least* ϵ. ARSMS *is* $(\tau, q_S, q_H, \epsilon)$-*unforgeable if no such adversary exists.*

Instantiations. Our robust-subgroup multi-signatures, i.e., RSMSP, RSMSP-zk, RSMS-pop, and RSMS-pop-zk can be extended with the following algorithms:

$\mathsf{Aggregate}(\{(m_i, J_i, \sigma_i, \mathsf{gpk}_i)\}_{i \in I})$: Output $\Sigma \leftarrow \prod_{i \in I} \sigma_i$.
$\mathsf{VerifyAgg}(\{(m_i, J_i, \mathsf{gpk}_i)\}_{i \in I}, \Sigma)$: For each $i \in I$, parse $\mathsf{gpk}_i = (\mathsf{gtag}_i, \mathcal{PK}_i)$ and compute $\mathsf{apk}_i \leftarrow \mathsf{KeyAgg}(J_i, \mathcal{PK}_i)$. If $e(\Sigma, g_2) = \prod_{i \in I} e(H_3(\mathsf{gtag}_i, m_i), \mathsf{apk}_i)$ output 1; else output 0.

We call the extended schemes ARSMSP, ARSMSP-zk, ARSMS-pop, ARSMS-pop-zk, respectively.

Theorem 11. *The schemes* ARSMS-pop-zk, ARSMSP-zk, ARSMS-pop *and finally* ARSMSP *are robust in the random oracle model.*

Proof. To show robustness, we only need to prove the robustness for aggregate signatures. Let $(\{J_i\}_{i \in K}, \Sigma) \leftarrow \mathsf{Aggregate}(\{(m_i, J_i, \sigma_i, \mathsf{gpk}_i)\}_{i \in I})$. From the instantiation of $\mathsf{Aggregate}$ and definition of robustness, we have $\Sigma = \prod_{i \in K} \sigma_i$, and for each $i \in K$, $\mathsf{VerifyMul}(m_i, J_i, \sigma_i, \mathsf{gpk}_i) = 1$. From the instantiation of $\mathsf{VerifyMul}$, we have $e(\sigma_i, g_2) = e(H_3(\mathsf{gtag}_i, m_i), \mathsf{apk}_i)$ where $\mathsf{gpk}_i = (\mathsf{gtag}_i, \mathcal{PK}_i)$ and $\mathsf{apk}_i \leftarrow \mathsf{KeyAgg}(J_i, \mathcal{PK}_i)$ for $i \in K$. Therefore

$$e(\Sigma, g_2) = \prod_{i \in K} e(H_3(\mathsf{gtag}_i, m_i), \mathsf{apk}_i),$$

which completes the proof.

Theorem 12. ARSMSP *and* ARSMSP-zk *are unforgeable under the computational* ψ-*co-CDH assumption in the random oracle model. Formally,*

1. ARSMSP *is* $(\tau, q_S, q_H, \epsilon)$-*unforgeable if* $q > 8q_H/\epsilon$ *and* ψ-*co-CDH is* $((\tau + (q_H + q_S + n) \cdot \tau_{\exp_1} + \ell \cdot \tau_{\exp_2}) \cdot 8q_H^2/\epsilon \cdot \ln(8q_H/\epsilon), \epsilon/(8q_H))$-*hard;*

2. ARSMSP-zk is $(\tau, q_S, q_H, \epsilon)$-unforgeable if $q > 8q_H/\epsilon$ and ψ-co-CDH is $(\tau + (q_H + 3q_S + n) \cdot \tau_{\exp_1} + (2q_S + \ell) \cdot \tau_{\exp_2}) \cdot 8q_H^2/\epsilon \cdot \ln(8q_H/\epsilon), \epsilon/(8q_H))$-hard.

where ℓ is the maximum number of signers involved in an aggregate signature, n is the maximum number of multi-signatures involved in an aggregate signature, and $\tau_{\exp_1}$ (resp. $\tau_{\exp_2}$) is the time required to compute one exponentiation in $\mathbb{G}_1$ (resp. $\mathbb{G}_2$).

Theorem 13. ARSMS-pop and ARSMS-pop-zk are unforgeable under the computational co-CDH assumption in the random oracle model. Formally,

1. ARSMS-pop is $(\tau, q_S, q_H, \epsilon)$-unforgeable if ψ-co-CDH is $(\tau + (q_H + q_S + \ell + n) \cdot \tau_{\exp_1}, \epsilon/q_H)$-hard.
2. ARSMS-pop-zk is $(\tau, q_S, q_H, \epsilon)$-unforgeable if ψ-co-CDH is $(\tau + (q_H + 5q_S + \ell + n) \cdot \tau_{\exp_1}, \epsilon/q_H)$-hard

where ℓ is the maximum number of signers involved in a single multi-signature, n is the maximum number of multi-signatures involved in an aggregate signature, and $\tau_{\exp_1}$ is the time required to compute one exponentiation in $\mathbb{G}_1$.

Compressibility. Apparently, ARSMS-pop and ARSMS-pop-zk are compressible and can be extended with the same Compress algorithm for RSMS-pop and RSMS-pop-zk.

6 Performance Evaluation

We implement the four multi-signature schemes, namelyRSMSP, RSMSP-zk, RSMS-pop and RSMS-pop-zk, using MCL library [25]. RSMSP and RSMSP-zk are implemented by swapping $\mathbb{G}_1$ and $\mathbb{G}_2$, i.e., putting the public keys on $\mathbb{G}_1$ and the signatures on $\mathbb{G}_2$. This is because VerifyMul and VerifyAgg involve reconstruction of the aggregate public keys which contains time-consuming exponentiation operations on the public keys. Putting public keys on $\mathbb{G}_1$ can mitigate this issue since the exponentiations on $\mathbb{G}_1$ are typically faster than the ones on $\mathbb{G}_2$. However, this will make Combine slower because the signature aggregations are now performed on $\mathbb{G}_2$. We note that Combine only needs to be run by a limited set of nodes like validators, but VerifyMul and VerifyAgg need to be run by any node that first obtains the multi-signatures. In addition, our RSMSP-zk scheme has optimised Combine using NIZKs which significantly improves the efficiency of Combine and offsets the loss. Therefore, switching $\mathbb{G}_1$ and $\mathbb{G}_2$ can provide better overall performance.

Performance evaluation of the Combine function. The algorithm Combine can be executed by any node in the network since it does not require any secret information. Combine only needs to be run once when computing the multi-signature from a set of individual signatures. Table 1 gives timing for combining a majority number $\lfloor \ell/2 \rfloor + 1$ of individual signatures from a group of size ℓ with $\ell = 64, 128, 256$. RSMSP-zk (resp. RSMS-pop-zk) is the optimised version of RSMSP (resp. RSMS-pop) by validating an individual signature using NIZK proofs instead of pairing equations. This optimisation makes Combine in RSMSP-zk (resp. RSMS-pop-zk) 2x faster than RSMSP (resp. RSMS-pop).

Table 1. Performance evaluation and comparison of the Combine function. The columns of Combine give the timings for combining a threshold number $\lfloor \ell/2 \rfloor + 1$ of individual signatures from a group of size ℓ with $\ell = 64, 128, 256$. That is, 33 (resp. 65, 129) individual signatures from a group of 64 (resp. 128, 256) members.

Protocol	Curve	Combine (ms)		
		64	128	256
RSMSP	BN256	44.720	89.576	176.031
	BLS12-381	51.803	96.384	190.928
	BN384	50.561	95.561	188.863
RSMSP-zk	BN256	26.228	51.951	101.077
	BLS12-381	26.943	52.931	105.625
	BN384	26.993	53.579	106.625
RSMS-pop	BN256	37.278	73.962	146.960
	BLS12-381	42.156	80.008	159.054
	BN384	42.880	80.214	159.365
RSMS-pop-zk	BN256	18.713	37.138	72.602
	BLS12-381	19.828	38.554	76.972
	BN384	19.212	37.994	76.048

Performance comparison with ECDSA. We shall compare the performance of the four multi-signature schemes with ECDSA signatures, in order to show that it is feasible to replace ECDSA with multi-signatures. The performance of ECDSA depends on the optimisations implemented in different libraries. The secp256k1 curve is used in Bitcoin for ECDSA signatures. The OpenSSL implementation of secp256k1 is not well optimised which leads to the low efficiency of ECDSA signing and verification operations. The Sodium library [5] provides a particularly efficient implementation of ECDSA over the curve Ed25519.

As shown in Table 2, the size of a multi-signature that combines/aggregates n individual signatures are constant, regardless of n. In comparison, n ECDSA signatures is of $64n$ bytes. We take consensus as an example. Suppose each committee has 200 validators and a notarisation of a new block requires at least 101 signatures. With ECDSA signatures, this accounts for 6.464 KB storage overhead for each block, while it is 48 Byte for RSMS-pop/RSMS-pop-zk and 96 bytes for RSMSP/RSMSP-zk.

In terms of the size of the public key for each entity, the constructions RSMS-pop and RSMS-pop-zk incurs the extra overhead introduced by the use of proof-of-possession for preventing rogue-key attacks. The public keys and PoPs only need to be verified once and stored in the blockchain for future reference. In comparison, the public keys in RSMSP and RSMSP-zk are 66% smaller than RSMS-pop and RSMS-pop-zk. For 200 validators, this means saving 19.2 KB for storing public keys.

Table 2. Signature size comparison between multi-signatures and ECDSA. The Multi-signature column gives the size of the multi-signature that combines n signatures.

Protocol	Library	Curve	Security Level (bits)	Public key (Byte)	Multi-signature (Byte)
RSMSP/RSMSP-zk	MCL	BN256	100	32	64
		BLS12-381	128	48	96
		BN384	128	48	96
RSMS-pop/RSMS-pop-zk	MCL	BN256	100	96	32
		BLS12-381	128	144	48
		BN384	128	144	48
ECDSA	Sodium	Ed25519	128	32	$64 \cdot n$
	OpenSSL	secp256k1	128	33	

In Table 3, we compare the efficiency of the four multi-signature schemes with ECDSA. The Sign column measures the timing for creating an individual signature which are less than 1 ms for all four multi-signature schemes.

The VerifyMul columns in Table 3 present the timings for verifying a multi-signature signed by a threshold (or majority) number of members from a group of ℓ members with $\ell = 64, 128, 256$. The threshold is set to be $\lfloor \ell/2 \rfloor + 1$. When using ECDSA for the same purpose as multi-signatures, this is equivalent to $\lfloor \ell/2 \rfloor + 1$ ECDSA signatures. From the table we can see that RSMS-pop and RSMS-pop-zk outperforms ECDSA and RSMSP and RSMSP-zk in terms of the verification time for a multi-signature. This is because VerifyMul in RSMS-pop and RSMS-pop-zk mainly involves computing two pairings which is almost constant. In comparison, VerifyMul in RSMS-pop and RSMS-pop-zk requires computing a sequence of exponentiations on the public keys in order to reconstruct the aggregate public keys for the subgroup.

The VerifyAgg columns in Table 3 give the timings for verifying an aggregate signature signed by k groups ($k = 64, 128, 256$) where each group consists of 128 members and a majority number (i.e., 65) of members signed. When using ECDSA for the same purpose, this corresponds to $65 \cdot k$ ECDSA signatures. For all four multi-signature schemes, the timing for verifying k multi-signatures using VerifyAgg is less than $k \cdot t$ where t is the time for verifying a multi-signature using VerifyMul. This is because VerifyAgg functions as a batch verification which saves $k - 1$ pairing computations. Similar to VerifyMul, RSMS-pop and RSMS-pop-zk outperforms RSMSP and RSMSP-zk and ECDSA in terms of the verification of aggregate signatures.

Table 3. Performance comparison between multi-signatures and ECDSA. The Sign column gives the timings for generating an individual signature. The columns of VerifyMul give the timings for verifying a multi-signature signed by a threshold number of members from a group of size ℓ with $\ell = 64, 128, 256$. The threshold number is set to be $\lfloor \ell/2 \rfloor + 1$. That is, 33 (resp. 65, 129) members from a group of 64 (resp. 128, 256) members. The columns of VerifyAgg give the timings for verifying an aggregate signature signed by 64 (or 128, 256) groups where each group consists of 128 members and a threshold number (i.e., 65) of members signed.

Protocol	Curve	Sign (ms)	VerifyMul (ms)			VerifyAgg (ms)		
			64	128	256	64×128	128×128	256×128
RSMSP	BN256	0.301	4.708	8.191	15.216	491.361	981.562	1963.130
	BLS12-381	0.311	4.824	8.249	15.235	498.063	1048.156	1971.246
	BN384	0.314	4.823	8.280	15.388	497.357	992.479	1972.311
RSMSP-zk	BN256	0.553	Same as above					
	BLS12-381	0.570						
	BN384	0.577						
RSMS-pop	BN256	0.172	1.153	1.193	1.275	48.674	98.982	198.468
	BLS12-381	0.178	1.229	1.267	1.352	51.117	103.633	207.195
	BN384	0.177	1.225	1.263	1.344	50.987	101.798	204.420
RSMS-pop-zk	BN256	0.463	Same as above					
	BLS12-381	0.474						
	BN384	0.474						
ECDSA	Ed25519	0.028	2.040	4.031	8.266	259.574	522.685	1053.570
	secp256k1	1.418	40.484	78.195	155.240	5203.854	10355.712	20790.631

References

1. Ethereum 2.0 Specifications. https://github.com/ethereum/eth2.0-specs
2. Andresen, G.: Bitcoin improvement proposal (BIP)0011 (2011). https://en.bitcoin.it/wiki/BIP_0011
3. Bagherzandi, A., Cheon, J.H., Jarecki, S.: Multisignatures secure under the discrete logarithm assumption and a generalized forking lemma. In: ACM CCS, pp. 449–458 (2008)
4. Bellare, M., Neven, G.: Multi-signatures in the plain public-key model and a general forking lemma. In: CCS 2006, pp. 390–399 (2006)
5. Bernstein, D.J., Denis, F.: Libsodium - a modern, portable, easy to use crypto library (2019). https://github.com/jedisct1/libsodium
6. Boldyreva, A.: Threshold signatures, multisignatures and blind signatures based on the Gap-Diffie-Hellman-Group signature scheme. In: Desmedt, Y.G. (ed.) PKC 2003. LNCS, vol. 2567, pp. 31–46. Springer, Heidelberg (2003). https://doi.org/10.1007/3-540-36288-6_3
7. Boldyreva, A., Gentry, C., O'Neill, A., Yum, D.H.: Ordered multisignatures and identity-based sequential aggregate signatures, with applications to secure routing. In: CCS 2007, pp. 276–285 (2007)

8. Boneh, D., Drijvers, M., Neven, G.: Compact multi-signatures for smaller blockchains. In: Peyrin, T., Galbraith, S. (eds.) ASIACRYPT 2018. LNCS, vol. 11273, pp. 435–464. Springer, Cham (2018). https://doi.org/10.1007/978-3-030-03329-3_15

9. Boneh, D., Gentry, C., Lynn, B., Shacham, H.: Aggregate and verifiably encrypted signatures from bilinear maps. In: Biham, E. (ed.) EUROCRYPT 2003. LNCS, vol. 2656, pp. 416–432. Springer, Heidelberg (2003). https://doi.org/10.1007/3-540-39200-9_26

10. Celo: Celo Blockchain. https://github.com/celo-org/celo-blockchain

11. Chaum, D., Pedersen, T.P.: Wallet databases with observers. In: Brickell, E.F. (ed.) CRYPTO 1992. LNCS, vol. 740, pp. 89–105. Springer, Heidelberg (1993). https://doi.org/10.1007/3-540-48071-4_7

12. Codechain: Codechain Foundry. https://github.com/CodeChain-io/foundry/blob/bls-consensus-signature/key/src/bls.rs

13. Devegili, A.J., Scott, M., Dahab, R.: Implementing cryptographic pairings over Barreto-Naehrig curves. In: Takagi, T., Okamoto, T., Okamoto, E., Okamoto, T. (eds.) Pairing 2007. LNCS, vol. 4575, pp. 197–207. Springer, Heidelberg (2007). https://doi.org/10.1007/978-3-540-73489-5_10

14. Drijvers, M., Gorbunov, S., Neven, G., Wee, H.: Pixel: multi-signatures for consensus. In: Capkun, S., Roesner, F. (eds.) 29th USENIX Security Symposium, USENIX Security 2020, 12–14 August 2020, pp. 2093–2110 (2020)

15. Elrond, T.: A highly scalable public blockchain via adaptive state sharding and secure proof of stake (2019). https://elrond.com/assets/files/elrond-whitepaper.pdf

16. Gabizon, A., et al.: PLUMO: towards scalable, interoperable blockchains using ultra light validation systems. In: The 3rd ZKProof Workshop (2020)

17. Gaži, P., Kiayias, A., Zindros, D.: Proof-of-stake sidechains. In: 2019 IEEE Symposium on Security and Privacy (SP), pp. 139–156 (2019)

18. Pereira, G.C.C.F., Simplicío, M.A., Jr., Naehrig, M., Barreto, P.S.L.M.: A family of implementation-friendly BN elliptic curves. J. Syst. Softw. **84**(8), 1319–1326 (2011)

19. Hanke, T., Movahedi, M., Williams, D.: DFINITY technology overview series, consensus system. CoRR abs/1805.04548 (2018). http://arxiv.org/abs/1805.04548

20. Harmony, T.: Technical Whitepaper - version 2.0. https://harmony.one/whitepaper.pdf

21. Lu, S., Ostrovsky, R., Sahai, A., Shacham, H., Waters, B.: Sequential aggregate signatures and multisignatures without random oracles. In: Vaudenay, S. (ed.) EUROCRYPT 2006. LNCS, vol. 4004, pp. 465–485. Springer, Heidelberg (2006). https://doi.org/10.1007/11761679_28

22. Lysyanskaya, A., Micali, S., Reyzin, L., Shacham, H.: Sequential aggregate signatures from trapdoor permutations. In: Cachin, C., Camenisch, J.L. (eds.) EUROCRYPT 2004. LNCS, vol. 3027, pp. 74–90. Springer, Heidelberg (2004). https://doi.org/10.1007/978-3-540-24676-3_5

23. Maxwell, G., Poelstra, A., Seurin, Y., Wuille, P.: Simple Schnorr multi-signatures with applications to Bitcoin. Des. Codes Crypt. **87**(9), 2139–2164 (2019). https://doi.org/10.1007/s10623-019-00608-x

24. Micali, S., Ohta, K., Reyzin, L.: Accountable-subgroup multisignatures: extended abstract. In: CCS 2001, pp. 245–254 (2001)

25. Mistunari, S.: MCL - a portable and fast pairing-based cryptography library (2019). https://github.com/herumi/mcl

26. Pointcheval, D., Stern, J.: Security arguments for digital signatures and blind signatures. J. Cryptol. **13**, 361–396 (2000)
27. Ristenpart, T., Yilek, S.: The power of proofs-of-possession: securing multiparty signatures against rogue-key attacks. In: Naor, M. (ed.) EUROCRYPT 2007. LNCS, vol. 4515, pp. 228–245. Springer, Heidelberg (2007). https://doi.org/10.1007/978-3-540-72540-4_13
28. Tendermint: Aggregate BLS signatures for votes. https://github.com/tendermint/tendermint/issues/1319

Subversion-Resilient Enhanced Privacy ID

Antonio Faonio[1]([✉]), Dario Fiore[2], Luca Nizzardo[4], and Claudio Soriente[3]

[1] EURECOM, Sophia Antipolis, France
faonio@eurecom.fr
[2] IMDEA Software Institute, Madrid, Spain
dario.fiore@imdea.org
[3] NEC Labs Europe, Madrid, Spain
claudio.soriente@neclab.eu
[4] Protocol Labs, Madrid, Spain
luca@proto.ai

Abstract. Anonymous attestation for secure hardware platforms leverages tailored group signature schemes and assumes the hardware to be trusted. Yet, there is an increasing concern on the trustworthiness of hardware components and embedded systems. A subverted hardware may, for example, use its signatures to exfiltrate identifying information or even the signing key. We focus on Enhanced Privacy ID (EPID)—a popular anonymous attestation scheme used in commodity secure hardware platforms like Intel SGX. We define and instantiate a *subversion resilient* EPID scheme (or SR-EPID). In a nutshell, SR-EPID provides the same functionality and security guarantees of the original EPID, despite potentially subverted hardware. In our design, a "sanitizer" ensures no covert channel between the hardware and the outside world both during enrollment and during attestation (i.e., when signatures are produced). We design a practical SR-EPID scheme secure against adaptive corruptions and based on a novel combination of malleable NIZKs and hash functions modeled as random oracles. Our approach has a number of advantages over alternative designs. Namely, the sanitizer bears no secret information—hence, a memory leak does not erode security. Also, we keep the signing protocol non-interactive, thereby minimizing latency during signature generation.

1 Introduction

Anonymous attestation is a key feature of secure hardware platforms, such as Intel SGX[1] or the Trusted Computing Group's Trusted Platform Module[2]. It allows a verifier to authenticate a party as member of a trusted set, while keeping the party itself anonymous (within that set). This functionality is realized by

---

[1] https://www.intel.com/content/www/us/en/architecture-and-technology/software-guard-extensions.html.

[2] https://trustedcomputinggroup.org/resource/tpm-library-specification/.

S. D. Galbraith (Ed.): CT-RSA 2022, LNCS 13161, pp. 562–588, 2022.
https://doi.org/10.1007/978-3-030-95312-6_23

using a privacy-enhanced flavor of group signatures in which signatures cannot be traced, not even by the group manager.

Given such realization paradigm, the security of anonymous attestation schemes is grounded on the trustworthiness of the signer. In particular, anonymity and unforgeability definitions assume that the signer is trusted and does not exfiltrate any information via its signatures. Yet, in most applications, the signer is a small piece of hardware with closed-source firmware (e.g., a smart card) to which a user has only black-box access. In such a scenario, trusting the hardware to behave honestly may be too strong of an assumption for at least two reasons. First, having only black-box access to a piece of hardware makes it virtually impossible to verify whether the hardware provides the claimed guarantees of security and privacy. Second, recent news on state-level adversaries corrupting security services[3] have shown that subverted hardware is a realistic threat. In the context of anonymous attestation, if the hardware gets subverted (e.g., via firmware bugs or backdoors), it may output valid, innocent-looking signatures that, in reality, covertly encode identifying information (e.g., using special nonces). Such signatures may allow a remote adversary to trace the signer, thereby breaking anonymity. Using a similar channel, a subverted signer could also exfiltrate its secret key, and this would enable an external adversary to frame an honest signer, for example by signing bogus messages on its behalf.

1.1 Our Contribution

We continue the study of subversion-resilient anonymous attestation and we focus on Enhanced Privacy ID (EPID) [9,10], an anonymous attestation scheme that is currently deployed on commodity trusted execution environments like Intel SGX. Our contribution is twofold: we first formalize the notion of *Subversion-Resilient EPID* (SR-EPID), and we propose a realization in bilinear groups.

The Model of Subversion-Resilient EPID. Enhanced Privacy ID is essentially a privacy-enhanced group signature where the group manager cannot trace a signature but signers can be revoked. In the context of remote attestation, a group member is instantiated by its signing component (the "signer"), which is typically a piece of hardware.

To counter subverted signers, our idea is to enhance the model by adding a "sanitizer" party whose goal is to ensure that no covert channel is established between a potentially subverted signer and external adversaries.[4] In practical application scenarios, the sanitizer could run on the same host of the signer (e.g., on a phone to sanitize signatures issued by the SIM card), or on a separate one (e.g., on a corporate firewall to sanitize signatures issued by local machines).

Compared to a subversion-resilient anonymous attestation scheme that uses split-signatures [11], our approach comes with multiple benefits. First, signature

---

[3] https://snowdenarchive.cjfe.org/.

[4] Adding a party between the potentially subverted signer and the outside world is necessary, as the signer could exfiltrate arbitrary information otherwise [11].

generation is non-interactive and the communication flow is unidirectional from the signer to the sanitizer, on to the verifier. Thus, our design decreases signing latency and provides more flexibility as the sanitization of a signature does not need to be done online. Another benefit of our design is the fact that the sanitizer holds no secret. This means that if a memory leak occurs on the sanitizer, one has nothing to recover but public information. Differently, in a split signature approach, security properties no longer hold if the TPM is subverted and the key share of its host is leaked.

The idea of adding a sanitizer to mitigate subversion attacks in anonymous attestation is inspired by that of using a cryptographic reverse firewall of Mironov and Stephens-Davidowitz [29]. Besides subversion-resilient unforgeability (as in Ateniese, Magri and Venturi [3]), in an EPID scheme we have to guarantee additional properties such as anonymity and non-frameability, as well as to deal with the complications of supporting revocation. Formalizing all these properties in rigorous definitions is a significant contribution of this paper.

We acknowledge that adding a sanitizer in this unidirectional communication channel also comes with the drawback that, when the signer is honest (i.e., not subverted), then for anonymity to hold we still need the sanitizer to be trusted. This is an inherent limitation of our model since the sanitizer is the last to speak in the protocol and can always establish a channel with the adversary[5]. Since our sanitizer does not hold a secret, a potential way to reduce trust on it can be to distribute its re-randomization procedure across multiple parties. Designing such a protocol does not seem straightforward as one should consider, for example, rushing adversaries and therefore it is left as future work.

As a byproduct of our new definitions of SR-EPID, we obtain a careful formalization of the notion of unforgeability for (non-subversion-resilient) EPID schemes, or more broadly, for group signature schemes with both key-revocation mechanisms and a blind join protocol. Compared to the previous definition of [10], ours formalizes several technical aspects that in [10] were essentially expressed only in words and left to the reader's interpretation. See the full version of this paper [20] for more details.

Our SR-EPID in Bilinear Groups. Our next contribution is an efficient construction of a SR-EPID based on bilinear pairings. Our starting point is the classical blueprint of group signature schemes where: (I) the group manager holds the secret key of a signature scheme; (II) during the join protocol the group manager creates a blind signature σ_y on a value y private to the prospective group member, and both σ and y are the group member's secret key; (III) a signature σ_M on message M is a signature of knowledge for M of a σ_y that verifies for y and the group public key. (IV) Finally, to support revocation and linkability, a signature σ_M is bound to an arbitrary basename B and contains a pseudo-random token $R_B = f_y(B)$. Without knowing y the token looks random (and thus hides the signer's identity) but, at the same time, can be efficiently checked

---

[5] This is not the case for the unforgeability and non-frameability properties for which we do consider the case of malicious sanitizers for honest signers.

against a revoked key y^*. That is, the verifier checks if $R_B = f_{y^*}(B)$ for all the y^* in the revocation list. Similarly, a signer that allows for linkability of its signatures may accept to produce multiple signatures on the same basename; such signatures could be easily linked as they carry the same token.

Our first idea to contrast subversion attacks is to let the sanitizer re-randomize every signature σ_M produced by the signer, sanitizing in this way the (possibly malicious) randomness chosen by the signer encodes a covert channel. We achieve this by employing re-randomizable NIZKs in step (III).

This is not the only possible attack vector between a subverted signer and an external adversary. For example, the signer may come with an hardcoded value y known to the external adversary so that all the (valid) signatures produced by the signer can be easily traced. To counter this class of attacks we let the sanitizer contribute with its randomness to the choice of y during the join protocol. Even further, we require the sanitizer to re-randomize any message sent to the group manager during the join protocol. Finally, another potential attack is that at any moment after the join protocol, the signer may switch to creating signatures by using a hardcoded secret $y', \sigma_{y'}$. As above, an external party equipped with y' could track those signatures. To contrast this class of attacks, we require the signer to produce, along with every signature σ_M, a proof π_σ that is verified by the sanitizer using a dedicated verification token and that ensures that the signer is using the same secret y used in the join protocol; if the check passes, the sanitizer strips off π_σ and returns a re-randomization of σ_M. Our model diverges from the cryptographic reverse firewall framework of [29] because of the verification token mechanism. Looking ahead, this is not simply a limitation of our scheme but more generally we can show that EPID schemes that admit secret-key based revocation cannot have a cryptographic reverse firewall, we give more details in Sect. 2.2.

The description above gives an high-level overview of the main ideas that we introduced in the protocol to counter subversion attacks. A significant technical contribution in the design of our construction is a set of techniques that we introduced to reconcile our extensive use of malleable NIZKs (and in particular, Groth-Sahai proofs [26]) with the goal of obtaining an efficient SR-EPID scheme. The main problem to prove security of our scheme is that we need the NIZK to be malleable and to have a flavor of simulation-extractable soundness.[6] In the EPID of [10], simulation-extractable soundness is also needed, but it is obtained for free by using Fiat-Shamir (Faust et al. [21]). In our case, this approach is not viable because the Fiat-Shamir compiler breaks any chance for re-randomizability. One could use a re-randomizable and (controlled) simulation-extractable NIZK (Chase et al. [16]), but in practice these tools are very expensive—they would require hundreds of pairings for verification and hundreds of group elements for the proofs. To overcome this problem, we propose a combination of (plain) GS proofs with the random oracle model. Briefly speaking, we use the random oracle

---

[6] In fact, on one hand we have to extract the witness from the adversary's forgery, while on the other hand we rely on zero-knowledge to disable any covert channel from subverted signers.

to generate the common reference string that will be used by the GS proof system and use the property that, in perfectly-hiding mode, this CRS can be created from a uniform random string[7]. In this way we can program the random oracle to produce extractable common reference strings for the forged signature made by the adversary and for the messages in the join protocol with corrupted members, and program the random oracle to have perfectly-hiding common reference strings for all the material that the reduction needs to simulate. Our technique is a reminiscence of techniques based on programmable hash functions [14] and linearly homomorphic signatures [27]. However, our ROM-based technique enables for more efficient schemes with *unbounded* simulation soundness. The resulting scheme provides the same functionality of EPID, tolerates subverted signers, and features signatures that are shorter than the ones in [10] for reasonable sizes of the revocation list: ours have $28 + 2n$ group elements whereas EPID signatures have $8+5n$, where n is the size of the revocation list (i.e., ours are shorter already for $n \geq 7$).

1.2   Related Work

Subversion-resilient signatures and Cryptographic Reverse Firewalls. Ateniese et al. [3] study subversion-resilient signature schemes and show that unique signatures as well as the use of a cryptographic reverse firewall (RF) of [29] ensure unforgeability despite a subverted signing algorithm. Chakraborty et al. [15] show how to use RF in multi-party settings where the adversary can fully corrupt all but one party, while the remaining parties are corrupt in a functionality-preserving way. Ganesh, Magri and Venturi [24] study the security properties of RF for the concrete case of interactive proof systems. Chen et al. [17] introduce malleable smooth projective hash functions and show how to use them in a modular way to construct RF for several cryptographic protocols.

Our scheme could be interpreted as a new EPID scheme equipped with a cryptographic reverse firewall for the *join protocol* that allows a new party to join the group, and a cryptograhic reverse firewall that protects the signatures sent by the signer. However, as mentioned in Sect. 1.1, there are some technical details that differentiate our model to the cryptographic reverse firewall framework.

Subversion-resilient anonymous attestation. Camenisch et al. [12] provide a Universally Composable (UC) definition for Direct Anonymous Attestation (DAA) that guarantees privacy despite a subverted TPM. The DAA scheme presented in [12] leverages dual-mode signatures of Camenisch and Lehmann [13] and builds upon the ideas of Bellare and Sandhu [7] to provide a signature scheme where the signing key is split between the host and the TPM. Later on, Camenisch *et al.* [11] build on the same idea of [12] and show a UC-secure DAA scheme that requires only minor changes to the TPM 2.0 interface and tolerates a subverted TPM by splitting the signing key between the host and the TPM.

---

[7] In particular, we need cryptographic hash functions that allow to hash directly on $\mathbb{G}_1$ and on $\mathbb{G}_2$, see Galbraith *et al.* [23].

We argue that splitting the signing key between the potentially subverted hardware (e.g., the TPM) and the host to achieve resilience to subversions is viable in scenarios where (i) the channel between the two parties has low latency—because of the interactive nature of the signing protocol—and (ii) the user can trust the host. Both conditions holds for TPM scenarios. In particular, a TPM is soldered to the motherboard of the host and has a high-speed bus to the main processor. Also, the TPM manufacturer is usually different from the one of the main processor—hence, the user may trust the latter but not the former. In case of TEEs such as Intel SGX, we note that there is no real separation between the TEE and the main processor. Thus, it would be hard to justify an untrusted TEE and a trusted processor since, in reality, they lie on the same die and are shipped by the same manufacturer. As such, the entity in charge of preventing the TEE from exfiltrating information (i.e., the one holding a share of the signing key) must be placed elsewhere along the channel between the TEE and the verifier, thereby paying a latency penalty to generate signatures.

We think that our solution is more suitable for TEE platforms like Intel SGX. In particular, the non-interactive nature of the signing protocol allows us to place the sanitizer "away" from the signer, without impact on performance. Thus, the sanitizer may be instantiated by a co-processor next to the TEE, or it may run on a company gateway that sanitizes attestations produced by hosts within the company network before they are sent out. As the sanitizer and the potentially subverted hardware may run on different platforms, they may come from different manufacturers. For example, one could pick an AMD or Risc-V processor to sanitize an Intel-based TEE such as SGX. A sanitizer may even be built by combining different COTS hardware as [28].

Other models for subversion resilience. Fischlin and Mazaheri introduce "self-guarding" cryptographic protocols [22] based on the assumption of a secure initial phase where the algorithm was genuine. Kleptographic attacks, introduced by Young and Yung [32], assume subverted implementations of standard cryptographic primitives. Later on, Bellare et al. [6] and Russell et al. [30] studied subverted symmetric encryption schemes and subverted key-generation routines, respectively. Russell et al. [31] propose for the first time an IND-CPA-secure encryption scheme that remains secure even in case of a subversion-capable adversary. Ateniese et al. [2] introduce an "immunizer" that takes as input a cryptographic primitive and augments it with subversion resilience. They introduce an immunizer in the plain model for a number of deterministic primitives (with a randomized key generation routine). Chow et al. [18], construct secure digital signature schemes in the presence of kleptographic attacks, by leveraging an offline phase to test the potentially subverted implementation in a black-box manner.

2   Subversion-Resilient Enhanced Privacy ID

Background on EPID. Enhanced Privacy ID is essentially a privacy-enhanced group signature scheme. Compared to classic group signatures (see Bellare *et al.* [5]), EPID drops the ability of the group manager to trace signatures, and adds novel revocation mechanisms. In particular, EPID allows to revoke a group member by adding its private key to a revocation list named PrivRL; while verifying a signature σ, the verification algorithm checks that none of the private keys in PrivRL may have produced σ. In case the secret key of a misbehaving group member did not leak, EPID can still revoke that member by using one of its signatures. That is, EPID accounts for an additional revocation list, named SigRL, containing signatures of revoked members.

Security notions for EPID include anonymity and unforgeability. Informally, anonymity ensures that signatures are not traceable by any party, including the group manager. Unforgeability ensures that only non-revoked group members can generate valid signatures. We note that EPID does not account for pseudonymous signatures. The latter allow for a sort of controlled linkability as each signature is bound to a "basename", and one can easily tell—via a Link algorithm— whether two signatures on the same basename where produced by the same group member. This signature mode is actually available in DAA and in the version of EPID used by Intel SGX. Further, DAA defines a security property tailored to pseudonymous signatures called *non-frameability*. Informally, non-frameability ensures that an adversary that corrupts the group manager cannot create a signature on a message M and basename bsn, that links to a signature of an honest group member. Given the usefulness of pseudonymous signatures in real-world deployments, we decide to include them—along with a definition of non-frameability—in our definition of subversion-resilient EPID. The study of subversion-resilient non-frameability can be found in the full version [20].

2.1 Subversion-Resilient EPID

For simplicity, we assume each signer to be paired with a sanitizer and we denote a pair of signer-sanitizer as a "platform".[8] In the security experiments we denote with $\mathcal{I}$ the issuer, with $\mathcal{S}$ the sanitizer, with $\mathcal{M}$ the signer, and with $\mathcal{P}$ the platform. Very often we refer to the signer as the "hardware" or the "machine" (thus the letter $\mathcal{M}$ for our notation). We assume group members to be platforms and gear security definition towards them.[9] Our notion of SR-EPID is designed so that (i) the sanitizer participates to the join protocol obtaining a verification token as output, and (ii) the sanitizer sanitizes signatures to avoid covert channel based on maliciously-sampled randomness using such verification token. The resulting syntax is a generalization of EPID that adds a Sanitize algorithm and modifies the original Join and Sig algorithms.

Syntax of Subversion-Resilient EPID. We denote by $\langle d, e, f \rangle \leftarrow P_{\mathcal{A},\mathcal{B},\mathcal{C}}\langle a, b, c \rangle$ an interactive protocol P between parties $\mathcal{A}$, $\mathcal{B}$ and $\mathcal{C}$ where a, b, c (resp. d, e, f) are

---

[8] In practical deployments a sanitizer may sanitize signatures of multiple signers and a single signer may have multiple sanitizers.

[9] For example, the anonymity definition focuses on an adversary that must tell which, out of two platforms, outputs the challenge signature.

the local inputs (resp. outputs) of $\mathcal{A}$, $\mathcal{B}$ and $\mathcal{C}$, respectively. An SR-EPID consists of an interactive protocol Join and algorithms: Init, Setup, Sig, Ver, Sanitize. All the algorithms (and the protocol) but Init take as input public parameters (generated by Init); for readability reasons, we keep this input implicit.

$\mathsf{Init}(1^\lambda) \rightarrow \mathsf{pub}$. This algorithm takes as input the security parameter λ and outputs public parameters pub.

$\mathsf{Setup}(\mathsf{pub}) \rightarrow (\mathsf{gpk}, \mathsf{isk})$. This algorithm takes the public parameters pub and outputs a group public key gpk and an issuing secret key isk for the issuer $\mathcal{I}$.

$\mathsf{Join}_{\mathcal{I}, \mathcal{S}_i, \mathcal{M}_i}\langle(\mathsf{gpk}, \mathsf{isk}), \mathsf{gpk}, \mathsf{gpk})\rangle \rightarrow \langle b, (b, \mathsf{svt}_i), \mathsf{sk}_i\rangle$. This is a protocol between the issuer $\mathcal{I}$, a sanitizer $\mathcal{S}_i$ and a signer $\mathcal{M}_i$. The issuer inputs $(\mathsf{gpk}, \mathsf{isk})$, while the other parties only input gpk. At the end of the protocol, $\mathcal{I}$ obtains a bit b indicating if the protocol terminated successfully, $\mathcal{M}_i$ obtains private key sk_i, and $\mathcal{S}_i$ obtains a sanitizer verification token svt_i and the same bit b of $\mathcal{I}$.

$\mathsf{Sig}(\mathsf{gpk}, \mathsf{sk}_i, \mathsf{bsn}, M, \mathsf{SigRL}) \rightarrow \bot/(\sigma, \pi_\sigma)$. The signing algorithm takes as input $\mathsf{gpk}, \mathsf{sk}_i$, a basename bsn, a message M, and a signature based revocation list SigRL. It outputs a signature σ and a proof π_σ, or an error $\bot$.

$\mathsf{Ver}(\mathsf{gpk}, \mathsf{bsn}, M, \sigma, \mathsf{SigRL}, \mathsf{PrivRL}) \rightarrow 0/1$. The verification algorithm takes as input gpk, bsn, M, σ, a signature based revocation list SigRL, and a private key based revocation list PrivRL. It outputs a bit.

$\mathsf{Sanitize}(\mathsf{gpk}, \mathsf{bsn}, M, (\sigma, \pi_\sigma), \mathsf{SigRL}, \mathsf{svt}_i) \rightarrow \bot/\sigma'$. The sanitization algorithm takes as input gpk, a basename bsn, a message M, a signature σ with corresponding proof π_σ, a signature based revocation list SigRL, and a sanitizer verification token svt_i. It outputs either $\bot$ or a sanitized signature σ'.

$\mathsf{Link}(\mathsf{gpk}, \mathsf{bsn}, M_1, \sigma_1, M_2, \sigma_2) \rightarrow 0/1$. The linking algorithm takes as input gpk, a basename bsn, and two tuples M_1, σ_1 and M_2, σ_2 and output a bit.

The last algorithm outputs 1 if the two signatures were generated by the same signer using the same basename (we call such property *linking correctness*).

In our syntax, we assume PrivRL to be a set of private keys $\{\mathsf{sk}_i\}_i$, and SigRL to be a set of triples $\{(\mathsf{bsn}_i, M_i, \sigma_i)\}_i$, each consisting of a basename, a message and a signature. We define two forms of correctness. To keep the syntax more light we let $\mathsf{Sig}(\mathsf{gpk}, \mathsf{sk}, \mathsf{bsn}, M)$ be equal to $\mathsf{Sig}(\mathsf{gpk}, \mathsf{sk}, \mathsf{bsn}, M, \emptyset)$, and $\mathsf{Ver}(\mathsf{gpk}, \mathsf{bsn}, M, \sigma)$ be equal to $\mathsf{Ver}(\mathsf{gpk}, \mathsf{bsn}, M, \sigma, \emptyset, \emptyset)$.

Definition 1 (Correctness, without revocation lists). *We say that an SR-EPID scheme satisfies standard correctness if for any* $\mathsf{pub} \leftarrow \mathsf{Init}(1^\lambda)$, *any* $(\mathsf{gpk}, \mathsf{gsk}) \leftarrow \mathsf{Setup}(\mathsf{pub})$, *any* $\langle b, (b, \mathsf{svt}), \mathsf{sk}\rangle \leftarrow \mathsf{Join}\langle(\mathsf{gpk}, \mathsf{gsk}), \mathsf{gpk}, \mathsf{gpk})\rangle$ *such that* $b = 1$, *and for any* bsn, M, $(\sigma, \pi_\sigma) \leftarrow \mathsf{Sig}(\mathsf{gpk}, \mathsf{sk}, \mathsf{bsn}, M)$, *and any* $\sigma' \leftarrow \mathsf{Sanitize}(\mathsf{gpk}, \mathsf{bsn}, M, (\sigma, \pi_\sigma), \mathsf{svt})$ *we have that both* $\mathsf{Ver}(\mathsf{gpk}, \mathsf{bsn}, M, \sigma) = 1$ *and* $\mathsf{Ver}(\mathsf{gpk}, \mathsf{bsn}, M, \sigma') = 1$.

Let $\Sigma_{\mathsf{gpk}, \mathsf{sk}}$ be the set of triples for any basename, message and signature where the signature algorithm can produce the signature with input gpk and the secret key sk (thus enumerating over all possible basenames and messages).

Definition 2 (Correctness, with revocation lists). *We say that an SR-EPID scheme satisfies correctness if for any* pub $\leftarrow$ Init(1^λ), *any* (gpk, gsk) $\leftarrow$ Setup(pub), *any* $\langle b, (b, \mathsf{svt}), \mathsf{sk} \rangle \leftarrow$ Join$\langle$(gpk, gsk), gpk, gpk)$\rangle$ *such that* $b = 1$, *and for any* bsn, M, *for any* PrivRL *and* SigRL, *any* $(\sigma_0, \pi_\sigma) \leftarrow$ Sig(gpk, sk, bsn, M, SigRL) *and any* $\sigma_1 \leftarrow$ Sanitize(gpk, bsn, M, (σ_0, π_σ), SigRL, svt) *we have:*

$$\Sigma_{\mathsf{gpk,sk}} \cap \mathsf{SigRL} = \emptyset \Rightarrow \sigma_0 \neq \bot \tag{1}$$

$$\mathsf{sk} \notin \mathsf{PrivRL} \Rightarrow \forall b' \in \{0, 1\} : \mathsf{Ver}(\mathsf{gpk}, \mathsf{bsn}, M, \sigma_{b'}, \mathsf{SigRL}, \mathsf{PrivRL}) = 1 \tag{2}$$

2.2   Subversion-Resilient Security

The security of an SR-EPID scheme is defined by three main properties, namely anonymity, unforgeability, and non-frameability. We consider subverted signers that can arbitrarily behave during the join protocol and, in particular, abort the execution of the protocol. However, once the join protocol is completed we assume that signers, although subverted, maintain a correct "input-output behavior". That is, a subverted signer produces a valid signature to a message and basename, namely a signature that verifies if the signer were not revoked, but that could be arbitrarily (and maliciously) distributed over the set of all valid signatures. We formalize this idea in the following assumption.

Assumption 1. Let Π be a SR-EPID. We assume that for any public parameter pub, any adversary $\mathcal{A}$, any gpk and auxiliary information aux, and any (possibly adaptively chosen) sequence of tuples $(\mathsf{bsn}_1, M_1), \ldots, (\mathsf{bsn}_q, M_q)$, let $\langle b, (b', \mathsf{svt}), \mathsf{state}_1 \rangle$ be a possible output of the join protocol Join$_{\mathcal{A},\mathcal{S},\mathcal{M}}\langle$(gpk, aux), gpk, (gpk, aux))$\rangle$ conditioned on $b' = 1$ or a possible output of the join protocol Join$_{\mathcal{I},\mathcal{A},\mathcal{M}}\langle$(gpk, aux), gpk, (gpk, aux))$\rangle$ conditioned on $b = 1$ and let $\sigma_i, \mathsf{state}_i \leftarrow \mathcal{M}_i(\mathsf{state}_{i-1}, M_i, \mathsf{bsn}_i)$ for $i = 1, \ldots, q$ then $\forall i \in [q] : \mathsf{Ver}(\mathsf{gpk}, M_1, \mathsf{bsn}_1, \sigma_i) = 1$.

The assumption models the fact that, if signers can be subverted, a signer should be considered safe as long as it does not return errors when it comes to generating signatures. The occurrence of such an error should alert a sanitizer anyway. First, such an error can occur if one of the signatures produced by the signer was included in the signature based revocation list: if the list was honestly created, it means that the signer has been revoked; if the list was maliciously crafted, then the signature request may constitute an attempt to deanonymize the signer. Second, if the errors are arbitrary then they inevitably enable to signal any kind of information from the signer.

Macros for the Join Protocol and Signature generation. As mentioned, the join protocol is a three-party protocol with the sanitizer being in the middle. To simplify the already heavy notation, we define the macro Join($\mathcal{M}$, state$_{\mathcal{S}}$, state$_{\mathcal{M}}$, $\gamma_{\mathcal{I}}$) which identifies one full round of the join protocol from the issuer point of view with an honest sanitizer and a machine $\mathcal{M}$. In more detail, the macro takes as input the description of the (possibly subverted) machine $\mathcal{M}$, the state of the sanitizer $\text{state}_\mathcal{S}$, the state of the machine $\text{state}_\mathcal{M}$ and the message sent by the issuer $\gamma_\mathcal{I}$, and it identifies the following set of actions:

$\underline{\text{Join}(\mathcal{M}, \text{state}_\mathcal{S}, \text{state}_\mathcal{M}, \gamma_\mathcal{I})}$:
1. $(\gamma'_\mathcal{S}, \text{state}'_\mathcal{S}) \leftarrow \mathcal{S}.\text{Join}(\text{gpk}, \text{state}_\mathcal{S}, \gamma_\mathcal{I})$;
2. $(\gamma_\mathcal{M}, \text{state}'_\mathcal{M}) \leftarrow \mathcal{M}.\text{Join}(\text{gpk}, \text{state}_\mathcal{M}, \gamma'_\mathcal{S})$;
3. $(\gamma_\mathcal{S}, \text{state}''_\mathcal{S}) \leftarrow \mathcal{S}.\text{Join}(\text{gpk}, \text{state}'_\mathcal{M}, \gamma_\mathcal{M})$;
4. Output $(\text{state}''_\mathcal{S}, \text{state}'_\mathcal{M}, \gamma_\mathcal{S})$.

Notice the procedures additionally take as input the group public key gpk, which we keep implicit. Similarly, the signature procedure is a two-phase protocol between the signer and the sanitizer for which we define the macro:

$\underline{\text{Sig}(\mathcal{M}, \text{state}_\mathcal{M}, \text{svt}, \text{bsn}, M, \text{SigRL})}$:
1. $(\sigma', \pi'_\sigma, \text{state}'_\mathcal{M}) \leftarrow \mathcal{M}.\text{Sig}(\text{state}_\mathcal{M}, \text{bsn}, M, \text{SigRL})$;
2. if $\text{svt} \neq \bot$ then $\sigma \leftarrow \text{Sanitize}(\text{gpk}, \text{bsn}, M^*, (\sigma', \pi'_\sigma), \text{SigRL}, \text{svt})$;
3. else $\sigma \leftarrow \sigma'$;
4. Output $(\text{state}'_\mathcal{M}, \sigma)$.

The macro additionally checks in step 2 that svt is a valid string. We use this check to discriminate the case when the sanitizer is corrupted.

Subversion-Resilient Anonymity. This notion formalizes the idea that an adversarial issuer cannot identify a group member through the signatures it produces. Recall that we assume a signer $\mathcal{M}_i$ to be paired with a sanitizer $\mathcal{S}_i$; we denote the platform constituted by $\mathcal{M}_i$ and $\mathcal{S}_i$ with $\mathcal{P}_i$. We assume $\mathcal{M}_i$ to be subverted, i.e., it runs an adversarially specified program, while $\mathcal{S}_i$ is honest. The case when both $\mathcal{M}_i$ and $\mathcal{S}_i$ are corrupted is meaningless for anonymity since the adversary controls all the relevant parties. The remaining case in which $\mathcal{M}_i$ is honest but $\mathcal{S}_i$ is corrupted is also hopeless for anonymity since a corrupted sanitizer could always maul the outputs of the signer in order to reveal its identity.

We formalize subversion-resilient anonymity for SR-EPID in a security experiment that appears in Fig. 1, and we formally define anonymity as follows.

Definition 3. *Consider the experiment described in Fig. 1. We say that an SR-EPID Π is anonymous if and only if for any PPT adversary $\mathcal{A}$:*

$$\mathbf{Adv}^{\text{anon}}_{\mathcal{A},\Pi}(\lambda) := |\Pr\left[\mathbf{Exp}^{\text{anon}}_{\mathcal{A},\Pi}(\lambda, 0) = 1\right] - \Pr\left[\mathbf{Exp}^{\text{anon}}_{\mathcal{A},\Pi}(\lambda, 1) = 1\right]| \in \text{negl}(\lambda).$$

Here we provide an intuitive explanation of the anonymity experiment. The idea is that the adversary plays the role of the issuer, i.e., it selects the group public key, and it can do the following: (1) ask platforms with subverted signers to join the system; (2) ask platforms with subverted signers to sign messages; (3) corrupt platforms. For (1), it means that the adversary specifies the code of a signer $\mathcal{M}_i$ that, together with an honest sanitizer $\mathcal{S}_i$, run the Join protocol with the adversary playing the role of the issuer. For (2), a subverted signer $\mathcal{M}_i$ produced a signature that is sanitized by $\mathcal{S}_i$ and then delivered to the adversary. Finally, (3) models a full corruption of the platform in which the adversary learns the secret key sk_i obtained by $\mathcal{M}_i$ at the end of its Join protocol.

The adversary can choose two platforms $(\mathcal{P}_{i_0}, \mathcal{P}_{i_1})$, a basename bsn^*, and a message M^* and it receives a *sanitized* signature on M^*, bsn^* produced by one of the two platforms. The goal of the adversary is to figure out which platform produced the signature. In order to avoid trivial attacks the two "challenge" platforms must be non-corrupted and none of their signatures can be included in the SigRL used to produce the challenge signature. Further, if the adversary has previously requested a signature with bsn^* form either platform, the challenger aborts. Similarly, after seeing the challenge signature, the adversary may not ask for a signature by any of the challenge platforms on basename bsn^*.

Technical details. The structure is the one depicted earlier: the adversary chooses the group public key on input the public parameters and then starts interacting with the oracle $\mathcal{C}$. The experiment maintains lists $L_{join}, L_{usr}, L_{corr}$ to book-keep information on the state of the Join protocol sessions, and the list of non-corrupted and corrupted platforms, respectively. Also, it maintains a flag Bad, initialized to false, which is turned to true whenever the adversary violates the rules of the experiments (see below). At some point the adversary outputs a message M^*, a basename bsn^*, and two indices i_0, i_1, along with a signature revocation list SigRL^*; it receives a sanitized signature generated using the sub-verted signer $\mathcal{M}_{i_b}$. In line 8 of $\mathbf{Exp}_{\mathcal{A},\Pi}^{anon}(\lambda, b)$ we ensure that the adversary did not previously query for a signature with basename bsn^* by one of the challenge platforms; if that is the case, the adversary could trivially win by using the Link algorithm. In line 11 of $\mathbf{Exp}_{\mathcal{A},\Pi}^{anon}(\lambda, b)$ we ensure that both challenge platforms generate valid signatures, after sanitization. Indeed if a difference would occur (e.g., one of them is $\perp$), the adversary could trivially win the game. For example, this would be the case if the SigRL chosen by $\mathcal{A}$ would contain a signature from, e.g., $\mathcal{M}_{i_0}$. Similar checks are done in lines 16–20 of the $\mathcal{C}$ oracle upon a signing query that involves one of the challenge platforms, say $i_{1-\beta}$. The code of those lines essentially ensure that the queried basename is not the challenge one, and that the other challenge platform i_β would generate a signature on the same message M that is valid iff so is the one generated by $i_{1-\beta}$. Again if such a difference would occur the adversary could trivially distinguish and win the experiment. Similarly to the other case, this could occur if the queried SigRL contains a signature of (only) one of the challenge platforms.

We stress that the mechanism that uses the verification tokens is necessary[10]. Indeed, consider the definition above where the svt and the proof π_σ are missing: An attacker can first performs two join protocols one with a subverted machine $\tilde{\mathcal{M}}$ with hardcoded a secret key $\tilde{\mathsf{sk}}$ that during joining time acts honestly, thus

---

[10] Here is where our model diverges from the cryptographic reverse firewall framework of [29].

Experiment $\mathbf{Exp}^{\text{anon}}_{\mathcal{A},\Pi}(\lambda, b)$

1 : $L_{join}, L_{usr}, L_{corr} \leftarrow \emptyset$; $post \leftarrow 0$; Bad $\leftarrow$ true
2 : pub $\leftarrow$ Init(1^λ); gpk $\leftarrow \mathcal{A}(\text{pub})$;
3 : $(\text{bsn}^*, M^*, i_0, i_1, \text{SigRL}^*) \leftarrow \mathcal{A}(\text{gpk})^{\mathcal{C}(\text{gpk}, \cdot)}$; $post \leftarrow 1$;
4 : **if** $(i_0, *, *, *, *) \notin L_{usr} \vee (i_1, *, *, *, *) \notin L_{usr}$ **then** Bad$\leftarrow$true;
5 : **if** VerSigRL(gpk, SigRL*) $= 0$ **then** Bad$\leftarrow$true
6 : **for** $j = 0, 1$ **do** :
7 :   Retrieve $(i_j, \mathcal{M}_{i_j}, \text{state}_{i_j}, \text{svt}_{i_j}, B_{i_j})$ from L_{usr};
8 :   **if** bsn$^* \in B_{i_j}$ **then** Bad$\leftarrow$true
9 : $(\text{state}'_{i_j}, \sigma_j) \leftarrow \text{Sig}(\mathcal{M}_{i_j}, \text{state}_{i_j}, \text{svt}_{i_j}, \text{bsn}, M, \text{SigRL})$;
10 :   Update $(i_j, \mathcal{M}_{i_j}, \text{state}'_{i_j}, \text{svt}_{i_j}, B_{i_j} \cup \{\text{bsn}^*\})$ in L_{usr};
11 : **if** $\perp \in \{\sigma_0, \sigma_1\}$ **then** Bad$\leftarrow$true **else** $\sigma^* \leftarrow \sigma_b$;
12 : $b' \leftarrow \mathcal{A}(\sigma^*)^{\mathcal{C}(\text{gpk}, \cdot)}$;
13 : **if** Bad $=$ false **return** b'; **else return** $\tilde{b} \leftarrow_\$ \{0, 1\}$.

Oracle $\mathcal{C}(\text{gsk}, \cdot)$

1 : **Upon query** $(\text{join}, i, \gamma_\mathcal{I})$:
2 :   Retrieve $(i, \mathcal{M}_i, \text{state}_\mathcal{S}, \text{state}_\mathcal{M})$ from L_{join},;
3 :   If not find parse $\gamma_\mathcal{I} = \mathcal{M}_i$ and add $(i, \mathcal{M}_i, \perp, \perp)$ in L_{join} and **return** ;
4 : $(\text{state}''_\mathcal{S}, \text{state}'_\mathcal{M}, \gamma_\mathcal{S}) \leftarrow \text{Join}(\mathcal{M}_i, \text{state}_\mathcal{S}, \text{state}_\mathcal{M}, \gamma_\mathcal{I})$;
5 :   Store $(i, \mathcal{M}_i, \text{state}''_\mathcal{S}, \text{state}'_\mathcal{M})$ in L_{join};
6 :   **if** $\gamma_\mathcal{S} = $ concluded **then**
7 : $\text{svt}_i \leftarrow \text{state}''_\mathcal{S}$, store $(i, \mathcal{M}_i, \text{state}'_\mathcal{M}, \text{svt}_i, \emptyset)$ in L_{usr}; **return** $(\gamma_\mathcal{S}, \text{svt}_i)$;
8 :   **else return** $\gamma_\mathcal{S}$.
9 : **Upon query** $(\text{sign}, i, \text{bsn}, M, \text{SigRL})$:
10 :   **if** $(i, *, *, *, *) \notin L_{usr}$ **then** Bad$\leftarrow$true;
11 :   **else** retrieve $(i, \mathcal{M}_i, \text{state}_i, \text{svt}_i, B_i) \in L_{usr}$;
12 : $(\text{state}'_i, \sigma) \leftarrow \text{Sig}(\mathcal{M}_i, \text{state}_i, \text{svt}_i, \text{bsn}, M, \text{SigRL})$;
13 :   Update $(i, \mathcal{M}_i, \text{state}'_i, \text{svt}_i, B_i \cup \{\text{bsn}\})$;
14 :   **if** $post = 0$ or $i \notin \{i_0, i_1\}$ **then return** σ
15 :   **else** let $i = i_\beta$ and $\beta \in \{0, 1\}$;
16 :   **if** bsn $= $ bsn* **then** Bad$\leftarrow$true;
17 :   Let $i = i_{1-\beta}$, retrieve $(i_\beta, \mathcal{M}_{i_\beta}, \text{state}_{i_\beta}, \text{svt}_{i_\beta}, B_{i_\beta}) \in L_{usr}$;
18 : $(\text{state}'_{i_\beta}, \tilde{\sigma}) \leftarrow \text{Sig}(\mathcal{M}_{i_\beta}, \text{state}_{i_\beta}, \text{svt}_{i_\beta}, \text{bsn}, M, \text{SigRL})$;
19 :   Update $(i_\beta, \mathcal{M}_{i_\beta}, \text{state}'_{i_\beta}, \text{svt}_{i_\beta}, B_{i_\beta} \cup \{\text{bsn}\})$ in L_{usr};
20 :   **if** $\perp \in \{\sigma, \tilde{\sigma}\}$ **then** Bad$\leftarrow$true; **endif return** σ;
21 : **Upon query** $(\text{corrupt}, i)$:
22 :   **if** $post = 1 \wedge i \in \{i_0, i_1\}$ **then** Bad$\leftarrow$true;
23 :   **else** retrieve $(i, \mathcal{M}_i, \text{state}_i, \text{svt}_i)$ from L_{usr};
24 :   move the tuple from L_{usr} to L_{cor};
25 :   **return** $(\text{state}_i, \text{svt}_i)$.

Fig. 1. Subversion-resilient anonymity experiment.

obtaining a new fresh secret key, but that computes valid signature using the hardcoded secret key. Suppose the scheme has a secret-key based revocation mechanism, then the adversary that knows $\tilde{\mathsf{sk}}$ can easily distinguish the subverted machine from an honest machine. In particular, it could verify the challenge signature using the revocation list $\{\tilde{\mathsf{sk}}\}$. The sanitizer, which only posses public information, has no way to identify that a different secret key has been used and avoid this attack. We formalize the above intuition in the full version of this paper. Another aspect of the anonymity experiment that we would like to point out is that the adversary receives the verification token immediately after the Join protocol is over. This models the fact the adversary could have access to the internal state of an honest sanitizer (except for its random tape), and this does not break anonymity.

Subversion-Resilient Unforgeability. This notion formalizes the idea that an adversary who does not control the issuer cannot generate signatures on new messages on behalf of non-corrupted platforms. To model subversion attacks, we let the platform signer $\mathcal{M}_i$ be an adversarially specified program. The sanitizer $\mathcal{S}_i$ is instead honest (unless the platform is fully corrupted).

Here we provide an intuition of the notion. The adversary receives the group public key, and it can do the following: (1) ask platforms with subverted signers to join the system; (2) ask corrupted platforms to join the system; (3) ask platforms with subverted signer to sign messages; (4) corrupt platforms. For (1), it means that the adversary specifies the code of a signer $\mathcal{M}_i$ and that signer together with sanitizer $\mathcal{S}_i$, run the Join protocol where both the issuer and $\mathcal{S}_i$ are controlled by the challenger. For (2), the adversary runs the Join protocol with the challenger playing the role of the issuer, whereas both the signer $\mathcal{M}_i$ and the sanitizer $\mathcal{S}_i$ are fully controlled by the adversary. For (3), the adversary asks a platform that joined the system to create a signature using the subverted signing algorithm (specified in $\mathcal{M}_i$ at Join time), this signature is sanitized by $\mathcal{S}_i$ and given to the adversary. Finally, (4) simply models a full corruption of the platform in which the adversary learns the secret key sk_i obtained by $\mathcal{M}_i$ at the end of its Join protocol[11].

The adversary's goal is to produce a valid signature on a basename-message tuple bsn^*, M^*. On the one hand, we cannot require the tuple bsn^*, M^* to be fresh, since it is reasonable to assume that multiple platforms may sign the same bsn^*, M^*. On the other hand, strong unforgeability is impossible, as we require that the signatures must be valid before and after sanitization. To satisfy these two apparently contrasting requirements simultaneously, we instead require that the adversary's forgery does not link to any of the other queried signatures on the same basename-message tuple. This essentially guarantees that the forgery is not a trivial rerandomization of signature obtained through a signing query.

---

[11] Here the corruption is *adaptive* in the sense that the platform first joined honestly and later can be corrupted by the adversary but we assume *secure erasure* of the previous states of the sanitizer.

Since an SR-EPID is a (kind of) group signature and in the above game the adversary may have learnt the secret keys of some group members, we add some additional checks to formalize what is a forgery, so to avoid trivial unavoidable attacks. Intuitively, we want that the signature must verify with respect to a private-key revocation list PrivRL* (resp. signature-based revocation list SigRL*) that includes the secret keys of (resp. a signature from) all corrupted group members. These corrupted group members include both the ones that honestly joined the system and were later corrupted, and those that were already corrupted (i.e., adversarially controlled) at join time. Modeling which keys should be revoked is not straightforward though. The first issue is that in case of a corrupted platform joining the group, the challenger does not know what is the key obtained by the adversary. Essentially, unless we revoke exactly that key or a signature produced with that key, the adversary is able to create valid signatures on any message of its choice. The second issue is similar and involves cases when a platform with a subverted signer joins the group: the challenger obtains a secret key sk_i from the signer $\mathcal{M}_i$ at the end of the Join protocol, but $\mathcal{M}_i$ is subverted and thus we have no guarantee that sk_i is the "real" secret key.[12] To define forgeries, we solve these issues by assuming the existence of an extractor that, by knowing a trapdoor and seeing the transcript of the Join protocol between the issuer and the sanitizer, can extract a token uniquely linkable (via an efficient procedure) to the secret key that is supposed to correspond to such transcript. This definition is close to the notion of uniquely identifiable transcripts used by [8] for DAA schemes. We stress that the extractor does not exist in the real world and is only an artifact of the security definition.[13] A practical interpretation of our definition is that unforgeability is guaranteed under the assumption that the revocation system is "perfect", namely that one revokes all the secret keys, or signatures produced by those secret keys, that an adversary obtained by interacting with the issuer in the Join protocol.

Definition 4. *Consider the experiment described in Fig. 2. We say that an SR-EPID Π is unforgeable if there exist PPT algorithms* CheckTK, CheckSig, *and a PPT extractor* $\mathcal{E} = (\mathcal{E}_0, \mathcal{E}_1)$ *such that the following properties hold:*

1. *For any pair of keys* (gpk, isk) *in the support of* Setup(pub) *and for any (even adversarial)* tk, sk_1, sk_2 *it holds* (CheckTK(gpk, sk_1, tk) = 1 $\wedge$ CheckTK(gpk, sk_2, tk) = 1) $\Rightarrow$ $sk_1 = sk_2$. *(Namely, any* tk *is associated to one and only one* sk.*)*

2. *For any pair of keys* (gpk, isk) *in the support of* Setup(pub) *and for any (even adversarial)* tk, sk, M, bsn, σ, SigRL, PrivRL *such that* Ver(gpk, bsn, M, σ, SigRL, PrivRL) = 1 *and* Ver(gpk, bsn, M, σ, SigRL, PrivRL $\cup$ {sk}) = 0, *it is always the case that* CheckTK(gpk, sk, tk) = 0 $\vee$ CheckSig(gpk, tk, σ) = 1. *(Namely, the token* tk *and the algorithm* CheckSig *allow to verify if a signature comes from a specific secret key.)*

---

[12] For instance, $\mathcal{M}_i$ may store locally only an obfuscated or encrypted version of the secret key.

[13] More precisely, an extractor does not exist if in the real world the Init algorithm is realized in a trusted manner, akin to CRS generation in NIZK proof systems.

3. *For any PPT adversary $\mathcal{A}$,* $\mathbf{Adv}^{\mathrm{unf}}_{\mathcal{A},\mathcal{E},\Pi}(\lambda) := \Pr\left[\mathbf{Exp}^{\mathrm{unf}}_{\mathcal{A},\mathcal{E},\Pi}(\lambda) = 1\right] \in \mathsf{negl}(\lambda).$

4. *The distribution* $\{\mathsf{pub} \xleftarrow{\$} \mathsf{Init}(1^\lambda)\}_{\lambda \in \mathbb{N}}$ *and* $\{\mathsf{pub}|\mathsf{pub}, \mathsf{tp} \xleftarrow{\$} \mathcal{E}_0(1^\lambda)\}_{\lambda \in \mathbb{N}}$ *are computationally indistinguishable.*

Technical details. Besides the use of the extractor, the security experiment is rather technical in some of its parts. Here we explain the main technicalities. As mentioned earlier, the structure of the experiment is that the adversary receives the group public key and then starts interacting with the oracle. The experiment maintains lists $L_{join}, L_{usr}, L_{corr}, L_{msg}$ to bookkeep information on the state of the Join protocol sessions, the list of uncorrupted and corrupted platforms respectively, and the list of the messages on which the adversary obtained signatures. After interacting with the oracle, the adversary outputs a message M^*, a basename bsn^*, a signature σ^* and revocation lists $\mathsf{PrivRL}^*, \mathsf{SigRL}^*$. The adversary wins if either event (4), or the conjunction of events (1), (2) and (3) occur. Intuitively, event (4) means that the adversary has "fooled" the extractor. Namely, the adversary produced a secret key sk (provided in the private-key revocation list PrivRL^*) that the algorithm $\mathsf{CheckTK}$ recognizes as associated to a token tk extracted by $\mathcal{E}_1$, but sk is not a valid signing key. In other words, our definition requires that any secret key[14] extracted by $\mathcal{E}_1$ should be valid. For the other winning case, events (2) and (3) are a generalization of the classical winning condition of digital signatures, i.e. where the adversary returns a valid signature on a new message. The conjunction of event (2) and (3) are more general than the classical unforgeability notion because instead of considering as *new* just the message, we also include the basename, and, more importantly, the fact that the forged signature apparently comes from a machine that either has never been set up or that has never signed the basename-message tuple. Event (1) instead is there to avoid trivial attacks due to the possibility of corrupting group members. Basically, (1) ensures that for any corrupted platform we have either its secret key in PrivRL^* or a signature produced by that platform in SigRL^*. For the latter statement to be efficiently checkable in the experiment we require the existence of an algorithm $\mathsf{CheckSig}$ for this purpose and that works with the token tk extracted by $\mathcal{E}_1$. With `honest_join` queries the adversary specifies the code of a signer $\mathcal{M}_i$, which then runs the Join protocol with an honest issuer and an honest sanitizer controlled by the challenger. At the end, if the issuer accepts, we extract a secret-key token tk_i from the transcript τ of the Join protocol, and we store information about $\mathcal{M}_i$, its state, the verification token and the extracted secret-key token. The verification token svt_i is also returned to the adversary. With `dishonestP_join` queries the adversary can let a fully corrupted platform (i.e., both $\mathcal{M}_i$ and $\mathcal{S}_i$ are under its control) join the group. In this case, the adversary runs the join protocol with the honest issuer controlled by the challenger: the oracle allows the adversary to start a Join session and then sends one message, γ, at a time; lines 9–11 formalize this step-by-step execution of the honest issuer on each message sent by the adversary on behalf

---

[14] Precisely, $\mathcal{E}$ extracts a token tk linked to sk.

Experiment $\mathbf{Exp}^{unf}_{\mathcal{A},\mathcal{E},\Pi}(\lambda)$:

1 : $L_{join}, L_{usr}, L_{corr}, L_{msg} \leftarrow \emptyset$; $(pub, tp) \leftarrow \mathcal{E}_0(1^\lambda)$; $(gpk, gsk) \overset{\$}{\leftarrow} \mathsf{Setup}(pub)$;

2 : $(bsn^*, M^*, \sigma^*, \mathsf{PrivRL}^*, \mathsf{SigRL}^*) \leftarrow \mathcal{A}(gpk)^{\mathcal{C}(sk,\cdot)}$;

3 : $R \leftarrow \{tk_i : (i, *, *, *, tk_i) \in L_{corr}\}$;

4 : **return** 1 if and only if $((1) \wedge (2) \wedge (3)) \vee (4)$:

5 :   (1) $\forall tk \in R : (\exists sk \in \mathsf{PrivRL}^* : \mathsf{CheckTK}(gpk, sk, tk) = 1)$

              OR $(\exists \sigma \in \mathsf{SigRL}^* : \mathsf{CheckSig}(gpk, tk, \sigma) = 1)$

6 :   (2) $\mathsf{Ver}(gpk, bsn^*, M^*, \sigma^*, \mathsf{SigRL}^*, \mathsf{PrivRL}^*) = 1$

7 :   (3) $\forall(*, bsn^*, M^*, \sigma) \in L_{msg} : \mathsf{Link}(gpk, bsn^*, M^*, \sigma^*, M^*, \sigma) = 0$

8 :   (4) $\exists sk \in \mathsf{PrivRL}^*$ and $tk \in R$ such that $\mathsf{CheckTK}(gpk, sk, tk) = 1$

          but $\mathsf{CheckSK}(gpk, sk) = 0$.

Oracle $\mathcal{C}(gsk, \cdot)$

---

1 : **Upon query** $(\mathsf{honest\_join}, i, \mathcal{M}_i)$:

2 :   **if** $\exists(i, *, *, *, *) \in L_{usr} \cup L_{corr}$ **then return** $\perp$;

3 : $\langle b, (b, svt_i), state_i \rangle \leftarrow \mathsf{Join}_{\mathcal{C}, \mathcal{C}, \mathcal{M}_i}\langle (gpk, isk), gpk, gpk \rangle$;

4 :   let τ be the issuer-sanitizer transcript

5 :   **if** $b = 1$ **then** $tk_i \leftarrow \mathcal{E}_1(tp, \tau)$; $L_{usr} \leftarrow L_{usr} \cup (i, \mathcal{M}_i, state_i, svt_i, tk_i)$;

6 :   **return** svt_i

7 : **Upon query** $(\mathsf{dishonestP\_join}, i, \gamma)$:

8 :   **if** $(i, *, *, *) \notin L_{join}$, **then** $L_{join} \leftarrow L_{join} \cup (i, (gpk, gsk), \xi, \xi)$;

9 :   Retrieve $(i, state_\mathcal{I}, \xi, \tau)$ from L_{join};

10 : $(\gamma_\mathcal{I}, state'_\mathcal{I}) \leftarrow \mathcal{I}.\mathsf{Join}(state_\mathcal{I}, \gamma)$; $state_\mathcal{I} \leftarrow state'_\mathcal{I}$; $\tau \leftarrow \tau \| (\gamma, \gamma_\mathcal{I})$;

11 :   Update $(i, state_\mathcal{I}, \xi, \tau)$ in L_{join};

12 :   **if** $\gamma_\mathcal{I} = $ concluded, **then** $tk_i \leftarrow \mathcal{E}_1(tp, \tau)$; store $(i, \perp, \perp, \perp, tk_i)$ in L_{corr}.

13 : **Upon query** $(\mathsf{dishonestS\_join}, i, \mathcal{U}, \gamma)$: /* $\mathcal{U} \in \{\mathcal{I}, \mathcal{M}\}$

14 :   **if** $(i, *, *, *) \notin L_{join}$ **then** $L_{join} \leftarrow L_{join} \cup (i, (gpk, gsk), \xi, \xi)$;

15 :   Retrieve $(i, state_\mathcal{I}, state_\mathcal{M}, \tau)$ from L_{join};

16 : $(\gamma_\mathcal{U}, state'_\mathcal{U}) \leftarrow \mathcal{U}.\mathsf{Join}(state_\mathcal{U}, \gamma)$; $state_\mathcal{U} \leftarrow state'_\mathcal{U}$; **if** $\mathcal{U} = \mathcal{I}$ **then** $\tau \leftarrow \tau \| (\gamma, \gamma_\mathcal{I})$;

17 :   Update $(i, state_\mathcal{I}, state_\mathcal{M}, \tau)$ in L_{join};

18 :   **if** $\mathcal{U} = \mathcal{I} \wedge \gamma_\mathcal{I} = $ concluded, **then** :

19 : $tk_i \leftarrow \mathcal{E}_1(tp, \tau)$; $sk_i \leftarrow state_\mathcal{M}$; store $(i, \Pi.\mathcal{M}, sk_i, \perp, tk_i)$ in L_{usr}.

20 : **Upon query** $(\mathsf{sign}, i, bsn, M, \mathsf{SigRL})$:

21 :   Retrieve the tuple $(i, \mathcal{M}_i, state_i, svt_i, tk_i)$ from L_{usr}; **if** not found **return** $\perp$;

22 : $(state'_i, \sigma) \leftarrow \mathsf{Sig}(\mathcal{M}_i, state_i, svt_i, bsn, M, \mathsf{SigRL})$;

23 : $L_{msg} \leftarrow L_{msg} \cup (i, bsn, M, \sigma)$; Update$(i, \mathcal{M}_i, state'_i, svt_i, tk_i)$; **return** σ.

24 : **Upon query** $(\mathsf{corrupt}, i)$:

25 :   Retrieve tuple$(i, \mathcal{M}_i, state_i, svt_i, tk_i)$ from L_{usr}; Move the tuple from L_{usr} to L_{cor};

26 :   **return** $state_i$.

Fig. 2. Subversion-resilient unforgeability experiment. The algorithm $\mathsf{CheckSK}(gpk, sk)$ is a shorthand for the following process: sample a random message, generate a signature on it using sk and output 1 iff the signature verifies. The symbol ξ denotes the empty string.

of $\mathcal{S}_i$. At the end, if the issuer accepts, we extract a secret-key token tk_i from the transcript τ of the Join protocol, and we store this token in the list L_{corr} of corrupted users. With $\mathtt{dishonestS\_join}$ queries we consider the case in which the adversary fully controls the sanitizer but the signer is not subverted. In this case, the oracle allows the adversary to run in the Join protocol with the honest issuer and honest signer. This is done by letting the adversary send messages to either $\mathcal{M}$ or $\mathcal{I}$; lines 15–17 formalize this step-by-step execution of the honest issuer and honest signer on each message γ sent by the corrupted sanitizer. At the end, if the issuer accepts, we extract a secret-key token tk_i from the transcript τ of the Join protocol, and we store all the relevant information in the list L_{usr} of honest platforms. Note that in this case we do not necessarily know the verification token since this is received by the sanitizer, which is the adversary. For $\mathtt{sign}$ queries, the oracle first checks that the platform has joined the system and if so it lets the (possibly subverted) signer $\mathcal{M}_i$ generate a signature σ' and corresponding proof π'_σ. Next, if $\mathsf{svt}_i \neq \bot$ the signature is sanitized and given to the adversary, otherwise a non-sanitized signature is returned. Notice that the case $\mathsf{svt}_i = \bot$ (when i is in L_{usr}) can occur only if the platform joined the system using a $\mathtt{dishonestS\_join}$ query, in which case the sanitizer is controlled by the adversary but – we recall – the signer is not subverted. Finally $\mathtt{corrupt}$ queries allow the adversary to corrupt an existing platform, which may have joined through either a $\mathtt{honest\_join}$ or $\mathtt{dishonestS\_join}$ query. As a result, the adversary learns the internal state of the signer, which is supposed to contain the secret key (note that the state of the sanitizer, that is the verification token, was already returned after the Join).

Subversion-Resilient Unforgeability in the Random Oracle Model. To capture also constructions in the random oracle model (ROM) we provide a suitable adaptation of the unforgeability definition. A dedicated ROM-based definition is needed in order to consider extractors that may simulate, and program, the random oracle. The ROM definition is the same as Definition 4, except that condition (3) accounts for the ROM-programmability granted to the extractor.

Comparison with Unforgeability of EPID. The notion of unforgeability defined above closely follows the one defined for EPID in [9], with the following main differences. First, in [9] there is no sanitizer. Second, in [9] the adversary cannot specify a subverted signer, namely $\mathtt{honest\_join}$ and $\mathtt{sign}$ queries are executed according to the protocol description. Third, valid forgeries in [9] include fresh signatures on messages already signed by the oracle. Such a forgery is not valid in our case since signatures are sanitizable (essentially re-randomizable).

Notice that the unforgeability definition of [9] requires the adversary to return the secret key obtained via $\mathtt{dishonest\_join}$ queries (called Join of type (i) in [9]). Nevertheless, the definition does not enforce at any point that the adversary is returning the correct key. It is possible that the authors are implicitly making the assumption that the adversary is honest at this stage, and this what seems to be used in the security proof (where the reduction does not even look at the key returned by the adversary but uses the key extracted from the PoK made by $\mathcal{A}$

during the Join protocol). This is a quite strong assumption. If this assumption is not made we can show an attack. $\mathcal{A}$ first performs a `dishonest_join` query by playing honestly (the same works if this query is `honest_join` followed by `corrupt`), it obtains a key sk_1. Next $\mathcal{A}$ performs another `dishonest_join` query where it plays honestly in the Join protocol, it obtains another key sk_2 but returns to the challenger sk_1. When it comes to the forgery step, from the point of view of the challenger the key that must be in PrivRL^* is sk_1 (maybe twice). This means that technically sk_2 is not revoked and thus the adversary can use it to create a signature that would pass the forgery checks and win the game. Note that this attack works even if the forgery checks ensure that all sk in PrivRL^* must be "valid" (this check was proposed as part of the Revoke algorithm of the EPID construction).

In our definition of unforgeability we avoid the above attack by requiring a security property of the Join protocol. Specifically, the join protocol is such that, if the execution of the protocol ends successfully, then the platform must have learnt one (and only one) secret key. We formalize this by requiring the existence on an extractor that can find this key by only looking at the transcript. In this way, we avoid the unrealistic requirement that the adversary *surrenders* all the corrupted secret keys. Notice that the existence of the extractor is only for definitional purpose, namely, only to asses the security statement that "unforgeability holds if all the corrupted secret keys are revoked".

3   Building Blocks

An asymmetric bilinear group generator is an algorithm $\mathcal{G}$ that upon input a security parameter 1^λ produces a tuple $\mathsf{bgp} = (p, \mathbb{G}_1, \mathbb{G}_2, \mathbb{G}_T, e, \mathcal{P}_1, \mathcal{P}_2)$, where $\mathbb{G}_1, \mathbb{G}_2$ and $\mathbb{G}_T$ are groups of prime order $p \geq 2^\lambda$, the elements $\mathcal{P}_1, \mathcal{P}_2$ are generators of $\mathbb{G}_1, \mathbb{G}_2$ respectively, $e : \mathbb{G}_1 \times \mathbb{G}_2 \to \mathbb{G}_T$ is an efficiently computable, non-degenerate bilinear map. In our construction we use Type-3 groups in which it is assumed that there is no efficiently computable isomorphism between $\mathbb{G}_1$ and $\mathbb{G}_2$. We use the bracket notation introduced in [19]. Elements in $\mathbb{G}_i$, are denoted in implicit notation as $[a]_i := a\mathcal{P}_i$, where $i \in \{1, 2, T\}$ and $\mathcal{P}_T := e(\mathcal{P}_1, \mathcal{P}_2)$. Given $a, b \in \mathbb{Z}_q$ we distinguish between $[ab]_i$, namely the group element whose discrete logarithm base $\mathcal{P}_i$ is ab, and $[a]_i \cdot b$, namely the execution of the multiplication of $[a]_i$ and b, and $[a]_1 \cdot [b]_2 = [a \cdot b]_T$, namely the execution of a pairing between $[a]_1$ and $[b]_2$. Vectors and matrices are denoted in boldface. We extend the pairing operation to vectors and matrices as $e([\mathbf{A}]_1, [\mathbf{B}]_2) = [\mathbf{A}^\top \cdot \mathbf{B}]_T$. All the algorithms take implicitly as input the public parameters bgp.

Structure-Preserving Signatures. A signature scheme over groups generated by $\mathcal{G}$ is a triple of efficient algorithms (KGen, Sig, Ver). Algorithm KGen outputs a public verification key vk and a secret signing key sk. Algorithm Sig takes as input a signing key and a message m in the message space, and outputs a signature σ. Algorithm Ver takes as input a verification key vk, a message m and a signature σ, and returns either 1 or 0 (i.e., "accept" or "reject", respectively). The scheme

(KGen, Sig, Ver) is correct if for every correctly generated key-pair vk, sk, and for every message m in the message space, we have $\mathsf{Ver}(vk, m, \mathsf{Sig}(sk, m)) = 1$. We consider the standard notion of existential unforgeability under chosen-messages attacks. For space reason, formal definition is omitted from the manuscript. Finally, a signature scheme over groups generated by $\mathcal{G}$ is *structure-preserving* [1] if (1) the verification key, the messages, and signatures consist of solely elements of $\mathbb{G}_1, \mathbb{G}_2$, and (2) the verification algorithm evaluates the signature by deciding group membership of elements in the signature and by evaluating pairing product equations.

Non-Interactive Zero-Knowledge Proof of Knowledge. A non-interactive zero-knowledge (NIZK) proof system for a relation $\mathcal{R}$ is a tuple $\mathcal{NIZK} = (\mathsf{Init}, \mathsf{P}, \mathsf{V})$ of PPT algorithms such that: Init on input the security parameter outputs a (uniformly random) common reference string $\mathsf{crs} \in \{0,1\}^\lambda$; $\mathsf{P}(\mathsf{crs}, x, w)$, given $(x, w) \in \mathcal{R}$, outputs a proof π; $\mathsf{V}(\mathsf{crs}, x, \pi)$, given instance x and proof π outputs 0 (reject) or 1 (accept). In this paper we consider the notion of *NIZK with labels*, that are NIZKs where P and V additionally take as input a label $L \in \mathcal{L}$ (e.g., a binary string). A NIZK (with labels) is *correct* if for every $\mathsf{crs} \xleftarrow{\$} \mathsf{Init}(1^\lambda)$, any label $L \in \mathcal{L}$, and any $(x, w) \in \mathcal{R}$, we have $\mathsf{V}(\mathsf{crs}, L, x, \mathsf{P}(\mathsf{crs}, L, x, w)) = 1$. As for security we consider the standard notions of adaptive composable zero-knowledge and adaptive perfect knowledge soundness [25].

Malleable and Re-Randomizable NIZKs. We use the definitional framework of Chase et al. [16] for malleable proof systems. For space reason we introduce only informally the framework here. A malleable NIZK comes with an NP relationship $\mathcal{R}$ and a set of *allowable* transformations $\mathcal{T}$. An allowable transformation $T = (T_x, T_w) \in \mathcal{T}$ maps tuple $(x, w) \in \mathcal{R}$ to another tuple $(T_x(x), T_w(w)) \in \mathcal{R}$, namely, the transformations are closed under $\mathcal{R}$. Additionally, a malleable NIZK has an algorithm ZKEval that upon input x, π and transformation T returns a new proof π' which is a valid proof for the instance $T_x(x)$. The work of [16] defines the notion of *strong derivation privacy* which informally states that, for any tuple x, π and transformation T adaptively chosen by the adversary, the proof π' is indistinguishable from a fresh simulated proof for the statement $T_x(x)$. In the special case of a malleable NIZK where the allowable transformation is the identity function we simply say that it is a *re-randomizable NIZK* and we omit the transformation from the inputs of ZKEval.

4   Our SR-EPID Construction

An Overview of Our Scheme. We elaborate further on the overview from Sect. 1.1. Recall that our construction follows the classical template similar to many group signature schemes to prove in zero-knowledge the knowledge of a signature originated by the issuer. In particular: (I) The issuer $\mathcal{I}$ keeps a secret key isk of a (structure-preserving) signature scheme. (II) The secret key of a platform is a signature σ_{sp} on a Pedersen commitment $[t]_1$ whose opening $\mathbf{y}$ is known to the signer only. Following the description given in Sect. 1.1, the conjunction of σ_{sp} and $[t]_1$ forms a blind signature on $\mathbf{y}$. (III) The signer generates a signature on a message M and basename bsn by creating a NIZK with label (bsn, M) of the knowledge of a valid signature σ_{sp} made by $\mathcal{I}$ on message a commitment $[t]_1$ and the knowledge of the opening of such commitment to a value $\mathbf{y}$. To realize the NIZK, our idea is to use a random oracle H to hash the string bsn, M and use the output string as the common-reference string of a (malleable) NIZK for the knowledge of the σ_{sp}, the commitment $[t]_1$ and the opening $\mathbf{y} = (y_0, y_1)$. Furthermore, to be able to re-randomize the signature, we make use the re-randomizable NIZK. (IV) To support revocation and linkability the final signature additionally contains the pseudorandom value $[c_1]_1 := \mathsf{K}(\mathsf{bsn}) \cdot y_0$, where K is a random oracle. More in details, linkability is trivially obtained, as two signatures by the same signer and for the same basename share the same value for $[c_1]_1$, while for (signature-based) revocation we additionally let the signer prove that all the revoked signatures contain a $[c_1]_1$ of the form $\mathsf{K}(\mathsf{bsn}) \cdot y_0'$ where $y_0' \neq y_0$.

Specific Building Blocks. Our scheme makes use of the following building blocks:

- A structure-preserving signature scheme $\mathcal{SS} = (\mathsf{KGen}_{sp}, \mathsf{Sig}_{sp}, \mathsf{Ver}_{sp})$ where messages are elements of $\mathbb{G}_1$ and signatures are in $\mathbb{G}_1^{\ell_1} \times \mathbb{G}_2^{\ell_2}$.
- An re-randomizable NIZK $\mathcal{NIZK}_{\mathsf{sign}}$ for the relationship $\mathcal{R}_{\mathsf{sign}}$ defined as:

$$\left\{ \begin{array}{c} (\mathsf{gpk}, [\mathbf{b}]_1, \mathsf{SigRL}), \\ ([t]_1, \sigma_{sp}, [\mathbf{y}]_2) \end{array} : \begin{array}{c} [\mathbf{b}]_1 \in span([1, y_0]_1^\mathsf{T}) \\ [t]_\mathsf{t} = [\mathbf{h}^\mathsf{T} \cdot \mathbf{y}]_\mathsf{t} \\ \mathsf{Ver}_{sp}(\mathsf{pk}_{sp}, [t]_1, \sigma_{sp}) = 1 \\ \forall i : [\mathbf{b}_i]_1 \notin span([1, y_0]_1^\mathsf{T}) \end{array} \right\}$$

where $\mathsf{SigRL} = \{[\mathbf{b}_i]_1\}_{i=1}^r$, $\mathsf{gpk} = ([\mathbf{h}]_1, \mathsf{pk}_{sp})$, and $\mathbf{y} = (y_0, y_1)^\mathsf{T}$. To simplify the exposition, in the description of the protocol below we omit gpk (the public key of the scheme) from the instance and we consider $([\mathbf{b}]_1, \mathsf{SigRL})$ as an instance for the relation.
- A malleable and re-randomizable NIZK $\mathcal{NIZK}_{\mathsf{com}}$ for the following relationship $\mathcal{R}_{\mathsf{com}}$ and set of transformations $\mathcal{T}_{\mathsf{com}}$ defined below:

$$\mathcal{R}_{\mathsf{com}} := \{(([\mathbf{h}]_1, [t]_1), [\mathbf{y}]_2 : [t]_\mathsf{t} = e([\mathbf{h}]_1, [\mathbf{y}]_2)\}$$

$$\mathcal{T}_{\mathsf{com}} := \left\{ T = (T_x, T_w) : \begin{array}{c} T_x([\mathbf{h}]_1, [t]_1) = [\mathbf{h}]_1, [t + h_2 \cdot y']_1 \\ T_w([\mathbf{y}]_2) = [y_0, y_1 + y']_2^\mathsf{T} \end{array} \right\}$$

Namely, the relation proves the knowledge of the opening of a Pedersen's commitment (in $\mathbb{G}_1$) whose commitment key is $[\mathbf{h}]_1$. The transformation allows to re-randomize the commitment by adding fresh randomness.
- A $\mathcal{NIZK}_{\mathsf{svt}}$ for the relation $\mathcal{R}_{\mathsf{svt}} = \{[x, xy, z, zy]_1, y : x, y, z \in \mathbb{Z}_p\}$.
- Three cryptographic hash functions H, J and K modeled as random oracles, where $\mathsf{H} : \{0,1\}^* \to \{0,1\}^\lambda$, $\mathsf{J} : \{0,1\}^* \to \{0,1\}^\lambda$ and $\mathsf{K} : \{0,1\}^\lambda \to \mathbb{G}_1$.

Our SR-EPID Scheme. We describe our scheme based on building block described above. For an instantiation and its efficiency see the full version [20].

$\mathsf{Init}(1^\lambda) \to \mathsf{pub}$: Generate description of a type-3 bilinear group $\mathsf{bgp} \xleftarrow{\$} \mathcal{G}(1^\lambda)$, the common reference string $\mathsf{crs_{svt}} \xleftarrow{\$} \mathcal{NIZK_{svt}}.\mathsf{Init(bgp)}$, and sample $\mathbf{h} \xleftarrow{\$} \mathbb{Z}_p^2$. Output $\mathsf{pub} = (\mathsf{bgp}, \mathsf{crs_{svt}}, [\mathbf{h}]_1)^{15}$

$\mathsf{Setup(pub)} \to (\mathsf{gpk}, \mathsf{isk})$: sample $(\mathsf{sk}_{sp}, \mathsf{pk}_{sp}) \xleftarrow{\$} \mathsf{KGen}_{sp}(\mathsf{bgp})$, and set $\mathsf{isk} := \mathsf{sk}_{sp}$, $\mathsf{gpk} := \mathsf{pk}_{sp}$.

$\mathsf{Join}_{\mathcal{I},\mathcal{S},\mathcal{M}}\langle(\mathsf{gpk}, \mathsf{isk}), \mathsf{gpk}, \mathsf{gpk}\rangle \to \langle b, (b, \mathsf{svt}), (\mathsf{sk}, \mathsf{svt})\rangle$: the platform $\mathcal{P} = (\mathcal{M}, \mathcal{S})$ and issuer $\mathcal{I}$ start an interactive protocol that proceeds as described below:

1. $\mathcal{I}$ samples $id \xleftarrow{\$} \{0,1\}^\lambda$, sends id to $\mathcal{S}$ and $\mathcal{M}$. Parties compute $\mathsf{crs_{com}} \leftarrow \mathsf{J}(id)$.

2. $\mathcal{M}$ samples $y_{0,\mathcal{M}}, c_\mathcal{M} \xleftarrow{\$} \mathbb{Z}_p$, set $\mathsf{svt}' := [c_\mathcal{M}, c_\mathcal{M} y_{0,\mathcal{M}}]_1$ and sends svt' to $\mathcal{S}$.

3. $\mathcal{S}$ parses $\mathsf{svt}' = (\mathsf{svt}'_0, \mathsf{svt}'_1)$, checks that $\mathsf{svt}'_0, \mathsf{svt}'_1 \neq [0]_1$ and if so it sets

$$\mathsf{svt} := c_\mathcal{S} \cdot (\mathsf{svt}' + ([0]_1, y_{0,\mathcal{S}} \cdot \mathsf{svt}'_0)) = [c_\mathcal{S} c_\mathcal{M}, c_\mathcal{S} c_\mathcal{M}(y_{0,\mathcal{S}} + y_{0,\mathcal{M}})]_1$$

and sends $(y_{0,\mathcal{S}}, \mathsf{svt}, [c_\mathcal{S}]_2)$ to $\mathcal{M}$.

4. $\mathcal{M}$ does as described below:
   - Parse $\mathsf{svt}' = (\mathsf{svt}'_0, \mathsf{svt}'_1)$, $\mathsf{svt} = (\mathsf{svt}_0, \mathsf{svt}_1)$ and assert $e(\mathsf{svt}'_0, [c_\mathcal{S}]_2) = e(\mathsf{svt}_0, [1]_2)$ and $e(\mathsf{svt}'_1 + [c_\mathcal{M} \cdot y_{0,\mathcal{S}}], [c_\mathcal{S}]_2) = e(\mathsf{svt}_1, [1]_2)$
   - Set $y_0 = y_{0,\mathcal{M}} + y_{0,\mathcal{S}}$, sample $y_{1,\mathcal{M}} \xleftarrow{\$} \mathbb{Z}_p$ and compute $[t_\mathcal{M}]_1 := (y_0, y_{1,\mathcal{M}}) \cdot [\mathbf{h}]_1$;
   - $\pi_\mathcal{M} \leftarrow \mathcal{NIZK_{com}}.\mathsf{P}(\mathsf{crs_{com}}, ([\mathbf{h}]_1, [t_\mathcal{M}]_1), [y_0, y_{1,\mathcal{M}}]_2)$;
   - Send $([t_\mathcal{M}]_1, \pi_\mathcal{M})$ to $\mathcal{S}$.

5. $\mathcal{S}$ checks $\mathcal{NIZK_{com}}.\mathsf{V}(\mathsf{crs_{com}}, ([\mathbf{h}]_1, [t_\mathcal{M}]_1), \pi_\mathcal{M}) = 1$; if the check passes:
   - Sample $y_{1,\mathcal{S}} \xleftarrow{\$} \mathbb{Z}_p$ and set $[t]_1 := [t_\mathcal{M} + h_2 \cdot y_{1,\mathcal{S}}]_1$;
   - Compute $\pi_\mathcal{S} \leftarrow \mathcal{NIZK_{com}}.\mathsf{ZKEval}(\mathsf{crs_{com}}, \pi_\mathcal{M}, [y_{1,\mathcal{S}}]_1)$;
   - Send $y_{1,\mathcal{S}}$ to $\mathcal{M}$ and $([t]_1, \pi_\mathcal{S})$ to $\mathcal{I}$.

6. $\mathcal{I}$ checks $\mathcal{NIZK_{com}}.\mathsf{V}(\mathsf{crs_{com}}, ([\mathbf{h}]_1, [t]_1), \pi_\mathcal{S}) = 1$, and if the check passes then $\mathcal{I}$ computes $\sigma_{sp} \leftarrow \mathsf{Sig}_{sp}(\mathsf{sk}_{sp}, [t]_1)$ and sends σ_{sp} to $\mathcal{M}$ (through $\mathcal{S}$).

7. $\mathcal{M}$ does as described below:
   - Compute $y_1 = y_{1,\mathcal{M}} + y_{1,\mathcal{S}}$, $y_0 = y_{0,\mathcal{M}} + y_{0,\mathcal{S}}$, and set $\mathbf{y} := (y_0, y_1)^\mathsf{T}$;
   - Verify (1) $[\mathbf{h}]_1^\mathsf{T} \cdot \mathbf{y} = [t]_1$ and (2) $\mathsf{Ver}_{sp}(\mathsf{pk}_{sp}, [t]_1, \sigma_{sp}) = 1$
   - If so, send the special message $\mathtt{completed}$ to $\mathcal{I}$ (through $\mathcal{S}$) and output $\mathsf{sk} := ([t]_1, \sigma_{sp}, \mathbf{y})$ and svt.

8. $\mathcal{S}$ outputs svt.

9. If $\mathcal{I}$ receives the special message $\mathtt{completed}$ then outputs it.

---

[15] Notice that we could consider a stronger model of subversion where the adversary could additionally subvert the public parameters. Our scheme, indeed, could be proved secure under this stronger model if we generate $[\mathbf{h}]_1$ using the ROM and use $\mathcal{NIZK_{svt}}$ with subversion-resistant soundness [4].

$\mathsf{Sig}(\mathsf{gpk}, \mathsf{sk}, \mathsf{svt}, \mathsf{bsn}, M, \mathsf{SigRL}) \rightarrow (\sigma, \pi_\sigma)$: On input $\mathsf{gpk}, \mathsf{sk} = ([t]_1, \sigma_{sp}, \mathbf{y})$, the base name $\mathsf{bsn} \in \{0, 1\}^\lambda$, the message $M \in \{0, 1\}^m$, and a signature revocation list $\mathsf{SigRL} = \{(\mathsf{bsn}_i, M_i, \sigma_i)\}_{i \in [n]}$, generate a signature σ and a proof π_σ as follows:

    1. Set $[c]_1 \leftarrow \mathsf{K}(\mathsf{bsn})$ and set $[\mathbf{c}]_1 := [c, c \cdot y_0]_1$;

    2. Compute $\pi \leftarrow \Pi_{\mathsf{sign}}.\mathsf{P}(\mathsf{H}(\mathsf{bsn}, M), ([\mathbf{c}]_1, \mathsf{SigRL}), ([t]_1, [\sigma_{sp}]_1, [\mathbf{y}]_2))$;

    3. Compute $\pi_\sigma \leftarrow \Pi_{\mathsf{svt}}.\mathsf{P}(\mathsf{crs}_{\mathsf{svt}}, (\mathsf{svt}, [\mathbf{c}]_1), y_0)$;

    4. Output $\sigma := ([\mathbf{c}]_1, \pi)$ and π_σ.

$\mathsf{Sanitize}(\mathsf{gpk}, \mathsf{bsn}, M, (\sigma, \pi_\sigma), \mathsf{SigRL}, \mathsf{svt})$: Parse $\sigma = ([\mathbf{c}]_1, \pi)$ and proceed as follows:

    1. If $\Pi_{\mathsf{sign}}.\mathsf{V}(\mathsf{crs}_{\mathsf{sign}}, \mathsf{H}(\mathsf{bsn}, M), ([\mathbf{c}]_1, \mathsf{SigRL}), \pi) = 0$ or $\Pi_{\mathsf{svt}}.\mathsf{V}(\mathsf{crs}_{\mathsf{svt}}, (\mathsf{svt}, [\mathbf{c}]_1), \pi_\sigma) = 0$ then output $\bot$.

    2. Re-randomize π by computing $\pi' \leftarrow \Pi_{\mathsf{sign}}.\mathsf{ZKEval}(\mathsf{H}(\mathsf{bsn}, M), ([\mathbf{c}]_1, \mathsf{SigRL}), \pi)$

    3. Output $\sigma' := ([\mathbf{c}]_1, \pi')$.

$\mathsf{Ver}(\mathsf{gpk}, \mathsf{bsn}, M, \sigma, \mathsf{PrivRL}, \mathsf{SigRL})$: Parse $\sigma = ([\mathbf{c}]_1, \pi)$ and $\mathsf{PrivRL} := \{f_1, \dots, f_{n_1}\}$. Return 1 if and only if:

    1. $\mathsf{K}(\mathsf{bsn}) = [c]_1$,

    2. $\Pi_{\mathsf{sign}}.\mathsf{V}(\mathsf{H}(\mathsf{bsn}, M), ([\mathbf{c}]_1, \mathsf{SigRL}), \pi)$ and

    3. for $\forall \mathsf{sk} \in \mathsf{PrivRL}$: let $\mathsf{sk} = ([t]_1, \sigma_{sp}, (y_0, y_1))$ check $(-y_0, 1) \cdot [\mathbf{c}]_1 \neq [0]_1$.

$\mathsf{Link}(\mathsf{gpk}, \mathsf{bsn}, M_1, \sigma_1, M_2, \sigma_2)$: Parse $\sigma_i = ([\mathbf{c}_i]_1, \pi_i)$ for $i = 1, 2$. Return 1 if and only if $[\mathbf{c}_1]_1 = [\mathbf{c}_2]_1$ and both signatures are valid, i.e., $\mathsf{Ver}(\mathsf{gpk}, \mathsf{bsn}, M_1, \sigma_1) = 1$ and $\mathsf{Ver}(\mathsf{gpk}, \mathsf{bsn}, M_2, \sigma_2) = 1$.

Remark 1 (On correctness without verification list). Additionally, we assume that for any $\mathsf{crs}, (\mathsf{gpk}, [\mathbf{b}]_1, \mathsf{SigRL})$ and π if $\mathcal{NIZK}_{\mathsf{sign}}.\mathcal{V}(\mathsf{crs}, (\mathsf{gpk}, [\mathbf{b}]_1, \mathsf{SigRL}), \pi) = 1$ then $\mathcal{NIZK}_{\mathsf{sign}}.\mathcal{V}(\mathsf{crs}, (\mathsf{gpk}, [\mathbf{b}]_1, \emptyset), \pi) = 1$. We notice that, by only minor modifications of the verification algorithm, this property holds for GS-NIZK proof system for the relation $\mathcal{R}_{\mathsf{sign}}$. The reason is that GS-NIZK is a commit-and-prove NIZK system where each group element of the witness is committed separately, and where there are different pieces of proof for each of the equation in the conjunction defined by the relation.

Assumption 2 (XDH Assumption). Given a bilinear group description $\mathsf{bgp} \xleftarrow{\$} \mathcal{G}(1^\lambda)$, we say that the *External Diffie-Hellman* (XDH) assumption holds in $\mathbb{G}_\beta$ where $\beta \in \{1, 2\}$ if the distribution $[x, y, xy]_\beta$ and the distribution $[x, y, z]_\beta$ where $(x, y, z) \xleftarrow{\$} \mathbb{Z}_p^3$ are computationally indistinguishable.

Theorem 1. *If $\mathcal{SS}$ is EUF-CM secure, both $\mathcal{NIZK}_{\mathsf{sign}}$ and $\mathcal{NIZK}_{\mathsf{com}}$ are adaptive extractable sound, perfect composable zero-knowledge and strong derivation private, $\mathcal{NIZK}_{\mathsf{svt}}$ is adaptive extractable sound, composable zero-knowledge, and both the XDH assumption holds in $\mathbb{G}_1$ and the Assumption 1 holds, the SP-EPID presented above is unforgeable in the ROM.*

To prove unforgeability we need to define an extractor: the main idea is to program the random oracle J to output strings (used as common reference strings in the protocol) that come with extraction trapdoors. Recall that by the properties of the NIZK, such strings are indistinguishable from random strings. Then, whenever required, the extractor can run the NIZK extractor over the NIZK proof provided by the platform during the join protocol to obtain a value $[\mathbf{y}]_2$. Finally, looking at the transcript of the join protocol, the extractor can produce the token $\mathsf{tk} = ([t]_1, \sigma_{sp}, [\mathbf{y}]_2)$. Notice that the created token looks almost like the secret key with the only difference that, in the secret key, the value $\mathbf{y}$ is given in $\mathbb{Z}_q^2$.[16] It is clear that the token is uniquely linked to the secret key.

With this extractor, we proceed with a sequence of hybrid experiments to prove unforgeability. In the first part of the hybrid argument we exploit the programmability of the random oracle to puncture the tuple (bsn^*, M^*) selected by the adversary for its forgery. In particular, we reach a stage where we can always extract the witnesses from valid signatures for (bsn^*, M^*), while for all the other basename-message tuples the challenger can always send to the adversary simulated signatures. To reach this point, we make use of the strong derivation privacy property of the NIZK proof system (which states that re-randomization of valid proofs are indistinguishable from brand-new simulated proofs for the same statement). Specifically, we can switch from signatures produced by the subverted hardware and re-randomized by the challenger of the experiment to signatures directly simulated by the challenger. The latter cutoff any possible channels that the subverted machines can setup with the adversary using biased randomness. At this point we can define the set $\mathcal{Q}_{sp}$ of all the messages $[t]_1$ signed by the challenger (impersonating the issuer) using the structure-preserving signature scheme. Notice that our definition allows the adversary to query the challenger for a signature on the message (bsn^*, M^*) itself. As the signatures for such basename-message tuple are always extractable, the challenger has no chances to simulate such signatures. However, by the security definition, the adversary is bound to output a forgery that does not link to any of the signatures for (bsn^*, M^*) output by the challenger. We exploit this property together with the fact that two not-linkable signatures must have different value for y_0, to show that the forged signature must be produced with a witness that contains a fresh value $[t^*]_1$ that is not in $\mathcal{Q}_{sp}$. More technically, we can reduce this to the binding property of the Pedersen's commitment scheme that we use.

Now, we can divide the set of the adversaries in two classes: the ones which produce a forged signature where $[t^*]_1$ is in $\mathcal{Q}_{sp}$ and the ones where $[t^*]_1$ is not in $\mathcal{Q}_{sp}$. For the latter, we can easily reduce to the unforgeability of the structure preserving signature scheme. For the former, instead, we need to proceed with more caution. First of all, we are assured by the previous step that adversaries from the first class of adversaries would never query the signature oracle on (bsn^*, M^*). Secondly, we use the puncturing technique again, however, this time we select the platform (let it be the platform number j^*) that is linked to the

---

[16] In our concrete instantiation we use GS-NIZK proof system, for which extraction in the source groups is more natural and efficient.

forged signature. By the definition of the class of adversaries this platform always exists. For this platform we switch the common-reference string used in the join protocol to be zero-knowledge. Once we are in zero-knowledge mode, we can use strong derivation privacy to make sure that the join protocol does not leak any information about the secret key that the platform computes (even if the machine is corrupted). At this point the secret key of the j^*-th platform is apparently completely hidden from the view of the adversary, in fact: (1) all the signatures are simulated and (2) the join protocol of the j-th platform is simulated. However, the j^*-th platform is still using a subverted machine, which, although cannot communicate anymore using biased randomness with the outside adversary, still receives the secret key. We show that we can substitute this subverted machine with a *well-behaving* machine that might abort during the join protocol but that, if it does not so then it always sign every basename-message tuple received (here we rely on Assumption 1). The last step is to show that such forgery would break the hiding property of the Pedersen's commitment scheme that we make use of.

Theorem 2. *If $\mathcal{NIZK}_{\mathsf{sign}}$ and $\mathcal{NIZK}_{\mathsf{com}}$ are strongly derivation private, adaptively extractable sound and adaptively composable perfect zero-knowledge, both the XDH assumption in $\mathbb{G}_1$ holds and the Assumption 1 holds, and $\mathcal{NIZK}_{\mathsf{svt}}$ is adaptively sound, then the SR-EPID described above is anonymous in the ROM.*

First we notice that adaptive corruption and selective corruption for anonymity are equivalent up to a polynomial degradation of the advantage of the adversary. In particular, we can assume that the adversary corrupts all the platforms but the i_1-th and the i_2-th platforms used for the challenge of security game. The idea of the reduction is to switch to zero-knowledge the common reference strings used in the join protocols for the platforms i_1 and i_2 by programming the random oracle. Similarly, switch to zero-knowledge and simulate all the signatures output by the two platforms (again by programming the random oracle). Thus using the strong derivation privacy property of $\mathcal{NIZK}_{\mathsf{sign}}$ and $\mathcal{NIZK}_{\mathsf{com}}$ to make sure that no information about the platform keys is exfiltrated. Notice that at this point the machines cannot communicate any information using biased randomness, on the other hand, they could still communicate using valid/invalid signatures. Although, the definition of anonymity disallows telling apart i_1 from i_2 using this channel, for technical reasons, in the last step of the proof (when we reduce to XDH) we need to completely disconnect the subverted machines and, again, substitute them with well-behaving machines, thus here we need to rely on Assumption 1. At this point the element $y_0^{(1)}$ (resp. $y_0^{(2)}$) of the key $\mathbf{y}^{(1)}$ of the platform i_1 (resp. key $\mathbf{y}^{(2)}$ of the platform i_2) are almost hidden to the view of the adversary. However, the challenge signature $\sigma = ([\mathbf{c}^*]_1, \pi)$ still contains the value $[c_1^*]_1 = \mathsf{K}(\mathsf{bsn}^*) \cdot y_0^{(b)}$. The last step of the proof of anonymity is to change the way the challenge signature is computed. In particular, the value above is computed as $\mathsf{K}(\mathsf{bsn}^*) \cdot x$ for a uniformly sampled x. This step is proved indistinguishable using the XDH assumption on $\mathbb{G}_1$.

Acknowledgements. This work has received funding in part from the European Research Council (ERC) under the European Union's Horizon 2020 research and innovation program under project PICOCRYPT (grant agreement No. 101001283), by the Spanish Government under projects SCUM (ref. RTI2018-102043-B-I00), CRYPTOEPIC (ref. EUR2019-103816), and SECURITAS (ref. RED2018-102321-T), and by the Madrid Regional Government under project BLOQUES (ref. S2018/TCS-4339). This work has been supported by SPATIAL project. SPATIAL has received funding from the European Union's Horizon 2020 research and innovation programme under grant agreement No. 101021808. This work has been partially funded by the EU H2020-SU-ICT-03-2018 Project No. 830929 CyberSec4Europe. The first author was a postdoctoral fellow at the IMDEA Software Institute where he performed the research leading to this paper.

References

1. Abe, M., Fuchsbauer, G., Groth, J., Haralambiev, K., Ohkubo, M.: Structure-preserving signatures and commitments to group elements. In: Rabin, T. (ed.) CRYPTO 2010. LNCS, vol. 6223, pp. 209–236. Springer, Heidelberg (2010). https://doi.org/10.1007/978-3-642-14623-7_12

2. Ateniese, G., Francati, D., Magri, B., Venturi, D.: Public immunization against complete subversion without random oracles. In: Deng, R.H., Gauthier-Umaña, V., Ochoa, M., Yung, M. (eds.) ACNS 2019. LNCS, vol. 11464, pp. 465–485. Springer, Cham (2019). https://doi.org/10.1007/978-3-030-21568-2_23

3. Ateniese, G., Magri, B., Venturi, D.: Subversion-resilient signature schemes. In: ACM CCS 2015 (2015)

4. Bellare, M., Fuchsbauer, G., Scafuro, A.: NIZKs with an untrusted CRS: security in the face of parameter subversion. In: Cheon, J.H., Takagi, T. (eds.) ASIACRYPT 2016, Part II. LNCS, vol. 10032, pp. 777–804. Springer, Heidelberg (2016). https://doi.org/10.1007/978-3-662-53890-6_26

5. Bellare, M., Micciancio, D., Warinschi, B.: Foundations of group signatures: formal definitions, simplified requirements, and a construction based on general assumptions. In: Biham, E. (ed.) EUROCRYPT 2003. LNCS, vol. 2656, pp. 614–629. Springer, Heidelberg (2003). https://doi.org/10.1007/3-540-39200-9_38

6. Bellare, M., Paterson, K.G., Rogaway, P.: Security of symmetric encryption against mass surveillance. In: Garay, J.A., Gennaro, R. (eds.) CRYPTO 2014, Part I. LNCS, vol. 8616, pp. 1–19. Springer, Heidelberg (2014). https://doi.org/10.1007/978-3-662-44371-2_1

7. Bellare, M., Sandhu, R.: The security of practical two-party RSA signature schemes. Cryptology ePrint Archive, Report 2001/060 (2001). https://eprint.iacr.org/2001/060

8. Bernhard, D., Fuchsbauer, G., Ghadafi, E., Smart, N.P., Warinschi, B.: Anonymous attestation with user-controlled linkability. Int. J. Inf. Secur. **12**(3), 219–249 (2013)

9. Brickell, E., Li, J.: Enhanced privacy ID: a direct anonymous attestation scheme with enhanced revocation capabilities. In: ACM WPES (2007)

10. Brickell, E., Li, J.: Enhanced privacy ID: a direct anonymous attestation scheme with enhanced revocation capabilities. IEEE Trans. Dependable Sec. Comput. **9**(3), 345–360 (2011)

11. Camenisch, J., Chen, L., Drijvers, M., Lehmann, A., Novick, D., Urian, R.: One TPM to bind them all: fixing TPM 2.0 for provably secure anonymous attestation. In: 2017 IEEE S&P, pp. 901–920 (2017)
12. Camenisch, J., Drijvers, M., Lehmann, A.: Anonymous attestation with subverted TPMs. In: Katz, J., Shacham, H. (eds.) CRYPTO 2017, Part III. LNCS, vol. 10403, pp. 427–461. Springer, Cham (2017). https://doi.org/10.1007/978-3-319-63697-9_15
13. Camenisch, J., Lehmann, A.: (Un)linkable pseudonyms for governmental databases. In: ACM CCS 2015 (2015)
14. Catalano, D., Fiore, D., Nizzardo, L.: Programmable hash functions go private: constructions and applications to (homomorphic) signatures with shorter public keys. In: Gennaro, R., Robshaw, M. (eds.) CRYPTO 2015, Part II. LNCS, vol. 9216, pp. 254–274. Springer, Heidelberg (2015). https://doi.org/10.1007/978-3-662-48000-7_13
15. Chakraborty, S., Dziembowski, S., Nielsen, J.B.: Reverse firewalls for actively secure MPCs. In: Micciancio, D., Ristenpart, T. (eds.) CRYPTO 2020, Part II. LNCS, vol. 12171, pp. 732–762. Springer, Cham (2020). https://doi.org/10.1007/978-3-030-56880-1_26
16. Chase, M., Kohlweiss, M., Lysyanskaya, A., Meiklejohn, S.: Malleable proof systems and applications. In: Pointcheval, D., Johansson, T. (eds.) EUROCRYPT 2012. LNCS, vol. 7237, pp. 281–300. Springer, Heidelberg (2012). https://doi.org/10.1007/978-3-642-29011-4_18
17. Chen, R., Mu, Y., Yang, G., Susilo, W., Guo, F., Zhang, M.: Cryptographic reverse firewall via malleable smooth projective hash functions. In: Cheon, J.H., Takagi, T. (eds.) ASIACRYPT 2016. LNCS, vol. 10031, pp. 844–876. Springer, Heidelberg (2016). https://doi.org/10.1007/978-3-662-53887-6_31
18. Chow, S.S.M., Russell, A., Tang, Q., Yung, M., Zhao, Y., Zhou, H.-S.: Let a non-barking watchdog bite: cliptographic signatures with an offline watchdog. In: Lin, D., Sako, K. (eds.) PKC 2019, Part I. LNCS, vol. 11442, pp. 221–251. Springer, Cham (2019). https://doi.org/10.1007/978-3-030-17253-4_8
19. Escala, A., Herold, G., Kiltz, E., Ràfols, C., Villar, J.: An algebraic framework for Diffie-Hellman assumptions. In: Canetti, R., Garay, J.A. (eds.) CRYPTO 2013, Part II. LNCS, vol. 8043, pp. 129–147. Springer, Heidelberg (2013). https://doi.org/10.1007/978-3-642-40084-1_8
20. Faonio, A., Fiore, D., Nizzardo, L., Soriente, C.: Subversion-resilient enhanced privacy ID. Cryptology ePrint Archive (2020). https://ia.cr/2020/1450
21. Faust, S., Kohlweiss, M., Marson, G.A., Venturi, D.: On the non-malleability of the Fiat-Shamir transform. In: Galbraith, S., Nandi, M. (eds.) INDOCRYPT 2012. LNCS, vol. 7668, pp. 60–79. Springer, Heidelberg (2012). https://doi.org/10.1007/978-3-642-34931-7_5
22. Fischlin, M., Mazaheri, S.: Self-guarding cryptographic protocols against algorithm substitution attacks (2018)
23. Galbraith, S.D., Paterson, K.G., Smart, N.P.: Pairings for cryptographers. Discret. Appl. Math. **156**(16), 3113–3121 (2008)
24. Ganesh, C., Magri, B., Venturi, D.: Cryptographic reverse firewalls for interactive proof systems. Theor. Comput. Sci. **855**, 104–132 (2021)
25. Groth, J.: Simulation-sound NIZK proofs for a practical language and constant size group signatures. In: Lai, X., Chen, K. (eds.) ASIACRYPT 2006. LNCS, vol. 4284, pp. 444–459. Springer, Heidelberg (2006). https://doi.org/10.1007/11935230_29

26. Groth, J., Sahai, A.: Efficient non-interactive proof systems for bilinear groups. In: Smart, N. (ed.) EUROCRYPT 2008. LNCS, vol. 4965, pp. 415–432. Springer, Heidelberg (2008). https://doi.org/10.1007/978-3-540-78967-3_24

27. Libert, B., Peters, T., Joye, M., Yung, M.: Non-malleability from malleability: simulation-sound quasi-adaptive NIZK proofs and CCA2-secure encryption from homomorphic signatures. In: Nguyen, P.Q., Oswald, E. (eds.) EUROCRYPT 2014. LNCS, vol. 8441, pp. 514–532. Springer, Heidelberg (2014). https://doi.org/10.1007/978-3-642-55220-5_29

28. Mavroudis, V., Cerulli, A., Svenda, P., Cvrcek, D., Klinec, D., Danezis, G.: A touch of evil: high-assurance cryptographic hardware from untrusted components. In: ACM CCS, pp. 1583–1600 (2017)

29. Mironov, I., Stephens-Davidowitz, N.: Cryptographic reverse firewalls. In: Oswald, E., Fischlin, M. (eds.) EUROCRYPT 2015, Part II. LNCS, vol. 9057, pp. 657–686. Springer, Heidelberg (2015). https://doi.org/10.1007/978-3-662-46803-6_22

30. Russell, A., Tang, Q., Yung, M., Zhou, H.-S.: Cliptography: clipping the power of kleptographic attacks. In: Cheon, J.H., Takagi, T. (eds.) ASIACRYPT 2016, Part II. LNCS, vol. 10032, pp. 34–64. Springer, Heidelberg (2016). https://doi.org/10.1007/978-3-662-53890-6_2

31. Russell, A., Tang, Q., Yung, M., Zhou, H.S.: Generic semantic security against a kleptographic adversary. In: ACM CCS 2017 (2017)

32. Young, A., Yung, M.: The dark side of "black-box" cryptography or: should we trust capstone? In: Koblitz, N. (ed.) CRYPTO 1996. LNCS, vol. 1109, pp. 89–103. Springer, Heidelberg (1996). https://doi.org/10.1007/3-540-68697-5_8

PriBank: Confidential Blockchain Scaling Using Short Commit-and-Proof NIZK Argument

Kristian Gjøsteen, Mayank Raikwar, and Shuang Wu[✉]

Norwegian University of Science and Technology, NTNU, Trondheim, Norway
{kristian.gjosteen,mayank.raikwar,shuang.wu}@ntnu.no

Abstract. Decentralized financial applications demand fast, cheap, and privacy-preserving cryptocurrency systems to facilitate high transaction volumes and provide privacy for users. Off-chain Layer-2 scaling solutions such as Plasma, ZK-Rollup, NOCUST are appealing innovations devised to enable the scalability and extensibility account-based blockchains that support smart contracts. The essential idea is simple yet powerful: move expensive computations off-chain and commit the abbreviated transaction data on-chain. Nevertheless, these solutions do not provide privacy for the users' balances and off-chain transaction data. In this paper, we propose *PriBank*, a novel privacy-preserving cryptocurrency system that enables private balances and transaction values on top of these Layer-2 scaling solutions. To construct PriBank system, we propose a Commit-and-Prove short NIZK argument for quadratic arithmetic programs. The Commit-and-Prove short NIZK argument is built on top of the existing zero-knowledge proof scheme: Bulletproof. It allows a prover to commit to an arbitrary set of witnesses by Pedersen commitments before proving, which may be of independent interest. We construct security models and definitions for Layer-2 privacy-preserving scaling solutions and analyse the security of our scheme under the security model. We also implement and evaluate the system, and present a comparative analysis with the existing solutions.

Keywords: Blockchain · Privacy · Scalability · Commitments · Zero-knowledge proofs · Smart contract

1 Introduction

Blockchain-based cryptocurrencies enable a peer-to-peer digital transfer of values by keeping an immutable, distributed but globally synchronised public ledger, the *blockchain*. However, the transactions in many of these blockchain-based systems such as Bitcoin [26], Ethereum [33] are public. Current blockchains are not suitable for daily financial transactions due to their privacy and scalability issues. For instance, the average throughput of Bitcoin is 4.6 transactions per second while Visa does around 1,700 transactions per second on average. Privacy and scalability, however, are hard to achieve at the same time. Since adding privacy and confidentiality for a blockchain inevitably adds more computation and data to the blockchain that results in reducing the transaction throughput and increasing the transaction fees and hence downgrading the scalability of the system.

There are many anonymous cryptocurrencies ranging from Zcash [30], Monero [32] based on Bitcoin-like blockchains, to works [7,8,20,23,31] built on top of the smart contracts. The systems built on these models can have private user balances, private and anonymous transactions. While most of the systems focus on improving privacy, a few (none) of them discuss the scalability of their designs. Monero employs anonymity sets in a ring structure to achieve privacy, however, these privacy sets are fairly small. Zcash and Monero rely on recording every transaction in the history to perform further transactions, this model is called unspent transaction output (UTXO) model. Zcash and its follow-up designs [7,20,23] inherit the same limitation of the UTXO model and also employ a zk-SNARK proof algorithm that has a sophisticated structured common reference string (CRS) requisite more trust for the parties to set up the system. Account-based systems [8,15] where transaction take place between accounts also incorporate zero-knowledge proof for privacy. The transactions in these systems are directly sent to the blockchain resulting in computation overload. All these systems do not achieve scalability due to the expensive blockchain transactions.

Many constructions such as Plasma [29], NOCUST [21], ZK-Rollup [19] aim to improve the scalability of blockchain by moving a large amount of data and computation off-chain through an untrusted operator. The operator puts a short summary of the transactions on-chain. The blockchain scaling designs following this architecture are called Layer-2 scaling solutions. Plasma/NOCUST claim to decrease the transaction cost nearly to zero. However, these systems send less data to the blockchain but they suffer from the problem of mass exit and long waiting time in case of withdraw (Detailed explanation in Sect. 1.2). Moreover, users need to keep online and monitor the behaviour of the operator and other users in case of a dispute. Dziembowski et al. [16] proved that mass exit is inevitable in these systems. ZK-Rollup is designed to avoid these issues by submitting a zero-knowledge proof with extra data to the blockchain, but it has less throughput and needs a trusted setup. We follow the similar scalability approach as ZK-Rollup but without trusted setup, and above all, provide privacy.

Based on the above observations, one possible approach to balance privacy and scalability is to build privacy on the top of these scaling architectures. However, it is not simply adapting the cryptographic techniques used in anonymous cryptocurrencies to the blockchain scaling solutions. First, the fundamental architecture difference of having an operator or not gives different security and threat models. Second, the goal of introducing an off-chain operator is to outsource the computation, while if the transactions are private, the operator needs to compute on private data. Third, the operator is supposed to send as minimal data as possible to the blockchain as long as the data can represent a unique and correct transaction history. While if the transactions are encrypted, inevitably it is more complex to "compress" the data and still be able to prove its correctness. Meanwhile, the overall cost 'to build privacy on scaling solutions' method is unknown, and is still a worthwhile question to be asked and to be investigated.

Motivated by the above, the contributions of this paper are as follows:

1. We construct an efficient Commit-and-Prove NIZK protocol for quadratic arithmetic program by modifying the Bulletproof protocol [9]. Our Commit-and-Prove NIZK protocol can be of independent interest (Sect. 3).
2. We formally define a privacy-preserving cryptocurrency system built on the top of layer-2 scaling and further, we present a security model of the system (Sect. 4).
3. We construct a privacy-preserving cryptocurrency system **PriBank** where the large computation of the user transactions is delegated to an off-chain operator while keeping the users' balances and transaction values private. Users trust the operator for confidentiality, but the system is trust-less for its integrity (Sect. 5).
4. We provide a security analysis of the system (Sect. 6) and implement the Commit-and-Prove NIZK protocol of PriBank in *Go* and further evaluate the performance of the protocol (Sect. 7).

Furthermore, in our system, the computation load and data sent to the blockchain is quadratic to the number of users in the worst case. The zero-knowledge argument for inner-product in our system allows a prover to commit to a subset of witness by Pedersen commitment, compared with Bulletproof where all the witness are committed by vector Pedersen commitment.

1.1 Overview of PriBank

The PriBank system aims to enhance the privacy of blockchain-based cryptocurrency scaling approaches, and concurrently manages the computation and data overload at a practical level. There are three types of entities in PriBank: *Users*, *Bank (Operator)*, and a *Smart Contract* running on the blockchain. The users make the transactions with other users of the system through the bank operator. From a privacy perspective, the operator serves as a bank on top of a blockchain where users' transactions and balances are hidden from other entities apart from the bank. The bank operator maintains users' balances and transactions, keeps them private, and periodically submits commitments to the users' data and zero-knowledge proofs to the smart contract. The smart contract validates the operator's commitments and proofs and records them on the blockchain only if they are valid. The difference between the traditional bank and PriBank is that PriBank is not trusted to execute users' requests honestly, yet the bank can do no harm apart from leaking user's information. As an additional benefit in the current regulatory climate, the information that the operator holds enables auditing of transactions, which is important to prevent financial crimes.

PriBank system operates in terms of *epochs*. An epoch is divided into three phases: *Transaction* phase, *Commit* phase and *Exit* phase. The beginning of an epoch is the *Transaction* phase which consists of three processes: *Register*, *Deposit* and *Transfer*. These process can run parallel. The operator collects all the transaction data in the *Transaction* phase, and sends the commitments and proofs to the smart contract in the *Commit* phase. At the end of epoch is the *Exit* phase where users can withdraw or exit the system with the balances that smart contract has confirmed during the *Commit* phase. Moreover, during the *Transaction* phase, a user can make multiple transactions to another user, but only the final balance is uploaded to the blockchain. Figure 1 depicts a general overview of PriBank.

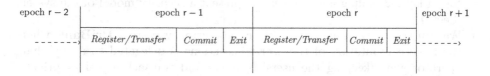

Fig. 1. An overview of PriBank system

PriBank Workflow: A general working flow of PriBank is as follows:

- Firstly, a smart contract is set up on the blockchain. It includes all the public parameters in the system. Then user register and deposit funds in the system through this smart contract.
- After registration, a user sends a plain text transaction to the operator using a secure channel. The operator then commits to the transaction value and generates its proof. Then, it returns the commitment and proof to the user along with a collection of all the transactions commitments made for this user within a specific period and asks for a signature on the collection. The user checks that the collection is valid, and if so signs the transaction collection.
- Through above operation, the operator collects a list of transaction commitments of a user and also gets the user's signature on them. At the end of a period, the operator updates each user's balance, submits the balance commitments and the lists of transaction commitments from the users along with a zero-knowledge proof to the smart contract on blockchain. The balances of users in the system are represented in the form of their commitments.
- Upon receiving the data from the operator, the smart contract verifies the signatures and the zero-knowledge proof, and updates the new balance commitment for each user if the data passes all the verification checks.
- The withdrawal or exit process are on the blockchain between the smart contract and users. The users have the necessary proof that they received from the operator beforehand for the withdrawal. They submit the requests and the proof to the smart contract. The smart contract checks the proof and processes the withdrawal or exit.

Functionality: PriBank processes the user transactions in an off-chain manner through an operator and smart contract, hence amortizes the cost incurred in the parent blockchain. As PriBank is deployed alongside the parent blockchain, the parent blockchain has a global view of user accounts. The parent blockchain should be account-based, smart-contract enabled (e.g. Ethereum [33]), and operated by an honest majority. Furthermore, PriBank operations should take place under the partially synchronous network where messages between two entities should reach within an upper bound delay. Users of PriBank should also be online at least once in each epoch to send or receive transactions in the system.

Verifiable Operation Through Commit-and-Prove Zero-Knowledge Proof. For the correct execution of the PriBank workflow, we build a commit-and-prove zero-knowledge proof system. The commit-and-prove approach in zero-knowledge proofs dates back to the works of Kilian [22] and Canetti et al. [11], following by the works [3,5,10]. The algorithms are zero-knowledge proof in which the prover proves statements about values that are committed. In *PriBank*, this proof system is built over an arithmetic circuit that represents the computation of the bank operator. We commit to the circuit wires and then prove that they satisfy the circuit. We use Pedersen commitment scheme to represent users' balances and transactions privately, these values are part of the wires of the circuit. For the other secret wires, we use the vector Pedersen commitment to shrink the size of the overall commitment to being logarithmic in the circuit size. We also use the signature and zero-knowledge proof verification in the smart contract that guarantees the correctness and verifiability of the updates from the bank operator. Details about the arithmetic circuit and mentioned commitment schemes are given in Sect. 2.

1.2 Related Work

The problem of scalability in blockchain has become more urgent recently. A large amount of work has been done to address this issue and many solutions have been proposed [4,14,21,25,29]. The majority of these solutions support off-chain interactions and computations. In these off-chain solutions, a large number of transactions take place off-chain through an operator who puts a short summary of these transactions on-chain. However, some of these systems are vulnerable to mass exit. In a mass exit scenario, the operator goes rogue and users of the systems need to send ownership proofs of their assets to the main chain, in order to exit the system with their respective assets. This event causes congestion on the main chain and the users might not be able to exit the system in time.

Apart from the problem of mass-exit, some of these solutions do not provide integrity of the transactions. Moreover, some solutions do incorporate zero-knowledge proofs to achieve the integrity of blockchain and off-chain systems. Nevertheless, transaction data in all these systems are public and therefore fail to address the privacy implications of blockchain.

In the blockchain context there are different privacy notions, ranging from privacy of transaction amounts [8,23,30] and transacting parties [15,17] to the privacy of embedded functional calls in a smart contract [7]. Different solutions have been proposed to achieve meaningful privacy notions. Several of these solutions employ advanced cryptographic techniques such as zero-knowledge proofs [30], ring signature [32], homomorphic encryption [34] and mixing techniques [6,24] to achieve various forms of privacy. Financial systems zkLedger [27], Solidus [12],

RSCoin [13] also achieve privacy of their transactions, but banks regulate the supply of funds and a blockchain is used to make transactions.

Hawk [23] is the first framework to construct privacy-preserving smart contracts. Hawk combines the idea of Zcash and multi-party computation that achieves on-chain privacy through the use of zero-knowledge proofs. The on-chain privacy is guaranteed by a party that performs off-chain computation, generates a cryptographic zk-SNARKs proof, and puts these results on-chain.

A zk-SNARK provides a succinct cryptographic proof attesting to the correctness of a computation. However, the use of zk-SNARK puts a bound on the number of participants (in Hawk) due to its trusted setup and circuit-dependent CRS. Ledger-based construction, Zexe [7], follows the similar idea of performing off-chain computation using zk-SNARKs and subsequently produces privacy-preserving transactions. In addition to Hawk, Zexe also hides which computations were performed off-chain, but both suffer from limitation of zk-SNARKs.

To build a privacy-preserving ledger system along with stateful computations in the smart contract, several new constructions have been proposed such as zKay [31], Zether [8], and Kachina [20]. All these constructions extend Ethereum with privacy-preserving currency or data. zKay achieves privacy of data using encryption and correctness using NIZK proof of encryption. zKay presents a new language that extends Ethereum smart contracts with private data types. Zether, on the other hand, proposes a privacy-preserving payment mechanism using ElGamal encryption and zero-knowledge proofs (Bulletproof-based range proofs). Kachina realizes a large class of privacy-preserving smart contracts. Kachina uses NIZK proofs and state oracles to establish the desired privacy-preserving smart contract. The security model of Kachina is based on Universal Composition (UC) model, encompassing the other mentioned models. However, many find UC hard to work with.

Quisquis [17] is a hybrid construction of UTXO and account-based model that provides a provably secure notion of anonymity. It achieves this notion by combining a DDH-based updatable public key system with NIZK proofs.

Although all the above-described privacy-preserving constructions achieve various privacy notions, none of the constructions explicitly provide scalability analysis. Furthermore, many of these constructions provide implementations without integrity and do not have a proper security model. Moreover, even some of these constructions involve off-chain transactions that might result in better scalability, but fail to mention and analyse it. To the best of our knowledge, PriBank is the only construction that enables a useful form of privacy along with scalability in account-based blockchain with a proper security model.

Tables 1 and 2 compare PriBank with the existing popular schemes for scalability and privacy, respectively. In these tables, '✓' denotes that the respective system has the corresponding feature, and '✗' denotes that the scheme lacks that feature. Table 1 compares PriBank with existing scalable off-chain systems. Table 2 compares PriBank with the existing privacy-preserving systems. However, schemes such as Monero and Zcash do not have a concept of off-chain third party, therefore they achieve stronger privacy notions. Irrespective of that, we compare our PriBank scheme to all these systems. '✗*' denotes that Zether itself

Table 1. Comparison Matrix for different off-chain systems.

Scheme		Plasma [29]	ZK-Rollup [19]	State Channel [25]	Our Scheme
Security	No Mass Exit Assumption	✗	✓	✓	✓
	No Watch Tower Assumption	✗	✓	✗	✓
	Cryptographic Primitives	Standard	New	Standard	Standard
Usability	Withdraw Time	1 week	10 min	1 confirmation	1 epoch
	Transaction Finalization Time	1 confirmation	1 confirmation	Instant	1 confirmation
	User Verification	✗	✗	✓	✓
Performance	Cost of Transaction	Very low	Very low	Low	Low
	No Collateral Required	✓	✓	✗	✓

Table 2. Comparison Matrix for different privacy-preserving systems.

Scheme		Monero [32]	Zcash [30]	Zexe [7]	Zether [8]	Quisquis [17]	Our Scheme
Privacy	Confidential Transaction	✓	✓	✓	✓	✓	✓
	Confidential User Address	✓	✓	✓	✗*	✓	✓
	Anonymity Set	Small	Large	Large	Small	Small	Large
Security	Security Model	✗	✗	✓*	✓*	✗	✓
	Cryptographic Primitives	Standard	Standard	New	New	Standard	Standard
Performance	Transaction Size	2–∞ KB	2 KB	0.945–∞ KB	1.472 KB	13.4 KB	0.033–1.9 KB
	No Trusted Setup Required	✗	✗	✗	✓	✓	✓

docs not provide anonymity, however, another construction Anonymous Zether does provide anonymity, though with extra cost. '✓*' denotes that the scheme does not provide extensive security analysis.

2 Preliminaries

Notation: Throughout the paper, we use bold font to denote vectors, i.e. $a \in \mathbb{Z}_p^n$ is a vector with elements $a_1, ..., a_n \in \mathbb{Z}_p$. The inner product between two vectors a, b is denoted by $\langle a, b \rangle$. The Hadamard product or entry wise multiplication of two vectors a, b is denoted by $a \circ b = (a_1 \cdot b_1, ..., a_n \cdot b_n) \in \mathbb{Z}_p^n$. We denote slices of a vector as: $a_{[:l]} = (a_1, ..., a_l) \in \mathbb{Z}_p^l, a_{[l:]} = (a_{l+1}, ..., a_n) \in \mathbb{Z}_p^{n-l}$.

2.1 Commitment Schemes

A commitment scheme allows one to commit to a chosen value (or chosen statement) while keeping it secret, with the ability to only reveal the commitment to the committed value later. A commitment schemes has Hiding and blinding properties. In PriBank, commitment schemes are used to commit to user's balance or transaction data. For the construction, we use Pedersen commitment [28] and Vector Pedersen commitment scheme.

- Given a group $\mathbb{G}$ of order q and two generators g, h of group $\mathbb{G}$, a *Pedersen commitment* for a value $a \in \mathbb{Z}_q$ is defined as $C_a = g^a h^r \in \mathbb{G}$, where $r \xleftarrow{\$} \mathbb{Z}_q$.
- Given a group $\mathbb{G}$ of order q, $g := (g_1, ..., g_n), h \leftarrow \mathbb{G}$ and a vector $a := (a_1, ..., a_n)$, a *vector Pedersen commitment* is $C_a = \prod_{i=1}^n g_i^{a_i} h^r \in \mathbb{G}, r \xleftarrow{\$} \mathbb{Z}_q$.

In Sect. 3.2, we are using the commitment scheme in slightly different way. We are constructing a collection of Pedersen commitments that are using the same randomness over different generators of the group.

2.2   Quadratic Arithmetic Program

We represent the operations that the bank operator do to compute the new balances from the old balances and transaction history into an arithmetic circuit satisfaction problem. The circuit gives the necessary range checks as well. The work of Gennaro et al. [18] shows how to further translate an arithmetic circuit satisfaction problem to a *Quadratic Arithmetic Program (QAP)*, where the circuit is reduced to a polynomial equation.

Definition 1 (Quadratic Arithmetic Program [18]**).** *A quadratic arithmetic program (QAP) Q over a field $\mathbb{Z}_p$ consists of three sets of polynomials $V = \{v_k(x) : k \in \{0, ..., n\}\}, U = \{u_k(x) : k \in \{0, ..., n\}\}, W = \{w_k(x) : k \in \{0, ..., n\}\}$ and a target polynomial $z(X)$, all are defined over $\mathbb{Z}_p$.*

Let a circuit C, where all the wires including inputs, outputs and inner circuit wires variables are labelled $a_0, a_1, ..., a_n$ (where $a_0 = 1$). A QAP Q is said to compute C if the following holds:

$a_1, ..., a_n \in \mathbb{Z}_p^n$ is a valid assignment to the wires variables of C iff there exist $h(X)$ such that

$$\sum_{i=1}^{n} a_i u_i(X) \cdot \sum_{i=1}^{n} a_i v_i(X) = \sum_{i=1}^{n} a_i w_i(X) + h(X)z(X)$$

The size of QAP is n, and degree is $deg(z(X))$, which is also the number of gates in the circuit C. The polynomials $u_k(X), v_k(X), w_k(X)$ have degree at most $deg(z(X)) - 1$.

2.3   Commit-and-Prove Zero-Knowledge Argument

A zero-knowledge argument is a protocol in which a prover wants to convince a verifier that a statement is true without revealing any private information. A commit-and-prove zero-knowledge argument is a zero-knowledge argument in which a prover proves statements about values that are committed. It allows a prover to commit to the secrets it holds before the prover knows what it is going to prove. For instance, a prover makes a commitment to a user's balance, later it can convince the verifier that this balance is in or out of a certain range.

We follow the notation of [9]. A commit-and-prove argument consists of three PPT algorithms $(\mathcal{G}, \mathcal{P}, \mathcal{V})$. These are the common reference generator $\mathcal{G}$, the interactive prover $\mathcal{P}$ and verifier $\mathcal{V}$. Take input as 1^λ, $\mathcal{G}$ outputs the common reference σ. The communication transcript between $\mathcal{P}$ and $\mathcal{V}$ when interacting on inputs s and t is denoted by $tr \leftarrow \langle \mathcal{P}(s), \mathcal{V}(t) \rangle$. We write the output of the protocol as $\langle \mathcal{P}(s), \mathcal{V}(t) \rangle = b$. If verifier accepts, $b = 0$, otherwise $b = 1$.

The language of commit-and-prove zero-knowledge argument proving is defined over a polynomial time decidable relation R and a commitment scheme $\mathsf{Com} = (\mathsf{Setup}, \mathsf{Commit}, \mathsf{VerCommit})$. R is defined over $\mathcal{D}_\sigma \times \mathcal{D}_x \times \mathcal{D}_u \times \mathcal{D}_w$: given a common reference σ, for a triple (x, u, w), we call x the statement, u the committed witness and w the non-committed witness. Define $\mathcal{R}^{\mathsf{Com}}$ as a family of relations that every relation $\mathbf{R} \in \mathcal{R}^{\mathsf{Com}}_\lambda$ can be represented by a tuple (σ, c, r, x, u, w). Let $\mathcal{L}$ be the language associated with $\mathbf{R}$, i.e.,

$$\mathcal{L}_\sigma = \{\sigma, c, x \mid \exists w, u, r \text{ s.t. } \mathsf{VerCommit}(c, u, r) = 1 \wedge R(\sigma, x, u, w) = 1\}$$

The commit-and-prove argument algorithm that we define has completeness, special soundness and perfect zero-knowledge. The formal definitions are given in Appendix F.

3   Commit-and-Prove Short NIZK Argument for Quadratic Arithmetic Program

In this section, we introduce the construction of commit-prove short interactive zero-knowledge proof for the quadratic arithmetic program. The protocol is lying on three sub-protocols: a zero-knowledge argument for a product of Pedersen commitments; a zero-knowledge argument for the inner product of a collection of Pedersen commitments and a public vector; a zero-knowledge argument for the inner product of a vector Pedersen Commitment and a public vector. We describe the sub-protocols at the beginning and then describe how we combine them and build the final protocol.

3.1   Zero-Knowledge Argument of Knowledge for Product of Pedersen Commitments

Consider two Pedersen commitments $c_a = g^a h^{r_a}$ and $c_b = g^b h^{r_b}$, the following Protocol 3.1 is to prove a Pedersen commitment c is committed to the product of a and b, i.e. $c = g^{ab} h^t$ (Fig. 2).

Protocol Input: $(g, h, c, c_a, c_b \in \mathbb{G}; a, b, r_a, r_b, t \in \mathbb{Z}_p)$
Protocol Output: ($\mathcal{V}$ accepts or $\mathcal{V}$ rejects)

$\mathcal{P}$'s input:$(g, h, a, b, r_a, r_b, t)$
$\mathcal{V}$'s input:(g, h, c_a, c_b, c)

1. $\mathcal{P}$ chooses randoms $\alpha, \beta, r_1, r_2, s_0, s_1$ and computes
   $d_1 = g^\alpha h^{r_1}$, $d_2 = g^\beta h^{r_2}$, $c_0 = g^{\alpha b + \beta a} h^{s_0}$, $c_1 = g^{\alpha\beta} h^{s_1}$.
   $\mathcal{P}$ sends (d_1, d_2, c_0, c_1) to $\mathcal{V}$.

2. $\mathcal{V}$: $x \xleftarrow{\$} \mathbb{Z}_p$, sends x to $\mathcal{P}$.

3. $\mathcal{P}$ computes $\theta_a = \alpha - ax$, $\theta_b = \beta - bx$, $\theta_1 = r_1 - r_a x$, $\theta_2 = r_2 - r_b x$ $\theta_{ab} = x^2 t - x s_0 + s_1$ then sends $\theta_a, \theta_b, \theta_1, \theta_2$ to $\mathcal{V}$.

4. $\mathcal{V}$ checks $c_a^x g^{\theta_a} h^{\theta_1} = d_1$, $c_b^x g^{\theta_b} h^{\theta_2} = d_2$, $g^{\theta_a \theta_b} h^{\theta_{ab}} c_0^x = c^{x^2} c_1$, output 1 if all the equations hold otherwise output 0.

Fig. 2. Protocol 3.1

We prove the protocol has perfect completeness, computational soundness and perfect zero-knowledge in Appendix B.

3.2 Zero-Knowledge Argument for Inner Product of Pedersen Commitments and a Public Vector

Consider a vector $a = (a_1, ..., a_n)$ and a collection of Pedersen commitments $\{c_i\}_{i=1}^n$ where $c_i = g^{a_i} h_i^\gamma$. These Pedersen commitments are commitments to the elements of a using the same randomness γ but over different generators h_i. We give a zero-knowledge argument Protocol 3.2 that claims c is a Pedersen commitment that commits to the inner product between a and a public vector b, i.e. $c = g^{\sum_{i=1}^n a_i b_i} h^t$ (Fig. 3).

Statement: Vector b, Pedersen commitments $\{c_i\}_{i=1}^n$ and generators $g, \{h_i\}_{i=1}^n$
Prover's Witness: Openings a, γ and t
Protocol Input: $(\{h_i\}_{i=1}^n, \{c_i\}_{i=1}^n, g, c \in \mathbb{G}; a, b \in \mathbb{Z}_p^n; \gamma, t \in \mathbb{Z}_p)$
Protocol Output: ($\mathcal{V}$ accepts or $\mathcal{V}$ rejects)

$\mathcal{P}$'s input:$(\{h_i\}_{i=1}^n, g, a, b, \gamma, t)$
$\mathcal{V}$'s input:$(\{h_i\}_{i=1}^n, g, c, \{c_i\}_{i=1}^n)$

1. $\mathcal{P}$ chooses randoms $\alpha, \beta, t \xleftarrow{\$} \mathbb{Z}_p$, computes
$$c_0 = h^\gamma, \quad \tau = \prod_{i=1}^n h_i^{b_i}, \quad \Omega = \tau^\gamma h^{-t},$$
$$d_1 = h^\alpha, \quad d_2 = \tau^\alpha h^\beta \text{ and sends}$$
(c_0, Ω, d_1, d_2) to $\mathcal{V}$.

2. $\mathcal{V}$ chooses a challenge $x \xleftarrow{\$} \mathbb{Z}_p$ and sends it to $\mathcal{P}$.
3. $\mathcal{P}$ computes $\theta_1 = \alpha - x\gamma, \theta_2 = \beta + xt$.
4. $\mathcal{V}$ computes $\tau = \prod_{i=1}^n h_i^{b_i}$, output accept if and only if
$$c = \frac{\prod_{i=1}^n c_i^{b_i}}{\Omega} \wedge d_1 = c_0^x h^{\theta_1} \wedge d_2 = \Omega^x \tau^{\theta_1} h^{\theta_2}$$

Fig. 3. Protocol 3.2

We prove the argument of knowledge presented in Protocol 3.2 has perfect completeness, computational soundness and perfect special honest-verifier zero-knowledge in Appendix C.

3.3 Zero-Knowledge Argument of Knowledge for Inner Product of Vector Pedersen Commitment and Public Vector

Consider a vector Pedersen commitment $c_a = \prod_{i=1}^n g_i^{a_i} h^{r_a}$ that commits to $a :=$ $(a_1, ..., a_n)$. We give a zero-knowledge argument protocol that claims c_{ab} is a Pedersen commitment that commits to the inner product between a and a public vector b, i.e. $c_{ab} = g^{\sum_{i=1}^n a_i b_i} h^{r_{ab}}$.

This algorithm is a variant of the inner product argument construction in Bulletproof [9]. We modify it to have the zero-knowledge property which we will use to build PriBank system. We prove the argument of knowledge presented in Protocol 3.3 has perfect completeness, computational knowledge soundness and perfect special honest-verifier zero-knowledge. The proofs for completeness and honest-verifier zero-knowledge are in Appendix D. The soundness proof follows the proof of Bulletproof and can be found in the full version of the paper (Fig. 4).

Statement: Generators vector $g: = \{g_1, ..., g_n\}$, generator h, vector $b: = \{b_1, ..., b_n\}$,

vector Pedersen commitment $c_a = \prod\limits_{i=1}^{n} g_i^{a_i} h^{r_a}$ and $c_{ab} = g^{\sum\limits_{i=1}^{n} a_i b_i} h^{r_{ab}}$

Prover's Witness: Openings for the commitments a, r_a, r_{ab}

$\mathcal{V}$ randomly chooses a challenge x' and sends it to $\mathcal{P}$. Let $c = c_a c_{ab}^{x'}$, $r = r_a + r_{ab} x'$, $u = g^{x'}$ and runs the following protocol Prove on input (g, u, h, a, b, c, r).

Protocol Prove:

Input: $(g \in \mathbb{G}^n, u, h, c \in \mathbb{G}; a, b \in \mathbb{Z}_p^n, r \in \mathbb{Z}_p)$ Output: ($\mathcal{V}$ accepts or $\mathcal{V}$ rejects)

$\mathcal{P}$'s input:(g, u, h, c, a, b)

$\mathcal{V}$'s input:(g, u, h, c, b)

if $n = 1$ ($a := \{a_1\}, g := \{g_1\}$):

1. $\mathcal{P}$ chooses randomness $\alpha_1, \alpha_2 \xleftarrow{\$} \mathbb{Z}_p$, computes and sends $d = g_1^{\alpha_1} u^{\alpha_1 b_1} h^{\alpha_2}$ to $\mathcal{V}$.

2. $\mathcal{V}$ chooses $x \xleftarrow{\$} \mathbb{Z}_p$ challenge x, sends it to the $\mathcal{P}$.

3. $\mathcal{P}$ computes $\theta_1 = \alpha_1 - x a_1, \theta_2 = \alpha_2 - xr$, sends θ_1 and θ_2 to $\mathcal{V}$

4. $\mathcal{V}$ accepts if $c^x g_1^{\theta_1} u^{b_1 \theta_1} h^{\theta_2} = d$, otherwise it rejects.

if $n > 1$:

1. Let $n' = \frac{n}{2}$, $\mathcal{P}$ chooses random $r_1 \xleftarrow{\$} \mathbb{Z}_p$ and $r_2 \xleftarrow{\$} \mathbb{Z}_p$, computes L, R as follows and sends L, R to $\mathcal{V}$.

$$L = g_{[n':]}^{a_{[:n']}} \cdot u^{\langle a_{[:n']}, b_{[n':]} \rangle} \cdot h^{r_1} \in \mathbb{G}$$

$$R = g_{[:n']}^{a_{[n':]}} \cdot u^{\langle a_{[n':]}, b_{[:n']} \rangle} \cdot h^{r_2} \in \mathbb{G}$$

2. $\mathcal{V}$ chooses challenge x and sends it to the prover, i.e.

$$\mathcal{V} \to \mathcal{P} : x \xleftarrow{\$} \mathbb{Z}_p$$

3. Both $\mathcal{P}$ and $\mathcal{V}$ compute

$$g' = g_{[:n']}^{x^{-1}} \circ g_{[n':]}^{x} \in \mathbb{G}^{n'}$$

$$b' = x^{-1} b_{[:n']} + x b_{[n':]} \in \mathbb{Z}_p^{n'}$$

$$c' = c \cdot L^{x^2} \cdot R^{x^{-2}} \in \mathbb{G}$$

4. $\mathcal{P}$ computes:

$$a' = x a_{[:n']} + x^{-1} a_{[n':]}$$

$$r = r + x^2 r_1 + x^{-2} r_2$$

5. Recursively run Prove on input $(g', u, h, c', a', b', r)$

Fig. 4. Protocol 3.3

3.4 Commit-and-Prove Zero-Knowledge Argument for QAP

We give a commit-and-prove zero-knowledge argument Protocol 3.4 for the satisfiability of a QAP for an arithmetic circuit C. For wires in the circuit $\{a_i\}_{i=0}^n$, we denote the input witnesses are $\{a_i\}_{i=0}^k$, the inner circuit witnesses are $\{a_i\}_{i=k+1}^l$ and the statements wires are $\{a_i\}_{i=l+1}^n$. The quadratic arithmetic program, Pedersen commitment and vector Pedersen commitment give a relation of the form $\boldsymbol{R} = (\mathbb{G}, \mathbb{Z}_p, k, l, \{u_i(X), v_i(X), w_i(X)\}_{i=0}^n, z(X),$ $\{a_i\}_{i=0}^n, c_l, \{c_i\}_{i=1}^k, \{a_i\}_{i=1}^l, \gamma, r)$ *such that with* $a_0 = 1$

$$\sum_{i=1}^n a_i u_i(X) \cdot \sum_{i=1}^n a_i v_i(X) = \sum_{i=1}^n a_i w_i(X) + h(X) z(X) \ \wedge \ \{c_i = g^{a_i} h_i^\gamma\}_{i=1}^k$$

$$\wedge \ c_l = h^r \prod_{i=k+1}^l g_i^{a_i} \wedge c_h = h^t \prod_{i=0}^{n-2} g_i^{e_i}$$

where $e_0, ..., e_{n-2}$ *are the coefficients of* $h(X)$ *(Fig. 5).*

Statements: A collection of Pedersen commitments $c_1, ..., c_k$ that commit to $a_1, ..., a_k$, two vector Pedersen commitments c_l and c_h that commit to $a_{k+1}, ..., a_l$ and the coefficients of polynomial $h(x) = e_0 + e_1 x + ... + e_{n-2} x^{n-2}$, the public values $a_{l+1}, ..., a_n$
Witnesses: $a_1, ..., a_l, \gamma, r, t, e_0, ..., e_{n-2}$
Input: $(g, h, \{h_i\}_{i=1}^k, \{c_i\}_{i=1}^k, c_l, c_h \in \mathbb{G}, \boldsymbol{g} \in \mathbb{G}^{n-2}; \{a_i\}_{i=1}^n, \gamma, r, t, \{e_i\}_{i=1}^{n-2} \in \mathbb{Z}_p)$
Output: ($\mathcal{V}$ accepts or $\mathcal{V}$ rejects)

$\mathcal{P}$'s input: $(g, h, \{h_i\}_{i=1}^k, \{c_i\}_{i=1}^k, c_l, c_h, \boldsymbol{g}, \{a_i\}_{i=1}^l, \gamma, r, t, \{e_i\}_{i=1}^{n-2})$
$\mathcal{V}$'s input: $(g, h, \{h_i\}_{i=1}^k, \{c_i\}_{i=1}^k, c_l, c_h, \boldsymbol{g})$

---

1. $\mathcal{V}$ sends challenge $x_1 \xleftarrow{\$} \mathbb{Z}_p$ to the $\mathcal{P}$, computes $\{u_i(x_1), v_i(x_1), w_i(x_1)\}_{i=0}^m$.

2. $\mathcal{P}$ chooses $t_u, t_v, t_w \xleftarrow{\$} \mathbb{Z}_p$ and computes

$$c_u = g^{\sum_{i=1}^k a_i u_i(x_1)} h^{t_u}, \quad c_v = g^{\sum_{i=1}^k a_i v_i(x_1)} h^{t_v}, \quad c_w = g^{\sum_{i=1}^k a_i w_i(x_1)} h^{t_w}$$

as the inner product between Pedersen commitments $\{c_i\}_{i=1}^k$ and $\{u_i(x_1)\}_{i=1}^k, \{v_i(x_1)\}_{i=1}^k, \{w_i(x_1)\}_{i=1}^k$ respectively. Run protocol 3.2 to give the proof of the correct constructions.

3. $\mathcal{P}$ chooses $s_u, s_v, s_w \xleftarrow{\$} \mathbb{Z}_p$ and computes

$$c_u = g^{\sum_{i=k+1}^l a_i u_i(x_1)} h^{s_u},$$

$$c_v = g^{\sum_{i=k+1}^l a_i v_i(x_1)} h^{s_v}$$

$$c_w = g^{\sum_{i=k+1}^l a_i w_i(x_1)} h^{s_w}$$

as the inner product of vector Pedersen commitment c_l between $\{u_i(x_1)\}_{i=k+1}^l$, $\{v_i(x_1)\}_{i=k+1}^l$ and $\{w_i(x_1)\}_{i=k+1}^l$ respectively. $\mathcal{P}$ also chooses $s_h \xleftarrow{\$} \mathbb{Z}_p$ and computes $c_{hz} = g^{h(x_1) z(x_1)} h^{s_h}$, which is an inner product of vector Pedersen commitment and public vector $z(x_1), x_1 z(x_1), ..., x_1^{n-2} z(x_1)$. Run Protocol 3.3 to give a proof for the above constructions.

4. $\mathcal{P}$ computes

$$c_a = c_u \cdot c_u \cdot g^{\sum_{i=l+1}^n a_i u_i(x_1)},$$

$$c_b = c_v \cdot c_v \cdot g^{\sum_{i=l+1}^n a_i v_i(x_1)},$$

$$c_c = c_w \cdot c_w \cdot g^{\sum_{i=l+1}^n a_i w_i(x_1)} \cdot c_{hz}$$

Run Protocol 3.1 to prove c_c commits to the product of the committed values of c_a and c_b.

Fig. 5. Protocol 3.4

We prove the protocol has perfect completeness, computational soundness and perfect special honest verifier zero-knowledge in Appendix E.

4   Blockchain-Based Bank Protocol

In this algorithm we isolate the blockchain functionality. The transactions/data that are sent to blockchains are denoted by trans, when a trans is accepted by the blockchain, the public state, bank state and users' states are all updated.

Definition 2 (BBank). *A blockchain-based bank protocol **BBank** is a tuple of algorithms* (Setup, KeyGen, EstablishBank, NewUser, Deposit, Withdraw, Pay, Commit) *with the following syntax and semantics*

- **Setup.** *The algorithm **Setup** generates the public parameters* pp, *to be distributed off-chain.*
- **KeyGen.** *The algorithm **KeyGen** takes the public parameters* pp *and generates the key pair for users or for a bank.*
- **EstablishBank.** *The algorithm establishes a bank, it takes the public parameters and a key pair as inputs, generates the initial state of the bank* $\mathsf{TempSt_b}$ *and a transaction* trans. *Once the transaction* trans *is accepted by the blockchain, it launches the smart contract.*

  $(\mathsf{trans}, \mathsf{TempSt_b}) \leftarrow \mathsf{EstablishBank}(\mathsf{pk_b}, \mathsf{sk_b}, \mathsf{pp})$
- **NewUser.** *This algorithm is performed by a user to register on the smart contract, but without any deposit for her account yet. It takes the public parameters and the key pair of a user as inputs, outputs* trans *and the initial state of this user.*

  $(\mathsf{trans}, \mathsf{Tempst_u}) \leftarrow \mathsf{NewUser}(\mathsf{pk_b}, \mathsf{sk_u}, \mathsf{pk_u}, \mathsf{pp})$
- **Deposit.** *The protocol is run by the operator and a user to deposit money on smart contract. It takes* pp, *the key pairs and states of a user and a bank, epoch counter, deposit value as inputs, outputs a* trans *and temporary states of user and bank. Once the transaction* trans *get accepted by the smart contract, the user gets a commitment for her initial balance.*

  $(\mathsf{trans}, \mathsf{TempSt_b}, \mathsf{TempSt_u}) \leftarrow \mathsf{Deposit}(\mathsf{pk_b}, \mathsf{sk_b}, \mathsf{pk_u}, \mathsf{sk_u}, \mathsf{St_b}, \mathsf{St_u}, \mathsf{pp}, \mathsf{v}, \mathsf{epoch})$
- **Withdraw.** *The algorithm is performed by a registered user who wants to exit the PriBank. It takes* pp, *the key pairs of a user, generates a* trans *and updates the temporary states of this user and the bank.*

  $(\mathsf{trans}, \mathsf{TempSt_b}, \mathsf{TempSt_u}) \leftarrow \mathsf{Withdraw}(\mathsf{pk_u}, \mathsf{sk_u}, \mathsf{St_b}, \mathsf{St_u}, \mathsf{pp}, \mathsf{v}, \mathsf{epoch})$
- **Pay.** *The protocol is run by the bank and a user (payer) to send transactions to other users. It takes the public key of the receiver, the key pair of the payer and the bank, the temporary states of the payer and the bank, the epoch counter and the transferred value as inputs, and then it updates the temporary states of both user and bank.*

  $(\mathsf{TempSt'_p}, \mathsf{TempSt'_b}) \leftarrow \mathsf{Pay}(\mathsf{pk_b}, \mathsf{sk_b}, \mathsf{pk_p}, \mathsf{sk_p}, \mathsf{pk_r}, \mathsf{TempSt_p}, \mathsf{TempSt_{bank}}, \mathsf{pp}, \mathsf{v}, \mathsf{epoch})$
- **Commit.** *The algorithm is performed by the bank. It takes the public state, the key pair of the bank, the state and temporary state of the bank as inputs and generates a* trans *and updates the temporary state of the bank.*

  $(\mathsf{trans}, \mathsf{TempSt'_b}) \leftarrow \mathsf{Commit}(\mathsf{pk_b}, \mathsf{sk_b}, \mathsf{St_b}, \mathsf{TempSt_b}, \mathsf{epoch})$
- **Contract.** *The algorithm takes the public parameters, a* trans, *the public state, all users' states and bank public states as inputs and then updates all of them.*

  $(\mathsf{St'_b}, \{\mathsf{St'_u}\}, \mathsf{TempSt'_b}, \{\mathsf{TempSt'_u}\}) \leftarrow \mathsf{Contract}(\{\mathsf{St_u}\}, \{\mathsf{TempSt_u}\}, \mathsf{St_b}, \mathsf{TempSt_b}, \mathsf{trans}, \mathsf{pp})$

4.1 Security Definition

We define two security definitions for the blockchain-based bank protocol; transaction indistinguishability and overdraft safety. Informally speaking,
transaction indistinguishability is from typical left-or-right setting used for
indistinguishability-based definitions, it specifies an adversary cannot distinguish
two confidential transactions. Overdraft safety says the honest users are guaranteed to be able to withdraw all their funds from the system.

  We firstly describe the experiment that defines the security of the above two
security definitions, and the formal definitions for security follow behind. Given a
(candidate) blockchain-based bank scheme Π, an adversary $\mathcal{A}$, and the security
parameter λ, the (probabilistic) experiment consists of interactions between $\mathcal{A}$
and the experiment. We assume the adversary $\mathcal{A}$ has full control of the network,
we also assume that the adversary forwards the transactions to the blockchain
on time (i.e. send query $\mathbf{Q} = \mathbf{Contract}$ on time, we explain the query below).
The experiment accepts different types of queries from the adversary. Figure 6
describes each type of query $\mathbf{Q}$.

4.2 Transaction Indistinguishability

Informally, transaction indistinguishability specifies an experiment where an
adversary sends two different transactions to the ledger. Only one will be
recorded, while the adversary is not able to distinguish which one of these two
is recorded. This security property could indicate the anonymity of the users as
well as the privacy of the transaction values, depending on leakage.

  Transaction indistinguishability is defined by an experiment Tx-IND, which
involves a polynomial-time adversary $\mathcal{A}$ attempting to break a given (candidate) BBANK scheme. We now describe the Tx-IND experiment mentioned above.
Given a (candidate) BBANK scheme Π, an adversary $\mathcal{A}$, and security parameter
λ, the (probabilistic) experiment Tx-IND$(\Pi, \mathcal{A}, \lambda)$ proceeds as the adversary is
capable of sending the listed queries in the experiment described in the previous
section, while the adversary is not allowed to send reveal query for the secret key
of the bank. In addition, the adversary sends the challenge queries we describe
next. In the challenge epoch, the experiment randomly chooses $b \leftarrow \{0,1\}$,
the adversary sends many challenge queries as $\mathbf{Q} = \mathbf{Challenge}(\mathbf{Q_0}, \mathbf{Q_1})$; for
each challenge query, these two queries leaks some information and the exper-
iment only performs Q_b. After finishing the queries, the adversary sends query
$\mathbf{Q} = \mathbf{Commit}$ and gets the output trans$_b$. At the end, the adversary outputs
$b' \in \{0,1\}$. The adversary wins the game if $b' = b$. During the challenge epoch,
we require the queries sent by the adversary to be *Public Consistent* as defined.

Definition 3 (Leakage Function). *A leakage function* Leakage *takes the output from the experiment as input, and the function outputs the leaked information
about the related queries.*

  $\eta \leftarrow$ Leakage$(\mathbf{Q})$

Definition 4 (Public Consistent). *To avoid an adversary winning the experiment trivially, we require the query pairs for* **Commit** *and* **Pay.User** *must be jointly consistent with respect to public information and* $\mathcal{A}$'s *view, namely,*

- *For all the users that the adversary controls (adversary has asked* **Reveal** *query for them), their states in the two banks should be consistent.*
- *If one of the queries* $\mathbf{Q}_0$ *and* $\mathbf{Q}_1$ *is not legitimate, the other query will not proceed by the experiment as well.*
- *The leaked information of* $\mathbf{Q}_0$ *and* $\mathbf{Q}_1$ *should be the same, i.e.,* Leakage($\mathbf{Q}_0$) = Leakage($\mathbf{Q}_1$)

$\mathbf{Q} = (\mathbf{KeyGen})$

1. Compute $(pk, sk) := \mathsf{KeyGen}(\mathsf{pp})$
2. Add (sk, pk) to the key list KeyList
3. Output the public key pk

$\mathbf{Q} = (\mathbf{EstablishBank}, pk)$

1. If (pk, sk) is not in KeyList, output $\perp$.
2. Start a bank instance (trans, TempSt$_b$) $\leftarrow$ EstablishBank(pk$_b$, sk$_b$, pp)
3. Store key pair and the temporary state of the bank, initiate the bank epoch counter as $n = 1$
4. Output trans

$\mathbf{Q} = (\mathbf{NewUser}, \mathsf{pk}, \mathsf{sk})$

1. If (pk, sk) is not in KeyList, outpt $\perp$.
2. Compute (trans, Tempst$_u$) $\leftarrow$ NewUser (pk$_b$, sk$_u$, pk$_u$, pp)
3. Store the temporary state of the user (pk, sk, TempSt$_u$)
4. Output trans

$\mathbf{Q} = (\mathbf{Deposit}, \mathsf{pk}_{user}, \mathsf{v}, \mathsf{epoch})$

1. If (pk$_u$, sk$_u$, TempSt$_u$) is not recorded, output $\perp$
2. Execute i-th instance of deposit protocol (trans, TempSt$_b$, TempSt$_u$) $\leftarrow$ Deposit (pk$_b$, sk$_b$, pk$_u$, sk$_u$, St$_b$, pp, v, epoch), when the bank/user sends m, sends (i, m) to $\mathcal{A}$.
3. Output trans

$\mathbf{Q} = (\mathbf{Pay}, \mathsf{pk}_p, \mathsf{pk}_r, \mathsf{v})$

1. If pk$_p$ or pk$_r$ is not in the KeyList, output $\perp$

2.Execute the ith pay protocol instance (TempSt$'_p$, TempSt$'_b$) $\leftarrow$ Pay(pk$_b$, sk$_b$, pk$_p$, sk$_p$, pk$_r$, TempSt$_p$, TempSt$_{bank}$, pp, v, epoch), when the bank/ user send m, send (i, m) to $\mathcal{A}$.

$\mathbf{Q} = (\mathbf{Send}, i, m)$

1. If $(i, \mathsf{TempSt}_b, \mathsf{TempSt}_u, \mathsf{trans})$ is recorded, send $\perp$ to adversary.
2. Send m to the ith instance. If the ith instance outputs $\perp$, record $(i, \perp)$ and sends $(i, \perp)$ to the adversary. If the ith instance outputs (TempSt$_b$, TempSt$_u$, trans), then record $(i, \mathsf{TempSt}_b, \mathsf{TempSt}_u, \mathsf{trans})$ and output trans. If the instance sends a message m', send (i, m') to the adversary.

$\mathbf{Q} = (\mathbf{Commit}, \mathsf{epoch})$

1. Compute (trans, TempSt$'_b$) $\leftarrow$ Commit (pk$_b$, sk$_b$, St$_b$, TempSt$_b$, epoch)
2. Output trans

$\mathbf{Q} = (\mathbf{Withdraw}, \mathsf{pk}_u, \mathsf{v})$

1. Compute (trans, TempSt$_b$, TempSt$_u$) $\leftarrow$ Withdraw(pk$_u$, sk$_u$, St$_b$, St$_u$, pp, v, epoch)
2. Output trans

$\mathbf{Q} = (\mathbf{Contract}, \mathsf{trans})$

1. Compute (St$'_b$, {St$'_u$}, TempSt$'_b$, {TempSt$'_u$}) $\leftarrow$ Contract({St$_u$}, {TempSt$_u$}, St$_b$, TempSt$_b$, trans, pp)
2. Output {St$'_u$}, St$'_b$

$\mathbf{Q} = (\mathbf{Reveal}, \mathsf{pk})$

Output the secret key and the state of the user/bank who owns pk, i.e., output Sk$_u$, St$_u$

Fig. 6. Query description in blockchain-bank experiment

Definition 5. *Let* Π = (Setup, KeyGen, EstablishBank, NewUser, Deposit, Withdraw, Pay, Commit, Contract) *be a candidate* BBANK *scheme and* λ *is the security parameter. We define the advantage of an adversary* $\mathcal{A}$ *in the* Tx − IND *experiment as follows,*

$$\mathsf{Adv}^{\mathsf{Tx\text{-}IND}}_{\Pi,\mathcal{A}(\lambda)} = |2\Pr[b = b'] - 1|$$

4.3 Overdraft Safety

Informally, overdraft safety specifies that an honest user can withdraw all the balance that she owns according to her state in the withdraw phase of any epoch. This security requirement prohibits an adversary to withdraw more than what it has, since otherwise there must be an honest user who cannot withdraw all of his balance because of the lack of the funds in the smart contract.

Overdraft safety is defined by an experiment Overdraft, which involves a polynomial-time adversary $\mathcal{A}$ attempting to break a given (candidate) BBANK scheme. We now describe the Overdraft experiment mentioned above. Given a BBANK scheme Π, an adversary $\mathcal{A}$, and security parameter λ, the (probabilistic) experiment Overdraft($\Pi, \mathcal{A}, \lambda$) proceeds as the adversary is capable of sending all the queries in the experiment that we define in the beginning of this section. In addition, adversary can send $\mathbf{Q} = \mathbf{Reveal}$ for the secret key and state of the bank. In the challenge epoch, the adversary wins if in a certain epoch, there is an honest user who tries and fails to withdraw all his balance within one epoch.

Definition 6. *Let* Π = (Setup, KeyGen, EstablishBank, NewUser, Deposit, Withdraw, Pay, Commit, Contract) *be a candidate* BBANK *scheme and* λ *is the security parameter. We define the advantage of an adversary* $\mathcal{A}$ *in the* Overdraft *game as*

$$\mathsf{Adv}^{\mathsf{Overdraft}}_{\Pi,\mathcal{A}(\lambda)} = Pr[\exists \mathsf{u} \in \mathcal{U} \text{ such that } \bot \leftarrow \mathsf{Withdraw}(\mathsf{b_{max}}, \mathsf{pk_u}, \mathsf{v})]$$

5 PriBank: Privacy-Preserving Scaling Construction

We present the construction of algorithms of PriBank in Fig. 7 with a brief descriptions as follows. A taxonomy of symbols is provided in Appendix G.

- **Proof of commitment.** Operator commits to a user's balance, transaction values, a randomness using Pedersen commitment, ComProve algorithm. A user verifies these commitments using ComVerify algorithm.
- **NIZK for updated balance.** Operator collects all transactions of the users in one epoch, computes the new commitments for users' updated balances and gives NIZK proof using ProBal. The verification algorithms is VeriBal.
- **Signature.** To provide the authenticity of data exchanged between users and operator, standard digital signatures are used in PriBank.

$\mathsf{ProBal}(\{c\}, \{c'\}, \{c_v\}, \{c_{t_i}\}, \{d_i\}, \{v_{ij}\}, g,$
$h, \gamma, c_0, \{h_i\}, \{h'_i\}, \{t_i\}, \{b_i\}, \{b'_i\}, C)$

Take $(\{d_i\}, \{t_i\}, \{b_i\}, \{b'_i\}, \{v_{ij}\})$ as inputs of the circuit C, compute all the inner wires of C as $a_{k+1}, ..., a_l$
set $\{c_k\} = \langle \{c_i\}, \{c'_i\}, \{c_v\}, \{c_{t_i}\}\rangle$
Compute c_l as described in protocol 3.4
Run protocol 3.4 as a prover, generate proof π_{zk}
return : π_{zk}

$\mathsf{VeriBal}(\{c\}, \{c'\}, \{c_v\}, \{c_{t_i}\}, g, h, \gamma, c_0,$
$\{h_i\}, \{h'_i\}, , C, \pi_{zk}) \rightarrow \{0, 1\}$:
Run protocol 3.4 as a verifier, generate
$\mathsf{b} \in \{0, 1\}$
return : b

$\mathsf{ComProve}(h^\gamma, h_i^\gamma, \gamma, h_i)$:
$\alpha \leftarrow \mathbb{Z}_p$
Compute $d = h^\alpha, d' = h_i^\alpha$
$x \leftarrow \mathsf{Hash}(h, h_i, h^\gamma, h_i^\gamma, d, d')$
Compute $\theta \leftarrow \theta - x\gamma$.
return : $\pi \leftarrow (d, d', \theta)$.

$\mathsf{ComVerify}(g, h, h_i, c_0, c_i, b_i, \pi)$:
Compute $x \leftarrow \mathsf{H}(h, h_i, h^\gamma, c_0, d, d')$
Let $c' = c_i / g^{b_i}$.
if $c_0^x h^\theta = d \wedge c'^x h^\theta = d'$ then
    return 1
else
    return 0

$\mathsf{Sign}(m, sk_E) \rightarrow \sigma_E$
$\mathsf{VerifySig}(m, \sigma_E, pk_E) \rightarrow \{0, 1\}$

Fig. 7. PriBank Construction Algorithms, including syntax for digital signatures.

Following, we provide a brief description of the main processes of PriBank:

Register. To register an account, a user u_i sends a request Reg consisting of signature σ_{b_i} on its balance b_i to the operator during an epoch r. The operator returns a randomness t_i with its commitment proofs and signature on these values. Further, user verifies all the details and accordingly sends a registration request to the smart contract along with a deposit transaction. The smart contract verifies the request and registers the user accordingly (Fig. 8). After a send/receive transaction, the user's balance becomes private in later epochs.

Operator O
$\{\mathsf{Reg} : pk_i, b_i, \sigma_{b_i}\} \leftarrow$
If $\mathsf{VerifySig}(b_i, \sigma_{b_i}, pk_i)$

1. $t_i \xleftarrow{\$} \mathbb{Z}_p, c_{t_i} \leftarrow g^{t_i} h_{t_i}^\gamma$
2. $\pi_1 \leftarrow \mathsf{ComProve}(c_0, h_{t_i}^\gamma,$
   $\gamma, h_{t_i})$
3. $m := \{c_{t_i}, r, pk_i\}$
4. $\sigma_o \leftarrow \mathsf{Sign}(m, sk_o)$
5. Send $\{m, \sigma_o, t_i, \pi_1\}$
   to $U \rightarrow$

User U
$d_1 \leftarrow \mathsf{VerifySig}(m, \sigma_o, pk_o)$
$d_2 \leftarrow \mathsf{ComVerify}(g, h, h_{t_i},$
$c_0, c_{t_i}, t_i, \pi_1)$
If $d_1 \wedge d_2$:

1. $\sigma_i \leftarrow \mathsf{Sign}(\langle m, \sigma_o\rangle, sk_i)$
2. Send $\{\mathsf{Reg} : m, \sigma_o, \sigma_i, b_i\}$
   to $SC \rightarrow$

Smart Contract SC
$d_1 \leftarrow \mathsf{VerifySig}(m, \sigma_o, pk_o)$
$d_2 \leftarrow \mathsf{VerifySig}(\langle m, \sigma_o\rangle,$
$\sigma_i, pk_i)$
If $d_1 \wedge d_2$:

1. $c_{b_i} \leftarrow g^{b_i} c_0$
2. $\mathsf{Record}(c_{t_i}, c_{b_i}, pk_i)$
3. $B \leftarrow B + b_i$

Fig. 8. User registration

Transfer. In each epoch r, each user u_i needs to get a fresh randomness t_i from the operator. The randomness is computed in similar way as in registration. To agree on the randomness computed by the operator, a user sends $\sigma_i \leftarrow \mathsf{Sign}(\langle m, \sigma_o \rangle, sk_i)$ to the operator and the operator verifies the signature by $\mathsf{VerifySig}(\langle m, \sigma_o \rangle, \sigma_i, pk_i)$ and records c_{t_i}, t_i. This randomness allows users to compute their balances $d_i = t_i - b_i$ during the end of the epoch, where d_i is published by the operator. The user u_i can compute the correctness of his balance by the published d_i before the end of the epoch. The randomness t_i is used as a 'mask' for the user's balance. The necessity of this randomness is for the balance to be sealed by the operator. Therefore, if a user receives some transactions that it doesn't know the transaction value, then, the user cannot compute its balance directly from its own transaction history.

Operator O
Transaction lists: $\mathcal{T}_r$, $\mathcal{CT}_r$

User U
Transaction lists: $\mathcal{T}_r$, $\mathcal{CT}_r$
$\mathsf{Tx}'_{ij} : (pk_i, pk_j, v_{ij}, \mathsf{Null}, r, n, \sigma_{ij})$
$\leftarrow$ Send Tx'_{ij} to O

$d \leftarrow \mathsf{ValidateTx}(\mathsf{Tx}'_{ij}, b_i)$
If $\neg(\mathsf{Online}(u_i) \wedge \mathsf{Online}(u_j) \wedge d)$: abort
$b_i' \leftarrow b_i - v_{ij}$, $\quad c_i' \leftarrow g^{b_i} h_i^{\gamma}$, $\quad c_{ij} \leftarrow g^{v_{ij}} h_{ij}^{\gamma}$
Let $\mathsf{Tx}_{ij} : (pk_i, pk_j, v_{ij}, c_{ij}, r, n)$, $\mathsf{CTx}_{ij} : (pk_j, c_{ij})$
$\mathcal{CT}'_r = \{\mathsf{CTx}_{ik} | \mathsf{CTx}_{ik} \in \mathcal{CT}_r \wedge k \neq j\} \cup \{\mathsf{CTx}'_{ij}\}$
$\pi \leftarrow \mathsf{ComProve}(c_0, h_{ij}^{\gamma}, \gamma)$, $m := \{\pi, \mathcal{CT}'_r\}$
$\sigma_o \leftarrow \mathsf{Sign}(m, sk_o)$
Send $\{m, \sigma_o\}$ to $U \rightarrow$

Check if $\mathcal{CT}'_r$ is the correct history
$d_1 \leftarrow \mathsf{VerifySig}(m, pk_o, \sigma_o)$
$b_i' \leftarrow b_i - v_{ij}$
$d_2 \leftarrow \mathsf{ComVerify}(g, h, h_{ij}, c_0, c_{ij}, v_{ij}, \pi)$
If $d_1 \wedge d_2 : \sigma_i \leftarrow \mathsf{Sign}(\mathcal{CT}', sk_i)$
$\leftarrow$ Send σ_i to O

$d_1 \leftarrow \mathsf{VerifySig}(\mathcal{CT}', \sigma_i, pk_i)$
If d_1; Update transaction lists
$\mathcal{T}_r \leftarrow \{\mathsf{Tx}_{ik} | \mathsf{Tx}_{ik} \in \mathcal{T}_r \wedge k \neq j\} \cup \{\mathsf{Tx}_{ij}\}$
$\mathcal{CT}_r \leftarrow \mathcal{CT}'_r$

Fig. 9. Transfer

If a user wants to send transactions in an epoch, he/she needs to keep records of two transaction lists $\mathcal{T}_r$ and $\mathcal{CT}_r$, the operator keeps records of these two lists for each user. The list $\mathcal{T}_r$ contains the plain transactions that user sent in epoch r, while $\mathcal{CT}$ only contains the confidential abbreviated transactions, i.e. $\mathcal{CT} = \{\mathsf{CTx}_{ij} | \mathsf{CTx}_{ij} : (pk_j, C_{ij})\}$ To send a transaction, a user sends the plain transaction to the operator. The operator checks its validation, commits to the transaction value, signs the transaction, and gives a proof of commitment. Meanwhile, the operator aggregates all the transactions sent by the user in this epoch, signs the confidential transaction list, and sends it to the user. If the user agrees to the confidential transaction list, he/she returns its signature on the list. Henceforth, a user confirms all its sent transactions in this epoch. Before the end of one epoch, the operator collects all the confidential lists of each user and sends them to the smart contract. The smart contract checks these lists and records the transactions accordingly. Figure 9 depicts the transfer process.

Commit. Before the end of an epoch, the operator collects all the confidential transaction lists of the users, compute the new balance and its commitments for each user i.e. $c_i = g^{b_i} h_i^{\gamma}$. Further, it computes $d_i = b_i - t_i, \forall i \in \{1, ..., N\}$ where t_i is the randomness that the operator agrees on with each user during the start of epoch. In case where a user has some receiving transactions during an epoch but the user did not agree on a randomness with the operator, the operator sets $d_i = \bot$. Subsequently, it generates a zero-knowledge proof for the correct computation by $\pi \leftarrow \mathsf{ProvBal}(\{\mathcal{CT}_r\}, \{c_i\}, \{d_i\})$, where the inputs are the confidential transaction lists, the balance commitments in the previous epoch, the updated balance commitments, the randomness commitments and d_i of all users. Finally, it submits the following data to the smart contract:

User Index	$\mathcal{CT}$ and Sig	t_i and Sig	Balance	d
u_1	$\mathcal{CT}_1^{\tau}, \sigma_1$	c_{t_1}, σ_{t_1}	c_1	d_1
$\vdots$	$\vdots$	$\vdots$	$\vdots$	$\vdots$
u_i	$\bot, \bot$	$c_{t_i}, \bot$	c_i	d_i
$\vdots$	$\vdots$	$\vdots$	$\vdots$	$\vdots$
u_N	$\mathcal{CT}_N^{\tau}, \sigma_N$	c_{t_N}, σ_{t_N}	c_N	d_N
Operator signature on the above data: σ_o				
zero-knowledge proof: π				

Upon receiving the data submitted by the operator, the smart contract checks the validation of each signature by $\mathsf{VerifySig}(m, \sigma_i, pk_i)$ and the validation of the zero-knowledge proof $\mathsf{VerifyBal}(\{\mathcal{CT}_r\}, \{c_i\}, \{d_i\})$. For every user u_i who did not agree on a randomness with the operator in this epoch, smart contract updates this user's balance commitment as his/her balance commitment in the previous epoch and for the other users who have send transaction with value C_{ji} to this user, it updates their balance commitments as $c_j = c_i \cdot C_{ji}$.

Exit. At the end of every epoch, a user who wants to exit the system can send a request to smart contract during the exit phase. The smart contract transfers the funds back to the user if the request is valid. The user who wants to exit gets the randomness and its proof of the latest randomness commitment that it agreed on with the operator. Generate the request as $\{\mathsf{exit}, pk_i, t_i, \pi, \sigma_i\}$ where σ_i is the user's signature on the request. Upon receiving the request, the smart contract verifies the signatures and verifies the proof of the most recently committed randomness by $\mathsf{ComVerify}(g, h, h_{t_i}, c_0, c_{t_i}, t_i, \pi)$. Transfer user's balance $b_i = t_i - d_i$ if all the verification get accepted.

6 Security Proof

6.1 Proof for Transaction Indistinguishability

We describe a simulation experiment $\mathbf{Exp}_{sim}$ in which the adversary $\mathcal{A}$ interacts with an experiment as in the Tx-IND experiment. While the answer of the experiment to the challenge queries is independent of b, therefor the $\mathcal{A}$'s advantage in the $\mathbf{Exp}_{sim}$ is 0. We further prove that the simulation experiment is indistinguishable from the real experiment $\mathbf{Exp}_{real}$.

$\mathbf{Exp}_{sim}$. In the challenge phase, how the simulated experiment answers the queries from the adversary is different from the $\mathbf{Exp}_{sim}$ as follows,

- $Q = (\mathbf{Commit}, \mathsf{epoch})$
  1. The operator collects all the transaction lists in this epoch, calculates the new balance for each user. Then the operator computes the balance masks as $d = t - b$ for users that the adversary has asked real key query before and select random values as balance masks for honest users.
  2. Simulate a zero-knowledge proof for the statement.
  3. Output trans.

Experiment $\mathbf{Exp}_1$. The experiment $\mathbf{Exp}_1$ modifies the real experiment by simulating the zero-knowledge proof. Since the zk-SNARK system is perfect honest-verifier zero knowledge, the distribution of the simulated proof is identical to the proof computed in a real experiment. Hence, the advantage of distinguishability of the adversary for experiments $\mathbf{Exp}_{real}$ and $\mathbf{Exp}_1$ is 0.

Experiment $\mathbf{Exp}_2$. The experiment $\mathbf{Exp}_2$ modifies $\mathbf{Exp}_1$ by replacing all the commitments for honest users' balances, randomness t_i and transactions values by commitments to random values. Precisely, in the real experiment, every time a user sends a transaction to the operator, the operator hides the transaction value by making a commitment to it (Fig. 9) and publishes the commitment on the blockchain later. In $\mathbf{Exp}_2$, the operator commits to a random value instead of the transaction value, by Lemma 1 (see below), $|\mathsf{Adv}^{\mathbf{Exp}_1} - \mathsf{Adv}^{\mathbf{Exp}_2}| \le q \cdot \mathsf{Adv}^{\mathbf{DDH}}$.

Experiment $\mathbf{Exp}_{sim}$. $\mathbf{Exp}_{sim}$ modifies $\mathbf{Exp}_2$ by replacing all the balance masks d_i for honest users to random values. Since the adversary does not know the honest users' t_i and these values are also random, hence the distributions for d_i in Exp_{sim} is indistinguishable.

As argued above, the responses of the adversary $\mathcal{A}$ to $\mathbf{Exp}_{sim}$ is independent of b, so that $\mathsf{Adv}^{\mathbf{Exp}_{sim}} = 0$. Then, by summing over $\mathcal{A}$'s advantages in the hybrid experiments, we can bound $\mathcal{A}$'s advantage in $\mathbf{Exp}_{real}$ by

$$\mathsf{Adv}^{\mathbf{Exp}_{real}} \le q \cdot \mathsf{Adv}^{\mathbf{DDH}}$$

Lemma 1. *Let Adv^{DDH} be the advantage of an adversary in DDH problem. Then after q $\mathbf{Pay}.\mathbf{User}$ queries, $|\mathsf{Adv}^{\mathbf{Exp}_2} - \mathsf{Adv}^{\mathbf{Exp}_1}| \le q \cdot \mathsf{Adv}^{\mathbf{DDH}}$*

Proof. In the challenge phase of the experiment, when the adversary sends the query Commit, the experiment replies with a trans that includes all the commitments for the transaction values and all the commitments for users' balances in the current epoch. While in $\mathbf{Exp}_2$, the commitments for the transactions and balances of honest users are actually commitments to the random values. We argue the two experiments are indistinguishable.

In $\mathbf{Exp}_1$, a commitment for a transaction from u_i to u_j is $c_{ij} = g^v h_{ij}^\gamma$ where v is the transaction value that known by the adversary, h_{ij} is a random generator such that the commitment key is unknown, γ is a secret held by the operator, while h^γ is publicly known. In $\mathbf{Exp}_2$, a commitment for such a transaction is computed as $c = g^v h_{ij}^s$ where s is uniformly selected from $\mathbb{Z}_p$. If an adversary can distinguish the tuple $(h^\gamma, h_{ij}, g^v h_{ij}^\gamma)$ from $(h^\gamma, h_{ij}, g^v h_{ij}^s)$, it can also solve the DDH tuple $(h^\gamma, h_{ij}, h_{ij}^z)$. The similar argument applies to the commitments for users' balances and the commitments for agreed randomness t_i. Hence, we have $q \cdot \mathsf{Adv}^{\mathbf{DDH}} \geq |\mathsf{Adv}^{\mathbf{Exp}_1} - \mathsf{Adv}^{\mathbf{Exp}_2}|$ where q is the total number of commitments. □

6.2 Proof for Overdraft Safety

Assuming the challenge epoch is n, the output of the experiment for query $\mathbf{Q} = \mathbf{Commit}$ is trans_n. At the end of this epoch, an honest user u_i fails to withdraw her total balance b_i. b_i is the balance recorded in the state of u_i. It is computed by the user's balance in the previous epoch being deduced by the user's spending and being added by the user's receiving in the current epoch. The experiment is performed under a setting that the signature forgery is impossible.

In the exit phase, an honest user u_i submits an exit request $\{\mathsf{exit}, pk_i', t_i, \pi, \sigma_i\}$, the smart contract accepts the request only if $1 \leftarrow \mathsf{ComVerify}(g, h, h_{t_i}, c_0, c_{t_i}, t_i, \pi)$. Suppose ComVerify fails, it indicates the proof π is incorrect. While we observe that the same algorithm with the same parameter is run by the user before the operator commits to blockchain (due to randomness agreement), since the user is honest, it should abort the execution in the transfer phase and refuse to sign the randomness commitment at that point.

Apart from the failure of ComVerify, a user can also fail to withdraw in the case that $b_i \neq b_i'$, i.e., the user withdraws less than what she believes to have. This can be the result of $b_i \neq t_i - d_i$ or the lack of funds in the smart contract. In the earlier case, it indicates the soundness of zero-knowledge proof is broken. In the later case, it implies that there must be at least one adversary, say u_j, who withdraws more than what it has, namely, $b_j \geq t_j - d_j$, which also indicates the soundness of zero-knowledge is broken.

7 Implementation and Evaluation

We evaluate the usability of the commit-and-prove zero-knowledge proof of *PriBank* and give its implementation in *Go*. We use elliptic curve secp256k1 with 128-bit security, the balances and transactions are 8-bits length, we test the proof size per user, transaction size, the proof generation time, verification time, the time for pre-processing. We do not deploy optimization on the implementation, therefore the performance in terms of time is not desirable that results in "low" cost of transaction instead of "Very low" cost similar to ZK-Rollup as depicted in Table 1. Particularly, the pre-processing to generate a QAP takes too long to perform further experiments on more users cases. We refer to the work [2,9] for optimization and faster implementation. The experiments were performed on 2 × 24 Xeon 2.4 GHz cores. The code of the implementation can be found in [1].

The commitment sent by the operator to the smart contract includes balance and transaction commitments, balance mask d, two signatures for each user, and a proof. The computation circuit of the operator allows each user in the system to send a transaction to every other user, Therefore, for an n user circuit the maximum transaction number is $n(n-1)$. Assuming a user can send a transaction with a zero value, the total commitment size of the operator is computed based on the maximum transaction number. While the number of transactions that have positive value might be much less, we measure the transaction size in a case where we assume a user send non-zero transactions to half of the other users in one epoch. Following, we depict the proof size, transaction size, and circuit gate numbers dependency of users in Fig. 10.

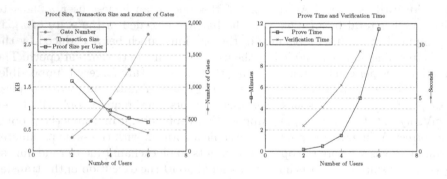

Fig. 10. Experimental results

8   Conclusion

Our goal in this work was to implement privacy over an account-based blockchain system. We formally defined a blockchain-based bank model along with security definitions. Following that, we presented a novel privacy-preserving cryptocurrency system PriBank, for that, we constructed an efficient Commit-and-Prove NIZK protocol. Our construction achieves privacy together with scalability in the blockchain which has not been achieved by the previous schemes. As most of the schemes are concerned with achieving privacy or scalability alone, hence, we compared our scheme separately with the popular privacy and scalability solutions. We provided a detailed security analysis and performance evaluation.

Future Directions. There are various ways to adapt and extend this work. One possibility is to reduce the complexity of the data which is sent to the smart contract in each epoch, henceforth increasing the efficiency of the overall system. Another direction of work is to build more efficient proof algorithm to reduce the verification complexity.

A   Commit-Prove Zero-Knowledge Proof Construction

Circuit: The arithmetic circuit C of the zero-knowledge proof is in Fig. 11

Inputs:

- Transaction values v_{ij} where $i, j \in 1, .., N, i \neq j$

- Users' randomness $\{t_i\}_{i=1}^{N}$

- Users' balances of the previous epoch b_i^{r-1} and the updated balance b_i^r
- User's balance mask $d_i, i \in \{1, ..., N\}$
- Total balance of the contract B

The circuit check the following constraints for the inputs:
$$b_i^r = b_i^{r-1} - \sum_{j=1}^{N} v_{ij} + \sum_{j=1}^{N} v_{ji} \wedge b_i^r = t_i - d_i \wedge B = \sum_{i=1}^{N} b_i^r \wedge v_{ij} \geq 0 \wedge b_i^{r-1} - \sum_{j=0}^{N} v_{ij} \geq 0$$

Fig. 11. Circuit

B   Proof of Protocol 3.1

Proof. **Soundness.** By the rewinding, the prover, the extractor $\mathcal{X}$ gets two valid transcripts that have the same commitments:
$(d_1, d_2, c_0, c_1, x, \theta_a, \theta_b, \theta_1, \theta_2, \theta_{ab})$, $(d_1, d_2, c_0, c_1, x', \theta_a', \theta_b', \theta_1', \theta_2', \theta_{ab}')$ from the verification, we get equations

$$c_a^x g^{\theta_a} h^{\theta_1} = d_1 \qquad c_a^{x'} g^{\theta_a'} h^{\theta_1'} = d_1$$

By the binding property of Pedersen commitment, This implies $a = \frac{\theta_a' - \theta_a}{x - x'}$, by the same technique, $\mathcal{X}$ can compute $b = \frac{\theta_b' - \theta_b}{x - x'}$ and α, β.

Next, assume c is a commitment that committed to z, we will prove $z = ab$. Assume $c_0 = g^u h^{r_{c0}}, c_1 = g^v h^{r_{c1}}$, observe that $g^{\theta_a \theta_b} h^{\theta_{ab}} c_0^x = c^{x^2} c_1$, it implies

$$g^{abx^2 - (\alpha\beta + b\alpha)x + \alpha\beta + ux} h^{\theta_{ab} + xr_{c0}} = g^{zx^2 + v} h^{r_c x^2 + r_{c1}}$$

Since $a, b, \alpha, \beta, u, v$ are all predefine value, either $\mathcal{X}$ can extract non-trivial relation between g, h or $u = \alpha b + \beta a$ and the extractor can extract $z = ab = \frac{\theta_a \theta_b - \theta_a' \theta_b' + (\alpha b + \beta a)(x - x')}{x^2 - x'^2}$.

Perfect special honest-verifier zero-knowledge. The simulator randomly chooses $\theta_1, \theta_2, \theta_a, \theta_b, \theta_{ab}, u, r \leftarrow \mathbb{Z}_p$ and randomly chooses a challenge $x \leftarrow \mathbb{Z}_p$, it computes $d_1 = c_a^x g^{\theta_a} h^{\theta_1}$, $d_2 = c_b^x g^{\theta_b} h^{\theta_2}$, $c_0 = g^u h^r$, $c_1 = g^{\theta_a \theta_b} h^{\theta_{ab}} c_0^x / c^{x^2}$. Thus the simulator produces a valid transcript $(d_1, d_2, c_0, c_1, x, \theta_a, \theta_b, \theta_1, \theta_2, \theta_{ab})$ that has the identical probability distributions with the real proof.   □

C   Proof of Protocol 3.2

Proof. **Soundness.** For an accepting transcripts $(c_0, \Omega, d_1, d_2, x, \theta_1, \theta_2)$, assume that

$$c_0 = h^\gamma, \Omega = \tau^u h^{-v}, d_1 = h^\alpha, d_2 = \tau^\delta h^\beta$$

since $d_1 = c_0^x h^{\theta_1}, d_2 = \Omega^x \tau^{\theta_1} h^{\theta_2}$ we have

$$h^{x\gamma + \theta_1} = h^\alpha, \quad \tau^{ux + \theta_1} h^{\theta_2 - vx} = \tau^\delta h^\beta$$

If $u \neq \gamma$ then it means $\theta_1 = \frac{\delta\gamma - u\alpha}{\gamma - u}$ and $x = \frac{\alpha - \delta}{\gamma - u}$ or the cheating prover is able to compute the Pedersen commitment key $\log_g h$. Since α, δ, γ are pre-defined values, $\Pr[x = \frac{\alpha - \delta}{u - \gamma}] = \frac{1}{p}$.

Since in the verification, $c = \prod_{i=1}^{n} c_i^{b_i} / \Omega$, assume $c = g^w h^t$, this implies

$$g^w h^t = g^{\sum_{i=1}^{n} a_i b_i} h^v$$

Hence, either $w = \sum_{i=1}^{n} a_i b_i$ or the prover is able to compute the discrete logarithm.

□

Perfect special honest-verifier zero-knowledge. The simulator randomly chooses $\gamma, \theta_1, \theta_2 \leftarrow \mathbb{Z}_p$ and computes $c_0 = h^\gamma, \Omega = \prod_{i=1}^{n} c_i^{b_i} / c$. Then the simulator chooses a challenge randomly $x \leftarrow \mathbb{Z}_p$ and computes $d_1 = c_0^x h^{\theta_1}, d_2 = \Omega^x \tau^{\theta_1} h^{\theta_2}$. The transcript $trs = (c_0, d_1, d_2, x, \theta_1, \theta_2)$ is a valid transcript that has the identical probability distributions with the real proof.

D   Proof of Protocol 3.3

Proof. We follow the proof of [9] for the soundness, and give our proof for the zero-knowledge property.

Soundness. We firstly construct an extractor $\mathcal{X}_1$ of protocol **Prove**, then construct an extractor $\mathcal{X}_2$ for protocol 3.3. For $\mathcal{X}_1$, we use an inductive argument showing that in each step, we either extract a witness or a discrete log relation. If $n = |g| = 1$, rewinding $\mathcal{P}$ to get 2 transcripts with the same randomness used by $\mathcal{P}$ but different challenges from $\mathcal{V}$, assume the witness of $\mathcal{P}$ are (a_1, c, r), $d = g_1^{t_1} u^{t_2} h^{t_3}$, the transcripts are

$$tr := (d, x, \theta_1, \theta_2)$$
$$tr' := (d, x', \theta_1', \theta_2')$$

then we get $g_1^{a_1 x + \theta_1} u^{cx + b_1 \theta_1} h^{\theta_2 + xr} = g_1^{a_1 x' + \theta_1'} u^{cx' + b_1 \theta_1'} h^{\theta_2' + x'r} = d$.

Since a_1, c, d are predefined value, either extractor can compute

$$\log_{g_1} u + \log_{g_1} h = \frac{\theta_1 - \theta_1'}{b_1 \theta_1' + \theta_2' - b_1 \theta_1 - \theta_2}$$

or $a_1 = \frac{\theta_1 - \theta_1'}{x' - x}$ and $c = a_1 b_1$

Next, on the k-th recursive step that on input$(g, u, h, c, \boldsymbol{b})$, assume that the $(k+1)$th recursive step has input$(\boldsymbol{g}', u, h, c', \boldsymbol{b}')$ and the witness can be extracted from this recursive are $r', \boldsymbol{a}', \langle \boldsymbol{a}', \boldsymbol{b}' \rangle$. We show that with the witness of the $(k+1)$th recursive step, an extractor can effectively compute a witness of the k-th recursive step or a non-trivial discrete logarithm relation between the generators.

On k-th recursive step, the extractor runs the prover to get L and R. Then, by rewinding the prover four times and giving it four different challenges x_1, x_2, x_3, x_4, the extractor obtains four $\boldsymbol{a}_i' \in \mathbb{Z}_p^{n'}$ such that

$$c \cdot L^{x_i^2} \cdot R^{x_i^{-2}} = \left(\boldsymbol{g}_{[:n']}^{x_i^{-1}} \circ \boldsymbol{g}_{[n':]}^{x_i^2} \right)^{\boldsymbol{a}_i'} h^{r_i'} u^{\langle \boldsymbol{a}_i', \boldsymbol{b}_i' \rangle} \quad \text{for } i = 1, ..., 4 \tag{1}$$

compute $v_1, v_2, v_3 \in \mathbb{Z}_p$ such that

$$\sum_{i=1}^{3} v_i x_i^2 = 1, \qquad \sum_{i=1}^{3} v_i = 0, \qquad \sum_{i=1}^{3} v_i x_i^{-2} = 0 \tag{2}$$

Then taking a linear combination of the first three equations with v_1, v_2, v_3 as the coefficients,

$$c^{v_i} \cdot L^{x_i^2 v_i} \cdot R^{x_i^{-2} v_i} = (\boldsymbol{g}_{[:n']}^{x_i^{-1}} \boldsymbol{g}_{[n':]}^{x_i})^{\boldsymbol{a}_i' v_i} h^{v_i r_i'} u^{\langle \boldsymbol{a}_i', \boldsymbol{b}_i' \rangle v_i} \text{ for } i - 1, 2, 3$$

we can compute

$L = \boldsymbol{g}^{\boldsymbol{a}_L} h^{r_L} u^{s_L}$, where

$$r_L = \sum_{i=1}^{3} v_i r_i', \quad \boldsymbol{a}_{L[:n']} = \sum_{i=1}^{3} x_i^{-1} \boldsymbol{a}_i' v_i, \quad \boldsymbol{a}_{L[n':]} = \sum_{i=1}^{3} x_i \boldsymbol{a}_i' v_i, \quad s_L = \sum_{i=1}^{3} \langle \boldsymbol{a}_i', \boldsymbol{b}_i' \rangle v_i$$

Repeating this process with different combinations (compute v_1, v_2, v_3 of Eq. 2 with different summations), we can also compute R, c such that

$$R = \boldsymbol{g}^{\boldsymbol{a}_R} h^{r_R} u^{s_R}$$
$$c = \boldsymbol{g}^{\boldsymbol{a}_c} h^{r_c} u^{s_c}$$

Now, we can rewrite Eq. 1, for each $x \in \{x_1, x_2, x_3, x_4\}$ as

$$\boldsymbol{g}^{\boldsymbol{a}_L x^2 + \boldsymbol{a}_c + \boldsymbol{a}_R x^{-2}} h^{x^2 r_L + r_c + x^{-2} r_R} u^{x^2 s_L + s_c + x^{-2} s_R} = \boldsymbol{g}_{[:n']}^{\boldsymbol{a}' \cdot x^{-1}} \boldsymbol{g}_{[n':]}^{\boldsymbol{a}' \cdot x} h^{r'} u^{\langle \boldsymbol{a}', \boldsymbol{b}' \rangle}$$

This implies that

$$a' \cdot x^{-1} = x^2 a_{L[:n']} + a_{c[:n']} + x^{-2} a_{R[:n']}$$
$$a' \cdot x = x^2 a_{L[n':]} + a_{c[n':]} + x^{-2} a_{R[n':]}$$
$$\langle a', b' \rangle = x^2 s_L + s_c + x^{-2} s_R$$

Either the extractor can obtain a non-trivial discrete logarithm relation between the generators (g, h, u) if these equations do not hold, or we can deduce that for each challenge $x \in \{x_1, x_2, x_3, x_4\}$

$$x^3 a_{L[:n']} + x(a_{c[:n']} - a_{L[n':]}) + x^{-1}(a_{R[:n']} - a_{c[n':]}) - x^{-3} a_{R[n':]} = 0$$

The only way the above equation hold for all challenges is if

$$a_{L[:n']} = a_{R[n':]} = 0, \quad a_{c[:n']} = a_{L[n':]}, \quad a_{R[:n']} = a_{c[n':]}$$

Thus $a' = x a_{c[:n']} + x^{-1} a_{c[n':]}$ Using these values we can see that:

$$x^2 s_L + s_c + x^{-2} s_R = \langle a', b' \rangle$$
$$= \langle a_{c[:n']}, b_{[n':]} \rangle \cdot x^2 + \langle a_c, b \rangle + \langle a_{c[n':]}, b_{[:n']} \rangle \cdot x^{-2}$$

Since the relation holds for all $x \in \{x_1, x_2, x_3, x_4\}$, it must be that

$$\langle a_c, b \rangle = s_c$$

The extractor, thus, either extracts a discrete logarithm relation between the generators, or the witness a_c.

We now show that at the beginning of the protocol 3.3, on input (c_a, c_{ab}, g, b), the extractor $\mathcal{X}_2$ runs $\mathcal{P}$ with challenge x and uses $\mathcal{X}_1$ to obtain a witness a, r such that $c_a c_{ab}^x = g^a g^{x\langle a, b \rangle} h^r$. Rewinding $\mathcal{P}$ with a different challenge x' and $\mathcal{X}_1$ extracts new witness a', r' such that $c_a c_{ab}^{x'} = g^{a'} g^{x\langle a', b \rangle} h^{r'}$. Then we get

$$g^{s(x-x')} h^{r_{ab}(x-x')} = g^{a-a'} g^{x\langle a,b \rangle - x'\langle a',b \rangle} h^{r-r'}$$

Unless $a = a'$ we get a not trivial discrete log relation between g, h and g. Otherwise we get $s = \langle a, b \rangle, r_{ab} = \frac{r-r'}{x-x'}, r_a = r - \frac{x(r-r')}{x-x'}$.   □

Perfect Zero-Knowledge. The simulator chooses randomly a vector $a \in \mathbb{Z}_p^n$ as witness and we show it can generate a valid transcripts for this vector.

For each recursive step when a prover asks for L, R, the simulator chooses randomly $r_1, r_2 \in \mathbb{Z}_p^*$, and computes

$$L = g_{[n':]}^{a_{[:n']}} \cdot u^{\langle a_{[:n']}, b_{[n':]} \rangle} \cdot h^{r_1} \in \mathbb{G}$$
$$R = g_{[:n']}^{a_{[n':]}} \cdot u^{\langle a_{[n':]}, b_{[:n']} \rangle} \cdot h^{r_2} \in \mathbb{G}$$

Assume that at the last recursive step the input commitment is c', the challenge is x. The simulator randomly choose $\theta_1, \theta_2 \in \mathbb{Z}_p^*$, compute $d = c'^x g_1^{\theta_1} u^{b_1 \theta_1} h^{\theta_2}$.

The transcript $trs = (c, L_1, R_1, x_1, L_2, R_2, x_2, ..., d, x, \theta_1, \theta_2)$ is a valid transcript that has the identical probability distributions with the real proof.

E   Proof of Protocol 3.4

Proof. **Soundness.** A valid transcript of protocol 3.4 consists of 8 sub-transcripts: three transcripts of Protocol 3.1 on statements

$$(\{c_1\}_{i=1}^k, \{h_i\}_{i=1}^k, g, h, c_u, \{u_i(x_1)\}_{i=1}^k);$$
$$(\{c_1\}_{i=1}^k, \{h_i\}_{i=1}^k, g, h, c_v, \{v_i(x_1)\}_{i=1}^k);$$
$$(\{c_1\}_{i=1}^k, \{h_i\}_{i=1}^k, g, h, c_w, \{w_i(x_1)\}_{i=1}^k)$$

respectively; four transcripts of Protocol 3.2 on statements $(g, b := \{u_{k+1}(x_1), ..., u_l(x_1)\}, c_l, c_u)$, $(g, b := \{v_{k+1}(x_1), ..., v_l(x_1)\}, c_l, c_v)$, $(g, b := \{w_{k+1}(x_1), ..., u_l(x_1)\}, c_l, c_w)$ and $(g, b := \{xz(x_1), ..., x^{n-2}z(x_1)\}, c_h, c_{hz})$ respectively; one transcript of Protocol 3.3 on statement (c_a, c_b, c_c).

The soundness of protocol 3.1 implies

$$c_u = g^{\sum_{i=1}^k a_i u_i(x_1)} h^{t_u}, \quad c_v = g^{\sum_{i=1}^k a_i v_i(x_1)} h^{t_v}, \quad c_w = g^{\sum_{i=1}^k a_i u_i(x_1)} h^{t_w}$$

The soundness of protocol 3.3 implies

$$c_u = g^{\sum_{i=k+1}^l a_i u_i(x_1)} h^{s_u}, \quad c_v = g^{\sum_{i=k+1}^l a_i v_i(x_1)} h^{s_v},$$

$$c_w = g^{\sum_{i=k+1}^l a_i w_i(x_1)} h^{s_w}, \quad c_{hz} = g^{h(x_1)z(x_1)} h^{s_h}$$

The knowledge extractor described in the proof of Protocol 3.1 can extract a, r_a and b, r_b such that

$$c_a = c_u \cdot c_u \cdot g^{\sum_{i=l+1}^n a_i u_i(x_1)} = g^a h^{r_a}$$

$$c_b = c_v \cdot c_v \cdot g^{\sum_{i=l+1}^n a_i v_i(x_1)} = g^b h^{r_b}$$

$$c_c = c_w \cdot c_w \cdot g^{\sum_{i=l+1}^n a_i w_i(x_1)} \cdot c_{hz} = g^{ab} h^{r_c}$$

which means

$$\sum_{i=1}^n a_i u_i(x_1) \cdot \sum_{i=1}^n a_i v_i(x_1) = \sum_{i=1}^n a_i w_i(x_1) + h(x_1)z(x_1)$$

Apart from the challenge x_1, all the variables in the above equation are predefined, therefore either the prover can compute the non-trivial discrete logarithm relation between the generators or $\sum_{i=1}^n a_i u_i(X) \cdot \sum_{i=1}^n a_i v_i(X) = \sum_{i=1}^n a_i w_i(X) + h(X)z(X)$.

Perfect special honest-verifier zero-knowledge. The zero-knowledge property follows by the zero-knowledge properties of the sub-protocols. The simulator can utilize the sub-protocols' simulator to produce a valid transcript without knowing the witnesses.   □

F   Definitions for Commit-and-Prove Zero-Knowledge Proof

Definition 7 (Perfect Completeness). *The triple $(\mathcal{G}, \mathcal{V}, \mathcal{P})$ has perfect completeness if for all non-uniform PPT adversary $\mathcal{A}$ such that*

$$\Pr \left[\begin{matrix} (\sigma, c, r, x, u, w) \notin \mathcal{R}_\lambda^{\mathsf{Com}} \\ \text{or } \langle \mathcal{P}(\sigma, c, r, x, u, w), \mathcal{V}(\sigma, c, x) \rangle = 1 \end{matrix} \middle| \begin{matrix} \sigma \leftarrow \mathcal{G}(1^\lambda) \\ (c, r, x, u, w) \leftarrow \mathcal{A}(\sigma) \end{matrix} \right] = 1$$

Definition 8 (Computational Soundness). *$(\mathcal{G}, \mathcal{V}, \mathcal{P})$ has computational soundness if it is not possible to prove a false statement where no witness exist, i.e. for all non-uniform polynomial time interactive adversary $\mathcal{A}_1, \mathcal{A}_2$, the function $\mathsf{negl}(\lambda)$ is negligible.*

$$\Pr \left[\begin{matrix} \mathcal{A}_1(tr) = 1 \ (i.e. \ tr \ is \ accepting) \wedge \\ (\sigma, c, r, x, u, w) \notin \mathcal{R}_\lambda^{\mathsf{Com}}) \end{matrix} \middle| \begin{matrix} \sigma \leftarrow \mathcal{G}(1^\lambda) \\ (c, x, s) \leftarrow \mathcal{A}_2(\sigma) \end{matrix} \right] \leq \mathsf{negl}(\lambda)$$

Definition 9 (Computational Knowledge Soundness). *$(\mathcal{G}, \mathcal{V}, \mathcal{P})$ has computational knowledge soundness if for all deterministic polynomial time $\mathcal{P}^*$, there exists an polynomial time knowledge extractor $\mathcal{E}$ such that for all non-uniform polynomial time interactive adversary $\mathcal{A}_1, \mathcal{A}_2$, the function $\mathsf{negl}(\lambda)$ is negligible.*

$$\left| \begin{matrix} \Pr \left[\mathcal{A}_1(tr) = 1 \middle| \begin{matrix} \sigma \leftarrow \mathcal{G}(1^\lambda), (c, x, s) \leftarrow \mathcal{A}_2(\sigma) \\ tr \leftarrow \langle \mathcal{P}^*(\sigma, c, x, s), \mathcal{V}(\sigma, c, x) \rangle \end{matrix} \right] - \\ \\ \Pr \left[\begin{matrix} \mathcal{A}_1(tr) = 1 \wedge \\ (tr \ is \ accepting \ i.e. \ (\sigma, c, r, x, u, w) \in \mathcal{R}_\lambda^{\mathsf{Com}}) \end{matrix} \middle| \begin{matrix} \sigma \leftarrow \mathcal{G}(1^\lambda) \\ (c, x, s) \leftarrow \mathcal{A}_2(\sigma) \\ (tr, w) \leftarrow \mathcal{E}^{\mathcal{O}}(\sigma, c, x) \end{matrix} \right] \end{matrix} \right| \leq \mathsf{negl}(\lambda)$$

where the oracle is given by $\mathcal{O} = \langle \mathcal{P}^*(\sigma, c, x, s), \mathcal{V}(\sigma, c, x) \rangle$.

The oracle $\mathcal{O}$ permits rewinding to a specific point and resuming with fresh randomness for the verifier from this point onwards. Informally, if there is an adversary that can produce an argument that satisfies the verifier with some probability, then there exists an emulator that can extract the witness. The value s is the internal state of $\mathcal{P}^*$, including randomness. The emulator is permitted to rewind the interaction between the prover and verifier to any move, then resuming with fresh randomness for the verifier.

Definition 10 (Perfect Special Honest-Verifier Zero-Knowledge). *A triple $(\mathcal{G}, \mathcal{P}, \mathcal{V})$ is a perfect special honest verifier zero knowledge argument of knowledge for $\mathcal{R}_\lambda^{\mathsf{Com}}$ if there exists a probabilistic polynomial time simulator $\mathcal{S}$ such that for all pairs of interactive adversaries $\mathcal{A}_1, \mathcal{A}_2$*

$$\Pr\left[(\sigma, c, r, x, u, w) \in \mathcal{R}_\lambda^{\mathsf{Com}} \text{ and } \mathcal{A}_1(tr) = 1 \,\middle|\, \begin{array}{l} \sigma \leftarrow \mathcal{G}(1^\lambda), (c, x, r, u, w, \rho) \leftarrow \mathcal{A}_2(\sigma) \\ tr \leftarrow \langle \mathcal{P}^*(\sigma, c, x, r, u, w), \mathcal{V}(\sigma, c, x; \rho) \rangle \end{array}\right]$$

$$= \Pr\left[(\sigma, c, r, x, u, w) \in \mathcal{R}_\lambda^{\mathsf{Com}} \text{ and } \mathcal{A}_1(tr) = 1 \,\middle|\, \begin{array}{l} \sigma \leftarrow \mathcal{G}(1^\lambda), (c, x, r, u, w, \rho) \leftarrow \mathcal{A}_2(\sigma) \\ tr \leftarrow \mathcal{S}(\sigma, c, x, \rho) \end{array}\right]$$

where ρ is the randomness used by the verifier.

Definition 11 (Commit-and-Prove Zero-knowledge Argument of Knowledge). *The triple $(\mathcal{S}, \mathcal{P}, \mathcal{V})$ is a commit-and-prove zero-knowledge argument of knowledge for a family of relations $\mathcal{R}^{\mathsf{Com}}$ if it satisfies the perfect completeness, perfect special honest-verifier zero-knowledge and computational soundness or computational knowledge soundness.*

G   Notations

- Op : the operator
- SC : the smart contract
- r : the epoch number
- pk_i : the public key of user u_i
- b_i : the balance of user u_i
- c_i : the commitment for the balance of user u_i
- t_i : the randomness of user u_i
- c_{t_i} : the commitment for the randomness t_i
- v_{ij} : the value of transaction that is sent from u_i to u_j
- σ : a signature
- B : the total balance in the smart contract.
- Tx'_{ij}:$(pk_i, pk_j, v_{ij}, \mathsf{Null}, r, n, \sigma_{ij})$: The plain transaction sent by user to the operator.

- Tx_{ij}:$(pk_i, pk_j, v_{ij}, \mathsf{c}_{ij}, r, n, \sigma_{ij})$: The plain transaction after that the operator commits to the value and replace the Null with the commitment.
- CTx_{ij} : (pk_j, c_{ij}) The abbreviated confidential transaction that sends value from u_i to u_j
- $\mathcal{T}r$: the plain transaction list
- $\mathcal{CT}_r$: the abbreviated confidential transaction list
- H : a collision resistant hash function
- $\{x_i\}_{i=1}^N$: a set of values $\{x_1, ..., x_N\}$, we use curly brackets to indicates a set of values.

References

1. Pribank in Go
2. libsnark: a C++ library for zkSNARK proofs

3. Agrawal, S., Ganesh, C., Mohassel, P.: Non-interactive zero-knowledge proofs for composite statements. In: Shacham, H., Boldyreva, A. (eds.) CRYPTO 2018. LNCS, vol. 10993, pp. 643–673. Springer, Cham (2018). https://doi.org/10.1007/978-3-319-96878-0_22

4. Back, A., et al.: Enabling blockchain innovations with pegged sidechains, vol. 72 (2014). http://www.opensciencereview.com/papers/123/enablingblockchain-innovations-with-pegged-sidechains

5. Benarroch, D., Campanelli, M., Fiore, D., Kolonelos, D.: Zero-knowledge proofs for set membership: efficient, succinct, modular. IACR Cryptol. ePrint Arch. **2019**, 1255 (2019)

6. Bonneau, J., Narayanan, A., Miller, A., Clark, J., Kroll, J.A., Felten, E.W.: Mixcoin: anonymity for bitcoin with accountable mixes. In: Christin, N., Safavi-Naini, R. (eds.) FC 2014. LNCS, vol. 8437, pp. 486–504. Springer, Heidelberg (2014). https://doi.org/10.1007/978-3-662-45472-5_31

7. Bowe, S., Chiesa, A., Green, M., Miers, I., Mishra, P., Wu, H.: Zexe: enabling decentralized private computation. In: 2020 IEEE Symposium on Security and Privacy (SP), pp. 947–964 (2020). https://doi.org/10.1109/SP40000.2020.00050

8. Bünz, B., Agrawal, S., Zamani, M., Boneh, D.: Zether: towards privacy in a smart contract world. In: Bonneau, J., Heninger, N. (eds.) FC 2020. LNCS, vol. 12059, pp. 423–443. Springer, Cham (2020). https://doi.org/10.1007/978-3-030-51280-4_23

9. Bünz, B., Bootle, J., Boneh, D., Poelstra, A., Wuille, P., Maxwell, G.: Bulletproofs: short proofs for confidential transactions and more. In: 2018 IEEE Symposium on Security and Privacy (SP), pp. 315–334. IEEE (2018)

10. Campanelli, M., Fiore, D., Querol, A.: LegoSNARK: modular design and composition of succinct zero-knowledge proofs. In: Proceedings of the 2019 ACM SIGSAC Conference on Computer and Communications Security, pp. 2075–2092 (2019)

11. Canetti, R., Lindell, Y., Ostrovsky, R., Sahai, A.: Universally composable two-party and multi-party secure computation. In: Proceedings of the Thiry-fourth Annual ACM Symposium on Theory of Computing, pp. 494–503 (2002)

12. Cecchetti, E., Zhang, F., Ji, Y., Kosba, A., Juels, A., Shi, E.: Solidus: confidential distributed ledger transactions via PVORM. In: Proceedings of 2017 ACM SIGSAC Conference on Computer and Communications Security, pp. 701–717 (2017)

13. Danezis, G., Meiklejohn, S.: Centrally banked cryptocurrencies. arXiv preprint arXiv:1505.06895 (2015)

14. Decker, C., Wattenhofer, R.: A fast and scalable payment network with bitcoin duplex micropayment channels. In: Pelc, A., Schwarzmann, A.A. (eds.) SSS 2015. LNCS, vol. 9212, pp. 3–18. Springer, Cham (2015). https://doi.org/10.1007/978-3-319-21741-3_1

15. Diamond, B.E.: Many-out-of-many proofs and applications to anonymous zether. In: 2021 IEEE Symposium on Security and Privacy (SP), pp. 1800–1817. IEEE Computer Society, Los Alamitos, May 2021. https://doi.org/10.1109/SP40001.2021.00026

16. Dziembowski, S., Fabiański, G., Faust, S., Riahi, S.: Lower bounds for off-chain protocols: exploring the limits of plasma. In: 12th Innovations in Theoretical Computer Science Conference (ITCS 2021) (2021)

17. Fauzi, P., Meiklejohn, S., Mercer, R., Orlandi, C.: Quisquis: a new design for anonymous cryptocurrencies. In: Galbraith, S.D., Moriai, S. (eds.) ASIACRYPT 2019. LNCS, vol. 11921, pp. 649–678. Springer, Cham (2019). https://doi.org/10.1007/978-3-030-34578-5_23

18. Gennaro, R., Gentry, C., Parno, B., Raykova, M.: Quadratic span programs and succinct NIZKs without PCPs. In: Johansson, T., Nguyen, P.Q. (eds.) EURO-CRYPT 2013. LNCS, vol. 7881, pp. 626–645. Springer, Heidelberg (2013). https://doi.org/10.1007/978-3-642-38348-9_37

19. Gluchowski, A.: Zk rollup: scaling with zero-knowledge proofs. Matter Labs (2019)

20. Kerber, T., Kiayias, A., Kohlweiss, M.: Kachina-foundations of private smart contracts. In: 2021 IEEE 34th Computer Security Foundations Symposium (CSF), pp. 1–16. IEEE (2021)

21. Khalil, R., Zamyatin, A., Felley, G., Moreno-Sanchez, P., Gervais, A.: Commit-chains: secure, scalable off-chain payments. Cryptology ePrint Archive, Report 2018/642 (2018)

22. Kilian, J.: Uses of Randomness in Algorithms and Protocols. Massachusetts Institute of Technology (1990)

23. Kosba, A., Miller, A., Shi, E., Wen, Z., Papamanthou, C.: Hawk: the blockchain model of cryptography and privacy-preserving smart contracts. In: 2016 IEEE Symposium on Security and Privacy (SP), pp. 839–858 (2016). https://doi.org/10.1109/SP.2016.55

24. Maxwell, G.: CoinJoin: bitcoin privacy for the real world. In: Post on Bitcoin Forum (2013)

25. Miller, A., Bentov, I., Kumaresan, R., McCorry, P.: Sprites: payment channels that go faster than lightning. CoRR arXiv:1702.05812 306 (2017)

26. Nakamoto, S.: Bitcoin: a peer-to-peer electronic cash system (2009). http://bitcoin.org/bitcoin.pdf

27. Narula, N., Vasquez, W., Virza, M.: zkLedger: privacy-preserving auditing for distributed ledgers. In: 15th {USENIX} Symposium on Networked Systems Design and Implementation ({NSDI} 18), pp. 65–80 (2018)

28. Pedersen, T.P.: Non-interactive and information-theoretic secure verifiable secret sharing. In: Feigenbaum, J. (ed.) CRYPTO 1991. LNCS, vol. 576, pp. 129–140. Springer, Heidelberg (1992). https://doi.org/10.1007/3-540-46766-1_9

29. Poon, J., Buterin, V.: Plasma: scalable autonomous smart contracts. White paper (2017)

30. Sasson, E.B., et al.: Zerocash: decentralized anonymous payments from bitcoin. In: 2014 IEEE Symposium on Security and Privacy, pp. 459–474. IEEE (2014)

31. Steffen, S., Bichsel, B., Gersbach, M., Melchior, N., Tsankov, P., Vechev, M.: zkay: specifying and enforcing data privacy in smart contracts. In: Proceedings of the 2019 ACM SIGSAC Conference on Computer and Communications Security, pp. 1759–1776 (2019)

32. The Monero Project: Monero (2014). https://web.getmonero.org

33. Wood, G.: Ethereum: a secure decentralised generalised transaction ledger. Yellow Paper (2014)

34. Zyskind, G., Nathan, O., et al.: Decentralizing privacy: using blockchain to protect personal data. In: 2015 IEEE Security and Privacy Workshops, pp. 180–184. IEEE (2015)

Author Index

Printed in the United States
by Baker & Taylor Publisher Services